PETERSON'S COLLEGES FOR STUDENTS WITH LEARNING DISABILITIES OR AD/HD

8TH EDITION

PETERSON'S

A ⓝelnet COMPANY

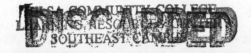

PETERSON'S
A ⓝelnet COMPANY

About Peterson's, a Nelnet company

Peterson's (www.petersons.com) is a leading provider of education information and advice, with books and online resources focusing on education search, test preparation, and financial aid. Its Web site offers searchable databases and interactive tools for contacting educational institutions, online practice tests and instruction, and planning tools for securing financial aid. Peterson's serves 110 million education consumers annually.

For more information, contact Peterson's, 2000 Lenox Drive, Lawrenceville, NJ 08648; 800-338-3282; or find us on the World Wide Web at www.petersons.com/about.

ISSN 1525-3813
ISBN-13: 978-0-7689-2506-7
ISBN-10: 0-7689-2506-1

Printed in the United States of America

10 9 8 7 6 5 4 3 2 1   09 08 07

Eighth Edition

CONTENTS

FOREWORD

Welcome to *Peterson's Colleges for Students with Learning Disabilities or AD/HD.*

Choosing a college that will provide the education and social life to suit his or her particular needs is a challenge for any student. For the student with LD or AD/HD, there are additional factors to take into account, but overall the process is more similar to that of other students than it is dissimilar. A successful college search depends on making the right match between your aspirations, an environment in which you feel comfortable, and the availability of support services. That being said, it is still no easy task to wade through all the literature and Web pages that describe support services, and that is why this directory exists. While all the information about support services cannot be captured in a few pages, it is still very valuable to have the basic information in a single publication.

Let me tell you a few things about the process you are undertaking. Once you have narrowed your search using this book, Web sites, and other materials, there is no substitute for meeting with the people who run the programs that provide support services. These people rarely try to talk you into attending a school that is not right for you. They tell you what support they do and do not provide so you can make an informed decision. I talk to hundreds of prospective students and their parents every year, and they occasionally come armed with a list of questions that they think will allow them to get at the "truth" about the support services provided at my school. They quickly learn that I have nothing to hide. I readily own up to what services are not provided. I tell them about the additional challenges of a large, competitive school. I tell them about other schools and what support they provide. Those of us who run support programs are every bit as invested as you are in finding you the right school. That is why, even though we don't like surveys,

we filled out the surveys used to create the profiles in this book. That is also why I and several of my colleagues consulted with Peterson's during the revision of this guide. I would like to thank Scott Lissner (Ohio State University), Ross Pollack (Manhattan College), and Emily Singer (The Catholic University of America) for their work on this guide.

So far in this preface, I have been referring to the reader as "you," the prospective student. That is because I want to empower you to "own" this search, to ask the questions you want to ask, and to make decisions for yourself. That is not to say that your parents' opinions are not valuable; they are. However, we in this field often see something we call the "stereophonic effect" when a student and his or her parents come into our offices. One parent sits on either side of the student, and we look directly at the student and ask a question. Immediately, there are competing answers from the left and right side of the prospective student but nothing from the center channel. This worries us, as we have all seen students whose only visits to our offices are the first one they make as a prospective student and then the one they make after they are in deep academic trouble. While some schools do more to monitor a student's academic progress than others, all students benefit from a clear understanding of their cognitive strengths and weaknesses and the ability to know when they need help. This is not a concept unique to students with LD or AD/HD.

I believe you will find this guide to be helpful in your college search. Good luck with your search, and maybe I will see you in Ann Arbor soon.

Sam Goodin is the Director of Services for Students with Disabilities at the University of Michigan. He is also a former President of the Association on Higher Education and Disability (AHEAD).

A NOTE FROM THE PETERSON'S EDITORS

Peterson's is pleased to present this eighth edition of *Colleges for Students with Learning Disabilities or AD/HD*. With comprehensive profiles of LD programs at more than 900 colleges in the U.S. and Canada, valuable advice from LD professionals, plus worksheets and checklists to keep you organized, this guide is an indispensable tool for LD students and their parents embarking on a college search.

First, you will want to read through the insightful articles in **What You Need to Know about College LD Programs** in the front of the guide, written by specialists in the field of learning disabilities. You will learn what directors of college LD programs and consultants in the private sector have to say about legal considerations, documentation, the distinctions between K–12 and higher education requirements, the transition from high school to college, the college experience, and more. In addition, there are samples of forms that are typically used in college disability support services (DSS) offices and checklists to keep you organized and on schedule.

"How to Use This Guide" explains how the book is organized and what information can be found in it, including descriptions of each section of the school profiles. There are explanations of the research procedures Peterson's used to obtain the profile information and the criteria that determined which schools are included in the book.

In **Profiles of College LD Programs** you will find in-depth information on specific schools' programs, including enrollment, staff and services, written policies, contacts, and more. To make it easier for you to locate the appropriate program, the profiles are divided into four categories: Four-Year Colleges with Structured/Proactive Programs, Four-Year Colleges with Self-Directed/Decentralized Programs, Two-Year Colleges with Structured/Proactive Programs, and Two-Year Colleges with Self-Directed/Decentralized Programs.

Finally, there are the **Indexes**: a Majors Index that lets you know which schools offer a degree in your academic area of interest (even the best LD services are worthless if you can't study what you're interested in!) and alphabetical and geographical indexes for easy reference.

Peterson's publishes a full line of resources that help guide students and parents through the college admission process. Peterson's publications can be found at your local bookstore, library, and high school guidance office—or visit us on the Web at www.petersons.com.

We welcome any comments or suggestions you may have about this publication and invite you to complete our online survey at www.petersons.com/booksurvey. Or you can fill out the survey at the back of this book, tear it out, and mail it to us at:

Publishing Department
Peterson's, a Nelnet company
2000 Lenox Drive
Lawrenceville, NJ 08648

Your feedback will help us make your educational dreams possible.

The editors at Peterson's wish you great success in your college search!

WHAT YOU NEED TO KNOW ABOUT COLLEGE LD PROGRAMS

DISTINCTIONS BETWEEN K–12 AND HIGHER EDUCATION REQUIREMENTS

The transition from high school to college is an experience that should be carefully planned for all students. Students with a learning disability (LD) who have received services during their K–12 school experiences have many factors to consider, and they must all be addressed thoughtfully.

There are many differences, some tangible and some more subtle, between the K–12 school experience and college, and it is important for students with learning disabilities to plan ahead so that they can make a good college choice. Self-understanding is vital as an LD student moves from the high school to the college setting. It is essential for students to understand what their disability is and how it impacts their learning in order to choose an institution where they can be successful.

During the K–12 experience, students generally have family and school personnel to guide them along the way. The college experience, even for those who stay near home, requires personal responsibility and independence on the part of the student. For the first time in their lives, students have to plan their own time and complete papers and projects without prompting and without automatic academic support. Most importantly, they have to learn how to be productive in the face of personal freedom that they have not experienced before.

The mission of colleges and universities is very different from that of K–12 institutions. Colleges are not required by law to seek out students with disabilities, and they are not required to do whatever it takes to help students succeed in a college setting. Colleges and universities are only required to provide "reasonable accommodations" to those students who identify themselves as learning disabled. The move from high school to college shifts from a model that fosters success to a model that provides access.

SELF-ADVOCACY

The Individuals with Disabilities Education Act (IDEA) protects the LD student during the K–12 school years. This means that it is the school's responsibility to seek out and identify students with disabilities and then serve them in the least restrictive environment possible. Under the IDEA, students and their families are guided through the education process. An Individual Education Plan (IEP) is developed and written for the student and carried out by the school each year. In addition, there is support in place. Students generally work with a guidance counselor

to plan their courses each year. Students with learning disabilities can also usually rely on a resource teacher, a special education teacher, or a guidance counselor to tell their teachers what kind of academic support is needed. For example, if a student needs extended time on an exam, it will be arranged through these support services.

This is not the case at most colleges. The majority of colleges offer reasonable accommodations as required by law and possibly some additional academic support. Many do not have trained learning disability specialists, and, if they do, they generally serve in an academic counseling role for many students. When LD students arrive at college, it is up to them to identify themselves to the Office for Disability Services and arrange for the help that they need. This is quite different from students knowing the help that they need will be there when they need it.

A new term that students are introduced to during the college admissions process is "disclosure." Students are expected from the very beginning to let others know about their learning disability if they want or need help. Students should understand and express the area(s) of their learning disability (e.g., written language), academic and personal strengths and weaknesses, the type of academic support they received in high school, and what areas they think they will need help with in college. They should learn to explain what accommodations they are requesting and why, and anything else that will help them get admitted and have a good college experience. Once college begins, the Disability Service Provider will help the student learn how to approach faculty members and others on campus.

THE ADMISSION PROCESS

In kindergarten through the twelfth grade, students with learning disabilities have others to advocate for them. When applying to colleges, students must fill out their own applications, write their own essays, and make their own case for why they are a good match for a particular institution. Though colleges cannot discriminate, they also are only required to accept students who are "otherwise qualified" for admittance to their institution. They are not required to overlook poor grades and test scores in order to admit a student; however, if there are compelling explanations for the low grades and test scores, this information may be taken into consideration during the admissions process. If you choose to write an essay about the impact of your learning disability on your high school education, it is best to make it a separate essay and still write the essay being asked for in the application. It may be important to help a school understand things about your high school experience that can be attributed to your disability. But it is essential to show that, like other students, you have something to offer to the college experience.

Colleges usually have basic admissions requirements that students must meet to be admitted. They are as follows:

- 4 units of English;
- 3 units of mathematics (geometry, algebra I, algebra II);
- 3 units of science (including a laboratory science);
- 2 units of foreign language (sometimes 3);
- 3 units of social studies;
- 1 unit of practical arts;
- 2 units of health and physical education;
- a minimum grade point average;
- rank in high school class; and
- a minimum ACT Assessment or SAT score.

These are only basic requirements, and they will differ from institution to institution. It is important to know that while colleges often consider extenuating circumstances, they are not *required* to consider them. If, for example, a student is identified with a learning disability in the middle of high school and has received poor grades up until then, a college will usually consider the improvement that may come after identification. If this has happened to you, you should draw attention to this fact in a short essay. Colleges care about improvement and what made it happen. They also want to know how you will use the resources of the college to continue to get good grades.

COURSE SUBSTITUTIONS

Colleges are in no way required to waive any course requirements. They are not required to substitute for any requirements. Very few colleges make a commitment to waive or substitute for a requirement before a student has been accepted by a school and has decided to enroll. Many factors are taken into consideration, and most schools have a policy and process in place that determines whether a waiver or substitution will be granted. This is rarely a decision that disability services personnel make independently. It usually involves faculty members and/or administrators and a committee process.

One reason that this decision needs to be made carefully is that colleges do not want to—and are not required to—waive or substitute courses in a student's major academic area. There are exceptions. For example, if a student is majoring in chemistry and is doing well but has had a very difficult time learning a second language, a substitution may be granted. The college would consider if foreign language acquisition was affected by the student's learning disability and if there was enough evidence that the student would not be able to learn a language well enough to show proficiency. In a case like this, the college could ask the student to take substitute courses for the language. These course options could include culture classes, linguistics, or even computer classes.

Students who have a history of performing poorly in mathematics should know that substitutions for the mathematics requirement are rare and, again, must be tied to the functional limitations of a disability.

Students should never choose a college hoping that a specific requirement will be substituted for or waived. A student can choose a major with a minimal number of courses in a particular area, but students should look at a college curriculum with the idea that they will take all the required courses.

ACADEMIC SUPPORT

Colleges, by law, have the right to have their own eligibility standards or guidelines in place. Once accepted by a college, a student must submit his or her documentation to the Office for Disability Services in order to determine if he or she is eligible for services. The burden rests on the student to provide adequate documentation. Most disability services offices only review the documentation of admitted students, so students usually don't know before they are accepted if their documentation will be accepted. It is in the student's best interest to ask if a college will review documentation before admittance to allow for time to update or amend the documentation as necessary, as sometimes even if students have been served throughout elementary, middle, and high school, their documentation may be rejected by a specific college.

What academic support a student receives in college is directly related to the functional limitations and rationale described in his or her provided documentation. For example, if there is evidence that a student has a learning disability in the area of reading and is a slow reader because of it, the student may be eligible for a reader and extended time on exams. If the student has a learning disability in math and asks for extended time on English tests with essay questions, it may not be granted.

ADAPTIVE TECHNOLOGY AND ALTERNATIVE MEDIA

Students often leave high school with very little experience using adaptive technology, such as programs that help students read and write. There is a wide variety of this type of technology. Be sure to find out if your high school has any options in this area. You may also want to explore this on your own. Some frequently used programs are Inspiration; WYNN; Read & Write Gold; and Kurzweil. In college, you may also have the opportunity (dependant on your documentation) to use books in electronic and audio formats. For example, some students benefit from listening to a book while reading it. This can be accomplished in a number of different ways. If you have used books on tape in the past or have a significant Reading Disability, you should ask whether a school can make books in alternative formats available to you.

SUCCESS AND THE LD STUDENT

The adjustment to college life is difficult for most students. Students with learning disabilities who have been served throughout their schooling are used to having remedial services and guidance. In general, colleges do not offer remediation. College settings may have developmental courses, but the grades students receive in these courses often do not count toward graduation. Students who go on to college must be prepared for the rigors of the admissions process and then the course work, once they are admitted. In the K–12 arena, students and their families are used to the support given by the school and the structure that is provided. Parents are used to communicating with teachers, helping to shape their child's school experience. This type of communication changes at the college level, where students, not parents, are expected to communicate their own needs and work directly with the Office for Disability Services and faculty members to get the services they need.

The responsibility for success rests with the student. Students with learning disabilities should do their research carefully and be sure that the kind of support that they need is in place at the postsecondary institutions they are considering. It is critical that students evaluate the type of help they have received in high school and what type of academic support they will need in college. By carefully considering the factors that should be in place for a successful college experience ahead of time, students have a good chance of choosing a college where they can be successful.

Lydia S. Block, Ph.D., is an educational consultant in Columbus, Ohio. She also is the Learning Specialist in the Learning Disabilities Assistance Center at Ohio Wesleyan University in Delaware, Ohio. Dr. Block works with students with LD, ADD, head injuries, and other disabilities.

THE COLLEGE EXPERIENCE

As with any major life change, starting college is both exciting and frightening at the same time. High school students often find the transition to college academically challenging and emotionally draining. The transition from high school to college for students with disabilities can be even more stressful because of their disabilities. One of the biggest challenges faced by all new students is negotiating the maze of requirements and services available to them. As a new arrival with learning disabilities or AD/HD, you may find additional bumps and turns in your road to a successful education. In addition to the normal maze of information that any new student receives, you also must be aware of the procedures required to ensure that your needed accommodations are provided.

STEP 1: BECOME FAMILIAR WITH YOUR DISABILITY

College is a time of change, and you will now be required to take on more responsibility for your education. More specifically, YOU must become your own advocate. You can do this by becoming proficient at realistically assessing and understanding your strengths, weaknesses, needs, interests, and preferences. Make sure you are comfortable communicating your strengths and weaknesses as well as the accommodations that you are requesting. One way you can do this is by reading your documentation and going through it with your teacher or psychologist to make sure that you understand it.

STEP 2: CONTACT THE DISABILITY SERVICES OFFICE

Contact the Disability Services Office and request any materials that you may need to start the registration process. This information may also be available on their Web site. One of the documents they will most likely send you will contain the documentation guidelines. Make sure that the documentation you have meets their requirements. You may need to request copies of evaluation results from your testing service provider or new and/or additional pieces of information. Preparing this documentation can take time, and delays can hold up receiving appropriate accommodations. Provide this information to the Disability Services Office as early as possible. This allows plenty of time for the office to review the information and become familiar with your accommodation needs.

If possible, arrange a visit to the Disability Services Office prior to your arrival on campus. This visit will allow you the opportunity to become familiar with the office and its services, the campus, the accommodation procedures, and other university resources, and it can alleviate the stress associated with dealing with a new environment. It also will give you the opportunity to ask questions, such as:

- What is the application process for students with learning disabilities?
- What are the services available to students with learning disabilities?
- What documentation is required?
- What will I need to do to receive these services once you have my documentation?
- Are there any additional fees for services?
- Are there other classes available for students with learning disabilities (e.g., study skills)?
- Do you have any course substitution policies or a reduced course load option?
- Do you have tutors? Content tutors or skills tutors? Are they trained to work with students with learning disabilities?
- How do I arrange for note-takers?
- Can I get my books on tape or in an electronic format?
- During orientation, are there placement tests given for which I will need accommodations?
- Is there a Learning Resource Center on campus?
- Is coaching available either on campus or privately?

STEP 3: TIME MANAGEMENT

In preparation for college, be aware of your individual needs when selecting classes and planning your course schedule. Organization is essential to staying focused. It is important to prioritize and think carefully about what academic and social opportunities you would like to explore and their time commitments. A reduced course load may be a viable option to help you acclimate to college life. The Disability Services Office will help determine if this is an appropriate accommodation for you. When choosing a class schedule, avoid classes that accentuate your weaknesses, particularly in your first term. You will want to work with the Disability Services Office and your academic adviser when selecting classes. Use this opportunity to try new experiences. You may find something new that stimulates your interest. To stay focused, try the following:

- When planning your schedule, try to leave time between classes, as well as time for yourself.

- There are many activities available—budget your time wisely.
- Use your free time between classes to study.
- Keep a "To Do" list daily and cross things off when they are done.
- Assign priorities to your tasks.
- Learn to say no to friends, phone calls, and unexpected interruptions.
- Carry a calendar with classes, appointments, and homework due dates.

STEP 4: RESPONSIBILITIES

Once you are enrolled in college, you are considered to be an adult responsible for meeting the requirements for your education, seeking support services available to you on campus, and interacting with the appropriate members of the college community to discuss your academic progress and any issues or concerns that may arise.

Therefore, you must become comfortable being your own self-advocate. In college, you are expected to participate in the processes associated with your education, and you need to be able to define your individual learning style, strengths, and weaknesses. You must compensate for these strengths and weaknesses, with the help of the Disability Services Office, while defining preferences and choices for learning. The Disability Services Office can assist you in interpreting documentation and in defining strategies for approaching and communicating with faculty members.

Meeting with faculty members frequently will serve to further enhance your education. To make sure you understand the information they give you, prepare for these meetings in advance. Here are some guidelines to follow:

- Make an appointment (try to do it early in the semester).
- Be on time for the appointment.
- Introduce yourself.
- Tell the instructor the class in which you are enrolled.
- Show an interest in the class.
- Be calm and courteous (don't interrupt, and make sure to know the difference between passive, aggressive, and assertive responses).
- Bring with you accommodations information, information on learning disabilities, and/or course materials you want to discuss.
- Be prepared to solve problems or look for alternative answers.
- Leave the instructor with a positive impression.

It is important for you to remember that the purpose of accommodations is to give you an opportunity to demonstrate mastery of course content and information being tested by minimizing or eliminating the impact of the disability. It is not to give you an unfair advantage. Each person plays a vital role in this process.

Student Responsibilities

- Meet the essential qualifications and institutional standards.
- Disclose the disability in a timely manner to the Disability Services Office.
- Provide appropriate documentation.
- Inform the Disability Services Office of accommodation needs.
- Request accommodations.
- Talk with professors about accommodations in the classroom, as needed. Bring the accommodation letter and any additional documents (i.e., note-taker announcement, recorded lecture policy) to the faculty member.
- Discuss with the faculty member how the accommodations are going to be implemented, and explain the situation. Contact should be maintained throughout the semester.
- Inform the Disability Services Office of barriers to a successful education.

Disability Services Office Responsibilities

- Inform students of office location and procedures for requesting accommodations.
- Accept and evaluate verifying documentation.
- Maintain accurate documentation for each student.
- Approve and provide appropriate accommodations.
- Provide notification to individuals as directed by the student.
- Protect student's privacy and confidentiality.
- Provide equal access to programs and services.

Faculty Responsibilities

- Make sure that each course, viewed in its entirety, is accessible (e.g., content, texts and materials, assessment method, online instruction, and time requirements).
- Support and implement reasonable accommodations (modifications) as identified in a letter from the Disability Services Office and presented by the student.
- Consult with the Disability Services Office if requests conflict with course objectives/requirements.
- Maintain CONFIDENTIALITY.
- Submit book lists to bookstore as early as possible.
- Include announcement on syllabus directing students to the Disability Services Office if they have need for an accommodation related to a disability.
- Contact the Disability Services Office if any of the academic adjustments results in a fundamental alteration of the course, if at any point in time you feel as though students' requests are unreasonable, or if you are not notified in a timely manner.

Being a college student with a learning disability takes persistence, patience, perseverance, and desire, along with solid communication skills. Many students encounter problems in college as a result of ignorance about the services available to them and/or poor communication between themselves and their college. It is of paramount importance, therefore, to be informed about your learning disability and then actively seek out the services available at your chosen institution. This assuages problems and lessens the stress you may encounter.

The bottom line is to be proactive in the process. Knowing where to go and what services are available through the Disability Services Office will ease the transition from high school to college. Even if you decide not to avail yourself of the services, it is still important to be prepared with all of the required information. Remember though that these services are not retroactive. It is your education, and the choice to use or not use services should not be taken lightly. It cannot be stressed strongly enough that identifying yourself to the Disability Services Office and providing them with the appropriate documentation enhances the institution's ability to provide timely services to meet your individual needs. You should know that the dedicated people who work in the field continually strive to improve the services of their institutions, to hone their individual skills in the field, and to educate the public overall—all to better serve your needs as a student with learning disabilities. Best of luck with this exciting time ahead of you!

Emily Singer is the Director of Disability Support Services at The Catholic University of America.

CHECKLIST FOR SUCCESSFUL TRANSITION

If you can check off each statement below, your transition from high school to college will be much smoother. If there are items that you have not yet completed, it is important that you do so as soon as possible before the start of your college enrollment.

❑ I understand my disability; I can discuss my strengths, weaknesses, and needs in detail, and I am able to identify accommodations and services that will provide me with an equal opportunity to succeed in college.

❑ I am currently attending my IEP meetings.

❑ At the time of application, my documentation will meet the criteria for each of the colleges I apply to.

❑ I can manage my time effectively, which includes going to class on time, balancing study time, and completing assignments by the due date.

❑ I have visited the colleges that I would like to attend, seen the campuses, and met with members of the disability services staff regarding documentation guidelines and possible accommodations.

❑ I am signed up for an orientation session at the college I have been accepted to and plan to attend.

LEGAL CONSIDERATIONS FOR LEARNING DISABILITY PROGRAMS

Perhaps the largest legal issue facing students with learning disabilities (LD) or attention deficit hyperactivity disorder (AD/HD) and their families is the different laws that govern schools serving K–12 vs. schools in the postsecondary education arena. Until a student goes on to college or turns 21, he or she is protected by the Individuals with Disabilities Education Act (IDEA). Once a student enters college, the Rehabilitation Act of 1973, Section 504, and the Americans with Disabilities Act (ADA) take over.

LAWS GOVERNING K–12 EDUCATION

The Individuals with Disabilities Education Act (IDEA) specifically requires that K–12 schools seek out students with disabilities and give them whatever help they need to be successful in the school setting. For this reason, students are evaluated at no charge by the school if a disability is suspected and may have Individual Education Plans (IEPs) formulated by the school. Some students will receive intervention to see how they respond to different types of educational support but may never actually be tested or identified as having a learning disability. They receive tutoring and other academic support during their school day as their IEP or their intervention plan dictates. Transition services are also required by IDEA. The school is required to have a transition statement in the student's IEP by the time he or she is 16 and to have a plan in place. It is important for parents to request that a transition plan be in place. It is this plan that helps ensure that the student has had the appropriate courses for college entrance and also helps the school and the family plan for the future.

High school students with learning disabilities or AD/HD are entitled to take college entrance exams (for instance, the ACT or SAT) with accommodations if they qualify. These accommodations can include a reader, a scribe, extended time, or additional breaks as needed. Until recently, the scores of students with disabilities were "flagged" by the testing agencies to show that the test had been taken with special accommodations. This is no longer the case. Students can now take these tests without being concerned that they will be discriminated against during the admissions process.

LAWS GOVERNING POSTSECONDARY EDUCATION

Colleges are not required to seek out students with learning disabilities and do not have to provide any diagnostic services. They also are only required to provide "reasonable accommodations." Students with learning disabilities or AD/HD may be entitled to reasonable academic support based on legislation that was passed in 1973. The Rehabilitation Act of 1973, Section 504, was the first civil rights law that specifically addressed individuals with disabilities. It was also the first law that addressed students with disabilities in postsecondary settings. The law mandates that all colleges and universities in the United States that receive any federal financial assistance cannot discriminate in the recruitment, admission, or treatment of students with disabilities. This law allows students with documented disabilities to request modifications, academic support, or auxiliary aids that allow them to participate in and benefit from all of the activities and programs that colleges offer. The law states:

> "No otherwise qualified handicapped individual in the United States shall, solely by reason of his handicap, be excluded from participation in, be denied the benefits of, or be subjected to discrimination under any program or activity receiving financial assistance."

Under the provisions of Section 504, colleges and universities may not:

- Limit the number of students with disabilities they admit;
- Ask questions on application materials that require the student to disclose a disability;
- Ask students to take preadmissions tests without academic assistance for which they may be eligible;
- Exclude a student who is qualified from a particular major or course of study;
- Counsel students with disabilities out of a particular program due to the disability;
- Have rules or policies that discriminate against students with disabilities; or
- Limit eligibility to students with disabilities for scholarships, financial assistance, fellowships, internships, or assistantships.

In 1990, the Americans with Disabilities Act (ADA) was passed, further ensuring that students with disabilities are entitled to accommodation in college.

Students should be able to disclose their disability when they apply to college without fear of discrimination. Some students who readily fit the admissions criteria for a particular school may choose not to disclose their disability. Even so, it is still important to communicate with the Office for Disability Services directly to determine if a college has appropriate services for the applicant. Once accepted, it is important to contact the Office for Disability Services immediately to determine eligibility for services and find out how they can be accessed.

Personnel Who Enforce These Laws

Each campus has an individual or individuals who have expertise in Section 504 and/or the ADA. On some campuses, particularly small ones, the Director of Disability Services may also be the ADA/504 Coordinator. On many campuses, the Director of Disability Services is also the 504 Coordinator, and the ADA Coordinator is a separate position. This information should be posted on the college Web site. If it is not, students should call the college to find out how these positions are staffed.

Eligibility Guidelines

There is no guidance under IDEA, Section 504, or the ADA that requires colleges to accept documentation that does not meet their guidelines. Each college has the right to develop its own guidelines and adhere to them. It is for this reason that even schools within the same state may have different criteria for determining eligibility for learning disability services.

Where Records Are Kept

The Office for Disability Services should be the primary place on campus where all documentation for learning disabilities is kept. Medical records that include information about medication may also be kept at the Student Health Center. Disability services offices are required to keep documentation of a disability in a separate file from the documentation of day-to-day interactions that a student has with the office.

Mandated Services

One of the major legal issues for colleges and universities is ensuring they have services in place that ensure equal access to the materials and instruction in the academic environment and whatever else is necessary to access all other programs and services on campus. Examples of these services are:

- Extra time on exams;
- Permitting tests to be individually proctored, read orally, dictated, or taken on a computer;
- The use of a system to provide notes;
- The opportunity to register to vote; and
- The provision of materials in alternate media.

In college, academic support services are offered in the following ways:

Readers

- Readers can be asked to repeat information.
- Readers can only read what is on the written page; they cannot be asked to reword material.

Scribes

- Scribes can write down exactly what a student says; they cannot organize or reword the student's ideas.
- It is up to the student to review what is written and direct the scribe to make corrections.

Note-takers

- A note-taker can be a recruited volunteer from the class.
- A note-taker can be a hired student worker.
- Students are required to attend classes even when notes are taken for them.

Adaptive Technology

- Adaptive technology includes computer hardware and software that allows students to access materials. This technology may enlarge print, actually read material out loud, type for students as they speak, highlight material, and even (to some degree) organize written material.

Voter Registration

The Motor Voter Registration Act requires all public institutions to offer all students with disabilities the opportunity to register to vote.

Additional Services

Many colleges also offer services beyond what the law states. Schools with learning centers in place and developmental courses often offer tutoring and study-skills workshops. It is important for students to ask about all of the services offered on a campus. There are often many offices that provide help, and students should learn about all of them. Campuses that offer more than what is required by law often have campus climates that are conducive to learning for all students.

Confidentiality

Throughout students' K–12 school careers, the material that is generated regarding their disability has been kept confidential. The Family Educational Rights Privacy Act of 1974 (FERPA), also known as the Buckley Amendment, governs K–12 schools but has implications for college settings as well. Always remember that diagnostic information is private and sensitive and should be handled accordingly by the institution. Students may request to review their own files; however, the office cannot forward documentation to another institution or professional. It is a good idea for students to keep copies of any information that they give the Disability Services Provider. They may need it later.

Grievance Procedures

Most colleges have a grievance procedure in place to handle concerns and complaints from students. Generally, if students feel that they have been denied a reasonable academic accommodation, they should first meet with the Disability Services Director. If the complaint cannot be resolved at that level, students should be informed of the process that is in place for filing a formal grievance and the specific time frame for filing. Complaints generally must be filed on a university-provided form and must include a written statement of the facts of the discriminatory incident in question. From that point on, the university then investigates the complaint.

RIGHTS FOR THE LD OR AD/HD STUDENT

Students with LD or AD/HD are afforded protections under civil rights laws. They should not be discriminated against based on their disability. Most college campuses welcome students with disabilities and have policies and procedures in place that make requesting academic accommodations a smooth process. It is important to know what policies and procedures are in place at a college and who on campus has the responsibility for making sure that students with disabilities can access what they need to get the same education as their peers without disabilities.

_____

Lydia S. Block, Ph.D., is an educational consultant in Columbus, Ohio. She also is a Learning Specialist in the Learning Disabilities Assistance Center at Ohio Wesleyan University in Delaware, Ohio. Dr. Block works with students with LD, AD/HD, head injuries, and other disabilities.

DOCUMENTATION REQUIRED FOR COLLEGE ELIGIBILITY

I was organizing my thoughts on documentation and considering what was most important to communicate. I thought through numerous presentations and conversations, and one family's story stuck in my mind as particularly representative. While each student is unique, I believe the following story of Tabatha (not her real name) is representative of the rigors surrounding documentation at the college level.

THE HIGH SCHOOL-TO-COLLEGE DISCONNECT

My first contact with Tabatha's family came when her mother called me with a complaint. She said that her daughter had just been told by our Office for Disability Services that she no longer had a learning disability and would not be eligible for services as she moved into her first year of college.

Back in Elementary School

In the third grade, Tabatha was identified as having a specific learning disability impacting language, primarily reading and writing. Based on school performance, observations, and a full battery of psychoeducational tests, Tabatha was found to be eligible for special education services under the Individuals with Disabilities Education Act (IDEA). For three years, there were annual IEP meetings. Then, at the end of sixth grade, she was reevaluated.

Tabatha's learning behaviors were observed in class. Her school performance and progress, as represented by such indicators as homework, classroom tests, proficiency tests, and systemwide achievement tests, was reviewed. In addition, the teachers and special educators who had worked most closely with Tabatha provided input. Her performance had clearly improved, but it was still lagging in a few areas. Tabatha was eligible for continued special education services.

High School

Three years and IEPs later, Tabatha was completing ninth grade and her third evaluation. Happily, after six years of services and support, the review of classroom and standardized achievement tests showed she was now performing above grade level. Both Tabatha and her family were delighted to hear this. Satisfaction and pride changed to concern and panic as the team explained that Tabatha would no longer be eligible for special education services.

After some lengthy discussions with the high school, the family's concerns were addressed by developing a 504 Plan under Section 504 of the Rehabilitation Act. The plan identified accommodations (modifications to policies and procedures), including additional time to complete assignments, additional time to take tests, the opportunity to take tests in a different setting that minimized distractions, and access to a computer for essay tests and written work. With these modifications, Tabatha was successful in high school and was accepted by three of the four colleges to which she applied.

On to College

Once Tabatha selected a college, she and her parents registered for an August orientation session, paid her deposit, and began to plan for the fall. Tabatha contacted the Office for Disability Services, arranged an appointment during orientation, and had a copy of her "special education file" sent. The file included the paperwork from all three reviews, her seven IEPs, and her 504 Plan.

At the meeting, Tabatha was asked if she had any documentation she had not sent in. She was not positive but didn't think so; mostly, she wanted to know why the counselor was asking. The counselor said that the only diagnostic tests given were from third grade. "Tests that old don't tell us much about your current needs and limitations," the counselor added.

"Weren't all of the IEPs and the evaluations from sixth and ninth grade sent?" Tabatha asked.

The counselor explained that neither of these evaluations contained any diagnostic tests (intelligence/aptitude, achievement, and cognitive process) used to diagnose a learning disability and determine its impact on adults. In addition, the ninth grade evaluation suggested that there were no longer any functional limitations since she was performing above grade level.

"I have always taken my tests with extra time!" Tabatha exclaimed. The counselor said that they would provide accommodations through January to allow her to update her documentation.

Tabatha left the meeting upset. She talked to her mother, who then went to speak to the counselor. The counselor repeated the explanations that he had given to Tabatha. Tabatha's mother then pointed to the 504 Plan and said that she was told 504 applied to colleges. Didn't the college have to accept Tabatha's 504 Plan?

The counselor said that a plan developed by a high school or even one from another college does not automatically apply. Eligibility at the college level is based on documentation demonstrating that there is a current substantial limitation and identifying current impacts or limitations that are connected to the accommodations requested. The counselor added that every college has some latitude in establishing what documentation it wants. The counselor referred Tabatha and her mother to the office Web site, where the college's documentation guidelines were published.

WHAT DO YOU NEED?

Tabatha's story highlights several critical points about documentation at the college level. Typically, an IEP or 504 Plan will not be sufficient. Depending on the age, approach, and level of details included in your last eligibility evaluation, it may not be enough. So what is enough?

What Does the Government Say?

The U.S. Department of Education's Office for Civil Rights, which is the primary enforcement agency for college access under Section 504 and the Americans with Disabilities Act (ADA), has produced an excellent booklet focused on the transition to college, entitled *Students with Disabilities Preparing for Postsecondary Education: Know Your Rights and Responsibilities* (http://www.ed.gov/ocr/transition.html). The points made about documentation are:

> "Schools may set reasonable standards for documentation. Some schools require more documentation than others. They may require you to provide documentation prepared by an appropriate professional, such as a medical doctor, psychologist, or other qualified diagnostician. The required documentation may include one or more of the following: a diagnosis of your current disability, the date of the diagnosis, how the diagnosis was reached, the credentials of the professional, how your disability affects a major life activity, and how the disability affects your academic performance. The documentation should provide enough information for you and your school to decide what is an appropriate academic adjustment.

> "Although an Individual Education Plan (IEP) or Section 504 Plan, if you have one, may help identify services that have been effective for you, it generally is not sufficient documentation. This is because postsecondary education presents different demands than high school education, and what you need to meet these new demands may be different. Also, in some cases, the nature of a disability may change.

> "If the documentation that you have does not meet the postsecondary school's requirements, a school official must tell you in a timely manner what additional documentation you need to provide. You may need a new evaluation in order to provide the required documentation."[1]

Six Elements of Comprehensive Documentation

Based on a review of decisions by the Office for Civil Rights, here are six core elements of documentation. You can use these elements to review existing documentation or to guide an evaluator in updating your documentation.

1. **A diagnostic statement identifying the condition(s).** Documentation should contain a clear statement identifying the disability. It is helpful if classification codes from the current editions of either the Diagnostic Statistical Manual (DSM) or the International Classifications of Disease (ICD) are included. The dates of the original diagnosis and any evaluations performed by referring professionals should be included, along with a date and description of the current evaluation being forwarded.

2. **Current functional impact of the condition(s).** The current functional impact on physical (including mobility dexterity, and endurance), perceptual, cognitive (including attention, distractibility, and communication), and behavioral abilities should be described as narrative. When formal or informal testing is used, the detailed results should be included. The combination of narrative and test results should provide a sense of severity, information on variability (over time, circumstance, or content), and potential environmental triggers.

3. **Treatments, medications, and assistive devices/services currently prescribed or in use.** This should include a description of treatments, medications, assistive devices, accommodations, and/or assistive services in current use and their estimated effectiveness in minimizing the impact of the condition(s). Also include any significant side effects that may impact physical, perceptual, behavioral, or cognitive performance.

4. **The expected progression or stability of the impacts described over time.** This description should provide an estimate of the change in the functional impacts of the condition(s) over time and/or recommendations concerning the predictable need for reevaluation of the condition(s). If the condition is variable

---

[1] U.S. Department of Education, Office for Civil Rights, *Students with Disabilities Preparing for Postsecondary Education: Know Your Rights and Responsibilities,* Washington, D.C., 2002.

(based on known cycles or environmental triggers), is the student under self-care for flare-ups or episodes?

5. **Recommended accommodations and services.** Recommendations should be logically connected to the impact of the condition. When connections are not obvious, they should be explained. Recommendations are not prescriptions and need to be evaluated by the college in the context of the student's academic program.

6. **Credentials of the evaluator.** If not clear from the letterhead or forms, the credentials of the evaluator should be included. If the evaluator's credentials are not those typically associated with diagnosis of the disability in question (for example, a general practitioner diagnosing attention deficit disorder), then a brief description of the evaluator's experience with this type of diagnosis should be included.

These six underlying elements for comprehensive documentation can be presented in a number of ways. You will recall that, according to the Office for Civil Rights, "Schools may set reasonable standards for documentation. Some schools require more documentation than others." So how do you know if your documentaion will be acceptable? If you know what colleges you are likely to attend, you should research their specific documentation requirements. Often, you can get these from the college's Web site. If you cannot find this information on the Web, you should contact the office and ask them to mail you a copy of their documentation guidelines. They will keep your request confidential.

The Highest Common Denominator

A psychoeducational battery consisting of standardized tests measuring aptitude, achievement, and cognitive processing is the most commonly accepted approach to identifying and quantifying the current functional impacts of a learning disability (the second of the six elements listed). Documentation containing such a battery is likely to meet the minimum standards for documentation at any institution and provides a foundation for anticipating accommodations in new settings and identifying compensatory strategies or tools you might use to minimize the impacts of your disability.

While the specific tests comprising a psychoeducational battery vary based on your educational history, there are five components that any complete battery should include:

1. **Adult referenced testing.** For tests relying on a norm or comparison group for interpretation, versions of the tests using an "adult" reference group may be considered necessary to show current impact (e.g., the Wechsler Adult Intelligence Scale vs. the Wechsler Intelligence Scale for Children). Typically, adult referenced tests begin to be administered around age 14.

2. **A measure of aptitude.** Commonly accepted aptitude measures include the Wechsler Adult Intelligence Scale, Woodcock-Johnson Psychoeducational Battery's Tests of Cognitive Ability, Kaufman Adolescent and Adult Intelligence Test, or Stanford-Binet Intelligence Scale.

3. **A standardized measure of academic achievement.** Commonly accepted achievement batteries include the Stanford Test of Academic Skills, Woodcock-Johnson Psycho-educational Battery's Tests of Achievement, and the Wechsler Individual Achievement Tests. An evaluation of achievement can also be based on a collection of measures focused on specific areas of achievement, such as the Nelson-Denny Reading Skills Test, the Stanford Diagnostic Mathematics Test, the Test of Written Language, or the Woodcock Reading Mastery Tests.

4. **Measures of cognitive processes impacted.** Standardized tests that measure cognitive processes, such as memory, perception, auditory and visual processing, processing speed, or executive functioning, that are affected by the condition should be included. Commonly used instruments include the Detroit Tests of Learning Aptitude, subtests on the Wechsler Adult Intelligence Scale, and the Woodcock-Johnson Psychoeducational Battery's Tests of Cognitive Ability.

5. **Clinical observations.** This includes a narrative provided by the professional administering the tests that discusses test choice, testing conditions, and the individual's behaviors during testing.

Alternatives

There are a number of approaches to evaluating a learning disability that do not include a traditional psychoeducational evaluation. For example, a growing number of evaluators are moving away from using aptitude/achievement discrepancies in diagnosing adults and do not include achievement testing. In addition, many public schools are moving toward observational evaluations and RTI (Response to Intervention) instead of evaluations based on psychometric tests.

What is often missing from the documentation provided by these alternative evaluation approaches is a clear and descriptive narrative of what was observed by the evaluator. For example, in the documentation provided by Tabatha, the evaluator indicated where observations were made (e.g., in the classroom), what was looked at (classroom testing, proficiency tests, etc.), and that she was no longer eligible for special education services but would have these accommodations under a 504 Plan. There were no descriptions of what was observed in her testing behaviors in response to testing conditions that indicated that extended time was needed. There was no discussion of what about her writing by hand supported the use of a computer as an aid. A rationale connecting observations to accommodations and services can provide colleges with the kind of information from which they need to work.

In order to receive accommodations, your documentation must demonstrate that you have a disability as defined by the ADA and Section 504: "A mental or physical impairment that substantially limits one or more of the major live activities..." (28 CFR Part 36, Sec. 104). It is important to remember that there are many cases where a learning disability, attention deficit disorder, or other condition is present and causes some difficulties but is not a substantial limitation. However, once the documentation has indicated that you have a disability, you are guaranteed equal treatment. For accommodations (extended testing time, books on tape, and other modifications or auxiliary aids), the documentation needs to identify current impacts of the disability that are rationally related to the requests you make.

L. Scott Lissner, M.A., is the University ADA Coordinator at The Ohio State University.

THROUGH THE EYES OF AN LD DIRECTOR: CRITICAL STEPS FOR COLLEGE SUCCESS

In one of many stories passed on throughout the ages, a local villager completed the arduous trek necessary to reach an esteemed Wise Man. The villager asked why one cannot cover the world in leather so one will never step on another thorn. The Wise Man replied, "There is no need to cover the world when one can achieve the same goal by covering the soles of one's feet with leather."

If students follow the advice dispensed by the many wise men and women located within collegiate support service offices, their transition to the postsecondary world will take shape without stepping on too many thorns.

K–12 THORNS

During the K–12 years, avoiding all academic thorns and simplifying all tasks to the lowest common denominator should be avoided when composing Individual Education Plans (IEP). Academic adjustments, auxiliary aids, and class selection must be based on clear and precise correlating strands stemming from comprehensive diagnostic evaluations. Having difficulty with particular course work in and of itself does not guarantee that antecedent variables stemming from a disability are in play. Cookie-cutter IEPs, in which the same set of accommodations is in place for all classes (a manifestation of the new generation of computerized, scantron-like IEPs), do not necessarily hold forth on the collegiate level. Collegiate support service personnel will not rubber-stamp high school IEPs.

Postgraduation summertime osmosis does not exist. Accommodations that maximized a student's potential in the high school world may disintegrate on the collegiate level. High school students who enjoyed 36 hours of teacher-driven class time and approximately 12 hours of at-home independent study each week must adapt to the mere 12 to 15 hours of collegiate professorial contact and budget 3 hours of study for each hour of class.

TRANSITIONING TO COLLEGE: SUMMER CLASSES

Families who expect the collegiate world to give carte blanche accommodations do have a litmus test. Summer classes offered throughout the country's two- and four-year postsecondary institutions are a wonderful venue to gauge a student's readiness for college. Enrolling in a summer class allows for a realistic shakedown of a student's skill base, alongside the possibility of parlaying the summer credits toward high school or postsecondary degrees. The compressed schedule of a summer class (typically, a sixteen-week class is completed in five to six weeks) ratchets up the workload to a level shadowing the time management and classroom skills necessary for a single class, surrounded by four additional courses within a standard fall/spring term. If the class is completed during the summer preceding the senior year, compensatory plans, based upon the summer class experience, can be developed and implemented throughout the student's final year in high school.

During the summer class, most students with learning disabilities discover the significant differences in the types of accommodations provided, the mode in which accommodations are carried out, and the new roles dictated to parents and students in the collegiate setting. If the student is planning to live on campus during college, it is important for parents to refrain from intervening during the summer school project, as parental structure will be nonexistent within the college dormitory setting. Students, not parents, are required to initiate contact with support service personnel in order to receive accommodations while concurrently creating lines of communication with faculty members.

STUDENT/FACULTY RELATIONSHIP

The student-faculty relationship is a cornerstone to a student's successful postsecondary transition. Faculty contact should be conducted within a faculty member's office during office hours, as impromptu discussions in the hall prior to or after class lack the confidentiality and time necessary for realistic advances with classroom material. Early in the semester (within the first week), students should hone in on information not detailed in the syllabus, which may pertain to specific accommodations they will be need. Academic accommodations will be based upon a range of variables, such as the types of exams to be administered. For example, if documentation supports the need for a word processor, this accommodation should be enlisted for an essay exam, but will have no relevance during a multiple-choice test. Throughout the semester, it is a good idea for students to discuss reading assignments prior to, not after, due dates with their professors. Most professors gladly review written assignments and return them with insightful feedback if they are handed in prior to the deadline (despite this extremely helpful point not usually being detailed on the syllabus).

COLLEGE COURSE SELECTION

Understanding a professor's teaching style and how it interacts with one's learning style makes the course selection process uniquely important, as inefficient class/ professor selection in and of itself can lead to a catastrophic transition process. This is a variable given scant consideration throughout the K–12 learning continuum. While multimodality teaching, utilizing listening, speaking, reading, and writing, is the buzzword during K–12 education, students are likely to encounter a college professor utilizing a single-modality format (lecture), especially when classes are held in a theater-sized lecture hall. Thus, a visual learner should, whenever possible, seek out a whiteboard aficionado, while an auditory learner should seek the comfort of a strictly auditory lecture hall platform.

A second piece of a student's learning style revolves around course requirements. A strong writer would certainly prefer a course requiring three papers, while a strong reader would long for three multiple-choice exams. Students should not be swayed by student feedback surrounding the perceived difficulty level of a professor, as the tough professor may have been evaluated by an individual with an opposing learning style.

Securing preferred classes requires advance planning. Most schools offer multiple orientation dates during the late spring or early summer months. Creating first-semester schedules is a component of most of these orientations. Students who attend the earliest orientation have the pick of the litter for choosing professors, while students attending the last session may find it difficult to create an optimal set of classes. If final exams, proms, or graduation conflicts with early orientation dates, student should ask if it is possible to register early and attend a later orientation.

The selection of courses (although, as many undergraduates point out, one selects professors, not courses) is an active, not passive, process. Collaboration with support service personnel will help make the selection process a success.

COURSE SUBSTITUTIONS

Students should not presume course substitutions will be an option, but they may inquire about the possibility of this academic adjustment. For example, say a student is accepted at Peterson's College and enrolls as a psychology major. As a junior, the student is required to complete a statistics course. Because documentation supplied to the support service office detailed a math disability, the student is convinced that a course substitution will be granted, and he will not be mandated to complete the statistics course. However, if Peterson's College deemed the statistics course to be an integral component of the psychology curriculum, the statistics course might be listed as a course ineligible for completion off campus and one that can never be substituted. The downside of neglecting a preadmission discussion on course substitutions is significant and may encompass changing majors or transferring to another school.

SUPPORT SERVICE OFFICE

Attending a comprehensive, structured program does not transfer all responsibilities from the student to the school. The student is the conduit between classroom and dormitory life and support service personnel. Time is everything when it comes to problem solving within the support service office. Most support service personnel are quite competent when it comes to solving problems that may arise, *if* the problems are brought to the support service personnel within 48 hours (or two class periods) of the mishap. For example, a student's note taker had the flu, and the student received no notes for the two-week period prior to an exam. The student believed the professor would automatically locate a replacement, while the support service office continued to assume all was well, as the note taker did not contact the office. The student took the exam, did poorly, and proceeded to complain to the support service office. If the student had contacted the professor or support service office in a timely manner, a substitute note taker would have been located and/or the test postponed.

Students should plan to visit the support service office during orientation or, if logistics allow, over the summer months prior to the start of classes. If students create a bond with the staff under a stress-free environment, there is a greater likelihood that those seeking assistance to remedy a problem in the midst of a semester will visit the support service office in a timely manner.

Ross Pollack, M.Ed., Ed.D., is Director of the Specialized Resource Center/ADA Coordinator at Manhattan College. He is one of four members of the New York State Department of Education's Standing Committee concerning the Task Force on Postsecondary Education and Disabilities.

DISABILITY SERVICES FORMS

Here are examples of two forms that are typically used by students with learning disabilities in college. The first is a checklist given to a newly admitted student by the college's Disability Services office. The second is an academic adjustment form to be given to a faculty member to request aids and/or academic adjustments for a specific class.

DISABILITY SERVICES INTAKE CHECKLIST

After you are admitted to the institution and have mailed in your deposit, you will need to begin your registration process for Disability Services.

❑ **1.** Contact DS to request an intake packet.

❑ **2.** Complete the information form and return it to the office with a copy of your documentation of your disability.

❑ **3.** When the intake form and documentation are received, DS will contact you with an update designating your file's status as approved or incomplete. Please be patient; we have many files to review.

❑ **4.** Once your file is "approved," call to schedule an intake appointment. This can be done at any time after the documentation is approved.

❑ **5.** At the intake appointment, you will
  - discuss the accommodations and services that you are eligible to use.
  - discuss the policies and procedures that you will need to follow in order to access your accommodations
  - discuss other possible resources that are available to you.

❑ **6.** Once you have registered for classes, you will
  - submit an Accommodation Request Form with your schedule to DS.
  - receive a copy of your accommodation letter to share with your professors.

❑ **7.** In college, **it is the student's responsibility to disclose his or her disability to instructors.** If you do not receive your accommodation letter at the intake appointment, it will be available to pick up within 72 hours of your appointment. This letter lists your accommodations for your courses.

  If you plan to disclose your disability to your professor(s) and use your accommodations in your class(es), then you must meet with your professor(s) to go over the accommodation letter with him or her.

  Depending on your accommodations, you may also be required to complete additional paperwork.

❑ **8.** Each semester, you need to complete a request form to obtain your accommodation letter. You can do this by turning in a hard copy of the form with an attached schedule. You will need to meet with a staff member if there are any changes to the accommodations.

You can meet with your DSS coordinator at any time throughout the semester to discuss your progress and your needs. Just call or send an e-mail to make an appointment.

SPECIALIZED RESOURCE CENTER (SRC)
Miguel Hall Room 300 / ext. 7101 or 7409 / FAX ext. 7808
ACADEMIC ADJUSTMENT/AUXILIARY AID FORM

FACULTY: Academic adjustments/auxiliary aids should not alter the integrity of your curricular components. The SRC counts on your input to maintain its efficacy, regarding the SRC's mandate to create an environment built on *equal access* for all students. The best plan of action is typically created during office hours, with a faculty member and student in attendance, without the intervention of the SRC; think of the academic adjustments/ auxiliary aids on this form as guideposts. ALL ADJUSTMENTS/AIDS ARE FOR THE CLASS AND SEMESTER SPECIFIED BELOW. PLEASE DO NOT CARRY OVER ADJUSTMENTS/AIDS TO OTHER CLASSES OR SEMESTERS.

PROFESSOR _____

COURSE _____

DATE _____ **SEMESTER** _____

The aforementioned student has provided documentation of a disability, which may affect his or her perfor- mance in your class. In accordance with federal laws, Section 504 of the 1973 Rehabilitation Act and the Americans with Disabilities Act (ADA), the following auxiliary aids and/or academic adjustments are requested:

_____ extended time (2X) for tests/quizzes   _____ dictionary or spell checker

_____ calculator   _____ reader

_____ scribe   _____ note-taker

_____ word processor

_____ other_____

_____ other_____

*   *   *   *   *   *

I understand the need to grant faculty two weeks notice for academic adjustments and auxiliary aids. Otherwise, it is not guaranteed the academic adjustments and auxiliary aids will be received on a timely basis.

_____   _____
student signature   date

I understand and agree with the academic adjustment(s)/auxiliary aid(s) listed above. I am aware that it is my responsibility to contact the SRC if there are any problems or concerns with the implementation of these items.

_____   _____
student signature   date

HOW TO USE THIS GUIDE

In the following pages you'll find detailed information about learning disabilities (LD) and attention deficit/hyperactivity disorder (AD/HD) programs and services at specific colleges. It should be noted that all institutions of higher learning offer accommodations as mandated by law, and they should be evaluated based on an individual's needs and interests. Any school considered a good fit should not necessarily be eliminated from consideration based on its non-inclusion in this guide. However, the schools that are profiled in this book have indicated that they offer more extensive services or accommodations above and beyond what is required by law.

The profiles are organized into two primary divisions: four-year colleges, followed by two-year colleges. These two primary divisions are further subdivided into Colleges with Structured/Proactive Programs—programs offering more comprehensive services for students with LD or AD/HD, and Colleges with Self-Directed/Decentralized Programs—programs that may be less structured but do still provide a considerable number of special services to students with LD or AD/HD. The four sections of individual college profiles are presented in this order: Four-Year Colleges with Structured/Proactive Programs; Four-Year Colleges with Self-Directed/Decentralized Programs; Two-Year Colleges with Structured/Proactive Programs; Two-Year Colleges with Self-Directed/Decentralized Programs.

STRUCTURED/PROACTIVE PROGRAMS VS. SELF-DIRECTED/ DECENTRALIZED PROGRAMS

Schools are classified as either Structured/Proactive or Self-Directed/Decentralized. Structured/Proactive Programs are more likely to have separate admissions processes and charge fees. These programs' services go well beyond those that are legally mandated, and the student is provided with a more structured environment that includes low staff-student ratios. Self-Directed/Decentralized Programs usually have no separate admissions processes, and eligibility for services must be established by the provision of disability documentation that meets institutional standards. Self-Directed/Decentralized Programs' services may be coordinated through the Disability Services Office and are based on need as specified by the student's documentation. Services may also be provided by other offices throughout the campus, and some services offered are not mandated by laws. In addition, student progress is usually not monitored.

While all programs offer students with appropriate documentation academic adjustments and auxiliary aids, utilizing these support mechanisms will vary, falling within these two distinct categories. Structured/Proactive Programs are intrinsically school-centered decision-making organizations, as compared to Self-Directed/Decentralized Programs where support service decisions remain within the students' domain. Students with a tendency to cocoon themselves or wait until the eleventh hour to seek assistance when faced with academically induced stress will find a comfort zone associated with Structured/Proactive Programs. Extra program fees, separate applications, and a limit to the number of students accepted into the program allow Structured/Proactive Programs to maintain a student-to-staff ratio indicative of a structured format. Students in a Self-Directed/Decentralized Program line the continuum of support services from once-a-semester visits for academic adjustments to daily visits in order to receive a more comprehensive level of support.

COLLEGE PROFILE LISTINGS

Each profile starts with the college name, address, and contact information. Additional information may include the following:

Learning Disabilities Program or Unit Information

Here you'll find the program or unit name (when provided by the school) and the number of students served by the program or unit during the 2006–07 academic year, followed by the numbers of full-time and/or part-time staff members. The providers of services to the students (academic advisers, coaches, counselors, diagnostic specialists, graduate assistants/students, LD specialists, professional tutors, regular education teachers, remediation/learning, skill tutors, strategy tutors, special education tutors, teacher trainees, and/or trained peer tutors), as well as whether the service is provided as part of the LD program or unit and/or through a collaborative provider located on or off campus, completes this section.

Orientation

Schools offering orientation for new undergraduate students with LD have the program's required or optional status, the length of the program, and when the special orientation occurs listed here.

Summer Program

Schools offering summer programs to help students prepare for the demands of college have the program's required or optional status, the length of the program, whether or not degree credit is earned, and to whom the program is available is listed here. The curriculum focus and cost may also appear.

Unique Aids and Services

Unique aids and services, which include advocates, career counseling, faculty training, parent workshops, a personal coach, priority registration, support groups, and weekly meetings with faculty are enumerated.

Subject-Area Tutoring

Subject-area tutoring, when available, is described as offered one-on-one, via small groups, and/or via class-size groups. Information is also provided on how the tutoring is provided (through the LD program or unit and/or collaboratively on- or off-campus) and how the tutoring is delivered (computer-based instruction, graduate, LD specialists, professional tutors, and trained peer tutors).

Assistive Technology

This section lists the types of assistive technology, such as digital textbooks/e-text, learning support software, and scanning, that are provided by the LD program or unit and where they are located in the school. It is also indicated whether technology training is provided to incoming students.

Diagnostic Testing

This section includes indications of diagnostic testing availability to undergraduate students through the LD program or unit and/or collaboratively on or off campus. The tests offered may include any of the following: auditory, handwriting, intelligence, learning strategies, learning styles, math, motor skills, neuropsychological, personality, reading, social skills, spelling, spoken language, study skills, written language, and visual processing.

Basic Skills Remediation

Basic skills remediation, when available, is described as offered one-on-one, via small groups, and/or via class-size groups. Information is also provided on how the basic skills remediation is provided (through the LD program or unit and/or collaboratively on or off campus) and how the basic skills remediation is delivered (computer-based instruction, graduate, LD specialists, professional tutors, regular education teachers, special education teachers, teacher trainees, and trained peer tutors). Basic skills remediation areas include auditory processing, computer skills, handwriting, learning strategies, math, motor skills, reading, social skills, spelling, spoken language, study skills, time management, visual processing, and written language.

Enrichment

Enrichment programs, when available, may be provided through the LD program or unit and/or collaboratively on or off campus. It will also be noted if the enrichment course/program is offered for credit. Enrichment programs include career planning, college survival skills, health and nutrition, learning strategies, math, medication management, oral communication skills, practical computer skills, reading, self-advocacy, stress management, study skills, test-taking, time management, vocabulary development, and written composition skills.

Student Organization

The name of any student organization for students with LD and the number of undergraduate student members are displayed here.

Fees

Listed here, if applicable, are costs (and reasons for variances) for non-mandated services, summer programs, orientation, and diagnostic testing.

Application

Information is given here pertaining to additional registration components, whether they are required or recommended for participation in the program or unit, and to whom the information should be sent upon application and upon acceptance. Deadlines for applying to the program or unit are also provided.

Written Policies

This section lists where students can find official policies regarding general/basic LD accommodations, substitutions and waivers of admissions requirements, substitutions and waivers of graduation requirements, course substitutions, reduced course loads, and grade forgiveness.

CRITERIA FOR INCLUSION IN THIS BOOK

To be included in this guide, an institution must have full accreditation or be a candidate for accreditation (preaccreditation) status by an institutional or specialized accrediting body recognized by the U.S. Department of Education or the Council for Higher Education Accreditation (CHEA). Institutional accrediting bodies, which review each institution as a whole, include the six regional associations of schools and colleges (Middle States, New England, North Central, Northwest, Southern, and Western), each of which is responsible for a specified portion of the United States and its territories. Other institutional accrediting bodies are national in scope and accredit specific kinds of institutions (e.g., Bible colleges, independent colleges, and rabbinical and Talmudic schools). Program registration by the New York State Board of Regents is considered to be the equivalent of institutional accreditation, since the board requires that all programs offered by an institution meet its standards before recognition is granted. A Canadian institution must be chartered and authorized to grant degrees by the provincial government, affiliated with a chartered institution, or accredited by a recognized U.S. accrediting body This guide also includes institutions outside the United States that are accredited by these U.S. accrediting bodies. There are recognized specialized or professional accrediting bodies in more than forty different fields, each of which is authorized to accredit institutions for specific programs in its particular field. For specialized institutions that offer programs in one field only, we designate this to be the equivalent of institutional accreditation. A full explanation of the accrediting process and complete information on recognized, institutional (regional and national) and specialized accrediting bodies can be found online at www.chea.org or at www.ed.gov/admins/finaid/accred/index.html.

RESEARCH PROCEDURES

The data contained in the **College Profile Listings** were researched between spring and summer 2007 through Peterson's Learning Disabilities Online Survey. Questionnaires were sent to the more than 3,800 colleges that meet the criteria for inclusion in this guide. All data included in this edition have been submitted by officials (usually admission officers, institutional research personnel, or LD program coordinators) at the colleges themselves. All usable information received in time for publication has been included. The omission of any particular item from a profile listing signifies that either the item is not applicable to that institution or that data were not available. Because of the comprehensive editorial review that takes place in our offices and because all material comes directly from college officials, Peterson's has every reason to believe that the information presented in this guide is accurate at the time of printing. However, students should check with a specific college or university at the time of application to verify data, which may have changed since the publication of this volume.

PROFILES OF COLLEGE
LD PROGRAMS

FOUR-YEAR COLLEGES WITH STRUCTURED/PROACTIVE PROGRAMS

Adelphi University
Learning Disabilities Program

One South Avenue

PO Box 701

Garden City, NY 11530-0701

http://academics.adelphi.edu/ldprog/

Contact: Susan Spencer, Assistant Dean and Director. Phone: 516-877-4710. Fax: 516-877-4711. E-mail: ldprogram@adelphi.edu.

Learning Disabilities Program Approximately 140 registered undergraduate students were served during 2006–07. The program or unit includes 16 full-time staff members. Academic advisers, counselors, LD specialists, professional tutors, remediation/learning specialists, skill tutors, special education teachers, and strategy tutors are provided through the program or unit. Academic advisers are provided collaboratively through on-campus or off-campus services.

Orientation The program or unit offers a mandatory 5-week orientation for new students during summer prior to enrollment.

Summer Program To help prepare for the demands of college, there is a mandatory 5-week summer program prior to entering the school available to high school graduates that focuses on life skills and/or college life adjustment, self-advocacy, study skills, test-taking skills, and time management. Degree credit will be earned. The program accepts students from out-of-state.

Unique Aids and Services Aids, services, or accommodations include faculty training, parent workshops, priority registration, support groups, counseling.

Assistive Technology Assistive technology is located in campus labs, the DSS office, a special lab and includes digital textbooks/e-text, learning support software, and scanning. Technology training is provided to incoming students.

Subject-Area Tutoring Tutoring is offered in small groups for most subjects. Tutoring is provided collaboratively through on-campus or off-campus services via computer-based instruction, graduate assistants/students, and trained peer tutors.

Diagnostic Testing Testing is provided through the program or unit for learning strategies, learning styles, reading, and written language. Testing for auditory processing, intelligence, neuropsychological, personality, and visual processing is provided collaboratively through on-campus or off-campus services.

Basic Skills Remediation Remediation is offered one-on-one for learning strategies, study skills, time management, and written language. Remediation is provided through the program or unit via LD specialists, special education teachers, and other.

Enrichment Enrichment programs are available through the program or unit for career planning, college survival skills, learning strategies, oral communication skills, self-advocacy, stress management, study skills, test taking, time management, vocabulary development, and written composition skills. Programs for career planning, college survival skills, math, and practical computer skills are provided collaboratively through on-campus or off-campus services.

Fees *LD Program or Service* fee is $6000. *Summer Program* fee is $1700. *Orientation* fee is $1700.

Application For admittance to the program or unit, students are required to apply to the program directly, provide a psychoeducational report (2 years old or less), provide documentation of high school services, and provide a comprehensive diagnostic report. Upon application, materials documenting need for services should be sent only to the LD program or unit. Upon acceptance, documentation of need for services should be sent only to the LD program or unit. *Application deadline (institutional):* Continuous. *Application deadline (LD program):* 3/1 for fall. Rolling/continuous for spring.

Written Policies Written policies regarding general/basic LD accommodations and substitutions and waivers of admissions requirements are available on the program Web site. Written policies regarding course substitutions, general/basic LD accommodations, reduced course loads, and substitutions and waivers of admissions requirements are available through the program or unit directly.

Alliance University College

630, 833-4th Avenue SW

Calgary, AB T2P 3T5

Canada

http://www.auc-nuc.ca/

Contact: Terry G. Symes, Learning Services Coordinator. Phone: 403-410-2000 Ext. 2937. Fax: 403-571-2556. E-mail: tsymes@auc-nuc.ca.

Approximately 25 registered undergraduate students were served during 2006–07. The program or unit includes 1 full-time staff member. Academic advisers, counselors, diagnostic specialists, LD specialists, professional tutors, regular education teachers, remediation/learning specialists, skill tutors, strategy tutors, and trained peer tutors are provided through the program or unit.

Orientation The program or unit offers an optional 1-day orientation for new students before registration, before classes begin, during summer prior to enrollment, during registration, after classes begin, and individually by special arrangement.

Unique Aids and Services Aids, services, or accommodations include advocates, career counseling, support groups, and weekly meetings with faculty.

Assistive Technology Assistive technology is located in a special lab and includes digital textbooks/e-text, learning support software, and scanning. Technology training is provided to incoming students.

Subject-Area Tutoring Tutoring is offered one-on-one and in small groups for most subjects. Tutoring is provided through the program or unit via computer-based instruction, LD specialists, professional tutors, and trained peer tutors. Tutoring is also provided collaboratively through on-campus or off-campus services via graduate assistants/students.

Diagnostic Testing Testing is provided through the program or unit for handwriting, intelligence, learning strategies, learning styles, math, personality, reading, social skills, spelling, spoken language, study skills, and written language. Testing for auditory processing, motor skills, neuropsychological, and visual processing is provided collaboratively through on-campus or off-campus services.

Basic Skills Remediation Remediation is offered one-on-one and in small groups for handwriting, learning strategies, math, reading, spelling, spoken language, study skills, and time management. Remediation is provided through the program or unit via LD specialists, professional tutors, and trained peer tutors.

Enrichment Enrichment programs are available through the program or unit for college survival skills, health and nutrition, learning strategies, math, oral communication skills, reading, self-

Alliance University College (continued)

advocacy, stress management, study skills, test taking, time management, and vocabulary development. Programs for career planning, oral communication skills, and written composition skills are provided collaboratively through on-campus or off-campus services.

Application For admittance to the program or unit, students are required to provide documentation of high school services. It is recommended that students provide a psychoeducational report (4 years old or less). Upon application, materials documenting need for services should be sent only to the LD program or unit. Upon acceptance, documentation of need for services should be sent only to the LD program or unit. *Application deadline (LD program):* Rolling/continuous for fall and rolling/continuous for spring.

Written Policies Written policies regarding general/basic LD accommodations and reduced course loads are available through the program or unit directly.

American International College
Supportive Learning Services

1000 State Street

Springfield, MA 01109-3189

http://www.aic.edu/

Contact: Mrs. Anne M. Midura, Office Manager. Phone: 413-205-3426. Fax: 413-205-3908. E-mail: anne.midura@ aic.edu. Head of LD Program: Prof. Mary M. Saltus, Coordinator. Phone: 413-205-3426. Fax: 413-204-3908. E-mail: mary.saltus@aic.edu.

Supportive Learning Services Approximately 95 registered undergraduate students were served during 2006–07. The program or unit includes 12 full-time staff members. LD specialists and professional tutors are provided through the program or unit.

Orientation The program or unit offers a mandatory 2-hour orientation for new students during the college orientation.

Subject-Area Tutoring Tutoring is offered one-on-one and in small groups for all subjects. Tutoring is provided through the program or unit via LD specialists and professional tutors.

Enrichment Enrichment programs are available through the program or unit for learning strategies, study skills, test taking, time management, and written composition skills. Programs for career planning, college survival skills, and written composition skills are provided collaboratively through on-campus or off-campus services. Credit is offered for college survival skills.

Fees *LD Program or Service* fee is $395 to $3171 (fee varies according to level/tier of service).

Application For admittance to the program or unit, students are required to provide a psychoeducational report (3 years old or less), provide documentation of high school services, and provide documentation of skill level testing. Upon application, materials documenting need for services should be sent only to the LD program or unit. *Application deadline (institutional):* Continuous. *Application deadline (LD program):* Rolling/continuous for fall and rolling/continuous for spring.

Written Policies Written policy regarding reduced course loads is outlined in the school's catalog/handbook. Written policy regarding general/basic LD accommodations is available through the program or unit directly.

American University
Academic Support Center

4400 Massachusetts Avenue, NW

Washington, DC 20016-8001

http://www.american.edu/asc

Contact: Ms. Nancy Sydnor-Greenberg, Coordinator, Learning Services Program. Phone: 202-885-3360. Fax: 202-885-1042. E-mail: asc@american.edu. Head of LD Program: Kathy Schwartz Kathy Schwartz, Director, Academic Support Center. Phone: 202-885-3360. Fax: 202-885-1042. E-mail: asc@american.edu.

Academic Support Center Approximately 300 registered undergraduate students were served during 2006–07. The program or unit includes 6 full-time and 6 part-time staff members. Graduate assistants/students, LD specialists, and trained peer tutors are provided through the program or unit. Academic advisers are provided collaboratively through on-campus or off-campus services.

Unique Aids and Services Aids, services, or accommodations include priority registration.

Assistive Technology Assistive technology is located in campus labs, the DSS office and includes digital textbooks/e-text and scanning. Technology training is provided to incoming students.

Subject-Area Tutoring Tutoring is offered one-on-one for all subjects. Tutoring is provided collaboratively through on-campus or off-campus services via trained peer tutors.

Enrichment Enrichment programs are available through the program or unit for college survival skills, learning strategies, reading, self-advocacy, study skills, test taking, time management, and written composition skills. Programs for career planning, math, medication management, and stress management are provided collaboratively through on-campus or off-campus services.

Fees *LD Program or Service* fee is $2000 (fee varies according to level/tier of service).

Application For admittance to the program or unit, students are required to apply to the program directly and provide a psychoeducational or neuropsychological report. Upon application, materials documenting need for services should be sent only to the LD program or unit. Upon acceptance, documentation of need for services should be sent only to the LD program or unit. *Application deadline (institutional):* 1/15. *Application deadline (LD program):* 1/15 for fall.

Written Policies Written policy regarding general/basic LD accommodations is available on the program Web site. Written policy regarding general/basic LD accommodations is outlined in the school's catalog/handbook. Written policies regarding general/basic LD accommodations and substitutions and waivers of admissions requirements are available through the program or unit directly.

Barry University
The Center for Advanced Learning Program (CAL)

11300 Northeast Second Avenue

Miami Shores, FL 33161-6695

http://www.barry.edu/

Contact: Ms. Kim Martinez, Coordinator of Center for Advanced Learning Program. Phone: 305-899-3461. Fax: 305-899-3778. E-mail: kmartinez@mail.barry.edu.

The Center for Advanced Learning Program (CAL) Approximately 45 registered undergraduate students were served during 2006–07. The program or unit includes 1 full-time and 15 part-time staff members. Academic advisers, counselors, LD specialists, and professional tutors are provided through the program or unit. Academic advisers and diagnostic specialists are provided collaboratively through on-campus or off-campus services.

Orientation The program or unit offers a mandatory half-day orientation for new students before classes begin.

Unique Aids and Services Aids, services, or accommodations include advocates, career counseling, and priority registration.

Subject-Area Tutoring Tutoring is offered one-on-one and in small groups for most subjects. Tutoring is provided through the program or unit via professional tutors.

Diagnostic Testing Testing is provided through the program or unit for learning strategies, learning styles, and study skills.

Basic Skills Remediation Remediation is offered in class-size groups for computer skills, math, reading, study skills, time management, and written language. Remediation is provided through the program or unit.

Enrichment Enrichment programs are available through the program or unit for career planning, college survival skills, learning strategies, stress management, study skills, test taking, and time management. Programs for career planning, math, stress management, study skills, test taking, time management, vocabulary development, and written composition skills are provided collaboratively through on-campus or off-campus services. Credit is offered for college survival skills, learning strategies, study skills, test taking, and time management.

Fees *LD Program or Service* fee is $6000.

Application For admittance to the program or unit, students are required to apply to the program directly, provide a psychoeducational report (3 years old or less), provide documentation of high school services, and provide a letter of recommendation, personal statement, and have a personal interview. Upon application, materials documenting need for services should be sent only to the LD program or unit. Upon acceptance, documentation of need for services should be sent only to the LD program or unit. *Application deadline (institutional):* Continuous. *Application deadline (LD program):* 8/15 for fall. 12/15 for spring.

Written Policies Written policies regarding course substitutions and general/basic LD accommodations are available on the program Web site. Written policies regarding course substitutions and general/basic LD accommodations are outlined in the school's catalog/handbook. Written policies regarding course substitutions and general/basic LD accommodations are available through the program or unit directly.

Beacon College
Office of Academic Affairs

105 East Main Street

Leesburg, FL 34748

http://www.beaconcollege.edu

Contact: Admissions Office. Phone: 352-787-7249. Fax: 352-787-0721. E-mail: admissions@beaconcollege.edu. Head of LD Program: Dr. Johnny Good, Vice President of Academic Affairs. Phone: 352-787-2193. Fax: 352-787-0721. E-mail: jgood@beaconcollege.edu.

Office of Academic Affairs Approximately 112 registered undergraduate students were served during 2006–07. The program or unit includes 35 full-time staff members. Academic advisers, counselors, LD specialists, professional tutors, regular education teachers, remediation/learning specialists, skill tutors, special education teachers, and strategy tutors are provided through the program or unit. Academic advisers, counselors, LD specialists, professional tutors, regular education teachers, remediation/learning specialists, skill tutors, special education teachers, and strategy tutors are provided collaboratively through on-campus or off-campus services.

Orientation The program or unit offers a mandatory orientation for new students before classes begin, after classes begin, and as part of College Success Class.

Summer Program an optional summer program prior to entering the school.

Unique Aids and Services Aids, services, or accommodations include advocates, career counseling, faculty training, parent workshops, personal coach, support groups, and weekly meetings with faculty.

Assistive Technology Assistive technology is located in campus labs, the Mentoring Center and includes digital textbooks/e-text, learning support software, and scanning. Technology training is provided to incoming students.

Subject-Area Tutoring Tutoring is offered one-on-one, in small groups, and in class-size groups for all subjects. Tutoring is provided through the program or unit via computer-based instruction, LD specialists, and professional tutors. Tutoring is also provided collaboratively through on-campus or off-campus services via computer-based instruction, LD specialists, and professional tutors.

Basic Skills Remediation Remediation is offered one-on-one, in small groups, and in class-size groups for auditory processing, computer skills, handwriting, learning strategies, math, motor skills, reading, social skills, spelling, spoken language, study skills, time management, visual processing, and written language. Remediation is provided through the program or unit via computer-based instruction, LD specialists, professional tutors, regular education teachers, and special education teachers. Remediation is also provided collaboratively through on-campus or off-campus services via computer-based instruction, LD specialists, professional tutors, regular education teachers, and special education teachers.

Enrichment Enrichment programs are available through the program or unit for career planning, college survival skills, health and nutrition, learning strategies, math, oral communication skills, practical computer skills, reading, self-advocacy, stress management, study skills, test taking, time management, vocabulary development, and written composition skills. Programs for career planning, college survival skills, health and nutrition, learning strategies, math, oral communication skills, practical computer skills, reading, self-

Beacon College (continued)

advocacy, stress management, study skills, test taking, time management, vocabulary development, and written composition skills are provided collaboratively through on-campus or off-campus services. Credit is offered for career planning, health and nutrition, math, oral communication skills, practical computer skills, reading, vocabulary development, and written composition skills.

Application For admittance to the program or unit, students are required to provide a psychoeducational report (3 years old or less) and provide WAIS. Upon application, materials documenting need for services should be sent only to admissions with institutional application materials. Upon acceptance, documentation of need for services should be sent only to admissions. *Application deadline (LD program):* Rolling/continuous for fall and rolling/continuous for spring.

Written Policies Written policy regarding general/basic LD accommodations is available on the program Web site. Written policies regarding course substitutions, general/basic LD accommodations, grade forgiveness, reduced course loads, substitutions and waivers of admissions requirements, and substitutions and waivers of graduation requirements are outlined in the school's catalog/handbook.

Brenau University
Learning Center

500 Washington Street SE

Gainesville, GA 30501

http://www.brenau.edu/learningcenter

Contact: Dr. Vincent Jeffrey Yamilkoski, Professor of Education and Director of Learning Disabilities. Phone: 770-534-6134. Fax: 770-297-5883. E-mail: vyamilkoski@lib.brenau.edu.

Learning Center Approximately 40 registered undergraduate students were served during 2006–07. The program or unit includes 2 full-time and 12 part-time staff members. Academic advisers, coaches, LD specialists, professional tutors, remediation/learning specialists, skill tutors, and strategy tutors are provided through the program or unit. Academic advisers, counselors, and diagnostic specialists are provided collaboratively through on-campus or off-campus services.

Orientation The program or unit offers a mandatory 1-hour orientation for new students during registration.

Unique Aids and Services Aids, services, or accommodations include advocates, career counseling, faculty training, personal coach, priority registration, and support groups.

Assistive Technology Assistive technology includes digital textbooks/e-text and scanning.

Subject-Area Tutoring Tutoring is offered one-on-one for all subjects. Tutoring is provided through the program or unit via LD specialists and professional tutors. Tutoring is also provided collaboratively through on-campus or off-campus services via computer-based instruction.

Diagnostic Testing Testing for auditory processing, intelligence, learning strategies, learning styles, math, personality, reading, social skills, spelling, spoken language, and written language is provided collaboratively through on-campus or off-campus services.

Basic Skills Remediation Remediation is offered one-on-one for auditory processing, computer skills, learning strategies, math, reading, spoken language, study skills, time management, visual processing, and written language. Remediation is provided through the program or unit via LD specialists and professional tutors.

Enrichment Enrichment programs are available through the program or unit for college survival skills, learning strategies, math, oral communication skills, practical computer skills, reading, self-advocacy, stress management, study skills, test taking, time management, vocabulary development, and written composition skills. Programs for career planning, college survival skills, health and nutrition, math, medication management, practical computer skills, stress management, study skills, test taking, time management, and written composition skills are provided collaboratively through on-campus or off-campus services. Credit is offered for college survival skills, learning strategies, practical computer skills, and study skills.

Student Organization Brenau Organization for Learning Disabilities (BOLD) consists of 10 members.

Fees *LD Program or Service* fee is $900 to $5400 (fee varies according to level/tier of service). *Diagnostic Testing* fee is $400.

Application For admittance to the program or unit, students are required to provide a psychoeducational report (3 years old or less). It is recommended that students provide documentation of high school services. Upon application, materials documenting need for services should be sent only to admissions with institutional application materials. Upon acceptance, documentation of need for services should be sent only to the LD program or unit. *Application deadline (institutional):* Continuous. *Application deadline (LD program):* Rolling/continuous for fall and rolling/continuous for spring.

Written Policies Written policies regarding general/basic LD accommodations and reduced course loads are available on the program Web site. Written policies regarding general/basic LD accommodations and substitutions and waivers of admissions requirements are outlined in the school's catalog/handbook. Written policies regarding general/basic LD accommodations and reduced course loads are available through the program or unit directly.

College of Mount St. Joseph
Project EXCEL

5701 Delhi Road

Cincinnati, OH 45233-1670

http://www.msj.edu/academics/departments/excel

Contact: Jane Pohlman, Director of Project EXCEL. Phone: 513-244-4623. Fax: 513-244-4222. E-mail: jane_pohlman@mail.msj.edu.

Project EXCEL Approximately 108 registered undergraduate students were served during 2006–07. The program or unit includes 6 full-time and 11 part-time staff members. Academic advisers, LD specialists, and professional tutors are provided through the program or unit. Academic advisers and counselors are provided collaboratively through on-campus or off-campus services.

Orientation The program or unit offers a mandatory 1-semester orientation for new students during the fall semester of the freshman year (in the form of a course, EXC 103).

Assistive Technology Assistive technology is located in campus labs, the DSS office and includes scanning.

Subject-Area Tutoring Tutoring is offered one-on-one and in small groups for most subjects. Tutoring is provided through the program or unit via computer-based instruction, LD specialists, and professional tutors.

Basic Skills Remediation Remediation is offered one-on-one and in small groups for computer skills, learning strategies, math, study skills, time management, and written language. Remediation is provided through the program or unit via computer-based instruction, LD specialists, and professional tutors.

Enrichment Enrichment programs are available through the program or unit for college survival skills, learning strategies, math, reading, self-advocacy, study skills, test taking, time management, and written composition skills. Programs for career planning, health and nutrition, math, practical computer skills, stress management, and written composition skills are provided collaboratively through on-campus or off-campus services. Credit is offered for career planning, learning strategies, math, practical computer skills, study skills, and written composition skills.

Fees *LD Program or Service* fee is $1700 to $3500 (fee varies according to level/tier of service).

Application For admittance to the program or unit, students are required to apply to the program directly and provide a psychoeducational report (3 years old or less). It is recommended that students provide documentation of high school services. Upon application, materials documenting need for services should be sent only to the LD program or unit. Upon acceptance, documentation of need for services should be sent only to the LD program or unit. *Application deadline (institutional): 8/15. Application deadline (LD program):* Rolling/continuous for fall and rolling/continuous for spring.

Written Policies Written policy regarding general/basic LD accommodations is available on the program Web site. Written policy regarding general/basic LD accommodations is available through the program or unit directly.

Concordia College–New York
Concordia Connection

171 White Plains Road

Bronxville, NY 10708-1998

http://www.concordia.onlinecommunity.com/
attendingconcordia/ldstudents.htm

Contact: Dr. George Groth, Director of Concordia Connection. Phone: 914-337-9300 Ext. 2361. Fax: 914-395-4500. E-mail: ghg@concordia-ny.edu.

Concordia Connection Approximately 32 registered undergraduate students were served during 2006–07. The program or unit includes 1 full-time and 4 part-time staff members. Counselors, LD specialists, skill tutors, special education teachers, and strategy tutors are provided through the program or unit.

Orientation The program or unit offers a mandatory 1-day orientation for new students before classes begin.

Unique Aids and Services Aids, services, or accommodations include career counseling and support groups.

Subject-Area Tutoring Tutoring is offered one-on-one and in small groups for most subjects. Tutoring is provided through the program or unit via LD specialists, professional tutors, and trained peer tutors. Tutoring is also provided collaboratively through on-campus or off-campus services via trained peer tutors.

Diagnostic Testing Testing is provided through the program or unit for learning strategies, learning styles, math, personality, reading, social skills, spelling, study skills, and written language.

Basic Skills Remediation Remediation is offered one-on-one and in small groups for learning strategies, math, reading, study skills, time management, and written language. Remediation is provided through the program or unit via LD specialists, professional tutors, special education teachers, and trained peer tutors.

Enrichment Enrichment programs are available through the program or unit for college survival skills, stress management, study skills, time management, and written composition skills.

Fees *LD Program or Service* fee is $2750 to $5500 (fee varies according to level/tier of service).

Application For admittance to the program or unit, students are required to provide a psychoeducational report and provide documentation of high school services. Upon application, materials documenting need for services should be sent only to admissions with institutional application materials. Upon acceptance, documentation of need for services should be sent only to admissions. *Application deadline (institutional): 3/15. Application deadline (LD program):* Rolling/continuous for fall and rolling/continuous for spring.

Written Policies Written policies regarding course substitutions, general/basic LD accommodations, reduced course loads, substitutions and waivers of admissions requirements, and substitutions and waivers of graduation requirements are available through the program or unit directly.

Edinboro University of Pennsylvania
Office for Students with Disabilities

Edinboro, PA 16444

http://www.edinboro.edu/

Contact: Ms. Kathleen K. Strosser, Assistant Director of Office for Students with Disabilities. Phone: 814-732-1399. Fax: 814-732-1120. E-mail: strosser@edinboro.edu.

Office for Students with Disabilities Approximately 235 registered undergraduate students were served during 2006–07. The program or unit includes 2 full-time and 2 part-time staff members. Academic advisers, graduate assistants/students, LD specialists, and other are provided through the program or unit. Academic advisers and counselors are provided collaboratively through on-campus or off-campus services.

Unique Aids and Services Aids, services, or accommodations include priority registration.

Assistive Technology Assistive technology is located in the DSS office and includes learning support software.

Subject-Area Tutoring Tutoring is offered in small groups for some subjects. Tutoring is provided collaboratively through on-campus or off-campus services via trained peer tutors.

Edinboro University of Pennsylvania (continued)

Basic Skills Remediation Remediation is offered one-on-one for learning strategies, study skills, time management, and written language. Remediation is provided through the program or unit via graduate assistants/students, professional tutors, and trained peer tutors.

Enrichment Enrichment programs are available through the program or unit for self-advocacy, study skills, test taking, time management, and written composition skills. Programs for career planning, college survival skills, and health and nutrition are provided collaboratively through on-campus or off-campus services.

Student Organization Delta Alpha Pi Honor Society consists of 30 members.

Fees *LD Program or Service* fee is $306 to $876 (fee varies according to level/tier of service).

Application For admittance to the program or unit, students are required to provide a psychoeducational report (3 years old or less). It is recommended that students provide documentation of high school services. Upon application, materials documenting need for services should be sent to both admissions and the LD program or unit. Upon acceptance, documentation of need for services should be sent only to the LD program or unit. *Application deadline (institutional):* 4/1. *Application deadline (LD program):* Rolling/continuous for fall and rolling/continuous for spring.

Written Policies Written policies regarding course substitutions and general/basic LD accommodations are available through the program or unit directly.

Fairleigh Dickinson University, College at Florham

The Regional Center for College Students with Learning Disabilities

285 Madison Avenue

Madison, NJ 07940-1099

http://www.fdu.edu/studentsvcs/rcsld.html

Contact: Mrs. Grace Hottinger, Admissions Coordinator. Phone: 201-692-2087. Fax: 201-692-2813. E-mail: graceh@fdu.edu. Head of LD Program: Dr. Mary Lupiani Farrell, Project Director. Phone: 201-692-2087. Fax: 201-692-2813. E-mail: farrell@fdu.edu.

The Regional Center for College Students with Learning Disabilities Approximately 150 registered undergraduate students were served during 2006–07. The program or unit includes 7 full-time and 2 part-time staff members. Counselors, LD specialists, professional tutors, remediation/learning specialists, skill tutors, and strategy tutors are provided through the program or unit. LD specialists and professional tutors are provided collaboratively through on-campus or off-campus services.

Summer Program To help prepare for the demands of college, there is an optional 2-week summer program prior to entering the school available to rising seniors, high school graduates that focuses on computing skills, study skills, test-taking skills, and time management. The program is available to students attending other colleges.

Unique Aids and Services Aids, services, or accommodations include career counseling and priority registration.

Assistive Technology Assistive technology is located in campus labs, a special lab and includes digital textbooks/e-text and learning support software. Technology training is provided to incoming students.

Subject-Area Tutoring Tutoring is offered in small groups for most subjects. Tutoring is provided through the program or unit via LD specialists and professional tutors. Tutoring is also provided collaboratively through on-campus or off-campus services via LD specialists and professional tutors.

Diagnostic Testing Testing is provided through the program or unit for auditory processing, intelligence, learning strategies, math, motor skills, reading, spelling, spoken language, study skills, visual processing, and written language.

Basic Skills Remediation Remediation is offered in small groups for math, reading, study skills, time management, and written language. Remediation is provided through the program or unit via LD specialists and special education teachers.

Enrichment Enrichment programs are available through the program or unit for career planning, college survival skills, learning strategies, practical computer skills, self-advocacy, study skills, test taking, time management, and written composition skills. Credit is offered for learning strategies, self-advocacy, and study skills.

Fees *Summer Program* fee is $800.

Application For admittance to the program or unit, students are required to apply to the program directly, provide a psychoeducational report (2 years old or less), and provide documentation of high school services. Upon application, materials documenting need for services should be sent only to the LD program or unit. Upon acceptance, documentation of need for services should be sent only to the LD program or unit. *Application deadline (institutional):* Continuous. *Application deadline (LD program):* Rolling/continuous for fall and rolling/continuous for spring.

Written Policies Written policies regarding course substitutions, general/basic LD accommodations, grade forgiveness, reduced course loads, substitutions and waivers of admissions requirements, and substitutions and waivers of graduation requirements are available through the program or unit directly.

Fairleigh Dickinson University, Metropolitan Campus

Regional Center for College Students with Learning Disabilities

1000 River Road

Teaneck, NJ 07666-1914

http://www.fdu.edu/studentsvcs/rcsld.html

Contact: Mr. Vincent John Varrassi, Campus Director: Metropolitan Campus, Teaneck, NJ. Phone: 201-692-2716. Fax: 201-692-2813. E-mail: varrassi@fdu.edu. Head of LD Program: Dr. Mary Lupiani Farrell, Project Director/University Director. Phone: 201-692-2716. Fax: 201-692-2716. E-mail: graceh@fdu.edu.

Regional Center for College Students with Learning Disabilities Approximately 64 registered undergraduate students were served during 2006–07. The program or unit includes 4 full-time and 3 part-time staff members. LD specialists, professional tutors, and special education teachers are provided through the program or unit.

Orientation The program or unit offers a mandatory 1-day orientation for new students before registration.

Summer Program To help prepare for the demands of college, there is an optional 2-week (day only) summer program prior to entering the school available to rising seniors, high school graduates that focuses on self-advocacy, study skills, and time management. The program is available to students attending other colleges.

Unique Aids and Services Aids, services, or accommodations include faculty training and priority registration.

Assistive Technology Assistive technology is located in campus labs, a special lab and includes digital textbooks/e-text, scanning, and text-to-speech software. Technology training is provided to incoming students.

Subject-Area Tutoring Tutoring is offered in small groups for some subjects. Tutoring is provided through the program or unit via LD specialists and professional tutors. Tutoring is also provided collaboratively through on-campus or off-campus services via LD specialists and professional tutors.

Diagnostic Testing Testing is provided through the program or unit for auditory processing, intelligence, learning strategies, math, neuropsychological, reading, spelling, spoken language, study skills, visual processing, and written language.

Basic Skills Remediation Remediation is offered in small groups for learning strategies, math, reading, time management, and written language. Remediation is provided through the program or unit via LD specialists and professional tutors.

Enrichment Enrichment programs are available through the program or unit for college survival skills, learning strategies, practical computer skills, self-advocacy, study skills, test taking, time management, and written composition skills. Programs for career planning, math, medication management, reading, and stress management are provided collaboratively through on-campus or off-campus services. Credit is offered for learning strategies and study skills.

Fees *Diagnostic Testing* fee is applicable.

Application For admittance to the program or unit, students are required to apply to the program directly, provide a psychoeducational report (2 years old or less), and provide documentation of high school services. Upon application, materials documenting need for services should be sent only to the LD program or unit. Upon acceptance, documentation of need for services should be sent only to the LD program or unit. *Application deadline (institutional):* Continuous. *Application deadline (LD program):* Rolling/continuous for fall and rolling/continuous for spring.

Written Policies Written policies regarding course substitutions, general/basic LD accommodations, grade forgiveness, reduced course loads, substitutions and waivers of admissions requirements, and substitutions and waivers of graduation requirements are available through the program or unit directly.

Gannon University
Program for Students with Learning Disabilities (PSLD)

University Square
Erie, PA 16541-0001
http://www.gannon.edu/departmental/psld/default.asp
Contact: Sr. Joyce Lowrey SSJ, Director. Phone: 814-871-5326. Fax: 814-871-7499. E-mail: lowrey001@gannon.edu.

Program for Students with Learning Disabilities (PSLD)
Approximately 65 registered undergraduate students were served during 2006–07. The program or unit includes 4 full-time and 6 part-time staff members. Academic advisers, coaches, counselors, diagnostic specialists, graduate assistants/students, LD specialists, professional tutors, regular education teachers, remediation/learning specialists, skill tutors, special education teachers, strategy tutors, and trained peer tutors are provided through the program or unit. Academic advisers and counselors are provided collaboratively through on-campus or off-campus services.

Unique Aids and Services Aids, services, or accommodations include advocates, career counseling, personal coach, and weekly meetings with faculty.

Assistive Technology Assistive technology is located in PSLD area and includes scanning and Kurzweil Reader. Technology training is provided to incoming students.

Subject-Area Tutoring Tutoring is offered one-on-one for most subjects. Tutoring is provided through the program or unit via computer-based instruction, graduate assistants/students, LD specialists, professional tutors, and trained peer tutors.

Basic Skills Remediation Remediation is offered one-on-one for computer skills, learning strategies, math, reading, study skills, time management, and written language. Remediation is provided through the program or unit via computer-based instruction, graduate assistants/students, LD specialists, professional tutors, regular education teachers, special education teachers, and trained peer tutors.

Enrichment Enrichment programs are available through the program or unit for college survival skills, learning strategies, math, oral communication skills, practical computer skills, reading, self-advocacy, stress management, study skills, test taking, time management, and written composition skills. Programs for career planning, college survival skills, health and nutrition, math, medication management, oral communication skills, practical computer skills, stress management, and study skills are provided collaboratively through on-campus or off-campus services. Credit is offered for college survival skills, learning strategies, reading, self-advocacy, stress management, study skills, test taking, time management, and written composition skills.

Fees *LD Program or Service* fee is $600.

Application For admittance to the program or unit, students are required to apply to the program directly and provide a psychoeducational report (4 years old or less). It is recommended that students provide documentation of high school services. Upon application, materials documenting need for services should be sent only to admissions with institutional application materials. Upon acceptance, documentation of need for services should be sent only to the LD program or unit. *Application deadline (institutional):* Continuous. *Application deadline (LD program):* Rolling/continuous for fall and rolling/continuous for spring.

Gannon University (continued)

Written Policies Written policies regarding course substitutions, general/basic LD accommodations, and substitutions and waivers of graduation requirements are available on the program Web site. Written policy regarding general/basic LD accommodations is outlined in the school's catalog/handbook. Written policies regarding course substitutions, general/basic LD accommodations, and substitutions and waivers of graduation requirements are available through the program or unit directly.

Georgian Court University
The Learning Center

900 Lakewood Avenue

Lakewood, NJ 08701-2697

http://www.georgian.edu/learningcenter/index.htm

Contact: Mrs. Patricia Cohen, Director of The Learning Center Program. Phone: 732-987-2659. E-mail: cohenp@ georgian.edu.

The Learning Center Approximately 30 registered undergraduate students were served during 2006–07. The program or unit includes 3 full-time and 3 part-time staff members. Academic advisers, counselors, diagnostic specialists, LD specialists, professional tutors, regular education teachers, skill tutors, and strategy tutors are provided through the program or unit.

Orientation The program or unit offers a mandatory 3-hour orientation for new students.

Subject-Area Tutoring Tutoring is offered one-on-one. Tutoring is provided through the program or unit via professional tutors.

Diagnostic Testing Testing is provided through the program or unit for auditory processing, intelligence, learning strategies, learning styles, math, personality, reading, social skills, spelling, study skills, and written language.

Basic Skills Remediation Remediation is offered one-on-one for learning strategies, social skills, study skills, and time management. Remediation is provided through the program or unit via regular education teachers.

Enrichment Enrichment programs are available through the program or unit for college survival skills, learning strategies, math, oral communication skills, reading, self-advocacy, stress management, study skills, test taking, time management, and written composition skills.

Fees *LD Program or Service* fee is $3000. *Diagnostic Testing* fee is $200 to $350.

Application For admittance to the program or unit, students are required to apply to the program directly and provide documentation of high school services. It is recommended that students provide a psychoeducational report (5 years old or less). Upon application, materials documenting need for services should be sent to both admissions and the LD program or unit. *Application deadline (institutional):* 8/1. *Application deadline (LD program):* 8/1 for fall. 1/1 for spring.

Written Policies Written policy regarding general/basic LD accommodations is available through the program or unit directly.

Graceland University
Student Disability Services and Chance Program

1 University Place

Lamoni, IA 50140

http://www.graceland.edu/show.cfm?durki=179

Contact: Susan Johnson Knotts, Director of Chance Program and Student Disability Services. Phone: 641-784-5421. Fax: 641-784-5446. E-mail: knotts@ graceland.edu.

Student Disability Services and Chance Program Approximately 70 registered undergraduate students were served during 2006–07. The program or unit includes 2 full-time staff members and 1 part-time staff member. Academic advisers and remediation/learning specialists are provided through the program or unit. Counselors, skill tutors, strategy tutors, and trained peer tutors are provided collaboratively through on-campus or off-campus services.

Unique Aids and Services Aids, services, or accommodations include advocates, career counseling, and faculty training.

Assistive Technology Assistive technology is located in a special lab and includes digital textbooks/e-text and scanning.

Subject-Area Tutoring Tutoring is offered one-on-one and in small groups for most subjects. Tutoring is provided through the program or unit via LD specialists. Tutoring is also provided collaboratively through on-campus or off-campus services via computer-based instruction and trained peer tutors.

Basic Skills Remediation Remediation is offered one-on-one for auditory processing, learning strategies, math, reading, spelling, study skills, time management, visual processing, written language, and language comprehension. Remediation is provided through the program or unit via LD specialists. Remediation is also provided collaboratively through on-campus or off-campus services via regular education teachers.

Enrichment Enrichment programs are available through the program or unit for career planning, college survival skills, learning strategies, practical computer skills, reading, self-advocacy, stress management, study skills, test taking, time management, vocabulary development, and written composition skills. Programs for career planning, college survival skills, health and nutrition, learning strategies, math, stress management, study skills, test taking, time management, vocabulary development, and written composition skills are provided collaboratively through on-campus or off-campus services. Credit is offered for career planning, college survival skills, health and nutrition, learning strategies, math, stress management, study skills, test taking, time management, vocabulary development, and written composition skills.

Fees *LD Program or Service* fee is $0 to $1350 (fee varies according to level/tier of service).

Application For admittance to the program or unit, students are required to apply to the program directly and provide a psychoeducational report (4 years old or less). It is recommended that students provide documentation of high school services. Upon application, materials documenting need for services should be sent only to admissions with institutional application materials. Upon acceptance, documentation of need for services should be sent only to admissions. *Application deadline (institutional):* Continuous. *Application deadline (LD program):* Rolling/continuous for fall and rolling/continuous for spring.

Written Policies Written policy regarding general/basic LD accommodations is outlined in the school's catalog/handbook. Written policies regarding course substitutions, general/basic LD accommodations, grade forgiveness, reduced course loads, substitutions and waivers of admissions requirements, and substitutions and waivers of graduation requirements are available through the program or unit directly.

Grambling State University
Student Counseling Services

PO Box 607
Grambling, LA 71245
http://www.gram.edu/

Contact: Dr. Coleen M. Speed, Director of Student Counseling Services. Phone: 318-274-3277 Ext. 3338. Fax: 318-274-3114 Ext. 3338. E-mail: speedc@gram.edu.

Student Counseling Services Approximately 45 registered undergraduate students were served during 2006–07. Academic advisers, coaches, counselors, graduate assistants/students, professional tutors, regular education teachers, and other are provided through the program or unit. Diagnostic specialists and LD specialists are provided collaboratively through on-campus or off-campus services.
Fees *LD Program or Service* fee varies according to academic program and disability.
Application For admittance to the program or unit, students are required to apply to the program directly, provide a psychoeducational report (6 years old or less), provide documentation of high school services, and provide recent diagnostic report. Upon application, materials documenting need for services should be sent only to the LD program or unit. Upon acceptance, documentation of need for services should be sent only to the LD program or unit. *Application deadline (institutional):* 6/30. *Application deadline (LD program):* Rolling/continuous for fall and rolling/continuous for spring.
Written Policies Written policies regarding course substitutions, general/basic LD accommodations, grade forgiveness, reduced course loads, substitutions and waivers of admissions requirements, and substitutions and waivers of graduation requirements are outlined in the school's catalog/handbook.

Hofstra University
Program for Academic Learning Skills (PALS)

100 Hofstra University
Hempstead, NY 11549
http://www.hofstra.edu/pals

Contact: PALS Information Line. Phone: 516-463-5761. Fax: 516-463-4049. E-mail: pals@hofstra.edu. Head of LD Program: Jayne Brownell Jayne Brownell, Assistant Vice President for Student Affairs. Phone: 516-463-7074. Fax: 516-463-2447. E-mail: pals@hofstra.edu.

Program for Academic Learning Skills (PALS) Approximately 81 registered undergraduate students were served during

2006–07. The program or unit includes 4 full-time staff members. Academic advisers, graduate assistants/students, LD specialists, remediation/learning specialists, skill tutors, and strategy tutors are provided through the program or unit. Academic advisers and professional tutors are provided collaboratively through on-campus or off-campus services.
Orientation The program or unit offers an optional 1-hour orientation for new students after classes begin.
Summer Program To help prepare for the demands of college, there is an optional 3-week summer program prior to entering the school available to rising seniors, high school graduates that focuses on self-advocacy, study skills, test-taking skills, and time management. The program is available to students attending other colleges.
Assistive Technology Assistive technology is located in computer labs and includes digital textbooks/e-text and Kurzweil Reader voice activated computer. Technology training is provided to incoming students.
Subject-Area Tutoring Tutoring is offered one-on-one for all subjects. Tutoring is provided collaboratively through on-campus or off-campus services via graduate assistants/students, professional tutors, and trained peer tutors.
Enrichment Enrichment programs are available through the program or unit for college survival skills, learning strategies, self-advocacy, study skills, test taking, time management, vocabulary development, and written composition skills. Programs for career planning, math, oral communication skills, practical computer skills, and reading are provided collaboratively through on-campus or off-campus services.
Fees *LD Program or Service* fee is $0 to $8000 (fee varies according to course level). *Summer Program* fee is $2000.
Application For admittance to the program or unit, students are required to provide a psychoeducational report (2 years old or less) and provide WAIS-III, achievement test results, full report, childhood history of AD/HD. Upon application, materials documenting need for services should be sent only to admissions with institutional application materials. Upon acceptance, documentation of need for services should be sent to both admissions and the LD program or unit. *Application deadline (institutional):* Continuous. *Application deadline (LD program):* Rolling/continuous for fall and rolling/continuous for spring.
Written Policies Written policies regarding course substitutions and general/basic LD accommodations are available on the program Web site. Written policies regarding course substitutions and general/basic LD accommodations are outlined in the school's catalog/handbook. Written policy regarding general/basic LD accommodations is available through the program or unit directly.

Iona College
College Assistance Program (CAP)

715 North Avenue
New Rochelle, NY 10801-1890
http://www.iona.edu/academic/support/cap/index.cfm

Contact: Mrs. Linda Refsland, Director. Phone: 914-633-2159. Fax: 914-633-2011. E-mail: capinformation@iona.edu. Head of LD Program: Mrs. Linda Refsland,

Iona College (continued)

Director. Phone: 914-633-2159. Fax: 914-633-2011. E-mail: capinformation@iona,edu.

College Assistance Program (CAP) Approximately 75 registered undergraduate students were served during 2006–07. The program or unit includes 2 full-time and 10 part-time staff members. Counselors, LD specialists, and skill tutors are provided through the program or unit.

Summer Program To help prepare for the demands of college, there is a mandatory 2-week summer program prior to entering the school that focuses on life skills and/or college life adjustment, self-advocacy, study skills, test-taking skills, and time management.

Unique Aids and Services Aids, services, or accommodations include priority registration.

Assistive Technology Assistive technology is located in the DSS office, a special lab and includes digital textbooks/e-text and learning support software. Technology training is provided to incoming students.

Subject-Area Tutoring Tutoring is offered one-on-one and in small groups for most subjects. Tutoring is provided through the program or unit via graduate assistants/students, professional tutors, and trained peer tutors. Tutoring is also provided collaboratively through on-campus or off-campus services via graduate assistants/students, professional tutors, and trained peer tutors.

Basic Skills Remediation Remediation is offered one-on-one for auditory processing, learning strategies, study skills, time management, visual processing, and written language. Remediation is provided through the program or unit via LD specialists.

Enrichment Enrichment programs are available through the program or unit for career planning, college survival skills, learning strategies, self-advocacy, stress management, study skills, test taking, time management, vocabulary development, and written composition skills. Programs for career planning, oral communication skills, practical computer skills, stress management, and written composition skills are provided collaboratively through on-campus or off-campus services.

Fees *LD Program or Service* fee is $3000. *Summer Program* fee is $750.

Application For admittance to the program or unit, students are required to apply to the program directly, provide a psychoeducational report (2 years old or less), provide documentation of high school services, and provide WAIS report, standardized achievement test scores. Upon application, materials documenting need for services should be sent only to the LD program or unit. *Application deadline (institutional):* 2/15. *Application deadline (LD program):* Rolling/continuous for fall and rolling/continuous for spring.

Written Policies Written policy regarding general/basic LD accommodations is available on the program Web site. Written policy regarding general/basic LD accommodations is outlined in the school's catalog/handbook. Written policy regarding general/basic LD accommodations is available through the program or unit directly.

King's College
FASP—Academics Studies Program

133 North River Street
Wilkes-Barre, PA 18711-0801
http://www.kings.edu/academics/academicskillscenter.htm#4

Contact: Ms. Jacintha A. Burke, Director of Academics Skills Center. Phone: 570-208-5800. Fax: 570-825-9049. E-mail: jaburke@kings.edu. Head of LD Program: Ms. Sheri Yech, Learning Differences Coordinator. Phone: 570-208-5900 Ext. 534. Fax: 570-825-9049. E-mail: sheriyech@kings.edu.

FASP—Academics Studies Program Approximately 35 registered undergraduate students were served during 2006–07. The program or unit includes 3 full-time staff members. LD specialists are provided through the program or unit. Academic advisers, regular education teachers, trained peer tutors, and other are provided collaboratively through on-campus or off-campus services.

Orientation The program or unit offers a mandatory 1-day orientation for new students before classes begin.

Summer Program To help prepare for the demands of college, there is an optional 5-week summer program prior to entering the school available to high school graduates that focuses on life skills and/or college life adjustment, self-advocacy, specific subject tutoring, study skills, test-taking skills, and time management. Degree credit will be earned. The program accepts students from out-of-state.

Unique Aids and Services Aids, services, or accommodations include career counseling, priority registration, and weekly meetings with faculty.

Assistive Technology Assistive technology is located in the DSS office and includes digital textbooks/e-text and scanning. Technology training is provided to incoming students.

Subject-Area Tutoring Tutoring is offered one-on-one and in small groups for most subjects. Tutoring is provided through the program or unit via LD specialists. Tutoring is also provided collaboratively through on-campus or off-campus services via trained peer tutors.

Diagnostic Testing Testing is provided through the program or unit for learning strategies, math, reading, spelling, study skills, and written language.

Enrichment Enrichment programs are available through the program or unit for college survival skills, learning strategies, medication management, self-advocacy, study skills, test taking, and time management. Programs for career planning, math, oral communication skills, practical computer skills, reading, and written composition skills are provided collaboratively through on-campus or off-campus services. Credit is offered for career planning and math.

Fees *LD Program or Service* fee is $500 to $1300 (fee varies according to level/tier of service). *Summer Program* fee is $650.

Application For admittance to the program or unit, students are required to apply to the program directly, provide a psychoeducational report (2 years old or less), and provide documentation of high school services. Upon application, materials documenting need for services should be sent to both admissions and the LD program or unit. Upon acceptance, documentation of need for services should be sent only to the LD program or unit. *Application deadline (institutional):* Continuous. *Application deadline (LD program):* Rolling/continuous for fall and rolling/continuous for spring.

Written Policies Written policy regarding general/basic LD accommodations is available on the program Web site. Written policy regarding general/basic LD accommodations is outlined in the school's catalog/handbook. Written policy regarding reduced course loads is available through the program or unit directly.

Loras College
Loras Learning Disabilities Program

1450 Alta Vista

Dubuque, IA 52004-0178

http://depts.loras.edu/LD/

Contact: Ms. Rochelle Fury, LD Secretary. Phone: 563-588-7134. Fax: 563-588-7071. E-mail: rochelle.fury@ loras.edu. Head of LD Program: Ms. Dianne Gibson, Director of Learning Disabilities Program. Phone: 563-588-7223. Fax: 563-588-7071. E-mail: dianne.gibson@ loras.edu.

Loras Learning Disabilities Program Approximately 65 registered undergraduate students were served during 2006–07. The program or unit includes 4 full-time staff members. Academic advisers, diagnostic specialists, LD specialists, remediation/learning specialists, skill tutors, strategy tutors, and trained peer tutors are provided through the program or unit. Academic advisers, counselors, and skill tutors are provided collaboratively through on-campus or off-campus services.

Unique Aids and Services Aids, services, or accommodations include priority registration, credit class for first-year students.

Assistive Technology Assistive technology is located in laptop computer issued to the student and includes digital textbooks/e-text, scanning, and books from Recording for the Blind and Dyslexic. Technology training is provided to incoming students.

Subject-Area Tutoring Tutoring is offered one-on-one and in small groups for all subjects. Tutoring is provided through the program or unit via LD specialists and trained peer tutors. Tutoring is also provided collaboratively through on-campus or off-campus services via trained peer tutors.

Diagnostic Testing Testing is provided through the program or unit for intelligence, math, reading, spelling, and written language. Testing for intelligence, math, personality, reading, spelling, and written language is provided collaboratively through on-campus or off-campus services.

Basic Skills Remediation Remediation is offered one-on-one and in class-size groups for learning strategies, reading, study skills, time management, and written language. Remediation is provided through the program or unit via LD specialists. Remediation is also provided collaboratively through on-campus or off-campus services via professional tutors, regular education teachers, trained peer tutors, and other.

Enrichment Enrichment programs are available through the program or unit for career planning, college survival skills, learning strategies, oral communication skills, practical computer skills, reading, self-advocacy, stress management, study skills, test taking, time management, vocabulary development, and written composition skills. Programs for career planning, college survival skills, health and nutrition, math, medication management, oral communication skills, practical computer skills, and written composition skills are provided collaboratively through on-campus or off-campus services.

Fees *LD Program or Service* fee is $3345 to $3895 (fee varies according to level/tier of service).

Application For admittance to the program or unit, students are required to provide a psychoeducational report (3 years old or less) and provide a personal essay. It is recommended that students provide documentation of high school services. Upon application, materials documenting need for services should be sent only to

admissions with institutional application materials. *Application deadline (institutional):* Continuous. *Application deadline (LD program):* 11/15 for fall. Rolling/continuous for spring.

Written Policies Written policies regarding course substitutions, general/basic LD accommodations, substitutions and waivers of admissions requirements, and substitutions and waivers of graduation requirements are available through the program or unit directly.

Louisiana College
Program to Assist Student Success (PASS)

1140 College Drive

Pineville, LA 71359-0001

http://www.lacollege.edu/

Contact: Betty P. Matthews, Program Director. Phone: 318-487-7629. Fax: 318-487-7285. E-mail: matthews@ lacollege.edu.

Program to Assist Student Success (PASS) Approximately 30 registered undergraduate students were served during 2006–07. The program or unit includes 1 full-time and 2 part-time staff members. Academic advisers, diagnostic specialists, LD specialists, professional tutors, regular education teachers, remediation/learning specialists, skill tutors, special education teachers, and trained peer tutors are provided through the program or unit.

Unique Aids and Services Aids, services, or accommodations include schedule planning, cooperative efforts with professors.

Assistive Technology Assistive technology is located in the PASS Department and includes digital textbooks/e-text and tapes.

Subject-Area Tutoring Tutoring is offered one-on-one for all subjects. Tutoring is provided through the program or unit via LD specialists, professional tutors, and trained peer tutors.

Enrichment Enrichment programs are available through the program or unit for math, study skills, test taking, and time management. Credit is offered for math.

Fees *LD Program or Service* fee is $450 to $850 (fee varies according to level/tier of service).

Application For admittance to the program or unit, students are required to apply to the program directly. It is recommended that students provide a psychoeducational report, provide documentation of high school services, and provide professionally prepared identification of disability. Upon application, materials documenting need for services should be sent only to the LD program or unit. Upon acceptance, documentation of need for services should be sent only to the LD program or unit. *Application deadline (LD program):* Rolling/continuous for fall and rolling/continuous for spring.

Written Policies Written policy regarding general/basic LD accommodations is outlined in the school's catalog/handbook. Written policy regarding general/basic LD accommodations is available through the program or unit directly.

Lynn University
Institute for Achievement and Learning, Comprehensive Support Program, Metamorphosis Program

3601 North Military Trail

Boca Raton, FL 33431-5598

http://www.lynn.edu/

Contact: Admissions. Phone: 561-237-7900. Fax: 561-237-7100. E-mail: admission@lynn.edu. Head of LD Program: Dr. Marsha Anne Glines, Dean of Institute for Achievement and Learning. Phone: 561-237-7881. Fax: 561-237-7100. E-mail: mglines@lynn.edu.

Institute for Achievement and Learning, Comprehensive Support Program, Metamorphosis Program Approximately 350 registered undergraduate students were served during 2006–07. The program or unit includes 10 full-time and 45 part-time staff members. Academic advisers, coaches, counselors, diagnostic specialists, graduate assistants/students, LD specialists, professional tutors, regular education teachers, remediation/learning specialists, strategy tutors, teacher trainees, and other are provided through the program or unit.

Orientation The program or unit offers a mandatory 1-day orientation for new students before classes begin.

Unique Aids and Services Aids, services, or accommodations include advocates, career counseling, faculty training.

Assistive Technology Assistive technology is located in campus labs, the DSS office, a special lab, the library and includes digital textbooks/e-text, learning support software, scanning, and Kurzweil Reader, books on CD, Dragon Naturally Speaking, audio recorders, Read & Write Gold software. Technology training is provided to incoming students.

Subject-Area Tutoring Tutoring is offered for all subjects. Tutoring is provided through the program or unit via computer-based instruction, LD specialists, professional tutors, and other. Tutoring is also provided collaboratively through on-campus or off-campus services via computer-based instruction, LD specialists, professional tutors, and other.

Diagnostic Testing Testing is provided through the program or unit for learning strategies, learning styles, personality, study skills, and other services. Testing for math, personality, study skills, written language, and other services is provided collaboratively through on-campus or off-campus services.

Enrichment Enrichment programs are available through the program or unit for career planning, college survival skills, health and nutrition, learning strategies, oral communication skills, practical computer skills, self-advocacy, stress management, study skills, test taking, time management, written composition skills, and other. Programs for career planning, college survival skills, health and nutrition, learning strategies, oral communication skills, practical computer skills, self-advocacy, stress management, study skills, test taking, time management, written composition skills, and other are provided collaboratively through on-campus or off-campus services.

Fees *LD Program or Service* fee is $8400 to $11,750 (fee varies according to level/tier of service).

Application For admittance to the program or unit, students are required to provide a psychoeducational report (3 years old or less). It is recommended that students provide documentation of high school services. Upon application, materials documenting need for services should be sent only to the LD program or unit. *Application deadline (institutional):* Continuous. *Application deadline (LD program):* Rolling/continuous for fall and rolling/continuous for spring.

Written Policies Written policy regarding general/basic LD accommodations is available on the program Web site. Written policy regarding general/basic LD accommodations is outlined in the school's catalog/handbook. Written policy regarding general/basic LD accommodations is available through the program or unit directly.

Marist College
Learning Disabilities Support Program

3399 North Road

Poughkeepsie, NY 12601-1387

http://www.marist.edu/

Contact: Ms. Gale Canale, Learning Disabilities Program Contact. Phone: 845-575-3274. Fax: 845-575-3011. E-mail: gale.canale@marist.edu. Head of LD Program: Director Learning Disabilities Support Program. Phone: 845-575-3274. Fax: 845-575-3011.

Learning Disabilities Support Program Approximately 75 registered undergraduate students were served during 2006–07. The program or unit includes 3 full-time and 3 part-time staff members. LD specialists, special education teachers, and trained peer tutors are provided through the program or unit.

Unique Aids and Services Aids, services, or accommodations include career counseling.

Assistive Technology Assistive technology is located in the DSS office, the library and includes digital textbooks/e-text.

Subject-Area Tutoring Tutoring is offered one-on-one and in small groups for most subjects. Tutoring is provided through the program or unit via LD specialists and trained peer tutors.

Basic Skills Remediation Remediation is offered one-on-one for learning strategies, study skills, time management, written language, and assistive technology. Remediation is provided through the program or unit via LD specialists and trained peer tutors.

Enrichment Enrichment programs are available through the program or unit for career planning, learning strategies, self-advocacy, stress management, study skills, test taking, time management, and written composition skills. Programs for math and written composition skills are provided collaboratively through on-campus or off-campus services.

Fees *LD Program or Service* fee is $3400.

Application For admittance to the program or unit, students are required to apply to the program directly, provide a psychoeducational report (3 years old or less), provide documentation of high school services, and provide achievement testing results in reading, writing and mathematics. Upon application, materials documenting need for services should be sent only to the LD program or unit. Upon acceptance, documentation of need for services should be sent only to the LD program or unit. *Application deadline (institutional):* 2/15. *Application deadline (LD program):* 2/15 for fall. 2/15 for spring.

Written Policies Written policy regarding general/basic LD accommodations is available on the program Web site. Written policy regarding general/basic LD accommodations is outlined in the school's catalog/handbook. Written policy regarding substitutions and waivers of admissions requirements is available through the program or unit directly.

Marshall University
HELP Program

One John Marshall Drive

Huntington, WV 25755

http://www.marshall.edu/help

Contact: Ms. Diane F. Williams, Coordinator of College H.E.L.P. Phone: 304-696-6314. Fax: 304-696-6312. E-mail: williamd@marshall.edu. Head of LD Program: Mrs. Lynne M. Weston, Director, H.E.L.P. Phone: 304-696-6316. Fax: 304-696-3231. E-mail: weston@marshall.edu.

HELP Program Approximately 200 registered undergraduate students were served during 2006–07. The program or unit includes 11 full-time and 60 part-time staff members. Academic advisers, coaches, diagnostic specialists, graduate assistants/students, LD specialists, professional tutors, remediation/learning specialists, skill tutors, and strategy tutors are provided through the program or unit. Academic advisers and counselors are provided collaboratively through on-campus or off-campus services.

Orientation The program or unit offers a mandatory 1-day orientation for new students before registration, before classes begin, and during summer prior to enrollment.

Summer Program To help prepare for the demands of college, there is a mandatory 5-week summer program prior to entering the school available to rising sophomores, high school graduates that focuses on computing skills, life skills and/or college life adjustment, self-advocacy, specific subject tutoring, study skills, test-taking skills, and time management. Degree credit will be earned. The program accepts students from out-of-state and is available to students attending other colleges.

Unique Aids and Services Aids, services, or accommodations include advocates, personal coach, priority registration, and support groups.

Assistive Technology Assistive technology is located in the H.E.L.P. Building and includes learning support software and scanning.

Subject-Area Tutoring Tutoring is offered one-on-one for all subjects. Tutoring is provided through the program or unit via computer-based instruction, graduate assistants/students, LD specialists, and professional tutors.

Diagnostic Testing Testing is provided through the program or unit for auditory processing, handwriting, intelligence, learning strategies, learning styles, math, neuropsychological, reading, spelling, study skills, visual processing, written language, and other services.

Basic Skills Remediation Remediation is offered one-on-one for auditory processing, computer skills, handwriting, learning strategies, math, reading, spelling, study skills, time management, visual processing, and written language. Remediation is provided through the program or unit via computer-based instruction and LD specialists.

Enrichment Enrichment programs are available through the program or unit for career planning, college survival skills, learning strategies, math, practical computer skills, reading, self-advocacy, stress management, study skills, test taking, time management, vocabulary development, and written composition skills.

Student Organization HELPERS consists of 15 members.

Fees *LD Program or Service* fee is $325 to $525 (fee varies according to level/tier of service). *Summer Program* fee is $1200 to $2200. *Orientation* fee is $75. *Diagnostic Testing* fee is $500 to $1000.

Application For admittance to the program or unit, students are required to apply to the program directly, provide a psychoeducational report (3 years old or less), and provide 2 letters of recommendation and a 1-page essay. It is recommended that students provide documentation of high school services. Upon application, materials documenting need for services should be sent only to the LD program or unit. *Application deadline (institutional):* Continuous. *Application deadline (LD program):* Rolling/continuous for fall and rolling/continuous for spring.

Written Policies Written policies regarding course substitutions and general/basic LD accommodations are available on the program Web site. Written policy regarding substitutions and waivers of admissions requirements is available through the program or unit directly.

Marymount Manhattan College
Program for Academic Access

221 East 71st Street

New York, NY 10021-4597

http://www.mmm.edu/

Contact: Dr. Jacquelyn Bonomo, Assistant Director of Program for Academic Access. Phone: 212-774-0724. Fax: 212-517-0419. E-mail: jbonomo@mmm.edu. Head of LD Program: Dr. Ann Jablon, Director of Program for Academic Access. Phone: 212-774-0721. E-mail: ajablon@mmm.edu.

Program for Academic Access Approximately 40 registered undergraduate students were served during 2006–07. The program or unit includes 1 full-time and 3 part-time staff members. Diagnostic specialists and LD specialists are provided through the program or unit.

Orientation The program or unit offers a mandatory half-day orientation for new students before classes begin and during summer prior to enrollment.

Unique Aids and Services Aids, services, or accommodations include career counseling, priority registration, weekly meetings with faculty, one workshop per semester.

Assistive Technology Assistive technology is located in program offices and includes learning support software and Kurzweil reading software. Technology training is provided to incoming students.

Subject-Area Tutoring Tutoring is offered one-on-one for all subjects. Tutoring is provided collaboratively through on-campus or off-campus services via professional tutors and trained peer tutors.

Marymount Manhattan College (continued)

Diagnostic Testing Testing is provided through the program or unit for learning strategies, reading, spelling, and study skills. Testing for intelligence, personality, spoken language, and written language is provided collaboratively through on-campus or off-campus services.

Basic Skills Remediation Remediation is offered one-on-one and in class-size groups for math, reading, spelling, study skills, time management, and written language. Remediation is provided through the program or unit via LD specialists. Remediation is also provided collaboratively through on-campus or off-campus services via computer-based instruction and regular education teachers.

Enrichment Enrichment programs are available through the program or unit for college survival skills, learning strategies, reading, self-advocacy, study skills, test taking, time management, vocabulary development, and written composition skills. Programs for career planning, college survival skills, health and nutrition, learning strategies, math, oral communication skills, practical computer skills, stress management, and written composition skills are provided collaboratively through on-campus or off-campus services. Credit is offered for health and nutrition, learning strategies, math, oral communication skills, practical computer skills, and written composition skills.

Fees *LD Program or Service* fee is $4000.

Application For admittance to the program or unit, students are required to provide a psychoeducational report (3 years old or less) and provide short essay on academic and career goals. Upon application, materials documenting need for services should be sent only to the LD program or unit. *Application deadline (institutional):* Continuous. *Application deadline (LD program):* Rolling/continuous for fall and rolling/continuous for spring.

Written Policies Written policies regarding general/basic LD accommodations and reduced course loads are available on the program Web site. Written policy regarding general/basic LD accommodations is outlined in the school's catalog/handbook. Written policies regarding general/basic LD accommodations and reduced course loads are available through the program or unit directly.

McDaniel College

2 College Hill
Westminster, MD 21157-4390
http://www.mcdaniel.edu/859.htm

Contact: Mr. Kevin Selby, Director Student Academic Support Services. Phone: 410-857-2479. Fax: 410-386-4617. E-mail: kselby@mcdaniel.edu.

Approximately 155 registered undergraduate students were served during 2006–07. The program or unit includes 3 full-time and 4 part-time staff members. Academic advisers, counselors, graduate assistants/students, LD specialists, skill tutors, strategy tutors, and trained peer tutors are provided through the program or unit. Academic advisers, counselors, diagnostic specialists, and trained peer tutors are provided collaboratively through on-campus or off-campus services.

Orientation The program or unit offers an optional 1-day orientation for new students during summer prior to enrollment.

Unique Aids and Services Aids, services, or accommodations include career counseling and priority registration.

Assistive Technology Assistive technology is located in the DSS office and includes learning support software.

Subject-Area Tutoring Tutoring is offered one-on-one and in small groups for some subjects. Tutoring is provided through the program or unit via graduate assistants/students and LD specialists. Tutoring is also provided collaboratively through on-campus or off-campus services via trained peer tutors.

Diagnostic Testing Testing is provided through the program or unit for learning strategies, learning styles, spoken language, study skills, and written language.

Basic Skills Remediation Remediation is offered one-on-one for learning strategies, math, social skills, study skills, and written language. Remediation is provided through the program or unit via computer-based instruction, graduate assistants/students, LD specialists, and professional tutors. Remediation is also provided collaboratively through on-campus or off-campus services via professional tutors.

Enrichment Enrichment programs are available through the program or unit for career planning, college survival skills, learning strategies, math, oral communication skills, self-advocacy, stress management, study skills, test taking, time management, vocabulary development, and written composition skills. Programs for career planning, college survival skills, health and nutrition, math, medication management, and written composition skills are provided collaboratively through on-campus or off-campus services.

Fees *LD Program or Service* fee is $0 to $2000 (fee varies according to level/tier of service).

Application For admittance to the program or unit, students are required to provide a psychoeducational report (3 years old or less). It is recommended that students provide documentation of high school services. Upon application, materials documenting need for services should be sent only to the LD program or unit. Upon acceptance, documentation of need for services should be sent only to the LD program or unit. *Application deadline (institutional):* 2/1. *Application deadline (LD program):* Rolling/continuous for fall.

Written Policies Written policy regarding general/basic LD accommodations is available on the program Web site. Written policies regarding course substitutions, general/basic LD accommodations, and substitutions and waivers of graduation requirements are available through the program or unit directly.

Mercyhurst College
Learning Differences Program

501 East 38th Street
Erie, PA 16546
http://www.mercyhurst.edu/

Contact: Ms. Dianne D. Rogers, Director. Phone: 814-824-2450. Fax: 814-824-2589. E-mail: drogers@mercyhurst.edu.

Learning Differences Program Approximately 80 registered undergraduate students were served during 2006–07. The program or unit includes 3 full-time and 7 part-time staff members. Academic advisers, coaches, counselors, graduate assistants/students, LD specialists, skill tutors, strategy tutors, and trained peer tutors are provided through the program or unit. Academic advisers, counselors, graduate assistants/students, remediation/learning specialists, skill tutors, strategy tutors, and trained peer tutors are provided collaboratively through on-campus or off-campus services.

Orientation The program or unit offers an optional 1-day orientation for new students before registration, before classes begin, during summer prior to enrollment, and individually by special arrangement.

Summer Program To help prepare for the demands of college, there is an optional 3-week summer program prior to entering the school available to rising seniors that focuses on life skills and/or college life adjustment, self-advocacy, specific subject tutoring, study skills, test-taking skills, and time management. Degree credit will be earned. The program accepts students from out-of-state.

Unique Aids and Services Aids, services, or accommodations include career counseling, priority registration, support groups, progress reports.

Assistive Technology Assistive technology is located in campus labs, the DSS office and includes digital textbooks/e-text, learning support software, and scanning. Technology training is provided to incoming students.

Subject-Area Tutoring Tutoring is offered one-on-one, in small groups, and in class-size groups for all subjects. Tutoring is provided through the program or unit via graduate assistants/students, LD specialists, and trained peer tutors. Tutoring is also provided collaboratively through on-campus or off-campus services via graduate assistants/students, trained peer tutors, and other.

Basic Skills Remediation Remediation is offered in small groups and in class-size groups for computer skills, math, reading, and written language. Remediation is provided collaboratively through on-campus or off-campus services.

Enrichment Programs for career planning, college survival skills, health and nutrition, learning strategies, math, practical computer skills, reading, self-advocacy, stress management, study skills, test taking, time management, and written composition skills are provided collaboratively through on-campus or off-campus services.

Student Organization Learning Differences Program consists of 80 members.

Fees *LD Program or Service* fee is $2000. *Summer Program* fee is $1800 to $2000.

Application For admittance to the program or unit, students are required to apply to the program directly, provide a psychoeducational report (3 years old or less), provide documentation of high school services, and provide personal interview. Upon application, materials documenting need for services should be sent to both admissions and the LD program or unit. Upon acceptance, documentation of need for services should be sent only to the LD program or unit. *Application deadline (institutional):* Continuous. *Application deadline (LD program):* Rolling/continuous for fall and rolling/continuous for spring.

Written Policies Written policy regarding general/basic LD accommodations is available on the program Web site. Written policies regarding general/basic LD accommodations, grade forgiveness, and reduced course loads are outlined in the school's catalog/handbook. Written policies regarding course substitutions, general/basic LD accommodations, grade forgiveness, reduced course loads, substitutions and waivers of admissions requirements, and substitutions and waivers of graduation requirements are available through the program or unit directly.

Metropolitan College of New York
Student Services—Program for Students with Special Needs

75 Varick Street
New York, NY 10013-1919
http://www.metropolitan.edu/
Contact: Suleyni Monero. E-mail: smonero@mcny.edu.

Student Services—Program for Students with Special Needs Approximately 10 registered undergraduate students were served during 2006–07. The program or unit includes 1 full-time staff member. Academic advisers, coaches, counselors, diagnostic specialists, graduate assistants/students, LD specialists, professional tutors, regular education teachers, remediation/learning specialists, skill tutors, special education teachers, strategy tutors, teacher trainees, trained peer tutors, and other are provided through the program or unit.

Summer Program available to rising sophomores, rising juniors, high school graduates.

Unique Aids and Services Aids, services, or accommodations include advocates and career counseling.

Assistive Technology Technology training is provided to incoming students.

Subject-Area Tutoring Tutoring is offered for most subjects. Tutoring is provided collaboratively through on-campus or off-campus services via professional tutors, trained peer tutors, and other.

Basic Skills Remediation Remediation is offered one-on-one for computer skills, math, reading, spelling, study skills, and time management. Remediation is provided through the program or unit via LD specialists. Remediation is also provided collaboratively through on-campus or off-campus services via computer-based instruction, professional tutors, trained peer tutors, and other.

Enrichment Programs for career planning, college survival skills, health and nutrition, learning strategies, math, practical computer skills, reading, study skills, test taking, time management, written composition skills, and other are provided collaboratively through on-campus or off-campus services.

Application For admittance to the program or unit, students are required to apply to the program directly and provide a psychoeducational report (1 year old or less). Upon application, materials documenting need for services should be sent only to the LD program or unit. Upon acceptance, documentation of need for services should be sent only to the LD program or unit. *Application deadline (institutional):* 8/15. *Application deadline (LD program):* Rolling/continuous for fall and rolling/continuous for spring.

Written Policies Written policy regarding general/basic LD accommodations is available through the program or unit directly.

Mitchell College
Learning Resource Center

437 Pequot Avenue
New London, CT 06320-4498
http://www.mitchell.edu/

Mitchell College (continued)

Contact: Ms. Jennifer Mauro, Admissions Liaison. Phone: 860-701-7719. Fax: 860-701-5469. E-mail: mauro_j@ mitchell.edu. Head of LD Program: Dr. Peter F. Love, Director of the Learning Resource Center. Phone: 860-701-5071. Fax: 860-701-5469. E-mail: love_p@ mitchell.edu.

Learning Resource Center Approximately 250 registered undergraduate students were served during 2006–07. The program or unit includes 28 full-time and 10 part-time staff members. Academic advisers, coaches, LD specialists, professional tutors, remediation/ learning specialists, skill tutors, and strategy tutors are provided through the program or unit. Academic advisers, LD specialists, professional tutors, remediation/learning specialists, skill tutors, and strategy tutors are provided collaboratively through on-campus or off-campus services.

Orientation The program or unit offers an optional half-day orientation for new students immediately prior to the general college new student orientation.

Summer Program To help prepare for the demands of college, there is an optional 5-week summer program prior to entering the school available to high school graduates that focuses on life skills and/or college life adjustment, self-advocacy, specific subject tutoring, study skills, test-taking skills, and time management. Degree credit will be earned. The program accepts students from out-of-state and is available to students attending other colleges.

Unique Aids and Services Aids, services, or accommodations include advocates, career counseling, faculty training, parent workshops, and support groups.

Assistive Technology Assistive technology includes digital textbooks/e-text, learning support software, and scanning.

Subject-Area Tutoring Tutoring is offered one-on-one, in small groups, and in class-size groups for all subjects. Tutoring is provided through the program or unit via professional tutors.

Basic Skills Remediation Remediation is offered one-on-one, in small groups, and in class-size groups for auditory processing, computer skills, learning strategies, math, reading, study skills, time management, visual processing, and written language. Remediation is provided through the program or unit via LD specialists and professional tutors.

Enrichment Enrichment programs are available through the program or unit for learning strategies, math, reading, self-advocacy, stress management, study skills, test taking, time management, vocabulary development, and written composition skills. Programs for career planning, college survival skills, health and nutrition, oral communication skills, practical computer skills, stress management, study skills, test taking, and time management are provided collaboratively through on-campus or off-campus services. Credit is offered for oral communication skills, practical computer skills, vocabulary development, and written composition skills.

Fees *LD Program or Service* fee is $3250 to $6500 (fee varies according to level/tier of service). *Summer Program* fee is $4000. *Orientation* fee is $4000.

Application For admittance to the program or unit, students are required to apply to the program directly, provide a psychoeducational report (3 years old or less), and provide documentation of high school services. Upon application, materials documenting need for services should be sent only to admissions with institutional application materials. *Application deadline (institutional):* Continuous. *Application deadline (LD program):* Rolling/continuous for fall and rolling/continuous for spring.

Written Policies Written policies regarding course substitutions, general/basic LD accommodations, reduced course loads, substitutions and waivers of admissions requirements, and substitutions and waivers of graduation requirements are outlined in the school's catalog/handbook. Written policies regarding course substitutions, general/basic LD accommodations, reduced course loads, substitutions and waivers of admissions requirements, and substitutions and waivers of graduation requirements are available through the program or unit directly.

Morningside College
Focus

1501 Morningside Avenue
Sioux City, IA 51106

http://www.morningsidecollege.net/student_life/LD/index.cfm

Contact: Ms. Karmen Ten Napel, Director of Focus. Phone: 800-831-0806 Ext. 5191. Fax: 712-274-5101. E-mail: tennapel@morningside.edu.

Focus Approximately 24 registered undergraduate students were served during 2006–07. The program or unit includes 2 full-time staff members and 1 part-time staff member. Coaches, LD specialists, remediation/learning specialists, special education teachers, and strategy tutors are provided through the program or unit. Academic advisers, counselors, diagnostic specialists, graduate assistants/ students, professional tutors, regular education teachers, skill tutors, teacher trainees, and trained peer tutors are provided collaboratively through on-campus or off-campus services.

Orientation The program or unit offers an optional 2-day orientation for new students before classes begin.

Unique Aids and Services Aids, services, or accommodations include advocates, career counseling, faculty training, personal coach, and support groups.

Assistive Technology Assistive technology is located in the DSS office and includes digital textbooks/e-text, scanning, and WYNN software, Dragon Naturally Speaking. Technology training is provided to incoming students.

Subject-Area Tutoring Tutoring is offered one-on-one and in small groups for all subjects. Tutoring is provided through the program or unit via LD specialists and professional tutors. Tutoring is also provided collaboratively through on-campus or off-campus services via graduate assistants/students, professional tutors, and trained peer tutors.

Basic Skills Remediation Remediation is offered in small groups for learning strategies, math, reading, study skills, time management, and written language. Remediation is provided through the program or unit via LD specialists. Remediation is also provided collaboratively through on-campus or off-campus services via professional tutors, regular education teachers, and trained peer tutors.

Enrichment Enrichment programs are available through the program or unit for learning strategies, oral communication skills, reading, self-advocacy, stress management, study skills, test taking, time management, vocabulary development, and written composition skills. Programs for career planning, college survival skills, math, practical computer skills, and stress management are provided collaboratively through on-campus or off-campus services.

Student Organization Mentoring Program consists of 15 members.

Fees *LD Program or Service* fee is $825 to $1550 (fee varies according to level/tier of service).

Application For admittance to the program or unit, students are required to apply to the program directly, provide a psychoeducational report (5 years old or less), and provide documentation of high school services. Upon application, materials documenting need for services should be sent only to the LD program or unit. *Application deadline (institutional):* Continuous. *Application deadline (LD program):* Rolling/continuous for fall and rolling/continuous for spring.

Written Policies Written policy regarding general/basic LD accommodations is outlined in the school's catalog/handbook. Written policies regarding course substitutions and substitutions and waivers of graduation requirements are available through the program or unit directly.

Muskingum College
PLUS Program

163 Stormont Street
New Concord, OH 43762
http://www.muskingum.edu/home/cal/index.html
Contact: Michelle Butler, Administrative Assistant. Phone: 740-826-8280. Fax: 740-826-8285. E-mail: butler@muskingum.edu. Head of LD Program: Dr. Eileen Henry, Executive Director of Center for Advancement of Learning. Phone: 740-826-8284. Fax: 740-826-8285. E-mail: ehenry@muskingum.edu.

PLUS Program Approximately 175 registered undergraduate students were served during 2006–07. The program or unit includes 17 full-time and 5 part-time staff members. Professional tutors are provided through the program or unit.

Orientation The program or unit offers a mandatory afternoon-long orientation for new students before classes begin.

Summer Program To help prepare for the demands of college, there is an optional 2-week summer program prior to entering the school available to rising seniors, high school graduates that focuses on computing skills, self-advocacy, specific subject tutoring, study skills, test-taking skills, and time management. The program accepts students from out-of-state and is available to students attending other colleges.

Unique Aids and Services Aids, services, or accommodations include priority registration.

Subject-Area Tutoring Tutoring is offered one-on-one and in small groups for all subjects. Tutoring is provided through the program or unit via professional tutors.

Enrichment Enrichment programs are available through the program or unit for career planning, learning strategies, study skills, test taking, and time management.

Student Organization ChatBack consists of 25 members.

Fees *LD Program or Service* fee is $2425 to $4850 (fee varies according to level/tier of service). *Summer Program* fee is $2400.

Application For admittance to the program or unit, students are required to provide a psychoeducational report (3 years old or less). It is recommended that students provide documentation of high school services. Upon application, materials documenting need for services should be sent only to the LD program or unit. *Application deadline (LD program):* Rolling/continuous for fall and rolling/continuous for spring.

Written Policies Written policies regarding general/basic LD accommodations and reduced course loads are available through the program or unit directly.

Notre Dame College
Academic Support Center for Students with Learning Differences (ASC)

4545 College Road
South Euclid, OH 44121-4293
http://www.notredamecollege.edu/campus_life/AcademicSupportCenter.html
Contact: Ms. Gretchen Noetzel Walsh, Director of Academic Support Center for Students with Learning Differences. Phone: 216-373-5185. Fax: 216-373-5187. E-mail: gwalsh@ndc.edu.

Academic Support Center for Students with Learning Differences (ASC) Approximately 24 registered undergraduate students were served during 2006–07. The program or unit includes 1 full-time and 10 part-time staff members. Academic advisers, counselors, LD specialists, professional tutors, skill tutors, special education teachers, and strategy tutors are provided through the program or unit. Counselors and diagnostic specialists are provided collaboratively through on-campus or off-campus services.

Orientation The program or unit offers a mandatory 2-day orientation for new students during summer prior to enrollment.

Summer Program To help prepare for the demands of college, there is an optional 5-week summer program prior to entering the school available to rising seniors, high school graduates that focuses on self-advocacy, study skills, test-taking skills, and time management. The program accepts students from out-of-state and is available to students attending other colleges.

Unique Aids and Services Aids, services, or accommodations include advocates, career counseling, faculty training, priority registration, support groups, Transfer to Action Groups with the Cleveland Clinic at NDC.

Assistive Technology Assistive technology is located in the Academic Support Center and includes digital textbooks/e-text, learning support software, scanning, and Kurzweil, Read & Write Gold, Naturally Speaking, Inspiration. Technology training is provided to incoming students.

Subject-Area Tutoring Tutoring is offered one-on-one and in small groups for most subjects. Tutoring is provided through the program or unit via computer-based instruction, LD specialists, and professional tutors.

Basic Skills Remediation Remediation is offered one-on-one for learning strategies, math, reading, social skills, study skills, time management, and written language. Remediation is provided through the program or unit via computer-based instruction, LD specialists, professional tutors, regular education teachers, and special education teachers.

Enrichment Enrichment programs are available through the program or unit for college survival skills, learning strategies, math, oral communication skills, practical computer skills, reading, self-advocacy, stress management, study skills, test taking, time management, vocabulary development, written composition skills, and other. Programs for career planning, health and nutrition, math, and

Notre Dame College (continued)

stress management are provided collaboratively through on-campus or off-campus services. Credit is offered for health and nutrition, math, oral communication skills, and practical computer skills.

Fees *LD Program or Service fee is $3000.*

Application For admittance to the program or unit, students are required to provide a psychoeducational report (3 years old or less). It is recommended that students provide documentation of high school services. Upon application, materials documenting need for services should be sent only to the LD program or unit. Upon acceptance, documentation of need for services should be sent only to the LD program or unit. *Application deadline (institutional):* Continuous. *Application deadline (LD program):* Rolling/continuous for fall and rolling/continuous for spring.

Written Policies Written policy regarding general/basic LD accommodations is available on the program Web site. Written policies regarding general/basic LD accommodations and substitutions and waivers of admissions requirements are outlined in the school's catalog/handbook. Written policy regarding reduced course loads is available through the program or unit directly.

Reinhardt College
Academic Support Office

7300 Reinhardt College Circle

Waleska, GA 30183-2981

http://www.reinhardt.edu/

Contact: Ms. Sylvia R. Robertson, Director of Academic Support Office. Phone: 770-720-5567. Fax: 770-720-5602. E-mail: srr@reinhardt.edu.

Academic Support Office Approximately 100 registered undergraduate students were served during 2006–07. The program or unit includes 4 full-time staff members. Academic advisers, LD specialists, regular education teachers, remediation/learning specialists, special education teachers, strategy tutors, and other are provided through the program or unit. Counselors and diagnostic specialists are provided collaboratively through on-campus or off-campus services.

Orientation The program or unit offers a mandatory 1-day orientation for new students before classes begin.

Unique Aids and Services Aids, services, or accommodations include priority registration.

Assistive Technology Assistive technology includes digital textbooks/e-text.

Subject-Area Tutoring Tutoring is offered in small groups for most subjects. Tutoring is provided through the program or unit via LD specialists and other.

Enrichment Enrichment programs are available through the program or unit for self-advocacy, test taking, time management, and written composition skills. Programs for career planning, college survival skills, health and nutrition, learning strategies, oral communication skills, stress management, and time management are provided collaboratively through on-campus or off-campus services. Credit is offered for college survival skills, health and nutrition, learning strategies, and oral communication skills.

Fees *LD Program or Service fee is $990 to $11,880 (fee varies according to level/tier of service).*

Application For admittance to the program or unit, students are required to apply to the program directly, provide a psychoeducational report (3 years old or less), provide documentation of high school services, and provide 3 letters of reference. Upon application, materials documenting need for services should be sent only to admissions with institutional application materials. Upon acceptance, documentation of need for services should be sent only to admissions. *Application deadline (institutional):* Continuous. *Application deadline (LD program):* Rolling/continuous for fall and rolling/continuous for spring.

Written Policies Written policy regarding general/basic LD accommodations is outlined in the school's catalog/handbook.

Roosevelt University
Disability Services, Learning and Support Services Program(LSSP)

430 South Michigan Avenue

Chicago, IL 60605-1394

http://www.roosevelt.edu/dss/default.htm

Contact: Nancy Litke, Director Academic Success Center. Phone: 312-341-3810. Fax: 312-341-2471. E-mail: nlitke@roosevelt.edu.

Disability Services, Learning and Support Services Program(LSSP) Approximately 28 registered undergraduate students were served during 2006–07. The program or unit includes 1 full-time and 3 part-time staff members. Academic advisers, coaches, LD specialists, professional tutors, remediation/learning specialists, skill tutors, and strategy tutors are provided through the program or unit. Academic advisers, counselors, graduate assistants/students, professional tutors, skill tutors, and strategy tutors are provided collaboratively through on-campus or off-campus services.

Orientation The program or unit offers an optional orientation for new students individually by special arrangement.

Unique Aids and Services Aids, services, or accommodations include advocates, career counseling, support groups, and weekly meetings with faculty.

Assistive Technology Assistive technology is located in the DSS office, the campus library and includes learning support software and scanning. Technology training is provided to incoming students.

Subject-Area Tutoring Tutoring is offered one-on-one and in small groups for most subjects. Tutoring is provided through the program or unit via computer-based instruction, graduate assistants/students, LD specialists, professional tutors, and trained peer tutors. Tutoring is also provided collaboratively through on-campus or off-campus services via computer-based instruction, graduate assistants/students, professional tutors, and trained peer tutors.

Basic Skills Remediation Remediation is offered one-on-one and in small groups for auditory processing, computer skills, learning strategies, math, reading, social skills, spelling, spoken language, study skills, time management, visual processing, and written language. Remediation is provided through the program or unit via computer-based instruction, LD specialists, and professional tutors. Remediation is also provided collaboratively through on-campus or off-campus services via computer-based instruction and professional tutors.

Enrichment Enrichment programs are available through the program or unit for career planning, college survival skills, learning strategies, math, oral communication skills, practical computer skills, reading, self-advocacy, stress management, study skills, test taking, time management, vocabulary development, and written composition skills. Programs for career planning, college survival skills, health and nutrition, learning strategies, math, oral communication skills, practical computer skills, reading, self-advocacy, stress management, study skills, test taking, time management, and written composition skills are provided collaboratively through on-campus or off-campus services.

Fees *LD Program or Service* fee is $1000.

Application For admittance to the program or unit, students are required to apply to the program directly and provide a psychoeducational report. It is recommended that students provide documentation of high school services. Upon application, materials documenting need for services should be sent only to the LD program or unit. Upon acceptance, documentation of need for services should be sent only to the LD program or unit. *Application deadline (institutional): 8/15. Application deadline (LD program):* Rolling/continuous for fall and rolling/continuous for spring.

Written Policies Written policies regarding course substitutions, general/basic LD accommodations, reduced course loads, substitutions and waivers of admissions requirements, and substitutions and waivers of graduation requirements are available on the program Web site. Written policies regarding course substitutions, general/basic LD accommodations, reduced course loads, substitutions and waivers of admissions requirements, and substitutions and waivers of graduation requirements are available through the program or unit directly.

St. Gregory's University
Partners in Learning

1900 West MacArthur Drive

Shawnee, OK 74804-2499

http://www.stgregorys.edu/Default.aspx?tabid=122

Contact: Ms. H.L. Watson, Director of Partners in Learning. Phone: 405-878-5103. Fax: 405-878-5198. E-mail: hlwatson@stgregorys.edu.

Partners in Learning Approximately 24 registered undergraduate students were served during 2006–07. The program or unit includes 2 full-time and 50 part-time staff members. Academic advisers, counselors, graduate assistants/students, LD specialists, and trained peer tutors are provided through the program or unit. Academic advisers, counselors, graduate assistants/students, LD specialists, regular education teachers, remediation/learning specialists, and trained peer tutors are provided collaboratively through on-campus or off-campus services.

Unique Aids and Services Aids, services, or accommodations include advocates, career counseling, and faculty training.

Assistive Technology Assistive technology is located in Partners in Learning Study Rooms and includes digital textbooks/e-text, learning support software, and scanning. Technology training is provided to incoming students.

Subject-Area Tutoring Tutoring is offered one-on-one and in small groups for all subjects. Tutoring is provided through the program or unit via graduate assistants/students and trained peer tutors. Tutoring is also provided collaboratively through on-campus or off-campus services via graduate assistants/students and trained peer tutors.

Basic Skills Remediation Remediation is offered in class-size groups for reading. Remediation is provided collaboratively through on-campus or off-campus services via regular education teachers.

Enrichment Programs for career planning, college survival skills, learning strategies, practical computer skills, reading, self-advocacy, stress management, study skills, test taking, time management, and written composition skills are provided collaboratively through on-campus or off-campus services.

Fees *LD Program or Service* fee is $7000.

Application For admittance to the program or unit, students are required to apply to the program directly, provide a psychoeducational report (3 years old or less), and provide documentation of high school services. Upon application, materials documenting need for services should be sent to both admissions and the LD program or unit. Upon acceptance, documentation of need for services should be sent only to the LD program or unit. *Application deadline (institutional):* Continuous. *Application deadline (LD program):* Rolling/continuous for fall and rolling/continuous for spring.

Written Policies Written policy regarding general/basic LD accommodations is available on the program Web site. Written policy regarding general/basic LD accommodations is outlined in the school's catalog/handbook. Written policy regarding substitutions and waivers of admissions requirements is available through the program or unit directly.

St. Thomas Aquinas College
Pathways

125 Route 340

Sparkill, NY 10976

http://www.stac.edu/

Contact: Dr. Richard F. Heath, Director of Pathways. Phone: 845-398-4230. Fax: 845-398-4229. E-mail: pathways@stac.edu.

Pathways Approximately 80 registered undergraduate students were served during 2006–07. The program or unit includes 4 full-time and 7 part-time staff members. Academic advisers, LD specialists, professional tutors, strategy tutors, and other are provided through the program or unit. Academic advisers and trained peer tutors are provided collaboratively through on-campus or off-campus services.

Orientation The program or unit offers a mandatory 4-day/3-night (residential) orientation for new students before classes begin and during summer prior to enrollment.

Unique Aids and Services Aids, services, or accommodations include priority registration, twice weekly individual mentoring.

Assistive Technology Assistive technology is located in the Pathways Office and includes learning support software and scanning.

Subject-Area Tutoring Tutoring is offered one-on-one and in small groups for most subjects. Tutoring is provided through the program or unit via professional tutors and other. Tutoring is also provided collaboratively through on-campus or off-campus services via graduate assistants/students and trained peer tutors.

St. Thomas Aquinas College (continued)

Basic Skills Remediation Remediation is offered one-on-one, in small groups, and in class-size groups for learning strategies, study skills, and time management. Remediation is provided through the program or unit via professional tutors and other. Remediation is also provided collaboratively through on-campus or off-campus services via graduate assistants/students and trained peer tutors.

Fees *LD Program or Service* fee is $3400. *Orientation* fee is $500 to $700.

Application For admittance to the program or unit, students are required to apply to the program directly and provide a psychoeducational report (3 years old or less). It is recommended that students provide documentation of high school services. Upon application, materials documenting need for services should be sent only to the LD program or unit. *Application deadline (institutional):* Continuous. *Application deadline (LD program):* Rolling/continuous for fall.

Written Policies Written policies regarding course substitutions, general/basic LD accommodations, substitutions and waivers of admissions requirements, and substitutions and waivers of graduation requirements are available through the program or unit directly.

Schreiner University
Learning Support Services

2100 Memorial Boulevard

Kerrville, TX 78028-5697

http://www.schreiner.edu/academics/lss.html

Contact: Dr. Jude D. Gallik, Director. Phone: 830-792-7257. Fax: 830-792-7294. E-mail: jgallik@schreiner.edu.

Learning Support Services Approximately 80 registered undergraduate students were served during 2006–07. The program or unit includes 4 full-time and 22 part-time staff members. Academic advisers, counselors, LD specialists, and professional tutors are provided through the program or unit. Academic advisers are provided collaboratively through on-campus or off-campus services.

Subject-Area Tutoring Tutoring is offered one-on-one and in small groups for all subjects. Tutoring is provided through the program or unit via professional tutors.

Enrichment Programs for career planning and college survival skills are provided collaboratively through on-campus or off-campus services.

Fees *LD Program or Service* fee is $6300.

Application For admittance to the program or unit, students are required to provide a psychoeducational report (1 year old or less) and provide WAIS III, achievement tests, and disability statement. It is recommended that students provide documentation of high school services. Upon application, materials documenting need for services should be sent only to the LD program or unit. *Application deadline (LD program):* 4/1 for fall. 11/15 for spring.

Written Policies Written policies regarding general/basic LD accommodations and substitutions and waivers of admissions requirements are available on the program Web site. Written policies regarding general/basic LD accommodations and substitutions and waivers of admissions requirements are outlined in the school's catalog/handbook. Written policies regarding course substitutions and substitutions and waivers of graduation requirements are available through the program or unit directly.

Southern Illinois University Carbondale
Clinical Center Achieve Program

Carbondale, IL 62901-4701

http://www.siu.edu/~achieve

Contact: Mr. Roger Pugh, Learning Skills Specialist. Phone: 618-453-2369 Ext. 10. Fax: 618-453-3711. E-mail: rpugh@siu.edu. Head of LD Program: Mrs. Sally Dedecker, Coordinator. Phone: 618-453-6131 Ext. 41. Fax: 618-453-3711. E-mail: lukidawg@siu.edu.

Clinical Center Achieve Program Approximately 150 registered undergraduate students were served during 2006–07. The program or unit includes 6 full-time and 150 part-time staff members. Diagnostic specialists, graduate assistants/students, LD specialists, professional tutors, remediation/learning specialists, skill tutors, special education teachers, strategy tutors, teacher trainees, and trained peer tutors are provided through the program or unit. Academic advisers, coaches, counselors, diagnostic specialists, and regular education teachers are provided collaboratively through on-campus or off-campus services.

Orientation The program or unit offers a mandatory 2-day orientation for new students before classes begin.

Summer Program To help prepare for the demands of college, there is a mandatory 2-day summer program prior to entering the school available to high school graduates that focuses on life skills and/or college life adjustment and self-advocacy. The program accepts students from out-of-state.

Unique Aids and Services Aids, services, or accommodations include advocates, career counseling, faculty training, and support groups.

Assistive Technology Assistive technology is located in a special lab and includes audio recorded books.

Subject-Area Tutoring Tutoring is offered one-on-one and in small groups for all subjects. Tutoring is provided through the program or unit via computer-based instruction, graduate assistants/students, LD specialists, professional tutors, and trained peer tutors.

Diagnostic Testing Testing is provided through the program or unit for auditory processing, handwriting, intelligence, learning strategies, learning styles, math, motor skills, neuropsychological, reading, spelling, spoken language, visual processing, written language, and other services. Testing for auditory processing, neuropsychological, personality, study skills, and visual processing is provided collaboratively through on-campus or off-campus services.

Basic Skills Remediation Remediation is offered one-on-one and in small groups for computer skills, learning strategies, math, reading, spelling, spoken language, study skills, time management, written language, and organization and test-taking. Remediation is provided through the program or unit via computer-based instruction, graduate assistants/students, LD specialists, professional tutors, special education teachers, teacher trainees, and trained peer tutors.

Enrichment Enrichment programs are available through the program or unit for career planning, college survival skills, learning strategies, math, practical computer skills, reading, self-advocacy, study skills, test taking, time management, vocabulary development, and written composition skills. Programs for health and nutrition, oral communication skills, reading, stress management, study skills, test taking, time management, and written composition skills are provided collaboratively through on-campus or off-campus services. Credit is offered for oral communication skills and practical computer skills.

Fees *LD Program or Service* fee is $500 to $5600 (fee varies according to level/tier of service). *Diagnostic Testing* fee is $500 to $1000.

Application For admittance to the program or unit, students are required to apply to the program directly, provide a psychoeducational report, and provide documentation of high school services. It is recommended that students provide diagnostic reports (reports that are several years old are accepted if complete). Upon application, materials documenting need for services should be sent only to the LD program or unit. Upon acceptance, documentation of need for services should be sent only to the LD program or unit. *Application deadline (institutional):* Continuous. *Application deadline (LD program):* Rolling/continuous for fall and rolling/continuous for spring.

Written Policies Written policy regarding general/basic LD accommodations is available on the program Web site. Written policy regarding general/basic LD accommodations is outlined in the school's catalog/handbook. Written policies regarding course substitutions, general/basic LD accommodations, reduced course loads, substitutions and waivers of admissions requirements, and substitutions and waivers of graduation requirements are available through the program or unit directly.

The University of Arizona
The Strategic Alternative Learning Techniques (SALT) Center

Tucson, AZ 85721

http://www.salt.arizona.edu

Contact: Susan Donaldson, Assistant to the Director. Phone: 520-621-1427. Fax: 520-626-6072. E-mail: sdonalds@u.arizona.edu. Head of LD Program: Dr. Jeff M. Orgera, Director. Phone: 520-621-1427. Fax: 520-626-6072. E-mail: jorgera@u.arizona.edu.

The Strategic Alternative Learning Techniques (SALT) Center Approximately 565 registered undergraduate students were served during 2006–07. The program or unit includes 26 full-time and 2 part-time staff members. Coaches, counselors, graduate assistants/students, LD specialists, remediation/learning specialists, skill tutors, strategy tutors, trained peer tutors, and other are provided through the program or unit. Academic advisers and counselors are provided collaboratively through on-campus or off-campus services.

Orientation The program or unit offers a mandatory 1-day orientation for new students before registration and during summer prior to enrollment.

Unique Aids and Services Aids, services, or accommodations include advocates, parent workshops, and support groups.

Assistive Technology Assistive technology is located in campus labs, the DSS office, Computer Resource Lab in SALT Center and includes learning support software, scanning, and Inspiration, Kurzweil, voice recognition software. Technology training is provided to incoming students.

Subject-Area Tutoring Tutoring is offered one-on-one, in small groups, and in class-size groups for most subjects. Tutoring is provided through the program or unit via computer-based instruction, graduate assistants/students, and trained peer tutors.

Enrichment Enrichment programs are available through the program or unit for career planning, college survival skills, health and nutrition, learning strategies, math, oral communication skills, reading, self-advocacy, stress management, study skills, test taking, time management, vocabulary development, and written composition skills. Programs for career planning, college survival skills, health and nutrition, learning strategies, math, medication management, oral communication skills, practical computer skills, stress management, study skills, test taking, time management, vocabulary development, and written composition skills are provided collaboratively through on-campus or off-campus services.

Student Organization Associated Students with Disabilities consists of 50 members.

Fees *LD Program or Service* fee is $1800 to $4200 (fee varies according to level/tier of service). *Orientation* fee is $50 to $80.

Application For admittance to the program or unit, students are required to apply to the program directly and provide responses to three essays, interview, and application. It is recommended that students provide a psychoeducational report (3 years old or less) and provide documentation of high school services. Upon application, materials documenting need for services should be sent only to the LD program or unit. Upon acceptance, documentation of need for services should be sent only to the LD program or unit. *Application deadline (institutional):* 4/1. *Application deadline (LD program):* Rolling/continuous for fall and rolling/continuous for spring.

Written Policies Written policies regarding general/basic LD accommodations and substitutions and waivers of admissions requirements are available on the program Web site. Written policy regarding substitutions and waivers of admissions requirements is outlined in the school's catalog/handbook. Written policies regarding course substitutions, general/basic LD accommodations, reduced course loads, and substitutions and waivers of graduation requirements are available through the program or unit directly.

University of California, Irvine
Disability Services Center

Irvine, CA 92697

http://www.disability.uci.edu

Contact: Dr. Jan Serrantino, Director. Phone: 949-824-7494. Fax: 949-824-3083. E-mail: dsc@uci.edu.

Disability Services Center Approximately 400 registered undergraduate students were served during 2006–07. The program or unit includes 6 full-time and 15 part-time staff members. Counselors are provided through the program or unit. Counselors are provided collaboratively through on-campus or off-campus services.

Orientation The program or unit offers a mandatory 2-hour orientation for new students before classes begin.

Summer Program To help prepare for the demands of college, there is an optional summer program prior to entering the school.

Unique Aids and Services Aids, services, or accommodations include career counseling, priority registration, and support groups.

University of California, Irvine (continued)

Assistive Technology Assistive technology is located in the DSS office and includes digital textbooks/e-text, learning support software, and scanning. Technology training is provided to incoming students.

Subject-Area Tutoring Tutoring is offered in small groups for most subjects. Tutoring is provided collaboratively through on-campus or off-campus services via graduate assistants/students, professional tutors, and trained peer tutors.

Enrichment Programs for career planning, college survival skills, health and nutrition, learning strategies, math, medication management, oral communication skills, self-advocacy, stress management, study skills, test taking, time management, and written composition skills are provided collaboratively through on-campus or off-campus services.

Application For admittance to the program or unit, students are required to apply to the program directly and provide a psychoeducational report (3 years old or less). It is recommended that students provide documentation of high school services. Upon application, materials documenting need for services should be sent only to the LD program or unit. Upon acceptance, documentation of need for services should be sent only to the LD program or unit. *Application deadline (institutional): 11/30. Application deadline (LD program):* Rolling/continuous for fall and rolling/continuous for spring.

Written Policies Written policy regarding general/basic LD accommodations is available on the program Web site. Written policy regarding general/basic LD accommodations is available through the program or unit directly.

The University of North Carolina at Chapel Hill
Academic Success Program for Students with LD/ADHD

Chapel Hill, NC 27599

http://www.unc.edu/depts/lds

Contact: Dr. Theresa Laurie Maitland, Director. Phone: 919-962-7227. Fax: 919-962-3674. E-mail: lds@unc.edu.

Academic Success Program for Students with LD/ADHD

Approximately 380 registered undergraduate students were served during 2006–07. The program or unit includes 4 full-time and 3 part-time staff members. Academic advisers, coaches, LD specialists, special education teachers, strategy tutors, and other are provided through the program or unit. Academic advisers, coaches, counselors, diagnostic specialists, graduate assistants/students, professional tutors, remediation/learning specialists, and skill tutors are provided collaboratively through on-campus or off-campus services.

Unique Aids and Services Aids, services, or accommodations include personal coach, priority registration, individual meetings with LD specialists.

Assistive Technology Assistive technology is located in the DSS office and includes digital textbooks/e-text and scanning. Technology training is provided to incoming students.

Subject-Area Tutoring Tutoring is offered one-on-one and in small groups for all subjects. Tutoring is provided collaboratively through on-campus or off-campus services via graduate assistants/students, professional tutors, and trained peer tutors.

Basic Skills Remediation Remediation is offered one-on-one and in small groups for learning strategies, math, reading, study skills, time management, and written language. Remediation is provided through the program or unit via LD specialists. Remediation is also provided collaboratively through on-campus or off-campus services via regular education teachers.

Enrichment Enrichment programs are available through the program or unit for college survival skills, learning strategies, medication management, reading, self-advocacy, stress management, study skills, test taking, time management, written composition skills, and other. Programs for career planning, college survival skills, health and nutrition, math, medication management, oral communication skills, practical computer skills, reading, stress management, study skills, test taking, time management, vocabulary development, written composition skills, and other are provided collaboratively through on-campus or off-campus services.

Application For admittance to the program or unit, students are required to apply to the program directly, provide a psychoeducational report (3 years old or less), and provide evaluation of attention and co-morbid issues (for AD/HD). It is recommended that students provide documentation of high school services. Upon application, materials documenting need for services should be sent only to admissions with institutional application materials. Upon acceptance, documentation of need for services should be sent only to the LD program or unit. *Application deadline (institutional): 1/15. Application deadline (LD program):* Rolling/continuous for fall and rolling/continuous for spring.

Written Policies Written policy regarding general/basic LD accommodations is available on the program Web site. Written policy regarding general/basic LD accommodations is available through the program or unit directly.

University of the Ozarks
Jones Learning Center

415 North College Avenue

Clarksville, AR 72830-2880

http://www.ozarks.edu/jlc/

Contact: Ms. Julia H. Frost, Director. Phone: 479-979-1403. Fax: 479-979-1429. E-mail: jlc@ozarks.edu.

Jones Learning Center Approximately 78 registered undergraduate students were served during 2006–07. The program or unit includes 21 full-time staff members and 1 part-time staff member. Academic advisers, diagnostic specialists, LD specialists, professional tutors, remediation/learning specialists, and trained peer tutors are provided through the program or unit. Academic advisers and regular education teachers are provided collaboratively through on-campus or off-campus services.

Orientation The program or unit offers a mandatory 3-day orientation for new students before classes begin and during summer prior to enrollment.

Unique Aids and Services Aids, services, or accommodations include priority registration, a program coordinator assigned to each student.

Assistive Technology Assistive technology is located in campus labs, a special lab and includes digital textbooks/e-text and scanning. Technology training is provided to incoming students.

Subject-Area Tutoring Tutoring is offered one-on-one and in small groups for all subjects. Tutoring is provided through the program or unit via LD specialists, professional tutors, and trained peer tutors.

Diagnostic Testing Testing is provided through the program or unit for auditory processing, intelligence, learning styles, math, reading, spelling, study skills, visual processing, and written language.

Basic Skills Remediation Remediation is offered one-on-one and in small groups for learning strategies, math, reading, study skills, time management, and written language. Remediation is provided through the program or unit via LD specialists and professional tutors.

Enrichment Enrichment programs are available through the program or unit for college survival skills, learning strategies, math, reading, self-advocacy, stress management, study skills, test taking, time management, and written composition skills. Programs for career planning and practical computer skills are provided collaboratively through on-campus or off-campus services. Credit is offered for career planning.

Student Organization Learning Center Ambassadors consists of 16 members.

Fees *LD Program or Service* fee is $15,500. *Diagnostic Testing* fee is $450 to $750.

Application For admittance to the program or unit, students are required to apply to the program directly, provide a psychoeducational report (5 years old or less), and provide results of on-campus psychoeducational evaluation. It is recommended that students provide documentation of high school services. Upon application, materials documenting need for services should be sent only to the LD program or unit. *Application deadline (institutional):* Continuous. *Application deadline (LD program):* Rolling/continuous for fall and rolling/continuous for spring.

Written Policies Written policies regarding general/basic LD accommodations and substitutions and waivers of admissions requirements are available on the program Web site. Written policies regarding general/basic LD accommodations and substitutions and waivers of admissions requirements are outlined in the school's catalog/handbook. Written policies regarding course substitutions, reduced course loads, and substitutions and waivers of admissions requirements are available through the program or unit directly.

University of Wisconsin–Oshkosh
Project Success

800 Algoma Boulevard

Oshkosh, WI 54901

http://www.uwosh.edu/success

Contact: Dr. William R. Kitz, Director. Phone: 920-424-1033. Fax: 920-424-0858. E-mail: kitz@uwosh.edu.

Project Success Approximately 200 registered undergraduate students were served during 2006–07. The program or unit includes 3 full-time and 50 part-time staff members. Diagnostic specialists, graduate assistants/students, LD specialists, remediation/learning specialists, skill tutors, special education teachers, strategy tutors, teacher trainees, and trained peer tutors are provided through the program or unit. Academic advisers, counselors, remediation/learning specialists, skill tutors, strategy tutors, teacher trainees, and trained peer tutors are provided collaboratively through on-campus or off-campus services.

Orientation The program or unit offers a mandatory 1-day orientation for new students before registration, before classes begin, and during summer prior to enrollment.

Summer Program To help prepare for the demands of college, there is a mandatory 6-week summer program prior to entering the school available to high school graduates that focuses on life skills and/or college life adjustment, self-advocacy, specific subject tutoring, study skills, and test-taking skills. Degree credit will be earned. The program accepts students from out-of-state.

Unique Aids and Services Aids, services, or accommodations include advocates.

Assistive Technology Assistive technology is located in campus labs, the DSS office, a special lab and includes digital textbooks/e-text and scanning. Technology training is provided to incoming students.

Subject-Area Tutoring Tutoring is offered one-on-one and in small groups for most subjects. Tutoring is provided through the program or unit via computer-based instruction, graduate assistants/students, LD specialists, professional tutors, and trained peer tutors. Tutoring is also provided collaboratively through on-campus or off-campus services via computer-based instruction and trained peer tutors.

Diagnostic Testing Testing is provided through the program or unit for math, reading, spelling, spoken language, and written language.

Basic Skills Remediation Remediation is offered one-on-one, in small groups, and in class-size groups for computer skills, handwriting, learning strategies, math, reading, spelling, study skills, time management, and written language. Remediation is provided through the program or unit via computer-based instruction, graduate assistants/students, LD specialists, professional tutors, special education teachers, teacher trainees, and trained peer tutors. Remediation is also provided collaboratively through on-campus or off-campus services via computer-based instruction.

Enrichment Enrichment programs are available through the program or unit for college survival skills, learning strategies, math, oral communication skills, practical computer skills, reading, self-advocacy, study skills, test taking, time management, vocabulary development, and written composition skills. Programs for career planning, college survival skills, health and nutrition, math, oral communication skills, practical computer skills, reading, stress management, study skills, test taking, time management, vocabulary development, and written composition skills are provided collaboratively through on-campus or off-campus services. Credit is offered for college survival skills, math, practical computer skills, reading, study skills, and written composition skills.

Application For admittance to the program or unit, students are required to apply to the program directly, provide a psychoeducational report (3 years old or less), and provide documentation of high school services. Upon application, materials documenting need for services should be sent only to the LD program or unit. Upon acceptance, documentation of need for services should be sent only to the LD program or unit. *Application deadline (institutional):* Continuous. *Application deadline (LD program):* Rolling/continuous for fall and rolling/continuous for spring.

University of Wisconsin–Oshkosh (continued)

Written Policies Written policies regarding course substitutions, general/basic LD accommodations, grade forgiveness, reduced course loads, substitutions and waivers of admissions requirements, and substitutions and waivers of graduation requirements are available through the program or unit directly.

Ursuline College
FOCUS Program

2550 Lander Road

Pepper Pike, OH 44124-4398

http://www.ursuline.edu/

Contact: Ms. Annette Gromada, Learning Disabilities Specialist. Phone: 440-449-2046. E-mail: agromada@ursuline.edu.

FOCUS Program Approximately 12 registered undergraduate students were served during 2006–07. The program or unit includes 2 full-time and 5 part-time staff members. Academic advisers, coaches, counselors, LD specialists, professional tutors, regular education teachers, remediation/learning specialists, and strategy tutors are provided through the program or unit.

Orientation The program or unit offers a mandatory varying length orientation for new students before classes begin, during registration, after classes begin, and individually by special arrangement.

Unique Aids and Services Aids, services, or accommodations include career counseling, faculty training, parent workshops, personal coach, priority registration, support groups, weekly meetings with faculty, testing accommodations.

Assistive Technology Assistive technology is located in the DSS office and includes learning support software. Technology training is provided to incoming students.

Subject-Area Tutoring Tutoring is offered one-on-one, in small groups, and in class-size groups for some subjects. Tutoring is provided through the program or unit via computer-based instruction, LD specialists, and professional tutors. Tutoring is also provided collaboratively through on-campus or off-campus services via computer-based instruction, graduate assistants/students, and professional tutors.

Diagnostic Testing Testing is provided through the program or unit for learning strategies, learning styles, math, reading, study skills, and written language. Testing for auditory processing, motor skills, neuropsychological, personality, social skills, and visual processing is provided collaboratively through on-campus or off-campus services.

Basic Skills Remediation Remediation is offered one-on-one, in small groups, and in class-size groups for computer skills, learning strategies, math, reading, social skills, spoken language, study skills, time management, visual processing, and written language. Remediation is provided through the program or unit via computer-based instruction, LD specialists, and professional tutors. Remediation is also provided collaboratively through on-campus or off-campus services via computer-based instruction, professional tutors, and regular education teachers.

Enrichment Enrichment programs are available through the program or unit for college survival skills, learning strategies, medication management, oral communication skills, self-advocacy, stress management, study skills, test taking, time management, and writ-

ten composition skills. Programs for career planning, college survival skills, health and nutrition, learning strategies, math, practical computer skills, reading, stress management, study skills, test taking, time management, vocabulary development, and written composition skills are provided collaboratively through on-campus or off-campus services.

Fees *LD Program or Service* fee is $1350. *Diagnostic Testing* fee is $0 to $500.

Application For admittance to the program or unit, students are required to apply to the program directly and provide a psychoeducational report (3 years old or less). Upon application, materials documenting need for services should be sent only to the LD program or unit. *Application deadline (institutional):* Continuous. *Application deadline (LD program):* Rolling/continuous for fall and rolling/continuous for spring.

Written Policies Written policy regarding general/basic LD accommodations is outlined in the school's catalog/handbook. Written policy regarding general/basic LD accommodations is available through the program or unit directly.

West Virginia Wesleyan College
Learning Center

59 College Avenue

Buckhannon, WV 26201

http://www.wvwc.edu/stu/sass

Contact: Dr. Shawn Mahoney Kuba, Director of the Learning Center. Phone: 304-473-8563. Fax: 304-473-8497. E-mail: kuba_s@wvwc.edu.

Learning Center Approximately 90 registered undergraduate students were served during 2006–07. The program or unit includes 7 full-time and 10 part-time staff members. Academic advisers, counselors, diagnostic specialists, LD specialists, professional tutors, remediation/learning specialists, skill tutors, special education teachers, strategy tutors, and trained peer tutors are provided through the program or unit. Academic advisers and counselors are provided collaboratively through on-campus or off-campus services.

Orientation The program or unit offers a mandatory 4-hour orientation for new students before registration and on the first day of first-year orientation.

Unique Aids and Services Aids, services, or accommodations include faculty training, parent workshops, personal coach, priority registration, support groups, weekly meetings with faculty, weekly conference with LD adviser, test lab, mentor advising program.

Assistive Technology Assistive technology is located in a special lab, the campus library and includes digital textbooks/e-text, learning support software, scanning, and Kurzweil text-to-voice, Dragon Professional voice-to-text, Inspiration. Technology training is provided to incoming students.

Subject-Area Tutoring Tutoring is offered one-on-one and in small groups for all subjects. Tutoring is provided through the program or unit via computer-based instruction, LD specialists, professional tutors, and trained peer tutors.

Diagnostic Testing Testing is provided through the program or unit for learning strategies, learning styles, math, reading, spelling, spoken language, study skills, visual processing, and written language.

Basic Skills Remediation Remediation is offered one-on-one for auditory processing, learning strategies, math, reading, social skills, spelling, spoken language, study skills, time management, visual processing, written language, and Lindamood-Bell and Mentor Adv. Remediation is provided through the program or unit via LD specialists, professional tutors, regular education teachers, and special education teachers.

Enrichment Enrichment programs are available through the program or unit for college survival skills, learning strategies, math, medication management, oral communication skills, practical computer skills, reading, self-advocacy, stress management, study skills, test taking, time management, vocabulary development, written composition skills, and other. Programs for career planning, health and nutrition, medication management, oral communication skills, practical computer skills, and stress management are provided collaboratively through on-campus or off-campus services. Credit is offered for career planning, college survival skills, health and nutrition, learning strategies, practical computer skills, and study skills.

Fees *LD Program or Service* fee is $600 to $3200 (fee varies according to course level and level/tier of service).

Application For admittance to the program or unit, students are required to provide a psychoeducational report (2 years old or less). It is recommended that students apply to the program directly, provide documentation of high school services, and provide recommendation of services and accommodations that will be helpful to student success. Upon application, materials documenting need for services should be sent only to the LD program or unit. Upon acceptance, documentation of need for services should be sent only to the LD program or unit. *Application deadline (LD program):* Rolling/continuous for fall and rolling/continuous for spring.

Written Policies Written policy regarding general/basic LD accommodations is available on the program Web site. Written policy regarding general/basic LD accommodations is available through the program or unit directly.

FOUR-YEAR COLLEGES WITH SELF-DIRECTED/DECENTRALIZED PROGRAMS

Abilene Christian University
Alpha Academic Services

ACU Box 29100

Abilene, TX 79699-9100

http://www.acu.edu/alpha

Contact: Mrs. Jamie Jimenez, Administrative Assistant. Phone: 325-674-2667. Fax: 325-674-6847. E-mail: jimenezj@acu.edu.

Alpha Academic Services Approximately 140 registered undergraduate students were served during 2006–07. The program or unit includes 6 full-time and 15 part-time staff members. Academic advisers, coaches, counselors, graduate assistants/students, professional tutors, skill tutors, strategy tutors, and trained peer tutors are provided through the program or unit. Academic advisers, counselors, diagnostic specialists, and regular education teachers are provided collaboratively through on-campus or off-campus services.

Orientation The program or unit offers a mandatory 2-hour orientation for new students after classes begin and individually by special arrangement.

Unique Aids and Services Aids, services, or accommodations include career counseling.

Assistive Technology Assistive technology is located in the DSS office, the library and includes learning support software and scanning. Technology training is provided to incoming students.

Subject-Area Tutoring Tutoring is offered one-on-one, in small groups, and in class-size groups for most subjects. Tutoring is provided through the program or unit via professional tutors and trained peer tutors. Tutoring is also provided collaboratively through on-campus or off-campus services via graduate assistants/students and trained peer tutors.

Diagnostic Testing Testing is provided through the program or unit for learning strategies, learning styles, and study skills. Testing for intelligence, math, neuropsychological, personality, reading, social skills, spelling, spoken language, visual processing, and written language is provided collaboratively through on-campus or off-campus services.

Basic Skills Remediation Remediation is offered one-on-one, in small groups, and in class-size groups for learning strategies, math, reading, spelling, spoken language, study skills, time management, and written language. Remediation is provided through the program or unit via graduate assistants/students and professional tutors. Remediation is also provided collaboratively through on-campus or off-campus services via computer-based instruction and regular education teachers.

Enrichment Enrichment programs are available through the program or unit for learning strategies, reading, self-advocacy, stress management, study skills, test taking, time management, vocabulary development, and written composition skills. Programs for career planning, college survival skills, health and nutrition, practical computer skills, reading, stress management, study skills, test taking, time management, vocabulary development, and written composition skills are provided collaboratively through on-campus or off-campus services.

Fees *Diagnostic Testing* fee is $250.

Application For admittance to the program or unit, students are required to apply to the program directly and provide a psychoeducational report (3 years old or less). It is recommended that students provide documentation of high school services. Upon application, materials documenting need for services should be sent to both admissions and the LD program or unit. Upon acceptance, documentation of need for services should be sent only to the LD program or unit. *Application deadline (institutional): 8/1. Application deadline (LD program): 8/1 for fall. 12/1 for spring.*

Written Policies Written policy regarding general/basic LD accommodations is available through the program or unit directly.

Academy of Art University
Classroom Services

79 New Montgomery Street

San Francisco, CA 94105-3410

http://cs.academyart.edu

Contact: Classroom Services Office. Phone: 415-618-3775. Fax: 415-618-3805. E-mail: classroomservices@academyart.edu. Head of LD Program: Ms. Andrea Drillings, Classroom Services Director. Phone: 415-618-3775. Fax: 415-618-3805. E-mail: classroomservices@academyart.edu.

Classroom Services The program or unit includes 3 full-time staff members and 1 part-time staff member. Strategy tutors are provided through the program or unit. Academic advisers, coaches, professional tutors, and skill tutors are provided collaboratively through on-campus or off-campus services.

Unique Aids and Services Aids, services, or accommodations include career counseling, faculty training, personal coach, support groups, and weekly meetings with faculty.

Assistive Technology Assistive technology is located in the DSS office, the library and includes audio books, CCTV scanner. Technology training is provided to incoming students.

Subject-Area Tutoring Tutoring is offered one-on-one and in small groups for all subjects. Tutoring is provided through the program or unit via LD specialists. Tutoring is also provided collaboratively through on-campus or off-campus services via professional tutors.

Basic Skills Remediation Remediation is available for learning strategies, study skills, and time management. Remediation is provided through the program or unit via LD specialists. Remediation is also provided collaboratively through on-campus or off-campus services.

Enrichment Enrichment programs are available through the program or unit for college survival skills, learning strategies, self-advocacy, stress management, study skills, test taking, and time management. Programs for career planning, college survival skills, learning strategies, oral communication skills, practical computer skills, self-advocacy, stress management, study skills, test taking, time management, and written composition skills are provided collaboratively through on-campus or off-campus services.

Application For admittance to the program or unit, students are required to provide a psychoeducational report. Upon application, materials documenting need for services should be sent only to the LD program or unit. Upon acceptance, documentation of need for services should be sent only to the LD program or unit. *Application deadline (institutional):* Continuous. *Application deadline (LD program):* Rolling/continuous for fall and rolling/continuous for spring.

Academy of Art University (continued)

Written Policies Written policy regarding general/basic LD accommodations is outlined in the school's catalog/handbook. Written policy regarding general/basic LD accommodations is available through the program or unit directly.

Acadia University
Disability/Access

Wolfville, NS B4P 2R6

Canada

http://www.acadiau.ca/

Contact: Jill Davies, Academic Support Coordinator. Phone: 902-585-1127. E-mail: jill.davies@acadiau.ca.

Disability/Access Approximately 130 registered undergraduate students were served during 2006–07. The program or unit includes 2 full-time staff members and 1 part-time staff member. Counselors and LD specialists are provided collaboratively through on-campus or off-campus services.

Assistive Technology Assistive technology is located in a special lab, the student's individual personal computer and includes digital textbooks/e-text, learning support software, and scanning. Technology training is provided to incoming students.

Subject-Area Tutoring Tutoring is offered one-on-one for most subjects. Tutoring is provided through the program or unit via trained peer tutors.

Diagnostic Testing Testing is provided through the program or unit for personality and study skills. Testing for intelligence, learning styles, math, neuropsychological, reading, spelling, visual processing, and written language is provided collaboratively through on-campus or off-campus services.

Basic Skills Remediation Remediation is offered one-on-one and in small groups for learning strategies, reading, study skills, time management, and written language. Remediation is provided through the program or unit via LD specialists. Remediation is also provided collaboratively through on-campus or off-campus services via trained peer tutors.

Fees *Diagnostic Testing* fee is applicable.

Application For admittance to the program or unit, students are required to provide a psychoeducational report (3 years old or less). Upon application, materials documenting need for services should be sent only to admissions with institutional application materials. Upon acceptance, documentation of need for services should be sent only to the LD program or unit. *Application deadline (institutional):* 7/1. *Application deadline (LD program):* Rolling/continuous for fall and rolling/continuous for spring.

Written Policies Written policy regarding general/basic LD accommodations is available on the program Web site. Written policy regarding general/basic LD accommodations is available through the program or unit directly.

Adams State College

208 Edgemont Boulevard

Alamosa, CO 81102

http://www2.adams.edu/ada/

Contact: Gregory Elliott, Director, Counseling & Career Center. Phone: 719-587-7746. Fax: 719-587-7522. E-mail: gregg_elliott@adams.edu.

Approximately 50 registered undergraduate students were served during 2006–07. The program or unit includes 2 part-time staff members. Counselors are provided through the program or unit. Academic advisers, counselors, graduate assistants/students, and trained peer tutors are provided collaboratively through on-campus or off-campus services.

Assistive Technology Assistive technology is located in campus labs and includes digital textbooks/e-text.

Subject-Area Tutoring Tutoring is offered one-on-one and in small groups for most subjects. Tutoring is provided collaboratively through on-campus or off-campus services via graduate assistants/students and trained peer tutors.

Enrichment Programs for career planning, learning strategies, stress management, study skills, time management, and written composition skills are provided collaboratively through on-campus or off-campus services.

Application For admittance to the program or unit, students are required to provide a psychoeducational report (3 years old or less) and provide documentation of high school services. Upon application, materials documenting need for services should be sent only to the LD program or unit. Upon acceptance, documentation of need for services should be sent only to the LD program or unit. *Application deadline (institutional):* 8/1. *Application deadline (LD program):* Rolling/continuous for fall and rolling/continuous for spring.

Written Policies Written policy regarding general/basic LD accommodations is available on the program Web site.

Alabama Agricultural and Mechanical University
Special Student Services

4900 Meridian Street

Huntsville, AL 35811

http://www.aamu.edu/

Contact: Ms. Sanoyia L. Williams, Director of Special Student Services. Phone: 256-372-4263. Fax: 256-372-4263. E-mail: sanoyia.williams@aamu.edu.

Special Student Services Approximately 45 registered undergraduate students were served during 2006–07. The program or unit includes 1 full-time staff member. Graduate assistants/students are provided through the program or unit. Academic advisers, coaches, counselors, diagnostic specialists, LD specialists, professional tutors, remediation/learning specialists, skill tutors, strategy tutors, and trained peer tutors are provided collaboratively through on-campus or off-campus services.

Summer Program To help prepare for the demands of college, there is an optional summer program prior to entering the school available to high school graduates that focuses on life skills and/or college life adjustment, specific subject tutoring, study skills, test-taking skills, and time management. The program accepts students from out-of-state and is available to students attending other colleges.

Subject-Area Tutoring Tutoring is offered in small groups for most subjects. Tutoring is provided collaboratively through on-campus or off-campus services via graduate assistants/students and trained peer tutors.

Basic Skills Remediation Remediation is offered in class-size groups for math and reading. Remediation is provided collaboratively through on-campus or off-campus services via graduate assistants/students and trained peer tutors.

Enrichment Programs for career planning, college survival skills, math, reading, stress management, study skills, test taking, time management, and written composition skills are provided collaboratively through on-campus or off-campus services. Credit is offered for college survival skills.

Application For admittance to the program or unit, students are required to provide a psychoeducational report (3 years old or less). It is recommended that students provide documentation of high school services. Upon application, materials documenting need for services should be sent to both admissions and the LD program or unit. Upon acceptance, documentation of need for services should be sent only to the LD program or unit. *Application deadline (institutional):* 7/15.

Written Policies Written policy regarding general/basic LD accommodations is available on the program Web site. Written policy regarding general/basic LD accommodations is outlined in the school's catalog/handbook. Written policy regarding general/basic LD accommodations is available through the program or unit directly.

Albany State University
Regents Center for Learning Disorders at Georgia Southern University

504 College Drive
Albany, GA 31705-2717
http://services.georgiasouthern.edu/rcld/

Contact: Dr. Beverly M. Sermons, Liaison/Consultant for RCLD at Georgia Southern. Phone: 912-681-5380. Fax: 912-681-0100. E-mail: beverly.sermons@gsu.edu. Head of LD Program: Dr. Stephanie Harris Jolly, Director of Counseling, Testing, and Disability Student Services. Phone: 229-430-4742. Fax: 229-430-3826. E-mail: stephanie.harris-jolly@asurams.edu.

Regents Center for Learning Disorders at Georgia Southern University Approximately 5 registered undergraduate students were served during 2006–07. Diagnostic specialists, LD specialists, and remediation/learning specialists are provided collaboratively through on-campus or off-campus services.

Orientation The program or unit offers an optional orientation for new students.

Summer Program To help prepare for the demands of college, there is an optional summer program prior to entering the school.

Unique Aids and Services Aids, services, or accommodations include career counseling, parent workshops, and support groups.

Assistive Technology Assistive technology is located in the DSS office and includes scanning. Technology training is provided to incoming students.

Subject-Area Tutoring Tutoring is offered one-on-one for some subjects. Tutoring is provided through the program or unit via trained peer tutors.

Diagnostic Testing Testing is provided through the program or unit for math, reading, and written language.

Basic Skills Remediation Remediation is offered one-on-one for math, reading, study skills, time management, and written language. Remediation is provided through the program or unit via trained peer tutors.

Enrichment Enrichment programs are available through the program or unit for career planning, college survival skills, health and nutrition, learning strategies, math, reading, study skills, time management, and written composition skills.

Fees *LD Program or Service* fee is $500 (fee varies according to level/tier of service). *Diagnostic Testing* fee is $15.

Application For admittance to the program or unit, students are required to provide a psychoeducational report (3 years old or less) and provide documentation of high school services. Upon application, materials documenting need for services should be sent only to the LD program or unit. Upon acceptance, documentation of need for services should be sent only to the LD program or unit. *Application deadline (institutional):* 7/1. *Application deadline (LD program):* Rolling/continuous for fall and rolling/continuous for spring.

Written Policies Written policies regarding general/basic LD accommodations, substitutions and waivers of admissions requirements, and substitutions and waivers of graduation requirements are available through the program or unit directly.

Albertson College of Idaho
Disabled Student Services

2112 Cleveland Boulevard
Caldwell, ID 83605-4494
http://www.albertson.edu/

Contact: Ms. Lynette Allen, Learning Support & Disability Services Coordinator. Phone: 208-459-5683. Fax: 208-459-5849. E-mail: lallen@albertson.edu.

Disabled Student Services Approximately 15 registered undergraduate students were served during 2006–07. The program or unit includes 1 full-time staff member. Remediation/learning specialists are provided through the program or unit. Academic advisers, coaches, counselors, and remediation/learning specialists are provided collaboratively through on-campus or off-campus services.

Orientation The program or unit offers an optional half-day orientation for new students during registration and after classes begin.

Unique Aids and Services Aids, services, or accommodations include career counseling.

Assistive Technology Assistive technology is located in campus labs and includes digital textbooks/e-text and learning support software. Technology training is provided to incoming students.

Subject-Area Tutoring Tutoring is offered one-on-one and in small groups for some subjects. Tutoring is provided collaboratively through on-campus or off-campus services via graduate assistants/students.

Albertson College of Idaho (continued)

Basic Skills Remediation Remediation is offered one-on-one for computer skills, learning strategies, math, reading, study skills, time management, and written language. Remediation is provided collaboratively through on-campus or off-campus services via graduate assistants/students and other.

Enrichment Programs for career planning and study skills are provided collaboratively through on-campus or off-campus services. Credit is offered for study skills.

Application For admittance to the program or unit, students are required to provide a psychoeducational report (3 years old or less). It is recommended that students apply to the program directly and provide documentation of high school services. Upon application, materials documenting need for services should be sent only to the LD program or unit. Upon acceptance, documentation of need for services should be sent to both admissions and the LD program or unit. *Application deadline (institutional): 6/1. Application deadline (LD program):* Rolling/continuous for fall and rolling/continuous for spring.

Written Policies Written policies regarding general/basic LD accommodations and reduced course loads are available on the program Web site. Written policies regarding general/basic LD accommodations and reduced course loads are outlined in the school's catalog/handbook.

Albion College
Learning Support Center

611 East Porter Street

Albion, MI 49224-1831

http://www.albion.edu/asc/lsc/disabilities.asp

Contact: Dr. Pamela Schwartz, Campus Disability Officer and Director Learning Support Center. Phone: 517-629-0825. Fax: 517-629-0504. E-mail: pschwartz@albion.edu.

Learning Support Center Approximately 160 registered undergraduate students were served during 2006–07. The program or unit includes 2 full-time and 2 part-time staff members. Coaches, LD specialists, and remediation/learning specialists are provided through the program or unit. Academic advisers, counselors, diagnostic specialists, graduate assistants/students, skill tutors, strategy tutors, and trained peer tutors are provided collaboratively through on-campus or off-campus services.

Orientation The program or unit offers a mandatory 1- to 2-hour orientation for new students individually by special arrangement.

Unique Aids and Services Aids, services, or accommodations include personal coach.

Assistive Technology Assistive technology is located in campus labs, the DSS office and includes digital textbooks/e-text, learning support software, and scanning. Technology training is provided to incoming students.

Subject-Area Tutoring Tutoring is offered one-on-one and in small groups for all subjects. Tutoring is provided through the program or unit via LD specialists. Tutoring is also provided collaboratively through on-campus or off-campus services via trained peer tutors.

Diagnostic Testing Testing is provided through the program or unit for learning strategies, learning styles, math, reading, and study skills.

Application For admittance to the program or unit, students are required to provide a psychoeducational report (5 years old or less). It is recommended that students provide documentation of high school services. Upon acceptance, documentation of need for services should be sent only to the LD program or unit. *Application deadline (institutional): 3/1. Application deadline (LD program):* Rolling/continuous for fall and rolling/continuous for spring.

Written Policies Written policies regarding general/basic LD accommodations and reduced course loads are available on the program Web site. Written policy regarding general/basic LD accommodations is available through the program or unit directly.

Albright College
Academic Support Services

13th and Bern Streets, PO Box 15234

Reading, PA 19612-5234

http://www.albright.edu/

Contact: Dr. Tiffenia D. Archie, Assistant Academic Dean and Director of Academic Support. Phone: 610-921-7662. Fax: 610-921-7554. E-mail: tarchie@alb.edu.

Academic Support Services Approximately 40 registered undergraduate students were served during 2006–07. The program or unit includes 1 full-time staff member. Graduate assistants/students, LD specialists, remediation/learning specialists, and trained peer tutors are provided through the program or unit. Academic advisers and skill tutors are provided collaboratively through on-campus or off-campus services.

Unique Aids and Services Aids, services, or accommodations include advocates, career counseling, priority registration, support groups, extended time, notes.

Subject-Area Tutoring Tutoring is offered in small groups. Tutoring is provided through the program or unit via trained peer tutors.

Application For admittance to the program or unit, students are required to provide a psychoeducational report (3 years old or less). It is recommended that students provide documentation of high school services. Upon application, materials documenting need for services should be sent only to the LD program or unit. *Application deadline (institutional):* Continuous. *Application deadline (LD program):* Rolling/continuous for fall and rolling/continuous for spring.

Written Policies Written policies regarding general/basic LD accommodations, substitutions and waivers of admissions requirements, and substitutions and waivers of graduation requirements are available on the program Web site. Written policies regarding general/basic LD accommodations, grade forgiveness, substitutions and waivers of admissions requirements, and substitutions and waivers of graduation requirements are outlined in the school's catalog/handbook. Written policies regarding course substitutions, reduced course loads, and substitutions and waivers of graduation requirements are available through the program or unit directly.

Alderson-Broaddus College

1 College Hill Drive
Philippi, WV 26416
http://www.ab.edu/

Contact: Ms. D Colantone, 504 Coordinator. Phone: 304-457-6274. Fax: 304-457-6239. E-mail: colantonedm@mail.ab.edu.

Approximately 26 registered undergraduate students were served during 2006–07. Services are provided through the program or unit.
Assistive Technology Assistive technology is located in campus labs.
Subject-Area Tutoring Tutoring is offered one-on-one, in small groups, and in class-size groups for most subjects. Tutoring is provided through the program or unit via graduate assistants/students, trained peer tutors, and other.
Basic Skills Remediation Remediation is offered one-on-one, in small groups, and in class-size groups for learning strategies, math, reading, study skills, time management, and written language. Remediation is provided through the program or unit via regular education teachers, trained peer tutors, and other.
Enrichment Programs for career planning, health and nutrition, and stress management are provided collaboratively through on-campus or off-campus services. Credit is offered for college survival skills, learning strategies, math, oral communication skills, practical computer skills, reading, study skills, test taking, time management, vocabulary development, written composition skills, and other.
Application For admittance to the program or unit, students are required to provide documentation of high school services. Upon acceptance, documentation of need for services should be sent only to the LD program or unit. *Application deadline (institutional):* Continuous. *Application deadline (LD program):* Rolling/continuous for fall and rolling/continuous for spring.
Written Policies Written policies regarding course substitutions, general/basic LD accommodations, reduced course loads, and substitutions and waivers of admissions requirements are available on the program Web site. Written policies regarding course substitutions, general/basic LD accommodations, reduced course loads, and substitutions and waivers of admissions requirements are outlined in the school's catalog/handbook.

Alma College
The Center for Student Development

614 West Superior Street
Alma, MI 48801-1599
http://www.alma.edu/

Contact: Ms. Stacey Graham, Assistant Director for Student Development. Phone: 989-463-7225. Fax: 989-463-7353. E-mail: graham@alma.edu.

The Center for Student Development Approximately 75 registered undergraduate students were served during 2006–07. The program or unit includes 1 full-time staff member. Academic advisers and counselors are provided collaboratively through on-campus or off-campus services.

Unique Aids and Services Aids, services, or accommodations include career counseling and priority registration.
Assistive Technology Assistive technology is located in campus labs, the DSS office and includes digital textbooks/e-text and scanning.
Subject-Area Tutoring Tutoring is offered one-on-one, in small groups, and in class-size groups for most subjects. Tutoring is provided through the program or unit via trained peer tutors. Tutoring is also provided collaboratively through on-campus or off-campus services via other.
Diagnostic Testing Testing is provided through the program or unit for learning styles, personality, and study skills. Testing for auditory processing, handwriting, intelligence, learning strategies, math, motor skills, neuropsychological, reading, social skills, spelling, spoken language, visual processing, and written language is provided collaboratively through on-campus or off-campus services.
Enrichment Programs for career planning, college survival skills, learning strategies, math, medication management, reading, stress management, study skills, test taking, time management, and written composition skills are provided collaboratively through on-campus or off-campus services.
Application For admittance to the program or unit, students are required to provide a psychoeducational report (5 years old or less). It is recommended that students provide documentation of high school services. Upon acceptance, documentation of need for services should be sent only to the LD program or unit. *Application deadline (institutional):* Continuous. *Application deadline (LD program):* Rolling/continuous for fall and rolling/continuous for spring.
Written Policies Written policy regarding general/basic LD accommodations is available on the program Web site. Written policy regarding general/basic LD accommodations is outlined in the school's catalog/handbook.

Alvernia College
Student Support Services

400 Saint Bernardine Street
Reading, PA 19607-1799
http://www.alvernia.edu

Contact: Jennifer P. Reimert, Associate Registrar/ADA Coordinator. Phone: 610-796-8436. Fax: 610-796-8295.

Student Support Services Approximately 55 registered undergraduate students were served during 2006–07. The program or unit includes 1 full-time staff member. Academic advisers, graduate assistants/students, LD specialists, and regular education teachers are provided collaboratively through on-campus or off-campus services.
Assistive Technology Assistive technology is located in campus labs, a special lab and includes scanning and JAWS, Kurzweil (purchase pending). Technology training is provided to incoming students.
Subject-Area Tutoring Tutoring is offered one-on-one for most subjects. Tutoring is provided collaboratively through on-campus or off-campus services via computer-based instruction, graduate assistants/students, trained peer tutors, and other.

Alvernia College (continued)

Diagnostic Testing Testing for auditory processing, handwriting, intelligence, learning strategies, learning styles, math, motor skills, neuropsychological, personality, reading, social skills, spelling, spoken language, study skills, visual processing, and written language is provided collaboratively through on-campus or off-campus services.

Basic Skills Remediation Remediation is available for computer skills, learning strategies, motor skills, reading, study skills, time management, and written language. Remediation is provided collaboratively through on-campus or off-campus services.

Application For admittance to the program or unit, students are required to provide documentation of high school services. It is recommended that students provide a psychoeducational report (5 years old or less). Upon application, materials documenting need for services should be sent only to the LD program or unit. Upon acceptance, documentation of need for services should be sent only to the LD program or unit. *Application deadline (institutional):* Continuous. *Application deadline (LD program):* Rolling/continuous for fall and rolling/continuous for spring.

Written Policies Written policy regarding general/basic LD accommodations is available on the program Web site. Written policy regarding general/basic LD accommodations is outlined in the school's catalog/handbook. Written policies regarding grade forgiveness and reduced course loads are available through the program or unit directly.

Amherst College
Academic Support Services

PO Box 5000

Amherst, MA 01002-5000

http://www.amherst.edu/

Contact: Dean Charri Boykin-East, Senior Associate Dean of Students. Phone: 413-542-2529. E-mail: cjboykineast@ amherst.edu.

Academic Support Services Approximately 22 registered undergraduate students were served during 2006–07. The program or unit includes 1 part-time staff member. Academic advisers, counselors, and trained peer tutors are provided collaboratively through on-campus or off-campus services.

Subject-Area Tutoring Tutoring is offered one-on-one for some subjects. Tutoring is provided collaboratively through on-campus or off-campus services via trained peer tutors.

Application For admittance to the program or unit, students are required to provide a psychoeducational report (3 years old or less). Upon acceptance, documentation of need for services should be sent only to the LD program or unit. *Application deadline (institutional):* 1/1. *Application deadline (LD program):* Rolling/continuous for fall and rolling/continuous for spring.

Written Policies Written policy regarding general/basic LD accommodations is available through the program or unit directly.

Anderson University

1100 East Fifth Street

Anderson, IN 46012-3495

http://www.anderson.edu/

Contact: Teresa J. Coplin, Director of Disabled Student Services. Phone: 765-641-4223. E-mail: tdcoplin@ anderson.edu.

Approximately 50 registered undergraduate students were served during 2006–07. The program or unit includes 1 full-time and 1 part-time staff member. Academic advisers, coaches, counselors, LD specialists, regular education teachers, and remediation/learning specialists are provided through the program or unit. Academic advisers, counselors, regular education teachers, and trained peer tutors are provided collaboratively through on-campus or off-campus services.

Orientation The program or unit offers an optional orientation for new students individually by special arrangement.

Unique Aids and Services Aids, services, or accommodations include advocates and career counseling.

Assistive Technology Assistive technology is located in the DSS office.

Subject-Area Tutoring Tutoring is offered one-on-one and in small groups for most subjects. Tutoring is provided through the program or unit via LD specialists and trained peer tutors. Tutoring is also provided collaboratively through on-campus or off-campus services via computer-based instruction.

Basic Skills Remediation Remediation is available for learning strategies, spelling, spoken language, study skills, time management, and written language. Remediation is provided through the program or unit via LD specialists and trained peer tutors.

Enrichment Enrichment programs are available through the program or unit for college survival skills, learning strategies, self-advocacy, study skills, test taking, time management, and written composition skills. Programs for career planning, health and nutrition, math, and stress management are provided collaboratively through on-campus or off-campus services. Credit is offered for career planning, college survival skills, health and nutrition, and study skills.

Application For admittance to the program or unit, students are required to provide a psychoeducational report (3 years old or less) and provide documentation of high school services. Upon application, materials documenting need for services should be sent only to the LD program or unit. *Application deadline (institutional):* 7/1. *Application deadline (LD program):* Rolling/continuous for fall and rolling/continuous for spring.

Written Policies Written policy regarding general/basic LD accommodations is available on the program Web site. Written policy regarding general/basic LD accommodations is outlined in the school's catalog/handbook.

Anderson University
Academic Services Center

316 Boulevard

Anderson, SC 29621-4035

http://www.ac.edu/

Contact: Mrs. Linda W. Carlson, Director of Academic Services. Phone: 864-231-2026. Fax: 864-231-5782. E-mail: lcarlson@andersonuniversity.edu.

Academic Services Center Approximately 13 registered undergraduate students were served during 2006–07.

Assistive Technology Assistive technology is located in the DSS office and includes books on tape or CD.

Application For admittance to the program or unit, students are required to provide a psychoeducational report (3 years old or less). It is recommended that students provide documentation of high school services. Upon application, materials documenting need for services should be sent only to admissions with institutional application materials. Upon acceptance, documentation of need for services should be sent only to the LD program or unit. *Application deadline (institutional): 7/1. Application deadline (LD program):* Rolling/continuous for fall and rolling/continuous for spring.

Written Policies Written policy regarding general/basic LD accommodations is available on the program Web site. Written policy regarding general/basic LD accommodations is outlined in the school's catalog/handbook. Written policies regarding course substitutions and substitutions and waivers of graduation requirements are available through the program or unit directly.

Angelo State University

2601 West Avenue N
San Angelo, TX 76909
http://www.angelo.edu/

Contact: Mr. Nolen Mears, Associate Dean of Student Services. Phone: 325-942-2191. Fax: 325-942-2126. E-mail: nolen.mears@angelo.edu.

Assistive Technology Assistive technology is located in the DSS office, the library and includes digital textbooks/e-text.

Diagnostic Testing Testing for auditory processing, intelligence, learning styles, math, neuropsychological, personality, reading, and visual processing is provided collaboratively through on-campus or off-campus services.

Basic Skills Remediation Remediation is available for math and written language.

Enrichment Programs for career planning, college survival skills, health and nutrition, learning strategies, math, medication management, oral communication skills, practical computer skills, reading, self-advocacy, stress management, study skills, test taking, time management, vocabulary development, and written composition skills are provided collaboratively through on-campus or off-campus services.

Fees *Diagnostic Testing* fee is $20.

Application For admittance to the program or unit, students are required to apply to the program directly and provide a psychoeducational report (3 years old or less). It is recommended that students provide documentation of high school services. Upon acceptance, documentation of need for services should be sent to both admissions and the LD program or unit. *Application deadline (institutional):* 8/15. *Application deadline (LD program):* Rolling/continuous for fall and rolling/continuous for spring.

Written Policies Written policies regarding course substitutions, general/basic LD accommodations, substitutions and waivers of admissions requirements, and substitutions and waivers of gradua-tion requirements are available on the program Web site. Written policies regarding course substitutions, general/basic LD accommodations, substitutions and waivers of admissions requirements, and substitutions and waivers of graduation requirements are outlined in the school's catalog/handbook.

Aquinas College
Student Affairs and Student Learning Services

4210 Harding Road
Nashville, TN 37205-2005
http://www.aquinascollege.edu/studentaffairs

Contact: Mrs. Suzette Telli, Director of Student Affairs. Phone: 615-297-7545 Ext. 436. Fax: 615-297-7970. E-mail: tellis@aquinascollege.edu.

Student Affairs and Student Learning Services Approximately 6 registered undergraduate students were served during 2006–07. The program or unit includes 2 full-time and 3 part-time staff members. Professional tutors, skill tutors, and trained peer tutors are provided through the program or unit. Academic advisers are provided collaboratively through on-campus or off-campus services.

Subject-Area Tutoring Tutoring is offered one-on-one and in small groups for most subjects. Tutoring is provided through the program or unit via professional tutors and trained peer tutors.

Diagnostic Testing Testing for auditory processing, intelligence, math, reading, visual processing, and written language is provided collaboratively through on-campus or off-campus services.

Basic Skills Remediation Remediation is offered in small groups for learning strategies, study skills, and time management. Remediation is provided through the program or unit via professional tutors.

Enrichment Enrichment programs are available through the program or unit for college survival skills, learning strategies, study skills, test taking, and time management. Credit is offered for college survival skills and learning strategies.

Fees *Diagnostic Testing* fee is $75 to $250.

Application For admittance to the program or unit, students are required to apply to the program directly and provide a psychoeducational report (5 years old or less). It is recommended that students provide documentation of high school services. Upon acceptance, documentation of need for services should be sent only to the LD program or unit. *Application deadline (institutional):* Continuous. *Application deadline (LD program):* Rolling/continuous for fall and rolling/continuous for spring.

Written Policies Written policy regarding general/basic LD accommodations is available on the program Web site. Written policy regarding general/basic LD accommodations is outlined in the school's catalog/handbook.

Argosy University, Chicago

20 South Clark Street, Suite 300
Chicago, IL 60603
http://www.argosyu.edu/

Argosy University, Chicago (continued)

Contact: Amy Herrick, Director of Student Services. Phone: 312-777-7637. Fax: 312-777-7750. E-mail: aherrick@ argosyu.edu.

Subject-Area Tutoring Tutoring is offered one-on-one for most subjects. Tutoring is provided collaboratively through on-campus or off-campus services via graduate assistants/students, professional tutors, and trained peer tutors.

Application For admittance to the program or unit, students are required to apply to the program directly and provide a psychoeducational report. Upon application, materials documenting need for services should be sent only to the LD program or unit. Upon acceptance, documentation of need for services should be sent only to the LD program or unit. *Application deadline (LD program):* Rolling/continuous for fall and rolling/continuous for spring.

Written Policies Written policy regarding general/basic LD accommodations is outlined in the school's catalog/handbook.

Argosy University, Nashville
Disability Services Office

341 Cool Springs Boulevard, Suite 210

Franklin, TN 37067-7226

http://www.argosyu.edu/

Contact: Mrs. Stacy Barger, Director of Student Services. Phone: 615-525-2800 Ext. 2814. Fax: 615-525-2900. E-mail: sbarger@argosyu.edu.

Disability Services Office The program or unit includes 1 full-time staff member. Academic advisers and regular education teachers are provided through the program or unit.

Application For admittance to the program or unit, students are required to apply to the program directly and provide a psychoeducational report (3 years old or less). Upon acceptance, documentation of need for services should be sent only to the LD program or unit. *Application deadline (LD program):* Rolling/continuous for fall and rolling/continuous for spring.

Written Policies Written policy regarding general/basic LD accommodations is available on the program Web site. Written policy regarding general/basic LD accommodations is outlined in the school's catalog/handbook.

Argosy University, Twin Cities
Student Services

1515 Central Parkway

Eagan, MN 55121

http://www.argosyu.edu/

Contact: Ms. Amy Sudbeck, Assistant Director of Student Services. Phone: 651-846-3392. E-mail: asudbeck@ argosyu.edu.

Student Services Approximately 20 registered undergraduate students were served during 2006–07. The program or unit includes 1

part-time staff member. Academic advisers, counselors, graduate assistants/students, professional tutors, and trained peer tutors are provided collaboratively through on-campus or off-campus services.

Unique Aids and Services Aids, services, or accommodations include career counseling.

Subject-Area Tutoring Tutoring is offered one-on-one and in small groups for most subjects. Tutoring is provided collaboratively through on-campus or off-campus services via graduate assistants/students, professional tutors, and trained peer tutors.

Diagnostic Testing Testing for intelligence, learning strategies, learning styles, math, neuropsychological, personality, reading, social skills, spelling, study skills, and written language is provided collaboratively through on-campus or off-campus services.

Basic Skills Remediation Remediation is offered one-on-one for math, reading, study skills, and time management. Remediation is provided collaboratively through on-campus or off-campus services via graduate assistants/students, regular education teachers, and trained peer tutors.

Enrichment Programs for career planning, stress management, study skills, test taking, and time management are provided collaboratively through on-campus or off-campus services.

Application For admittance to the program or unit, students are required to apply to the program directly and provide a psychoeducational report (3 years old or less). Upon application, materials documenting need for services should be sent only to the LD program or unit. Upon acceptance, documentation of need for services should be sent only to the LD program or unit. *Application deadline (institutional):* Continuous. *Application deadline (LD program):* Rolling/continuous for fall and rolling/continuous for spring.

Written Policies Written policy regarding general/basic LD accommodations is available on the program Web site. Written policies regarding course substitutions, general/basic LD accommodations, and substitutions and waivers of admissions requirements are outlined in the school's catalog/handbook.

Arizona State University at the West campus
Disability Resource Center

PO Box 37100, 4701 West Thunderbird Road

Phoenix, AZ 85069-7100

http://www.west.asu.edu/drc

Contact: Dr. Adele Darr, Director. Phone: 602-543-8145. Fax: 602-543-8169. E-mail: adele.darr@asu.edu.

Disability Resource Center Approximately 42 registered undergraduate students were served during 2006–07. The program or unit includes 1 full-time staff member. LD specialists are provided through the program or unit. Academic advisers, coaches, counselors, diagnostic specialists, graduate assistants/students, professional tutors, regular education teachers, remediation/learning specialists, skill tutors, special education teachers, strategy tutors, teacher trainees, and trained peer tutors are provided collaboratively through on-campus or off-campus services.

Orientation The program or unit offers an optional 3-hour orientation for new students before classes begin and individually by special arrangement.

Unique Aids and Services Aids, services, or accommodations include advocates, career counseling, personal coach, priority registration, and support groups.

Assistive Technology Assistive technology is located in campus labs, the DSS office, a special lab and includes digital textbooks/e-text, learning support software, and scanning. Technology training is provided to incoming students.

Subject-Area Tutoring Tutoring is offered in small groups for all subjects. Tutoring is provided collaboratively through on-campus or off-campus services via computer-based instruction and trained peer tutors.

Diagnostic Testing Testing for auditory processing, intelligence, learning strategies, learning styles, math, personality, reading, spelling, spoken language, visual processing, and written language is provided collaboratively through on-campus or off-campus services.

Basic Skills Remediation Remediation is offered one-on-one and in small groups for computer skills, learning strategies, math, reading, study skills, and time management. Remediation is provided collaboratively through on-campus or off-campus services via computer-based instruction, LD specialists, and trained peer tutors.

Enrichment Programs for career planning, college survival skills, health and nutrition, learning strategies, math, practical computer skills, reading, self-advocacy, stress management, study skills, test taking, time management, and written composition skills are provided collaboratively through on-campus or off-campus services. Credit is offered for practical computer skills.

Fees *Diagnostic Testing* fee is $450.

Application For admittance to the program or unit, students are required to provide a psychoeducational report (3 years old or less). It is recommended that students provide documentation of high school services. Upon application, materials documenting need for services should be sent only to the LD program or unit. Upon acceptance, documentation of need for services should be sent only to the LD program or unit. *Application deadline (institutional):* Continuous. *Application deadline (LD program):* Rolling/continuous for fall and rolling/continuous for spring.

Written Policies Written policies regarding course substitutions, general/basic LD accommodations, grade forgiveness, reduced course loads, substitutions and waivers of admissions requirements, and substitutions and waivers of graduation requirements are available on the program Web site. Written policies regarding general/basic LD accommodations and grade forgiveness are outlined in the school's catalog/handbook. Written policies regarding course substitutions, general/basic LD accommodations, reduced course loads, substitutions and waivers of admissions requirements, and substitutions and waivers of graduation requirements are available through the program or unit directly.

The Art Institute of Houston
Department of Student Affairs

1900 Yorktown

Houston, TX 77056-4115

http://www.aih.artinstitutes.edu/

Contact: Tom Wilbeck, Director of Counseling Services/Disabilities Coordinator. Phone: 713-623-2040 Ext. 4118. Fax: 713-966-2776. E-mail: twilbeck@aii.edu.

Department of Student Affairs Approximately 80 registered undergraduate students were served during 2006–07. The program or unit includes 1 full-time staff member. Counselors are provided through the program or unit.

Unique Aids and Services Aids, services, or accommodations include faculty training, personal coach, and support groups.

Assistive Technology Assistive technology is located in the DSS office. Technology training is provided to incoming students.

Subject-Area Tutoring Tutoring is offered one-on-one, in small groups, and in class-size groups for all subjects. Tutoring is provided collaboratively through on-campus or off-campus services via computer-based instruction, graduate assistants/students, professional tutors, and trained peer tutors.

Basic Skills Remediation Remediation is offered one-on-one, in small groups, and in class-size groups for computer skills, learning strategies, math, reading, social skills, study skills, time management, and written language. Remediation is provided collaboratively through on-campus or off-campus services via professional tutors, regular education teachers, and trained peer tutors.

Enrichment Enrichment programs are available through the program or unit for career planning, health and nutrition, learning strategies, medication management, oral communication skills, stress management, study skills, test taking, time management, and written composition skills. Programs for career planning, college survival skills, health and nutrition, learning strategies, math, practical computer skills, reading, stress management, study skills, test taking, time management, and written composition skills are provided collaboratively through on-campus or off-campus services. Credit is offered for college survival skills.

Application For admittance to the program or unit, students are required to provide a psychoeducational report (3 years old or less). It is recommended that students provide documentation of high school services. Upon application, materials documenting need for services should be sent to both admissions and the LD program or unit. Upon acceptance, documentation of need for services should be sent to both admissions and the LD program or unit. *Application deadline (institutional):* Continuous. *Application deadline (LD program):* Rolling/continuous for fall and rolling/continuous for spring.

Written Policies Written policy regarding general/basic LD accommodations is outlined in the school's catalog/handbook.

The Art Institute of Pittsburgh
Disability Services

420 Boulevard of the Allies

Pittsburgh, PA 15219

http://www.aip.artinstitutes.edu/

Contact: Barron Whited, Counselor/Disability Services Coordinator. Phone: 412-291-6290. Fax: 412-263-3805. E-mail: bwhited@aii.edu.

Disability Services Approximately 110 registered undergraduate students were served during 2006–07. The program or unit includes 1 full-time staff member. Academic advisers, counselors, remediation/learning specialists, and trained peer tutors are provided collaboratively through on-campus or off-campus services.

The Art Institute of Pittsburgh (continued)

Unique Aids and Services Aids, services, or accommodations include faculty training.

Subject-Area Tutoring Tutoring is offered one-on-one and in small groups for most subjects. Tutoring is provided collaboratively through on-campus or off-campus services via graduate assistants/ students and trained peer tutors.

Basic Skills Remediation Remediation is offered in class-size groups for math and written language. Remediation is provided collaboratively through on-campus or off-campus services via computer-based instruction and regular education teachers.

Application For admittance to the program or unit, students are required to provide a psychoeducational report. It is recommended that students provide documentation of high school services. Upon application, materials documenting need for services should be sent only to the LD program or unit. Upon acceptance, documentation of need for services should be sent only to the LD program or unit. *Application deadline (institutional):* Continuous. *Application deadline (LD program):* Rolling/continuous for fall and rolling/continuous for spring.

Written Policies Written policies regarding course substitutions, general/basic LD accommodations, substitutions and waivers of admissions requirements, and substitutions and waivers of graduation requirements are outlined in the school's catalog/handbook.

The Art Institute of Seattle
Disability Services Office

2323 Elliott Avenue

Seattle, WA 98121-1642

http://www.artinstitutes.edu/seattle/students_disability.asp

Contact: Ms. Karen Ehnat, Director of Disability Services. Phone: 206-239-2308. Fax: 206-441-3475. E-mail: ehnatk@ aii.edu.

Disability Services Office Approximately 60 registered undergraduate students were served during 2006–07. The program or unit includes 1 full-time staff member. Academic advisers, counselors, regular education teachers, skill tutors, strategy tutors, and trained peer tutors are provided collaboratively through on-campus or off-campus services.

Assistive Technology Assistive technology is located in campus labs, the DSS office and includes digital textbooks/e-text, learning support software, and scanning.

Subject-Area Tutoring Tutoring is offered one-on-one and in small groups for most subjects. Tutoring is provided collaboratively through on-campus or off-campus services via trained peer tutors and other.

Basic Skills Remediation Remediation is offered one-on-one for study skills and time management. Remediation is provided through the program or unit. Remediation is also provided collaboratively through on-campus or off-campus services.

Application For admittance to the program or unit, students are required to provide a psychoeducational report and provide results of current testing at the adult level. It is recommended that students provide documentation of high school services. Upon application, materials documenting need for services should be sent only to the LD program or unit. Upon acceptance, documentation of need for

services should be sent only to the LD program or unit. *Application deadline (institutional):* Continuous. *Application deadline (LD program):* Rolling/continuous for fall and rolling/continuous for spring.

Written Policies Written policy regarding general/basic LD accommodations is available on the program Web site. Written policy regarding general/basic LD accommodations is outlined in the school's catalog/handbook. Written policies regarding course substitutions, general/basic LD accommodations, and reduced course loads are available through the program or unit directly.

Asbury College
Support Program for Students with Learning Disabilities

1 Macklem Drive

Wilmore, KY 40390-1198

http://www.asbury.edu/

Contact: Ms. Lynn D. Gagle, Director, Support Program for Students with Learning Disabilities. Phone: 859-858-3511 Ext. 2203. Fax: 859-858-3921. E-mail: lynn.gagle@ asbury.edu.

Support Program for Students with Learning Disabilities Approximately 28 registered undergraduate students were served during 2006–07. The program or unit includes 1 part-time staff member. Academic advisers, counselors, and trained peer tutors are provided collaboratively through on-campus or off-campus services.

Orientation The program or unit offers an optional varying length orientation for new students individually by special arrangement.

Unique Aids and Services Aids, services, or accommodations include advocates and support groups.

Assistive Technology Assistive technology is located in the library.

Subject-Area Tutoring Tutoring is offered one-on-one for all subjects. Tutoring is provided collaboratively through on-campus or off-campus services via trained peer tutors.

Diagnostic Testing Testing for intelligence, learning strategies, neuropsychological, personality, study skills, and written language is provided collaboratively through on-campus or off-campus services.

Basic Skills Remediation Remediation is available for learning strategies, social skills, study skills, time management, and written language. Remediation is provided collaboratively through on-campus or off-campus services via LD specialists and trained peer tutors.

Enrichment Programs for career planning, college survival skills, learning strategies, medication management, and self-advocacy are provided collaboratively through on-campus or off-campus services. Credit is offered for learning strategies and self-advocacy.

Application For admittance to the program or unit, students are required to apply to the program directly, provide a psychoeducational report (1 year old or less), and provide physician or psychiatrist diagnosis. It is recommended that students provide documentation of high school services. Upon application, materials documenting need for services should be sent only to the LD program or unit. Upon acceptance, documentation of need for services should be sent only to the LD program or unit. *Application deadline (institutional):* Continuous. *Application deadline (LD program):* Rolling/continuous for fall and rolling/continuous for spring.

Written Policies Written policies regarding course substitutions, general/basic LD accommodations, and substitutions and waivers of admissions requirements are outlined in the school's catalog/handbook. Written policies regarding course substitutions, general/basic LD accommodations, reduced course loads, and substitutions and waivers of admissions requirements are available through the program or unit directly.

Ashland University
Classroom Support Services

401 College Avenue

Ashland, OH 44805-3702

http://www.ashland.edu/dss

Contact: Ms. Suzanne Guisasola Salvo, Director Classroom Support Services. Phone: 419-289-5904. Fax: 419-289-5294. E-mail: ssalvo@ashland.edu.

Classroom Support Services Approximately 120 registered undergraduate students were served during 2006–07. The program or unit includes 3 full-time staff members. LD specialists, remediation/learning specialists, strategy tutors, and other are provided through the program or unit. LD specialists, remediation/learning specialists, and other are provided collaboratively through on-campus or off-campus services.

Orientation The program or unit offers a mandatory orientation for new students before classes begin, after classes begin, and individually by special arrangement.

Unique Aids and Services Aids, services, or accommodations include career counseling, faculty training, priority registration, and weekly meetings with faculty.

Assistive Technology Assistive technology is located in the DSS office, a special lab and includes digital textbooks/e-text, learning support software, scanning, and textbooks taped by community volunteers.

Subject-Area Tutoring Tutoring is offered one-on-one and in small groups for most subjects. Tutoring is provided through the program or unit via LD specialists and trained peer tutors. Tutoring is also provided collaboratively through on-campus or off-campus services via trained peer tutors.

Basic Skills Remediation Remediation is offered one-on-one for auditory processing, learning strategies, social skills, spelling, spoken language, study skills, time management, visual processing, and written language. Remediation is provided through the program or unit via LD specialists. Remediation is also provided collaboratively through on-campus or off-campus services via LD specialists.

Enrichment Enrichment programs are available through the program or unit for career planning, college survival skills, learning strategies, oral communication skills, reading, self-advocacy, stress management, study skills, test taking, time management, and written composition skills. Programs for career planning, college survival skills, learning strategies, oral communication skills, self-advocacy, stress management, study skills, test taking, time management, and written composition skills are provided collaboratively through on-campus or off-campus services.

Application For admittance to the program or unit, students are required to provide a psychoeducational report (5 years old or less), provide documentation of high school services, and provide medical documentation. It is recommended that students apply to the program directly. Upon acceptance, documentation of need for services should be sent only to the LD program or unit. *Application deadline (institutional):* Continuous. *Application deadline (LD program):* Rolling/continuous for fall and rolling/continuous for spring.

Written Policies Written policy regarding general/basic LD accommodations is available on the program Web site. Written policy regarding general/basic LD accommodations is outlined in the school's catalog/handbook. Written policies regarding general/basic LD accommodations and reduced course loads are available through the program or unit directly.

Athabasca University
Access to Students with Disabilities Office

1 University Drive

Athabasca, AB T9S 3A3

Canada

http://www.athabascau.ca/asd

Contact: Mr. Martin Reaney, Professional Support Services Coordinator. Phone: 780-497-3424 Ext. 3424. Fax: 780-421-2546. E-mail: asd@athabascau.ca.

Access to Students with Disabilities Office The program or unit includes 3 full-time staff members. Services are provided through the program or unit. Academic advisers, counselors, and LD specialists are provided collaboratively through on-campus or off-campus services.

Assistive Technology Assistive technology is located in campus labs, the DSS office and includes digital textbooks/e-text and scanning.

Enrichment Enrichment programs are available through the program or unit for learning strategies. Programs for career planning, college survival skills, health and nutrition, learning strategies, study skills, time management, and written composition skills are provided collaboratively through on-campus or off-campus services.

Application For admittance to the program or unit, students are required to provide a psychoeducational report. It is recommended that students provide documentation of high school services and provide documentation of accommodations provided through postsecondary support service providers. Upon application, materials documenting need for services should be sent only to the LD program or unit. Upon acceptance, documentation of need for services should be sent only to the LD program or unit. *Application deadline (institutional):* Continuous. *Application deadline (LD program):* Rolling/continuous for fall and rolling/continuous for spring.

Written Policies Written policies regarding general/basic LD accommodations, grade forgiveness, and reduced course loads are available on the program Web site. Written policy regarding general/basic LD accommodations is outlined in the school's catalog/handbook. Written policies regarding general/basic LD accommodations, grade forgiveness, and reduced course loads are available through the program or unit directly.

Athens State University
Counseling and Career Services: Services to Students with Disabilities

300 North Beaty Street

Athens, AL 35611

http://www.athens.edu/counseling/disability.php

Contact: Ms. Maureen J. Chemsak, Director of Counseling and Disability Services. Phone: 256-233-8285. Fax: 256-233-6520. E-mail: maureen.chemsak@athens.edu.

Counseling and Career Services: Services to Students with Disabilities Approximately 25 registered undergraduate students were served during 2006–07. The program or unit includes 1 part-time staff member. Counselors are provided collaboratively through on-campus or off-campus services.

Unique Aids and Services Aids, services, or accommodations include career counseling and priority registration.

Assistive Technology Assistive technology is located in campus labs, the DSS office, the library.

Application For admittance to the program or unit, students are required to provide information from prior college. It is recommended that students provide documentation of high school services. Upon application, materials documenting need for services should be sent only to the LD program or unit. Upon acceptance, documentation of need for services should be sent only to the LD program or unit. *Application deadline (institutional):* Continuous. *Application deadline (LD program):* Rolling/continuous for fall and rolling/continuous for spring.

Written Policies Written policy regarding general/basic LD accommodations is available on the program Web site. Written policy regarding general/basic LD accommodations is outlined in the school's catalog/handbook.

Auburn University Montgomery
Center for Special Services

PO Box 244023

Montgomery, AL 36124-4023

http://www.aum.edu/Academics/Student_Services/Center_for_Special_Services/

Contact: Miss Keyonna L. Dailey, Student Services Coordinator. Phone: 334-244-3631. Fax: 334-244-3907. E-mail: kdailey2@mail.aum.edu. Head of LD Program: Mrs. Tamara J. Massey-Garrett, Director. Phone: 334-244-3631. Fax: 334-244-3907. E-mail: tmassey2@mail.aum.edu.

Center for Special Services Approximately 60 registered undergraduate students were served during 2006–07. The program or unit includes 4 full-time and 2 part-time staff members. Trained peer tutors and other are provided through the program or unit. Professional tutors, remediation/learning specialists, trained peer tutors, and other are provided collaboratively through on-campus or off-campus services.

Summer Program To help prepare for the demands of college, there is an optional 1-week summer program prior to entering the school available to rising seniors, high school graduates that focuses on life skills and/or college life adjustment, self-advocacy, specific subject tutoring, study skills, test-taking skills, and time management. The program accepts students from out-of-state and is available to students attending other colleges.

Unique Aids and Services Aids, services, or accommodations include career counseling, faculty training, priority registration, testing accommodations.

Assistive Technology Assistive technology is located in campus labs, the DSS office and includes digital textbooks/e-text, learning support software, and scanning.

Subject-Area Tutoring Tutoring is offered one-on-one for some subjects. Tutoring is provided collaboratively through on-campus or off-campus services via professional tutors and trained peer tutors.

Basic Skills Remediation Remediation is offered in class-size groups for math, reading, and written language. Remediation is provided collaboratively through on-campus or off-campus services via regular education teachers.

Enrichment Programs for career planning, college survival skills, learning strategies, self-advocacy, stress management, study skills, test taking, and time management are provided collaboratively through on-campus or off-campus services.

Application For admittance to the program or unit, students are required to provide a psychoeducational report (3 years old or less). Upon application, materials documenting need for services should be sent only to the LD program or unit. Upon acceptance, documentation of need for services should be sent only to the LD program or unit. *Application deadline (institutional):* Continuous. *Application deadline (LD program):* Rolling/continuous for fall and rolling/continuous for spring.

Written Policies Written policies regarding course substitutions, general/basic LD accommodations, and grade forgiveness are available on the program Web site. Written policy regarding grade forgiveness is outlined in the school's catalog/handbook. Written policies regarding course substitutions and general/basic LD accommodations are available through the program or unit directly.

Augsburg College
Center for Learning and Adaptive Student Services (CLASS)

2211 Riverside Avenue

Minneapolis, MN 55454-1351

http://www.augsburg.edu/classprogram

Contact: CLASS Assistant. Phone: 612-330-1053. Fax: 612-330-1137. E-mail: class@augsburg.edu. Head of LD Program: Director of CLASS. Phone: 612-330-1648. Fax: 612-330-1137. E-mail: class@augsburg.edu.

Center for Learning and Adaptive Student Services (CLASS) Approximately 150 registered undergraduate students were served during 2006–07. The program or unit includes 7 full-time staff members. LD specialists, skill tutors, and strategy tutors are provided through the program or unit. Academic advisers, coaches, counselors, diagnostic specialists, graduate assistants/students, regular education teachers, remediation/learning specialists, special education teachers, teacher trainees, and trained peer tutors are provided collaboratively through on-campus or off-campus services.

Orientation The program or unit offers an optional orientation for new students before classes begin, after classes begin, and during other times.

Unique Aids and Services Aids, services, or accommodations include weekly meetings with disability specialist.

Assistive Technology Assistive technology is located in campus labs, the DSS office, a special lab and includes scanning and dictation software, AlphaSmart, Recording for the Blind and Dyslexic books. Technology training is provided to incoming students.

Basic Skills Remediation Remediation is offered one-on-one for learning strategies, study skills, and time management. Remediation is provided through the program or unit via LD specialists.

Enrichment Enrichment programs are available through the program or unit for learning strategies, self-advocacy, study skills, test taking, and time management. Program for career planning is provided collaboratively through on-campus or off-campus services.

Application For admittance to the program or unit, students are required to apply to the program directly and provide a psychoeducational report (3 years old or less). It is recommended that students provide documentation of high school services. Upon application, materials documenting need for services should be sent only to the LD program or unit. Upon acceptance, documentation of need for services should be sent only to the LD program or unit. *Application deadline (institutional):* 8/15. *Application deadline (LD program):* Rolling/continuous for fall and rolling/continuous for spring.

Written Policies Written policy regarding general/basic LD accommodations is available on the program Web site. Written policy regarding general/basic LD accommodations is outlined in the school's catalog/handbook. Written policies regarding course substitutions and general/basic LD accommodations are available through the program or unit directly.

Aurora University
Learning Center

347 South Gladstone Avenue

Aurora, IL 60506-4892

http://www.aurora.edu/learningcenter/

Contact: Susan Lausier, Disabilities Services Coordinator. Phone: 630-844-5267. Fax: 630-844-3688. E-mail: slausier@aurora.edu. Head of LD Program: Mr. Eric Schwarze, Director of the Learning Center. Phone: 630-844-5521. Fax: 630-844-5463. E-mail: eschwarz@aurora.edu.

Learning Center Approximately 25 registered undergraduate students were served during 2006–07. The program or unit includes 3 full-time and 4 part-time staff members. Professional tutors, skill tutors, strategy tutors, and trained peer tutors are provided through the program or unit. Academic advisers and counselors are provided collaboratively through on-campus or off-campus services.

Unique Aids and Services Aids, services, or accommodations include advocates, testing accommodations, note-takers, typical classroom accommodations.

Assistive Technology Assistive technology is located in campus labs, the DSS office and includes digital textbooks/e-text, learning support software, and scanning. Technology training is provided to incoming students.

Subject-Area Tutoring Tutoring is offered one-on-one and in small groups for all subjects. Tutoring is provided through the program or unit via computer-based instruction, professional tutors, and trained peer tutors.

Basic Skills Remediation Remediation is offered one-on-one for computer skills, learning strategies, math, reading, spelling, study skills, time management, and written language. Remediation is provided through the program or unit via computer-based instruction and professional tutors.

Enrichment Enrichment programs are available through the program or unit for college survival skills, learning strategies, practical computer skills, study skills, test taking, and time management. Programs for career planning and health and nutrition are provided collaboratively through on-campus or off-campus services.

Application For admittance to the program or unit, students are required to provide a psychoeducational report (3 years old or less). It is recommended that students provide documentation of high school services. Upon acceptance, documentation of need for services should be sent only to the LD program or unit. *Application deadline (institutional):* 5/1. *Application deadline (LD program):* Rolling/continuous for fall and rolling/continuous for spring.

Written Policies Written policy regarding general/basic LD accommodations is available on the program Web site. Written policy regarding general/basic LD accommodations is outlined in the school's catalog/handbook. Written policy regarding general/basic LD accommodations is available through the program or unit directly.

Austin College
Academic Skills Center

900 North Grand Avenue

Sherman, TX 75090-4400

http://www.austincollege.edu/Info.asp?1854

Contact: Ms. Laura Marquez, Director of Academic Skills Center. Phone: 903-813-2454. Fax: 903-813-3188. E-mail: lmarquez@austincollege.edu.

Academic Skills Center Approximately 21 registered undergraduate students were served during 2006–07. The program or unit includes 1 full-time staff member. LD specialists are provided through the program or unit. Academic advisers, coaches, counselors, professional tutors, and trained peer tutors are provided collaboratively through on-campus or off-campus services.

Unique Aids and Services Aids, services, or accommodations include career counseling.

Assistive Technology Assistive technology is located in the DSS office and includes digital textbooks/e-text, learning support software, and scanning.

Subject-Area Tutoring Tutoring is offered one-on-one and in small groups for most subjects. Tutoring is provided collaboratively through on-campus or off-campus services via trained peer tutors.

Enrichment Programs for career planning, health and nutrition, learning strategies, self-advocacy, stress management, study skills, test taking, time management, and written composition skills are provided collaboratively through on-campus or off-campus services.

Austin College (continued)

Application For admittance to the program or unit, students are required to provide a psychoeducational report (3 years old or less). Upon application, materials documenting need for services should be sent only to the LD program or unit. Upon acceptance, documentation of need for services should be sent only to the LD program or unit. *Application deadline (institutional): 5/1. Application deadline (LD program):* Rolling/continuous for fall and rolling/continuous for spring.

Written Policies Written policies regarding general/basic LD accommodations and substitutions and waivers of graduation requirements are available on the program Web site. Written policies regarding course substitutions, general/basic LD accommodations, and substitutions and waivers of graduation requirements are outlined in the school's catalog/handbook. Written policies regarding course substitutions, general/basic LD accommodations, and substitutions and waivers of graduation requirements are available through the program or unit directly.

Avila University

11901 Wornall Road

Kansas City, MO 64145-1698

http://www.avila.edu/

Contact: Ms. Suzanne R. Franklin, Director, Learning Center. Phone: 816-501-3666. Fax: 816-501-2461. E-mail: sue.franklin@avila.edu.

Approximately 20 registered undergraduate students were served during 2006–07. The program or unit includes 1 full-time and 2 part-time staff members. Professional tutors, skill tutors, and strategy tutors are provided through the program or unit. Academic advisers, coaches, counselors, diagnostic specialists, professional tutors, skill tutors, trained peer tutors, and other are provided collaboratively through on-campus or off-campus services.

Unique Aids and Services Aids, services, or accommodations include career counseling and priority registration.

Assistive Technology Assistive technology is located in campus labs, the DSS office and includes digital textbooks/e-text and learning support software. Technology training is provided to incoming students.

Subject-Area Tutoring Tutoring is offered one-on-one, in small groups, and in class-size groups for most subjects. Tutoring is provided collaboratively through on-campus or off-campus services via computer-based instruction, graduate assistants/students, professional tutors, and trained peer tutors.

Basic Skills Remediation Remediation is offered one-on-one, in small groups, and in class-size groups for auditory processing, computer skills, learning strategies, math, reading, spelling, spoken language, study skills, time management, visual processing, written language, and biology, chemistry, anatomy/physiology. Remediation is provided collaboratively through on-campus or off-campus services via computer-based instruction, graduate assistants/students, professional tutors, and trained peer tutors.

Enrichment Enrichment programs are available through the program or unit for college survival skills, learning strategies, math, oral communication skills, self-advocacy, stress management, study skills, test taking, time management, vocabulary development, and written composition skills. Programs for career planning, college

survival skills, health and nutrition, learning strategies, math, oral communication skills, practical computer skills, reading, self-advocacy, stress management, study skills, test taking, time management, vocabulary development, and written composition skills are provided collaboratively through on-campus or off-campus services. Credit is offered for learning strategies, study skills, and written composition skills.

Student Organization Disability Advocacy Group (DAG) consists of 12 members.

Application For admittance to the program or unit, students are required to apply to the program directly, provide a psychoeducational report (3 years old or less), and provide documentation of high school services. Upon acceptance, documentation of need for services should be sent only to the LD program or unit. *Application deadline (institutional):* Continuous. *Application deadline (LD program):* Rolling/continuous for fall and rolling/continuous for spring.

Written Policies Written policies regarding course substitutions, general/basic LD accommodations, substitutions and waivers of admissions requirements, and substitutions and waivers of graduation requirements are available on the program Web site. Written policies regarding course substitutions, general/basic LD accommodations, substitutions and waivers of admissions requirements, and substitutions and waivers of graduation requirements are available through the program or unit directly.

Baker College of Allen Park
Special Needs Department

4500 Enterprise Drive

Allen Park, MI 48101

https://www.baker.edu/departments/academic/counseling/specialneeds.cfm

Contact: Chip Evans, Academic Advisor/Special Needs Coordinator. Phone: 313-425-3738. Fax: 313-425-3777.

Special Needs Department Approximately 12 registered undergraduate students were served during 2006–07. The program or unit includes 1 full-time staff member. Academic advisers and counselors are provided through the program or unit. Counselors, diagnostic specialists, skill tutors, and strategy tutors are provided collaboratively through on-campus or off-campus services.

Unique Aids and Services Aids, services, or accommodations include advocates, career counseling, and faculty training.

Assistive Technology Assistive technology is located in campus labs and includes digital textbooks/e-text, learning support software, and scanning.

Subject-Area Tutoring Tutoring is offered one-on-one and in small groups for some subjects. Tutoring is provided collaboratively through on-campus or off-campus services via computer-based instruction, graduate assistants/students, professional tutors, and trained peer tutors.

Application For admittance to the program or unit, students are required to apply to the program directly and provide a psychoeducational report (3 years old or less). It is recommended that students provide documentation of high school services. Upon application, materials documenting need for services should be sent only to the

LD program or unit. Upon acceptance, documentation of need for services should be sent only to the LD program or unit. *Application deadline (institutional): 9/24. Application deadline (LD program):* 9/15 for fall. 3/20 for spring.

Written Policies Written policy regarding general/basic LD accommodations is available on the program Web site. Written policy regarding general/basic LD accommodations is outlined in the school's catalog/handbook. Written policy regarding general/basic LD accommodations is available through the program or unit directly.

Ball State University
Disabled Student Development

2000 University Avenue
Muncie, IN 47306-1099
http://www.bsu.edu/dsd/

Contact: Mr. Larry Markle, Director. Phone: 765-285-5293. Fax: 765-285-5295. E-mail: dsd@bsu.edu.

Disabled Student Development Approximately 300 registered undergraduate students were served during 2006–07. Academic advisers, counselors, graduate assistants/students, regular education teachers, skill tutors, strategy tutors, and trained peer tutors are provided collaboratively through on-campus or off-campus services.

Orientation The program or unit offers an optional 2-hour orientation for new students after classes begin.

Unique Aids and Services Aids, services, or accommodations include priority registration.

Assistive Technology Assistive technology is located in a special lab and includes digital textbooks/e-text, learning support software, and scanning. Technology training is provided to incoming students.

Subject-Area Tutoring Tutoring is offered one-on-one, in small groups, and in class-size groups for most subjects. Tutoring is provided collaboratively through on-campus or off-campus services via computer-based instruction, graduate assistants/students, and trained peer tutors.

Basic Skills Remediation Remediation is offered one-on-one and in small groups for learning strategies, study skills, and time management. Remediation is provided collaboratively through on-campus or off-campus services via graduate assistants/students and trained peer tutors.

Enrichment Programs for career planning, learning strategies, study skills, time management, and written composition skills are provided collaboratively through on-campus or off-campus services.

Application For admittance to the program or unit, students are required to provide a psychoeducational report (3 years old or less). Upon acceptance, documentation of need for services should be sent only to the LD program or unit. *Application deadline (institutional):* Continuous. *Application deadline (LD program):* Rolling/continuous for fall and rolling/continuous for spring.

Written Policies Written policy regarding general/basic LD accommodations is available on the program Web site. Written policy regarding general/basic LD accommodations is outlined in the school's catalog/handbook. Written policies regarding course substitutions, reduced course loads, and substitutions and waivers of graduation requirements are available through the program or unit directly.

The Baptist College of Florida

5400 College Drive
Graceville, FL 32440-1898
http://www.baptistcollege.edu/

Contact: Stephanie Orr, Administrative Assistant to Senior Vice President. Phone: 800-328-2660 Ext. 465. Fax: 850-263-7506. E-mail: sworr@baptistcollege.edu.

Approximately 15 registered undergraduate students were served during 2006–07. The program or unit includes 1 full-time and 4 part-time staff members. Academic advisers are provided through the program or unit. Counselors, regular education teachers, and skill tutors are provided collaboratively through on-campus or off-campus services.

Unique Aids and Services Aids, services, or accommodations include career counseling.

Subject-Area Tutoring Tutoring is offered one-on-one for all subjects. Tutoring is provided collaboratively through on-campus or off-campus services via trained peer tutors.

Basic Skills Remediation Remediation is offered one-on-one and in class-size groups for computer skills, math, reading, and written language. Remediation is provided collaboratively through on-campus or off-campus services via regular education teachers and trained peer tutors.

Application It is recommended that students provide documentation of high school services. Upon acceptance, documentation of need for services should be sent only to the LD program or unit. *Application deadline (institutional): 8/11. Application deadline (LD program):* Rolling/continuous for fall and rolling/continuous for spring.

Written Policies Written policy regarding general/basic LD accommodations is outlined in the school's catalog/handbook.

Bard College
Academic Resources Center

PO Box 5000
Annandale-on-Hudson, NY 12504
http://inside.bard.edu/academicresources/academics/services.shtml

Contact: Dr. Lucille C. Larney, Academic Support Specialist. Phone: 845-758-6822 Ext. 6637. Fax: 845-758-7646. E-mail: larney@bard.edu.

Academic Resources Center Approximately 123 registered undergraduate students were served during 2006–07. The program or unit includes 1 full-time staff member. Academic advisers, professional tutors, skill tutors, strategy tutors, and other are provided through the program or unit. Academic advisers, counselors, professional tutors, skill tutors, strategy tutors, trained peer tutors, and other are provided collaboratively through on-campus or off-campus services.

Orientation The program or unit offers an optional orientation for new students individually by special arrangement.

Bard College (continued)

Unique Aids and Services Aids, services, or accommodations include faculty training, personal coach, support groups, weekly meetings with faculty, test and classroom accommodations, academic advising and counseling.

Assistive Technology Assistive technology is located in the Academic Resources Center and includes digital textbooks/e-text, learning support software, and scanning. Technology training is provided to incoming students.

Subject-Area Tutoring Tutoring is offered one-on-one and in small groups for all subjects. Tutoring is provided through the program or unit via LD specialists, professional tutors, and other. Tutoring is also provided collaboratively through on-campus or off-campus services via computer-based instruction, professional tutors, trained peer tutors, and other.

Basic Skills Remediation Remediation is offered one-on-one and in small groups for auditory processing, learning strategies, math, reading, social skills, study skills, time management, and written language. Remediation is provided through the program or unit via LD specialists, professional tutors, and other. Remediation is also provided collaboratively through on-campus or off-campus services via computer-based instruction, professional tutors, trained peer tutors, and other.

Enrichment Enrichment programs are available through the program or unit for college survival skills, learning strategies, reading, self-advocacy, stress management, study skills, test taking, time management, written composition skills, and other. Programs for career planning, college survival skills, health and nutrition, learning strategies, math, medication management, practical computer skills, reading, stress management, study skills, test taking, time management, vocabulary development, written composition skills, and other are provided collaboratively through on-campus or off-campus services. Credit is offered for written composition skills.

Application For admittance to the program or unit, students are required to provide a psychoeducational report (3 years old or less) and provide disability registration form. It is recommended that students provide documentation of high school services. Upon application, materials documenting need for services should be sent only to admissions with institutional application materials. Upon acceptance, documentation of need for services should be sent only to the LD program or unit. *Application deadline (institutional): 1/15. Application deadline (LD program):* Rolling/continuous for fall and rolling/continuous for spring.

Written Policies Written policy regarding general/basic LD accommodations is available on the program Web site. Written policy regarding general/basic LD accommodations is outlined in the school's catalog/handbook.

Bates College
Dean of Students Office: Learning Differences Office

Andrews Road
Lewiston, ME 04240-6028
http://www.bates.edu/dos

Contact: Ms. Holly L. Gurney, Associate Dean of Students.
Phone: 207-786-6220. Fax: 207-753-6971. E-mail:
hgurney@bates.edu.

Dean of Students Office: Learning Differences Office
Approximately 178 registered undergraduate students were served during 2006–07. The program or unit includes 1 full-time and 1 part-time staff member. Academic advisers, coaches, counselors, LD specialists, professional tutors, skill tutors, and strategy tutors are provided through the program or unit. Academic advisers, counselors, diagnostic specialists, professional tutors, remediation/learning specialists, and skill tutors are provided collaboratively through on-campus or off-campus services.

Unique Aids and Services Aids, services, or accommodations include weekly meetings with faculty, time management/organization meetings with LD staff.

Assistive Technology Assistive technology is located in the DSS office, a special lab, the individual student's computer and includes digital textbooks/e-text, learning support software, and scanning. Technology training is provided to incoming students.

Subject-Area Tutoring Tutoring is offered one-on-one and in small groups for most subjects. Tutoring is provided through the program or unit via LD specialists and professional tutors. Tutoring is also provided collaboratively through on-campus or off-campus services via professional tutors and trained peer tutors.

Diagnostic Testing Testing for auditory processing, handwriting, intelligence, learning styles, neuropsychological, reading, spelling, spoken language, visual processing, and written language is provided collaboratively through on-campus or off-campus services.

Basic Skills Remediation Remediation is offered one-on-one for computer skills, handwriting, learning strategies, reading, social skills, study skills, and time management. Remediation is provided through the program or unit via LD specialists.

Enrichment Enrichment programs are available through the program or unit for learning strategies, reading, self-advocacy, stress management, study skills, test taking, time management, and written composition skills. Programs for career planning, college survival skills, health and nutrition, learning strategies, math, reading, stress management, study skills, test taking, time management, and written composition skills are provided collaboratively through on-campus or off-campus services.

Fees *Diagnostic Testing* fee is applicable.

Application For admittance to the program or unit, students are required to provide a psychoeducational report and provide documentation of high school services. Upon acceptance, documentation of need for services should be sent only to the LD program or unit. *Application deadline (institutional): 1/1. Application deadline (LD program):* Rolling/continuous for fall and rolling/continuous for spring.

Written Policies Written policy regarding general/basic LD accommodations is available on the program Web site. Written policy regarding general/basic LD accommodations is outlined in the school's catalog/handbook. Written policy regarding general/basic LD accommodations is available through the program or unit directly.

Baylor University
Office of Access and Learning Accommodation

Waco, TX 76798
http://www.baylor.edu/oala

Contact: Dae Vasek, Director. Phone: 254-710-3605. Fax: 254-710-3608. E-mail: dae_vasek@baylor.edu.

Office of Access and Learning Accommodation Approximately 375 registered undergraduate students were served during 2006–07. The program or unit includes 4 full-time staff members. Academic advisers, counselors, graduate assistants/students, strategy tutors, and trained peer tutors are provided through the program or unit. Academic advisers and strategy tutors are provided collaboratively through on-campus or off-campus services.

Unique Aids and Services Aids, services, or accommodations include advocates, faculty training, and priority registration.

Assistive Technology Assistive technology is located in the DSS office and includes digital textbooks/e-text, learning support software, and scanning.

Subject-Area Tutoring Tutoring is offered one-on-one, in small groups, and in class-size groups. Tutoring is provided through the program or unit via graduate assistants/students, professional tutors, and trained peer tutors. Tutoring is also provided collaboratively through on-campus or off-campus services via professional tutors.

Enrichment Enrichment programs are available through the program or unit for career planning, college survival skills, health and nutrition, learning strategies, oral communication skills, practical computer skills, reading, self-advocacy, stress management, study skills, test taking, and time management. Program for study skills is provided collaboratively through on-campus or off-campus services. Credit is offered for career planning, college survival skills, health and nutrition, learning strategies, oral communication skills, practical computer skills, reading, self-advocacy, stress management, study skills, test taking, and time management.

Application For admittance to the program or unit, students are required to apply to the program directly and provide a psychoeducational report (3 years old or less). It is recommended that students provide documentation of high school services. Upon application, materials documenting need for services should be sent only to the LD program or unit. Upon acceptance, documentation of need for services should be sent only to the LD program or unit. *Application deadline (institutional): 2/1. Application deadline (LD program):* Rolling/continuous for fall and rolling/continuous for spring.

Written Policies Written policy regarding general/basic LD accommodations is available on the program Web site. Written policies regarding general/basic LD accommodations and reduced course loads are available through the program or unit directly.

Belmont Abbey College
Office of Academic Assistance

100 Belmont-Mt. Holly Road

Belmont, NC 28012-1802

http://www.belmontabbeycollege.edu/academics/
CareerSupport/disability.aspx

Contact: Ms. Stacey Davis, Director of Academic Assistance. Phone: 704-825-6776. Fax: 704-825-6727. E-mail: staceydavis@bac.edu.

Office of Academic Assistance Approximately 35 registered undergraduate students were served during 2006–07. The program or unit includes 1 full-time staff member. Coaches, counselors, LD specialists, and professional tutors are provided collaboratively through on-campus or off-campus services.

Unique Aids and Services Aids, services, or accommodations include priority registration.

Assistive Technology Assistive technology is located in campus labs and includes learning support software. Technology training is provided to incoming students.

Subject-Area Tutoring Tutoring is offered in small groups for some subjects. Tutoring is provided collaboratively through on-campus or off-campus services via professional tutors.

Basic Skills Remediation Remediation is offered one-on-one for learning strategies, reading, study skills, time management, and written language. Remediation is provided through the program or unit via LD specialists.

Enrichment Programs for career planning, college survival skills, learning strategies, stress management, study skills, test taking, and time management are provided collaboratively through on-campus or off-campus services.

Application For admittance to the program or unit, students are required to provide a psychoeducational report (3 years old or less). It is recommended that students provide documentation of high school services. Upon application, materials documenting need for services should be sent only to admissions with institutional application materials. Upon acceptance, documentation of need for services should be sent only to the LD program or unit. *Application deadline (institutional): 8/1. Application deadline (LD program):* Rolling/continuous for fall and rolling/continuous for spring.

Written Policies Written policy regarding general/basic LD accommodations is available on the program Web site. Written policy regarding general/basic LD accommodations is available through the program or unit directly.

Bemidji State University
Disability Services Office

1500 Birchmont Drive, NE

Bemidji, MN 56601-2699

http://www.bemidjistate.edu/disabilities/

Contact: Kathi Hagen, Coordinator, Disability Services Office. Phone: 218-755-3883. Fax: 218-755-4116. E-mail: khagen@bemidjistate.edu.

Disability Services Office Approximately 111 registered undergraduate students were served during 2006–07. The program or unit includes 1 full-time staff member. Academic advisers are provided through the program or unit. Academic advisers, coaches, counselors, regular education teachers, skill tutors, strategy tutors, and trained peer tutors are provided collaboratively through on-campus or off-campus services.

Orientation The program or unit offers an optional 1-hour per week (for entire semester) orientation for new students after classes begin.

Summer Program To help prepare for the demands of college, there is an optional 1-week summer program prior to entering the school available to rising sophomores that focuses on computing skills, life skills and/or college life adjustment, self-advocacy, study skills, test-taking skills, and time management. The program accepts students from out-of-state and is available to students attending other colleges.

Bemidji State University (continued)

Unique Aids and Services Aids, services, or accommodations include career counseling, faculty training, personal coach, priority registration, and support groups.

Assistive Technology Assistive technology is located in the DSS office, the library and includes scanning.

Subject-Area Tutoring Tutoring is offered one-on-one and in small groups for most subjects. Tutoring is provided through the program or unit via computer-based instruction and trained peer tutors. Tutoring is also provided collaboratively through on-campus or off-campus services via computer-based instruction, LD specialists, and trained peer tutors.

Basic Skills Remediation Remediation is offered in class-size groups for learning strategies, math, reading, social skills, study skills, and time management. Remediation is provided collaboratively through on-campus or off-campus services.

Enrichment Enrichment programs are available through the program or unit for college survival skills, self-advocacy, stress management, study skills, test taking, time management, and written composition skills. Programs for career planning, college survival skills, health and nutrition, learning strategies, math, reading, study skills, and time management are provided collaboratively through on-campus or off-campus services. Credit is offered for career planning and study skills.

Fees *Summer Program* fee is $75.

Application For admittance to the program or unit, students are required to apply to the program directly, provide a psychoeducational report (5 years old or less), and provide testing results and recommendations if applicable. It is recommended that students provide documentation of high school services. Upon application, materials documenting need for services should be sent to both admissions and the LD program or unit. Upon acceptance, documentation of need for services should be sent only to the LD program or unit. *Application deadline (institutional):* Continuous. *Application deadline (LD program):* Rolling/continuous for fall and rolling/continuous for spring.

Written Policies Written policies regarding course substitutions, general/basic LD accommodations, grade forgiveness, reduced course loads, substitutions and waivers of admissions requirements, and substitutions and waivers of graduation requirements are available through the program or unit directly.

Benedictine College
Academic Assistance Center

1020 North 2nd Street

Atchison, KS 66002-1499

http://www.benedictine.edu/

Contact: Ms. Camille Osborn, Director of General Studies Center. Phone: 913-367-5340 Ext. 2517. Fax: 913-367-5462. E-mail: cosborn@benedictine.edu.

Academic Assistance Center Approximately 30 registered undergraduate students were served during 2006–07. The program or unit includes 5 part-time staff members. Counselors and trained peer tutors are provided through the program or unit. Academic advisers, counselors, and trained peer tutors are provided collaboratively through on-campus or off-campus services.

Orientation The program or unit offers a mandatory orientation for new students before classes begin, during registration, after classes begin, and individually by special arrangement.

Unique Aids and Services Aids, services, or accommodations include advocates and weekly meetings with faculty.

Assistive Technology Assistive technology includes digital textbooks/e-text.

Subject-Area Tutoring Tutoring is offered one-on-one and in small groups for most subjects. Tutoring is provided through the program or unit via computer-based instruction and trained peer tutors.

Basic Skills Remediation Remediation is offered in class-size groups for learning strategies, study skills, and time management. Remediation is provided through the program or unit via regular education teachers.

Enrichment Enrichment programs are available through the program or unit for college survival skills and study skills. Programs for career planning, health and nutrition, learning strategies, stress management, and study skills are provided collaboratively through on-campus or off-campus services. Credit is offered for college survival skills.

Application For admittance to the program or unit, students are required to provide a psychoeducational report (3 years old or less). It is recommended that students provide documentation of high school services. Upon application, materials documenting need for services should be sent only to admissions with institutional application materials. Upon acceptance, documentation of need for services should be sent only to admissions. *Application deadline (LD program):* Rolling/continuous for fall and rolling/continuous for spring.

Written Policies Written policy regarding general/basic LD accommodations is available through the program or unit directly.

Bentley College
Counseling and Student Development

175 Forest Street

Waltham, MA 02452-4705

http://ecampus.bentley.edu/dept/counsel/

Contact: Mr. Christopher Kennedy, Coordinator of Disability Services. Phone: 781-891-2274. Fax: 781-891-2474. E-mail: ckennedy@bentley.edu.

Counseling and Student Development Approximately 125 registered undergraduate students were served during 2006–07. The program or unit includes 1 full-time staff member. Academic advisers, coaches, LD specialists, skill tutors, and strategy tutors are provided through the program or unit. Academic advisers, counselors, diagnostic specialists, professional tutors, regular education teachers, remediation/learning specialists, skill tutors, special education teachers, strategy tutors, teacher trainees, and trained peer tutors are provided collaboratively through on-campus or off-campus services.

Summer Program To help prepare for the demands of college, there is a mandatory 1-week summer program prior to entering the school available to high school graduates that focuses on life skills and/or college life adjustment. The program accepts students from out-of-state.

Unique Aids and Services Aids, services, or accommodations include advocates, career counseling, faculty training, parent workshops, personal coach, priority registration, support groups, and weekly meetings with faculty.

Assistive Technology Assistive technology is located in the library and includes digital textbooks/e-text, learning support software, and scanning. Technology training is provided to incoming students.

Subject-Area Tutoring Tutoring is offered one-on-one for most subjects. Tutoring is provided through the program or unit via LD specialists. Tutoring is also provided collaboratively through on-campus or off-campus services via computer-based instruction, graduate assistants/students, professional tutors, and trained peer tutors.

Enrichment Enrichment programs are available through the program or unit for college survival skills, learning strategies, self-advocacy, stress management, study skills, test taking, and time management. Programs for career planning, college survival skills, health and nutrition, math, medication management, oral communication skills, practical computer skills, reading, stress management, study skills, test taking, time management, and written composition skills are provided collaboratively through on-campus or off-campus services.

Application For admittance to the program or unit, students are required to provide a psychoeducational report (3 years old or less). It is recommended that students provide documentation of high school services. Upon application, materials documenting need for services should be sent only to admissions with institutional application materials. Upon acceptance, documentation of need for services should be sent only to the LD program or unit. *Application deadline (institutional):* 2/1. *Application deadline (LD program):* Rolling/continuous for fall and rolling/continuous for spring.

Written Policies Written policies regarding course substitutions, general/basic LD accommodations, grade forgiveness, reduced course loads, and substitutions and waivers of graduation requirements are available on the program Web site. Written policies regarding course substitutions, general/basic LD accommodations, grade forgiveness, reduced course loads, and substitutions and waivers of graduation requirements are outlined in the school's catalog/handbook.

Bethany University
Educational Support Services

800 Bethany Drive

Scotts Valley, CA 95066-2820

http://www.bethany.edu/

Contact: Cynthia S.T. FitzGerald, Director of Educational Support Services. Phone: 831-438-3800 Ext. 3946. Fax: 831-439-9983. E-mail: cfitz@fc.bethany.edu.

Educational Support Services Approximately 44 registered undergraduate students were served during 2006–07. The program or unit includes 1 full-time and 6 part-time staff members. Academic advisers, counselors, graduate assistants/students, LD specialists, regular education teachers, remediation/learning specialists, skill tutors, strategy tutors, teacher trainees, and trained peer tutors are provided through the program or unit. Academic advisers, skill tutors, strategy tutors, and trained peer tutors are provided collaboratively through on-campus or off-campus services.

Unique Aids and Services Aids, services, or accommodations include advocates, faculty training, peer tutors in the Student Individualized Learning Center, weekly meeting with educational therapist.

Assistive Technology Assistive technology is located in the library, Student Individualized Learning Center and includes ZoomText.

Subject-Area Tutoring Tutoring is offered one-on-one and in small groups for all subjects. Tutoring is provided through the program or unit via graduate assistants/students, LD specialists, professional tutors, and trained peer tutors. Tutoring is also provided collaboratively through on-campus or off-campus services via computer-based instruction, graduate assistants/students, and trained peer tutors.

Basic Skills Remediation Remediation is offered in small groups and in class-size groups for computer skills, learning strategies, math, reading, spelling, study skills, time management, and written language. Remediation is provided through the program or unit via graduate assistants/students, LD specialists, teacher trainees, and trained peer tutors. Remediation is also provided collaboratively through on-campus or off-campus services via graduate assistants/students, regular education teachers, special education teachers, and trained peer tutors.

Enrichment Enrichment programs are available through the program or unit for college survival skills, learning strategies, reading, stress management, study skills, test taking, time management, vocabulary development, and written composition skills. Programs for career planning, health and nutrition, math, oral communication skills, practical computer skills, reading, self-advocacy, stress management, study skills, test taking, time management, and written composition skills are provided collaboratively through on-campus or off-campus services. Credit is offered for college survival skills, learning strategies, math, oral communication skills, practical computer skills, stress management, study skills, test taking, time management, and written composition skills.

Application For admittance to the program or unit, students are required to apply to the program directly, provide a psychoeducational report (3 years old or less), and provide professional documentation of 504/ADA issues and recommended accommodations. It is recommended that students provide documentation of high school services. Upon acceptance, documentation of need for services should be sent only to the LD program or unit. *Application deadline (institutional):* 7/31. *Application deadline (LD program):* Rolling/continuous for fall and rolling/continuous for spring.

Written Policies Written policies regarding course substitutions, general/basic LD accommodations, grade forgiveness, reduced course loads, substitutions and waivers of admissions requirements, and substitutions and waivers of graduation requirements are available on the program Web site. Written policies regarding course substitutions, general/basic LD accommodations, grade forgiveness, reduced course loads, substitutions and waivers of admissions requirements, and substitutions and waivers of graduation requirements are outlined in the school's catalog/handbook.

Bethel College
Academic Support Center

1001 West McKinley Avenue

Mishawaka, IN 46545-5591

http://www.bethelcollege.edu

Contact: Dr. Carolyn L. Arthur, Director of the Academic Support Center. Phone: 574-257-3356. Fax: 574-257-3434. E-mail: arthurc@bethelcollege.edu.

Academic Support Center Approximately 50 registered undergraduate students were served during 2006–07. The program or unit includes 2 full-time staff members. LD specialists and remediation/learning specialists are provided through the program or unit. Academic advisers, coaches, counselors, diagnostic specialists, and regular education teachers are provided collaboratively through on-campus or off-campus services.

Unique Aids and Services Aids, services, or accommodations include weekly accountability meetings with Director of the ASC.

Assistive Technology Assistive technology is located in the DSS office and includes textbooks in audio format.

Subject-Area Tutoring Tutoring is offered one-on-one for most subjects. Tutoring is provided through the program or unit via LD specialists and trained peer tutors.

Basic Skills Remediation Remediation is offered one-on-one for math, reading, study skills, and time management. Remediation is provided through the program or unit via LD specialists and trained peer tutors.

Enrichment Enrichment programs are available through the program or unit for college survival skills, learning strategies, reading, stress management, study skills, test taking, time management, vocabulary development, and written composition skills. Programs for career planning, college survival skills, math, and stress management are provided collaboratively through on-campus or off-campus services.

Application For admittance to the program or unit, students are required to provide a psychoeducational report (3 years old or less) and provide documentation of high school services. Upon application, materials documenting need for services should be sent only to admissions with institutional application materials. Upon acceptance, documentation of need for services should be sent to both admissions and the LD program or unit. *Application deadline (institutional): 8/6. Application deadline (LD program):* Rolling/continuous for fall and rolling/continuous for spring.

Written Policies Written policy regarding general/basic LD accommodations is outlined in the school's catalog/handbook. Written policies regarding course substitutions and substitutions and waivers of graduation requirements are available through the program or unit directly.

Bethel University
Disability Services

3900 Bethel Drive

St. Paul, MN 55112-6999

http://www.bethel.edu/Disability

Contact: Ms. Kathleen J. McGillivray, Director of Disability Services. Phone: 651-635-8759. Fax: 651-638-6351. E-mail: k-mcgillivray@bethel.edu.

Disability Services Approximately 52 registered undergraduate students were served during 2006–07. The program or unit includes 1 full-time and 5 part-time staff members. Academic advisers, coaches, diagnostic specialists, professional tutors, special education teachers, and other are provided through the program or unit. Academic advisers, coaches, diagnostic specialists, graduate assistants/students, LD specialists, remediation/learning specialists, and strategy tutors are provided collaboratively through on-campus or off-campus services.

Unique Aids and Services Aids, services, or accommodations include advocates, faculty training, and weekly meetings with faculty.

Assistive Technology Assistive technology includes digital textbooks/e-text.

Subject-Area Tutoring Tutoring is offered one-on-one and in small groups for some subjects. Tutoring is provided collaboratively through on-campus or off-campus services via computer-based instruction, LD specialists, and other.

Enrichment Programs for career planning, college survival skills, learning strategies, study skills, test taking, time management, and written composition skills are provided collaboratively through on-campus or off-campus services. Credit is offered for college survival skills.

Application For admittance to the program or unit, students are required to provide a psychoeducational report. It is recommended that students provide documentation of high school services. Upon acceptance, documentation of need for services should be sent only to the LD program or unit. *Application deadline (institutional): 8/1. Application deadline (LD program):* Rolling/continuous for fall and rolling/continuous for spring.

Written Policies Written policy regarding general/basic LD accommodations is available on the program Web site. Written policy regarding general/basic LD accommodations is outlined in the school's catalog/handbook. Written policy regarding general/basic LD accommodations is available through the program or unit directly.

Bishop's University
Special Needs, Counseling Services

2600 College Street

Sherbrooke, QC J1M 0C8

Canada

http://www.ubishops.ca/

Contact: Linda Nyiri, Special Needs Assistant. Phone: 819-822-9600 Ext. 2434. Fax: 819-822-9605. E-mail: lnyiri@ubishops.ca. Head of LD Program: Sandy-Lee Ward, Counsellor. Phone: 819-822-9695. Fax: 819-822-9605. E-mail: slward@ubishops.ca.

Special Needs, Counseling Services Approximately 80 registered undergraduate students were served during 2006–07. The program or unit includes 3 part-time staff members. Counselors, diagnostic specialists, skill tutors, strategy tutors, trained peer tutors, and other are provided through the program or unit. Academic advisers are provided collaboratively through on-campus or off-campus services.

Orientation The program or unit offers an optional orientation for new students before classes begin, during registration, and individually by special arrangement.

Unique Aids and Services Aids, services, or accommodations include advocates and career counseling.

Assistive Technology Assistive technology is located in a special lab and includes digital textbooks/e-text, learning support software, and scanning. Technology training is provided to incoming students.

Subject-Area Tutoring Tutoring is offered one-on-one for all subjects. Tutoring is provided through the program or unit via trained peer tutors.

Diagnostic Testing Testing is provided through the program or unit for intelligence, learning strategies, learning styles, math, reading, spelling, study skills, visual processing, and written language.

Basic Skills Remediation Remediation is available for learning strategies, reading, study skills, and time management. Remediation is provided through the program or unit via LD specialists. Remediation is also provided collaboratively through on-campus or off-campus services via trained peer tutors.

Enrichment Enrichment programs are available through the program or unit for career planning, college survival skills, learning strategies, reading, stress management, study skills, test taking, and time management. Programs for college survival skills, health and nutrition, math, medication management, oral communication skills, practical computer skills, and written composition skills are provided collaboratively through on-campus or off-campus services.

Student Organization Bishop's University Special Needs Association.

Application For admittance to the program or unit, students are required to apply to the program directly and provide a psychoeducational report (3 years old or less). It is recommended that students provide documentation of high school services. Upon application, materials documenting need for services should be sent only to the LD program or unit. Upon acceptance, documentation of need for services should be sent only to the LD program or unit. *Application deadline (institutional): 3/1. Application deadline (LD program):* Rolling/continuous for fall and rolling/continuous for spring.

Written Policies Written policy regarding general/basic LD accommodations is outlined in the school's catalog/handbook.

Bluefield State College
Student Support Services

219 Rock Street

Bluefield, WV 24701-2198

http://www.bluefieldstate.edu/

Contact: Ms. Carolyn T. Kirby, Director of Student Support Services. Phone: 304-327-4098. Fax: 304-327-4448. E-mail: ckirby@bluefieldstate.edu.

Student Support Services Approximately 5 registered undergraduate students were served during 2006–07. Academic advisers, counselors, professional tutors, and trained peer tutors are provided collaboratively through on-campus or off-campus services.

Assistive Technology Assistive technology is located in the DSS office and includes scanning.

Subject-Area Tutoring Tutoring is offered one-on-one and in small groups for all subjects. Tutoring is provided collaboratively through on-campus or off-campus services via professional tutors and trained peer tutors.

Basic Skills Remediation Remediation is offered in class-size groups for math, reading, and written language. Remediation is provided collaboratively through on-campus or off-campus services via regular education teachers.

Enrichment Programs for career planning, college survival skills, health and nutrition, learning strategies, math, oral communication skills, practical computer skills, reading, stress management, study skills, test taking, time management, and written composition skills are provided collaboratively through on-campus or off-campus services.

Student Organization People First consists of 10 members.

Application For admittance to the program or unit, students are required to apply to the program directly and provide a psychoeducational report (2 years old or less). It is recommended that students provide documentation of high school services. Upon application, materials documenting need for services should be sent only to the LD program or unit. Upon acceptance, documentation of need for services should be sent only to the LD program or unit. *Application deadline (institutional):* Continuous. *Application deadline (LD program):* 10/31 for fall. 3/30 for spring.

Written Policies Written policy regarding general/basic LD accommodations is available on the program Web site. Written policy regarding general/basic LD accommodations is outlined in the school's catalog/handbook. Written policy regarding general/basic LD accommodations is available through the program or unit directly.

Boston Architectural College
Advising Department

320 Newbury Street

Boston, MA 02115-2795

http://www.the-bac.edu/

Contact: Ms. Jenifer A. Marshall, Director of Advising. Phone: 617-585-0259. Fax: 617-585-0141. E-mail: jenifer.marshall@the-bac.edu.

Advising Department Approximately 40 registered undergraduate students were served during 2006–07. Academic advisers, regular education teachers, remediation/learning specialists, and skill tutors are provided through the program or unit.

Unique Aids and Services Aids, services, or accommodations include advocates and career counseling.

Assistive Technology Assistive technology is located in campus labs, the DSS office and includes digital textbooks/e-text.

Subject-Area Tutoring Tutoring is offered one-on-one and in small groups for most subjects. Tutoring is provided through the program or unit via graduate assistants/students, LD specialists, professional tutors, and trained peer tutors. Tutoring is also provided collaboratively through on-campus or off-campus services via computer-based instruction, graduate assistants/students, professional tutors, and trained peer tutors.

Boston Architectural College (continued)

Basic Skills Remediation Remediation is available for computer skills, learning strategies, math, reading, spoken language, study skills, time management, and written language.

Enrichment Enrichment programs are available through the program or unit for learning strategies, oral communication skills, self-advocacy, stress management, study skills, test taking, time management, and written composition skills. Programs for career planning, college survival skills, learning strategies, math, oral communication skills, reading, stress management, study skills, test taking, time management, and written composition skills are provided collaboratively through on-campus or off-campus services.

Application For admittance to the program or unit, students are required to apply to the program directly and provide a psychoeducational report (5 years old or less). It is recommended that students provide documentation of high school services. Upon acceptance, documentation of need for services should be sent only to the LD program or unit. *Application deadline (institutional):* Continuous. *Application deadline (LD program):* Rolling/continuous for fall and rolling/continuous for spring.

Written Policies Written policy regarding general/basic LD accommodations is available on the program Web site. Written policy regarding general/basic LD accommodations is outlined in the school's catalog/handbook. Written policy regarding general/basic LD accommodations is available through the program or unit directly.

Boston College

140 Commonwealth Avenue

Chestnut Hill, MA 02467-3800

http://www.bc.edu/connors

Contact: Dr. Kathleen Duggan, Assistant Director of Academic Development Center. Fax: 617-552-6075.

Approximately 400 registered undergraduate students were served during 2006–07. The program or unit includes 2 full-time staff members and 1 part-time staff member. Coaches, graduate assistants/students, LD specialists, strategy tutors, and trained peer tutors are provided through the program or unit. Academic advisers and counselors are provided collaboratively through on-campus or off-campus services.

Summer Program To help prepare for the demands of college, there is 6-week summer program prior to entering the school available to high school graduates that focuses on self-advocacy, specific subject tutoring, study skills, and time management. Degree credit will be earned. The program accepts students from out-of-state.

Unique Aids and Services Aids, services, or accommodations include personal coach and priority registration.

Subject-Area Tutoring Tutoring is offered one-on-one for most subjects. Tutoring is provided through the program or unit via professional tutors and trained peer tutors. Tutoring is also provided collaboratively through on-campus or off-campus services via graduate assistants/students, professional tutors, and trained peer tutors.

Enrichment Programs for career planning, college survival skills, health and nutrition, learning strategies, math, medication management, reading, self-advocacy, stress management, study skills, test taking, time management, and written composition skills are provided collaboratively through on-campus or off-campus services.

Application For admittance to the program or unit, students are required to provide a psychoeducational report (4 years old or less). It is recommended that students provide documentation of high school services. Upon application, materials documenting need for services should be sent only to admissions with institutional application materials. Upon acceptance, documentation of need for services should be sent only to the LD program or unit. *Application deadline (institutional):* 1/1.

Written Policies Written policy regarding general/basic LD accommodations is outlined in the school's catalog/handbook. Written policies regarding course substitutions, general/basic LD accommodations, reduced course loads, and substitutions and waivers of graduation requirements are available through the program or unit directly.

Bradley University
Center for Learning Assistance

1501 West Bradley Avenue

Peoria, IL 61625-0002

http://www.bradley.edu/students/support/learn.html

Contact: Dr. Deborah J. Fischer, Director, Center for Learning Assistance. Phone: 309-677-2845. Fax: 309-677-3654. E-mail: djfisch@bradley.edu.

Center for Learning Assistance Approximately 115 registered undergraduate students were served during 2006–07. The program or unit includes 3 full-time and 2 part-time staff members. Remediation/learning specialists and trained peer tutors are provided through the program or unit. Remediation/learning specialists and trained peer tutors are provided collaboratively through on-campus or off-campus services.

Unique Aids and Services Aids, services, or accommodations include faculty training.

Assistive Technology Assistive technology is located in a special lab and includes learning support software and scanning.

Subject-Area Tutoring Tutoring is offered one-on-one and in small groups for some subjects. Tutoring is provided through the program or unit via trained peer tutors. Tutoring is also provided collaboratively through on-campus or off-campus services via graduate assistants/students and trained peer tutors.

Diagnostic Testing Testing is provided through the program or unit for learning strategies, learning styles, reading, and study skills. Testing for learning styles, reading, and study skills is provided collaboratively through on-campus or off-campus services.

Basic Skills Remediation Remediation is offered one-on-one and in class-size groups for learning strategies, math, reading, study skills, time management, and written language. Remediation is provided through the program or unit via trained peer tutors. Remediation is also provided collaboratively through on-campus or off-campus services via trained peer tutors.

Enrichment Enrichment programs are available through the program or unit for college survival skills, learning strategies, math, reading, stress management, study skills, test taking, and time management. Programs for career planning, college survival skills, learning strategies, practical computer skills, reading, stress management, study skills, test taking, time management, and written composition skills are provided collaboratively through on-campus or off-campus services.

Application For admittance to the program or unit, students are required to provide a psychoeducational report (3 years old or less). It is recommended that students provide documentation of high school services. Upon acceptance, documentation of need for services should be sent only to the LD program or unit. *Application deadline (institutional):* Continuous. *Application deadline (LD program):* Rolling/continuous for fall and rolling/continuous for spring.

Written Policies Written policy regarding general/basic LD accommodations is available on the program Web site. Written policy regarding general/basic LD accommodations is outlined in the school's catalog/handbook.

Brandeis University

415 South Street
Waltham, MA 02454-9110
http://www.brandeis.edu/
Contact: Ms. Beth Rodgers-Kay, Director, Disabilities Services & Support. Phone: 781-736-3470. E-mail: brodgers@brandeis.edu.

The program or unit includes 1 full-time staff member. LD specialists are provided through the program or unit. Academic advisers and trained peer tutors are provided collaboratively through on-campus or off-campus services.

Application For admittance to the program or unit, students are required to provide a psychoeducational report (3 years old or less). It is recommended that students provide documentation of high school services. Upon acceptance, documentation of need for services should be sent only to the LD program or unit. *Application deadline (institutional):* 1/15. *Application deadline (LD program):* Rolling/continuous for fall.

Written Policies Written policy regarding general/basic LD accommodations is available on the program Web site. Written policies regarding course substitutions and general/basic LD accommodations are available through the program or unit directly.

Brandon University

270 18th Street
Brandon, MB R7A 6A9
Canada
http://www.brandonu.ca/
Contact: Dr. Janet Wright, Executive Dean, Student & International Affairs/University Registrar. Phone: 204-727-9635. Fax: 204-725-2143. E-mail: wrightj@brandonu.ca.

Approximately 50 registered undergraduate students were served during 2006–07.

Unique Aids and Services Aids, services, or accommodations include career counseling and priority registration.

Assistive Technology Assistive technology is located in a special lab and includes digital textbooks/e-text and learning support software.

Subject-Area Tutoring Tutoring is offered one-on-one and in small groups for all subjects. Tutoring is provided collaboratively through on-campus or off-campus services via trained peer tutors.

Basic Skills Remediation Remediation is offered one-on-one and in small groups for computer skills, learning strategies, math, spelling, study skills, time management, and written language. Remediation is provided collaboratively through on-campus or off-campus services.

Application For admittance to the program or unit, students are required to provide a psychoeducational report (3 years old or less). It is recommended that students provide documentation of high school services. Upon application, materials documenting need for services should be sent only to the LD program or unit. Upon acceptance, documentation of need for services should be sent to both admissions and the LD program or unit. *Application deadline (institutional):* Continuous. *Application deadline (LD program):* Rolling/continuous for fall and rolling/continuous for spring.

Written Policies Written policy regarding general/basic LD accommodations is available on the program Web site. Written policy regarding general/basic LD accommodations is outlined in the school's catalog/handbook. Written policy regarding general/basic LD accommodations is available through the program or unit directly.

Brevard College
Office for Students with Special Needs and Disabilities

400 North Broad Street
Brevard, NC 28712-3306
http://www.brevard.edu/
Contact: Ms. Susan Kuehn, Director of Office for Students with Special Needs and Disabilities. Phone: 828-884-8131. Fax: 828-884-3790. E-mail: skuehn@brevard.edu.

Office for Students with Special Needs and Disabilities Approximately 55 registered undergraduate students were served during 2006–07. The program or unit includes 1 full-time staff member. Academic advisers, counselors, professional tutors, remediation/learning specialists, and trained peer tutors are provided collaboratively through on-campus or off-campus services.

Unique Aids and Services Aids, services, or accommodations include priority registration.

Assistive Technology Assistive technology is located in campus labs, the DSS office and includes digital textbooks/e-text, scanning, and tape recorders. Technology training is provided to incoming students.

Subject-Area Tutoring Tutoring is offered one-on-one and in small groups for most subjects. Tutoring is provided collaboratively through on-campus or off-campus services via professional tutors and trained peer tutors.

Diagnostic Testing Testing for learning strategies, learning styles, reading, and visual processing is provided collaboratively through on-campus or off-campus services.

Basic Skills Remediation Remediation is offered one-on-one for computer skills, math, reading, study skills, time management, visual processing, and written language. Remediation is provided collaboratively through on-campus or off-campus services via professional tutors, regular education teachers, and trained peer tutors.

Brevard College (continued)

Enrichment Enrichment programs are available through the program or unit for self-advocacy. Programs for career planning, college survival skills, health and nutrition, learning strategies, math, medication management, oral communication skills, practical computer skills, reading, stress management, study skills, test taking, time management, vocabulary development, and written composition skills are provided collaboratively through on-campus or off-campus services. Credit is offered for college survival skills, health and nutrition, math, oral communication skills, practical computer skills, reading, stress management, time management, and vocabulary development.

Application For admittance to the program or unit, students are required to provide a psychoeducational report (3 years old or less). It is recommended that students provide documentation of high school services. Upon application, materials documenting need for services should be sent only to the LD program or unit. Upon acceptance, documentation of need for services should be sent only to the LD program or unit. *Application deadline (institutional):* Continuous. *Application deadline (LD program):* Rolling/continuous for fall and rolling/continuous for spring.

Written Policies Written policies regarding course substitutions, general/basic LD accommodations, reduced course loads, substitutions and waivers of admissions requirements, and substitutions and waivers of graduation requirements are available on the program Web site. Written policies regarding course substitutions, general/basic LD accommodations, reduced course loads, substitutions and waivers of admissions requirements, and substitutions and waivers of graduation requirements are available through the program or unit directly.

Brewton-Parker College
Disability Support Services

Highway 280

Mt. Vernon, GA 30445-0197

http://www.bpc.edu/studentlife/Counseling/disability.htm

Contact: Mrs. Juanita Kissell, Director of Counseling Services. Phone: 912-583-3219. E-mail: jkissell@bpc.edu.

Disability Support Services Approximately 20 registered undergraduate students were served during 2006–07. The program or unit includes 1 full-time staff member. Counselors are provided through the program or unit. Regular education teachers and trained peer tutors are provided collaboratively through on-campus or off-campus services.

Assistive Technology Assistive technology is located in the DSS office.

Subject-Area Tutoring Tutoring is offered one-on-one, in small groups, and in class-size groups for most subjects. Tutoring is provided collaboratively through on-campus or off-campus services via professional tutors and trained peer tutors.

Basic Skills Remediation Remediation is offered in small groups and in class-size groups for learning strategies, math, reading, spelling, study skills, time management, and written language. Remediation is provided collaboratively through on-campus or off-campus services via regular education teachers, special education teachers, and trained peer tutors.

Enrichment Enrichment programs are available through the program or unit for career planning, stress management, study skills, test taking, and time management. Programs for college survival skills, learning strategies, math, reading, and written composition skills are provided collaboratively through on-campus or off-campus services. Credit is offered for college survival skills, math, reading, and written composition skills.

Application For admittance to the program or unit, students are required to provide a psychoeducational report (3 years old or less). It is recommended that students apply to the program directly and provide documentation of high school services. Upon application, materials documenting need for services should be sent only to the LD program or unit. Upon acceptance, documentation of need for services should be sent only to the LD program or unit. *Application deadline (institutional):* Continuous. *Application deadline (LD program):* Rolling/continuous for fall and rolling/continuous for spring.

Written Policies Written policy regarding general/basic LD accommodations is available on the program Web site. Written policy regarding general/basic LD accommodations is outlined in the school's catalog/handbook. Written policy regarding general/basic LD accommodations is available through the program or unit directly.

Briar Cliff University
Student Support Services

3303 Rebecca Street

Sioux City, IA 51104-0100

http://www.briarcliff.edu/

Contact: Sr. Jean Ann Beringer OSF, Director of Student Support Services. Phone: 712-279-5232. Fax: 712-279-5366. E-mail: jean.beringer@briarcliff.edu.

Student Support Services Approximately 5 registered undergraduate students were served during 2006–07. The program or unit includes 1 part-time staff member. Counselors, skill tutors, and trained peer tutors are provided through the program or unit.

Application For admittance to the program or unit, students are required to apply to the program directly and provide a psychoeducational report (3 years old or less). It is recommended that students provide documentation of high school services. Upon application, materials documenting need for services should be sent only to the LD program or unit. Upon acceptance, documentation of need for services should be sent only to the LD program or unit. *Application deadline (institutional):* Continuous. *Application deadline (LD program):* Rolling/continuous for fall and rolling/continuous for spring.

Written Policies Written policies regarding course substitutions, general/basic LD accommodations, and reduced course loads are available on the program Web site. Written policies regarding course substitutions, general/basic LD accommodations, reduced course loads, substitutions and waivers of admissions requirements, and substitutions and waivers of graduation requirements are available through the program or unit directly.

Bridgewater College
Academic Support and Disability Services

402 East College Street

Bridgewater, VA 22812-1599

http://www.bridgewater.edu

Contact: Dr. Chip Studwell, Director of Academic Support and Disability Services. Phone: 540-828-5370. Fax: 540-828-5757. E-mail: cstudwel@bridgewater.edu.

Academic Support and Disability Services Approximately 80 registered undergraduate students were served during 2006–07. The program or unit includes 2 full-time staff members. Academic advisers and trained peer tutors are provided through the program or unit.

Unique Aids and Services Aids, services, or accommodations include career counseling and priority registration.

Assistive Technology Assistive technology is located in the Academic Support Center and includes digital textbooks/e-text and scanning.

Subject-Area Tutoring Tutoring is provided collaboratively through on-campus or off-campus services via trained peer tutors.

Application For admittance to the program or unit, students are required to provide a psychoeducational report (2 years old or less) and provide scheduled meeting with Director in May/June prior to starting college. Upon acceptance, documentation of need for services should be sent to both admissions and the LD program or unit. *Application deadline (institutional):* Continuous.

Written Policies Written policies regarding course substitutions and general/basic LD accommodations are available on the program Web site.

British Columbia Institute of Technology
Disability Resource Centre

3700 Willingdon Avenue

Burnaby, BC V5G 3H2

Canada

http://www.bcit.ca/drc

Contact: Dr. Derek McLauchlan, Learning Specialist. Phone: 604-432-8930. Fax: 604-431-0724. E-mail: derek_mclauchlan@bcit.ca.

Disability Resource Centre Approximately 420 registered undergraduate students were served during 2006–07. The program or unit includes 6 full-time staff members. Academic advisers, counselors, diagnostic specialists, LD specialists, remediation/learning specialists, and strategy tutors are provided through the program or unit. Academic advisers and strategy tutors are provided collaboratively through on-campus or off-campus services.

Summer Program To help prepare for the demands of college, there is an optional 1- to 4-day summer program prior to entering the school that focuses on computing skills, study skills, test-taking skills, and time management. The program accepts students from out-of-state.

Unique Aids and Services Aids, services, or accommodations include career counseling.

Assistive Technology Assistive technology is located in the DSS office, a special lab and includes digital textbooks/e-text, learning support software, scanning, and Kurzweil, taped texts, enlarged notes. Technology training is provided to incoming students.

Subject-Area Tutoring Tutoring is offered one-on-one for all subjects. Tutoring is provided through the program or unit via trained peer tutors. Tutoring is also provided collaboratively through on-campus or off-campus services via trained peer tutors.

Basic Skills Remediation Remediation is offered one-on-one for learning strategies, study skills, and time management. Remediation is provided through the program or unit via LD specialists.

Enrichment Enrichment programs are available through the program or unit for career planning and learning strategies. Programs for career planning, college survival skills, health and nutrition, learning strategies, stress management, study skills, test taking, and time management are provided collaboratively through on-campus or off-campus services.

Fees *Summer Program* fee is $500 Canadian dollars.

Application For admittance to the program or unit, students are required to provide a psychoeducational report. It is recommended that students provide documentation of high school services. Upon application, materials documenting need for services should be sent only to the LD program or unit. Upon acceptance, documentation of need for services should be sent only to the LD program or unit. *Application deadline (LD program):* Rolling/continuous for fall and rolling/continuous for spring.

Written Policies Written policy regarding general/basic LD accommodations is available on the program Web site.

Brock University
Services for Students with disABILITIES

500 Glenridge Avenue

St. Catharines, ON L2S 3A1

Canada

http://www.brocku.ca/sdc/disABILITIES

Contact: Ms. Judith Ann Brooder, Manager, Services for Students with disABILITIES. Phone: 905-688-5550 Ext. 3240. Fax: 905-688-7260. E-mail: jbrooder@brocku.ca.

Services for Students with disABILITIES Approximately 300 registered undergraduate students were served during 2006–07. The program or unit includes 5 full-time and 5 part-time staff members. Counselors, graduate assistants/students, LD specialists, remediation/learning specialists, skill tutors, and strategy tutors are provided through the program or unit. Academic advisers, counselors, diagnostic specialists, skill tutors, and trained peer tutors are provided collaboratively through on-campus or off-campus services.

Orientation The program or unit offers an optional 1-day orientation for new students before classes begin, during summer prior to enrollment, during registration, and individually by special arrangement.

Summer Program To help prepare for the demands of college, there is an optional 3-day summer program prior to entering the school available to high school graduates that focuses on computing skills, life skills and/or college life adjustment, self-advocacy, study skills, test-taking skills, and time management. The program accepts students from out-of-state.

Brock University (continued)

Unique Aids and Services Aids, services, or accommodations include faculty training and priority registration.

Assistive Technology Assistive technology is located in the DSS office and includes digital textbooks/e-text, learning support software, and scanning. Technology training is provided to incoming students.

Subject-Area Tutoring Tutoring is offered one-on-one for some subjects. Tutoring is provided through the program or unit via graduate assistants/students and LD specialists. Tutoring is also provided collaboratively through on-campus or off-campus services via graduate assistants/students, LD specialists, professional tutors, and trained peer tutors.

Diagnostic Testing Testing is provided through the program or unit for intelligence, learning strategies, learning styles, math, personality, reading, spelling, spoken language, study skills, visual processing, and written language. Testing for auditory processing, handwriting, intelligence, learning strategies, learning styles, math, motor skills, neuropsychological, personality, reading, social skills, spelling, spoken language, study skills, visual processing, and written language is provided collaboratively through on-campus or off-campus services.

Enrichment Enrichment programs are available through the program or unit for career planning, college survival skills, learning strategies, oral communication skills, practical computer skills, reading, self-advocacy, stress management, study skills, test taking, time management, vocabulary development, and written composition skills. Programs for career planning, college survival skills, health and nutrition, learning strategies, medication management, oral communication skills, reading, self-advocacy, stress management, study skills, test taking, time management, vocabulary development, and written composition skills are provided collaboratively through on-campus or off-campus services.

Fees *Summer Program* fee is $40. *Orientation* fee is $40. *Diagnostic Testing* fee is $0 to $3000.

Application For admittance to the program or unit, students are required to provide a psychoeducational report. It is recommended that students provide documentation of high school services. Upon application, materials documenting need for services should be sent only to the LD program or unit. Upon acceptance, documentation of need for services should be sent only to the LD program or unit. *Application deadline (institutional):* 4/1. *Application deadline (LD program):* Rolling/continuous for fall and rolling/continuous for spring.

Written Policies Written policy regarding general/basic LD accommodations is available on the program Web site. Written policy regarding general/basic LD accommodations is outlined in the school's catalog/handbook. Written policy regarding general/basic LD accommodations is available through the program or unit directly.

Brown University
Disability Support Services
Providence, RI 02912
http://www.brown.edu/dss
Contact: Catherine J. Axe, Director. Phone: 401-863-9588. Fax: 401-863-1999. E-mail: dss@brown.edu.

Disability Support Services Approximately 160 registered undergraduate students were served during 2006–07. The program or unit

includes 1 full-time and 2 part-time staff members. Academic advisers, coaches, counselors, diagnostic specialists, LD specialists, professional tutors, and skill tutors are provided collaboratively through on-campus or off-campus services.

Orientation The program or unit offers a mandatory 3- to 5-hour orientation for new students before classes begin and after classes begin.

Unique Aids and Services Aids, services, or accommodations include career counseling, personal coach, and support groups.

Assistive Technology Assistive technology is located in the DSS office, libraries and includes digital textbooks/e-text, learning support software, and scanning.

Subject-Area Tutoring Tutoring is offered one-on-one and in small groups for some subjects. Tutoring is provided collaboratively through on-campus or off-campus services via graduate assistants/students, professional tutors, and trained peer tutors.

Diagnostic Testing Testing for auditory processing, handwriting, intelligence, learning strategies, learning styles, math, motor skills, neuropsychological, personality, reading, social skills, spelling, spoken language, study skills, visual processing, and written language is provided collaboratively through on-campus or off-campus services.

Basic Skills Remediation Remediation is offered one-on-one for learning strategies, reading, spelling, study skills, time management, and written language. Remediation is provided collaboratively through on-campus or off-campus services via professional tutors.

Enrichment Enrichment programs are available through the program or unit for self-advocacy. Programs for career planning, learning strategies, math, oral communication skills, practical computer skills, reading, self-advocacy, stress management, study skills, test taking, time management, and written composition skills are provided collaboratively through on-campus or off-campus services.

Fees *Diagnostic Testing* fee is $300 to $2000.

Application For admittance to the program or unit, students are required to provide a psychoeducational report (3 years old or less). It is recommended that students provide documentation of high school services. Upon application, materials documenting need for services should be sent only to admissions with institutional application materials. Upon acceptance, documentation of need for services should be sent only to the LD program or unit. *Application deadline (institutional):* 1/1. *Application deadline (LD program):* Rolling/continuous for fall and rolling/continuous for spring.

Written Policies Written policies regarding general/basic LD accommodations and reduced course loads are available on the program Web site. Written policy regarding general/basic LD accommodations is outlined in the school's catalog/handbook. Written policies regarding general/basic LD accommodations and reduced course loads are available through the program or unit directly.

Bryn Mawr College
Access Services
101 North Merion Avenue
Bryn Mawr, PA 19010-2899
http://www.brynmawr.edu/access_services
Contact: Stephanie Bell, Coordinator. Phone: 610-526-7351. Fax: 610-526-7451. E-mail: sbell@brynmawr.edu.

Access Services Approximately 35 registered undergraduate students were served during 2006–07. The program or unit includes 1 part-time staff member. LD specialists are provided through the program or unit. Graduate assistants/students are provided collaboratively through on-campus or off-campus services.

Subject-Area Tutoring Tutoring is offered one-on-one, in small groups, and in class-size groups for some subjects. Tutoring is provided collaboratively through on-campus or off-campus services via graduate assistants/students and trained peer tutors.

Diagnostic Testing Testing for auditory processing, intelligence, math, motor skills, neuropsychological, personality, reading, spelling, spoken language, visual processing, and written language is provided collaboratively through on-campus or off-campus services.

Enrichment Enrichment programs are available through the program or unit for learning strategies, self-advocacy, study skills, test taking, and time management. Programs for career planning, college survival skills, health and nutrition, learning strategies, medication management, stress management, study skills, test taking, time management, and written composition skills are provided collaboratively through on-campus or off-campus services.

Fees *Diagnostic Testing* fee is $850 to $3500.

Application For admittance to the program or unit, students are required to provide a psychoeducational report. Upon acceptance, documentation of need for services should be sent only to the LD program or unit. *Application deadline (institutional):* 1/15.

Written Policies Written policy regarding general/basic LD accommodations is available on the program Web site. Written policies regarding general/basic LD accommodations and reduced course loads are outlined in the school's catalog/handbook. Written policies regarding course substitutions and general/basic LD accommodations are available through the program or unit directly.

Buena Vista University
Center for Academic Excellence

610 West Fourth Street
Storm Lake, IA 50588

http://www.bvu.edu/departments/academicaffairs/cae/

Contact: Donna S. Musel, Director, Center for Academic Excellence. Phone: 712-749-1237. Fax: 712-749-2037. E-mail: museld@bvu.edu.

Center for Academic Excellence Approximately 50 registered undergraduate students were served during 2006–07. The program or unit includes 1 full-time staff member. Academic advisers, skill tutors, strategy tutors, and trained peer tutors are provided through the program or unit. Academic advisers, counselors, diagnostic specialists, and regular education teachers are provided collaboratively through on-campus or off-campus services.

Unique Aids and Services Aids, services, or accommodations include faculty training and priority registration.

Assistive Technology Assistive technology is located in the DSS office, the student's laptop computer and includes digital textbooks/e-text and scanning. Technology training is provided to incoming students.

Subject-Area Tutoring Tutoring is offered one-on-one and in small groups for all subjects. Tutoring is provided collaboratively through on-campus or off-campus services via trained peer tutors.

Basic Skills Remediation Remediation is offered one-on-one and in small groups for reading, spelling, study skills, time management, and written language. Remediation is provided collaboratively through on-campus or off-campus services.

Enrichment Programs for stress management, study skills, test taking, and time management are provided collaboratively through on-campus or off-campus services. Credit is offered for math, vocabulary development, and written composition skills.

Application For admittance to the program or unit, students are required to provide documentation of disability. It is recommended that students provide a psychoeducational report and provide documentation of high school services. Upon acceptance, documentation of need for services should be sent only to the LD program or unit. *Application deadline (LD program):* Rolling/continuous for fall and rolling/continuous for spring.

Written Policies Written policy regarding general/basic LD accommodations is available on the program Web site. Written policy regarding general/basic LD accommodations is outlined in the school's catalog/handbook. Written policies regarding general/basic LD accommodations and reduced course loads are available through the program or unit directly.

Buffalo State College, State University of New York
Disability Services for Students

1300 Elmwood Avenue
Buffalo, NY 14222-1095

http://www.buffalostate.edu/offices/disabilityservices

Contact: Mrs. Marianne R. Savino, Director, Disability Services. Phone: 716-878-4500. Fax: 716-878-3804. E-mail: savinomr@buffalostate.edu.

Disability Services for Students Approximately 385 registered undergraduate students were served during 2006–07. The program or unit includes 4 full-time and 2 part-time staff members. Academic advisers, counselors, graduate assistants/students, and other are provided through the program or unit. Academic advisers, counselors, diagnostic specialists, graduate assistants/students, professional tutors, remediation/learning specialists, skill tutors, strategy tutors, trained peer tutors, and other are provided collaboratively through on-campus or off-campus services.

Unique Aids and Services Aids, services, or accommodations include advocates, career counseling, faculty training, priority registration, and support groups.

Assistive Technology Assistive technology is located in campus labs, the DSS office, the library and includes digital textbooks/e-text, learning support software, and other adaptive equipment and software. Technology training is provided to incoming students.

Subject-Area Tutoring Tutoring is offered one-on-one and in small groups for most subjects. Tutoring is provided collaboratively through on-campus or off-campus services via computer-based instruction, graduate assistants/students, professional tutors, trained peer tutors, and other.

Basic Skills Remediation Remediation is offered one-on-one and in small groups for computer skills, learning strategies, math, reading, social skills, spelling, spoken language, study skills, time

Buffalo State College, State University of New York (continued)
management, visual processing, and written language. Remediation is provided collaboratively through on-campus or off-campus services via computer-based instruction, graduate assistants/students, professional tutors, trained peer tutors, and other.

Enrichment Enrichment programs are available through the program or unit for career planning, self-advocacy, stress management, and test taking. Programs for career planning, college survival skills, health and nutrition, learning strategies, math, medication management, oral communication skills, practical computer skills, reading, self-advocacy, stress management, study skills, test taking, time management, vocabulary development, written composition skills, and other are provided collaboratively through on-campus or off-campus services. Credit is offered for college survival skills, oral communication skills, practical computer skills, and reading.

Student Organization Abilities Support Group consists of 25 members.

Application For admittance to the program or unit, students are required to provide a psychoeducational report (2 years old or less) and provide full psychoeducational evaluation including strengths, weaknesses, and prior support provided. It is recommended that students provide documentation of high school services. Upon application, materials documenting need for services should be sent only to the LD program or unit. Upon acceptance, documentation of need for services should be sent only to the LD program or unit. *Application deadline (institutional):* Continuous. *Application deadline (LD program):* Rolling/continuous for fall and rolling/continuous for spring.

Written Policies Written policies regarding course substitutions, general/basic LD accommodations, reduced course loads, substitutions and waivers of admissions requirements, and substitutions and waivers of graduation requirements are available on the program Web site. Written policies regarding course substitutions, general/basic LD accommodations, reduced course loads, substitutions and waivers of admissions requirements, and substitutions and waivers of graduation requirements are outlined in the school's catalog/handbook. Written policies regarding course substitutions, general/basic LD accommodations, reduced course loads, substitutions and waivers of admissions requirements, and substitutions and waivers of graduation requirements are available through the program or unit directly.

California State University, Fullerton
Disabled Student Services

PO Box 34080
Fullerton, CA 92834-9480
http://www.fullerton.edu/disabledservices

Contact: Mr. Doug Liverpool, Learning Disability/Mental Health Specialist. Phone: 714-278-3112. Fax: 714-278-2408. E-mail: dliverpool@fullerton.edu. Head of LD Program: Mr. Paul Miller, Director, Disabled Student Services. Phone: 714-278-3112. Fax: 714-278-2408. E-mail: pmiller@fullerton.edu.

Disabled Student Services Approximately 350 registered undergraduate students were served during 2006–07. The program or unit

includes 1 full-time staff member. Diagnostic specialists and LD specialists are provided through the program or unit. Academic advisers, coaches, counselors, diagnostic specialists, LD specialists, skill tutors, and trained peer tutors are provided collaboratively through on-campus or off-campus services.

Unique Aids and Services Aids, services, or accommodations include advocates, faculty training, and priority registration.

Assistive Technology Assistive technology is located in campus labs, the DSS office, a special lab and includes digital textbooks/e-text, learning support software, and scanning. Technology training is provided to incoming students.

Diagnostic Testing Testing is provided through the program or unit for intelligence and other services. Testing for intelligence and other services is provided collaboratively through on-campus or off-campus services.

Enrichment Enrichment programs are available through the program or unit for self-advocacy. Programs for career planning, college survival skills, health and nutrition, learning strategies, math, medication management, self-advocacy, stress management, study skills, time management, and written composition skills are provided collaboratively through on-campus or off-campus services.

Application For admittance to the program or unit, students are required to apply to the program directly, provide a psychoeducational report, and provide cognitive/achievement testing. Upon application, materials documenting need for services should be sent only to the LD program or unit. *Application deadline (institutional):* 11/30. *Application deadline (LD program):* Rolling/continuous for fall and rolling/continuous for spring.

Written Policies Written policy regarding general/basic LD accommodations is available on the program Web site. Written policy regarding grade forgiveness is outlined in the school's catalog/handbook. Written policies regarding course substitutions, general/basic LD accommodations, substitutions and waivers of admissions requirements, and substitutions and waivers of graduation requirements are available through the program or unit directly.

California State University, Northridge
Center on Disabilities

18111 Nordhoff Street
Northridge, CA 91330
http://www.csun.edu/cod

Contact: Dr. Jennifer Zvi, Learning Disabilities Specialist. Phone: 818-677-2684. Fax: 818-477-4929. E-mail: jennifer.zvi@csun.edu.

Center on Disabilities Approximately 300 registered undergraduate students were served during 2006–07. The program or unit includes 1 full-time and 1 part-time staff member. Academic advisers, coaches, counselors, diagnostic specialists, LD specialists, skill tutors, and strategy tutors are provided through the program or unit. Academic advisers, coaches, counselors, diagnostic specialists, LD specialists, skill tutors, and strategy tutors are provided collaboratively through on-campus or off-campus services.

Unique Aids and Services Aids, services, or accommodations include career counseling, personal coach, priority registration, and support groups.

Assistive Technology Assistive technology is located in campus labs, special library study rooms and includes digital textbooks/e-text, learning support software, and scanning.

Subject-Area Tutoring Tutoring is offered for some subjects.

Diagnostic Testing Testing is provided through the program or unit for auditory processing, handwriting, intelligence, learning strategies, learning styles, math, motor skills, neuropsychological, reading, spelling, visual processing, and written language. Testing for learning strategies, learning styles, personality, spoken language, and study skills is provided collaboratively through on-campus or off-campus services.

Basic Skills Remediation Remediation is available for computer skills, learning strategies, math, study skills, time management, and written language. Remediation is provided collaboratively through on-campus or off-campus services via graduate assistants/students.

Enrichment Programs for career planning, college survival skills, health and nutrition, learning strategies, math, practical computer skills, self-advocacy, stress management, study skills, test taking, time management, and written composition skills are provided collaboratively through on-campus or off-campus services.

Application It is recommended that students apply to the program directly, provide a psychoeducational report (3 years old or less), and provide documentation of high school services. Upon application, materials documenting need for services should be sent to both admissions and the LD program or unit. Upon acceptance, documentation of need for services should be sent only to the LD program or unit. *Application deadline (institutional): 11/30. Application deadline (LD program):* Rolling/continuous for fall and rolling/continuous for spring.

Written Policies Written policy regarding general/basic LD accommodations is available on the program Web site. Written policy regarding general/basic LD accommodations is outlined in the school's catalog/handbook. Written policy regarding general/basic LD accommodations is available through the program or unit directly.

California State University, Sacramento
Services to Students with Disabilities

6000 J Street

Sacramento, CA 95819-6048

http://www.csus.edu/sswd/sswd.html

Contact: Mrs. Jamie Jones, Learning Disabilities Specialist. Phone: 916-278-6721. Fax: 916-278-7825. E-mail: jamie.j.jones@csus.edu. Head of LD Program: Judy Dean, Director of Services to Students with Disabilities. Phone: 916-278-6955. Fax: 916-278-7825. E-mail: deanj@csus.edu.

Services to Students with Disabilities Approximately 450 registered undergraduate students were served during 2006–07. The program or unit includes 2 full-time staff members. Counselors, diagnostic specialists, LD specialists, remediation/learning specialists, strategy tutors, and other are provided through the program or unit. Academic advisers, coaches, graduate assistants/students, professional tutors, regular education teachers, skill tutors, and trained peer tutors are provided collaboratively through on-campus or off-campus services.

Unique Aids and Services Aids, services, or accommodations include priority registration.

Assistive Technology Assistive technology is located in campus labs, a special lab and includes digital textbooks/e-text, learning support software, and scanning. Technology training is provided to incoming students.

Subject-Area Tutoring Tutoring is offered one-on-one, in small groups, and in class-size groups for most subjects. Tutoring is provided through the program or unit via LD specialists. Tutoring is also provided collaboratively through on-campus or off-campus services via computer-based instruction, graduate assistants/students, professional tutors, and trained peer tutors.

Diagnostic Testing Testing is provided through the program or unit for learning strategies, learning styles, and study skills. Testing for auditory processing, intelligence, math, personality, reading, social skills, spelling, spoken language, visual processing, and written language is provided collaboratively through on-campus or off-campus services.

Basic Skills Remediation Remediation is offered one-on-one, in small groups, and in class-size groups for computer skills, learning strategies, math, reading, spoken language, study skills, time management, and written language. Remediation is provided through the program or unit via LD specialists. Remediation is also provided collaboratively through on-campus or off-campus services via computer-based instruction, graduate assistants/students, professional tutors, regular education teachers, trained peer tutors, and other.

Enrichment Enrichment programs are available through the program or unit for college survival skills, learning strategies, math, practical computer skills, self-advocacy, stress management, study skills, test taking, and time management. Programs for career planning, health and nutrition, math, medication management, oral communication skills, practical computer skills, reading, stress management, vocabulary development, and written composition skills are provided collaboratively through on-campus or off-campus services. Credit is offered for college survival skills, learning strategies, math, practical computer skills, self-advocacy, stress management, study skills, test taking, and time management.

Application For admittance to the program or unit, students are required to apply to the program directly, provide a psychoeducational report (5 years old or less), provide documentation of high school services, and provide adult-normed assessment only. Upon application, materials documenting need for services should be sent to both admissions and the LD program or unit. Upon acceptance, documentation of need for services should be sent only to the LD program or unit. *Application deadline (institutional): 8/1. Application deadline (LD program):* Rolling/continuous for fall and rolling/continuous for spring.

Written Policies Written policy regarding general/basic LD accommodations is available on the program Web site. Written policies regarding course substitutions and general/basic LD accommodations are available through the program or unit directly.

California State University, San Bernardino
Services to Students with Disabilities

5500 University Parkway

San Bernardino, CA 92407-2397

http://enrollment.csusb.edu/~ssd

Contact: Dr. Doron A. Dula, Learning Disabilities Specialist. Phone: 909-537-5238. Fax: 909-537-7090. E-mail: ddula@csusb.edu. Head of LD Program: Dr. Beth Jaworski, Director. Phone: 909-537-5238. Fax: 909-537-7090. E-mail: bjaworsk@csusb.edu.

Services to Students with Disabilities Approximately 65 registered undergraduate students were served during 2006–07. The program or unit includes 1 full-time staff member. Counselors, diagnostic specialists, and LD specialists are provided through the program or unit. Academic advisers, diagnostic specialists, graduate assistants/students, skill tutors, and strategy tutors are provided collaboratively through on-campus or off-campus services.
Unique Aids and Services Aids, services, or accommodations include priority registration.
Assistive Technology Assistive technology is located in special lab (lab also provides assistive technology training) and includes digital textbooks/e-text, scanning, and speech-to-text software.
Subject-Area Tutoring Tutoring is offered in small groups for some subjects. Tutoring is provided collaboratively through on-campus or off-campus services via graduate assistants/students.
Enrichment Programs for career planning, college survival skills, health and nutrition, math, practical computer skills, reading, stress management, time management, and written composition skills are provided collaboratively through on-campus or off-campus services.
Application For admittance to the program or unit, students are required to apply to the program directly, provide a psychoeducational report (3 years old or less), and provide concomitant medical/psychiatric for past and current treatment. It is recommended that students provide documentation of high school services. Upon application, materials documenting need for services should be sent only to the LD program or unit. Upon acceptance, documentation of need for services should be sent only to the LD program or unit. *Application deadline (institutional):* Continuous. *Application deadline (LD program):* Rolling/continuous for fall and rolling/continuous for spring.
Written Policies Written policy regarding general/basic LD accommodations is available through the program or unit directly.

California State University, Stanislaus
Disability Resource Services

801 West Monte Vista Avenue

Turlock, CA 95382

http://web.csustan.edu/DRS/

Contact: Mr. Lee Bettencourt, Interim Director. Phone: 209-667-3159. Fax: 209-667-3585. E-mail: lbettencourt@csustan.edu.

Disability Resource Services Approximately 83 registered undergraduate students were served during 2006–07. The program or unit includes 1 full-time staff member. Counselors are provided through the program or unit. Academic advisers, counselors, and regular education teachers are provided collaboratively through on-campus or off-campus services.
Assistive Technology Assistive technology is located in the DSS office, the library and includes digital textbooks/e-text.
Subject-Area Tutoring Tutoring is offered one-on-one and in small groups for most subjects. Tutoring is provided collaboratively through on-campus or off-campus services via graduate assistants/students and trained peer tutors.
Basic Skills Remediation Remediation is offered one-on-one, in small groups, and in class-size groups for learning strategies, math, study skills, time management, and written language. Remediation is provided collaboratively through on-campus or off-campus services via graduate assistants/students, regular education teachers, and trained peer tutors.
Enrichment Enrichment programs are available through the program or unit for college survival skills, learning strategies, self-advocacy, stress management, study skills, test taking, and time management. Programs for career planning, health and nutrition, medication management, and written composition skills are provided collaboratively through on-campus or off-campus services.
Application For admittance to the program or unit, students are required to provide a psychoeducational report (3 years old or less). It is recommended that students provide documentation of high school services. Upon application, materials documenting need for services should be sent only to the LD program or unit. Upon acceptance, documentation of need for services should be sent only to the LD program or unit. *Application deadline (institutional):* 7/1. *Application deadline (LD program):* Rolling/continuous for fall and rolling/continuous for spring.
Written Policies Written policies regarding course substitutions, general/basic LD accommodations, substitutions and waivers of admissions requirements, and substitutions and waivers of graduation requirements are available on the program Web site. Written policies regarding course substitutions, general/basic LD accommodations, substitutions and waivers of admissions requirements, and substitutions and waivers of graduation requirements are outlined in the school's catalog/handbook. Written policies regarding course substitutions, general/basic LD accommodations, substitutions and waivers of admissions requirements, and substitutions and waivers of graduation requirements are available through the program or unit directly.

Calvin College
Student Academic Services (SAS)

3201 Burton Street, SE

Grand Rapids, MI 49546-4388

http://www.calvin.edu/academic/sas

Contact: June De Boer, Coordinator of Services to Students with Disabilities. Phone: 616-526-6113. Fax: 616-526-7066. E-mail: jed4@calvin.edu. Head of LD Program: Karen

Broekstra, Coordinator of Services to Students with Disabilities. Phone: 616-526-6113. Fax: 616-526-7066. E-mail: kbroekst@calvin.edu.

Student Academic Services (SAS) Approximately 400 registered undergraduate students were served during 2006–07. The program or unit includes 3 full-time staff members. LD specialists are provided through the program or unit. Academic advisers, coaches, counselors, diagnostic specialists, skill tutors, strategy tutors, and trained peer tutors are provided collaboratively through on-campus or off-campus services.

Orientation The program or unit offers an optional 1-hour orientation for new students before classes begin and individually by special arrangement.

Unique Aids and Services Aids, services, or accommodations include advocates, career counseling, faculty training, personal coach, priority registration, and support groups.

Assistive Technology Assistive technology is located in campus labs, the DSS office, a special lab and includes digital textbooks/e-text, learning support software, scanning, and books on tape/CD-ROM. Technology training is provided to incoming students.

Subject-Area Tutoring Tutoring is offered one-on-one, in small groups, and in class-size groups for most subjects. Tutoring is provided collaboratively through on-campus or off-campus services via trained peer tutors.

Diagnostic Testing Testing is provided through the program or unit for personality. Testing for auditory processing, handwriting, intelligence, learning strategies, learning styles, math, motor skills, neuropsychological, personality, reading, social skills, spelling, spoken language, study skills, visual processing, written language, and other services is provided collaboratively through on-campus or off-campus services.

Enrichment Programs for career planning, college survival skills, health and nutrition, learning strategies, math, medication management, oral communication skills, reading, self-advocacy, stress management, study skills, test taking, time management, and written composition skills are provided collaboratively through on-campus or off-campus services.

Fees *Diagnostic Testing* fee is applicable.

Application For admittance to the program or unit, students are required to provide a psychoeducational report (3 years old or less). It is recommended that students provide documentation of high school services. Upon application, materials documenting need for services should be sent only to the LD program or unit. Upon acceptance, documentation of need for services should be sent only to the LD program or unit. *Application deadline (institutional):* 8/15. *Application deadline (LD program):* Rolling/continuous for fall and rolling/continuous for spring.

Written Policies Written policy regarding grade forgiveness is outlined in the school's catalog/handbook. Written policy regarding general/basic LD accommodations is available through the program or unit directly.

Cameron University
Disability Services

2800 West Gore Boulevard
Lawton, OK 73505-6377
http://www.cameron.edu/disabled_services

Contact: Dr. Jennifer A. Pruchnicki, Director of Student Development. Phone: 580-581-2209. Fax: 580-581-2564. E-mail: jpruchni@cameron.edu.

Disability Services Approximately 35 registered undergraduate students were served during 2006–07. The program or unit includes 3 full-time staff members. Academic advisers, counselors, regular education teachers, and remediation/learning specialists are provided collaboratively through on-campus or off-campus services.

Assistive Technology Assistive technology is located in campus labs, the DSS office and includes digital textbooks/e-text, learning support software, and scanning.

Subject-Area Tutoring Tutoring is offered one-on-one and in small groups for most subjects. Tutoring is provided collaboratively through on-campus or off-campus services via professional tutors and trained peer tutors.

Basic Skills Remediation Remediation is available for math, reading, and written language. Remediation is provided collaboratively through on-campus or off-campus services via regular education teachers.

Enrichment Program for career planning is provided collaboratively through on-campus or off-campus services.

Application For admittance to the program or unit, students are required to apply to the program directly. It is recommended that students provide a psychoeducational report (3 years old or less) and provide documentation of high school services. Upon application, materials documenting need for services should be sent only to the LD program or unit. Upon acceptance, documentation of need for services should be sent only to the LD program or unit. *Application deadline (institutional):* Continuous. *Application deadline (LD program):* Rolling/continuous for fall and rolling/continuous for spring.

Written Policies Written policy regarding general/basic LD accommodations is available on the program Web site. Written policy regarding general/basic LD accommodations is outlined in the school's catalog/handbook. Written policies regarding course substitutions and general/basic LD accommodations are available through the program or unit directly.

Cape Breton University
AccessAbility Centre

Box 5300
1250 Grand Lake Road
Sydney, NS B1P 6L2
Canada
http://www.cbu.ca/

Contact: Mr. Mel Clarke, Disability Resource Facilitator. Phone: 902-563-1404. Fax: 902-563-1216. E-mail: mel_clarke@cbu.ca.

AccessAbility Centre Approximately 60 registered undergraduate students were served during 2006–07. The program or unit includes 2 full-time and 12 part-time staff members. Professional tutors, regular education teachers, skill tutors, special education teachers, strategy tutors, teacher trainees, and trained peer tutors are provided through the program or unit. Academic advisers, counselors, diagnostic specialists, and remediation/learning specialists are provided collaboratively through on-campus or off-campus services.

Cape Breton University (continued)

Orientation The program or unit offers an optional orientation for new students before registration, before classes begin, and individually by special arrangement.

Unique Aids and Services Aids, services, or accommodations include advocates, career counseling, and personal coach.

Assistive Technology Assistive technology is located in the DSS office, a special lab and includes digital textbooks/e-text and learning support software. Technology training is provided to incoming students.

Subject-Area Tutoring Tutoring is offered one-on-one and in small groups for most subjects. Tutoring is provided through the program or unit via graduate assistants/students and trained peer tutors.

Diagnostic Testing Testing for auditory processing, handwriting, intelligence, learning strategies, learning styles, math, motor skills, neuropsychological, personality, reading, social skills, spelling, spoken language, study skills, visual processing, and written language is provided collaboratively through on-campus or off-campus services.

Basic Skills Remediation Remediation is offered one-on-one for social skills, spelling, spoken language, study skills, time management, and written language. Remediation is provided through the program or unit via LD specialists. Remediation is also provided collaboratively through on-campus or off-campus services via graduate assistants/students, regular education teachers, and teacher trainees.

Enrichment Programs for career planning, college survival skills, health and nutrition, learning strategies, math, oral communication skills, practical computer skills, reading, self-advocacy, stress management, study skills, test taking, time management, vocabulary development, written composition skills, and other are provided collaboratively through on-campus or off-campus services.

Fees *Diagnostic Testing* fee is $600 Canadian dollars.

Application For admittance to the program or unit, students are required to provide a psychoeducational report (3 years old or less). It is recommended that students provide documentation of high school services. Upon application, materials documenting need for services should be sent to both admissions and the LD program or unit. Upon acceptance, documentation of need for services should be sent to both admissions and the LD program or unit. *Application deadline (institutional):* 8/1. *Application deadline (LD program):* Rolling/continuous for fall and rolling/continuous for spring.

Written Policies Written policies regarding general/basic LD accommodations, reduced course loads, and substitutions and waivers of admissions requirements are available through the program or unit directly.

Cardinal Stritch University
Academic Support Center

6801 North Yates Road

Milwaukee, WI 53217-3985

http://www.stritch.edu/

Contact: Dr. Marcia L. Laskey, Director Academic Support Center. Phone: 414-410-4168 Ext. 4168. Fax: 414-410-4239. E-mail: mllaskey@stritch.edu.

Academic Support Center Approximately 40 registered undergraduate students were served during 2006–07. The program or unit

includes 4 full-time and 4 part-time staff members. LD specialists, professional tutors, remediation/learning specialists, and strategy tutors are provided through the program or unit.

Orientation The program or unit offers a mandatory 30-minute orientation for new students individually by special arrangement.

Unique Aids and Services Aids, services, or accommodations include advocates, priority registration, and weekly meetings with faculty.

Assistive Technology Assistive technology is located in the Academic Support Center, the library and includes books on tape/CD.

Subject-Area Tutoring Tutoring is offered one-on-one for most subjects. Tutoring is provided through the program or unit via LD specialists and professional tutors.

Basic Skills Remediation Remediation is offered one-on-one and in class-size groups for computer skills, learning strategies, math, reading, social skills, study skills, time management, visual processing, and written language. Remediation is provided through the program or unit via LD specialists and professional tutors.

Enrichment Enrichment programs are available through the program or unit for college survival skills, learning strategies, math, oral communication skills, reading, self-advocacy, stress management, study skills, test taking, time management, and written composition skills. Program for career planning is provided collaboratively through on-campus or off-campus services.

Application For admittance to the program or unit, students are required to provide a psychoeducational report and provide documentation from a licensed professional with test results included. Upon application, materials documenting need for services should be sent only to the LD program or unit. Upon acceptance, documentation of need for services should be sent only to the LD program or unit. *Application deadline (institutional):* 8/1. *Application deadline (LD program):* Rolling/continuous for fall and rolling/continuous for spring.

Written Policies Written policy regarding general/basic LD accommodations is outlined in the school's catalog/handbook. Written policy regarding general/basic LD accommodations is available through the program or unit directly.

Carleton University
The Paul Menton Center

1125 Colonel By Drive

Ottawa, ON K1S 5B6

Canada

http://www.carleton.ca/pmc/

Contact: Dr. Nancy McIntyre, Coordinator of Learning Disabilities. Phone: 613-520-6608. Fax: 613-520-3995. E-mail: nancy_mcintyre@carleton.ca.

The Paul Menton Center Approximately 250 registered undergraduate students were served during 2006–07. The program or unit includes 3 full-time staff members and 1 part-time staff member. Coaches, counselors, LD specialists, remediation/learning specialists, strategy tutors, and other are provided through the program or unit. Academic advisers, counselors, diagnostic specialists, graduate assistants/students, professional tutors, skill tutors, and trained peer tutors are provided collaboratively through on-campus or off-campus services.

Orientation The program or unit offers an optional half-day orientation for new students before classes begin and individually by special arrangement.

Unique Aids and Services Aids, services, or accommodations include career counseling.

Assistive Technology Assistive technology is located in the DSS office, a special lab and includes digital textbooks/e-text, learning support software, scanning, and writing organization, reading software, voice-to-text software, digital recorders. Technology training is provided to incoming students.

Diagnostic Testing Testing is provided through the program or unit for study skills. Testing for auditory processing, handwriting, intelligence, learning strategies, learning styles, math, motor skills, neuropsychological, personality, reading, social skills, spelling, spoken language, visual processing, written language, and other services is provided collaboratively through on-campus or off-campus services.

Enrichment Enrichment programs are available through the program or unit for college survival skills, learning strategies, oral communication skills, practical computer skills, reading, self-advocacy, stress management, study skills, test taking, time management, vocabulary development, written composition skills, and other. Programs for career planning, health and nutrition, learning strategies, medication management, stress management, study skills, test taking, time management, and written composition skills are provided collaboratively through on-campus or off-campus services.

Fees *Diagnostic Testing* fee is $200 to $1500.

Application For admittance to the program or unit, students are required to provide a psychoeducational report (3 years old or less). It is recommended that students provide documentation of high school services. Upon application, materials documenting need for services should be sent only to the LD program or unit. Upon acceptance, documentation of need for services should be sent only to the LD program or unit. *Application deadline (institutional):* 6/1. *Application deadline (LD program):* Rolling/continuous for fall and rolling/continuous for spring.

Written Policies Written policy regarding general/basic LD accommodations is available on the program Web site. Written policy regarding general/basic LD accommodations is available through the program or unit directly.

Carlow University
Office of Disability Services

3333 Fifth Avenue

Pittsburgh, PA 15213-3165

http://www.carlow.edu/

Contact: Ms. Joan Arlene House, Director of Disability Services. Phone: 412-578-6257. Fax: 412-578-6257. E-mail: houseja@carlow.edu.

Office of Disability Services Approximately 25 registered undergraduate students were served during 2006–07. The program or unit includes 1 full-time staff member. Skill tutors are provided collaboratively through on-campus or off-campus services.

Unique Aids and Services Aids, services, or accommodations include career counseling.

Assistive Technology Assistive technology is located in campus labs, the DSS office and includes digital textbooks/e-text and scanning. Technology training is provided to incoming students.

Subject-Area Tutoring Tutoring is offered one-on-one and in small groups for most subjects. Tutoring is provided collaboratively through on-campus or off-campus services via professional tutors and trained peer tutors.

Basic Skills Remediation Remediation is offered one-on-one and in small groups for learning strategies, math, reading, study skills, and time management. Remediation is provided collaboratively through on-campus or off-campus services via professional tutors and trained peer tutors.

Enrichment Enrichment programs are available through the program or unit for self-advocacy. Programs for career planning, college survival skills, health and nutrition, learning strategies, math, reading, stress management, study skills, test taking, time management, and written composition skills are provided collaboratively through on-campus or off-campus services.

Student Organization Total Respect Equality and Awareness Through Education (TREAT) consists of 10 members.

Application For admittance to the program or unit, students are required to provide a psychoeducational report (3 years old or less). Upon application, materials documenting need for services should be sent only to the LD program or unit. Upon acceptance, documentation of need for services should be sent only to the LD program or unit. *Application deadline (institutional):* 7/1. *Application deadline (LD program):* Rolling/continuous for fall.

Written Policies Written policies regarding course substitutions and general/basic LD accommodations are available on the program Web site. Written policies regarding course substitutions and general/basic LD accommodations are outlined in the school's catalog/handbook. Written policies regarding course substitutions and general/basic LD accommodations are available through the program or unit directly.

Carnegie Mellon University
Disability Resources

5000 Forbes Avenue

Pittsburgh, PA 15213-3891

http://hr.web.cmu.edu/dsrg/

Contact: Mr. Larry Powell, Manager. Phone: 412-268-2013. Fax: 412-268-2853. E-mail: lpowell@andrew.cmu.edu.

Disability Resources Approximately 129 registered undergraduate students were served during 2006–07. The program or unit includes 2 full-time staff members. LD specialists are provided through the program or unit. Academic advisers, counselors, graduate assistants/students, LD specialists, and trained peer tutors are provided collaboratively through on-campus or off-campus services.

Assistive Technology Assistive technology is located in the DSS office and includes scanning.

Subject-Area Tutoring Tutoring is offered one-on-one, in small groups, and in class-size groups for most subjects. Tutoring is provided collaboratively through on-campus or off-campus services via trained peer tutors.

Basic Skills Remediation Remediation is offered one-on-one, in small groups, and in class-size groups for computer skills, learning strategies, math, reading, study skills, time management, and written language. Remediation is provided collaboratively through on-campus or off-campus services via trained peer tutors.

Carnegie Mellon University (continued)

Enrichment Programs for career planning, college survival skills, health and nutrition, learning strategies, math, medication management, stress management, study skills, test taking, time management, vocabulary development, and written composition skills are provided collaboratively through on-campus or off-campus services.
Student Organization SMAART.
Application It is recommended that students provide a psychoeducational report (5 years old or less) and provide a neuropsychological report. Upon acceptance, documentation of need for services should be sent only to the LD program or unit. *Application deadline (institutional):* 1/1. *Application deadline (LD program):* Rolling/continuous for fall and rolling/continuous for spring.
Written Policies Written policy regarding general/basic LD accommodations is available on the program Web site. Written policies regarding course substitutions, grade forgiveness, reduced course loads, substitutions and waivers of admissions requirements, and substitutions and waivers of graduation requirements are outlined in the school's catalog/handbook. Written policy regarding general/basic LD accommodations is available through the program or unit directly.

Carroll College
Disabled Services

100 North East Avenue

Waukesha, WI 53186-5593

http://www.cc.edu/wyc

Contact: Ms. Andrea K. Broman, Disability Services Coordinator. Phone: 262-524-7335. Fax: 262-524-6892. E-mail: abroman@cc.edu.

Disabled Services Approximately 27 registered undergraduate students were served during 2006–07. The program or unit includes 1 full-time staff member. Coaches, counselors, LD specialists, regular education teachers, skill tutors, special education teachers, strategy tutors, teacher trainees, and trained peer tutors are provided through the program or unit. Academic advisers, counselors, diagnostic specialists, LD specialists, and remediation/learning specialists are provided collaboratively through on-campus or off-campus services.
Unique Aids and Services Aids, services, or accommodations include career counseling, faculty training, and personal coach.
Assistive Technology Assistive technology is located in the DSS office and includes scanning and Kurzweil.
Subject-Area Tutoring Tutoring is offered one-on-one and in small groups for most subjects. Tutoring is provided through the program or unit via trained peer tutors. Tutoring is also provided collaboratively through on-campus or off-campus services via professional tutors.
Diagnostic Testing Testing is provided through the program or unit for learning strategies, learning styles, and study skills. Testing for auditory processing, handwriting, intelligence, learning strategies, learning styles, math, motor skills, neuropsychological, personality, reading, social skills, spelling, spoken language, study skills, visual processing, and written language is provided collaboratively through on-campus or off-campus services.

Basic Skills Remediation Remediation is offered one-on-one and in small groups for learning strategies, math, reading, social skills, study skills, and time management. Remediation is provided through the program or unit. Remediation is also provided collaboratively through on-campus or off-campus services via computer-based instruction and trained peer tutors.
Enrichment Enrichment programs are available through the program or unit for learning strategies, self-advocacy, study skills, test taking, and time management. Programs for career planning, college survival skills, math, practical computer skills, self-advocacy, stress management, study skills, test taking, time management, and written composition skills are provided collaboratively through on-campus or off-campus services.
Application For admittance to the program or unit, students are required to apply to the program directly and provide a psychoeducational report (10 years old or less). It is recommended that students provide documentation of high school services. Upon application, materials documenting need for services should be sent only to the LD program or unit. Upon acceptance, documentation of need for services should be sent only to the LD program or unit. *Application deadline (institutional):* Continuous. *Application deadline (LD program):* Rolling/continuous for fall and rolling/continuous for spring.
Written Policies Written policies regarding general/basic LD accommodations and substitutions and waivers of graduation requirements are available on the program Web site. Written policy regarding general/basic LD accommodations is outlined in the school's catalog/handbook. Written policies regarding course substitutions, general/basic LD accommodations, and reduced course loads are available through the program or unit directly.

Carroll College
Academic Resource Center

1601 North Benton Avenue

Helena, MT 59625-0002

http://www.carroll.edu/

Contact: Mrs. Joan M. Stottlemyer, Director of Academic Resource Center. Phone: 406-447-4504. Fax: 406-447-5476. E-mail: jstottle@carroll.edu.

Academic Resource Center Approximately 40 registered undergraduate students were served during 2006–07. The program or unit includes 1 part-time staff member. Academic advisers, counselors, and other are provided collaboratively through on-campus or off-campus services.
Unique Aids and Services Aids, services, or accommodations include extended time on tests, note-taking.
Subject-Area Tutoring Tutoring is offered one-on-one, in small groups, and in class-size groups for some subjects. Tutoring is provided through the program or unit via trained peer tutors and other. Tutoring is also provided collaboratively through on-campus or off-campus services via trained peer tutors and other.
Basic Skills Remediation Remediation is offered one-on-one for learning strategies, study skills, and time management. Remediation is provided through the program or unit. Remediation is also provided collaboratively through on-campus or off-campus services.

Application For admittance to the program or unit, students are required to apply to the program directly and provide a psychoeducational report (3 years old or less). It is recommended that students provide documentation of high school services and provide documentation from psychologist, psychiatrist, LD specialist, counselor. Upon acceptance, documentation of need for services should be sent only to the LD program or unit. *Application deadline (institutional): 6/1. Application deadline (LD program):* Rolling/continuous for fall and rolling/continuous for spring.
Written Policies Written policies regarding general/basic LD accommodations and reduced course loads are available on the program Web site. Written policies regarding general/basic LD accommodations and reduced course loads are outlined in the school's catalog/handbook. Written policies regarding general/basic LD accommodations and reduced course loads are available through the program or unit directly.

Carson-Newman College

1646 Russell Avenue, PO Box 557
Jefferson City, TN 37760
http://www.cn.edu/
Contact: Laura Wadlington, Coordinator for Students with Disabilities. Phone: 865-471-3270. E-mail: lwadlington@cn.edu.

Approximately 20 registered undergraduate students were served during 2006–07. The program or unit includes 1 part-time staff member. Academic advisers, counselors, regular education teachers, remediation/learning specialists, and trained peer tutors are provided collaboratively through on-campus or off-campus services.
Subject-Area Tutoring Tutoring is offered one-on-one, in small groups, and in class-size groups.
Basic Skills Remediation Remediation is offered in class-size groups for math, reading, study skills, and written language. Remediation is provided collaboratively through on-campus or off-campus services via regular education teachers and other.
Application For admittance to the program or unit, students are required to provide a psychoeducational report (3 years old or less) and provide a request for specific accommodations. It is recommended that students provide documentation of high school services. Upon acceptance, documentation of need for services should be sent only to the LD program or unit. *Application deadline (institutional): 8/1. Application deadline (LD program):* Rolling/continuous for fall.
Written Policies Written policy regarding general/basic LD accommodations is outlined in the school's catalog/handbook. Written policies regarding course substitutions and substitutions and waivers of graduation requirements are available through the program or unit directly.

Carthage College

2001 Alford Park Drive
Kenosha, WI 53140
http://www.carthage.edu/

Contact: Diane Schowalter, Learning Specialist. Phone: 262-551-5802. E-mail: dschowalter1@carthage.edu.

Approximately 160 registered undergraduate students were served during 2006–07. The program or unit includes 1 full-time staff member. Academic advisers, diagnostic specialists, and other are provided collaboratively through on-campus or off-campus services.
Assistive Technology Assistive technology includes digital textbooks/e-text.
Subject-Area Tutoring Tutoring is offered one-on-one for most subjects. Tutoring is provided collaboratively through on-campus or off-campus services via other.
Diagnostic Testing Testing is provided through the program or unit for auditory processing, intelligence, math, reading, spelling, visual processing, written language, and other services.
Application For admittance to the program or unit, students are required to provide a psychoeducational report (3 years old or less) and provide documentation of high school services. Upon application, materials documenting need for services should be sent only to the LD program or unit. Upon acceptance, documentation of need for services should be sent only to the LD program or unit. *Application deadline (institutional):* Continuous. *Application deadline (LD program):* Rolling/continuous for fall and rolling/continuous for spring.
Written Policies Written policy regarding general/basic LD accommodations is available on the program Web site. Written policy regarding general/basic LD accommodations is outlined in the school's catalog/handbook. Written policies regarding course substitutions and substitutions and waivers of admissions requirements are available through the program or unit directly.

The Catholic University of America
Disability Support Services

Cardinal Station
Washington, DC 20064
http://disabilityservices.cua.edu
Contact: Ms. Emily Singer, Director of Disability Support Services. Phone: 202-319-5211. Fax: 202-319-5126. E-mail: cua-disabilityservices@cua.edu.

Disability Support Services Approximately 175 registered undergraduate students were served during 2006–07. The program or unit includes 2 full-time staff members. LD specialists and remediation/learning specialists are provided through the program or unit. Academic advisers, counselors, graduate assistants/students, remediation/learning specialists, skill tutors, strategy tutors, and trained peer tutors are provided collaboratively through on-campus or off-campus services.
Unique Aids and Services Aids, services, or accommodations include faculty training and priority registration.
Assistive Technology Assistive technology is located in campus labs, the DSS office and includes digital textbooks/e-text, learning support software, and scanning.
Subject-Area Tutoring Tutoring is offered one-on-one and in small groups for most subjects. Tutoring is provided collaboratively through on-campus or off-campus services via graduate assistants/students, trained peer tutors, and other.

The Catholic University of America (continued)

Basic Skills Remediation Remediation is offered one-on-one for learning strategies, reading, study skills, time management, and written language. Remediation is provided collaboratively through on-campus or off-campus services via LD specialists.

Application For admittance to the program or unit, students are required to apply to the program directly and provide a psychoeducational report (3 years old or less). Upon acceptance, documentation of need for services should be sent only to the LD program or unit. *Application deadline (institutional):* 2/15. *Application deadline (LD program):* Rolling/continuous for fall and rolling/continuous for spring.

Written Policies Written policies regarding course substitutions and general/basic LD accommodations are available on the program Web site. Written policies regarding course substitutions and general/basic LD accommodations are outlined in the school's catalog/handbook. Written policies regarding course substitutions and general/basic LD accommodations are available through the program or unit directly.

Cedar Crest College
Academic Services

100 College Drive

Allentown, PA 18104-6196

http://www.cedarcrest.edu/

Contact: Karen A. Schoenborn, Disabilities Specialist. Phone: 610-606-4628 Ext. 4628. Fax: 610-606-4673. E-mail: kschoen@cedarcrest.edu.

Academic Services Approximately 65 registered undergraduate students were served during 2006–07. The program or unit includes 1 full-time and 1 part-time staff member. Academic advisers, professional tutors, skill tutors, strategy tutors, and trained peer tutors are provided through the program or unit. Academic advisers, coaches, counselors, diagnostic specialists, and regular education teachers are provided collaboratively through on-campus or off-campus services.

Unique Aids and Services Aids, services, or accommodations include career counseling and priority registration.

Subject-Area Tutoring Tutoring is offered one-on-one and in small groups for most subjects. Tutoring is provided through the program or unit via professional tutors and trained peer tutors.

Basic Skills Remediation Remediation is offered one-on-one and in small groups for computer skills, learning strategies, math, reading, spelling, study skills, time management, and written language. Remediation is provided through the program or unit via computer-based instruction and professional tutors.

Application For admittance to the program or unit, students are required to apply to the program directly. It is recommended that students provide a psychoeducational report (5 years old or less) and provide documentation of high school services. Upon application, materials documenting need for services should be sent only to the LD program or unit. Upon acceptance, documentation of need for services should be sent only to the LD program or unit. *Application deadline (institutional):* Continuous. *Application deadline (LD program):* Rolling/continuous for fall and rolling/continuous for spring.

Written Policies Written policy regarding general/basic LD accommodations is available on the program Web site. Written policy regarding general/basic LD accommodations is outlined in the school's catalog/handbook. Written policy regarding general/basic LD accommodations is available through the program or unit directly.

Charleston Southern University
Office of Disability Services

PO Box 118087

Charleston, SC 29423-8087

http://www.charlestonsouthern.edu/

Contact: Dr. Ruben Berry, Dean, Student Success Center. Phone: 843-863-7170. Fax: 843-863-8030. E-mail: rberry@csuniv.edu.

Office of Disability Services Approximately 70 registered undergraduate students were served during 2006–07. The program or unit includes 1 full-time staff member. Counselors and LD specialists are provided through the program or unit. Academic advisers, coaches, diagnostic specialists, professional tutors, and trained peer tutors are provided collaboratively through on-campus or off-campus services.

Orientation The program or unit offers an optional orientation for new students individually by special arrangement.

Unique Aids and Services Aids, services, or accommodations include faculty training, personal counseling by appointment.

Subject-Area Tutoring Tutoring is offered one-on-one for most subjects. Tutoring is provided collaboratively through on-campus or off-campus services via trained peer tutors.

Basic Skills Remediation Remediation is offered one-on-one for learning strategies, social skills, study skills, and time management. Remediation is provided through the program or unit. Remediation is also provided collaboratively through on-campus or off-campus services via trained peer tutors.

Enrichment Programs for career planning, college survival skills, learning strategies, stress management, study skills, test taking, and time management are provided collaboratively through on-campus or off-campus services.

Application For admittance to the program or unit, students are required to apply to the program directly and provide a psychoeducational report (3 years old or less). It is recommended that students provide documentation of high school services. Upon application, materials documenting need for services should be sent only to admissions with institutional application materials. Upon acceptance, documentation of need for services should be sent only to the LD program or unit. *Application deadline (institutional):* Continuous. *Application deadline (LD program):* Rolling/continuous for fall and rolling/continuous for spring.

Written Policies Written policy regarding general/basic LD accommodations is available on the program Web site. Written policies regarding course substitutions, general/basic LD accommodations, and reduced course loads are available through the program or unit directly.

Christopher Newport University

1 University Place
Newport News, VA 23606-2998
http://www.cnu.edu/

Contact: Coordinator of Disability Services. E-mail: advise@cnu.edu.

The program or unit includes 1 full-time staff member. Academic advisers are provided collaboratively through on-campus or off-campus services.

Orientation The program or unit offers an optional orientation for new students individually by special arrangement.

Enrichment Programs for career planning, college survival skills, learning strategies, math, self-advocacy, stress management, study skills, test taking, time management, and written composition skills are provided collaboratively through on-campus or off-campus services.

Application For admittance to the program or unit, students are required to apply to the program directly and provide a psychoeducational report (3 years old or less). It is recommended that students provide documentation of high school services. Upon acceptance, documentation of need for services should be sent only to the LD program or unit. *Application deadline (institutional): 3/1. Application deadline (LD program):* Rolling/continuous for fall and rolling/continuous for spring.

Written Policies Written policies regarding course substitutions, general/basic LD accommodations, substitutions and waivers of admissions requirements, and substitutions and waivers of graduation requirements are available on the program Web site. Written policies regarding course substitutions, general/basic LD accommodations, substitutions and waivers of admissions requirements, and substitutions and waivers of graduation requirements are outlined in the school's catalog/handbook. Written policies regarding course substitutions, general/basic LD accommodations, substitutions and waivers of admissions requirements, and substitutions and waivers of graduation requirements are available through the program or unit directly.

Cincinnati Christian University
Academic Support Office

2700 Glenway Avenue
PO Box 04320
Cincinnati, OH 45204-3200
http://www.ccuniversity.edu/

Contact: Mrs. Cindi L. Cooper, Academic Support Director. Phone: 513-244-8420. Fax: 513-244-8123. E-mail: cindi.cooper@ccuniversity.edu.

Academic Support Office The program or unit includes 1 full-time staff member. Academic advisers, counselors, graduate assistants/students, skill tutors, and other are provided collaboratively through on-campus or off-campus services.

Assistive Technology Assistive technology is located in campus labs, the DSS office and includes digital textbooks/e-text and scanning. Technology training is provided to incoming students.

Subject-Area Tutoring Tutoring is offered one-on-one and in small groups for most subjects. Tutoring is provided through the program or unit via graduate assistants/students and other. Tutoring is also provided collaboratively through on-campus or off-campus services via graduate assistants/students.

Basic Skills Remediation Remediation is offered one-on-one and in small groups for study skills, time management, and written language. Remediation is provided through the program or unit. Remediation is also provided collaboratively through on-campus or off-campus services.

Enrichment Enrichment programs are available through the program or unit for career planning, learning strategies, study skills, test taking, time management, and written composition skills.

Application For admittance to the program or unit, students are required to provide a psychoeducational report (5 years old or less). It is recommended that students provide documentation of high school services. Upon acceptance, documentation of need for services should be sent only to the LD program or unit. *Application deadline (institutional): 7/1. Application deadline (LD program):* Rolling/continuous for fall and rolling/continuous for spring.

Written Policies Written policy regarding general/basic LD accommodations is available on the program Web site. Written policy regarding general/basic LD accommodations is available through the program or unit directly.

Claremont McKenna College
Dean of Students Office

500 East 9th Street
Claremont, CA 91711
http://www.claremontmckenna.edu/directory/dean-students.asp

Contact: Mr. Jefferson Huang, Dean of Students. Phone: 909-621-8114. Fax: 909-621-8495. E-mail: jefferson.huang@claremontmckenna.edu.

Dean of Students Office Approximately 45 registered undergraduate students were served during 2006–07. The program or unit includes 1 full-time and 3 part-time staff members. Academic advisers, coaches, counselors, diagnostic specialists, LD specialists, professional tutors, regular education teachers, skill tutors, strategy tutors, and other are provided collaboratively through on-campus or off-campus services.

Unique Aids and Services Aids, services, or accommodations include career counseling and weekly meetings with faculty.

Subject-Area Tutoring Tutoring is offered one-on-one, in small groups, and in class-size groups for most subjects. Tutoring is provided collaboratively through on-campus or off-campus services via computer-based instruction, LD specialists, and trained peer tutors.

Basic Skills Remediation Remediation is offered one-on-one for auditory processing, computer skills, handwriting, learning strategies, math, motor skills, reading, social skills, spelling, spoken language, study skills, time management, visual processing, written language, and others. Remediation is provided collaboratively through on-campus or off-campus services via LD specialists.

Claremont McKenna College (continued)

Enrichment Programs for career planning, learning strategies, math, oral communication skills, practical computer skills, reading, self-advocacy, stress management, study skills, test taking, time management, written composition skills, and other are provided collaboratively through on-campus or off-campus services.

Application For admittance to the program or unit, students are required to provide a psychoeducational report (3 years old or less). It is recommended that students provide documentation of high school services. Upon application, materials documenting need for services should be sent only to admissions with institutional application materials. Upon acceptance, documentation of need for services should be sent only to the LD program or unit. *Application deadline (institutional):* 1/2. *Application deadline (LD program):* Rolling/continuous for fall and rolling/continuous for spring.

Written Policies Written policy regarding general/basic LD accommodations is available on the program Web site. Written policy regarding general/basic LD accommodations is outlined in the school's catalog/handbook.

Clark University
Disability Services Department

950 Main Street

Worcester, MA 01610-1477

http://www.clarku.edu/offices/aac/ada/

Contact: Jane Daigneault, Coordinator of Disability Services. Phone: 508-793-7468. Fax: 508-421-3700. E-mail: jdaigneault@clarku.edu.

Disability Services Department Approximately 142 registered undergraduate students were served during 2006–07. The program or unit includes 1 full-time staff member. LD specialists are provided through the program or unit. Academic advisers and regular education teachers are provided collaboratively through on-campus or off-campus services.

Orientation The program or unit offers an optional 2-day orientation for new students before registration and before classes begin.

Unique Aids and Services Aids, services, or accommodations include career counseling.

Fees *Orientation* fee is $250.

Application For admittance to the program or unit, students are required to provide a psychoeducational report (3 years old or less). Upon acceptance, documentation of need for services should be sent only to the LD program or unit. *Application deadline (institutional):* 1/15. *Application deadline (LD program):* Rolling/continuous for fall and rolling/continuous for spring.

Written Policies Written policy regarding general/basic LD accommodations is available on the program Web site.

Clayton State University
Disability Resource Center

5900 North Lee Street

Morrow, GA 30260-0285

http://adminservices.clayton.edu/disability/

Contact: Karen Blackburn, Support Services Coordinator. Phone: 678-466-5445. Fax: 678-466-5467. E-mail: disabilityresourcecenter@clayton.edu.

Disability Resource Center Approximately 25 registered undergraduate students were served during 2006–07. The program or unit includes 3 full-time staff members. Skill tutors and strategy tutors are provided through the program or unit. Diagnostic specialists and trained peer tutors are provided collaboratively through on-campus or off-campus services.

Orientation The program or unit offers a mandatory 1- to 2-hour orientation for new students after documentation is accepted and intake is complete.

Unique Aids and Services Aids, services, or accommodations include priority registration.

Assistive Technology Assistive technology is located in the DSS office, the student's laptop computer and includes digital textbooks/e-text, learning support software, and scanning. Technology training is provided to incoming students.

Subject-Area Tutoring Tutoring is offered for some subjects. Tutoring is provided collaboratively through on-campus or off-campus services via computer-based instruction and trained peer tutors.

Diagnostic Testing Testing for auditory processing, handwriting, intelligence, learning styles, math, motor skills, neuropsychological, personality, reading, spelling, spoken language, study skills, visual processing, and written language is provided collaboratively through on-campus or off-campus services.

Enrichment Enrichment programs are available through the program or unit for career planning, learning strategies, self-advocacy, study skills, test taking, and time management. Programs for career planning, college survival skills, health and nutrition, study skills, test taking, time management, and written composition skills are provided collaboratively through on-campus or off-campus services.

Fees *Diagnostic Testing* fee is $500.

Application For admittance to the program or unit, students are required to provide a psychoeducational report and provide documentation of high school services. Upon application, materials documenting need for services should be sent only to the LD program or unit. Upon acceptance, documentation of need for services should be sent only to the LD program or unit. *Application deadline (institutional):* 7/17.

Written Policies Written policy regarding general/basic LD accommodations is available on the program Web site. Written policies regarding general/basic LD accommodations and reduced course loads are available through the program or unit directly.

Clemson University

Clemson, SC 29634

http://www.clemson.edu/

Contact: Arlene Casey Stewart EdD, Director, Student Disability Services. Phone: 864-656-6848. Fax: 864-656-6849. E-mail: astewar@clemson.edu.

The program or unit includes 4 full-time staff members and 1 part-time staff member. Coaches, LD specialists, and other are provided through the program or unit. Academic advisers, coaches, counselors, diagnostic specialists, graduate assistants/students, regular education teachers, remediation/learning specialists, trained peer tutors, and other are provided collaboratively through on-campus or off-campus services.

Unique Aids and Services Aids, services, or accommodations include career counseling, faculty training, and priority registration.

Assistive Technology Assistive technology is located in campus labs, the DSS office, a special lab and includes digital textbooks/e-text. Technology training is provided to incoming students.

Subject-Area Tutoring Tutoring is offered in small groups for most subjects. Tutoring is provided collaboratively through on-campus or off-campus services via graduate assistants/students and trained peer tutors.

Diagnostic Testing Testing is provided through the program or unit for learning strategies, learning styles, and study skills. Testing for intelligence, learning strategies, learning styles, math, personality, reading, spelling, spoken language, study skills, visual processing, written language, and other services is provided collaboratively through on-campus or off-campus services.

Enrichment Enrichment programs are available through the program or unit for career planning, learning strategies, self-advocacy, study skills, test taking, and time management. Programs for career planning, college survival skills, health and nutrition, learning strategies, math, medication management, practical computer skills, self-advocacy, stress management, study skills, test taking, and time management are provided collaboratively through on-campus or off-campus services. Credit is offered for college survival skills.

Fees *Diagnostic Testing* fee is $350.

Application For admittance to the program or unit, students are required to apply to the program directly and provide a psychoeducational report (3 years old or less). Upon application, materials documenting need for services should be sent only to the LD program or unit. Upon acceptance, documentation of need for services should be sent only to the LD program or unit. *Application deadline (institutional):* 5/1. *Application deadline (LD program):* Rolling/continuous for fall and rolling/continuous for spring.

Written Policies Written policies regarding course substitutions, general/basic LD accommodations, and reduced course loads are available on the program Web site. Written policies regarding course substitutions and general/basic LD accommodations are outlined in the school's catalog/handbook. Written policies regarding course substitutions, general/basic LD accommodations, and reduced course loads are available through the program or unit directly.

The Cleveland Institute of Art
Academic Services Office

11141 East Boulevard

Cleveland, OH 44106-1700

http://www.cia.edu/

Contact: Ms. Jill Milenski, Associate Director of Academic Services. Phone: 216-421-7462. Fax: 216-754-2557. E-mail: jmilenski@gate.cia.edu.

Academic Services Office Approximately 20 registered undergraduate students were served during 2006–07. The program or unit

includes 2 part-time staff members. Academic advisers and trained peer tutors are provided through the program or unit. Counselors, diagnostic specialists, and LD specialists are provided collaboratively through on-campus or off-campus services.

Unique Aids and Services Aids, services, or accommodations include advocates.

Assistive Technology Assistive technology is located in a special lab and includes learning support software, scanning, and voice recognition software, WYNN Wizard text-to-speech software. Technology training is provided to incoming students.

Subject-Area Tutoring Tutoring is offered one-on-one, in small groups, and in class-size groups for some subjects. Tutoring is provided through the program or unit via computer-based instruction and trained peer tutors. Tutoring is also provided collaboratively through on-campus or off-campus services via computer-based instruction.

Basic Skills Remediation Remediation is offered in class-size groups for learning strategies, study skills, and time management. Remediation is provided collaboratively through on-campus or off-campus services.

Enrichment Programs for career planning, learning strategies, study skills, test taking, time management, and written composition skills are provided collaboratively through on-campus or off-campus services.

Application For admittance to the program or unit, students are required to provide a psychoeducational report. It is recommended that students provide documentation of high school services. Upon application, materials documenting need for services should be sent only to the LD program or unit. Upon acceptance, documentation of need for services should be sent only to the LD program or unit. *Application deadline (institutional):* Continuous. *Application deadline (LD program):* Rolling/continuous for fall and rolling/continuous for spring.

Written Policies Written policy regarding general/basic LD accommodations is outlined in the school's catalog/handbook.

Coastal Carolina University
Disability Services

PO Box 261954

Conway, SC 29528-6054

http://www.coastal.edu/counseling/disabilityservices.html

Contact: Wendy Woodsby. Phone: 843-349-2307. Fax: 843-349-2898.

Disability Services Approximately 200 registered undergraduate students were served during 2006–07. The program or unit includes 1 full-time staff member. Counselors are provided through the program or unit. Academic advisers, coaches, counselors, professional tutors, and trained peer tutors are provided collaboratively through on-campus or off-campus services.

Unique Aids and Services Aids, services, or accommodations include career counseling, faculty training, parent workshops, priority registration, and support groups.

Subject-Area Tutoring Tutoring is offered one-on-one for some subjects. Tutoring is provided collaboratively through on-campus or off-campus services via trained peer tutors.

Coastal Carolina University (continued)

Diagnostic Testing Testing for auditory processing, handwriting, intelligence, learning strategies, learning styles, math, motor skills, neuropsychological, personality, reading, social skills, spelling, spoken language, study skills, visual processing, and written language is provided collaboratively through on-campus or off-campus services.

Enrichment Enrichment programs are available through the program or unit for college survival skills, health and nutrition, medication management, oral communication skills, reading, self-advocacy, stress management, study skills, test taking, and time management. Programs for career planning, college survival skills, health and nutrition, learning strategies, math, oral communication skills, practical computer skills, reading, self-advocacy, stress management, time management, vocabulary development, and written composition skills are provided collaboratively through on-campus or off-campus services. Credit is offered for college survival skills, health and nutrition, and oral communication skills.

Application For admittance to the program or unit, students are required to provide a psychoeducational report (3 years old or less), provide documentation of high school services, and provide medical report, if applicable. Upon application, materials documenting need for services should be sent only to the LD program or unit. Upon acceptance, documentation of need for services should be sent only to the LD program or unit. *Application deadline (institutional):* 8/15. *Application deadline (LD program):* Rolling/continuous for fall and rolling/continuous for spring.

Written Policies Written policies regarding course substitutions, general/basic LD accommodations, and substitutions and waivers of graduation requirements are available on the program Web site. Written policies regarding course substitutions, general/basic LD accommodations, and reduced course loads are available through the program or unit directly.

Coe College
Academic Achievement Program

1220 1st Avenue, NE

Cedar Rapids, IA 52402-5092

http://www.public.coe.edu/departments

Contact: Lois Kabela-Coates, Director, Academic Achievement. Phone: 319-399-8547. E-mail: lkabela@coe.edu.

Academic Achievement Program Approximately 20 registered undergraduate students were served during 2006–07. The program or unit includes 3 full-time staff members and 1 part-time staff member. Academic advisers, counselors, remediation/learning specialists, skill tutors, and trained peer tutors are provided through the program or unit.

Orientation The program or unit offers an optional orientation for new students before registration, before classes begin, after classes begin, and individually by special arrangement.

Unique Aids and Services Aids, services, or accommodations include career counseling.

Assistive Technology Assistive technology is located in campus labs, the DSS office and includes digital textbooks/e-text and scanning. Technology training is provided to incoming students.

Subject-Area Tutoring Tutoring is offered one-on-one and in small groups for most subjects. Tutoring is provided through the program or unit via LD specialists and trained peer tutors.

Diagnostic Testing Testing is provided through the program or unit for learning styles, reading, and study skills.

Basic Skills Remediation Remediation is offered one-on-one and in small groups for math, reading, study skills, and time management. Remediation is provided through the program or unit via computer-based instruction and LD specialists.

Enrichment Enrichment programs are available through the program or unit for career planning, college survival skills, learning strategies, math, reading, self-advocacy, study skills, test taking, and time management. Programs for career planning, health and nutrition, medication management, oral communication skills, practical computer skills, reading, stress management, and written composition skills are provided collaboratively through on-campus or off-campus services. Credit is offered for oral communication skills, reading, study skills, and written composition skills.

Application For admittance to the program or unit, students are required to provide a psychoeducational report (5 years old or less). It is recommended that students apply to the program directly and provide documentation of high school services. Upon application, materials documenting need for services should be sent only to the LD program or unit. Upon acceptance, documentation of need for services should be sent only to the LD program or unit. *Application deadline (institutional):* 3/1. *Application deadline (LD program):* Rolling/continuous for fall and rolling/continuous for spring.

Written Policies Written policy regarding general/basic LD accommodations is available on the program Web site. Written policies regarding general/basic LD accommodations and reduced course loads are available through the program or unit directly.

Colby College

Mayflower Hill

Waterville, ME 04901-8840

http://www.colby.edu/dos/

Contact: Mr. Mark R. Serdjenian, Associate Dean of Students for Academics. Phone: 207-859-4255. Fax: 207-859-4262. E-mail: mrserdje@colby.edu.

Approximately 120 registered undergraduate students were served during 2006–07. The program or unit includes 1 part-time staff member. Academic advisers, counselors, diagnostic specialists, skill tutors, and trained peer tutors are provided collaboratively through on-campus or off-campus services.

Assistive Technology Assistive technology is located in the library and includes scanning.

Subject-Area Tutoring Tutoring is offered one-on-one for all subjects. Tutoring is provided collaboratively through on-campus or off-campus services via trained peer tutors.

Diagnostic Testing Testing for auditory processing, learning strategies, learning styles, and visual processing is provided collaboratively through on-campus or off-campus services.

Enrichment Programs for career planning, health and nutrition, and stress management are provided collaboratively through on-campus or off-campus services.

Fees *Diagnostic Testing* fee is $500.

Application For admittance to the program or unit, students are required to provide a psychoeducational report (5 years old or less). Upon application, materials documenting need for services should be sent only to admissions with institutional application materials. Upon acceptance, documentation of need for services should be sent only to the LD program or unit. *Application deadline (institutional):* 1/1. *Application deadline (LD program):* Rolling/continuous for fall and rolling/continuous for spring.

Written Policies Written policies regarding course substitutions, general/basic LD accommodations, reduced course loads, and substitutions and waivers of graduation requirements are available on the program Web site. Written policies regarding course substitutions, general/basic LD accommodations, reduced course loads, and substitutions and waivers of graduation requirements are outlined in the school's catalog/handbook. Written policies regarding course substitutions, general/basic LD accommodations, reduced course loads, and substitutions and waivers of graduation requirements are available through the program or unit directly.

Colgate University
Academic Support and Disability Services

13 Oak Drive

Hamilton, NY 13346-1386

http://offices.colgate.edu/disabilities

Contact: Director of Academic Support and Disability Services. Phone: 315-228-7375. Fax: 315-228-7975. E-mail: lwaldman@mail.colgate.edu.

Academic Support and Disability Services Approximately 200 registered undergraduate students were served during 2006–07. The program or unit includes 1 full-time staff member. Remediation/learning specialists are provided through the program or unit. Academic advisers, coaches, counselors, diagnostic specialists, professional tutors, regular education teachers, strategy tutors, and trained peer tutors are provided collaboratively through on-campus or off-campus services.

Unique Aids and Services Aids, services, or accommodations include services as determined on a case-by-case, course-by-course basis.

Assistive Technology Assistive technology is located in the library, Information Technology Center and includes tools, aids, and devices determined on a case-by-case basis.

Subject-Area Tutoring Tutoring is offered one-on-one, in small groups, and in class-size groups for most subjects. Tutoring is provided through the program or unit via LD specialists. Tutoring is also provided collaboratively through on-campus or off-campus services via computer-based instruction, graduate assistants/students, professional tutors, and trained peer tutors.

Enrichment Enrichment programs are available through the program or unit for career planning, college survival skills, learning strategies, math, medication management, oral communication skills, practical computer skills, reading, self-advocacy, stress management, study skills, test taking, time management, vocabulary development, written composition skills, and other. Programs for career planning, college survival skills, health and nutrition, learning strategies, math, medication management, oral communication skills,

practical computer skills, stress management, study skills, test taking, time management, vocabulary development, written composition skills, and other are provided collaboratively through on-campus or off-campus services.

Application For admittance to the program or unit, students are required to provide a psychoeducational report. It is recommended that students provide documentation of high school services. Upon acceptance, documentation of need for services should be sent only to the LD program or unit. *Application deadline (institutional):* 1/15. *Application deadline (LD program):* Rolling/continuous for fall and rolling/continuous for spring.

Written Policies Written policy regarding general/basic LD accommodations is available on the program Web site. Written policy regarding general/basic LD accommodations is outlined in the school's catalog/handbook. Written policy regarding general/basic LD accommodations is available through the program or unit directly.

College of Charleston
Center for Disability Services/SNAP

66 George Street

Charleston, SC 29424-0001

http://www.cofc.edu/~cds

Contact: Mrs. Bobbie Lindstrom, Director. Phone: 843-953-1431. Fax: 843-953-7731. E-mail: lindstromb@cofc.edu.

Center for Disability Services/SNAP Approximately 350 registered undergraduate students were served during 2006–07. The program or unit includes 2 full-time staff members and 1 part-time staff member. Academic advisers, coaches, and strategy tutors are provided through the program or unit. Academic advisers, counselors, diagnostic specialists, graduate assistants/students, professional tutors, skill tutors, strategy tutors, and trained peer tutors are provided collaboratively through on-campus or off-campus services.

Orientation The program or unit offers an optional half-day orientation for new students individually by special arrangement and the day before classes begin (for students approved for services).

Unique Aids and Services Aids, services, or accommodations include career counseling, personal coach, and priority registration.

Assistive Technology Assistive technology is located in the DSS office and includes digital textbooks/e-text, scanning, and speech-to-text. Technology training is provided to incoming students.

Subject-Area Tutoring Tutoring is offered one-on-one and in small groups for most subjects. Tutoring is provided collaboratively through on-campus or off-campus services via graduate assistants/students, professional tutors, and trained peer tutors.

Diagnostic Testing Testing for auditory processing, intelligence, learning styles, math, personality, reading, spelling, study skills, visual processing, and written language is provided collaboratively through on-campus or off-campus services.

Basic Skills Remediation Remediation is offered one-on-one and in class-size groups for learning strategies, study skills, and time management. Remediation is provided collaboratively through on-campus or off-campus services via graduate assistants/students, professional tutors, and trained peer tutors.

College of Charleston (continued)

Enrichment Enrichment programs are available through the program or unit for self-advocacy and time management. Programs for career planning, college survival skills, learning strategies, stress management, study skills, test taking, time management, and written composition skills are provided collaboratively through on-campus or off-campus services.

Fees *Diagnostic Testing* fee is $400 to $900.

Application For admittance to the program or unit, students are required to apply to the program directly and provide a psychoeducational report (3 years old or less). It is recommended that students provide documentation of high school services. Upon acceptance, documentation of need for services should be sent only to the LD program or unit. *Application deadline (institutional):* 4/1. *Application deadline (LD program):* Rolling/continuous for fall and rolling/continuous for spring.

Written Policies Written policies regarding course substitutions and general/basic LD accommodations are outlined in the school's catalog/handbook. Written policy regarding reduced course loads is available through the program or unit directly.

College of Mount Saint Vincent
Disabled Student Services

6301 Riverdale Avenue

Riverdale, NY 10471-1093

http://www.mountsaintvincent.edu/

Contact: Mr. Thomas Allen Brady, Director, Center for Academic Excellence. Phone: 718-405-3273. Fax: 718-405-3715. E-mail: thomas.brady@ mountsaintvincent.edu.

Disabled Student Services Approximately 30 registered undergraduate students were served during 2006–07. The program or unit includes 1 full-time and 5 part-time staff members. Diagnostic specialists and LD specialists are provided through the program or unit. Academic advisers, counselors, graduate assistants/students, professional tutors, regular education teachers, remediation/learning specialists, and skill tutors are provided collaboratively through on-campus or off-campus services.

Unique Aids and Services Aids, services, or accommodations include advocates and personal coach.

Assistive Technology Assistive technology is located in the DSS office and includes digital textbooks/e-text and scanning.

Subject-Area Tutoring Tutoring is offered one-on-one for most subjects. Tutoring is provided through the program or unit via LD specialists, professional tutors, and trained peer tutors.

Basic Skills Remediation Remediation is offered one-on-one and in class-size groups for learning strategies, math, reading, study skills, time management, and written language. Remediation is provided through the program or unit via LD specialists and professional tutors. Remediation is also provided collaboratively through on-campus or off-campus services via trained peer tutors.

Application For admittance to the program or unit, students are required to apply to the program directly and provide a psychoeducational report (3 years old or less). It is recommended that students provide documentation of high school services. Upon application,

materials documenting need for services should be sent only to the LD program or unit. Upon acceptance, documentation of need for services should be sent only to the LD program or unit. *Application deadline (institutional):* Continuous. *Application deadline (LD program):* Rolling/continuous for fall and rolling/continuous for spring.

Written Policies Written policies regarding course substitutions and substitutions and waivers of admissions requirements are available on the program Web site. Written policies regarding course substitutions and substitutions and waivers of admissions requirements are outlined in the school's catalog/handbook. Written policy regarding general/basic LD accommodations is available through the program or unit directly.

College of Saint Elizabeth
Disability Services

2 Convent Road

Morristown, NJ 07960-6989

http://www.cse.edu/

Contact: Mr. William H. Moesch, Coordinator, Disability Services. Phone: 973-290-4261. Fax: 973-290-4244. E-mail: wmoesch@cse.edu.

Disability Services Approximately 35 registered undergraduate students were served during 2006–07. The program or unit includes 1 part-time staff member. Diagnostic specialists are provided through the program or unit. Counselors, professional tutors, and other are provided collaboratively through on-campus or off-campus services.

Unique Aids and Services Aids, services, or accommodations include career counseling, case manager meetings.

Assistive Technology Assistive technology is located in campus labs, the Academic Skills Center and includes digital textbooks/e-text and scanning.

Subject-Area Tutoring Tutoring is offered one-on-one, in small groups, and in class-size groups for all subjects. Tutoring is provided collaboratively through on-campus or off-campus services via professional tutors.

Basic Skills Remediation Remediation is offered in small groups and in class-size groups for learning strategies, math, reading, study skills, and written language. Remediation is provided collaboratively through on-campus or off-campus services via professional tutors and other.

Enrichment Programs for career planning, health and nutrition, learning strategies, math, medication management, reading, self-advocacy, stress management, study skills, test taking, time management, and written composition skills are provided collaboratively through on-campus or off-campus services.

Application For admittance to the program or unit, students are required to apply to the program directly, provide a psychoeducational report (4 years old or less), and provide psychological and educational evaluations, medical evaluations. Upon application, materials documenting need for services should be sent only to the LD program or unit. Upon acceptance, documentation of need for services should be sent only to the LD program or unit. *Application deadline (institutional):* 8/15. *Application deadline (LD program):* Rolling/continuous for fall and rolling/continuous for spring.

Written Policies Written policies regarding course substitutions, general/basic LD accommodations, grade forgiveness, reduced course loads, substitutions and waivers of admissions requirements, and substitutions and waivers of graduation requirements are outlined in the school's catalog/handbook.

College of St. Joseph
Project Success

71 Clement Road

Rutland, VT 05701-3899

http://www.csj.edu/

Contact: Mrs. Charlotte Gillam, Director of Project Success. Phone: 802-776-5239. Fax: 802-776-5258. E-mail: cgillam@csj.edu.

Project Success Approximately 40 registered undergraduate students were served during 2006–07. The program or unit includes 1 full-time staff member. Diagnostic specialists, LD specialists, skill tutors, and trained peer tutors are provided through the program or unit.

Unique Aids and Services Aids, services, or accommodations include career counseling.

Assistive Technology Assistive technology is located in a special lab and includes scanning.

Subject-Area Tutoring Tutoring is offered one-on-one and in small groups for some subjects. Tutoring is provided through the program or unit via LD specialists, professional tutors, and trained peer tutors.

Basic Skills Remediation Remediation is offered one-on-one, in small groups, and in class-size groups for learning strategies, math, reading, study skills, time management, and written language. Remediation is provided through the program or unit via LD specialists, professional tutors, and trained peer tutors.

Enrichment Enrichment programs are available through the program or unit for learning strategies, math, study skills, time management, and written composition skills. Programs for career planning, college survival skills, learning strategies, math, study skills, time management, and written composition skills are provided collaboratively through on-campus or off-campus services. Credit is offered for career planning, college survival skills, learning strategies, math, study skills, time management, and written composition skills.

Application For admittance to the program or unit, students are required to provide documentation of high school services. It is recommended that students provide a psychoeducational report (3 years old or less). Upon application, materials documenting need for services should be sent to both admissions and the LD program or unit. Upon acceptance, documentation of need for services should be sent to both admissions and the LD program or unit. *Application deadline (institutional):* Continuous. *Application deadline (LD program):* Rolling/continuous for fall and rolling/continuous for spring.

Written Policies Written policy regarding general/basic LD accommodations is available on the program Web site. Written policy regarding general/basic LD accommodations is outlined in the school's catalog/handbook.

College of Saint Mary
Achievement Center, ADA Services

1901 South 72nd Street

Omaha, NE 68124-2377

http://csm.edu/Student_Life_and_Services/CSM_Achievement_Center/ADA/

Contact: Ms. Jennifer Yarns, Assistant Director of Achievement Center, Retention & ADA Services. Phone: 402-399-2366. Fax: 402-366-2439. E-mail: jyarns@csm.edu.

Achievement Center, ADA Services Approximately 20 registered undergraduate students were served during 2006–07. The program or unit includes 1 part-time staff member. Counselors, diagnostic specialists, remediation/learning specialists, special education teachers, and trained peer tutors are provided collaboratively through on-campus or off-campus services.

Summer Program To help prepare for the demands of college, there is 3-day summer program prior to entering the school available to high school graduates that focuses on life skills and/or college life adjustment, self-advocacy, study skills, and time management. The program accepts students from out-of-state.

Unique Aids and Services Aids, services, or accommodations include meetings with ADA coordinator.

Assistive Technology Assistive technology is located in testing room and includes ReadPlease Plus, Dragon Naturally Speaking software.

Subject-Area Tutoring Tutoring is offered one-on-one and in small groups. Tutoring is provided collaboratively through on-campus or off-campus services via computer-based instruction and trained peer tutors.

Diagnostic Testing Testing for auditory processing, learning strategies, neuropsychological, reading, spelling, visual processing, and written language is provided collaboratively through on-campus or off-campus services.

Basic Skills Remediation Remediation is offered one-on-one for learning strategies, study skills, and time management. Remediation is provided collaboratively through on-campus or off-campus services via computer-based instruction, professional tutors, and trained peer tutors.

Enrichment Programs for career planning, health and nutrition, learning strategies, and study skills are provided collaboratively through on-campus or off-campus services. Credit is offered for learning strategies and study skills.

Fees *Diagnostic Testing* fee is applicable.

Application For admittance to the program or unit, students are required to apply to the program directly and provide documentation from expert of definitive clinical diagnosis. It is recommended that students provide a psychoeducational report (5 years old or less) and provide documentation of high school services. Upon application, materials documenting need for services should be sent only to the LD program or unit. Upon acceptance, documentation of need for services should be sent only to the LD program or unit. *Application deadline (institutional):* Continuous. *Application deadline (LD program):* Rolling/continuous for fall and rolling/continuous for spring.

Written Policies Written policy regarding general/basic LD accommodations is available through the program or unit directly.

The College of Saint Rose
Services for Students with Disabilities

432 Western Avenue

Albany, NY 12203-1419

http://www.strose.edu/Academic_Programs/
Academic_Support/special_services.asp

Contact: Mrs. Kelly A. Hermann, Assistant Director for Special Services. Phone: 518-337-2335. Fax: 518-458-5330. E-mail: hermannk@strose.edu. Head of LD Program: Ms. Carol Schour, Assistant Vice President for Student Affairs. Phone: 518-458-5305. Fax: 518-485-3822. E-mail: schourc@strose.edu.

Services for Students with Disabilities Approximately 70 registered undergraduate students were served during 2006–07. The program or unit includes 1 full-time staff member. Graduate assistants/students and trained peer tutors are provided through the program or unit. Academic advisers, counselors, diagnostic specialists, remediation/learning specialists, and skill tutors are provided collaboratively through on-campus or off-campus services.

Unique Aids and Services Aids, services, or accommodations include career counseling.

Assistive Technology Assistive technology is located in campus labs, the Academic Support Center, the library and includes digital textbooks/e-text, learning support software, scanning, and Kurzweil screen reader. Technology training is provided to incoming students.

Subject-Area Tutoring Tutoring is offered one-on-one, in small groups, and in class-size groups for most subjects. Tutoring is provided through the program or unit via computer-based instruction, graduate assistants/students, and trained peer tutors.

Diagnostic Testing Testing for auditory processing, handwriting, intelligence, learning strategies, learning styles, math, motor skills, neuropsychological, personality, reading, social skills, spelling, spoken language, visual processing, and written language is provided collaboratively through on-campus or off-campus services.

Basic Skills Remediation Remediation is offered one-on-one for learning strategies, math, reading, study skills, time management, and written language. Remediation is provided through the program or unit via computer-based instruction and graduate assistants/students.

Enrichment Enrichment programs are available through the program or unit for college survival skills, learning strategies, math, study skills, test taking, and time management. Programs for career planning, oral communication skills, reading, stress management, and written composition skills are provided collaboratively through on-campus or off-campus services. Credit is offered for stress management.

Student Organization Disabilities Club consists of 8 members.

Fees *Diagnostic Testing* fee is applicable.

Application For admittance to the program or unit, students are required to provide a psychoeducational report (3 years old or less). It is recommended that students provide documentation of high school services. Upon acceptance, documentation of need for services should be sent only to the LD program or unit. *Application deadline (institutional):* 2/1. *Application deadline (LD program):* Rolling/continuous for fall and rolling/continuous for spring.

Written Policies Written policy regarding general/basic LD accommodations is available on the program Web site. Written policy regarding general/basic LD accommodations is available through the program or unit directly.

The College of St. Scholastica
Disability Resource Center

1200 Kenwood Avenue

Duluth, MN 55811-4199

http://www.css.edu/disability.xml

Contact: Heather Angelle, MSW, Coordinator for Students with Disabilities. Phone: 218-723-6645. Fax: 218-723-6482. E-mail: hangelle@css.edu.

Disability Resource Center Approximately 60 registered undergraduate students were served during 2006–07. The program or unit includes 1 full-time and 1 part-time staff member. Academic advisers are provided through the program or unit. Academic advisers, counselors, and skill tutors are provided collaboratively through on-campus or off-campus services.

Unique Aids and Services Aids, services, or accommodations include priority registration, double time on all in-class assignments and examinations, distraction reduced environment.

Assistive Technology Assistive technology is located in campus labs, various locations offered through an outside company and includes digital textbooks/e-text and Dragon Naturally Speaking.

Subject-Area Tutoring Tutoring is offered one-on-one and in small groups for most subjects. Tutoring is provided collaboratively through on-campus or off-campus services via computer-based instruction, graduate assistants/students, and trained peer tutors.

Application For admittance to the program or unit, students are required to apply to the program directly and provide a psychoeducational report (3 years old or less). Upon application, materials documenting need for services should be sent only to the LD program or unit. Upon acceptance, documentation of need for services should be sent only to the LD program or unit. *Application deadline (institutional):* Continuous. *Application deadline (LD program):* Rolling/continuous for fall and rolling/continuous for spring.

Written Policies Written policy regarding general/basic LD accommodations is available on the program Web site. Written policy regarding general/basic LD accommodations is available through the program or unit directly.

College of Staten Island of the City University of New York

2800 Victory Boulevard

Staten Island, NY 10314-6600

http://www.csi.cuny.edu/

Contact: Ms. Margaret Venditti, Director of Disability Services. Phone: 718-982-2510. Fax: 718-982-2117. E-mail: venditti@mail.csi.cuny.edu.

Approximately 190 registered undergraduate students were served during 2006–07. The program or unit includes 2 full-time and 13

part-time staff members. Academic advisers, counselors, professional tutors, regular education teachers, and trained peer tutors are provided collaboratively through on-campus or off-campus services.
Orientation The program or unit offers an optional 2-hour orientation for new students before classes begin and individually by special arrangement.
Unique Aids and Services Aids, services, or accommodations include advocates, career counseling, faculty training, priority registration, and support groups.
Assistive Technology Assistive technology is located in campus labs, the DSS office and includes digital textbooks/e-text, learning support software, and scanning.
Subject-Area Tutoring Tutoring is offered one-on-one and in small groups for most subjects. Tutoring is provided through the program or unit via computer-based instruction, professional tutors, and trained peer tutors. Tutoring is also provided collaboratively through on-campus or off-campus services via computer-based instruction, professional tutors, and trained peer tutors.
Basic Skills Remediation Remediation is offered one-on-one, in small groups, and in class-size groups for math, reading, and written language. Remediation is provided through the program or unit via professional tutors and trained peer tutors. Remediation is also provided collaboratively through on-campus or off-campus services via professional tutors and regular education teachers.
Enrichment Enrichment programs are available through the program or unit for college survival skills, learning strategies, math, oral communication skills, reading, self-advocacy, stress management, study skills, test taking, time management, and written composition skills. Programs for career planning, college survival skills, health and nutrition, learning strategies, math, practical computer skills, reading, stress management, study skills, test taking, time management, and written composition skills are provided collaboratively through on-campus or off-campus services. Credit is offered for career planning, college survival skills, health and nutrition, practical computer skills, study skills, test taking, time management, and written composition skills.
Student Organization Organization of Unique Individuals (OUI) consists of 25 members.
Application For admittance to the program or unit, students are required to provide a psychoeducational report (3 years old or less). It is recommended that students provide documentation of high school services. Upon application, materials documenting need for services should be sent only to the LD program or unit. Upon acceptance, documentation of need for services should be sent only to the LD program or unit. *Application deadline (institutional):* Continuous. *Application deadline (LD program):* Rolling/continuous for fall and rolling/continuous for spring.
Written Policies Written policy regarding general/basic LD accommodations is available on the program Web site. Written policy regarding general/basic LD accommodations is outlined in the school's catalog/handbook. Written policy regarding general/basic LD accommodations is available through the program or unit directly.

College of the Atlantic
Academic Services

105 Eden Street
Bar Harbor, ME 04609-1198
http://www.coa.edu/

Contact: Dr. Ken E. Hill, Academic Dean. Phone: 207-288-5015 Ext. 241. E-mail: khill@coa.edu.

Academic Services Approximately 19 registered undergraduate students were served during 2006–07. The program or unit includes 1 full-time and 5 part-time staff members. Counselors are provided through the program or unit. Academic advisers, counselors, diagnostic specialists, LD specialists, professional tutors, regular education teachers, remediation/learning specialists, skill tutors, and strategy tutors are provided collaboratively through on-campus or off-campus services.
Unique Aids and Services Aids, services, or accommodations include advocates, support groups, and weekly meetings with faculty.
Assistive Technology Assistive technology includes digital textbooks/e-text.
Subject-Area Tutoring Tutoring is offered one-on-one, in small groups, and in class-size groups for some subjects. Tutoring is provided collaboratively through on-campus or off-campus services via LD specialists, professional tutors, and trained peer tutors.
Basic Skills Remediation Remediation is offered one-on-one, in small groups, and in class-size groups for computer skills, learning strategies, math, social skills, spoken language, study skills, time management, and written language. Remediation is provided collaboratively through on-campus or off-campus services via LD specialists, professional tutors, regular education teachers, and trained peer tutors.
Enrichment Program for study skills is provided collaboratively through on-campus or off-campus services.
Application It is recommended that students provide a psychoeducational report and provide documentation of high school services. Upon application, materials documenting need for services should be sent only to the LD program or unit. Upon acceptance, documentation of need for services should be sent only to the LD program or unit. *Application deadline (institutional):* 2/15. *Application deadline (LD program):* Rolling/continuous for fall and rolling/continuous for spring.
Written Policies Written policy regarding general/basic LD accommodations is outlined in the school's catalog/handbook.

The College of William and Mary
Disability Services

PO Box 8795
Williamsburg, VA 23187-8795
http://www.wm.edu/deanofstudents/disable/

Contact: Assistant Dean of Students. Phone: 757-221-2510. Fax: 757-221-2538.

Disability Services Approximately 40 registered undergraduate students were served during 2006–07. The program or unit includes 1 full-time staff member. LD specialists and regular education teachers are provided collaboratively through on-campus or off-campus services.
Assistive Technology Assistive technology is located in the DSS office and includes scanning. Technology training is provided to incoming students.
Diagnostic Testing Testing for study skills is provided collaboratively through on-campus or off-campus services.

The College of William and Mary (continued)

Enrichment Programs for career planning, college survival skills, health and nutrition, learning strategies, medication management, self-advocacy, stress management, study skills, test taking, time management, and written composition skills are provided collaboratively through on-campus or off-campus services.

Student Organization Inter-Ability Action Coalition consists of 20 members.

Application For admittance to the program or unit, students are required to provide a psychoeducational report (3 years old or less) and provide documentation as specified in 'Documentation of Disability" (see Web site for details). Upon application, materials documenting need for services should be sent only to the LD program or unit. Upon acceptance, documentation of need for services should be sent only to the LD program or unit. *Application deadline (institutional):* 1/1.

Written Policies Written policies regarding course substitutions and general/basic LD accommodations are available on the program Web site. Written policies regarding course substitutions and general/ basic LD accommodations are outlined in the school's catalog/ handbook.

Colorado Technical University
Office of Vice President of Education

4435 North Chestnut Street
Colorado Springs, CO 80907-3896
http://www.coloradotech.edu
Contact: Dr. Wally G. Astor, Vice President of Education. Phone: 719-590-6892. Fax: 719-590-6869. E-mail: wastor@coloradotech.edu.

Office of Vice President of Education Approximately 8 registered undergraduate students were served during 2006–07. Academic advisers and regular education teachers are provided collaboratively through on-campus or off-campus services.

Orientation The program or unit offers an optional orientation for new students individually by special arrangement.

Unique Aids and Services Aids, services, or accommodations include career counseling.

Assistive Technology Assistive technology includes digital textbooks/e-text.

Subject-Area Tutoring Tutoring is offered one-on-one for most subjects. Tutoring is provided collaboratively through on-campus or off-campus services via other.

Enrichment Program for career planning is provided collaboratively through on-campus or off-campus services.

Application For admittance to the program or unit, students are required to apply to the program directly and provide documentation of high school services. It is recommended that students provide a psychoeducational report (3 years old or less). Upon application, materials documenting need for services should be sent only to admissions with institutional application materials. *Application deadline (LD program):* Rolling/continuous for fall and rolling/continuous for spring.

Written Policies Written policy regarding general/basic LD accommodations is outlined in the school's catalog/handbook. Written policy regarding general/basic LD accommodations is available through the program or unit directly.

Columbus State University

4225 University Avenue
Columbus, GA 31907-5645
http://www.colstate.edu/
Contact: Mrs. Joy Golden Norman, Disability Services Coordinator. Phone: 706-565-3628. Fax: 706-569-3096. E-mail: norman_joy@colstate.edu.

The program or unit includes 1 full-time staff member. Academic advisers and LD specialists are provided through the program or unit. Academic advisers and LD specialists are provided collaboratively through on-campus or off-campus services.

Unique Aids and Services Aids, services, or accommodations include advocates, personal coach, priority registration, and weekly meetings with faculty.

Assistive Technology Assistive technology is located in a special lab and includes digital textbooks/e-text, learning support software, and scanning.

Subject-Area Tutoring Tutoring is offered one-on-one and in small groups for most subjects. Tutoring is provided through the program or unit via computer-based instruction and trained peer tutors.

Application For admittance to the program or unit, students are required to provide a psychoeducational report (3 years old or less). It is recommended that students provide documentation of high school services. Upon application, materials documenting need for services should be sent only to the LD program or unit. Upon acceptance, documentation of need for services should be sent only to the LD program or unit. *Application deadline (institutional):* 7/1. *Application deadline (LD program):* Rolling/continuous for fall and rolling/continuous for spring.

Written Policies Written policies regarding course substitutions, general/basic LD accommodations, reduced course loads, substitutions and waivers of admissions requirements, and substitutions and waivers of graduation requirements are available on the program Web site. Written policies regarding general/basic LD accommodations and reduced course loads are outlined in the school's catalog/ handbook.

Concordia University
ADA and Academic Support

800 North Columbia Avenue
Seward, NE 68434-1599
http://www.cune.edu/academicsupport
Contact: Mrs. Tanya Jarchow, ADA & Academic Support, Director. Phone: 402-643-7377. E-mail: tanya.jarchow@cune.edu.

ADA and Academic Support Approximately 7 registered undergraduate students were served during 2006–07. The program or unit includes 1 full-time and 2 part-time staff members. Academic advisers and diagnostic specialists are provided through the program or unit. Trained peer tutors are provided collaboratively through on-campus or off-campus services.

Unique Aids and Services Aids, services, or accommodations include advocates, career counseling, and faculty training.

Assistive Technology Assistive technology is located in the Library Learning Commons Lab and includes learning support software. Technology training is provided to incoming students.

Subject-Area Tutoring Tutoring is offered one-on-one and in small groups for most subjects. Tutoring is provided through the program or unit via LD specialists and trained peer tutors.

Basic Skills Remediation Remediation is offered one-on-one for learning strategies, study skills, time management, and written language. Remediation is provided through the program or unit via LD specialists.

Enrichment Enrichment programs are available through the program or unit for college survival skills, learning strategies, self-advocacy, study skills, test taking, and time management. Programs for career planning, health and nutrition, and medication management are provided collaboratively through on-campus or off-campus services.

Application For admittance to the program or unit, students are required to provide a psychoeducational report (5 years old or less). It is recommended that students provide documentation of high school services. Upon application, materials documenting need for services should be sent only to the LD program or unit. Upon acceptance, documentation of need for services should be sent only to the LD program or unit. *Application deadline (institutional):* 8/1. *Application deadline (LD program):* Rolling/continuous for fall and rolling/continuous for spring.

Written Policies Written policies regarding general/basic LD accommodations and reduced course loads are available through the program or unit directly.

Concordia University College of Alberta

7128 Ada Boulevard, NW

Edmonton, AB T5B 4E4

Canada

http://www.concordia.ab.ca/

Contact: Ms. Tatiana Pitchko, Coordinator, Student Events and Services. Phone: 780-479-9242. E-mail: tpitchko@concordia.ab.ca.

The program or unit includes 1 full-time staff member. Academic advisers, counselors, diagnostic specialists, professional tutors, skill tutors, and strategy tutors are provided collaboratively through on-campus or off-campus services.

Orientation The program or unit offers an optional half-day orientation for new students after classes begin.

Unique Aids and Services Aids, services, or accommodations include career counseling and personal coach.

Assistive Technology Assistive technology is located in the assistive technology room and includes learning support software and scanning. Technology training is provided to incoming students.

Subject-Area Tutoring Tutoring is offered one-on-one for most subjects. Tutoring is provided collaboratively through on-campus or off-campus services via professional tutors.

Basic Skills Remediation Remediation is offered one-on-one for learning strategies, study skills, time management, and written language. Remediation is provided collaboratively through on-campus or off-campus services via LD specialists.

Enrichment Programs for career planning, college survival skills, health and nutrition, learning strategies, stress management, study skills, test taking, time management, and written composition skills are provided collaboratively through on-campus or off-campus services.

Application For admittance to the program or unit, students are required to provide a psychoeducational report (3 years old or less) and provide documentation of high school services. Upon application, materials documenting need for services should be sent only to the LD program or unit. Upon acceptance, documentation of need for services should be sent only to the LD program or unit. *Application deadline (institutional):* 6/30. *Application deadline (LD program):* Rolling/continuous for fall and rolling/continuous for spring.

Written Policies Written policy regarding general/basic LD accommodations is available on the program Web site. Written policy regarding general/basic LD accommodations is outlined in the school's catalog/handbook. Written policy regarding general/basic LD accommodations is available through the program or unit directly.

Concord University
Office of Disability Services

Vermillion Street, PO Box 1000

Athens, WV 24712-1000

http://www.concord.edu/Pages/resources/Pages/ADA/ADA.html

Contact: Ms. Nancy Ellison, Disability Services Coordinator. Phone: 304-384-6086. Fax: 304-384-6064. E-mail: ods@concord.edu.

Office of Disability Services Approximately 62 registered undergraduate students were served during 2006–07. Academic advisers, counselors, remediation/learning specialists, skill tutors, and trained peer tutors are provided collaboratively through on-campus or off-campus services.

Orientation The program or unit offers an optional orientation for new students individually by special arrangement.

Unique Aids and Services Aids, services, or accommodations include advocates, career counseling, and priority registration.

Assistive Technology Assistive technology is located in the library and includes learning support software, scanning, and recorded textbooks. Technology training is provided to incoming students.

Subject-Area Tutoring Tutoring is offered one-on-one and in small groups for most subjects. Tutoring is provided through the program or unit via other. Tutoring is also provided collaboratively through on-campus or off-campus services via computer-based instruction, trained peer tutors, and other.

Basic Skills Remediation Remediation is offered one-on-one, in small groups, and in class-size groups for computer skills, learning strategies, math, reading, social skills, study skills, time management, and written language. Remediation is provided through the program or unit. Remediation is also provided collaboratively through on-campus or off-campus services via computer-based instruction, trained peer tutors, and other.

Enrichment Enrichment programs are available through the program or unit for college survival skills and written composition skills. Programs for career planning, college survival skills, health and nutrition, math, oral communication skills, reading, vocabulary

Concord University (continued)

development, written composition skills, and other are provided collaboratively through on-campus or off-campus services. Credit is offered for health and nutrition, math, oral communication skills, reading, vocabulary development, and written composition skills.

Application For admittance to the program or unit, students are required to provide a psychoeducational report (3 years old or less). It is recommended that students provide documentation of high school services. Upon acceptance, documentation of need for services should be sent only to the LD program or unit. *Application deadline (institutional):* Continuous. *Application deadline (LD program):* Rolling/continuous for fall and rolling/continuous for spring.

Written Policies Written policy regarding general/basic LD accommodations is available on the program Web site. Written policy regarding general/basic LD accommodations is outlined in the school's catalog/handbook. Written policy regarding general/basic LD accommodations is available through the program or unit directly.

Coppin State University
Disability Support Services Program

2500 West North Avenue

Baltimore, MD 21216-3698

http://www.coppin.edu/

Contact: Ms. Patricia A. Johnson, Counselor. Phone: 410-951-3944. Fax: 410-951-3511. E-mail: patjohnson@coppin.edu. Head of LD Program: Dr. Janet D Spry, Director of Rehabilitation Counseling/Disability Support Services Program. Phone: 410-951-3614. Fax: 410-951-3511. E-mail: jspry@coppin.edu.

Disability Support Services Program Approximately 25 registered undergraduate students were served during 2006–07. The program or unit includes 1 full-time staff member. Academic advisers, counselors, graduate assistants/students, and trained peer tutors are provided collaboratively through on-campus or off-campus services.

Summer Program To help prepare for the demands of college, there is an optional 6-week summer program prior to entering the school available to high school graduates that focuses on life skills and/or college life adjustment, specific subject tutoring, study skills, test-taking skills, and time management. The program accepts students from out-of-state.

Unique Aids and Services Aids, services, or accommodations include advocates, priority registration, and support groups.

Assistive Technology Assistive technology is located in campus labs, the DSS office and includes digital textbooks/e-text and learning support software. Technology training is provided to incoming students.

Subject-Area Tutoring Tutoring is offered one-on-one for some subjects. Tutoring is provided collaboratively through on-campus or off-campus services via computer-based instruction and graduate assistants/students.

Diagnostic Testing Testing for learning strategies, learning styles, math, and social skills is provided collaboratively through on-campus or off-campus services.

Basic Skills Remediation Remediation is offered one-on-one and in small groups for computer skills, math, social skills, study skills, time management, and written language. Remediation is provided collaboratively through on-campus or off-campus services via computer-based instruction, graduate assistants/students, and professional tutors.

Enrichment Enrichment programs are available through the program or unit for medication management. Programs for career planning, college survival skills, health and nutrition, learning strategies, math, oral communication skills, reading, self-advocacy, stress management, study skills, test taking, time management, and vocabulary development are provided collaboratively through on-campus or off-campus services. Credit is offered for career planning, college survival skills, health and nutrition, learning strategies, math, oral communication skills, reading, self-advocacy, stress management, study skills, test taking, time management, and vocabulary development.

Application For admittance to the program or unit, students are required to apply to the program directly, provide a psychoeducational report (3 years old or less), and provide documentation of high school services. Upon application, materials documenting need for services should be sent only to the LD program or unit. Upon acceptance, documentation of need for services should be sent to both admissions and the LD program or unit. *Application deadline (LD program):* Rolling/continuous for fall and rolling/continuous for spring.

Written Policies Written policies regarding course substitutions, grade forgiveness, reduced course loads, and substitutions and waivers of graduation requirements are outlined in the school's catalog/handbook. Written policies regarding course substitutions, general/basic LD accommodations, grade forgiveness, reduced course loads, substitutions and waivers of admissions requirements, and substitutions and waivers of graduation requirements are available through the program or unit directly.

Cornell University
Student Disability Services

Ithaca, NY 14853-0001

http://www.clt.cornell.edu/campus/sds

Contact: Michele D. Fish, Associate Director. Phone: 607-254-4545. Fax: 607-255-1562. E-mail: clt_sds@cornell.edu. Head of LD Program: Katherine Fahey, Director. Phone: 607-254-4545. Fax: 607-255-1562. E-mail: clt_sds@cornell.edu.

Student Disability Services Approximately 279 registered undergraduate students were served during 2006–07. The program or unit includes 3 full-time and 2 part-time staff members. Academic advisers, coaches, counselors, professional tutors, skill tutors, strategy tutors, and trained peer tutors are provided collaboratively through on-campus or off-campus services.

Orientation The program or unit offers an optional 1-hour orientation for new students before classes begin.

Assistive Technology Assistive technology is located in campus labs, the DSS office and includes digital textbooks/e-text. Technology training is provided to incoming students.

Subject-Area Tutoring Tutoring is offered one-on-one, in small groups, and in class-size groups for some subjects. Tutoring is provided collaboratively through on-campus or off-campus services via computer-based instruction, graduate assistants/students, professional tutors, and trained peer tutors.

Enrichment Programs for college survival skills, health and nutrition, learning strategies, math, reading, study skills, test taking, time management, and written composition skills are provided collaboratively through on-campus or off-campus services. Credit is offered for college survival skills, health and nutrition, learning strategies, math, and study skills.

Student Organization Cornell Union for Disability Awareness consists of 40 members.

Application For admittance to the program or unit, students are required to apply to the program directly, provide a psychoeducational report, and provide request for disability services & accommodations form. Upon acceptance, documentation of need for services should be sent only to the LD program or unit. *Application deadline (institutional):* 1/1. *Application deadline (LD program):* Rolling/continuous for fall and rolling/continuous for spring.

Written Policies Written policies regarding course substitutions and general/basic LD accommodations are available on the program Web site. Written policy regarding course substitutions is outlined in the school's catalog/handbook. Written policy regarding general/basic LD accommodations is available through the program or unit directly.

Cornerstone University
Cornerstone Learning Center (CLC)

1001 East Beltline Avenue, NE

Grand Rapids, MI 49525-5897

http://www.cornerstone.edu/

Contact: Mrs. Anna M. Maddox, Director. Phone: 616-222-1596. Fax: 616-222-1595. E-mail: anna_m_maddox@cornerstone.edu.

Cornerstone Learning Center (CLC) Approximately 75 registered undergraduate students were served during 2006–07. The program or unit includes 3 full-time staff members and 1 part-time staff member. Academic advisers, diagnostic specialists, LD specialists, professional tutors, remediation/learning specialists, skill tutors, special education teachers, strategy tutors, and trained peer tutors are provided through the program or unit. Academic advisers, coaches, counselors, diagnostic specialists, regular education teachers, remediation/learning specialists, and trained peer tutors are provided collaboratively through on-campus or off-campus services.

Unique Aids and Services Aids, services, or accommodations include faculty training, personal coach, and support groups.

Assistive Technology Assistive technology includes digital textbooks/e-text.

Subject-Area Tutoring Tutoring is offered one-on-one, in small groups, and in class-size groups for all subjects. Tutoring is provided through the program or unit via trained peer tutors. Tutoring is also provided collaboratively through on-campus or off-campus services via computer-based instruction and trained peer tutors.

Basic Skills Remediation Remediation is offered one-on-one, in small groups, and in class-size groups for computer skills, learning strategies, math, reading, spelling, study skills, time management,

written language, and English as a Second Language (ESL). Remediation is provided through the program or unit via teacher trainees and trained peer tutors. Remediation is also provided collaboratively through on-campus or off-campus services via graduate assistants/students, regular education teachers, special education teachers, and trained peer tutors.

Enrichment Enrichment programs are available through the program or unit for college survival skills, learning strategies, reading, stress management, study skills, test taking, time management, and written composition skills. Programs for career planning, health and nutrition, math, medication management, stress management, time management, and written composition skills are provided collaboratively through on-campus or off-campus services. Credit is offered for college survival skills, learning strategies, math, and written composition skills.

Application For admittance to the program or unit, students are required to apply to the program directly, provide a psychoeducational report (2 years old or less), provide documentation of high school services, and provide registration with the Health Center for students taking medications. Upon application, materials documenting need for services should be sent only to the LD program or unit. Upon acceptance, documentation of need for services should be sent to both admissions and the LD program or unit. *Application deadline (institutional):* Continuous. *Application deadline (LD program):* Rolling/continuous for fall and rolling/continuous for spring.

Written Policies Written policies regarding course substitutions and general/basic LD accommodations are available on the program Web site. Written policies regarding course substitutions, general/basic LD accommodations, and reduced course loads are outlined in the school's catalog/handbook. Written policies regarding general/basic LD accommodations and reduced course loads are available through the program or unit directly.

Daemen College
The Learning Center

4380 Main Street

Amherst, NY 14226-3592

http://www.daemen.edu/offices/learningcenter

Contact: Ms. Danielle D. LaMarre, Assistant Coordinator. Phone: 716-839-8333. Fax: 716-839-8516. E-mail: dlamarre@daemen.edu. Head of LD Program: Dr. Kathleen Boone, Associate Dean and EE/AA Officer. Phone: 716-839-8301. Fax: 716-839-8279. E-mail: kboone@daemen.edu.

The Learning Center Approximately 70 registered undergraduate students were served during 2006–07. The program or unit includes 2 full-time staff members. Professional tutors, skill tutors, strategy tutors, and trained peer tutors are provided through the program or unit. Academic advisers are provided collaboratively through on-campus or off-campus services.

Assistive Technology Assistive technology is located in the DSS office and includes digital textbooks/e-text, learning support software, and scanning. Technology training is provided to incoming students.

Daemen College (continued)

Subject-Area Tutoring Tutoring is offered one-on-one, in small groups, and in class-size groups for most subjects. Tutoring is provided through the program or unit via professional tutors and trained peer tutors.

Basic Skills Remediation Remediation is offered one-on-one, in small groups, and in class-size groups for learning strategies, math, reading, study skills, time management, and written language. Remediation is provided through the program or unit via professional tutors and trained peer tutors. Remediation is also provided collaboratively through on-campus or off-campus services via regular education teachers.

Enrichment Programs for learning strategies, self-advocacy, study skills, test taking, and time management are provided collaboratively through on-campus or off-campus services.

Application For admittance to the program or unit, students are required to provide a psychoeducational report. It is recommended that students provide documentation of high school services. Upon application, materials documenting need for services should be sent only to the LD program or unit. Upon acceptance, documentation of need for services should be sent only to the LD program or unit. *Application deadline (institutional):* Continuous. *Application deadline (LD program):* Rolling/continuous for fall and rolling/continuous for spring.

Written Policies Written policies regarding general/basic LD accommodations, substitutions and waivers of admissions requirements, and substitutions and waivers of graduation requirements are available on the program Web site. Written policies regarding general/basic LD accommodations, substitutions and waivers of admissions requirements, and substitutions and waivers of graduation requirements are outlined in the school's catalog/handbook. Written policy regarding general/basic LD accommodations is available through the program or unit directly.

Dalhousie University
Student Accessibility Services

Halifax, NS B3H 4R2

Canada

http://www.studentaccessibility.dal.ca

Contact: Mr. Paul M. Szymanowski, Advisor. Phone: 902-494-2836. Fax: 902-494-2042. E-mail: access@dal.ca.

Student Accessibility Services Approximately 300 registered undergraduate students were served during 2006–07. The program or unit includes 2 full-time and 2 part-time staff members. Counselors are provided through the program or unit. Academic advisers, LD specialists, professional tutors, skill tutors, strategy tutors, and other are provided collaboratively through on-campus or off-campus services.

Unique Aids and Services Aids, services, or accommodations include career counseling, faculty training, regular meetings for students at high risk.

Assistive Technology Assistive technology is located in the DSS office, library learning common and includes digital textbooks/e-text, learning support software, and scanning. Technology training is provided to incoming students.

Subject-Area Tutoring Tutoring is offered for most subjects. Tutoring is provided collaboratively through on-campus or off-campus services via professional tutors and other.

Diagnostic Testing Testing for auditory processing, handwriting, intelligence, learning strategies, learning styles, math, motor skills, neuropsychological, personality, reading, social skills, spelling, spoken language, study skills, visual processing, written language, and other services is provided collaboratively through on-campus or off-campus services.

Basic Skills Remediation Remediation is offered one-on-one and in small groups for computer skills, learning strategies, reading, study skills, time management, and written language. Remediation is provided collaboratively through on-campus or off-campus services via graduate assistants/students, professional tutors, trained peer tutors, and other.

Enrichment Enrichment programs are available through the program or unit for self-advocacy. Programs for career planning, college survival skills, learning strategies, oral communication skills, stress management, study skills, test taking, time management, written composition skills, and other are provided collaboratively through on-campus or off-campus services. Credit is offered for career planning, college survival skills, and written composition skills.

Fees *Diagnostic Testing* fee is $1600 to $2000.

Application For admittance to the program or unit, students are required to provide a psychoeducational report (3 years old or less). It is recommended that students apply to the program directly and provide documentation of high school services. Upon application, materials documenting need for services should be sent only to the LD program or unit. Upon acceptance, documentation of need for services should be sent only to the LD program or unit. *Application deadline (institutional):* 6/1. *Application deadline (LD program):* Rolling/continuous for fall and rolling/continuous for spring.

Written Policies Written policies regarding general/basic LD accommodations and substitutions and waivers of admissions requirements are available on the program Web site. Written policies regarding general/basic LD accommodations and substitutions and waivers of admissions requirements are outlined in the school's catalog/handbook. Written policies regarding general/basic LD accommodations and substitutions and waivers of graduation requirements are available through the program or unit directly.

Dallas Baptist University
Disabled Student Services

3000 Mountain Creek Parkway

Dallas, TX 75211-9299

http://www.dbu.edu

Contact: Mr. Mark Hale, Associate Vice President for Student Affairs. Phone: 214-333-5101. Fax: 214-333-6962. E-mail: markh@dbu.edu.

Disabled Student Services Approximately 80 registered undergraduate students were served during 2006–07. The program or unit includes 1 full-time staff member. Academic advisers, coaches, counselors, graduate assistants/students, regular education teachers, remediation/learning specialists, trained peer tutors, and other are provided collaboratively through on-campus or off-campus services.

Assistive Technology Assistive technology is located in campus labs, the DSS office and includes digital textbooks/e-text, learning support software, and audio books. Technology training is provided to incoming students.

Subject-Area Tutoring Tutoring is offered one-on-one, in small groups, and in class-size groups for some subjects. Tutoring is provided collaboratively through on-campus or off-campus services via trained peer tutors.

Enrichment Programs for career planning, college survival skills, health and nutrition, learning strategies, math, practical computer skills, stress management, study skills, test taking, time management, and written composition skills are provided collaboratively through on-campus or off-campus services.

Application For admittance to the program or unit, students are required to provide a psychoeducational report (2 years old or less). It is recommended that students provide documentation of high school services. Upon application, materials documenting need for services should be sent only to the LD program or unit. Upon acceptance, documentation of need for services should be sent to both admissions and the LD program or unit. *Application deadline (institutional):* Continuous. *Application deadline (LD program):* Rolling/continuous for fall and rolling/continuous for spring.

Written Policies Written policy regarding general/basic LD accommodations is available on the program Web site. Written policy regarding general/basic LD accommodations is outlined in the school's catalog/handbook.

Basic Skills Remediation Remediation is offered in class-size groups for learning strategies, math, reading, study skills, time management, and written language. Remediation is provided collaboratively through on-campus or off-campus services via computer-based instruction, regular education teachers, and trained peer tutors.

Enrichment Enrichment programs are available through the program or unit for college survival skills, learning strategies, self-advocacy, study skills, test taking, and time management. Programs for career planning, college survival skills, health and nutrition, learning strategies, math, practical computer skills, reading, stress management, study skills, test taking, time management, vocabulary development, and written composition skills are provided collaboratively through on-campus or off-campus services. Credit is offered for college survival skills and learning strategies.

Application For admittance to the program or unit, students are required to apply to the program directly and provide a psychoeducational report (3 years old or less). It is recommended that students provide documentation of high school services. Upon acceptance, documentation of need for services should be sent only to the LD program or unit. *Application deadline (institutional):* 4/1. *Application deadline (LD program):* Rolling/continuous for fall.

Written Policies Written policy regarding general/basic LD accommodations is available on the program Web site. Written policies regarding course substitutions, general/basic LD accommodations, reduced course loads, and substitutions and waivers of graduation requirements are available through the program or unit directly.

Delaware State University
Office of Disabilities Services

1200 North DuPont Highway

Dover, DE 19901-2277

http://www.desu.edu

Contact: Mrs. Laura H. Kurtz, Director, Office of Disabilities Services. Phone: 302-857-6388. Fax: 302-857-6386. E-mail: lkurtz@desu.edu.

Office of Disabilities Services Approximately 60 registered undergraduate students were served during 2006–07. The program or unit includes 2 full-time and 2 part-time staff members. Coaches, diagnostic specialists, LD specialists, skill tutors, and strategy tutors are provided through the program or unit. Academic advisers, counselors, diagnostic specialists, trained peer tutors, and other are provided collaboratively through on-campus or off-campus services.

Unique Aids and Services Aids, services, or accommodations include advocates and priority registration.

Subject-Area Tutoring Tutoring is offered one-on-one, in small groups, and in class-size groups for most subjects. Tutoring is provided through the program or unit via LD specialists. Tutoring is also provided collaboratively through on-campus or off-campus services via computer-based instruction, trained peer tutors, and other.

Diagnostic Testing Testing is provided through the program or unit for learning strategies, learning styles, math, reading, spelling, and study skills. Testing for learning strategies, learning styles, math, reading, study skills, and written language is provided collaboratively through on-campus or off-campus services.

DePaul University
Productive Learning Strategies (PLuS) Program

1 East Jackson Boulevard

Chicago, IL 60604-2287

http://condor.depaul.edu/~plus/

Contact: Ms. Judith R. Kolar, Acting Director, Productive Learning Strategies (PLuS) Program. Phone: 773-325-1677. Fax: 773-325-4673. E-mail: jkolar@depaul.edu.

Productive Learning Strategies (PLuS) Program Approximately 240 registered undergraduate students were served during 2006–07. The program or unit includes 2 full-time and 6 part-time staff members. Academic advisers, coaches, diagnostic specialists, graduate assistants/students, LD specialists, remediation/learning specialists, skill tutors, special education teachers, and strategy tutors are provided through the program or unit. Academic advisers, counselors, diagnostic specialists, graduate assistants/students, professional tutors, regular education teachers, skill tutors, teacher trainees, and trained peer tutors are provided collaboratively through on-campus or off-campus services.

Orientation The program or unit offers a mandatory 1- to 1.5-hour orientation for new students before classes begin, during summer prior to enrollment, individually by special arrangement, and during the university orientation dates.

Unique Aids and Services Aids, services, or accommodations include advocates, career counseling, faculty training, personal coach, priority registration, organization/time management.

DePaul University (continued)

Subject-Area Tutoring Tutoring is offered one-on-one for some subjects. Tutoring is provided through the program or unit via graduate assistants/students and LD specialists. Tutoring is also provided collaboratively through on-campus or off-campus services via graduate assistants/students and trained peer tutors.

Basic Skills Remediation Remediation is offered one-on-one for learning strategies, math, reading, social skills, spelling, spoken language, study skills, time management, written language, and organizational skills. Remediation is provided through the program or unit via graduate assistants/students, LD specialists, and special education teachers. Remediation is also provided collaboratively through on-campus or off-campus services via graduate assistants/students and trained peer tutors.

Enrichment Enrichment programs are available through the program or unit for career planning, college survival skills, learning strategies, oral communication skills, reading, self-advocacy, study skills, test taking, time management, vocabulary development, and written composition skills. Programs for career planning, college survival skills, health and nutrition, math, practical computer skills, stress management, test taking, and written composition skills are provided collaboratively through on-campus or off-campus services.

Fees *LD Program or Service* fee is $350 to $600 (fee varies according to level/tier of service).

Application For admittance to the program or unit, students are required to apply to the program directly and provide a psychoeducational report (5 years old or less). It is recommended that students provide documentation of high school services and provide an academic performance report from a specialist working with the student. Upon acceptance, documentation of need for services should be sent only to the LD program or unit. *Application deadline (institutional):* Continuous. *Application deadline (LD program):* Rolling/continuous for fall and rolling/continuous for spring.

Written Policies Written policy regarding general/basic LD accommodations is available on the program Web site.

Dominican University
Dean of Students Office

7900 West Division Street

River Forest, IL 60305-1099

http://www.dom.edu/

Contact: Trudi Goggin, Dean of Students. Phone: 708-524-6824. Fax: 708-524-6659. E-mail: tgoggin@dom.edu.

Dean of Students Office Approximately 20 registered undergraduate students were served during 2006–07. Counselors, diagnostic specialists, and skill tutors are provided collaboratively through on-campus or off-campus services.

Unique Aids and Services Aids, services, or accommodations include advocates.

Assistive Technology Assistive technology is located in campus labs and includes digital textbooks/e-text, learning support software, and scanning. Technology training is provided to incoming students.

Subject-Area Tutoring Tutoring is offered one-on-one and in small groups for some subjects. Tutoring is provided collaboratively through on-campus or off-campus services via other.

Basic Skills Remediation Remediation is offered in small groups for learning strategies, study skills, and time management. Remediation is provided collaboratively through on-campus or off-campus services via regular education teachers.

Application For admittance to the program or unit, students are required to provide a psychoeducational report (3 years old or less). It is recommended that students provide documentation of high school services. Upon acceptance, documentation of need for services should be sent only to the LD program or unit. *Application deadline (institutional):* Continuous. *Application deadline (LD program):* Rolling/continuous for fall and rolling/continuous for spring.

Written Policies Written policies regarding course substitutions, general/basic LD accommodations, and substitutions and waivers of admissions requirements are outlined in the school's catalog/handbook. Written policies regarding course substitutions, general/basic LD accommodations, and substitutions and waivers of admissions requirements are available through the program or unit directly.

Drake University
Student Disability Services

2507 University Avenue

Des Moines, IA 50311-4516

http://www.drake.edu/

Contact: Mrs. Michelle Leigh Laughlin, Student Disability Services Coordinator. Phone: 515-271-1835. Fax: 515-271-1855. E-mail: michelle.laughlin@drake.edu.

Student Disability Services Approximately 97 registered undergraduate students were served during 2006–07. The program or unit includes 1 full-time staff member. Counselors, strategy tutors, and other are provided through the program or unit. Academic advisers, diagnostic specialists, regular education teachers, skill tutors, strategy tutors, and trained peer tutors are provided collaboratively through on-campus or off-campus services.

Unique Aids and Services Aids, services, or accommodations include advocates and faculty training.

Subject-Area Tutoring Tutoring is offered one-on-one, in small groups, and in class-size groups for some subjects. Tutoring is provided collaboratively through on-campus or off-campus services via computer-based instruction and trained peer tutors.

Enrichment Enrichment programs are available through the program or unit for self-advocacy, stress management, study skills, test taking, and time management. Programs for career planning, health and nutrition, learning strategies, self-advocacy, stress management, study skills, test taking, time management, and written composition skills are provided collaboratively through on-campus or off-campus services.

Application For admittance to the program or unit, students are required to apply to the program directly and provide a psychoeducational report (3 years old or less). It is recommended that students provide documentation of high school services. Upon application, materials documenting need for services should be sent only to the LD program or unit. Upon acceptance, documentation of need for services should be sent only to the LD program or unit. *Application deadline (institutional):* 3/1. *Application deadline (LD program):* Rolling/continuous for fall and rolling/continuous for spring.

Written Policies Written policies regarding course substitutions, general/basic LD accommodations, and reduced course loads are outlined in the school's catalog/handbook. Written policies regarding course substitutions, general/basic LD accommodations, and reduced course loads are available through the program or unit directly.

Drury University
Disability Services

900 North Benton Avenue

Springfield, MO 65802

http://www.drury.edu/

Contact: Mr. Lawrence Anderson, Coordinator of Disability Services. Phone: 417-873-7457. Fax: 417-873-6833. E-mail: landerso@drury.edu.

Disability Services Approximately 35 registered undergraduate students were served during 2006–07. The program or unit includes 1 full-time and 1 part-time staff member. Counselors, graduate assistants/students, and skill tutors are provided through the program or unit. Academic advisers, diagnostic specialists, and skill tutors are provided collaboratively through on-campus or off-campus services.
Orientation The program or unit offers an optional 1-hour orientation for new students.
Unique Aids and Services Aids, services, or accommodations include priority registration.
Assistive Technology Assistive technology is located in the DSS office and includes digital textbooks/e-text, learning support software, and scanning. Technology training is provided to incoming students.
Subject-Area Tutoring Tutoring is offered one-on-one for most subjects. Tutoring is provided through the program or unit via trained peer tutors. Tutoring is also provided collaboratively through on-campus or off-campus services via trained peer tutors.
Enrichment Enrichment programs are available through the program or unit for self-advocacy, test taking, and time management. Programs for career planning, math, self-advocacy, and written composition skills are provided collaboratively through on-campus or off-campus services.
Application For admittance to the program or unit, students are required to provide a psychoeducational report (3 years old or less). It is recommended that students provide documentation of high school services. Upon application, materials documenting need for services should be sent to both admissions and the LD program or unit. Upon acceptance, documentation of need for services should be sent only to the LD program or unit. *Application deadline (institutional):* 8/1. *Application deadline (LD program):* Rolling/continuous for fall and rolling/continuous for spring.
Written Policies Written policies regarding course substitutions and general/basic LD accommodations are available through the program or unit directly.

Duke University
Office of Services for Students with Disabilities

Durham, NC 27708-0586

http://www.duke.edu/web/skills

Contact: Ms. Donna Hall, Director, Academic Resource Center. Phone: 919-684-5917. Fax: 919-684-8934. E-mail: dhall@duke.edu.

Office of Services for Students with Disabilities Approximately 45 registered undergraduate students were served during 2006–07. The program or unit includes 3 full-time staff members. Academic advisers, coaches, counselors, LD specialists, skill tutors, and trained peer tutors are provided collaboratively through on-campus or off-campus services.
Assistive Technology Assistive technology is located in campus labs, the DSS office and includes digital textbooks/e-text and learning support software.
Subject-Area Tutoring Tutoring is offered one-on-one for some subjects. Tutoring is provided collaboratively through on-campus or off-campus services via trained peer tutors.
Enrichment Programs for career planning, college survival skills, learning strategies, study skills, test taking, time management, and written composition skills are provided collaboratively through on-campus or off-campus services.
Application For admittance to the program or unit, students are required to provide a psychoeducational report (3 years old or less). It is recommended that students provide documentation of high school services. Upon application, materials documenting need for services should be sent only to the LD program or unit. Upon acceptance, documentation of need for services should be sent only to the LD program or unit. *Application deadline (institutional):* 1/2. *Application deadline (LD program):* 6/10 for fall. 11/10 for spring.
Written Policies Written policy regarding general/basic LD accommodations is available on the program Web site.

Earlham College
Center for Academic Enrichment

801 National Road West

Richmond, IN 47374-4095

http://www.earlham.edu/~sas/support

Contact: Donna Keesling, Director of the Center for Academic Enrichment. Phone: 765-983-1341. Fax: 765-973-2120. E-mail: keesldo@earlham.edu.

Center for Academic Enrichment Approximately 67 registered undergraduate students were served during 2006–07. The program or unit includes 1 full-time and 1 part-time staff member. Academic advisers, counselors, and trained peer tutors are provided through the program or unit. Academic advisers, counselors, and trained peer tutors are provided collaboratively through on-campus or off-campus services.
Assistive Technology Assistive technology is located in public labs and one small private lab and includes digital textbooks/e-text and scan-read technology, voice-to-text technology. Technology training is provided to incoming students.

Earlham College (continued)

Subject-Area Tutoring Tutoring is offered one-on-one and in small groups for most subjects. Tutoring is provided through the program or unit via trained peer tutors. Tutoring is also provided collaboratively through on-campus or off-campus services via trained peer tutors.

Enrichment Programs for career planning, health and nutrition, medication management, stress management, study skills, test taking, time management, and written composition skills are provided collaboratively through on-campus or off-campus services.

Application For admittance to the program or unit, students are required to provide a psychoeducational report. Upon acceptance, documentation of need for services should be sent only to the LD program or unit. *Application deadline (institutional): 2/15. Application deadline (LD program):* Rolling/continuous for fall and rolling/continuous for spring.

Written Policies Written policy regarding general/basic LD accommodations is available on the program Web site. Written policy regarding general/basic LD accommodations is outlined in the school's catalog/handbook. Written policies regarding course substitutions and general/basic LD accommodations are available through the program or unit directly.

East Carolina University
Disability Support Services

East 5th Street

Greenville, NC 27858-4353

http://www.ecu.edu/dss

Contact: Ms. Liz Johnston, Director of Disability Support Services. Phone: 252-737-1016. Fax: 252-737-1025. E-mail: johnstone@ecu.edu. Head of LD Program: Ms. Diane Majewski, Associate Director of Disability Support Services. Phone: 252-737-1016. Fax: 252-737-1025. E-mail: majewskid@ecu.edu.

Disability Support Services Approximately 500 registered undergraduate students were served during 2006–07. The program or unit includes 4 full-time staff members. Coaches, graduate assistants/students, and LD specialists are provided through the program or unit. Academic advisers, counselors, diagnostic specialists, professional tutors, regular education teachers, remediation/learning specialists, skill tutors, special education teachers, strategy tutors, teacher trainees, trained peer tutors, and other are provided collaboratively through on-campus or off-campus services.

Unique Aids and Services Aids, services, or accommodations include faculty training and personal coach.

Assistive Technology Assistive technology is located in campus labs, the DSS office and includes digital textbooks/e-text, learning support software, and scanning. Technology training is provided to incoming students.

Subject-Area Tutoring Tutoring is offered one-on-one, in small groups, and in class-size groups for most subjects. Tutoring is provided through the program or unit via computer-based instruction, graduate assistants/students, and LD specialists. Tutoring is also provided collaboratively through on-campus or off-campus services via computer-based instruction and graduate assistants/students.

Basic Skills Remediation Remediation is offered one-on-one for computer skills, learning strategies, math, reading, study skills, time management, and written language. Remediation is provided through the program or unit via graduate assistants/students and LD specialists.

Application For admittance to the program or unit, students are required to provide a psychoeducational report (3 years old or less) and provide other documentation (contact office for details). Upon application, materials documenting need for services should be sent only to the LD program or unit. Upon acceptance, documentation of need for services should be sent only to the LD program or unit. *Application deadline (institutional): 3/15. Application deadline (LD program):* Rolling/continuous for fall and rolling/continuous for spring.

Written Policies Written policies regarding general/basic LD accommodations, grade forgiveness, substitutions and waivers of admissions requirements, and substitutions and waivers of graduation requirements are available on the program Web site. Written policies regarding general/basic LD accommodations, grade forgiveness, substitutions and waivers of admissions requirements, and substitutions and waivers of graduation requirements are outlined in the school's catalog/handbook. Written policy regarding general/basic LD accommodations is available through the program or unit directly.

Eastern Connecticut State University
Office of AccesAbility Services

83 Windham Street

Willimantic, CT 06226-2295

http://www.easternct.edu

Contact: Dr. Pamela J. Starr, Coordinator/Counselor. Phone: 860-465-0189. Fax: 860-465-0136. E-mail: starrp@easternct.edu.

Office of AccesAbility Services Approximately 80 registered undergraduate students were served during 2006–07. The program or unit includes 1 full-time and 1 part-time staff member. Counselors, trained peer tutors, and other are provided through the program or unit. Trained peer tutors are provided collaboratively through on-campus or off-campus services.

Orientation The program or unit offers an optional orientation for new students before registration, before classes begin, during summer prior to enrollment, during registration, after classes begin, and individually by special arrangement.

Unique Aids and Services Aids, services, or accommodations include faculty training and priority registration.

Subject-Area Tutoring Tutoring is offered one-on-one and in small groups. Tutoring is provided through the program or unit via trained peer tutors. Tutoring is also provided collaboratively through on-campus or off-campus services via trained peer tutors.

Enrichment Enrichment programs are available through the program or unit for learning strategies, self-advocacy, study skills, test taking, time management, and other. Programs for career planning, college survival skills, health and nutrition, learning strategies, math, medication management, oral communication skills, practical computer skills, reading, stress management, study skills, test taking, time management, vocabulary development, written composition skills, and other are provided collaboratively through on-campus or off-campus services. Credit is offered for oral communication skills, practical computer skills, reading, vocabulary development, written composition skills, and other.

Application For admittance to the program or unit, students are required to apply to the program directly and provide a psychoeducational report. It is recommended that students provide documentation of high school services. Upon application, materials documenting need for services should be sent only to the LD program or unit. Upon acceptance, documentation of need for services should be sent only to the LD program or unit. *Application deadline (institutional): 5/1. Application deadline (LD program):* Rolling/continuous for fall and rolling/continuous for spring.

Written Policies Written policy regarding general/basic LD accommodations is available on the program Web site. Written policies regarding course substitutions, reduced course loads, and substitutions and waivers of graduation requirements are outlined in the school's catalog/handbook. Written policies regarding course substitutions, general/basic LD accommodations, and reduced course loads are available through the program or unit directly.

Eastern Mennonite University
Student Disability Support Services

1200 Park Road

Harrisonburg, VA 22802-2462

http://www.emu.edu/academicsupport/

Contact: Ms. Joyce Coryell Hedrick, Coordinator, Student Disability Support Services. Phone: 540-432-4233. Fax: 540-432-4631. E-mail: hedrickj@emu.edu.

Student Disability Support Services Approximately 72 registered undergraduate students were served during 2006–07. The program or unit includes 1 part-time staff member. Academic advisers, coaches, counselors, skill tutors, strategy tutors, and trained peer tutors are provided through the program or unit. Academic advisers, counselors, diagnostic specialists, regular education teachers, remediation/learning specialists, trained peer tutors, and other are provided collaboratively through on-campus or off-campus services.

Orientation The program or unit offers a mandatory orientation for new students during summer prior to enrollment, during registration, after classes begin, and individually by special arrangement.

Unique Aids and Services Aids, services, or accommodations include advocates, career counseling, faculty training, personal coach, priority registration, support groups, weekly meetings with faculty, mental health counseling.

Assistive Technology Assistive technology is located in campus labs, the DSS office, a special lab and includes digital textbooks/e-text, learning support software, scanning, and voice recognition software. Technology training is provided to incoming students.

Subject-Area Tutoring Tutoring is offered one-on-one, in small groups, and in class-size groups for most subjects. Tutoring is provided through the program or unit via computer-based instruction and trained peer tutors. Tutoring is also provided collaboratively through on-campus or off-campus services via computer-based instruction, trained peer tutors, and other.

Diagnostic Testing Testing is provided through the program or unit for learning strategies, learning styles, and reading. Testing for auditory processing, handwriting, intelligence, learning strategies, learning styles, math, motor skills, neuropsychological, personality, reading, social skills, spelling, spoken language, study skills, visual processing, written language, and other services is provided collaboratively through on-campus or off-campus services.

Basic Skills Remediation Remediation is offered one-on-one, in small groups, and in class-size groups for computer skills, learning strategies, math, reading, social skills, study skills, time management, written language, and organizational management. Remediation is provided through the program or unit via trained peer tutors and other. Remediation is also provided collaboratively through on-campus or off-campus services via computer-based instruction, regular education teachers, teacher trainees, trained peer tutors, and other.

Enrichment Enrichment programs are available through the program or unit for career planning, college survival skills, learning strategies, math, practical computer skills, reading, self-advocacy, stress management, study skills, test taking, time management, and written composition skills. Programs for career planning, college survival skills, health and nutrition, learning strategies, math, medication management, oral communication skills, practical computer skills, reading, stress management, and written composition skills are provided collaboratively through on-campus or off-campus services. Credit is offered for reading and written composition skills.

Student Organization Student Disability Awareness Committee.

Fees *Diagnostic Testing* fee is $0 to $500.

Application For admittance to the program or unit, students are required to apply to the program directly, provide a psychoeducational report (3 years old or less), and provide a psychoeducational report based on adult norms (3 years old or less). It is recommended that students provide documentation of high school services. Upon application, materials documenting need for services should be sent only to the LD program or unit. Upon acceptance, documentation of need for services should be sent only to the LD program or unit. *Application deadline (institutional):* Continuous. *Application deadline (LD program):* Rolling/continuous for fall and rolling/continuous for spring.

Written Policies Written policy regarding general/basic LD accommodations is outlined in the school's catalog/handbook. Written policies regarding course substitutions, general/basic LD accommodations, reduced course loads, substitutions and waivers of admissions requirements, and substitutions and waivers of graduation requirements are available through the program or unit directly.

Eastern Michigan University
Access Services Office

Ypsilanti, MI 48197

http://www.emich.edu/access_services/

Contact: Mr. Donald J. Anderson, Director. Phone: 734-487-2470. Fax: 734-487-5784. E-mail: donald.anderson@emich.edu.

Access Services Office Approximately 350 registered undergraduate students were served during 2006–07. The program or unit includes 2 full-time staff members. Graduate assistants/students are

Eastern Michigan University (continued)

provided through the program or unit. Academic advisers, coaches, counselors, trained peer tutors, and other are provided collaboratively through on-campus or off-campus services.

Unique Aids and Services Aids, services, or accommodations include priority registration.

Assistive Technology Assistive technology is located in a special lab and includes digital textbooks/e-text and scanning. Technology training is provided to incoming students.

Subject-Area Tutoring Tutoring is offered one-on-one and in small groups for some subjects. Tutoring is provided collaboratively through on-campus or off-campus services via graduate assistants/students and trained peer tutors.

Diagnostic Testing Testing for auditory processing, intelligence, learning strategies, learning styles, math, motor skills, neuropsychological, personality, reading, spelling, spoken language, study skills, visual processing, and written language is provided collaboratively through on-campus or off-campus services.

Enrichment Programs for career planning, college survival skills, health and nutrition, learning strategies, math, reading, stress management, study skills, test taking, time management, and written composition skills are provided collaboratively through on-campus or off-campus services.

Fees *Diagnostic Testing* fee is $50 to $1000.

Application For admittance to the program or unit, students are required to provide a psychoeducational report (5 years old or less). Upon acceptance, documentation of need for services should be sent only to the LD program or unit. *Application deadline (LD program):* Rolling/continuous for fall and rolling/continuous for spring.

Written Policies Written policy regarding general/basic LD accommodations is available on the program Web site. Written policy regarding general/basic LD accommodations is outlined in the school's catalog/handbook.

Eastern Nazarene College
Center for Academic Services

23 East Elm Avenue

Quincy, MA 02170-2999

http://enc.edu/goto/counseling/academic_services.htm

Contact: Bill Boozang, Director of Academic Services. Phone: 617-745-3722. Fax: 617-745-3915. E-mail: bill.boozang@enc.edu.

Center for Academic Services Approximately 35 registered undergraduate students were served during 2006–07. The program or unit includes 2 full-time staff members. Academic advisers, coaches, regular education teachers, skill tutors, strategy tutors, teacher trainees, trained peer tutors, and other are provided collaboratively through on-campus or off-campus services.

Unique Aids and Services Aids, services, or accommodations include advocates, career counseling, personal coach, and weekly meetings with faculty.

Subject-Area Tutoring Tutoring is offered one-on-one and in small groups for all subjects. Tutoring is provided through the program or unit via graduate assistants/students and trained peer tutors.

Basic Skills Remediation Remediation is offered one-on-one, in small groups, and in class-size groups for learning strategies, math, reading, study skills, time management, and written language. Remediation is provided through the program or unit via computer-based instruction, graduate assistants/students, regular education teachers, teacher trainees, and trained peer tutors.

Enrichment Enrichment programs are available through the program or unit for college survival skills, learning strategies, math, practical computer skills, reading, self-advocacy, study skills, test taking, time management, vocabulary development, and written composition skills. Programs for career planning, college survival skills, health and nutrition, learning strategies, medication management, oral communication skills, reading, self-advocacy, stress management, study skills, test taking, and time management are provided collaboratively through on-campus or off-campus services. Credit is offered for career planning, college survival skills, health and nutrition, learning strategies, math, oral communication skills, reading, study skills, test taking, time management, vocabulary development, and written composition skills.

Application For admittance to the program or unit, students are required to provide a psychoeducational report (3 years old or less) and provide documentation of high school services. Upon application, materials documenting need for services should be sent only to the LD program or unit. Upon acceptance, documentation of need for services should be sent only to the LD program or unit. *Application deadline (institutional):* 9/1. *Application deadline (LD program):* Rolling/continuous for fall and rolling/continuous for spring.

Written Policies Written policy regarding general/basic LD accommodations is outlined in the school's catalog/handbook.

East Stroudsburg University of Pennsylvania
Office of Disability Services

200 Prospect Street

East Stroudsburg, PA 18301-2999

http://www3.esu.edu/academics/disabilityservices/index.asp

Contact: Ms. Kristen Laga, Assistive Technology Specialist and Outreach Coordinator. Phone: 570-422-3954. Fax: 570-422-3898. E-mail: klaga@po-box.esu.edu. Head of LD Program: Dr. Edith Fisher Miller, Professor and Director of Disability Services. Phone: 570-422-3954. Fax: 570-422-3898. E-mail: emiller@po-box.esu.edu.

Office of Disability Services Approximately 181 registered undergraduate students were served during 2006–07. The program or unit includes 2 full-time staff members and 1 part-time staff member. Academic advisers, graduate assistants/students, and LD specialists are provided through the program or unit. Academic advisers, counselors, professional tutors, regular education teachers, and trained peer tutors are provided collaboratively through on-campus or off-campus services.

Unique Aids and Services Aids, services, or accommodations include priority registration.

Assistive Technology Assistive technology is located in campus labs, the DSS office and includes digital textbooks/e-text, learning support software, scanning, and text-to-speech programs, speech-to-text programs, reading pen. Technology training is provided to incoming students.

Subject-Area Tutoring Tutoring is offered one-on-one and in small groups for most subjects. Tutoring is provided collaboratively through on-campus or off-campus services via professional tutors and trained peer tutors.

Enrichment Enrichment programs are available through the program or unit for career planning, college survival skills, learning strategies, oral communication skills, reading, self-advocacy, stress management, study skills, test taking, time management, and other.

Student Organization Delta Alpha Pi Honor Society consists of 30 members.

Application For admittance to the program or unit, students are required to provide a psychoeducational report (3 years old or less). It is recommended that students provide documentation of high school services. Upon application, materials documenting need for services should be sent only to the LD program or unit. Upon acceptance, documentation of need for services should be sent only to the LD program or unit. *Application deadline (institutional):* 4/1. *Application deadline (LD program):* Rolling/continuous for fall and rolling/continuous for spring.

Written Policies Written policy regarding general/basic LD accommodations is available on the program Web site.

Eckerd College
Disability Support Services

4200 54th Avenue South

St. Petersburg, FL 33711

http://www.eckerd.edu/counselinghealth/dss/index.php

Contact: Dr. Scott C. Strader, Director, Counseling & Disability Support Services. Phone: 727-864-8248. Fax: 727-864-8323. E-mail: stradesc@eckerd.edu.

Disability Support Services Approximately 100 registered undergraduate students were served during 2006–07. The program or unit includes 1 full-time and 1 part-time staff member. Coaches, counselors, and LD specialists are provided through the program or unit. Academic advisers, diagnostic specialists, and graduate assistants/students are provided collaboratively through on-campus or off-campus services.

Assistive Technology Assistive technology is located in the library and includes digital textbooks/e-text.

Subject-Area Tutoring Tutoring is offered one-on-one and in small groups for some subjects. Tutoring is provided collaboratively through on-campus or off-campus services via graduate assistants/students and professional tutors.

Enrichment Enrichment programs are available through the program or unit for college survival skills, learning strategies, stress management, study skills, and time management. Programs for career planning, health and nutrition, oral communication skills, practical computer skills, and written composition skills are provided collaboratively through on-campus or off-campus services. Credit is offered for written composition skills.

Application For admittance to the program or unit, students are required to provide a psychoeducational report (3 years old or less). Upon acceptance, documentation of need for services should be sent only to the LD program or unit. *Application deadline (institutional):* Continuous. *Application deadline (LD program):* Rolling/continuous for fall and rolling/continuous for spring.

Written Policies Written policy regarding general/basic LD accommodations is available on the program Web site. Written policies regarding course substitutions, general/basic LD accommodations, and substitutions and waivers of graduation requirements are available through the program or unit directly.

Elmira College
Disability Services

One Park Place

Elmira, NY 14901

http://www.elmira.edu/

Contact: Ms. Carolyn Draht, Managing Director of Teacher Education Programs and Education Services. Phone: 607-735-1922. E-mail: cdraht@elmira.edu.

Disability Services Approximately 80 registered undergraduate students were served during 2006–07. The program or unit includes 2 full-time staff members. Graduate assistants/students, skill tutors, strategy tutors, and trained peer tutors are provided through the program or unit. Academic advisers, coaches, counselors, diagnostic specialists, graduate assistants/students, regular education teachers, and teacher trainees are provided collaboratively through on-campus or off-campus services.

Unique Aids and Services Aids, services, or accommodations include career counseling and priority registration.

Assistive Technology Assistive technology is located in campus labs, the Tutorial Center and includes digital textbooks/e-text. Technology training is provided to incoming students.

Subject-Area Tutoring Tutoring is offered one-on-one, in small groups, and in class-size groups for most subjects. Tutoring is provided collaboratively through on-campus or off-campus services via graduate assistants/students and trained peer tutors.

Application For admittance to the program or unit, students are required to provide a psychoeducational report (3 years old or less). It is recommended that students provide documentation of high school services. Upon acceptance, documentation of need for services should be sent only to the LD program or unit. *Application deadline (institutional):* 4/15. *Application deadline (LD program):* 8/1 for fall. 12/1 for spring.

Written Policies Written policy regarding general/basic LD accommodations is available on the program Web site. Written policy regarding general/basic LD accommodations is outlined in the school's catalog/handbook. Written policy regarding general/basic LD accommodations is available through the program or unit directly.

Elms College
Office of Disability Services

291 Springfield Street

Chicopee, MA 01013-2839

http://www.elms.edu/

Contact: Ms. Anne Marie Smith, Coordinator of Disability Services. Phone: 413-265-2333. Fax: 413-594-3951. E-mail: smitha@elms.edu.

Office of Disability Services Approximately 77 registered undergraduate students were served during 2006–07. The program or unit includes 1 part-time staff member. Coaches, regular education teachers, trained peer tutors, and other are provided through the program or unit. Coaches, regular education teachers, trained peer tutors, and other are provided collaboratively through on-campus or off-campus services.

Unique Aids and Services Aids, services, or accommodations include close monitoring of progress.

Assistive Technology Assistive technology is located in campus labs, the DSS office and includes digital textbooks/e-text, learning support software, and scanning. Technology training is provided to incoming students.

Subject-Area Tutoring Tutoring is offered one-on-one for most subjects. Tutoring is provided collaboratively through on-campus or off-campus services via professional tutors and trained peer tutors.

Diagnostic Testing Testing for intelligence, math, reading, and written language is provided collaboratively through on-campus or off-campus services.

Enrichment Enrichment programs are available through the program or unit for learning strategies, self-advocacy, study skills, test taking, and time management. Programs for career planning, college survival skills, health and nutrition, and medication management are provided collaboratively through on-campus or off-campus services.

Fees *Diagnostic Testing* fee is $750 to $1500.

Application For admittance to the program or unit, students are required to provide a psychoeducational report. It is recommended that students provide documentation of high school services and provide any other supporting documentation on functional limitation of disability and requesting accommodation. Upon application, materials documenting need for services should be sent only to the LD program or unit. Upon acceptance, documentation of need for services should be sent only to the LD program or unit. *Application deadline (institutional):* Continuous. *Application deadline (LD program):* Rolling/continuous for fall and rolling/continuous for spring.

Written Policies Written policies regarding course substitutions, general/basic LD accommodations, reduced course loads, and substitutions and waivers of admissions requirements are available on the program Web site. Written policies regarding course substitutions, general/basic LD accommodations, reduced course loads, and substitutions and waivers of admissions requirements are available through the program or unit directly.

Elon University
Disabilities Services

2700 Campus Box

Elon, NC 27244-2010

http://www.elon.edu/

Contact: Ms. Priscilla K. Lipe, Disabilities Services Coordinator. Phone: 336-278-6500. Fax: 336-278-6514. E-mail: plipe@elon.edu.

Disabilities Services Approximately 222 registered undergraduate students were served during 2006–07. The program or unit includes 1 full-time staff member. Academic advisers and LD specialists are provided through the program or unit. Academic advisers, coaches, counselors, and regular education teachers are provided collaboratively through on-campus or off-campus services.

Unique Aids and Services Aids, services, or accommodations include priority registration.

Subject-Area Tutoring Tutoring is offered one-on-one and in small groups for most subjects. Tutoring is provided collaboratively through on-campus or off-campus services via trained peer tutors.

Basic Skills Remediation Remediation is offered in class-size groups for written language. Remediation is provided collaboratively through on-campus or off-campus services via regular education teachers.

Enrichment Programs for career planning, oral communication skills, practical computer skills, self-advocacy, and stress management are provided collaboratively through on-campus or off-campus services. Credit is offered for career planning.

Application For admittance to the program or unit, students are required to provide a psychoeducational report (4 years old or less). Upon acceptance, documentation of need for services should be sent only to the LD program or unit. *Application deadline (institutional):* 1/10. *Application deadline (LD program):* Rolling/continuous for fall and rolling/continuous for spring.

Written Policies Written policy regarding general/basic LD accommodations is available on the program Web site. Written policies regarding course substitutions, general/basic LD accommodations, and reduced course loads are available through the program or unit directly.

Embry-Riddle Aeronautical University
Disability Support Services

600 South Clyde Morris Boulevard

Daytona Beach, FL 32114-3900

http://www.erau.edu/db/studentlife/disabilitysup/index.html

Contact: Mrs. Olivia Vanessa Lloyd, Director. Phone: 386-226-7916. Fax: 386-226-6071. E-mail: lloydv@erau.edu.

Disability Support Services Approximately 120 registered undergraduate students were served during 2006–07. The program or unit includes 3 full-time staff members. Academic advisers, counselors, LD specialists, professional tutors, regular education teachers, remediation/learning specialists, and trained peer tutors are provided collaboratively through on-campus or off-campus services.

Unique Aids and Services Aids, services, or accommodations include advocates, personal coach, priority registration, weekly meeting with disability advocate.

Assistive Technology Assistive technology is located in campus labs, the DSS office, the library and includes digital textbooks/e-text, learning support software, and scanning. Technology training is provided to incoming students.

Subject-Area Tutoring Tutoring is offered one-on-one for most subjects. Tutoring is provided collaboratively through on-campus or off-campus services via trained peer tutors.

Basic Skills Remediation Remediation is offered one-on-one for computer skills, learning strategies, math, reading, social skills, study skills, and time management. Remediation is provided collaboratively through on-campus or off-campus services via regular education teachers and trained peer tutors.

Enrichment Enrichment programs are available through the program or unit for college survival skills, learning strategies, oral communication skills, reading, self-advocacy, stress management, study skills, test taking, time management, and written composition skills. Credit is offered for college survival skills and oral communication skills.

Application For admittance to the program or unit, students are required to provide a psychoeducational report (4 years old or less). It is recommended that students provide documentation of high school services. Upon application, materials documenting need for services should be sent only to the LD program or unit. Upon acceptance, documentation of need for services should be sent only to the LD program or unit. *Application deadline (institutional):* Continuous. *Application deadline (LD program):* Rolling/continuous for fall and rolling/continuous for spring.

Written Policies Written policies regarding course substitutions, general/basic LD accommodations, reduced course loads, and substitutions and waivers of admissions requirements are available on the program Web site. Written policies regarding course substitutions, general/basic LD accommodations, reduced course loads, and substitutions and waivers of admissions requirements are available through the program or unit directly.

Emory University
Office of Disability Services

1380 South Oxford Road

Atlanta, GA 30322-1100

http://www.ods.emory.edu

Contact: Jessalyn P. Smiley, Coordinator. Phone: 404-727-6016. Fax: 404-727-1126. E-mail: jessalyn.p.smiley@emory.edu. Head of LD Program: Gloria Y. Weaver, Director. Phone: 404-727-6016. Fax: 404-727-1126. E-mail: gloria.weaver@emory.edu.

Office of Disability Services Approximately 250 registered undergraduate students were served during 2006–07. The program or unit includes 2 full-time and 3 part-time staff members. Academic advisers, coaches, counselors, diagnostic specialists, LD specialists, and trained peer tutors are provided collaboratively through on-campus or off-campus services.

Assistive Technology Assistive technology is located in campus labs and includes digital textbooks/e-text and learning support software.

Subject-Area Tutoring Tutoring is offered one-on-one, in small groups, and in class-size groups for most subjects. Tutoring is provided collaboratively through on-campus or off-campus services via trained peer tutors.

Diagnostic Testing Testing for auditory processing, handwriting, intelligence, learning strategies, learning styles, math, motor skills, neuropsychological, personality, reading, social skills, spelling, spoken language, study skills, visual processing, and written language is provided collaboratively through on-campus or off-campus services.

Enrichment Programs for career planning, college survival skills, health and nutrition, learning strategies, math, practical computer skills, stress management, study skills, test taking, time management, and written composition skills are provided collaboratively through on-campus or off-campus services.

Fees *Diagnostic Testing* fee is $450 to $2000.

Application For admittance to the program or unit, students are required to provide a psychoeducational report (3 years old or less) and provide self-identification to program. Upon acceptance, documentation of need for services should be sent only to the LD program or unit. *Application deadline (institutional):* 1/15. *Application deadline (LD program):* Rolling/continuous for fall and rolling/continuous for spring.

Written Policies Written policies regarding course substitutions, general/basic LD accommodations, grade forgiveness, reduced course loads, and substitutions and waivers of graduation requirements are available on the program Web site. Written policies regarding course substitutions, general/basic LD accommodations, grade forgiveness, reduced course loads, and substitutions and waivers of graduation requirements are outlined in the school's catalog/handbook. Written policy regarding general/basic LD accommodations is available through the program or unit directly.

Eugene Lang College The New School for Liberal Arts
Student Disability Services

65 West 11th Street

New York, NY 10011-8601

http://www.newschool.edu/studentservices/disability/

Contact: Mr. Jason Luchs, Assistant Director Student Disability Services. Phone: 212-229-5626 Ext. 3135. Fax: 212-229-1090. E-mail: sds@newschool.edu.

Student Disability Services Approximately 20 registered undergraduate students were served during 2006–07. The program or unit includes 2 full-time staff members and 1 part-time staff member. Academic advisers, counselors, and other are provided collaboratively through on-campus or off-campus services.

Assistive Technology Assistive technology is located in campus labs and includes digital textbooks/e-text, learning support software, and scanning.

Enrichment Programs for career planning, college survival skills, health and nutrition, learning strategies, self-advocacy, stress management, study skills, test taking, time management, and written composition skills are provided collaboratively through on-campus or off-campus services.

Eugene Lang College The New School for Liberal Arts (continued)

Application For admittance to the program or unit, students are required to apply to the program directly, provide a psychoeducational report (3 years old or less), and provide other documentation (contact office for guidelines). Upon acceptance, documentation of need for services should be sent only to the LD program or unit. *Application deadline (institutional): 2/1. Application deadline (LD program):* Rolling/continuous for fall and rolling/continuous for spring.

Written Policies Written policy regarding general/basic LD accommodations is available on the program Web site. Written policy regarding general/basic LD accommodations is outlined in the school's catalog/handbook. Written policy regarding general/basic LD accommodations is available through the program or unit directly.

Everglades University

6151 Lake Osprey Drive

Sarasota, FL 34240

http://www.evergladesuniversity.edu/

Contact: John Hoatson. Phone: 941-907-2262. E-mail: jhoatson@evergladesuniverstiy.edu.

Academic advisers are provided collaboratively through on-campus or off-campus services.

Subject-Area Tutoring Tutoring is offered one-on-one and in small groups for all subjects. Tutoring is provided collaboratively through on-campus or off-campus services via computer-based instruction, trained peer tutors, and other.

Enrichment Programs for career planning and study skills are provided collaboratively through on-campus or off-campus services.

Application Upon application, materials documenting need for services should be sent only to admissions with institutional application materials. Upon acceptance, documentation of need for services should be sent to both admissions and the LD program or unit. *Application deadline (LD program):* Rolling/continuous for fall.

Written Policies Written policy regarding general/basic LD accommodations is outlined in the school's catalog/handbook.

Fairfield University
Academic and Disability Support Services

1073 North Benson Road

Fairfield, CT 06824-5195

http://www.fairfield.edu/x2008.html

Contact: Susan Birge, Assistant Vice President/Director of Counseling & Psychological Services. Phone: 203-254-4000 Ext. 2146. Fax: 203-254-5545. E-mail: sbirge@ mail.fairfield.edu.

Academic and Disability Support Services Approximately 70 registered undergraduate students were served during 2006–07. The program or unit includes 1 full-time and 2 part-time staff members. Graduate assistants/students, LD specialists, skill tutors,

strategy tutors, and trained peer tutors are provided through the program or unit. Academic advisers, coaches, counselors, diagnostic specialists, and trained peer tutors are provided collaboratively through on-campus or off-campus services.

Unique Aids and Services Aids, services, or accommodations include faculty training.

Assistive Technology Assistive technology is located in the DSS office, a special lab, the library and includes digital textbooks/ e-text. Technology training is provided to incoming students.

Subject-Area Tutoring Tutoring is offered one-on-one and in small groups for most subjects. Tutoring is provided through the program or unit via graduate assistants/students and trained peer tutors. Tutoring is also provided collaboratively through on-campus or off-campus services via trained peer tutors.

Basic Skills Remediation Remediation is offered one-on-one for reading, study skills, time management, and written language. Remediation is provided through the program or unit via graduate assistants/students, LD specialists, and trained peer tutors. Remediation is also provided collaboratively through on-campus or off-campus services via trained peer tutors.

Enrichment Enrichment programs are available through the program or unit for learning strategies, reading, self-advocacy, study skills, test taking, and time management. Programs for career planning, college survival skills, health and nutrition, math, reading, stress management, study skills, and written composition skills are provided collaboratively through on-campus or off-campus services.

Application For admittance to the program or unit, students are required to provide a psychoeducational report. It is recommended that students provide documentation of high school services. Upon acceptance, documentation of need for services should be sent only to the LD program or unit. *Application deadline (institutional):* 1/15. *Application deadline (LD program):* Rolling/continuous for fall.

Written Policies Written policy regarding general/basic LD accommodations is available on the program Web site. Written policy regarding general/basic LD accommodations is outlined in the school's catalog/handbook. Written policy regarding general/basic LD accommodations is available through the program or unit directly.

Farmingdale State College

2350 Broadhollow Road

Farmingdale, NY 11735

http://www.farmingdale.edu/

Contact: Ms. Malka Edelman, Director. Phone: 631-420-2411. Fax: 631-420-2163. E-mail: malka.edelman@ farmingdale.edu.

Approximately 195 registered undergraduate students were served during 2006–07. The program or unit includes 1 full-time and 2 part-time staff members. Counselors and LD specialists are provided through the program or unit. Academic advisers, counselors, LD specialists, professional tutors, skill tutors, and trained peer tutors are provided collaboratively through on-campus or off-campus services.

Orientation The program or unit offers an optional morning-long orientation for new students before classes begin and after classes begin.

Subject-Area Tutoring Tutoring is offered one-on-one and in small groups for some subjects. Tutoring is provided through the program or unit via LD specialists. Tutoring is also provided collaboratively through on-campus or off-campus services via professional tutors and trained peer tutors.

Enrichment Programs for career planning, college survival skills, health and nutrition, learning strategies, math, self-advocacy, test taking, written composition skills, and other are provided collaboratively through on-campus or off-campus services.

Application For admittance to the program or unit, students are required to provide a psychoeducational report (3 years old or less) and provide documentation of high school services. Upon acceptance, documentation of need for services should be sent only to the LD program or unit. *Application deadline (institutional):* Continuous. *Application deadline (LD program):* Rolling/continuous for fall and rolling/continuous for spring.

Written Policies Written policy regarding general/basic LD accommodations is outlined in the school's catalog/handbook. Written policies regarding course substitutions, general/basic LD accommodations, reduced course loads, and substitutions and waivers of graduation requirements are available through the program or unit directly.

Fashion Institute of Technology
FIT-ABLE

Seventh Avenue at 27th Street

New York, NY 10001-5992

http://www.fitnyc.edu/

Contact: Ms. Susan Altman, Learning Disabilities Coordinator. Phone: 212-217-8228. Fax: 212-217-3133. E-mail: susan_altman@fitnyc.edu. Head of LD Program: Ms. Elizabeth Holly Mortensen, Coordinator for Disability Services. Phone: 212-217-8900. Fax: 212-217-3133. E-mail: elizabeth_mortensen@fitnyc.edu.

FIT-ABLE Approximately 120 registered undergraduate students were served during 2006–07. The program or unit includes 1 full-time and 3 part-time staff members. Counselors, LD specialists, professional tutors, skill tutors, strategy tutors, trained peer tutors, and other are provided through the program or unit.

Orientation The program or unit offers an optional orientation for new students after classes begin and individually by special arrangement.

Unique Aids and Services Aids, services, or accommodations include career counseling and support groups.

Assistive Technology Assistive technology is located in campus labs, the DSS office, the library and includes digital textbooks/e-text, learning support software, and scanning. Technology training is provided to incoming students.

Subject-Area Tutoring Tutoring is offered one-on-one for all subjects. Tutoring is provided through the program or unit via computer-based instruction, LD specialists, professional tutors, and trained peer tutors. Tutoring is also provided collaboratively through on-campus or off-campus services via professional tutors and trained peer tutors.

Basic Skills Remediation Remediation is offered in class-size groups for learning strategies, study skills, and time management. Remediation is provided through the program or unit via LD specialists and professional tutors.

Enrichment Enrichment programs are available through the program or unit for career planning, college survival skills, self-advocacy, stress management, study skills, test taking, and time management.

Application For admittance to the program or unit, students are required to provide a psychoeducational report (3 years old or less). It is recommended that students provide documentation of high school services. Upon acceptance, documentation of need for services should be sent only to the LD program or unit. *Application deadline (institutional):* 2/1. *Application deadline (LD program):* Rolling/continuous for fall.

Written Policies Written policy regarding general/basic LD accommodations is available on the program Web site. Written policy regarding general/basic LD accommodations is outlined in the school's catalog/handbook. Written policy regarding general/basic LD accommodations is available through the program or unit directly.

Fayetteville State University
Disabled Student Services

1200 Murchison Road

Fayetteville, NC 28301-4298

http://www.uncfsu.edu/studentaffairs/CFPD/cfpdservices.htm

Contact: Mr. Fred Sapp Jr., Director of the Center for Personal Development. Phone: 910-672-1222. Fax: 910-672-1389. E-mail: fsapp@uncfsu.edu.

Disabled Student Services Approximately 40 registered undergraduate students were served during 2006–07. The program or unit includes 2 full-time staff members. Counselors and diagnostic specialists are provided through the program or unit. Academic advisers, diagnostic specialists, graduate assistants/students, LD specialists, professional tutors, regular education teachers, remediation/learning specialists, skill tutors, special education teachers, strategy tutors, and trained peer tutors are provided collaboratively through on-campus or off-campus services.

Unique Aids and Services Aids, services, or accommodations include career counseling and priority registration.

Assistive Technology Assistive technology is located in campus labs, the DSS office, the library and includes digital textbooks/e-text, learning support software, and scanning. Technology training is provided to incoming students.

Subject-Area Tutoring Tutoring is offered in small groups for all subjects. Tutoring is provided collaboratively through on-campus or off-campus services via graduate assistants/students, professional tutors, and trained peer tutors.

Diagnostic Testing Testing is provided through the program or unit for personality and study skills. Testing for auditory processing, intelligence, learning strategies, learning styles, math, motor skills, neuropsychological, reading, and visual processing is provided collaboratively through on-campus or off-campus services.

Fayetteville State University (continued)

Basic Skills Remediation Remediation is offered in small groups for learning strategies, math, reading, study skills, and time management. Remediation is provided collaboratively through on-campus or off-campus services via graduate assistants/students, professional tutors, regular education teachers, and trained peer tutors.

Enrichment Enrichment programs are available through the program or unit for college survival skills and health and nutrition. Programs for career planning, college survival skills, learning strategies, reading, stress management, study skills, test taking, and time management are provided collaboratively through on-campus or off-campus services.

Application For admittance to the program or unit, students are required to apply to the program directly and provide a psychoeducational report (5 years old or less). Upon acceptance, documentation of need for services should be sent only to the LD program or unit. *Application deadline (institutional):* 7/1. *Application deadline (LD program):* Rolling/continuous for fall and rolling/continuous for spring.

Written Policies Written policy regarding general/basic LD accommodations is available on the program Web site. Written policy regarding course substitutions is outlined in the school's catalog/handbook.

Ferrum College
Office of Academic Disability Services

PO Box 1000
Ferrum, VA 24088-9001
http://www.ferrum.edu/arc/disabilities.htm
Contact: Linda Albrecht, Coordinator of Disability Services. Phone: 540-365-4273. E-mail: lalbrecht@ferrum.edu. Head of LD Program: Nancy S. Beach, Director of Disability Services. Phone: 540-365-4262. E-mail: nbeach@ferrum.edu.

Office of Academic Disability Services Approximately 40 registered undergraduate students were served during 2006–07. The program or unit includes 1 full-time and 1 part-time staff member. LD specialists and strategy tutors are provided through the program or unit. Academic advisers, coaches, remediation/learning specialists, skill tutors, and trained peer tutors are provided collaboratively through on-campus or off-campus services.

Summer Program To help prepare for the demands of college, there is an optional 2-week summer program prior to entering the school that focuses on computing skills, life skills and/or college life adjustment, specific subject tutoring, and time management. Degree credit will be earned. The program accepts students from out-of-state.

Unique Aids and Services Aids, services, or accommodations include faculty training, advocacy and support meetings with specialist (may be arranged by student as needed).

Assistive Technology Assistive technology is located in the DSS office, a special lab and includes digital textbooks/e-text and scanning. Technology training is provided to incoming students.

Subject-Area Tutoring Tutoring is offered one-on-one, in small groups, and in class-size groups for some subjects. Tutoring is provided collaboratively through on-campus or off-campus services via computer-based instruction and trained peer tutors.

Basic Skills Remediation Remediation is offered in class-size groups for math, reading, and written language. Remediation is provided collaboratively through on-campus or off-campus services via computer-based instruction and other.

Application For admittance to the program or unit, students are required to provide a psychoeducational report. Upon acceptance, documentation of need for services should be sent only to the LD program or unit. *Application deadline (institutional):* Continuous.

Written Policies Written policy regarding general/basic LD accommodations is available on the program Web site. Written policies regarding course substitutions, general/basic LD accommodations, grade forgiveness, reduced course loads, substitutions and waivers of admissions requirements, and substitutions and waivers of graduation requirements are outlined in the school's catalog/handbook. Written policies regarding course substitutions, general/basic LD accommodations, grade forgiveness, reduced course loads, substitutions and waivers of admissions requirements, and substitutions and waivers of graduation requirements are available through the program or unit directly.

Fitchburg State College
Disability Services

160 Pearl Street
Fitchburg, MA 01420-2697
http://www.fsc.edu/disabilities

Contact: Dawn K. Stevenson, MEd, OTR/L, Director of Disability Services. Phone: 978-664-3427. Fax: 978-665-4799. E-mail: dstevenson@fsc.edu.

Disability Services Approximately 230 registered undergraduate students were served during 2006–07. The program or unit includes 2 full-time and 2 part-time staff members. Coaches, counselors, graduate assistants/students, and other are provided through the program or unit. Academic advisers, coaches, counselors, graduate assistants/students, LD specialists, skill tutors, strategy tutors, trained peer tutors, and other are provided collaboratively through on-campus or off-campus services.

Orientation The program or unit offers an optional varying length orientation for new students individually by special arrangement.

Unique Aids and Services Aids, services, or accommodations include advocates, career counseling, personal coach, priority registration, prevocational skill development.

Assistive Technology Assistive technology is located in campus labs, the DSS office, a special lab, the library, classrooms, other specialized locations by arrangement and includes digital textbooks/e-text, learning support software, scanning, and screen magnification, CCTVs, Recording for the Blind and Dyslexic players, digital tape recorders, ergonomic and alternative input devices. Technology training is provided to incoming students.

Subject-Area Tutoring Tutoring is offered one-on-one and in small groups for most subjects. Tutoring is provided through the program or unit via computer-based instruction, graduate assistants/students, and other. Tutoring is also provided collaboratively through on-campus or off-campus services via computer-based instruction, graduate assistants/students, professional tutors, trained peer tutors, and other.

Diagnostic Testing Testing is provided through the program or unit for learning strategies, learning styles, motor skills, social skills, study skills, visual processing, and other services. Testing for learning strategies, learning styles, motor skills, social skills, and study skills is provided collaboratively through on-campus or off-campus services.

Enrichment Enrichment programs are available through the program or unit for career planning, college survival skills, learning strategies, medication management, practical computer skills, self-advocacy, stress management, study skills, test taking, time management, and other. Programs for career planning, college survival skills, health and nutrition, learning strategies, math, oral communication skills, practical computer skills, reading, self-advocacy, stress management, study skills, test taking, time management, vocabulary development, and written composition skills are provided collaboratively through on-campus or off-campus services. Credit is offered for college survival skills, health and nutrition, oral communication skills, practical computer skills, reading, and written composition skills.

Student Organization Delta Alpha Pi International Honor Society and Celebrating Everyone's Differences consists of 45 members.

Application For admittance to the program or unit, students are required to apply to the program directly and provide a psychoeducational report (3 years old or less). It is recommended that students provide documentation of high school services and provide documentation on emotional, attentional, and communication disorders as detailed on Web site. Upon application, materials documenting need for services should be sent only to admissions with institutional application materials. Upon acceptance, documentation of need for services should be sent only to the LD program or unit. *Application deadline (LD program):* Rolling/continuous for fall and rolling/continuous for spring.

Written Policies Written policies regarding general/basic LD accommodations and substitutions and waivers of admissions requirements are available on the program Web site. Written policies regarding general/basic LD accommodations, grade forgiveness, reduced course loads, and substitutions and waivers of admissions requirements are outlined in the school's catalog/handbook. Written policies regarding course substitutions, general/basic LD accommodations, reduced course loads, and substitutions and waivers of admissions requirements are available through the program or unit directly.

Flagler College
Special Programs

74 King Street

PO Box 1027

St. Augustine, FL 32085-1027

http://www.flagler.edu/

Contact: Debbie Kamm-Larew, Director of Special Programs. Phone: 904-819-6460. Fax: 904-824-6017. E-mail: dkamm@flagler.edu.

Special Programs Approximately 35 registered undergraduate students were served during 2006–07. The program or unit includes 1 full-time staff member. LD specialists and strategy tutors are

provided through the program or unit. Academic advisers, counselors, professional tutors, and regular education teachers are provided collaboratively through on-campus or off-campus services.

Orientation The program or unit offers an optional orientation for new students individually by special arrangement.

Unique Aids and Services Aids, services, or accommodations include career counseling.

Assistive Technology Assistive technology is located in the DSS office, the library, open access labs and includes digital textbooks/e-text, learning support software, and scanning. Technology training is provided to incoming students.

Enrichment Enrichment programs are available through the program or unit for learning strategies, self-advocacy, study skills, and time management. Programs for career planning, college survival skills, math, reading, stress management, and written composition skills are provided collaboratively through on-campus or off-campus services.

Application For admittance to the program or unit, students are required to provide a psychoeducational report (3 years old or less). It is recommended that students provide documentation of high school services. Upon acceptance, documentation of need for services should be sent only to the LD program or unit. *Application deadline (institutional):* 3/1. *Application deadline (LD program):* Rolling/continuous for fall and rolling/continuous for spring.

Written Policies Written policies regarding course substitutions and general/basic LD accommodations are outlined in the school's catalog/handbook. Written policy regarding reduced course loads is available through the program or unit directly.

Florida Atlantic University
Office for Students with Disabilities

777 Glades Road, PO Box 3091

Boca Raton, FL 33431-0991

http://www.osd.fau.edu

Contact: Mrs. Nicole Rokos, Director. Phone: 561-297-3880. Fax: 561-297-2184. E-mail: nrokos@fau.edu.

Office for Students with Disabilities Approximately 475 registered undergraduate students were served during 2006–07. The program or unit includes 8 full-time and 3 part-time staff members. Graduate assistants/students, LD specialists, remediation/learning specialists, skill tutors, strategy tutors, trained peer tutors, and other are provided through the program or unit. Academic advisers, counselors, diagnostic specialists, professional tutors, regular education teachers, skill tutors, and trained peer tutors are provided collaboratively through on-campus or off-campus services.

Unique Aids and Services Aids, services, or accommodations include advocates, career counseling, and support groups.

Assistive Technology Assistive technology is located in the DSS office and includes learning support software, scanning, and Kurzweil 3000, Dragon Naturally Speaking. Technology training is provided to incoming students.

Subject-Area Tutoring Tutoring is offered one-on-one and in small groups for some subjects. Tutoring is provided through the program or unit via LD specialists. Tutoring is also provided collaboratively through on-campus or off-campus services via computer-based instruction, graduate assistants/students, and trained peer tutors.

Florida Atlantic University (continued)

Basic Skills Remediation Remediation is offered one-on-one for computer skills, learning strategies, study skills, time management, and standardized test preparation. Remediation is provided through the program or unit via LD specialists. Remediation is also provided collaboratively through on-campus or off-campus services via trained peer tutors.

Enrichment Enrichment programs are available through the program or unit for learning strategies, practical computer skills, reading, self-advocacy, study skills, test taking, time management, written composition skills, and other. Programs for career planning, college survival skills, health and nutrition, learning strategies, math, oral communication skills, reading, stress management, study skills, test taking, time management, vocabulary development, written composition skills, and other are provided collaboratively through on-campus or off-campus services. Credit is offered for career planning, college survival skills, health and nutrition, learning strategies, oral communication skills, practical computer skills, and study skills.

Student Organization There is a student organization consisting of 19 members.

Application For admittance to the program or unit, students are required to apply to the program directly and provide a psychoeducational report (3 years old or less). It is recommended that students provide documentation of high school services and provide a letter from transferring institution of higher education regarding accommodations received. Upon acceptance, documentation of need for services should be sent only to the LD program or unit. *Application deadline (institutional): 6/1. Application deadline (LD program):* Rolling/continuous for fall and rolling/continuous for spring.

Written Policies Written policies regarding course substitutions, general/basic LD accommodations, substitutions and waivers of admissions requirements, and substitutions and waivers of graduation requirements are available on the program Web site. Written policy regarding general/basic LD accommodations is outlined in the school's catalog/handbook. Written policies regarding course substitutions, general/basic LD accommodations, substitutions and waivers of admissions requirements, and substitutions and waivers of graduation requirements are available through the program or unit directly.

Florida College
Advising Office

119 North Glen Arven Avenue
Temple Terrace, FL 33617
http://www.floridacollege.edu/

Contact: Dr. Steve Walker, Director of Advising. Phone: 813-988-5131. Fax: 813-899-6772. E-mail: walkers@floridacollege.edu.

Advising Office Approximately 12 registered undergraduate students were served during 2006–07. The program or unit includes 2 part-time staff members. Academic advisers are provided through the program or unit.

Unique Aids and Services Aids, services, or accommodations include career counseling and weekly meetings with faculty.

Subject-Area Tutoring Tutoring is offered one-on-one and in small groups for some subjects. Tutoring is provided collaboratively through on-campus or off-campus services via computer-based instruction and trained peer tutors.

Basic Skills Remediation Remediation is offered in class-size groups for computer skills, learning strategies, math, reading, study skills, time management, and written language. Remediation is provided collaboratively through on-campus or off-campus services via computer-based instruction and regular education teachers.

Enrichment Programs for career planning, college survival skills, health and nutrition, learning strategies, math, practical computer skills, reading, study skills, test taking, time management, and written composition skills are provided collaboratively through on-campus or off-campus services. Credit is offered for health and nutrition, math, practical computer skills, reading, study skills, test taking, time management, and written composition skills.

Application For admittance to the program or unit, students are required to apply to the program directly. It is recommended that students provide a psychoeducational report (3 years old or less) and provide documentation of high school services. Upon acceptance, documentation of need for services should be sent only to admissions. *Application deadline (institutional): 8/1. Application deadline (LD program):* Rolling/continuous for fall and rolling/continuous for spring.

Written Policies Written policy regarding general/basic LD accommodations is available through the program or unit directly.

Florida Gulf Coast University
The Office of Adaptive Services

10501 FGCU Boulevard South
Fort Myers, FL 33965-6565
http://www.fgcu.edu/adaptive

Contact: Ms. Cori Bright, Director of Adaptive Services. Phone: 239-590-7956 Ext. 7956. Fax: 239-590-7975. E-mail: cbright@fgcu.edu.

The Office of Adaptive Services Approximately 278 registered undergraduate students were served during 2006–07. The program or unit includes 2 full-time and 4 part-time staff members. Diagnostic specialists, graduate assistants/students, LD specialists, professional tutors, remediation/learning specialists, skill tutors, and strategy tutors are provided through the program or unit. Academic advisers, coaches, counselors, graduate assistants/students, regular education teachers, special education teachers, teacher trainees, and trained peer tutors are provided collaboratively through on-campus or off-campus services.

Unique Aids and Services Aids, services, or accommodations include career counseling, faculty training, priority registration, and support groups.

Assistive Technology Assistive technology is located in campus labs, the DSS office and includes learning support software and scanning.

Subject-Area Tutoring Tutoring is offered one-on-one for all subjects. Tutoring is provided through the program or unit via graduate assistants/students, LD specialists, professional tutors, and trained peer tutors. Tutoring is also provided collaboratively through on-campus or off-campus services via computer-based instruction.

Diagnostic Testing Testing is provided through the program or unit for handwriting, learning strategies, learning styles, and study skills. Testing for auditory processing, intelligence, math, motor skills, neuropsychological, personality, reading, social skills, spelling, spoken language, visual processing, and written language is provided collaboratively through on-campus or off-campus services.

Basic Skills Remediation Remediation is offered one-on-one for computer skills, learning strategies, math, reading, spelling, study skills, time management, and written language. Remediation is provided through the program or unit via graduate assistants/students, LD specialists, and professional tutors. Remediation is also provided collaboratively through on-campus or off-campus services via computer-based instruction, regular education teachers, special education teachers, teacher trainees, and trained peer tutors.

Enrichment Enrichment programs are available through the program or unit for learning strategies, reading, self-advocacy, stress management, study skills, test taking, time management, vocabulary development, and written composition skills. Programs for career planning, college survival skills, health and nutrition, math, medication management, oral communication skills, and practical computer skills are provided collaboratively through on-campus or off-campus services.

Fees *Diagnostic Testing* fee is $300 to $3000.

Application For admittance to the program or unit, students are required to apply to the program directly and provide a psychoeducational report (3 years old or less). It is recommended that students provide documentation of high school services. Upon application, materials documenting need for services should be sent to both admissions and the LD program or unit. Upon acceptance, documentation of need for services should be sent only to the LD program or unit. *Application deadline (institutional):* 8/1. *Application deadline (LD program):* Rolling/continuous for fall and rolling/continuous for spring.

Written Policies Written policies regarding general/basic LD accommodations and substitutions and waivers of admissions requirements are available on the program Web site. Written policy regarding general/basic LD accommodations is outlined in the school's catalog/handbook. Written policies regarding course substitutions, general/basic LD accommodations, grade forgiveness, reduced course loads, substitutions and waivers of admissions requirements, and substitutions and waivers of graduation requirements are available through the program or unit directly.

Florida Institute of Technology
Academic Support Services

150 West University Boulevard
Melbourne, FL 32901-6975
http://www.fit.edu/asc
Contact: Mr. Rodney Bowers, Director of Academic Support Services. Phone: 321-674-7110. Fax: 321-674-8072. E-mail: rbowers@fit.edu.

Academic Support Services Approximately 41 registered undergraduate students were served during 2006–07. The program or unit includes 4 full-time and 4 part-time staff members. Professional tutors, remediation/learning specialists, and skill tutors are provided through the program or unit. Academic advisers, counselors, diagnostic specialists, graduate assistants/students, and professional tutors are provided collaboratively through on-campus or off-campus services.

Subject-Area Tutoring Tutoring is offered one-on-one and in small groups for most subjects. Tutoring is provided through the program or unit via graduate assistants/students, professional tutors, and trained peer tutors.

Diagnostic Testing Testing for auditory processing, intelligence, learning strategies, learning styles, motor skills, neuropsychological, personality, social skills, visual processing, and written language is provided collaboratively through on-campus or off-campus services.

Basic Skills Remediation Remediation is offered in class-size groups for learning strategies, math, study skills, time management, and written language. Remediation is provided collaboratively through on-campus or off-campus services via regular education teachers.

Enrichment Programs for career planning, health and nutrition, math, stress management, test taking, time management, and written composition skills are provided collaboratively through on-campus or off-campus services. Credit is offered for college survival skills, learning strategies, practical computer skills, study skills, time management, and written composition skills.

Fees *Diagnostic Testing* fee is $200.

Application For admittance to the program or unit, students are required to provide a psychoeducational report (3 years old or less). It is recommended that students provide documentation of high school services. Upon acceptance, documentation of need for services should be sent only to the LD program or unit. *Application deadline (institutional):* Continuous. *Application deadline (LD program):* Rolling/continuous for fall and rolling/continuous for spring.

Written Policies Written policy regarding general/basic LD accommodations is available on the program Web site. Written policy regarding general/basic LD accommodations is available through the program or unit directly.

Florida International University
Disability Resource Center

11200 S.W. 8th Street
Miami, FL 33199
http://drc.fiu.edu/
Contact: Mrs. Amanda Niguidula, Interim Director of The Disability Resource Center. Phone: 305-348-3532. Fax: 305-348-3852. E-mail: xniguidu@fiu.edu.

Disability Resource Center Approximately 142 registered undergraduate students were served during 2006–07. The program or unit includes 5 full-time staff members. Counselors, diagnostic specialists, and professional tutors are provided through the program or unit.

Unique Aids and Services Aids, services, or accommodations include career counseling and priority registration.

Assistive Technology Assistive technology is located in campus labs, the DSS office, the library and includes digital textbooks/e-text and learning support software. Technology training is provided to incoming students.

Subject-Area Tutoring Tutoring is offered in small groups for some subjects. Tutoring is provided collaboratively through on-campus or off-campus services via computer-based instruction and professional tutors.

Florida International University (continued)

Diagnostic Testing Testing for auditory processing, intelligence, math, motor skills, neuropsychological, personality, reading, spelling, and visual processing is provided collaboratively through on-campus or off-campus services.

Basic Skills Remediation Remediation is offered in small groups for math and reading. Remediation is provided collaboratively through on-campus or off-campus services via computer-based instruction and professional tutors.

Enrichment Enrichment programs are available through the program or unit for career planning and self-advocacy. Programs for career planning, health and nutrition, math, practical computer skills, reading, stress management, study skills, test taking, time management, and written composition skills are provided collaboratively through on-campus or off-campus services. Credit is offered for practical computer skills.

Student Organization Step-Up consists of 15 members.

Fees *Diagnostic Testing* fee is $250.

Application For admittance to the program or unit, students are required to provide a psychoeducational report (10 years old or less). Upon application, materials documenting need for services should be sent only to the LD program or unit. Upon acceptance, documentation of need for services should be sent only to the LD program or unit. *Application deadline (institutional):* Continuous. *Application deadline (LD program):* Rolling/continuous for fall and rolling/continuous for spring.

Written Policies Written policies regarding course substitutions, general/basic LD accommodations, grade forgiveness, reduced course loads, substitutions and waivers of admissions requirements, and substitutions and waivers of graduation requirements are available on the program Web site.

Fontbonne University
The Kinkel Center for Academic Resources

6800 Wydown Boulevard
St. Louis, MO 63105-3098
http://www.fontbonne.edu/campusdepartments/thekinkelcenter.htm

Contact: Dr. Jane Daily Snyder, Director of Academic Resources. Phone: 314-719-3627. Fax: 314-719-3614. E-mail: jsnyder@fontbonne.edu.

The Kinkel Center for Academic Resources Approximately 56 registered undergraduate students were served during 2006–07. The program or unit includes 4 full-time and 11 part-time staff members. Counselors, professional tutors, skill tutors, strategy tutors, and trained peer tutors are provided collaboratively through on-campus or off-campus services.

Unique Aids and Services Aids, services, or accommodations include career counseling and faculty training.

Assistive Technology Assistive technology is located in a special lab and includes scanning. Technology training is provided to incoming students.

Subject-Area Tutoring Tutoring is offered one-on-one and in small groups for all subjects. Tutoring is provided collaboratively through on-campus or off-campus services via professional tutors and trained peer tutors.

Basic Skills Remediation Remediation is offered one-on-one, in small groups, and in class-size groups for computer skills, learning strategies, math, reading, spoken language, study skills, time management, and written language. Remediation is provided collaboratively through on-campus or off-campus services via professional tutors and trained peer tutors.

Enrichment Programs for career planning, college survival skills, health and nutrition, learning strategies, math, oral communication skills, practical computer skills, reading, stress management, study skills, test taking, time management, and written composition skills are provided collaboratively through on-campus or off-campus services. Credit is offered for health and nutrition, oral communication skills, practical computer skills, and reading.

Application For admittance to the program or unit, students are required to apply to the program directly, provide a psychoeducational report (3 years old or less), and provide documentation of high school services. Upon acceptance, documentation of need for services should be sent only to the LD program or unit. *Application deadline (institutional):* 8/1. *Application deadline (LD program):* Rolling/continuous for fall and rolling/continuous for spring.

Written Policies Written policy regarding general/basic LD accommodations is available on the program Web site. Written policy regarding general/basic LD accommodations is outlined in the school's catalog/handbook. Written policy regarding general/basic LD accommodations is available through the program or unit directly.

Fort Hays State University
Disability Student Services

600 Park Street
Hays, KS 67601-4099
http://www.fhsu.edu/disability

Contact: Ms. Carol Solko-Olliff, Director of Services for Students with Disabilities. Phone: 785-628-4276. Fax: 785-628-4113. E-mail: csolko@fhsu.edu.

Disability Student Services Approximately 30 registered undergraduate students were served during 2006–07. The program or unit includes 3 full-time staff members and 1 part-time staff member. Academic advisers, counselors, diagnostic specialists, graduate assistants/students, regular education teachers, strategy tutors, and trained peer tutors are provided collaboratively through on-campus or off-campus services.

Unique Aids and Services Aids, services, or accommodations include advocates, career counseling, notes, test-taking accommodations.

Assistive Technology Assistive technology is located in campus labs, the DSS office, a special lab, the library and includes digital textbooks/e-text, learning support software, and scanning.

Subject-Area Tutoring Tutoring is offered one-on-one for most subjects. Tutoring is provided collaboratively through on-campus or off-campus services via computer-based instruction, graduate assistants/students, and trained peer tutors.

Diagnostic Testing Testing for auditory processing, intelligence, learning strategies, learning styles, math, neuropsychological, personality, reading, spoken language, study skills, and written language is provided collaboratively through on-campus or off-campus services.

Enrichment Programs for career planning, college survival skills, health and nutrition, learning strategies, math, oral communication skills, practical computer skills, stress management, study skills, test taking, time management, vocabulary development, and written composition skills are provided collaboratively through on-campus or off-campus services. Credit is offered for career planning, health and nutrition, learning strategies, math, oral communication skills, practical computer skills, stress management, study skills, test taking, time management, vocabulary development, and written composition skills.

Student Organization Creating Access for Today's Students (CATS) consists of 1 member.

Application It is recommended that students provide documentation of high school services. Upon application, materials documenting need for services should be sent only to the LD program or unit. Upon acceptance, documentation of need for services should be sent only to the LD program or unit. *Application deadline (institutional):* Continuous. *Application deadline (LD program):* Rolling/continuous for fall and rolling/continuous for spring.

Written Policies Written policy regarding general/basic LD accommodations is available on the program Web site. Written policies regarding general/basic LD accommodations and reduced course loads are available through the program or unit directly.

and written composition skills. Programs for career planning, health and nutrition, learning strategies, math, stress management, and written composition skills are provided collaboratively through on-campus or off-campus services.

Application For admittance to the program or unit, students are required to apply to the program directly and provide a psychoeducational report (3 years old or less). It is recommended that students provide documentation of high school services. Upon application, materials documenting need for services should be sent only to admissions with institutional application materials. Upon acceptance, documentation of need for services should be sent only to the LD program or unit. *Application deadline (institutional):* 5/15. *Application deadline (LD program):* Rolling/continuous for fall and rolling/continuous for spring.

Written Policies Written policies regarding course substitutions, general/basic LD accommodations, substitutions and waivers of admissions requirements, and substitutions and waivers of graduation requirements are available on the program Web site. Written policies regarding general/basic LD accommodations and substitutions and waivers of admissions requirements are outlined in the school's catalog/handbook. Written policies regarding course substitutions, general/basic LD accommodations, reduced course loads, substitutions and waivers of admissions requirements, and substitutions and waivers of graduation requirements are available through the program or unit directly.

Framingham State College
Academic Support Services

100 State Street, PO Box 9101

Framingham, MA 01701-9101

http://www.framingham.edu/CASA/academicsupport.htm

Contact: LaDonna Bridges, Director, Academic Support. Phone: 508-626-4906. Fax: 508-626-4913. E-mail: lbridges@frc.mass.edu.

Academic Support Services Approximately 300 registered undergraduate students were served during 2006–07. The program or unit includes 1 full-time staff member. Academic advisers, professional tutors, skill tutors, and trained peer tutors are provided collaboratively through on-campus or off-campus services.

Orientation The program or unit offers an optional 2-hour orientation for new students individually by special arrangement.

Unique Aids and Services Aids, services, or accommodations include faculty training.

Assistive Technology Assistive technology is located in Center for Academic Support and Advising and includes digital textbooks/e-text, learning support software, and scanning.

Subject-Area Tutoring Tutoring is offered one-on-one and in small groups for most subjects. Tutoring is provided collaboratively through on-campus or off-campus services via professional tutors and trained peer tutors.

Basic Skills Remediation Remediation is offered one-on-one and in small groups for learning strategies, reading, study skills, time management, and written language. Remediation is provided through the program or unit. Remediation is also provided collaboratively through on-campus or off-campus services.

Enrichment Enrichment programs are available through the program or unit for college survival skills, learning strategies, math, reading, self-advocacy, study skills, test taking, time management,

Franciscan University of Steubenville

1235 University Boulevard

Steubenville, OH 43952-1763

http://www.franciscan.edu/

Contact: Mrs. Rose D. Kline, Director of Student Academic Services. Phone: 740-284-5358. Fax: 740-284-7095. E-mail: rkline@franciscan.edu.

Approximately 45 registered undergraduate students were served during 2006–07. The program or unit includes 2 full-time staff members and 1 part-time staff member. Academic advisers, coaches, counselors, graduate assistants/students, LD specialists, remediation/learning specialists, skill tutors, special education teachers, strategy tutors, trained peer tutors, and other are provided through the program or unit. Academic advisers, counselors, regular education teachers, remediation/learning specialists, skill tutors, and trained peer tutors are provided collaboratively through on-campus or off-campus services.

Orientation The program or unit offers an optional 2-hour orientation for new students after classes begin and individually by special arrangement.

Unique Aids and Services Aids, services, or accommodations include advocates, faculty training, and priority registration.

Assistive Technology Assistive technology is located in the DSS office and includes digital textbooks/e-text and scanning.

Subject-Area Tutoring Tutoring is offered one-on-one and in small groups for most subjects. Tutoring is provided through the program or unit via LD specialists, professional tutors, and trained peer tutors. Tutoring is also provided collaboratively through on-campus or off-campus services via graduate assistants/students and trained peer tutors.

Franciscan University of Steubenville (continued)

Basic Skills Remediation Remediation is offered one-on-one and in small groups for learning strategies, math, reading, study skills, time management, and written language. Remediation is provided through the program or unit via computer-based instruction, LD specialists, professional tutors, and trained peer tutors. Remediation is also provided collaboratively through on-campus or off-campus services via professional tutors and trained peer tutors.

Enrichment Enrichment programs are available through the program or unit for college survival skills, learning strategies, reading, self-advocacy, stress management, study skills, test taking, time management, and written composition skills. Programs for career planning, college survival skills, learning strategies, stress management, study skills, test taking, time management, and written composition skills are provided collaboratively through on-campus or off-campus services.

Application For admittance to the program or unit, students are required to provide a psychoeducational report (3 years old or less). Upon application, materials documenting need for services should be sent only to the LD program or unit. Upon acceptance, documentation of need for services should be sent only to the LD program or unit. *Application deadline (institutional):* Continuous. *Application deadline (LD program):* Rolling/continuous for fall and rolling/continuous for spring.

Written Policies Written policy regarding general/basic LD accommodations is available on the program Web site. Written policies regarding general/basic LD accommodations and reduced course loads are outlined in the school's catalog/handbook. Written policies regarding general/basic LD accommodations and reduced course loads are available through the program or unit directly.

Franklin College
Academic Resource Center

101 Branigin Boulevard

Franklin, IN 46131-2623

http://www.franklincollege.edu/ARCweb/ADA.htm

Contact: Beth Tidball, Director of Academic Resources. Phone: 317-738-8286. Fax: 317-738-8284. E-mail: btidball@ franklincollege.edu.

Academic Resource Center Approximately 15 registered undergraduate students were served during 2006–07. The program or unit includes 1 part-time staff member. Academic advisers, coaches, counselors, regular education teachers, and trained peer tutors are provided collaboratively through on-campus or off-campus services.

Subject-Area Tutoring Tutoring is offered one-on-one and in small groups for some subjects. Tutoring is provided collaboratively through on-campus or off-campus services via trained peer tutors.

Basic Skills Remediation Remediation is offered one-on-one, in small groups, and in class-size groups for learning strategies, math, reading, study skills, time management, and written language. Remediation is provided collaboratively through on-campus or off-campus services via regular education teachers and trained peer tutors.

Enrichment Programs for career planning, college survival skills, health and nutrition, learning strategies, math, stress management, study skills, test taking, time management, and written composition

skills are provided collaboratively through on-campus or off-campus services. Credit is offered for career planning, college survival skills, health and nutrition, learning strategies, math, and study skills.

Application For admittance to the program or unit, students are required to provide a psychoeducational report (3 years old or less). It is recommended that students provide documentation of high school services. Upon acceptance, documentation of need for services should be sent only to the LD program or unit. *Application deadline (institutional):* Continuous. *Application deadline (LD program):* Rolling/continuous for fall and rolling/continuous for spring.

Written Policies Written policies regarding course substitutions and substitutions and waivers of graduation requirements are outlined in the school's catalog/handbook. Written policy regarding general/basic LD accommodations is available through the program or unit directly.

Franklin Pierce University
Academic Services

20 College Road, PO Box 60

Rindge, NH 03461-0060

http://www.fpc.edu

Contact: Patricia Moore, Coordinator. Phone: 603-899-4100 Ext. 4044. Fax: 603-899-4395. E-mail: moorep@fpc.edu.

Academic Services Approximately 50 registered undergraduate students were served during 2006–07. The program or unit includes 4 full-time staff members and 1 part-time staff member. LD specialists, remediation/learning specialists, skill tutors, and trained peer tutors are provided through the program or unit.

Unique Aids and Services Aids, services, or accommodations include weekly meetings with faculty.

Subject-Area Tutoring Tutoring is offered in small groups for most subjects. Tutoring is provided through the program or unit via trained peer tutors.

Basic Skills Remediation Remediation is offered in small groups for learning strategies, math, reading, study skills, time management, and written language. Remediation is provided through the program or unit via LD specialists and trained peer tutors.

Application For admittance to the program or unit, students are required to provide a psychoeducational report (3 years old or less). It is recommended that students provide documentation of high school services. Upon application, materials documenting need for services should be sent to both admissions and the LD program or unit. Upon acceptance, documentation of need for services should be sent only to the LD program or unit. *Application deadline (institutional):* Continuous. *Application deadline (LD program):* Rolling/continuous for fall and rolling/continuous for spring.

Written Policies Written policies regarding general/basic LD accommodations and reduced course loads are available on the program Web site. Written policies regarding general/basic LD accommodations and reduced course loads are outlined in the school's catalog/handbook.

Franklin University
Office of Disability Services

201 South Grant Avenue

Columbus, OH 43215-5399

http://www.franklin.edu

Contact: Ms. Carla H. Waugh, Disability Services Coordinator. Phone: 614-947-6753. Fax: 614-255-9518. E-mail: waughc@franklin.edu.

Office of Disability Services Approximately 35 registered undergraduate students were served during 2006–07. The program or unit includes 1 full-time staff member. Academic advisers, coaches, regular education teachers, trained peer tutors, and other are provided collaboratively through on-campus or off-campus services.

Assistive Technology Assistive technology is located in the DSS office and includes digital textbooks/e-text.

Subject-Area Tutoring Tutoring is offered one-on-one and in small groups for some subjects. Tutoring is provided collaboratively through on-campus or off-campus services via computer-based instruction and trained peer tutors.

Basic Skills Remediation Remediation is offered one-on-one and in small groups for computer skills, learning strategies, math, study skills, and written language. Remediation is provided collaboratively through on-campus or off-campus services via trained peer tutors.

Enrichment Programs for learning strategies, math, reading, study skills, and written composition skills are provided collaboratively through on-campus or off-campus services. Credit is offered for learning strategies.

Application For admittance to the program or unit, students are required to provide a psychoeducational report (3 years old or less). It is recommended that students provide documentation of high school services. Upon application, materials documenting need for services should be sent only to the LD program or unit. Upon acceptance, documentation of need for services should be sent only to the LD program or unit. *Application deadline (LD program):* Rolling/continuous for fall and rolling/continuous for spring.

Written Policies Written policies regarding general/basic LD accommodations, grade forgiveness, and reduced course loads are available on the program Web site. Written policies regarding general/basic LD accommodations, grade forgiveness, and reduced course loads are outlined in the school's catalog/handbook.

Franklin W. Olin College of Engineering
Office of Student Life

Olin Way

Needham, MA 02492-1200

http://www.olin.edu/

Contact: Ms. Alison Black, Assistant Dean of Student Life. Phone: 781-292-2327. Fax: 781-292-2325. E-mail: alison.black@olin.edu.

Office of Student Life Approximately 9 registered undergraduate students were served during 2006–07. The program or unit includes 1 full-time staff member. Academic advisers and counselors are provided through the program or unit. Academic advisers, counselors, and diagnostic specialists are provided collaboratively through on-campus or off-campus services.

Unique Aids and Services Aids, services, or accommodations include career counseling, faculty training, parent workshops, personal coach, and weekly meetings with faculty.

Assistive Technology Assistive technology is located in the Information Technology Department and includes digital textbooks/e-text. Technology training is provided to incoming students.

Subject-Area Tutoring Tutoring is offered one-on-one for most subjects. Tutoring is provided through the program or unit via trained peer tutors.

Diagnostic Testing Testing for auditory processing, handwriting, intelligence, learning strategies, learning styles, math, motor skills, neuropsychological, personality, reading, social skills, spelling, spoken language, study skills, visual processing, and written language is provided collaboratively through on-campus or off-campus services.

Basic Skills Remediation Remediation is offered one-on-one for first-year courses. Remediation is provided collaboratively through on-campus or off-campus services via regular education teachers.

Enrichment Enrichment programs are available through the program or unit for college survival skills, learning strategies, and time management. Programs for career planning, health and nutrition, math, medication management, oral communication skills, practical computer skills, reading, self-advocacy, stress management, study skills, and test taking are provided collaboratively through on-campus or off-campus services.

Fees *Diagnostic Testing* fee is applicable.

Application For admittance to the program or unit, students are required to provide documentation of high school services. It is recommended that students provide a psychoeducational report (3 years old or less). Upon application, materials documenting need for services should be sent only to the LD program or unit. Upon acceptance, documentation of need for services should be sent only to the LD program or unit. *Application deadline (institutional):* 1/6. *Application deadline (LD program):* 7/31 for fall. 11/30 for spring.

Written Policies Written policies regarding course substitutions, general/basic LD accommodations, reduced course loads, substitutions and waivers of admissions requirements, and substitutions and waivers of graduation requirements are available on the program Web site. Written policies regarding course substitutions, general/basic LD accommodations, reduced course loads, and substitutions and waivers of graduation requirements are outlined in the school's catalog/handbook.

Freed-Hardeman University
Office of Disability Services

158 East Main Street

Henderson, TN 38340-2399

http://www.fhu.edu/

Contact: Mrs. Nadine McNeal, Director of Disability Services. Phone: 731-989-6644. Fax: 731-989-6679. E-mail: nmcneal@fhu.edu.

Office of Disability Services Approximately 50 registered undergraduate students were served during 2006–07. The program or unit includes 1 full-time and 1 part-time staff member. Coaches, coun-

Freed-Hardeman University (continued)

selors, graduate assistants/students, professional tutors, regular education teachers, skill tutors, strategy tutors, and trained peer tutors are provided through the program or unit. Academic advisers, graduate assistants/students, professional tutors, regular education teachers, special education teachers, and trained peer tutors are provided collaboratively through on-campus or off-campus services.

Unique Aids and Services Aids, services, or accommodations include advocates, faculty training, parent workshops, and personal coach.

Assistive Technology Assistive technology is located in campus labs, library labs and includes digital textbooks/e-text. Technology training is provided to incoming students.

Subject-Area Tutoring Tutoring is offered one-on-one, in small groups, and in class-size groups for all subjects. Tutoring is provided through the program or unit via trained peer tutors and other. Tutoring is also provided collaboratively through on-campus or off-campus services via graduate assistants/students and trained peer tutors.

Enrichment Enrichment programs are available through the program or unit for learning strategies, medication management, self-advocacy, stress management, study skills, and time management. Program for career planning is provided collaboratively through on-campus or off-campus services.

Application For admittance to the program or unit, students are required to provide a psychoeducational report. It is recommended that students apply to the program directly and provide documentation of high school services. Upon application, materials documenting need for services should be sent to both admissions and the LD program or unit. Upon acceptance, documentation of need for services should be sent only to the LD program or unit. *Application deadline (institutional):* Continuous. *Application deadline (LD program):* Rolling/continuous for fall and rolling/continuous for spring.

Written Policies Written policies regarding general/basic LD accommodations and substitutions and waivers of admissions requirements are available on the program Web site. Written policies regarding general/basic LD accommodations and substitutions and waivers of admissions requirements are outlined in the school's catalog/handbook. Written policies regarding general/basic LD accommodations and grade forgiveness are available through the program or unit directly.

Fresno Pacific University
Services for Students with Disabilities

1717 South Chestnut Avenue

Fresno, CA 93702-4709

http://www.fresno.edu/studentlife/office/disability_services/

Contact: Mr. Don R. Sparks, Assistant Dean of Student Development Programs. Phone: 559-453-3696. Fax: 559-453-7147. E-mail: drsparks@fresno.edu.

Services for Students with Disabilities Approximately 30 registered undergraduate students were served during 2006–07. The program or unit includes 1 part-time staff member. Services are provided through the program or unit. Academic advisers, trained peer tutors, and other are provided collaboratively through on-campus or off-campus services.

Summer Program To help prepare for the demands of college, there is an optional 3-week summer program prior to entering the school available to high school graduates that focuses on study skills, test-taking skills, and time management. The program accepts students from out-of-state.

Unique Aids and Services Aids, services, or accommodations include advocates and career counseling.

Assistive Technology Assistive technology is located in the DSS office, a special lab and includes digital textbooks/e-text.

Subject-Area Tutoring Tutoring is offered one-on-one and in small groups for most subjects. Tutoring is provided collaboratively through on-campus or off-campus services via trained peer tutors.

Fees *Summer Program* fee is $400.

Application For admittance to the program or unit, students are required to apply to the program directly. It is recommended that students provide a psychoeducational report (3 years old or less) and provide documentation of high school services. Upon acceptance, documentation of need for services should be sent only to the LD program or unit. *Application deadline (institutional):* Continuous. *Application deadline (LD program):* Rolling/continuous for fall and rolling/continuous for spring.

Written Policies Written policy regarding general/basic LD accommodations is available on the program Web site. Written policy regarding general/basic LD accommodations is outlined in the school's catalog/handbook.

Friends University
Cross Cultural Programs and Services

2100 West University Street

Wichita, KS 67213

http://www.friends.edu/

Contact: Ms. Jaclyn Hugg, Cross Cultural Programs & Services. Phone: 316-295-5675. Fax: 316-295-5675. E-mail: hugg@friends.edu.

Cross Cultural Programs and Services Approximately 20 registered undergraduate students were served during 2006–07. The program or unit includes 1 full-time staff member. Academic advisers, counselors, professional tutors, regular education teachers, and trained peer tutors are provided collaboratively through on-campus or off-campus services.

Unique Aids and Services Aids, services, or accommodations include extended time on tests and assignments.

Assistive Technology Assistive technology is located in the DSS office and includes books on CD.

Subject-Area Tutoring Tutoring is offered one-on-one and in small groups for most subjects. Tutoring is provided collaboratively through on-campus or off-campus services via professional tutors and trained peer tutors.

Enrichment Programs for career planning, health and nutrition, learning strategies, math, and written composition skills are provided collaboratively through on-campus or off-campus services. Credit is offered for learning strategies.

Student Organization Multicultural Student Assembly.

Application For admittance to the program or unit, students are required to apply to the program directly. It is recommended that students provide a psychoeducational report (3 years old or less) and provide documentation of high school services. Upon application, materials documenting need for services should be sent only to the LD program or unit. Upon acceptance, documentation of need for services should be sent only to the LD program or unit. *Application deadline (LD program):* Rolling/continuous for fall and rolling/continuous for spring.

Written Policies Written policy regarding general/basic LD accommodations is available on the program Web site. Written policy regarding general/basic LD accommodations is outlined in the school's catalog/handbook. Written policy regarding general/basic LD accommodations is available through the program or unit directly.

Furman University
Disability Services

3300 Poinsett Highway

Greenville, SC 29613

http://www.furman.edu/disability/index.htm

Contact: Gina Parris, Coordinator of Disability Services. Phone: 864-294-2322. Fax: 864-294-3044. E-mail: gina.parris@furman.edu.

Disability Services Approximately 95 registered undergraduate students were served during 2006–07. The program or unit includes 1 full-time and 1 part-time staff member. Services are provided through the program or unit. Academic advisers, coaches, counselors, diagnostic specialists, regular education teachers, and trained peer tutors are provided collaboratively through on-campus or off-campus services.

Unique Aids and Services Aids, services, or accommodations include priority registration.

Assistive Technology Assistive technology is located in the DSS office, the library and includes digital textbooks/e-text and scanning.

Subject-Area Tutoring Tutoring is offered one-on-one for most subjects. Tutoring is provided collaboratively through on-campus or off-campus services via trained peer tutors.

Application For admittance to the program or unit, students are required to provide a psychoeducational report (3 years old or less). It is recommended that students provide documentation of high school services. Upon application, materials documenting need for services should be sent only to the LD program or unit. Upon acceptance, documentation of need for services should be sent only to the LD program or unit. *Application deadline (institutional):* 1/15. *Application deadline (LD program):* Rolling/continuous for fall and rolling/continuous for spring.

Written Policies Written policies regarding course substitutions, general/basic LD accommodations, and substitutions and waivers of graduation requirements are available on the program Web site. Written policies regarding course substitutions and substitutions and waivers of graduation requirements are outlined in the school's catalog/handbook. Written policies regarding course substitutions, general/basic LD accommodations, reduced course loads, and substitutions and waivers of graduation requirements are available through the program or unit directly.

Gallaudet University
Office for Students with Disabilities

800 Florida Avenue, NE

Washington, DC 20002-3625

http://depts.gallaudet.edu/OSWD/index.htm

Contact: Dr. Patricia Marie Tesar, Director, Office for Students with Disabilities. Phone: 202-651-5652 Ext. 3127. Fax: 202-651-5887. E-mail: patricia.tesar@gallaudet.edu.

Office for Students with Disabilities Approximately 75 registered undergraduate students were served during 2006–07. The program or unit includes 6 full-time staff members. Academic advisers, coaches, counselors, diagnostic specialists, graduate assistants/students, LD specialists, professional tutors, regular education teachers, remediation/learning specialists, skill tutors, special education teachers, strategy tutors, teacher trainees, trained peer tutors, and other are provided through the program or unit.

Orientation The program or unit offers an optional 3-day orientation for new students before classes begin, during summer prior to enrollment, during registration, after classes begin, and individually by special arrangement.

Summer Program To help prepare for the demands of college, there is an optional 3-week (specific to math) summer program prior to entering the school that focuses on computing skills and specific subject tutoring. The program accepts students from out-of-state.

Unique Aids and Services Aids, services, or accommodations include advocates, career counseling, faculty training, parent workshops, priority registration, support groups, and weekly meetings with faculty.

Assistive Technology Assistive technology is located in campus labs, the DSS office and includes learning support software and scanning. Technology training is provided to incoming students.

Subject-Area Tutoring Tutoring is offered one-on-one for most subjects. Tutoring is provided collaboratively through on-campus or off-campus services via trained peer tutors.

Diagnostic Testing Testing for auditory processing, handwriting, intelligence, learning strategies, learning styles, math, motor skills, neuropsychological, personality, reading, social skills, spelling, spoken language, study skills, visual processing, written language, and other services is provided collaboratively through on-campus or off-campus services.

Basic Skills Remediation Remediation is offered one-on-one for computer skills, learning strategies, math, reading, social skills, study skills, time management, and written language. Remediation is provided through the program or unit via graduate assistants/students and trained peer tutors. Remediation is also provided collaboratively through on-campus or off-campus services via special education teachers and trained peer tutors.

Enrichment Programs for career planning, college survival skills, math, reading, self-advocacy, stress management, study skills, test taking, time management, and written composition skills are provided collaboratively through on-campus or off-campus services.

Fees *Summer Program* fee is $1500. *Diagnostic Testing* fee is $550.

Application For admittance to the program or unit, students are required to apply to the program directly, provide a psychoeducational report (3 years old or less), and provide psychoeducational adult testing results that meet Gallaudet University documentation

Gallaudet University (continued)

standards. It is recommended that students provide documentation of high school services. Upon application, materials documenting need for services should be sent only to the LD program or unit. Upon acceptance, documentation of need for services should be sent only to the LD program or unit. *Application deadline (LD program):* Rolling/continuous for fall and rolling/continuous for spring.

Written Policies Written policies regarding general/basic LD accommodations and reduced course loads are available on the program Web site. Written policies regarding general/basic LD accommodations and reduced course loads are outlined in the school's catalog/handbook. Written policies regarding course substitutions, general/basic LD accommodations, reduced course loads, substitutions and waivers of admissions requirements, and substitutions and waivers of graduation requirements are available through the program or unit directly.

Gardner-Webb University
Noel Program for Students with Disabilities

PO Box 997

Boiling Springs, NC 28017

http://noel.gardner-webb.edu/

Contact: Ms. Cheryl Jenks Potter, Director of Noel Program for Students with Disabilities. Phone: 704-406-4270 Ext. 4271. Fax: 704-406-3524. E-mail: disabilityservices@ gardner-webb.edu.

Noel Program for Students with Disabilities Approximately 101 registered undergraduate students were served during 2006–07. The program or unit includes 9 full-time staff members and 1 part-time staff member. Academic advisers, coaches, counselors, graduate assistants/students, LD specialists, remediation/learning specialists, skill tutors, strategy tutors, and trained peer tutors are provided through the program or unit. Academic advisers, counselors, diagnostic specialists, LD specialists, remediation/learning specialists, skill tutors, and trained peer tutors are provided collaboratively through on-campus or off-campus services.
Orientation The program or unit offers an optional 2-hour orientation for new students before classes begin.
Unique Aids and Services Aids, services, or accommodations include career counseling, priority registration, support groups, weekly meetings with faculty, readers, note-takers.
Assistive Technology Assistive technology is located in campus labs, the DSS office, the library and includes digital textbooks/e-text, learning support software, scanning, and books on tape, books scanned on CD. Technology training is provided to incoming students.
Subject-Area Tutoring Tutoring is offered one-on-one, in small groups, and in class-size groups for all subjects. Tutoring is provided collaboratively through on-campus or off-campus services via graduate assistants/students and trained peer tutors.
Basic Skills Remediation Remediation is offered in class-size groups for math, reading, and written language. Remediation is provided collaboratively through on-campus or off-campus services via regular education teachers.

Enrichment Enrichment programs are available through the program or unit for career planning, college survival skills, learning strategies, self-advocacy, stress management, study skills, test taking, and time management. Programs for career planning, college survival skills, math, reading, self-advocacy, stress management, test taking, time management, and written composition skills are provided collaboratively through on-campus or off-campus services.
Application For admittance to the program or unit, students are required to provide a psychoeducational report (3 years old or less). Upon application, materials documenting need for services should be sent only to the LD program or unit. Upon acceptance, documentation of need for services should be sent only to the LD program or unit. *Application deadline (institutional):* Continuous. *Application deadline (LD program):* Rolling/continuous for fall and rolling/continuous for spring.
Written Policies Written policies regarding course substitutions, general/basic LD accommodations, reduced course loads, and substitutions and waivers of admissions requirements are available on the program Web site. Written policy regarding general/basic LD accommodations is outlined in the school's catalog/handbook. Written policies regarding course substitutions, general/basic LD accommodations, reduced course loads, and substitutions and waivers of admissions requirements are available through the program or unit directly.

Geneva College
Academic Counseling Center and Educational Support Services (ACCESS)

3200 College Avenue

Beaver Falls, PA 15010-3599

http://www.geneva.edu/page/access

Contact: Mrs. Nancy I. Smith, Director of Academic Counseling Center & Educational Support Services (ACCESS). Phone: 724-847-5566. Fax: 724-847-6991. E-mail: nismith@geneva.edu.

Academic Counseling Center and Educational Support Services (ACCESS) Approximately 76 registered undergraduate students were served during 2006–07. The program or unit includes 1 full-time and 1 part-time staff member. LD specialists, remediation/learning specialists, and trained peer tutors are provided through the program or unit. LD specialists, regular education teachers, remediation/learning specialists, and trained peer tutors are provided collaboratively through on-campus or off-campus services.
Orientation The program or unit offers an optional orientation for new students before classes begin, during summer prior to enrollment, and individually by special arrangement.
Unique Aids and Services Aids, services, or accommodations include career counseling, personal coach, and priority registration.
Assistive Technology Assistive technology is located in campus labs, the DSS office and includes learning support software. Technology training is provided to incoming students.
Subject-Area Tutoring Tutoring is offered one-on-one and in small groups for most subjects. Tutoring is provided through the program or unit via computer-based instruction, graduate assistants/ students, and trained peer tutors.

Diagnostic Testing Testing is provided through the program or unit for learning strategies, learning styles, and study skills. Testing for auditory processing, intelligence, learning styles, math, motor skills, neuropsychological, reading, social skills, spelling, and visual processing is provided collaboratively through on-campus or off-campus services.

Basic Skills Remediation Remediation is offered in class-size groups for math, reading, and written language. Remediation is provided through the program or unit via regular education teachers. Remediation is also provided collaboratively through on-campus or off-campus services via regular education teachers.

Enrichment Enrichment programs are available through the program or unit for learning strategies, reading, self-advocacy, study skills, test taking, and time management. Programs for career planning, college survival skills, math, medication management, practical computer skills, reading, stress management, and written composition skills are provided collaboratively through on-campus or off-campus services. Credit is offered for practical computer skills.

Student Organization Delta Alpha Pi International Honor Society consists of 10 members.

Application For admittance to the program or unit, students are required to provide a psychoeducational report (3 years old or less). It is recommended that students provide documentation of high school services. Upon application, materials documenting need for services should be sent only to the LD program or unit. Upon acceptance, documentation of need for services should be sent only to the LD program or unit. *Application deadline (institutional):* Continuous. *Application deadline (LD program):* Rolling/continuous for fall and rolling/continuous for spring.

Written Policies Written policy regarding general/basic LD accommodations is available on the program Web site. Written policy regarding general/basic LD accommodations is outlined in the school's catalog/handbook. Written policy regarding general/basic LD accommodations is available through the program or unit directly.

Georgetown College
Student Wellness Center Disability Services

400 East College Street
Georgetown, KY 40324-1696
http://spider.georgetowncollege.edu/stuwellness/disability.htm

Contact: Ms. Lora M. Helton, Administrative Assistant. Phone: 502-863-8201. Fax: 502-868-7717. E-mail: lora_helton@georgetowncollege.edu. Head of LD Program: Dr. Edward O. Marshall, Director. Phone: 502-863-7074. Fax: 502-868-7717. E-mail: edward_marshall@georgetowncollege.edu.

Student Wellness Center Disability Services Approximately 50 registered undergraduate students were served during 2006–07. The program or unit includes 1 full-time and 1 part-time staff member. Academic advisers, counselors, graduate assistants/students, regular education teachers, and trained peer tutors are provided collaboratively through on-campus or off-campus services.

Unique Aids and Services Aids, services, or accommodations include advocates.

Assistive Technology Assistive technology is located in campus labs, a special lab.

Basic Skills Remediation Remediation is offered in class-size groups for study skills, time management, and written language. Remediation is provided collaboratively through on-campus or off-campus services via regular education teachers and trained peer tutors.

Enrichment Programs for career planning, college survival skills, health and nutrition, learning strategies, math, oral communication skills, practical computer skills, stress management, study skills, time management, vocabulary development, and written composition skills are provided collaboratively through on-campus or off-campus services.

Student Organization The Achievers consists of 8 members.

Application For admittance to the program or unit, students are required to provide a psychoeducational report (3 years old or less). It is recommended that students provide documentation of high school services. Upon acceptance, documentation of need for services should be sent only to the LD program or unit. *Application deadline (institutional):* 8/1. *Application deadline (LD program):* Rolling/continuous for fall and rolling/continuous for spring.

Written Policies Written policy regarding general/basic LD accommodations is available on the program Web site. Written policy regarding general/basic LD accommodations is outlined in the school's catalog/handbook. Written policy regarding general/basic LD accommodations is available through the program or unit directly.

The George Washington University
Disability Support Services

2121 Eye Street, NW
Washington, DC 20052
http://gwired.gwu.edu/dss

Contact: Ms. Christy Willis, Director. Phone: 202-994-8250. Fax: 202-994-7610. E-mail: cwillis@gwu.edu. Head of LD Program: Ms. Susan McMenamin, Associate Director. Phone: 202-994-8250. Fax: 202-994-7610. E-mail: susanmcm@gwu.edu.

Disability Support Services Approximately 353 registered undergraduate students were served during 2006–07. The program or unit includes 6 full-time and 4 part-time staff members. LD specialists and strategy tutors are provided through the program or unit. Academic advisers, counselors, graduate assistants/students, professional tutors, skill tutors, and trained peer tutors are provided collaboratively through on-campus or off-campus services.

Orientation The program or unit offers a mandatory 2-hour orientation for new students after classes begin.

Unique Aids and Services Aids, services, or accommodations include advocates, career counseling, faculty training, priority registration, support groups, and weekly meetings with faculty.

Assistive Technology Assistive technology is located in a special lab and includes digital textbooks/e-text, learning support software, and scanning. Technology training is provided to incoming students.

Subject-Area Tutoring Tutoring is offered one-on-one for all subjects. Tutoring is provided collaboratively through on-campus or off-campus services via computer-based instruction, graduate assistants/students, professional tutors, and trained peer tutors.

The George Washington University (continued)

Enrichment Enrichment programs are available through the program or unit for career planning, college survival skills, learning strategies, oral communication skills, reading, self-advocacy, stress management, study skills, test taking, time management, and written composition skills. Programs for career planning, college survival skills, health and nutrition, learning strategies, math, practical computer skills, stress management, study skills, test taking, time management, and written composition skills are provided collaboratively through on-campus or off-campus services.

Application For admittance to the program or unit, students are required to provide a psychoeducational report (3 years old or less). It is recommended that students provide documentation of high school services. Upon acceptance, documentation of need for services should be sent only to the LD program or unit. *Application deadline (institutional):* 1/15. *Application deadline (LD program):* Rolling/continuous for fall and rolling/continuous for spring.

Written Policies Written policy regarding general/basic LD accommodations is available on the program Web site. Written policy regarding reduced course loads is outlined in the school's catalog/handbook. Written policies regarding course substitutions and general/basic LD accommodations are available through the program or unit directly.

Georgia College & State University
Office of Disability Services

Hancock Street

Milledgeville, GA 31061

http://www.gcsu.edu

Contact: Mr. Robert M. Chambers, Assistant Director of Equity for Disability Services. Phone: 478-445-5931. Fax: 478-445-1287. E-mail: mike.chambers@gcsu.edu.

Office of Disability Services Approximately 125 registered undergraduate students were served during 2006–07. The program or unit includes 1 full-time staff member. Services are provided through the program or unit. Academic advisers, counselors, graduate assistants/students, LD specialists, professional tutors, regular education teachers, remediation/learning specialists, and special education teachers are provided collaboratively through on-campus or off-campus services.

Unique Aids and Services Aids, services, or accommodations include advocates, faculty training, and priority registration.

Assistive Technology Assistive technology is located in campus labs, the DSS office and includes digital textbooks/e-text and learning support software. Technology training is provided to incoming students.

Subject-Area Tutoring Tutoring is offered one-on-one and in small groups for some subjects. Tutoring is provided collaboratively through on-campus or off-campus services via graduate assistants/students and trained peer tutors.

Diagnostic Testing Testing for auditory processing, handwriting, intelligence, learning strategies, learning styles, math, motor skills, neuropsychological, personality, reading, social skills, spelling, spoken language, study skills, visual processing, written language, and other services is provided collaboratively through on-campus or off-campus services.

Basic Skills Remediation Remediation is offered one-on-one, in small groups, and in class-size groups for math, reading, and written language. Remediation is provided through the program or unit. Remediation is also provided collaboratively through on-campus or off-campus services via special education teachers.

Enrichment Programs for career planning, college survival skills, health and nutrition, math, practical computer skills, reading, stress management, and written composition skills are provided collaboratively through on-campus or off-campus services. Credit is offered for math and practical computer skills.

Fees *Diagnostic Testing* fee is $500.

Application For admittance to the program or unit, students are required to apply to the program directly. It is recommended that students provide a psychoeducational report (3 years old or less) and provide documentation of high school services. Upon application, materials documenting need for services should be sent only to the LD program or unit. *Application deadline (institutional):* 4/1. *Application deadline (LD program):* Rolling/continuous for fall and rolling/continuous for spring.

Written Policies Written policies regarding course substitutions, general/basic LD accommodations, reduced course loads, substitutions and waivers of admissions requirements, and substitutions and waivers of graduation requirements are available on the program Web site.

Glenville State College

200 High Street

Glenville, WV 26351-1200

http://www.glenville.edu/

Contact: Dr. Kathy Butler, Vice President for Academic Affairs. Phone: 304-462-4100. Fax: 304-462-8619. E-mail: kathy.butler@glenville.edu.

Approximately 21 registered undergraduate students were served during 2006–07. The program or unit includes 2 full-time staff members. Academic advisers, counselors, and trained peer tutors are provided through the program or unit.

Unique Aids and Services Aids, services, or accommodations include advocates and career counseling.

Subject-Area Tutoring Tutoring is offered one-on-one and in small groups for all subjects. Tutoring is provided collaboratively through on-campus or off-campus services via trained peer tutors.

Application For admittance to the program or unit, students are required to apply to the program directly, provide a psychoeducational report (3 years old or less), provide documentation of high school services, and provide psychological report or medical report with original signatures. Upon application, materials documenting need for services should be sent only to the LD program or unit. Upon acceptance, documentation of need for services should be sent only to the LD program or unit. *Application deadline (institutional):* Continuous. *Application deadline (LD program):* Rolling/continuous for fall and rolling/continuous for spring.

Written Policies Written policy regarding general/basic LD accommodations is available on the program Web site. Written policy regarding general/basic LD accommodations is outlined in the school's catalog/handbook.

Gonzaga University
Disability Resources, Education, and Access Management

502 East Boone Avenue

Spokane, WA 99258

http://www.gonzaga.edu/Campus-Resources/
Offices-and-Services-A-Z/
Disability-Resources-Education-and-Access-Management/
default.asp

Contact: Angela M. Merritt, Assistant Director of Disability Resources, Education, and Access Management. Phone: 509-323-4134. Fax: 509-323-5523. E-mail: merritt@gonzaga.edu. Head of LD Program: Kathryne M. Shearer, Director, Disability Resources, Education, and Access Management. Phone: 509-323-4134. Fax: 509-323-5523. E-mail: shearer@gonzaga.edu.

Disability Resources, Education, and Access Management Approximately 70 registered undergraduate students were served during 2006–07. The program or unit includes 4 full-time staff members. Graduate assistants/students are provided through the program or unit. Academic advisers, counselors, diagnostic specialists, skill tutors, and strategy tutors are provided collaboratively through on-campus or off-campus services.

Orientation The program or unit offers a mandatory 2-hour orientation for new students individually by special arrangement.

Unique Aids and Services Aids, services, or accommodations include advocates, career counseling, faculty training, and priority registration.

Assistive Technology Assistive technology is located in the DSS office and includes digital textbooks/e-text, learning support software, scanning, and speech-to-text software. Technology training is provided to incoming students.

Enrichment Enrichment programs are available through the program or unit for self-advocacy. Programs for career planning, college survival skills, health and nutrition, learning strategies, medication management, stress management, study skills, test taking, time management, and written composition skills are provided collaboratively through on-campus or off-campus services. Credit is offered for written composition skills.

Application For admittance to the program or unit, students are required to provide a psychoeducational report. It is recommended that students provide documentation of high school services. Upon application, materials documenting need for services should be sent only to the LD program or unit. Upon acceptance, documentation of need for services should be sent only to the LD program or unit. *Application deadline (institutional):* 2/1. *Application deadline (LD program):* Rolling/continuous for fall and rolling/continuous for spring.

Written Policies Written policy regarding general/basic LD accommodations is available on the program Web site. Written policy regarding general/basic LD accommodations is outlined in the school's catalog/handbook. Written policies regarding course substitutions, general/basic LD accommodations, reduced course loads, and substitutions and waivers of graduation requirements are available through the program or unit directly.

Gordon College
Academic Support Center

255 Grapevine Road

Wenham, MA 01984-1899

http://www.gordon.edu/

Contact: Ann Seavey, Director, Academic Support Center. Phone: 978-927-2300 Ext. 4746. Fax: 978-867-4678. E-mail: ann.seavey@gordon.edu. Head of LD Program: Ann Seavey, Director, Academic Support Center. Fax: 978-867-4648.

Academic Support Center Approximately 100 registered undergraduate students were served during 2006–07. The program or unit includes 2 full-time and 3 part-time staff members. Academic advisers, coaches, counselors, LD specialists, professional tutors, remediation/learning specialists, skill tutors, strategy tutors, and trained peer tutors are provided through the program or unit. Academic advisers, coaches, counselors, diagnostic specialists, professional tutors, skill tutors, and strategy tutors are provided collaboratively through on-campus or off-campus services.

Orientation The program or unit offers an optional 1-hour orientation for new students individually by special arrangement.

Unique Aids and Services Aids, services, or accommodations include advocates, faculty training, personal coach, priority registration, support groups, weekly meetings with faculty, regular meetings with tutors and/or staff.

Assistive Technology Assistive technology is located in a special lab and includes digital textbooks/e-text, learning support software, and scanning. Technology training is provided to incoming students.

Subject-Area Tutoring Tutoring is offered one-on-one, in small groups, and in class-size groups for most subjects. Tutoring is provided through the program or unit via LD specialists, professional tutors, and trained peer tutors.

Enrichment Enrichment programs are available through the program or unit for college survival skills, learning strategies, math, self-advocacy, stress management, study skills, test taking, time management, and written composition skills. Programs for career planning and college survival skills are provided collaboratively through on-campus or off-campus services.

Application Upon application, materials documenting need for services should be sent to both admissions and the LD program or unit. Upon acceptance, documentation of need for services should be sent only to the LD program or unit. *Application deadline (institutional):* Continuous. *Application deadline (LD program):* Rolling/continuous for fall and rolling/continuous for spring.

Written Policies Written policy regarding general/basic LD accommodations is available on the program Web site. Written policy regarding general/basic LD accommodations is outlined in the school's catalog/handbook.

Goshen College
Academic Support Center

1700 South Main Street

Goshen, IN 46526-4794

http://www.goshen.edu/studentlife/asc.php

Goshen College (continued)

Contact: Mrs. Lois Martin, Director. Phone: 574-535-7576. Fax: 574-535-1589. E-mail: lmartin@goshen.edu.

Academic Support Center Approximately 27 registered undergraduate students were served during 2006–07. The program or unit includes 1 full-time and 43 part-time staff members. Remediation/learning specialists and trained peer tutors are provided through the program or unit. Diagnostic specialists are provided collaboratively through on-campus or off-campus services.

Assistive Technology Assistive technology is located in campus labs, the library and includes scanning and FM noise filtration system. Technology training is provided to incoming students.

Subject-Area Tutoring Tutoring is offered one-on-one and in small groups for most subjects. Tutoring is provided through the program or unit via trained peer tutors.

Enrichment Enrichment programs are available through the program or unit for college survival skills, learning strategies, reading, self-advocacy, stress management, study skills, test taking, time management, and written composition skills. Programs for career planning, health and nutrition, medication management, and stress management are provided collaboratively through on-campus or off-campus services.

Application For admittance to the program or unit, students are required to apply to the program directly and provide a psychoeducational report (3 years old or less). It is recommended that students provide documentation of high school services. Upon acceptance, documentation of need for services should be sent only to the LD program or unit. *Application deadline (institutional):* 8/15.

Written Policies Written policy regarding general/basic LD accommodations is available through the program or unit directly.

Grace College
The Learning Center

200 Seminary Drive

Winona Lake, IN 46590-1294

http://www.grace.edu/

Contact: Mrs. Peggy S. Underwood, Director. Phone: 574-372-5100 Ext. 6422. E-mail: underwps@grace.edu.

The Learning Center Approximately 28 registered undergraduate students were served during 2006–07. The program or unit includes 2 full-time staff members and 1 part-time staff member. Skill tutors, strategy tutors, trained peer tutors, and other are provided through the program or unit. Academic advisers, coaches, regular education teachers, and special education teachers are provided collaboratively through on-campus or off-campus services.

Unique Aids and Services Aids, services, or accommodations include career counseling, faculty training, and personal coach.

Assistive Technology Assistive technology is located in the Learning Center and includes learning support software, scanning, and Kurzweil, Intelligent Tutor.

Subject-Area Tutoring Tutoring is offered one-on-one and in small groups for most subjects. Tutoring is provided through the program or unit via trained peer tutors.

Diagnostic Testing Testing is provided through the program or unit.

Basic Skills Remediation Remediation is offered one-on-one and in class-size groups for auditory processing, computer skills, learning strategies, math, reading, spelling, study skills, time management, visual processing, written language, and others. Remediation is provided through the program or unit via trained peer tutors. Remediation is also provided collaboratively through on-campus or off-campus services via regular education teachers.

Enrichment Enrichment programs are available through the program or unit for college survival skills, learning strategies, self-advocacy, study skills, test taking, and time management. Program for career planning is provided collaboratively through on-campus or off-campus services.

Application For admittance to the program or unit, students are required to provide a psychoeducational report (5 years old or less) and provide documentation of high school services. Upon application, materials documenting need for services should be sent only to admissions with institutional application materials. Upon acceptance, documentation of need for services should be sent only to the LD program or unit. *Application deadline (institutional):* 8/1. *Application deadline (LD program):* Rolling/continuous for fall and rolling/continuous for spring.

Written Policies Written policies regarding general/basic LD accommodations and grade forgiveness are outlined in the school's catalog/handbook. Written policy regarding general/basic LD accommodations is available through the program or unit directly.

Green Mountain College
Jose M. Calhoun Learning Center

One College Circle

Poultney, VT 05764-1199

http://www.greenmtn.edu/

Contact: Ms. Raina L. Robins, Director of Academic Support Services. Phone: 802-287-8287. Fax: 802-287-8288. E-mail: robinsr@greenmtn.edu.

Jose M. Calhoun Learning Center Approximately 80 registered undergraduate students were served during 2006–07. The program or unit includes 3 full-time staff members and 1 part-time staff member. Remediation/learning specialists and trained peer tutors are provided through the program or unit.

Subject-Area Tutoring Tutoring is offered one-on-one and in small groups for most subjects. Tutoring is provided through the program or unit via trained peer tutors.

Enrichment Enrichment programs are available through the program or unit for college survival skills, learning strategies, math, practical computer skills, reading, self-advocacy, stress management, study skills, test taking, time management, and written composition skills. Programs for career planning, health and nutrition, medication management, practical computer skills, stress management, and written composition skills are provided collaboratively through on-campus or off-campus services.

Application For admittance to the program or unit, students are required to provide a psychoeducational report (3 years old or less). It is recommended that students apply to the program directly and provide documentation of high school services. Upon application, materials documenting need for services should be sent only to the LD program or unit. Upon acceptance, documentation of need for services should be sent only to the LD program or unit. *Application deadline (institutional):* Continuous. *Application deadline (LD program):* Rolling/continuous for fall and rolling/continuous for spring.

Written Policies Written policy regarding general/basic LD accommodations is available on the program Web site. Written policy regarding general/basic LD accommodations is outlined in the school's catalog/handbook. Written policy regarding general/basic LD accommodations is available through the program or unit directly.

Greensboro College
Office of Disability Services

815 West Market Street

Greensboro, NC 27401-1875

http://www.gborocollege.edu/academics_new/disability.php

Contact: Ms. Julie Yindra, Learning Disabilities Specialist. Phone: 336-272-7102 Ext. 591. Fax: 336-271-6634. E-mail: jyindra@gborocollege.edu.

Office of Disability Services Approximately 170 registered undergraduate students were served during 2006–07. The program or unit includes 1 full-time and 1 part-time staff member. Academic advisers, counselors, diagnostic specialists, LD specialists, remediation/learning specialists, and strategy tutors are provided through the program or unit. Academic advisers, coaches, professional tutors, regular education teachers, remediation/learning specialists, skill tutors, and trained peer tutors are provided collaboratively through on-campus or off-campus services.

Orientation The program or unit offers an optional orientation for new students before classes begin, during summer prior to enrollment, during registration, and individually by special arrangement.

Unique Aids and Services Aids, services, or accommodations include advocates, career counseling, faculty training, and weekly meetings with faculty.

Assistive Technology Assistive technology is located in a special lab and includes scanning and voice-to-text. Technology training is provided to incoming students.

Subject-Area Tutoring Tutoring is offered one-on-one for most subjects. Tutoring is provided through the program or unit via computer-based instruction and LD specialists. Tutoring is also provided collaboratively through on-campus or off-campus services via computer-based instruction, graduate assistants/students, professional tutors, and trained peer tutors.

Diagnostic Testing Testing is provided through the program or unit for learning strategies, learning styles, and study skills. Testing for auditory processing, handwriting, intelligence, math, motor skills, neuropsychological, personality, reading, spoken language, visual processing, and written language is provided collaboratively through on-campus or off-campus services.

Basic Skills Remediation Remediation is offered one-on-one for learning strategies, math, reading, study skills, time management, written language, and self-advocacy skills. Remediation is provided through the program or unit via computer-based instruction and LD specialists. Remediation is also provided collaboratively through on-campus or off-campus services via professional tutors.

Enrichment Enrichment programs are available through the program or unit for college survival skills, learning strategies, medication management, reading, self-advocacy, stress management, study

skills, test taking, and time management. Programs for career planning, health and nutrition, math, and written composition skills are provided collaboratively through on-campus or off-campus services. Credit is offered for college survival skills.

Fees *Diagnostic Testing* fee is applicable.

Application For admittance to the program or unit, students are required to provide a psychoeducational report (3 years old or less) and provide additional documentation based on the nature and scope of the disability. It is recommended that students provide documentation of high school services. Upon application, materials documenting need for services should be sent only to the LD program or unit. Upon acceptance, documentation of need for services should be sent only to the LD program or unit. *Application deadline (LD program):* Rolling/continuous for fall and rolling/continuous for spring.

Written Policies Written policies regarding course substitutions, general/basic LD accommodations, and substitutions and waivers of graduation requirements are outlined in the school's catalog/handbook. Written policies regarding course substitutions, general/basic LD accommodations, and substitutions and waivers of graduation requirements are available through the program or unit directly.

Grinnell College
Academic Advising Office

1121 Park Street

Grinnell, IA 50112-1690

http://www.grinnell.edu/offices/studentaffairs/acadadvising/disabilityservices/

Contact: Ms. Joyce M. Stern, Dean for Student Academic Support & Advising. Phone: 641-269-3702. Fax: 641-269-3710. E-mail: sternjm@grinnell.edu.

Academic Advising Office Approximately 38 registered undergraduate students were served during 2006–07. The program or unit includes 2 full-time staff members. Academic advisers, counselors, diagnostic specialists, professional tutors, skill tutors, strategy tutors, trained peer tutors, and other are provided collaboratively through on-campus or off-campus services.

Orientation The program or unit offers an optional 1-hour orientation for new students before classes begin and during new student orientation.

Assistive Technology Assistive technology is located in the student's personal computer as needed and includes digital textbooks/e-text. Technology training is provided to incoming students.

Subject-Area Tutoring Tutoring is offered one-on-one, in small groups, and in class-size groups for all subjects. Tutoring is provided collaboratively through on-campus or off-campus services via graduate assistants/students, professional tutors, and trained peer tutors.

Diagnostic Testing Testing for reading is provided collaboratively through on-campus or off-campus services.

Basic Skills Remediation Remediation is offered one-on-one and in small groups for math, reading, study skills, time management, and written language. Remediation is provided collaboratively through on-campus or off-campus services via professional tutors.

Grinnell College (continued)

Enrichment Programs for career planning, learning strategies, math, reading, stress management, study skills, test taking, time management, vocabulary development, and written composition skills are provided collaboratively through on-campus or off-campus services.

Application For admittance to the program or unit, students are required to provide a psychoeducational report. It is recommended that students provide documentation of high school services. Upon application, materials documenting need for services should be sent only to the LD program or unit. Upon acceptance, documentation of need for services should be sent only to the LD program or unit. *Application deadline (institutional):* 1/20. *Application deadline (LD program):* Rolling/continuous for fall and rolling/continuous for spring.

Written Policies Written policy regarding general/basic LD accommodations is available on the program Web site. Written policy regarding general/basic LD accommodations is outlined in the school's catalog/handbook.

Gustavus Adolphus College
Disability Services

800 West College Avenue
St. Peter, MN 56082-1498
http://www.gustavus.edu
Contact: Ms. Laurie L. Bickett, Disability Services Coordinator. Phone: 507-933-6286. Fax: 507-933-6207. E-mail: lbickett@gustavus.edu.

Disability Services Approximately 29 registered undergraduate students were served during 2006–07. The program or unit includes 1 part-time staff member. LD specialists are provided through the program or unit. Academic advisers, coaches, counselors, and trained peer tutors are provided collaboratively through on-campus or off-campus services.

Unique Aids and Services Aids, services, or accommodations include advocates and priority registration.

Assistive Technology Assistive technology is located in the library and includes digital textbooks/e-text, learning support software, and scanning.

Subject-Area Tutoring Tutoring is offered one-on-one and in small groups for most subjects. Tutoring is provided through the program or unit via LD specialists. Tutoring is also provided collaboratively through on-campus or off-campus services via trained peer tutors.

Basic Skills Remediation Remediation is available for auditory processing, learning strategies, reading, study skills, time management, visual processing, written language, and others.

Enrichment Enrichment programs are available through the program or unit for learning strategies, medication management, reading, self-advocacy, stress management, study skills, test taking, time management, vocabulary development, and written composition skills. Programs for career planning, college survival skills, health and nutrition, learning strategies, math, medication management, oral communication skills, practical computer skills, reading, self-advocacy, stress management, study skills, test taking, time management, vocabulary development, and written composition skills are provided collaboratively through on-campus or off-campus services.

Application For admittance to the program or unit, students are required to provide a psychoeducational report (3 years old or less). It is recommended that students provide documentation of high school services. Upon application, materials documenting need for services should be sent only to the LD program or unit. Upon acceptance, documentation of need for services should be sent only to the LD program or unit. *Application deadline (institutional):* 4/1. *Application deadline (LD program):* Rolling/continuous for fall and rolling/continuous for spring.

Written Policies Written policies regarding course substitutions, general/basic LD accommodations, substitutions and waivers of admissions requirements, and substitutions and waivers of graduation requirements are available on the program Web site. Written policies regarding substitutions and waivers of admissions requirements and substitutions and waivers of graduation requirements are outlined in the school's catalog/handbook. Written policies regarding course substitutions, general/basic LD accommodations, reduced course loads, substitutions and waivers of admissions requirements, and substitutions and waivers of graduation requirements are available through the program or unit directly.

Hamilton College

198 College Hill Road
Clinton, NY 13323-1296
http://www.hamilton.edu/
Contact: Mr. Allen Harrison Jr., Associate Dean of Students for Diversity and Accessibility. Phone: 315-859-4021. Fax: 315-859-4077. E-mail: aharriso@hamilton.edu.

Approximately 80 registered undergraduate students were served during 2006–07. The program or unit includes 1 part-time staff member. Academic advisers, coaches, counselors, diagnostic specialists, skill tutors, trained peer tutors, and other are provided collaboratively through on-campus or off-campus services.

Subject-Area Tutoring Tutoring is offered one-on-one and in small groups for most subjects. Tutoring is provided collaboratively through on-campus or off-campus services via trained peer tutors and other.

Application For admittance to the program or unit, students are required to provide a psychoeducational report (3 years old or less). Upon acceptance, documentation of need for services should be sent to both admissions and the LD program or unit. *Application deadline (institutional):* 1/1. *Application deadline (LD program):* Rolling/continuous for fall and rolling/continuous for spring.

Written Policies Written policy regarding general/basic LD accommodations is available on the program Web site. Written policy regarding general/basic LD accommodations is outlined in the school's catalog/handbook.

Hamline University
Disabilities Services

1536 Hewitt Avenue

St. Paul, MN 55104-1284

http://www.hamline.edu/hamline_info/offices_services/
student_relations/studentaffairs/disabilities_services/
disability_services.html

Contact: Deb Holtz JD, Director of Disability Services.
Phone: 651-523-2521. Fax: 651-523-2403. E-mail:
dholtz02@gw.hamline.edu.

Disabilities Services Approximately 80 registered undergraduate students were served during 2006–07. The program or unit includes 1 full-time and 1 part-time staff member. Counselors, LD specialists, remediation/learning specialists, and strategy tutors are provided through the program or unit. Academic advisers, counselors, regular education teachers, skill tutors, and strategy tutors are provided collaboratively through on-campus or off-campus services.

Unique Aids and Services Aids, services, or accommodations include priority registration.

Assistive Technology Assistive technology is located in the DSS office and includes digital textbooks/e-text and scanning.

Subject-Area Tutoring Tutoring is offered one-on-one for most subjects. Tutoring is provided collaboratively through on-campus or off-campus services via graduate assistants/students and trained peer tutors.

Basic Skills Remediation Remediation is offered in class-size groups for learning strategies, reading, spoken language, study skills, time management, and written language. Remediation is provided collaboratively through on-campus or off-campus services via regular education teachers.

Enrichment Programs for career planning, health and nutrition, and written composition skills are provided collaboratively through on-campus or off-campus services.

Application It is recommended that students provide a psychoeducational report (4 years old or less) and provide documentation of high school services. Upon application, materials documenting need for services should be sent only to the LD program or unit. Upon acceptance, documentation of need for services should be sent only to the LD program or unit. *Application deadline (institutional):* Continuous. *Application deadline (LD program):* Rolling/continuous for fall and rolling/continuous for spring.

Written Policies Written policy regarding general/basic LD accommodations is available on the program Web site. Written policies regarding course substitutions, general/basic LD accommodations, grade forgiveness, reduced course loads, substitutions and waivers of admissions requirements, and substitutions and waivers of graduation requirements are available through the program or unit directly.

Hampden-Sydney College
Office of Academic Success

PO Box 667

Hampden-Sydney, VA 23943

http://www.hsc.edu/academics/success/

Contact: Mrs. Elizabeth McCormack Ford, Associate Dean for Academic Support. Phone: 434-223-6286. Fax: 434-223-6347. E-mail: eford@hsc.edu.

Office of Academic Success Approximately 100 registered undergraduate students were served during 2006–07. The program or unit includes 1 full-time and 1 part-time staff member. Diagnostic specialists are provided through the program or unit. Academic advisers, counselors, and trained peer tutors are provided collaboratively through on-campus or off-campus services.

Subject-Area Tutoring Tutoring is offered one-on-one and in small groups for most subjects. Tutoring is provided through the program or unit via professional tutors and trained peer tutors. Tutoring is also provided collaboratively through on-campus or off-campus services via trained peer tutors.

Enrichment Enrichment programs are available through the program or unit for college survival skills, learning strategies, stress management, study skills, test taking, and time management. Programs for career planning, college survival skills, health and nutrition, learning strategies, oral communication skills, and stress management are provided collaboratively through on-campus or off-campus services. Credit is offered for oral communication skills.

Application For admittance to the program or unit, students are required to provide a psychoeducational report (3 years old or less). It is recommended that students provide documentation of high school services. Upon acceptance, documentation of need for services should be sent only to the LD program or unit. *Application deadline (institutional):* 3/1. *Application deadline (LD program):* Rolling/continuous for fall and rolling/continuous for spring.

Written Policies Written policies regarding course substitutions, general/basic LD accommodations, reduced course loads, and substitutions and waivers of graduation requirements are available on the program Web site. Written policies regarding course substitutions, general/basic LD accommodations, reduced course loads, and substitutions and waivers of graduation requirements are outlined in the school's catalog/handbook. Written policies regarding course substitutions, general/basic LD accommodations, reduced course loads, and substitutions and waivers of graduation requirements are available through the program or unit directly.

Hampshire College
Center for Academic Support and Advising (CASA)

893 West Street

Amherst, MA 01002

http://www.hampshire.edu/cms/index.php?id=3369

Contact: Mr. Joel Dansky, Disabilities Services Coordinator. Phone: 413-559-5423. Fax: 413-559-6098. E-mail: jdansky@hampshire.edu.

Center for Academic Support and Advising (CASA) Approximately 80 registered undergraduate students were served during 2006–07. The program or unit includes 1 part-time staff member. LD specialists, skill tutors, and strategy tutors are provided through the program or unit. Academic advisers, counselors, LD specialists, skill tutors, strategy tutors, and trained peer tutors are provided collaboratively through on-campus or off-campus services.

Hampshire College (continued)

Orientation The program or unit offers an optional orientation for new students individually by special arrangement.

Unique Aids and Services Aids, services, or accommodations include advocates, career counseling.

Assistive Technology Assistive technology is located in a special lab, the campus network and includes digital textbooks/e-text, scanning, and voice recognition software, graphic organizer. Technology training is provided to incoming students.

Basic Skills Remediation Remediation is offered one-on-one for learning strategies, math, study skills, time management, and written language. Remediation is provided through the program or unit via LD specialists. Remediation is also provided collaboratively through on-campus or off-campus services via LD specialists and regular education teachers.

Enrichment Enrichment programs are available through the program or unit for college survival skills, oral communication skills, reading, self-advocacy, stress management, study skills, test taking, and time management. Programs for career planning, college survival skills, health and nutrition, learning strategies, math, medication management, oral communication skills, practical computer skills, reading, stress management, study skills, test taking, time management, and written composition skills are provided collaboratively through on-campus or off-campus services.

Application For admittance to the program or unit, students are required to provide a psychoeducational report (3 years old or less) and provide Request for Accommodations(available through Center for Academic Support & Advising. It is recommended that students provide documentation of high school services. Upon acceptance, documentation of need for services should be sent only to the LD program or unit. *Application deadline (institutional): 1/15. Application deadline (LD program):* Rolling/continuous for fall and rolling/continuous for spring.

Written Policies Written policy regarding general/basic LD accommodations is available on the program Web site. Written policy regarding general/basic LD accommodations is outlined in the school's catalog/handbook. Written policies regarding general/basic LD accommodations and reduced course loads are available through the program or unit directly.

Harding University
Student Support Services

915 E. Market Avenue

Searcy, AR 72149-0001

http://www.harding.edu/

Contact: Mrs. Teresa J. McLeod, Disabilities Director. Phone: 501-279-4019. Fax: 501-279-5702. E-mail: tmcleod@harding.edu.

Student Support Services Approximately 150 registered undergraduate students were served during 2006–07. The program or unit includes 6 full-time and 16 part-time staff members. Academic advisers, counselors, graduate assistants/students, LD specialists, and trained peer tutors are provided through the program or unit. Academic advisers, coaches, and diagnostic specialists are provided collaboratively through on-campus or off-campus services.

Unique Aids and Services Aids, services, or accommodations include career counseling, personal coach, and priority registration.

Assistive Technology Assistive technology is located in TRIO Student Support Services Office and includes learning support software and scanning. Technology training is provided to incoming students.

Subject-Area Tutoring Tutoring is offered one-on-one, in small groups, and in class-size groups for most subjects. Tutoring is provided through the program or unit via computer-based instruction, graduate assistants/students, and trained peer tutors. Tutoring is also provided collaboratively through on-campus or off-campus services via LD specialists.

Basic Skills Remediation Remediation is offered one-on-one, in small groups, and in class-size groups for learning strategies, math, reading, spelling, study skills, time management, and written language. Remediation is provided collaboratively through on-campus or off-campus services via computer-based instruction, graduate assistants/students, regular education teachers, trained peer tutors, and other.

Enrichment Programs for career planning, college survival skills, learning strategies, math, reading, stress management, study skills, test taking, time management, vocabulary development, and written composition skills are provided collaboratively through on-campus or off-campus services.

Application For admittance to the program or unit, students are required to apply to the program directly, provide a psychoeducational report (3 years old or less), and provide psychological evaluation. It is recommended that students provide documentation of high school services. Upon acceptance, documentation of need for services should be sent only to the LD program or unit. *Application deadline (institutional):* 6/1. *Application deadline (LD program):* Rolling/continuous for fall and rolling/continuous for spring.

Written Policies Written policy regarding general/basic LD accommodations is available on the program Web site. Written policy regarding general/basic LD accommodations is outlined in the school's catalog/handbook. Written policy regarding reduced course loads is available through the program or unit directly.

Harrington College of Design
Student Services/Academic Advising

200 West Madison Street

Chicago, IL 60606

http://www.interiordesign.edu/

Contact: Susan J. Kirkman, Vice President of Academics/Dean of Education. Phone: 312-697-8030. Fax: 312-697-8115. E-mail: skirkman@interiordesign.edu.

Student Services/Academic Advising Approximately 25 registered undergraduate students were served during 2006–07. The program or unit includes 1 part-time staff member. Academic advisers, coaches, graduate assistants/students, and professional tutors are provided collaboratively through on-campus or off-campus services.

Unique Aids and Services Aids, services, or accommodations include career counseling, priority registration, tutoring and open lab assistance.

Subject-Area Tutoring Tutoring is offered one-on-one and in small groups for all subjects. Tutoring is provided collaboratively through on-campus or off-campus services via graduate assistants/students, trained peer tutors, and other.

Basic Skills Remediation Remediation is offered one-on-one for computer skills, math, and written language. Remediation is provided collaboratively through on-campus or off-campus services via graduate assistants/students and other.

Enrichment Programs for career planning, college survival skills, health and nutrition, learning strategies, math, practical computer skills, self-advocacy, stress management, study skills, test taking, time management, written composition skills, and other are provided collaboratively through on-campus or off-campus services.

Application For admittance to the program or unit, students are required to provide documentation of high school services. It is recommended that students provide a psychoeducational report and provide any post high school testing or accommodations. Upon application, materials documenting need for services should be sent only to the LD program or unit. Upon acceptance, documentation of need for services should be sent only to the LD program or unit. *Application deadline (institutional):* Continuous. *Application deadline (LD program):* Rolling/continuous for fall and rolling/continuous for spring.

Written Policies Written policy regarding general/basic LD accommodations is outlined in the school's catalog/handbook.

Hartwick College
Academic Center for Excellence/Learning Support Specialist

One Hartwick Drive

Oneonta, NY 13820-4020

http://www.hartwick.edu/x5544.xml

Contact: Ms. Patty Jacobsen, Learning Support Specialist. Phone: 607-431-4435. Fax: 607-431-4412. E-mail: ace@hartwick.edu.

Academic Center for Excellence/Learning Support Specialist Approximately 50 registered undergraduate students were served during 2006–07. The program or unit includes 1 full-time staff member. LD specialists are provided through the program or unit. Counselors are provided collaboratively through on-campus or off-campus services.

Assistive Technology Assistive technology is located in the DSS office, the library and includes digital textbooks/e-text, learning support software, and scanning. Technology training is provided to incoming students.

Subject-Area Tutoring Tutoring is offered one-on-one, in small groups, and in class-size groups for most subjects. Tutoring is provided collaboratively through on-campus or off-campus services via trained peer tutors.

Application For admittance to the program or unit, students are required to apply to the program directly, provide a psychoeducational report (3 years old or less), and provide documentation as specified on Web site: http://www.hartwick.edu/x5544.xml. It is recommended that students provide documentation of high school services. Upon acceptance, documentation of need for services should be

sent only to the LD program or unit. *Application deadline (institutional):* 2/15. *Application deadline (LD program):* Rolling/continuous for fall and rolling/continuous for spring.

Written Policies Written policies regarding course substitutions, general/basic LD accommodations, and substitutions and waivers of admissions requirements are available on the program Web site. Written policy regarding general/basic LD accommodations is available through the program or unit directly.

Haskell Indian Nations University
Disability Support Services

155 Indian Avenue, #5031

Lawrence, KS 66046-4800

http://www.haskell.edu/

Contact: Mr. Perry R. Graves, Disability Support Services Coordinator. Phone: 785-749-8470 Ext. 258. Fax: 785-749-8473. E-mail: pgraves@haskell.edu.

Disability Support Services Approximately 12 registered undergraduate students were served during 2006–07. The program or unit includes 1 full-time staff member. LD specialists are provided through the program or unit. LD specialists, regular education teachers, and trained peer tutors are provided collaboratively through on-campus or off-campus services.

Unique Aids and Services Aids, services, or accommodations include advocates.

Assistive Technology Assistive technology is located in library's computer lab and includes digital textbooks/e-text, scanning, and speech-to-text software. Technology training is provided to incoming students.

Subject-Area Tutoring Tutoring is offered in small groups for some subjects. Tutoring is provided collaboratively through on-campus or off-campus services via trained peer tutors.

Application For admittance to the program or unit, students are required to apply to the program directly and provide a psychoeducational report (3 years old or less). It is recommended that students provide documentation of high school services. Upon application, materials documenting need for services should be sent only to the LD program or unit. Upon acceptance, documentation of need for services should be sent only to the LD program or unit. *Application deadline (LD program):* Rolling/continuous for fall and rolling/continuous for spring.

Written Policies Written policies regarding general/basic LD accommodations and reduced course loads are available on the program Web site. Written policies regarding general/basic LD accommodations and reduced course loads are available through the program or unit directly.

Haverford College
Office of Disabilities Services

370 Lancaster Avenue

Haverford, PA 19041-1392

http://www.haverford.edu/ods/ods

Haverford College (continued)

Contact: Dr. Richard E. Webb, Coordinator of Disabilities Services. Phone: 610-896-1290. Fax: 610-896-2969.

Office of Disabilities Services Approximately 25 registered undergraduate students were served during 2006–07. The program or unit includes 2 part-time staff members. Diagnostic specialists are provided through the program or unit. Academic advisers, coaches, counselors, diagnostic specialists, and trained peer tutors are provided collaboratively through on-campus or off-campus services.

Assistive Technology Assistive technology is located in campus labs, a special lab and includes digital textbooks/e-text and scanning.

Subject-Area Tutoring Tutoring is offered one-on-one for most subjects. Tutoring is provided collaboratively through on-campus or off-campus services via trained peer tutors.

Application For admittance to the program or unit, students are required to provide a psychoeducational report (3 years old or less). It is recommended that students provide documentation of high school services. Upon acceptance, documentation of need for services should be sent only to the LD program or unit. *Application deadline (institutional):* 1/15. *Application deadline (LD program):* Rolling/continuous for fall and rolling/continuous for spring.

Written Policies Written policies regarding course substitutions, general/basic LD accommodations, reduced course loads, and substitutions and waivers of graduation requirements are available on the program Web site. Written policy regarding general/basic LD accommodations is outlined in the school's catalog/handbook. Written policies regarding general/basic LD accommodations and substitutions and waivers of graduation requirements are available through the program or unit directly.

Henderson State University
Disability Resource Center

1100 Henderson Street

Arkadelphia, AR 71999-0001

http://www.hsu.edu/disability/

Contact: Ms. Vickie Faust, Assistant Director. Phone: 870-230-5475. Fax: 870-230-5473. E-mail: faustv@hsu.edu.

Disability Resource Center Approximately 40 registered undergraduate students were served during 2006–07. The program or unit includes 4 full-time staff members. Academic advisers, counselors, LD specialists, skill tutors, strategy tutors, trained peer tutors, and other are provided through the program or unit. Academic advisers, counselors, diagnostic specialists, LD specialists, regular education teachers, and remediation/learning specialists are provided collaboratively through on-campus or off-campus services.

Unique Aids and Services Aids, services, or accommodations include career counseling, priority registration, and support groups.

Assistive Technology Assistive technology is located in the DSS office, the library and includes digital textbooks/e-text, learning support software, and scanning. Technology training is provided to incoming students.

Subject-Area Tutoring Tutoring is offered one-on-one and in small groups for some subjects. Tutoring is provided through the program or unit via graduate assistants/students and trained peer tutors. Tutoring is also provided collaboratively through on-campus or off-campus services via computer-based instruction, graduate assistants/students, and trained peer tutors.

Basic Skills Remediation Remediation is offered one-on-one, in small groups, and in class-size groups for computer skills, learning strategies, math, reading, social skills, study skills, time management, and written language. Remediation is provided through the program or unit via trained peer tutors. Remediation is also provided collaboratively through on-campus or off-campus services via computer-based instruction, graduate assistants/students, and regular education teachers.

Enrichment Enrichment programs are available through the program or unit for career planning, college survival skills, learning strategies, math, practical computer skills, self-advocacy, stress management, study skills, test taking, time management, and written composition skills. Programs for career planning, college survival skills, health and nutrition, math, oral communication skills, practical computer skills, reading, study skills, vocabulary development, and written composition skills are provided collaboratively through on-campus or off-campus services. Credit is offered for college survival skills, math, oral communication skills, practical computer skills, reading, and written composition skills.

Application For admittance to the program or unit, students are required to apply to the program directly and provide a psychoeducational report (4 years old or less). It is recommended that students provide documentation of high school services. Upon application, materials documenting need for services should be sent only to the LD program or unit. Upon acceptance, documentation of need for services should be sent only to the LD program or unit. *Application deadline (institutional):* 7/15. *Application deadline (LD program):* Rolling/continuous for fall and rolling/continuous for spring.

Written Policies Written policies regarding course substitutions, general/basic LD accommodations, and substitutions and waivers of graduation requirements are available on the program Web site. Written policy regarding general/basic LD accommodations is outlined in the school's catalog/handbook. Written policies regarding course substitutions, general/basic LD accommodations, and substitutions and waivers of graduation requirements are available through the program or unit directly.

Heritage Christian University

PO Box HCU

Florence, AL 35630

http://www.hcu.edu/

Contact: Mr. Bill Bagents, Dean of Students. Phone: 256-766-6610 Ext. 221. Fax: 256-766-9289. E-mail: bbagents@hcu.edu.

Approximately 1 registered undergraduate students were served during 2006–07. Academic advisers, counselors, and remediation/learning specialists are provided collaboratively through on-campus or off-campus services.

Subject-Area Tutoring Tutoring is offered one-on-one and in small groups for all subjects. Tutoring is provided collaboratively through on-campus or off-campus services via other.

Diagnostic Testing Testing for handwriting, math, reading, spelling, and spoken language is provided collaboratively through on-campus or off-campus services.

Basic Skills Remediation Remediation is offered one-on-one and in small groups for math, reading, spelling, and written language. Remediation is provided collaboratively through on-campus or off-campus services.

Application Upon application, materials documenting need for services should be sent only to admissions with institutional application materials. *Application deadline (institutional):* Continuous.

Written Policies Written policy regarding general/basic LD accommodations is outlined in the school's catalog/handbook.

High Point University
Academic Services Center

University Station, Montlieu Avenue

High Point, NC 27262-3598

http://www.highpoint.edu/academics/asc/

Contact: Ms. Irene Ingersoll, Assistant Director of the Academic Services Center/Disability Coordinator. Phone: 336-841-9037. Fax: 336-841-5123. E-mail: iingerso@highpoint.edu.

Academic Services Center Approximately 180 registered undergraduate students were served during 2006–07. The program or unit includes 3 full-time and 30 part-time staff members. Graduate assistants/students, LD specialists, remediation/learning specialists, teacher trainees, and trained peer tutors are provided through the program or unit. Academic advisers, counselors, graduate assistants/students, LD specialists, regular education teachers, remediation/learning specialists, skill tutors, teacher trainees, and trained peer tutors are provided collaboratively through on-campus or off-campus services.

Summer Program To help prepare for the demands of college, there is an optional 4-week summer program prior to entering the school available to high school graduates that focuses on life skills and/or college life adjustment, specific subject tutoring, study skills, test-taking skills, and time management. Degree credit will be earned. The program accepts students from out-of-state.

Unique Aids and Services Aids, services, or accommodations include career counseling, faculty training, priority registration, and weekly meetings with faculty.

Assistive Technology Assistive technology is located in the DSS office, the library and includes digital textbooks/e-text, learning support software, and scanning.

Subject-Area Tutoring Tutoring is offered one-on-one and in small groups for most subjects. Tutoring is provided through the program or unit via computer-based instruction, graduate assistants/students, LD specialists, and trained peer tutors. Tutoring is also provided collaboratively through on-campus or off-campus services via graduate assistants/students, LD specialists, and trained peer tutors.

Basic Skills Remediation Remediation is offered one-on-one and in small groups for computer skills, learning strategies, math, reading, spelling, study skills, and time management. Remediation is provided through the program or unit via graduate assistants/students and trained peer tutors. Remediation is also provided collaboratively through on-campus or off-campus services via graduate assistants/students and trained peer tutors.

Enrichment Enrichment programs are available through the program or unit for college survival skills, learning strategies, math, practical computer skills, stress management, study skills, test taking, time management, vocabulary development, and written composition skills. Programs for career planning, college survival skills, health and nutrition, learning strategies, math, reading, stress management, study skills, test taking, time management, vocabulary development, and written composition skills are provided collaboratively through on-campus or off-campus services. Credit is offered for college survival skills, health and nutrition, learning strategies, reading, stress management, study skills, test taking, and time management.

Fees *Summer Program* fee is $2205 to $3151.

Application For admittance to the program or unit, students are required to provide a psychoeducational report (3 years old or less). It is recommended that students provide documentation of high school services. Upon application, materials documenting need for services should be sent only to the LD program or unit. Upon acceptance, documentation of need for services should be sent only to the LD program or unit. *Application deadline (institutional):* 8/15. *Application deadline (LD program):* Rolling/continuous for fall and rolling/continuous for spring.

Written Policies Written policies regarding course substitutions, general/basic LD accommodations, reduced course loads, and substitutions and waivers of graduation requirements are available on the program Web site. Written policies regarding course substitutions, general/basic LD accommodations, reduced course loads, substitutions and waivers of admissions requirements, and substitutions and waivers of graduation requirements are available through the program or unit directly.

Hope College
Academic Support Center and Disabled Student Services

141 East 12th Street, PO Box 9000

Holland, MI 49422-9000

http://www.hope.edu/

Contact: Ms. Jeanne Lindell, Coordinator of Academic Support Services for Students with Disabilities. Phone: 616-395-7830. Fax: 616-395-7617. E-mail: asc@hope.edu.

Academic Support Center and Disabled Student Services Approximately 32 registered undergraduate students were served during 2006–07. The program or unit includes 2 full-time staff members. Academic advisers are provided through the program or unit. Academic advisers, counselors, diagnostic specialists, LD specialists, regular education teachers, skill tutors, special education teachers, strategy tutors, trained peer tutors, and other are provided collaboratively through on-campus or off-campus services.

Orientation The program or unit offers an optional varying length orientation for new students individually by special arrangement.

Unique Aids and Services Aids, services, or accommodations include priority registration, support groups, and weekly meetings with faculty.

Hope College (continued)

Assistive Technology Assistive technology is located in a special lab and includes digital textbooks/e-text, learning support software, and scanning. Technology training is provided to incoming students.

Subject-Area Tutoring Tutoring is offered one-on-one, in small groups, and in class-size groups for most subjects. Tutoring is provided through the program or unit via LD specialists. Tutoring is also provided collaboratively through on-campus or off-campus services via trained peer tutors.

Basic Skills Remediation Remediation is offered one-on-one for learning strategies, reading, study skills, and time management. Remediation is provided collaboratively through on-campus or off-campus services.

Enrichment Enrichment programs are available through the program or unit for college survival skills, health and nutrition, learning strategies, oral communication skills, self-advocacy, stress management, study skills, test taking, time management, and other. Programs for career planning, college survival skills, learning strategies, math, reading, stress management, study skills, test taking, time management, written composition skills, and other are provided collaboratively through on-campus or off-campus services.

Application For admittance to the program or unit, students are required to provide a psychoeducational report (3 years old or less). Upon acceptance, documentation of need for services should be sent only to the LD program or unit. *Application deadline (institutional):* Continuous. *Application deadline (LD program):* Rolling/continuous for fall and rolling/continuous for spring.

Written Policies Written policy regarding general/basic LD accommodations is available on the program Web site.

Houghton College
Student Academic Services

One Willard Avenue
Houghton, NY 14744
http://www.houghton.edu/
Contact: Dr. Susan M. Hice, Director of Student Academic Services. Phone: 585-567-9262. Fax: 585-567-9500. E-mail: susan.hice@houghton.edu.

Student Academic Services Approximately 35 registered undergraduate students were served during 2006–07. The program or unit includes 4 part-time staff members. Counselors, diagnostic specialists, and LD specialists are provided through the program or unit. Academic advisers, counselors, and trained peer tutors are provided collaboratively through on-campus or off-campus services.

Unique Aids and Services Aids, services, or accommodations include weekly meetings with faculty.

Assistive Technology Assistive technology is located in the DSS office and includes digital textbooks/e-text and scanning. Technology training is provided to incoming students.

Subject-Area Tutoring Tutoring is offered one-on-one, in small groups, and in class-size groups for most subjects. Tutoring is provided collaboratively through on-campus or off-campus services via trained peer tutors.

Diagnostic Testing Testing is provided through the program or unit for reading and study skills. Testing for learning strategies, learning styles, reading, spelling, and study skills is provided collaboratively through on-campus or off-campus services.

Basic Skills Remediation Remediation is offered one-on-one for learning strategies, study skills, and time management. Remediation is provided through the program or unit via LD specialists. Remediation is also provided collaboratively through on-campus or off-campus services via graduate assistants/students and trained peer tutors.

Application For admittance to the program or unit, students are required to apply to the program directly, provide a psychoeducational report (3 years old or less), and provide complete psychological evaluation/diagnosis, which meets our documentation requirements. Upon application, materials documenting need for services should be sent only to the LD program or unit. Upon acceptance, documentation of need for services should be sent only to the LD program or unit. *Application deadline (institutional):* Continuous. *Application deadline (LD program):* Rolling/continuous for fall and rolling/continuous for spring.

Written Policies Written policies regarding general/basic LD accommodations and substitutions and waivers of graduation requirements are available on the program Web site. Written policies regarding general/basic LD accommodations and substitutions and waivers of graduation requirements are outlined in the school's catalog/handbook. Written policies regarding course substitutions, general/basic LD accommodations, reduced course loads, and substitutions and waivers of graduation requirements are available through the program or unit directly.

Houston Baptist University
Enrichment Center

7502 Fondren Road
Houston, TX 77074-3298
http://www.hbu.edu/
Contact: Sebron Williams EdD, Director of Academic Testing. Phone: 281-649-3000 Ext. 3285. E-mail: swilliams@hbu.edu.

Enrichment Center Approximately 15 registered undergraduate students were served during 2006–07. Counselors are provided through the program or unit. Academic advisers and counselors are provided collaboratively through on-campus or off-campus services.

Unique Aids and Services Aids, services, or accommodations include career counseling.

Subject-Area Tutoring Tutoring is offered one-on-one for some subjects. Tutoring is provided collaboratively through on-campus or off-campus services via professional tutors and trained peer tutors.

Diagnostic Testing Testing is provided through the program or unit for auditory processing, intelligence, learning strategies, learning styles, math, neuropsychological, personality, reading, study skills, visual processing, and written language. Testing for auditory processing, intelligence, learning strategies, learning styles, math, neuropsychological, personality, reading, study skills, visual processing, and written language is provided collaboratively through on-campus or off-campus services.

Basic Skills Remediation Remediation is offered one-on-one and in class-size groups for learning strategies, reading, social skills, study skills, time management, and written language. Remediation is provided through the program or unit via LD specialists and other. Remediation is also provided collaboratively through on-campus or off-campus services.

Enrichment Programs for career planning, college survival skills, learning strategies, math, medication management, oral communication skills, reading, self-advocacy, stress management, study skills, test taking, time management, vocabulary development, written composition skills, and other are provided collaboratively through on-campus or off-campus services.

Application Upon acceptance, documentation of need for services should be sent only to the LD program or unit. *Application deadline (institutional):* Continuous. *Application deadline (LD program):* Rolling/continuous for fall and rolling/continuous for spring.

Written Policies Written policy regarding general/basic LD accommodations is outlined in the school's catalog/handbook.

Hunter College of the City University of New York
Office of AccessABILITY

695 Park Avenue

New York, NY 10021-5085

http://studentservices.hunter.cuny.edu/access.htm

Contact: Mr. Don Cohen, Counselor. Phone: 212-650-3580. Fax: 212-650-3449. E-mail: don.cohen@hunter.cuny.edu. Head of LD Program: Ms. Sudi Shayesteh, Director, Office of AccessABILITY. Phone: 212-650-3581. Fax: 212-650-3449. E-mail: sudi.shayesteh@hunter.cuny.edu.

Office of AccessABILITY Approximately 145 registered undergraduate students were served during 2006–07. The program or unit includes 6 full-time and 6 part-time staff members. Academic advisers, counselors, graduate assistants/students, LD specialists, professional tutors, skill tutors, strategy tutors, trained peer tutors, and other are provided through the program or unit. Academic advisers, counselors, professional tutors, skill tutors, strategy tutors, and trained peer tutors are provided collaboratively through on-campus or off-campus services.

Unique Aids and Services Aids, services, or accommodations include career counseling, personal coach, priority registration, and support groups.

Assistive Technology Assistive technology is located in the Access and Technology Center and includes digital textbooks/e-text, learning support software, scanning, and voice recognition software. Technology training is provided to incoming students.

Subject-Area Tutoring Tutoring is offered one-on-one and in small groups for most subjects. Tutoring is provided through the program or unit via computer-based instruction, graduate assistants/students, LD specialists, and trained peer tutors. Tutoring is also provided collaboratively through on-campus or off-campus services via graduate assistants/students, professional tutors, and trained peer tutors.

Enrichment Enrichment programs are available through the program or unit for career planning, college survival skills, learning strategies, oral communication skills, practical computer skills, reading, self-advocacy, stress management, study skills, test taking, and time management. Programs for career planning, college survival skills, health and nutrition, learning strategies, math, oral communication skills, practical computer skills, reading, stress manage-

ment, study skills, test taking, time management, vocabulary development, and written composition skills are provided collaboratively through on-campus or off-campus services. Credit is offered for college survival skills.

Student Organization PossAbilities Club consists of 10 members.

Application For admittance to the program or unit, students are required to apply to the program directly and provide a psychoeducational report (5 years old or less). It is recommended that students provide documentation of high school services. Upon acceptance, documentation of need for services should be sent only to the LD program or unit. *Application deadline (institutional):* 3/15. *Application deadline (LD program):* Rolling/continuous for fall and rolling/continuous for spring.

Written Policies Written policies regarding general/basic LD accommodations and reduced course loads are available on the program Web site. Written policies regarding course substitutions and general/basic LD accommodations are available through the program or unit directly.

Huntington University
Learning Center

2303 College Avenue

Huntington, IN 46750-1299

http://www.huntington.edu/students/learning_center/disabilities.htm

Contact: Mrs. Kris Chafin, Director of Learning Assistance. Phone: 260-359-4290. Fax: 260-359-4144. E-mail: kchafin@huntington.edu.

Learning Center Approximately 15 registered undergraduate students were served during 2006–07. The program or unit includes 1 part-time staff member. Coaches and counselors are provided through the program or unit. Academic advisers, counselors, and trained peer tutors are provided collaboratively through on-campus or off-campus services.

Unique Aids and Services Aids, services, or accommodations include personal coach.

Assistive Technology Assistive technology is located in the DSS office and includes digital textbooks/e-text, learning support software, and scanning. Technology training is provided to incoming students.

Subject-Area Tutoring Tutoring is offered one-on-one and in small groups for some subjects. Tutoring is provided through the program or unit via trained peer tutors. Tutoring is also provided collaboratively through on-campus or off-campus services via computer-based instruction.

Diagnostic Testing Testing is provided through the program or unit for study skills.

Basic Skills Remediation Remediation is offered one-on-one for computer skills, learning strategies, math, spoken language, study skills, time management, and written language. Remediation is provided through the program or unit via computer-based instruction and trained peer tutors.

Enrichment Enrichment programs are available through the program or unit for college survival skills, math, practical computer skills, self-advocacy, stress management, study skills, test taking,

Huntington University (continued)

time management, and written composition skills. Programs for career planning, health and nutrition, learning strategies, and stress management are provided collaboratively through on-campus or off-campus services.

Application For admittance to the program or unit, students are required to provide a psychoeducational report (4 years old or less). It is recommended that students provide documentation of high school services. Upon application, materials documenting need for services should be sent only to the LD program or unit. Upon acceptance, documentation of need for services should be sent only to the LD program or unit. *Application deadline (institutional):* 8/1. *Application deadline (LD program):* Rolling/continuous for fall and rolling/continuous for spring.

Written Policies Written policies regarding course substitutions, general/basic LD accommodations, reduced course loads, substitutions and waivers of admissions requirements, and substitutions and waivers of graduation requirements are available through the program or unit directly.

Husson College
Office of Student Affairs

One College Circle
Bangor, ME 04401-2999
http://www.husson.edu/

Contact: Mr. John Rubino, Dean of the College. Phone: 207-941-7107. Fax: 207-941-7190. E-mail: rubinoj@husson.edu.

Office of Student Affairs Approximately 12 registered undergraduate students were served during 2006–07. Academic advisers, coaches, counselors, diagnostic specialists, graduate assistants/students, LD specialists, professional tutors, regular education teachers, remediation/learning specialists, skill tutors, and trained peer tutors are provided collaboratively through on-campus or off-campus services.

Subject-Area Tutoring Tutoring is offered one-on-one and in small groups for some subjects. Tutoring is provided collaboratively through on-campus or off-campus services via professional tutors and trained peer tutors.

Basic Skills Remediation Remediation is offered one-on-one and in small groups for learning strategies, math, study skills, time management, and written language. Remediation is provided collaboratively through on-campus or off-campus services via regular education teachers and trained peer tutors.

Enrichment Programs for career planning, college survival skills, health and nutrition, learning strategies, math, medication management, reading, self-advocacy, stress management, study skills, test taking, time management, and written composition skills are provided collaboratively through on-campus or off-campus services.

Application For admittance to the program or unit, students are required to provide a psychoeducational report (3 years old or less) and provide documentation of high school services. Upon acceptance, documentation of need for services should be sent to both admissions and the LD program or unit. *Application deadline (institutional):* 9/1. *Application deadline (LD program):* Rolling/continuous for fall and rolling/continuous for spring.

Written Policies Written policy regarding general/basic LD accommodations is outlined in the school's catalog/handbook.

Idaho State University
ADA Disabilities and Resource Center

921 South 8th Avenue
Pocatello, ID 83209
http://www.isu.edu/ada4isu/

Contact: Dennis Toney, Director. Phone: 208-282-3599. Fax: 208-282-4617. E-mail: tonedenn@isu.edu.

ADA Disabilities and Resource Center Approximately 120 registered undergraduate students were served during 2006–07. Diagnostic specialists, graduate assistants/students, professional tutors, skill tutors, and strategy tutors are provided collaboratively through on-campus or off-campus services.

Assistive Technology Assistive technology is located in the DSS office and includes digital textbooks/e-text and scanning.

Subject-Area Tutoring Tutoring is offered one-on-one, in small groups, and in class-size groups for some subjects. Tutoring is provided collaboratively through on-campus or off-campus services via computer-based instruction, graduate assistants/students, professional tutors, and trained peer tutors.

Diagnostic Testing Testing for auditory processing, handwriting, intelligence, learning strategies, learning styles, math, neuropsychological, personality, reading, spelling, spoken language, study skills, visual processing, and written language is provided collaboratively through on-campus or off-campus services.

Basic Skills Remediation Remediation is offered one-on-one, in small groups, and in class-size groups for computer skills, learning strategies, math, study skills, time management, and written language. Remediation is provided collaboratively through on-campus or off-campus services via computer-based instruction, graduate assistants/students, professional tutors, and trained peer tutors.

Enrichment Programs for career planning, college survival skills, health and nutrition, learning strategies, math, oral communication skills, practical computer skills, reading, self-advocacy, study skills, test taking, time management, and written composition skills are provided collaboratively through on-campus or off-campus services. Credit is offered for college survival skills, health and nutrition, learning strategies, math, oral communication skills, practical computer skills, reading, study skills, test taking, time management, and written composition skills.

Fees *Diagnostic Testing* fee is $100.

Application For admittance to the program or unit, students are required to provide a psychoeducational report (3 years old or less). Upon acceptance, documentation of need for services should be sent only to the LD program or unit. *Application deadline (institutional):* 8/1. *Application deadline (LD program):* Rolling/continuous for fall and rolling/continuous for spring.

Written Policies Written policy regarding general/basic LD accommodations is available on the program Web site. Written policy regarding general/basic LD accommodations is outlined in the school's catalog/handbook. Written policy regarding general/basic LD accommodations is available through the program or unit directly.

The Illinois Institute of Art–Schaumburg
Disability Services

1000 Plaza Drive
Schaumburg, IL 60173
http://www.ilis.artinstitutes.edu/

Contact: Larry Disch, MA, Counselor/Disability Services Coordinator. Phone: 800-314-3450 Ext. 4541. Fax: 847-619-7145. E-mail: ldisch@aii.edu.

Disability Services Approximately 45 registered undergraduate students were served during 2006–07. The program or unit includes 1 part-time staff member. Academic advisers, counselors, regular education teachers, and trained peer tutors are provided collaboratively through on-campus or off-campus services.

Unique Aids and Services Aids, services, or accommodations include faculty training.

Assistive Technology Assistive technology is located in the library and includes digital textbooks/e-text, learning support software, and scanning.

Subject-Area Tutoring Tutoring is offered one-on-one and in small groups for most subjects. Tutoring is provided collaboratively through on-campus or off-campus services via trained peer tutors and other.

Basic Skills Remediation Remediation is offered one-on-one, in small groups, and in class-size groups for computer skills, learning strategies, math, reading, study skills, time management, and written language. Remediation is provided collaboratively through on-campus or off-campus services via regular education teachers and trained peer tutors.

Enrichment Enrichment programs are available through the program or unit for college survival skills, health and nutrition, learning strategies, self-advocacy, stress management, study skills, test taking, and time management. Programs for career planning, college survival skills, health and nutrition, learning strategies, math, self-advocacy, stress management, study skills, test taking, and time management are provided collaboratively through on-campus or off-campus services.

Application For admittance to the program or unit, students are required to provide a psychoeducational report. It is recommended that students provide documentation of high school services. Upon acceptance, documentation of need for services should be sent only to the LD program or unit. *Application deadline (institutional):* Continuous. *Application deadline (LD program):* Rolling/continuous for fall and rolling/continuous for spring.

Written Policies Written policy regarding general/basic LD accommodations is available on the program Web site. Written policy regarding general/basic LD accommodations is outlined in the school's catalog/handbook. Written policy regarding general/basic LD accommodations is available through the program or unit directly.

Illinois State University
Disability Concerns

Normal, IL 61790-2200
http://www.disabilityconcerns.ilstu.edu/

Contact: Ms. Sheryl J. Hogan, Coordinator of Learning Disability Services. Phone: 309-438-5853. Fax: 309-438-7713. E-mail: sjhogan@ilstu.edu. Head of LD Program: Ms. Ann M. Caldwell, Director. Phone: 309-438-5853. Fax: 309-438-7713. E-mail: amcaldw@ilstu.edu.

Disability Concerns Approximately 175 registered undergraduate students were served during 2006–07. The program or unit includes 5 full-time staff members and 1 part-time staff member. Graduate assistants/students, LD specialists, and strategy tutors are provided through the program or unit. Academic advisers, counselors, diagnostic specialists, skill tutors, strategy tutors, and trained peer tutors are provided collaboratively through on-campus or off-campus services.

Orientation The program or unit offers a mandatory orientation for new students individually by special arrangement.

Unique Aids and Services Aids, services, or accommodations include career counseling and faculty training.

Assistive Technology Assistive technology is located in campus labs, the DSS office, a special lab and includes digital textbooks/e-text. Technology training is provided to incoming students.

Subject-Area Tutoring Tutoring is offered one-on-one and in small groups for some subjects. Tutoring is provided collaboratively through on-campus or off-campus services via trained peer tutors.

Diagnostic Testing Testing for intelligence is provided collaboratively through on-campus or off-campus services.

Basic Skills Remediation Remediation is offered one-on-one for learning strategies, study skills, and time management. Remediation is provided through the program or unit via LD specialists.

Enrichment Enrichment programs are available through the program or unit for learning strategies, self-advocacy, study skills, test taking, and time management. Programs for career planning, college survival skills, health and nutrition, learning strategies, practical computer skills, stress management, study skills, test taking, time management, and written composition skills are provided collaboratively through on-campus or off-campus services.

Fees *Diagnostic Testing* fee is $400.

Application For admittance to the program or unit, students are required to apply to the program directly, provide a psychoeducational report, and provide documentation of high school services. Upon application, materials documenting need for services should be sent only to the LD program or unit. Upon acceptance, documentation of need for services should be sent only to the LD program or unit. *Application deadline (institutional): 3/1. Application deadline (LD program):* Rolling/continuous for fall and rolling/continuous for spring.

Written Policies Written policy regarding general/basic LD accommodations is available on the program Web site.

Illinois Wesleyan University
Office of the Associate Provost

PO Box 2900
Bloomington, IL 61702-2900
http://www.iwu.edu/

Contact: Dr. Roger Schanitter, Associate Provost. Phone: 309-556-3255. E-mail: rschnait@iwu.edu.

Office of the Associate Provost Approximately 20 registered undergraduate students were served during 2006–07. The program

Illinois Wesleyan University (continued)

or unit includes 2 part-time staff members. Academic advisers, coaches, counselors, diagnostic specialists, skill tutors, and trained peer tutors are provided collaboratively through on-campus or off-campus services.

Unique Aids and Services Aids, services, or accommodations include extended examination time.

Subject-Area Tutoring Tutoring is offered one-on-one and in small groups for some subjects. Tutoring is provided collaboratively through on-campus or off-campus services via trained peer tutors.

Basic Skills Remediation Remediation is offered one-on-one for learning strategies, study skills, time management, and written language. Remediation is provided collaboratively through on-campus or off-campus services via trained peer tutors and other.

Application For admittance to the program or unit, students are required to provide a psychoeducational report. It is recommended that students provide documentation of high school services. Upon acceptance, documentation of need for services should be sent only to the LD program or unit. *Application deadline (LD program):* Rolling/continuous for fall and rolling/continuous for spring.

Written Policies Written policies regarding course substitutions, general/basic LD accommodations, and substitutions and waivers of graduation requirements are available on the program Web site. Written policy regarding general/basic LD accommodations is outlined in the school's catalog/handbook.

Immaculata University
Learning Support Specialist's Office

1145 King Road
Immaculata, PA 19345

http://www.immaculata.edu

Contact: Dr. Janet F. Kane, Dean, College of Undergraduate Studies. Phone: 610-647-4400 Ext. 3019. Fax: 610-640-0836. E-mail: jkane@immaculta.edu.

Learning Support Specialist's Office Approximately 40 registered undergraduate students were served during 2006–07. The program or unit includes 2 part-time staff members. Academic advisers, coaches, counselors, graduate assistants/students, professional tutors, regular education teachers, skill tutors, and trained peer tutors are provided collaboratively through on-campus or off-campus services.

Assistive Technology Assistive technology is located in Office of Academic Affairs and includes text enlargement.

Subject-Area Tutoring Tutoring is offered one-on-one and in small groups for most subjects. Tutoring is provided collaboratively through on-campus or off-campus services via computer-based instruction, graduate assistants/students, professional tutors, and trained peer tutors.

Enrichment Programs for career planning, college survival skills, health and nutrition, learning strategies, math, practical computer skills, stress management, study skills, time management, and written composition skills are provided collaboratively through on-campus or off-campus services.

Application For admittance to the program or unit, students are required to provide a psychoeducational report (5 years old or less) and provide documentation of high school services. Upon application, materials documenting need for services should be sent only to the LD program or unit. Upon acceptance, documentation of need for services should be sent only to the LD program or unit. *Application deadline (institutional):* Continuous. *Application deadline (LD program):* Rolling/continuous for fall and rolling/continuous for spring.

Written Policies Written policies regarding general/basic LD accommodations and reduced course loads are available through the program or unit directly.

Indiana University Bloomington
Disability Services for Students

107 S. Indiana Avenue
Bloomington, IN 47405-7000

http://www.indiana.edu/~iubdss

Contact: S. Whitney Manchester, Learning Disabilities Coordinator. Phone: 812-855-7578. Fax: 812-855-7650. E-mail: wmanches@indiana.edu. Head of LD Program: Martha P. Jacques Engstrom, Director. Phone: 812-855-7578. Fax: 812-855-7650. E-mail: mjacques@indiana.edu.

Disability Services for Students Approximately 686 registered undergraduate students were served during 2006–07. The program or unit includes 3 full-time staff members.

Orientation The program or unit offers a mandatory 2-hour orientation for new students before classes begin.

Assistive Technology Assistive technology is located in the DSS office, the Adaptive Technology Center in the main library and includes digital textbooks/e-text and learning support software.

Basic Skills Remediation Remediation is offered one-on-one for study skills and time management. Remediation is provided through the program or unit via LD specialists.

Application For admittance to the program or unit, students are required to apply to the program directly, provide a psychoeducational report (3 years old or less), and provide an evaluation after age 16 with adult normed tests. It is recommended that students provide documentation of high school services. Upon acceptance, documentation of need for services should be sent only to the LD program or unit. *Application deadline (institutional):* Continuous. *Application deadline (LD program):* Rolling/continuous for fall and rolling/continuous for spring.

Written Policies Written policies regarding course substitutions, general/basic LD accommodations, grade forgiveness, reduced course loads, substitutions and waivers of admissions requirements, and substitutions and waivers of graduation requirements are available on the program Web site. Written policies regarding course substitutions, general/basic LD accommodations, grade forgiveness, reduced course loads, substitutions and waivers of admissions requirements, and substitutions and waivers of graduation requirements are available through the program or unit directly.

Indiana University of Pennsylvania

Disability Support Services, Advising and Testing Center

Indiana, PA 15705-1087

http://www.iup.edu/advisingtesting/DisabilitySupport/

Contact: Dr. Todd A. Van Wieren, Assistant Director, Disability Support Services. Phone: 724-357-4067. Fax: 724-357-2889. E-mail: toddvw@iup.edu. Head of LD Program: Dr. Catherine M Dugan, Director, Advising & Testing Center. Phone: 724-357-4067. Fax: 724-357-2889. E-mail: cmdugan@iup.edu.

Disability Support Services, Advising and Testing Center Approximately 300 registered undergraduate students were served during 2006–07. The program or unit includes 3 full-time and 3 part-time staff members. Academic advisers and graduate assistants/students are provided collaboratively through on-campus or off-campus services.

Orientation The program or unit offers a mandatory 1-hour orientation for new students.

Unique Aids and Services Aids, services, or accommodations include advocates, career counseling, priority registration, and weekly meetings with faculty.

Assistive Technology Assistive technology is located in campus labs, the DSS office and includes learning support software and scanning.

Subject-Area Tutoring Tutoring is offered in class-size groups for some subjects. Tutoring is provided collaboratively through on-campus or off-campus services via trained peer tutors.

Diagnostic Testing Testing for auditory processing, intelligence, learning styles, math, motor skills, personality, reading, spelling, spoken language, visual processing, and written language is provided collaboratively through on-campus or off-campus services.

Basic Skills Remediation Remediation is offered in class-size groups for learning strategies, math, reading, study skills, time management, and written language. Remediation is provided collaboratively through on-campus or off-campus services via regular education teachers.

Enrichment Programs for career planning, college survival skills, health and nutrition, learning strategies, math, oral communication skills, practical computer skills, reading, study skills, test taking, time management, and vocabulary development are provided collaboratively through on-campus or off-campus services. Credit is offered for career planning, college survival skills, health and nutrition, learning strategies, math, oral communication skills, practical computer skills, reading, study skills, test taking, time management, and vocabulary development.

Fees *Diagnostic Testing* fee is $100.

Application For admittance to the program or unit, students are required to provide a psychoeducational report (3 years old or less). It is recommended that students provide documentation of high school services. Upon application, materials documenting need for services should be sent only to the LD program or unit. Upon acceptance, documentation of need for services should be sent only to the LD program or unit. *Application deadline (institutional):* Continuous. *Application deadline (LD program):* Rolling/continuous for fall and rolling/continuous for spring.

Written Policies Written policy regarding general/basic LD accommodations is available on the program Web site. Written policy regarding general/basic LD accommodations is available through the program or unit directly.

Indiana University–Purdue University Fort Wayne

Services for Students with Disabilities (SSD)

2101 East Coliseum Boulevard

Fort Wayne, IN 46805-1499

http://www.ipfw.edu/ssd/

Contact: Ms. Julie Schrader-Gettys, Accommodation Specialist. Phone: 260-481-6950. Fax: 260-481-6018. E-mail: schradej@ipfw.edu. Head of LD Program: Mr. Eric J. Wagenfeld, Director. Phone: 260-481-6658. Fax: 260-481-6018. E-mail: wagenfee@ipfw.edu.

Services for Students with Disabilities (SSD) Approximately 200 registered undergraduate students were served during 2006–07. The program or unit includes 3 full-time and 10 part-time staff members. Counselors, LD specialists, skill tutors, and strategy tutors are provided through the program or unit. Academic advisers, coaches, counselors, diagnostic specialists, regular education teachers, skill tutors, and strategy tutors are provided collaboratively through on-campus or off-campus services.

Unique Aids and Services Aids, services, or accommodations include personal coach and priority registration.

Assistive Technology Assistive technology is located in campus labs, the DSS office and includes digital textbooks/e-text, learning support software, and scanning. Technology training is provided to incoming students.

Subject-Area Tutoring Tutoring is offered one-on-one, in small groups, and in class-size groups for most subjects. Tutoring is provided collaboratively through on-campus or off-campus services via trained peer tutors.

Basic Skills Remediation Remediation is offered in class-size groups for learning strategies, math, reading, spelling, study skills, time management, and written language. Remediation is provided through the program or unit via LD specialists. Remediation is also provided collaboratively through on-campus or off-campus services via regular education teachers and trained peer tutors.

Student Organization Dasel.

Application For admittance to the program or unit, students are required to apply to the program directly and provide a psychoeducational report. It is recommended that students provide documentation of high school services. Upon application, materials documenting need for services should be sent only to the LD program or unit. Upon acceptance, documentation of need for services should be sent only to the LD program or unit. *Application deadline (institutional):* 8/1. *Application deadline (LD program):* Rolling/continuous for fall and rolling/continuous for spring.

Written Policies Written policy regarding general/basic LD accommodations is available through the program or unit directly.

Indiana University–Purdue University Indianapolis
Adaptive Educational Services

355 North Lansing

Indianapolis, IN 46202-2896

http://www.iupui.edu/~sldweb/aes/

Contact: Ms. Pamela A. King, Director. Phone: 317-274-3241. Fax: 317-278-2051. E-mail: pking@iupui.edu.

Adaptive Educational Services Approximately 400 registered undergraduate students were served during 2006–07. The program or unit includes 6 full-time staff members. Academic advisers, coaches, counselors, diagnostic specialists, graduate assistants/students, LD specialists, professional tutors, regular education teachers, remediation/learning specialists, skill tutors, special education teachers, strategy tutors, teacher trainees, and trained peer tutors are provided collaboratively through on-campus or off-campus services.
Unique Aids and Services Aids, services, or accommodations include career counseling.
Assistive Technology Assistive technology includes digital textbooks/e-text.
Application For admittance to the program or unit, students are required to apply to the program directly and provide a psychoeducational report (3 years old or less). It is recommended that students provide documentation of high school services. Upon application, materials documenting need for services should be sent only to the LD program or unit. Upon acceptance, documentation of need for services should be sent only to the LD program or unit. *Application deadline (institutional):* 6/1. *Application deadline (LD program):* Rolling/continuous for fall and rolling/continuous for spring.

Indiana University Southeast
Office of Disability Services

4201 Grant Line Road

New Albany, IN 47150-6405

http://www.ius.edu/SSDis

Contact: Mrs. Hannah Lea Wallace, Coordinator of Disability Services. Phone: 812-941-2243. Fax: 812-941-2542. E-mail: wallaceh@ius.edu.

Office of Disability Services Approximately 200 registered undergraduate students were served during 2006–07. The program or unit includes 1 full-time staff member. Academic advisers and counselors are provided through the program or unit. Academic advisers, coaches, diagnostic specialists, graduate assistants/students, professional tutors, regular education teachers, remediation/learning specialists, skill tutors, and trained peer tutors are provided collaboratively through on-campus or off-campus services.
Unique Aids and Services Aids, services, or accommodations include career counseling and support groups.
Assistive Technology Assistive technology is located in a special lab and includes digital textbooks/e-text. Technology training is provided to incoming students.

Subject-Area Tutoring Tutoring is offered one-on-one, in small groups, and in class-size groups for most subjects. Tutoring is provided collaboratively through on-campus or off-campus services via computer-based instruction, graduate assistants/students, professional tutors, and trained peer tutors.
Basic Skills Remediation Remediation is offered one-on-one, in small groups, and in class-size groups for learning strategies, math, and study skills. Remediation is provided collaboratively through on-campus or off-campus services via professional tutors, regular education teachers, and special education teachers.
Enrichment Programs for career planning, college survival skills, learning strategies, math, study skills, and written composition skills are provided collaboratively through on-campus or off-campus services.
Application For admittance to the program or unit, students are required to provide a psychoeducational report (3 years old or less). It is recommended that students provide documentation of high school services. Upon acceptance, documentation of need for services should be sent only to the LD program or unit. *Application deadline (institutional):* Continuous. *Application deadline (LD program):* Rolling/continuous for fall and rolling/continuous for spring.
Written Policies Written policy regarding general/basic LD accommodations is available on the program Web site. Written policies regarding course substitutions, general/basic LD accommodations, and substitutions and waivers of graduation requirements are available through the program or unit directly.

Ithaca College
Academic Support Services for Students with Disabilities

100 Job Hall

Ithaca, NY 14850-7020

http://www.ithaca.edu/acssd/

Contact: Ms. Cathy Howe, Administrative Assistant. Phone: 607-274-1005. Fax: 607-274-3957. E-mail: chowe@ithaca.edu. Head of LD Program: Ms. Leslie Schettino, Director of Academic Support Services. Phone: 607-274-1005. Fax: 607-274-3957. E-mail: lschettino@ithaca.edu.

Academic Support Services for Students with Disabilities Approximately 440 registered undergraduate students were served during 2006–07. The program or unit includes 2 full-time staff members and 1 part-time staff member. Counselors are provided through the program or unit. Academic advisers, counselors, diagnostic specialists, professional tutors, and trained peer tutors are provided collaboratively through on-campus or off-campus services.
Unique Aids and Services Aids, services, or accommodations include advocates, career counseling, faculty training, priority registration, and weekly meetings with faculty.
Assistive Technology Assistive technology is located in campus labs, a special lab and includes digital textbooks/e-text, learning support software, and scanning.
Subject-Area Tutoring Tutoring is offered one-on-one for some subjects. Tutoring is provided collaboratively through on-campus or off-campus services via trained peer tutors.

Enrichment Enrichment programs are available through the program or unit for self-advocacy, study skills, test taking, and time management. Programs for career planning, college survival skills, health and nutrition, learning strategies, math, medication management, oral communication skills, practical computer skills, stress management, and written composition skills are provided collaboratively through on-campus or off-campus services.

Application For admittance to the program or unit, students are required to provide a psychoeducational report (3 years old or less). It is recommended that students provide documentation of high school services. Upon acceptance, documentation of need for services should be sent only to the LD program or unit. *Application deadline (institutional): 2/1. Application deadline (LD program):* Rolling/continuous for fall and rolling/continuous for spring.

Written Policies Written policy regarding general/basic LD accommodations is available on the program Web site. Written policy regarding general/basic LD accommodations is outlined in the school's catalog/handbook. Written policies regarding course substitutions and general/basic LD accommodations are available through the program or unit directly.

Jacksonville University
Student Disability Support Services

2800 University Boulevard North

Jacksonville, FL 32211-3394

http://www.ju.edu/

Contact: Dr. John A. Balog, Vice President for Student Life. Phone: 904-256-7067 Ext. 7067. Fax: 904-256-7066 Ext. 7066. E-mail: jbalog@ju.edu.

Student Disability Support Services Approximately 35 registered undergraduate students were served during 2006–07. The program or unit includes 1 full-time staff member. Academic advisers, counselors, regular education teachers, skill tutors, and trained peer tutors are provided through the program or unit.

Unique Aids and Services Aids, services, or accommodations include career counseling and faculty training.

Subject-Area Tutoring Tutoring is offered one-on-one and in small groups for all subjects. Tutoring is provided collaboratively through on-campus or off-campus services via trained peer tutors and other.

Enrichment Programs for career planning, college survival skills, health and nutrition, learning strategies, math, reading, stress management, study skills, test taking, time management, and written composition skills are provided collaboratively through on-campus or off-campus services.

Application For admittance to the program or unit, students are required to provide a psychoeducational report (3 years old or less). Upon acceptance, documentation of need for services should be sent only to the LD program or unit. *Application deadline (institutional):* Continuous. *Application deadline (LD program):* Rolling/continuous for fall and rolling/continuous for spring.

Written Policies Written policies regarding general/basic LD accommodations, substitutions and waivers of admissions requirements, and substitutions and waivers of graduation requirements are outlined in the school's catalog/handbook. Written policies regarding course substitutions, general/basic LD accommodations, reduced

course loads, substitutions and waivers of admissions requirements, and substitutions and waivers of graduation requirements are available through the program or unit directly.

John Brown University
Student Support Services

2000 West University Street

Siloam Springs, AR 72761-2121

http://www.jbu.edu/academics/academic_affairs/sss/services/disability/index.asp

Contact: Ms. Rebecca J. Lambert, Director of Student Support Services. Phone: 479-524-7217. Fax: 479-238-8750. E-mail: blambert@jbu.edu.

Student Support Services Approximately 50 registered undergraduate students were served during 2006–07. The program or unit includes 2 full-time and 3 part-time staff members. Academic advisers, coaches, graduate assistants/students, LD specialists, remediation/learning specialists, and trained peer tutors are provided through the program or unit. Academic advisers and counselors are provided collaboratively through on-campus or off-campus services.

Unique Aids and Services Aids, services, or accommodations include career counseling and faculty training.

Assistive Technology Assistive technology is located in a special lab and includes digital textbooks/e-text and learning support software. Technology training is provided to incoming students.

Subject-Area Tutoring Tutoring is offered one-on-one, in small groups, and in class-size groups for most subjects. Tutoring is provided through the program or unit via LD specialists and trained peer tutors.

Diagnostic Testing Testing is provided through the program or unit for learning strategies, learning styles, and study skills.

Basic Skills Remediation Remediation is available for computer skills, learning strategies, math, reading, study skills, and time management. Remediation is provided through the program or unit via LD specialists and professional tutors.

Enrichment Enrichment programs are available through the program or unit for college survival skills, learning strategies, math, practical computer skills, reading, self-advocacy, stress management, study skills, test taking, and time management. Programs for career planning, stress management, and written composition skills are provided collaboratively through on-campus or off-campus services.

Application For admittance to the program or unit, students are required to apply to the program directly. It is recommended that students provide a psychoeducational report (3 years old or less) and provide documentation of high school services. Upon acceptance, documentation of need for services should be sent only to the LD program or unit. *Application deadline (institutional):* Continuous. *Application deadline (LD program):* Rolling/continuous for fall and rolling/continuous for spring.

Written Policies Written policy regarding general/basic LD accommodations is available on the program Web site. Written policy regarding general/basic LD accommodations is outlined in the school's catalog/handbook. Written policy regarding general/basic LD accommodations is available through the program or unit directly.

John F. Kennedy University
Office of Disability Services for Students

100 Ellinwood Way

Pleasant Hill, CA 94523-4817

http://www.jfku.edu/

Contact: Lisa Noshay-Petro, Director of Office of Disability Services for Students. Phone: 925-969-3362. E-mail: ods@jfku.edu.

Office of Disability Services for Students Approximately 50 registered undergraduate students were served during 2006–07. The program or unit includes 1 full-time and 2 part-time staff members. Academic advisers are provided collaboratively through on-campus or off-campus services.
Unique Aids and Services Aids, services, or accommodations include career counseling and priority registration.
Assistive Technology Assistive technology is located in the DSS office and includes digital textbooks/e-text, learning support software, and scanning. Technology training is provided to incoming students.
Basic Skills Remediation Remediation is offered one-on-one and in small groups for learning strategies, reading, and written language. Remediation is provided collaboratively through on-campus or off-campus services via professional tutors.
Enrichment Programs for career planning, health and nutrition, learning strategies, stress management, study skills, test taking, and written composition skills are provided collaboratively through on-campus or off-campus services. Credit is offered for health and nutrition and stress management.
Application For admittance to the program or unit, students are required to apply to the program directly and provide a psychoeducational report. It is recommended that students provide documentation of high school services. Upon application, materials documenting need for services should be sent only to the LD program or unit. Upon acceptance, documentation of need for services should be sent only to the LD program or unit. *Application deadline (LD program):* Rolling/continuous for fall and rolling/continuous for spring.
Written Policies Written policies regarding general/basic LD accommodations and substitutions and waivers of admissions requirements are outlined in the school's catalog/handbook. Written policies regarding general/basic LD accommodations and substitutions and waivers of admissions requirements are available through the program or unit directly.

Johnson & Wales University
Center for Academic Support

901 West Trade Street, Suite 175

Charlotte, NC 28202

http://www.jwu.edu/charlotte/cas/

Contact: Mrs. Susan Robb Flaherty, Director, Center for Academic Support. Phone: 980-598-1510. Fax: 980-598-1505. E-mail: susan.flaherty@jwu.edu.

Center for Academic Support Approximately 200 registered undergraduate students were served during 2006–07. The program or unit includes 4 full-time and 5 part-time staff members. LD specialists, professional tutors, and trained peer tutors are provided through the program or unit.
Orientation The program or unit offers an optional 90-minute orientation for new students during registration.
Unique Aids and Services Aids, services, or accommodations include faculty training and priority registration.
Assistive Technology Assistive technology is located in the DSS office and includes digital textbooks/e-text and scanning. Technology training is provided to incoming students.
Subject-Area Tutoring Tutoring is offered one-on-one and in small groups for most subjects. Tutoring is provided through the program or unit via professional tutors and trained peer tutors.
Basic Skills Remediation Remediation is offered one-on-one for learning strategies, math, reading, study skills, time management, and written language. Remediation is provided through the program or unit via LD specialists.
Enrichment Enrichment programs are available through the program or unit for learning strategies, math, reading, self-advocacy, study skills, test taking, time management, vocabulary development, and written composition skills. Programs for career planning, college survival skills, health and nutrition, and stress management are provided collaboratively through on-campus or off-campus services.
Application For admittance to the program or unit, students are required to provide a psychoeducational report (3 years old or less). It is recommended that students provide documentation of high school services. Upon application, materials documenting need for services should be sent only to the LD program or unit. Upon acceptance, documentation of need for services should be sent only to the LD program or unit. *Application deadline (institutional):* Continuous. *Application deadline (LD program):* Rolling/continuous for fall and rolling/continuous for spring.
Written Policies Written policies regarding general/basic LD accommodations and reduced course loads are available on the program Web site. Written policies regarding general/basic LD accommodations and reduced course loads are outlined in the school's catalog/handbook. Written policy regarding general/basic LD accommodations is available through the program or unit directly.

Johnson & Wales University
The Center for Academic Support

8 Abbott Park Place

Providence, RI 02903-3703

http://www.jwu.edu

Contact: Ms. Meryl Ann Berstein, Director of Center for Academic Support. Phone: 401-598-4689. Fax: 401-598-4657.

The Center for Academic Support Approximately 600 registered undergraduate students were served during 2006–07. The program or unit includes 7 full-time and 32 part-time staff members. Counselors, LD specialists, professional tutors, remediation/learning specialists, skill tutors, special education teachers, strategy tutors, and trained peer tutors are provided through the program or unit. Academic advisers, counselors, and regular education teachers are provided collaboratively through on-campus or off-campus services.

Orientation The program or unit offers an optional 2-hour orientation for new students before classes begin.

Unique Aids and Services Aids, services, or accommodations include advocates, faculty training, priority registration, and support groups.

Assistive Technology Assistive technology is located in the DSS office, libraries and includes digital textbooks/e-text, learning support software, and scanning. Technology training is provided to incoming students.

Subject-Area Tutoring Tutoring is offered one-on-one, in small groups, and in class-size groups for all subjects. Tutoring is provided through the program or unit via computer-based instruction, graduate assistants/students, LD specialists, professional tutors, and trained peer tutors. Tutoring is also provided collaboratively through on-campus or off-campus services via computer-based instruction, graduate assistants/students, LD specialists, professional tutors, and trained peer tutors.

Basic Skills Remediation Remediation is offered one-on-one and in small groups for learning strategies, math, reading, spoken language, study skills, time management, and written language. Remediation is provided through the program or unit via computer-based instruction, graduate assistants/students, LD specialists, professional tutors, regular education teachers, special education teachers, and trained peer tutors. Remediation is also provided collaboratively through on-campus or off-campus services via computer-based instruction, graduate assistants/students, LD specialists, professional tutors, regular education teachers, special education teachers, and trained peer tutors.

Student Organization Conversation Group consists of 6 members.

Application For admittance to the program or unit, students are required to provide a psychoeducational report (3 years old or less). It is recommended that students provide documentation of high school services. Upon acceptance, documentation of need for services should be sent only to the LD program or unit. *Application deadline (institutional):* Continuous. *Application deadline (LD program):* Rolling/continuous for fall and rolling/continuous for spring.

Written Policies Written policy regarding general/basic LD accommodations is available on the program Web site. Written policies regarding course substitutions, general/basic LD accommodations, and reduced course loads are outlined in the school's catalog/handbook. Written policies regarding course substitutions, general/basic LD accommodations, and reduced course loads are available through the program or unit directly.

Johnson & Wales University

7150 Montview Boulevard
Denver, CO 80220
http://www.jwu.edu/

Contact: Ms. Joyce L. Scott, Disability Services Coordinator. Phone: 303-256-9451. Fax: 303-256-9476. E-mail: jscott@jwu.edu.

The program or unit includes 3 full-time staff members and 1 part-time staff member. Academic advisers, counselors, professional tutors, and trained peer tutors are provided through the program or unit. Regular education teachers are provided collaboratively through on-campus or off-campus services.

Unique Aids and Services Aids, services, or accommodations include career counseling, faculty training, e-mail contact with faculty.

Assistive Technology Assistive technology is located in campus labs, a special lab and includes digital textbooks/e-text. Technology training is provided to incoming students.

Subject-Area Tutoring Tutoring is offered one-on-one and in small groups for all subjects. Tutoring is provided through the program or unit via computer-based instruction, professional tutors, and trained peer tutors. Tutoring is also provided collaboratively through on-campus or off-campus services via computer-based instruction.

Basic Skills Remediation Remediation is offered one-on-one for computer skills, learning strategies, math, reading, spelling, study skills, time management, and written language. Remediation is provided through the program or unit via computer-based instruction, professional tutors, and trained peer tutors. Remediation is also provided collaboratively through on-campus or off-campus services via regular education teachers and trained peer tutors.

Enrichment Enrichment programs are available through the program or unit for learning strategies, math, practical computer skills, reading, self-advocacy, stress management, study skills, test taking, time management, and written composition skills. Programs for career planning, college survival skills, and practical computer skills are provided collaboratively through on-campus or off-campus services. Credit is offered for career planning, college survival skills, and practical computer skills.

Application For admittance to the program or unit, students are required to provide a psychoeducational report. Upon application, materials documenting need for services should be sent only to the LD program or unit. Upon acceptance, documentation of need for services should be sent only to the LD program or unit. *Application deadline (institutional):* Continuous. *Application deadline (LD program):* Rolling/continuous for fall and rolling/continuous for spring.

Written Policies Written policies regarding general/basic LD accommodations and reduced course loads are available through the program or unit directly.

Johnson & Wales University
Department of Student Success

1701 Northeast 127th Street
North Miami, FL 33181
http://www.jwu.edu/florida/stu_succ.htm

Contact: Dr. Martha Sacks, Director of Student Success. Phone: 305-892-7046. Fax: 305-892-5399. E-mail: martha.sacks@jwu.edu.

Department of Student Success Approximately 95 registered undergraduate students were served during 2006–07. The program or unit includes 3 full-time and 10 part-time staff members. Counselors, LD specialists, professional tutors, and trained peer tutors are provided through the program or unit. Academic advisers are provided collaboratively through on-campus or off-campus services.

Unique Aids and Services Aids, services, or accommodations include career counseling and priority registration.

Johnson & Wales University (continued)

Subject-Area Tutoring Tutoring is offered one-on-one and in small groups for all subjects. Tutoring is provided through the program or unit via professional tutors and trained peer tutors.

Basic Skills Remediation Remediation is offered one-on-one for computer skills, learning strategies, math, reading, spelling, study skills, time management, and written language. Remediation is provided through the program or unit via professional tutors and trained peer tutors.

Enrichment Enrichment programs are available through the program or unit for learning strategies, math, stress management, study skills, test taking, time management, and written composition skills.

Application For admittance to the program or unit, students are required to provide a psychoeducational report (3 years old or less). It is recommended that students provide documentation of high school services. Upon application, materials documenting need for services should be sent only to the LD program or unit. Upon acceptance, documentation of need for services should be sent only to the LD program or unit. *Application deadline (institutional):* Continuous. *Application deadline (LD program):* Rolling/continuous for fall and rolling/continuous for spring.

Written Policies Written policy regarding general/basic LD accommodations is outlined in the school's catalog/handbook. Written policies regarding general/basic LD accommodations, grade forgiveness, reduced course loads, substitutions and waivers of admissions requirements, and substitutions and waivers of graduation requirements are available through the program or unit directly.

Johnson State College
Academic Support Services

337 College Hill

Johnson, VT 05656-9405

http://www.jsc.edu/Academics/AcademicSupport/default.aspx

Contact: Mr. Clyde Stats, Student Development Coordinator. Phone: 802-635-1263. Fax: 802-635-1454. E-mail: statsc@jsc.vsc.edu. Head of LD Program: Ms. Dian Duranleau, Learning Specialist. Phone: 802-635-1264. Fax: 802-635-1454. E-mail: duranled@jsc.vsc.edu.

Academic Support Services Approximately 94 registered undergraduate students were served during 2006–07. The program or unit includes 7 full-time staff members. Academic advisers, counselors, and LD specialists are provided through the program or unit. Professional tutors, skill tutors, and trained peer tutors are provided collaboratively through on-campus or off-campus services.

Summer Program To help prepare for the demands of college, there is a mandatory 1-day summer program prior to entering the school available to high school graduates that focuses on life skills and/or college life adjustment. Degree credit will be earned. The program accepts students from out-of-state.

Unique Aids and Services Aids, services, or accommodations include career counseling, priority registration, note-takers, extended time/alternate location on exams.

Assistive Technology Assistive technology is located in the DSS office and includes digital textbooks/e-text, learning support software, and scanning.

Subject-Area Tutoring Tutoring is offered one-on-one and in small groups for most subjects. Tutoring is provided through the program or unit via graduate assistants/students, professional tutors, trained peer tutors, and other.

Diagnostic Testing Testing is provided through the program or unit for learning styles, math, reading, and written language.

Basic Skills Remediation Remediation is offered in class-size groups for learning strategies, math, spelling, study skills, time management, and written language. Remediation is provided collaboratively through on-campus or off-campus services via regular education teachers.

Enrichment Enrichment programs are available through the program or unit for career planning, college survival skills, learning strategies, math, reading, self-advocacy, study skills, test taking, time management, vocabulary development, and written composition skills. Programs for career planning, stress management, vocabulary development, and written composition skills are provided collaboratively through on-campus or off-campus services.

Fees *Summer Program* fee is $150.

Application For admittance to the program or unit, students are required to provide a psychoeducational report (3 years old or less). It is recommended that students provide documentation of high school services. Upon application, materials documenting need for services should be sent only to the LD program or unit. Upon acceptance, documentation of need for services should be sent only to the LD program or unit. *Application deadline (institutional):* Continuous. *Application deadline (LD program):* Rolling/continuous for fall and rolling/continuous for spring.

Written Policies Written policies regarding course substitutions, general/basic LD accommodations, and substitutions and waivers of graduation requirements are available on the program Web site. Written policies regarding course substitutions and substitutions and waivers of graduation requirements are outlined in the school's catalog/handbook. Written policies regarding general/basic LD accommodations and reduced course loads are available through the program or unit directly.

Kansas State University
Disability Support Services

Manhattan, KS 66506

http://www.ksu.edu/dss

Contact: Ms. Andrea Blair, Learning Disabilities Specialist. Phone: 785-532-6441. Fax: 785-532-6457. E-mail: andreab@ksu.edu.

Disability Support Services Approximately 400 registered undergraduate students were served during 2006–07. The program or unit includes 1 full-time staff member. Graduate assistants/students and LD specialists are provided through the program or unit.

Orientation The program or unit offers an optional 2-hour orientation for new students before classes begin.

Unique Aids and Services Aids, services, or accommodations include faculty training, priority registration, and support groups.

Assistive Technology Assistive technology is located in the university library (Media Development Center) and includes digital textbooks/e-text, learning support software, and scanning. Technology training is provided to incoming students.

Subject-Area Tutoring Tutoring is offered one-on-one and in small groups for some subjects. Tutoring is provided through the program or unit via trained peer tutors.

Enrichment Enrichment programs are available through the program or unit for study skills and time management. Programs for career planning, college survival skills, learning strategies, math, stress management, and study skills are provided collaboratively through on-campus or off-campus services.

Application For admittance to the program or unit, students are required to apply to the program directly and provide a psychoeducational report (3 years old or less). It is recommended that students provide documentation of high school services. Upon acceptance, documentation of need for services should be sent only to the LD program or unit. *Application deadline (institutional):* Continuous. *Application deadline (LD program):* Rolling/continuous for fall.

Written Policies Written policies regarding course substitutions and general/basic LD accommodations are available on the program Web site. Written policies regarding course substitutions and general/basic LD accommodations are outlined in the school's catalog/handbook. Written policies regarding course substitutions and general/basic LD accommodations are available through the program or unit directly.

Kendall College
Academic Success Center

900 North Branch Street

Chicago, IL 60622

http://www.kendall.edu/

Contact: Ms. Erin M. Shelley, Director, Academic Success Center. Phone: 312-752-22036. Fax: 312-752-2237. E-mail: eshelley@kendall.edu.

Academic Success Center Approximately 20 registered undergraduate students were served during 2006–07. The program or unit includes 1 full-time and 5 part-time staff members. LD specialists, professional tutors, remediation/learning specialists, skill tutors, and strategy tutors are provided through the program or unit. Academic advisers and counselors are provided collaboratively through on-campus or off-campus services.

Orientation The program or unit offers a mandatory orientation for new students before classes begin, during registration, and individually by special arrangement.

Unique Aids and Services Aids, services, or accommodations include advocates, career counseling, and personal coach.

Assistive Technology Assistive technology is located in the Academic Success Center and includes digital textbooks/e-text, learning support software, and scanning. Technology training is provided to incoming students.

Subject-Area Tutoring Tutoring is offered one-on-one and in small groups for all subjects. Tutoring is provided through the program or unit via computer-based instruction, LD specialists, professional tutors, and trained peer tutors.

Basic Skills Remediation Remediation is offered one-on-one, in small groups, and in class-size groups for computer skills, learning strategies, math, reading, spelling, study skills, time management, and written language. Remediation is provided through the program or unit via computer-based instruction, LD specialists, professional tutors, special education teachers, and trained peer tutors.

Enrichment Enrichment programs are available through the program or unit for career planning, college survival skills, health and nutrition, learning strategies, math, oral communication skills, practical computer skills, reading, self-advocacy, stress management, study skills, test taking, time management, vocabulary development, and written composition skills. Programs for career planning, health and nutrition, math, oral communication skills, practical computer skills, reading, self-advocacy, stress management, study skills, test taking, time management, vocabulary development, and written composition skills are provided collaboratively through on-campus or off-campus services. Credit is offered for math and practical computer skills.

Application For admittance to the program or unit, students are required to apply to the program directly and provide a psychoeducational report (5 years old or less). It is recommended that students provide documentation of high school services. Upon application, materials documenting need for services should be sent only to the LD program or unit. Upon acceptance, documentation of need for services should be sent only to the LD program or unit. *Application deadline (institutional):* Continuous. *Application deadline (LD program):* Rolling/continuous for fall and rolling/continuous for spring.

Written Policies Written policies regarding course substitutions, general/basic LD accommodations, grade forgiveness, reduced course loads, substitutions and waivers of admissions requirements, and substitutions and waivers of graduation requirements are outlined in the school's catalog/handbook.

Kennesaw State University
Disabled Student Support Services

1000 Chastain Road

Kennesaw, GA 30144-5591

http://www.kennesaw.edu/stu_dev/dsss

Contact: Ms. Carol J. Pope, Assistant Director for Disabled Student Support Services. Phone: 770-423-6443. Fax: 770-423-6667. E-mail: cpope@kennesaw.edu.

Disabled Student Support Services Approximately 125 registered undergraduate students were served during 2006–07. The program or unit includes 1 full-time and 1 part-time staff member. Academic advisers, counselors, LD specialists, remediation/learning specialists, skill tutors, and strategy tutors are provided through the program or unit. Academic advisers, counselors, and diagnostic specialists are provided collaboratively through on-campus or off-campus services.

Summer Program To help prepare for the demands of college, there is an optional 2-day summer program prior to entering the school available to rising seniors, high school graduates that focuses on life skills and/or college life adjustment, self-advocacy, study skills, test-taking skills, and time management. The program accepts students from out-of-state and is available to students attending other colleges.

Unique Aids and Services Aids, services, or accommodations include advocates, career counseling, priority registration, and support groups.

Assistive Technology Assistive technology is located in the DSS office, a special lab and includes digital textbooks/e-text, learning support software, and scanning. Technology training is provided to incoming students.

Kennesaw State University (continued)

Subject-Area Tutoring Tutoring is offered one-on-one and in small groups for some subjects. Tutoring is provided through the program or unit via LD specialists. Tutoring is also provided collaboratively through on-campus or off-campus services via computer-based instruction, graduate assistants/students, and trained peer tutors.

Diagnostic Testing Testing is provided through the program or unit for learning strategies, learning styles, social skills, and study skills. Testing for auditory processing, handwriting, intelligence, math, motor skills, neuropsychological, personality, reading, spelling, spoken language, visual processing, and written language is provided collaboratively through on-campus or off-campus services.

Basic Skills Remediation Remediation is offered one-on-one and in small groups for computer skills, learning strategies, social skills, study skills, and time management. Remediation is provided through the program or unit via LD specialists.

Enrichment Enrichment programs are available through the program or unit for college survival skills, learning strategies, practical computer skills, self-advocacy, stress management, study skills, test taking, time management, and written composition skills. Programs for career planning, health and nutrition, math, practical computer skills, stress management, and written composition skills are provided collaboratively through on-campus or off-campus services.

Student Organization Disabled Students Organization consists of 20 members.

Fees *Diagnostic Testing* fee is $500.

Application For admittance to the program or unit, students are required to apply to the program directly and provide a psychoeducational report (3 years old or less). It is recommended that students provide documentation of high school services. Upon application, materials documenting need for services should be sent only to the LD program or unit. Upon acceptance, documentation of need for services should be sent only to the LD program or unit. *Application deadline (institutional): 5/18. Application deadline (LD program):* Rolling/continuous for fall and rolling/continuous for spring.

Written Policies Written policy regarding general/basic LD accommodations is available on the program Web site. Written policy regarding general/basic LD accommodations is available through the program or unit directly.

Kentucky Wesleyan College

3000 Frederica Street, PO Box 1039
Owensboro, KY 42302-1039
http://www.kwc.edu/

Contact: Mr. Donald C. Schmied, Registrar. Phone: 270-852-3118. Fax: 270-852-3190. E-mail: dschmied@kwc.edu.

Approximately 5 registered undergraduate students were served during 2006–07. The program or unit includes 1 full-time and 1 part-time staff member. Skill tutors are provided through the program or unit. Regular education teachers and trained peer tutors are provided collaboratively through on-campus or off-campus services.

Subject-Area Tutoring Tutoring is offered one-on-one for most subjects. Tutoring is provided collaboratively through on-campus or off-campus services via computer-based instruction and trained peer tutors.

Enrichment Program for career planning is provided collaboratively through on-campus or off-campus services. Credit is offered for college survival skills, learning strategies, math, reading, study skills, test taking, and written composition skills.

Application For admittance to the program or unit, students are required to apply to the program directly and provide a psychoeducational report (2 years old or less). It is recommended that students provide documentation of high school services. Upon acceptance, documentation of need for services should be sent only to the LD program or unit. *Application deadline (LD program):* Rolling/continuous for fall and rolling/continuous for spring.

Kenyon College
Disability Services

Gambier, OH 43022-9623
http://www.kenyon.edu/x24732.xml

Contact: Mrs. Erin F. Salva, Coordinator of Disability Services. Phone: 740-427-5453. Fax: 740-427-5702. E-mail: salvae@kenyon.edu.

Disability Services Approximately 90 registered undergraduate students were served during 2006–07. The program or unit includes 1 full-time staff member. Academic advisers and counselors are provided collaboratively through on-campus or off-campus services.

Unique Aids and Services Aids, services, or accommodations include priority registration, weekly meetings with Coordinator of DS.

Assistive Technology Assistive technology is located in campus labs, the DSS office, the student's individual computer and includes scanning. Technology training is provided to incoming students.

Subject-Area Tutoring Tutoring is offered one-on-one for most subjects.

Application For admittance to the program or unit, students are required to provide a psychoeducational report. Upon acceptance, documentation of need for services should be sent only to the LD program or unit. *Application deadline (institutional):* 1/15.

Written Policies Written policy regarding general/basic LD accommodations is available on the program Web site. Written policy regarding general/basic LD accommodations is outlined in the school's catalog/handbook. Written policies regarding course substitutions, general/basic LD accommodations, and reduced course loads are available through the program or unit directly.

Keuka College
Academic Success at Keuka (ASK)

Keuka Park, NY 14478-0098
http://www.keuka.edu/info

Contact: Ms. Jennifer Robinson, Assistant Director, ASK. Phone: 315-279-5636. Fax: 315-279-5626. E-mail: jrobins@mail.keuka.edu. Head of LD Program: Ms. Carole K. Lillis, Director, ASK. Phone: 315-279-5636. Fax: 315-279-5626. E-mail: clillis@mail.keuka.edu.

Academic Success at Keuka (ASK) Approximately 85 registered undergraduate students were served during 2006–07. The program or unit includes 3 full-time and 3 part-time staff members. LD specialists, professional tutors, remediation/learning specialists, skill tutors, strategy tutors, and trained peer tutors are provided through the program or unit. Academic advisers and coaches are provided collaboratively through on-campus or off-campus services.

Unique Aids and Services Aids, services, or accommodations include advocates, career counseling, priority registration, support groups, and weekly meetings with faculty.

Assistive Technology Assistive technology is located in the DSS office and includes digital textbooks/e-text, learning support software, and scanning. Technology training is provided to incoming students.

Subject-Area Tutoring Tutoring is offered one-on-one and in small groups for all subjects. Tutoring is provided through the program or unit via graduate assistants/students, LD specialists, professional tutors, and trained peer tutors.

Basic Skills Remediation Remediation is offered one-on-one, in small groups, and in class-size groups for computer skills, learning strategies, math, reading, study skills, time management, and written language. Remediation is provided through the program or unit via LD specialists, professional tutors, regular education teachers, and trained peer tutors.

Enrichment Enrichment programs are available through the program or unit for college survival skills, learning strategies, oral communication skills, reading, self-advocacy, study skills, test taking, time management, and written composition skills. Programs for career planning, health and nutrition, math, medication management, oral communication skills, practical computer skills, reading, stress management, vocabulary development, and written composition skills are provided collaboratively through on-campus or off-campus services.

Application For admittance to the program or unit, students are required to provide a psychoeducational report (3 years old or less) and provide documentation of high school services. Upon application, materials documenting need for services should be sent only to the LD program or unit. Upon acceptance, documentation of need for services should be sent only to the LD program or unit. *Application deadline (institutional):* Continuous. *Application deadline (LD program):* Rolling/continuous for fall and rolling/continuous for spring.

Written Policies Written policy regarding general/basic LD accommodations is available on the program Web site. Written policy regarding general/basic LD accommodations is outlined in the school's catalog/handbook. Written policy regarding general/basic LD accommodations is available through the program or unit directly.

The King's University College

9125 50th Street

Edmonton, AB T6B 2H3

Canada

http://www.kingsu.ca/

Contact: Ms. Megan Edwards, Student Life Assistant. Phone: 800-661-8582. Fax: 780-465-3534. E-mail: megan.edwards@kingsu.ca.

Approximately 25 registered undergraduate students were served during 2006–07. The program or unit includes 1 full-time staff member. Academic advisers and trained peer tutors are provided collaboratively through on-campus or off-campus services.

Orientation The program or unit offers an optional orientation for new students individually by special arrangement.

Unique Aids and Services Aids, services, or accommodations include career counseling.

Subject-Area Tutoring Tutoring is offered one-on-one for most subjects. Tutoring is provided collaboratively through on-campus or off-campus services via trained peer tutors.

Application For admittance to the program or unit, students are required to provide a psychoeducational report (5 years old or less). It is recommended that students provide documentation of high school services. Upon application, materials documenting need for services should be sent only to the LD program or unit. Upon acceptance, documentation of need for services should be sent only to the LD program or unit. *Application deadline (institutional):* Continuous. *Application deadline (LD program):* Rolling/continuous for fall and rolling/continuous for spring.

Written Policies Written policy regarding general/basic LD accommodations is outlined in the school's catalog/handbook. Written policy regarding general/basic LD accommodations is available through the program or unit directly.

Kutztown University of Pennsylvania
Disability Services Office

15200 Kutztown Road

Kutztown, PA 19530-0730

http://www.kutztown.edu/

Contact: Mrs. Patricia J. Richter, Director of Disability Services for the Americans with Disabilities Act. Phone: 610-683-4108. Fax: 610-683-1520. E-mail: richter@kutztown.edu.

Disability Services Office Approximately 280 registered undergraduate students were served during 2006–07. The program or unit includes 3 full-time staff members. Academic advisers, coaches, counselors, graduate assistants/students, LD specialists, skill tutors, strategy tutors, and trained peer tutors are provided collaboratively through on-campus or off-campus services.

Orientation The program or unit offers a mandatory orientation for new students before classes begin, during summer prior to enrollment, and individually by special arrangement.

Summer Program To help prepare for the demands of college, there is an optional 1-week summer program prior to entering the school available to high school graduates that focuses on life skills and/or college life adjustment, self-advocacy, study skills, test-taking skills, and time management. Degree credit will be earned. The program accepts students from out-of-state.

Unique Aids and Services Aids, services, or accommodations include advocates, faculty training, priority registration, and support groups.

Assistive Technology Assistive technology is located in campus labs, a special lab, the library and includes digital textbooks/e-text and scanning.

Kutztown University of Pennsylvania (continued)

Subject-Area Tutoring Tutoring is offered one-on-one and in small groups for all subjects. Tutoring is provided collaboratively through on-campus or off-campus services via computer-based instruction and trained peer tutors.

Enrichment Programs for career planning, college survival skills, health and nutrition, learning strategies, self-advocacy, stress management, study skills, test taking, time management, and written composition skills are provided collaboratively through on-campus or off-campus services.

Student Organization The Phoenix Group consists of 12 members.

Application For admittance to the program or unit, students are required to provide a psychoeducational report and provide updated documentation (4 years old or less). It is recommended that students provide documentation of high school services. Upon application, materials documenting need for services should be sent only to the LD program or unit. Upon acceptance, documentation of need for services should be sent to both admissions and the LD program or unit. *Application deadline (institutional):* Continuous. *Application deadline (LD program):* Rolling/continuous for fall and rolling/continuous for spring.

Written Policies Written policy regarding general/basic LD accommodations is available on the program Web site. Written policy regarding general/basic LD accommodations is outlined in the school's catalog/handbook. Written policies regarding course substitutions and general/basic LD accommodations are available through the program or unit directly.

Kuyper College
Academic Support Office

3333 East Beltline, NE

Grand Rapids, MI 49525-9749

http://www.kuyper.edu/

Contact: Andrew Zwart, Academic Support Coordinator. Phone: 616-988-3688. Fax: 616-988-3608. E-mail: azwart@kuyper.edu.

Academic Support Office Approximately 45 registered undergraduate students were served during 2006–07. The program or unit includes 1 part-time staff member. Graduate assistants/students, LD specialists, strategy tutors, and trained peer tutors are provided through the program or unit. Academic advisers, coaches, counselors, and diagnostic specialists are provided collaboratively through on-campus or off-campus services.

Summer Program To help prepare for the demands of college, there is a mandatory 1-week summer program prior to entering the school available to high school graduates that focuses on study skills, test-taking skills, and time management. The program accepts students from out-of-state.

Unique Aids and Services Aids, services, or accommodations include support groups.

Assistive Technology Assistive technology is located in the DSS office and includes digital textbooks/e-text.

Subject-Area Tutoring Tutoring is offered one-on-one and in small groups for all subjects. Tutoring is provided collaboratively through on-campus or off-campus services via graduate assistants/students and trained peer tutors.

Diagnostic Testing Testing for auditory processing, intelligence, learning styles, neuropsychological, personality, reading, spelling, study skills, visual processing, and written language is provided collaboratively through on-campus or off-campus services.

Basic Skills Remediation Remediation is offered one-on-one and in class-size groups for computer skills, learning strategies, reading, spelling, study skills, time management, and written language. Remediation is provided through the program or unit via special education teachers. Remediation is also provided collaboratively through on-campus or off-campus services via regular education teachers.

Enrichment Enrichment programs are available through the program or unit for learning strategies, reading, time management, and written composition skills. Programs for career planning, learning strategies, stress management, study skills, test taking, time management, and written composition skills are provided collaboratively through on-campus or off-campus services.

Fees *Diagnostic Testing* fee is $400.

Application It is recommended that students apply to the program directly, provide a psychoeducational report (3 years old or less), and provide documentation of high school services. Upon application, materials documenting need for services should be sent only to the LD program or unit. Upon acceptance, documentation of need for services should be sent only to the LD program or unit. *Application deadline (institutional):* Continuous. *Application deadline (LD program):* 8/15 for fall. 12/15 for spring.

Written Policies Written policy regarding general/basic LD accommodations is available on the program Web site. Written policy regarding general/basic LD accommodations is outlined in the school's catalog/handbook.

Laboratory Institute of Merchandising
Disability Services

12 East 53rd Street

New York, NY 10022-5268

http://www.limcollege.edu/

Contact: Dr. Ellen Simpao, Director of Counseling. Phone: 212-752-1530 Ext. 229. Fax: 212-752-5319. E-mail: esimpao@limcollege.edu.

Disability Services Approximately 35 registered undergraduate students were served during 2006–07. The program or unit includes 1 part-time staff member. Counselors are provided through the program or unit. Academic advisers, counselors, regular education teachers, and trained peer tutors are provided collaboratively through on-campus or off-campus services.

Unique Aids and Services Aids, services, or accommodations include career counseling, parent workshops, priority registration, and weekly meetings with faculty.

Subject-Area Tutoring Tutoring is offered one-on-one and in small groups for some subjects. Tutoring is provided collaboratively through on-campus or off-campus services via professional tutors and trained peer tutors.

Basic Skills Remediation Remediation is offered one-on-one, in small groups, and in class-size groups for learning strategies, math, reading, spelling, study skills, time management, and written language. Remediation is provided collaboratively through on-campus or off-campus services via computer-based instruction, professional tutors, regular education teachers, and trained peer tutors.

Enrichment Enrichment programs are available through the program or unit for career planning, college survival skills, health and nutrition, learning strategies, medication management, self-advocacy, stress management, study skills, test taking, time management, and other. Programs for career planning, college survival skills, health and nutrition, learning strategies, math, oral communication skills, practical computer skills, reading, self-advocacy, stress management, study skills, test taking, time management, vocabulary development, written composition skills, and other are provided collaboratively through on-campus or off-campus services. Credit is offered for math, oral communication skills, practical computer skills, and written composition skills.

Application For admittance to the program or unit, students are required to provide documentation of high school services. It is recommended that students provide a psychoeducational report (3 years old or less) and provide neuropsychological reports. Upon application, materials documenting need for services should be sent only to the LD program or unit. Upon acceptance, documentation of need for services should be sent only to the LD program or unit. *Application deadline (institutional):* Continuous. *Application deadline (LD program):* Rolling/continuous for fall and rolling/continuous for spring.

Written Policies Written policy regarding general/basic LD accommodations is available on the program Web site. Written policy regarding general/basic LD accommodations is outlined in the school's catalog/handbook. Written policy regarding general/basic LD accommodations is available through the program or unit directly.

LaGrange College
Counseling Center/Learning Disabilities Accommodations

601 Broad Street
LaGrange, GA 30240-2999
http://www.lagrange.edu/
Contact: Mrs. Pamela Tremblay, Director of Counseling/Learning Disabilities Coordinator. Phone: 706-880-8313. E-mail: ptremblay@lagrange.edu.

Counseling Center/Learning Disabilities Accommodations
Approximately 25 registered undergraduate students were served during 2006–07. The program or unit includes 1 full-time staff member. Academic advisers and counselors are provided through the program or unit.

Unique Aids and Services Aids, services, or accommodations include academic and personal counseling.

Subject-Area Tutoring Tutoring is offered one-on-one for some subjects. Tutoring is provided through the program or unit via other. Tutoring is also provided collaboratively through on-campus or off-campus services via trained peer tutors.

Basic Skills Remediation Remediation is offered one-on-one for study skills and time management. Remediation is provided through the program or unit.

Enrichment Enrichment programs are available through the program or unit for college survival skills, health and nutrition, learning strategies, stress management, study skills, test taking, and time management.

Application For admittance to the program or unit, students are required to provide a psychoeducational report (4 years old or less). It is recommended that students provide documentation of high school services. Upon acceptance, documentation of need for services should be sent to both admissions and the LD program or unit. *Application deadline (institutional):* Continuous. *Application deadline (LD program):* Rolling/continuous for fall and rolling/continuous for spring.

Written Policies Written policy regarding general/basic LD accommodations is available on the program Web site. Written policy regarding general/basic LD accommodations is outlined in the school's catalog/handbook. Written policy regarding general/basic LD accommodations is available through the program or unit directly.

Lake Erie College
Office of Academic Services

391 West Washington Street
Painesville, OH 44077-3389
http://www.lec.edu/
Contact: Dr. Susan Culotta, Assistant Professor of Psychology, Coordinator of Academic Support Services. Phone: 440-375-7182. Fax: 440-375-7005. E-mail: sculotta@lec.edu.

Office of Academic Services The program or unit includes 2 full-time staff members and 1 part-time staff member. Academic advisers, coaches, counselors, professional tutors, regular education teachers, and trained peer tutors are provided through the program or unit.

Subject-Area Tutoring Tutoring is offered one-on-one for most subjects. Tutoring is provided through the program or unit via professional tutors and trained peer tutors.

Basic Skills Remediation Remediation is offered one-on-one for math, reading, spelling, spoken language, study skills, time management, visual processing, and written language. Remediation is provided through the program or unit via professional tutors, regular education teachers, and trained peer tutors.

Enrichment Enrichment programs are available through the program or unit for math. Programs for career planning, college survival skills, health and nutrition, learning strategies, math, stress management, study skills, test taking, and time management are provided collaboratively through on-campus or off-campus services.

Application For admittance to the program or unit, students are required to provide documentation of high school services. Upon application, materials documenting need for services should be sent only to admissions with institutional application materials. Upon acceptance, documentation of need for services should be sent only to the LD program or unit. *Application deadline (LD program):* Rolling/continuous for fall and rolling/continuous for spring.

Written Policies Written policies regarding general/basic LD accommodations and substitutions and waivers of admissions requirements are available on the program Web site. Written policy regarding grade forgiveness is outlined in the school's catalog/handbook. Written policy regarding general/basic LD accommodations is available through the program or unit directly.

Lakeland College
Hayssen Academic Resource Center

PO Box 359

Sheboygan, WI 53082-0359

http://www1.lakeland.edu/hayssen

Contact: Dr. Paul M. White, Director of Hayssen Academic Resource Center. Phone: 920-565-1412. Fax: 920-565-1389. E-mail: whitepm@lakeland.edu.

Hayssen Academic Resource Center Approximately 40 registered undergraduate students were served during 2006–07. The program or unit includes 2 full-time staff members and 1 part-time staff member. Academic advisers, professional tutors, remediation/learning specialists, skill tutors, strategy tutors, and trained peer tutors are provided through the program or unit. Academic advisers, coaches, counselors, diagnostic specialists, regular education teachers, and remediation/learning specialists are provided collaboratively through on-campus or off-campus services.

Unique Aids and Services Aids, services, or accommodations include faculty training.

Assistive Technology Assistive technology is located in campus labs, the DSS office, a special lab and includes digital textbooks/e-text, learning support software, and scanning. Technology training is provided to incoming students.

Subject-Area Tutoring Tutoring is offered one-on-one and in small groups for all subjects. Tutoring is provided through the program or unit via computer-based instruction, professional tutors, and trained peer tutors.

Diagnostic Testing Testing is provided through the program or unit for learning strategies, learning styles, math, reading, and study skills.

Basic Skills Remediation Remediation is offered one-on-one and in class-size groups for learning strategies, math, reading, spelling, study skills, time management, and written language. Remediation is provided through the program or unit via professional tutors and trained peer tutors. Remediation is also provided collaboratively through on-campus or off-campus services via computer-based instruction and regular education teachers.

Enrichment Enrichment programs are available through the program or unit for college survival skills, learning strategies, math, reading, self-advocacy, stress management, study skills, test taking, time management, and written composition skills. Programs for career planning, college survival skills, health and nutrition, learning strategies, math, medication management, oral communication skills, practical computer skills, reading, stress management, study skills, test taking, time management, vocabulary development, and written composition skills are provided collaboratively through on-campus or off-campus services. Credit is offered for career planning, college survival skills, learning strategies, math, practical computer skills, reading, study skills, test taking, time management, vocabulary development, and written composition skills.

Application For admittance to the program or unit, students are required to apply to the program directly and provide a psychoeducational report (3 years old or less). It is recommended that students provide documentation of high school services. Upon application, materials documenting need for services should be sent to both admissions and the LD program or unit. Upon acceptance, docu-

mentation of need for services should be sent only to the LD program or unit. *Application deadline (institutional):* Continuous. *Application deadline (LD program):* Rolling/continuous for fall and rolling/continuous for spring.

Written Policies Written policy regarding general/basic LD accommodations is available on the program Web site. Written policy regarding general/basic LD accommodations is outlined in the school's catalog/handbook. Written policies regarding course substitutions, general/basic LD accommodations, reduced course loads, substitutions and waivers of admissions requirements, and substitutions and waivers of graduation requirements are available through the program or unit directly.

Lake Superior State University
Disability Services, Resource Center for Students with Disabilities (RCSD)

650 W Easterday Avenue

Sault Sainte Marie, MI 49783

http://www.lssu.edu/disability/

Contact: Ms. Victoria Diane Fox, Disability Services Coordinator. Phone: 906-635-2355. Fax: 906-635-7564. E-mail: vfox@lssu.edu. Head of LD Program: Dr. Ken Peress, Vice President Student Affairs. Phone: 906-632-6841 Ext. 2634. Fax: 906-635-7510. E-mail: kperess@lssu.edu.

Disability Services, Resource Center for Students with Disabilities (RCSD) Approximately 155 registered undergraduate students were served during 2006–07. The program or unit includes 1 full-time staff member. Academic advisers and LD specialists are provided through the program or unit. Academic advisers, counselors, LD specialists, regular education teachers, remediation/learning specialists, skill tutors, strategy tutors, and trained peer tutors are provided collaboratively through on-campus or off-campus services.

Unique Aids and Services Aids, services, or accommodations include career counseling, faculty training, and priority registration.

Assistive Technology Assistive technology is located in the DSS office, a special lab and includes digital textbooks/e-text, learning support software, scanning, and scanning pens, AlphaSmart keyboards, large font keyboards, tape recorders, FM hearing helpers.

Subject-Area Tutoring Tutoring is offered one-on-one, in small groups, and in class-size groups for all subjects. Tutoring is provided collaboratively through on-campus or off-campus services via computer-based instruction, graduate assistants/students, professional tutors, and trained peer tutors.

Basic Skills Remediation Remediation is offered one-on-one and in class-size groups for computer skills, math, reading, study skills, time management, and written language. Remediation is provided through the program or unit via LD specialists and trained peer tutors. Remediation is also provided collaboratively through on-campus or off-campus services via computer-based instruction, regular education teachers, and trained peer tutors.

Enrichment Enrichment programs are available through the program or unit for self-advocacy. Programs for career planning, college survival skills, learning strategies, math, practical computer skills, reading, stress management, study skills, test taking, and time management are provided collaboratively through on-campus or off-campus services.

Application For admittance to the program or unit, students are required to apply to the program directly. It is recommended that students provide a psychoeducational report (3 years old or less), provide documentation of high school services, and provide recommendations for post-secondary accommodations from either IEP or psychoeducational report. Upon application, materials documenting need for services should be sent only to the LD program or unit. Upon acceptance, documentation of need for services should be sent only to the LD program or unit. *Application deadline (institutional): 8/15. Application deadline (LD program):* Rolling/continuous for fall and rolling/continuous for spring.

Written Policies Written policy regarding course substitutions is outlined in the school's catalog/handbook. Written policies regarding general/basic LD accommodations and reduced course loads are available through the program or unit directly.

Lamar University
Services for Students with Disabilities

4400 Martin Luther King Parkway
Beaumont, TX 77710
http://dept.lamar.edu/sfswd
Contact: Mrs. Callie Faye Trahan, Director of Services for Students with Disabilities. Phone: 409-880-8347. Fax: 409-880-2225. E-mail: callie.trahan@lamar.edu.

Services for Students with Disabilities Approximately 150 registered undergraduate students were served during 2006–07. The program or unit includes 2 full-time and 2 part-time staff members. Academic advisers, counselors, graduate assistants/students, regular education teachers, remediation/learning specialists, skill tutors, and strategy tutors are provided collaboratively through on-campus or off-campus services.

Orientation The program or unit offers an optional 2-hour orientation for new students before classes begin, individually by special arrangement, and after registration.

Unique Aids and Services Aids, services, or accommodations include career counseling, faculty training, and priority registration.

Assistive Technology Assistive technology is located in campus labs, the DSS office and includes digital textbooks/e-text, learning support software, and scanning. Technology training is provided to incoming students.

Subject-Area Tutoring Tutoring is offered one-on-one and in small groups for some subjects. Tutoring is provided collaboratively through on-campus or off-campus services via computer-based instruction, graduate assistants/students, trained peer tutors, and other.

Basic Skills Remediation Remediation is offered in class-size groups for auditory processing, computer skills, handwriting, learning strategies, math, reading, study skills, time management, and written language. Remediation is provided collaboratively through on-campus or off-campus services via computer-based instruction, graduate assistants/students, regular education teachers, trained peer tutors, and other.

Enrichment Programs for career planning, health and nutrition, learning strategies, math, oral communication skills, practical computer skills, reading, self-advocacy, stress management, study skills, test taking, time management, and written composition skills are provided collaboratively through on-campus or off-campus services. Credit is offered for health and nutrition, learning strategies, math, oral communication skills, practical computer skills, reading, study skills, time management, and written composition skills.

Student Organization Students with Alternative Abilities consists of 10 members.

Application For admittance to the program or unit, students are required to apply to the program directly and provide a psychoeducational report (3 years old or less). It is recommended that students provide documentation of high school services. Upon application, materials documenting need for services should be sent only to the LD program or unit. Upon acceptance, documentation of need for services should be sent only to the LD program or unit. *Application deadline (institutional): 8/1. Application deadline (LD program):* Rolling/continuous for fall and rolling/continuous for spring.

Written Policies Written policy regarding grade forgiveness is available on the program Web site. Written policies regarding course substitutions, general/basic LD accommodations, and grade forgiveness are outlined in the school's catalog/handbook. Written policies regarding course substitutions, general/basic LD accommodations, and reduced course loads are available through the program or unit directly.

Lancaster Bible College
Disability Services Office, Reaching Academic Potential (RAP)

901 Eden Road, PO Box 83403
Lancaster, PA 17608-3403
http://www.lbc.edu/
Contact: Dr. Shirley Tucker, Director, Disability Services Office. Phone: 717-560-8200 Ext. 5383. Fax: 717-560-8213. E-mail: stucker@lbc.edu.

Disability Services Office, Reaching Academic Potential (RAP) Approximately 25 registered undergraduate students were served during 2006–07. The program or unit includes 2 full-time and 14 part-time staff members. Academic advisers, professional tutors, regular education teachers, remediation/learning specialists, skill tutors, strategy tutors, teacher trainees, and trained peer tutors are provided through the program or unit. Academic advisers, professional tutors, regular education teachers, remediation/learning specialists, skill tutors, strategy tutors, teacher trainees, and trained peer tutors are provided collaboratively through on-campus or off-campus services.

Subject-Area Tutoring Tutoring is offered one-on-one and in small groups for most subjects. Tutoring is provided through the program or unit via professional tutors and trained peer tutors. Tutoring is also provided collaboratively through on-campus or off-campus services via professional tutors and trained peer tutors.

Diagnostic Testing Testing for auditory processing, intelligence, learning styles, math, neuropsychological, personality, reading, social skills, spelling, visual processing, and written language is provided collaboratively through on-campus or off-campus services.

Lancaster Bible College (continued)

Basic Skills Remediation Remediation is offered one-on-one and in class-size groups for learning strategies, math, study skills, time management, and written language. Remediation is provided collaboratively through on-campus or off-campus services via regular education teachers, teacher trainees, and trained peer tutors.

Enrichment Enrichment programs are available through the program or unit for college survival skills, learning strategies, self-advocacy, study skills, test taking, time management, and written composition skills. Programs for career planning, college survival skills, learning strategies, self-advocacy, study skills, test taking, time management, and written composition skills are provided collaboratively through on-campus or off-campus services. Credit is offered for college survival skills.

Fees *Diagnostic Testing* fee is $750 to $1500.

Application For admittance to the program or unit, students are required to provide a psychoeducational report (3 years old or less) and provide documentation from medical professionals. It is recommended that students provide documentation of high school services. Upon acceptance, documentation of need for services should be sent only to the LD program or unit. *Application deadline (institutional):* Continuous. *Application deadline (LD program):* Rolling/continuous for fall and rolling/continuous for spring.

Written Policies Written policies regarding course substitutions, general/basic LD accommodations, and reduced course loads are available through the program or unit directly.

Langston University
Office of Disability Services

PO Box 907

Langston, OK 73050-0907

http://www.lunet.edu/

Contact: Ms. Stephanie M. Adams, ADA Compliance Officer. Phone: 405-466-3444. Fax: 405-466-3447. E-mail: smadams@lunet.edu.

Office of Disability Services Approximately 60 registered undergraduate students were served during 2006–07. The program or unit includes 1 full-time staff member. Academic advisers and counselors are provided through the program or unit. Academic advisers, counselors, professional tutors, skill tutors, strategy tutors, and trained peer tutors are provided collaboratively through on-campus or off-campus services.

Unique Aids and Services Aids, services, or accommodations include faculty training and weekly meetings with faculty.

Subject-Area Tutoring Tutoring is offered one-on-one and in small groups for most subjects. Tutoring is provided collaboratively through on-campus or off-campus services via graduate assistants/students, professional tutors, and trained peer tutors.

Basic Skills Remediation Remediation is offered one-on-one, in small groups, and in class-size groups for math, reading, spelling, visual processing, and written language. Remediation is provided collaboratively through on-campus or off-campus services via computer-based instruction, graduate assistants/students, professional tutors, regular education teachers, and trained peer tutors.

Application For admittance to the program or unit, students are required to provide a psychoeducational report (2 years old or less) and provide documentation of high school services. Upon applica-

tion, materials documenting need for services should be sent only to the LD program or unit. Upon acceptance, documentation of need for services should be sent only to the LD program or unit. *Application deadline (institutional):* Continuous. *Application deadline (LD program):* Rolling/continuous for fall and rolling/continuous for spring.

Written Policies Written policies regarding general/basic LD accommodations and substitutions and waivers of admissions requirements are outlined in the school's catalog/handbook. Written policies regarding general/basic LD accommodations and substitutions and waivers of admissions requirements are available through the program or unit directly.

Lawrence University
Student Academic Services

PO Box 599

Appleton, WI 54912-0599

http://www.lawrence.edu/

Contact: Mr. Geoff C. Gajewski, Associate Dean of Student Academic Services. Phone: 920-832-6530. Fax: 920-832-6884. E-mail: geoffrey.c.gajewski@lawrence.edu.

Student Academic Services Approximately 25 registered undergraduate students were served during 2006–07. The program or unit includes 2 part-time staff members. Academic advisers, skill tutors, strategy tutors, and trained peer tutors are provided through the program or unit. Counselors are provided collaboratively through on-campus or off-campus services.

Unique Aids and Services Aids, services, or accommodations include academic accommodations as needed.

Assistive Technology Assistive technology is located in the Center for Teaching and Learning and includes scanning.

Subject-Area Tutoring Tutoring is offered one-on-one and in small groups for all subjects. Tutoring is provided through the program or unit via trained peer tutors.

Basic Skills Remediation Remediation is offered one-on-one and in small groups for computer skills, learning strategies, math, reading, spelling, spoken language, study skills, time management, and written language. Remediation is provided through the program or unit via trained peer tutors.

Enrichment Enrichment programs are available through the program or unit for college survival skills, learning strategies, math, oral communication skills, practical computer skills, reading, self-advocacy, stress management, study skills, test taking, time management, vocabulary development, and written composition skills. Programs for career planning, health and nutrition, and medication management are provided collaboratively through on-campus or off-campus services.

Application For admittance to the program or unit, students are required to provide a psychoeducational report (3 years old or less). It is recommended that students provide documentation of high school services. Upon acceptance, documentation of need for services should be sent only to the LD program or unit. *Application deadline (institutional):* 1/15. *Application deadline (LD program):* Rolling/continuous for fall and rolling/continuous for spring.

Written Policies Written policy regarding general/basic LD accommodations is available on the program Web site. Written policy regarding general/basic LD accommodations is outlined in the school's catalog/handbook. Written policies regarding course substitutions, general/basic LD accommodations, reduced course loads, substitutions and waivers of admissions requirements, and substitutions and waivers of graduation requirements are available through the program or unit directly.

Lebanon Valley College
Office of Disability Services

101 North College Avenue
Annville, PA 17003-1400
http://www.lvc.edu/disability-services/?bhjs=-1

Contact: Dr. Yvonne Foster, Director of Disability Services. Phone: 717-867-6071. Fax: 717-867-6091. E-mail: foster@lvc.edu.

Office of Disability Services Approximately 110 registered undergraduate students were served during 2006–07. The program or unit includes 2 full-time staff members. Academic advisers, LD specialists, skill tutors, and strategy tutors are provided through the program or unit. Academic advisers, counselors, and trained peer tutors are provided collaboratively through on-campus or off-campus services.

Unique Aids and Services Aids, services, or accommodations include career counseling, faculty training, priority registration, extended time on exams in distraction-reduced room, peer notetakers.

Assistive Technology Assistive technology includes books on tape.

Subject-Area Tutoring Tutoring is offered one-on-one for most subjects. Tutoring is provided collaboratively through on-campus or off-campus services via trained peer tutors.

Basic Skills Remediation Remediation is offered one-on-one for learning strategies, social skills, study skills, and time management. Remediation is provided through the program or unit via LD specialists.

Application For admittance to the program or unit, students are required to provide a psychoeducational report (3 years old or less). It is recommended that students provide documentation of high school services. Upon acceptance, documentation of need for services should be sent only to the LD program or unit. *Application deadline (institutional):* Continuous. *Application deadline (LD program):* Rolling/continuous for fall and rolling/continuous for spring.

Written Policies Written policy regarding general/basic LD accommodations is available on the program Web site. Written policy regarding general/basic LD accommodations is outlined in the school's catalog/handbook. Written policies regarding course substitutions, general/basic LD accommodations, reduced course loads, and substitutions and waivers of graduation requirements are available through the program or unit directly.

Lehigh University
Academic Support Services

27 Memorial Drive West
Bethlehem, PA 18015-3094
http://www.lehigh.edu/~inacsup/disabilities/

Contact: Dean Cheryl A. Ashcroft, Assistant Dean of Students. Phone: 610-758-4152. Fax: 610-758-5293. E-mail: caa4@lehigh.edu.

Academic Support Services Approximately 157 registered undergraduate students were served during 2006–07. The program or unit includes 2 full-time staff members. Coaches, graduate assistants/students, LD specialists, and strategy tutors are provided through the program or unit. Academic advisers, counselors, professional tutors, skill tutors, strategy tutors, and trained peer tutors are provided collaboratively through on-campus or off-campus services.

Orientation The program or unit offers a mandatory 1-hour orientation for new students before classes begin, individually by special arrangement, and during new student orientation.

Unique Aids and Services Aids, services, or accommodations include career counseling, faculty training, parent workshops, personal coach, support groups, peer mentors.

Assistive Technology Assistive technology is located in the library and includes digital textbooks/e-text, scanning, and Kurzweil software. Technology training is provided to incoming students.

Subject-Area Tutoring Tutoring is offered one-on-one and in small groups for some subjects. Tutoring is provided collaboratively through on-campus or off-campus services via graduate assistants/students, professional tutors, and trained peer tutors.

Basic Skills Remediation Remediation is offered one-on-one and in small groups for learning strategies, study skills, and time management. Remediation is provided through the program or unit via LD specialists. Remediation is also provided collaboratively through on-campus or off-campus services via graduate assistants/students and professional tutors.

Enrichment Enrichment programs are available through the program or unit for college survival skills, learning strategies, self-advocacy, study skills, test taking, and time management. Programs for career planning, college survival skills, health and nutrition, learning strategies, math, stress management, study skills, test taking, time management, and written composition skills are provided collaboratively through on-campus or off-campus services.

Student Organization Peer Mentors consists of 20 members.

Application For admittance to the program or unit, students are required to provide a psychoeducational report (3 years old or less). It is recommended that students apply to the program directly and provide documentation of high school services. Upon acceptance, documentation of need for services should be sent only to the LD program or unit. *Application deadline (institutional):* 1/1. *Application deadline (LD program):* 8/3 for fall. Rolling/continuous for spring.

Written Policies Written policies regarding course substitutions, general/basic LD accommodations, and substitutions and waivers of graduation requirements are available on the program Web site. Written policy regarding general/basic LD accommodations is outlined in the school's catalog/handbook. Written policies regarding course substitutions, general/basic LD accommodations, and substitutions and waivers of graduation requirements are available through the program or unit directly.

Le Moyne College
Disability Support Services

1419 Salt Springs Road

Syracuse, NY 13214

http://www.lemoyne.edu/academic_advisement/
disability_support/

Contact: Jennifer Reddy. Phone: 315-445-4118. Fax: 315-445-6014. E-mail: asc@lemoyne.edu. Head of LD Program: Roger Purdy, EdM, Director of Disability Support Services. Phone: 315-445-4118. Fax: 315-445-6014. E-mail: purdyrg@lemoyne.edu.

Disability Support Services Approximately 125 registered undergraduate students were served during 2006–07. The program or unit includes 2 full-time staff members. Academic advisers, graduate assistants/students, LD specialists, and other are provided through the program or unit. Academic advisers, coaches, counselors, professional tutors, skill tutors, and trained peer tutors are provided collaboratively through on-campus or off-campus services.

Unique Aids and Services Aids, services, or accommodations include note-takers, alternative testing arrangements.

Assistive Technology Assistive technology is located in campus labs, the DSS office and includes digital textbooks/e-text, scanning, and Kurzweil, Inspiration, ZoomText, Premier, Co:Writer, CCTV, Dragon Naturally Speaking, Duxbury, JAWS, ABBYY, OmniPage. Technology training is provided to incoming students.

Subject-Area Tutoring Tutoring is offered one-on-one, in small groups, and in class-size groups for some subjects. Tutoring is provided through the program or unit via professional tutors and trained peer tutors. Tutoring is also provided collaboratively through on-campus or off-campus services via computer-based instruction, professional tutors, and trained peer tutors.

Basic Skills Remediation Remediation is offered one-on-one, in small groups, and in class-size groups for computer skills, learning strategies, math, reading, study skills, time management, and written language. Remediation is provided through the program or unit via trained peer tutors and other. Remediation is also provided collaboratively through on-campus or off-campus services via computer-based instruction, professional tutors, regular education teachers, trained peer tutors, and other.

Enrichment Enrichment programs are available through the program or unit for reading, self-advocacy, and written composition skills. Programs for career planning, college survival skills, learning strategies, math, oral communication skills, practical computer skills, reading, stress management, study skills, test taking, time management, vocabulary development, and written composition skills are provided collaboratively through on-campus or off-campus services.

Application For admittance to the program or unit, students are required to provide a psychoeducational report (5 years old or less) and provide review of documentation (a meeting is required). It is recommended that students provide documentation of high school services. Upon acceptance, documentation of need for services should be sent only to the LD program or unit. *Application deadline (institutional): 2/1. Application deadline (LD program): Rolling/continuous for fall and rolling/continuous for spring.*

Written Policies Written policy regarding general/basic LD accommodations is available on the program Web site. Written policy regarding general/basic LD accommodations is outlined in the school's catalog/handbook. Written policies regarding course substitutions and general/basic LD accommodations are available through the program or unit directly.

LeTourneau University
Office of Students with Disability

PO Box 7001

Longview, TX 75607-7001

http://www.letu.edu/

Contact: Dr. William Howard Franklin, Dean of Student Services. Phone: 903-233-4460. Fax: 903-233-4402. E-mail: billfranklin@letu.edu.

Office of Students with Disability Approximately 50 registered undergraduate students were served during 2006–07. The program or unit includes 1 full-time staff member. Counselors, graduate assistants/students, regular education teachers, and trained peer tutors are provided through the program or unit.

Assistive Technology Assistive technology is located in the Resource Center and includes learning support software, scanning, and PDF textbooks.

Subject-Area Tutoring Tutoring is offered one-on-one, in small groups, and in class-size groups for most subjects. Tutoring is provided collaboratively through on-campus or off-campus services via graduate assistants/students and trained peer tutors.

Basic Skills Remediation Remediation is offered one-on-one and in small groups for learning strategies, math, reading, social skills, study skills, time management, and written language. Remediation is provided collaboratively through on-campus or off-campus services via graduate assistants/students and trained peer tutors.

Enrichment Programs for career planning, college survival skills, health and nutrition, learning strategies, math, reading, stress management, study skills, test taking, time management, and written composition skills are provided collaboratively through on-campus or off-campus services. Credit is offered for college survival skills and written composition skills.

Application For admittance to the program or unit, students are required to apply to the program directly and provide a psychoeducational report (1 year old or less). It is recommended that students provide documentation of high school services. Upon application, materials documenting need for services should be sent only to the LD program or unit. Upon acceptance, documentation of need for services should be sent only to the LD program or unit. *Application deadline (institutional): 8/1. Application deadline (LD program): Rolling/continuous for fall and rolling/continuous for spring.*

Written Policies Written policies regarding course substitutions, general/basic LD accommodations, and reduced course loads are available through the program or unit directly.

Lewis University
Leckrone Academic Resource Center

One University Parkway

Romeoville, IL 60446

http://www.lewisu.edu/

Contact: Ms. Denise Rich, Academic Skills Coordinator. Phone: 815-836-5284. Fax: 815-838-4614. E-mail: richde@lewisu.edu.

Leckrone Academic Resource Center Approximately 75 registered undergraduate students were served during 2006–07. The program or unit includes 3 full-time staff members. Academic advisers, graduate assistants/students, skill tutors, and strategy tutors are provided through the program or unit. Academic advisers, coaches, and counselors are provided collaboratively through on-campus or off-campus services.

Unique Aids and Services Aids, services, or accommodations include career counseling and priority registration.

Assistive Technology Assistive technology is located in campus labs. Technology training is provided to incoming students.

Subject-Area Tutoring Tutoring is offered one-on-one and in small groups for most subjects. Tutoring is provided through the program or unit via trained peer tutors. Tutoring is also provided collaboratively through on-campus or off-campus services via trained peer tutors.

Diagnostic Testing Testing for auditory processing, intelligence, math, neuropsychological, personality, and reading is provided collaboratively through on-campus or off-campus services.

Enrichment Programs for career planning, college survival skills, health and nutrition, learning strategies, self-advocacy, study skills, test taking, time management, and written composition skills are provided collaboratively through on-campus or off-campus services.

Application For admittance to the program or unit, students are required to provide a psychoeducational report (5 years old or less) and provide documentation of high school services. Upon application, materials documenting need for services should be sent only to admissions with institutional application materials. Upon acceptance, documentation of need for services should be sent only to the LD program or unit. *Application deadline (institutional): 8/1. Application deadline (LD program):* Rolling/continuous for fall and rolling/continuous for spring.

Written Policies Written policy regarding general/basic LD accommodations is available on the program Web site. Written policy regarding general/basic LD accommodations is outlined in the school's catalog/handbook.

Liberty University
Office of Disability Academic Support

1971 University Boulevard

Lynchburg, VA 24502

https://www.liberty.edu/academics/index.cfm?PID=12863

Contact: Mr. Denny McHaney, Coordinator of Disability Academic Support. Phone: 434-582-2159. Fax: 434-582-7567. E-mail: wdmchane@liberty.edu.

Office of Disability Academic Support Approximately 120 registered undergraduate students were served during 2006–07. The program or unit includes 3 part-time staff members. LD specialists are provided through the program or unit. Academic advisers and trained peer tutors are provided collaboratively through on-campus or off-campus services.

Unique Aids and Services Aids, services, or accommodations include advocates and priority registration.

Assistive Technology Assistive technology is located in a special lab and includes scanning. Technology training is provided to incoming students.

Subject-Area Tutoring Tutoring is offered one-on-one and in small groups for some subjects. Tutoring is provided collaboratively through on-campus or off-campus services via trained peer tutors.

Basic Skills Remediation Remediation is offered in class-size groups for learning strategies, math, reading, spelling, study skills, and time management. Remediation is provided collaboratively through on-campus or off-campus services via regular education teachers.

Enrichment Program for career planning is provided collaboratively through on-campus or off-campus services. Credit is offered for college survival skills, learning strategies, math, reading, stress management, study skills, test taking, time management, and written composition skills.

Application For admittance to the program or unit, students are required to provide a psychoeducational report (4 years old or less) and provide documentation of high school services. Upon application, materials documenting need for services should be sent only to the LD program or unit. Upon acceptance, documentation of need for services should be sent only to the LD program or unit. *Application deadline (institutional): 6/30. Application deadline (LD program):* Rolling/continuous for fall and rolling/continuous for spring.

Written Policies Written policy regarding general/basic LD accommodations is available on the program Web site. Written policies regarding course substitutions, general/basic LD accommodations, and substitutions and waivers of graduation requirements are outlined in the school's catalog/handbook. Written policy regarding general/basic LD accommodations is available through the program or unit directly.

Lincoln University
Office of Student Services

PO Box 179

Lincoln University, PA 19352

http://www.lincoln.edu/

Contact: Ms. Rita Myers, Director of Student Services. Phone: 484-365-7229. Fax: 484-365-7971. E-mail: rmyers@lincoln.edu.

Office of Student Services Approximately 26 registered undergraduate students were served during 2006–07. The program or unit includes 2 full-time staff members and 1 part-time staff member. Academic advisers, graduate assistants/students, and trained peer tutors are provided through the program or unit. Academic advisers, counselors, graduate assistants/students, professional tutors, regular

Lincoln University (continued)

education teachers, remediation/learning specialists, skill tutors, strategy tutors, and trained peer tutors are provided collaboratively through on-campus or off-campus services.

Unique Aids and Services Aids, services, or accommodations include faculty training and priority registration.

Assistive Technology Assistive technology is located in campus labs, the DSS office and includes digital textbooks/e-text, learning support software, and scanning. Technology training is provided to incoming students.

Subject-Area Tutoring Tutoring is offered one-on-one, in small groups, and in class-size groups for most subjects. Tutoring is provided through the program or unit via graduate assistants/students and trained peer tutors. Tutoring is also provided collaboratively through on-campus or off-campus services via computer-based instruction, graduate assistants/students, professional tutors, and trained peer tutors.

Basic Skills Remediation Remediation is offered one-on-one, in small groups, and in class-size groups for computer skills, math, reading, study skills, and time management. Remediation is provided through the program or unit via trained peer tutors. Remediation is also provided collaboratively through on-campus or off-campus services via professional tutors and trained peer tutors.

Enrichment Enrichment programs are available through the program or unit for self-advocacy. Programs for career planning, college survival skills, health and nutrition, learning strategies, math, oral communication skills, practical computer skills, reading, study skills, and time management are provided collaboratively through on-campus or off-campus services.

Application For admittance to the program or unit, students are required to apply to the program directly and provide a psychoeducational report (3 years old or less). It is recommended that students provide documentation of high school services. Upon acceptance, documentation of need for services should be sent only to the LD program or unit. *Application deadline (institutional):* Continuous. *Application deadline (LD program):* Rolling/continuous for fall and rolling/continuous for spring.

Written Policies Written policy regarding general/basic LD accommodations is available on the program Web site. Written policies regarding course substitutions, general/basic LD accommodations, and reduced course loads are available through the program or unit directly.

Lindenwood University
Campus Accessibility Services

209 South Kingshighway
St. Charles, MO 63301-1695
http://www.lindenwood.edu/
Contact: Ms. Tonie J. Isenhour, Coordinator for Campus Accessibility Services. Phone: 636-949-4784. E-mail: tisenhour@lindenwood.edu.

Campus Accessibility Services Approximately 30 registered undergraduate students were served during 2006–07. The program or unit includes 1 full-time staff member. Academic advisers are provided through the program or unit. Academic advisers and other are provided collaboratively through on-campus or off-campus services.

Assistive Technology Assistive technology is located in campus labs and includes digital textbooks/e-text and scanning.

Subject-Area Tutoring Tutoring is offered one-on-one and in small groups for most subjects. Tutoring is provided collaboratively through on-campus or off-campus services via other.

Basic Skills Remediation Remediation is offered in class-size groups for computer skills, learning strategies, math, reading, study skills, time management, and written language. Remediation is provided collaboratively through on-campus or off-campus services.

Enrichment Programs for career planning, college survival skills, learning strategies, math, practical computer skills, reading, study skills, test taking, time management, and written composition skills are provided collaboratively through on-campus or off-campus services. Credit is offered for college survival skills, learning strategies, math, practical computer skills, reading, study skills, test taking, time management, and written composition skills.

Application For admittance to the program or unit, students are required to provide a psychoeducational report (3 years old or less). Upon acceptance, documentation of need for services should be sent only to the LD program or unit. *Application deadline (institutional):* Continuous. *Application deadline (LD program):* Rolling/continuous for fall and rolling/continuous for spring.

Written Policies Written policy regarding general/basic LD accommodations is available on the program Web site. Written policy regarding general/basic LD accommodations is outlined in the school's catalog/handbook.

Long Island University, Brooklyn Campus

One University Plaza
Brooklyn, NY 11201-8423
http://www.liu.edu/
Contact: Mrs. Phyllis Brown-Richardson, Learning Disabilities Specialist. Phone: 718-488-1044. Fax: 718-834-6045. E-mail: phyllisbrown-richardson@liu.edu. Head of LD Program: Prof. Jeff Lambert, Director of Special Educational Services. Phone: 718-488-1044. Fax: 718-834-6045. E-mail: jlambert@liu.edu.

Approximately 50 registered undergraduate students were served during 2006–07. The program or unit includes 8 full-time and 12 part-time staff members. Academic advisers, counselors, graduate assistants/students, LD specialists, regular education teachers, skill tutors, strategy tutors, and trained peer tutors are provided collaboratively through on-campus or off-campus services.

Orientation The program or unit offers an optional orientation for new students before classes begin, after classes begin, and individually by special arrangement.

Unique Aids and Services Aids, services, or accommodations include advocates, career counseling, and faculty training.

Subject-Area Tutoring Tutoring is offered one-on-one and in small groups. Tutoring is provided collaboratively through on-campus or off-campus services via computer-based instruction, graduate assistants/students, LD specialists, and trained peer tutors.

Basic Skills Remediation Remediation is offered one-on-one and in small groups. Remediation is provided collaboratively through on-campus or off-campus services via computer-based instruction, graduate assistants/students, LD specialists, regular education teachers, and trained peer tutors.

Enrichment Programs for career planning, college survival skills, learning strategies, math, oral communication skills, practical computer skills, self-advocacy, stress management, study skills, test taking, time management, vocabulary development, and written composition skills are provided collaboratively through on-campus or off-campus services.

Application For admittance to the program or unit, students are required to provide a psychoeducational report (3 years old or less). It is recommended that students apply to the program directly and provide documentation of high school services. Upon application, materials documenting need for services should be sent only to the LD program or unit. Upon acceptance, documentation of need for services should be sent only to the LD program or unit. *Application deadline (institutional):* Continuous. *Application deadline (LD program):* Rolling/continuous for fall and rolling/continuous for spring.

Loyola Marymount University
Disability Support Services

One LMU Drive

Los Angeles, CA 90045-2659

http://www.lmu.edu/dss

Contact: Ms. Priscilla F. Levine, Director, Disability Support Services. Phone: 310-338-4535. Fax: 310-338-7657. E-mail: plevine@lmu.edu.

Disability Support Services Approximately 171 registered undergraduate students were served during 2006–07. The program or unit includes 2 full-time and 4 part-time staff members. Graduate assistants/students are provided through the program or unit. Counselors and diagnostic specialists are provided collaboratively through on-campus or off-campus services.

Orientation The program or unit offers a mandatory 1-hour orientation for new students after classes begin and individually by special arrangement.

Unique Aids and Services Aids, services, or accommodations include advocates, faculty training, and priority registration.

Assistive Technology Assistive technology is located in the DSS office, the library and includes scanning and screen readers. Technology training is provided to incoming students.

Subject-Area Tutoring Tutoring is offered one-on-one for most subjects. Tutoring is provided collaboratively through on-campus or off-campus services via computer-based instruction, graduate assistants/students, professional tutors, and trained peer tutors.

Enrichment Programs for career planning, college survival skills, health and nutrition, learning strategies, math, medication management, reading, stress management, study skills, test taking, time management, and written composition skills are provided collaboratively through on-campus or off-campus services.

Application For admittance to the program or unit, students are required to apply to the program directly and provide a psychoeducational report (3 years old or less). It is recommended that students provide documentation of high school services and provide letters from teachers, counselor, and previous standardized test scores/results. Upon application, materials documenting need for services should be sent only to the LD program or unit. Upon acceptance,

documentation of need for services should be sent only to the LD program or unit. *Application deadline (institutional):* 1/15. *Application deadline (LD program):* Rolling/continuous for fall and rolling/continuous for spring.

Written Policies Written policy regarding general/basic LD accommodations is available on the program Web site. Written policy regarding general/basic LD accommodations is outlined in the school's catalog/handbook. Written policy regarding general/basic LD accommodations is available through the program or unit directly.

Loyola University Chicago
Services for Students with Disabilities

820 North Michigan Avenue

Chicago, IL 60611-2196

http://www.luc.edu/depts/lac/disabilities

Contact: Coordinator. Phone: 773-508-7714. Fax: 773-508-3810.

Services for Students with Disabilities Approximately 160 registered undergraduate students were served during 2006–07. The program or unit includes 2 full-time staff members. Academic advisers, coaches, counselors, graduate assistants/students, regular education teachers, remediation/learning specialists, and trained peer tutors are provided collaboratively through on-campus or off-campus services.

Assistive Technology Assistive technology is located in the library and includes learning support software. Technology training is provided to incoming students.

Subject-Area Tutoring Tutoring is offered one-on-one and in small groups for most subjects. Tutoring is provided collaboratively through on-campus or off-campus services via graduate assistants/students and trained peer tutors.

Basic Skills Remediation Remediation is offered one-on-one, in small groups, and in class-size groups for learning strategies, study skills, and time management. Remediation is provided through the program or unit. Remediation is also provided collaboratively through on-campus or off-campus services via graduate assistants/students, LD specialists, and other.

Enrichment Programs for career planning, college survival skills, health and nutrition, learning strategies, math, oral communication skills, practical computer skills, self-advocacy, stress management, study skills, test taking, time management, and written composition skills are provided collaboratively through on-campus or off-campus services. Credit is offered for career planning, college survival skills, health and nutrition, math, oral communication skills, practical computer skills, study skills, test taking, and time management.

Application For admittance to the program or unit, students are required to provide a psychoeducational report (3 years old or less) and provide documentation by a professional in the area of LD-testing results, previous accommodations. It is recommended that students provide documentation of high school services. Upon application, materials documenting need for services should be sent only to admissions with institutional application materials. Upon acceptance, documentation of need for services should be sent only to the LD program or unit. *Application deadline (institutional):* 4/1. *Application deadline (LD program):* Rolling/continuous for fall and rolling/continuous for spring.

Loyola University Chicago (continued)

Written Policies Written policy regarding general/basic LD accommodations is available on the program Web site. Written policy regarding general/basic LD accommodations is outlined in the school's catalog/handbook. Written policy regarding general/basic LD accommodations is available through the program or unit directly.

Loyola University New Orleans

6363 Saint Charles Avenue

New Orleans, LA 70118-6195

http://www.loyno.edu/

Contact: Ms. Sarah Mead Smith, Director of Disability Services. Phone: 504-865-2990. Fax: 504-865-3543. E-mail: ssmith@loyno.edu.

The program or unit includes 1 full-time and 1 part-time staff member. Counselors, diagnostic specialists, LD specialists, and remediation/learning specialists are provided through the program or unit. Counselors, diagnostic specialists, LD specialists, remediation/learning specialists, and trained peer tutors are provided collaboratively through on-campus or off-campus services.

Unique Aids and Services Aids, services, or accommodations include advocates, priority registration, academic counseling and registration advising by learning specialists.

Assistive Technology Assistive technology is located in the DSS office and includes digital textbooks/e-text and scanning.

Subject-Area Tutoring Tutoring is offered one-on-one and in small groups for most subjects. Tutoring is provided through the program or unit via trained peer tutors. Tutoring is also provided collaboratively through on-campus or off-campus services via trained peer tutors.

Diagnostic Testing Testing for learning strategies, math, and reading is provided collaboratively through on-campus or off-campus services.

Enrichment Programs for career planning, college survival skills, learning strategies, practical computer skills, stress management, study skills, test taking, time management, vocabulary development, and written composition skills are provided collaboratively through on-campus or off-campus services. Credit is offered for career planning, college survival skills, learning strategies, practical computer skills, study skills, and written composition skills.

Application Upon acceptance, documentation of need for services should be sent only to the LD program or unit. *Application deadline (institutional):* 1/15. *Application deadline (LD program):* Rolling/continuous for fall.

Written Policies Written policy regarding general/basic LD accommodations is available on the program Web site. Written policies regarding course substitutions, general/basic LD accommodations, grade forgiveness, reduced course loads, substitutions and waivers of admissions requirements, and substitutions and waivers of graduation requirements are available through the program or unit directly.

Lynchburg College
Support Services

1501 Lakeside Drive

Lynchburg, VA 24501-3199

http://www.lynchburg.edu/disabilityservices.xml

Contact: Shawn Marie Arnold, Support Services Coordinator. Phone: 434-544-8687. Fax: 434-544-8485. E-mail: arnold_sm@lynchburg.edu.

Support Services Approximately 207 registered undergraduate students were served during 2006–07. The program or unit includes 1 full-time staff member. Academic advisers and trained peer tutors are provided through the program or unit. Coaches, counselors, regular education teachers, skill tutors, and strategy tutors are provided collaboratively through on-campus or off-campus services.

Orientation The program or unit offers an optional orientation for new students during summer prior to enrollment.

Unique Aids and Services Aids, services, or accommodations include career counseling, personal coach, priority registration.

Assistive Technology Assistive technology is located in a special lab and includes learning support software.

Subject-Area Tutoring Tutoring is offered one-on-one and in small groups for most subjects. Tutoring is provided collaboratively through on-campus or off-campus services via graduate assistants/students, professional tutors, and trained peer tutors.

Enrichment Enrichment programs are available through the program or unit for self-advocacy. Programs for college survival skills, learning strategies, oral communication skills, stress management, study skills, test taking, time management, and written composition skills are provided collaboratively through on-campus or off-campus services. Credit is offered for career planning, college survival skills, learning strategies, oral communication skills, stress management, study skills, test taking, time management, and written composition skills.

Application For admittance to the program or unit, students are required to provide a psychoeducational report (3 years old or less). It is recommended that students provide documentation of high school services. Upon acceptance, documentation of need for services should be sent only to the LD program or unit. *Application deadline (institutional):* Continuous. *Application deadline (LD program):* 7/15 for fall. 12/1 for spring.

Written Policies Written policies regarding course substitutions, general/basic LD accommodations, grade forgiveness, reduced course loads, substitutions and waivers of admissions requirements, and substitutions and waivers of graduation requirements are available on the program Web site. Written policies regarding course substitutions, general/basic LD accommodations, grade forgiveness, reduced course loads, substitutions and waivers of admissions requirements, and substitutions and waivers of graduation requirements are outlined in the school's catalog/handbook. Written policies regarding course substitutions, general/basic LD accommodations, grade forgiveness, reduced course loads, substitutions and waivers of admissions requirements, and substitutions and waivers of graduation requirements are available through the program or unit directly.

Macalester College
Disability Student Services

1600 Grand Avenue

St. Paul, MN 55105-1899

http://www.macalester.edu/disability

Contact: Irene Kao, Assistant Dean of Students/Coordinator for Disability Student Services. Phone: 651-696-6136. Fax: 651-696-6630. E-mail: kao@macalester.edu.

Disability Student Services Approximately 100 registered undergraduate students were served during 2006–07. The program or unit includes 1 full-time staff member. LD specialists are provided through the program or unit. Academic advisers, coaches, counselors, diagnostic specialists, professional tutors, skill tutors, strategy tutors, and trained peer tutors are provided collaboratively through on-campus or off-campus services.

Unique Aids and Services Aids, services, or accommodations include advocates.

Assistive Technology Assistive technology is located in the DSS office, a special lab and includes learning support software and scanning.

Subject-Area Tutoring Tutoring is offered one-on-one for some subjects. Tutoring is provided collaboratively through on-campus or off-campus services via trained peer tutors.

Enrichment Enrichment programs are available through the program or unit for self-advocacy. Programs for career planning, health and nutrition, learning strategies, math, oral communication skills, reading, stress management, study skills, test taking, time management, vocabulary development, and written composition skills are provided collaboratively through on-campus or off-campus services.

Application For admittance to the program or unit, students are required to provide a psychoeducational report (3 years old or less). It is recommended that students apply to the program directly. Upon application, materials documenting need for services should be sent only to the LD program or unit. Upon acceptance, documentation of need for services should be sent only to the LD program or unit. *Application deadline (institutional):* 1/15.

Written Policies Written policy regarding general/basic LD accommodations is available on the program Web site. Written policy regarding general/basic LD accommodations is outlined in the school's catalog/handbook. Written policies regarding course substitutions and reduced course loads are available through the program or unit directly.

MacMurray College

447 East College Avenue

Jacksonville, IL 62650

http://www.mac.edu/

Contact: Mr. Randy Myers, Director of Special Services. Phone: 217-479-7123. Fax: 217-291-0702. E-mail: randy.myers@mac.edu.

Approximately 5 registered undergraduate students were served during 2006–07. The program or unit includes 2 full-time staff members. Academic advisers, coaches, LD specialists, remediation/learning specialists, skill tutors, and trained peer tutors are provided through the program or unit.

Unique Aids and Services Aids, services, or accommodations include advocates and career counseling.

Subject-Area Tutoring Tutoring is offered one-on-one and in small groups. Tutoring is provided through the program or unit via computer-based instruction, graduate assistants/students, and trained peer tutors. Tutoring is also provided collaboratively through on-campus or off-campus services via computer-based instruction, graduate assistants/students, and trained peer tutors.

Basic Skills Remediation Remediation is offered one-on-one and in class-size groups for computer skills, learning strategies, math, reading, study skills, time management, and written language. Remediation is provided through the program or unit via computer-based instruction, regular education teachers, and trained peer tutors. Remediation is also provided collaboratively through on-campus or off-campus services via computer-based instruction, regular education teachers, and trained peer tutors.

Enrichment Programs for career planning, college survival skills, health and nutrition, learning strategies, math, oral communication skills, practical computer skills, reading, self-advocacy, stress management, study skills, test taking, time management, and written composition skills are provided collaboratively through on-campus or off-campus services.

Application It is recommended that students provide a psychoeducational report (3 years old or less) and provide documentation of high school services. Upon application, materials documenting need for services should be sent only to admissions with institutional application materials. Upon acceptance, documentation of need for services should be sent only to admissions. *Application deadline (institutional):* Continuous. *Application deadline (LD program):* Rolling/continuous for fall and rolling/continuous for spring.

Written Policies Written policies regarding general/basic LD accommodations and reduced course loads are available through the program or unit directly.

Maine College of Art
Student Affairs

97 Spring Street

Portland, ME 04101-3987

http://www.meca.edu/

Contact: Ms. Daisy D. Wilson, Director of Student Affairs. Phone: 207-879-5742 Ext. 235. Fax: 207-772-5069. E-mail: dwilson@meca.edu.

Student Affairs Approximately 35 registered undergraduate students were served during 2006–07. The program or unit includes 2 full-time staff members and 1 part-time staff member. Academic advisers, counselors, professional tutors, and trained peer tutors are provided through the program or unit. Academic advisers, diagnostic specialists, professional tutors, and regular education teachers are provided collaboratively through on-campus or off-campus services.

Unique Aids and Services Aids, services, or accommodations include ADA accommodations advising to faculty.

Assistive Technology Assistive technology is located in Academic Adviser's office and includes books on tape or CD.

Subject-Area Tutoring Tutoring is offered one-on-one and in small groups for all subjects. Tutoring is provided through the program or unit via computer-based instruction, graduate assistants/

Maine College of Art (continued)

students, LD specialists, and professional tutors. Tutoring is also provided collaboratively through on-campus or off-campus services via computer-based instruction, graduate assistants/students, LD specialists, and professional tutors.

Enrichment Enrichment programs are available through the program or unit for self-advocacy, test taking, time management, vocabulary development, and written composition skills. Programs for career planning, college survival skills, health and nutrition, learning strategies, math, stress management, study skills, time management, vocabulary development, and written composition skills are provided collaboratively through on-campus or off-campus services.

Application For admittance to the program or unit, students are required to apply to the program directly and provide documentation of high school services. It is recommended that students provide a psychoeducational report (2 years old or less). Upon application, materials documenting need for services should be sent only to admissions with institutional application materials. Upon acceptance, documentation of need for services should be sent only to the LD program or unit. *Application deadline (institutional):* Continuous. *Application deadline (LD program):* Rolling/continuous for fall and rolling/continuous for spring.

Written Policies Written policy regarding general/basic LD accommodations is available on the program Web site. Written policy regarding general/basic LD accommodations is outlined in the school's catalog/handbook. Written policies regarding course substitutions, general/basic LD accommodations, grade forgiveness, and reduced course loads are available through the program or unit directly.

Maine Maritime Academy

Castine, ME 04420

http://www.mma.edu

Contact: Prof. Donald A. Dobbin MSC, Associate Academic Dean. Phone: 207-326-2370 Ext. 370. Fax: 207-326-2218. E-mail: ddobb@mma.edu.

Approximately 38 registered undergraduate students were served during 2006–07. The program or unit includes 1 full-time staff member. Academic advisers, skill tutors, and strategy tutors are provided through the program or unit. Skill tutors and strategy tutors are provided collaboratively through on-campus or off-campus services.

Assistive Technology Assistive technology is located in campus labs and includes digital textbooks/e-text.

Subject-Area Tutoring Tutoring is offered in small groups for some subjects. Tutoring is provided collaboratively through on-campus or off-campus services via graduate assistants/students and trained peer tutors.

Diagnostic Testing Testing for auditory processing, handwriting, intelligence, math, motor skills, neuropsychological, reading, spelling, visual processing, and written language is provided collaboratively through on-campus or off-campus services.

Basic Skills Remediation Remediation is offered one-on-one for math, reading, spelling, study skills, and written language. Remediation is provided through the program or unit via regular education teachers. Remediation is also provided collaboratively through on-campus or off-campus services via regular education teachers and trained peer tutors.

Application For admittance to the program or unit, students are required to apply to the program directly and provide a psychoeducational report (3 years old or less). Upon application, materials documenting need for services should be sent only to admissions with institutional application materials. Upon acceptance, documentation of need for services should be sent only to the LD program or unit. *Application deadline (institutional):* 7/1. *Application deadline (LD program):* Rolling/continuous for fall and rolling/continuous for spring.

Written Policies Written policies regarding general/basic LD accommodations and reduced course loads are available through the program or unit directly.

Manhattan College
Specialized Resource Center

Manhattan College Parkway

Riverdale, NY 10471

http://www.manhattan.edu/sprscent

Contact: Dr. Ross Pollack, ADA Coordinator. Phone: 718-862-7101. Fax: 718-862-7808. E-mail: ross.pollack@manhattan.edu.

Specialized Resource Center Approximately 125 registered undergraduate students were served during 2006–07. The program or unit includes 1 full-time and 1 part-time staff member. LD specialists are provided through the program or unit. Academic advisers, counselors, graduate assistants/students, professional tutors, skill tutors, strategy tutors, and trained peer tutors are provided collaboratively through on-campus or off-campus services.

Assistive Technology Assistive technology is located in the DSS office and includes technology based on individualized determination.

Subject-Area Tutoring Tutoring is offered one-on-one and in small groups for most subjects. Tutoring is provided collaboratively through on-campus or off-campus services via graduate assistants/students, professional tutors, and trained peer tutors.

Enrichment Programs for career planning and college survival skills are provided collaboratively through on-campus or off-campus services.

Application For admittance to the program or unit, students are required to provide a psychoeducational report. It is recommended that students provide documentation of high school services. Upon application, materials documenting need for services should be sent only to the LD program or unit. Upon acceptance, documentation of need for services should be sent only to the LD program or unit. *Application deadline (institutional):* 4/15. *Application deadline (LD program):* Rolling/continuous for fall and rolling/continuous for spring.

Written Policies Written policies regarding course substitutions, general/basic LD accommodations, reduced course loads, and substitutions and waivers of graduation requirements are available on the program Web site.

Manhattanville College

HELP Center

2900 Purchase Street
Purchase, NY 10577-2132
http://www.manhattanville.edu/

Contact: Ms. Eleanor K. Schwartz, HELP Center Coordinator. Phone: 914-323-5313. Fax: 914-323-5493. E-mail: help@mville.edu. Head of LD Program: Ms. Jean Baldassare, Director of Disability Services. Phone: 914-323-7127. E-mail: baldassarej@mville.edu.

HELP Center Approximately 45 registered undergraduate students were served during 2006–07. The program or unit includes 1 full-time and 7 part-time staff members. Academic advisers, LD specialists, professional tutors, remediation/learning specialists, skill tutors, special education teachers, and strategy tutors are provided through the program or unit. Academic advisers, counselors, graduate assistants/students, and trained peer tutors are provided collaboratively through on-campus or off-campus services.

Orientation The program or unit offers individually by special arrangement.

Unique Aids and Services Aids, services, or accommodations include support groups.

Assistive Technology Assistive technology is located in campus labs, a special lab and includes learning support software, scanning, and Kurzweil.

Subject-Area Tutoring Tutoring is offered one-on-one for most subjects. Tutoring is provided through the program or unit via computer-based instruction, LD specialists, and professional tutors. Tutoring is also provided collaboratively through on-campus or off-campus services via computer-based instruction, graduate assistants/students, and trained peer tutors.

Basic Skills Remediation Remediation is offered one-on-one for learning strategies, reading, spelling, study skills, time management, and written language. Remediation is provided through the program or unit via computer-based instruction, LD specialists, professional tutors, and special education teachers.

Enrichment Enrichment programs are available through the program or unit for learning strategies, reading, self-advocacy, study skills, test taking, time management, vocabulary development, and written composition skills. Programs for career planning, college survival skills, learning strategies, math, oral communication skills, stress management, and written composition skills are provided collaboratively through on-campus or off-campus services. Credit is offered for written composition skills.

Fees *LD Program or Service* fee varies according to level/tier of service.

Application For admittance to the program or unit, students are required to provide a psychoeducational report (5 years old or less). It is recommended that students provide documentation of high school services. Upon acceptance, documentation of need for services should be sent only to the LD program or unit. *Application deadline (institutional):* 3/1. *Application deadline (LD program):* Rolling/continuous for fall and rolling/continuous for spring.

Written Policies Written policy regarding general/basic LD accommodations is available on the program Web site. Written policies regarding general/basic LD accommodations and reduced course loads are outlined in the school's catalog/handbook. Written policies regarding general/basic LD accommodations and reduced course loads are available through the program or unit directly.

Mannes College The New School for Music

Student Disability Services

150 West 85th Street
New York, NY 10024-4402
http://www.newschool.edu/studentservices/disability/

Contact: Mr. Jason Luchs, Assistant Director of Student Disability Services. Phone: 212-229-5626 Ext. 3135. Fax: 212-229-1090. E-mail: luchsj@newschool.edu.

Student Disability Services Approximately 5 registered undergraduate students were served during 2006–07. The program or unit includes 1 full-time and 1 part-time staff member. Academic advisers, counselors, and other are provided collaboratively through on-campus or off-campus services.

Assistive Technology Assistive technology is located in campus labs and includes digital textbooks/e-text, learning support software, and scanning.

Enrichment Programs for career planning, college survival skills, health and nutrition, learning strategies, self-advocacy, stress management, study skills, test taking, time management, and written composition skills are provided collaboratively through on-campus or off-campus services.

Application For admittance to the program or unit, students are required to apply to the program directly and provide a psychoeducational report (3 years old or less). Upon acceptance, documentation of need for services should be sent only to the LD program or unit. *Application deadline (institutional):* 12/1. *Application deadline (LD program):* Rolling/continuous for fall and rolling/continuous for spring.

Written Policies Written policy regarding general/basic LD accommodations is available on the program Web site. Written policy regarding general/basic LD accommodations is outlined in the school's catalog/handbook. Written policy regarding general/basic LD accommodations is available through the program or unit directly.

Marian College

Learning and Counseling Center/ Academic Support Services Program

3200 Cold Spring Road
Indianapolis, IN 46222-1997
http://studentlife.marian.edu/learning_counseling.asp

Contact: Ms. Marjorie Batic, Director of Academic Support Services. Phone: 317-955-6150. Fax: 317-955-6415. E-mail: mbatic@marian.edu.

Learning and Counseling Center/Academic Support Services Program Approximately 50 registered undergraduate students were served during 2006–07. The program or unit includes 1 full-time and 1 part-time staff member. Graduate assistants/students, professional tutors, and remediation/learning specialists are provided through the program or unit. Academic advisers, coaches, counselors, LD specialists, regular education teachers, skill tutors, strategy tutors, and trained peer tutors are provided collaboratively through on-campus or off-campus services.

Marian College (continued)

Summer Program an optional summer program prior to entering the school.

Unique Aids and Services Aids, services, or accommodations include career counseling.

Subject-Area Tutoring Tutoring is offered one-on-one and in small groups for all subjects. Tutoring is provided through the program or unit via computer-based instruction, LD specialists, and professional tutors. Tutoring is also provided collaboratively through on-campus or off-campus services via trained peer tutors.

Diagnostic Testing Testing is provided through the program or unit for intelligence, learning strategies, learning styles, math, motor skills, personality, reading, spelling, and study skills. Testing for auditory processing, handwriting, intelligence, motor skills, neuropsychological, personality, social skills, spelling, spoken language, visual processing, and written language is provided collaboratively through on-campus or off-campus services.

Basic Skills Remediation Remediation is offered one-on-one, in small groups, and in class-size groups for learning strategies, math, reading, study skills, time management, and organization, test-taking, note-taking. Remediation is provided through the program or unit via computer-based instruction, LD specialists, and professional tutors. Remediation is also provided collaboratively through on-campus or off-campus services via regular education teachers and teacher trainees.

Enrichment Enrichment programs are available through the program or unit for college survival skills, learning strategies, math, medication management, oral communication skills, reading, stress management, study skills, test taking, time management, and written composition skills. Programs for career planning, health and nutrition, and practical computer skills are provided collaboratively through on-campus or off-campus services. Credit is offered for college survival skills, health and nutrition, practical computer skills, and vocabulary development.

Application For admittance to the program or unit, students are required to provide a psychoeducational report (3 years old or less). It is recommended that students provide documentation of high school services and provide a neuropsychological report. Upon acceptance, documentation of need for services should be sent only to the LD program or unit. *Application deadline (institutional):* 8/1. *Application deadline (LD program):* Rolling/continuous for fall and rolling/continuous for spring.

Written Policies Written policy regarding general/basic LD accommodations is outlined in the school's catalog/handbook. Written policies regarding course substitutions, general/basic LD accommodations, reduced course loads, substitutions and waivers of admissions requirements, and substitutions and waivers of graduation requirements are available through the program or unit directly.

Marietta College
Academic Resource Center

215 Fifth Street

Marietta, OH 45750-4000

http://mcnet.marietta.edu/~arc/students.html

Contact: Barbi Cheadle, Disabilities Specialist. Phone: 740-376-4700. Fax: 740-376-4406. E-mail: bkc001@ marietta.edu. Head of LD Program: Debra R. Higgins,

Director of the Academic Resource Center. Phone: 740-376-4700. Fax: 740-376-4406. E-mail: higginsd@ marietta.edu.

Academic Resource Center Approximately 50 registered undergraduate students were served during 2006–07. The program or unit includes 2 full-time staff members. LD specialists, skill tutors, strategy tutors, and trained peer tutors are provided through the program or unit. Academic advisers, coaches, counselors, regular education teachers, and other are provided collaboratively through on-campus or off-campus services.

Assistive Technology Assistive technology is located in the DSS office and includes digital textbooks/e-text, scanning, and text-to-speech software, speech recognition software. Technology training is provided to incoming students.

Subject-Area Tutoring Tutoring is offered one-on-one and in small groups for all subjects. Tutoring is provided through the program or unit via trained peer tutors.

Enrichment Enrichment programs are available through the program or unit for college survival skills, learning strategies, study skills, test taking, and time management. Programs for career planning, college survival skills, learning strategies, and written composition skills are provided collaboratively through on-campus or off-campus services.

Application For admittance to the program or unit, students are required to provide a psychoeducational report (3 years old or less) and provide test evaluations. It is recommended that students provide documentation of high school services. Upon acceptance, documentation of need for services should be sent to both admissions and the LD program or unit. *Application deadline (institutional):* 5/1. *Application deadline (LD program):* Rolling/continuous for fall and rolling/continuous for spring.

Written Policies Written policy regarding general/basic LD accommodations is available on the program Web site. Written policy regarding general/basic LD accommodations is outlined in the school's catalog/handbook.

Marquette University
Office of Disability Services

PO Box 1881

Milwaukee, WI 53201-1881

http://www.marquette.edu/oses/disability

Contact: Ms. Heidi Vering, Coordinator, Disability Services. Phone: 414-288-1645. Fax: 414-288-5799. E-mail: heidi.vering@marquette.edu.

Office of Disability Services Approximately 50 registered undergraduate students were served during 2006–07. The program or unit includes 1 full-time and 1 part-time staff member. Graduate assistants/ students and strategy tutors are provided through the program or unit. Academic advisers, regular education teachers, strategy tutors, trained peer tutors, and other are provided collaboratively through on-campus or off-campus services.

Assistive Technology Assistive technology is located in the library and includes digital textbooks/e-text and Kurzweil 3000. Technology training is provided to incoming students.

Subject-Area Tutoring Tutoring is offered in small groups for most subjects. Tutoring is provided collaboratively through on-campus or off-campus services via graduate assistants/students and trained peer tutors.

Basic Skills Remediation Remediation is available for learning strategies, study skills, and time management. Remediation is provided collaboratively through on-campus or off-campus services via trained peer tutors and other.

Enrichment Programs for career planning, health and nutrition, learning strategies, stress management, study skills, test taking, time management, and written composition skills are provided collaboratively through on-campus or off-campus services. Credit is offered for career planning.

Application For admittance to the program or unit, students are required to provide a psychoeducational report (5 years old or less). It is recommended that students provide documentation of high school services. Upon application, materials documenting need for services should be sent only to the LD program or unit. Upon acceptance, documentation of need for services should be sent only to the LD program or unit. *Application deadline (institutional):* 12/1. *Application deadline (LD program):* Rolling/continuous for fall and rolling/continuous for spring.

Written Policies Written policies regarding course substitutions, general/basic LD accommodations, and substitutions and waivers of graduation requirements are available on the program Web site. Written policies regarding course substitutions and substitutions and waivers of graduation requirements are outlined in the school's catalog/handbook. Written policies regarding course substitutions, general/basic LD accommodations, and substitutions and waivers of graduation requirements are available through the program or unit directly.

Marymount University
Disability Support Services

2807 North Glebe Road

Arlington, VA 22207-4299

http://www.marymount.edu/studentlife/disability/

Contact: Ms. Kelly L. DeSenti, Director of Disability Support Services. Phone: 703-284-1615. Fax: 703-524-8763. E-mail: kelly.desenti@marymount.edu.

Disability Support Services Approximately 111 registered undergraduate students were served during 2006–07. The program or unit includes 1 full-time staff member. Academic advisers, counselors, remediation/learning specialists, skill tutors, strategy tutors, and trained peer tutors are provided collaboratively through on-campus or off-campus services.

Unique Aids and Services Aids, services, or accommodations include weekly meetings with DSS Director.

Assistive Technology Assistive technology is located in campus labs, the library, Tutoring Center and includes scanning and JAWS.

Subject-Area Tutoring Tutoring is offered one-on-one, in small groups, and in class-size groups for most subjects. Tutoring is provided collaboratively through on-campus or off-campus services via computer-based instruction, graduate assistants/students, trained peer tutors, and other.

Basic Skills Remediation Remediation is offered one-on-one, in small groups, and in class-size groups for learning strategies, math, reading, social skills, study skills, and time management. Remediation is provided through the program or unit. Remediation is also provided collaboratively through on-campus or off-campus services via computer-based instruction, regular education teachers, and other.

Enrichment Enrichment programs are available through the program or unit for career planning, self-advocacy, stress management, study skills, test taking, time management, and other. Programs for career planning, college survival skills, health and nutrition, learning strategies, math, medication management, practical computer skills, stress management, study skills, test taking, time management, and written composition skills are provided collaboratively through on-campus or off-campus services. Credit is offered for college survival skills, health and nutrition, practical computer skills, stress management, and written composition skills.

Application For admittance to the program or unit, students are required to provide a psychoeducational report (3 years old or less) and provide LD testing on the adult scales, DSM diagnosis as appropriate. Upon application, materials documenting need for services should be sent only to the LD program or unit. Upon acceptance, documentation of need for services should be sent only to the LD program or unit. *Application deadline (institutional):* Continuous. *Application deadline (LD program):* Rolling/continuous for fall and rolling/continuous for spring.

Written Policies Written policy regarding general/basic LD accommodations is available on the program Web site. Written policy regarding general/basic LD accommodations is outlined in the school's catalog/handbook. Written policies regarding course substitutions, general/basic LD accommodations, and substitutions and waivers of graduation requirements are available through the program or unit directly.

Marywood University
Office of Disability Services

2300 Adams Avenue

Scranton, PA 18509-1598

http://www.Marywood.edu/Disabilities/disabilityservices.html

Contact: Ms. Diane J. Taylor, MA, NCC, Associate Director of Academic Success for Student Support Services. Phone: 570-340-6045 Ext. 2335. Fax: 570-340-6028. E-mail: dtaylor@marywood.edu.

Office of Disability Services Approximately 50 registered undergraduate students were served during 2006–07. The program or unit includes 1 full-time staff member. Academic advisers, counselors, and trained peer tutors are provided collaboratively through on-campus or off-campus services.

Orientation The program or unit offers an optional varying length orientation for new students before classes begin, during summer prior to enrollment, and individually by special arrangement.

Unique Aids and Services Aids, services, or accommodations include career counseling, faculty training, and weekly meetings with faculty.

Assistive Technology Assistive technology is located in campus labs and includes digital textbooks/e-text and computer software. Technology training is provided to incoming students.

Marywood University (continued)

Subject-Area Tutoring Tutoring is offered one-on-one and in small groups for all subjects. Tutoring is provided through the program or unit via LD specialists. Tutoring is also provided collaboratively through on-campus or off-campus services via computer-based instruction, professional tutors, and trained peer tutors.

Enrichment Enrichment programs are available through the program or unit for college survival skills, learning strategies, self-advocacy, stress management, study skills, and time management. Programs for career planning, college survival skills, health and nutrition, math, oral communication skills, practical computer skills, reading, test taking, and written composition skills are provided collaboratively through on-campus or off-campus services.

Application For admittance to the program or unit, students are required to provide a psychoeducational report (3 years old or less), provide documentation of high school services, and provide psycho-educational evaluation. Upon application, materials documenting need for services should be sent to both admissions and the LD program or unit. Upon acceptance, documentation of need for services should be sent only to the LD program or unit. *Application deadline (institutional):* Continuous. *Application deadline (LD program):* Rolling/continuous for fall and rolling/continuous for spring.

Written Policies Written policies regarding course substitutions, general/basic LD accommodations, grade forgiveness, reduced course loads, substitutions and waivers of admissions requirements, and substitutions and waivers of graduation requirements are available through the program or unit directly.

Massachusetts College of Liberal Arts
Learning Services Center

375 Church Street

North Adams, MA 01247-4100

http://www.mcla.edu/Academics/Academic_Resources/Learning_Services_Center/disabled.php

Contact: Claire Devereaux Smith, Assistant Director of Learning Services/Coordinator of Academic Support. Phone: 413-662-5318. Fax: 413-662-5319. E-mail: claire.smith@mcla.edu. Head of LD Program: Theresa Miller, Director of Learning Services. Phone: 413-662-5309. Fax: 413-662-5319. E-mail: theresa.miller@mcla.edu.

Learning Services Center Approximately 90 registered undergraduate students were served during 2006–07. The program or unit includes 1 full-time staff member. Academic advisers, counselors, and LD specialists are provided through the program or unit. Trained peer tutors are provided collaboratively through on-campus or off-campus services.

Summer Program To help prepare for the demands of college, there is an optional 4-week summer program prior to entering the school available to high school graduates that focuses on study skills. The program accepts students from out-of-state.

Unique Aids and Services Aids, services, or accommodations include priority registration.

Assistive Technology Assistive technology is located in campus labs, the DSS office and includes learning support software, scanning, and digital texts only if available from the publisher.

Subject-Area Tutoring Tutoring is offered in small groups for some subjects. Tutoring is provided collaboratively through on-campus or off-campus services via trained peer tutors.

Diagnostic Testing Testing for intelligence, math, reading, and written language is provided collaboratively through on-campus or off-campus services.

Basic Skills Remediation Remediation is offered in class-size groups for learning strategies and math. Remediation is provided collaboratively through on-campus or off-campus services via regular education teachers.

Application For admittance to the program or unit, students are required to provide a psychoeducational report (3 years old or less). It is recommended that students provide documentation of high school services. Upon application, materials documenting need for services should be sent only to admissions with institutional application materials. Upon acceptance, documentation of need for services should be sent only to the LD program or unit. *Application deadline (institutional):* Continuous. *Application deadline (LD program):* 10/18 for fall. 3/1 for spring.

Written Policies Written policy regarding general/basic LD accommodations is available on the program Web site. Written policy regarding course substitutions is available through the program or unit directly.

McMaster University
Centre for Student Development, Assistive Technology, Learning and Academic Support (ATLAS) Program

1280 Main Street West

Hamilton, ON L8S 4M2

Canada

http://csd.mcmaster.ca/atlas/

Contact: Ms. Indrani Reddy, Learning Disabilities Coordinator. Phone: 905-525-9140 Ext. 24354. Fax: 905-528-3749. E-mail: reddyin@mcmaster.ca.

Centre for Student Development, Assistive Technology, Learning and Academic Support (ATLAS) Program Approximately 125 registered undergraduate students were served during 2006–07. The program or unit includes 3 full-time staff members and 1 part-time staff member. Diagnostic specialists, LD specialists, remediation/learning specialists, trained peer tutors, and other are provided through the program or unit. Academic advisers, counselors, and diagnostic specialists are provided collaboratively through on-campus or off-campus services.

Summer Program To help prepare for the demands of college, there is an optional 3-day summer program prior to entering the school available to high school graduates that focuses on life skills and/or college life adjustment, self-advocacy, study skills, test-taking skills, and time management. The program is available to students attending other colleges.

Assistive Technology Assistive technology is located in the DSS office and includes digital textbooks/e-text, learning support software, and scanning. Technology training is provided to incoming students.

Subject-Area Tutoring Tutoring is offered one-on-one for some subjects. Tutoring is provided through the program or unit via computer-based instruction, LD specialists, and trained peer tutors.
Diagnostic Testing Testing is provided through the program or unit for learning strategies, learning styles, math, reading, spelling, spoken language, study skills, visual processing, and written language. Testing for auditory processing, intelligence, learning strategies, math, motor skills, neuropsychological, personality, visual processing, and written language is provided collaboratively through on-campus or off-campus services.
Basic Skills Remediation Remediation is offered one-on-one for auditory processing, computer skills, learning strategies, reading, social skills, spelling, study skills, time management, visual processing, and written language. Remediation is provided through the program or unit via computer-based instruction, LD specialists, and trained peer tutors.
Enrichment Enrichment programs are available through the program or unit for learning strategies, math, oral communication skills, practical computer skills, reading, self-advocacy, stress management, study skills, test taking, time management, vocabulary development, and written composition skills. Programs for career planning, college survival skills, health and nutrition, medication management, and stress management are provided collaboratively through on-campus or off-campus services.
Fees *Diagnostic Testing* fee is $0 to $1800.
Application For admittance to the program or unit, students are required to provide a psychoeducational report. It is recommended that students provide documentation of high school services. Upon acceptance, documentation of need for services should be sent only to the LD program or unit. *Application deadline (LD program):* 11/1 for fall. 6/1 for spring.
Written Policies Written policy regarding general/basic LD accommodations is available on the program Web site. Written policy regarding general/basic LD accommodations is outlined in the school's catalog/handbook.

McNeese State University
Services for Students with Disabilities

4205 Ryan Street

Lake Charles, LA 70609

http://www.mcneese.edu/administration/vpsse/swd/

Contact: Mr. Timothy W. Delaney, Director. Phone: 337-475-5916. Fax: 337-475-5878. E-mail: ssd@mcneese.edu.

Services for Students with Disabilities Approximately 62 registered undergraduate students were served during 2006–07. The program or unit includes 2 full-time and 2 part-time staff members. Graduate assistants/students and other are provided through the program or unit. Academic advisers, counselors, diagnostic specialists, graduate assistants/students, and professional tutors are provided collaboratively through on-campus or off-campus services.
Unique Aids and Services Aids, services, or accommodations include faculty training.
Assistive Technology Assistive technology is located in campus labs and includes scanning.

Subject-Area Tutoring Tutoring is offered in small groups for some subjects. Tutoring is provided through the program or unit via graduate assistants/students. Tutoring is also provided collaboratively through on-campus or off-campus services via computer-based instruction, LD specialists, and professional tutors.
Diagnostic Testing Testing for auditory processing, intelligence, personality, reading, spelling, study skills, visual processing, and written language is provided collaboratively through on-campus or off-campus services.
Basic Skills Remediation Remediation is offered in class-size groups for learning strategies, math, reading, study skills, and written language. Remediation is provided collaboratively through on-campus or off-campus services via graduate assistants/students, regular education teachers, and teacher trainees.
Application For admittance to the program or unit, students are required to apply to the program directly, provide a psychoeducational report (3 years old or less), and provide other documentation. Upon application, materials documenting need for services should be sent only to the LD program or unit. Upon acceptance, documentation of need for services should be sent only to the LD program or unit. *Application deadline (institutional):* Continuous. *Application deadline (LD program):* Rolling/continuous for fall and rolling/continuous for spring.
Written Policies Written policy regarding general/basic LD accommodations is available on the program Web site.

Mercer University
Disability Support Services

1400 Coleman Avenue

Macon, GA 31207-0003

http://www.mercer.edu/stu_support/swd.htm

Contact: Ms. Carole S. Burrowbridge, Disability Support Services Coordinator. Phone: 478-301-2778 Ext. 478. Fax: 478-301-2127. E-mail: burrowbrid_c@mercer.edu.

Disability Support Services Approximately 55 registered undergraduate students were served during 2006–07. Academic advisers, counselors, diagnostic specialists, LD specialists, and trained peer tutors are provided collaboratively through on-campus or off-campus services.
Unique Aids and Services Aids, services, or accommodations include faculty training and priority registration.
Assistive Technology Assistive technology is located in the DSS office, the library, the Tutoring Center and includes digital textbooks/e-text, learning support software, and scanning.
Subject-Area Tutoring Tutoring is offered in small groups for some subjects. Tutoring is provided collaboratively through on-campus or off-campus services via trained peer tutors.
Diagnostic Testing Testing for auditory processing, handwriting, intelligence, learning strategies, learning styles, math, motor skills, neuropsychological, personality, reading, social skills, spelling, spoken language, study skills, visual processing, written language, and other services is provided collaboratively through on-campus or off-campus services.
Enrichment Programs for career planning, college survival skills, health and nutrition, learning strategies, medication management, self-advocacy, stress management, study skills, test taking, time management, and written composition skills are provided collaboratively through on-campus or off-campus services.

Mercer University (continued)

Student Organization Delta Sigma Omicron consists of 6 members.

Fees *Diagnostic Testing* fee is applicable.

Application For admittance to the program or unit, students are required to provide a psychoeducational report. It is recommended that students provide documentation of high school services. Upon acceptance, documentation of need for services should be sent only to the LD program or unit. *Application deadline (institutional):* 7/1. *Application deadline (LD program):* Rolling/continuous for fall and rolling/continuous for spring.

Written Policies Written policy regarding general/basic LD accommodations is available on the program Web site. Written policies regarding course substitutions, general/basic LD accommodations, reduced course loads, substitutions and waivers of admissions requirements, and substitutions and waivers of graduation requirements are available through the program or unit directly.

Mercy College of Health Sciences
Student Services/Student Enrichment Program

928 Sixth Avenue

Des Moines, IA 50309-1239

http://www.mchs.edu/

Contact: Susan J. Rhoades, Dean, Enrollment & Student Services. Phone: 515-643-3180. E-mail: srhoades@mercydesmoines.org.

Student Services/Student Enrichment Program Approximately 15 registered undergraduate students were served during 2006–07. The program or unit includes 1 part-time staff member. Academic advisers, regular education teachers, remediation/learning specialists, and skill tutors are provided collaboratively through on-campus or off-campus services.

Subject-Area Tutoring Tutoring is offered one-on-one and in small groups for some subjects. Tutoring is provided collaboratively through on-campus or off-campus services via trained peer tutors.

Enrichment Credit is offered for college survival skills, learning strategies, math, medication management, stress management, study skills, test taking, and time management.

Application It is recommended that students provide documentation of high school services. Upon acceptance, documentation of need for services should be sent only to admissions. *Application deadline (institutional):* Continuous. *Application deadline (LD program):* Rolling/continuous for fall.

Written Policies Written policy regarding general/basic LD accommodations is outlined in the school's catalog/handbook. Written policy regarding general/basic LD accommodations is available through the program or unit directly.

Michigan State University
Resource Center for Persons with Disabilities

East Lansing, MI 48824

http://www.rcpd.msu.edu

Contact: Elaine High, Learning Disabilities Specialist. Phone: 517-353-9642. Fax: 517-432-3191. E-mail: high@msu.edu. Head of LD Program: Mr. Michael J. Hudson, Director. Phone: 517-353-9642 Ext. 229. E-mail: mjh@msu.edu.

Resource Center for Persons with Disabilities Approximately 533 registered undergraduate students were served during 2006–07. The program or unit includes 2 full-time staff members and 1 part-time staff member. Coaches, diagnostic specialists, LD specialists, remediation/learning specialists, skill tutors, and strategy tutors are provided through the program or unit. Academic advisers, counselors, professional tutors, and trained peer tutors are provided collaboratively through on-campus or off-campus services.

Orientation The program or unit offers an optional 2.5-hour orientation for new students before classes begin.

Unique Aids and Services Aids, services, or accommodations include faculty training and priority registration.

Assistive Technology Assistive technology is located in campus labs, the DSS office and includes digital textbooks/e-text, learning support software, and scanning. Technology training is provided to incoming students.

Subject-Area Tutoring Tutoring is offered one-on-one and in small groups for some subjects. Tutoring is provided collaboratively through on-campus or off-campus services via trained peer tutors.

Diagnostic Testing Testing is provided through the program or unit for learning strategies, learning styles, and study skills. Testing for intelligence, math, personality, reading, and spelling is provided collaboratively through on-campus or off-campus services.

Basic Skills Remediation Remediation is offered one-on-one, in small groups, and in class-size groups for learning strategies, reading, spelling, study skills, and time management. Remediation is provided through the program or unit via LD specialists. Remediation is also provided collaboratively through on-campus or off-campus services via LD specialists.

Enrichment Program for math is provided collaboratively through on-campus or off-campus services. Credit is offered for math.

Student Organization Council of Students with Disabilities consists of 151 members.

Fees *Diagnostic Testing* fee is $250.

Application For admittance to the program or unit, students are required to apply to the program directly and provide a psychoeducational report (4 years old or less). It is recommended that students provide documentation of high school services. Upon acceptance, documentation of need for services should be sent only to the LD program or unit. *Application deadline (institutional):* Continuous. *Application deadline (LD program):* Rolling/continuous for fall and rolling/continuous for spring.

Written Policies Written policy regarding general/basic LD accommodations is available on the program Web site.

Middle Tennessee State University
Disabled Student Services

1301 East Main Street

Murfreesboro, TN 37132

http://www.mtsu.edu/~dssemail/

Contact: Janet Norman, Assistant Director. Phone: 615-904-8246. Fax: 615-898-4893. E-mail: jnorman@mtsu.edu.

Disabled Student Services Approximately 450 registered undergraduate students were served during 2006–07. The program or unit includes 4 full-time and 25 part-time staff members. LD specialists are provided through the program or unit. Academic advisers, counselors, graduate assistants/students, regular education teachers, remediation/learning specialists, special education teachers, and trained peer tutors are provided collaboratively through on-campus or off-campus services.

Unique Aids and Services Aids, services, or accommodations include priority registration.

Assistive Technology Assistive technology is located in campus labs, the DSS office, a special lab and includes digital textbooks/e-text, learning support software, and scanning.

Subject-Area Tutoring Tutoring is offered one-on-one and in small groups for some subjects. Tutoring is provided collaboratively through on-campus or off-campus services via graduate assistants/students and trained peer tutors.

Basic Skills Remediation Remediation is offered in class-size groups for learning strategies, math, reading, and written language. Remediation is provided collaboratively through on-campus or off-campus services via computer-based instruction, graduate assistants/students, regular education teachers, and trained peer tutors.

Enrichment Enrichment programs are available through the program or unit for college survival skills. Programs for career planning, learning strategies, math, reading, and written composition skills are provided collaboratively through on-campus or off-campus services. Credit is offered for learning strategies, math, reading, and written composition skills.

Student Organization Sigma Delta Sigma consists of 25 members.

Application For admittance to the program or unit, students are required to provide a psychoeducational report (2 years old or less). Upon application, materials documenting need for services should be sent only to the LD program or unit. Upon acceptance, documentation of need for services should be sent only to the LD program or unit. *Application deadline (institutional):* 7/1. *Application deadline (LD program):* Rolling/continuous for fall and rolling/continuous for spring.

Written Policies Written policy regarding general/basic LD accommodations is available on the program Web site. Written policy regarding general/basic LD accommodations is available through the program or unit directly.

Midland Lutheran College
Academic Support Services

900 North Clarkson Street

Fremont, NE 68025-4200

http://www.mlc.edu

Contact: Dr. Lori Moseman, Director of Academic Support Services. Phone: 402-941-6257. Fax: 402-727-6223. E-mail: moseman@mlc.edu.

Academic Support Services Approximately 10 registered undergraduate students were served during 2006–07. The program or unit includes 2 full-time staff members. Academic advisers, counselors, skill tutors, trained peer tutors, and other are provided collaboratively through on-campus or off-campus services.

Assistive Technology Assistive technology is located in the Learning Center and includes digital textbooks/e-text, learning support software, and scanning.

Subject-Area Tutoring Tutoring is offered one-on-one and in small groups for most subjects. Tutoring is provided collaboratively through on-campus or off-campus services via trained peer tutors and other.

Basic Skills Remediation Remediation is offered one-on-one and in small groups for learning strategies, study skills, and time management. Remediation is provided collaboratively through on-campus or off-campus services via special education teachers, trained peer tutors, and other.

Enrichment Enrichment programs are available through the program or unit for learning strategies, self-advocacy, stress management, study skills, test taking, and time management. Program for stress management is provided collaboratively through on-campus or off-campus services.

Application For admittance to the program or unit, students are required to apply to the program directly and provide a psychoeducational report (5 years old or less). It is recommended that students provide documentation of high school services. Upon application, materials documenting need for services should be sent only to the LD program or unit. Upon acceptance, documentation of need for services should be sent only to the LD program or unit. *Application deadline (institutional):* Continuous. *Application deadline (LD program):* Rolling/continuous for fall and rolling/continuous for spring.

Written Policies Written policy regarding general/basic LD accommodations is outlined in the school's catalog/handbook. Written policy regarding general/basic LD accommodations is available through the program or unit directly.

Millersville University of Pennsylvania
Office of Learning Services

PO Box 1002

Millersville, PA 17551-0302

http://www.millersville.edu/~ols

Contact: Mrs. Sherlynn Bessick, Director of Office of Learning Services. Phone: 717-872-3178. Fax: 717-871-2129. E-mail: learning.services@millersville.edu.

Millersville University of Pennsylvania (continued)

Office of Learning Services Approximately 200 registered undergraduate students were served during 2006–07. The program or unit includes 2 full-time and 20 part-time staff members. Graduate assistants/students, skill tutors, strategy tutors, teacher trainees, trained peer tutors, and other are provided through the program or unit. Academic advisers, counselors, graduate assistants/students, skill tutors, strategy tutors, trained peer tutors, and other are provided collaboratively through on-campus or off-campus services.

Unique Aids and Services Aids, services, or accommodations include career counseling, faculty training, priority registration, specialty workshops (AD/HD, autism, critical thinking).

Assistive Technology Assistive technology is located in campus labs, the DSS office, a special lab and includes digital textbooks/e-text and learning support software.

Subject-Area Tutoring Tutoring is offered one-on-one and in small groups for most subjects. Tutoring is provided through the program or unit via computer-based instruction, graduate assistants/students, and trained peer tutors. Tutoring is also provided collaboratively through on-campus or off-campus services via computer-based instruction, graduate assistants/students, and trained peer tutors.

Basic Skills Remediation Remediation is offered one-on-one and in small groups for learning strategies, math, study skills, time management, written language, and critical thinking, note-taking. Remediation is provided through the program or unit via computer-based instruction, graduate assistants/students, and trained peer tutors. Remediation is also provided collaboratively through on-campus or off-campus services via computer-based instruction, graduate assistants/students, and trained peer tutors.

Enrichment Enrichment programs are available through the program or unit for career planning, college survival skills, learning strategies, math, self-advocacy, study skills, test taking, time management, and written composition skills. Programs for career planning, college survival skills, health and nutrition, learning strategies, math, medication management, oral communication skills, practical computer skills, stress management, and written composition skills are provided collaboratively through on-campus or off-campus services. Credit is offered for health and nutrition.

Application For admittance to the program or unit, students are required to apply to the program directly, provide a psychoeducational report (3 years old or less), and provide documentation of high school services. Upon acceptance, documentation of need for services should be sent to both admissions and the LD program or unit. *Application deadline (institutional):* Continuous. *Application deadline (LD program):* Rolling/continuous for fall and rolling/continuous for spring.

Written Policies Written policy regarding general/basic LD accommodations is available on the program Web site. Written policy regarding general/basic LD accommodations is outlined in the school's catalog/handbook. Written policy regarding general/basic LD accommodations is available through the program or unit directly.

Minneapolis College of Art and Design
Individualized Academic Success Program

2501 Stevens Avenue South

Minneapolis, MN 55404-4347

http://www.mcad.edu/

Contact: Ms. Margaret Anne McGee, Learning Center Director. Phone: 612-874-3633. Fax: 612-874-3702. E-mail: margaret_mcgee@mcad.edu.

Individualized Academic Success Program Approximately 15 registered undergraduate students were served during 2006–07. The program or unit includes 1 full-time and 10 part-time staff members. Graduate assistants/students, LD specialists, skill tutors, strategy tutors, and trained peer tutors are provided through the program or unit. Academic advisers and counselors are provided collaboratively through on-campus or off-campus services.

Unique Aids and Services Aids, services, or accommodations include career counseling, personal coach, and weekly meetings with faculty.

Assistive Technology Assistive technology is located in a special lab and includes digital textbooks/e-text, learning support software, and scanning. Technology training is provided to incoming students.

Subject-Area Tutoring Tutoring is offered one-on-one for all subjects. Tutoring is provided through the program or unit via computer-based instruction, graduate assistants/students, LD specialists, and trained peer tutors.

Basic Skills Remediation Remediation is offered one-on-one for computer skills, learning strategies, reading, study skills, time management, and written language. Remediation is provided through the program or unit via graduate assistants/students and trained peer tutors.

Application For admittance to the program or unit, students are required to provide a psychoeducational report (3 years old or less) and provide documentation of high school services. It is recommended that students provide a diagnostic letter from learning disability professional. Upon application, materials documenting need for services should be sent to both admissions and the LD program or unit. Upon acceptance, documentation of need for services should be sent only to the LD program or unit. *Application deadline (institutional):* 6/1. *Application deadline (LD program):* Rolling/continuous for fall and rolling/continuous for spring.

Written Policies Written policy regarding general/basic LD accommodations is outlined in the school's catalog/handbook.

Minnesota State University Mankato
Office of Disability Services

228 Wiecking Center

Mankato, MN 56001

http://www.mnsu.edu/dso/

Contact: Beth L. Claussen, Disability Accommodation Specialist. Phone: 507-389-5436. Fax: 507-389-1199. E-mail: beth.claussen@mnsu.edu.

Office of Disability Services Approximately 122 registered undergraduate students were served during 2006–07. The program or unit includes 2 full-time and 4 part-time staff members. Graduate assistants/students are provided through the program or unit. Academic advisers, coaches, counselors, LD specialists, regular education teachers, skill tutors, strategy tutors, and trained peer tutors are provided collaboratively through on-campus or off-campus services.

Unique Aids and Services Aids, services, or accommodations include advocates, faculty training, priority registration, alternative testing, note-takers, texts in alternate format.

Assistive Technology Assistive technology is located in campus labs, the DSS office, a special lab and includes digital textbooks/e-text, learning support software, and scanning. Technology training is provided to incoming students.

Subject-Area Tutoring Tutoring is offered one-on-one and in small groups for most subjects. Tutoring is provided collaboratively through on-campus or off-campus services via graduate assistants/students, LD specialists, and trained peer tutors.

Basic Skills Remediation Remediation is offered one-on-one and in small groups for computer skills, learning strategies, math, reading, study skills, time management, and written language. Remediation is provided through the program or unit via LD specialists. Remediation is also provided collaboratively through on-campus or off-campus services via computer-based instruction, graduate assistants/students, professional tutors, and trained peer tutors.

Enrichment Enrichment programs are available through the program or unit for self-advocacy. Programs for career planning, college survival skills, health and nutrition, learning strategies, practical computer skills, stress management, study skills, test taking, and time management are provided collaboratively through on-campus or off-campus services.

Application For admittance to the program or unit, students are required to provide a psychoeducational report (3 years old or less) and provide diagnostic summary report. It is recommended that students provide documentation of high school services. Upon acceptance, documentation of need for services should be sent only to the LD program or unit. *Application deadline (institutional):* Continuous. *Application deadline (LD program):* Rolling/continuous for fall and rolling/continuous for spring.

Written Policies Written policies regarding course substitutions, general/basic LD accommodations, reduced course loads, and substitutions and waivers of graduation requirements are available on the program Web site. Written policies regarding course substitutions, general/basic LD accommodations, reduced course loads, and substitutions and waivers of graduation requirements are outlined in the school's catalog/handbook. Written policies regarding course substitutions, general/basic LD accommodations, reduced course loads, and substitutions and waivers of graduation requirements are available through the program or unit directly.

Minnesota State University Moorhead
Disability Services

1104 7th Avenue South

Moorhead, MN 56563-0002

http://www.mnstate.edu/disability/

Contact: Mr. Greg Toutges, Coordinator of Disability Services. Phone: 218-477-5859. Fax: 218-477-2430. E-mail: toutges@mnstate.edu.

Disability Services Approximately 90 registered undergraduate students were served during 2006–07. The program or unit includes 1 full-time and 5 part-time staff members. Academic advisers, coaches, counselors, diagnostic specialists, graduate assistants/students, LD specialists, professional tutors, regular education teachers, remediation/learning specialists, skill tutors, special education teachers, strategy tutors, teacher trainees, and trained peer tutors are provided collaboratively through on-campus or off-campus services.

Orientation The program or unit offers a mandatory 1-hour orientation for new students individually by special arrangement.

Unique Aids and Services Aids, services, or accommodations include career counseling, priority registration, support groups, note-taking services, test accommodations.

Assistive Technology Assistive technology includes digital textbooks/e-text.

Subject-Area Tutoring Tutoring is offered one-on-one and in class-size groups for some subjects. Tutoring is provided collaboratively through on-campus or off-campus services via graduate assistants/students and trained peer tutors.

Enrichment Enrichment programs are available through the program or unit for self-advocacy, test taking, time management, and other. Programs for career planning, college survival skills, health and nutrition, learning strategies, math, medication management, oral communication skills, practical computer skills, reading, stress management, study skills, vocabulary development, and written composition skills are provided collaboratively through on-campus or off-campus services. Credit is offered for career planning, college survival skills, math, oral communication skills, practical computer skills, reading, stress management, and study skills.

Application For admittance to the program or unit, students are required to apply to the program directly and provide a psychoeducational report (3 years old or less). It is recommended that students provide documentation of high school services. Upon application, materials documenting need for services should be sent only to the LD program or unit. Upon acceptance, documentation of need for services should be sent only to the LD program or unit. *Application deadline (institutional):* 8/7. *Application deadline (LD program):* Rolling/continuous for fall and rolling/continuous for spring.

Written Policies Written policy regarding general/basic LD accommodations is available on the program Web site. Written policy regarding general/basic LD accommodations is available through the program or unit directly.

Mississippi University for Women
Academic Support Services

1100 College Street, MUW-1600

Columbus, MS 39701-9998

http://www.muw.edu/academicsupport/

Contact: Mrs. Carol H. Frazier, Director, Academic Support Services. Phone: 662-329-7138. Fax: 662-241-6035. E-mail: cfrazier@muw.edu.

Academic Support Services Approximately 10 registered undergraduate students were served during 2006–07. The program or unit includes 2 full-time staff members. Academic advisers, counselors, regular education teachers, and trained peer tutors are provided collaboratively through on-campus or off-campus services.

Assistive Technology Assistive technology is located in the DSS office, a special lab and includes digital textbooks/e-text and scanning.

Subject-Area Tutoring Tutoring is offered one-on-one and in small groups for some subjects. Tutoring is provided collaboratively through on-campus or off-campus services via computer-based instruction and graduate assistants/students.

Basic Skills Remediation Remediation is offered one-on-one, in small groups, and in class-size groups for learning strategies, math, reading, study skills, time management, and written language. Remediation is provided collaboratively through on-campus or off-campus services via computer-based instruction and regular education teachers.

Application For admittance to the program or unit, students are required to provide a psychoeducational report (3 years old or less). Upon application, materials documenting need for services should be sent only to the LD program or unit. Upon acceptance, documentation of need for services should be sent only to the LD program or unit. *Application deadline (LD program):* Rolling/continuous for fall and rolling/continuous for spring.

Written Policies Written policy regarding general/basic LD accommodations is available on the program Web site. Written policy regarding general/basic LD accommodations is available through the program or unit directly.

Missouri State University
Learning Diagnostic Clinic

901 South National

Springfield, MO 65804-0094

http://psychology.missouristate.edu/ldc/

Contact: Dr. Steve Capps, Director Learning Diagnostic Clinic. Phone: 417-836-4787. Fax: 417-836-5475. E-mail: stevencapps@missouristate.edu.

Learning Diagnostic Clinic Approximately 225 registered undergraduate students were served during 2006–07. The program or unit includes 4 full-time and 15 part-time staff members. Academic

advisers, counselors, diagnostic specialists, graduate assistants/students, LD specialists, professional tutors, skill tutors, strategy tutors, and trained peer tutors are provided through the program or unit.

Assistive Technology Assistive technology is located in campus labs.

Diagnostic Testing Testing is provided through the program or unit for handwriting, intelligence, math, motor skills, neuropsychological, personality, reading, spelling, visual processing, and written language.

Enrichment Enrichment programs are available through the program or unit for stress management, study skills, test taking, and time management.

Fees *LD Program or Service* fee is $0 to $1250 (fee varies according to level/tier of service). *Diagnostic Testing* fee is $150 to $500.

Application For admittance to the program or unit, students are required to apply to the program directly and provide a psychoeducational report (5 years old or less). Upon application, materials documenting need for services should be sent only to the LD program or unit. Upon acceptance, documentation of need for services should be sent only to the LD program or unit. *Application deadline (institutional):* 7/20. *Application deadline (LD program):* Rolling/continuous for fall and rolling/continuous for spring.

Written Policies Written policy regarding general/basic LD accommodations is available on the program Web site. Written policy regarding reduced course loads is outlined in the school's catalog/handbook. Written policy regarding general/basic LD accommodations is available through the program or unit directly.

Molloy College
Disability Support Services/Success Through Expanded Education Program (DSS/STEEP)

1000 Hempstead Avenue

Rockville Centre, NY 11571-5002

http://students.molloy.edu/admissions/steep.asp

Contact: Prof. Barbara B. Merola, Coordinator of DSS/STEEP. Phone: 516-678-5000 Ext. 6381. Fax: 516-255-4837. E-mail: bmerola@molloy.edu.

Disability Support Services/Success Through Expanded Education Program (DSS/STEEP) Approximately 75 registered undergraduate students were served during 2006–07. The program or unit includes 1 full-time staff member. Academic advisers, counselors, diagnostic specialists, and LD specialists are provided through the program or unit. Academic advisers, professional tutors, and trained peer tutors are provided collaboratively through on-campus or off-campus services.

Unique Aids and Services Aids, services, or accommodations include advocates, career counseling, faculty training, and personal coach.

Assistive Technology Assistive technology is located in the DSS office.

Subject-Area Tutoring Tutoring is offered one-on-one and in small groups for most subjects. Tutoring is provided through the program or unit via LD specialists. Tutoring is also provided collaboratively through on-campus or off-campus services via graduate assistants/students, professional tutors, and trained peer tutors.

Basic Skills Remediation Remediation is offered in class-size groups for learning strategies, math, study skills, time management, and written language. Remediation is provided collaboratively through on-campus or off-campus services via regular education teachers.

Enrichment Enrichment programs are available through the program or unit for college survival skills, learning strategies, oral communication skills, reading, self-advocacy, stress management, study skills, test taking, time management, and vocabulary development. Programs for career planning, health and nutrition, math, practical computer skills, and written composition skills are provided collaboratively through on-campus or off-campus services.

Application For admittance to the program or unit, students are required to provide a psychoeducational report (3 years old or less). It is recommended that students provide documentation of high school services. Upon application, materials documenting need for services should be sent only to admissions with institutional application materials. Upon acceptance, documentation of need for services should be sent only to the LD program or unit. *Application deadline (institutional):* Continuous. *Application deadline (LD program):* Rolling/continuous for fall and rolling/continuous for spring.

Written Policies Written policy regarding general/basic LD accommodations is available on the program Web site. Written policy regarding general/basic LD accommodations is outlined in the school's catalog/handbook. Written policy regarding general/basic LD accommodations is available through the program or unit directly.

Monmouth College
Office of Academic Affairs

700 East Broadway

Monmouth, IL 61462-1998

http://www.monm.edu/

Contact: Dean Marta Tucker, Associate Academic Dean. Phone: 309-457-2325. Fax: 309-457-2310. E-mail: marta@monm.edu.

Office of Academic Affairs Approximately 15 registered undergraduate students were served during 2006–07. Academic advisers, coaches, counselors, regular education teachers, trained peer tutors, and other are provided collaboratively through on-campus or off-campus services.

Assistive Technology Assistive technology is located in Melinger Teaching and Learning Center and includes learning support software and scanning.

Subject-Area Tutoring Tutoring is offered one-on-one and in small groups for most subjects. Tutoring is provided collaboratively through on-campus or off-campus services via graduate assistants/students and trained peer tutors.

Diagnostic Testing Testing for auditory processing, handwriting, intelligence, learning strategies, learning styles, math, motor skills, neuropsychological, personality, reading, social skills, spelling, spoken language, study skills, visual processing, written language, and other services is provided collaboratively through on-campus or off-campus services.

Enrichment Programs for career planning, college survival skills, learning strategies, oral communication skills, stress management, study skills, test taking, and time management are provided collaboratively through on-campus or off-campus services.

Fees *Diagnostic Testing* fee is applicable.

Application For admittance to the program or unit, students are required to provide a psychoeducational report (5 years old or less) and provide documentation of high school services. Upon application, materials documenting need for services should be sent only to admissions with institutional application materials. Upon acceptance, documentation of need for services should be sent to both admissions and the LD program or unit. *Application deadline (institutional):* Continuous. *Application deadline (LD program):* Rolling/continuous for fall and rolling/continuous for spring.

Monmouth University
Department of Disability Services for Students

400 Cedar Avenue

West Long Branch, NJ 07764-1898

http://www.monmouth.edu/

Contact: Ms. Carolyne Chirichello, Assistant Director/LD Specialist. Phone: 732-571-3460. Fax: 732-263-5126. E-mail: cchirich@monmouth.edu. Head of LD Program: Mr. Skip Carey, Director of Disability Services. Phone: 732-571-3460. Fax: 732-263-5126. E-mail: jcarey@monmouth.edu.

Department of Disability Services for Students Approximately 187 registered undergraduate students were served during 2006–07. The program or unit includes 4 full-time staff members. LD specialists are provided through the program or unit. Counselors and other are provided collaboratively through on-campus or off-campus services.

Orientation The program or unit offers an optional 1.5-hour orientation for new students during the first week of fall semester classes.

Unique Aids and Services Aids, services, or accommodations include priority registration.

Assistive Technology Assistive technology is located in the DSS office and includes digital textbooks/e-text.

Subject-Area Tutoring Tutoring is offered one-on-one for some subjects. Tutoring is provided collaboratively through on-campus or off-campus services via professional tutors and trained peer tutors.

Application For admittance to the program or unit, students are required to provide a psychoeducational report (3 years old or less). It is recommended that students provide documentation of high school services. Upon acceptance, documentation of need for services should be sent to both admissions and the LD program or unit. *Application deadline (institutional):* 3/1. *Application deadline (LD program):* Rolling/continuous for fall and rolling/continuous for spring.

Written Policies Written policy regarding general/basic LD accommodations is available on the program Web site. Written policy regarding general/basic LD accommodations is outlined in the school's catalog/handbook. Written policy regarding general/basic LD accommodations is available through the program or unit directly.

Montana State University
Disability, Re-entry, and Veteran Services

Bozeman, MT 59717

http://www.montana.edu/wwwres

Contact: Brenda K. York, Director. Phone: 406-994-2824. Fax: 406-994-3943. E-mail: byork@montana.edu.

Disability, Re-entry, and Veteran Services Approximately 210 registered undergraduate students were served during 2006–07. The program or unit includes 3 full-time staff members. Academic advisers, counselors, diagnostic specialists, and LD specialists are provided through the program or unit. Academic advisers, professional tutors, remediation/learning specialists, skill tutors, strategy tutors, and trained peer tutors are provided collaboratively through on-campus or off-campus services.
Orientation The program or unit offers an optional orientation for new students after classes begin.
Unique Aids and Services Aids, services, or accommodations include priority registration, extended time.
Assistive Technology Assistive technology is located in campus labs, the DSS office and includes digital textbooks/e-text, learning support software, and scanning. Technology training is provided to incoming students.
Subject-Area Tutoring Tutoring is offered one-on-one for some subjects. Tutoring is provided collaboratively through on-campus or off-campus services via professional tutors and trained peer tutors.
Basic Skills Remediation Remediation is offered one-on-one, in small groups, and in class-size groups for computer skills, learning strategies, math, reading, study skills, time management, and written language. Remediation is provided collaboratively through on-campus or off-campus services via professional tutors and trained peer tutors.
Enrichment Programs for career planning, college survival skills, health and nutrition, learning strategies, math, practical computer skills, reading, stress management, study skills, test taking, time management, and written composition skills are provided collaboratively through on-campus or off-campus services.
Application For admittance to the program or unit, students are required to provide a psychoeducational report (5 years old or less). It is recommended that students provide documentation of high school services. Upon application, materials documenting need for services should be sent only to the LD program or unit. Upon acceptance, documentation of need for services should be sent only to the LD program or unit. *Application deadline (institutional):* Continuous. *Application deadline (LD program):* Rolling/continuous for fall and rolling/continuous for spring.
Written Policies Written policies regarding course substitutions, general/basic LD accommodations, and substitutions and waivers of graduation requirements are available on the program Web site. Written policies regarding course substitutions, general/basic LD accommodations, reduced course loads, and substitutions and waivers of graduation requirements are available through the program or unit directly.

Montana State University–Billings
Disability Support Services

1500 University Drive
Billings, MT 59101-0298

http://www.msubillings.edu

Contact: Ms. Trudy Ilene Carey, Interim Coordinator. Phone: 406-657-2283. Fax: 406-657-1658. E-mail: tcarey@msubillings.edu.

Disability Support Services Approximately 125 registered undergraduate students were served during 2006–07. The program or unit includes 2 full-time and 2 part-time staff members. Services are provided through the program or unit. Services are provided collaboratively through on-campus or off-campus services.
Unique Aids and Services Aids, services, or accommodations include priority registration, alternative tests, note-takers, taped lectures.
Assistive Technology Assistive technology is located in the DSS office, the library and includes digital textbooks/e-text, learning support software, and scanning.
Application For admittance to the program or unit, students are required to provide a psychoeducational report (5 years old or less). It is recommended that students provide documentation of high school services. Upon application, materials documenting need for services should be sent only to the LD program or unit. Upon acceptance, documentation of need for services should be sent only to the LD program or unit. *Application deadline (institutional):* 7/1. *Application deadline (LD program):* Rolling/continuous for fall and rolling/continuous for spring.
Written Policies Written policy regarding general/basic LD accommodations is available on the program Web site. Written policy regarding general/basic LD accommodations is outlined in the school's catalog/handbook. Written policy regarding general/basic LD accommodations is available through the program or unit directly.

Montana Tech of The University of Montana

1300 West Park Street
Butte, MT 59701-8997

http://www.mtech.edu/

Contact: Counselor/Disability Services Coordinator. Phone: 406-496-3730. Fax: 406-496-3731. Head of LD Program: Paul Beatty, Dean of Students. Phone: 406-496-4198. Fax: 406-496-4757. E-mail: pbeatty@mtech.edu.

Approximately 10 registered undergraduate students were served during 2006–07. The program or unit includes 1 part-time staff member. Academic advisers, counselors, LD specialists, professional tutors, regular education teachers, and skill tutors are provided collaboratively through on-campus or off-campus services.
Summer Program To help prepare for the demands of college, there is an optional 2-week summer program prior to entering the school.

Unique Aids and Services Aids, services, or accommodations include career counseling, weekly meetings with retention specialist, mentor program.

Subject-Area Tutoring Tutoring is offered one-on-one for most subjects. Tutoring is provided collaboratively through on-campus or off-campus services via trained peer tutors.

Basic Skills Remediation Remediation is available for math, study skills, time management, and written language. Remediation is provided collaboratively through on-campus or off-campus services via professional tutors, regular education teachers, and trained peer tutors.

Enrichment Programs for career planning, college survival skills, learning strategies, math, stress management, study skills, and time management are provided collaboratively through on-campus or off-campus services.

Application For admittance to the program or unit, students are required to provide a psychoeducational report and provide documentation from a certified professional specifying the disability and recommended accommodations. Upon acceptance, documentation of need for services should be sent only to the LD program or unit. *Application deadline (institutional):* Continuous. *Application deadline (LD program):* Rolling/continuous for fall and rolling/continuous for spring.

Written Policies Written policy regarding general/basic LD accommodations is available on the program Web site. Written policy regarding general/basic LD accommodations is outlined in the school's catalog/handbook.

Moravian College
Office of Learning Services

1200 Main Street
Bethlehem, PA 18018-6650

http://www.moravian.edu/

Contact: Mrs. Laurie Morgan Roth, Director of Learning Services. Phone: 610-861-1510. Fax: 610-625-7935. E-mail: melmr01@moravian.edu.

Office of Learning Services Approximately 29 registered undergraduate students were served during 2006–07. The program or unit includes 1 full-time and 1 part-time staff member. Skill tutors and strategy tutors are provided through the program or unit. Diagnostic specialists and other are provided collaboratively through on-campus or off-campus services.

Assistive Technology Assistive technology is located in campus labs and includes learning support software.

Subject-Area Tutoring Tutoring is offered one-on-one and in small groups for most subjects. Tutoring is provided through the program or unit via trained peer tutors. Tutoring is also provided collaboratively through on-campus or off-campus services via trained peer tutors.

Enrichment Enrichment programs are available through the program or unit for college survival skills, learning strategies, study skills, test taking, and time management. Programs for career planning, health and nutrition, math, medication management, stress management, and written composition skills are provided collaboratively through on-campus or off-campus services.

Application For admittance to the program or unit, students are required to provide a psychoeducational report (3 years old or less). It is recommended that students provide documentation of high school services. Upon acceptance, documentation of need for services should be sent only to the LD program or unit. *Application deadline (institutional):* 3/1. *Application deadline (LD program):* Rolling/continuous for fall and rolling/continuous for spring.

Written Policies Written policies regarding course substitutions and general/basic LD accommodations are available through the program or unit directly.

Mount Holyoke College
Office of Learning Skills

50 College Street
South Hadley, MA 01075

http://www.mtholyoke.edu/offices/dos/12583.shtml

Contact: Dr. John Martin Body III, Associate Dean for Learning Skills. Phone: 413-538-2504. E-mail: jbody@mtholyoke.edu.

Office of Learning Skills Approximately 125 registered undergraduate students were served during 2006–07. The program or unit includes 2 part-time staff members. Academic advisers, coaches, diagnostic specialists, graduate assistants/students, LD specialists, and strategy tutors are provided through the program or unit.

Assistive Technology Assistive technology is located in a special lab and includes text-to-speech reading software, speech recognition software. Technology training is provided to incoming students.

Subject-Area Tutoring Tutoring is offered one-on-one, in small groups, and in class-size groups for most subjects. Tutoring is provided collaboratively through on-campus or off-campus services via graduate assistants/students and trained peer tutors.

Diagnostic Testing Testing is provided through the program or unit for intelligence, learning strategies, learning styles, math, reading, spelling, spoken language, study skills, visual processing, and written language.

Enrichment Enrichment programs are available through the program or unit for college survival skills, learning strategies, medication management, practical computer skills, self-advocacy, study skills, test taking, time management, and written composition skills. Programs for career planning, health and nutrition, oral communication skills, stress management, and written composition skills are provided collaboratively through on-campus or off-campus services.

Student Organization ADAPT consists of 10 members.

Fees *Diagnostic Testing* fee is $25 to $650.

Application For admittance to the program or unit, students are required to provide a psychoeducational report (3 years old or less). It is recommended that students provide documentation of high school services. Upon acceptance, documentation of need for services should be sent only to the LD program or unit. *Application deadline (institutional):* 1/15. *Application deadline (LD program):* Rolling/continuous for fall and rolling/continuous for spring.

Written Policies Written policies regarding course substitutions, general/basic LD accommodations, reduced course loads, and substitutions and waivers of graduation requirements are available on the program Web site. Written policies regarding course substitutions, general/basic LD accommodations, reduced course loads, and substitutions and waivers of graduation requirements are outlined in the school's catalog/handbook.

Mount St. Mary's University
Department of Learning Services

16300 Old Emmitsburg Road

Emmitsburg, MD 21727-7799

http://www.msmary.edu

Contact: Mrs. Denise L. Marjarum, Director of Learning Services. Phone: 301-447-5006. Fax: 301-447-5918. E-mail: marjarum@msmary.edu.

Department of Learning Services Approximately 130 registered undergraduate students were served during 2006–07. The program or unit includes 3 full-time and 2 part-time staff members. Graduate assistants/students, LD specialists, skill tutors, strategy tutors, and trained peer tutors are provided through the program or unit. Academic advisers, counselors, and regular education teachers are provided collaboratively through on-campus or off-campus services.

Unique Aids and Services Aids, services, or accommodations include note-takers, interpreters.

Assistive Technology Assistive technology is located in the DSS office and includes learning support software and scanning. Technology training is provided to incoming students.

Subject-Area Tutoring Tutoring is offered one-on-one and in small groups for all subjects. Tutoring is provided through the program or unit via graduate assistants/students and trained peer tutors.

Diagnostic Testing Testing is provided through the program or unit for learning strategies, learning styles, and study skills.

Basic Skills Remediation Remediation is offered one-on-one for learning strategies, math, study skills, time management, and written language. Remediation is provided through the program or unit via graduate assistants/students, LD specialists, and trained peer tutors.

Enrichment Enrichment programs are available through the program or unit for college survival skills, learning strategies, self-advocacy, study skills, test taking, and time management. Programs for career planning, health and nutrition, math, medication management, practical computer skills, stress management, and written composition skills are provided collaboratively through on-campus or off-campus services.

Application For admittance to the program or unit, students are required to provide a psychoeducational report (3 years old or less). Upon application, materials documenting need for services should be sent only to the LD program or unit. Upon acceptance, documentation of need for services should be sent only to the LD program or unit. *Application deadline (institutional):* Continuous. *Application deadline (LD program):* Rolling/continuous for fall and rolling/continuous for spring.

Written Policies Written policy regarding general/basic LD accommodations is available on the program Web site. Written policy regarding general/basic LD accommodations is outlined in the school's catalog/handbook. Written policies regarding course substitutions, general/basic LD accommodations, and substitutions and waivers of admissions requirements are available through the program or unit directly.

Mount Saint Vincent University
Disability Services

166 Bedford Highway

Halifax, NS B3M 2J6

Canada

http://www.msvu.ca/

Contact: Mrs. Kim Elizabeth Musgrave, Coordinator of Disability Services. Phone: 902-457-6323. Fax: 902-445-2201. E-mail: kim.musgrave@msvu.ca.

Disability Services Approximately 50 registered undergraduate students were served during 2006–07. The program or unit includes 3 full-time staff members. Counselors and graduate assistants/students are provided through the program or unit. Academic advisers, counselors, diagnostic specialists, graduate assistants/students, and LD specialists are provided collaboratively through on-campus or off-campus services.

Orientation The program or unit offers an optional 1-hour orientation for new students before classes begin and during summer prior to enrollment.

Unique Aids and Services Aids, services, or accommodations include advocates, career counseling, faculty training, personal coach, and support groups.

Assistive Technology Assistive technology is located in the DSS office, the library and includes digital textbooks/e-text and scanning. Technology training is provided to incoming students.

Subject-Area Tutoring Tutoring is offered for some subjects.

Diagnostic Testing Testing is provided through the program or unit for learning strategies, learning styles, and study skills.

Basic Skills Remediation Remediation is offered one-on-one for learning strategies, reading, social skills, study skills, time management, and written language. Remediation is provided through the program or unit via graduate assistants/students and LD specialists. Remediation is also provided collaboratively through on-campus or off-campus services via graduate assistants/students and other.

Enrichment Enrichment programs are available through the program or unit for career planning, college survival skills, learning strategies, oral communication skills, reading, self-advocacy, stress management, study skills, test taking, and time management. Programs for career planning, college survival skills, health and nutrition, learning strategies, medication management, oral communication skills, reading, stress management, study skills, test taking, time management, and written composition skills are provided collaboratively through on-campus or off-campus services.

Application For admittance to the program or unit, students are required to provide a psychoeducational report (3 years old or less). It is recommended that students provide documentation of high school services. Upon application, materials documenting need for services should be sent to both admissions and the LD program or unit. Upon acceptance, documentation of need for services should be sent only to the LD program or unit. *Application deadline (institutional):* 3/15. *Application deadline (LD program):* Rolling/continuous for fall and rolling/continuous for spring.

Written Policies Written policy regarding general/basic LD accommodations is available on the program Web site. Written policies regarding general/basic LD accommodations, reduced course loads, substitutions and waivers of admissions requirements, and substitutions and waivers of graduation requirements are outlined in the school's catalog/handbook. Written policy regarding general/basic LD accommodations is available through the program or unit directly.

Mount Union College
Disability Support Services

1972 Clark Avenue

Alliance, OH 44601-3993

http://www.muc.edu/academics/disability_support_services

Contact: Karen A. Saracusa, Director. Phone: 330-823-7372. E-mail: saracuka@muc.edu.

Disability Support Services Approximately 33 registered undergraduate students were served during 2006–07. The program or unit includes 1 full-time staff member. Academic advisers are provided collaboratively through on-campus or off-campus services.

Orientation The program or unit offers an optional 1-hour orientation for new students during new student orientation.

Assistive Technology Assistive technology is located in the DSS office and includes digital textbooks/e-text.

Subject-Area Tutoring Tutoring is offered in small groups for most subjects. Tutoring is provided collaboratively through on-campus or off-campus services via trained peer tutors.

Application For admittance to the program or unit, students are required to provide a psychoeducational report. It is recommended that students provide documentation of high school services. Upon application, materials documenting need for services should be sent only to the LD program or unit. Upon acceptance, documentation of need for services should be sent only to the LD program or unit. *Application deadline (institutional):* Continuous. *Application deadline (LD program):* Rolling/continuous for fall and rolling/continuous for spring.

Written Policies Written policy regarding general/basic LD accommodations is available on the program Web site. Written policies regarding course substitutions and substitutions and waivers of graduation requirements are outlined in the school's catalog/handbook. Written policies regarding course substitutions, general/basic LD accommodations, and substitutions and waivers of graduation requirements are available through the program or unit directly.

Mount Vernon Nazarene University

800 Martinsburg Road

Mount Vernon, OH 43050-9500

http://www.mvnu.edu/

Contact: Mr. David Leedy, Disability Services Coordinator. Phone: 740-392-6868 Ext. 4548. Fax: 740-392-6332. E-mail: david.leedy@mvnu.edu.

The program or unit includes 1 full-time staff member. LD specialists are provided through the program or unit.

Assistive Technology Assistive technology is located in the DSS office and includes digital textbooks/e-text.

Application For admittance to the program or unit, students are required to apply to the program directly and provide a psychoeducational report (5 years old or less). It is recommended that students provide documentation of high school services. Upon acceptance, documentation of need for services should be sent only to the LD program or unit. *Application deadline (institutional):* 5/1. *Application deadline (LD program):* Rolling/continuous for fall and rolling/continuous for spring.

Written Policies Written policies regarding course substitutions, general/basic LD accommodations, reduced course loads, and substitutions and waivers of graduation requirements are available on the program Web site. Written policies regarding course substitutions, general/basic LD accommodations, reduced course loads, and substitutions and waivers of graduation requirements are outlined in the school's catalog/handbook. Written policies regarding course substitutions, general/basic LD accommodations, reduced course loads, and substitutions and waivers of graduation requirements are available through the program or unit directly.

Multnomah Bible College and Biblical Seminary
Disabled Student Services

8435 Northeast Glisan Street

Portland, OR 97220-5898

http://www.multnomah.edu/

Contact: Mr. David Wayne Jongeward, Associate Academic Dean. Phone: 503-251-6423. Fax: 503-251-6449. E-mail: djongeward@multnomah.edu.

Disabled Student Services Approximately 6 registered undergraduate students were served during 2006–07. Services are provided through the program or unit. Academic advisers, coaches, counselors, graduate assistants/students, and regular education teachers are provided collaboratively through on-campus or off-campus services.

Unique Aids and Services Aids, services, or accommodations include advocates, faculty training, test-taking accommodations.

Assistive Technology Assistive technology is located in the Information Technology Department and includes learning support software and scanning.

Subject-Area Tutoring Tutoring is offered one-on-one and in small groups for most subjects. Tutoring is provided collaboratively through on-campus or off-campus services via computer-based instruction, graduate assistants/students, and trained peer tutors.

Application For admittance to the program or unit, students are required to apply to the program directly and provide a psychoeducational report (3 years old or less). It is recommended that students provide documentation of high school services. Upon application, materials documenting need for services should be sent to both admissions and the LD program or unit. Upon acceptance, documentation of need for services should be sent only to the LD program or unit. *Application deadline (institutional):* 7/15. *Application deadline (LD program):* Rolling/continuous for fall and rolling/continuous for spring.

Written Policies Written policies regarding general/basic LD accommodations and substitutions and waivers of admissions requirements are available through the program or unit directly.

Murray State University
Services for Students with Learning Disabilities; Student Support Services

113 Sparks Hall

Murray, KY 42071

http://www.murraystate.edu/secsv/SSLD

Contact: Cindy Clemson, Coordinator of Services for Students with Learning Disabilities. Phone: 270-809-2018. Fax: 270-809-4339. E-mail: cindy.clemson@murraystate.edu. Head of LD Program: Annazette McCane, Director of Equal Opportunity. Phone: 270-809-3155. Fax: 270-809-6887. E-mail: annazette.mccane@murraystate.edu.

Services for Students with Learning Disabilities; Student Support Services Approximately 385 registered undergraduate students were served during 2006–07. The program or unit includes 7 full-time staff members. Academic advisers, coaches, graduate assistants/students, LD specialists, skill tutors, strategy tutors, and trained peer tutors are provided through the program or unit. Academic advisers, counselors, diagnostic specialists, graduate assistants/students, remediation/learning specialists, skill tutors, strategy tutors, and trained peer tutors are provided collaboratively through on-campus or off-campus services.

Orientation The program or unit offers a mandatory 1-semester orientation for new students through a freshman orientation course.

Summer Program To help prepare for the demands of college, there is an optional 3-day summer program prior to entering the school available to high school graduates that focuses on life skills and/or college life adjustment, self-advocacy, study skills, and time management. The program accepts students from out-of-state.

Unique Aids and Services Aids, services, or accommodations include advocates, career counseling, faculty training, priority registration, support groups, regular meetings with faculty.

Assistive Technology Assistive technology is located in the DSS office and includes digital textbooks/e-text and scanning. Technology training is provided to incoming students.

Subject-Area Tutoring Tutoring is offered one-on-one for most subjects. Tutoring is provided through the program or unit via computer-based instruction, graduate assistants/students, LD specialists, and trained peer tutors. Tutoring is also provided collaboratively through on-campus or off-campus services via computer-based instruction, graduate assistants/students, and trained peer tutors.

Diagnostic Testing Testing is provided through the program or unit for learning strategies, learning styles, and study skills. Testing for auditory processing, handwriting, intelligence, learning strategies, learning styles, math, neuropsychological, personality, reading, social skills, spelling, spoken language, study skills, and written language is provided collaboratively through on-campus or off-campus services.

Basic Skills Remediation Remediation is offered in class-size groups for learning strategies, math, reading, spelling, spoken language, study skills, time management, and written language. Remediation is provided collaboratively through on-campus or off-campus services via computer-based instruction, graduate assistants/students, and regular education teachers.

Enrichment Enrichment programs are available through the program or unit for college survival skills, learning strategies, self-advocacy, study skills, test taking, time management, and vocabulary development. Programs for career planning, college survival skills, health and nutrition, learning strategies, math, medication management, oral communication skills, practical computer skills, reading, self-advocacy, stress management, study skills, test taking, time management, vocabulary development, and written composition skills are provided collaboratively through on-campus or off-campus services. Credit is offered for career planning, college survival skills, health and nutrition, learning strategies, math, oral communication skills, practical computer skills, reading, self-advocacy, stress management, study skills, test taking, time management, vocabulary development, and written composition skills.

Fees *LD Program or Service* fee is $225 to $1125 (fee varies according to level/tier of service). *Summer Program* fee is $100. *Diagnostic Testing* fee is $25 to $400.

Application For admittance to the program or unit, students are required to apply to the program directly and provide a psychoeducational report (3 years old or less). It is recommended that students provide documentation of high school services. Upon acceptance, documentation of need for services should be sent only to the LD program or unit. *Application deadline (LD program):* Rolling/continuous for fall and rolling/continuous for spring.

Written Policies Written policies regarding course substitutions, general/basic LD accommodations, grade forgiveness, reduced course loads, substitutions and waivers of admissions requirements, and substitutions and waivers of graduation requirements are available on the program Web site. Written policies regarding course substitutions, general/basic LD accommodations, grade forgiveness, reduced course loads, substitutions and waivers of admissions requirements, and substitutions and waivers of graduation requirements are outlined in the school's catalog/handbook. Written policies regarding course substitutions, general/basic LD accommodations, grade forgiveness, reduced course loads, substitutions and waivers of admissions requirements, and substitutions and waivers of graduation requirements are available through the program or unit directly.

Naropa University

2130 Arapahoe Avenue

Boulder, CO 80302-6697

http://www.naropa.edu/

Contact: Robert D. Cillo, Dean of Students. Phone: 303-546-3506. Fax: 303-245-4795. E-mail: bcillo@naropa.edu.

Approximately 5 registered undergraduate students were served during 2006–07. The program or unit includes 1 part-time staff member. LD specialists and other are provided through the program or unit.

Unique Aids and Services Aids, services, or accommodations include advocates.

Application For admittance to the program or unit, students are required to provide assessments from professionals in field. It is recommended that students apply to the program directly, provide a psychoeducational report (2 years old or less), and provide documentation of high school services. Upon application, materials documenting need for services should be sent only to the LD program or unit. Upon acceptance, documentation of need for services should be sent only to the LD program or unit. *Application deadline (institutional):* 1/15. *Application deadline (LD program):* Rolling/continuous for fall and rolling/continuous for spring.

Written Policies Written policy regarding general/basic LD accommodations is available on the program Web site. Written policy regarding general/basic LD accommodations is outlined in the school's catalog/handbook.

National-Louis University
Department of Diversity, Access and Equity

122 South Michigan Avenue

Chicago, IL 60603

http://www.nl.edu

Contact: Erin H. Haulotte, Director of Diversity & Employment. Phone: 847-947-5491. Fax: 847-947-5610. E-mail: erin.haulotte@nl.edu.

Department of Diversity, Access and Equity Approximately 80 registered undergraduate students were served during 2006–07. The program or unit includes 2 full-time staff members. Academic advisers, coaches, counselors, diagnostic specialists, graduate assistants/students, LD specialists, professional tutors, regular education teachers, skill tutors, and strategy tutors are provided collaboratively through on-campus or off-campus services.
Unique Aids and Services Aids, services, or accommodations include priority registration.
Assistive Technology Assistive technology is located in campus labs, the DSS office and includes digital textbooks/e-text and learning support software.
Subject-Area Tutoring Tutoring is offered for most subjects.
Enrichment Programs for career planning, learning strategies, math, oral communication skills, practical computer skills, reading, study skills, test taking, and written composition skills are provided collaboratively through on-campus or off-campus services.
Application For admittance to the program or unit, students are required to apply to the program directly and provide a psychoeducational report (5 years old or less). It is recommended that students provide documentation of high school services. Upon application, materials documenting need for services should be sent only to the LD program or unit. Upon acceptance, documentation of need for services should be sent only to the LD program or unit. *Application deadline (institutional):* Continuous. *Application deadline (LD program):* Rolling/continuous for fall and rolling/continuous for spring.
Written Policies Written policies regarding course substitutions, general/basic LD accommodations, grade forgiveness, reduced course loads, substitutions and waivers of admissions requirements, and substitutions and waivers of graduation requirements are available on the program Web site. Written policies regarding course substitutions, general/basic LD accommodations, grade forgiveness, reduced course loads, substitutions and waivers of admissions requirements, and substitutions and waivers of graduation requirements are outlined in the school's catalog/handbook. Written policies regarding course substitutions, general/basic LD accommodations, grade forgiveness, reduced course loads, substitutions and waivers of admissions requirements, and substitutions and waivers of graduation requirements are available through the program or unit directly.

Nebraska Methodist College
Student Developmental Services

720 N. 87th Street

Omaha, NE 68114

http://www.methodistcollege.edu/

Contact: Ms. Carol Moore, Academic Skills Specialist. Phone: 402-354-7214. E-mail: carol.moore@methodistcollege.edu.

Student Developmental Services Approximately 2 registered undergraduate students were served during 2006–07. The program or unit includes 1 part-time staff member. Remediation/learning specialists are provided through the program or unit.
Unique Aids and Services Aids, services, or accommodations include weekly meetings with faculty.
Subject-Area Tutoring Tutoring is offered one-on-one for most subjects. Tutoring is provided collaboratively through on-campus or off-campus services via trained peer tutors.
Basic Skills Remediation Remediation is offered one-on-one for learning strategies, math, study skills, time management, and visual processing. Remediation is provided collaboratively through on-campus or off-campus services via trained peer tutors.
Enrichment Enrichment programs are available through the program or unit for college survival skills, learning strategies, math, self-advocacy, stress management, study skills, test taking, and time management.
Application For admittance to the program or unit, students are required to provide a psychoeducational report (3 years old or less). It is recommended that students provide documentation of high school services. Upon acceptance, documentation of need for services should be sent only to the LD program or unit. *Application deadline (institutional):* 4/1. *Application deadline (LD program):* Rolling/continuous for fall and rolling/continuous for spring.

Neumann College
John C. Ford Academic Resource Center

One Neumann Drive

Aston, PA 19014-1298

http://www.neumann.edu/academics/arc/services.asp

Contact: Mr. P. Vincent Riley, Disabilities Services Coordinator. Phone: 610-361-5471. Fax: 610-358-4564. E-mail: rileyv@neumann.edu. Head of LD Program: Ms. Theresa Albany Huke, Director, Academic Resources. Phone: 610-361-5249. Fax: 610-358-4564. E-mail: huket@neumann.edu.

John C. Ford Academic Resource Center Approximately 80 registered undergraduate students were served during 2006–07. The program or unit includes 2 full-time and 5 part-time staff members. Academic advisers, graduate assistants/students, professional tutors, remediation/learning specialists, skill tutors, strategy tutors, and trained peer tutors are provided through the program or unit. Academic advisers, counselors, LD specialists, professional tutors, regular education teachers, remediation/learning specialists, and skill tutors are provided collaboratively through on-campus or off-campus services.

Neumann College (continued)

Unique Aids and Services Aids, services, or accommodations include advocates, career counseling, faculty training, parent workshops, personal coach, and priority registration.

Assistive Technology Assistive technology is located in the DSS office and includes scanning.

Subject-Area Tutoring Tutoring is offered one-on-one and in small groups for most subjects. Tutoring is provided through the program or unit via computer-based instruction, graduate assistants/students, LD specialists, professional tutors, and trained peer tutors. Tutoring is also provided collaboratively through on-campus or off-campus services via professional tutors.

Basic Skills Remediation Remediation is offered in small groups and in class-size groups for learning strategies, math, reading, study skills, time management, and written language. Remediation is provided through the program or unit via regular education teachers. Remediation is also provided collaboratively through on-campus or off-campus services via computer-based instruction and regular education teachers.

Enrichment Enrichment programs are available through the program or unit for college survival skills, learning strategies, math, reading, stress management, study skills, test taking, time management, vocabulary development, and written composition skills. Programs for career planning, college survival skills, health and nutrition, learning strategies, math, reading, stress management, study skills, test taking, time management, vocabulary development, and written composition skills are provided collaboratively through on-campus or off-campus services. Credit is offered for college survival skills, health and nutrition, learning strategies, math, reading, stress management, study skills, test taking, time management, vocabulary development, and written composition skills.

Application For admittance to the program or unit, students are required to apply to the program directly and provide a psychoeducational report (5 years old or less). It is recommended that students provide documentation of high school services. Upon acceptance, documentation of need for services should be sent only to the LD program or unit. *Application deadline (institutional):* 4/1. *Application deadline (LD program):* Rolling/continuous for fall and rolling/continuous for spring.

Written Policies Written policy regarding general/basic LD accommodations is available on the program Web site. Written policy regarding general/basic LD accommodations is outlined in the school's catalog/handbook. Written policy regarding general/basic LD accommodations is available through the program or unit directly.

Neumont University
Student Services

2755 East Cottonwood Parkway, Suite 600
Salt Lake City, UT 84121
http://www.neumont.edu/

Contact: Erin McCormack, Student Services Administrator. Phone: 801-302-2844. E-mail: erin.mccormack@neumont.edu.

Student Services Approximately 6 registered undergraduate students were served during 2006–07. The program or unit includes 1 full-time staff member. Academic advisers are provided through the program or unit.

Unique Aids and Services Aids, services, or accommodations include career counseling and priority registration.

Assistive Technology Assistive technology is located in the DSS office and includes digital textbooks/e-text.

Subject-Area Tutoring Tutoring is offered one-on-one and in small groups for all subjects. Tutoring is provided collaboratively through on-campus or off-campus services via trained peer tutors.

Application For admittance to the program or unit, students are required to apply to the program directly and provide a psychoeducational report (3 years old or less). It is recommended that students provide documentation of high school services. Upon application, materials documenting need for services should be sent only to the LD program or unit. Upon acceptance, documentation of need for services should be sent only to the LD program or unit. *Application deadline (institutional):* Continuous. *Application deadline (LD program):* Rolling/continuous for fall and rolling/continuous for spring.

Written Policies Written policy regarding general/basic LD accommodations is outlined in the school's catalog/handbook. Written policy regarding general/basic LD accommodations is available through the program or unit directly.

New Jersey City University
Project Mentor: Regional Center for Students with Learning Disabilities

2039 Kennedy Boulevard
Jersey City, NJ 07305-1597
http://www.njcu.edu/pmentor

Contact: Ms. Leah Jackson, Coordinator, Project Mentor: Regional Center for Students with Learning Disabilities. Phone: 201-200-2091. Fax: 201-200-3083. E-mail: ljackson1@njcu.edu. Head of LD Program: Ms. Jennifer Aitken, Director and Project Mentor: Regional Center for Students with Learning Disabilities. Phone: 201-200-2091. Fax: 201-200-2575. E-mail: jaitken@njcu.edu.

Project Mentor: Regional Center for Students with Learning Disabilities Approximately 115 registered undergraduate students were served during 2006–07. The program or unit includes 2 full-time and 8 part-time staff members. Academic advisers, diagnostic specialists, graduate assistants/students, LD specialists, professional tutors, and strategy tutors are provided through the program or unit. Academic advisers are provided collaboratively through on-campus or off-campus services.

Orientation The program or unit offers a mandatory 1-semester orientation for new students during summer prior to enrollment and during the fall semester (1 degree credit).

Summer Program To help prepare for the demands of college, there is a mandatory 4-week summer program prior to entering the school available to high school graduates that focuses on computing skills, life skills and/or college life adjustment, self-advocacy, study skills, test-taking skills, and time management. Degree credit will be earned.

Unique Aids and Services Aids, services, or accommodations include faculty training, parent workshops, weekly meetings with mentors.

Assistive Technology Assistive technology is located in campus labs, the DSS office, the library and includes digital textbooks/e-text, learning support software, and portable word processors (AlphaSmart/Dana). Technology training is provided to incoming students.

Subject-Area Tutoring Tutoring is offered one-on-one and in small groups for some subjects. Tutoring is provided through the program or unit via graduate assistants/students and professional tutors.

Diagnostic Testing Testing is provided through the program or unit for learning strategies, learning styles, math, written language, and other services.

Basic Skills Remediation Remediation is offered in small groups and in class-size groups for learning strategies, math, reading, spelling, study skills, time management, and written language. Remediation is provided through the program or unit via graduate assistants/students, professional tutors, and teacher trainees.

Enrichment Enrichment programs are available through the program or unit for career planning, college survival skills, learning strategies, math, oral communication skills, practical computer skills, reading, self-advocacy, stress management, study skills, test taking, time management, and written composition skills. Programs for career planning, college survival skills, stress management, study skills, test taking, and time management are provided collaboratively through on-campus or off-campus services. Credit is offered for practical computer skills.

Student Organization Project Eye-to-Eye consists of 7 members.

Fees *Diagnostic Testing* fee is $0 to $575.

Application For admittance to the program or unit, students are required to apply to the program directly, provide a psychoeducational report, provide documentation of high school services, and provide high school transcript, letters of recommendation. Upon application, materials documenting need for services should be sent only to the LD program or unit. Upon acceptance, documentation of need for services should be sent only to the LD program or unit. *Application deadline (institutional):* 4/1. *Application deadline (LD program):* 5/15 for fall. Rolling/continuous for spring.

Written Policies Written policy regarding general/basic LD accommodations is available on the program Web site. Written policy regarding general/basic LD accommodations is outlined in the school's catalog/handbook.

The New School: A University
Student Disability Services

66 West 12th Street
New York, NY 10011
http://www.newschool.edu/studentservices/disability/

Contact: Mr. Jason Luchs, Assistant Director of Student Disability Services. Phone: 212-229-5626 Ext. 3135. Fax: 212-229-1090. E-mail: luchsj@newschool.edu.

Student Disability Services Approximately 8 registered undergraduate students were served during 2006–07. The program or unit includes 2 full-time staff members and 1 part-time staff member. Academic advisers and counselors are provided collaboratively through on-campus or off-campus services.

Assistive Technology Assistive technology is located in campus labs and includes digital textbooks/e-text, learning support software, and scanning.

Enrichment Programs for career planning, health and nutrition, self-advocacy, stress management, and time management are provided collaboratively through on-campus or off-campus services.

Application For admittance to the program or unit, students are required to apply to the program directly and provide a psychoeducational report (3 years old or less). Upon acceptance, documentation of need for services should be sent only to the LD program or unit. *Application deadline (LD program):* Rolling/continuous for fall and rolling/continuous for spring.

New York University
Henry and Lucy Moses Center for Students with Disabilities

70 Washington Square South
New York, NY 10012-1019
http://www.nyu.edu/csd

Contact: Ms. Lakshmi Clark-McClendon, Coordinator of Services for Students with Learning Disabilities and AD/HD. Phone: 212-998-4980. Fax: 212-995-4114. E-mail: lc83@nyu.edu.

Henry and Lucy Moses Center for Students with Disabilities Approximately 301 registered undergraduate students were served during 2006–07. The program or unit includes 1 full-time and 6 part-time staff members. Graduate assistants/students, LD specialists, remediation/learning specialists, skill tutors, and strategy tutors are provided through the program or unit. Academic advisers, coaches, counselors, diagnostic specialists, LD specialists, professional tutors, and trained peer tutors are provided collaboratively through on-campus or off-campus services.

Orientation The program or unit offers an optional 2- to 3-hour orientation for new students before classes begin and after classes begin.

Summer Program To help prepare for the demands of college, there is an optional summer program prior to entering the school available to high school graduates that focuses on life skills and/or college life adjustment and self-advocacy.

Unique Aids and Services Aids, services, or accommodations include career counseling, faculty training, priority registration, support groups.

Assistive Technology Assistive technology is located in campus labs, the DSS office, a special lab and includes digital textbooks/e-text, learning support software, scanning, and speech-to-text, text-to-speech software. Technology training is provided to incoming students.

Subject-Area Tutoring Tutoring is offered one-on-one and in small groups for all subjects. Tutoring is provided collaboratively through on-campus or off-campus services via graduate assistants/students, professional tutors, and trained peer tutors.

Basic Skills Remediation Remediation is offered one-on-one for auditory processing, learning strategies, reading, study skills, time management, visual processing, and written language. Remediation is provided through the program or unit via graduate assistants/students and LD specialists. Remediation is also provided collaboratively through on-campus or off-campus services.

New York University (continued)

Enrichment Enrichment programs are available through the program or unit for learning strategies, reading, self-advocacy, stress management, study skills, test taking, time management, and written composition skills. Programs for career planning, college survival skills, health and nutrition, learning strategies, math, medication management, oral communication skills, practical computer skills, stress management, study skills, test taking, time management, vocabulary development, and written composition skills are provided collaboratively through on-campus or off-campus services.
Student Organization Cultivating a Community for Disabled Students at NYU.
Application For admittance to the program or unit, students are required to provide a psychoeducational report (3 years old or less) and provide current neuropsychological or psychoeducational evaluation. It is recommended that students provide documentation of high school services. Upon application, materials documenting need for services should be sent only to the LD program or unit. Upon acceptance, documentation of need for services should be sent only to the LD program or unit. *Application deadline (institutional): 1/15. Application deadline (LD program):* Rolling/continuous for fall and rolling/continuous for spring.
Written Policies Written policies regarding course substitutions, general/basic LD accommodations, reduced course loads, and substitutions and waivers of graduation requirements are available on the program Web site. Written policies regarding course substitutions, general/basic LD accommodations, reduced course loads, and substitutions and waivers of graduation requirements are available through the program or unit directly.

Niagara University
Office of Academic Support

Niagara Falls, NY 14109

http://www.niagara.edu/oas/

Contact: Ms. Diane E. Stoelting, Coordinator of Specialized Support Services. Phone: 716-286-8076. Fax: 716-286-8063. E-mail: ds@niagara.edu.

Office of Academic Support Approximately 90 registered undergraduate students were served during 2006–07. The program or unit includes 2 full-time staff members and 1 part-time staff member. Academic advisers, counselors, regular education teachers, remediation/learning specialists, skill tutors, trained peer tutors, and other are provided collaboratively through on-campus or off-campus services.
Unique Aids and Services Aids, services, or accommodations include weekly meetings with the Coordinator of Specialized Support Services.
Assistive Technology Assistive technology is located in the DSS office and includes digital textbooks/e-text and scanning. Technology training is provided to incoming students.
Subject-Area Tutoring Tutoring is offered in small groups for some subjects. Tutoring is provided collaboratively through on-campus or off-campus services via trained peer tutors.
Basic Skills Remediation Remediation is offered in class-size groups for math, reading, study skills, and written language. Remediation is provided collaboratively through on-campus or off-campus services via regular education teachers.

Enrichment Programs for career planning, college survival skills, learning strategies, self-advocacy, stress management, study skills, test taking, and time management are provided collaboratively through on-campus or off-campus services.
Application For admittance to the program or unit, students are required to provide a psychoeducational report (3 years old or less). It is recommended that students provide documentation of high school services. Upon application, materials documenting need for services should be sent only to the LD program or unit. Upon acceptance, documentation of need for services should be sent only to the LD program or unit. *Application deadline (institutional): 8/1. Application deadline (LD program):* Rolling/continuous for fall and rolling/continuous for spring.
Written Policies Written policies regarding course substitutions, general/basic LD accommodations, and reduced course loads are available on the program Web site. Written policies regarding course substitutions, general/basic LD accommodations, and reduced course loads are available through the program or unit directly.

Nipissing University
Disability Services, Enhanced Services Program

100 College Drive, Box 5002

North Bay, ON P1B 8L7

Canada

http://www.nipissingu.ca/disabilityservices/

Contact: Mr. Mike Walker, Learning Strategist. Phone: 705-474-3450 Ext. 4333. Fax: 705-495-2850. E-mail: mikew@nipissingu.ca. Head of LD Program: Mr. Daniel Pletzer, Manager of Counseling and Disability Services. Phone: 705-474-3450 Ext. 4493. Fax: 705-495-2850. E-mail: danp@nipissingu.ca.

Disability Services, Enhanced Services Program Approximately 130 registered undergraduate students were served during 2006–07. The program or unit includes 3 full-time staff members. LD specialists, remediation/learning specialists, skill tutors, strategy tutors, and other are provided through the program or unit. Academic advisers, counselors, diagnostic specialists, professional tutors, skill tutors, and trained peer tutors are provided collaboratively through on-campus or off-campus services.
Orientation The program or unit offers an optional 3-day orientation for new students before classes begin and individually by special arrangement.
Summer Program To help prepare for the demands of college, there is an optional ongoing during the summer for assessment and 1-week intensive summer program prior to entering the school available to high school graduates that focuses on computing skills, life skills and/or college life adjustment, self-advocacy, specific subject tutoring, study skills, test-taking skills, and time management.
Unique Aids and Services Aids, services, or accommodations include career counseling, support groups, test/examination and learning environment accommodations.
Assistive Technology Assistive technology is located in campus labs, the DSS office and includes digital textbooks/e-text, learning support software, and scanning. Technology training is provided to incoming students.

Subject-Area Tutoring Tutoring is offered one-on-one for most subjects. Tutoring is provided collaboratively through on-campus or off-campus services via professional tutors and trained peer tutors.

Diagnostic Testing Testing is provided through the program or unit for learning strategies, learning styles, math, personality, reading, spelling, study skills, and written language. Testing for auditory processing, intelligence, math, motor skills, neuropsychological, personality, reading, social skills, spelling, spoken language, visual processing, and written language is provided collaboratively through on-campus or off-campus services.

Basic Skills Remediation Remediation is offered one-on-one and in small groups for computer skills, learning strategies, social skills, study skills, time management, and written language. Remediation is provided through the program or unit via LD specialists. Remediation is also provided collaboratively through on-campus or off-campus services.

Enrichment Enrichment programs are available through the program or unit for college survival skills, learning strategies, oral communication skills, practical computer skills, reading, self-advocacy, stress management, study skills, test taking, time management, and written composition skills. Programs for career planning, college survival skills, health and nutrition, learning strategies, math, medication management, oral communication skills, reading, self-advocacy, stress management, study skills, test taking, and written composition skills are provided collaboratively through on-campus or off-campus services. Credit is offered for career planning, college survival skills, health and nutrition, learning strategies, oral communication skills, reading, self-advocacy, stress management, study skills, test taking, time management, and written composition skills.

Student Organization Disability Orientation Issues Team (DOIT) consists of 35 members.

Fees *Diagnostic Testing* fee is $0 to $1800.

Application For admittance to the program or unit, students are required to provide a psychoeducational report (3 years old or less). It is recommended that students provide documentation of high school services and provide transition plan. Upon application, materials documenting need for services should be sent to both admissions and the LD program or unit. Upon acceptance, documentation of need for services should be sent only to the LD program or unit. *Application deadline (institutional):* 6/1. *Application deadline (LD program):* Rolling/continuous for fall and rolling/continuous for spring.

Written Policies Written policies regarding general/basic LD accommodations and substitutions and waivers of admissions requirements are available on the program Web site. Written policy regarding substitutions and waivers of admissions requirements is outlined in the school's catalog/handbook. Written policies regarding general/basic LD accommodations and reduced course loads are available through the program or unit directly.

Norfolk State University

700 Park Avenue

Norfolk, VA 23504

http://www.nsu.edu/

Contact: Marian Shepherd, Disability Services Coordinator. Phone: 757-823-2014. Fax: 757-823-2689. E-mail: mshepherd@nsu.edu. Head of LD Program: Mrs. Beverly

Harris, Director Disability Services/ADA Coordinator. Phone: 757-823-2409. Fax: 757-823-2689. E-mail: bbharris@nsu.edu.

The program or unit includes 3 full-time staff members and 1 part-time staff member. Counselors are provided through the program or unit.

Unique Aids and Services Aids, services, or accommodations include priority registration and support groups.

Assistive Technology Assistive technology is located in campus labs, the DSS office, a special lab, the library and includes digital textbooks/e-text, learning support software, and scanning. Technology training is provided to incoming students.

Subject-Area Tutoring Tutoring is offered one-on-one and in small groups for most subjects. Tutoring is provided collaboratively through on-campus or off-campus services via graduate assistants/students and trained peer tutors.

Enrichment Programs for career planning, college survival skills, learning strategies, practical computer skills, and self-advocacy are provided collaboratively through on-campus or off-campus services.

Application For admittance to the program or unit, students are required to apply to the program directly and provide documentation of high school services. Upon application, materials documenting need for services should be sent only to the LD program or unit. Upon acceptance, documentation of need for services should be sent only to the LD program or unit. *Application deadline (LD program):* Rolling/continuous for fall and rolling/continuous for spring.

Written Policies Written policies regarding general/basic LD accommodations, grade forgiveness, and reduced course loads are available on the program Web site. Written policies regarding general/basic LD accommodations, grade forgiveness, and reduced course loads are outlined in the school's catalog/handbook. Written policies regarding general/basic LD accommodations and reduced course loads are available through the program or unit directly.

North Carolina School of the Arts
Counseling and Disability Services

1533 South Main Street

PO Box 12189

Winston-Salem, NC 27127-2188

http://www.ncarts.edu/studentlife/disability.htm

Contact: Dr. Thomas L. Murray Jr., Director of Counseling and Disability Services. Phone: 336-770-3277. Fax: 336-770-1492. E-mail: murrayt@ncarts.edu.

Counseling and Disability Services Approximately 40 registered undergraduate students were served during 2006–07. The program or unit includes 2 full-time staff members. Counselors, LD specialists, remediation/learning specialists, skill tutors, special education teachers, and strategy tutors are provided through the program or unit. Diagnostic specialists, professional tutors, and regular education teachers are provided collaboratively through on-campus or off-campus services.

Summer Program available to rising juniors, high school graduates.

North Carolina School of the Arts (continued)

Assistive Technology Assistive technology is located in the Learning Specialist's Office and includes digital textbooks/e-text, learning support software, and scanning.

Subject-Area Tutoring Tutoring is offered one-on-one and in class-size groups for most subjects. Tutoring is provided through the program or unit via LD specialists.

Basic Skills Remediation Remediation is offered one-on-one for auditory processing, computer skills, learning strategies, reading, social skills, spelling, study skills, time management, visual processing, and written language. Remediation is provided through the program or unit via LD specialists.

Enrichment Enrichment programs are available through the program or unit for written composition skills.

Application For admittance to the program or unit, students are required to apply to the program directly, provide a psychoeducational report (3 years old or less), and provide results of psychological evaluation conducted within the past 3 years. It is recommended that students provide documentation of high school services. Upon application, materials documenting need for services should be sent only to admissions with institutional application materials. Upon acceptance, documentation of need for services should be sent only to the LD program or unit. *Application deadline (institutional): 3/1. Application deadline (LD program):* Rolling/continuous for fall and rolling/continuous for spring.

Written Policies Written policies regarding general/basic LD accommodations and substitutions and waivers of admissions requirements are available on the program Web site. Written policies regarding general/basic LD accommodations and substitutions and waivers of admissions requirements are outlined in the school's catalog/handbook.

North Carolina State University
Disability Services Office

Raleigh, NC 27695

http://www.ncsu.edu/dso

Contact: Mark Newmiller, Assistant Director. Phone: 919-513-3766. Fax: 919-513-2840. E-mail: mark_newmiller@ncsu.edu.

Disability Services Office Approximately 650 registered undergraduate students were served during 2006–07. The program or unit includes 6 full-time and 2 part-time staff members. Academic advisers, coaches, counselors, diagnostic specialists, graduate assistants/students, LD specialists, professional tutors, regular education teachers, remediation/learning specialists, skill tutors, special education teachers, strategy tutors, teacher trainees, trained peer tutors, and other are provided collaboratively through on-campus or off-campus services.

Unique Aids and Services Aids, services, or accommodations include priority registration.

Assistive Technology Assistive technology is located in campus labs, the DSS office, a special lab and includes digital textbooks/e-text, learning support software, and scanning. Technology training is provided to incoming students.

Subject-Area Tutoring Tutoring is offered one-on-one, in small groups, and in class-size groups for some subjects. Tutoring is provided collaboratively through on-campus or off-campus services via computer-based instruction, graduate assistants/students, and trained peer tutors.

Enrichment Enrichment programs are available through the program or unit for time management. Programs for career planning, college survival skills, health and nutrition, learning strategies, stress management, study skills, test taking, time management, and written composition skills are provided collaboratively through on-campus or off-campus services.

Application For admittance to the program or unit, students are required to apply to the program directly and provide a psychoeducational report (3 years old or less). Upon acceptance, documentation of need for services should be sent only to the LD program or unit. *Application deadline (institutional): 2/1. Application deadline (LD program):* Rolling/continuous for fall and rolling/continuous for spring.

Written Policies Written policies regarding course substitutions, general/basic LD accommodations, grade forgiveness, reduced course loads, substitutions and waivers of admissions requirements, and substitutions and waivers of graduation requirements are available on the program Web site. Written policies regarding course substitutions, general/basic LD accommodations, grade forgiveness, reduced course loads, substitutions and waivers of admissions requirements, and substitutions and waivers of graduation requirements are outlined in the school's catalog/handbook. Written policies regarding course substitutions, general/basic LD accommodations, grade forgiveness, reduced course loads, substitutions and waivers of admissions requirements, and substitutions and waivers of graduation requirements are available through the program or unit directly.

North Central College
Academic Support Services

30 North Brainard Street, PO Box 3063

Naperville, IL 60566-7063

http://www.noctrl.edu/

Contact: Jennifer L. Pippen, Assistant Director of Academic Support. Phone: 630-637-5264. Fax: 630-637-5462. E-mail: jlpippen@noctrl.edu.

Academic Support Services Approximately 70 registered undergraduate students were served during 2006–07. The program or unit includes 1 full-time and 2 part-time staff members. Academic advisers, counselors, LD specialists, skill tutors, strategy tutors, and trained peer tutors are provided through the program or unit.

Orientation The program or unit offers an optional 2-hour orientation for new students during summer prior to enrollment.

Unique Aids and Services Aids, services, or accommodations include advocates.

Assistive Technology Assistive technology is located in the DSS office, the library and includes digital textbooks/e-text and scanning. Technology training is provided to incoming students.

Subject-Area Tutoring Tutoring is offered one-on-one and in small groups for most subjects. Tutoring is provided through the program or unit via computer-based instruction, LD specialists, and trained peer tutors.

Basic Skills Remediation Remediation is offered one-on-one, in small groups, and in class-size groups for learning strategies, math, social skills, study skills, time management, and written language. Remediation is provided through the program or unit via LD specialists, regular education teachers, trained peer tutors, and other.
Enrichment Enrichment programs are available through the program or unit for learning strategies, self-advocacy, test taking, time management, and written composition skills. Programs for career planning, college survival skills, learning strategies, math, stress management, study skills, test taking, time management, and written composition skills are provided collaboratively through on-campus or off-campus services.
Application It is recommended that students apply to the program directly, provide a psychoeducational report (3 years old or less), and provide documentation of high school services. Upon acceptance, documentation of need for services should be sent only to the LD program or unit. *Application deadline (institutional):* Continuous. *Application deadline (LD program):* Rolling/continuous for fall and rolling/continuous for spring.
Written Policies Written policy regarding general/basic LD accommodations is available on the program Web site. Written policies regarding course substitutions, general/basic LD accommodations, reduced course loads, and substitutions and waivers of graduation requirements are available through the program or unit directly.

North Central University
Student Success Center (SSC)

910 Elliot Avenue

Minneapolis, MN 55404-1322

http://www.northcentral.edu/ssc/disability/

Contact: Ms. Rachel C. Gray, Assistant Director, Student Success Center. Phone: 612-343-4402. Fax: 612-343-4771. E-mail: rcgray@northcentral.edu. Head of LD Program: Mr. Todd J. Monger, Director, Student Success Center. Phone: 612-343-4458. Fax: 612-343-4771. E-mail: tjmonger@northcentral.edu.

Student Success Center (SSC) Approximately 35 registered undergraduate students were served during 2006–07. The program or unit includes 1 full-time and 1 part-time staff member. Counselors, graduate assistants/students, and regular education teachers are provided through the program or unit. Skill tutors, strategy tutors, and trained peer tutors are provided collaboratively through on-campus or off-campus services.
Summer Program an optional summer program prior to entering the school.
Unique Aids and Services Aids, services, or accommodations include advocates, career counseling, faculty training, and personal coach.
Assistive Technology Assistive technology is located in the Student Success Center and includes digital textbooks/e-text, learning support software, and scanning. Technology training is provided to incoming students.
Subject-Area Tutoring Tutoring is offered one-on-one and in small groups for most subjects. Tutoring is provided through the program or unit via computer-based instruction, trained peer tutors, and other.

Basic Skills Remediation Remediation is offered one-on-one for learning strategies, math, study skills, and time management. Remediation is provided through the program or unit via regular education teachers, trained peer tutors, and other.
Enrichment Enrichment programs are available through the program or unit for career planning, college survival skills, learning strategies, math, self-advocacy, stress management, study skills, test taking, time management, and other.
Application It is recommended that students apply to the program directly, provide a psychoeducational report (3 years old or less), provide documentation of high school services, and provide professional assessment and recommendations. Upon application, materials documenting need for services should be sent to both admissions and the LD program or unit. Upon acceptance, documentation of need for services should be sent only to the LD program or unit. *Application deadline (LD program):* Rolling/continuous for fall and rolling/continuous for spring.
Written Policies Written policies regarding general/basic LD accommodations and substitutions and waivers of admissions requirements are available on the program Web site. Written policies regarding general/basic LD accommodations, substitutions and waivers of admissions requirements, and substitutions and waivers of graduation requirements are outlined in the school's catalog/handbook. Written policies regarding course substitutions, general/basic LD accommodations, and substitutions and waivers of admissions requirements are available through the program or unit directly.

North Dakota State University
Disability Services

1301 North University Avenue

Fargo, ND 58105

http://www.ndsu.edu/counseling/disability.shtml

Contact: Bunnie Johnson-Messelt, Coordinator of Disability Services. Phone: 701-231-7671. Fax: 701-231-6318. E-mail: bunnie.johnson-messelt@ndsu.edu.

Disability Services Approximately 65 registered undergraduate students were served during 2006–07. LD specialists are provided through the program or unit. Academic advisers, counselors, and diagnostic specialists are provided collaboratively through on-campus or off-campus services.
Assistive Technology Assistive technology is located in campus labs, a special lab and includes digital textbooks/e-text and scanning. Technology training is provided to incoming students.
Subject-Area Tutoring Tutoring is offered one-on-one and in small groups for most subjects. Tutoring is provided collaboratively through on-campus or off-campus services via graduate assistants/students and trained peer tutors.
Basic Skills Remediation Remediation is offered in class-size groups for math, reading, study skills, and English. Remediation is provided collaboratively through on-campus or off-campus services via graduate assistants/students and regular education teachers.
Application It is recommended that students provide a psychoeducational report (3 years old or less) and provide documentation of high school services. Upon application, materials documenting need for services should be sent to both admissions and the LD program

North Dakota State University (continued)

or unit. Upon acceptance, documentation of need for services should be sent only to the LD program or unit. *Application deadline (institutional):* 8/15. *Application deadline (LD program):* Rolling/continuous for fall and rolling/continuous for spring.

Written Policies Written policies regarding course substitutions, general/basic LD accommodations, grade forgiveness, reduced course loads, substitutions and waivers of admissions requirements, and substitutions and waivers of graduation requirements are available on the program Web site.

Northeastern University
Disability Resource Center and Learning Disability Program

360 Huntington Avenue
Boston, MA 02115-5096
http://www.drc.neu.edu

Contact: Ms. Debbi Hines Auerbach, Service Coordinator. Phone: 617-373-2675. Fax: 617-373-7800. E-mail: d.auerbach@neu.edu. Head of LD Program: G. Ruth Kukiela Bork, Dean and Director, Disability Resource Center. Phone: 617-373-2675. Fax: 617-373-7800. E-mail: r.bork@neu.edu.

Disability Resource Center and Learning Disability Program Approximately 300 registered undergraduate students were served during 2006–07. The program or unit includes 4 full-time and 2 part-time staff members. Counselors, LD specialists, remediation/learning specialists, skill tutors, strategy tutors, trained peer tutors, and other are provided through the program or unit. Academic advisers, counselors, diagnostic specialists, graduate assistants/students, LD specialists, regular education teachers, remediation/learning specialists, skill tutors, strategy tutors, and trained peer tutors are provided collaboratively through on-campus or off-campus services.

Orientation The program or unit offers 2.5-day orientation for new students before registration.

Unique Aids and Services Aids, services, or accommodations include advocates, career counseling, and faculty training.

Assistive Technology Assistive technology is located in the DSS office, a special lab and includes digital textbooks/e-text, learning support software, scanning, and Kurzweil, Inspiration. Technology training is provided to incoming students.

Subject-Area Tutoring Tutoring is offered one-on-one and in small groups for most subjects. Tutoring is provided through the program or unit via graduate assistants/students, LD specialists, and trained peer tutors. Tutoring is also provided collaboratively through on-campus or off-campus services via graduate assistants/students, LD specialists, and trained peer tutors.

Diagnostic Testing Testing for neuropsychological is provided collaboratively through on-campus or off-campus services.

Basic Skills Remediation Remediation is offered in class-size groups for math and written language. Remediation is provided through the program or unit via regular education teachers. Remediation is also provided collaboratively through on-campus or off-campus services via regular education teachers.

Enrichment Enrichment programs are available through the program or unit for self-advocacy, study skills, time management, and written composition skills. Programs for career planning, college

survival skills, health and nutrition, learning strategies, oral communication skills, practical computer skills, reading, self-advocacy, stress management, study skills, test taking, time management, and written composition skills are provided collaboratively through on-campus or off-campus services.

Fees *LD Program or Service* fee is $0 to $2300 (fee varies according to level/tier of service). *Diagnostic Testing* fee is $0 to $1800.

Application For admittance to the program or unit, students are required to provide a psychoeducational report (3 years old or less). It is recommended that students provide documentation of high school services. Upon application, materials documenting need for services should be sent only to the LD program or unit. Upon acceptance, documentation of need for services should be sent only to the LD program or unit. *Application deadline (institutional):* 1/15. *Application deadline (LD program):* Rolling/continuous for fall and rolling/continuous for spring.

Written Policies Written policies regarding course substitutions, general/basic LD accommodations, and reduced course loads are available on the program Web site. Written policy regarding reduced course loads is outlined in the school's catalog/handbook. Written policies regarding course substitutions, general/basic LD accommodations, and reduced course loads are available through the program or unit directly.

Northern Illinois University
Center for Access-Ability Resources (CAAR)

De Kalb, IL 60115-2854

http://www.niu.edu/caar

Contact: Mr. Garth Rubin, Coordinator. Phone: 815-753-1303. Fax: 815-753-9570. E-mail: grubin@niu.edu. Head of LD Program: Ms. Nancy J. Kasinski, Director. Phone: 815-753-9734. Fax: 815-753-9570. E-mail: nancyk@niu.edu.

Center for Access-Ability Resources (CAAR) Approximately 190 registered undergraduate students were served during 2006–07. The program or unit includes 1 full-time and 5 part-time staff members. Coaches, counselors, graduate assistants/students, and LD specialists are provided through the program or unit. Academic advisers, coaches, counselors, regular education teachers, and trained peer tutors are provided collaboratively through on-campus or off-campus services.

Orientation The program or unit offers a mandatory 1- to 5-hour orientation for new students during summer prior to enrollment, individually by special arrangement, and during the year, upon notification of need.

Unique Aids and Services Aids, services, or accommodations include career counseling, faculty training, personal coach, priority registration, and support groups.

Assistive Technology Assistive technology is located in campus labs, the DSS office and includes digital textbooks/e-text and scanning. Technology training is provided to incoming students.

Subject-Area Tutoring Tutoring is offered one-on-one and in small groups for some subjects. Tutoring is provided collaboratively through on-campus or off-campus services via computer-based instruction, graduate assistants/students, and trained peer tutors.

Diagnostic Testing Testing for auditory processing, handwriting, intelligence, learning styles, math, personality, reading, spelling, spoken language, study skills, visual processing, written language, and other services is provided collaboratively through on-campus or off-campus services.

Basic Skills Remediation Remediation is offered one-on-one and in small groups for auditory processing, learning strategies, math, reading, social skills, spoken language, study skills, and time management. Remediation is provided through the program or unit via graduate assistants/students. Remediation is also provided collaboratively through on-campus or off-campus services via graduate assistants/students, regular education teachers, trained peer tutors, and other.

Enrichment Enrichment programs are available through the program or unit for career planning, college survival skills, learning strategies, self-advocacy, study skills, test taking, and time management. Programs for career planning, college survival skills, health and nutrition, learning strategies, oral communication skills, practical computer skills, stress management, study skills, test taking, time management, and written composition skills are provided collaboratively through on-campus or off-campus services. Credit is offered for career planning, college survival skills, health and nutrition, learning strategies, oral communication skills, and study skills.

Fees *Diagnostic Testing* fee is $0 to $400.

Application For admittance to the program or unit, students are required to provide a psychoeducational report (3 years old or less). It is recommended that students provide documentation of high school services. Upon application, materials documenting need for services should be sent only to the LD program or unit. Upon acceptance, documentation of need for services should be sent only to the LD program or unit. *Application deadline (institutional):* 8/1.

Written Policies Written policies regarding course substitutions, general/basic LD accommodations, reduced course loads, substitutions and waivers of admissions requirements, and substitutions and waivers of graduation requirements are available on the program Web site. Written policies regarding course substitutions, general/basic LD accommodations, reduced course loads, substitutions and waivers of admissions requirements, and substitutions and waivers of graduation requirements are available through the program or unit directly.

Northern Michigan University

1401 Presque Isle Avenue

Marquette, MI 49855-5301

http://www.nmu.edu/

Contact: Ms. Lynn Walden, Coordinator of Disability Services. Phone: 906-227-1700. Fax: 906-227-1714. E-mail: lwalden@nmu.edu.

Approximately 150 registered undergraduate students were served during 2006–07. The program or unit includes 1 full-time and 1 part-time staff member. LD specialists are provided through the program or unit. Academic advisers, counselors, LD specialists, professional tutors, remediation/learning specialists, trained peer tutors, and other are provided collaboratively through on-campus or off-campus services.

Unique Aids and Services Aids, services, or accommodations include note-takers, meetings with appropriate agencies and caseworkers.

Assistive Technology Assistive technology is located in the DSS office and includes digital textbooks/e-text, learning support software, and scanning. Technology training is provided to incoming students.

Subject-Area Tutoring Tutoring is offered one-on-one and in small groups for some subjects. Tutoring is provided collaboratively through on-campus or off-campus services via computer-based instruction, graduate assistants/students, and trained peer tutors.

Basic Skills Remediation Remediation is offered in class-size groups for learning strategies, math, reading, study skills, time management, and written language. Remediation is provided collaboratively through on-campus or off-campus services via computer-based instruction, graduate assistants/students, regular education teachers, and trained peer tutors.

Enrichment Programs for career planning, college survival skills, health and nutrition, learning strategies, math, oral communication skills, stress management, study skills, test taking, time management, and written composition skills are provided collaboratively through on-campus or off-campus services. Credit is offered for college survival skills, stress management, study skills, test taking, and time management.

Application For admittance to the program or unit, students are required to apply to the program directly and provide a psychoeducational report (3 years old or less). It is recommended that students provide documentation of high school services. Upon application, materials documenting need for services should be sent only to the LD program or unit. *Application deadline (institutional):* Continuous. *Application deadline (LD program):* Rolling/continuous for fall and rolling/continuous for spring.

Written Policies Written policy regarding general/basic LD accommodations is available on the program Web site. Written policy regarding general/basic LD accommodations is available through the program or unit directly.

Northern State University
Office of Disability Services

1200 South Jay Street

Aberdeen, SD 57401-7198

http://www.northern.edu/disability_services/index.htm

Contact: Ms. Karen Gerety, Director of Disability Services. Phone: 605-626-2371. Fax: 605-626-3399. E-mail: geretyk@northern.edu.

Office of Disability Services Approximately 40 registered undergraduate students were served during 2006–07. The program or unit includes 1 full-time and 1 part-time staff member. Graduate assistants/students are provided through the program or unit. Academic advisers, counselors, regular education teachers, and trained peer tutors are provided collaboratively through on-campus or off-campus services.

Summer Program To help prepare for the demands of college, there is an optional 2-month summer program prior to entering the school available to high school graduates that focuses on life skills and/or college life adjustment, specific subject tutoring, study skills, and time management. The program is available to students attending other colleges.

Northern State University (continued)

Unique Aids and Services Aids, services, or accommodations include priority registration.

Assistive Technology Assistive technology is located in the library and includes learning support software. Technology training is provided to incoming students.

Subject-Area Tutoring Tutoring is offered one-on-one and in small groups for most subjects. Tutoring is provided collaboratively through on-campus or off-campus services via graduate assistants/students and trained peer tutors.

Basic Skills Remediation Remediation is offered in class-size groups for math, reading, and written language. Remediation is provided collaboratively through on-campus or off-campus services via computer-based instruction and regular education teachers.

Enrichment Programs for career planning, college survival skills, learning strategies, math, reading, study skills, time management, vocabulary development, and written composition skills are provided collaboratively through on-campus or off-campus services.

Application For admittance to the program or unit, students are required to apply to the program directly, provide a psychoeducational report (3 years old or less), and provide documentation of high school services. Upon application, materials documenting need for services should be sent only to the LD program or unit. Upon acceptance, documentation of need for services should be sent only to the LD program or unit. *Application deadline (institutional):* 9/1. *Application deadline (LD program):* Rolling/continuous for fall and rolling/continuous for spring.

Written Policies Written policies regarding general/basic LD accommodations, reduced course loads, and substitutions and waivers of graduation requirements are available on the program Web site. Written policies regarding general/basic LD accommodations, reduced course loads, and substitutions and waivers of graduation requirements are outlined in the school's catalog/handbook. Written policies regarding general/basic LD accommodations and reduced course loads are available through the program or unit directly.

North Georgia College & State University
Student Disability Resources

82 College Circle

Dahlonega, GA 30597

http://www.ngcsu.edu/Learning/ATallant/disaccom.shtml

Contact: Mrs. Elizabeth Powell McIntosh, Coordinator, Student Disability Resources. Phone: 706-867-2782. Fax: 706-867-2882. E-mail: emcintosh@ngcsu.edu.

Student Disability Resources Approximately 180 registered undergraduate students were served during 2006–07. The program or unit includes 1 full-time staff member. Academic advisers, coaches, counselors, skill tutors, strategy tutors, and trained peer tutors are provided through the program or unit. Academic advisers, coaches, counselors, diagnostic specialists, skill tutors, strategy tutors, and trained peer tutors are provided collaboratively through on-campus or off-campus services.

Unique Aids and Services Aids, services, or accommodations include career counseling and priority registration.

Assistive Technology Assistive technology is located in campus labs, the DSS office, a special lab and includes digital textbooks/e-text and learning support software. Technology training is provided to incoming students.

Subject-Area Tutoring Tutoring is offered one-on-one and in small groups for some subjects. Tutoring is provided collaboratively through on-campus or off-campus services via computer-based instruction and trained peer tutors.

Diagnostic Testing Testing is provided through the program or unit for learning strategies, learning styles, social skills, and study skills. Testing for auditory processing, handwriting, intelligence, learning strategies, learning styles, math, motor skills, neuropsychological, personality, reading, social skills, spelling, spoken language, study skills, visual processing, and written language is provided collaboratively through on-campus or off-campus services.

Basic Skills Remediation Remediation is available for learning strategies, reading, study skills, and time management. Remediation is provided collaboratively through on-campus or off-campus services via computer-based instruction and trained peer tutors.

Enrichment Enrichment programs are available through the program or unit for career planning, college survival skills, learning strategies, math, oral communication skills, reading, self-advocacy, stress management, study skills, test taking, time management, and written composition skills. Programs for career planning, college survival skills, health and nutrition, learning strategies, math, medication management, oral communication skills, practical computer skills, reading, self-advocacy, stress management, study skills, test taking, time management, and written composition skills are provided collaboratively through on-campus or off-campus services. Credit is offered for learning strategies, oral communication skills, reading, self-advocacy, stress management, study skills, test taking, and time management.

Fees *Diagnostic Testing* fee is $500.

Application For admittance to the program or unit, students are required to apply to the program directly and provide a psychoeducational report (3 years old or less). It is recommended that students provide documentation of high school services. Upon application, materials documenting need for services should be sent only to the LD program or unit. Upon acceptance, documentation of need for services should be sent only to admissions. *Application deadline (institutional):* 7/1. *Application deadline (LD program):* Rolling/continuous for fall and rolling/continuous for spring.

Written Policies Written policies regarding course substitutions, general/basic LD accommodations, grade forgiveness, reduced course loads, substitutions and waivers of admissions requirements, and substitutions and waivers of graduation requirements are available on the program Web site. Written policies regarding course substitutions, general/basic LD accommodations, grade forgiveness, reduced course loads, substitutions and waivers of admissions requirements, and substitutions and waivers of graduation requirements are outlined in the school's catalog/handbook.

Northwestern College

3003 Snelling Avenue North

St. Paul, MN 55113-1598

http://www.nwc.edu/

Contact: Mr. David Golias, Disabilities Office for Support Services Coordinator. Phone: 651-286-7446. E-mail: dpgolias@nwc.edu.

Academic advisers, remediation/learning specialists, trained peer tutors, and other are provided collaboratively through on-campus or off-campus services.
Orientation The program or unit offers an optional orientation for new students individually by special arrangement.
Assistive Technology Assistive technology is located in the DSS office.
Subject-Area Tutoring Tutoring is offered one-on-one for some subjects. Tutoring is provided collaboratively through on-campus or off-campus services via trained peer tutors.
Basic Skills Remediation Remediation is offered in class-size groups for learning strategies, math, study skills, and written language. Remediation is provided collaboratively through on-campus or off-campus services via computer-based instruction and regular education teachers.
Enrichment Program for career planning is provided collaboratively through on-campus or off-campus services.
Application For admittance to the program or unit, students are required to apply to the program directly and provide a psychoeducational report (4 years old or less). It is recommended that students provide documentation of high school services. Upon application, materials documenting need for services should be sent only to the LD program or unit. Upon acceptance, documentation of need for services should be sent only to the LD program or unit. *Application deadline (institutional):* 8/1. *Application deadline (LD program):* Rolling/continuous for fall and rolling/continuous for spring.

Northwestern Oklahoma State University

709 Oklahoma Boulevard
Alva, OK 73717-2799
http://www.nwosu.edu/stdserv/handbook/ADAforms.html
Contact: Daresa Poe, Secretary for Student Services. Phone: 580-327-8414. E-mail: ddpoe@nwosu.edu. Head of LD Program: Brad Franz, Dean of Student Affairs and Enrollment Management. Phone: 580-327-8415. E-mail: bmfranz@nwosu.edu.

Approximately 50 registered undergraduate students were served during 2006–07.
Assistive Technology Assistive technology includes digital textbooks/e-text.
Subject-Area Tutoring Tutoring is offered one-on-one and in small groups.
Enrichment Programs for career planning, learning strategies, and study skills are provided collaboratively through on-campus or off-campus services.
Application For admittance to the program or unit, students are required to apply to the program directly. *Application deadline (institutional):* Continuous. *Application deadline (LD program):* Rolling/continuous for fall and rolling/continuous for spring.
Written Policies Written policy regarding general/basic LD accommodations is available on the program Web site. Written policy regarding general/basic LD accommodations is outlined in the school's catalog/handbook.

Northwest Nazarene University
Academic Support Center

623 Holly Street
Nampa, ID 83686-5897
http://www.nnu.edu/
Contact: Mrs. Barbara Sosoka Howard, Adviser to Students with Learning Disabilities. Phone: 208-467-8669. Fax: 208-467-8469. E-mail: bshoward@nnu.edu.

Academic Support Center Approximately 12 registered undergraduate students were served during 2006–07. The program or unit includes 2 part-time staff members. Academic advisers, coaches, counselors, professional tutors, regular education teachers, remediation/learning specialists, skill tutors, strategy tutors, and trained peer tutors are provided through the program or unit.
Unique Aids and Services Aids, services, or accommodations include career counseling, personal coach, and weekly meetings with faculty.
Subject-Area Tutoring Tutoring is offered one-on-one and in small groups for most subjects. Tutoring is provided collaboratively through on-campus or off-campus services via LD specialists and trained peer tutors.
Basic Skills Remediation Remediation is offered one-on-one and in small groups for computer skills, learning strategies, math, reading, spelling, study skills, time management, and written language. Remediation is provided collaboratively through on-campus or off-campus services via regular education teachers and trained peer tutors.
Enrichment Programs for career planning, college survival skills, health and nutrition, learning strategies, math, oral communication skills, practical computer skills, reading, study skills, test taking, time management, and written composition skills are provided collaboratively through on-campus or off-campus services. Credit is offered for career planning, college survival skills, health and nutrition, learning strategies, math, oral communication skills, practical computer skills, reading, study skills, test taking, time management, and written composition skills.
Application For admittance to the program or unit, students are required to provide documentation of high school services and provide test results. Upon acceptance, documentation of need for services should be sent only to the LD program or unit. *Application deadline (institutional):* 8/15. *Application deadline (LD program):* Rolling/continuous for fall and rolling/continuous for spring.
Written Policies Written policy regarding general/basic LD accommodations is available on the program Web site. Written policy regarding general/basic LD accommodations is outlined in the school's catalog/handbook.

Northwood University
Learning Center

4000 Whiting Drive
Midland, MI 48640-2398
https://www.northwood.edu/sharedmedia/pdf/academics/fl/disabilityservices.pdf

Northwood University (continued)

Contact: Director, Learning Center. Phone: 561-478-5585. Fax: 561-681-7971.

Learning Center Approximately 6 registered undergraduate students were served during 2006–07. The program or unit includes 1 part-time staff member. Academic advisers, professional tutors, regular education teachers, and skill tutors are provided collaboratively through on-campus or off-campus services.

Orientation The program or unit offers an optional 1-hour orientation for new students before classes begin.

Unique Aids and Services Aids, services, or accommodations include advocates and career counseling.

Assistive Technology Assistive technology is located in campus labs, the DSS office and includes learning support software. Technology training is provided to incoming students.

Subject-Area Tutoring Tutoring is offered one-on-one, in small groups, and in class-size groups for some subjects. Tutoring is provided collaboratively through on-campus or off-campus services via computer-based instruction and professional tutors.

Basic Skills Remediation Remediation is offered one-on-one, in small groups, and in class-size groups for computer skills, math, study skills, time management, and written language. Remediation is provided collaboratively through on-campus or off-campus services via computer-based instruction, professional tutors, and regular education teachers.

Enrichment Programs for career planning, college survival skills, learning strategies, math, oral communication skills, practical computer skills, study skills, test taking, time management, and written composition skills are provided collaboratively through on-campus or off-campus services. Credit is offered for college survival skills, learning strategies, math, oral communication skills, practical computer skills, and written composition skills.

Application For admittance to the program or unit, students are required to provide a psychoeducational report (3 years old or less). Upon acceptance, documentation of need for services should be sent only to the LD program or unit. *Application deadline (institutional):* Continuous. *Application deadline (LD program):* Rolling/continuous for fall and rolling/continuous for spring.

Written Policies Written policy regarding general/basic LD accommodations is available on the program Web site. Written policy regarding general/basic LD accommodations is available through the program or unit directly.

Northwood University, Florida Campus
Learning Center

2600 North Military Trail

West Palm Beach, FL 33409-2911

http://www.northwood.edu/sharedmedia/pdf/academics/fl/disabilityservices.pdf

Contact: Director, Learning Center. Phone: 561-478-5585. Fax: 561-681-7971.

Learning Center Approximately 7 registered undergraduate students were served during 2006–07. The program or unit includes 1

part-time staff member. Skill tutors are provided through the program or unit. Academic advisers, professional tutors, and regular education teachers are provided collaboratively through on-campus or off-campus services.

Orientation The program or unit offers an optional 1-hour orientation for new students before classes begin.

Unique Aids and Services Aids, services, or accommodations include advocates and career counseling.

Assistive Technology Assistive technology is located in campus labs, the DSS office and includes learning support software. Technology training is provided to incoming students.

Subject-Area Tutoring Tutoring is offered one-on-one, in small groups, and in class-size groups for some subjects. Tutoring is provided through the program or unit via computer-based instruction. Tutoring is also provided collaboratively through on-campus or off-campus services via computer-based instruction and professional tutors.

Basic Skills Remediation Remediation is offered one-on-one, in small groups, and in class-size groups for computer skills, math, study skills, time management, and written language. Remediation is provided through the program or unit via computer-based instruction and regular education teachers. Remediation is also provided collaboratively through on-campus or off-campus services via computer-based instruction.

Enrichment Programs for career planning, math, practical computer skills, study skills, test taking, time management, and written composition skills are provided collaboratively through on-campus or off-campus services. Credit is offered for math, practical computer skills, study skills, test taking, time management, and written composition skills.

Application For admittance to the program or unit, students are required to provide a psychoeducational report (3 years old or less). Upon acceptance, documentation of need for services should be sent only to the LD program or unit. *Application deadline (institutional):* Continuous. *Application deadline (LD program):* Rolling/continuous for fall and rolling/continuous for spring.

Written Policies Written policy regarding general/basic LD accommodations is available on the program Web site. Written policy regarding general/basic LD accommodations is available through the program or unit directly.

Northwood University, Texas Campus
Student Support Center

1114 West FM 1382

Cedar Hill, TX 75104-1204

http://www.northwood.edu/

Contact: Ms. Paula J. Whitehead, Director, Student Support Center. Phone: 972-293-4075. E-mail: whitehea@northwood.edu.

Student Support Center Approximately 7 registered undergraduate students were served during 2006–07. The program or unit includes 1 full-time staff member. Academic advisers, counselors, regular education teachers, and trained peer tutors are provided collaboratively through on-campus or off-campus services.

Unique Aids and Services Aids, services, or accommodations include career counseling and weekly meetings with faculty.

Subject-Area Tutoring Tutoring is offered one-on-one for some subjects. Tutoring is provided collaboratively through on-campus or off-campus services via trained peer tutors.

Basic Skills Remediation Remediation is offered one-on-one for social skills, study skills, and time management. Remediation is provided through the program or unit.

Enrichment Enrichment programs are available through the program or unit for career planning, college survival skills, self-advocacy, stress management, study skills, test taking, and time management. Programs for career planning, health and nutrition, oral communication skills, practical computer skills, self-advocacy, study skills, time management, and written composition skills are provided collaboratively through on-campus or off-campus services. Credit is offered for career planning, oral communication skills, practical computer skills, and written composition skills.

Application For admittance to the program or unit, students are required to apply to the program directly and provide a psychoeducational report. Upon acceptance, documentation of need for services should be sent only to the LD program or unit. *Application deadline (institutional):* Continuous. *Application deadline (LD program):* 8/1 for fall. 11/1 for spring.

Written Policies Written policy regarding general/basic LD accommodations is available through the program or unit directly.

Notre Dame de Namur University
Program for Academic Success and Support

1500 Ralston Avenue

Belmont, CA 94002-1908

http://www.ndnu.edu/academics/acad-success-center/
tutorial-center/pass.aspx

Contact: Ms. Peggy Koshland Crane, Director of Academic Success Center and Program for Academic Support and Success. Phone: 650-508-3670. Fax: 650-508-3457. E-mail: mcrane@ndnu.edu.

Program for Academic Success and Support Approximately 40 registered undergraduate students were served during 2006–07. The program or unit includes 1 full-time and 2 part-time staff members. Diagnostic specialists, LD specialists, and remediation/ learning specialists are provided through the program or unit. Academic advisers, coaches, counselors, graduate assistants/students, professional tutors, skill tutors, and strategy tutors are provided collaboratively through on-campus or off-campus services.

Unique Aids and Services Aids, services, or accommodations include advocates, career counseling, and faculty training.

Assistive Technology Assistive technology is located in campus labs, the DSS office and includes digital textbooks/e-text, learning support software, and scanning. Technology training is provided to incoming students.

Subject-Area Tutoring Tutoring is offered one-on-one and in small groups for all subjects. Tutoring is provided through the program or unit via computer-based instruction, graduate assistants/ students, LD specialists, professional tutors, and trained peer tutors.

Diagnostic Testing Testing is provided through the program or unit for handwriting, learning strategies, learning styles, math, personality, reading, social skills, spelling, spoken language, study skills, written language, and other services. Testing for auditory processing, intelligence, motor skills, neuropsychological, and visual processing is provided collaboratively through on-campus or off-campus services.

Basic Skills Remediation Remediation is offered one-on-one and in small groups for auditory processing, computer skills, learning strategies, math, reading, social skills, study skills, time management, visual processing, written language, and others. Remediation is provided through the program or unit via computer-based instruction, LD specialists, and regular education teachers. Remediation is also provided collaboratively through on-campus or off-campus services via computer-based instruction, graduate assistants/students, professional tutors, teacher trainees, and trained peer tutors.

Enrichment Enrichment programs are available through the program or unit for college survival skills, learning strategies, math, oral communication skills, practical computer skills, reading, self-advocacy, study skills, test taking, time management, vocabulary development, written composition skills, and other. Programs for career planning, college survival skills, health and nutrition, learning strategies, math, medication management, oral communication skills, practical computer skills, reading, self-advocacy, stress management, study skills, test taking, time management, vocabulary development, written composition skills, and other are provided collaboratively through on-campus or off-campus services.

Fees *Diagnostic Testing* fee is $600 to $1200.

Application For admittance to the program or unit, students are required to provide documentation of high school services and provide medical diagnosis, mental health impairment documentation. It is recommended that students provide a psychoeducational report. Upon application, materials documenting need for services should be sent only to admissions with institutional application materials. Upon acceptance, documentation of need for services should be sent to both admissions and the LD program or unit. *Application deadline (institutional):* Continuous. *Application deadline (LD program):* 10/1 for fall. 2/1 for spring.

Written Policies Written policy regarding general/basic LD accommodations is available on the program Web site. Written policy regarding general/basic LD accommodations is outlined in the school's catalog/handbook. Written policies regarding course substitutions, substitutions and waivers of admissions requirements, and substitutions and waivers of graduation requirements are available through the program or unit directly.

Nova Scotia Agricultural College
Academic Support Centre

PO Box 550

Truro, NS B2N 5E3

Canada

http://nsac.ca/recruiting/studentlife/tutoring.asp

Contact: Ms. Judy M. Smith, Dean of Student Services. Phone: 902-893-7915. Fax: 902-893-6545. E-mail: jsmith@ nsac.ca.

Nova Scotia Agricultural College (continued)

Academic Support Centre Approximately 32 registered undergraduate students were served during 2006–07. The program or unit includes 1 full-time staff member. LD specialists and trained peer tutors are provided through the program or unit. Academic advisers, diagnostic specialists, LD specialists, and remediation/learning specialists are provided collaboratively through on-campus or off-campus services.

Orientation The program or unit offers an optional varying length orientation for new students after classes begin.

Unique Aids and Services Aids, services, or accommodations include disabilities resource facilitator.

Assistive Technology Assistive technology is located in the DSS office and includes digital textbooks/e-text and scanning. Technology training is provided to incoming students.

Subject-Area Tutoring Tutoring is offered one-on-one and in small groups for most subjects. Tutoring is provided through the program or unit via trained peer tutors.

Diagnostic Testing Testing is provided through the program or unit for math. Testing for auditory processing, learning strategies, learning styles, personality, reading, and visual processing is provided collaboratively through on-campus or off-campus services.

Basic Skills Remediation Remediation is offered one-on-one and in small groups for learning strategies, math, reading, study skills, and time management. Remediation is provided through the program or unit via computer-based instruction, LD specialists, and trained peer tutors.

Application For admittance to the program or unit, students are required to provide a psychoeducational report (6 years old or less) and provide documentation of high school services. It is recommended that students apply to the program directly. Upon application, materials documenting need for services should be sent only to admissions with institutional application materials. Upon acceptance, documentation of need for services should be sent only to the LD program or unit. *Application deadline (institutional):* 8/1. *Application deadline (LD program):* Rolling/continuous for fall and rolling/continuous for spring.

Written Policies Written policies regarding general/basic LD accommodations and reduced course loads are available through the program or unit directly.

Nova Southeastern University
Office of Student Disability Services

3301 College Avenue

Fort Lauderdale, FL 33314-7796

http://www.nova.edu/disabilityservices

Contact: Arlene Giczkowski, Director, Student Disability Services. Phone: 954-262-7189. Fax: 954-262-1390. E-mail: giczkows@nova.edu.

Office of Student Disability Services Approximately 40 registered undergraduate students were served during 2006–07. The program or unit includes 1 full-time staff member. LD specialists are provided through the program or unit. Academic advisers and LD specialists are provided collaboratively through on-campus or off-campus services.

Unique Aids and Services Aids, services, or accommodations include support groups.

Assistive Technology Assistive technology is located in a special lab and includes digital textbooks/e-text.

Subject-Area Tutoring Tutoring is offered one-on-one and in small groups for some subjects. Tutoring is provided collaboratively through on-campus or off-campus services via professional tutors and trained peer tutors.

Diagnostic Testing Testing is provided through the program or unit for learning strategies. Testing for auditory processing, handwriting, intelligence, learning styles, math, motor skills, neuropsychological, personality, reading, social skills, spelling, spoken language, visual processing, and written language is provided collaboratively through on-campus or off-campus services.

Basic Skills Remediation Remediation is available for written language.

Enrichment Programs for career planning, college survival skills, math, practical computer skills, self-advocacy, study skills, test taking, and time management are provided collaboratively through on-campus or off-campus services.

Fees *Diagnostic Testing* fee is applicable.

Application For admittance to the program or unit, students are required to provide a psychoeducational report (3 years old or less). It is recommended that students provide documentation of high school services. Upon acceptance, documentation of need for services should be sent only to the LD program or unit. *Application deadline (institutional):* Continuous. *Application deadline (LD program):* Rolling/continuous for fall and rolling/continuous for spring.

Written Policies Written policy regarding general/basic LD accommodations is available on the program Web site. Written policy regarding general/basic LD accommodations is outlined in the school's catalog/handbook. Written policies regarding course substitutions, general/basic LD accommodations, reduced course loads, and substitutions and waivers of graduation requirements are available through the program or unit directly.

NSCAD University
Office of Student and Academic Services

5163 Duke Street

Halifax, NS B3J 3J6

Canada

http://www.nscad.ca/

Contact: Ms. Bernadette Kehoe, Coordinator of Financial Aid and Student Counselling. Phone: 902-494-8130. Fax: 902-425-2987. E-mail: bkehoe@nscad.ns.ca. Head of LD Program: Mr. Bill Travis, Disability Resource Facilitator. Phone: 902-494-8313. Fax: 902-425-2987. E-mail: btravis@nscad.ca.

Office of Student and Academic Services Approximately 47 registered undergraduate students were served during 2006–07. The program or unit includes 1 full-time staff member. Academic advisers and counselors are provided through the program or unit. Counselors, LD specialists, and skill tutors are provided collaboratively through on-campus or off-campus services.

Assistive Technology Assistive technology is located in campus labs, the DSS office and includes learning support software and scanning. Technology training is provided to incoming students.

Subject-Area Tutoring Tutoring is offered one-on-one for some subjects. Tutoring is provided through the program or unit via computer-based instruction. Tutoring is also provided collaboratively through on-campus or off-campus services via computer-based instruction and LD specialists.

Enrichment Programs for learning strategies, oral communication skills, stress management, study skills, test taking, time management, and written composition skills are provided collaboratively through on-campus or off-campus services.

Application It is recommended that students provide a psychoeducational report (3 years old or less) and provide documentation of high school services. Upon acceptance, documentation of need for services should be sent only to the LD program or unit. *Application deadline (institutional):* 5/15. *Application deadline (LD program):* 9/20 for fall. 1/18 for spring.

Written Policies Written policy regarding general/basic LD accommodations is available through the program or unit directly.

Oak Hills Christian College
Assisted Learning Program

1600 Oak Hills Road, SW

Bemidji, MN 56601-8832

http://www.oakhills.edu

Contact: Assisted Learning Program Director. Phone: 218-751-8670. Fax: 218-751-8825.

Assisted Learning Program Approximately 18 registered undergraduate students were served during 2006–07. The program or unit includes 2 part-time staff members. Academic advisers, counselors, diagnostic specialists, graduate assistants/students, regular education teachers, skill tutors, and trained peer tutors are provided collaboratively through on-campus or off-campus services.

Unique Aids and Services Aids, services, or accommodations include advocates, faculty training, personal coach, and weekly meetings with faculty.

Assistive Technology Assistive technology is located in the DSS office, a special lab and includes digital textbooks/e-text, learning support software, and scanning. Technology training is provided to incoming students.

Subject-Area Tutoring Tutoring is offered one-on-one and in small groups for some subjects. Tutoring is provided through the program or unit via trained peer tutors. Tutoring is also provided collaboratively through on-campus or off-campus services via trained peer tutors.

Diagnostic Testing Testing is provided through the program or unit for learning strategies, learning styles, and personality.

Basic Skills Remediation Remediation is offered in class-size groups for math and written language. Remediation is provided collaboratively through on-campus or off-campus services via regular education teachers.

Enrichment Enrichment programs are available through the program or unit for learning strategies, study skills, test taking, and time management. Program for oral communication skills is provided collaboratively through on-campus or off-campus services.

Application For admittance to the program or unit, students are required to provide a psychoeducational report (5 years old or less). It is recommended that students provide documentation of high school services. Upon application, materials documenting need for services should be sent to both admissions and the LD program or unit. Upon acceptance, documentation of need for services should be sent to both admissions and the LD program or unit. *Application deadline (institutional):* Continuous. *Application deadline (LD program):* Rolling/continuous for fall and rolling/continuous for spring.

Written Policies Written policies regarding general/basic LD accommodations, substitutions and waivers of admissions requirements, and substitutions and waivers of graduation requirements are available on the program Web site. Written policies regarding general/basic LD accommodations, substitutions and waivers of admissions requirements, and substitutions and waivers of graduation requirements are outlined in the school's catalog/handbook.

Oakland University
Office of Disability Support Services

Rochester, MI 48309-4401

http://www2.oakland.edu/oakland/ouportal/index.asp?site=20

Contact: Office of Disability Support Services. Phone: 248-370-3266. Fax: 248-370-4989. E-mail: dss@oakland.edu.

Office of Disability Support Services Approximately 200 registered undergraduate students were served during 2006–07. The program or unit includes 2 full-time and 2 part-time staff members. Academic advisers, diagnostic specialists, and trained peer tutors are provided collaboratively through on-campus or off-campus services.

Unique Aids and Services Aids, services, or accommodations include advocates, career counseling, and priority registration.

Assistive Technology Assistive technology is located in campus labs, the DSS office, a special lab and includes digital textbooks/e-text, learning support software, and scanning. Technology training is provided to incoming students.

Subject-Area Tutoring Tutoring is offered one-on-one and in small groups for most subjects. Tutoring is provided collaboratively through on-campus or off-campus services via trained peer tutors.

Diagnostic Testing Testing for auditory processing, intelligence, learning strategies, learning styles, math, reading, spelling, spoken language, study skills, and written language is provided collaboratively through on-campus or off-campus services.

Basic Skills Remediation Remediation is offered one-on-one and in small groups for auditory processing, learning strategies, math, reading, spelling, study skills, time management, and written language. Remediation is provided collaboratively through on-campus or off-campus services via graduate assistants/students and trained peer tutors.

Enrichment Programs for career planning, college survival skills, health and nutrition, learning strategies, math, practical computer skills, reading, self-advocacy, stress management, study skills, test taking, time management, vocabulary development, and written composition skills are provided collaboratively through on-campus or off-campus services. Credit is offered for career planning, college survival skills, reading, stress management, and written composition skills.

Oakland University (continued)

Fees *Diagnostic Testing* fee is $100.

Application For admittance to the program or unit, students are required to apply to the program directly, provide a psychoeducational report (3 years old or less), and provide all assessment scores, histories, and reports if submitting IEP as temporary documentation. Upon acceptance, documentation of need for services should be sent only to the LD program or unit. *Application deadline (institutional):* Continuous.

Written Policies Written policies regarding general/basic LD accommodations and reduced course loads are available through the program or unit directly.

Occidental College
Center for Academic Excellence

1600 Campus Road
Los Angeles, CA 90041-3314
http://www.departments.oxy.edu/cae/

Contact: Prof. Diana C. Linden PhD, Educational Specialist, Disabilities Services Provider. Phone: 323-259-2573. Fax: 323-259-1402. E-mail: linden@oxy.edu. Head of LD Program: Prof. Thomas Burkdall PhD, Professor of English Writing, Director Center for Academic Excellence. E-mail: tlburk@oxy.edu.

Center for Academic Excellence Approximately 80 registered undergraduate students were served during 2006–07. The program or unit includes 1 full-time and 1 part-time staff member. Academic advisers, coaches, diagnostic specialists, LD specialists, and strategy tutors are provided through the program or unit.

Orientation The program or unit offers an optional 1-hour orientation for new students before registration and before classes begin.

Unique Aids and Services Aids, services, or accommodations include personal coach and priority registration.

Assistive Technology Assistive technology is located in the DSS office, a special lab and includes digital textbooks/e-text, scanning, and voice-to-text/screen readers. Technology training is provided to incoming students.

Subject-Area Tutoring Tutoring is offered one-on-one for most subjects. Tutoring is provided through the program or unit via LD specialists and trained peer tutors.

Diagnostic Testing Testing is provided through the program or unit for learning strategies, learning styles, reading, study skills, and written language. Testing for intelligence, learning strategies, learning styles, neuropsychological, and reading is provided collaboratively through on-campus or off-campus services.

Enrichment Enrichment programs are available through the program or unit for learning strategies, reading, self-advocacy, study skills, test taking, time management, and written composition skills. Programs for career planning, college survival skills, medication management, and stress management are provided collaboratively through on-campus or off-campus services.

Student Organization Learning Differences Association consists of 10 members.

Application For admittance to the program or unit, students are required to provide a psychoeducational report (3 years old or less). Upon application, materials documenting need for services should be sent to both admissions and the LD program or unit. Upon

acceptance, documentation of need for services should be sent only to the LD program or unit. *Application deadline (institutional):* 1/10. *Application deadline (LD program):* Rolling/continuous for fall and rolling/continuous for spring.

Written Policies Written policy regarding general/basic LD accommodations is available on the program Web site. Written policies regarding general/basic LD accommodations and substitutions and waivers of admissions requirements are available through the program or unit directly.

Oglethorpe University
Learning Resources Center (LRC)

4484 Peachtree Road, NE
Atlanta, GA 30319-2797
http://www.oglethorpe.edu/

Contact: Dr. Jon Michael Saulson, Director, Learning Resources Center. Phone: 404-364-8869. Fax: 404-364-8894. E-mail: jsaulson@oglethorpe.edu.

Learning Resources Center (LRC) Approximately 40 registered undergraduate students were served during 2006–07. The program or unit includes 1 part-time staff member. Academic advisers, coaches, counselors, graduate assistants/students, professional tutors, skill tutors, and trained peer tutors are provided through the program or unit. Diagnostic specialists, LD specialists, and remediation/learning specialists are provided collaboratively through on-campus or off-campus services.

Summer Program To help prepare for the demands of college, there is an optional 1-week summer program prior to entering the school available to high school graduates that focuses on life skills and/or college life adjustment. The program accepts students from out-of-state.

Unique Aids and Services Aids, services, or accommodations include faculty training, priority registration, and support groups.

Assistive Technology Assistive technology is located in the DSS office, AMAC via Athens, Georgia and includes digital textbooks/e-text and learning support software. Technology training is provided to incoming students.

Subject-Area Tutoring Tutoring is offered one-on-one and in small groups for some subjects. Tutoring is provided collaboratively through on-campus or off-campus services via computer-based instruction, graduate assistants/students, professional tutors, and trained peer tutors.

Diagnostic Testing Testing is provided through the program or unit for handwriting, learning strategies, math, reading, spelling, study skills, and written language. Testing for auditory processing, intelligence, learning styles, motor skills, neuropsychological, personality, social skills, spoken language, and visual processing is provided collaboratively through on-campus or off-campus services.

Enrichment Enrichment programs are available through the program or unit for math, reading, self-advocacy, study skills, test taking, time management, and written composition skills. Programs for career planning, college survival skills, health and nutrition, learning strategies, math, medication management, oral communication skills, practical computer skills, reading, stress management, study skills, test taking, time management, vocabulary development, and written composition skills are provided collaboratively through on-campus or off-campus services.

Application For admittance to the program or unit, students are required to provide a psychoeducational report (3 years old or less). It is recommended that students provide documentation of high school services. Upon application, materials documenting need for services should be sent only to the LD program or unit. Upon acceptance, documentation of need for services should be sent only to the LD program or unit. *Application deadline (institutional):* Continuous. *Application deadline (LD program):* Rolling/continuous for fall and rolling/continuous for spring.

Written Policies Written policies regarding course substitutions and reduced course loads are outlined in the school's catalog/handbook. Written policy regarding general/basic LD accommodations is available through the program or unit directly.

The Ohio State University
Office for Disability Services

Enarson Hall, 154 W. 12th Avenue
Columbus, OH 43210
http://www.ods.osu.edu

Contact: Ms. Lois J. Burke, Director. Phone: 614-292-3307. Fax: 614-292-4190. E-mail: burke.4@osu.edu.

Office for Disability Services Approximately 400 registered undergraduate students were served during 2006–07. The program or unit includes 6 full-time staff members. Counselors and other are provided through the program or unit. Counselors and other are provided collaboratively through on-campus or off-campus services.

Orientation The program or unit offers a mandatory 90-minute orientation for new students before classes begin, after classes begin, and individually by special arrangement.

Unique Aids and Services Aids, services, or accommodations include priority registration.

Assistive Technology Assistive technology is located in the DSS office and includes digital textbooks/e-text, learning support software, and scanning. Technology training is provided to incoming students.

Diagnostic Testing Testing is provided through the program or unit for auditory processing, intelligence, math, reading, spelling, study skills, visual processing, and written language. Testing for auditory processing, intelligence, math, reading, spelling, spoken language, visual processing, and written language is provided collaboratively through on-campus or off-campus services.

Enrichment Enrichment programs are available through the program or unit for self-advocacy. Programs for career planning, learning strategies, medication management, stress management, study skills, test taking, time management, and written composition skills are provided collaboratively through on-campus or off-campus services. Credit is offered for learning strategies and study skills.

Fees *Diagnostic Testing* fee is $300.

Application For admittance to the program or unit, students are required to provide a psychoeducational report (3 years old or less). It is recommended that students provide documentation of high school services and provide most recent psychoeducational testing (ability and achievement). Upon application, materials documenting need for services should be sent only to the LD program or unit. Upon acceptance, documentation of need for services should be

sent only to the LD program or unit. *Application deadline (institutional):* 2/1. *Application deadline (LD program):* Rolling/continuous for fall and rolling/continuous for spring.

Written Policies Written policy regarding general/basic LD accommodations is available on the program Web site. Written policies regarding course substitutions and general/basic LD accommodations are available through the program or unit directly.

The Ohio State University at Lima
Office for Disability Services

4240 Campus Drive
Lima, OH 45804
http://www.lima.osu.edu/

Contact: Mrs. Karen M. Meyer, Coordinator for Disability Services. Phone: 419-995-8453. Fax: 419-995-8483. E-mail: meyer.193@osu.edu.

Office for Disability Services Approximately 25 registered undergraduate students were served during 2006–07. The program or unit includes 1 full-time and 1 part-time staff member. LD specialists are provided through the program or unit. Services are provided collaboratively through on-campus or off-campus services.

Unique Aids and Services Aids, services, or accommodations include priority registration and support groups.

Assistive Technology Assistive technology is located in campus labs, the DSS office and includes digital textbooks/e-text.

Subject-Area Tutoring Tutoring is offered one-on-one for most subjects. Tutoring is provided through the program or unit via LD specialists. Tutoring is also provided collaboratively through on-campus or off-campus services via trained peer tutors.

Basic Skills Remediation Remediation is offered one-on-one for learning strategies, math, study skills, and time management. Remediation is provided through the program or unit via LD specialists. Remediation is also provided collaboratively through on-campus or off-campus services via trained peer tutors.

Application For admittance to the program or unit, students are required to apply to the program directly, provide a psychoeducational report (5 years old or less), and provide documentation of high school services. Upon application, materials documenting need for services should be sent only to the LD program or unit. Upon acceptance, documentation of need for services should be sent only to the LD program or unit. *Application deadline (institutional):* 2/1. *Application deadline (LD program):* Rolling/continuous for fall and rolling/continuous for spring.

Written Policies Written policies regarding general/basic LD accommodations and substitutions and waivers of admissions requirements are available on the program Web site. Written policy regarding general/basic LD accommodations is outlined in the school's catalog/handbook. Written policies regarding course substitutions, general/basic LD accommodations, grade forgiveness, reduced course loads, substitutions and waivers of admissions requirements, and substitutions and waivers of graduation requirements are available through the program or unit directly.

Ohio University–Chillicothe
Institutional Equity

571 West Fifth Street, PO Box 629

Chillicothe, OH 45601-0629

http://www.chillicothe.ohiou.edu/students

Contact: Dr. Diane Diekroger, Coordinator of Student Support. Phone: 740-774-7717. Fax: 740-774-7295. E-mail: diekroge@ohio.edu.

Institutional Equity Approximately 50 registered undergraduate students were served during 2006–07. The program or unit includes 1 full-time and 2 part-time staff members. Counselors, graduate assistants/students, and other are provided through the program or unit. Academic advisers, diagnostic specialists, regular education teachers, and trained peer tutors are provided collaboratively through on-campus or off-campus services.

Summer Program To help prepare for the demands of college, there is an optional 5-week summer program prior to entering the school available to rising sophomores, high school graduates that focuses on life skills and/or college life adjustment, study skills, test-taking skills, and time management. Degree credit will be earned. The program accepts students from out-of-state and is available to students attending other colleges.

Unique Aids and Services Aids, services, or accommodations include advocates.

Assistive Technology Assistive technology is located in campus labs and includes scanning and voice activated computer.

Subject-Area Tutoring Tutoring is offered one-on-one for all subjects. Tutoring is provided collaboratively through on-campus or off-campus services via trained peer tutors.

Basic Skills Remediation Remediation is offered in class-size groups for math and written language. Remediation is provided collaboratively through on-campus or off-campus services via regular education teachers.

Fees *Summer Program* fee is $417.

Application For admittance to the program or unit, students are required to provide documentation of high school services. It is recommended that students provide a psychoeducational report (1 year old or less). Upon application, materials documenting need for services should be sent only to the LD program or unit. Upon acceptance, documentation of need for services should be sent only to the LD program or unit. *Application deadline (LD program):* Rolling/continuous for fall and rolling/continuous for spring.

Written Policies Written policy regarding general/basic LD accommodations is outlined in the school's catalog/handbook. Written policy regarding general/basic LD accommodations is available through the program or unit directly.

Ohio Wesleyan University
Learning Disabilities Assistance Center

61 South Sandusky Street

Delaware, OH 43015

http://arc.owu.edu/

Contact: Dr. Lydia Susan Block, Learning Specialist. Phone: 740-368-3857. Fax: 740-368-3499. E-mail: lsblock@owu.edu.

Learning Disabilities Assistance Center Approximately 250 registered undergraduate students were served during 2006–07. The program or unit includes 1 full-time staff member. LD specialists, skill tutors, strategy tutors, and other are provided collaboratively through on-campus or off-campus services.

Assistive Technology Assistive technology is located in the DSS office, the library and includes digital textbooks/e-text, learning support software, and scanning.

Subject-Area Tutoring Tutoring is offered one-on-one, in small groups, and in class-size groups for some subjects. Tutoring is provided collaboratively through on-campus or off-campus services via other.

Basic Skills Remediation Remediation is offered in small groups for learning strategies, study skills, and time management. Remediation is provided collaboratively through on-campus or off-campus services.

Enrichment Programs for career planning, college survival skills, learning strategies, math, medication management, reading, study skills, time management, and written composition skills are provided collaboratively through on-campus or off-campus services. Credit is offered for college survival skills.

Application For admittance to the program or unit, students are required to provide a psychoeducational report (3 years old or less). It is recommended that students provide documentation of high school services. Upon acceptance, documentation of need for services should be sent only to the LD program or unit. *Application deadline (institutional):* 3/1.

Written Policies Written policies regarding course substitutions, general/basic LD accommodations, and reduced course loads are available through the program or unit directly.

Oklahoma State University
Student Disability Services

Stillwater, OK 74078

http://sds.okstate.edu

Contact: Mr. Michael Shuttic, Coordinator of Student Disability Services and ADA Compliance. Phone: 405-744-7116. Fax: 405-744-8380. E-mail: m.shuttic@okstate.edu.

Student Disability Services Approximately 160 registered undergraduate students were served during 2006–07. The program or unit includes 4 full-time and 2 part-time staff members. Graduate assistants/students and strategy tutors are provided through the program or unit. Academic advisers, counselors, diagnostic specialists, remediation/learning specialists, skill tutors, strategy tutors, and trained peer tutors are provided collaboratively through on-campus or off-campus services.

Summer Program To help prepare for the demands of college, there is an optional 1- or 2-day summer program prior to entering the school.

Unique Aids and Services Aids, services, or accommodations include advocates, career counseling, and faculty training.

Assistive Technology Assistive technology is located in campus labs, the DSS office, the individual student's computer and includes digital textbooks/e-text and scanning. Technology training is provided to incoming students.

Subject-Area Tutoring Tutoring is offered one-on-one and in small groups for most subjects. Tutoring is provided collaboratively through on-campus or off-campus services via computer-based instruction, graduate assistants/students, professional tutors, and trained peer tutors.

Diagnostic Testing Testing is provided through the program or unit for learning strategies and learning styles. Testing for auditory processing, intelligence, learning strategies, learning styles, math, motor skills, neuropsychological, reading, spelling, spoken language, study skills, visual processing, and written language is provided collaboratively through on-campus or off-campus services.

Basic Skills Remediation Remediation is available for learning strategies, math, study skills, time management, and written language. Remediation is provided collaboratively through on-campus or off-campus services via graduate assistants/students, regular education teachers, and trained peer tutors.

Enrichment Programs for career planning, college survival skills, learning strategies, math, stress management, study skills, test taking, and time management are provided collaboratively through on-campus or off-campus services. Credit is offered for college survival skills, learning strategies, and math.

Fees *Diagnostic Testing* fee is $150 to $350.

Application For admittance to the program or unit, students are required to provide a psychoeducational report. It is recommended that students provide documentation of high school services. Upon application, materials documenting need for services should be sent only to the LD program or unit. Upon acceptance, documentation of need for services should be sent only to the LD program or unit. *Application deadline (institutional):* Continuous. *Application deadline (LD program):* Rolling/continuous for fall and rolling/continuous for spring.

Written Policies Written policies regarding course substitutions, general/basic LD accommodations, and substitutions and waivers of graduation requirements are available on the program Web site. Written policies regarding course substitutions and substitutions and waivers of graduation requirements are outlined in the school's catalog/handbook. Written policies regarding course substitutions, general/basic LD accommodations, and substitutions and waivers of graduation requirements are available through the program or unit directly.

Old Dominion University
Disability Services

5115 Hampton Boulevard
Norfolk, VA 23529

http://studentaffairs.odu.edu/disabilityservices/

Contact: Ms. Sheryn Davis Milton, Director of Disability Services. Phone: 757-683-4655. Fax: 757-683-5356. E-mail: smilton@odu.edu.

Disability Services Approximately 275 registered undergraduate students were served during 2006–07. The program or unit includes 3 full-time and 2 part-time staff members. Counselors, graduate assistants/students, LD specialists, remediation/learning specialists, and strategy tutors are provided through the program or unit. Academic advisers, counselors, and skill tutors are provided collaboratively through on-campus or off-campus services.

Orientation The program or unit offers an optional 1-hour orientation for new students after classes begin.

Summer Program To help prepare for the demands of college, there is an optional 2-day/1-night summer program prior to entering the school available to rising juniors, rising seniors, high school graduates that focuses on life skills and/or college life adjustment and self-advocacy. The program accepts students from out-of-state and is available to students attending other colleges.

Unique Aids and Services Aids, services, or accommodations include faculty training, priority registration, and support groups.

Assistive Technology Assistive technology is located in campus labs, the DSS office, a special lab and includes digital textbooks/e-text, learning support software, and scanning.

Subject-Area Tutoring Tutoring is offered one-on-one and in small groups for some subjects. Tutoring is provided collaboratively through on-campus or off-campus services via graduate assistants/students, professional tutors, and trained peer tutors.

Diagnostic Testing Testing is provided through the program or unit for learning strategies, learning styles, and study skills.

Basic Skills Remediation Remediation is offered in class-size groups for learning strategies, math, spelling, study skills, time management, and written language. Remediation is provided collaboratively through on-campus or off-campus services via professional tutors and regular education teachers.

Enrichment Enrichment programs are available through the program or unit for college survival skills, learning strategies, study skills, test taking, and time management. Programs for career planning, college survival skills, health and nutrition, learning strategies, stress management, study skills, test taking, and time management are provided collaboratively through on-campus or off-campus services. Credit is offered for career planning and college survival skills.

Fees *Summer Program* fee is $75.

Application For admittance to the program or unit, students are required to apply to the program directly, provide a psychoeducational report (3 years old or less), and provide learning disability psychoeducational testing report. It is recommended that students provide documentation of high school services. Upon acceptance, documentation of need for services should be sent only to the LD program or unit. *Application deadline (institutional):* 3/15. *Application deadline (LD program):* Rolling/continuous for fall and rolling/continuous for spring.

Written Policies Written policy regarding general/basic LD accommodations is available on the program Web site. Written policies regarding general/basic LD accommodations and grade forgiveness are outlined in the school's catalog/handbook. Written policy regarding course substitutions is available through the program or unit directly.

Oral Roberts University
Student Resources

7777 South Lewis Avenue
Tulsa, OK 74171-0001
http://www.oru.edu/

Oral Roberts University (continued)

Contact: Mr. Danny Ray Ziriax, Director of Student Resources. Phone: 918-495-7018. Fax: 918-495-7879. E-mail: dziriax@oru.edu.

Student Resources Approximately 25 registered undergraduate students were served during 2006–07. The program or unit includes 2 full-time staff members. LD specialists and special education teachers are provided through the program or unit. Academic advisers, counselors, professional tutors, regular education teachers, remediation/learning specialists, and trained peer tutors are provided collaboratively through on-campus or off-campus services.

Unique Aids and Services Aids, services, or accommodations include advocates, career counseling, and faculty training.

Assistive Technology Assistive technology is located in the DSS office and includes learning support software and scanning.

Subject-Area Tutoring Tutoring is offered in small groups for most subjects. Tutoring is provided collaboratively through on-campus or off-campus services via computer-based instruction and trained peer tutors.

Basic Skills Remediation Remediation is offered in class-size groups for math, reading, and written language. Remediation is provided collaboratively through on-campus or off-campus services via computer-based instruction and trained peer tutors.

Enrichment Programs for career planning, college survival skills, health and nutrition, learning strategies, math, oral communication skills, practical computer skills, reading, study skills, test taking, time management, vocabulary development, and written composition skills are provided collaboratively through on-campus or off-campus services. Credit is offered for college survival skills, health and nutrition, learning strategies, math, oral communication skills, practical computer skills, reading, study skills, test taking, time management, vocabulary development, and written composition skills.

Application For admittance to the program or unit, students are required to apply to the program directly and provide a psychoeducational report (3 years old or less). It is recommended that students provide documentation of high school services. Upon application, materials documenting need for services should be sent only to the LD program or unit. Upon acceptance, documentation of need for services should be sent only to the LD program or unit. *Application deadline (institutional):* Continuous. *Application deadline (LD program):* Rolling/continuous for fall and rolling/continuous for spring.

Written Policies Written policy regarding general/basic LD accommodations is outlined in the school's catalog/handbook. Written policy regarding general/basic LD accommodations is available through the program or unit directly.

Oregon Institute of Technology
Services for Students with Disabilities

3201 Campus Drive
Klamath Falls, OR 97601-8801
http://www.oit.edu/index.html?method=disb
Contact: Mr. Ron Douglas McCutcheon OSM, Director of Campus Access and Equal Opportunity. Phone:

541-885-1031. Fax: 541-885-1072. E-mail: ron.mccutcheon@oit.edu.

Services for Students with Disabilities Approximately 46 registered undergraduate students were served during 2006–07. The program or unit includes 1 full-time staff member. Skill tutors, strategy tutors, and other are provided through the program or unit. Academic advisers, counselors, diagnostic specialists, LD specialists, regular education teachers, remediation/learning specialists, skill tutors, trained peer tutors, and other are provided collaboratively through on-campus or off-campus services.

Unique Aids and Services Aids, services, or accommodations include career counseling, faculty training, priority registration, support groups, weekly meetings with faculty, note-taking, faculty notes.

Assistive Technology Assistive technology is located in campus labs, the DSS office, a special lab and includes digital textbooks/e-text, learning support software, and scanning. Technology training is provided to incoming students.

Subject-Area Tutoring Tutoring is offered one-on-one and in small groups for most subjects. Tutoring is provided collaboratively through on-campus or off-campus services via computer-based instruction, trained peer tutors, and other.

Diagnostic Testing Testing is provided through the program or unit for learning styles and study skills. Testing for auditory processing, intelligence, learning styles, math, motor skills, neuropsychological, reading, spelling, study skills, visual processing, and written language is provided collaboratively through on-campus or off-campus services.

Enrichment Enrichment programs are available through the program or unit for college survival skills, learning strategies, oral communication skills, self-advocacy, stress management, study skills, test taking, time management, and other. Programs for career planning, college survival skills, health and nutrition, learning strategies, math, medication management, oral communication skills, practical computer skills, reading, self-advocacy, stress management, study skills, test taking, time management, vocabulary development, written composition skills, and other are provided collaboratively through on-campus or off-campus services. Credit is offered for other.

Fees *Diagnostic Testing* fee is applicable.

Application For admittance to the program or unit, students are required to provide a psychoeducational report (3 years old or less). It is recommended that students provide documentation of high school services. Upon application, materials documenting need for services should be sent only to the LD program or unit. Upon acceptance, documentation of need for services should be sent only to the LD program or unit. *Application deadline (institutional):* 10/1. *Application deadline (LD program):* Rolling/continuous for fall and rolling/continuous for spring.

Written Policies Written policy regarding general/basic LD accommodations is available on the program Web site. Written policy regarding general/basic LD accommodations is available through the program or unit directly.

Otis College of Art and Design
Students with Disabilities Services

9045 Lincoln Boulevard

Los Angeles, CA 90045-9785

http://intranet.otis.edu/StudentAffairs/SRC/disabilities.shtml

Contact: Dr. Carol D. Branch, Director, Learning Resources. Phone: 310-846-2554. Fax: 310-665-9158. E-mail: ananse@otis.edu.

Students with Disabilities Services Approximately 45 registered undergraduate students were served during 2006–07. The program or unit includes 2 full-time and 2 part-time staff members. Regular education teachers, skill tutors, strategy tutors, and trained peer tutors are provided through the program or unit. Academic advisers, counselors, diagnostic specialists, LD specialists, and remediation/learning specialists are provided collaboratively through on-campus or off-campus services.
Orientation The program or unit offers an optional 1-hour orientation for new students during registration and individually by special arrangement.
Unique Aids and Services Aids, services, or accommodations include career counseling and faculty training.
Assistive Technology Assistive technology is located in the Student Resources Center and includes digital textbooks/e-text, learning support software, and scanning. Technology training is provided to incoming students.
Subject-Area Tutoring Tutoring is offered one-on-one for most subjects. Tutoring is provided through the program or unit via computer-based instruction, graduate assistants/students, and trained peer tutors.
Enrichment Programs for career planning, college survival skills, learning strategies, math, self-advocacy, stress management, study skills, test taking, time management, and written composition skills are provided collaboratively through on-campus or off-campus services.
Application For admittance to the program or unit, students are required to apply to the program directly and provide a psychoeducational report (3 years old or less). It is recommended that students provide documentation of high school services. Upon application, materials documenting need for services should be sent only to admissions with institutional application materials. Upon acceptance, documentation of need for services should be sent only to the LD program or unit. *Application deadline (institutional):* Continuous. *Application deadline (LD program):* Rolling/continuous for fall and rolling/continuous for spring.
Written Policies Written policy regarding general/basic LD accommodations is available on the program Web site. Written policy regarding general/basic LD accommodations is outlined in the school's catalog/handbook. Written policies regarding course substitutions and general/basic LD accommodations are available through the program or unit directly.

Otterbein College
Academic Support Center—Office for Disability Services

1 Otterbein College

Westerville, OH 43081

http://www.otterbein.edu/academics/DS/index.asp

Contact: Ms. Leah M. Monaghan, Disability Services Coordinator. Phone: 614-823-1618. Fax: 614-823-1983. E-mail: lmonaghan@otterbein.edu.

Academic Support Center—Office for Disability Services Approximately 85 registered undergraduate students were served during 2006–07. The program or unit includes 1 full-time and 2 part-time staff members. Remediation/learning specialists are provided collaboratively through on-campus or off-campus services.
Orientation The program or unit offers an optional 1-hour orientation for new students before classes begin.
Unique Aids and Services Aids, services, or accommodations include priority registration.
Assistive Technology Assistive technology includes digital textbooks/e-text.
Subject-Area Tutoring Tutoring is offered one-on-one for most subjects. Tutoring is provided collaboratively through on-campus or off-campus services via trained peer tutors.
Basic Skills Remediation Remediation is offered in class-size groups for learning strategies, math, reading, study skills, time management, and written language. Remediation is provided collaboratively through on-campus or off-campus services via regular education teachers.
Enrichment Programs for career planning, college survival skills, learning strategies, math, reading, study skills, test taking, time management, vocabulary development, and written composition skills are provided collaboratively through on-campus or off-campus services.
Application For admittance to the program or unit, students are required to provide a psychoeducational report (3 years old or less). It is recommended that students provide documentation of high school services. Upon application, materials documenting need for services should be sent only to the LD program or unit. Upon acceptance, documentation of need for services should be sent only to the LD program or unit. *Application deadline (institutional):* 3/1. *Application deadline (LD program):* Rolling/continuous for fall and rolling/continuous for spring.
Written Policies Written policies regarding course substitutions, general/basic LD accommodations, and substitutions and waivers of graduation requirements are available through the program or unit directly.

Our Lady of the Lake University of San Antonio
Center for Academic Achievement

411 Southwest 24th Street

San Antonio, TX 78207-4689

http://www.ollusa.edu

Our Lady of the Lake University of San Antonio (continued)

Contact: Mrs. Theresa Gateley, Assistant Director, Center for Academic Achievement. Phone: 210-431-4114. Fax: 210-432-4463. E-mail: gatet@lake.ollusa.edu. Head of LD Program: Mrs. Susan Ramos-Sossaman, Director, Center for Academic Achievement. Phone: 210-434-6711 Ext. 2590. Fax: 210-432-4463. E-mail: ramos@lake.ollusa.edu.

Center for Academic Achievement Approximately 30 registered undergraduate students were served during 2006–07. The program or unit includes 2 full-time staff members. Academic advisers, counselors, diagnostic specialists, graduate assistants/students, professional tutors, regular education teachers, skill tutors, and trained peer tutors are provided collaboratively through on-campus or off-campus services.

Summer Program To help prepare for the demands of college, there is an optional 6-week summer program prior to entering the school available to high school graduates that focuses on specific subject tutoring. Degree credit will be earned. The program accepts students from out-of-state.

Unique Aids and Services Aids, services, or accommodations include advocates, career counseling, personal coach, and priority registration.

Assistive Technology Assistive technology is located in the DSS office and includes learning support software and scanning.

Subject-Area Tutoring Tutoring is offered one-on-one and in small groups for most subjects. Tutoring is provided collaboratively through on-campus or off-campus services via computer-based instruction, graduate assistants/students, professional tutors, and trained peer tutors.

Basic Skills Remediation Remediation is offered one-on-one and in small groups for computer skills, learning strategies, math, study skills, and time management. Remediation is provided collaboratively through on-campus or off-campus services via professional tutors and trained peer tutors.

Enrichment Programs for career planning, college survival skills, health and nutrition, learning strategies, math, oral communication skills, practical computer skills, stress management, study skills, test taking, time management, and written composition skills are provided collaboratively through on-campus or off-campus services.

Application For admittance to the program or unit, students are required to provide a psychoeducational report (3 years old or less). It is recommended that students provide documentation of high school services. Upon application, materials documenting need for services should be sent only to the LD program or unit. Upon acceptance, documentation of need for services should be sent only to the LD program or unit. *Application deadline (institutional):* 7/15. *Application deadline (LD program):* Rolling/continuous for fall and rolling/continuous for spring.

Written Policies Written policy regarding general/basic LD accommodations is available on the program Web site. Written policy regarding general/basic LD accommodations is outlined in the school's catalog/handbook. Written policies regarding course substitutions, general/basic LD accommodations, reduced course loads, and substitutions and waivers of graduation requirements are available through the program or unit directly.

Pacific Oaks College

5 Westmoreland Place
Pasadena, CA 91103
http://www.pacificoaks.edu/

Contact: Ms. Patricia Meda, CARE Director. Phone: 626-397-1338. E-mail: pmeda@pacificoaks.edu.

Approximately 17 registered undergraduate students were served during 2006–07. The program or unit includes 4 full-time staff members. LD specialists and remediation/learning specialists are provided through the program or unit. Services are provided collaboratively through on-campus or off-campus services.

Unique Aids and Services Aids, services, or accommodations include career counseling.

Assistive Technology Assistive technology is located in the DSS office and includes learning support software.

Subject-Area Tutoring Tutoring is offered one-on-one for some subjects. Tutoring is provided through the program or unit via other.

Basic Skills Remediation Remediation is offered one-on-one and in small groups for learning strategies, study skills, time management, and written language. Remediation is provided through the program or unit via LD specialists and other.

Enrichment Enrichment programs are available through the program or unit for career planning, college survival skills, learning strategies, stress management, study skills, time management, written composition skills, and other.

Application For admittance to the program or unit, students are required to apply to the program directly. Upon acceptance, documentation of need for services should be sent only to the LD program or unit. *Application deadline (LD program):* Rolling/continuous for fall and rolling/continuous for spring.

Written Policies Written policy regarding general/basic LD accommodations is available on the program Web site. Written policy regarding general/basic LD accommodations is outlined in the school's catalog/handbook.

Park University
Academic Support Services

8700 NW River Park Drive
Parkville, MO 64152-3795
http://www.park.edu/support/policy.asp

Contact: Debra McArthur, Director of Academic Support Services. Phone: 816-584-6330. Fax: 816-505-5445. E-mail: debra.mcarthur@park.edu.

Academic Support Services Approximately 50 registered undergraduate students were served during 2006–07. The program or unit includes 4 full-time and 20 part-time staff members. Professional tutors, remediation/learning specialists, skill tutors, and trained peer tutors are provided through the program or unit. Academic advisers are provided collaboratively through on-campus or off-campus services.

Subject-Area Tutoring Tutoring is offered one-on-one and in small groups for most subjects. Tutoring is provided through the program or unit via professional tutors and trained peer tutors.

Basic Skills Remediation Remediation is offered in small groups and in class-size groups for learning strategies, math, reading, study skills, and written language. Remediation is provided through the program or unit via professional tutors, regular education teachers, and trained peer tutors. Remediation is also provided collaboratively through on-campus or off-campus services via professional tutors and regular education teachers.

Enrichment Enrichment programs are available through the program or unit for college survival skills, learning strategies, math, reading, study skills, test taking, time management, and written composition skills. Programs for career planning, math, stress management, and written composition skills are provided collaboratively through on-campus or off-campus services.

Application For admittance to the program or unit, students are required to apply to the program directly and provide a psychoeducational report (3 years old or less). It is recommended that students provide documentation of high school services. Upon application, materials documenting need for services should be sent only to the LD program or unit. Upon acceptance, documentation of need for services should be sent only to the LD program or unit. *Application deadline (institutional):* 8/1. *Application deadline (LD program):* 7/1 for fall. 11/30 for spring.

Written Policies Written policy regarding general/basic LD accommodations is available on the program Web site. Written policy regarding general/basic LD accommodations is outlined in the school's catalog/handbook. Written policy regarding general/basic LD accommodations is available through the program or unit directly.

Parsons The New School for Design
Student Disability Services

66 Fifth Avenue

New York, NY 10011-8878

http://www.newschool.edu/studentservices/disability/

Contact: Mr. Jason Luchs, Assistant Director Student Disability Services. Phone: 212-229-5626 Ext. 3135. Fax: 212-229-1090. E-mail: luchsj@newschool.edu.

Student Disability Services Approximately 35 registered undergraduate students were served during 2006–07. The program or unit includes 1 full-time and 1 part-time staff member. Services are provided through the program or unit. Academic advisers, counselors, and other are provided collaboratively through on-campus or off-campus services.

Assistive Technology Assistive technology is located in campus labs and includes digital textbooks/e-text, learning support software, and scanning.

Enrichment Enrichment programs are available through the program or unit for self-advocacy. Programs for career planning, college survival skills, health and nutrition, learning strategies, self-advocacy, stress management, study skills, test taking, time management, and written composition skills are provided collaboratively through on-campus or off-campus services.

Application For admittance to the program or unit, students are required to apply to the program directly, provide a psychoeducational report, and provide documentation (contact office for specific guidelines). Upon acceptance, documentation of need for services

should be sent only to the LD program or unit. *Application deadline (institutional):* 3/1. *Application deadline (LD program):* Rolling/continuous for fall and rolling/continuous for spring.

Written Policies Written policy regarding general/basic LD accommodations is available on the program Web site. Written policy regarding general/basic LD accommodations is outlined in the school's catalog/handbook. Written policy regarding general/basic LD accommodations is available through the program or unit directly.

Paul Quinn College
Student Disabilities Services

3837 Simpson-Stuart Road

Dallas, TX 75241-4331

http://www.pqc.edu/

Contact: Ms. Shelly R. Bradford, Director of Learner Assessment Program. Phone: 214-376-7005. Fax: 214-371-5889. E-mail: sbradford@pqc.edu. Head of LD Program: Rev. Velda Turnley, Assistant to the Vice President of Academic Affairs. Phone: 214-302-3637. E-mail: vturnley@pqc.edu.

Student Disabilities Services Approximately 15 registered undergraduate students were served during 2006–07. The program or unit includes 2 full-time staff members. Counselors and LD specialists are provided through the program or unit. Academic advisers, coaches, diagnostic specialists, graduate assistants/students, professional tutors, regular education teachers, remediation/learning specialists, skill tutors, special education teachers, strategy tutors, teacher trainees, and trained peer tutors are provided collaboratively through on-campus or off-campus services.

Orientation The program or unit offers an optional 1-day orientation for new students before registration and individually by special arrangement.

Summer Program To help prepare for the demands of college, there is an optional 1-week summer program prior to entering the school available to rising sophomores, high school graduates that focuses on computing skills, life skills and/or college life adjustment, self-advocacy, study skills, test-taking skills, and time management. The program accepts students from out-of-state.

Unique Aids and Services Aids, services, or accommodations include advocates, career counseling, support groups, and weekly meetings with faculty.

Assistive Technology Assistive technology is located in a special lab and includes learning support software.

Subject-Area Tutoring Tutoring is offered one-on-one, in small groups, and in class-size groups for most subjects. Tutoring is provided collaboratively through on-campus or off-campus services via computer-based instruction, professional tutors, and trained peer tutors.

Basic Skills Remediation Remediation is offered in small groups and in class-size groups for computer skills, learning strategies, math, reading, social skills, study skills, time management, and written language. Remediation is provided collaboratively through on-campus or off-campus services via computer-based instruction, professional tutors, regular education teachers, special education teachers, teacher trainees, and trained peer tutors.

Paul Quinn College (continued)

Enrichment Programs for career planning, college survival skills, learning strategies, practical computer skills, self-advocacy, stress management, study skills, test taking, time management, and written composition skills are provided collaboratively through on-campus or off-campus services.

Application For admittance to the program or unit, students are required to provide a psychoeducational report and provide documentation of high school services. It is recommended that students apply to the program directly. Upon application, materials documenting need for services should be sent only to admissions with institutional application materials. Upon acceptance, documentation of need for services should be sent only to admissions. *Application deadline (institutional): 6/1. Application deadline (LD program):* Rolling/continuous for fall and rolling/continuous for spring.

Written Policies Written policies regarding course substitutions, general/basic LD accommodations, and substitutions and waivers of graduation requirements are outlined in the school's catalog/handbook. Written policies regarding course substitutions, general/basic LD accommodations, grade forgiveness, reduced course loads, substitutions and waivers of admissions requirements, and substitutions and waivers of graduation requirements are available through the program or unit directly.

Penn State Abington

1600 Woodland Road

Abington, PA 19001

http://www.equity.psu.edu/ods

Contact: Anne W. Prior, Disability Contact Liaison and Learning Center Director. Phone: 215-881-7537. Fax: 215-881-7317. E-mail: axp28@psu.edu.

Approximately 50 registered undergraduate students were served during 2006–07. The program or unit includes 1 part-time staff member.

Orientation The program or unit offers an optional 1-hour orientation for new students individually by special arrangement.

Unique Aids and Services Aids, services, or accommodations include priority registration, extended time for testing, note-takers.

Assistive Technology Assistive technology includes digital textbooks/e-text and scanning.

Application For admittance to the program or unit, students are required to apply to the program directly and provide a psychoeducational report (3 years old or less). Upon acceptance, documentation of need for services should be sent only to the LD program or unit. *Application deadline (institutional):* Continuous. *Application deadline (LD program):* Rolling/continuous for fall and rolling/continuous for spring.

Written Policies Written policies regarding course substitutions, general/basic LD accommodations, and reduced course loads are available on the program Web site. Written policies regarding course substitutions, general/basic LD accommodations, and reduced course loads are outlined in the school's catalog/handbook.

Piedmont College
Academic Support

PO Box 10

165 Central Avenue

Demorest, GA 30535-0010

http://www.piedmont.edu/

Contact: Debra K. Taylor, Director of Academic Support. Phone: 706-778-3000 Ext. 1359. Fax: 706-776-2811. E-mail: dtaylor@piedmont.edu.

Academic Support Approximately 20 registered undergraduate students were served during 2006–07. The program or unit includes 1 full-time staff member. Academic advisers, coaches, counselors, graduate assistants/students, skill tutors, strategy tutors, and trained peer tutors are provided collaboratively through on-campus or off-campus services.

Unique Aids and Services Aids, services, or accommodations include priority registration.

Assistive Technology Assistive technology includes books on tape.

Subject-Area Tutoring Tutoring is offered one-on-one and in small groups for some subjects. Tutoring is provided collaboratively through on-campus or off-campus services via graduate assistants/students and trained peer tutors.

Enrichment Programs for career planning, college survival skills, learning strategies, oral communication skills, practical computer skills, stress management, study skills, test taking, time management, and other are provided collaboratively through on-campus or off-campus services. Credit is offered for oral communication skills and practical computer skills.

Application For admittance to the program or unit, students are required to provide a psychoeducational report (3 years old or less). It is recommended that students provide documentation of high school services. Upon acceptance, documentation of need for services should be sent only to the LD program or unit. *Application deadline (institutional): 7/1. Application deadline (LD program):* Rolling/continuous for fall and rolling/continuous for spring.

Written Policies Written policy regarding general/basic LD accommodations is available on the program Web site. Written policy regarding general/basic LD accommodations is outlined in the school's catalog/handbook.

Pine Manor College
Brown Learning Resource Center

400 Heath Street

Chestnut Hill, MA 02467

http://www.pmc.edu/academic/LRC/lrc.html

Contact: Ms. Mary E. Walsh, Director of Brown Learning Resource Center. Phone: 617-731-7181. Fax: 617-731-7631. E-mail: walshmar@pmc.edu.

Brown Learning Resource Center Approximately 45 registered undergraduate students were served during 2006–07. The program or unit includes 5 full-time staff members and 1 part-time staff member. Coaches, LD specialists, professional tutors, skill tutors, and strategy tutors are provided through the program or unit. Academic advisers, counselors, and diagnostic specialists are provided collaboratively through on-campus or off-campus services.

Orientation The program or unit offers an optional 30-minute orientation for new students before registration, before classes begin, during summer prior to enrollment, individually by special arrangement, and during fall orientation.

Unique Aids and Services Aids, services, or accommodations include advocates, career counseling, faculty training, and priority registration.

Subject-Area Tutoring Tutoring is offered one-on-one for most subjects. Tutoring is provided through the program or unit via LD specialists and professional tutors.

Basic Skills Remediation Remediation is offered one-on-one for computer skills, learning strategies, math, reading, spelling, study skills, time management, and written language. Remediation is provided through the program or unit via LD specialists and professional tutors.

Enrichment Enrichment programs are available through the program or unit for reading, self-advocacy, stress management, study skills, test taking, time management, vocabulary development, and written composition skills. Programs for career planning, college survival skills, health and nutrition, learning strategies, math, medication management, oral communication skills, practical computer skills, stress management, study skills, test taking, time management, and written composition skills are provided collaboratively through on-campus or off-campus services.

Application For admittance to the program or unit, students are required to provide a psychoeducational report. It is recommended that students provide documentation of high school services. Upon application, materials documenting need for services should be sent to both admissions and the LD program or unit. Upon acceptance, documentation of need for services should be sent only to the LD program or unit. *Application deadline (institutional):* Continuous. *Application deadline (LD program):* Rolling/continuous for fall and rolling/continuous for spring.

Written Policies Written policy regarding general/basic LD accommodations is available on the program Web site. Written policy regarding general/basic LD accommodations is outlined in the school's catalog/handbook. Written policies regarding course substitutions, general/basic LD accommodations, reduced course loads, and substitutions and waivers of graduation requirements are available through the program or unit directly.

Pittsburg State University
The Learning Center

1701 South Broadway

Pittsburg, KS 66762

http://www.pittstate.edu/

Contact: Dr. Jamie G. Wood, Learning Center Director. Phone: 620-235-4193. Fax: 620-235-4193. E-mail: jwood@pittstate.edu.

The Learning Center Approximately 135 registered undergraduate students were served during 2006–07. The program or unit includes 1 full-time and 3 part-time staff members. Diagnostic specialists, graduate assistants/students, LD specialists, skill tutors,

strategy tutors, and trained peer tutors are provided through the program or unit. Academic advisers, coaches, counselors, and regular education teachers are provided collaboratively through on-campus or off-campus services.

Orientation The program or unit offers a mandatory 30- to 45-minute orientation for new students individually by special arrangement.

Unique Aids and Services Aids, services, or accommodations include advocates.

Assistive Technology Assistive technology is located in the DSS office and includes learning support software. Technology training is provided to incoming students.

Subject-Area Tutoring Tutoring is offered one-on-one and in small groups for most subjects. Tutoring is provided through the program or unit via graduate assistants/students. Tutoring is also provided collaboratively through on-campus or off-campus services via trained peer tutors.

Diagnostic Testing Testing is provided through the program or unit for handwriting, intelligence, math, reading, written language, and other services. Testing for personality is provided collaboratively through on-campus or off-campus services.

Basic Skills Remediation Remediation is available for computer skills, learning strategies, study skills, time management, and written language.

Enrichment Programs for career planning, college survival skills, and study skills are provided collaboratively through on-campus or off-campus services.

Application For admittance to the program or unit, students are required to provide a psychoeducational report and provide some official documentation of the learning disability. It is recommended that students provide documentation of high school services. Upon application, materials documenting need for services should be sent only to the LD program or unit. Upon acceptance, documentation of need for services should be sent only to the LD program or unit. *Application deadline (institutional):* Continuous. *Application deadline (LD program):* Rolling/continuous for fall and rolling/continuous for spring.

Written Policies Written policy regarding general/basic LD accommodations is available on the program Web site.

Point Loma Nazarene University
Special Academic Services

3900 Lomaland Drive

San Diego, CA 92106-2899

http://www.pointloma.edu/Special AcademicServices

Contact: Mrs. Patricia Louise Curley, Director, Special Academic Services. Phone: 619-849-2486. Fax: 619-849-7023. E-mail: patcurley@pointloma.edu.

Special Academic Services Approximately 69 registered undergraduate students were served during 2006–07. The program or unit includes 1 full-time staff member. Coaches, counselors, LD specialists, professional tutors, skill tutors, strategy tutors, and trained peer tutors are provided through the program or unit. Academic advisers, diagnostic specialists, graduate assistants/students, professional tutors,

Point Loma Nazarene University (continued)

regular education teachers, remediation/learning specialists, special education teachers, and teacher trainees are provided collaboratively through on-campus or off-campus services.

Assistive Technology Assistive technology is located in campus labs, the DSS office, a special lab and includes digital textbooks/e-text, learning support software, and scanning. Technology training is provided to incoming students.

Subject-Area Tutoring Tutoring is offered one-on-one and in small groups for most subjects. Tutoring is provided through the program or unit via trained peer tutors.

Basic Skills Remediation Remediation is offered one-on-one and in small groups for learning strategies, reading, study skills, time management, and written language. Remediation is provided through the program or unit via computer-based instruction, LD specialists, and trained peer tutors.

Enrichment Enrichment programs are available through the program or unit for college survival skills, learning strategies, reading, self-advocacy, study skills, test taking, time management, and written composition skills. Programs for career planning and health and nutrition are provided collaboratively through on-campus or off-campus services.

Application For admittance to the program or unit, students are required to apply to the program directly and provide a psychoeducational report (3 years old or less). It is recommended that students provide documentation of high school services. Upon application, materials documenting need for services should be sent only to the LD program or unit. Upon acceptance, documentation of need for services should be sent to both admissions and the LD program or unit. *Application deadline (institutional):* 3/1. *Application deadline (LD program):* Rolling/continuous for fall and rolling/continuous for spring.

Written Policies Written policies regarding course substitutions and general/basic LD accommodations are available on the program Web site. Written policies regarding course substitutions and general/basic LD accommodations are outlined in the school's catalog/handbook. Written policy regarding general/basic LD accommodations is available through the program or unit directly.

Portland State University
Disability Resource Center

PO Box 751
Portland, OR 97207-0751
http://www.ess.pdx.edu/uasc/drc
Contact: Accommodations Coordinator. Phone: 503-725-4100. Fax: 503-725-4103. E-mail: drc@pdx.edu.

Disability Resource Center Approximately 267 registered undergraduate students were served during 2006–07. The program or unit includes 2 full-time staff members. Coaches, counselors, graduate assistants/students, and LD specialists are provided through the program or unit. Academic advisers, counselors, diagnostic specialists, and professional tutors are provided collaboratively through on-campus or off-campus services.

Orientation The program or unit offers an optional 2-hour orientation for new students individually by special arrangement and during the intake process.

Unique Aids and Services Aids, services, or accommodations include career counseling, personal coach, priority registration, and support groups.

Assistive Technology Assistive technology is located in campus labs, a special lab and includes digital textbooks/e-text, learning support software, and scanning. Technology training is provided to incoming students.

Subject-Area Tutoring Tutoring is offered one-on-one and in small groups for some subjects. Tutoring is provided collaboratively through on-campus or off-campus services via trained peer tutors.

Enrichment Enrichment programs are available through the program or unit for self-advocacy, study skills, test taking, and time management. Programs for career planning, college survival skills, self-advocacy, stress management, study skills, test taking, time management, and written composition skills are provided collaboratively through on-campus or off-campus services.

Student Organization Disability Advocacy Cultural Association consists of 20 members.

Application For admittance to the program or unit, students are required to provide a psychoeducational report (3 years old or less) and provide documentation that meets PSU requirements. It is recommended that students provide documentation of high school services. Upon application, materials documenting need for services should be sent only to the LD program or unit. *Application deadline (institutional):* Continuous. *Application deadline (LD program):* Rolling/continuous for fall.

Written Policies Written policy regarding general/basic LD accommodations is available on the program Web site. Written policy regarding general/basic LD accommodations is available through the program or unit directly.

Prairie Bible Institute
Student Success Office

330 Sixth Avenue North, PO Box 4000
Three Hills, AB T0M 2N0
Canada
http://www.prairie.edu/currentstudents/academics/studentsuccess.asp
Contact: Mrs. Deanna Dyck, Director of Student Success & Career Services. Phone: 403-443-5511. E-mail: deanna.dyck@prairie.edu.

Student Success Office Approximately 5 registered undergraduate students were served during 2006–07. The program or unit includes 1 full-time staff member. Counselors, diagnostic specialists, and trained peer tutors are provided through the program or unit.

Unique Aids and Services Aids, services, or accommodations include personal coach and support groups.

Assistive Technology Assistive technology is located in the DSS office and includes learning support software.

Subject-Area Tutoring Tutoring is offered one-on-one and in small groups for most subjects. Tutoring is provided through the program or unit via computer-based instruction and trained peer tutors.

Diagnostic Testing Testing is provided through the program or unit for learning strategies, learning styles, personality, and study skills.

Basic Skills Remediation Remediation is offered one-on-one for learning strategies, study skills, time management, and written language. Remediation is provided through the program or unit via computer-based instruction and trained peer tutors.

Fees *LD Program or Service* fee is $0 to $125 Canadian dollars.

Application It is recommended that students apply to the program directly, provide a psychoeducational report (3 years old or less), and provide documentation of high school services. Upon application, materials documenting need for services should be sent only to admissions with institutional application materials. Upon acceptance, documentation of need for services should be sent only to admissions. *Application deadline (LD program):* Rolling/continuous for fall and rolling/continuous for spring.

Written Policies Written policy regarding general/basic LD accommodations is available on the program Web site. Written policies regarding general/basic LD accommodations and reduced course loads are available through the program or unit directly.

Prairie View A&M University
Office of Diagnostic Testing and Disability Services

PO Box 519

Prairie View, TX 77446-0519

http://www.pvamu.edu/

Contact: Dr. Kay F. Norman, Administrator for Diagnostic Testing and Disability Services. Phone: 936-261-6582. Fax: 936-857-3584. E-mail: kfnorman@pvamu.edu.

Office of Diagnostic Testing and Disability Services Approximately 102 registered undergraduate students were served during 2006–07. The program or unit includes 4 full-time and 3 part-time staff members. Academic advisers, counselors, diagnostic specialists, graduate assistants/students, LD specialists, and trained peer tutors are provided through the program or unit. Academic advisers, counselors, professional tutors, and skill tutors are provided collaboratively through on-campus or off-campus services.

Summer Program To help prepare for the demands of college, there is an optional 4-week summer program prior to entering the school available to high school graduates that focuses on life skills and/or college life adjustment, specific subject tutoring, test-taking skills, and time management. Degree credit will be earned. The program accepts students from out-of-state.

Unique Aids and Services Aids, services, or accommodations include advocates and career counseling.

Assistive Technology Assistive technology is located in the DSS office and includes learning support software and hardware, other devices and services.

Subject-Area Tutoring Tutoring is offered one-on-one and in small groups for most subjects. Tutoring is provided through the program or unit via graduate assistants/students and LD specialists. Tutoring is also provided collaboratively through on-campus or off-campus services via professional tutors and trained peer tutors.

Diagnostic Testing Testing is provided through the program or unit for intelligence, learning strategies, learning styles, math, reading, spelling, spoken language, and written language. Testing for learning strategies and study skills is provided collaboratively through on-campus or off-campus services.

Basic Skills Remediation Remediation is offered in small groups for computer skills, learning strategies, math, study skills, and time management. Remediation is provided through the program or unit via graduate assistants/students and LD specialists. Remediation is also provided collaboratively through on-campus or off-campus services via professional tutors and trained peer tutors.

Enrichment Enrichment programs are available through the program or unit for learning strategies, math, self-advocacy, and vocabulary development. Programs for career planning, college survival skills, health and nutrition, learning strategies, math, medication management, reading, stress management, study skills, test taking, time management, and written composition skills are provided collaboratively through on-campus or off-campus services.

Fees *Summer Program* fee is $0 to $250.

Application For admittance to the program or unit, students are required to apply to the program directly. It is recommended that students provide a psychoeducational report, provide documentation of high school services, and provide medical reports, mobility evaluations. Upon application, materials documenting need for services should be sent only to the LD program or unit. Upon acceptance, documentation of need for services should be sent only to the LD program or unit. *Application deadline (institutional):* 6/1. *Application deadline (LD program):* Rolling/continuous for fall and rolling/continuous for spring.

Written Policies Written policy regarding substitutions and waivers of graduation requirements is outlined in the school's catalog/handbook. Written policies regarding course substitutions, general/basic LD accommodations, reduced course loads, and substitutions and waivers of admissions requirements are available through the program or unit directly.

Pratt Institute
Disability Services Office

200 Willoughby Avenue

Brooklyn, NY 11205-3899

http://www.pratt.edu/disabilityservices

Contact: Ms. Mai Linda McDonald, Disability Services Coordinator. Phone: 718-636-3711. Fax: 718-399-4239. E-mail: mcdonald@pratt.edu.

Disability Services Office Approximately 118 registered undergraduate students were served during 2006–07. The program or unit includes 1 full-time and 2 part-time staff members. Skill tutors, teacher trainees, and other are provided through the program or unit. Academic advisers, coaches, counselors, diagnostic specialists, professional tutors, and strategy tutors are provided collaboratively through on-campus or off-campus services.

Unique Aids and Services Aids, services, or accommodations include advocates, career counseling, support groups, time management assistance, tutoring in subjects such as art history and English.

Assistive Technology Assistive technology is located in the Writing and Tutorial Center and includes learning support software, scanning, and Kurzweil 3000, Inspiration. Technology training is provided to incoming students.

Subject-Area Tutoring Tutoring is offered one-on-one for some subjects. Tutoring is provided through the program or unit via other. Tutoring is also provided collaboratively through on-campus or off-campus services via professional tutors, trained peer tutors, and other.

Pratt Institute (continued)

Diagnostic Testing Testing for intelligence, neuropsychological, and written language is provided collaboratively through on-campus or off-campus services.

Enrichment Programs for career planning, college survival skills, learning strategies, time management, and written composition skills are provided collaboratively through on-campus or off-campus services.

Fees *Diagnostic Testing* fee is applicable.

Application For admittance to the program or unit, students are required to provide complete documentation as prescribed by AHEAD. It is recommended that students provide documentation of high school services. Upon acceptance, documentation of need for services should be sent only to the LD program or unit. *Application deadline (institutional): 2/1. Application deadline (LD program):* Rolling/continuous for fall and rolling/continuous for spring.

Written Policies Written policy regarding general/basic LD accommodations is available on the program Web site. Written policy regarding general/basic LD accommodations is outlined in the school's catalog/handbook. Written policy regarding general/basic LD accommodations is available through the program or unit directly.

Presbyterian College
Office of the Provost

503 South Broad Street

Clinton, SC 29325

http://www.presby.edu/

Contact: Mrs. N. Susan Carbonneau, Senior Administrative Assistant. Phone: 864-833-8234. Fax: 864-833-8481. E-mail: scarbo@presby.edu. Head of LD Program: Dr. Daria Cronic, Associate Professor of Special Education/Coordinator of Disability Support Services. Phone: 864-833-8279. Fax: 864-833-8481. E-mail: dtcronic@presby.edu.

Office of the Provost Approximately 104 registered undergraduate students were served during 2006–07. The program or unit includes 3 part-time staff members. Academic advisers, regular education teachers, and other are provided collaboratively through on-campus or off-campus services.

Subject-Area Tutoring Tutoring is offered one-on-one and in small groups for most subjects. Tutoring is provided collaboratively through on-campus or off-campus services via graduate assistants/students and other.

Basic Skills Remediation Remediation is offered one-on-one and in small groups for learning strategies, study skills, time management, and written language. Remediation is provided collaboratively through on-campus or off-campus services via graduate assistants/students and other.

Enrichment Programs for career planning, college survival skills, learning strategies, study skills, time management, and written composition skills are provided collaboratively through on-campus or off-campus services.

Application For admittance to the program or unit, students are required to provide a psychoeducational report (3 years old or less). It is recommended that students provide documentation of high school services. Upon acceptance, documentation of need for ser-

vices should be sent only to the LD program or unit. *Application deadline (institutional): 5/1. Application deadline (LD program):* Rolling/continuous for fall and rolling/continuous for spring.

Written Policies Written policy regarding general/basic LD accommodations is outlined in the school's catalog/handbook. Written policy regarding general/basic LD accommodations is available through the program or unit directly.

Purdue University North Central
Student Support Services

1401 South US Highway 421

Westville, IN 46391-9542

http://www.pnc.edu/sa/sss.html

Contact: Jodi James, Disability Services Coordinator. Phone: 219-785-5374. Fax: 219-785-5589. E-mail: jjames@pnc.edu.

Student Support Services Approximately 40 registered undergraduate students were served during 2006–07. The program or unit includes 1 full-time staff member. Counselors and trained peer tutors are provided through the program or unit. Academic advisers and trained peer tutors are provided collaboratively through on-campus or off-campus services.

Unique Aids and Services Aids, services, or accommodations include career counseling and faculty training.

Assistive Technology Assistive technology is located in the DSS office and includes digital textbooks/e-text and scanning. Technology training is provided to incoming students.

Subject-Area Tutoring Tutoring is offered one-on-one and in small groups for most subjects. Tutoring is provided through the program or unit via trained peer tutors. Tutoring is also provided collaboratively through on-campus or off-campus services via trained peer tutors.

Basic Skills Remediation Remediation is offered in class-size groups for computer skills, learning strategies, math, reading, study skills, and time management. Remediation is provided through the program or unit via teacher trainees. Remediation is also provided collaboratively through on-campus or off-campus services via regular education teachers.

Enrichment Enrichment programs are available through the program or unit for career planning, learning strategies, math, reading, self-advocacy, stress management, study skills, test taking, and time management. Programs for career planning, college survival skills, health and nutrition, learning strategies, math, oral communication skills, practical computer skills, reading, stress management, study skills, test taking, vocabulary development, and written composition skills are provided collaboratively through on-campus or off-campus services. Credit is offered for health and nutrition, oral communication skills, practical computer skills, reading, vocabulary development, and written composition skills.

Application For admittance to the program or unit, students are required to provide a psychoeducational report (3 years old or less). It is recommended that students apply to the program directly and provide documentation of high school services. Upon application, materials documenting need for services should be sent only to the LD program or unit. Upon acceptance, documentation of need for services should be sent only to the LD program or unit. *Application deadline (institutional): 8/6. Application deadline (LD program):* Rolling/continuous for fall and rolling/continuous for spring.

Written Policies Written policies regarding course substitutions, general/basic LD accommodations, reduced course loads, substitutions and waivers of admissions requirements, and substitutions and waivers of graduation requirements are available on the program Web site.

Queens College of the City University of New York
Office of Special Services

65-30 Kissena Boulevard

Flushing, NY 11367-1597

http://www.qc.cuny.edu/

Contact: Mr. John Kiefer, Learning Disabilities Specialist. Phone: 718-997-5977. Fax: 718-997-5895.

Office of Special Services Approximately 700 registered undergraduate students were served during 2006–07. The program or unit includes 1 full-time staff member. Coaches, counselors, graduate assistants/students, LD specialists, remediation/learning specialists, and other are provided through the program or unit.

Orientation The program or unit offers a mandatory 45-minute orientation for new students individually by special arrangement.

Unique Aids and Services Aids, services, or accommodations include career counseling, faculty training, personal coach, and weekly meetings with faculty.

Assistive Technology Assistive technology is located in a special lab and includes digital textbooks/e-text, learning support software, scanning, and Braille, ZoomText, C-Print. Technology training is provided to incoming students.

Subject-Area Tutoring Tutoring is offered one-on-one for all subjects. Tutoring is provided through the program or unit via computer-based instruction, graduate assistants/students, and LD specialists. Tutoring is also provided collaboratively through on-campus or off-campus services via computer-based instruction, graduate assistants/students, LD specialists, and trained peer tutors.

Basic Skills Remediation Remediation is offered one-on-one for computer skills, learning strategies, math, reading, study skills, visual processing, and written language. Remediation is provided through the program or unit via computer-based instruction, graduate assistants/students, LD specialists, and trained peer tutors. Remediation is also provided collaboratively through on-campus or off-campus services via LD specialists and trained peer tutors.

Enrichment Enrichment programs are available through the program or unit for career planning, college survival skills, learning strategies, math, oral communication skills, practical computer skills, reading, self-advocacy, stress management, study skills, test taking, vocabulary development, written composition skills, and other. Programs for health and nutrition and medication management are provided collaboratively through on-campus or off-campus services.

Student Organization CDS Committee of Disabled Students consists of 10 members.

Application For admittance to the program or unit, students are required to apply to the program directly. It is recommended that students provide a psychoeducational report (3 years old or less).

Upon acceptance, documentation of need for services should be sent only to the LD program or unit. *Application deadline (institutional): 1/1. Application deadline (LD program):* Rolling/continuous for fall and rolling/continuous for spring.

Written Policies Written policies regarding general/basic LD accommodations and substitutions and waivers of admissions requirements are available on the program Web site. Written policies regarding general/basic LD accommodations and reduced course loads are outlined in the school's catalog/handbook. Written policies regarding course substitutions, general/basic LD accommodations, grade forgiveness, reduced course loads, substitutions and waivers of admissions requirements, and substitutions and waivers of graduation requirements are available through the program or unit directly.

Queen's University at Kingston
Disability Services Office

Kingston, ON K7L 3N6

Canada

http://www.queensu.ca/

Contact: Gail Camille Eaton-Smith, Learning Disabilities Strategist. Phone: 613-533-6467. Fax: 613-533-6740. E-mail: ge2@queensu.ca. Head of LD Program: Dr. Michael Condra, Director, Health Counselling & Disability Services. Phone: 613-533-2506. E-mail: condram@queensu.ca.

Disability Services Office Approximately 306 registered undergraduate students were served during 2006–07. The program or unit includes 2 full-time staff members. LD specialists and strategy tutors are provided through the program or unit. Academic advisers, diagnostic specialists, professional tutors, skill tutors, and trained peer tutors are provided collaboratively through on-campus or off-campus services.

Summer Program To help prepare for the demands of college, there is an optional 4-week online summer program prior to entering the school available to high school graduates that focuses on computing skills, life skills and/or college life adjustment, self-advocacy, study skills, and time management. The program is available to students attending other colleges.

Unique Aids and Services Aids, services, or accommodations include advocates and career counseling.

Assistive Technology Assistive technology is located in campus labs and includes digital textbooks/e-text, learning support software, and scanning. Technology training is provided to incoming students.

Subject-Area Tutoring Tutoring is offered one-on-one for all subjects. Tutoring is provided through the program or unit via computer-based instruction and LD specialists. Tutoring is also provided collaboratively through on-campus or off-campus services via computer-based instruction, graduate assistants/students, LD specialists, professional tutors, and trained peer tutors.

Diagnostic Testing Testing for handwriting, intelligence, learning strategies, math, motor skills, neuropsychological, personality, reading, social skills, spelling, spoken language, study skills, visual processing, and written language is provided collaboratively through on-campus or off-campus services.

Queen's University at Kingston (continued)

Basic Skills Remediation Remediation is offered one-on-one for learning strategies, reading, study skills, time management, and written language. Remediation is provided through the program or unit via LD specialists. Remediation is also provided collaboratively through on-campus or off-campus services via graduate assistants/students, professional tutors, teacher trainees, and trained peer tutors.
Fees *Summer Program* fee is $200. *Diagnostic Testing* fee is $1500.
Application For admittance to the program or unit, students are required to provide a psychoeducational report (3 years old or less). It is recommended that students provide documentation of high school services. Upon application, materials documenting need for services should be sent only to admissions with institutional application materials. Upon acceptance, documentation of need for services should be sent only to the LD program or unit. *Application deadline (institutional):* 2/16. *Application deadline (LD program):* Rolling/continuous for fall and rolling/continuous for spring.
Written Policies Written policies regarding general/basic LD accommodations and reduced course loads are available on the program Web site. Written policies regarding general/basic LD accommodations and reduced course loads are outlined in the school's catalog/handbook. Written policies regarding general/basic LD accommodations and reduced course loads are available through the program or unit directly.

Queens University of Charlotte
Student Disability Services

1900 Selwyn Avenue

Charlotte, NC 28274-0002

http://www.queens.edu/studentlife/resources/disability.asp

Contact: Ms. Sandra Lynn Rogelberg, Manager, Student Disability Services. Phone: 704-337-2508. Fax: 704-337-2325. E-mail: rogelbes@queens.edu.

Student Disability Services Approximately 35 registered undergraduate students were served during 2006–07. The program or unit includes 1 part-time staff member. Academic advisers, counselors, regular education teachers, and trained peer tutors are provided collaboratively through on-campus or off-campus services.
Unique Aids and Services Aids, services, or accommodations include career counseling and faculty training.
Assistive Technology Assistive technology is located in an allocated room and includes digital textbooks/e-text and Kurzweil 3000.
Subject-Area Tutoring Tutoring is offered one-on-one for most subjects. Tutoring is provided collaboratively through on-campus or off-campus services via trained peer tutors.
Application For admittance to the program or unit, students are required to provide a psychoeducational report (3 years old or less). Upon acceptance, documentation of need for services should be sent only to the LD program or unit. *Application deadline (institutional):* Continuous. *Application deadline (LD program):* Rolling/continuous for fall and rolling/continuous for spring.
Written Policies Written policy regarding general/basic LD accommodations is available on the program Web site.

Radford University
Disability Resource Office

PO Box 6890, RU Station

Radford, VA 24142

http://www.radford.edu/~dro

Contact: Ms. JoAnn Stephens Forrest, Coordinator. Phone: 540-831-6350. Fax: 540-831-6525. E-mail: jrstephe@radford.edu.

Disability Resource Office Approximately 315 registered undergraduate students were served during 2006–07. The program or unit includes 2 full-time staff members and 1 part-time staff member. Academic advisers, counselors, skill tutors, and strategy tutors are provided through the program or unit. Academic advisers, diagnostic specialists, graduate assistants/students, professional tutors, regular education teachers, skill tutors, strategy tutors, and trained peer tutors are provided collaboratively through on-campus or off-campus services.
Orientation The program or unit offers an optional orientation for new students during summer prior to enrollment and individually by special arrangement.
Assistive Technology Assistive technology is located in campus labs, the DSS office, the library and includes digital textbooks/e-text, learning support software, and scanning. Technology training is provided to incoming students.
Subject-Area Tutoring Tutoring is offered one-on-one and in small groups for most subjects. Tutoring is provided through the program or unit via graduate assistants/students. Tutoring is also provided collaboratively through on-campus or off-campus services via graduate assistants/students, professional tutors, trained peer tutors, and other.
Basic Skills Remediation Remediation is offered one-on-one for learning strategies, math, reading, study skills, time management, and written language. Remediation is provided through the program or unit via special education teachers. Remediation is also provided collaboratively through on-campus or off-campus services via graduate assistants/students, professional tutors, regular education teachers, and trained peer tutors.
Application For admittance to the program or unit, students are required to provide a psychoeducational report (3 years old or less), provide documentation of high school services, and provide personal interview and DRO registration. Upon acceptance, documentation of need for services should be sent only to the LD program or unit. *Application deadline (institutional):* 2/1. *Application deadline (LD program):* Rolling/continuous for fall and rolling/continuous for spring.
Written Policies Written policy regarding general/basic LD accommodations is available on the program Web site. Written policy regarding general/basic LD accommodations is outlined in the school's catalog/handbook. Written policy regarding general/basic LD accommodations is available through the program or unit directly.

Ramapo College of New Jersey

505 Ramapo Valley Road

Mahwah, NJ 07430-1680

http://www.ramapo.edu/

Contact: Ms. Nancy Carr, Director. Phone: 201-684-7513. Fax: 201-684-7004. E-mail: ncarr@ramapo.edu.

The program or unit includes 6 full-time and 3 part-time staff members. Academic advisers, counselors, graduate assistants/students, LD specialists, professional tutors, remediation/learning specialists, skill tutors, and trained peer tutors are provided through the program or unit. Academic advisers, counselors, professional tutors, regular education teachers, skill tutors, and trained peer tutors are provided collaboratively through on-campus or off-campus services.

Orientation The program or unit offers an optional 2-day orientation for new students before classes begin.

Summer Program To help prepare for the demands of college, there is an optional 1-week summer program prior to entering the school available to high school graduates that focuses on life skills and/or college life adjustment, self-advocacy, study skills, time management, and vocational skills. The program accepts students from out-of-state.

Unique Aids and Services Aids, services, or accommodations include advocates, career counseling, faculty training, parent workshops, priority registration, support groups, and weekly meetings with faculty.

Assistive Technology Assistive technology is located in a special lab and includes learning support software and scanning. Technology training is provided to incoming students.

Subject-Area Tutoring Tutoring is offered one-on-one for most subjects. Tutoring is provided through the program or unit via LD specialists, professional tutors, and trained peer tutors. Tutoring is also provided collaboratively through on-campus or off-campus services via professional tutors and trained peer tutors.

Basic Skills Remediation Remediation is offered one-on-one for computer skills, learning strategies, math, reading, study skills, and written language. Remediation is provided through the program or unit via computer-based instruction and trained peer tutors. Remediation is also provided collaboratively through on-campus or off-campus services via regular education teachers and trained peer tutors.

Enrichment Enrichment programs are available through the program or unit for career planning, self-advocacy, stress management, study skills, test taking, and time management. Programs for career planning, college survival skills, health and nutrition, math, practical computer skills, reading, stress management, study skills, vocabulary development, and written composition skills are provided collaboratively through on-campus or off-campus services. Credit is offered for career planning.

Student Organization OSS Student Coalition consists of 20 members.

Application For admittance to the program or unit, students are required to provide a psychoeducational report (3 years old or less). Upon acceptance, documentation of need for services should be sent only to the LD program or unit. *Application deadline (institutional):* 3/1. *Application deadline (LD program):* Rolling/continuous for fall and rolling/continuous for spring.

Written Policies Written policies regarding course substitutions, general/basic LD accommodations, and substitutions and waivers of graduation requirements are available on the program Web site. Written policy regarding general/basic LD accommodations is available through the program or unit directly.

Randolph College
Learning Resources Center and Disability Services

2500 Rivermont Avenue

Lynchburg, VA 24503-1526

http://www.rmwc.edu/academics/resources_lrc.asp

Contact: Mrs. Tina T. Barnes, Director of Learning Resources Center and Disability Services. Phone: 434-947-8132. Fax: 434-947-8999. E-mail: tbarnes@randolphcollege.edu.

Learning Resources Center and Disability Services Approximately 20 registered undergraduate students were served during 2006–07. The program or unit includes 1 full-time and 1 part-time staff member. LD specialists, strategy tutors, and trained peer tutors are provided through the program or unit. Academic advisers, coaches, counselors, regular education teachers, skill tutors, strategy tutors, and trained peer tutors are provided collaboratively through on-campus or off-campus services.

Unique Aids and Services Aids, services, or accommodations include advocates, career counseling, personal coach, priority registration, working with the student to determine appropriate outside agencies that can provide services.

Assistive Technology Assistive technology is located in campus labs, science labs and includes learning support software, scanning, and Kurzweil 3000. Technology training is provided to incoming students.

Subject-Area Tutoring Tutoring is offered one-on-one, in small groups, and in class-size groups for most subjects. Tutoring is provided through the program or unit via trained peer tutors. Tutoring is also provided collaboratively through on-campus or off-campus services via trained peer tutors.

Diagnostic Testing Testing is provided through the program or unit for learning styles and study skills. Testing for auditory processing, intelligence, learning strategies, math, motor skills, neuropsychological, personality, reading, social skills, spelling, spoken language, visual processing, written language, and other services is provided collaboratively through on-campus or off-campus services.

Basic Skills Remediation Remediation is offered one-on-one for computer skills, learning strategies, study skills, and time management. Remediation is provided through the program or unit via LD specialists and trained peer tutors. Remediation is also provided collaboratively through on-campus or off-campus services via LD specialists and trained peer tutors.

Enrichment Programs for career planning, college survival skills, health and nutrition, learning strategies, practical computer skills, stress management, study skills, test taking, time management, and written composition skills are provided collaboratively through on-campus or off-campus services.

Fees *Diagnostic Testing* fee is applicable.

Randolph College (continued)

Application For admittance to the program or unit, students are required to apply to the program directly and provide a psychoeducational report (3 years old or less). It is recommended that students provide documentation of high school services and provide documentation appropriate to the disability by a credentialed individual. Upon application, materials documenting need for services should be sent to both admissions and the LD program or unit. Upon acceptance, documentation of need for services should be sent only to the LD program or unit. *Application deadline (institutional):* 3/1. *Application deadline (LD program):* Rolling/continuous for fall and rolling/continuous for spring.

Written Policies Written policy regarding general/basic LD accommodations is available on the program Web site. Written policies regarding course substitutions, general/basic LD accommodations, substitutions and waivers of admissions requirements, and substitutions and waivers of graduation requirements are outlined in the school's catalog/handbook. Written policies regarding course substitutions, general/basic LD accommodations, substitutions and waivers of admissions requirements, and substitutions and waivers of graduation requirements are available through the program or unit directly.

Randolph-Macon College
Office for Disability Support Services

PO Box 5005

Ashland, VA 23005-5505

http://www.rmc.edu/directory/offices/hac/DSS/index.asp

Contact: Dr. Jack Trammell, Director of DSS. Phone: 804-752-7343. E-mail: dss@rmc.edu.

Office for Disability Support Services Approximately 50 registered undergraduate students were served during 2006–07. The program or unit includes 1 full-time staff member. Academic advisers, coaches, counselors, diagnostic specialists, professional tutors, skill tutors, strategy tutors, and trained peer tutors are provided collaboratively through on-campus or off-campus services.

Unique Aids and Services Aids, services, or accommodations include career counseling, faculty training, personal coach, support groups, and weekly meetings with faculty.

Assistive Technology Assistive technology is located in the DSS office and includes digital textbooks/e-text, learning support software, and scanning.

Subject-Area Tutoring Tutoring is offered one-on-one, in small groups, and in class-size groups. Tutoring is provided through the program or unit via LD specialists. Tutoring is also provided collaboratively through on-campus or off-campus services via computer-based instruction and trained peer tutors.

Enrichment Enrichment programs are available through the program or unit for college survival skills, learning strategies, oral communication skills, reading, study skills, test taking, and time management. Programs for career planning, college survival skills, health and nutrition, learning strategies, math, medication management, oral communication skills, practical computer skills, reading, self-advocacy, stress management, study skills, test taking, time management, and written composition skills are provided collaboratively through on-campus or off-campus services. Credit is offered for college survival skills and study skills.

Application For admittance to the program or unit, students are required to provide a psychoeducational report (3 years old or less). Upon acceptance, documentation of need for services should be sent only to the LD program or unit. *Application deadline (institutional):* 3/1. *Application deadline (LD program):* 6/1 for fall. Rolling/continuous for spring.

Written Policies Written policies regarding course substitutions, general/basic LD accommodations, and substitutions and waivers of graduation requirements are available on the program Web site. Written policies regarding course substitutions, general/basic LD accommodations, and substitutions and waivers of graduation requirements are outlined in the school's catalog/handbook. Written policy regarding general/basic LD accommodations is available through the program or unit directly.

Redeemer University College
Student Life Department—Services to Students with Disabilities

777 Garner Road East

Ancaster, ON L9K 1J4

Canada

http://www.redeemer.on.ca/

Contact: Nancy Hartholt, Special Needs Coordinator. Phone: 905-648-2131 Ext. 4220. Fax: 905-648-2134. E-mail: nhartholt@redeemer.ca.

Student Life Department—Services to Students with Disabilities Approximately 40 registered undergraduate students were served during 2006–07. The program or unit includes 1 part-time staff member. Services are provided through the program or unit. Academic advisers, counselors, and diagnostic specialists are provided collaboratively through on-campus or off-campus services.

Unique Aids and Services Aids, services, or accommodations include career counseling and support groups.

Assistive Technology Assistive technology includes digital textbooks/e-text.

Subject-Area Tutoring Tutoring is offered one-on-one, in small groups, and in class-size groups for all subjects. Tutoring is provided through the program or unit via trained peer tutors and other.

Diagnostic Testing Testing is provided through the program or unit for learning strategies, learning styles, and study skills. Testing for auditory processing, handwriting, intelligence, math, motor skills, neuropsychological, personality, reading, spelling, visual processing, and written language is provided collaboratively through on-campus or off-campus services.

Basic Skills Remediation Remediation is offered one-on-one, in small groups, and in class-size groups for computer skills, learning strategies, math, reading, spelling, study skills, time management, and written language. Remediation is provided through the program or unit via trained peer tutors and other.

Enrichment Enrichment programs are available through the program or unit for career planning, college survival skills, learning strategies, study skills, test taking, time management, and written composition skills.

Fees *Diagnostic Testing* fee is $1800.

Application For admittance to the program or unit, students are required to provide a psychoeducational report (3 years old or less). It is recommended that students apply to the program directly and provide documentation of high school services. Upon application, materials documenting need for services should be sent only to the LD program or unit. Upon acceptance, documentation of need for services should be sent only to the LD program or unit. *Application deadline (institutional):* 5/31. *Application deadline (LD program):* Rolling/continuous for fall and rolling/continuous for spring.

Written Policies Written policies regarding course substitutions, reduced course loads, substitutions and waivers of admissions requirements, and substitutions and waivers of graduation requirements are outlined in the school's catalog/handbook. Written policies regarding general/basic LD accommodations and substitutions and waivers of admissions requirements are available through the program or unit directly.

Rensselaer Polytechnic Institute
Disability Services for Students

110 8th Street

Troy, NY 12180-3590

http://www.rpi.edu/

Contact: Debra Hamilton, Assistant Dean of Students. Phone: 518-276-2746. Fax: 518-276-4839. E-mail: dss@rpi.edu.

Disability Services for Students Approximately 114 registered undergraduate students were served during 2006–07. The program or unit includes 2 part-time staff members. Counselors are provided through the program or unit. Academic advisers, counselors, LD specialists, remediation/learning specialists, and skill tutors are provided collaboratively through on-campus or off-campus services.

Orientation The program or unit offers an optional 1-hour orientation for new students before classes begin, individually by special arrangement, and immediately following regular summer orientation.

Assistive Technology Assistive technology is located in the library and includes digital textbooks/e-text, learning support software, and scanning. Technology training is provided to incoming students.

Subject-Area Tutoring Tutoring is offered one-on-one and in small groups for most subjects. Tutoring is provided collaboratively through on-campus or off-campus services via trained peer tutors.

Basic Skills Remediation Remediation is offered one-on-one and in small groups for learning strategies, reading, study skills, time management, and written language. Remediation is provided collaboratively through on-campus or off-campus services via LD specialists and trained peer tutors.

Application For admittance to the program or unit, students are required to provide a psychoeducational report (3 years old or less). It is recommended that students provide documentation of high school services. Upon acceptance, documentation of need for services should be sent only to the LD program or unit. *Application deadline (institutional):* 1/15. *Application deadline (LD program):* Rolling/continuous for fall and rolling/continuous for spring.

Written Policies Written policy regarding general/basic LD accommodations is available on the program Web site. Written policies regarding general/basic LD accommodations and reduced course loads are available through the program or unit directly.

Rhodes College
Office of Student Disability Services

2000 North Parkway

Memphis, TN 38112-1690

http://www.rhodes.edu/disability

Contact: Ms. Melissa Butler McCowen, Coordinator of Disability and Career Services. Phone: 901-843-3994. Fax: 901-843-3040. E-mail: mccowenm@rhodes.edu.

Office of Student Disability Services Approximately 35 registered undergraduate students were served during 2006–07. The program or unit includes 1 part-time staff member. Counselors are provided through the program or unit. Academic advisers, counselors, and trained peer tutors are provided collaboratively through on-campus or off-campus services.

Unique Aids and Services Aids, services, or accommodations include career counseling, academic support services.

Assistive Technology Assistive technology is located in the DSS office, a special lab and includes Kurzweil 3000 Scan/Read, Dragon Naturally Speaking Professional. Technology training is provided to incoming students.

Subject-Area Tutoring Tutoring is offered in small groups and in class-size groups for some subjects. Tutoring is provided collaboratively through on-campus or off-campus services via trained peer tutors and other.

Basic Skills Remediation Remediation is offered one-on-one and in small groups for learning strategies, study skills, and time management. Remediation is provided collaboratively through on-campus or off-campus services.

Enrichment Programs for career planning, college survival skills, health and nutrition, learning strategies, math, medication management, self-advocacy, stress management, study skills, test taking, time management, and written composition skills are provided collaboratively through on-campus or off-campus services.

Application For admittance to the program or unit, students are required to apply to the program directly, provide a psychoeducational report (3 years old or less), and provide documentation as specified in guide guidelines available on Web site: www.rhodes.edu/disability. It is recommended that students provide documentation of high school services. Upon application, materials documenting need for services should be sent only to the LD program or unit. Upon acceptance, documentation of need for services should be sent only to the LD program or unit. *Application deadline (institutional):* Continuous. *Application deadline (LD program):* Rolling/continuous for fall and rolling/continuous for spring.

Written Policies Written policies regarding general/basic LD accommodations and reduced course loads are available on the program Web site. Written policies regarding general/basic LD accommodations and reduced course loads are available through the program or unit directly.

Rice University
Disability Support Services

6100 Main Street
PO Box 1892
Houston, TX 77251-1892
http://www.dss.rice.edu

Contact: Ms. Jean Ashmore, Director, Disability Support Services. Phone: 713-348-5841. Fax: 713-348-5199. E-mail: adarice@rice.edu.

Disability Support Services Approximately 10 registered undergraduate students were served during 2006–07. The program or unit includes 2 full-time staff members. Academic advisers, coaches, counselors, and regular education teachers are provided collaboratively through on-campus or off-campus services.
Assistive Technology Assistive technology is located in a special lab and includes digital textbooks/e-text and scanning. Technology training is provided to incoming students.
Subject-Area Tutoring Tutoring is offered one-on-one, in small groups, and in class-size groups for most subjects. Tutoring is provided collaboratively through on-campus or off-campus services via graduate assistants/students and trained peer tutors.
Enrichment Programs for career planning, college survival skills, health and nutrition, learning strategies, medication management, oral communication skills, self-advocacy, stress management, study skills, test taking, time management, and written composition skills are provided collaboratively through on-campus or off-campus services.
Application For admittance to the program or unit, students are required to apply to the program directly and provide a psychoeducational report. It is recommended that students provide documentation of high school services. Upon acceptance, documentation of need for services should be sent only to the LD program or unit. *Application deadline (institutional):* 1/10. *Application deadline (LD program):* Rolling/continuous for fall and rolling/continuous for spring.
Written Policies Written policy regarding general/basic LD accommodations is available on the program Web site. Written policies regarding course substitutions, general/basic LD accommodations, and reduced course loads are available through the program or unit directly.

The Richard Stockton College of New Jersey
Learning Access Program

PO Box 195, Jimmie Leeds Road
Pomona, NJ 08240-0195
http://talon.stockton.edu/eyos/page.cfm?siteID=61&pageID=5

Contact: Ms. Frances H. Bottone, Director of the Wellness Center. Phone: 609-652-4988. Fax: 609-748-5550. E-mail: frances.bottone@stockton.edu.

Learning Access Program Approximately 300 registered undergraduate students were served during 2006–07. The program or unit includes 3 full-time staff members. Academic advisers, counselors,

diagnostic specialists, LD specialists, and remediation/learning specialists are provided through the program or unit. Academic advisers, counselors, diagnostic specialists, professional tutors, skill tutors, and trained peer tutors are provided collaboratively through on-campus or off-campus services.
Unique Aids and Services Aids, services, or accommodations include advocates, career counseling, faculty training, priority registration, interpreters.
Assistive Technology Assistive technology is located in campus labs, the DSS office, a special lab and includes digital textbooks/e-text, learning support software, scanning, and ZoomText.
Subject-Area Tutoring Tutoring is offered one-on-one for some subjects. Tutoring is provided through the program or unit via LD specialists. Tutoring is also provided collaboratively through on-campus or off-campus services via graduate assistants/students and trained peer tutors.
Enrichment Enrichment programs are available through the program or unit for career planning, learning strategies, self-advocacy, stress management, study skills, test taking, time management, and written composition skills. Programs for career planning, college survival skills, health and nutrition, learning strategies, math, medication management, practical computer skills, self-advocacy, stress management, study skills, test taking, time management, and written composition skills are provided collaboratively through on-campus or off-campus services.
Application It is recommended that students provide a psychoeducational report (5 years old or less) and provide documentation of high school services. Upon application, materials documenting need for services should be sent only to the LD program or unit. Upon acceptance, documentation of need for services should be sent to both admissions and the LD program or unit. *Application deadline (institutional):* 5/1. *Application deadline (LD program):* Rolling/continuous for fall and rolling/continuous for spring.
Written Policies Written policy regarding general/basic LD accommodations is available on the program Web site. Written policy regarding general/basic LD accommodations is outlined in the school's catalog/handbook.

Ringling College of Art and Design
Academic Resource Center

2700 North Tamiami Trail
Sarasota, FL 34234-5895
http://www.ringling.edu/Disabilities.397.0.html

Contact: Ms. Virginia B. DeMers, Director of Academic Resource Center. Phone: 941-359-7627 Ext. 7627. Fax: 941-359-6115. E-mail: vdemers@ringling.edu.

Academic Resource Center Approximately 40 registered undergraduate students were served during 2006–07. The program or unit includes 1 full-time and 1 part-time staff member. Professional tutors, remediation/learning specialists, skill tutors, strategy tutors, and trained peer tutors are provided through the program or unit. Academic advisers, counselors, and regular education teachers are provided collaboratively through on-campus or off-campus services.
Orientation The program or unit offers during the school orientation.

Assistive Technology Assistive technology is located in the DSS office and includes digital textbooks/e-text and learning support software.

Subject-Area Tutoring Tutoring is offered one-on-one and in small groups for some subjects. Tutoring is provided through the program or unit via LD specialists, professional tutors, and trained peer tutors.

Diagnostic Testing Testing is provided through the program or unit for learning styles.

Basic Skills Remediation Remediation is offered one-on-one and in class-size groups for learning strategies, spelling, study skills, time management, and written language. Remediation is provided through the program or unit via professional tutors, regular education teachers, and trained peer tutors. Remediation is also provided collaboratively through on-campus or off-campus services via regular education teachers.

Enrichment Enrichment programs are available through the program or unit for reading, study skills, test taking, time management, vocabulary development, and written composition skills. Programs for career planning, college survival skills, learning strategies, and written composition skills are provided collaboratively through on-campus or off-campus services.

Application For admittance to the program or unit, students are required to provide a psychoeducational report (3 years old or less) and provide intelligence and achievement testing with scores. It is recommended that students provide documentation of high school services. Upon application, materials documenting need for services should be sent only to the LD program or unit. Upon acceptance, documentation of need for services should be sent only to the LD program or unit. *Application deadline (institutional):* Continuous. *Application deadline (LD program):* Rolling/continuous for fall and rolling/continuous for spring.

Written Policies Written policy regarding general/basic LD accommodations is available on the program Web site. Written policy regarding general/basic LD accommodations is outlined in the school's catalog/handbook. Written policy regarding general/basic LD accommodations is available through the program or unit directly.

Ripon College
Student Support Services

300 Seward Street, PO Box 248

Ripon, WI 54971

http://www.ripon.edu/

Contact: Mr. Dan Krhin, Director of Student Support Services. Phone: 920-748-8107 Ext. 107. Fax: 920-748-8382. E-mail: krhind@ripon.edu.

Student Support Services Approximately 12 registered undergraduate students were served during 2006–07. The program or unit includes 2 full-time and 20 part-time staff members. Academic advisers, coaches, counselors, graduate assistants/students, LD specialists, skill tutors, and trained peer tutors are provided through the program or unit. Academic advisers, counselors, diagnostic specialists, LD specialists, and regular education teachers are provided collaboratively through on-campus or off-campus services.

Orientation The program or unit offers a mandatory 1-hour orientation for new students individually by special arrangement.

Unique Aids and Services Aids, services, or accommodations include advocates and career counseling.

Assistive Technology Assistive technology is located in a special lab and includes digital textbooks/e-text, learning support software, and scanning. Technology training is provided to incoming students.

Subject-Area Tutoring Tutoring is offered one-on-one for most subjects. Tutoring is provided through the program or unit via trained peer tutors.

Diagnostic Testing Testing for auditory processing, handwriting, intelligence, learning strategies, neuropsychological, reading, spelling, and written language is provided collaboratively through on-campus or off-campus services.

Basic Skills Remediation Remediation is available for math, reading, and written language. Remediation is provided through the program or unit via trained peer tutors. Remediation is also provided collaboratively through on-campus or off-campus services via computer-based instruction.

Enrichment Enrichment programs are available through the program or unit for career planning, college survival skills, learning strategies, math, practical computer skills, reading, self-advocacy, stress management, study skills, test taking, time management, and written composition skills. Programs for career planning, health and nutrition, math, medication management, oral communication skills, practical computer skills, stress management, vocabulary development, and written composition skills are provided collaboratively through on-campus or off-campus services.

Fees *Diagnostic Testing* fee is applicable.

Application For admittance to the program or unit, students are required to provide a psychoeducational report (3 years old or less) and provide documentation of high school services. Upon application, materials documenting need for services should be sent to both admissions and the LD program or unit. Upon acceptance, documentation of need for services should be sent to both admissions and the LD program or unit. *Application deadline (institutional):* Continuous. *Application deadline (LD program):* Rolling/continuous for fall and rolling/continuous for spring.

Written Policies Written policies regarding general/basic LD accommodations and substitutions and waivers of admissions requirements are available through the program or unit directly.

Rivier College
Office of Special Services

420 Main Street

Nashua, NH 03060-5086

http://www.rivier.edu

Contact: Kate Ricci, Coordinator of Special Services. Phone: 603-897-8497. Fax: 603-897-8816. E-mail: kricci@rivier.edu.

Office of Special Services Approximately 20 registered undergraduate students were served during 2006–07. The program or unit includes 1 full-time staff member. Academic advisers, diagnostic specialists, regular education teachers, and strategy tutors are provided collaboratively through on-campus or off-campus services.

Unique Aids and Services Aids, services, or accommodations include career counseling and priority registration.

Rivier College (continued)

Assistive Technology Assistive technology is located in campus labs, the DSS office, the library and includes digital textbooks/e-text and scanning. Technology training is provided to incoming students.

Subject-Area Tutoring Tutoring is offered in small groups for most subjects. Tutoring is provided collaboratively through on-campus or off-campus services via graduate assistants/students and trained peer tutors.

Enrichment Programs for career planning, college survival skills, self-advocacy, stress management, study skills, time management, and written composition skills are provided collaboratively through on-campus or off-campus services.

Application For admittance to the program or unit, students are required to provide a psychoeducational report (3 years old or less). It is recommended that students provide documentation of high school services and provide information from a medical doctor regarding medical issues. Upon application, materials documenting need for services should be sent to both admissions and the LD program or unit. Upon acceptance, documentation of need for services should be sent only to the LD program or unit. *Application deadline (institutional):* Continuous. *Application deadline (LD program):* 10/1 for fall. 2/1 for spring.

Written Policies Written policy regarding general/basic LD accommodations is available on the program Web site. Written policy regarding general/basic LD accommodations is outlined in the school's catalog/handbook. Written policies regarding course substitutions and reduced course loads are available through the program or unit directly.

Rochester Institute of Technology
Disability Services Office and Learning Support Services (LSS)

One Lomb Memorial Drive

Rochester, NY 14623-5603

http://www.rit.edu/dso

Contact: Mrs. Lisa A. Fraser, Chairperson of Learning Support Services. Phone: 585-475-5296. Fax: 585-475-6682. E-mail: lafldc@rit.edu. Head of LD Program: Ms. Susan Ackerman, Coordinator of Disability Services. Phone: 585-475-7804 V/TTY. Fax: 585-475-2215. E-mail: smacst@rit.edu.

Disability Services Office and Learning Support Services (LSS) Approximately 734 registered undergraduate students were served during 2006–07. The program or unit includes 9 full-time and 13 part-time staff members. Coaches, LD specialists, professional tutors, skill tutors, and strategy tutors are provided through the program or unit. Academic advisers, counselors, diagnostic specialists, graduate assistants/students, professional tutors, regular education teachers, skill tutors, and trained peer tutors are provided collaboratively through on-campus or off-campus services.

Orientation The program or unit offers a mandatory orientation for new students before classes begin.

Unique Aids and Services Aids, services, or accommodations include career counseling and priority registration.

Assistive Technology Assistive technology includes digital textbooks/e-text.

Subject-Area Tutoring Tutoring is offered one-on-one and in small groups for all subjects. Tutoring is provided collaboratively through on-campus or off-campus services via graduate assistants/students, professional tutors, and trained peer tutors.

Diagnostic Testing Testing for handwriting, learning strategies, learning styles, math, personality, reading, social skills, spelling, spoken language, study skills, written language, and other services is provided collaboratively through on-campus or off-campus services.

Enrichment Enrichment programs are available through the program or unit for college survival skills, learning strategies, self-advocacy, stress management, study skills, test taking, and time management. Programs for career planning, college survival skills, health and nutrition, learning strategies, math, medication management, oral communication skills, practical computer skills, reading, stress management, test taking, time management, vocabulary development, and written composition skills are provided collaboratively through on-campus or off-campus services. Credit is offered for career planning.

Fees *LD Program or Service* fee is $440 to $950 (fee varies according to level/tier of service).

Application For admittance to the program or unit, students are required to apply to the program directly and provide a psychoeducational report (3 years old or less). It is recommended that students provide documentation of high school services. Upon acceptance, documentation of need for services should be sent only to the LD program or unit. *Application deadline (institutional):* 2/1. *Application deadline (LD program):* Rolling/continuous for fall and rolling/continuous for spring.

Written Policies Written policy regarding general/basic LD accommodations is available on the program Web site. Written policy regarding general/basic LD accommodations is outlined in the school's catalog/handbook. Written policies regarding general/basic LD accommodations and reduced course loads are available through the program or unit directly.

Rockford College
Disability Support Services

5050 East State Street

Rockford, IL 61108-2393

http://www.rockford.edu

Contact: Ms. Lorri L. Hoover, Director Disability Support Services. Phone: 815-226-4022. Fax: 815-226-4161. E-mail: lhoover@rockford.edu. Head of LD Program: Jeanne Grey, Director Rockford College Learning Resource Center. Phone: 815-226-4088. E-mail: jgrey@rockford.edu.

Disability Support Services Approximately 40 registered undergraduate students were served during 2006–07. The program or unit includes 1 part-time staff member. Coaches, counselors, diagnostic specialists, graduate assistants/students, LD specialists, professional tutors, remediation/learning specialists, skill tutors, strategy tutors, trained peer tutors, and other are provided collaboratively through on-campus or off-campus services.

Orientation The program or unit offers a mandatory orientation for new students individually by special arrangement.

Unique Aids and Services Aids, services, or accommodations include priority registration and weekly meetings with faculty.

Assistive Technology Assistive technology is located in the DSS office and includes digital textbooks/e-text, learning support software, and scanning. Technology training is provided to incoming students.

Subject-Area Tutoring Tutoring is offered one-on-one for most subjects. Tutoring is provided collaboratively through on-campus or off-campus services via graduate assistants/students, LD specialists, professional tutors, and trained peer tutors.

Diagnostic Testing Testing for auditory processing, intelligence, learning strategies, learning styles, math, motor skills, neuropsychological, reading, social skills, spelling, spoken language, study skills, visual processing, and written language is provided collaboratively through on-campus or off-campus services.

Basic Skills Remediation Remediation is offered one-on-one and in small groups for computer skills, learning strategies, math, reading, spelling, study skills, time management, and written language. Remediation is provided collaboratively through on-campus or off-campus services via computer-based instruction, LD specialists, professional tutors, regular education teachers, and special education teachers.

Enrichment Programs for career planning, college survival skills, health and nutrition, learning strategies, math, practical computer skills, reading, self-advocacy, stress management, study skills, test taking, time management, and vocabulary development are provided collaboratively through on-campus or off-campus services. Credit is offered for health and nutrition, math, practical computer skills, and reading.

Application For admittance to the program or unit, students are required to apply to the program directly, provide a psychoeducational report, and provide documentation by a licensed professional. It is recommended that students provide documentation of high school services. Upon acceptance, documentation of need for services should be sent only to the LD program or unit. *Application deadline (institutional): 8/1. Application deadline (LD program): Rolling/continuous for fall and rolling/continuous for spring.*

Written Policies Written policy regarding general/basic LD accommodations is available on the program Web site. Written policies regarding course substitutions, general/basic LD accommodations, reduced course loads, substitutions and waivers of admissions requirements, and substitutions and waivers of graduation requirements are outlined in the school's catalog/handbook. Written policies regarding course substitutions, general/basic LD accommodations, reduced course loads, substitutions and waivers of admissions requirements, and substitutions and waivers of graduation requirements are available through the program or unit directly.

Rockhurst University
Access Services

1100 Rockhurst Road

Kansas City, MO 64110-2561

http://www.rockhurst.edu/

Contact: Ms. Sandra A. Waddell, Director of Access Services. Phone: 816-501-4689. Fax: 816-501-3481. E-mail: sandy.waddell@rockhurst.edu.

Access Services Approximately 45 registered undergraduate students were served during 2006–07. Academic advisers, graduate assistants/students, and trained peer tutors are provided collaboratively through on-campus or off-campus services.

Subject-Area Tutoring Tutoring is offered one-on-one, in small groups, and in class-size groups for most subjects. Tutoring is provided collaboratively through on-campus or off-campus services via graduate assistants/students and trained peer tutors.

Application For admittance to the program or unit, students are required to provide a psychoeducational report (3 years old or less). It is recommended that students provide documentation of high school services. Upon acceptance, documentation of need for services should be sent only to the LD program or unit. *Application deadline (institutional): 6/30. Application deadline (LD program): Rolling/continuous for fall and rolling/continuous for spring.*

Rocky Mountain College
Services for Academic Success

1511 Poly Drive

Billings, MT 59102-1796

http://www.rocky.edu/

Contact: Dr. Jane Van Dyk, Associate Vice President. Phone: 406-657-1128. Fax: 406-259-9751. E-mail: vandykj@rocky.edu.

Services for Academic Success Approximately 30 registered undergraduate students were served during 2006–07. The program or unit includes 4 full-time staff members. Academic advisers, coaches, counselors, LD specialists, professional tutors, remediation/learning specialists, skill tutors, strategy tutors, and trained peer tutors are provided through the program or unit.

Unique Aids and Services Aids, services, or accommodations include advocates, career counseling, personal coach, and weekly meetings with faculty.

Assistive Technology Assistive technology is located in the DSS office and includes scanning. Technology training is provided to incoming students.

Subject-Area Tutoring Tutoring is offered one-on-one and in small groups for most subjects. Tutoring is provided through the program or unit via LD specialists, professional tutors, and trained peer tutors. Tutoring is also provided collaboratively through on-campus or off-campus services via trained peer tutors.

Basic Skills Remediation Remediation is offered one-on-one, in small groups, and in class-size groups for math, reading, study skills, and written language. Remediation is provided through the program or unit via regular education teachers.

Enrichment Enrichment programs are available through the program or unit for career planning, learning strategies, math, reading, study skills, test taking, and written composition skills. Programs for career planning, college survival skills, health and nutrition, learning strategies, and reading are provided collaboratively through on-campus or off-campus services. Credit is offered for college survival skills, health and nutrition, learning strategies, math, reading, study skills, test taking, and written composition skills.

Application For admittance to the program or unit, students are required to apply to the program directly and provide a psychoeducational report (3 years old or less). It is recommended that students provide documentation of high school services. Upon application,

Rocky Mountain College (continued)

materials documenting need for services should be sent only to the LD program or unit. Upon acceptance, documentation of need for services should be sent only to the LD program or unit. *Application deadline (institutional):* Continuous. *Application deadline (LD program):* Rolling/continuous for fall and rolling/continuous for spring.

Written Policies Written policy regarding general/basic LD accommodations is available on the program Web site. Written policy regarding general/basic LD accommodations is outlined in the school's catalog/handbook. Written policy regarding general/basic LD accommodations is available through the program or unit directly.

Rowan University
Academic Success Center

201 Mullica Hill Road

Glassboro, NJ 08028-1701

http://www.rowan.edu/studentaffairs/asc/

Contact: Dr. Melissa J. Arnott-Cox, Director, Academic Success Center. Phone: 856-256-4260. Fax: 856-256-4438. E-mail: arnott@rowan.edu.

Academic Success Center Approximately 320 registered undergraduate students were served during 2006–07. The program or unit includes 3 full-time staff members. Coaches, graduate assistants/students, LD specialists, remediation/learning specialists, skill tutors, strategy tutors, and trained peer tutors are provided through the program or unit.

Orientation The program or unit offers an optional 4-week (approximately 6 hours) orientation for new students after classes begin and during the first week of classes.

Unique Aids and Services Aids, services, or accommodations include career counseling, faculty training, parent workshops, personal coach, priority registration, support groups, mentoring program.

Assistive Technology Assistive technology is located in campus labs, the DSS office, a special lab and includes digital textbooks/e-text, learning support software, and scanning. Technology training is provided to incoming students.

Subject-Area Tutoring Tutoring is offered one-on-one and in small groups for all subjects. Tutoring is provided through the program or unit via computer-based instruction, graduate assistants/students, LD specialists, and trained peer tutors. Tutoring is also provided collaboratively through on-campus or off-campus services via computer-based instruction and trained peer tutors.

Diagnostic Testing Testing is provided through the program or unit for learning strategies, learning styles, math, reading, study skills, and written language.

Basic Skills Remediation Remediation is offered in small groups and in class-size groups for computer skills, learning strategies, math, reading, social skills, study skills, time management, and written language. Remediation is provided through the program or unit via computer-based instruction, graduate assistants/students, LD specialists, and trained peer tutors. Remediation is also provided collaboratively through on-campus or off-campus services via graduate assistants/students, regular education teachers, and trained peer tutors.

Enrichment Enrichment programs are available through the program or unit for career planning, college survival skills, learning strategies, self-advocacy, stress management, study skills, test taking, and time management. Programs for career planning, college survival skills, health and nutrition, learning strategies, math, practical computer skills, reading, stress management, study skills, test taking, time management, and written composition skills are provided collaboratively through on-campus or off-campus services. Credit is offered for math, practical computer skills, reading, and written composition skills.

Application For admittance to the program or unit, students are required to provide a psychoeducational report (2 years old or less) and provide documentation of disability, and LD testing results. Upon application, materials documenting need for services should be sent only to the LD program or unit. Upon acceptance, documentation of need for services should be sent only to the LD program or unit. *Application deadline (institutional):* 1/31. *Application deadline (LD program):* Rolling/continuous for fall and rolling/continuous for spring.

Written Policies Written policy regarding general/basic LD accommodations is available on the program Web site. Written policy regarding substitutions and waivers of graduation requirements is outlined in the school's catalog/handbook. Written policies regarding course substitutions, general/basic LD accommodations, reduced course loads, and substitutions and waivers of graduation requirements are available through the program or unit directly.

Rush University

600 South Paulina

Chicago, IL 60612-3832

http://www.rushu.rush.edu/

Contact: Dr. Paul Jones, MD; Associate Provost of Student Affairs. Phone: 312-942-2819. Fax: 312-942-2778. E-mail: paul_jones@rush.edu.

Approximately 3 registered undergraduate students were served during 2006–07. Counselors and remediation/learning specialists are provided collaboratively through on-campus or off-campus services.

Unique Aids and Services Aids, services, or accommodations include career counseling.

Assistive Technology Assistive technology includes FM audio devices. Technology training is provided to incoming students.

Subject-Area Tutoring Tutoring is offered one-on-one and in small groups for all subjects. Tutoring is provided collaboratively through on-campus or off-campus services via trained peer tutors.

Diagnostic Testing Testing for auditory processing, intelligence, learning strategies, learning styles, neuropsychological, reading, social skills, and visual processing is provided collaboratively through on-campus or off-campus services.

Basic Skills Remediation Remediation is offered one-on-one for learning strategies, reading, social skills, study skills, and time management. Remediation is provided collaboratively through on-campus or off-campus services via LD specialists.

Fees *Diagnostic Testing* fee is $1500.

Application For admittance to the program or unit, students are required to provide a psychoeducational report (3 years old or less) and provide documentation of LD diagnosis. Upon acceptance, documentation of need for services should be sent only to the LD program or unit. *Application deadline (LD program):* Rolling/continuous for fall and rolling/continuous for spring.

Written Policies Written policies regarding general/basic LD accommodations, reduced course loads, substitutions and waivers of admissions requirements, and substitutions and waivers of graduation requirements are available on the program Web site. Written policies regarding general/basic LD accommodations, reduced course loads, substitutions and waivers of admissions requirements, and substitutions and waivers of graduation requirements are available through the program or unit directly.

Rutgers, The State University of New Jersey, Newark
Office of Disability Services

Newark, NJ 07102

http://disabilityservices.rutgers.edu

Contact: Mr. Nathan F. Levinson, Campus Coordinator for the Concerns of Students with Disabilities. Phone: 856-225-6219. Fax: 856-225-6231. E-mail: nathan.levinson@rutgers.edu. Head of LD Program: Dr. Gregory Allen Moorehead, Director, Student Disability Services. Phone: 732-932-2848. Fax: 732-932-2849. E-mail: drgreg@rci.rutgers.edu.

Office of Disability Services Approximately 50 registered undergraduate students were served during 2006–07. The program or unit includes 1 full-time staff member. Academic advisers, skill tutors, and strategy tutors are provided collaboratively through on-campus or off-campus services.

Unique Aids and Services Aids, services, or accommodations include career counseling.

Assistive Technology Assistive technology is located in the DSS office, Learning Centers, the library and includes digital textbooks/e-text, learning support software, and scanning. Technology training is provided to incoming students.

Subject-Area Tutoring Tutoring is offered one-on-one and in small groups for most subjects. Tutoring is provided collaboratively through on-campus or off-campus services via computer-based instruction, LD specialists, and trained peer tutors.

Diagnostic Testing Testing for intelligence and neuropsychological is provided collaboratively through on-campus or off-campus services.

Enrichment Programs for career planning, college survival skills, health and nutrition, learning strategies, medication management, practical computer skills, stress management, study skills, test taking, time management, and written composition skills are provided collaboratively through on-campus or off-campus services.

Fees *Diagnostic Testing* fee is $150 to $500.

Application For admittance to the program or unit, students are required to apply to the program directly and provide a psychoeducational report (4 years old or less). Upon application, materials documenting need for services should be sent to both admissions and the LD program or unit. Upon acceptance, documentation of need for services should be sent only to the LD program or unit. *Application deadline (institutional):* Continuous. *Application deadline (LD program):* Rolling/continuous for fall and rolling/continuous for spring.

Written Policies Written policies regarding course substitutions, general/basic LD accommodations, grade forgiveness, reduced course loads, substitutions and waivers of admissions requirements, and substitutions and waivers of graduation requirements are available on the program Web site.

Rutgers, The State University of New Jersey, New Brunswick
Office of Disability Services

New Brunswick, NJ 08901-1281

http://disabilityservices.rutgers.edu

Contact: Dr. Gregory Allen Moorehead, Director, Student Disability Services. Phone: 732-932-2848. Fax: 732-932-2849. E-mail: drgreg@rci.rutgers.edu.

Office of Disability Services Approximately 200 registered undergraduate students were served during 2006–07. The program or unit includes 3 full-time staff members. Services are provided through the program or unit. Academic advisers are provided collaboratively through on-campus or off-campus services.

Unique Aids and Services Aids, services, or accommodations include career counseling.

Assistive Technology Assistive technology is located in the DSS office, Learning Centers and includes digital textbooks/e-text, learning support software, and scanning. Technology training is provided to incoming students.

Subject-Area Tutoring Tutoring is offered one-on-one, in small groups, and in class-size groups for most subjects. Tutoring is provided collaboratively through on-campus or off-campus services via computer-based instruction, graduate assistants/students, and trained peer tutors.

Diagnostic Testing Testing for auditory processing, intelligence, learning strategies, learning styles, math, motor skills, neuropsychological, personality, reading, and visual processing is provided collaboratively through on-campus or off-campus services.

Enrichment Programs for career planning, college survival skills, health and nutrition, learning strategies, math, medication management, stress management, study skills, test taking, and time management are provided collaboratively through on-campus or off-campus services.

Application For admittance to the program or unit, students are required to apply to the program directly and provide a psychoeducational report (4 years old or less). Upon application, materials documenting need for services should be sent only to the LD program or unit. Upon acceptance, documentation of need for services should be sent only to the LD program or unit. *Application deadline (institutional):* Continuous. *Application deadline (LD program):* Rolling/continuous for fall and rolling/continuous for spring.

Written Policies Written policy regarding general/basic LD accommodations is available on the program Web site. Written policy regarding general/basic LD accommodations is available through the program or unit directly.

Ryerson University
The Access Centre

350 Victoria Street
Toronto, ON M5B 2K3
Canada

http://www.ryerson.ca/studentservices/accesscentre/

Contact: Ms. Tracy Machado, Front Desk and Intake Worker. Phone: 416-979-5290. Fax: 416-979-5094. E-mail: tmachad@ryerson.ca.

The Access Centre Counselors, diagnostic specialists, LD specialists, professional tutors, and trained peer tutors are provided through the program or unit. Academic advisers, counselors, graduate assistants/students, professional tutors, remediation/learning specialists, skill tutors, strategy tutors, and trained peer tutors are provided collaboratively through on-campus or off-campus services.

Unique Aids and Services Aids, services, or accommodations include advocates.

Assistive Technology Assistive technology is located in campus labs, a special lab, test/exam center and includes digital textbooks/e-text, learning support software, scanning, and services provided by or in conjunction with library and IT services. Technology training is provided to incoming students.

Subject-Area Tutoring Tutoring is offered one-on-one and in small groups for some subjects. Tutoring is provided collaboratively through on-campus or off-campus services via graduate assistants/students, LD specialists, professional tutors, and trained peer tutors.

Diagnostic Testing Testing is provided through the program or unit for auditory processing, intelligence, learning strategies, math, personality, reading, spelling, spoken language, visual processing, and written language. Testing for auditory processing, intelligence, learning strategies, learning styles, math, personality, reading, spelling, spoken language, study skills, visual processing, and written language is provided collaboratively through on-campus or off-campus services.

Basic Skills Remediation Remediation is offered in small groups and in class-size groups for learning strategies, reading, study skills, time management, and written language. Remediation is provided collaboratively through on-campus or off-campus services via graduate assistants/students, LD specialists, and professional tutors.

Fees *Diagnostic Testing* fee is $1000.

Application For admittance to the program or unit, students are required to provide a psychoeducational report (5 years old or less). It is recommended that students provide documentation of high school services. *Application deadline (institutional):* 2/15. *Application deadline (LD program):* Rolling/continuous for fall and rolling/continuous for spring.

Written Policies Written policy regarding general/basic LD accommodations is available on the program Web site.

The Sage Colleges
Disabilities Student Services

45 Ferry Street
Troy, NY 12180-4115
http://www.sage.edu

Contact: Ms. Katherine Norman, Director of Disabilities Services. Phone: 518-244-2208. Fax: 518-244-1764. E-mail: normak@sage.edu.

Disabilities Student Services Approximately 32 registered undergraduate students were served during 2006–07. The program or unit includes 1 full-time staff member. Counselors are provided through the program or unit. Academic advisers, coaches, counselors, diagnostic specialists, graduate assistants/students, LD specialists, and trained peer tutors are provided collaboratively through on-campus or off-campus services.

Orientation The program or unit offers an optional orientation for new students individually by special arrangement.

Unique Aids and Services Aids, services, or accommodations include advocates, career counseling, faculty training, and weekly meetings with faculty.

Assistive Technology Assistive technology is located in campus labs, the library and includes digital textbooks/e-text, learning support software, and scanning. Technology training is provided to incoming students.

Subject-Area Tutoring Tutoring is offered one-on-one for most subjects. Tutoring is provided collaboratively through on-campus or off-campus services via computer-based instruction, graduate assistants/students, LD specialists, and trained peer tutors.

Basic Skills Remediation Remediation is offered one-on-one for computer skills, learning strategies, math, reading, study skills, time management, and written language. Remediation is provided collaboratively through on-campus or off-campus services via computer-based instruction, LD specialists, and trained peer tutors.

Enrichment Programs for career planning, college survival skills, health and nutrition, learning strategies, math, medication management, oral communication skills, practical computer skills, reading, self-advocacy, stress management, study skills, test taking, time management, and written composition skills are provided collaboratively through on-campus or off-campus services.

Application For admittance to the program or unit, students are required to provide a psychoeducational report (3 years old or less). It is recommended that students provide documentation of high school services. Upon acceptance, documentation of need for services should be sent only to the LD program or unit. *Application deadline (LD program):* Rolling/continuous for fall and rolling/continuous for spring.

Written Policies Written policy regarding general/basic LD accommodations is available on the program Web site. Written policy regarding general/basic LD accommodations is outlined in the school's catalog/handbook. Written policies regarding course substitutions, general/basic LD accommodations, reduced course loads, and substitutions and waivers of graduation requirements are available through the program or unit directly.

Saginaw Valley State University
Disability Services

7400 Bay Road
University Center, MI 48710
http://www.svsu.edu/disabilityservices

Contact: Cynthia Woiderski, Director. Phone: 989-964-7000. Fax: 989-964-7258. E-mail: clbw@svsu.edu.

Disability Services Approximately 150 registered undergraduate students were served during 2006–07. The program or unit includes 1 full-time staff member. Academic advisers, counselors, and trained peer tutors are provided collaboratively through on-campus or off-campus services.

Unique Aids and Services Aids, services, or accommodations include peer mentors.

Assistive Technology Assistive technology is located in campus labs and includes digital textbooks/e-text and scanning. Technology training is provided to incoming students.

Subject-Area Tutoring Tutoring is offered one-on-one and in small groups for some subjects. Tutoring is provided collaboratively through on-campus or off-campus services via computer-based instruction and trained peer tutors.

Enrichment Programs for career planning, college survival skills, health and nutrition, practical computer skills, stress management, and written composition skills are provided collaboratively through on-campus or off-campus services.

Student Organization Ablers Club consists of 12 members.

Application For admittance to the program or unit, students are required to provide a psychoeducational report (3 years old or less). It is recommended that students provide documentation of high school services and provide transitional profile. Upon acceptance, documentation of need for services should be sent only to the LD program or unit. *Application deadline (institutional):* Continuous. *Application deadline (LD program):* Rolling/continuous for fall and rolling/continuous for spring.

Written Policies Written policy regarding general/basic LD accommodations is available on the program Web site.

St. Bonaventure University
Disability Support Services

Route 417

St. Bonaventure, NY 14778-2284

http://www.sbu.edu/go/academics/academic-support/teaching-and-learning-center/disability-support/index.htm

Contact: Jean Trevarton Ehman, Director, Teaching and Learning Center. Phone: 716-375-2066. Fax: 716-375-2072. E-mail: jehman@sbu.edu.

Disability Support Services Approximately 130 registered undergraduate students were served during 2006–07. The program or unit includes 1 full-time staff member. Graduate assistants/students and LD specialists are provided through the program or unit. Academic advisers, counselors, diagnostic specialists, and trained peer tutors are provided collaboratively through on-campus or off-campus services.

Unique Aids and Services Aids, services, or accommodations include advocates, career counseling, faculty training, personal coach, weekly meetings with faculty, peer mentors.

Subject-Area Tutoring Tutoring is offered one-on-one and in small groups for most subjects. Tutoring is provided through the program or unit via LD specialists. Tutoring is also provided collaboratively through on-campus or off-campus services via graduate assistants/students, professional tutors, and trained peer tutors.

Enrichment Enrichment programs are available through the program or unit for learning strategies, self-advocacy, study skills, test taking, and time management. Programs for career planning, college survival skills, math, stress management, and written composition skills are provided collaboratively through on-campus or off-campus services. Credit is offered for college survival skills.

Application For admittance to the program or unit, students are required to provide a psychoeducational report (3 years old or less). It is recommended that students provide documentation of high school services. Upon application, materials documenting need for services should be sent only to the LD program or unit. Upon acceptance, documentation of need for services should be sent only to the LD program or unit. *Application deadline (institutional):* 4/15. *Application deadline (LD program):* Rolling/continuous for fall and rolling/continuous for spring.

Written Policies Written policy regarding general/basic LD accommodations is outlined in the school's catalog/handbook. Written policies regarding course substitutions, general/basic LD accommodations, reduced course loads, and substitutions and waivers of graduation requirements are available through the program or unit directly.

St. Cloud State University
Student Disability Services

720 4th Avenue South

St. Cloud, MN 56301-4498

http://www.stcloudstate.edu/sds

Contact: Owen Zimpel, Director of Student Disability Services. Phone: 320-308-3117. Fax: 320-308-5100. E-mail: ojzimpel@stcloudstate.edu.

Student Disability Services Approximately 163 registered undergraduate students were served during 2006–07. The program or unit includes 6 full-time and 2 part-time staff members. Graduate assistants/students and other are provided through the program or unit. Academic advisers, counselors, special education teachers, and trained peer tutors are provided collaboratively through on-campus or off-campus services.

Orientation The program or unit offers an optional orientation for new students individually by special arrangement.

Unique Aids and Services Aids, services, or accommodations include priority registration and support groups.

Assistive Technology Assistive technology is located in the DSS office, a special lab and includes digital textbooks/e-text.

Subject-Area Tutoring Tutoring is offered one-on-one for some subjects. Tutoring is provided through the program or unit via other.

Basic Skills Remediation Remediation is offered one-on-one for learning strategies, social skills, and time management. Remediation is provided through the program or unit via graduate assistants/students.

Enrichment Enrichment programs are available through the program or unit for learning strategies, self-advocacy, test taking, and time management. Programs for career planning, college survival skills, health and nutrition, reading, stress management, study skills, and written composition skills are provided collaboratively through on-campus or off-campus services.

St. Cloud State University (continued)

Application For admittance to the program or unit, students are required to apply to the program directly and provide a psychoeducational report (3 years old or less). It is recommended that students provide documentation of high school services. Upon acceptance, documentation of need for services should be sent only to the LD program or unit. *Application deadline (institutional): 6/1. Application deadline (LD program):* Rolling/continuous for fall and rolling/continuous for spring.

Written Policies Written policy regarding general/basic LD accommodations is available on the program Web site. Written policy regarding general/basic LD accommodations is available through the program or unit directly.

St. Francis Xavier University
Program for Students with Disabilities

Box 5000

Antigonish, NS B2G 2W5

Canada

http://www.stfx.ca/campus/stu-serv/counselling/

Contact: Ms. Mary Ellen Clancy, Coordinator, Program for Students with Disabilities. Phone: 902-867-2370. Fax: 902-867-2406. E-mail: mclancy@stfx.ca.

Program for Students with Disabilities Approximately 98 registered undergraduate students were served during 2006–07. The program or unit includes 3 full-time and 2 part-time staff members. Academic advisers, coaches, counselors, LD specialists, professional tutors, regular education teachers, remediation/learning specialists, skill tutors, strategy tutors, and trained peer tutors are provided through the program or unit. Academic advisers, coaches, diagnostic specialists, teacher trainees, and trained peer tutors are provided collaboratively through on-campus or off-campus services.

Orientation The program or unit offers an optional 3-hour (varies as needed) orientation for new students before registration, before classes begin, during summer prior to enrollment, during registration, after classes begin, and individually by special arrangement.

Unique Aids and Services Aids, services, or accommodations include advocates, career counseling, faculty training, parent workshops, personal coach, and support groups.

Assistive Technology Assistive technology is located in the DSS office and includes digital textbooks/e-text, learning support software, and scanning. Technology training is provided to incoming students.

Subject-Area Tutoring Tutoring is offered one-on-one and in small groups for most subjects. Tutoring is provided through the program or unit via LD specialists, professional tutors, and trained peer tutors. Tutoring is also provided collaboratively through on-campus or off-campus services via professional tutors and trained peer tutors.

Basic Skills Remediation Remediation is offered one-on-one and in small groups for auditory processing, computer skills, learning strategies, math, social skills, study skills, time management, visual processing, and written language. Remediation is provided through the program or unit via computer-based instruction, LD specialists, professional tutors, regular education teachers, and trained

peer tutors. Remediation is also provided collaboratively through on-campus or off-campus services via computer-based instruction, professional tutors, teacher trainees, and trained peer tutors.

Enrichment Enrichment programs are available through the program or unit for career planning, college survival skills, learning strategies, math, medication management, oral communication skills, practical computer skills, self-advocacy, stress management, study skills, test taking, time management, vocabulary development, and written composition skills. Programs for career planning, college survival skills, health and nutrition, learning strategies, math, medication management, oral communication skills, practical computer skills, reading, self-advocacy, stress management, study skills, test taking, time management, vocabulary development, and written composition skills are provided collaboratively through on-campus or off-campus services.

Student Organization Disabilities at "X" consists of 30 members.

Application For admittance to the program or unit, students are required to provide a psychoeducational report (5 years old or less). It is recommended that students provide documentation of high school services. Upon application, materials documenting need for services should be sent only to the LD program or unit. Upon acceptance, documentation of need for services should be sent only to the LD program or unit. *Application deadline (institutional):* Continuous. *Application deadline (LD program):* Rolling/continuous for fall and rolling/continuous for spring.

Written Policies Written policy regarding general/basic LD accommodations is available on the program Web site. Written policies regarding general/basic LD accommodations and reduced course loads are available through the program or unit directly.

Saint John's University
Academic Advising

PO Box 2000

Collegeville, MN 56321

http://www.csbsju.edu/

Contact: Susan R. Douma, Director of Academic Advising. Phone: 320-363-2248. Fax: 320-363-2714. E-mail: sdouma@csbsju.edu.

Academic Advising Approximately 100 registered undergraduate students were served during 2006–07. The program or unit includes 1 part-time staff member. Academic advisers and counselors are provided through the program or unit. Academic advisers, counselors, and other are provided collaboratively through on-campus or off-campus services.

Unique Aids and Services Aids, services, or accommodations include advocates, career counseling, and priority registration.

Assistive Technology Assistive technology is located in campus labs, the DSS office, residential halls and includes digital textbooks/e-text and scanning.

Subject-Area Tutoring Tutoring is offered one-on-one and in small groups for all subjects. Tutoring is provided collaboratively through on-campus or off-campus services via other.

Enrichment Enrichment programs are available through the program or unit for self-advocacy and other. Programs for career planning, health and nutrition, math, practical computer skills, reading, self-advocacy, stress management, written composition skills, and other are provided collaboratively through on-campus or off-campus services.

Application For admittance to the program or unit, students are required to provide a psychoeducational report (3 years old or less) and provide other documentation (varies depending on disability). It is recommended that students provide documentation of high school services. Upon application, materials documenting need for services should be sent to both admissions and the LD program or unit. Upon acceptance, documentation of need for services should be sent only to the LD program or unit. *Application deadline (institutional):* Continuous. *Application deadline (LD program):* Rolling/continuous for fall.

Written Policies Written policies regarding course substitutions, general/basic LD accommodations, and substitutions and waivers of admissions requirements are available through the program or unit directly.

Saint Joseph's College

U.S. Highway 231, PO Box 890
Rensselaer, IN 47978
http://www.saintjoe.edu/sss/counseling/ld_support.html
Contact: Dr. Leslie Frere, Director of Counseling and Health Services. Phone: 219-866-6116. Fax: 219-866-6355. E-mail: lfrere@saintjoe.edu.

The program or unit includes 1 full-time staff member. Counselors are provided through the program or unit.

Subject-Area Tutoring Tutoring is offered one-on-one for most subjects. Tutoring is provided collaboratively through on-campus or off-campus services via trained peer tutors.

Basic Skills Remediation Remediation is offered one-on-one and in small groups for learning strategies, study skills, and time management. Remediation is provided collaboratively through on-campus or off-campus services via LD specialists.

Enrichment Programs for college survival skills and other are provided collaboratively through on-campus or off-campus services. Credit is offered for college survival skills and other.

Application For admittance to the program or unit, students are required to provide a psychoeducational report. It is recommended that students provide documentation of high school services. Upon application, materials documenting need for services should be sent only to admissions with institutional application materials. Upon acceptance, documentation of need for services should be sent only to the LD program or unit. *Application deadline (institutional):* Continuous. *Application deadline (LD program):* Rolling/continuous for fall and rolling/continuous for spring.

Written Policies Written policy regarding general/basic LD accommodations is available on the program Web site. Written policy regarding general/basic LD accommodations is outlined in the school's catalog/handbook.

St. Lawrence University
Academic Services for Students with Special Needs

Canton, NY 13617-1455
http://www.stlawu.edu/needs/

Contact: Mr. John Meagher, Director, Office of Academic Services for Students with Special Needs. Phone: 315-229-5164. E-mail: jmeagher@stlawu.edu.

Academic Services for Students with Special Needs
Approximately 110 registered undergraduate students were served during 2006–07. The program or unit includes 1 full-time and 1 part-time staff member. Academic advisers, counselors, diagnostic specialists, skill tutors, and trained peer tutors are provided through the program or unit. Academic advisers, coaches, counselors, teacher trainees, and trained peer tutors are provided collaboratively through on-campus or off-campus services.

Assistive Technology Assistive technology is located in the DSS office and includes learning support software and scanning. Technology training is provided to incoming students.

Subject-Area Tutoring Tutoring is offered one-on-one, in small groups, and in class-size groups for most subjects. Tutoring is provided collaboratively through on-campus or off-campus services via graduate assistants/students and trained peer tutors.

Enrichment Programs for career planning, health and nutrition, learning strategies, stress management, study skills, test taking, time management, and written composition skills are provided collaboratively through on-campus or off-campus services.

Application For admittance to the program or unit, students are required to provide a psychoeducational report (3 years old or less) and provide documentation of high school services. Upon acceptance, documentation of need for services should be sent only to the LD program or unit. *Application deadline (institutional):* 2/1. *Application deadline (LD program):* Rolling/continuous for fall and rolling/continuous for spring.

Written Policies Written policy regarding general/basic LD accommodations is available on the program Web site. Written policy regarding general/basic LD accommodations is outlined in the school's catalog/handbook. Written policy regarding general/basic LD accommodations is available through the program or unit directly.

Saint Leo University
Office of Disability Services

PO Box 6665
Saint Leo, FL 33574-6665
http://www.saintleo.edu/

Contact: Dr. Mary E. Sloan, Director of Disability Services. Phone: 352-588-5464. Fax: 352-588-8605. E-mail: mary.sloan@saintleo.edu.

Office of Disability Services Approximately 50 registered undergraduate students were served during 2006–07. The program or unit includes 1 full-time staff member. LD specialists are provided through the program or unit. Academic advisers, coaches, counselors, professional tutors, and regular education teachers are provided collaboratively through on-campus or off-campus services.

Unique Aids and Services Aids, services, or accommodations include faculty training, personal coach, and priority registration.

Subject-Area Tutoring Tutoring is offered one-on-one and in small groups for most subjects. Tutoring is provided collaboratively through on-campus or off-campus services via professional tutors and trained peer tutors.

Saint Leo University (continued)

Enrichment Enrichment programs are available through the program or unit for learning strategies, self-advocacy, stress management, study skills, test taking, and time management.

Application For admittance to the program or unit, students are required to provide a psychoeducational report (3 years old or less). Upon acceptance, documentation of need for services should be sent only to the LD program or unit. *Application deadline (institutional):* 8/15. *Application deadline (LD program):* Rolling/continuous for fall and rolling/continuous for spring.

Written Policies Written policies regarding course substitutions, general/basic LD accommodations, reduced course loads, substitutions and waivers of admissions requirements, and substitutions and waivers of graduation requirements are available on the program Web site. Written policies regarding course substitutions, general/basic LD accommodations, reduced course loads, substitutions and waivers of admissions requirements, and substitutions and waivers of graduation requirements are available through the program or unit directly.

St. Mary's College of Maryland
Academic Services

18952 East Fisher Road

St. Mary's City, MD 20686-3001

http://www.smcm.edu/academics/academicserv/disabilities.cfm

Contact: Dr. Nancy Brewer Danganan, Coordinator of Advising Programs. Phone: 240-895-4388. Fax: 240-895-4331. E-mail: nadanganan@smcm.edu.

Academic Services Approximately 65 registered undergraduate students were served during 2006–07. The program or unit includes 1 part-time staff member. Academic advisers and counselors are provided through the program or unit. Academic advisers, counselors, regular education teachers, and trained peer tutors are provided collaboratively through on-campus or off-campus services.

Unique Aids and Services Aids, services, or accommodations include career counseling.

Assistive Technology Assistive technology is located in the library and includes learning support software and books on tape/CD and digitally when available.

Subject-Area Tutoring Tutoring is offered one-on-one, in small groups, and in class-size groups for most subjects. Tutoring is provided collaboratively through on-campus or off-campus services via professional tutors, trained peer tutors, and other.

Basic Skills Remediation Remediation is offered one-on-one for learning strategies, study skills, and time management. Remediation is provided collaboratively through on-campus or off-campus services via trained peer tutors and other.

Enrichment Enrichment programs are available through the program or unit for learning strategies, study skills, test taking, and time management. Programs for career planning, college survival skills, health and nutrition, learning strategies, math, stress management, study skills, test taking, time management, and written composition skills are provided collaboratively through on-campus or off-campus services.

Application For admittance to the program or unit, students are required to provide a psychoeducational report (3 years old or less). It is recommended that students provide documentation of high school services. Upon application, materials documenting need for services should be sent to both admissions and the LD program or unit. Upon acceptance, documentation of need for services should be sent only to the LD program or unit. *Application deadline (institutional):* 1/15. *Application deadline (LD program):* Rolling/continuous for fall and rolling/continuous for spring.

Written Policies Written policy regarding general/basic LD accommodations is available on the program Web site. Written policies regarding course substitutions, general/basic LD accommodations, and substitutions and waivers of graduation requirements are available through the program or unit directly.

St. Norbert College
Academic Support Services

100 Grant Street

De Pere, WI 54115-2099

http://www.snc.edu/

Contact: Ms. Karen Goode-Bartholomew, Director of Academic Support Services. Phone: 920-403-1326. Fax: 920-403-4021. E-mail: karen.goode-bartholomew@snc.edu.

Academic Support Services Approximately 120 registered undergraduate students were served during 2006–07. The program or unit includes 2 full-time staff members. Coaches, remediation/learning specialists, skill tutors, strategy tutors, and trained peer tutors are provided through the program or unit. Academic advisers, counselors, diagnostic specialists, and graduate assistants/students are provided collaboratively through on-campus or off-campus services.

Unique Aids and Services Aids, services, or accommodations include career counseling, personal coach, and priority registration.

Subject-Area Tutoring Tutoring is offered one-on-one and in small groups for most subjects. Tutoring is provided through the program or unit via trained peer tutors.

Diagnostic Testing Testing is provided through the program or unit for learning styles, reading, and study skills.

Enrichment Enrichment programs are available through the program or unit for learning strategies, reading, stress management, study skills, test taking, time management, and vocabulary development. Programs for career planning, college survival skills, health and nutrition, learning strategies, math, medication management, reading, study skills, test taking, time management, and vocabulary development are provided collaboratively through on-campus or off-campus services. Credit is offered for college survival skills, math, reading, study skills, test taking, time management, and vocabulary development.

Application For admittance to the program or unit, students are required to provide a psychoeducational report (3 years old or less). Upon application, materials documenting need for services should be sent only to the LD program or unit. Upon acceptance, documentation of need for services should be sent only to the LD program or unit. *Application deadline (institutional):* Continuous. *Application deadline (LD program):* Rolling/continuous for fall and rolling/continuous for spring.

Written Policies Written policies regarding course substitutions, reduced course loads, and substitutions and waivers of graduation requirements are outlined in the school's catalog/handbook. Written policies regarding course substitutions, general/basic LD accommodations, reduced course loads, and substitutions and waivers of graduation requirements are available through the program or unit directly.

St. Thomas University
Department of Student Affairs

51 Dineen Drive

Fredericton, NB E3B 5G3

Canada

http://www.stu.ca

Contact: Mrs. Jane McGinn-Giberson, Director of the Student Affairs. Phone: 506-452-0638. Fax: 506-460-0319. E-mail: jmcginn@stu.ca. Head of LD Program: Mrs. Marina Nedashkivska, Coordinator of Services for Student Accessibility. Phone: 506-453-7207. Fax: 506-460-0319. E-mail: marina@stu.ca.

Department of Student Affairs Approximately 50 registered undergraduate students were served during 2006–07. The program or unit includes 1 full-time staff member. Academic advisers, coaches, and counselors are provided through the program or unit. Academic advisers, coaches, counselors, diagnostic specialists, graduate assistants/students, LD specialists, professional tutors, regular education teachers, skill tutors, strategy tutors, and trained peer tutors are provided collaboratively through on-campus or off-campus services.

Orientation The program or unit offers an optional 1-day or more orientation for new students before registration, before classes begin, during summer prior to enrollment, during registration, after classes begin, and individually by special arrangement.

Unique Aids and Services Aids, services, or accommodations include advocates, career counseling, faculty training, personal coach, priority registration, support groups, weekly meetings with faculty, scribes.

Assistive Technology Assistive technology is located in the DSS office, a special lab and includes digital textbooks/e-text, learning support software, and scanning. Technology training is provided to incoming students.

Subject-Area Tutoring Tutoring is offered one-on-one and in small groups for most subjects. Tutoring is provided through the program or unit via trained peer tutors. Tutoring is also provided collaboratively through on-campus or off-campus services via computer-based instruction, graduate assistants/students, professional tutors, and trained peer tutors.

Diagnostic Testing Testing for learning strategies, learning styles, reading, social skills, spoken language, study skills, visual processing, and written language is provided collaboratively through on-campus or off-campus services.

Basic Skills Remediation Remediation is offered one-on-one and in small groups for auditory processing, computer skills, learning strategies, math, reading, social skills, spelling, spoken language, study skills, time management, visual processing, and written language. Remediation is provided collaboratively through on-campus

or off-campus services via computer-based instruction, graduate assistants/students, LD specialists, professional tutors, regular education teachers, teacher trainees, and trained peer tutors.

Enrichment Programs for career planning, college survival skills, health and nutrition, learning strategies, math, oral communication skills, practical computer skills, reading, self-advocacy, stress management, study skills, test taking, time management, and written composition skills are provided collaboratively through on-campus or off-campus services.

Application It is recommended that students provide a psychoeducational report and provide documentation of high school services. Upon application, materials documenting need for services should be sent only to the LD program or unit. Upon acceptance, documentation of need for services should be sent only to the LD program or unit. *Application deadline (institutional): 8/31. Application deadline (LD program):* Rolling/continuous for fall and rolling/continuous for spring.

Written Policies Written policy regarding general/basic LD accommodations is available on the program Web site. Written policies regarding course substitutions, general/basic LD accommodations, grade forgiveness, reduced course loads, substitutions and waivers of admissions requirements, and substitutions and waivers of graduation requirements are outlined in the school's catalog/handbook. Written policies regarding course substitutions, grade forgiveness, reduced course loads, substitutions and waivers of admissions requirements, and substitutions and waivers of graduation requirements are available through the program or unit directly.

Saint Xavier University
Learning Center and Disability Services

3700 West 103rd Street

Chicago, IL 60655-3105

http://www.sxu.edu/learning_center/default.asp

Contact: Ms. Julie S. Ashley, Director, Learning Center and Disability Services. Phone: 773-298-3308. E-mail: ashley@sxu.edu.

Learning Center and Disability Services Approximately 60 registered undergraduate students were served during 2006–07. The program or unit includes 2 full-time staff members. LD specialists are provided through the program or unit. Counselors, professional tutors, skill tutors, and trained peer tutors are provided collaboratively through on-campus or off-campus services.

Unique Aids and Services Aids, services, or accommodations include career counseling and priority registration.

Assistive Technology Assistive technology is located in the DSS office and includes learning support software, scanning, and JAWS, Kurzweil, reading pen, Dragon Naturally Speaking. Technology training is provided to incoming students.

Subject-Area Tutoring Tutoring is offered one-on-one and in small groups for most subjects. Tutoring is provided collaboratively through on-campus or off-campus services via computer-based instruction, professional tutors, and trained peer tutors.

Enrichment Programs for career planning, college survival skills, learning strategies, practical computer skills, reading, stress management, study skills, test taking, and time management are provided collaboratively through on-campus or off-campus services. Credit is offered for health and nutrition, math, and written composition skills.

Saint Xavier University (continued)

Application For admittance to the program or unit, students are required to provide formal documentation, including testing, clinician's diagnosis, interpretation. It is recommended that students provide documentation of high school services. Upon acceptance, documentation of need for services should be sent only to the LD program or unit. *Application deadline (institutional):* Continuous. *Application deadline (LD program):* Rolling/continuous for fall and rolling/continuous for spring.

Written Policies Written policy regarding general/basic LD accommodations is available on the program Web site. Written policy regarding general/basic LD accommodations is outlined in the school's catalog/handbook. Written policies regarding course substitutions and general/basic LD accommodations are available through the program or unit directly.

Salve Regina University
Academic Development Center

100 Ochre Point Avenue

Newport, RI 02840-4192

http://www.salve.edu/offices/acdevel/index.cfm

Contact: Dr. Susan B. Pratt, Director, Academic Development Center. Phone: 401-341-2228. Fax: 401-341-2912. E-mail: susan.pratt@salve.edu.

Academic Development Center Approximately 65 registered undergraduate students were served during 2006–07. The program or unit includes 1 full-time and 2 part-time staff members. Diagnostic specialists, LD specialists, strategy tutors, and trained peer tutors are provided through the program or unit. Academic advisers, diagnostic specialists, LD specialists, professional tutors, regular education teachers, remediation/learning specialists, strategy tutors, and trained peer tutors are provided collaboratively through on-campus or off-campus services.

Assistive Technology Assistive technology is located in the DSS office and includes digital textbooks/e-text, scanning, and Dragon Naturally Speaking. Technology training is provided to incoming students.

Subject-Area Tutoring Tutoring is offered one-on-one for most subjects. Tutoring is provided through the program or unit via trained peer tutors. Tutoring is also provided collaboratively through on-campus or off-campus services via trained peer tutors.

Basic Skills Remediation Remediation is offered one-on-one for learning strategies, study skills, time management, and written language. Remediation is provided through the program or unit via LD specialists and other. Remediation is also provided collaboratively through on-campus or off-campus services via trained peer tutors.

Enrichment Enrichment programs are available through the program or unit for self-advocacy, stress management, study skills, test taking, and time management. Programs for reading, self-advocacy, stress management, and test taking are provided collaboratively through on-campus or off-campus services. Credit is offered for college survival skills, learning strategies, self-advocacy, stress management, study skills, test taking, time management, vocabulary development, and written composition skills.

Application For admittance to the program or unit, students are required to provide a psychoeducational report. It is recommended that students provide documentation of high school services. Upon acceptance, documentation of need for services should be sent only to the LD program or unit. *Application deadline (institutional):* 3/1. *Application deadline (LD program):* Rolling/continuous for fall and rolling/continuous for spring.

Written Policies Written policy regarding general/basic LD accommodations is available on the program Web site. Written policy regarding general/basic LD accommodations is outlined in the school's catalog/handbook. Written policy regarding general/basic LD accommodations is available through the program or unit directly.

San Diego State University

5500 Campanile Drive

San Diego, CA 92182

http://www.sa.sdsu.edu/dss/dss_home.html

Contact: Margo Behr, Coordinator of Learning Disabilities Program. Phone: 619-594-6473. Fax: 619-594-4315. E-mail: mbehr@mail.sdsu.edu.

Approximately 250 registered undergraduate students were served during 2006–07. The program or unit includes 2 full-time staff members and 1 part-time staff member. Counselors, diagnostic specialists, graduate assistants/students, LD specialists, professional tutors, and remediation/learning specialists are provided through the program or unit. Academic advisers, coaches, counselors, diagnostic specialists, and regular education teachers are provided collaboratively through on-campus or off-campus services.

Orientation The program or unit offers a mandatory 1-hour orientation for new students before using accommodations authorized by DSS program.

Unique Aids and Services Aids, services, or accommodations include advocates, career counseling, and priority registration.

Assistive Technology Assistive technology is located in a special lab and includes digital textbooks/e-text and scanning. Technology training is provided to incoming students.

Subject-Area Tutoring Tutoring is offered one-on-one and in small groups for some subjects. Tutoring is provided through the program or unit via graduate assistants/students and trained peer tutors. Tutoring is also provided collaboratively through on-campus or off-campus services via graduate assistants/students, professional tutors, and trained peer tutors.

Diagnostic Testing Testing is provided through the program or unit for auditory processing, intelligence, math, neuropsychological, reading, spelling, spoken language, visual processing, and written language. Testing for auditory processing and reading is provided collaboratively through on-campus or off-campus services.

Basic Skills Remediation Remediation is offered in class-size groups for math and written language. Remediation is provided through the program or unit via regular education teachers and trained peer tutors. Remediation is also provided collaboratively through on-campus or off-campus services via professional tutors, regular education teachers, and trained peer tutors.

Enrichment Enrichment programs are available through the program or unit for college survival skills, learning strategies, self-advocacy, study skills, test taking, time management, and written composition skills. Programs for career planning, college survival skills, health and nutrition, learning strategies, math, medication management, practical computer skills, reading, stress management, and written composition skills are provided collaboratively through on-campus or off-campus services. Credit is offered for college survival skills, math, study skills, test taking, time management, and written composition skills.

Application For admittance to the program or unit, students are required to apply to the program directly. It is recommended that students provide a psychoeducational report, provide documentation of high school services, and provide documentation from community college (for transfer students). Upon application, materials documenting need for services should be sent only to the LD program or unit. Upon acceptance, documentation of need for services should be sent only to the LD program or unit. *Application deadline (institutional):* 11/30. *Application deadline (LD program):* Rolling/continuous for fall and rolling/continuous for spring.

Written Policies Written policies regarding course substitutions, general/basic LD accommodations, and substitutions and waivers of graduation requirements are available on the program Web site. Written policies regarding course substitutions, substitutions and waivers of admissions requirements, and substitutions and waivers of graduation requirements are outlined in the school's catalog/handbook. Written policies regarding general/basic LD accommodations and substitutions and waivers of admissions requirements are available through the program or unit directly.

San Francisco State University
Disability Programs and Resource Center

1600 Holloway Avenue

San Francisco, CA 94132-1722

http://www.sfsu.edu/~dprc/

Contact: Zi Hengstler, Learning Specialist. Phone: 415-338-7878. Fax: 415-338-1041. E-mail: zibelle@sfsu.edu.

Disability Programs and Resource Center Approximately 300 registered undergraduate students were served during 2006–07. The program or unit includes 2 part-time staff members. Academic advisers, counselors, diagnostic specialists, LD specialists, and trained peer tutors are provided through the program or unit.

Unique Aids and Services Aids, services, or accommodations include priority registration.

Subject-Area Tutoring Tutoring is offered in small groups for most subjects. Tutoring is provided collaboratively through on-campus or off-campus services via trained peer tutors.

Enrichment Enrichment programs are available through the program or unit for self-advocacy. Programs for career planning and study skills are provided collaboratively through on-campus or off-campus services.

Application For admittance to the program or unit, students are required to apply to the program directly and provide a psychoeducational report (3 years old or less). It is recommended that students provide documentation of high school services. Upon acceptance, documentation of need for services should be sent only to the LD program or unit. *Application deadline (institutional):* Continuous. *Application deadline (LD program):* Rolling/continuous for fall and rolling/continuous for spring.

Written Policies Written policies regarding course substitutions, general/basic LD accommodations, reduced course loads, substitutions and waivers of admissions requirements, and substitutions and waivers of graduation requirements are available through the program or unit directly.

Santa Clara University
Disabilities Resources

500 El Camino Real

Santa Clara, CA 95053

http://www.scu.edu/advising/

Contact: Ann Ravenscroft, Director of Disabilities Resources. Phone: 408-554-4111. Fax: 408-554-5136. E-mail: eravenscroft@scu.edu.

Disabilities Resources Approximately 77 registered undergraduate students were served during 2006–07. The program or unit includes 2 full-time staff members. Academic advisers, graduate assistants/students, and LD specialists are provided through the program or unit. Academic advisers, counselors, regular education teachers, skill tutors, strategy tutors, and trained peer tutors are provided collaboratively through on-campus or off-campus services.

Orientation The program or unit offers a mandatory 2-hour orientation for new students before classes begin and individually by special arrangement.

Unique Aids and Services Aids, services, or accommodations include career counseling and priority registration.

Assistive Technology Assistive technology is located in campus labs and includes learning support software. Technology training is provided to incoming students.

Subject-Area Tutoring Tutoring is offered one-on-one and in small groups for most subjects. Tutoring is provided collaboratively through on-campus or off-campus services via computer-based instruction, graduate assistants/students, and trained peer tutors.

Application For admittance to the program or unit, students are required to apply to the program directly, provide a psychoeducational report (3 years old or less), and provide documentation from an appropriate professional. It is recommended that students provide documentation of high school services. Upon acceptance, documentation of need for services should be sent only to the LD program or unit. *Application deadline (institutional):* 1/15. *Application deadline (LD program):* Rolling/continuous for fall and rolling/continuous for spring.

Written Policies Written policies regarding course substitutions, general/basic LD accommodations, and substitutions and waivers of graduation requirements are available on the program Web site. Written policies regarding course substitutions, general/basic LD accommodations, and substitutions and waivers of graduation requirements are available through the program or unit directly.

Savannah College of Art and Design
Center for Student Counseling and Disabilities Services

342 Bull Street, PO Box 3146
Savannah, GA 31402-3146
http://www.scad.edu

Contact: Ms. Lita Clary, Coordinator for Disability Resource Services. Phone: 912-525-4665. Fax: 912-525-4955. E-mail: lclary@scad.edu.

Center for Student Counseling and Disabilities Services
Approximately 977 registered undergraduate students were served during 2006–07. The program or unit includes 5 full-time staff members. Counselors and LD specialists are provided through the program or unit. Academic advisers and skill tutors are provided collaboratively through on-campus or off-campus services.

Unique Aids and Services Aids, services, or accommodations include support groups.

Subject-Area Tutoring Tutoring is offered one-on-one and in small groups for some subjects. Tutoring is provided collaboratively through on-campus or off-campus services via trained peer tutors and other.

Basic Skills Remediation Remediation is offered one-on-one and in small groups for study skills, time management, and subject matter content. Remediation is provided collaboratively through on-campus or off-campus services via trained peer tutors.

Application Upon acceptance, documentation of need for services should be sent to both admissions and the LD program or unit. *Application deadline (institutional):* Continuous. *Application deadline (LD program):* Rolling/continuous for fall and rolling/continuous for spring.

Written Policies Written policy regarding general/basic LD accommodations is available through the program or unit directly.

School of the Art Institute of Chicago
The Disability and Learning Resource Center

37 South Wabash
Chicago, IL 60603-3103
http://www.artic.edu/saic/

Contact: Heather Walsh, Director, Disability and Learning Resource Center. Phone: 312-499-4278. Fax: 312-499-4290. E-mail: dlrc@saic.edu.

The Disability and Learning Resource Center Approximately 150 registered undergraduate students were served during 2006–07. The program or unit includes 2 full-time staff members and 1 part-time staff member. Graduate assistants/students, LD specialists, remediation/learning specialists, and strategy tutors are provided through the program or unit. Academic advisers, counselors, and trained peer tutors are provided collaboratively through on-campus or off-campus services.

Unique Aids and Services Aids, services, or accommodations include advocates, career counseling, faculty training, and priority registration.

Assistive Technology Assistive technology is located in the DSS office and includes digital textbooks/e-text, learning support software, and scanning. Technology training is provided to incoming students.

Basic Skills Remediation Remediation is offered one-on-one and in small groups for learning strategies, reading, study skills, time management, and written language. Remediation is provided through the program or unit via graduate assistants/students and LD specialists.

Enrichment Enrichment programs are available through the program or unit for college survival skills, learning strategies, study skills, test taking, time management, and written composition skills. Programs for career planning, college survival skills, health and nutrition, learning strategies, reading, study skills, test taking, time management, and written composition skills are provided collaboratively through on-campus or off-campus services. Credit is offered for reading and written composition skills.

Application For admittance to the program or unit, students are required to provide a psychoeducational report (3 years old or less). Upon application, materials documenting need for services should be sent only to the LD program or unit. Upon acceptance, documentation of need for services should be sent only to the LD program or unit. *Application deadline (institutional):* Continuous. *Application deadline (LD program):* Rolling/continuous for fall and rolling/continuous for spring.

Written Policies Written policy regarding general/basic LD accommodations is available on the program Web site. Written policy regarding general/basic LD accommodations is outlined in the school's catalog/handbook. Written policies regarding general/basic LD accommodations and reduced course loads are available through the program or unit directly.

School of Visual Arts
Learning Disabilities Office

209 East 23rd Street
New York, NY 10010-3994

http://schoolofvisualarts.edu/studentaffairs/
index.jsp?sid0=237&sid1=143

Contact: Ms. Colette Hughes, Learning Disabilities Coordinator. Phone: 212-592-2157. Fax: 212-627-1942. E-mail: chughes@sva.edu.

Learning Disabilities Office Approximately 150 registered undergraduate students were served during 2006–07. The program or unit includes 1 full-time and 1 part-time staff member. LD specialists, professional tutors, and remediation/learning specialists are provided through the program or unit. Academic advisers are provided collaboratively through on-campus or off-campus services.

Assistive Technology Assistive technology is located in campus labs and includes digital textbooks/e-text and learning support software.

Subject-Area Tutoring Tutoring is offered one-on-one. Tutoring is provided through the program or unit via LD specialists.

Basic Skills Remediation Remediation is offered one-on-one for learning strategies, reading, spelling, study skills, time management, and written language. Remediation is provided through the program or unit via LD specialists.

Enrichment Enrichment programs are available through the program or unit for learning strategies, reading, study skills, time management, vocabulary development, and written composition skills.

Application For admittance to the program or unit, students are required to apply to the program directly, provide a psychoeducational report, and provide documentation of high school services. Upon acceptance, documentation of need for services should be sent only to the LD program or unit. *Application deadline (institutional):* Continuous. *Application deadline (LD program):* Rolling/continuous for fall and rolling/continuous for spring.

Written Policies Written policy regarding general/basic LD accommodations is available on the program Web site. Written policy regarding general/basic LD accommodations is available through the program or unit directly.

Seattle Pacific University
Disability Support Services

3307 Third Avenue West

Seattle, WA 98119-1997

http://www.spu.edu/dss

Contact: Bethany Anderson, Program Coordinator for Disability Support Services. Phone: 206-281-2272. Fax: 206-286-7348. E-mail: disabilityservices@spu.edu.

Disability Support Services Approximately 30 registered undergraduate students were served during 2006–07. The program or unit includes 1 full-time staff member. Remediation/learning specialists are provided through the program or unit. Remediation/learning specialists are provided collaboratively through on-campus or off-campus services.

Unique Aids and Services Aids, services, or accommodations include extra time for exams, note-takers.

Assistive Technology Assistive technology is located in the DSS office, a special lab and includes digital textbooks/e-text and books on tape.

Subject-Area Tutoring Tutoring is offered one-on-one and in small groups for most subjects. Tutoring is provided collaboratively through on-campus or off-campus services via graduate assistants/students and trained peer tutors.

Basic Skills Remediation Remediation is offered one-on-one and in class-size groups for learning strategies, math, reading, spelling, study skills, time management, and written language. Remediation is provided collaboratively through on-campus or off-campus services via graduate assistants/students and regular education teachers.

Enrichment Enrichment programs are available through the program or unit for reading, self-advocacy, study skills, test taking, and time management. Programs for career planning, college survival skills, health and nutrition, learning strategies, math, medication management, reading, stress management, study skills, test taking, time management, and written composition skills are provided collaboratively through on-campus or off-campus services. Credit is offered for career planning, college survival skills, learning strategies, math, reading, study skills, test taking, and time management.

Application For admittance to the program or unit, students are required to provide a psychoeducational report (3 years old or less). Upon acceptance, documentation of need for services should be sent only to the LD program or unit. *Application deadline (institutional):* 2/1. *Application deadline (LD program):* Rolling/continuous for fall and rolling/continuous for spring.

Written Policies Written policies regarding course substitutions, general/basic LD accommodations, reduced course loads, and substitutions and waivers of graduation requirements are available on the program Web site. Written policies regarding course substitutions, general/basic LD accommodations, reduced course loads, and substitutions and waivers of graduation requirements are available through the program or unit directly.

Seton Hall University
Disability Support Services

400 South Orange Avenue

South Orange, NJ 07079-2697

http://www.shu.edu/

Contact: Dr. Linda R. Walter, Director. Phone: 973-313-6003. Fax: 973-761-9185. E-mail: walterli@shu.edu.

Disability Support Services Approximately 350 registered undergraduate students were served during 2006–07. The program or unit includes 4 full-time staff members and 1 part-time staff member. Diagnostic specialists, graduate assistants/students, LD specialists, professional tutors, remediation/learning specialists, skill tutors, and strategy tutors are provided through the program or unit. Academic advisers and counselors are provided collaboratively through on-campus or off-campus services.

Summer Program To help prepare for the demands of college, there is an optional summer program prior to entering the school available to high school graduates that focuses on life skills and/or college life adjustment, study skills, and time management. Degree credit will be earned.

Unique Aids and Services Aids, services, or accommodations include career counseling, faculty training, parent workshops, priority registration, and support groups.

Assistive Technology Assistive technology is located in campus labs, the DSS office and includes digital textbooks/e-text. Technology training is provided to incoming students.

Subject-Area Tutoring Tutoring is offered one-on-one and in small groups for most subjects. Tutoring is provided through the program or unit via computer-based instruction and LD specialists. Tutoring is also provided collaboratively through on-campus or off-campus services via computer-based instruction, graduate assistants/students, and trained peer tutors.

Diagnostic Testing Testing is provided through the program or unit for intelligence, reading, and other services. Testing for math, reading, and written language is provided collaboratively through on-campus or off-campus services.

Basic Skills Remediation Remediation is offered in small groups and in class-size groups for computer skills, learning strategies, math, social skills, study skills, time management, and written language. Remediation is provided through the program or unit via

Seton Hall University (continued)

special education teachers. Remediation is also provided collaboratively through on-campus or off-campus services via computer-based instruction and regular education teachers.

Enrichment Enrichment programs are available through the program or unit for college survival skills, learning strategies, medication management, oral communication skills, practical computer skills, self-advocacy, stress management, study skills, test taking, time management, and written composition skills. Programs for career planning, college survival skills, health and nutrition, math, medication management, oral communication skills, practical computer skills, reading, stress management, study skills, test taking, time management, and written composition skills are provided collaboratively through on-campus or off-campus services.

Fees *Diagnostic Testing* fee is applicable.

Application For admittance to the program or unit, students are required to provide a psychoeducational report (3 years old or less), provide documentation of high school services, and provide exam scores from educational and psychological assessments. Upon application, materials documenting need for services should be sent only to the LD program or unit. Upon acceptance, documentation of need for services should be sent only to the LD program or unit. *Application deadline (institutional):* 3/1. *Application deadline (LD program):* Rolling/continuous for fall.

Written Policies Written policies regarding course substitutions, general/basic LD accommodations, substitutions and waivers of admissions requirements, and substitutions and waivers of graduation requirements are available on the program Web site. Written policy regarding general/basic LD accommodations is outlined in the school's catalog/handbook. Written policies regarding course substitutions, general/basic LD accommodations, substitutions and waivers of admissions requirements, and substitutions and waivers of graduation requirements are available through the program or unit directly.

Seton Hill University
Office of Disability Services

Seton Hill Drive

Greensburg, PA 15601

http://www.setonhill.edu/

Contact: Ms. Teresa Ann Bassi, Director of Counseling, Disability and Health Services. Phone: 724-838-4295. Fax: 724-830-4733. E-mail: bassi@setonhill.edu. Head of LD Program: Ms. Kimberley Cook, Coordinator of Disability Services. Phone: 724-552-1607. Fax: 724-830-4733. E-mail: cook@setonhill.edu.

Office of Disability Services Approximately 40 registered undergraduate students were served during 2006–07. The program or unit includes 1 part-time staff member. Academic advisers, counselors, skill tutors, and strategy tutors are provided through the program or unit. Academic advisers, coaches, counselors, regular education teachers, skill tutors, strategy tutors, and trained peer tutors are provided collaboratively through on-campus or off-campus services.

Orientation The program or unit offers an optional 3-day orientation for new students before classes begin and after classes begin.

Summer Program To help prepare for the demands of college, there is an optional 3-day summer program prior to entering the school available to high school graduates that focuses on computing skills, life skills and/or college life adjustment, self-advocacy, study skills, test-taking skills, and time management. The program accepts students from out-of-state.

Unique Aids and Services Aids, services, or accommodations include career counseling, faculty training, personal coach, support groups, and weekly meetings with faculty.

Assistive Technology Assistive technology is located in campus labs, the DSS office, a special lab and includes digital textbooks/e-text, learning support software, and scanning. Technology training is provided to incoming students.

Subject-Area Tutoring Tutoring is offered one-on-one and in small groups for most subjects. Tutoring is provided collaboratively through on-campus or off-campus services via computer-based instruction and trained peer tutors.

Basic Skills Remediation Remediation is offered one-on-one, in small groups, and in class-size groups for auditory processing, computer skills, handwriting, learning strategies, math, social skills, spelling, study skills, time management, visual processing, and written language. Remediation is provided through the program or unit via LD specialists. Remediation is also provided collaboratively through on-campus or off-campus services via computer-based instruction, regular education teachers, and teacher trainees.

Enrichment Enrichment programs are available through the program or unit for medication management, self-advocacy, stress management, study skills, test taking, and time management. Programs for career planning, college survival skills, health and nutrition, learning strategies, math, medication management, oral communication skills, practical computer skills, stress management, study skills, test taking, time management, vocabulary development, and written composition skills are provided collaboratively through on-campus or off-campus services. Credit is offered for study skills and time management.

Application For admittance to the program or unit, students are required to provide a diagnostic report with recommendation. It is recommended that students provide a psychoeducational report (3 years old or less) and provide documentation of high school services. Upon application, materials documenting need for services should be sent only to the LD program or unit. Upon acceptance, documentation of need for services should be sent only to the LD program or unit. *Application deadline (institutional):* 8/15. *Application deadline (LD program):* Rolling/continuous for fall and rolling/continuous for spring.

Written Policies Written policy regarding general/basic LD accommodations is outlined in the school's catalog/handbook. Written policies regarding course substitutions, general/basic LD accommodations, reduced course loads, and substitutions and waivers of admissions requirements are available through the program or unit directly.

Sewanee: The University of the South
University Counseling Service

735 University Avenue

Sewanee, TN 37383-1000

http://www.sewanee.edu/

Contact: University Counseling Service. Phone: 931-598-1325. Fax: 931-598-1261. E-mail: parambo@ sewanee.edu.

University Counseling Service Approximately 35 registered undergraduate students were served during 2006–07. The program or unit includes 2 full-time staff members. Counselors and diagnostic specialists are provided through the program or unit. Academic advisers, coaches, regular education teachers, skill tutors, trained peer tutors, and other are provided collaboratively through on-campus or off-campus services.

Summer Program To help prepare for the demands of college, there is an optional summer program prior to entering the school.

Unique Aids and Services Aids, services, or accommodations include career counseling and weekly meetings with faculty.

Subject-Area Tutoring Tutoring is offered one-on-one, in small groups, and in class-size groups for some subjects. Tutoring is provided collaboratively through on-campus or off-campus services via graduate assistants/students, trained peer tutors, and other.

Enrichment Enrichment programs are available through the program or unit for career planning, college survival skills, learning strategies, medication management, stress management, study skills, test taking, and time management. Programs for health and nutrition, math, oral communication skills, practical computer skills, reading, self-advocacy, vocabulary development, and written composition skills are provided collaboratively through on-campus or off-campus services.

Application For admittance to the program or unit, students are required to provide a psychoeducational report (3 years old or less) and provide a neuropsychological report. It is recommended that students provide documentation of high school services. Upon acceptance, documentation of need for services should be sent only to the LD program or unit. *Application deadline (institutional): 2/1. Application deadline (LD program):* Rolling/continuous for fall and rolling/continuous for spring.

Written Policies Written policy regarding general/basic LD accommodations is outlined in the school's catalog/handbook. Written policy regarding general/basic LD accommodations is available through the program or unit directly.

Shippensburg University of Pennsylvania
Office of Disability Services

1871 Old Main Drive

Shippensburg, PA 17257-2299

http://webspace.ship.edu/ods

Contact: Paula Madey, Director, Office of Disability Services. Phone: 717-477-1329. Fax: 717-477-4065. E-mail: pdmade@ship.edu.

Office of Disability Services Approximately 475 registered undergraduate students were served during 2006–07. The program or unit includes 1 full-time and 1 part-time staff member. LD specialists are provided through the program or unit. Academic advisers, coaches, counselors, graduate assistants/students, LD specialists, professional tutors, remediation/learning specialists, skill tutors, strategy tutors, and trained peer tutors are provided collaboratively through on-campus or off-campus services.

Orientation The program or unit offers a mandatory 30-minute orientation for new students before registration, before classes begin, during summer prior to enrollment, during registration, after classes begin, and individually by special arrangement.

Unique Aids and Services Aids, services, or accommodations include career counseling and priority registration.

Assistive Technology Assistive technology is located in the DSS office, the library and includes Kurzweil 3000.

Subject-Area Tutoring Tutoring is offered one-on-one and in small groups for all subjects. Tutoring is provided collaboratively through on-campus or off-campus services via graduate assistants/students, LD specialists, professional tutors, trained peer tutors, and other.

Basic Skills Remediation Remediation is offered one-on-one and in small groups for learning strategies, math, reading, social skills, spelling, study skills, time management, visual processing, and written language. Remediation is provided collaboratively through on-campus or off-campus services via graduate assistants/students, LD specialists, professional tutors, trained peer tutors, and other.

Enrichment Programs for career planning, college survival skills, health and nutrition, learning strategies, math, reading, stress management, study skills, test taking, time management, and written composition skills are provided collaboratively through on-campus or off-campus services.

Application For admittance to the program or unit, students are required to apply to the program directly and provide recent evaluation. It is recommended that students provide a psychoeducational report (3 years old or less) and provide documentation of high school services. Upon acceptance, documentation of need for services should be sent only to the LD program or unit. *Application deadline (institutional):* Continuous. *Application deadline (LD program):* Rolling/continuous for fall and rolling/continuous for spring.

Written Policies Written policy regarding general/basic LD accommodations is available on the program Web site. Written policy regarding general/basic LD accommodations is outlined in the school's catalog/handbook. Written policies regarding course substitutions and general/basic LD accommodations are available through the program or unit directly.

Slippery Rock University of Pennsylvania
Office for Students with Disabilities

1 Morrow Way

Slippery Rock, PA 16057-1383

http://sru.edu

Slippery Rock University of Pennsylvania (continued)

Contact: Ms. Linda M. Smith, Director of Office for Students with Disabilities. Phone: 724-738-2203. Fax: 724-738-4399. E-mail: linda.smith@sru.edu.

Office for Students with Disabilities Approximately 400 registered undergraduate students were served during 2006–07. The program or unit includes 1 full-time staff member. Graduate assistants/students are provided through the program or unit. Graduate assistants/students are provided collaboratively through on-campus or off-campus services.

Unique Aids and Services Aids, services, or accommodations include priority registration.

Assistive Technology Assistive technology is located in the DSS office and includes scanning. Technology training is provided to incoming students.

Subject-Area Tutoring Tutoring is offered one-on-one for some subjects. Tutoring is provided collaboratively through on-campus or off-campus services via trained peer tutors.

Basic Skills Remediation Remediation is offered one-on-one for learning strategies, math, study skills, and time management. Remediation is provided collaboratively through on-campus or off-campus services via trained peer tutors.

Enrichment Programs for learning strategies, math, study skills, test taking, and time management are provided collaboratively through on-campus or off-campus services.

Application It is recommended that students provide documentation of high school services and provide psychological report (after admission). Upon acceptance, documentation of need for services should be sent only to the LD program or unit. *Application deadline (LD program):* Rolling/continuous for fall.

Written Policies Written policy regarding general/basic LD accommodations is available on the program Web site.

Southern Adventist University
Learning Success Services

PO Box 370
Collegedale, TN 37315-0370
http://lss.southern.edu

Contact: Ms. Sheila S. Smith, Disability Services Coordinator. Phone: 423-236-2574. Fax: 423-236-1838. E-mail: sssmith@southern.edu.

Learning Success Services Approximately 40 registered undergraduate students were served during 2006–07. The program or unit includes 3 full-time and 20 part-time staff members. Academic advisers, graduate assistants/students, skill tutors, strategy tutors, teacher trainees, and trained peer tutors are provided through the program or unit. Academic advisers, counselors, diagnostic specialists, and regular education teachers are provided collaboratively through on-campus or off-campus services.

Unique Aids and Services Aids, services, or accommodations include advocates, career counseling, faculty training, instruction on reducing test anxiety.

Assistive Technology Assistive technology is located in the DSS office, the individual student's personal computer and includes digital textbooks/e-text, scanning, and screen readers.

Subject-Area Tutoring Tutoring is offered one-on-one and in small groups for most subjects. Tutoring is provided through the program or unit via computer-based instruction, graduate assistants/students, trained peer tutors, and other.

Diagnostic Testing Testing for intelligence, math, personality, reading, spelling, written language, and other services is provided collaboratively through on-campus or off-campus services.

Basic Skills Remediation Remediation is offered one-on-one and in small groups for computer skills, learning strategies, math, reading, social skills, spelling, spoken language, study skills, time management, and written language. Remediation is provided through the program or unit via computer-based instruction, graduate assistants/students, regular education teachers, special education teachers, teacher trainees, trained peer tutors, and other.

Enrichment Enrichment programs are available through the program or unit for college survival skills, learning strategies, oral communication skills, reading, self-advocacy, stress management, study skills, test taking, time management, vocabulary development, written composition skills, and other. Programs for career planning, college survival skills, health and nutrition, medication management, and stress management are provided collaboratively through on-campus or off-campus services.

Fees *Diagnostic Testing* fee is applicable.

Application For admittance to the program or unit, students are required to provide a psychoeducational report (3 years old or less) and provide psychoeducational testing and DSM-IV diagnosis done on adult-normed instruments. It is recommended that students provide documentation of high school services. Upon application, materials documenting need for services should be sent only to the LD program or unit. Upon acceptance, documentation of need for services should be sent only to the LD program or unit. *Application deadline (institutional):* Continuous. *Application deadline (LD program):* Rolling/continuous for fall and rolling/continuous for spring.

Written Policies Written policy regarding general/basic LD accommodations is available on the program Web site. Written policy regarding general/basic LD accommodations is outlined in the school's catalog/handbook. Written policy regarding general/basic LD accommodations is available through the program or unit directly.

Southern Illinois University Edwardsville
Disability Support Services

Edwardsville, IL 62026-0001
http://www.siue.edu/DSS

Contact: Jim Boyle, Learning Disabilities Specialist. Phone: 618-650-3726 Ext. 2568. Fax: 618-650-5691. E-mail: jboyle@siue.edu.

Disability Support Services Approximately 88 registered undergraduate students were served during 2006–07. The program or unit includes 3 full-time staff members. Academic advisers, diagnostic specialists, and LD specialists are provided through the program or unit. Coaches, counselors, graduate assistants/students, professional tutors, regular education teachers, remediation/learning specialists, skill tutors, and trained peer tutors are provided collaboratively through on-campus or off-campus services.

Orientation The program or unit offers a mandatory 5-hour orientation for new students before classes begin.

Unique Aids and Services Aids, services, or accommodations include faculty training, priority registration, and support groups.

Assistive Technology Assistive technology is located in the DSS office.

Subject-Area Tutoring Tutoring is offered one-on-one and in small groups for most subjects. Tutoring is provided through the program or unit via LD specialists and professional tutors. Tutoring is also provided collaboratively through on-campus or off-campus services via computer-based instruction, graduate assistants/students, and trained peer tutors.

Diagnostic Testing Testing is provided through the program or unit for auditory processing, intelligence, learning styles, math, motor skills, neuropsychological, reading, social skills, spelling, spoken language, study skills, visual processing, and written language.

Basic Skills Remediation Remediation is offered in class-size groups for computer skills, learning strategies, math, reading, spelling, study skills, time management, and written language. Remediation is provided through the program or unit via LD specialists and professional tutors. Remediation is also provided collaboratively through on-campus or off-campus services via computer-based instruction, graduate assistants/students, regular education teachers, and trained peer tutors.

Enrichment Programs for career planning, college survival skills, health and nutrition, learning strategies, math, oral communication skills, practical computer skills, reading, self-advocacy, stress management, study skills, test taking, time management, vocabulary development, and written composition skills are provided collaboratively through on-campus or off-campus services. Credit is offered for career planning, college survival skills, health and nutrition, math, oral communication skills, practical computer skills, reading, study skills, vocabulary development, and written composition skills.

Student Organization New Horizons consists of 15 members.

Application For admittance to the program or unit, students are required to provide a psychoeducational report (3 years old or less) and provide documentation of high school services. Upon acceptance, documentation of need for services should be sent only to the LD program or unit. *Application deadline (institutional): 5/1. Application deadline (LD program):* Rolling/continuous for fall and rolling/continuous for spring.

Written Policies Written policy regarding general/basic LD accommodations is available on the program Web site. Written policies regarding general/basic LD accommodations and substitutions and waivers of admissions requirements are available through the program or unit directly.

Southern Nazarene University
Academic Center for Excellence, Disability Services

6729 Northwest 39th Expressway
Bethany, OK 73008
http://www.snu.edu/

Contact: Mrs. Erin Toler, Director of Disability Services. Phone: 405-491-6694. Fax: 405-717-6286. E-mail: etoler@snu.edu. Head of LD Program: Mrs. Loral McDonald Henck,

Director of Academic Center for Excellence. Phone: 405-789-6400 Ext. 6694. E-mail: lhenck@snu.edu.

Academic Center for Excellence, Disability Services Approximately 40 registered undergraduate students were served during 2006–07. The program or unit includes 1 full-time staff member. LD specialists, remediation/learning specialists, and trained peer tutors are provided through the program or unit. Academic advisers, counselors, diagnostic specialists, skill tutors, strategy tutors, and trained peer tutors are provided collaboratively through on-campus or off-campus services.

Unique Aids and Services Aids, services, or accommodations include advocates, career counseling, faculty training, and personal coach.

Assistive Technology Assistive technology is located in the DSS office and includes digital textbooks/e-text, learning support software, and scanning. Technology training is provided to incoming students.

Subject-Area Tutoring Tutoring is offered one-on-one and in small groups for some subjects. Tutoring is provided through the program or unit via trained peer tutors. Tutoring is also provided collaboratively through on-campus or off-campus services via computer-based instruction and trained peer tutors.

Diagnostic Testing Testing for intelligence, neuropsychological, visual processing, and written language is provided collaboratively through on-campus or off-campus services.

Basic Skills Remediation Remediation is offered one-on-one, in small groups, and in class-size groups for learning strategies, math, reading, study skills, time management, and written language. Remediation is provided through the program or unit via trained peer tutors. Remediation is also provided collaboratively through on-campus or off-campus services via computer-based instruction and trained peer tutors.

Enrichment Enrichment programs are available through the program or unit for learning strategies, reading, self-advocacy, stress management, study skills, test taking, time management, vocabulary development, and written composition skills. Programs for career planning, college survival skills, health and nutrition, math, medication management, oral communication skills, practical computer skills, self-advocacy, stress management, study skills, test taking, time management, and written composition skills are provided collaboratively through on-campus or off-campus services. Credit is offered for college survival skills, study skills, and written composition skills.

Fees *Diagnostic Testing* fee is $150 to $2000.

Application For admittance to the program or unit, students are required to provide a psychoeducational report (3 years old or less). It is recommended that students apply to the program directly, provide documentation of high school services, and provide testing evaluations/results. Upon application, materials documenting need for services should be sent only to the LD program or unit. Upon acceptance, documentation of need for services should be sent only to the LD program or unit. *Application deadline (institutional): 8/15. Application deadline (LD program):* Rolling/continuous for fall and rolling/continuous for spring.

Written Policies Written policy regarding general/basic LD accommodations is available on the program Web site. Written policies regarding course substitutions, substitutions and waivers of admissions requirements, and substitutions and waivers of graduation requirements are outlined in the school's catalog/handbook. Written policies regarding course substitutions, general/basic LD accommodations, substitutions and waivers of admissions requirements, and substitutions and waivers of graduation requirements are available through the program or unit directly.

Southern Oregon University
Disability Services for Students

1250 Siskiyou Boulevard
Ashland, OR 97520
http://www.sou.edu/access/dss

Contact: Ms. Theresa Lowrie, Director of Disability Services for Students. Phone: 541-552-6213. Fax: 541-552-8462. E-mail: lowriet@sou.edu.

Disability Services for Students Approximately 85 registered undergraduate students were served during 2006–07. The program or unit includes 1 full-time and 4 part-time staff members. Graduate assistants/students and other are provided through the program or unit. Academic advisers, counselors, LD specialists, regular education teachers, remediation/learning specialists, skill tutors, strategy tutors, and trained peer tutors are provided collaboratively through on-campus or off-campus services.

Unique Aids and Services Aids, services, or accommodations include priority registration.

Assistive Technology Assistive technology is located in campus labs, the DSS office, a special lab, equipment loaned to the individual student and includes digital textbooks/e-text, learning support software, and scanning. Technology training is provided to incoming students.

Subject-Area Tutoring Tutoring is offered one-on-one and in small groups for all subjects. Tutoring is provided collaboratively through on-campus or off-campus services via computer-based instruction, professional tutors, and trained peer tutors.

Basic Skills Remediation Remediation is offered in class-size groups for learning strategies, math, study skills, time management, and written language. Remediation is provided collaboratively through on-campus or off-campus services via computer-based instruction, regular education teachers, and trained peer tutors.

Enrichment Programs for career planning, college survival skills, health and nutrition, learning strategies, medication management, self-advocacy, stress management, study skills, test taking, and time management are provided collaboratively through on-campus or off-campus services. Credit is offered for career planning, college survival skills, learning strategies, stress management, study skills, test taking, and time management.

Student Organization Challenge Club consists of 12 members.

Application For admittance to the program or unit, students are required to provide a psychoeducational report (3 years old or less). It is recommended that students provide documentation of high school services. Upon acceptance, documentation of need for services should be sent only to the LD program or unit. *Application deadline (institutional):* Continuous. *Application deadline (LD program):* Rolling/continuous for fall and rolling/continuous for spring.

Written Policies Written policies regarding course substitutions and general/basic LD accommodations are available on the program Web site. Written policies regarding course substitutions, general/ basic LD accommodations, and substitutions and waivers of admissions requirements are available through the program or unit directly.

Southern University and Agricultural and Mechanical College
Office of Disability Services (ODS)

Baton Rouge, LA 70813
http://www.subr.edu/

Contact: Prof. Patricia Rowley Hebert, Coordinator, Office of Disability Services. Phone: 225-771-3950. Fax: 225-771-5652. E-mail: patricia_hebert@subr.edu.

Office of Disability Services (ODS) Approximately 243 registered undergraduate students were served during 2006–07. The program or unit includes 1 full-time and 3 part-time staff members. Academic advisers, coaches, counselors, graduate assistants/students, LD specialists, regular education teachers, remediation/learning specialists, skill tutors, special education teachers, teacher trainees, and trained peer tutors are provided collaboratively through on-campus or off-campus services.

Orientation The program or unit offers an optional varying length orientation for new students individually by special arrangement.

Unique Aids and Services Aids, services, or accommodations include advocates, career counseling, faculty training, and priority registration.

Assistive Technology Assistive technology is located in campus labs and includes learning support software and scanning.

Subject-Area Tutoring Tutoring is offered one-on-one and in small groups for most subjects. Tutoring is provided collaboratively through on-campus or off-campus services via computer-based instruction, graduate assistants/students, LD specialists, professional tutors, and trained peer tutors.

Basic Skills Remediation Remediation is offered in small groups for auditory processing, computer skills, learning strategies, math, reading, spelling, spoken language, study skills, time management, visual processing, and written language. Remediation is provided collaboratively through on-campus or off-campus services via computer-based instruction, graduate assistants/students, LD specialists, regular education teachers, special education teachers, teacher trainees, and trained peer tutors.

Enrichment Enrichment programs are available through the program or unit for career planning, college survival skills, health and nutrition, learning strategies, self-advocacy, stress management, study skills, and time management. Programs for career planning, college survival skills, health and nutrition, learning strategies, math, medication management, oral communication skills, practical computer skills, reading, stress management, study skills, test taking, time management, vocabulary development, and written composition skills are provided collaboratively through on-campus or off-campus services. Credit is offered for health and nutrition, oral communication skills, practical computer skills, and written composition skills.

Application For admittance to the program or unit, students are required to apply to the program directly and provide a psychoeducational report (3 years old or less). It is recommended that students provide documentation of high school services. Upon application, materials documenting need for services should be sent only to the LD program or unit. Upon acceptance, documentation of need for services should be sent only to the LD program or unit. *Application deadline (institutional):* 7/1. *Application deadline (LD program):* Rolling/continuous for fall and rolling/continuous for spring.

Written Policies Written policy regarding general/basic LD accommodations is available through the program or unit directly.

Southern Utah University
Disability Support Office

351 West University Boulevard

Cedar City, UT 84720-2498

http://www.suu.edu/

Contact: Mrs. Carmen Rosa Alldredge, Coordinator of Services for Students with Disabilities. Phone: 435-865-8022. Fax: 435-865-8235. E-mail: alldredge@suu.edu.

Disability Support Office Approximately 43 registered undergraduate students were served during 2006–07. The program or unit includes 2 full-time staff members. Academic advisers, coaches, counselors, diagnostic specialists, regular education teachers, remediation/learning specialists, skill tutors, and trained peer tutors are provided collaboratively through on-campus or off-campus services.

Orientation The program or unit offers an optional 2-day orientation for new students before registration, before classes begin, and every year for sophomores, juniors, and seniors.

Unique Aids and Services Aids, services, or accommodations include career counseling, faculty training, priority registration, and support groups.

Subject-Area Tutoring Tutoring is offered in small groups for most subjects. Tutoring is provided collaboratively through on-campus or off-campus services via computer-based instruction, graduate assistants/students, and trained peer tutors.

Basic Skills Remediation Remediation is offered in small groups for learning strategies, math, reading, spelling, study skills, time management, and written language. Remediation is provided collaboratively through on-campus or off-campus services via teacher trainees and trained peer tutors.

Enrichment Programs for career planning, college survival skills, health and nutrition, learning strategies, math, medication management, oral communication skills, practical computer skills, reading, self-advocacy, stress management, study skills, test taking, time management, vocabulary development, and written composition skills are provided collaboratively through on-campus or off-campus services. Credit is offered for career planning, college survival skills, health and nutrition, learning strategies, math, stress management, study skills, test taking, time management, and written composition skills.

Student Organization Elite Achievers Club consists of 12 members.

Fees *LD Program or Service* fee is $600 to $1800 (fee varies according to academic program).

Application For admittance to the program or unit, students are required to provide a psychoeducational report (3 years old or less). It is recommended that students provide documentation of high school services and provide educational psychological evaluation. Upon application, materials documenting need for services should be sent only to the LD program or unit. Upon acceptance, documentation of need for services should be sent only to the LD program or unit. *Application deadline (institutional):* 8/1. *Application deadline (LD program):* 7/1 for fall. 12/1 for spring.

Written Policies Written policies regarding general/basic LD accommodations, substitutions and waivers of admissions requirements, and substitutions and waivers of graduation requirements are available on the program Web site. Written policies regarding general/basic LD accommodations, substitutions and waivers of admissions requirements, and substitutions and waivers of graduation requirements are outlined in the school's catalog/handbook. Written policies regarding general/basic LD accommodations, substitutions and waivers of admissions requirements, and substitutions and waivers of graduation requirements are available through the program or unit directly.

South University

709 Mall Boulevard

Savannah, GA 31406-4805

http://www.southuniversity.edu/

Contact: Mrs. Lisa J. Breitberg, Counselor, Director of Disabilities. Phone: 912-201-8170. Fax: 912-201-8070. E-mail: lbreitberg@southuniversity.edu.

The program or unit includes 1 part-time staff member. Counselors, professional tutors, regular education teachers, remediation/learning specialists, skill tutors, and other are provided collaboratively through on-campus or off-campus services.

Unique Aids and Services Aids, services, or accommodations include career counseling, counseling support.

Assistive Technology Assistive technology is located in campus labs and includes Recording for the Blind and Dyslexic.

Subject-Area Tutoring Tutoring is offered one-on-one and in small groups for most subjects. Tutoring is provided collaboratively through on-campus or off-campus services via computer-based instruction, graduate assistants/students, professional tutors, and trained peer tutors.

Basic Skills Remediation Remediation is offered one-on-one, in small groups, and in class-size groups for learning strategies, math, study skills, time management, and written language. Remediation is provided collaboratively through on-campus or off-campus services via regular education teachers.

Enrichment Programs for career planning, college survival skills, health and nutrition, learning strategies, oral communication skills, self-advocacy, stress management, study skills, test taking, and time management are provided collaboratively through on-campus or off-campus services.

Application It is recommended that students provide a psychoeducational report (5 years old or less) and provide documentation of high school services. Upon application, materials documenting need for services should be sent only to the LD program or unit. Upon acceptance, documentation of need for services should be sent to both admissions and the LD program or unit. *Application deadline (institutional):* Continuous. *Application deadline (LD program):* Rolling/continuous for fall and rolling/continuous for spring.

Written Policies Written policies regarding general/basic LD accommodations and substitutions and waivers of admissions requirements are available on the program Web site. Written policies regarding general/basic LD accommodations and substitutions and waivers of admissions requirements are outlined in the school's catalog/handbook. Written policy regarding general/basic LD accommodations is available through the program or unit directly.

Southwest Baptist University
Special Services

1600 University Avenue

Bolivar, MO 65613-2597

http://www.sbuniv.edu/

Contact: Dana Steward, University Success Center Director. Phone: 417-328-1425. Fax: 417-328-2091. E-mail: dsteward@sbuniv.edu.

Special Services Approximately 18 registered undergraduate students were served during 2006–07. The program or unit includes 1 part-time staff member. Academic advisers, regular education teachers, and remediation/learning specialists are provided collaboratively through on-campus or off-campus services.

Unique Aids and Services Aids, services, or accommodations include peer mentoring.

Subject-Area Tutoring Tutoring is offered one-on-one, in small groups, and in class-size groups for some subjects. Tutoring is provided collaboratively through on-campus or off-campus services via trained peer tutors and other.

Basic Skills Remediation Remediation is offered in class-size groups for learning strategies, study skills, time management, written language, and math. Remediation is provided collaboratively through on-campus or off-campus services via regular education teachers and trained peer tutors.

Enrichment Programs for career planning, college survival skills, learning strategies, study skills, test taking, time management, and other are provided collaboratively through on-campus or off-campus services.

Application For admittance to the program or unit, students are required to provide a psychoeducational report (3 years old or less). It is recommended that students apply to the program directly and provide documentation of high school services. Upon application, materials documenting need for services should be sent only to the LD program or unit. Upon acceptance, documentation of need for services should be sent only to the LD program or unit. *Application deadline (institutional):* Continuous. *Application deadline (LD program):* Rolling/continuous for fall and rolling/continuous for spring.

Written Policies Written policy regarding general/basic LD accommodations is outlined in the school's catalog/handbook. Written policy regarding general/basic LD accommodations is available through the program or unit directly.

Southwestern Adventist University
Office for Students with Disabilities and Academic Support

100 Hillcrest Drive

Keene, TX 76059

http://www.swau.edu/

Contact: Mrs. Kim A. Hutchinson, Director of Students With Disabilities and Academic Support. Phone: 817-202-6255. E-mail: hutchinsonk@swau.edu.

Office for Students with Disabilities and Academic Support Approximately 20 registered undergraduate students were served during 2006–07. The program or unit includes 1 part-time staff member. Academic advisers, professional tutors, skill tutors, strategy tutors, and trained peer tutors are provided through the program or unit. Academic advisers, counselors, graduate assistants/students, regular education teachers, and trained peer tutors are provided collaboratively through on-campus or off-campus services.

Unique Aids and Services Aids, services, or accommodations include career counseling, faculty training, and personal coach.

Subject-Area Tutoring Tutoring is offered one-on-one for most subjects. Tutoring is provided through the program or unit via professional tutors and trained peer tutors.

Basic Skills Remediation Remediation is offered one-on-one for learning strategies, math, reading, study skills, time management, and written language. Remediation is provided through the program or unit via professional tutors and trained peer tutors. Remediation is also provided collaboratively through on-campus or off-campus services via regular education teachers.

Enrichment Enrichment programs are available through the program or unit for career planning, college survival skills, learning strategies, study skills, test taking, and time management. Programs for college survival skills, health and nutrition, math, oral communication skills, practical computer skills, and written composition skills are provided collaboratively through on-campus or off-campus services. Credit is offered for college survival skills, health and nutrition, math, oral communication skills, practical computer skills, and written composition skills.

Application For admittance to the program or unit, students are required to apply to the program directly and provide a psychoeducational report. It is recommended that students provide documentation of high school services. Upon application, materials documenting need for services should be sent only to the LD program or unit. Upon acceptance, documentation of need for services should be sent only to the LD program or unit. *Application deadline (LD program):* Rolling/continuous for fall and rolling/continuous for spring.

Written Policies Written policy regarding general/basic LD accommodations is available through the program or unit directly.

Southwestern College
Disability Services Office

100 College Street

Winfield, KS 67156-2499

http://www.sckans.edu/acsup

Contact: Dan Falk, Director of Disability Services. Phone: 620-229-6267. E-mail: dan.falk@sckans.edu.

Disability Services Office Approximately 12 registered undergraduate students were served during 2006–07. The program or unit includes 1 full-time staff member. Trained peer tutors and other are provided through the program or unit. Academic advisers, LD specialists, regular education teachers, trained peer tutors, and other are provided collaboratively through on-campus or off-campus services.

Assistive Technology Assistive technology is located in the DSS office and includes digital textbooks/e-text, learning support software, and scanning. Technology training is provided to incoming students.

Subject-Area Tutoring Tutoring is offered one-on-one. Tutoring is provided through the program or unit via trained peer tutors. Tutoring is also provided collaboratively through on-campus or off-campus services via trained peer tutors and other.

Basic Skills Remediation Remediation is offered one-on-one for learning strategies, study skills, and time management. Remediation is provided through the program or unit. Remediation is also provided collaboratively through on-campus or off-campus services.

Application For admittance to the program or unit, students are required to apply to the program directly, provide a psychoeducational report (3 years old or less), and provide documentation of high school services. Upon application, materials documenting need for services should be sent only to the LD program or unit. Upon acceptance, documentation of need for services should be sent only to the LD program or unit. *Application deadline (institutional):* 8/25. *Application deadline (LD program):* Rolling/continuous for fall and rolling/continuous for spring.

Written Policies Written policy regarding general/basic LD accommodations is available through the program or unit directly.

Southwestern University
Center for Academic Success

1001 East University Avenue

Georgetown, TX 78626

http://www.southwestern.edu/academic/acser-home.html

Contact: Ms. Kimele Carter, Academic and Access Resources Coordinator. Phone: 512-863-1286. Fax: 512-863-1744. E-mail: carterk@southwestern.edu.

Center for Academic Success Approximately 50 registered undergraduate students were served during 2006–07. The program or unit includes 4 full-time and 7 part-time staff members. Academic advisers and trained peer tutors are provided through the program or unit. Counselors and diagnostic specialists are provided collaboratively through on-campus or off-campus services.

Unique Aids and Services Aids, services, or accommodations include advocates, faculty training, priority registration, extended testing time.

Assistive Technology Assistive technology is located in the individual student's portable system and includes digital textbooks/e-text and scanning.

Subject-Area Tutoring Tutoring is offered one-on-one for some subjects. Tutoring is provided through the program or unit via trained peer tutors and other.

Basic Skills Remediation Remediation is offered one-on-one for learning strategies, reading, social skills, study skills, time management, written language, and other areas as needed. Remediation is provided through the program or unit via trained peer tutors and other.

Enrichment Enrichment programs are available through the program or unit for college survival skills, self-advocacy, and time management.

Student Organization Advocates consists of 15 members.

Application For admittance to the program or unit, students are required to provide a psychoeducational report (3 years old or less). It is recommended that students provide documentation of high school services. Upon application, materials documenting need for services should be sent only to admissions with institutional application materials. Upon acceptance, documentation of need for services should be sent only to the LD program or unit. *Application deadline (institutional):* 2/15. *Application deadline (LD program):* Rolling/continuous for fall and rolling/continuous for spring.

Written Policies Written policies regarding course substitutions, general/basic LD accommodations, reduced course loads, substitutions and waivers of admissions requirements, and substitutions and waivers of graduation requirements are available on the program Web site. Written policies regarding course substitutions, general/basic LD accommodations, reduced course loads, substitutions and waivers of admissions requirements, and substitutions and waivers of graduation requirements are outlined in the school's catalog/handbook. Written policies regarding course substitutions, general/basic LD accommodations, reduced course loads, substitutions and waivers of admissions requirements, and substitutions and waivers of graduation requirements are available through the program or unit directly.

Spalding University
Disability Services

851 South Fourth Street

Louisville, KY 40203-2188

http://www.spalding.edu

Contact: Kay Veter, Director of Student Success and Engagement. Phone: 502-585-9911 Ext. 2239. Fax: 502-588-7170. E-mail: kvetter@spalding.edu.

Disability Services Approximately 150 registered undergraduate students were served during 2006–07. The program or unit includes 1 full-time and 1 part-time staff member. Graduate assistants/students and LD specialists are provided through the program or unit. Academic advisers, coaches, counselors, diagnostic specialists, and professional tutors are provided collaboratively through on-campus or off-campus services.

Unique Aids and Services Aids, services, or accommodations include support groups.

Assistive Technology Assistive technology is located in campus labs, the DSS office, a special lab and includes digital textbooks/e-text, learning support software, and scanning. Technology training is provided to incoming students.

Subject-Area Tutoring Tutoring is offered one-on-one for most subjects. Tutoring is provided collaboratively through on-campus or off-campus services via computer-based instruction and graduate assistants/students.

Diagnostic Testing Testing for intelligence, learning strategies, learning styles, math, neuropsychological, personality, reading, social skills, study skills, and written language is provided collaboratively through on-campus or off-campus services.

Basic Skills Remediation Remediation is offered in class-size groups for math. Remediation is provided collaboratively through on-campus or off-campus services via computer-based instruction and regular education teachers.

Spalding University (continued)

Enrichment Enrichment programs are available through the program or unit for college survival skills, math, stress management, and written composition skills. Programs for career planning, college survival skills, math, stress management, and written composition skills are provided collaboratively through on-campus or off-campus services. Credit is offered for college survival skills and math.

Application For admittance to the program or unit, students are required to apply to the program directly and provide a psychoeducational report (4 years old or less). It is recommended that students provide documentation of high school services. Upon application, materials documenting need for services should be sent to both admissions and the LD program or unit. Upon acceptance, documentation of need for services should be sent only to the LD program or unit. *Application deadline (institutional):* Continuous. *Application deadline (LD program):* Rolling/continuous for fall and rolling/continuous for spring.

Written Policies Written policy regarding general/basic LD accommodations is outlined in the school's catalog/handbook. Written policy regarding general/basic LD accommodations is available through the program or unit directly.

Springfield College
Office of Student Support Services

263 Alden Street
Springfield, MA 01109-3797
http://www.spfldcol.edu/homepage/dept.nsf/studentSupport

Contact: Ms. Deb Dickens, Director of Student Support Services. Phone: 413-748-3768. Fax: 413-748-3937. E-mail: ddickens@spfldcol.edu.

Office of Student Support Services Approximately 125 registered undergraduate students were served during 2006–07. The program or unit includes 1 full-time and 1 part-time staff member. Academic advisers, coaches, and LD specialists are provided through the program or unit. Academic advisers and trained peer tutors are provided collaboratively through on-campus or off-campus services.

Unique Aids and Services Aids, services, or accommodations include advocates and personal coach.

Assistive Technology Assistive technology is located in campus labs, the DSS office and includes digital textbooks/e-text and scanning.

Subject-Area Tutoring Tutoring is offered one-on-one and in small groups for most subjects. Tutoring is provided through the program or unit via LD specialists. Tutoring is also provided collaboratively through on-campus or off-campus services via graduate assistants/students and trained peer tutors.

Basic Skills Remediation Remediation is offered one-on-one for computer skills, learning strategies, study skills, and time management. Remediation is provided through the program or unit via LD specialists.

Enrichment Enrichment programs are available through the program or unit for learning strategies, practical computer skills, self-advocacy, study skills, test taking, and time management. Programs for career planning, study skills, test taking, time management, and written composition skills are provided collaboratively through on-campus or off-campus services.

Application For admittance to the program or unit, students are required to provide a psychoeducational report (3 years old or less). It is recommended that students provide documentation of high school services. Upon acceptance, documentation of need for services should be sent only to the LD program or unit. *Application deadline (institutional):* 4/1. *Application deadline (LD program):* Rolling/continuous for fall and rolling/continuous for spring.

Written Policies Written policy regarding general/basic LD accommodations is available on the program Web site. Written policies regarding course substitutions, general/basic LD accommodations, reduced course loads, substitutions and waivers of admissions requirements, and substitutions and waivers of graduation requirements are outlined in the school's catalog/handbook. Written policy regarding general/basic LD accommodations is available through the program or unit directly.

State University of New York at Fredonia
Disability Support Services for Students

Fredonia, NY 14063-1136
http://www.fredonia.edu/tlc/dsshandbook.html

Contact: Mr. Adam D. Hino, Coordinator of Disability Support Services for Students. Phone: 716-673-3270. Fax: 716-673-3801. E-mail: adam.hino@fredonia.edu.

Disability Support Services for Students Approximately 66 registered undergraduate students were served during 2006–07. The program or unit includes 1 full-time staff member. Trained peer tutors and other are provided collaboratively through on-campus or off-campus services.

Assistive Technology Assistive technology is located in the DSS office and includes digital textbooks/e-text and scanning.

Subject-Area Tutoring Tutoring is offered one-on-one and in small groups for most subjects. Tutoring is provided through the program or unit via trained peer tutors.

Enrichment Enrichment programs are available through the program or unit for self-advocacy. Programs for oral communication skills and stress management are provided collaboratively through on-campus or off-campus services.

Application For admittance to the program or unit, students are required to provide a psychoeducational report. It is recommended that students provide documentation of high school services. Upon acceptance, documentation of need for services should be sent only to the LD program or unit. *Application deadline (institutional):* Continuous. *Application deadline (LD program):* Rolling/continuous for fall and rolling/continuous for spring.

Written Policies Written policy regarding general/basic LD accommodations is available on the program Web site. Written policy regarding general/basic LD accommodations is outlined in the school's catalog/handbook. Written policy regarding general/basic LD accommodations is available through the program or unit directly.

State University of New York College at Brockport
Office for Students with Disabilities

350 New Campus Drive

Brockport, NY 14420-2997

http://www.brockport.edu/osd/

Contact: Mrs. Maryellen Post, Coordinator. Phone: 585-395-5409. Fax: 585-395-5291. E-mail: mpost@brockport.edu.

Office for Students with Disabilities Approximately 150 registered undergraduate students were served during 2006–07. The program or unit includes 2 full-time staff members and 1 part-time staff member. Counselors and graduate assistants/students are provided through the program or unit. Academic advisers, counselors, diagnostic specialists, regular education teachers, skill tutors, and strategy tutors are provided collaboratively through on-campus or off-campus services.

Unique Aids and Services Aids, services, or accommodations include faculty training.

Assistive Technology Assistive technology is located in campus labs, the DSS office and includes digital textbooks/e-text and learning support software.

Subject-Area Tutoring Tutoring is offered one-on-one. Tutoring is provided collaboratively through on-campus or off-campus services via graduate assistants/students and trained peer tutors.

Basic Skills Remediation Remediation is offered one-on-one and in small groups for computer skills, learning strategies, study skills, time management, and note-taking skills. Remediation is provided collaboratively through on-campus or off-campus services via regular education teachers and other.

Enrichment Programs for career planning, college survival skills, health and nutrition, learning strategies, practical computer skills, stress management, study skills, test taking, time management, and written composition skills are provided collaboratively through on-campus or off-campus services.

Application For admittance to the program or unit, students are required to provide a psychoeducational report. It is recommended that students provide documentation of high school services. Upon acceptance, documentation of need for services should be sent only to the LD program or unit. *Application deadline (institutional):* Continuous. *Application deadline (LD program):* Rolling/continuous for fall and rolling/continuous for spring.

Written Policies Written policy regarding general/basic LD accommodations is available on the program Web site. Written policy regarding general/basic LD accommodations is outlined in the school's catalog/handbook. Written policies regarding course substitutions and general/basic LD accommodations are available through the program or unit directly.

State University of New York College at Cortland

PO Box 2000

Cortland, NY 13045

http://www.cortland.edu/

Contact: Ms. Ute G. Gomez, Coordinator, Student Disability Services. Phone: 607-753-2066. Fax: 607-753-5495. E-mail: gomezu@cortland.edu.

Approximately 300 registered undergraduate students were served during 2006–07. The program or unit includes 2 full-time staff members and 1 part-time staff member. Counselors are provided through the program or unit. Academic advisers, counselors, graduate assistants/students, professional tutors, skill tutors, and other are provided collaboratively through on-campus or off-campus services.

Orientation The program or unit offers an optional orientation for new students before classes begin and individually by special arrangement.

Unique Aids and Services Aids, services, or accommodations include career counseling, test-taking center.

Assistive Technology Assistive technology is located in a special lab and includes digital textbooks/e-text, learning support software, and books on tape, Kurzweil Reader. Technology training is provided to incoming students.

Subject-Area Tutoring Tutoring is offered one-on-one, in small groups, and in class-size groups for most subjects. Tutoring is provided through the program or unit via computer-based instruction and other. Tutoring is also provided collaboratively through on-campus or off-campus services via computer-based instruction, graduate assistants/students, professional tutors, and trained peer tutors.

Enrichment Programs for career planning, health and nutrition, learning strategies, medication management, practical computer skills, stress management, study skills, test taking, time management, and written composition skills are provided collaboratively through on-campus or off-campus services.

Application For admittance to the program or unit, students are required to apply to the program directly and provide a psychoeducational report (3 years old or less). It is recommended that students provide documentation of high school services. Upon acceptance, documentation of need for services should be sent only to the LD program or unit. *Application deadline (institutional):* Continuous. *Application deadline (LD program):* Rolling/continuous for fall and rolling/continuous for spring.

Written Policies Written policies regarding course substitutions, general/basic LD accommodations, substitutions and waivers of admissions requirements, and substitutions and waivers of graduation requirements are available on the program Web site. Written policy regarding general/basic LD accommodations is outlined in the school's catalog/handbook. Written policies regarding course substitutions, general/basic LD accommodations, reduced course loads, substitutions and waivers of admissions requirements, and substitutions and waivers of graduation requirements are available through the program or unit directly.

State University of New York College at Geneseo
Office of Disability Services

1 College Circle

Geneseo, NY 14454-1401

http://disability.geneseo.edu

Contact: Dr. Tabitha Buggie-Hunt, Director, Office of Disability Services. Phone: 585-245-5112. Fax: 585-245-5032. E-mail: tbuggieh@geneseo.edu.

Office of Disability Services Approximately 100 registered undergraduate students were served during 2006–07. The program or unit includes 1 full-time staff member.

Assistive Technology Assistive technology is located in the DSS office and includes digital textbooks/e-text and scanning.

Subject-Area Tutoring Tutoring is offered one-on-one and in small groups for most subjects. Tutoring is provided collaboratively through on-campus or off-campus services via trained peer tutors and other.

Application For admittance to the program or unit, students are required to provide a psychoeducational report (5 years old or less). Upon acceptance, documentation of need for services should be sent only to the LD program or unit. *Application deadline (institutional):* 1/15. *Application deadline (LD program):* Rolling/continuous for fall and rolling/continuous for spring.

Written Policies Written policies regarding course substitutions, general/basic LD accommodations, and substitutions and waivers of admissions requirements are available on the program Web site. Written policies regarding general/basic LD accommodations and substitutions and waivers of admissions requirements are available through the program or unit directly.

State University of New York College at Potsdam

44 Pierrepont Avenue

Potsdam, NY 13676

http://www.potsdam.edu/

Contact: Ms. Sharon House, Director of Accommodative Services. Phone: 315-267-3267. Fax: 315-267-3267. E-mail: housese@potsdam.edu.

Approximately 113 registered undergraduate students were served during 2006–07. The program or unit includes 1 full-time staff member. Academic advisers, counselors, and trained peer tutors are provided collaboratively through on-campus or off-campus services.

Unique Aids and Services Aids, services, or accommodations include career counseling and faculty training.

Assistive Technology Assistive technology is located in the DSS office, the library and includes digital textbooks/e-text and learning support software.

Subject-Area Tutoring Tutoring is offered one-on-one and in small groups for most subjects. Tutoring is provided collaboratively through on-campus or off-campus services via trained peer tutors.

Enrichment Programs for career planning, college survival skills, learning strategies, math, stress management, study skills, test taking, time management, and written composition skills are provided collaboratively through on-campus or off-campus services.

Application For admittance to the program or unit, students are required to provide a psychoeducational report. It is recommended that students provide documentation of high school services. Upon acceptance, documentation of need for services should be sent only to the LD program or unit. *Application deadline (institutional):* Continuous.

Written Policies Written policy regarding general/basic LD accommodations is available on the program Web site. Written policy regarding general/basic LD accommodations is outlined in the school's catalog/handbook. Written policy regarding general/basic LD accommodations is available through the program or unit directly.

State University of New York College of Environmental Science and Forestry
Office of Student Life

1 Forestry Drive

Syracuse, NY 13210-2779

http://www.esf.edu/

Contact: Mr. Thomas O. Slocum, Director of Career and Counseling Services. Phone: 315-470-6660. Fax: 315-470-4728. E-mail: toslocum@esf.edu.

Office of Student Life Approximately 33 registered undergraduate students were served during 2006–07. The program or unit includes 4 full-time staff members. Coaches, diagnostic specialists, LD specialists, professional tutors, remediation/learning specialists, skill tutors, special education teachers, strategy tutors, teacher trainees, and trained peer tutors are provided through the program or unit. Academic advisers, counselors, graduate assistants/students, and regular education teachers are provided collaboratively through on-campus or off-campus services.

Unique Aids and Services Aids, services, or accommodations include advocates and career counseling.

Assistive Technology Assistive technology is located in the DSS office and includes digital textbooks/e-text.

Subject-Area Tutoring Tutoring is offered one-on-one and in small groups for some subjects. Tutoring is provided through the program or unit via LD specialists. Tutoring is also provided collaboratively through on-campus or off-campus services via graduate assistants/students and trained peer tutors.

Application For admittance to the program or unit, students are required to provide a psychoeducational report (3 years old or less). It is recommended that students provide documentation of high school services. Upon acceptance, documentation of need for services should be sent only to the LD program or unit. *Application deadline (institutional):* 12/1. *Application deadline (LD program):* Rolling/continuous for fall and rolling/continuous for spring.

Written Policies Written policy regarding general/basic LD accommodations is outlined in the school's catalog/handbook. Written policy regarding reduced course loads is available through the program or unit directly.

Stephen F. Austin State University
Disability Services

1936 North Street

Nacogdoches, TX 75962

http://www2.sfasu.edu/disabilityservices/

Contact: Mr. Chuck Lopez, Director of Disability Services. Phone: 936-468-3004. Fax: 936-468-1368. E-mail: clopez@sfasu.edu.

Disability Services Approximately 65 registered undergraduate students were served during 2006–07. Counselors, graduate assistants/students, professional tutors, skill tutors, and strategy tutors are provided through the program or unit. Academic advisers, coaches, counselors, diagnostic specialists, graduate assistants/students, LD specialists, professional tutors, regular education teachers, remediation/learning specialists, skill tutors, special education teachers, strategy tutors, teacher trainees, and trained peer tutors are provided collaboratively through on-campus or off-campus services.

Unique Aids and Services Aids, services, or accommodations include career counseling, faculty training, personal coach, and priority registration.

Assistive Technology Assistive technology includes digital textbooks/e-text.

Subject-Area Tutoring Tutoring is offered one-on-one, in small groups, and in class-size groups for all subjects. Tutoring is provided through the program or unit via professional tutors and trained peer tutors. Tutoring is also provided collaboratively through on-campus or off-campus services via computer-based instruction, graduate assistants/students, professional tutors, and trained peer tutors.

Diagnostic Testing Testing is provided through the program or unit for learning strategies and learning styles. Testing for auditory processing, handwriting, intelligence, learning strategies, learning styles, math, motor skills, neuropsychological, personality, reading, social skills, spelling, spoken language, study skills, visual processing, and written language is provided collaboratively through on-campus or off-campus services.

Basic Skills Remediation Remediation is offered in class-size groups for learning strategies, math, reading, study skills, time management, and written language. Remediation is provided through the program or unit via trained peer tutors. Remediation is also provided collaboratively through on-campus or off-campus services via professional tutors, regular education teachers, trained peer tutors, and other.

Enrichment Enrichment programs are available through the program or unit for career planning, college survival skills, learning strategies, self-advocacy, stress management, study skills, test taking, and time management. Programs for career planning, college survival skills, health and nutrition, math, medication management, oral communication skills, practical computer skills, reading, self-advocacy, stress management, study skills, test taking, time management, vocabulary development, and written composition skills are provided collaboratively through on-campus or off-campus services. Credit is offered for college survival skills, learning strategies, math, oral communication skills, practical computer skills, reading, study skills, test taking, time management, vocabulary development, and written composition skills.

Fees *Diagnostic Testing* fee is $0 to $800.

Application For admittance to the program or unit, students are required to apply to the program directly and provide a psychoeducational report (3 years old or less). It is recommended that students provide documentation of high school services. Upon application, materials documenting need for services should be sent only to the LD program or unit. Upon acceptance, documentation of need for services should be sent only to the LD program or unit. *Application deadline (institutional):* Continuous. *Application deadline (LD program):* Rolling/continuous for fall and rolling/continuous for spring.

Written Policies Written policies regarding course substitutions, general/basic LD accommodations, and substitutions and waivers of graduation requirements are available on the program Web site. Written policy regarding general/basic LD accommodations is outlined in the school's catalog/handbook. Written policies regarding course substitutions, general/basic LD accommodations, and substitutions and waivers of graduation requirements are available through the program or unit directly.

Sterling College
Learning Support Service

PO Box 72

Craftsbury Common, VT 05827-0072

http://www.sterlingcollege.edu

Contact: Gwyn Harris, Director of Admissions. Phone: 800-648-3591 Ext. 1. Fax: 802-586-2596. E-mail: admissions@sterlingcollege.edu. Head of LD Program: Leland Peterson, Coordinator of Learning Support and Counseling Services. Phone: 802-586-7711 Ext. 120. Fax: 802-586-2596. E-mail: lpeterson@sterlingcollege.edu.

Learning Support Service Approximately 12 registered undergraduate students were served during 2006–07. The program or unit includes 1 full-time staff member. Counselors and strategy tutors are provided through the program or unit. Academic advisers and trained peer tutors are provided collaboratively through on-campus or off-campus services.

Unique Aids and Services Aids, services, or accommodations include career counseling, support groups, and weekly meetings with faculty.

Subject-Area Tutoring Tutoring is offered one-on-one and in small groups for some subjects. Tutoring is provided through the program or unit via other. Tutoring is also provided collaboratively through on-campus or off-campus services via professional tutors, trained peer tutors, and other.

Basic Skills Remediation Remediation is offered in small groups and in class-size groups for learning strategies, math, study skills, time management, and written language. Remediation is provided through the program or unit. Remediation is also provided collaboratively through on-campus or off-campus services via regular education teachers, trained peer tutors, and other.

Enrichment Enrichment programs are available through the program or unit for learning strategies, self-advocacy, stress management, study skills, and time management. Programs for career planning, health and nutrition, math, medication management, written composition skills, and other are provided collaboratively through on-campus or off-campus services. Credit is offered for career planning, health and nutrition, math, written composition skills, and other.

Sterling College (continued)

Application For admittance to the program or unit, students are required to provide a psychoeducational report (3 years old or less). Upon application, materials documenting need for services should be sent only to the LD program or unit. Upon acceptance, documentation of need for services should be sent to both admissions and the LD program or unit. *Application deadline (institutional):* Continuous. *Application deadline (LD program):* Rolling/continuous for fall and rolling/continuous for spring.

Written Policies Written policy regarding general/basic LD accommodations is outlined in the school's catalog/handbook. Written policy regarding general/basic LD accommodations is available through the program or unit directly.

Stetson University
Academic Resources Center

421 North Woodland Boulevard

DeLand, FL 32723

http://www.stetson.edu/academicsupport

Contact: Dr. Karen L. Cole, Director of Academic Resources Center. Phone: 386-822-7127. Fax: 386-822-7130. E-mail: kcole@stetson.edu.

Academic Resources Center Approximately 75 registered undergraduate students were served during 2006–07. The program or unit includes 1 full-time and 1 part-time staff member. Diagnostic specialists, graduate assistants/students, regular education teachers, skill tutors, and trained peer tutors are provided collaboratively through on-campus or off-campus services.

Orientation The program or unit offers an optional 1-hour orientation for new students through individual meetings during fall orientation program.

Unique Aids and Services Aids, services, or accommodations include advocates and faculty training.

Assistive Technology Assistive technology is located in the DSS office and includes alternate form textbooks.

Subject-Area Tutoring Tutoring is offered one-on-one and in small groups for most subjects. Tutoring is provided collaboratively through on-campus or off-campus services via graduate assistants/students and trained peer tutors.

Basic Skills Remediation Remediation is offered in small groups for learning strategies, reading, study skills, and time management. Remediation is provided through the program or unit via LD specialists and trained peer tutors. Remediation is also provided collaboratively through on-campus or off-campus services via LD specialists and trained peer tutors.

Enrichment Enrichment programs are available through the program or unit for college survival skills, learning strategies, math, practical computer skills, reading, stress management, study skills, test taking, and time management. Programs for career planning, health and nutrition, math, practical computer skills, stress management, study skills, test taking, time management, and written composition skills are provided collaboratively through on-campus or off-campus services.

Student Organization Association of Disability Advocates (ADA) consists of 15 members.

Application For admittance to the program or unit, students are required to provide a psychoeducational report (3 years old or less). It is recommended that students provide documentation of high school services. Upon acceptance, documentation of need for services should be sent only to the LD program or unit. *Application deadline (institutional):* 3/1. *Application deadline (LD program):* Rolling/continuous for fall and rolling/continuous for spring.

Written Policies Written policies regarding course substitutions, general/basic LD accommodations, and reduced course loads are available on the program Web site. Written policy regarding grade forgiveness is outlined in the school's catalog/handbook. Written policies regarding course substitutions, general/basic LD accommodations, and reduced course loads are available through the program or unit directly.

Stonehill College
Center for Academic Achievement

320 Washington Street

Easton, MA 02357-5510

http://www.stonehill.edu/academics/resource_center.htm

Contact: Ms. Autumn Grant, Director of the Center for Academic Achievement. Phone: 508-565-1033. Fax: 508-565-1492. E-mail: akimball@stonehill.edu.

Center for Academic Achievement Approximately 45 registered undergraduate students were served during 2006–07. The program or unit includes 1 full-time and 1 part-time staff member. LD specialists are provided through the program or unit. Academic advisers, counselors, diagnostic specialists, LD specialists, skill tutors, strategy tutors, and trained peer tutors are provided collaboratively through on-campus or off-campus services.

Orientation The program or unit offers individually by special arrangement.

Assistive Technology Assistive technology is located in campus labs, the DSS office and includes books on CD. Technology training is provided to incoming students.

Subject-Area Tutoring Tutoring is offered one-on-one and in small groups for most subjects. Tutoring is provided collaboratively through on-campus or off-campus services via trained peer tutors.

Diagnostic Testing Testing for learning styles, neuropsychological, and study skills is provided collaboratively through on-campus or off-campus services.

Basic Skills Remediation Remediation is offered one-on-one, in small groups, and in class-size groups for learning strategies, study skills, and time management. Remediation is provided through the program or unit. Remediation is also provided collaboratively through on-campus or off-campus services.

Enrichment Programs for career planning, college survival skills, health and nutrition, learning strategies, stress management, study skills, test taking, time management, and written composition skills are provided collaboratively through on-campus or off-campus services. Credit is offered for college survival skills.

Application For admittance to the program or unit, students are required to provide a psychoeducational report (3 years old or less). It is recommended that students provide documentation of high school services. Upon acceptance, documentation of need for services should be sent only to the LD program or unit. *Application deadline (institutional): 1/15. Application deadline (LD program):* Rolling/continuous for fall and rolling/continuous for spring.

Written Policies Written policies regarding course substitutions, general/basic LD accommodations, reduced course loads, substitutions and waivers of admissions requirements, and substitutions and waivers of graduation requirements are available through the program or unit directly.

Sweet Briar College
Academic Advising

Sweet Briar, VA 24595

http://www.dean.sbc.edu/advising.html

Contact: Dr. Alix Ingber, Director of Academic Advising. Phone: 434-381-6206. Fax: 434-381-6489. E-mail: ingber@sbc.edu.

Academic Advising Approximately 100 registered undergraduate students were served during 2006–07. The program or unit includes 1 full-time staff member. Academic advisers, coaches, counselors, diagnostic specialists, LD specialists, skill tutors, and strategy tutors are provided collaboratively through on-campus or off-campus services.

Unique Aids and Services Aids, services, or accommodations include career counseling.

Assistive Technology Assistive technology includes digital textbooks/e-text.

Subject-Area Tutoring Tutoring is offered one-on-one for all subjects. Tutoring is provided collaboratively through on-campus or off-campus services via computer-based instruction, professional tutors, and trained peer tutors.

Diagnostic Testing Testing for auditory processing, intelligence, learning strategies, learning styles, math, motor skills, neuropsychological, reading, spoken language, study skills, visual processing, and written language is provided collaboratively through on-campus or off-campus services.

Basic Skills Remediation Remediation is offered one-on-one for learning strategies, math, reading, spelling, time management, and written language. Remediation is provided collaboratively through on-campus or off-campus services via computer-based instruction and trained peer tutors.

Enrichment Programs for career planning, college survival skills, health and nutrition, learning strategies, math, reading, stress management, study skills, test taking, time management, and written composition skills are provided collaboratively through on-campus or off-campus services.

Fees *Diagnostic Testing* fee is $600.

Application For admittance to the program or unit, students are required to provide a psychoeducational report (5 years old or less). Upon application, materials documenting need for services should be sent only to admissions with institutional application materials. Upon acceptance, documentation of need for services should be sent only to the LD program or unit. *Application deadline (institutional): 2/1. Application deadline (LD program):* Rolling/continuous for fall and rolling/continuous for spring.

Written Policies Written policies regarding course substitutions, general/basic LD accommodations, grade forgiveness, substitutions and waivers of admissions requirements, and substitutions and waivers of graduation requirements are outlined in the school's catalog/handbook.

Syracuse University
Office of Disability Services

Syracuse, NY 13244

http://www.disabilityservices.syr.edu

Contact: Mr. Stephen H. Simon, Director, Office of Disability Services. Phone: 315-443-1128. Fax: 315-443-1312. E-mail: shsimon@syr.edu.

Office of Disability Services Approximately 460 registered undergraduate students were served during 2006–07. The program or unit includes 7 full-time and 24 part-time staff members. Counselors and skill tutors are provided through the program or unit. Academic advisers, counselors, diagnostic specialists, graduate assistants/students, strategy tutors, and trained peer tutors are provided collaboratively through on-campus or off-campus services.

Summer Program To help prepare for the demands of college, there is an optional 6-week summer program prior to entering the school available to high school graduates that focuses on life skills and/or college life adjustment, self-advocacy, specific subject tutoring, study skills, test-taking skills, and time management. Degree credit will be earned. The program accepts students from out-of-state.

Unique Aids and Services Aids, services, or accommodations include advocates, faculty training, parent workshops.

Assistive Technology Assistive technology is located in campus labs, the DSS office, a special lab, various locations on campus and includes digital textbooks/e-text, learning support software, and scanning. Technology training is provided to incoming students.

Subject-Area Tutoring Tutoring is offered one-on-one and in small groups for some subjects. Tutoring is provided collaboratively through on-campus or off-campus services via graduate assistants/students, professional tutors, and trained peer tutors.

Diagnostic Testing Testing is provided through the program or unit for learning styles and study skills. Testing for intelligence, learning strategies, learning styles, math, reading, spelling, study skills, and written language is provided collaboratively through on-campus or off-campus services.

Enrichment Enrichment programs are available through the program or unit for college survival skills, self-advocacy, stress management, and time management. Programs for career planning, college survival skills, health and nutrition, learning strategies, math, oral communication skills, reading, self-advocacy, stress management, study skills, test taking, time management, and written composition skills are provided collaboratively through on-campus or off-campus services. Credit is offered for health and nutrition, test taking, time management, and written composition skills.

Fees *Diagnostic Testing* fee is applicable.

Application For admittance to the program or unit, students are required to apply to the program directly and provide a psychoeducational report (5 years old or less). It is recommended that students provide documentation of high school services. Upon application, materials documenting need for services should be sent only to the

Syracuse University (continued)
LD program or unit. Upon acceptance, documentation of need for services should be sent only to the LD program or unit. *Application deadline (institutional):* 1/1. *Application deadline (LD program):* Rolling/continuous for fall and rolling/continuous for spring.
Written Policies Written policies regarding course substitutions, general/basic LD accommodations, grade forgiveness, reduced course loads, substitutions and waivers of admissions requirements, and substitutions and waivers of graduation requirements are available on the program Web site.

Taylor University
Academic Enrichment Center

236 West Reade Avenue

Upland, IN 46989-1001

http://www.taylor.edu/academics/supportservices/aec/disabilities.shtml

Contact: Dr. R. Edwin Welch, Coordinator of Academic Support Services. Phone: 765-998-5523. E-mail: edwelch@tayloru.edu.

Academic Enrichment Center Approximately 35 registered undergraduate students were served during 2006–07. The program or unit includes 1 full-time staff member. Services are provided through the program or unit. Regular education teachers and trained peer tutors are provided collaboratively through on-campus or off-campus services.
Unique Aids and Services Aids, services, or accommodations include priority registration.
Assistive Technology Assistive technology is located in the DSS office and includes digital textbooks/e-text, scanning, and speech-to-text and text-to-speech software. Technology training is provided to incoming students.
Subject-Area Tutoring Tutoring is offered one-on-one and in small groups for most subjects. Tutoring is provided collaboratively through on-campus or off-campus services via trained peer tutors.
Basic Skills Remediation Remediation is offered one-on-one and in small groups for learning strategies, math, reading, study skills, time management, and written language. Remediation is provided collaboratively through on-campus or off-campus services via regular education teachers.
Enrichment Enrichment programs are available through the program or unit for study skills, test taking, and time management. Programs for career planning, college survival skills, learning strategies, math, reading, study skills, test taking, time management, and written composition skills are provided collaboratively through on-campus or off-campus services. Credit is offered for learning strategies, math, reading, and study skills.
Application For admittance to the program or unit, students are required to apply to the program directly and provide a psychoeducational report (3 years old or less). It is recommended that students provide documentation of high school services. Upon acceptance, documentation of need for services should be sent only to the LD program or unit. *Application deadline (institutional):* Continuous. *Application deadline (LD program):* Rolling/continuous for fall and rolling/continuous for spring.

Written Policies Written policies regarding course substitutions, general/basic LD accommodations, and substitutions and waivers of graduation requirements are available on the program Web site. Written policies regarding course substitutions, general/basic LD accommodations, and substitutions and waivers of graduation requirements are available through the program or unit directly.

Temple University
Disability Resources and Services

1801 North Broad Street

Philadelphia, PA 19122-6096

http://www.temple.edu/disability

Contact: Ms. Vanessa L. Dash, Learning Disability Coordinator. Phone: 215-204-1280. Fax: 215-204-6794. E-mail: vdash@temple.edu. Head of LD Program: Mr. John Bennett, Director of Disability Resources & Services. Phone: 215-204-1280. Fax: 215-204-6794. E-mail: john.bennett@temple.edu.

Disability Resources and Services Approximately 600 registered undergraduate students were served during 2006–07. The program or unit includes 1 full-time staff member. LD specialists are provided through the program or unit. Academic advisers, coaches, counselors, regular education teachers, skill tutors, and strategy tutors are provided collaboratively through on-campus or off-campus services.
Unique Aids and Services Aids, services, or accommodations include career counseling.
Assistive Technology Assistive technology is located in campus labs, the DSS office and includes digital textbooks/e-text and scanning. Technology training is provided to incoming students.
Enrichment Programs for career planning, college survival skills, health and nutrition, learning strategies, math, medication management, stress management, study skills, test taking, time management, and written composition skills are provided collaboratively through on-campus or off-campus services.
Application For admittance to the program or unit, students are required to provide a psychoeducational report (5 years old or less). It is recommended that students provide documentation of high school services and provide a current evaluation. Upon acceptance, documentation of need for services should be sent only to the LD program or unit. *Application deadline (institutional):* 4/1. *Application deadline (LD program):* Rolling/continuous for fall and rolling/continuous for spring.
Written Policies Written policy regarding general/basic LD accommodations is available on the program Web site. Written policies regarding course substitutions, general/basic LD accommodations, and substitutions and waivers of graduation requirements are available through the program or unit directly.

Tennessee Wesleyan College

Academic Success Center/Disabilities Services

PO Box 40

Athens, TN 37371-0040

http://www.twcnet.edu

Contact: Dr. Catherine Bowen Emanuel, Special Needs Coordinator. Phone: 423-746-5305. Fax: 423-744-9968. E-mail: cemanuel@twcnet.edu.

Academic Success Center/Disabilities Services Approximately 16 registered undergraduate students were served during 2006–07. The program or unit includes 1 full-time staff member. Academic advisers, LD specialists, remediation/learning specialists, skill tutors, strategy tutors, and trained peer tutors are provided through the program or unit. Coaches and graduate assistants/students are provided collaboratively through on-campus or off-campus services.

Unique Aids and Services Aids, services, or accommodations include advocates and personal coach.

Assistive Technology Assistive technology is located in the DSS office and includes digital textbooks/e-text. Technology training is provided to incoming students.

Subject-Area Tutoring Tutoring is offered one-on-one for some subjects. Tutoring is provided collaboratively through on-campus or off-campus services via professional tutors and trained peer tutors.

Diagnostic Testing Testing for auditory processing, handwriting, intelligence, learning strategies, learning styles, math, motor skills, neuropsychological, personality, reading, spelling, spoken language, visual processing, and written language is provided collaboratively through on-campus or off-campus services.

Basic Skills Remediation Remediation is offered one-on-one for learning strategies, math, reading, spoken language, study skills, time management, and written language. Remediation is provided collaboratively through on-campus or off-campus services via LD specialists and trained peer tutors.

Enrichment Programs for career planning, college survival skills, health and nutrition, learning strategies, math, oral communication skills, practical computer skills, reading, stress management, study skills, test taking, time management, vocabulary development, and written composition skills are provided collaboratively through on-campus or off-campus services. Credit is offered for college survival skills.

Fees *Diagnostic Testing* fee is $350.

Application For admittance to the program or unit, students are required to provide a psychoeducational report (3 years old or less) and provide documentation of high school services. It is recommended that students apply to the program directly. Upon application, materials documenting need for services should be sent to both admissions and the LD program or unit. Upon acceptance, documentation of need for services should be sent to both admissions and the LD program or unit. *Application deadline (institutional):* 8/31. *Application deadline (LD program):* 9/20 for fall. 9/20 for spring.

Written Policies Written policy regarding general/basic LD accommodations is outlined in the school's catalog/handbook.

Texas A&M University

Disability Services

College Station, TX 77843

http://disability.tamu.edu

Contact: Dr. Anne Reber, Director of Disability Services. Phone: 979-845-1637. Fax: 979-458-1214. E-mail: disability@tamu.edu.

Disability Services Approximately 350 registered undergraduate students were served during 2006–07. The program or unit includes 9 full-time staff members. LD specialists are provided through the program or unit. Academic advisers, counselors, diagnostic specialists, graduate assistants/students, professional tutors, remediation/learning specialists, skill tutors, and strategy tutors are provided collaboratively through on-campus or off-campus services.

Unique Aids and Services Aids, services, or accommodations include advocates and priority registration.

Assistive Technology Assistive technology is located in campus labs, the DSS office, a special lab and includes digital textbooks/e-text, learning support software, and scanning.

Subject-Area Tutoring Tutoring is offered one-on-one, in small groups, and in class-size groups for some subjects. Tutoring is provided collaboratively through on-campus or off-campus services via computer-based instruction, graduate assistants/students, professional tutors, and trained peer tutors.

Diagnostic Testing Testing for auditory processing, intelligence, learning strategies, learning styles, math, neuropsychological, personality, reading, spelling, spoken language, study skills, visual processing, and written language is provided collaboratively through on-campus or off-campus services.

Basic Skills Remediation Remediation is offered in class-size groups for learning strategies, math, reading, study skills, time management, and written language. Remediation is provided collaboratively through on-campus or off-campus services via computer-based instruction, graduate assistants/students, professional tutors, and regular education teachers.

Enrichment Enrichment programs are available through the program or unit for learning strategies and self-advocacy. Programs for career planning, college survival skills, health and nutrition, learning strategies, math, oral communication skills, practical computer skills, reading, stress management, study skills, test taking, time management, and written composition skills are provided collaboratively through on-campus or off-campus services. Credit is offered for career planning, college survival skills, health and nutrition, math, oral communication skills, practical computer skills, stress management, study skills, test taking, time management, and written composition skills.

Fees *Diagnostic Testing* fee is $350 to $1000.

Application For admittance to the program or unit, students are required to provide a psychoeducational report (3 years old or less). It is recommended that students provide documentation of high school services. Upon acceptance, documentation of need for services should be sent only to the LD program or unit. *Application deadline (institutional):* 2/1. *Application deadline (LD program):* Rolling/continuous for fall and rolling/continuous for spring.

Written Policies Written policy regarding general/basic LD accommodations is available on the program Web site. Written policy regarding general/basic LD accommodations is outlined in the school's catalog/handbook. Written policy regarding general/basic LD accommodations is available through the program or unit directly.

Texas A&M University–Corpus Christi

6300 Ocean Drive
Corpus Christi, TX 78412-5503
http://www.tamucc.edu/

Contact: Ms. Rachel A. Cox, Director, Disability Services. Phone: 361-825-5816. Fax: 361-825-2536. E-mail: rachel.cox@tamucc.edu.

Approximately 25 registered undergraduate students were served during 2006–07. Services are provided collaboratively through on-campus or off-campus services.

Assistive Technology Assistive technology is located in campus labs, the DSS office and includes digital textbooks/e-text, learning support software, and scanning.

Subject-Area Tutoring Tutoring is offered one-on-one and in small groups for most subjects. Tutoring is provided collaboratively through on-campus or off-campus services via trained peer tutors.

Application For admittance to the program or unit, students are required to provide psychological evaluation. Upon application, materials documenting need for services should be sent only to the LD program or unit. Upon acceptance, documentation of need for services should be sent only to the LD program or unit. *Application deadline (institutional): 7/1. Application deadline (LD program):* Rolling/continuous for fall and rolling/continuous for spring.

Thiel College
Office of Special Needs (OSS)

75 College Avenue
Greenville, PA 16125-2181
http://www.thiel.edu/

Contact: Ms. Susan Cowan, Coordinator of Office of Special Needs. Phone: 724-589-2063. Fax: 724-589-2850. E-mail: scowan@thiel.edu.

Office of Special Needs (OSS) Approximately 40 registered undergraduate students were served during 2006–07. The program or unit includes 1 full-time staff member. Academic advisers, counselors, professional tutors, remediation/learning specialists, and trained peer tutors are provided collaboratively through on-campus or off-campus services.

Subject-Area Tutoring Tutoring is offered one-on-one. Tutoring is provided collaboratively through on-campus or off-campus services via trained peer tutors.

Basic Skills Remediation Remediation is offered in class-size groups for learning strategies, math, reading, study skills, time management, and written language. Remediation is provided collaboratively through on-campus or off-campus services via professional tutors, regular education teachers, trained peer tutors, and other.

Enrichment Programs for career planning, college survival skills, learning strategies, math, oral communication skills, reading, stress management, study skills, test taking, time management, and written composition skills are provided collaboratively through on-campus or off-campus services. Credit is offered for math, stress management, study skills, test taking, time management, and written composition skills.

Application For admittance to the program or unit, students are required to provide documentation from professional DSM-IV diagnosis. It is recommended that students provide documentation of high school services. Upon application, materials documenting need for services should be sent only to the LD program or unit. Upon acceptance, documentation of need for services should be sent only to the LD program or unit. *Application deadline (institutional): 6/30. Application deadline (LD program):* Rolling/continuous for fall and rolling/continuous for spring.

Written Policies Written policy regarding general/basic LD accommodations is outlined in the school's catalog/handbook. Written policy regarding general/basic LD accommodations is available through the program or unit directly.

Thomas Edison State College
Office of Students with Disabilities

101 West State Street
Trenton, NJ 08608-1176
http://www.tesc.edu/

Contact: Ms. Barbara E. Aikins, ADA Coordinator. Phone: 609-984-1141 Ext. 3415. Fax: 609-777-2956. E-mail: ada@tesc.edu.

Office of Students with Disabilities Approximately 22 registered undergraduate students were served during 2006–07. The program or unit includes 1 full-time staff member. Academic advisers and LD specialists are provided collaboratively through on-campus or off-campus services.

Assistive Technology Assistive technology includes books on tape.

Application For admittance to the program or unit, students are required to provide LD evaluation. It is recommended that students provide a psychoeducational report (5 years old or less) and provide documentation of high school services. Upon application, materials documenting need for services should be sent only to the LD program or unit. Upon acceptance, documentation of need for services should be sent only to the LD program or unit. *Application deadline (LD program):* Rolling/continuous for fall and rolling/continuous for spring.

Written Policies Written policy regarding general/basic LD accommodations is outlined in the school's catalog/handbook. Written policies regarding course substitutions, substitutions and waivers of admissions requirements, and substitutions and waivers of graduation requirements are available through the program or unit directly.

Towson University
Disability Support Services

8000 York Road
Towson, MD 21252-0001
http://www.new.towson.edu/dss
Contact: Susan Willemin, Director of Disability Support Services. Phone: 410-704-2638. Fax: 410-704-4247. E-mail: dssquestionbox@towson.edu.

Disability Support Services Approximately 400 registered undergraduate students were served during 2006–07. The program or unit includes 6 full-time and 2 part-time staff members. LD specialists and remediation/learning specialists are provided through the program or unit. Academic advisers, counselors, graduate assistants/students, LD specialists, remediation/learning specialists, skill tutors, strategy tutors, and trained peer tutors are provided collaboratively through on-campus or off-campus services.

Orientation The program or unit offers an optional 2-hour orientation for new students before classes begin and during orientation weekend for new students.

Unique Aids and Services Aids, services, or accommodations include priority registration.

Assistive Technology Assistive technology is located in campus labs, the DSS office and includes digital textbooks/e-text and scanning. Technology training is provided to incoming students.

Subject-Area Tutoring Tutoring is offered one-on-one, in small groups, and in class-size groups for most subjects. Tutoring is provided through the program or unit via LD specialists. Tutoring is also provided collaboratively through on-campus or off-campus services via graduate assistants/students, LD specialists, and trained peer tutors.

Basic Skills Remediation Remediation is offered one-on-one and in small groups for learning strategies, study skills, time management, written language, and test-taking strategies. Remediation is provided through the program or unit via LD specialists. Remediation is also provided collaboratively through on-campus or off-campus services via LD specialists.

Enrichment Enrichment programs are available through the program or unit for self-advocacy, study skills, test taking, and time management. Programs for career planning, health and nutrition, learning strategies, oral communication skills, self-advocacy, stress management, study skills, test taking, time management, and written composition skills are provided collaboratively through on-campus or off-campus services.

Application For admittance to the program or unit, students are required to apply to the program directly and provide a psychoeducational report (3 years old or less). It is recommended that students provide documentation of high school services. Upon application, materials documenting need for services should be sent to both admissions and the LD program or unit. Upon acceptance, documentation of need for services should be sent only to the LD program or unit. *Application deadline (institutional):* 2/15. *Application deadline (LD program):* Rolling/continuous for fall and rolling/continuous for spring.

Written Policies Written policy regarding general/basic LD accommodations is available on the program Web site. Written policy regarding general/basic LD accommodations is outlined in the school's catalog/handbook. Written policies regarding course substitutions, general/basic LD accommodations, and reduced course loads are available through the program or unit directly.

Trent University
Learning Integration Program

1600 West Bank Drive
Peterborough, ON K9J 7B8
Canada
http://www.Trentu.ca/disabilityservices
Contact: Ms. Eunice Lund-Lucas, Manager Disability Services. Phone: 705-748-1281. Fax: 705-748-1509. E-mail: elundlucas@trentu.ca.

Learning Integration Program Approximately 200 registered undergraduate students were served during 2006–07. The program or unit includes 3 full-time and 3 part-time staff members. Coaches, counselors, diagnostic specialists, LD specialists, professional tutors, remediation/learning specialists, and strategy tutors are provided through the program or unit. Academic advisers, counselors, graduate assistants/students, regular education teachers, skill tutors, and strategy tutors are provided collaboratively through on-campus or off-campus services.

Orientation The program or unit offers an optional 2-day orientation for new students during summer prior to enrollment.

Summer Program To help prepare for the demands of college, there is an optional 2 day on-site and 6-week online summer program prior to entering the school available to high school graduates that focuses on life skills and/or college life adjustment, self-advocacy, study skills, test-taking skills, and time management. The program accepts students from out-of-state and is available to students attending other colleges.

Unique Aids and Services Aids, services, or accommodations include advocates, career counseling, faculty training, parent workshops, and personal coach.

Assistive Technology Assistive technology is located in the DSS office, the library and includes digital textbooks/e-text, learning support software, and scanning. Technology training is provided to incoming students.

Subject-Area Tutoring Tutoring is offered one-on-one for most subjects. Tutoring is provided through the program or unit via professional tutors. Tutoring is also provided collaboratively through on-campus or off-campus services via trained peer tutors.

Diagnostic Testing Testing is provided through the program or unit for auditory processing, handwriting, intelligence, learning strategies, learning styles, math, motor skills, neuropsychological, personality, reading, social skills, spelling, spoken language, study skills, visual processing, and written language. Testing for learning styles, reading, spelling, study skills, and written language is provided collaboratively through on-campus or off-campus services.

Basic Skills Remediation Remediation is offered one-on-one for learning strategies, math, reading, social skills, study skills, time management, written language, and motivational issues. Remediation is provided through the program or unit via computer-based instruction, LD specialists, and professional tutors.

Enrichment Enrichment programs are available through the program or unit for college survival skills, health and nutrition, learning strategies, self-advocacy, stress management, study skills, test taking, and time management. Programs for career planning, learning strategies, math, medication management, reading, stress management, study skills, test taking, time management, and written composition skills are provided collaboratively through on-campus or off-campus services.

Trent University (continued)
Fees *Diagnostic Testing* fee is $1500.
Application For admittance to the program or unit, students are required to provide documentation of high school services. It is recommended that students provide a psychoeducational report. Upon application, materials documenting need for services should be sent to both admissions and the LD program or unit. Upon acceptance, documentation of need for services should be sent only to the LD program or unit. *Application deadline (institutional):* 6/1. *Application deadline (LD program):* Rolling/continuous for fall.
Written Policies Written policy regarding general/basic LD accommodations is available on the program Web site. Written policy regarding general/basic LD accommodations is outlined in the school's catalog/handbook.

Trevecca Nazarene University

333 Murfreesboro Road

Nashville, TN 37210-2877

http://www.trevecca.edu/academics/academic.support.ctr/ disability.services.html

Contact: Coordinator, Student Disability Services. Phone: 615-248-1463. Fax: 615-248-1717. E-mail: amurphy@ trevecca.edu.

Approximately 10 registered undergraduate students were served during 2006–07. The program or unit includes 1 full-time staff member. Academic advisers are provided through the program or unit. Academic advisers and trained peer tutors are provided collaboratively through on-campus or off-campus services.
Assistive Technology Assistive technology is located in campus labs, Academic Support Center and includes digital textbooks/e-text, learning support software, and scanning.
Subject-Area Tutoring Tutoring is offered one-on-one and in small groups for most subjects. Tutoring is provided collaboratively through on-campus or off-campus services via graduate assistants/students and trained peer tutors.
Basic Skills Remediation Remediation is offered in class-size groups for learning strategies, math, reading, study skills, time management, and written language. Remediation is provided collaboratively through on-campus or off-campus services via regular education teachers.
Application For admittance to the program or unit, students are required to provide a psychoeducational report. It is recommended that students provide documentation of high school services. Upon acceptance, documentation of need for services should be sent only to the LD program or unit. *Application deadline (institutional):* 7/1. *Application deadline (LD program):* Rolling/continuous for fall and rolling/continuous for spring.
Written Policies Written policy regarding general/basic LD accommodations is available on the program Web site. Written policy regarding general/basic LD accommodations is outlined in the school's catalog/handbook.

Trinity Baptist College

800 Hammond Boulevard

Jacksonville, FL 32221

http://www.tbc.edu/

Contact: Dr. Lois Schaefer, Associate Professor. Phone: 904-596-2506. Fax: 904-596-2531. E-mail: lschaefer@ tbc.edu.

Approximately 25 registered undergraduate students were served during 2006–07. The program or unit includes 2 full-time staff members. Diagnostic specialists, LD specialists, and special education teachers are provided through the program or unit. Academic advisers, counselors, professional tutors, regular education teachers, and special education teachers are provided collaboratively through on-campus or off-campus services.
Orientation The program or unit offers a mandatory 30-minute orientation for new students before classes begin, during registration, individually by special arrangement, and whenever the student is referred to the program because of difficulty with academic achievement.
Unique Aids and Services Aids, services, or accommodations include advocates, faculty training, meetings with faculty adviser/special education counselor.
Subject-Area Tutoring Tutoring is offered one-on-one and in small groups for most subjects. Tutoring is provided through the program or unit via LD specialists. Tutoring is also provided collaboratively through on-campus or off-campus services via trained peer tutors and other.
Diagnostic Testing Testing is provided through the program or unit for auditory processing, handwriting, intelligence, learning strategies, learning styles, reading, spoken language, study skills, and visual processing. Testing for reading, spelling, and study skills is provided collaboratively through on-campus or off-campus services.
Basic Skills Remediation Remediation is offered one-on-one and in small groups for auditory processing, handwriting, learning strategies, reading, spelling, study skills, time management, visual processing, and written language. Remediation is provided through the program or unit via LD specialists and special education teachers. Remediation is also provided collaboratively through on-campus or off-campus services via LD specialists, regular education teachers, special education teachers, teacher trainees, and trained peer tutors.
Enrichment Enrichment programs are available through the program or unit for college survival skills, learning strategies, reading, self-advocacy, stress management, study skills, test taking, and time management. Programs for career planning, college survival skills, learning strategies, practical computer skills, reading, self-advocacy, study skills, time management, vocabulary development, and written composition skills are provided collaboratively through on-campus or off-campus services.
Application For admittance to the program or unit, students are required to provide a psychoeducational report and provide testing completed by the college specialist in LD if other documentation is not available. It is recommended that students apply to the program directly and provide documentation of high school services. Upon application, materials documenting need for services should be sent to both admissions and the LD program or unit. Upon acceptance, documentation of need for services should be sent to both admissions and the LD program or unit. *Application deadline (institutional):* Continuous. *Application deadline (LD program):* Rolling/continuous for fall and rolling/continuous for spring.

Written Policies Written policies regarding general/basic LD accommodations, grade forgiveness, and reduced course loads are outlined in the school's catalog/handbook.

Trinity College
Counseling Center

300 Summit Street

Hartford, CT 06106-3100

http://www.trincoll.edu/StudentLife/HealthSafety/CounselingCenter/

Contact: Mr. Fred Alford, Dean of Students. Phone: 860-297-2157. E-mail: fred.alford@trincoll.edu. Head of LD Program: Dr. Randolph M. Lee, Director of the Counseling Center. Phone: 860-297-2413. Fax: 860-297-2428. E-mail: randolph.lee@trincoll.edu.

Counseling Center Counselors and other are provided through the program or unit. Counselors are provided collaboratively through on-campus or off-campus services.

Subject-Area Tutoring Tutoring is offered one-on-one for some subjects. Tutoring is provided collaboratively through on-campus or off-campus services via other.

Diagnostic Testing Testing is provided through the program or unit for intelligence and personality.

Application For admittance to the program or unit, students are required to provide a psychoeducational report (3 years old or less). It is recommended that students provide documentation of high school services. Upon application, materials documenting need for services should be sent only to the LD program or unit. Upon acceptance, documentation of need for services should be sent only to the LD program or unit. *Application deadline (institutional):* 1/1. *Application deadline (LD program):* Rolling/continuous for fall and rolling/continuous for spring.

Written Policies Written policies regarding general/basic LD accommodations and reduced course loads are available on the program Web site.

Trinity University
Disability Services for Students

One Trinity Place

San Antonio, TX 78212-7200

http://www.trinity.edu/dss

Contact: Coordinator of Disability Services. Phone: 210-999-7411. Fax: 210-999-7848. E-mail: dss@trinity.edu.

Disability Services for Students Approximately 75 registered undergraduate students were served during 2006–07. The program or unit includes 1 full-time staff member. Academic advisers and counselors are provided collaboratively through on-campus or off-campus services.

Unique Aids and Services Aids, services, or accommodations include advocates and priority registration.

Assistive Technology Assistive technology is located in the library and includes digital textbooks/e-text and scanning. Technology training is provided to incoming students.

Subject-Area Tutoring Tutoring is offered one-on-one for most subjects. Tutoring is provided collaboratively through on-campus or off-campus services via other.

Enrichment Enrichment programs are available through the program or unit for college survival skills, learning strategies, self-advocacy, stress management, study skills, test taking, and time management. Programs for career planning, college survival skills, learning strategies, practical computer skills, stress management, study skills, test taking, time management, and written composition skills are provided collaboratively through on-campus or off-campus services. Credit is offered for practical computer skills.

Application For admittance to the program or unit, students are required to apply to the program directly and provide a psychoeducational report (3 years old or less). Upon acceptance, documentation of need for services should be sent only to the LD program or unit. *Application deadline (institutional):* 2/1. *Application deadline (LD program):* Rolling/continuous for fall and rolling/continuous for spring.

Written Policies Written policies regarding general/basic LD accommodations and substitutions and waivers of graduation requirements are available on the program Web site. Written policies regarding course substitutions, general/basic LD accommodations, reduced course loads, and substitutions and waivers of graduation requirements are available through the program or unit directly.

Troy University
Adaptive Needs Program

University Avenue

Troy, AL 36082

http://www.troy.edu/

Contact: Deborah G. Sellers, Adaptive Needs Program Director. Phone: 334-670-3221. Fax: 334-670-3810. E-mail: dsellers@troy.edu.

Adaptive Needs Program Approximately 55 registered undergraduate students were served during 2006–07. The program or unit includes 2 full-time staff members. Academic advisers, graduate assistants/students, and skill tutors are provided through the program or unit.

Orientation The program or unit offers an optional 1- to 2-hour orientation for new students before registration and individually by special arrangement.

Unique Aids and Services Aids, services, or accommodations include career counseling, faculty training, priority registration, academic advising.

Assistive Technology Assistive technology is located in campus labs and includes access to computers.

Subject-Area Tutoring Tutoring is offered one-on-one and in small groups for some subjects. Tutoring is provided collaboratively through on-campus or off-campus services via computer-based instruction and trained peer tutors.

Basic Skills Remediation Remediation is offered in class-size groups for learning strategies, math, study skills, time management, and written language. Remediation is provided collaboratively through on-campus or off-campus services via regular education teachers and trained peer tutors.

Troy University (continued)

Enrichment Enrichment programs are available through the program or unit for self-advocacy. Programs for career planning, college survival skills, learning strategies, study skills, and test taking are provided collaboratively through on-campus or off-campus services. Credit is offered for career planning, college survival skills, learning strategies, study skills, and test taking.

Fees *Orientation* fee is $55.

Application For admittance to the program or unit, students are required to provide a psychoeducational report (3 years old or less) and provide documentation of high school services. Upon application, materials documenting need for services should be sent only to the LD program or unit. Upon acceptance, documentation of need for services should be sent only to the LD program or unit. *Application deadline (institutional):* Continuous. *Application deadline (LD program):* Rolling/continuous for fall and rolling/continuous for spring.

Written Policies Written policy regarding general/basic LD accommodations is available on the program Web site. Written policy regarding general/basic LD accommodations is available through the program or unit directly.

Truman State University
Disability Services

100 East Normal Street

Kirksville, MO 63501-4221

http://disabilityservices.truman.edu/

Contact: Mrs. Vicky L. Wehner RN, Coordinator. Phone: 660-785-4478. Fax: 660-785-4011. E-mail: vwehner@truman.edu.

Disability Services Approximately 105 registered undergraduate students were served during 2006–07. The program or unit includes 10 part-time staff members. Academic advisers, counselors, graduate assistants/students, LD specialists, professional tutors, remediation/learning specialists, skill tutors, strategy tutors, and trained peer tutors are provided through the program or unit. Academic advisers, coaches, counselors, diagnostic specialists, graduate assistants/students, LD specialists, professional tutors, regular education teachers, remediation/learning specialists, skill tutors, and trained peer tutors are provided collaboratively through on-campus or off-campus services.

Unique Aids and Services Aids, services, or accommodations include advocates, career counseling, faculty training, personal coach, and priority registration.

Assistive Technology Assistive technology is located in campus labs, the DSS office, a special lab and includes digital textbooks/e-text, scanning, and JAWS, Dragon Naturally Speaking.

Subject-Area Tutoring Tutoring is offered one-on-one, in small groups, and in class-size groups for most subjects. Tutoring is provided through the program or unit via graduate assistants/students. Tutoring is also provided collaboratively through on-campus or off-campus services via graduate assistants/students and trained peer tutors.

Basic Skills Remediation Remediation is offered one-on-one for learning strategies, math, study skills, and time management. Remediation is provided through the program or unit via computer-based instruction, graduate assistants/students, and trained peer tutors. Remediation is also provided collaboratively through on-campus or off-campus services via graduate assistants/students, regular education teachers, and trained peer tutors.

Enrichment Enrichment programs are available through the program or unit for college survival skills, learning strategies, self-advocacy, study skills, test taking, and time management. Programs for career planning, college survival skills, health and nutrition, math, medication management, oral communication skills, self-advocacy, stress management, study skills, test taking, time management, and written composition skills are provided collaboratively through on-campus or off-campus services. Credit is offered for oral communication skills.

Application For admittance to the program or unit, students are required to provide a psychoeducational report (3 years old or less) and provide medical documentation for chronic, psychiatric, or temporary physical disability. It is recommended that students provide documentation of high school services. Upon application, materials documenting need for services should be sent only to the LD program or unit. Upon acceptance, documentation of need for services should be sent only to the LD program or unit. *Application deadline (institutional):* 3/1. *Application deadline (LD program):* Rolling/continuous for fall and rolling/continuous for spring.

Written Policies Written policies regarding general/basic LD accommodations and reduced course loads are available through the program or unit directly.

Tufts University
Disability Services/Academic Services for Students with Disabilities

Medford, MA 02155

http://www.studentservices.tufts.edu/disabilityservices/

Contact: Sandra Baer, Program Director, Disability Services. Phone: 617-627-5571. Fax: 617-627-3971. E-mail: sandra.baer@tufts.edu.

Disability Services/Academic Services for Students with Disabilities Approximately 90 registered undergraduate students were served during 2006–07. The program or unit includes 1 full-time staff member. Academic advisers, coaches, diagnostic specialists, graduate assistants/students, LD specialists, remediation/learning specialists, skill tutors, special education teachers, strategy tutors, teacher trainees, and trained peer tutors are provided through the program or unit. Academic advisers, counselors, professional tutors, regular education teachers, special education teachers, teacher trainees, and trained peer tutors are provided collaboratively through on-campus or off-campus services.

Summer Program available to rising sophomores, rising juniors, rising seniors, high school graduates. The program accepts students from out-of-state and is available to students attending other colleges.

Assistive Technology Assistive technology is located in the DSS office and includes digital textbooks/e-text and scanning.

Subject-Area Tutoring Tutoring is offered one-on-one and in small groups for all subjects. Tutoring is provided through the program or unit via graduate assistants/students. Tutoring is also provided collaboratively through on-campus or off-campus services via graduate assistants/students and trained peer tutors.

Enrichment Enrichment programs are available through the program or unit for learning strategies, study skills, test taking, and time management. Programs for career planning, medication management, stress management, and written composition skills are provided collaboratively through on-campus or off-campus services.

Application For admittance to the program or unit, students are required to provide a psychoeducational report (5 years old or less) and provide documentation of high school services. Upon acceptance, documentation of need for services should be sent only to the LD program or unit. *Application deadline (institutional):* 1/1. *Application deadline (LD program):* Rolling/continuous for fall and rolling/continuous for spring.

Written Policies Written policy regarding general/basic LD accommodations is available on the program Web site. Written policies regarding course substitutions and general/basic LD accommodations are available through the program or unit directly.

Tyndale University College & Seminary

25 Ballyconnor Court

Toronto, ON M2M 4B3

Canada

http://www.tyndale.ca/

Contact: Ms. Sheila Stevens, Director of Counselling Services. E-mail: sstevens@tyndale.ca.

Approximately 10 registered undergraduate students were served during 2006–07. Academic advisers and counselors are provided collaboratively through on-campus or off-campus services.

Basic Skills Remediation Remediation is offered one-on-one for auditory processing, learning strategies, reading, spelling, study skills, and time management. Remediation is provided collaboratively through on-campus or off-campus services via computer-based instruction and professional tutors.

Enrichment Programs for career planning, college survival skills, health and nutrition, learning strategies, stress management, study skills, test taking, time management, and written composition skills are provided collaboratively through on-campus or off-campus services.

Application It is recommended that students provide a psychoeducational report (5 years old or less) and provide documentation of high school services. Upon application, materials documenting need for services should be sent only to admissions with institutional application materials. Upon acceptance, documentation of need for services should be sent only to admissions.

Written Policies Written policies regarding general/basic LD accommodations, grade forgiveness, reduced course loads, and substitutions and waivers of graduation requirements are available through the program or unit directly.

Union College
Teaching Learning Center

3800 South 48th Street

Lincoln, NE 68506-4300

http://www.ucollege.edu/tlc

Contact: Mrs. Debbie Forshee-Sweeney, Director. Phone: 402-486-2506. Fax: 402-486-2691. E-mail: deforshe@ucollege.edu.

Teaching Learning Center Approximately 75 registered undergraduate students were served during 2006–07. The program or unit includes 3 full-time staff members and 1 part-time staff member. Academic advisers, coaches, graduate assistants/students, LD specialists, professional tutors, remediation/learning specialists, skill tutors, special education teachers, and strategy tutors are provided through the program or unit. Counselors, diagnostic specialists, regular education teachers, and other are provided collaboratively through on-campus or off-campus services.

Orientation The program or unit offers a mandatory 3-hour orientation for new students after classes begin and individually by special arrangement.

Unique Aids and Services Aids, services, or accommodations include career counseling and faculty training.

Assistive Technology Assistive technology includes audio textbooks.

Subject-Area Tutoring Tutoring is offered one-on-one for most subjects. Tutoring is provided through the program or unit via LD specialists.

Diagnostic Testing Testing for auditory processing, intelligence, learning strategies, learning styles, math, neuropsychological, personality, reading, spelling, spoken language, study skills, and written language is provided collaboratively through on-campus or off-campus services.

Basic Skills Remediation Remediation is offered one-on-one and in class-size groups for computer skills, learning strategies, math, reading, social skills, spelling, study skills, time management, and written language. Remediation is provided through the program or unit via LD specialists.

Enrichment Enrichment programs are available through the program or unit for college survival skills, learning strategies, math, reading, self-advocacy, stress management, study skills, test taking, time management, and written composition skills. Programs for career planning, health and nutrition, math, oral communication skills, and practical computer skills are provided collaboratively through on-campus or off-campus services. Credit is offered for health and nutrition, math, oral communication skills, practical computer skills, and written composition skills.

Fees *LD Program or Service* fee is $0 to $495 (fee varies according to level/tier of service). *Diagnostic Testing* fee is $350.

Application For admittance to the program or unit, students are required to apply to the program directly, provide a psychoeducational report (3 years old or less), and provide documentation of high school services. Upon application, materials documenting need for services should be sent only to the LD program or unit. Upon acceptance, documentation of need for services should be sent only to the LD program or unit. *Application deadline (institutional):* Continuous. *Application deadline (LD program):* Rolling/continuous for fall and rolling/continuous for spring.

Union College (continued)

Written Policies Written policy regarding general/basic LD accommodations is available on the program Web site. Written policy regarding general/basic LD accommodations is available through the program or unit directly.

Unity College
Learning Resource Center

90 Quaker Hill Road
Unity, ME 04988
http://www.unity.edu/lrc/lrc.htm
Contact: Mr. Greg Perkins, Learning Specialist. Phone: 207-948-3131 Ext. 377. Fax: 207-948-6277. E-mail: gperkins@unity.edu.

Learning Resource Center Approximately 40 registered undergraduate students were served during 2006–07. The program or unit includes 2 full-time staff members. Academic advisers, LD specialists, remediation/learning specialists, strategy tutors, and trained peer tutors are provided through the program or unit. Academic advisers, counselors, regular education teachers, and trained peer tutors are provided collaboratively through on-campus or off-campus services.
Orientation The program or unit offers an optional orientation for new students individually by special arrangement.
Unique Aids and Services Aids, services, or accommodations include advocates.
Assistive Technology Assistive technology is located in the DSS office and includes digital textbooks/e-text, learning support software, and scanning.
Subject-Area Tutoring Tutoring is offered one-on-one and in small groups for most subjects. Tutoring is provided through the program or unit via LD specialists and trained peer tutors. Tutoring is also provided collaboratively through on-campus or off-campus services via trained peer tutors.
Basic Skills Remediation Remediation is offered one-on-one and in class-size groups for learning strategies, math, study skills, time management, and written language. Remediation is provided through the program or unit via LD specialists and trained peer tutors. Remediation is also provided collaboratively through on-campus or off-campus services via regular education teachers and trained peer tutors.
Enrichment Enrichment programs are available through the program or unit for college survival skills, learning strategies, math, reading, self-advocacy, stress management, study skills, test taking, time management, and written composition skills. Programs for career planning, college survival skills, health and nutrition, learning strategies, math, practical computer skills, stress management, time management, and written composition skills are provided collaboratively through on-campus or off-campus services.
Application For admittance to the program or unit, students are required to provide a psychoeducational report (3 years old or less) and provide documentation of high school services. Upon application, materials documenting need for services should be sent only to admissions with institutional application materials. Upon acceptance, documentation of need for services should be sent only to the LD program or unit. *Application deadline (institutional):* Continuous. *Application deadline (LD program):* Rolling/continuous for fall and rolling/continuous for spring.

Written Policies Written policy regarding general/basic LD accommodations is outlined in the school's catalog/handbook.

University at Albany, State University of New York
Disability Resource Center

1400 Washington Avenue
Albany, NY 12222-0001
http://www.albany.edu/studentlife/DSS/
Contact: Carolyn B. Malloch, Assistant Director, Disability Resource Center. Phone: 518-442-5566. Fax: 518-442-5400. E-mail: cmalloch@uamail.albany.edu.

Disability Resource Center Approximately 200 registered undergraduate students were served during 2006–07. The program or unit includes 2 full-time staff members. Coaches, LD specialists, skill tutors, and strategy tutors are provided through the program or unit. Academic advisers and counselors are provided collaboratively through on-campus or off-campus services.
Unique Aids and Services Aids, services, or accommodations include personal coach and priority registration.
Subject-Area Tutoring Tutoring is offered one-on-one, in small groups, and in class-size groups for most subjects. Tutoring is provided collaboratively through on-campus or off-campus services via graduate assistants/students and trained peer tutors.
Enrichment Enrichment programs are available through the program or unit for college survival skills, learning strategies, self-advocacy, study skills, and time management.
Application For admittance to the program or unit, students are required to provide a psychoeducational report (3 years old or less) and provide supporting testing documentation if course substitution is requested. It is recommended that students provide documentation of high school services. Upon application, materials documenting need for services should be sent only to the LD program or unit. Upon acceptance, documentation of need for services should be sent only to the LD program or unit. *Application deadline (institutional):* 3/1. *Application deadline (LD program):* Rolling/continuous for fall and rolling/continuous for spring.
Written Policies Written policy regarding general/basic LD accommodations is available on the program Web site. Written policies regarding course substitutions, general/basic LD accommodations, and substitutions and waivers of graduation requirements are outlined in the school's catalog/handbook.

University at Buffalo, the State University of New York
Disability Services

Capen Hall
Buffalo, NY 14260
http://www.ub-disability.buffalo.edu

Contact: Mr. Randy Borst, Director of Disability Services. Phone: 716-645-2608. Fax: 716-645-3116. E-mail: stu-disability@buffalo.edu.

Disability Services Approximately 150 registered undergraduate students were served during 2006–07. The program or unit includes 4 full-time staff members. Graduate assistants/students are provided through the program or unit. Academic advisers, counselors, graduate assistants/students, remediation/learning specialists, skill tutors, strategy tutors, and trained peer tutors are provided collaboratively through on-campus or off-campus services.

Unique Aids and Services Aids, services, or accommodations include career counseling.

Assistive Technology Assistive technology includes digital textbooks/e-text.

Subject-Area Tutoring Tutoring is offered one-on-one and in small groups for some subjects. Tutoring is provided collaboratively through on-campus or off-campus services via graduate assistants/students and trained peer tutors.

Basic Skills Remediation Remediation is offered one-on-one, in small groups, and in class-size groups for learning strategies, math, social skills, study skills, time management, and written language. Remediation is provided collaboratively through on-campus or off-campus services via graduate assistants/students, regular education teachers, and trained peer tutors.

Enrichment Enrichment programs are available through the program or unit for self-advocacy and time management. Programs for career planning, college survival skills, health and nutrition, learning strategies, math, medication management, oral communication skills, practical computer skills, reading, self-advocacy, stress management, study skills, test taking, time management, and written composition skills are provided collaboratively through on-campus or off-campus services. Credit is offered for career planning, college survival skills, health and nutrition, learning strategies, math, oral communication skills, and study skills.

Application For admittance to the program or unit, students are required to apply to the program directly and provide a psychoeducational report (3 years old or less). It is recommended that students provide documentation of high school services. Upon application, materials documenting need for services should be sent only to the LD program or unit. Upon acceptance, documentation of need for services should be sent only to the LD program or unit. *Application deadline (LD program):* Rolling/continuous for fall and rolling/continuous for spring.

Written Policies Written policies regarding course substitutions and general/basic LD accommodations are available through the program or unit directly.

The University of Akron

302 Buchtel Common
Akron, OH 44325
http://www.uakron.edu/

Contact: Amy Liikala Conwi, Associate Director, Office of Accessibility. Phone: 330-972-7928. Fax: 330-972-5422. E-mail: conwi@uakron.edu. Head of LD Program: Dr. Stacey Jeanne Moore, Director, Office of Accessibility. Phone: 330-972-7928. Fax: 330-972-5422. E-mail: staceyjm@uakron.edu.

The program or unit includes 6 full-time and 11 part-time staff members. Diagnostic specialists, graduate assistants/students, LD specialists, skill tutors, and strategy tutors are provided through the program or unit. Academic advisers, counselors, professional tutors, regular education teachers, remediation/learning specialists, teacher trainees, and trained peer tutors are provided collaboratively through on-campus or off-campus services.

Unique Aids and Services Aids, services, or accommodations include advocates, career counseling, faculty training, and priority registration.

Assistive Technology Assistive technology is located in campus labs, the DSS office and includes digital textbooks/e-text, learning support software, and scanning. Technology training is provided to incoming students.

Subject-Area Tutoring Tutoring is offered one-on-one and in small groups for most subjects. Tutoring is provided collaboratively through on-campus or off-campus services via computer-based instruction, graduate assistants/students, professional tutors, and trained peer tutors.

Diagnostic Testing Testing is provided through the program or unit for learning strategies and learning styles. Testing for auditory processing, intelligence, personality, social skills, study skills, visual processing, written language, and other services is provided collaboratively through on-campus or off-campus services.

Basic Skills Remediation Remediation is offered one-on-one and in small groups for computer skills, learning strategies, math, reading, spelling, study skills, time management, and written language. Remediation is provided through the program or unit via computer-based instruction, graduate assistants/students, LD specialists, and trained peer tutors. Remediation is also provided collaboratively through on-campus or off-campus services via computer-based instruction, graduate assistants/students, LD specialists, and trained peer tutors.

Enrichment Enrichment programs are available through the program or unit for college survival skills, learning strategies, self-advocacy, study skills, test taking, time management, vocabulary development, and written composition skills. Programs for career planning, college survival skills, health and nutrition, learning strategies, math, reading, stress management, study skills, test taking, time management, vocabulary development, and written composition skills are provided collaboratively through on-campus or off-campus services. Credit is offered for career planning and college survival skills.

Fees *Diagnostic Testing* fee is $30 to $100.

Application For admittance to the program or unit, students are required to provide a psychoeducational report. It is recommended that students provide documentation of high school services. Upon application, materials documenting need for services should be sent only to the LD program or unit. Upon acceptance, documentation of need for services should be sent only to the LD program or unit. *Application deadline (institutional):* 8/1. *Application deadline (LD program):* Rolling/continuous for fall and rolling/continuous for spring.

Written Policies Written policies regarding course substitutions, general/basic LD accommodations, substitutions and waivers of admissions requirements, and substitutions and waivers of graduation requirements are available on the program Web site. Written policies regarding course substitutions, general/basic LD accommodations, substitutions and waivers of admissions requirements, and substitutions and waivers of graduation requirements are outlined in the school's catalog/handbook. Written policies regarding course

The University of Akron (continued)

substitutions, general/basic LD accommodations, substitutions and waivers of admissions requirements, and substitutions and waivers of graduation requirements are available through the program or unit directly.

The University of Alabama
Office of Disability Services (ODS)

Tuscaloosa, AL 35487

http://www.ods.ua.edu

Contact: Ms. Judy Thorpe, Director, Office of Disability Services. Phone: 205-348-4285. Fax: 205-348-0804. E-mail: jthorpe@aalan.ua.edu.

Office of Disability Services (ODS) Approximately 150 registered undergraduate students were served during 2006–07. The program or unit includes 3 full-time staff members. Academic advisers, counselors, diagnostic specialists, regular education teachers, and trained peer tutors are provided collaboratively through on-campus or off-campus services.

Orientation The program or unit offers an optional 3-hour orientation for new students before classes begin.

Unique Aids and Services Aids, services, or accommodations include faculty training, parent workshops, and priority registration.

Assistive Technology Assistive technology is located in the DSS office, the main library and includes digital textbooks/e-text and scanning.

Subject-Area Tutoring Tutoring is offered one-on-one and in small groups for some subjects. Tutoring is provided collaboratively through on-campus or off-campus services via computer-based instruction and trained peer tutors.

Diagnostic Testing Testing for auditory processing, intelligence, learning strategies, learning styles, math, neuropsychological, personality, reading, spelling, study skills, visual processing, and written language is provided collaboratively through on-campus or off-campus services.

Enrichment Programs for career planning, college survival skills, health and nutrition, stress management, study skills, test taking, and written composition skills are provided collaboratively through on-campus or off-campus services. Credit is offered for health and nutrition and study skills.

Fees *Diagnostic Testing* fee is applicable.

Application For admittance to the program or unit, students are required to apply to the program directly and provide a psychoeducational report (3 years old or less). Upon application, materials documenting need for services should be sent only to the LD program or unit. Upon acceptance, documentation of need for services should be sent only to the LD program or unit. *Application deadline (LD program):* Rolling/continuous for fall and rolling/continuous for spring.

Written Policies Written policies regarding course substitutions, general/basic LD accommodations, and substitutions and waivers of graduation requirements are available on the program Web site.

The University of Alabama in Huntsville
PASS

301 Sparkman Drive

Huntsville, AL 35899

http://www.uah.edu/ARC/

Contact: Dr. Jared Dinehart, Disability Coordinator. Phone: 256-824-6203. Fax: 256-824-6672. E-mail: jared.dinehart@uah.edu.

PASS Approximately 160 registered undergraduate students were served during 2006–07. The program or unit includes 2 full-time and 3 part-time staff members. Graduate assistants/students, skill tutors, strategy tutors, and trained peer tutors are provided through the program or unit. Academic advisers, counselors, graduate assistants/students, regular education teachers, teacher trainees, and trained peer tutors are provided collaboratively through on-campus or off-campus services.

Unique Aids and Services Aids, services, or accommodations include advocates, career counseling, faculty training, and priority registration.

Subject-Area Tutoring Tutoring is offered one-on-one and in small groups for some subjects. Tutoring is provided through the program or unit via graduate assistants/students and trained peer tutors. Tutoring is also provided collaboratively through on-campus or off-campus services via computer-based instruction, graduate assistants/students, and trained peer tutors.

Diagnostic Testing Testing is provided through the program or unit for learning strategies, learning styles, and study skills. Testing for learning strategies, learning styles, personality, social skills, and study skills is provided collaboratively through on-campus or off-campus services.

Enrichment Enrichment programs are available through the program or unit for college survival skills, learning strategies, self-advocacy, study skills, test taking, and time management. Programs for career planning, college survival skills, health and nutrition, learning strategies, math, self-advocacy, stress management, study skills, test taking, time management, and written composition skills are provided collaboratively through on-campus or off-campus services.

Application For admittance to the program or unit, students are required to provide a psychoeducational report (5 years old or less). It is recommended that students provide documentation of high school services. Upon application, materials documenting need for services should be sent only to the LD program or unit. Upon acceptance, documentation of need for services should be sent only to the LD program or unit. *Application deadline (institutional):* 8/15. *Application deadline (LD program):* Rolling/continuous for fall and rolling/continuous for spring.

Written Policies Written policy regarding general/basic LD accommodations is available on the program Web site. Written policy regarding general/basic LD accommodations is outlined in the school's catalog/handbook. Written policies regarding course substitutions, general/basic LD accommodations, reduced course loads, substitutions and waivers of admissions requirements, and substitutions and waivers of graduation requirements are available through the program or unit directly.

University of Alaska Anchorage
Disability Support Services

3211 Providence Drive

Anchorage, AK 99508-8060

http://www.uaa.alaska.edu/

Contact: Ms. Kaela Parks, Director, Disability Support Services. Phone: 907-786-4535. Fax: 907-786-4531. E-mail: ankmk4@uaa.alaska.edu.

Disability Support Services Approximately 80 registered undergraduate students were served during 2006–07. Academic advisers, counselors, remediation/learning specialists, and trained peer tutors are provided collaboratively through on-campus or off-campus services.

Unique Aids and Services Aids, services, or accommodations include career counseling and priority registration.

Assistive Technology Assistive technology is located in campus labs, a special lab and includes digital textbooks/e-text, learning support software, scanning, and loaner equipment. Technology training is provided to incoming students.

Subject-Area Tutoring Tutoring is offered one-on-one for most subjects. Tutoring is provided collaboratively through on-campus or off-campus services via computer-based instruction, graduate assistants/students, and trained peer tutors.

Basic Skills Remediation Remediation is offered one-on-one and in class-size groups for computer skills, learning strategies, math, reading, spoken language, study skills, time management, and written language. Remediation is provided collaboratively through on-campus or off-campus services via computer-based instruction, graduate assistants/students, regular education teachers, and trained peer tutors.

Enrichment Programs for career planning, college survival skills, learning strategies, math, reading, stress management, study skills, test taking, time management, vocabulary development, and written composition skills are provided collaboratively through on-campus or off-campus services. Credit is offered for college survival skills, learning strategies, math, reading, stress management, study skills, test taking, time management, vocabulary development, and written composition skills.

Application For admittance to the program or unit, students are required to provide a psychoeducational report (3 years old or less) and provide an interview to discuss accommodation options. It is recommended that students provide documentation of high school services. Upon application, materials documenting need for services should be sent only to the LD program or unit. Upon acceptance, documentation of need for services should be sent only to the LD program or unit. *Application deadline (institutional):* 7/1. *Application deadline (LD program):* Rolling/continuous for fall and rolling/continuous for spring.

Written Policies Written policies regarding course substitutions, general/basic LD accommodations, grade forgiveness, reduced course loads, substitutions and waivers of admissions requirements, and substitutions and waivers of graduation requirements are available on the program Web site. Written policy regarding general/basic LD accommodations is outlined in the school's catalog/handbook. Written policies regarding course substitutions, general/basic LD accom-

modations, grade forgiveness, reduced course loads, substitutions and waivers of admissions requirements, and substitutions and waivers of graduation requirements are available through the program or unit directly.

University of Arkansas
Center for Educational Access

800 Hotz Hall

Fayetteville, AR 72701-1201

http://cea.uark.edu

Contact: Anne L. Jannarone, Director. Phone: 479-575-3104. Fax: 479-575-7445. E-mail: ada@uark.edu.

Center for Educational Access Approximately 300 registered undergraduate students were served during 2006–07. The program or unit includes 6 full-time and 15 part-time staff members. Diagnostic specialists and graduate assistants/students are provided through the program or unit. Academic advisers, coaches, counselors, graduate assistants/students, regular education teachers, remediation/learning specialists, skill tutors, strategy tutors, trained peer tutors, and other are provided collaboratively through on-campus or off-campus services.

Unique Aids and Services Aids, services, or accommodations include faculty training and priority registration.

Assistive Technology Assistive technology is located in campus labs, the DSS office and includes digital textbooks/e-text, learning support software, and scanning. Technology training is provided to incoming students.

Subject-Area Tutoring Tutoring is offered one-on-one, in small groups, and in class-size groups for some subjects. Tutoring is provided collaboratively through on-campus or off-campus services via computer-based instruction, graduate assistants/students, and trained peer tutors.

Diagnostic Testing Testing for auditory processing, intelligence, learning strategies, learning styles, math, motor skills, neuropsychological, personality, reading, spelling, spoken language, study skills, visual processing, and written language is provided collaboratively through on-campus or off-campus services.

Basic Skills Remediation Remediation is offered one-on-one, in small groups, and in class-size groups for computer skills, learning strategies, math, reading, spelling, spoken language, study skills, time management, visual processing, and written language. Remediation is provided collaboratively through on-campus or off-campus services via computer-based instruction, graduate assistants/students, regular education teachers, and trained peer tutors.

Enrichment Programs for career planning, college survival skills, health and nutrition, learning strategies, math, medication management, oral communication skills, practical computer skills, reading, self-advocacy, stress management, study skills, test taking, time management, and written composition skills are provided collaboratively through on-campus or off-campus services. Credit is offered for college survival skills.

Fees *Diagnostic Testing* fee is $300 to $500.

Application For admittance to the program or unit, students are required to apply to the program directly and provide a psychoeducational report. It is recommended that students provide documentation of high school services. Upon application, materials docu-

University of Arkansas (continued)

menting need for services should be sent only to the LD program or unit. *Application deadline (institutional): 8/15. Application deadline (LD program):* Rolling/continuous for fall and rolling/continuous for spring.

Written Policies Written policies regarding course substitutions, general/basic LD accommodations, substitutions and waivers of admissions requirements, and substitutions and waivers of graduation requirements are available on the program Web site. Written policies regarding course substitutions, grade forgiveness, substitutions and waivers of admissions requirements, and substitutions and waivers of graduation requirements are outlined in the school's catalog/handbook. Written policies regarding general/basic LD accommodations, grade forgiveness, and reduced course loads are available through the program or unit directly.

University of Arkansas at Fort Smith

PO Box 3649

Fort Smith, AR 72913-3649

http://www.uafortsmith.edu/

Contact: Mr. Roger A. Young, ADA Student Services Coordinator. Phone: 479-788-7577 Ext. 7577. Fax: 479-788-7587 Ext. 7587. E-mail: ryoung@uafortsmith.edu.

Approximately 73 registered undergraduate students were served during 2006–07. The program or unit includes 2 full-time staff members. Academic advisers, coaches, counselors, professional tutors, regular education teachers, remediation/learning specialists, skill tutors, and trained peer tutors are provided through the program or unit.

Orientation The program or unit offers a mandatory 1-hour orientation for new students individually by special arrangement.

Unique Aids and Services Aids, services, or accommodations include career counseling and priority registration.

Subject-Area Tutoring Tutoring is offered one-on-one and in small groups for all subjects. Tutoring is provided collaboratively through on-campus or off-campus services via computer-based instruction, graduate assistants/students, professional tutors, and trained peer tutors.

Basic Skills Remediation Remediation is offered one-on-one, in small groups, and in class-size groups for computer skills, learning strategies, math, reading, spelling, study skills, time management, and written language. Remediation is provided collaboratively through on-campus or off-campus services via computer-based instruction, graduate assistants/students, professional tutors, regular education teachers, and trained peer tutors.

Enrichment Enrichment programs are available through the program or unit for career planning. Programs for career planning, college survival skills, health and nutrition, learning strategies, math, oral communication skills, practical computer skills, reading, stress management, study skills, test taking, time management, and written composition skills are provided collaboratively through on-campus or off-campus services. Credit is offered for college survival skills and learning strategies.

Student Organization Students with Disabilities consists of 14 members.

Application For admittance to the program or unit, students are required to apply to the program directly and provide a psychoeducational report (5 years old or less). It is recommended that students provide documentation of high school services. Upon acceptance, documentation of need for services should be sent only to the LD program or unit. *Application deadline (institutional):* Continuous. *Application deadline (LD program):* Rolling/continuous for fall and rolling/continuous for spring.

Written Policies Written policy regarding general/basic LD accommodations is available on the program Web site. Written policies regarding course substitutions, general/basic LD accommodations, grade forgiveness, reduced course loads, substitutions and waivers of admissions requirements, and substitutions and waivers of graduation requirements are outlined in the school's catalog/handbook. Written policies regarding course substitutions, general/basic LD accommodations, grade forgiveness, reduced course loads, substitutions and waivers of admissions requirements, and substitutions and waivers of graduation requirements are available through the program or unit directly.

University of Baltimore
Disability Support Services

1420 North Charles Street

Baltimore, MD 21201-5779

http://www.ubalt.edu/disability

Contact: Ms. Jacquelyn Noelle Truelove-DeSimone, Director. Phone: 410-837-4141. Fax: 410-837-4932. E-mail: jtruelove@ubalt.edu.

Disability Support Services Approximately 65 registered undergraduate students were served during 2006–07. The program or unit includes 1 full-time staff member. Academic advisers, counselors, professional tutors, skill tutors, and other are provided collaboratively through on-campus or off-campus services.

Orientation The program or unit offers an optional 2-hour orientation for new students individually by special arrangement.

Unique Aids and Services Aids, services, or accommodations include career counseling, priority registration, weekly meetings with the DSS Director.

Assistive Technology Assistive technology is located in the DSS office and includes digital textbooks/e-text, learning support software, and scanning. Technology training is provided to incoming students.

Subject-Area Tutoring Tutoring is offered one-on-one and in small groups for most subjects. Tutoring is provided through the program or unit via graduate assistants/students. Tutoring is also provided collaboratively through on-campus or off-campus services via computer-based instruction, professional tutors, and trained peer tutors.

Basic Skills Remediation Remediation is offered one-on-one and in small groups for computer skills, learning strategies, math, study skills, time management, and written language. Remediation is provided collaboratively through on-campus or off-campus services via computer-based instruction, graduate assistants/students, professional tutors, and trained peer tutors.

Enrichment Enrichment programs are available through the program or unit for practical computer skills, self-advocacy, stress management, and test taking. Programs for career planning, college survival skills, health and nutrition, learning strategies, math, oral communication skills, practical computer skills, stress management, study skills, test taking, time management, and written composition skills are provided collaboratively through on-campus or off-campus services.

Application For admittance to the program or unit, students are required to provide a psychoeducational report (5 years old or less). Upon application, materials documenting need for services should be sent only to the LD program or unit. Upon acceptance, documentation of need for services should be sent only to the LD program or unit. *Application deadline (institutional): 2/15. Application deadline (LD program):* Rolling/continuous for fall and rolling/continuous for spring.

Written Policies Written policy regarding general/basic LD accommodations is available on the program Web site. Written policies regarding course substitutions and general/basic LD accommodations are available through the program or unit directly.

University of Calgary
Disability Resource Center

2500 University Drive, NW
Calgary, AB T2N 1N4
Canada
http://www.ucalgary.ca/drc
Contact: Judy Smith, Office Administrator. Phone: 403-220-8237. Fax: 403-210-1063. E-mail: jusmith@ucalgary.ca.

Disability Resource Center Approximately 320 registered undergraduate students were served during 2006–07. The program or unit includes 1 full-time and 1 part-time staff member. Diagnostic specialists and LD specialists are provided through the program or unit. Coaches, counselors, graduate assistants/students, professional tutors, strategy tutors, and trained peer tutors are provided collaboratively through on-campus or off-campus services.

Orientation The program or unit offers an optional 1-week orientation for new students before classes begin.

Summer Program To help prepare for the demands of college, there is an optional 1-week summer program prior to entering the school.

Unique Aids and Services Aids, services, or accommodations include career counseling, faculty training, and personal coach.

Assistive Technology Assistive technology is located in campus labs, a special lab and includes digital textbooks/e-text, learning support software, and scanning. Technology training is provided to incoming students.

Basic Skills Remediation Remediation is offered one-on-one for auditory processing, computer skills, learning strategies, reading, spelling, spoken language, study skills, time management, visual processing, and written language. Remediation is provided through the program or unit via computer-based instruction, graduate assistants/students, and LD specialists. Remediation is also provided collaboratively through on-campus or off-campus services via professional tutors and trained peer tutors.

Enrichment Enrichment programs are available through the program or unit for career planning, learning strategies, medication management, oral communication skills, reading, self-advocacy, stress management, study skills, time management, vocabulary develop-

ment, and written composition skills. Programs for college survival skills, health and nutrition, practical computer skills, and test taking are provided collaboratively through on-campus or off-campus services.

Fees *LD Program or Service* fee is $460 Canadian dollars. *Summer Program* fee is $460 Canadian dollars. *Orientation* fee is $460 Canadian dollars.

Application For admittance to the program or unit, students are required to provide a psychoeducational report (5 years old or less). Upon application, materials documenting need for services should be sent only to the LD program or unit. Upon acceptance, documentation of need for services should be sent only to the LD program or unit. *Application deadline (LD program):* Rolling/continuous for fall and rolling/continuous for spring.

Written Policies Written policy regarding general/basic LD accommodations is available on the program Web site. Written policy regarding general/basic LD accommodations is available through the program or unit directly.

University of California, Berkeley

Berkeley, CA 94720-1500
http://dsp.berkeley.edu/
Contact: Dr. Connie Chiba, Disability Services Coordinator. Phone: 510-642-0518. E-mail: cchiba@uclink.berkeley.edu.

Approximately 200 registered undergraduate students were served during 2006–07. The program or unit includes 2 full-time and 2 part-time staff members. LD specialists are provided through the program or unit.

Orientation The program or unit offers an optional 2- to 3-hour orientation for new students before classes begin.

Unique Aids and Services Aids, services, or accommodations include priority registration and support groups.

Assistive Technology Assistive technology is located in a special lab and includes digital textbooks/e-text, learning support software, and scanning. Technology training is provided to incoming students.

Subject-Area Tutoring Tutoring is offered one-on-one for some subjects. Tutoring is provided collaboratively through on-campus or off-campus services via trained peer tutors.

Enrichment Enrichment programs are available through the program or unit for career planning, college survival skills, learning strategies, reading, self-advocacy, study skills, test taking, and time management.

Student Organization Disabled Students' Union.

Application For admittance to the program or unit, students are required to provide a psychoeducational report. Upon application, materials documenting need for services should be sent only to admissions with institutional application materials. Upon acceptance, documentation of need for services should be sent only to the LD program or unit. *Application deadline (institutional): 11/30. Application deadline (LD program):* 11/30 for fall.

Written Policies Written policies regarding general/basic LD accommodations and reduced course loads are available on the program Web site. Written policies regarding course substitutions and substitutions and waivers of graduation requirements are available through the program or unit directly.

University of California, Los Angeles
Office for Students with Disabilities

405 Hilgard Avenue

Los Angeles, CA 90095

http://www.osd.ucla.edu

Contact: Dr. Julie Morris, Coordinator of Learning Disabilities Program. Phone: 310-794-5732. Fax: 310-825-9656. E-mail: jmorris@saonet.ucla.edu.

Office for Students with Disabilities Approximately 300 registered undergraduate students were served during 2006–07. The program or unit includes 2 full-time staff members and 1 part-time staff member. Counselors, diagnostic specialists, and LD specialists are provided through the program or unit. Academic advisers, counselors, diagnostic specialists, skill tutors, strategy tutors, and trained peer tutors are provided collaboratively through on-campus or off-campus services.

Orientation The program or unit offers an optional orientation for new students before classes begin.

Unique Aids and Services Aids, services, or accommodations include support groups.

Assistive Technology Assistive technology is located in campus labs and includes digital textbooks/e-text and scanning.

Subject-Area Tutoring Tutoring is offered one-on-one and in small groups for some subjects. Tutoring is provided collaboratively through on-campus or off-campus services via trained peer tutors.

Enrichment Enrichment programs are available through the program or unit for learning strategies, reading, test taking, time management, and written composition skills. Programs for study skills and written composition skills are provided collaboratively through on-campus or off-campus services.

Student Organization Disabled Student Union.

Application For admittance to the program or unit, students are required to provide a psychoeducational report (3 years old or less). It is recommended that students provide adult versions of tests for LD documentation. Upon acceptance, documentation of need for services should be sent only to the LD program or unit. *Application deadline (institutional):* 11/30. *Application deadline (LD program):* Rolling/continuous for fall and rolling/continuous for spring.

Written Policies Written policy regarding general/basic LD accommodations is available on the program Web site. Written policies regarding course substitutions, general/basic LD accommodations, and reduced course loads are available through the program or unit directly.

University of California, Santa Barbara
Disabled Students Program

Santa Barbara, CA 93106

http://www.sa.ucsb.edu/dsp

Contact: Disabled Students Program. Phone: 805-893-2668. Fax: 805-893-7127.

Disabled Students Program Approximately 200 registered undergraduate students were served during 2006–07. The program or unit includes 7 full-time staff members. LD specialists are provided through the program or unit. Academic advisers, coaches, counselors, diagnostic specialists, graduate assistants/students, professional tutors, regular education teachers, skill tutors, strategy tutors, and teacher trainees are provided collaboratively through on-campus or off-campus services.

Orientation The program or unit offers a mandatory 1- to 2-hour orientation for new students before classes begin and individually by special arrangement.

Unique Aids and Services Aids, services, or accommodations include advocates, priority registration, special exam accommodations, note-takers.

Assistive Technology Assistive technology is located in a special lab.

Subject-Area Tutoring Tutoring is offered in small groups for some subjects. Tutoring is provided collaboratively through on-campus or off-campus services via computer-based instruction, graduate assistants/students, and professional tutors.

Enrichment Enrichment programs are available through the program or unit for self-advocacy. Programs for career planning, college survival skills, health and nutrition, learning strategies, math, medication management, stress management, study skills, test taking, time management, and written composition skills are provided collaboratively through on-campus or off-campus services.

Application For admittance to the program or unit, students are required to apply to the program directly and provide documentation as specified on Web site: http://dsp.sa.ucsb.edu/GeneralInformation/Documentation.aspx. It is recommended that students provide a psychoeducational report (3 years old or less). Upon acceptance, documentation of need for services should be sent only to the LD program or unit. *Application deadline (institutional):* 11/30. *Application deadline (LD program):* Rolling/continuous for fall and rolling/continuous for spring.

Written Policies Written policy regarding general/basic LD accommodations is available on the program Web site.

University of Central Florida
Student Disability Services

4000 Central Florida Boulevard

Orlando, FL 32816

http://www.sds.sdes.ucf.edu

Contact: Ms. Pam Rea, Assistant Director. Phone: 407-823-2371. Fax: 407-823-2372. E-mail: prea@mail.ucf.edu. Head of LD Program: Dr. Philip N. Kalfin, Director. Phone: 407-823-2371. Fax: 407-823-2372. E-mail: pkalfin@mail.ucf.edu.

Student Disability Services Approximately 531 registered undergraduate students were served during 2006–07. The program or unit includes 6 full-time staff members. Remediation/learning specialists, skill tutors, strategy tutors, and other are provided collaboratively through on-campus or off-campus services.

Summer Program available to high school graduates.

Unique Aids and Services Aids, services, or accommodations include priority registration, note-takers, extended time on exams in a distraction reduced environment.

Assistive Technology Assistive technology is located in the DSS office and includes digital textbooks/e-text and scanning. Technology training is provided to incoming students.

Subject-Area Tutoring Tutoring is offered one-on-one, in small groups, and in class-size groups for some subjects. Tutoring is provided collaboratively through on-campus or off-campus services via graduate assistants/students and trained peer tutors.

Application For admittance to the program or unit, students are required to apply to the program directly and provide a psychoeducational report (3 years old or less). Upon application, materials documenting need for services should be sent only to admissions with institutional application materials. Upon acceptance, documentation of need for services should be sent only to the LD program or unit. *Application deadline (institutional):* 3/1. *Application deadline (LD program):* Rolling/continuous for fall and rolling/continuous for spring.

Written Policies Written policies regarding course substitutions, general/basic LD accommodations, reduced course loads, substitutions and waivers of admissions requirements, and substitutions and waivers of graduation requirements are available through the program or unit directly.

University of Central Missouri
Office of Accessibility Services

Warrensburg, MO 64093

http://www.ucmo.edu/access

Contact: Dr. Barbara J. Mayfield, Director, ADA and 504 Coordinator. Phone: 660-543-4421. Fax: 660-543-4724. E-mail: mayfield@ucmo.edu.

Office of Accessibility Services Approximately 180 registered undergraduate students were served during 2006–07. The program or unit includes 3 full-time and 20 part-time staff members. Academic advisers, graduate assistants/students, LD specialists, remediation/learning specialists, and strategy tutors are provided through the program or unit. Academic advisers, counselors, graduate assistants/students, regular education teachers, remediation/learning specialists, skill tutors, strategy tutors, trained peer tutors, and other are provided collaboratively through on-campus or off-campus services.

Orientation The program or unit offers an optional orientation for new students individually by special arrangement and during AE 1400 orientation course.

Unique Aids and Services Aids, services, or accommodations include advocates, career counseling, faculty training, priority registration, and support groups.

Assistive Technology Assistive technology is located in campus labs, the DSS office, a special lab and includes digital textbooks/e-text, learning support software, scanning, and Braille embosser. Technology training is provided to incoming students.

Subject-Area Tutoring Tutoring is offered in small groups for all subjects. Tutoring is provided collaboratively through on-campus or off-campus services via computer-based instruction, graduate assistants/students, and trained peer tutors.

Diagnostic Testing Testing for auditory processing, learning strategies, learning styles, personality, social skills, spoken language, study skills, and written language is provided collaboratively through on-campus or off-campus services.

Basic Skills Remediation Remediation is offered in small groups and in class-size groups for auditory processing, computer skills, learning strategies, math, reading, social skills, spoken language, study skills, time management, written language, and hearing. Remediation is provided collaboratively through on-campus or off-campus services via computer-based instruction, graduate assistants/students, professional tutors, and trained peer tutors.

Enrichment Enrichment programs are available through the program or unit for career planning, college survival skills, practical computer skills, self-advocacy, stress management, study skills, test taking, and time management. Programs for career planning, college survival skills, health and nutrition, learning strategies, math, oral communication skills, practical computer skills, reading, stress management, study skills, test taking, time management, vocabulary development, and written composition skills are provided collaboratively through on-campus or off-campus services. Credit is offered for career planning, college survival skills, health and nutrition, learning strategies, math, oral communication skills, practical computer skills, reading, stress management, study skills, test taking, time management, vocabulary development, and written composition skills.

Student Organization Fair Access Network for Students (FANS) consists of 12 members.

Application For admittance to the program or unit, students are required to apply to the program directly and provide a psychoeducational report (5 years old or less). It is recommended that students provide documentation of high school services. Upon application, materials documenting need for services should be sent only to the LD program or unit. Upon acceptance, documentation of need for services should be sent only to the LD program or unit. *Application deadline (institutional):* Continuous. *Application deadline (LD program):* Rolling/continuous for fall and rolling/continuous for spring.

Written Policies Written policy regarding general/basic LD accommodations is available on the program Web site. Written policy regarding general/basic LD accommodations is outlined in the school's catalog/handbook. Written policies regarding course substitutions, general/basic LD accommodations, grade forgiveness, reduced course loads, substitutions and waivers of admissions requirements, and substitutions and waivers of graduation requirements are available through the program or unit directly.

University of Central Oklahoma
Disability Support Services

100 North University Drive

Edmond, OK 73034-5209

http://www.ucok.edu/disability_support/

Contact: Kimberly Fields, Assistant Director. Phone: 405-974-2516. Fax: 405-974-3894. E-mail: kfields1@ucok.edu.

Disability Support Services Approximately 275 registered undergraduate students were served during 2006–07. The program or unit includes 4 full-time and 3 part-time staff members. Academic advisers, coaches, counselors, and LD specialists are provided through

University of Central Oklahoma (continued)

the program or unit. Academic advisers, coaches, counselors, regular education teachers, skill tutors, and strategy tutors are provided collaboratively through on-campus or off-campus services.

Orientation The program or unit offers an optional orientation for new students during registration and individually by special arrangement.

Unique Aids and Services Aids, services, or accommodations include support groups.

Assistive Technology Assistive technology is located in campus labs, the DSS office and includes digital textbooks/e-text and learning support software.

Enrichment Enrichment programs are available through the program or unit for career planning, college survival skills, learning strategies, oral communication skills, stress management, study skills, and time management. Programs for career planning, college survival skills, learning strategies, math, oral communication skills, stress management, study skills, and time management are provided collaboratively through on-campus or off-campus services.

Student Organization Students for an Accessible Society consists of 60 members.

Application For admittance to the program or unit, students are required to provide a psychoeducational report. It is recommended that students provide documentation of high school services. Upon acceptance, documentation of need for services should be sent only to the LD program or unit. *Application deadline (institutional):* Continuous. *Application deadline (LD program):* Rolling/continuous for fall.

Written Policies Written policy regarding general/basic LD accommodations is available on the program Web site. Written policies regarding general/basic LD accommodations and grade forgiveness are outlined in the school's catalog/handbook. Written policies regarding course substitutions, general/basic LD accommodations, reduced course loads, substitutions and waivers of admissions requirements, and substitutions and waivers of graduation requirements are available through the program or unit directly.

University of Cincinnati
Disability Services Office/Academic Excellence and Support Services

2624 Clifton Avenue
Cincinnati, OH 45221
http://www.uc.edu/sas/disability
Contact: Ms. Debra Spotts Merchant JD, Director. Phone: 513-556-6823. Fax: 513-556-1383. E-mail: debra.merchant@uc.edu.

Disability Services Office/Academic Excellence and Support Services Approximately 350 registered undergraduate students were served during 2006–07. The program or unit includes 6 full-time staff members. Counselors and graduate assistants/students are provided through the program or unit. Academic advisers, counselors, diagnostic specialists, graduate assistants/students, remediation/learning specialists, skill tutors, and trained peer tutors are provided collaboratively through on-campus or off-campus services.

Unique Aids and Services Aids, services, or accommodations include advocates, priority registration, support groups, one-on-one progress checks.

Assistive Technology Assistive technology is located in the DSS office and includes digital textbooks/e-text and scanning. Technology training is provided to incoming students.

Subject-Area Tutoring Tutoring is offered one-on-one and in small groups for most subjects. Tutoring is provided collaboratively through on-campus or off-campus services via graduate assistants/students, trained peer tutors, and other.

Basic Skills Remediation Remediation is offered in class-size groups for math, study skills, time management, and written language. Remediation is provided collaboratively through on-campus or off-campus services via regular education teachers and trained peer tutors.

Enrichment Enrichment programs are available through the program or unit for self-advocacy. Programs for career planning, college survival skills, health and nutrition, practical computer skills, stress management, study skills, test taking, time management, and written composition skills are provided collaboratively through on-campus or off-campus services. Credit is offered for career planning, college survival skills, practical computer skills, and written composition skills.

Application For admittance to the program or unit, students are required to apply to the program directly and provide a psychoeducational report (3 years old or less). It is recommended that students provide documentation of high school services. Upon application, materials documenting need for services should be sent only to the LD program or unit. Upon acceptance, documentation of need for services should be sent only to the LD program or unit. *Application deadline (institutional):* Continuous. *Application deadline (LD program):* Rolling/continuous for fall and rolling/continuous for spring.

Written Policies Written policy regarding general/basic LD accommodations is available on the program Web site. Written policy regarding course substitutions is available through the program or unit directly.

University of Colorado at Boulder
Academic Access and Resources

Boulder, CO 80309
http://www.colorado.edu/disabilityservices
Contact: Jim Cohn, Coordinator of Academic Resource Team. Phone: 303-492-8671. Fax: 303-492-5601. E-mail: dsinfo@spot.colorado.edu.

Academic Access and Resources Approximately 250 registered undergraduate students were served during 2006–07. The program or unit includes 3 full-time and 10 part-time staff members. Academic advisers, diagnostic specialists, LD specialists, skill tutors, and strategy tutors are provided through the program or unit. Academic advisers, counselors, diagnostic specialists, professional tutors, regular education teachers, remediation/learning specialists, strategy tutors, and trained peer tutors are provided collaboratively through on-campus or off-campus services.

Orientation The program or unit offers an optional 1.5-hour orientation for new students before classes begin and individually by special arrangement.

Colleges for Students with Learning Disabilities or AD/HD

Unique Aids and Services Aids, services, or accommodations include advocates, career counseling, faculty training, individualized meetings with students.

Assistive Technology Assistive technology is located in the DSS office and includes digital textbooks/e-text, learning support software, and scanning.

Subject-Area Tutoring Tutoring is offered for most subjects. Tutoring is provided collaboratively through on-campus or off-campus services via computer-based instruction, graduate assistants/ students, professional tutors, and trained peer tutors.

Diagnostic Testing Testing is provided through the program or unit for auditory processing, handwriting, intelligence, learning strategies, learning styles, math, neuropsychological, reading, spelling, spoken language, study skills, visual processing, and written language. Testing for auditory processing, intelligence, learning styles, math, neuropsychological, personality, reading, social skills, spelling, spoken language, visual processing, and written language is provided collaboratively through on-campus or off-campus services.

Enrichment Enrichment programs are available through the program or unit for career planning, college survival skills, learning strategies, oral communication skills, reading, self-advocacy, stress management, study skills, test taking, time management, and written composition skills. Programs for career planning, college survival skills, learning strategies, math, oral communication skills, practical computer skills, self-advocacy, stress management, study skills, test taking, time management, and written composition skills are provided collaboratively through on-campus or off-campus services.

Fees *Diagnostic Testing* fee is $500.

Application For admittance to the program or unit, students are required to provide a psychoeducational report (3 years old or less). Upon application, materials documenting need for services should be sent only to the LD program or unit. Upon acceptance, documentation of need for services should be sent only to the LD program or unit. *Application deadline (institutional): 1/15. Application deadline (LD program):* Rolling/continuous for fall and rolling/continuous for spring.

Written Policies Written policies regarding general/basic LD accommodations and substitutions and waivers of graduation requirements are available on the program Web site. Written policy regarding general/basic LD accommodations is outlined in the school's catalog/handbook. Written policies regarding general/basic LD accommodations, substitutions and waivers of admissions requirements, and substitutions and waivers of graduation requirements are available through the program or unit directly.

University of Connecticut
University Program for College Students with Learning Disabilities (UPLD)

Storrs, CT 06269

http://www.upld.uconn.edu

Contact: Dr. David R. Parker, Director, University Program for College Students with Learning Disabilities. Phone: 860-486-0178. Fax: 860-486-5799.

University Program for College Students with Learning Disabilities (UPLD) Approximately 170 registered undergraduate students were served during 2006–07. The program or unit includes

1 full-time and 4 part-time staff members. Graduate assistants/ students and LD specialists are provided through the program or unit. Academic advisers, coaches, counselors, and trained peer tutors are provided collaboratively through on-campus or off-campus services.

Application For admittance to the program or unit, students are required to provide a psychoeducational report (3 years old or less). It is recommended that students provide documentation of high school services. Upon acceptance, documentation of need for services should be sent only to the LD program or unit. *Application deadline (institutional): 2/1. Application deadline (LD program):* Rolling/continuous for fall and rolling/continuous for spring.

Written Policies Written policies regarding course substitutions and general/basic LD accommodations are available on the program Web site. Written policies regarding course substitutions and general/ basic LD accommodations are outlined in the school's catalog/ handbook. Written policies regarding course substitutions, general/ basic LD accommodations, and reduced course loads are available through the program or unit directly.

University of Dayton
LEAD: Disability Services

300 College Park

Dayton, OH 45469-1300

http://lead.udayton.edu/prospective/disability/index.htm

Contact: Ms. Brenda D. Cooper, Program Coordinator of LEAD: Disability Services. Phone: 937-229-2066. Fax: 937-229-3270. E-mail: brenda.cooper@notes.udayton.edu. Head of LD Program: Dr. Tim B. King, Director of LEAD Services. Phone: 937-229-2066. Fax: 937-229-3270. E-mail: tim.king@notes.udayton.edu.

LEAD: Disability Services Approximately 360 registered undergraduate students were served during 2006–07. The program or unit includes 3 full-time staff members and 1 part-time staff member. Counselors, LD specialists, remediation/learning specialists, and special education teachers are provided through the program or unit. Academic advisers, coaches, counselors, diagnostic specialists, regular education teachers, skill tutors, special education teachers, and trained peer tutors are provided collaboratively through on-campus or off-campus services.

Unique Aids and Services Aids, services, or accommodations include faculty training and priority registration.

Assistive Technology Assistive technology is located in campus labs, a special lab, the library and includes digital textbooks/e-text. Technology training is provided to incoming students.

Subject-Area Tutoring Tutoring is offered one-on-one, in small groups, and in class-size groups for all subjects. Tutoring is provided collaboratively through on-campus or off-campus services via computer-based instruction and trained peer tutors.

Basic Skills Remediation Remediation is offered one-on-one and in small groups for learning strategies, math, study skills, time management, and written language. Remediation is provided collaboratively through on-campus or off-campus services via trained peer tutors.

Enrichment Enrichment programs are available through the program or unit for self-advocacy, stress management, study skills, test taking, and time management. Programs for career planning, health

University of Dayton (continued)

and nutrition, learning strategies, math, practical computer skills, self-advocacy, stress management, study skills, test taking, time management, and written composition skills are provided collaboratively through on-campus or off-campus services.

Application For admittance to the program or unit, students are required to provide a psychoeducational report (5 years old or less). It is recommended that students provide documentation of high school services and provide diagnostic report/summary with corresponding codes. Upon application, materials documenting need for services should be sent to both admissions and the LD program or unit. Upon acceptance, documentation of need for services should be sent only to the LD program or unit. *Application deadline (institutional):* Continuous. *Application deadline (LD program):* Rolling/continuous for fall.

Written Policies Written policy regarding general/basic LD accommodations is available on the program Web site. Written policy regarding general/basic LD accommodations is outlined in the school's catalog/handbook. Written policy regarding general/basic LD accommodations is available through the program or unit directly.

University of Delaware
LD/ADHD Services, Academic Enrichment Center

Newark, DE 19716
http://www.aec.udel.edu

Contact: Ms. Catherine M. Conrad, Staff Assistant. Phone: 302-831-2805. Fax: 302-831-4128. E-mail: cmconrad@udel.edu. Head of LD Program: Ms. Lysbet J. Murray, Associate Director, Academic Enrichment Center. Phone: 302-831-3025. Fax: 302-831-4128. E-mail: lysbet@udel.edu.

LD/ADHD Services, Academic Enrichment Center Approximately 250 registered undergraduate students were served during 2006–07. The program or unit includes 2 full-time staff members and 1 part-time staff member. LD specialists are provided through the program or unit. Academic advisers, graduate assistants/students, skill tutors, and trained peer tutors are provided collaboratively through on-campus or off-campus services.

Assistive Technology Assistive technology is located in the library.

Subject-Area Tutoring Tutoring is offered one-on-one and in small groups for most subjects. Tutoring is provided collaboratively through on-campus or off-campus services via trained peer tutors.

Application For admittance to the program or unit, students are required to apply to the program directly, provide a psychoeducational report (3 years old or less), and provide evidence of current impact on academic performance. It is recommended that students provide documentation of high school services. Upon application, materials documenting need for services should be sent only to the LD program or unit. Upon acceptance, documentation of need for services should be sent only to the LD program or unit. *Application deadline (institutional):* 1/15. *Application deadline (LD program):* Rolling/continuous for fall and rolling/continuous for spring.

Written Policies Written policies regarding course substitutions and general/basic LD accommodations are available on the program Web site. Written policies regarding course substitutions and general/basic LD accommodations are available through the program or unit directly.

University of Detroit Mercy
UAS/Disability Support Services

4001 W McNichols Rd, PO Box 19900

Detroit, MI 48219-0900

http://www.udmercy.edu/uas/disability_support/

Contact: Emilie A. Gallegos, Director of UAS/Disability Support Services. Phone: 313-578-0310. Fax: 313-578-0342. E-mail: gallegem@udmercy.edu.

UAS/Disability Support Services Approximately 75 registered undergraduate students were served during 2006–07. The program or unit includes 2 full-time and 2 part-time staff members. Professional tutors, remediation/learning specialists, skill tutors, strategy tutors, and trained peer tutors are provided through the program or unit. Academic advisers, diagnostic specialists, and LD specialists are provided collaboratively through on-campus or off-campus services.

Unique Aids and Services Aids, services, or accommodations include advocates and faculty training.

Assistive Technology Assistive technology is located in the DSS office and includes digital textbooks/e-text, learning support software, and scanning.

Subject-Area Tutoring Tutoring is offered one-on-one and in small groups for most subjects. Tutoring is provided through the program or unit via computer-based instruction, graduate assistants/students, professional tutors, and trained peer tutors.

Diagnostic Testing Testing is provided through the program or unit for learning strategies, learning styles, math, personality, reading, spelling, and study skills. Testing for intelligence, motor skills, personality, reading, social skills, and written language is provided collaboratively through on-campus or off-campus services.

Basic Skills Remediation Remediation is offered one-on-one and in small groups for computer skills, learning strategies, math, reading, study skills, time management, and written language. Remediation is provided through the program or unit via computer-based instruction, graduate assistants/students, professional tutors, teacher trainees, and trained peer tutors.

Enrichment Enrichment programs are available through the program or unit for college survival skills, learning strategies, math, reading, stress management, study skills, test taking, time management, vocabulary development, and written composition skills. Programs for career planning, health and nutrition, math, and written composition skills are provided collaboratively through on-campus or off-campus services. Credit is offered for career planning, college survival skills, health and nutrition, learning strategies, reading, and vocabulary development.

Fees *Diagnostic Testing* fee is $0 to $300.

Application For admittance to the program or unit, students are required to provide a psychoeducational report (3 years old or less). It is recommended that students provide documentation of high school services. Upon application, materials documenting need for services should be sent only to the LD program or unit. Upon acceptance, documentation of need for services should be sent only to the LD program or unit. *Application deadline (LD program):* Rolling/continuous for fall and rolling/continuous for spring.

Written Policies Written policy regarding general/basic LD accommodations is available on the program Web site. Written policy regarding general/basic LD accommodations is outlined in the school's catalog/handbook. Written policies regarding course substitutions, general/basic LD accommodations, and reduced course loads are available through the program or unit directly.

University of Dubuque
Academic Support Center

2000 University Avenue

Dubuque, IA 52001-5099

http://www.dbq.edu/asc/disabilities.cfm

Contact: Susanna Robey, Director of Academic Resource Center. Phone: 563-589-3218. E-mail: srobey@dbq.edu.

Academic Support Center Approximately 25 registered undergraduate students were served during 2006–07. The program or unit includes 3 full-time staff members. Academic advisers and professional tutors are provided through the program or unit. Coaches, counselors, diagnostic specialists, graduate assistants/students, LD specialists, and regular education teachers are provided collaboratively through on-campus or off-campus services.

Unique Aids and Services Aids, services, or accommodations include advocates, career counseling, personal coach, and priority registration.

Assistive Technology Assistive technology is located in the Academic Support Center and includes digital textbooks/e-text, learning support software, and scanning. Technology training is provided to incoming students.

Subject-Area Tutoring Tutoring is offered one-on-one for most subjects. Tutoring is provided through the program or unit via computer-based instruction, graduate assistants/students, LD specialists, professional tutors, and trained peer tutors.

Basic Skills Remediation Remediation is offered one-on-one and in class-size groups for auditory processing, computer skills, handwriting, learning strategies, math, motor skills, reading, social skills, spelling, spoken language, study skills, time management, visual processing, and written language. Remediation is provided through the program or unit via computer-based instruction, graduate assistants/students, LD specialists, professional tutors, and regular education teachers.

Enrichment Enrichment programs are available through the program or unit for learning strategies, math, oral communication skills, practical computer skills, reading, study skills, test taking, time management, vocabulary development, and written composition skills. Programs for career planning, college survival skills, health and nutrition, self-advocacy, and stress management are provided collaboratively through on-campus or off-campus services. Credit is offered for oral communication skills and practical computer skills.

Application For admittance to the program or unit, students are required to provide a psychoeducational report (3 years old or less). It is recommended that students apply to the program directly, provide documentation of high school services, and provide physician report. Upon application, materials documenting need for services should be sent to both admissions and the LD program or unit. Upon acceptance, documentation of need for services should be sent only to the LD program or unit. *Application deadline (institutional):* Continuous. *Application deadline (LD program):* Rolling/continuous for fall and rolling/continuous for spring.

Written Policies Written policy regarding general/basic LD accommodations is available on the program Web site. Written policy regarding general/basic LD accommodations is outlined in the school's catalog/handbook. Written policy regarding substitutions and waivers of admissions requirements is available through the program or unit directly.

University of Evansville
Counseling Center

1800 Lincoln Avenue

Evansville, IN 47722

http://www.evansville.edu

Contact: Sylvia Buck, Director of Counseling/Coordinator of Disability Services. Phone: 812-488-2663. Fax: 812-488-2156. E-mail: sb79@evansville.edu.

Counseling Center Approximately 35 registered undergraduate students were served during 2006–07. The program or unit includes 2 full-time staff members. Counselors are provided through the program or unit. Trained peer tutors are provided collaboratively through on-campus or off-campus services.

Assistive Technology Assistive technology is located in the DSS office and includes digital textbooks/e-text.

Subject-Area Tutoring Tutoring is offered in small groups for some subjects. Tutoring is provided collaboratively through on-campus or off-campus services via trained peer tutors.

Enrichment Programs for career planning, stress management, time management, and written composition skills are provided collaboratively through on-campus or off-campus services.

Application For admittance to the program or unit, students are required to provide a psychoeducational report. It is recommended that students provide documentation of high school services. Upon application, materials documenting need for services should be sent only to the LD program or unit. Upon acceptance, documentation of need for services should be sent only to the LD program or unit. *Application deadline (institutional):* 2/1. *Application deadline (LD program):* Rolling/continuous for fall and rolling/continuous for spring.

Written Policies Written policy regarding general/basic LD accommodations is available on the program Web site. Written policy regarding general/basic LD accommodations is outlined in the school's catalog/handbook. Written policies regarding course substitutions and general/basic LD accommodations are available through the program or unit directly.

The University of Findlay
Office of Disability Services

1000 North Main Street

Findlay, OH 45840-3653

http://www.findlay.edu/offices/adminoffices/disabilityservices

Contact: Mrs. Lori B. Colchagoff, The Director of Disability Services. Phone: 419-434-5532. Fax: 419-434-5748. E-mail: lcolchagoff@findlay.edu.

The University of Findlay (continued)

Office of Disability Services Approximately 25 registered undergraduate students were served during 2006–07. The program or unit includes 1 full-time and 2 part-time staff members. Academic advisers, coaches, counselors, graduate assistants/students, regular education teachers, and trained peer tutors are provided through the program or unit. Academic advisers, coaches, counselors, graduate assistants/students, regular education teachers, and trained peer tutors are provided collaboratively through on-campus or off-campus services.

Unique Aids and Services Aids, services, or accommodations include advocates and faculty training.

Assistive Technology Assistive technology is located in campus labs, the DSS office and includes digital textbooks/e-text. Technology training is provided to incoming students.

Subject-Area Tutoring Tutoring is offered one-on-one and in small groups for most subjects. Tutoring is provided through the program or unit via computer-based instruction, graduate assistants/students, and trained peer tutors. Tutoring is also provided collaboratively through on-campus or off-campus services via graduate assistants/students.

Basic Skills Remediation Remediation is offered one-on-one and in small groups for learning strategies, social skills, study skills, and time management. Remediation is provided through the program or unit via graduate assistants/students and trained peer tutors.

Enrichment Enrichment programs are available through the program or unit for career planning, college survival skills, learning strategies, study skills, test taking, time management, and written composition skills. Programs for reading, stress management, and written composition skills are provided collaboratively through on-campus or off-campus services. Credit is offered for career planning, college survival skills, learning strategies, and reading.

Application For admittance to the program or unit, students are required to apply to the program directly, provide a psychoeducational report, and provide documentation of high school services. Upon application, materials documenting need for services should be sent only to the LD program or unit. Upon acceptance, documentation of need for services should be sent only to the LD program or unit. *Application deadline (institutional):* Continuous. *Application deadline (LD program):* Rolling/continuous for fall and rolling/continuous for spring.

Written Policies Written policy regarding general/basic LD accommodations is available on the program Web site. Written policy regarding general/basic LD accommodations is outlined in the school's catalog/handbook. Written policies regarding course substitutions, general/basic LD accommodations, reduced course loads, substitutions and waivers of admissions requirements, and substitutions and waivers of graduation requirements are available through the program or unit directly.

University of Great Falls

1301 Twentieth Street South

Great Falls, MT 59405

http://www.ugf.edu/

Contact: Kathy Meier, Learning Disabilities Specialists. Phone: 406-791-5213. Fax: 406-791-5220. E-mail: kmeier01@ugf.edu. Head of LD Program: Michelle Maloney,

Director of Student Support Services. Phone: 406-791-5212. Fax: 406-791-5220. E-mail: mmaloney01@ugf.edu.

Approximately 30 registered undergraduate students were served during 2006–07. The program or unit includes 3 full-time staff members. Counselors, diagnostic specialists, LD specialists, professional tutors, remediation/learning specialists, skill tutors, strategy tutors, and trained peer tutors are provided through the program or unit. Academic advisers, counselors, and LD specialists are provided collaboratively through on-campus or off-campus services.

Orientation The program or unit offers an optional orientation for new students after classes begin and individually by special arrangement.

Summer Program To help prepare for the demands of college, there is an optional 1-week summer program prior to entering the school available to high school graduates that focuses on computing skills, life skills and/or college life adjustment, specific subject tutoring, study skills, test-taking skills, and time management. The program accepts students from out-of-state.

Unique Aids and Services Aids, services, or accommodations include advocates, career counseling, faculty training, priority registration, support groups, and weekly meetings with faculty.

Assistive Technology Assistive technology is located in the DSS office and includes learning support software and scanning. Technology training is provided to incoming students.

Subject-Area Tutoring Tutoring is offered one-on-one, in small groups, and in class-size groups for all subjects. Tutoring is provided through the program or unit via LD specialists, professional tutors, and trained peer tutors. Tutoring is also provided collaboratively through on-campus or off-campus services via computer-based instruction and graduate assistants/students.

Diagnostic Testing Testing is provided through the program or unit for learning strategies, learning styles, reading, social skills, spelling, spoken language, and study skills. Testing for auditory processing, handwriting, intelligence, math, motor skills, visual processing, and written language is provided collaboratively through on-campus or off-campus services.

Basic Skills Remediation Remediation is offered one-on-one, in small groups, and in class-size groups for computer skills, learning strategies, math, reading, social skills, spelling, spoken language, study skills, time management, visual processing, and written language. Remediation is provided through the program or unit via LD specialists, professional tutors, and trained peer tutors. Remediation is also provided collaboratively through on-campus or off-campus services via computer-based instruction, graduate assistants/students, regular education teachers, special education teachers, and teacher trainees.

Enrichment Enrichment programs are available through the program or unit for career planning, college survival skills, health and nutrition, learning strategies, math, oral communication skills, practical computer skills, reading, self-advocacy, stress management, study skills, test taking, time management, vocabulary development, and written composition skills. Programs for career planning, college survival skills, health and nutrition, learning strategies, math, medication management, oral communication skills, practical computer skills, reading, self-advocacy, stress management, study skills, test taking, time management, vocabulary development, and written composition skills are provided collaboratively through on-campus or off-campus services. Credit is offered for practical computer skills and written composition skills.

Application For admittance to the program or unit, students are required to provide a psychoeducational report (3 years old or less) and provide documentation of high school services. Upon application, materials documenting need for services should be sent only to the LD program or unit. Upon acceptance, documentation of need for services should be sent only to the LD program or unit. *Application deadline (institutional):* 8/1. *Application deadline (LD program):* Rolling/continuous for fall and rolling/continuous for spring.

Written Policies Written policies regarding course substitutions, general/basic LD accommodations, grade forgiveness, reduced course loads, and substitutions and waivers of graduation requirements are outlined in the school's catalog/handbook. Written policy regarding general/basic LD accommodations is available through the program or unit directly.

University of Guelph
Centre for Students with Disabilities

Guelph, ON N1G 2W1

Canada

http://www.slcs.uoguelph.ca/csd

Contact: Carol Herriot, Learning Disability Specialist. Phone: 519-824-4120 Ext. 56208. Fax: 519-824-9689. E-mail: cherriot@uoguelph.ca.

Centre for Students with Disabilities Approximately 950 registered undergraduate students were served during 2006–07. The program or unit includes 10 full-time and 2 part-time staff members. Coaches and LD specialists are provided through the program or unit. Academic advisers, counselors, diagnostic specialists, professional tutors, skill tutors, and strategy tutors are provided collaboratively through on-campus or off-campus services.

Orientation The program or unit offers an optional 4-hour orientation for new students before classes begin.

Summer Program To help prepare for the demands of college, there is an optional 7-day summer program prior to entering the school available to high school graduates that focuses on computing skills, life skills and/or college life adjustment, self-advocacy, study skills, test-taking skills, and time management. The program is available to students attending other colleges.

Assistive Technology Assistive technology is located in campus labs and includes digital textbooks/e-text, learning support software, and scanning. Technology training is provided to incoming students.

Enrichment Enrichment programs are available through the program or unit for learning strategies, self-advocacy, test taking, and written composition skills. Programs for career planning, college survival skills, health and nutrition, medication management, practical computer skills, study skills, and written composition skills are provided collaboratively through on-campus or off-campus services. Credit is offered for college survival skills, learning strategies, oral communication skills, practical computer skills, reading, self-advocacy, stress management, study skills, test taking, and written composition skills.

Application For admittance to the program or unit, students are required to provide a psychoeducational report (3 years old or less). It is recommended that students provide documentation of high school services. Upon application, materials documenting need for services should be sent only to the LD program or unit. Upon

acceptance, documentation of need for services should be sent only to the LD program or unit. *Application deadline (institutional):* 3/1. *Application deadline (LD program):* Rolling/continuous for fall and rolling/continuous for spring.

Written Policies Written policy regarding general/basic LD accommodations is available through the program or unit directly.

University of Hartford
Learning Plus, L+

200 Bloomfield Avenue

West Hartford, CT 06117-1599

http://uhaweb.hartford.edu/LDSupport/

Contact: Ms. E. Lynne Golden, Director of Learning Plus. Phone: 860-768-4312. Fax: 860-768-4183. E-mail: golden@hartford.edu.

Learning Plus, L+ Approximately 175 registered undergraduate students were served during 2006–07. The program or unit includes 1 full-time and 6 part-time staff members. LD specialists, remediation/learning specialists, and strategy tutors are provided through the program or unit. Counselors, LD specialists, and remediation/learning specialists are provided collaboratively through on-campus or off-campus services.

Orientation The program or unit offers an optional 1-hour orientation for new students after classes begin and individually by special arrangement.

Assistive Technology Assistive technology is located in the DSS office and includes digital textbooks/e-text and learning support software.

Enrichment Enrichment programs are available through the program or unit for college survival skills, learning strategies, math, reading, self-advocacy, stress management, study skills, test taking, time management, and written composition skills. Programs for career planning, medication management, reading, stress management, study skills, test taking, time management, and written composition skills are provided collaboratively through on-campus or off-campus services. Credit is offered for test taking, time management, and written composition skills.

Application For admittance to the program or unit, students are required to provide a psychoeducational report (3 years old or less) and provide aptitude test results (WAIS III), achievement test results (WIAT or WJR), and information processing. It is recommended that students provide documentation of high school services. Upon acceptance, documentation of need for services should be sent only to the LD program or unit. *Application deadline (institutional):* Continuous. *Application deadline (LD program):* Rolling/continuous for fall and rolling/continuous for spring.

Written Policies Written policies regarding general/basic LD accommodations, substitutions and waivers of admissions requirements, and substitutions and waivers of graduation requirements are available on the program Web site. Written policies regarding general/basic LD accommodations, substitutions and waivers of admissions requirements, and substitutions and waivers of graduation requirements are outlined in the school's catalog/handbook. Written policies regarding course substitutions, general/basic LD accommodations, reduced course loads, substitutions and waivers of admissions requirements, and substitutions and waivers of graduation requirements are available through the program or unit directly.

University of Hawaii at Manoa
KOKUA Program

2500 Campus Road

Honolulu, HI 96822

http://www.uhm.hawaii.edu/

Contact: Ann Ito, Coordinator. Phone: 808-956-7511. E-mail: kokua@hawaii.edu.

KOKUA Program Approximately 250 registered undergraduate students were served during 2006–07. The program or unit includes 3 full-time staff members. Academic advisers and counselors are provided through the program or unit. Academic advisers, counselors, and regular education teachers are provided collaboratively through on-campus or off-campus services.

Orientation The program or unit offers an optional orientation for new students individually by special arrangement.

Unique Aids and Services Aids, services, or accommodations include advocates and priority registration.

Application For admittance to the program or unit, students are required to provide a psychoeducational report. It is recommended that students provide documentation of high school services. Upon application, materials documenting need for services should be sent only to the LD program or unit. Upon acceptance, documentation of need for services should be sent only to the LD program or unit. *Application deadline (institutional):* 5/1. *Application deadline (LD program):* Rolling/continuous for fall and rolling/continuous for spring.

University of Hawaii–West Oahu

96-129 Ala Ike

Pearl City, HI 96782-3366

http://www.uhwo.hawaii.edu/

Contact: Janice Takaki, Student Services Specialist. Phone: 808-454-4700. Fax: 808-453-6075. E-mail: takaki@hawaii.edu.

The program or unit includes 1 full-time staff member. Academic advisers are provided collaboratively through on-campus or off-campus services.

Assistive Technology Assistive technology is located in the DSS office and includes digital textbooks/e-text.

Application For admittance to the program or unit, students are required to provide a psychoeducational report. It is recommended that students provide documentation of high school services. Upon acceptance, documentation of need for services should be sent only to the LD program or unit. *Application deadline (institutional):* 8/1. *Application deadline (LD program):* Rolling/continuous for fall and rolling/continuous for spring.

Written Policies Written policy regarding general/basic LD accommodations is available through the program or unit directly.

University of Houston
Justin Dart, Jr. Center for Students with DisABILITIES

4800 Calhoun Road

Houston, TX 77204

http://www.uh.edu/csd

Contact: Scott Crain, Counselor. Phone: 713-743-5400. Fax: 713-743-5396. E-mail: wscrain@mail.uh.edu. Head of LD Program: Cheryl Amoruso, Director. Phone: 713-743-5400. Fax: 713-743-5396. E-mail: camoruso@mail.uh.edu.

Justin Dart, Jr. Center for Students with DisABILITIES Approximately 375 registered undergraduate students were served during 2006–07. The program or unit includes 6 full-time and 5 part-time staff members. Coaches, counselors, LD specialists, and strategy tutors are provided through the program or unit. Academic advisers, coaches, counselors, diagnostic specialists, graduate assistants/students, LD specialists, professional tutors, regular education teachers, remediation/learning specialists, skill tutors, special education teachers, strategy tutors, teacher trainees, and trained peer tutors are provided collaboratively through on-campus or off-campus services.

Orientation The program or unit offers a mandatory orientation for new students individually by special arrangement and during the 'Cougar Preview".

Unique Aids and Services Aids, services, or accommodations include career counseling, personal coach, priority registration, and support groups.

Assistive Technology Assistive technology is located in the DSS office and includes digital textbooks/e-text, scanning, and voice-to-text software, screen reading software, screen magnification software. Technology training is provided to incoming students.

Subject-Area Tutoring Tutoring is offered one-on-one, in small groups, and in class-size groups for most subjects. Tutoring is provided collaboratively through on-campus or off-campus services via computer-based instruction, graduate assistants/students, professional tutors, and trained peer tutors.

Diagnostic Testing Testing for auditory processing, intelligence, learning strategies, learning styles, math, motor skills, neuropsychological, personality, reading, social skills, spelling, spoken language, study skills, visual processing, and written language is provided collaboratively through on-campus or off-campus services.

Basic Skills Remediation Remediation is offered in small groups and in class-size groups for computer skills, learning strategies, math, reading, social skills, spelling, study skills, time management, and written language. Remediation is provided collaboratively through on-campus or off-campus services via graduate assistants/students, professional tutors, teacher trainees, and trained peer tutors.

Enrichment Enrichment programs are available through the program or unit for college survival skills, learning strategies, self-advocacy, study skills, test taking, and time management. Programs for career planning, college survival skills, health and nutrition, learning strategies, math, medication management, oral communication skills, practical computer skills, reading, self-advocacy, stress management, study skills, test taking, time management, vocabulary development, and written composition skills are provided collaboratively through on-campus or off-campus services.

Student Organization DisABLED Student Association (Delta Sigma Alpha) consists of 400 members.

Fees *Diagnostic Testing* fee is $250.

Application For admittance to the program or unit, students are required to provide a psychoeducational report (3 years old or less). It is recommended that students provide documentation of high school services and provide documentation of previous higher education accommodations. Upon application, materials documenting need for services should be sent only to the LD program or unit. Upon acceptance, documentation of need for services should be sent only to the LD program or unit. *Application deadline (institutional): 4/1. Application deadline (LD program):* Rolling/continuous for fall and rolling/continuous for spring.

Written Policies Written policies regarding course substitutions, general/basic LD accommodations, reduced course loads, substitutions and waivers of admissions requirements, and substitutions and waivers of graduation requirements are available on the program Web site. Written policies regarding course substitutions, general/basic LD accommodations, substitutions and waivers of admissions requirements, and substitutions and waivers of graduation requirements are outlined in the school's catalog/handbook. Written policies regarding course substitutions, general/basic LD accommodations, and reduced course loads are available through the program or unit directly.

University of Illinois at Urbana–Champaign
Division of Disability Resources and Educational Services (DRES)

601 East John Street
Champaign, IL 61820
http://www.disability.uiuc.edu

Contact: Ms. Karen L. Wold, Learning Disabilities Specialist. Phone: 217-333-8705. Fax: 217-333-0248. E-mail: kwold2@uiuc.edu.

Division of Disability Resources and Educational Services (DRES) Approximately 190 registered undergraduate students were served during 2006–07. The program or unit includes 2 full-time and 5 part-time staff members. Diagnostic specialists, graduate assistants/students, LD specialists, remediation/learning specialists, skill tutors, strategy tutors, and other are provided through the program or unit. Academic advisers, coaches, and counselors are provided collaboratively through on-campus or off-campus services.

Orientation The program or unit offers an optional orientation for new students individually by special arrangement.

Summer Program To help prepare for the demands of college, there is an optional summer program prior to entering the school that focuses on computing skills, life skills and/or college life adjustment, self-advocacy, study skills, test-taking skills, and time management. Degree credit will be earned. The program accepts students from out-of-state.

Unique Aids and Services Aids, services, or accommodations include advocates, career counseling, faculty training, personal coach, priority registration, support groups, individual counseling.

Assistive Technology Assistive technology is located in campus labs, the DSS office, department libraries and includes digital textbooks/e-text, learning support software, and scanning. Technology training is provided to incoming students.

Subject-Area Tutoring Tutoring is offered one-on-one and in small groups for most subjects. Tutoring is provided collaboratively through on-campus or off-campus services via trained peer tutors and other.

Basic Skills Remediation Remediation is offered one-on-one for learning strategies, reading, social skills, spelling, study skills, time management, written language, and compensatory strategies. Remediation is provided through the program or unit via LD specialists.

Enrichment Enrichment programs are available through the program or unit for career planning, college survival skills, learning strategies, oral communication skills, practical computer skills, reading, self-advocacy, stress management, study skills, test taking, time management, vocabulary development, and written composition skills. Programs for career planning, college survival skills, health and nutrition, learning strategies, math, medication management, oral communication skills, practical computer skills, reading, stress management, study skills, test taking, time management, and written composition skills are provided collaboratively through on-campus or off-campus services.

Student Organization Delta Sigma Omicron consists of 30 members.

Application For admittance to the program or unit, students are required to apply to the program directly and provide a psychoeducational report (3 years old or less). Upon application, materials documenting need for services should be sent only to the LD program or unit. Upon acceptance, documentation of need for services should be sent only to the LD program or unit. *Application deadline (institutional): 1/2. Application deadline (LD program):* Rolling/continuous for fall and rolling/continuous for spring.

Written Policies Written policies regarding course substitutions, general/basic LD accommodations, reduced course loads, substitutions and waivers of admissions requirements, and substitutions and waivers of graduation requirements are available on the program Web site. Written policies regarding course substitutions, general/basic LD accommodations, reduced course loads, substitutions and waivers of admissions requirements, and substitutions and waivers of graduation requirements are outlined in the school's catalog/handbook. Written policies regarding course substitutions, general/basic LD accommodations, reduced course loads, substitutions and waivers of admissions requirements, and substitutions and waivers of graduation requirements are available through the program or unit directly.

University of Kansas
Disability Resources

Lawrence, KS 66045
http://www.disability.ku.edu

Contact: Mr. Andrew Shoemaker, Learning Disabilities Specialist. Phone: 785-864-2620. Fax: 785-864-2817. E-mail: shoe@ku.edu.

Disability Resources Approximately 275 registered undergraduate students were served during 2006–07. The program or unit includes 1 full-time and 1 part-time staff member. Graduate assistants/students and LD specialists are provided through the program or unit. Academic advisers, counselors, diagnostic specialists, graduate

University of Kansas (continued)

assistants/students, LD specialists, regular education teachers, skill tutors, strategy tutors, and trained peer tutors are provided collaboratively through on-campus or off-campus services.

Orientation The program or unit offers an optional 30-minute orientation for new students as a part of the university's new student orientation session.

Unique Aids and Services Aids, services, or accommodations include career counseling and support groups.

Assistive Technology Assistive technology is located in campus labs, the DSS office and includes digital textbooks/e-text and scanning. Technology training is provided to incoming students.

Subject-Area Tutoring Tutoring is offered one-on-one and in small groups for some subjects. Tutoring is provided collaboratively through on-campus or off-campus services via graduate assistants/students, LD specialists, professional tutors, and trained peer tutors.

Diagnostic Testing Testing for auditory processing, handwriting, intelligence, learning strategies, learning styles, math, motor skills, neuropsychological, personality, reading, social skills, spelling, spoken language, study skills, visual processing, and written language is provided collaboratively through on-campus or off-campus services.

Basic Skills Remediation Remediation is available for learning strategies, study skills, and time management.

Enrichment Programs for career planning, college survival skills, health and nutrition, learning strategies, math, oral communication skills, practical computer skills, reading, self-advocacy, stress management, study skills, test taking, time management, and written composition skills are provided collaboratively through on-campus or off-campus services. Credit is offered for career planning and college survival skills.

Student Organization Able Hawks consists of 15 members.

Fees *Diagnostic Testing* fee is $250 to $1500.

Application For admittance to the program or unit, students are required to provide a psychoeducational report (3 years old or less). It is recommended that students provide documentation of high school services. Upon application, materials documenting need for services should be sent only to the LD program or unit. Upon acceptance, documentation of need for services should be sent only to the LD program or unit. *Application deadline (institutional):* 4/1. *Application deadline (LD program):* Rolling/continuous for fall and rolling/continuous for spring.

Written Policies Written policy regarding general/basic LD accommodations is available on the program Web site. Written policies regarding general/basic LD accommodations and reduced course loads are available through the program or unit directly.

University of Kentucky
Disability Resource Center

Lexington, KY 40506-0032

http://www.uky.edu/StudentAffairs/DisabilityResourceCenter/

Contact: Dr. Leisa Pickering, Cognitive Disabilities Consultant. Phone: 859-257-2754. Fax: 859-257-1980. E-mail: lmpick@email.uky.edu. Head of LD Program: Jacob Karnes Jr., Assistant Dean of Students. Phone: 859-257-2754. Fax: 859-257-1980. E-mail: jkarnes@email.uky.edu.

Disability Resource Center Approximately 620 registered undergraduate students were served during 2006–07. The program or unit

includes 1 full-time staff member. LD specialists and strategy tutors are provided through the program or unit. Academic advisers, counselors, graduate assistants/students, remediation/learning specialists, skill tutors, and strategy tutors are provided collaboratively through on-campus or off-campus services.

Unique Aids and Services Aids, services, or accommodations include advocates, career counseling, priority registration, support groups, faculty consultations as needed.

Assistive Technology Assistive technology is located in campus labs, the DSS office, a special lab and includes digital textbooks/e-text, scanning, and speech-to-text and text-to-speech software. Technology training is provided to incoming students.

Subject-Area Tutoring Tutoring is offered one-on-one and in small groups for some subjects. Tutoring is provided collaboratively through on-campus or off-campus services via graduate assistants/students, LD specialists, trained peer tutors, and other.

Diagnostic Testing Testing for auditory processing, intelligence, math, motor skills, neuropsychological, personality, reading, social skills, spelling, spoken language, visual processing, and written language is provided collaboratively through on-campus or off-campus services.

Basic Skills Remediation Remediation is offered in class-size groups for computer skills, learning strategies, math, study skills, time management, and written language. Remediation is provided collaboratively through on-campus or off-campus services via graduate assistants/students, trained peer tutors, and other.

Enrichment Programs for career planning, college survival skills, health and nutrition, learning strategies, math, medication management, oral communication skills, practical computer skills, stress management, study skills, test taking, time management, and written composition skills are provided collaboratively through on-campus or off-campus services. Credit is offered for health and nutrition, math, oral communication skills, practical computer skills, and written composition skills.

Fees *Diagnostic Testing* fee is $350 to $1000.

Application For admittance to the program or unit, students are required to apply to the program directly and provide a psychoeducational report (3 years old or less). Upon acceptance, documentation of need for services should be sent only to the LD program or unit. *Application deadline (institutional):* 2/15. *Application deadline (LD program):* Rolling/continuous for fall and rolling/continuous for spring.

Written Policies Written policy regarding general/basic LD accommodations is available on the program Web site. Written policy regarding general/basic LD accommodations is outlined in the school's catalog/handbook. Written policy regarding general/basic LD accommodations is available through the program or unit directly.

The University of Maine at Augusta
Learning Support Services

46 University Drive

Augusta, ME 04330-9410

http://www.uma.maine.edu

Contact: Mr. Donald T. Osier, Director of Learning Support Services. Phone: 207-621-3066. Fax: 207-621-3491. E-mail: donald.osier@maine.edu.

Learning Support Services Approximately 35 registered undergraduate students were served during 2006–07. The program or unit includes 3 full-time and 2 part-time staff members. Academic advisers, counselors, professional tutors, remediation/learning specialists, and trained peer tutors are provided collaboratively through on-campus or off-campus services.

Unique Aids and Services Aids, services, or accommodations include note-takers, extended time for tests.

Assistive Technology Assistive technology is located in the DSS office, the library and includes digital textbooks/e-text.

Subject-Area Tutoring Tutoring is offered one-on-one and in small groups for some subjects. Tutoring is provided collaboratively through on-campus or off-campus services via professional tutors and trained peer tutors.

Basic Skills Remediation Remediation is offered in class-size groups for math, reading, and written language. Remediation is provided collaboratively through on-campus or off-campus services via regular education teachers.

Application For admittance to the program or unit, students are required to provide a psychoeducational report (3 years old or less). It is recommended that students provide documentation of high school services. Upon application, materials documenting need for services should be sent only to the LD program or unit. Upon acceptance, documentation of need for services should be sent only to the LD program or unit. *Application deadline (institutional):* 8/31. *Application deadline (LD program):* Rolling/continuous for fall and rolling/continuous for spring.

Written Policies Written policies regarding general/basic LD accommodations and substitutions and waivers of graduation requirements are available on the program Web site. Written policies regarding general/basic LD accommodations and substitutions and waivers of graduation requirements are outlined in the school's catalog/handbook.

University of Maine at Fort Kent
Academic and Counseling Services

23 University Drive

Fort Kent, ME 04743-1292

http://www.umfk.maine.edu/acserv

Contact: Mr. Shawn Graham, Academic Counselor. Phone: 207-834-7532. Fax: 207-834-7870. E-mail: shawn.graham@maine.edu.

Academic and Counseling Services Approximately 20 registered undergraduate students were served during 2006–07. The program or unit includes 2 full-time and 2 part-time staff members. Academic advisers, counselors, professional tutors, remediation/learning specialists, skill tutors, and trained peer tutors are provided through the program or unit. Academic advisers, counselors, professional tutors, regular education teachers, remediation/learning specialists, and skill tutors are provided collaboratively through on-campus or off-campus services.

Summer Program an optional summer program prior to entering the school.

Assistive Technology Assistive technology is located in the DSS office, the library and includes digital textbooks/e-text, learning support software, and scanning. Technology training is provided to incoming students.

Subject-Area Tutoring Tutoring is offered one-on-one and in small groups for all subjects. Tutoring is provided through the program or unit via professional tutors and trained peer tutors. Tutoring is also provided collaboratively through on-campus or off-campus services via professional tutors and trained peer tutors.

Basic Skills Remediation Remediation is offered one-on-one, in small groups, and in class-size groups for computer skills, learning strategies, math, reading, study skills, time management, and written language. Remediation is provided through the program or unit via professional tutors and regular education teachers.

Application For admittance to the program or unit, students are required to provide a psychoeducational report (3 years old or less). Upon acceptance, documentation of need for services should be sent only to the LD program or unit. *Application deadline (LD program):* Rolling/continuous for fall and rolling/continuous for spring.

Written Policies Written policy regarding general/basic LD accommodations is available on the program Web site. Written policy regarding general/basic LD accommodations is outlined in the school's catalog/handbook.

University of Maine at Machias

9 O'Brien Avenue

Machias, ME 04654-1321

http://www.umm.maine.edu/

Contact: Ms. Jean Schild, Student Resources Coordinator. Phone: 207-255-1228. Fax: 207-255-4864. E-mail: schild@maine.edu.

Approximately 63 registered undergraduate students were served during 2006–07.

Unique Aids and Services Aids, services, or accommodations include personal coach, one-on-one services as needed.

Assistive Technology Assistive technology is located in the DSS office, the library and includes digital textbooks/e-text and scanning.

Subject-Area Tutoring Tutoring is offered one-on-one and in small groups for most subjects. Tutoring is provided collaboratively through on-campus or off-campus services via trained peer tutors.

Basic Skills Remediation Remediation is offered one-on-one and in small groups for learning strategies, study skills, and time management. Remediation is provided collaboratively through on-campus or off-campus services via LD specialists.

Enrichment Enrichment programs are available through the program or unit for college survival skills, learning strategies, self-advocacy, study skills, test taking, and time management. Programs for career planning, college survival skills, health and nutrition, math, practical computer skills, stress management, vocabulary devel-

University of Maine at Machias (continued)

opment, and written composition skills are provided collaboratively through on-campus or off-campus services. Credit is offered for college survival skills, vocabulary development, and written composition skills.

Application For admittance to the program or unit, students are required to provide a psychoeducational report (3 years old or less). *Application deadline (institutional): 8/15. Application deadline (LD program):* Rolling/continuous for fall and rolling/continuous for spring.

Written Policies Written policy regarding general/basic LD accommodations is available on the program Web site. Written policy regarding general/basic LD accommodations is outlined in the school's catalog/handbook.

University of Manitoba
Disability Services

Winnipeg, MB R3T 2N2

Canada

http://www.umanitoba.ca/

Contact: Ms. Carolyn Christie, Coordinator. Phone: 204-474-6213. E-mail: disability_services@umanitoba.ca.

Disability Services Approximately 150 registered undergraduate students were served during 2006–07. The program or unit includes 6 full-time staff members and 1 part-time staff member. LD specialists are provided through the program or unit. Academic advisers, coaches, counselors, diagnostic specialists, LD specialists, skill tutors, strategy tutors, and trained peer tutors are provided collaboratively through on-campus or off-campus services.

Unique Aids and Services Aids, services, or accommodations include advocates, career counseling, faculty training, personal coach, priority registration, and support groups.

Assistive Technology Assistive technology is located in the DSS office and includes digital textbooks/e-text, learning support software, and scanning. Technology training is provided to incoming students.

Subject-Area Tutoring Tutoring is offered one-on-one for most subjects. Tutoring is provided collaboratively through on-campus or off-campus services via trained peer tutors.

Diagnostic Testing Testing for auditory processing, intelligence, math, motor skills, neuropsychological, reading, spelling, visual processing, written language, and other services is provided collaboratively through on-campus or off-campus services.

Basic Skills Remediation Remediation is offered one-on-one, in small groups, and in class-size groups for learning strategies, math, reading, spelling, study skills, time management, and written language. Remediation is provided collaboratively through on-campus or off-campus services via LD specialists, professional tutors, and trained peer tutors.

Enrichment Enrichment programs are available through the program or unit for college survival skills, learning strategies, reading, self-advocacy, stress management, study skills, test taking, time management, and written composition skills. Programs for career planning, college survival skills, learning strategies, math, practical computer skills, reading, self-advocacy, stress management, study skills, test taking, time management, and written composition skills

are provided collaboratively through on-campus or off-campus services. Credit is offered for college survival skills, learning strategies, practical computer skills, reading, study skills, time management, and written composition skills.

Application For admittance to the program or unit, students are required to apply to the program directly and provide a psychoeducational report. It is recommended that students provide documentation of high school services. Upon application, materials documenting need for services should be sent only to the LD program or unit. Upon acceptance, documentation of need for services should be sent only to the LD program or unit. *Application deadline (institutional):* 7/1. *Application deadline (LD program):* Rolling/continuous for fall and rolling/continuous for spring.

Written Policies Written policy regarding general/basic LD accommodations is available on the program Web site. Written policies regarding general/basic LD accommodations, grade forgiveness, and reduced course loads are available through the program or unit directly.

University of Mary Hardin-Baylor
Counseling and Testing Center and the Meadows Center for Academic Excellence

900 College Street

Belton, TX 76513

http://www.umhb.edu/

Contact: Nate Williams, Director of Counseling and Testing. Phone: 254-295-4696. Fax: 254-295-4196. E-mail: nwilliams@umhb.edu.

Counseling and Testing Center and the Meadows Center for Academic Excellence Approximately 75 registered undergraduate students were served during 2006–07. The program or unit includes 3 full-time and 3 part-time staff members. Academic advisers, counselors, diagnostic specialists, regular education teachers, remediation/learning specialists, skill tutors, strategy tutors, trained peer tutors, and other are provided collaboratively through on-campus or off-campus services.

Unique Aids and Services Aids, services, or accommodations include advocates, career counseling, faculty training, and personal coach.

Assistive Technology Assistive technology is located in campus labs, the DSS office, the student's personal computer and includes digital textbooks/e-text.

Subject-Area Tutoring Tutoring is offered one-on-one and in small groups for most subjects. Tutoring is provided collaboratively through on-campus or off-campus services via computer-based instruction, graduate assistants/students, LD specialists, trained peer tutors, and other.

Diagnostic Testing Testing for handwriting, intelligence, learning strategies, learning styles, math, neuropsychological, personality, reading, social skills, spelling, study skills, written language, and other services is provided collaboratively through on-campus or off-campus services.

Basic Skills Remediation Remediation is offered one-on-one, in small groups, and in class-size groups for learning strategies, math, reading, social skills, spelling, study skills, time management, and written language. Remediation is provided collaboratively through on-campus or off-campus services via computer-based instruction, graduate assistants/students, LD specialists, regular education teachers, and trained peer tutors.

Enrichment Programs for career planning, college survival skills, health and nutrition, learning strategies, medication management, self-advocacy, stress management, study skills, test taking, and time management are provided collaboratively through on-campus or off-campus services.

Fees *Diagnostic Testing* fee is $50.

Application For admittance to the program or unit, students are required to provide a psychoeducational report (3 years old or less) and provide a diagnostic report from a professional qualified to make the respective diagnosis. It is recommended that students apply to the program directly. Upon acceptance, documentation of need for services should be sent only to the LD program or unit. *Application deadline (institutional):* Continuous. *Application deadline (LD program):* Rolling/continuous for fall and rolling/continuous for spring.

Written Policies Written policy regarding general/basic LD accommodations is outlined in the school's catalog/handbook. Written policy regarding general/basic LD accommodations is available through the program or unit directly.

University of Maryland, Baltimore County
Student Support Services

1000 Hilltop Circle

Baltimore, MD 21250

http://www.umbc.edu/

Contact: Ms. Valerie D. Valentine, Disabilities Specialist. Phone: 410-455-8496. Fax: 410-455-1028. E-mail: valerie@umbc.edu. Head of LD Program: Ms. Cynthia Hill, Associate Provost. Phone: 410-455-2459. Fax: 410-455-1028. E-mail: chill@umbc.edu.

Student Support Services Approximately 250 registered undergraduate students were served during 2006–07. The program or unit includes 5 full-time staff members and 1 part-time staff member. Counselors and skill tutors are provided through the program or unit. Academic advisers, counselors, remediation/learning specialists, and skill tutors are provided collaboratively through on-campus or off-campus services.

Orientation The program or unit offers before classes begin, during summer prior to enrollment, individually by special arrangement, and two weeks after receiving application for services.

Unique Aids and Services Aids, services, or accommodations include priority registration, support groups, and weekly meetings with faculty.

Assistive Technology Assistive technology is located in the DSS office and includes digital textbooks/e-text, learning support software, and scanning.

Subject-Area Tutoring Tutoring is offered one-on-one and in small groups for most subjects. Tutoring is provided through the program or unit via LD specialists and trained peer tutors.

Enrichment Enrichment programs are available through the program or unit for career planning, college survival skills, learning strategies, math, and written composition skills. Program for career planning is provided collaboratively through on-campus or off-campus services.

Application For admittance to the program or unit, students are required to apply to the program directly. It is recommended that students provide a psychoeducational report (2 years old or less) and provide documentation of high school services. Upon application, materials documenting need for services should be sent only to the LD program or unit. Upon acceptance, documentation of need for services should be sent only to the LD program or unit. *Application deadline (institutional):* 2/1. *Application deadline (LD program):* Rolling/continuous for fall and rolling/continuous for spring.

Written Policies Written policy regarding general/basic LD accommodations is available on the program Web site. Written policy regarding general/basic LD accommodations is available through the program or unit directly.

University of Mary Washington
Office of Disability Services

1301 College Avenue

Fredericksburg, VA 22401-5358

http://www.umw.edu/disability

Contact: Ms. Stephanie S. Smith, Director of Disability Services. Phone: 540-654-1266. Fax: 540-654-1163. E-mail: ssmith@umw.edu.

Office of Disability Services Approximately 85 registered undergraduate students were served during 2006–07. The program or unit includes 2 full-time staff members. Strategy tutors are provided through the program or unit. Academic advisers, regular education teachers, skill tutors, and trained peer tutors are provided collaboratively through on-campus or off-campus services.

Orientation The program or unit offers an optional 1-day orientation for new students before classes begin, during summer prior to enrollment, and individually by special arrangement.

Unique Aids and Services Aids, services, or accommodations include faculty training, parent workshops, and priority registration.

Assistive Technology Assistive technology is located in campus labs, the DSS office and includes digital textbooks/e-text and scanning.

Subject-Area Tutoring Tutoring is offered one-on-one for some subjects. Tutoring is provided collaboratively through on-campus or off-campus services via trained peer tutors.

Enrichment Enrichment programs are available through the program or unit for time management. Programs for career planning, college survival skills, learning strategies, oral communication skills, practical computer skills, stress management, study skills, test taking, time management, and written composition skills are provided collaboratively through on-campus or off-campus services.

Application For admittance to the program or unit, students are required to apply to the program directly and provide a psychoeducational report (3 years old or less). Upon acceptance, documenta-

University of Mary Washington (continued)

tion of need for services should be sent only to the LD program or unit. *Application deadline (institutional): 2/1. Application deadline (LD program):* Rolling/continuous for fall and rolling/continuous for spring.

Written Policies Written policies regarding course substitutions, general/basic LD accommodations, reduced course loads, and substitutions and waivers of graduation requirements are available on the program Web site. Written policies regarding course substitutions, general/basic LD accommodations, reduced course loads, and substitutions and waivers of graduation requirements are available through the program or unit directly.

University of Massachusetts Amherst
Disability Services

Amherst, MA 01003

http://www.umass.edu/disability/

Contact: Ms. Madeline L. Peters, Director Disability Services. Phone: 413-545-0892. Fax: 413-577-0122. E-mail: ds@educ.umass.edu.

Disability Services Approximately 400 registered undergraduate students were served during 2006–07. The program or unit includes 9 full-time and 20 part-time staff members. Graduate assistants/students, LD specialists, professional tutors, remediation/learning specialists, skill tutors, special education teachers, and strategy tutors are provided through the program or unit. Academic advisers, counselors, diagnostic specialists, graduate assistants/students, and trained peer tutors are provided collaboratively through on-campus or off-campus services.

Unique Aids and Services Aids, services, or accommodations include advocates, support groups, and weekly meetings with faculty.

Assistive Technology Assistive technology is located in campus labs and includes digital textbooks/e-text, learning support software, and scanning.

Subject-Area Tutoring Tutoring is offered one-on-one for some subjects. Tutoring is provided through the program or unit via graduate assistants/students, LD specialists, and professional tutors. Tutoring is also provided collaboratively through on-campus or off-campus services via computer-based instruction, graduate assistants/students, and trained peer tutors.

Diagnostic Testing Testing for auditory processing, intelligence, math, neuropsychological, personality, spoken language, visual processing, written language, and other services is provided collaboratively through on-campus or off-campus services.

Basic Skills Remediation Remediation is offered in small groups for learning strategies, reading, social skills, study skills, time management, visual processing, and written language. Remediation is provided through the program or unit via special education teachers.

Enrichment Enrichment programs are available through the program or unit for college survival skills, learning strategies, reading, self-advocacy, study skills, test taking, and time management. Programs for career planning, health and nutrition, medication management, oral communication skills, stress management, test taking, time management, and written composition skills are provided collaboratively through on-campus or off-campus services.

Fees *Diagnostic Testing* fee is applicable.

Application For admittance to the program or unit, students are required to provide a psychoeducational report (5 years old or less). It is recommended that students provide documentation of high school services. Upon application, materials documenting need for services should be sent only to admissions with institutional application materials. Upon acceptance, documentation of need for services should be sent only to the LD program or unit. *Application deadline (institutional): 1/15. Application deadline (LD program):* Rolling/continuous for fall and rolling/continuous for spring.

Written Policies Written policies regarding course substitutions, general/basic LD accommodations, substitutions and waivers of admissions requirements, and substitutions and waivers of graduation requirements are available on the program Web site.

University of Massachusetts Boston
Ross Center for Disability Services

100 Morrissey Boulevard

Boston, MA 02125-3393

http://www.rosscenter.umb.edu

Contact: Stacey M. Foskett, Assistant Director. Phone: 617-287-7400. Fax: 617-287-7466. E-mail: stacey.foskett@umb.edu. Head of LD Program: Virginia Perelson, Director. Phone: 617-287-7400. Fax: 617-287-7466. E-mail: virginia.perelson@umb.edu.

Ross Center for Disability Services Approximately 90 registered undergraduate students were served during 2006–07. The program or unit includes 1 full-time and 1 part-time staff member. Academic advisers, counselors, graduate assistants/students, skill tutors, and strategy tutors are provided through the program or unit. Academic advisers, counselors, graduate assistants/students, professional tutors, remediation/learning specialists, skill tutors, strategy tutors, and trained peer tutors are provided collaboratively through on-campus or off-campus services.

Unique Aids and Services Aids, services, or accommodations include priority registration, note-takers, testing accommodations.

Assistive Technology Assistive technology is located in the DSS office, a special lab and includes digital textbooks/e-text. Technology training is provided to incoming students.

Subject-Area Tutoring Tutoring is offered one-on-one and in small groups for all subjects. Tutoring is provided collaboratively through on-campus or off-campus services via computer-based instruction, graduate assistants/students, and trained peer tutors.

Enrichment Enrichment programs are available through the program or unit for college survival skills, learning strategies, self-advocacy, study skills, test taking, time management, and written composition skills. Programs for career planning, college survival skills, health and nutrition, learning strategies, math, oral communication skills, practical computer skills, reading, self-advocacy, stress management, study skills, test taking, time management, and written composition skills are provided collaboratively through on-campus or off-campus services.

Student Organization Center for Students with Disabilities consists of 25 members.

Application For admittance to the program or unit, students are required to provide a psychoeducational report (3 years old or less). Upon application, materials documenting need for services should be sent only to admissions with institutional application materials. Upon acceptance, documentation of need for services should be sent only to the LD program or unit. *Application deadline (institutional):* 6/1. *Application deadline (LD program):* Rolling/continuous for fall and rolling/continuous for spring.

Written Policies Written policy regarding general/basic LD accommodations is available on the program Web site. Written policy regarding substitutions and waivers of admissions requirements is outlined in the school's catalog/handbook. Written policy regarding general/basic LD accommodations is available through the program or unit directly.

University of Massachusetts Lowell
Office of Disability Services

1 University Avenue

Lowell, MA 01854-2881

http://www.uml.edu/student-services/disability/default.html

Contact: Dr. Chandrika Sharma, Director, Disability Services. Phone: 978-934-4574. Fax: 978-934-2032. E-mail: chandrika_sharma@uml.edu.

Office of Disability Services Approximately 350 registered undergraduate students were served during 2006–07. The program or unit includes 1 part-time staff member. Academic advisers, coaches, LD specialists, professional tutors, and skill tutors are provided collaboratively through on-campus or off-campus services.

Unique Aids and Services Aids, services, or accommodations include advocates, career counseling, faculty training, personal coach, and priority registration.

Assistive Technology Assistive technology is located in the DSS office and includes digital textbooks/e-text and learning support software. Technology training is provided to incoming students.

Subject-Area Tutoring Tutoring is offered in small groups for most subjects. Tutoring is provided collaboratively through on-campus or off-campus services via computer-based instruction, graduate assistants/students, LD specialists, professional tutors, and trained peer tutors.

Diagnostic Testing Testing is provided through the program or unit for learning strategies, learning styles, personality, study skills, and written language.

Basic Skills Remediation Remediation is offered in small groups for computer skills, learning strategies, math, study skills, and time management. Remediation is provided collaboratively through on-campus or off-campus services via graduate assistants/students, professional tutors, and trained peer tutors.

Enrichment Programs for career planning, college survival skills, health and nutrition, learning strategies, math, medication management, oral communication skills, practical computer skills, reading, self-advocacy, stress management, study skills, test taking, time management, and written composition skills are provided collaboratively through on-campus or off-campus services.

Application For admittance to the program or unit, students are required to provide a psychoeducational report and provide documentation of high school services. Upon application, materials documenting need for services should be sent only to admissions with institutional application materials. *Application deadline (institutional):* Continuous. *Application deadline (LD program):* Rolling/continuous for fall and rolling/continuous for spring.

Written Policies Written policies regarding course substitutions, general/basic LD accommodations, and reduced course loads are available on the program Web site.

University of Miami
Office of Disability Services

University of Miami Branch

Coral Gables, FL 33124

http://www.umarc.miami.edu

Contact: Accommodations Coordinator. Phone: 305-284-2374. Fax: 305-284-1999. E-mail: disabilityservices@miami.edu. Head of LD Program: Dr. Mykel Mangrum Billups, Director, Academic Resource Center. Phone: 305-284-2800. Fax: 305-284-1999. E-mail: disabilityservices@miami.edu.

Office of Disability Services Approximately 500 registered undergraduate students were served during 2006–07. The program or unit includes 3 full-time staff members. Graduate assistants/students, remediation/learning specialists, and skill tutors are provided through the program or unit. Graduate assistants/students, remediation/learning specialists, and skill tutors are provided collaboratively through on-campus or off-campus services.

Unique Aids and Services Aids, services, or accommodations include advocates.

Assistive Technology Assistive technology is located in the DSS office, the library and includes learning support software and scanning.

Subject-Area Tutoring Tutoring is offered one-on-one and in small groups for most subjects. Tutoring is provided through the program or unit via graduate assistants/students, professional tutors, and trained peer tutors. Tutoring is also provided collaboratively through on-campus or off-campus services via graduate assistants/students.

Basic Skills Remediation Remediation is offered one-on-one for computer skills, learning strategies, math, reading, social skills, spoken language, study skills, and time management. Remediation is provided through the program or unit via graduate assistants/students and trained peer tutors.

Enrichment Enrichment programs are available through the program or unit for college survival skills, learning strategies, reading, self-advocacy, stress management, study skills, test taking, time management, and written composition skills. Programs for stress management, study skills, test taking, time management, and written composition skills are provided collaboratively through on-campus or off-campus services.

Application For admittance to the program or unit, students are required to provide a psychoeducational report (3 years old or less) and provide complete, comprehensive, current psychoeducational

University of Miami (continued)

test report. Upon acceptance, documentation of need for services should be sent only to the LD program or unit. *Application deadline (institutional):* 2/1. *Application deadline (LD program):* Rolling/continuous for fall.

Written Policies Written policy regarding general/basic LD accommodations is available on the program Web site. Written policy regarding general/basic LD accommodations is available through the program or unit directly.

University of Michigan
Services for Students with Disabilities

Ann Arbor, MI 48109

http://www.umich.edu/~sswd/

Contact: Dr. Stuart Segal, Coordinator. Phone: 734-763-3000. Fax: 734-936-3947. E-mail: sssegal@umich.edu.

Services for Students with Disabilities Approximately 470 registered undergraduate students were served during 2006–07. The program or unit includes 2 full-time staff members. Graduate assistants/students and LD specialists are provided through the program or unit. Academic advisers, counselors, diagnostic specialists, and remediation/learning specialists are provided collaboratively through on-campus or off-campus services.

Orientation The program or unit offers an optional half-day orientation for new students before classes begin.

Unique Aids and Services Aids, services, or accommodations include advocates, personal coach, and priority registration.

Subject-Area Tutoring Tutoring is offered one-on-one for some subjects. Tutoring is provided collaboratively through on-campus or off-campus services via graduate assistants/students and trained peer tutors.

Diagnostic Testing Testing is provided through the program or unit for reading and study skills. Testing for auditory processing, handwriting, intelligence, learning strategies, learning styles, math, motor skills, neuropsychological, spelling, and written language is provided collaboratively through on-campus or off-campus services.

Basic Skills Remediation Remediation is offered one-on-one for learning strategies, math, study skills, time management, and written language. Remediation is provided through the program or unit via LD specialists. Remediation is also provided collaboratively through on-campus or off-campus services via graduate assistants/students, LD specialists, professional tutors, and trained peer tutors.

Enrichment Programs for career planning, college survival skills, study skills, time management, and written composition skills are provided collaboratively through on-campus or off-campus services.

Application For admittance to the program or unit, students are required to provide a psychoeducational report and provide psychological report to be evaluated by the university for significant discrepancies in test scores. Upon application, materials documenting need for services should be sent only to the LD program or unit. Upon acceptance, documentation of need for services should be sent only to the LD program or unit. *Application deadline (institutional):* 2/1. *Application deadline (LD program):* Rolling/continuous for fall and rolling/continuous for spring.

Written Policies Written policy regarding general/basic LD accommodations is available on the program Web site.

University of Minnesota, Duluth
Disability Services and Resources

10 University Drive

Duluth, MN 55812-2496

http://www.d.umn.edu/access/CognitivePro.html

Contact: Judith W. Bromen, Learning Disorders Program Coordinator. Phone: 218-726-7965. Fax: 218-726-6706. E-mail: jbromen@d.umn.edu.

Disability Services and Resources Approximately 115 registered undergraduate students were served during 2006–07. The program or unit includes 2 full-time staff members. Academic advisers, diagnostic specialists, and LD specialists are provided through the program or unit. Academic advisers, counselors, skill tutors, strategy tutors, and trained peer tutors are provided collaboratively through on-campus or off-campus services.

Orientation The program or unit offers an optional 1-day orientation for new students before classes begin.

Summer Program available to high school graduates.

Unique Aids and Services Aids, services, or accommodations include priority registration.

Assistive Technology Assistive technology is located in campus labs, the DSS office and includes digital textbooks/e-text, learning support software, and scanning.

Subject-Area Tutoring Tutoring is offered one-on-one, in small groups, and in class-size groups for some subjects. Tutoring is provided collaboratively through on-campus or off-campus services via trained peer tutors.

Diagnostic Testing Testing is provided through the program or unit for intelligence, math, reading, spelling, spoken language, and written language. Testing for auditory processing, intelligence, and spoken language is provided collaboratively through on-campus or off-campus services.

Basic Skills Remediation Remediation is offered in class-size groups for math, study skills, and written language. Remediation is provided collaboratively through on-campus or off-campus services via regular education teachers.

Enrichment Enrichment programs are available through the program or unit for learning strategies, self-advocacy, and time management. Programs for career planning, college survival skills, health and nutrition, learning strategies, math, practical computer skills, stress management, study skills, and written composition skills are provided collaboratively through on-campus or off-campus services. Credit is offered for health and nutrition, learning strategies, math, study skills, and written composition skills.

Student Organization Access for All consists of 8 members.

Fees *Orientation* fee is $50 to $65. *Diagnostic Testing* fee is $0 to $50.

Application For admittance to the program or unit, students are required to provide a psychoeducational report (3 years old or less). It is recommended that students provide documentation of high school services. Upon application, materials documenting need for services should be sent only to the LD program or unit. Upon acceptance, documentation of need for services should be sent only to the LD program or unit. *Application deadline (institutional):* 2/1. *Application deadline (LD program):* Rolling/continuous for fall and rolling/continuous for spring.

Written Policies Written policy regarding general/basic LD accommodations is available on the program Web site. Written policy regarding general/basic LD accommodations is outlined in the school's catalog/handbook. Written policy regarding general/basic LD accommodations is available through the program or unit directly.

University of Mississippi
Office of Student Disability Services

Oxford, MS 38677

http://www.olemiss.edu/depts/sds

Contact: Ms. Stacey Reycraft, Assistant Director and Disability Specialist. Phone: 662-915-7128. Fax: 662-915-5972. E-mail: sds@olemiss.edu.

Office of Student Disability Services Approximately 400 registered undergraduate students were served during 2006–07. The program or unit includes 5 full-time staff members. Services are provided collaboratively through on-campus or off-campus services.
Unique Aids and Services Aids, services, or accommodations include priority registration.
Assistive Technology Assistive technology is located in campus labs, the DSS office and includes digital textbooks/e-text, learning support software, scanning, and Dragon Dictate, Kurzweil, VictorReader, ZoomText. Technology training is provided to incoming students.
Application For admittance to the program or unit, students are required to apply to the program directly and provide a psychoeducational report (3 years old or less). Upon acceptance, documentation of need for services should be sent only to the LD program or unit. *Application deadline (institutional): 7/20. Application deadline (LD program):* Rolling/continuous for fall and rolling/continuous for spring.
Written Policies Written policy regarding general/basic LD accommodations is available on the program Web site. Written policy regarding general/basic LD accommodations is outlined in the school's catalog/handbook.

University of Missouri–Columbia
Office of Disability Services

Columbia, MO 65211

http://disabilityservices.missouri.edu

Contact: Mr. Matthew E. Buckley, Coordinator of Learning Programs. Phone: 573-882-4696. Fax: 573-882-5002. E-mail: disabilityservices@missouri.edu. Head of LD Program: Dr. Sarah Colby Weaver, Director. Phone: 573-882-4696. Fax: 573-882-5002. E-mail: disabilityservices@missouri.edu.

Office of Disability Services Approximately 606 registered undergraduate students were served during 2006–07. The program or unit includes 6 full-time staff members. Graduate assistants/students, LD specialists, remediation/learning specialists, skill tutors, and strategy tutors are provided through the program or unit. Academic advisers, coaches, counselors, diagnostic specialists, professional tutors, regular education teachers, teacher trainees, and trained peer tutors are provided collaboratively through on-campus or off-campus services.
Unique Aids and Services Aids, services, or accommodations include career counseling, faculty training, personal coach, priority registration, weekly meetings with faculty, extra testing time, private testing room, classroom note-takers, test-readers, test-scribes.
Assistive Technology Assistive technology includes digital textbooks/e-text.
Subject-Area Tutoring Tutoring is offered one-on-one, in small groups, and in class-size groups for most subjects. Tutoring is provided collaboratively through on-campus or off-campus services via graduate assistants/students, professional tutors, and trained peer tutors.
Diagnostic Testing Testing is provided through the program or unit for learning strategies, learning styles, and study skills. Testing for auditory processing, handwriting, intelligence, math, motor skills, neuropsychological, personality, reading, social skills, spelling, spoken language, visual processing, and written language is provided collaboratively through on-campus or off-campus services.
Basic Skills Remediation Remediation is offered one-on-one for learning strategies, study skills, and time management. Remediation is provided through the program or unit via LD specialists.
Enrichment Programs for career planning, college survival skills, health and nutrition, learning strategies, math, oral communication skills, practical computer skills, reading, self-advocacy, stress management, study skills, test taking, time management, and written composition skills are provided collaboratively through on-campus or off-campus services. Credit is offered for career planning, college survival skills, health and nutrition, learning strategies, math, oral communication skills, practical computer skills, reading, self-advocacy, stress management, study skills, test taking, time management, and written composition skills.
Fees *Diagnostic Testing* fee is $800 to $1200.
Application For admittance to the program or unit, students are required to provide a psychoeducational report (5 years old or less). Upon application, materials documenting need for services should be sent only to the LD program or unit. Upon acceptance, documentation of need for services should be sent only to the LD program or unit. *Application deadline (institutional):* Continuous. *Application deadline (LD program):* Rolling/continuous for fall and rolling/continuous for spring.
Written Policies Written policy regarding general/basic LD accommodations is available on the program Web site. Written policies regarding substitutions and waivers of admissions requirements and substitutions and waivers of graduation requirements are outlined in the school's catalog/handbook. Written policy regarding general/basic LD accommodations is available through the program or unit directly.

University of Missouri–Kansas City
Office of Services for Students with Disabilities

5100 Rockhill Road

Kansas City, MO 64110-2499

http://www.umkc.edu/disability

Contact: Mr. R. Scott Laurent, Coordinator. Phone: 816-235-5696. Fax: 816-235-6363. E-mail: disability@umkc.edu.

Office of Services for Students with Disabilities Approximately 100 registered undergraduate students were served during 2006–07. The program or unit includes 2 full-time and 6 part-time staff members. Skill tutors, strategy tutors, and other are provided through the program or unit. Academic advisers, counselors, diagnostic specialists, LD specialists, remediation/learning specialists, skill tutors, strategy tutors, and trained peer tutors are provided collaboratively through on-campus or off-campus services.

Unique Aids and Services Aids, services, or accommodations include career counseling, faculty training, and priority registration.

Assistive Technology Assistive technology is located in campus labs, the main library and includes digital textbooks/e-text and scanning. Technology training is provided to incoming students.

Subject-Area Tutoring Tutoring is offered in small groups and in class-size groups for some subjects. Tutoring is provided collaboratively through on-campus or off-campus services via graduate assistants/students and trained peer tutors.

Diagnostic Testing Testing for auditory processing, handwriting, intelligence, learning strategies, learning styles, math, motor skills, neuropsychological, personality, reading, social skills, spelling, spoken language, study skills, visual processing, written language, and other services is provided collaboratively through on-campus or off-campus services.

Basic Skills Remediation Remediation is offered one-on-one and in class-size groups for auditory processing, computer skills, handwriting, learning strategies, math, reading, social skills, spelling, study skills, time management, visual processing, and written language. Remediation is provided through the program or unit. Remediation is also provided collaboratively through on-campus or off-campus services via graduate assistants/students, LD specialists, and trained peer tutors.

Enrichment Enrichment programs are available through the program or unit for self-advocacy, test taking, and time management. Programs for career planning, college survival skills, health and nutrition, learning strategies, math, oral communication skills, practical computer skills, stress management, study skills, test taking, time management, and written composition skills are provided collaboratively through on-campus or off-campus services. Credit is offered for career planning, college survival skills, learning strategies, oral communication skills, practical computer skills, study skills, test taking, and time management.

Student Organization Eclectic Learners consists of 20 members.

Fees *Diagnostic Testing* fee is applicable.

Application For admittance to the program or unit, students are required to provide a psychoeducational report (3 years old or less). It is recommended that students provide documentation of high school services. Upon acceptance, documentation of need for ser-

vices should be sent only to the LD program or unit. *Application deadline (institutional):* Continuous. *Application deadline (LD program):* Rolling/continuous for fall and rolling/continuous for spring.

Written Policies Written policy regarding general/basic LD accommodations is available on the program Web site. Written policies regarding general/basic LD accommodations and reduced course loads are available through the program or unit directly.

University of Missouri–Rolla
Disability Support Services

1870 Miner Circle

Rolla, MO 65409-0910

http://campus.umr.edu/dss/

Contact: Ms. Connie Arthur, Student Disabilities Services Adviser. Phone: 573-341-4222. Fax: 573-341-6179. E-mail: dss@umr.edu.

Disability Support Services Approximately 122 registered undergraduate students were served during 2006–07. The program or unit includes 1 full-time staff member. Academic advisers, coaches, counselors, LD specialists, professional tutors, skill tutors, strategy tutors, and trained peer tutors are provided collaboratively through on-campus or off-campus services.

Orientation The program or unit offers a mandatory 5-day orientation for new students before classes begin.

Unique Aids and Services Aids, services, or accommodations include advocates, career counseling, priority registration, support groups, mentoring program.

Assistive Technology Assistive technology is located in campus labs, the DSS office, Testing Center and includes digital textbooks/e-text, learning support software, and scanning. Technology training is provided to incoming students.

Subject-Area Tutoring Tutoring is offered in small groups for some subjects. Tutoring is provided collaboratively through on-campus or off-campus services via computer-based instruction, graduate assistants/students, LD specialists, and trained peer tutors.

Diagnostic Testing Testing is provided through the program or unit for learning strategies, learning styles, study skills, and visual processing. Testing for personality and written language is provided collaboratively through on-campus or off-campus services.

Enrichment Enrichment programs are available through the program or unit for learning strategies, self-advocacy, stress management, study skills, test taking, and time management. Programs for career planning, college survival skills, oral communication skills, practical computer skills, reading, and written composition skills are provided collaboratively through on-campus or off-campus services.

Application For admittance to the program or unit, students are required to provide a psychoeducational report (3 years old or less). It is recommended that students apply to the program directly and provide documentation of high school services. Upon application, materials documenting need for services should be sent only to the LD program or unit. Upon acceptance, documentation of need for services should be sent only to the LD program or unit. *Application deadline (institutional):* 7/1. *Application deadline (LD program):* Rolling/continuous for fall and rolling/continuous for spring.

Written Policies Written policy regarding general/basic LD accommodations is available on the program Web site. Written policy regarding general/basic LD accommodations is outlined in the school's catalog/handbook.

University of Nebraska at Kearney
Academic Success Office

905 West 25th Street

Kearney, NE 68849-0001

http://www.unk.edu

Contact: Mr. David Lee Brandt, Assistant Director. Phone: 308-865-8214. Fax: 308-865-8286. E-mail: brandtdl@unk.edu. Head of LD Program: Dr. Gail Zeller, Director. Phone: 308-865-8988. Fax: 308-865-8286. E-mail: zellerg@unk.edu.

Academic Success Office Approximately 85 registered undergraduate students were served during 2006–07. The program or unit includes 3 full-time staff members and 1 part-time staff member. Trained peer tutors and other are provided through the program or unit. Academic advisers, counselors, trained peer tutors, and other are provided collaboratively through on-campus or off-campus services.

Assistive Technology Assistive technology is located in campus labs, the DSS office and includes learning support software and scanning. Technology training is provided to incoming students.

Subject-Area Tutoring Tutoring is offered one-on-one, in small groups, and in class-size groups for most subjects. Tutoring is provided through the program or unit via trained peer tutors. Tutoring is also provided collaboratively through on-campus or off-campus services via graduate assistants/students.

Basic Skills Remediation Remediation is offered one-on-one, in small groups, and in class-size groups for computer skills, learning strategies, math, reading, spelling, spoken language, study skills, time management, and written language. Remediation is provided collaboratively through on-campus or off-campus services via computer-based instruction, graduate assistants/students, regular education teachers, and trained peer tutors.

Enrichment Programs for career planning, college survival skills, health and nutrition, learning strategies, math, self-advocacy, stress management, study skills, test taking, time management, vocabulary development, and written composition skills are provided collaboratively through on-campus or off-campus services. Credit is offered for college survival skills, health and nutrition, learning strategies, math, stress management, study skills, test taking, time management, vocabulary development, and written composition skills.

Student Organization Collegians for Integration and Accessibility consists of 23 members.

Application For admittance to the program or unit, students are required to apply to the program directly, provide documentation of high school services, and provide signed statement from a qualified professional, the nature of the disability, how it was diagnosed. It is recommended that students provide a psychoeducational report (3 years old or less). Upon application, materials documenting need for services should be sent only to the LD program or unit. Upon

acceptance, documentation of need for services should be sent only to the LD program or unit. *Application deadline (institutional):* Continuous. *Application deadline (LD program):* Rolling/continuous for fall and rolling/continuous for spring.

Written Policies Written policy regarding general/basic LD accommodations is available on the program Web site. Written policy regarding general/basic LD accommodations is outlined in the school's catalog/handbook. Written policy regarding general/basic LD accommodations is available through the program or unit directly.

University of Nebraska at Omaha
Services for Students with disABILITIES

6001 Dodge Street

Omaha, NE 68182

http://www.unomaha.edu/disability/

Contact: Kate Benecke. Phone: 402-554-2872. E-mail: mbenecke@mail.unomaha.edu.

Services for Students with disABILITIES Approximately 45 registered undergraduate students were served during 2006–07. The program or unit includes 3 full-time staff members and 1 part-time staff member. Academic advisers, coaches, counselors, diagnostic specialists, graduate assistants/students, LD specialists, professional tutors, regular education teachers, remediation/learning specialists, skill tutors, special education teachers, strategy tutors, teacher trainees, and trained peer tutors are provided collaboratively through on-campus or off-campus services.

Unique Aids and Services Aids, services, or accommodations include advocates and priority registration.

Subject-Area Tutoring Tutoring is offered one-on-one, in small groups, and in class-size groups for most subjects. Tutoring is provided collaboratively through on-campus or off-campus services via computer-based instruction, graduate assistants/students, LD specialists, professional tutors, and trained peer tutors.

Enrichment Enrichment programs are available through the program or unit for self-advocacy. Programs for career planning, college survival skills, health and nutrition, learning strategies, math, reading, stress management, study skills, test taking, time management, and written composition skills are provided collaboratively through on-campus or off-campus services.

Student Organization Network for disABLED Students.

Application For admittance to the program or unit, students are required to provide a psychoeducational report (3 years old or less). It is recommended that students provide documentation of high school services. Upon application, materials documenting need for services should be sent only to the LD program or unit. Upon acceptance, documentation of need for services should be sent only to the LD program or unit. *Application deadline (institutional):* 8/1. *Application deadline (LD program):* Rolling/continuous for fall and rolling/continuous for spring.

University of Nebraska–Lincoln

14th and R Streets
Lincoln, NE 68588
http://www.unl.edu/

Contact: Ms. Veva Cheney, Director of Services for Students with Disabilities. Phone: 402-472-3787. Fax: 402-472-0080. E-mail: vcheney2@unl.edu.

The program or unit includes 3 full-time staff members and 1 part-time staff member. Academic advisers, counselors, and skill tutors are provided collaboratively through on-campus or off-campus services.

Unique Aids and Services Aids, services, or accommodations include priority registration, extended time on tests, note-taker in the classroom.

Assistive Technology Assistive technology is located in a special lab and includes digital textbooks/e-text and scanning. Technology training is provided to incoming students.

Subject-Area Tutoring Tutoring is offered one-on-one and in small groups for some subjects. Tutoring is provided collaboratively through on-campus or off-campus services via graduate assistants/students and trained peer tutors.

Diagnostic Testing Testing for auditory processing, intelligence, math, personality, reading, spelling, visual processing, and written language is provided collaboratively through on-campus or off-campus services.

Enrichment Programs for career planning, college survival skills, health and nutrition, self-advocacy, stress management, study skills, test taking, time management, and written composition skills are provided collaboratively through on-campus or off-campus services.

Fees *Diagnostic Testing* fee is $300 to $600.

Application For admittance to the program or unit, students are required to provide a psychoeducational report (3 years old or less). It is recommended that students provide documentation of high school services. Upon application, materials documenting need for services should be sent only to the LD program or unit. Upon acceptance, documentation of need for services should be sent only to the LD program or unit. *Application deadline (institutional):* 5/1. *Application deadline (LD program):* Rolling/continuous for fall and rolling/continuous for spring.

Written Policies Written policies regarding course substitutions, general/basic LD accommodations, reduced course loads, substitutions and waivers of admissions requirements, and substitutions and waivers of graduation requirements are available through the program or unit directly.

University of New Brunswick Fredericton
Student Accessibility Centre

PO Box 4400
Fredericton, NB E3B 5A3
Canada
http://www.unbf.ca/studentaccessibility/

Contact: Patricia Kirby, Coordinator, Services for Students with Disabilities. Phone: 506-453-3515. Fax: 506-453-4765. E-mail: pkirby@unb.ca.

Student Accessibility Centre Approximately 300 registered undergraduate students were served during 2006–07. The program or unit includes 4 full-time and 15 part-time staff members. Coaches, diagnostic specialists, graduate assistants/students, LD specialists, professional tutors, remediation/learning specialists, skill tutors, strategy tutors, and trained peer tutors are provided through the program or unit. Academic advisers, counselors, diagnostic specialists, regular education teachers, skill tutors, special education teachers, and teacher trainees are provided collaboratively through on-campus or off-campus services.

Orientation The program or unit offers an optional 2-day orientation for new students during summer prior to enrollment, after classes begin, and individually by special arrangement.

Unique Aids and Services Aids, services, or accommodations include advocates, career counseling, personal coach, and support groups.

Assistive Technology Assistive technology is located in the DSS office, a special lab, Harriet Irving Library and includes digital textbooks/e-text, learning support software, scanning, and Kurzweil 3000, Dragon Naturally Speaking. Technology training is provided to incoming students.

Subject-Area Tutoring Tutoring is offered one-on-one for all subjects. Tutoring is provided through the program or unit via computer-based instruction, graduate assistants/students, LD specialists, professional tutors, and trained peer tutors. Tutoring is also provided collaboratively through on-campus or off-campus services via computer-based instruction, graduate assistants/students, professional tutors, and trained peer tutors.

Diagnostic Testing Testing is provided through the program or unit for handwriting, learning strategies, learning styles, math, personality, reading, social skills, spelling, spoken language, study skills, visual processing, and written language. Testing for auditory processing, handwriting, intelligence, math, motor skills, and neuropsychological is provided collaboratively through on-campus or off-campus services.

Basic Skills Remediation Remediation is offered one-on-one for computer skills, learning strategies, math, reading, social skills, spelling, spoken language, study skills, time management, and written language. Remediation is provided through the program or unit via computer-based instruction, graduate assistants/students, LD specialists, professional tutors, teacher trainees, and trained peer tutors. Remediation is also provided collaboratively through on-campus or off-campus services via computer-based instruction, graduate assistants/students, professional tutors, regular education teachers, special education teachers, teacher trainees, and trained peer tutors.

Enrichment Enrichment programs are available through the program or unit for career planning, learning strategies, practical computer skills, self-advocacy, stress management, study skills, test taking, and time management. Programs for career planning, college survival skills, health and nutrition, math, medication management, oral communication skills, practical computer skills, reading, stress management, study skills, test taking, time management, and written composition skills are provided collaboratively through on-campus or off-campus services.

Application For admittance to the program or unit, students are required to apply to the program directly. It is recommended that students provide a psychoeducational report (5 years old or less) and provide documentation of high school services. Upon application, materials documenting need for services should be sent only to the LD program or unit. Upon acceptance, documentation of need for services should be sent only to the LD program or unit. *Application deadline (institutional):* 3/31. *Application deadline (LD program):* Rolling/continuous for fall and rolling/continuous for spring.

Written Policies Written policy regarding general/basic LD accommodations is available on the program Web site. Written policies regarding general/basic LD accommodations and grade forgiveness are outlined in the school's catalog/handbook. Written policies regarding general/basic LD accommodations, grade forgiveness, and reduced course loads are available through the program or unit directly.

University of New Brunswick Saint John
Student Services

PO Box 5050
Saint John, NB E2L 4L5
Canada
http://www.unbsj.ca/studentservices
Contact: Mr. Ken Craft, Student Development Coordinator. Phone: 506-648-5962. Fax: 506-648-5816. E-mail: kcraft@unbsj.ca.

Student Services Approximately 15 registered undergraduate students were served during 2006–07. The program or unit includes 1 full-time staff member. Academic advisers, counselors, skill tutors, and trained peer tutors are provided collaboratively through on-campus or off-campus services.

Unique Aids and Services Aids, services, or accommodations include advocates and career counseling.

Assistive Technology Assistive technology is located in the DSS office and includes digital textbooks/e-text and scanning. Technology training is provided to incoming students.

Basic Skills Remediation Remediation is offered one-on-one for learning strategies, reading, study skills, time management, and written language. Remediation is provided through the program or unit.

Enrichment Enrichment programs are available through the program or unit for college survival skills, learning strategies, reading, study skills, test taking, and time management. Programs for career planning, college survival skills, health and nutrition, learning strategies, math, medication management, oral communication skills, reading, self-advocacy, stress management, study skills, test taking, time management, and written composition skills are provided collaboratively through on-campus or off-campus services.

Application For admittance to the program or unit, students are required to provide a psychoeducational report. It is recommended that students provide documentation of high school services. Upon acceptance, documentation of need for services should be sent only to the LD program or unit. *Application deadline (LD program):* Rolling/continuous for fall and rolling/continuous for spring.

Written Policies Written policy regarding general/basic LD accommodations is available on the program Web site. Written policy regarding general/basic LD accommodations is outlined in the school's catalog/handbook. Written policy regarding general/basic LD accommodations is available through the program or unit directly.

University of New England
Disability Services

Hills Beach Road
Biddeford, ME 04005-9526
http://www.une.edu/studentlife/dsd/
Contact: Susan M. Church, Director Disability Services. Phone: 207-602-2815. Fax: 207-602-5971. E-mail: schurch@une.edu.

Disability Services Approximately 80 registered undergraduate students were served during 2006–07. The program or unit includes 2 full-time staff members. Academic advisers, counselors, professional tutors, remediation/learning specialists, skill tutors, strategy tutors, and trained peer tutors are provided collaboratively through on-campus or off-campus services.

Unique Aids and Services Aids, services, or accommodations include priority registration.

Assistive Technology Assistive technology is located in the DSS office and includes digital textbooks/e-text and scanning.

Subject-Area Tutoring Tutoring is offered in small groups for most subjects. Tutoring is provided collaboratively through on-campus or off-campus services via professional tutors and trained peer tutors.

Enrichment Enrichment programs are available through the program or unit for self-advocacy. Programs for career planning, college survival skills, learning strategies, math, reading, study skills, test taking, time management, and written composition skills are provided collaboratively through on-campus or off-campus services.

Application For admittance to the program or unit, students are required to provide a psychoeducational report (3 years old or less). It is recommended that students provide documentation of high school services. Upon application, materials documenting need for services should be sent only to the LD program or unit. Upon acceptance, documentation of need for services should be sent only to the LD program or unit. *Application deadline (institutional):* 2/15. *Application deadline (LD program):* Rolling/continuous for fall and rolling/continuous for spring.

Written Policies Written policies regarding course substitutions, general/basic LD accommodations, and reduced course loads are available on the program Web site. Written policies regarding course substitutions, general/basic LD accommodations, and reduced course loads are available through the program or unit directly.

University of New Hampshire
Disability Services for Students (DSS)

Durham, NH 03824
http://www.unh.edu/disabilityservices/disabilityservices.html
Contact: Katherine A. Berger, Assistant Director/Learning Disability Specialist. Phone: 603-862-0830. Fax: 603-862-4043. E-mail: kathy.berger@unh.edu. Head of LD Program: Maxine J. Little, Director. Phone: 603-862-2648. Fax: 603-862-4043. E-mail: maxine.little@unh.edu.

University of New Hampshire (continued)

Disability Services for Students (DSS) Approximately 243 registered undergraduate students were served during 2006–07. The program or unit includes 3 full-time and 3 part-time staff members. Academic advisers, coaches, counselors, LD specialists, and strategy tutors are provided through the program or unit. Academic advisers, coaches, counselors, diagnostic specialists, graduate assistants/students, LD specialists, professional tutors, regular education teachers, remediation/learning specialists, skill tutors, strategy tutors, and trained peer tutors are provided collaboratively through on-campus or off-campus services.

Unique Aids and Services Aids, services, or accommodations include advocates, priority registration.

Assistive Technology Assistive technology is located in the DSS office, a special lab and includes digital textbooks/e-text and scanning.

Subject-Area Tutoring Tutoring is offered one-on-one, in small groups, and in class-size groups for some subjects. Tutoring is provided collaboratively through on-campus or off-campus services via graduate assistants/students and trained peer tutors.

Basic Skills Remediation Remediation is offered one-on-one for learning strategies, study skills, and time management. Remediation is provided collaboratively through on-campus or off-campus services via trained peer tutors.

Enrichment Enrichment programs are available through the program or unit for self-advocacy, stress management, and other. Programs for career planning, college survival skills, health and nutrition, learning strategies, math, oral communication skills, practical computer skills, reading, self-advocacy, stress management, study skills, test taking, time management, written composition skills, and other are provided collaboratively through on-campus or off-campus services.

Application For admittance to the program or unit, students are required to apply to the program directly and provide a psychoeducational report (3 years old or less). It is recommended that students provide documentation of high school services and provide history, other scores and sub-test scores on information processing. Upon application, materials documenting need for services should be sent only to the LD program or unit. Upon acceptance, documentation of need for services should be sent only to the LD program or unit. *Application deadline (institutional):* 2/1. *Application deadline (LD program):* Rolling/continuous for fall and rolling/continuous for spring.

Written Policies Written policy regarding general/basic LD accommodations is available on the program Web site. Written policy regarding general/basic LD accommodations is outlined in the school's catalog/handbook. Written policy regarding general/basic LD accommodations is available through the program or unit directly.

University of New Hampshire at Manchester

400 Commercial Street
Manchester, NH 03101-1113
http://www.unhm.unh.edu/

Contact: Ms. Joy M. Breeden, Academic Counselor. Phone: 603-641-4170. Fax: 603-641-4125. E-mail: joy.breeden@unh.edu.

Approximately 7 registered undergraduate students were served during 2006–07. The program or unit includes 1 full-time staff member. Academic advisers, professional tutors, regular education teachers, skill tutors, strategy tutors, and trained peer tutors are provided collaboratively through on-campus or off-campus services.

Unique Aids and Services Aids, services, or accommodations include advocates and faculty training.

Assistive Technology Assistive technology is located in campus labs, a special lab and includes digital textbooks/e-text.

Subject-Area Tutoring Tutoring is offered one-on-one and in small groups for some subjects. Tutoring is provided through the program or unit via LD specialists. Tutoring is also provided collaboratively through on-campus or off-campus services via graduate assistants/students, professional tutors, and trained peer tutors.

Basic Skills Remediation Remediation is offered one-on-one and in small groups for learning strategies, math, reading, study skills, and time management. Remediation is provided through the program or unit via professional tutors and trained peer tutors. Remediation is also provided collaboratively through on-campus or off-campus services via graduate assistants/students, LD specialists, professional tutors, regular education teachers, and trained peer tutors.

Application For admittance to the program or unit, students are required to provide a psychoeducational report (3 years old or less). It is recommended that students provide documentation of high school services. Upon acceptance, documentation of need for services should be sent only to the LD program or unit. *Application deadline (institutional):* 6/15. *Application deadline (LD program):* Rolling/continuous for fall and rolling/continuous for spring.

Written Policies Written policies regarding course substitutions, general/basic LD accommodations, substitutions and waivers of admissions requirements, and substitutions and waivers of graduation requirements are available on the program Web site. Written policies regarding course substitutions, general/basic LD accommodations, substitutions and waivers of admissions requirements, and substitutions and waivers of graduation requirements are outlined in the school's catalog/handbook. Written policies regarding general/basic LD accommodations and reduced course loads are available through the program or unit directly.

University of New Haven
Disability Services and Resources

300 Orange Avenue
West Haven, CT 06516-1916
http://www.newhaven.edu/campuslife/disabilities.html
Contact: Ms. Linda Copney-Okeke, Director of Disability Services and Resources. Phone: 203-932-7332. Fax: 203-931-6082. E-mail: lcopney-okeke@newhaven.edu.

Disability Services and Resources Approximately 200 registered undergraduate students were served during 2006–07. The program or unit includes 1 full-time staff member. Academic advisers, counselors, graduate assistants/students, LD specialists, and skill tutors are provided through the program or unit. Academic advisers, counselors, diagnostic specialists, professional tutors, skill tutors, and strategy tutors are provided collaboratively through on-campus or off-campus services.

Unique Aids and Services Aids, services, or accommodations include career counseling and faculty training.
Assistive Technology Assistive technology is located in campus labs, the DSS office, the library and includes digital textbooks/e-text, learning support software, and scanning. Technology training is provided to incoming students.
Subject-Area Tutoring Tutoring is offered one-on-one and in small groups for most subjects. Tutoring is provided through the program or unit via graduate assistants/students. Tutoring is also provided collaboratively through on-campus or off-campus services via computer-based instruction, graduate assistants/students, and professional tutors.
Diagnostic Testing Testing is provided through the program or unit for learning strategies and learning styles. Testing for intelligence, math, personality, reading, spelling, study skills, visual processing, written language, and other services is provided collaboratively through on-campus or off-campus services.
Basic Skills Remediation Remediation is offered one-on-one, in small groups, and in class-size groups for computer skills, learning strategies, math, reading, study skills, and time management. Remediation is provided through the program or unit via graduate assistants/students. Remediation is also provided collaboratively through on-campus or off-campus services via graduate assistants/students, professional tutors, and regular education teachers.
Enrichment Enrichment programs are available through the program or unit for math, practical computer skills, self-advocacy, study skills, test taking, time management, and written composition skills. Programs for career planning, college survival skills, health and nutrition, learning strategies, math, oral communication skills, reading, stress management, study skills, test taking, time management, and written composition skills are provided collaboratively through on-campus or off-campus services. Credit is offered for math, oral communication skills, practical computer skills, reading, and written composition skills.
Application For admittance to the program or unit, students are required to provide a psychoeducational report. It is recommended that students provide documentation of high school services. Upon acceptance, documentation of need for services should be sent only to the LD program or unit. *Application deadline (institutional):* Continuous. *Application deadline (LD program):* Rolling/continuous for fall and rolling/continuous for spring.
Written Policies Written policies regarding course substitutions, general/basic LD accommodations, and reduced course loads are available through the program or unit directly.

University of New Mexico
Accessibility Services
Albuquerque, NM 87131-2039
https://as.unm.edu
Contact: Mrs. Nicole Hudson, Learning Disabilities Program Specialist. Phone: 505-277-3506. Fax: 505-277-8650. E-mail: nhudson@unm.edu. Head of LD Program: Ms. Joan E. Green, Director. Phone: 505-277-3506. Fax: 505-277-3750. E-mail: jegreen@unm.edu.

Accessibility Services Approximately 120 registered undergraduate students were served during 2006–07. The program or unit includes 1 full-time staff member. Graduate assistants/students, LD

specialists, professional tutors, skill tutors, and strategy tutors are provided through the program or unit. Academic advisers, coaches, counselors, professional tutors, and remediation/learning specialists are provided collaboratively through on-campus or off-campus services.
Assistive Technology Assistive technology is located in the DSS office, a special lab and includes digital textbooks/e-text, learning support software, and scanning. Technology training is provided to incoming students.
Subject-Area Tutoring Tutoring is offered one-on-one and in small groups for most subjects. Tutoring is provided through the program or unit via LD specialists, professional tutors, and trained peer tutors. Tutoring is also provided collaboratively through on-campus or off-campus services via computer-based instruction, graduate assistants/students, professional tutors, and trained peer tutors.
Basic Skills Remediation Remediation is offered one-on-one for social skills, study skills, and time management. Remediation is provided through the program or unit via computer-based instruction and LD specialists.
Enrichment Enrichment programs are available through the program or unit for learning strategies, self-advocacy, study skills, test taking, time management, and written composition skills. Programs for career planning, college survival skills, health and nutrition, math, stress management, study skills, test taking, time management, and written composition skills are provided collaboratively through on-campus or off-campus services.
Application For admittance to the program or unit, students are required to apply to the program directly and provide a psychoeducational report (3 years old or less). Upon acceptance, documentation of need for services should be sent only to the LD program or unit. *Application deadline (institutional):* 6/15. *Application deadline (LD program):* Rolling/continuous for fall and rolling/continuous for spring.
Written Policies Written policies regarding course substitutions, grade forgiveness, and substitutions and waivers of graduation requirements are available on the program Web site. Written policy regarding grade forgiveness is outlined in the school's catalog/handbook. Written policy regarding general/basic LD accommodations is available through the program or unit directly.

University of New Orleans
Office of Disability Services
Lake Front
New Orleans, LA 70148
http://www.ods.uno.edu
Contact: Mrs. Amy A. King, Assistant Director. Phone: 504-280-7284. Fax: 504-280-3998. E-mail: aaking@uno.edu. Head of LD Program: Dr. Janice Lyn, Associate Dean, Student Affairs, and Director, Office of Disability Services. Phone: 504-280-6222. Fax: 504-280-3975. E-mail: jlyn@uno.edu.

Office of Disability Services Approximately 100 registered undergraduate students were served during 2006–07. The program or unit includes 2 full-time staff members and 1 part-time staff member. Graduate assistants/students are provided through the program or

University of New Orleans (continued)

unit. Academic advisers, counselors, diagnostic specialists, professional tutors, regular education teachers, skill tutors, and trained peer tutors are provided collaboratively through on-campus or off-campus services.

Assistive Technology Assistive technology is located in campus labs, the DSS office and includes digital textbooks/e-text, learning support software, and scanning. Technology training is provided to incoming students.

Subject-Area Tutoring Tutoring is offered one-on-one and in small groups for some subjects. Tutoring is provided collaboratively through on-campus or off-campus services via trained peer tutors.

Enrichment Programs for career planning, college survival skills, health and nutrition, learning strategies, oral communication skills, practical computer skills, self-advocacy, stress management, study skills, test taking, and time management are provided collaboratively through on-campus or off-campus services. Credit is offered for college survival skills and oral communication skills.

Application For admittance to the program or unit, students are required to provide a psychoeducational report (3 years old or less) and provide documentation from an evaluator qualified to administer the psychoeducational testing. Upon application, materials documenting need for services should be sent only to the LD program or unit. Upon acceptance, documentation of need for services should be sent only to the LD program or unit. *Application deadline (institutional):* Continuous. *Application deadline (LD program):* Rolling/continuous for fall and rolling/continuous for spring.

Written Policies Written policies regarding course substitutions and general/basic LD accommodations are available on the program Web site. Written policies regarding course substitutions and general/basic LD accommodations are available through the program or unit directly.

The University of North Carolina at Asheville
Advising and Learning Support

One University Heights

Asheville, NC 28804-3299

http://www.unca.edu/disabilityservices

Contact: Mr. Ethan Fesperman, Disabilities Coordinator. Phone: 828-232-5050. Fax: 828-250-2346. E-mail: efesperm@unca.edu.

Advising and Learning Support Approximately 70 registered undergraduate students were served during 2006–07. The program or unit includes 1 full-time staff member. Academic advisers, coaches, counselors, regular education teachers, and trained peer tutors are provided collaboratively through on-campus or off-campus services.

Unique Aids and Services Aids, services, or accommodations include faculty training, priority registration, support groups, and weekly meetings with faculty.

Subject-Area Tutoring Tutoring is offered one-on-one for all subjects. Tutoring is provided collaboratively through on-campus or off-campus services via trained peer tutors.

Student Organization Equal Access consists of 10 members.

Application For admittance to the program or unit, students are required to provide a psychoeducational report (3 years old or less), provide documentation of high school services, and provide specific diagnosis. Upon application, materials documenting need for services should be sent only to the LD program or unit. Upon acceptance, documentation of need for services should be sent only to the LD program or unit. *Application deadline (institutional):* 2/15. *Application deadline (LD program):* Rolling/continuous for fall and rolling/continuous for spring.

Written Policies Written policy regarding general/basic LD accommodations is available on the program Web site. Written policy regarding general/basic LD accommodations is outlined in the school's catalog/handbook. Written policies regarding course substitutions and substitutions and waivers of graduation requirements are available through the program or unit directly.

The University of North Carolina at Charlotte
Office of Disability Services

9201 University City Boulevard

Charlotte, NC 28223-0001

http://www.ds.uncc.edu

Contact: JoAnn Fernald, Director of Disability Services. Phone: 704-687-4355. Fax: 704-687-3226. E-mail: dissrvcs@uncc.edu.

Office of Disability Services Approximately 600 registered undergraduate students were served during 2006–07. The program or unit includes 5 full-time staff members. Counselors, graduate assistants/students, LD specialists, and other are provided through the program or unit. Academic advisers, counselors, graduate assistants/students, professional tutors, skill tutors, strategy tutors, trained peer tutors, and other are provided collaboratively through on-campus or off-campus services.

Unique Aids and Services Aids, services, or accommodations include advocates, priority registration, individual meetings with trained counselors.

Assistive Technology Assistive technology is located in campus labs, the DSS office, a special lab and includes digital textbooks/e-text, learning support software, and scanning.

Subject-Area Tutoring Tutoring is offered one-on-one, in small groups, and in class-size groups for most subjects. Tutoring is provided collaboratively through on-campus or off-campus services via computer-based instruction, graduate assistants/students, professional tutors, and trained peer tutors.

Basic Skills Remediation Remediation is offered one-on-one and in small groups for learning strategies, study skills, time management, and written language. Remediation is provided collaboratively through on-campus or off-campus services via computer-based instruction, graduate assistants/students, professional tutors, trained peer tutors, and other.

Enrichment Enrichment programs are available through the program or unit for career planning, learning strategies, self-advocacy, test taking, and other. Programs for college survival skills, health and nutrition, learning strategies, math, medication management, oral communication skills, practical computer skills, reading, self-advocacy, stress management, study skills, test taking, time management, vocabulary development, written composition skills, and other are provided collaboratively through on-campus or off-campus services. Credit is offered for health and nutrition, math, and practical computer skills.

Application For admittance to the program or unit, students are required to apply to the program directly, provide a psychoeducational report (3 years old or less), and provide diagnosis and academic recommendations from the evaluator. Upon acceptance, documentation of need for services should be sent only to the LD program or unit. *Application deadline (institutional): 7/1. Application deadline (LD program):* Rolling/continuous for fall and rolling/continuous for spring.

Written Policies Written policies regarding course substitutions, general/basic LD accommodations, grade forgiveness, reduced course loads, substitutions and waivers of admissions requirements, and substitutions and waivers of graduation requirements are available on the program Web site. Written policies regarding course substitutions, general/basic LD accommodations, grade forgiveness, reduced course loads, substitutions and waivers of admissions requirements, and substitutions and waivers of graduation requirements are outlined in the school's catalog/handbook. Written policies regarding course substitutions, general/basic LD accommodations, reduced course loads, substitutions and waivers of admissions requirements, and substitutions and waivers of graduation requirements are available through the program or unit directly.

University of Northern British Columbia

3333 University Way

Prince George, BC V2N 4Z9

Canada

http://www.unbc.ca/

Contact: Maureen G. Hewlett, Disabilities Advisor/ Coordinator Disability Services. Phone: 250-960-6355. Fax: 250-960-5775. E-mail: hewlettm@unbc.ca.

The program or unit includes 3 full-time staff members. Academic advisers, coaches, diagnostic specialists, graduate assistants/students, LD specialists, professional tutors, regular education teachers, skill tutors, strategy tutors, and trained peer tutors are provided through the program or unit. Academic advisers, counselors, and diagnostic specialists are provided collaboratively through on-campus or off-campus services.

Orientation The program or unit offers an optional orientation for new students before classes begin, after classes begin, and individually by special arrangement.

Unique Aids and Services Aids, services, or accommodations include advocates, faculty training, personal coach, and support groups.

Assistive Technology Assistive technology is located in the DSS office and includes digital textbooks/e-text, learning support software, and scanning. Technology training is provided to incoming students.

Subject-Area Tutoring Tutoring is offered one-on-one and in small groups for most subjects. Tutoring is provided through the program or unit via computer-based instruction, graduate assistants/ students, LD specialists, professional tutors, and trained peer tutors.

Diagnostic Testing Testing is provided through the program or unit for auditory processing, handwriting, intelligence, learning strategies, learning styles, math, motor skills, personality, reading, social skills, spelling, study skills, visual processing, written language, and other services. Testing for auditory processing, intelligence, motor skills, neuropsychological, reading, visual processing, and written language is provided collaboratively through on-campus or off-campus services.

Basic Skills Remediation Remediation is offered one-on-one and in small groups for computer skills, learning strategies, reading, social skills, study skills, time management, and written language. Remediation is provided through the program or unit via computer-based instruction, graduate assistants/students, LD specialists, professional tutors, teacher trainees, and trained peer tutors.

Enrichment Enrichment programs are available through the program or unit for career planning, college survival skills, health and nutrition, learning strategies, medication management, oral communication skills, practical computer skills, reading, self-advocacy, stress management, study skills, test taking, time management, vocabulary development, written composition skills, and other. Programs for career planning, college survival skills, health and nutrition, math, medication management, and stress management are provided collaboratively through on-campus or off-campus services.

Student Organization Imperfection Club for Everyone (ICE) consists of 25 members.

Application For admittance to the program or unit, students are required to provide a psychoeducational report. It is recommended that students apply to the program directly and provide documentation of high school services. Upon acceptance, documentation of need for services should be sent only to the LD program or unit. *Application deadline (institutional): 3/1. Application deadline (LD program):* Rolling/continuous for fall and rolling/continuous for spring.

Written Policies Written policy regarding general/basic LD accommodations is available on the program Web site. Written policy regarding general/basic LD accommodations is outlined in the school's catalog/handbook. Written policies regarding general/basic LD accommodations, grade forgiveness, and reduced course loads are available through the program or unit directly.

University of Northern Iowa
Student Disability Services

1227 West 27th Street

Cedar Falls, IA 50614

http://www.uni.edu/disability

Contact: Jill L. Smith, Interim Coordinator. Phone: 319-273-2676. Fax: 319-276-6884. E-mail: jill.smith@ uni.edu.

Student Disability Services Approximately 180 registered undergraduate students were served during 2006–07. The program or unit includes 1 full-time staff member. LD specialists are provided through the program or unit. Academic advisers, counselors, diagnostic specialists, graduate assistants/students, regular education teachers, skill tutors, strategy tutors, and trained peer tutors are provided collaboratively through on-campus or off-campus services.

University of Northern Iowa (continued)

Unique Aids and Services Aids, services, or accommodations include career counseling, priority registration, weekly meetings with disability services staff.

Assistive Technology Assistive technology is located in campus labs and includes digital textbooks/e-text and scanning. Technology training is provided to incoming students.

Subject-Area Tutoring Tutoring is offered one-on-one and in small groups for most subjects. Tutoring is provided collaboratively through on-campus or off-campus services via graduate assistants/students, professional tutors, and trained peer tutors.

Diagnostic Testing Testing for intelligence, learning strategies, learning styles, math, personality, reading, spelling, study skills, and written language is provided collaboratively through on-campus or off-campus services.

Enrichment Programs for career planning, health and nutrition, learning strategies, self-advocacy, stress management, study skills, and time management are provided collaboratively through on-campus or off-campus services.

Fees *Diagnostic Testing* fee is $400.

Application For admittance to the program or unit, students are required to provide a psychoeducational report (3 years old or less). Upon acceptance, documentation of need for services should be sent only to the LD program or unit. *Application deadline (institutional): 8/15. Application deadline (LD program):* Rolling/continuous for fall and rolling/continuous for spring.

Written Policies Written policies regarding course substitutions, general/basic LD accommodations, substitutions and waivers of admissions requirements, and substitutions and waivers of graduation requirements are available on the program Web site. Written policies regarding course substitutions, substitutions and waivers of admissions requirements, and substitutions and waivers of graduation requirements are outlined in the school's catalog/handbook. Written policy regarding general/basic LD accommodations is available through the program or unit directly.

University of North Florida
Disability Resource Center

4567 St. Johns Bluff Road South
Jacksonville, FL 32224-2645

http://www.unf.edu/

Contact: Dr. Kristine W. Webb, Director. Phone: 904-620-2769. Fax: 904-620-3874. E-mail: kwebb@unf.edu.

Disability Resource Center Approximately 150 registered undergraduate students were served during 2006–07. The program or unit includes 4 full-time and 2 part-time staff members. Academic advisers, counselors, regular education teachers, remediation/learning specialists, skill tutors, strategy tutors, and trained peer tutors are provided collaboratively through on-campus or off-campus services.

Unique Aids and Services Aids, services, or accommodations include career counseling and priority registration.

Assistive Technology Assistive technology is located in the DSS office and includes learning support software and scanning. Technology training is provided to incoming students.

Subject-Area Tutoring Tutoring is offered one-on-one and in small groups for some subjects. Tutoring is provided collaboratively through on-campus or off-campus services via trained peer tutors.

Enrichment Programs for career planning, college survival skills, learning strategies, math, stress management, study skills, test taking, time management, vocabulary development, and written composition skills are provided collaboratively through on-campus or off-campus services.

Application For admittance to the program or unit, students are required to provide a psychoeducational report (3 years old or less). It is recommended that students provide documentation of high school services. Upon application, materials documenting need for services should be sent only to the LD program or unit. Upon acceptance, documentation of need for services should be sent only to the LD program or unit. *Application deadline (institutional): 7/2. Application deadline (LD program):* Rolling/continuous for fall and rolling/continuous for spring.

Written Policies Written policies regarding general/basic LD accommodations, substitutions and waivers of admissions requirements, and substitutions and waivers of graduation requirements are available on the program Web site. Written policies regarding course substitutions, general/basic LD accommodations, substitutions and waivers of admissions requirements, and substitutions and waivers of graduation requirements are available through the program or unit directly.

University of Notre Dame
Disability Services

Notre Dame, IN 46556

http://www.nd.edu/~osd

Contact: Mr. Scott Howland, Coordinator of Disability Services. Phone: 574-631-7141. Fax: 574-631-2133. E-mail: showland@nd.edu.

Disability Services Approximately 140 registered undergraduate students were served during 2006–07. The program or unit includes 1 full-time staff member. Services are provided through the program or unit. Academic advisers, counselors, diagnostic specialists, trained peer tutors, and other are provided collaboratively through on-campus or off-campus services.

Unique Aids and Services Aids, services, or accommodations include priority registration.

Assistive Technology Assistive technology is located in the DSS office and includes digital textbooks/e-text and scanning.

Subject-Area Tutoring Tutoring is offered one-on-one and in small groups for most subjects. Tutoring is provided collaboratively through on-campus or off-campus services via trained peer tutors.

Diagnostic Testing Testing for auditory processing, intelligence, neuropsychological, personality, reading, social skills, spelling, spoken language, study skills, visual processing, and written language is provided collaboratively through on-campus or off-campus services.

Enrichment Programs for career planning, health and nutrition, learning strategies, stress management, study skills, test taking, time management, and written composition skills are provided collaboratively through on-campus or off-campus services.

Student Organization Perspectives consists of 20 members.

Fees *Diagnostic Testing* fee is $750 to $1500.

Application For admittance to the program or unit, students are required to provide a psychoeducational report (3 years old or less). Upon acceptance, documentation of need for services should be sent only to the LD program or unit. *Application deadline (institutional):* 12/31. *Application deadline (LD program):* Rolling/continuous for fall and rolling/continuous for spring.

Written Policies Written policies regarding course substitutions, general/basic LD accommodations, and substitutions and waivers of graduation requirements are available on the program Web site. Written policy regarding general/basic LD accommodations is outlined in the school's catalog/handbook. Written policies regarding course substitutions, general/basic LD accommodations, and substitutions and waivers of graduation requirements are available through the program or unit directly.

University of Oregon
Disability Services

Eugene, OR 97403

http://ds.uoregon.edu

Contact: Mr. Steve Pickett, Director of Disability Services and Associate Director of Academic Advising. Phone: 541-346-1155. Fax: 541-346-6013. E-mail: spickett@uoregon.edu.

Disability Services Approximately 400 registered undergraduate students were served during 2006–07. The program or unit includes 4 full-time and 3 part-time staff members. Academic advisers, coaches, counselors, diagnostic specialists, graduate assistants/students, LD specialists, professional tutors, regular education teachers, remediation/learning specialists, skill tutors, and strategy tutors are provided collaboratively through on-campus or off-campus services.

Orientation The program or unit offers a mandatory varying length orientation for new students before registration, before classes begin, during summer prior to enrollment, during registration, after classes begin, and individually by special arrangement.

Unique Aids and Services Aids, services, or accommodations include faculty training, regularly scheduled appointments with a DS adviser.

Assistive Technology Assistive technology is located in a special lab and includes digital textbooks/e-text, learning support software, and scanning. Technology training is provided to incoming students.

Subject-Area Tutoring Tutoring is offered one-on-one and in small groups for most subjects. Tutoring is provided collaboratively through on-campus or off-campus services via computer-based instruction, graduate assistants/students, LD specialists, professional tutors, and trained peer tutors.

Diagnostic Testing Testing for auditory processing, handwriting, intelligence, learning strategies, learning styles, math, motor skills, neuropsychological, personality, reading, social skills, spelling, spoken language, study skills, visual processing, written language, and other services is provided collaboratively through on-campus or off-campus services.

Basic Skills Remediation Remediation is offered one-on-one and in small groups for auditory processing, computer skills, learning strategies, math, reading, spelling, spoken language, study skills, time management, visual processing, and written language. Remediation is provided collaboratively through on-campus or off-campus services via computer-based instruction, graduate assistants/students, LD specialists, professional tutors, regular education teachers, and trained peer tutors.

Enrichment Programs for career planning, college survival skills, health and nutrition, learning strategies, math, medication management, oral communication skills, practical computer skills, reading, self-advocacy, stress management, study skills, test taking, time management, vocabulary development, and written composition skills are provided collaboratively through on-campus or off-campus services.

Fees *Diagnostic Testing* fee is $500.

Application For admittance to the program or unit, students are required to provide assessment results appropriate to the disabling condition. It is recommended that students apply to the program directly, provide a psychoeducational report (3 years old or less), and provide documentation of high school services. Upon application, materials documenting need for services should be sent only to admissions with institutional application materials. Upon acceptance, documentation of need for services should be sent only to the LD program or unit. *Application deadline (institutional):* 1/15. *Application deadline (LD program):* Rolling/continuous for fall and rolling/continuous for spring.

Written Policies Written policies regarding general/basic LD accommodations and substitutions and waivers of admissions requirements are available on the program Web site. Written policies regarding course substitutions, general/basic LD accommodations, grade forgiveness, reduced course loads, substitutions and waivers of admissions requirements, and substitutions and waivers of graduation requirements are outlined in the school's catalog/handbook. Written policy regarding general/basic LD accommodations is available through the program or unit directly.

University of Pennsylvania
Student Disabilities Services

3451 Walnut Street

Philadelphia, PA 19104

http://www.vpul.upenn.edu/lrc/sds/index.html

Contact: Matthew F. Tominey, Director of Student Disabilities Services. Phone: 215-573-9235. Fax: 215-746-6326. E-mail: sdsmail@pobox.upenn.edu.

Student Disabilities Services Approximately 400 registered undergraduate students were served during 2006–07. The program or unit includes 5 full-time staff members and 1 part-time staff member. Diagnostic specialists, LD specialists, strategy tutors, and other are provided through the program or unit. Academic advisers, counselors, graduate assistants/students, remediation/learning specialists, skill tutors, trained peer tutors, and other are provided collaboratively through on-campus or off-campus services.

Orientation The program or unit offers an optional 2-hour orientation for new students before classes begin and individually by special arrangement.

Summer Program To help prepare for the demands of college, there is an optional 4-week summer program prior to entering the school. Degree credit will be earned.

Unique Aids and Services Aids, services, or accommodations include career counseling, faculty training, support groups.

Assistive Technology Assistive technology is located in campus labs, the DSS office and includes digital textbooks/e-text, learning support software, and scanning. Technology training is provided to incoming students.

University of Pennsylvania (continued)

Subject-Area Tutoring Tutoring is offered one-on-one and in small groups for some subjects. Tutoring is provided collaboratively through on-campus or off-campus services via graduate assistants/students and trained peer tutors.

Enrichment Enrichment programs are available through the program or unit for college survival skills, learning strategies, oral communication skills, reading, self-advocacy, stress management, study skills, test taking, time management, vocabulary development, written composition skills, and other. Programs for career planning, health and nutrition, math, medication management, oral communication skills, practical computer skills, stress management, written composition skills, and other are provided collaboratively through on-campus or off-campus services.

Student Organization Student Disabilities Services Student Advisory Board consists of 20 members.

Application For admittance to the program or unit, students are required to provide a psychoeducational report (3 years old or less). It is recommended that students provide documentation of high school services and provide related histories and medical documentation. Upon acceptance, documentation of need for services should be sent only to the LD program or unit. *Application deadline (institutional):* 1/1. *Application deadline (LD program):* Rolling/continuous for fall and rolling/continuous for spring.

Written Policies Written policies regarding course substitutions and general/basic LD accommodations are available on the program Web site. Written policies regarding course substitutions and general/basic LD accommodations are outlined in the school's catalog/handbook. Written policies regarding course substitutions and general/basic LD accommodations are available through the program or unit directly.

University of Pittsburgh
Disability Resources and Services

4200 Fifth Avenue
Pittsburgh, PA 15260
http://www.drs.pitt.edu

Contact: Leigh J. Culley, Coordinator of Services. Phone: 412-648-7890. Fax: 412-624-3346. E-mail: lculley@pitt.edu. Head of LD Program: Lynnett Van Slyke, Director. Phone: 412-648-7890. Fax: 412-624-3346. E-mail: vanslyke@pitt.edu.

Disability Resources and Services Approximately 380 registered undergraduate students were served during 2006–07. The program or unit includes 6 full-time staff members. LD specialists, remediation/learning specialists, skill tutors, and strategy tutors are provided through the program or unit. Academic advisers, coaches, counselors, diagnostic specialists, graduate assistants/students, professional tutors, regular education teachers, special education teachers, teacher trainees, and trained peer tutors are provided collaboratively through on-campus or off-campus services.

Assistive Technology Assistive technology is located in campus labs, the DSS office, a special lab and includes digital textbooks/e-text and scanning.

Subject-Area Tutoring Tutoring is offered one-on-one and in small groups for most subjects. Tutoring is provided collaboratively through on-campus or off-campus services via graduate assistants/students, professional tutors, and trained peer tutors.

Diagnostic Testing Testing for auditory processing, handwriting, intelligence, learning strategies, learning styles, math, motor skills, neuropsychological, personality, reading, social skills, spelling, spoken language, study skills, visual processing, and written language is provided collaboratively through on-campus or off-campus services.

Enrichment Enrichment programs are available through the program or unit for learning strategies, self-advocacy, study skills, test taking, and time management. Programs for career planning, college survival skills, health and nutrition, learning strategies, math, medication management, oral communication skills, reading, stress management, study skills, test taking, time management, vocabulary development, and written composition skills are provided collaboratively through on-campus or off-campus services.

Fees *Diagnostic Testing* fee is applicable.

Application For admittance to the program or unit, students are required to apply to the program directly and provide a psychoeducational report (5 years old or less). Upon application, materials documenting need for services should be sent only to the LD program or unit. Upon acceptance, documentation of need for services should be sent only to the LD program or unit. *Application deadline (institutional):* Continuous. *Application deadline (LD program):* Rolling/continuous for fall and rolling/continuous for spring.

Written Policies Written policies regarding course substitutions, general/basic LD accommodations, substitutions and waivers of admissions requirements, and substitutions and waivers of graduation requirements are available on the program Web site. Written policy regarding general/basic LD accommodations is outlined in the school's catalog/handbook. Written policies regarding course substitutions, general/basic LD accommodations, substitutions and waivers of admissions requirements, and substitutions and waivers of graduation requirements are available through the program or unit directly.

University of Pittsburgh at Bradford
Academic Success Center, Disability Resources and Services

300 Campus Drive
Bradford, PA 16701-2812
http://www.upb.pitt.edu/

Contact: Ms. Anna R. Ezzolo, Learning Development Specialist. Phone: 814-362-7609. Fax: 814-362-7607. E-mail: arj4@upb.pitt.edu. Head of LD Program: Dr. Gillian Boyce, Director of Academic Success Center. Phone: 814-362-7674. E-mail: boyce@exchange.upb.pitt.edu.

Academic Success Center, Disability Resources and Services Approximately 30 registered undergraduate students were served during 2006–07. The program or unit includes 2 full-time staff members and 1 part-time staff member. Remediation/learning specialists and trained peer tutors are provided through the program or unit. Academic advisers and counselors are provided collaboratively through on-campus or off-campus services.

Unique Aids and Services Aids, services, or accommodations include career counseling.

Assistive Technology Assistive technology is located in the DSS office, a special lab and includes digital textbooks/e-text, learning support software, and scanning. Technology training is provided to incoming students.

Subject-Area Tutoring Tutoring is offered one-on-one, in small groups, and in class-size groups for most subjects. Tutoring is provided collaboratively through on-campus or off-campus services via computer-based instruction and trained peer tutors.

Basic Skills Remediation Remediation is offered one-on-one and in small groups for auditory processing, computer skills, learning strategies, reading, social skills, study skills, time management, and visual processing. Remediation is provided through the program or unit via LD specialists.

Enrichment Enrichment programs are available through the program or unit for self-advocacy. Programs for career planning, college survival skills, learning strategies, math, oral communication skills, reading, stress management, study skills, test taking, time management, and written composition skills are provided collaboratively through on-campus or off-campus services. Credit is offered for college survival skills, learning strategies, and study skills.

Application For admittance to the program or unit, students are required to apply to the program directly and provide a psychoeducational report (3 years old or less). It is recommended that students provide documentation of high school services. Upon acceptance, documentation of need for services should be sent only to the LD program or unit. *Application deadline (institutional):* Continuous. *Application deadline (LD program):* Rolling/continuous for fall and rolling/continuous for spring.

Written Policies Written policy regarding general/basic LD accommodations is available on the program Web site. Written policy regarding general/basic LD accommodations is outlined in the school's catalog/handbook. Written policies regarding course substitutions, general/basic LD accommodations, and substitutions and waivers of graduation requirements are available through the program or unit directly.

University of Pittsburgh at Johnstown
Disability Services/Academic Support Center

450 Schoolhouse Road

Johnstown, PA 15904-2990

http://www.upj.pitt.edu/

Contact: Coordinator of Disability Services. Phone: 814-269-7001. Fax: 814-269-7177.

Disability Services/Academic Support Center Approximately 80 registered undergraduate students were served during 2006–07. The program or unit includes 1 full-time and 8 part-time staff members. Academic advisers, coaches, counselors, diagnostic specialists, graduate assistants/students, LD specialists, professional tutors, regular education teachers, skill tutors, strategy tutors, and trained peer tutors are provided through the program or unit. Academic advisers, coaches, counselors, diagnostic specialists, LD specialists, professional tutors, regular education teachers, skill tutors, strategy tutors, and trained peer tutors are provided collaboratively through on-campus or off-campus services.

Unique Aids and Services Aids, services, or accommodations include career counseling, priority registration, and weekly meetings with faculty.

Assistive Technology Assistive technology is located in campus labs and includes digital textbooks/e-text. Technology training is provided to incoming students.

Subject-Area Tutoring Tutoring is offered one-on-one, in small groups, and in class-size groups for most subjects. Tutoring is provided through the program or unit via LD specialists and trained peer tutors. Tutoring is also provided collaboratively through on-campus or off-campus services via professional tutors and trained peer tutors.

Diagnostic Testing Testing is provided through the program or unit for math. Testing for auditory processing, intelligence, learning strategies, learning styles, math, motor skills, neuropsychological, personality, reading, social skills, spelling, study skills, and visual processing is provided collaboratively through on-campus or off-campus services.

Basic Skills Remediation Remediation is offered one-on-one and in small groups for learning strategies, math, study skills, time management, and written language. Remediation is provided through the program or unit via trained peer tutors. Remediation is also provided collaboratively through on-campus or off-campus services via professional tutors and trained peer tutors.

Enrichment Programs for career planning, college survival skills, learning strategies, stress management, study skills, time management, and written composition skills are provided collaboratively through on-campus or off-campus services. Credit is offered for college survival skills.

Fees *Diagnostic Testing* fee is applicable.

Application For admittance to the program or unit, students are required to apply to the program directly and provide a psychoeducational report (3 years old or less). Upon application, materials documenting need for services should be sent only to the LD program or unit. Upon acceptance, documentation of need for services should be sent only to the LD program or unit. *Application deadline (institutional):* Continuous. *Application deadline (LD program):* Rolling/continuous for fall and rolling/continuous for spring.

Written Policies Written policy regarding general/basic LD accommodations is available on the program Web site. Written policy regarding general/basic LD accommodations is outlined in the school's catalog/handbook. Written policy regarding general/basic LD accommodations is available through the program or unit directly.

University of Portland
Office for Students with Disabilities

5000 North Willamette Boulevard

Portland, OR 97203-5798

http://www.up.edu/healthcenter/default.aspx?cid=547&pid=70&gd=yes

Contact: Ms. Melanie Gangle, Coordinator of Office for Students with Disabilities. Phone: 503-943-7134. Fax: 503-943-7199. E-mail: gangle@up.edu.

Office for Students with Disabilities Approximately 21 registered undergraduate students were served during 2006–07. The

University of Portland (continued)

program or unit includes 1 full-time staff member. Academic advisers, counselors, regular education teachers, skill tutors, and strategy tutors are provided collaboratively through on-campus or off-campus services.

Assistive Technology Assistive technology is located in a special lab and includes digital textbooks/e-text and learning support software.

Subject-Area Tutoring Tutoring is offered one-on-one, in small groups, and in class-size groups for some subjects. Tutoring is provided collaboratively through on-campus or off-campus services via computer-based instruction, graduate assistants/students, and trained peer tutors.

Enrichment Programs for career planning, college survival skills, health and nutrition, learning strategies, math, practical computer skills, reading, stress management, study skills, test taking, time management, and written composition skills are provided collaboratively through on-campus or off-campus services. Credit is offered for health and nutrition and stress management.

Application For admittance to the program or unit, students are required to provide a psychoeducational report and provide completed accommodation request form. It is recommended that students provide documentation of high school services. Upon acceptance, documentation of need for services should be sent only to the LD program or unit. *Application deadline (institutional): 6/1. Application deadline (LD program):* Rolling/continuous for fall and rolling/continuous for spring.

Written Policies Written policies regarding general/basic LD accommodations and reduced course loads are available on the program Web site.

University of Redlands
Disabled Student Services

1200 East Colton Avenue

PO Box 3080

Redlands, CA 92373-0999

http://www.redlands.edu/x3010.xml

Contact: Jen Ostermiller, Director of Academic Support and Disabled Student Services. Phone: 909-748-8108. Fax: 909-335-5297. E-mail: jen_ostermiller@redlands.edu.

Disabled Student Services Approximately 150 registered undergraduate students were served during 2006–07. The program or unit includes 1 full-time staff member. Academic advisers and counselors are provided through the program or unit. Academic advisers, counselors, diagnostic specialists, and trained peer tutors are provided collaboratively through on-campus or off-campus services.

Orientation The program or unit offers an optional orientation for new students individually by special arrangement.

Unique Aids and Services Aids, services, or accommodations include career counseling and faculty training.

Assistive Technology Assistive technology is located in the DSS office and includes digital textbooks/e-text.

Subject-Area Tutoring Tutoring is offered one-on-one for most subjects. Tutoring is provided collaboratively through on-campus or off-campus services via trained peer tutors.

Enrichment Enrichment programs are available through the program or unit for self-advocacy and time management. Programs for career planning, college survival skills, health and nutrition, learning strategies, practical computer skills, stress management, study skills, test taking, time management, vocabulary development, and written composition skills are provided collaboratively through on-campus or off-campus services. Credit is offered for career planning, college survival skills, learning strategies, practical computer skills, study skills, test taking, time management, and written composition skills.

Application For admittance to the program or unit, students are required to provide a psychoeducational report (3 years old or less). It is recommended that students provide documentation of high school services. Upon application, materials documenting need for services should be sent only to admissions with institutional application materials. Upon acceptance, documentation of need for services should be sent only to the LD program or unit. *Application deadline (institutional): 3/1. Application deadline (LD program):* Rolling/continuous for fall and rolling/continuous for spring.

Written Policies Written policies regarding course substitutions, general/basic LD accommodations, and reduced course loads are available on the program Web site. Written policies regarding course substitutions, general/basic LD accommodations, and reduced course loads are available through the program or unit directly.

University of Rhode Island
Disability Services for Students

Kingston, RI 02881

http://www.uri.edu/disability

Contact: Ms. Rosemary Lavigne MSC, Coordinator of Disability Services for Students. Phone: 401-874-2098. Fax: 401-874-5574. E-mail: rlavigne@uri.edu. Head of LD Program: Ms. Pamela A. Rohland, Director of Disability Services for Students. Phone: 401-874-2098. Fax: 401-874-2098. E-mail: rohland@uri.edu.

Disability Services for Students Approximately 400 registered undergraduate students were served during 2006–07. The program or unit includes 2 full-time and 2 part-time staff members. Graduate assistants/students, LD specialists, remediation/learning specialists, skill tutors, special education teachers, and strategy tutors are provided through the program or unit. Academic advisers, coaches, counselors, diagnostic specialists, graduate assistants/students, professional tutors, regular education teachers, skill tutors, strategy tutors, teacher trainees, trained peer tutors, and other are provided collaboratively through on-campus or off-campus services.

Orientation The program or unit offers an optional varying length orientation for new students before registration, during summer prior to enrollment, individually by special arrangement, and during the university first-year student orientation.

Unique Aids and Services Aids, services, or accommodations include advocates, career counseling, faculty training, priority registration, support groups, and weekly meetings with faculty.

Assistive Technology Assistive technology is located in campus labs, the DSS office and includes digital textbooks/e-text and scanning. Technology training is provided to incoming students.

Subject-Area Tutoring Tutoring is offered one-on-one and in small groups for some subjects. Tutoring is provided through the program or unit via LD specialists. Tutoring is also provided collaboratively through on-campus or off-campus services via computer-based instruction, graduate assistants/students, professional tutors, and trained peer tutors.

Basic Skills Remediation Remediation is offered one-on-one for learning strategies, study skills, time management, and written language. Remediation is provided through the program or unit via graduate assistants/students and LD specialists. Remediation is also provided collaboratively through on-campus or off-campus services via computer-based instruction, graduate assistants/students, professional tutors, and other.

Enrichment Enrichment programs are available through the program or unit for college survival skills, self-advocacy, stress management, study skills, test taking, and time management. Programs for career planning, college survival skills, health and nutrition, learning strategies, math, medication management, oral communication skills, practical computer skills, reading, self-advocacy, stress management, study skills, test taking, time management, and written composition skills are provided collaboratively through on-campus or off-campus services. Credit is offered for college survival skills, learning strategies, and written composition skills.

Application For admittance to the program or unit, students are required to apply to the program directly and provide a psychoeducational report (3 years old or less). Upon application, materials documenting need for services should be sent only to admissions with institutional application materials. Upon acceptance, documentation of need for services should be sent only to the LD program or unit. *Application deadline (institutional): 2/1. Application deadline (LD program):* Rolling/continuous for fall and rolling/continuous for spring.

Written Policies Written policies regarding course substitutions, general/basic LD accommodations, reduced course loads, substitutions and waivers of admissions requirements, and substitutions and waivers of graduation requirements are available on the program Web site. Written policies regarding course substitutions, general/basic LD accommodations, reduced course loads, substitutions and waivers of admissions requirements, and substitutions and waivers of graduation requirements are available through the program or unit directly.

University of Rio Grande
Department of Accessibility

218 North College Avenue

Rio Grande, OH 45674

http://www.rio.edu/

Contact: Marshall E. Kimmel, Counselor. Phone: 740-245-7339. Fax: 740-245-7446. E-mail: mkimmel@rio.edu.

Department of Accessibility Approximately 68 registered undergraduate students were served during 2006–07. The program or unit includes 1 full-time and 1 part-time staff member. Academic advisers, counselors, and LD specialists are provided through the program or unit. Coaches, diagnostic specialists, professional tutors,

regular education teachers, remediation/learning specialists, skill tutors, strategy tutors, and trained peer tutors are provided collaboratively through on-campus or off-campus services.

Orientation The program or unit offers an optional 1-semester (fall) orientation for new students before classes begin, during summer prior to enrollment, and individually by special arrangement.

Unique Aids and Services Aids, services, or accommodations include career counseling and support groups.

Assistive Technology Assistive technology is located in campus labs, the DSS office, a special lab and includes learning support software, scanning, and text-to-speech software. Technology training is provided to incoming students.

Subject-Area Tutoring Tutoring is offered one-on-one and in small groups for all subjects. Tutoring is provided collaboratively through on-campus or off-campus services via computer-based instruction and trained peer tutors.

Basic Skills Remediation Remediation is offered in class-size groups for learning strategies, math, reading, study skills, time management, and written language. Remediation is provided collaboratively through on-campus or off-campus services via computer-based instruction and regular education teachers.

Enrichment Enrichment programs are available through the program or unit for college survival skills, learning strategies, stress management, study skills, test taking, time management, and other. Programs for career planning, health and nutrition, learning strategies, math, medication management, oral communication skills, practical computer skills, reading, self-advocacy, study skills, test taking, time management, vocabulary development, and written composition skills are provided collaboratively through on-campus or off-campus services. Credit is offered for health and nutrition, math, practical computer skills, reading, and written composition skills.

Application For admittance to the program or unit, students are required to provide a psychoeducational report (3 years old or less). It is recommended that students provide documentation of high school services. Upon application, materials documenting need for services should be sent only to the LD program or unit. Upon acceptance, documentation of need for services should be sent only to the LD program or unit. *Application deadline (institutional):* Continuous. *Application deadline (LD program):* Rolling/continuous for fall and rolling/continuous for spring.

Written Policies Written policy regarding general/basic LD accommodations is outlined in the school's catalog/handbook. Written policies regarding course substitutions, general/basic LD accommodations, reduced course loads, and substitutions and waivers of admissions requirements are available through the program or unit directly.

University of St. Thomas
Enhancement Program—Disability Services

2115 Summit Avenue

St. Paul, MN 55105-1096

http://www.stthomas.edu/enhancementprog

Contact: Ms. Kimberly Schumann, Director. Phone: 651-962-6315. Fax: 651-962-5965. E-mail: kjschumann@stthomas.edu.

University of St. Thomas (continued)

Enhancement Program—Disability Services Approximately 150 registered undergraduate students were served during 2006–07. The program or unit includes 1 full-time and 1 part-time staff member. Academic advisers, counselors, graduate assistants/students, and LD specialists are provided through the program or unit. Academic advisers, counselors, diagnostic specialists, graduate assistants/students, remediation/learning specialists, skill tutors, strategy tutors, and trained peer tutors are provided collaboratively through on-campus or off-campus services.

Unique Aids and Services Aids, services, or accommodations include advocates, faculty training, note-takers, extended exam time, reader.

Assistive Technology Assistive technology is located in the library and includes digital textbooks/e-text, scanning, and audio texts from Recording for the Blind and Dyslexic.

Subject-Area Tutoring Tutoring is offered one-on-one, in small groups, and in class-size groups for most subjects. Tutoring is provided through the program or unit via graduate assistants/students and trained peer tutors. Tutoring is also provided collaboratively through on-campus or off-campus services via graduate assistants/students and trained peer tutors.

Basic Skills Remediation Remediation is offered one-on-one and in small groups for learning strategies, math, reading, spelling, study skills, time management, and written language. Remediation is provided through the program or unit via graduate assistants/students and trained peer tutors. Remediation is also provided collaboratively through on-campus or off-campus services via graduate assistants/students, trained peer tutors, and other.

Enrichment Enrichment programs are available through the program or unit for self-advocacy, stress management, study skills, test taking, time management, and written composition skills. Programs for career planning, health and nutrition, learning strategies, math, medication management, practical computer skills, reading, stress management, study skills, test taking, time management, and written composition skills are provided collaboratively through on-campus or off-campus services.

Application For admittance to the program or unit, students are required to provide a psychoeducational report (3 years old or less). Upon acceptance, documentation of need for services should be sent only to the LD program or unit. *Application deadline (institutional):* Continuous. *Application deadline (LD program):* Rolling/continuous for fall and rolling/continuous for spring.

Written Policies Written policies regarding course substitutions, general/basic LD accommodations, reduced course loads, and substitutions and waivers of graduation requirements are available through the program or unit directly.

University of St. Thomas
Counseling and Disability Services

3800 Montrose Boulevard
Houston, TX 77006-4696
http://v2.stthom.edu/Campus_Student_Life/
Health_Counseling/Disability_Services/Index.aqf

Contact: Debby Jones, MEd, LPC, Assistant Director of Counseling and Disability Services. Phone: 713-525-6953. Fax: 713-942-3474. E-mail: jonesdm@stthom.edu. Head of

LD Program: Dr. Rose Signorello, Executive Director of Counseling, Wellness and Disability Services. Phone: 713-525-3162. Fax: 713-942-3474. E-mail: signorr@stthom.edu.

Counseling and Disability Services Approximately 25 registered undergraduate students were served during 2006–07. The program or unit includes 2 full-time staff members. Counselors are provided through the program or unit. Academic advisers, counselors, diagnostic specialists, LD specialists, professional tutors, regular education teachers, skill tutors, and trained peer tutors are provided collaboratively through on-campus or off-campus services.

Unique Aids and Services Aids, services, or accommodations include priority registration.

Subject-Area Tutoring Tutoring is offered one-on-one for some subjects. Tutoring is provided collaboratively through on-campus or off-campus services via trained peer tutors.

Basic Skills Remediation Remediation is offered in class-size groups for math and written language. Remediation is provided collaboratively through on-campus or off-campus services via regular education teachers.

Enrichment Programs for career planning, college survival skills, health and nutrition, learning strategies, stress management, study skills, test taking, time management, and written composition skills are provided collaboratively through on-campus or off-campus services.

Application For admittance to the program or unit, students are required to apply to the program directly and provide a psychoeducational report. It is recommended that students provide documentation of high school services. Upon acceptance, documentation of need for services should be sent only to the LD program or unit. *Application deadline (institutional):* Continuous. *Application deadline (LD program):* Rolling/continuous for fall and rolling/continuous for spring.

Written Policies Written policy regarding general/basic LD accommodations is available on the program Web site. Written policy regarding general/basic LD accommodations is outlined in the school's catalog/handbook. Written policies regarding course substitutions, general/basic LD accommodations, and reduced course loads are available through the program or unit directly.

University of San Diego
Disability Services

5998 Alcala Park
San Diego, CA 92110-2492
http://www.sandiego.edu/disability

Contact: Dr. Donald Kirson, Director of Disability Services. Phone: 619-260-4655. Fax: 619-260-4699. E-mail: dkirson@sandiego.edu.

Disability Services Approximately 123 registered undergraduate students were served during 2006–07. The program or unit includes 1 full-time and 1 part-time staff member. LD specialists and other are provided through the program or unit.

Unique Aids and Services Aids, services, or accommodations include faculty training.

Assistive Technology Assistive technology is located in the DSS office and includes digital textbooks/e-text and scanning.

Enrichment Enrichment programs are available through the program or unit for learning strategies, self-advocacy, stress management, study skills, test taking, and time management.

Application For admittance to the program or unit, students are required to provide a psychoeducational report (3 years old or less) and provide psychoeducational report reflecting adult norms. Upon acceptance, documentation of need for services should be sent only to the LD program or unit. *Application deadline (institutional):* 1/15. *Application deadline (LD program):* Rolling/continuous for fall and rolling/continuous for spring.

Written Policies Written policy regarding general/basic LD accommodations is available on the program Web site. Written policy regarding general/basic LD accommodations is outlined in the school's catalog/handbook. Written policy regarding general/basic LD accommodations is available through the program or unit directly.

University of San Francisco
Student Disability Services

2130 Fulton Street

San Francisco, CA 94117-1080

http://www.usfca.edu/sds

Contact: Tom Merrell, Director of Student Disability Services. Phone: 415-422-2613. Fax: 415-422-5906. E-mail: sds@usfca.edu.

Student Disability Services Approximately 200 registered undergraduate students were served during 2006–07. The program or unit includes 2 full-time and 3 part-time staff members. Coaches, LD specialists, remediation/learning specialists, skill tutors, and strategy tutors are provided through the program or unit. Academic advisers, professional tutors, regular education teachers, and trained peer tutors are provided collaboratively through on-campus or off-campus services.

Unique Aids and Services Aids, services, or accommodations include advocates, career counseling, faculty training, personal coach, priority registration, support groups, and weekly meetings with faculty.

Assistive Technology Assistive technology is located in campus labs, the DSS office, a special lab, the individual student's personal computer and includes digital textbooks/e-text, learning support software, and scanning. Technology training is provided to incoming students.

Subject-Area Tutoring Tutoring is offered one-on-one, in small groups, and in class-size groups for most subjects. Tutoring is provided through the program or unit via LD specialists and professional tutors. Tutoring is also provided collaboratively through on-campus or off-campus services via computer-based instruction, graduate assistants/students, and trained peer tutors.

Basic Skills Remediation Remediation is offered one-on-one for learning strategies, math, reading, social skills, spelling, study skills, time management, and written language. Remediation is provided through the program or unit via LD specialists and trained peer tutors. Remediation is also provided collaboratively through on-campus or off-campus services via graduate assistants/students, professional tutors, teacher trainees, and trained peer tutors.

Enrichment Enrichment programs are available through the program or unit for career planning, college survival skills, learning strategies, oral communication skills, practical computer skills, read-

ing, self-advocacy, stress management, study skills, test taking, time management, and written composition skills. Programs for career planning, college survival skills, learning strategies, math, practical computer skills, reading, stress management, study skills, test taking, time management, and written composition skills are provided collaboratively through on-campus or off-campus services. Credit is offered for career planning, college survival skills, learning strategies, math, practical computer skills, reading, stress management, study skills, test taking, time management, and written composition skills.

Application For admittance to the program or unit, students are required to provide a psychoeducational report (5 years old or less) and provide an intake interview. It is recommended that students provide documentation of high school services. Upon application, materials documenting need for services should be sent only to admissions with institutional application materials. Upon acceptance, documentation of need for services should be sent only to the LD program or unit. *Application deadline (institutional):* 2/1. *Application deadline (LD program):* Rolling/continuous for fall and rolling/continuous for spring.

Written Policies Written policies regarding course substitutions, general/basic LD accommodations, reduced course loads, substitutions and waivers of admissions requirements, and substitutions and waivers of graduation requirements are available on the program Web site. Written policies regarding course substitutions, general/basic LD accommodations, substitutions and waivers of admissions requirements, and substitutions and waivers of graduation requirements are outlined in the school's catalog/handbook. Written policies regarding course substitutions, general/basic LD accommodations, reduced course loads, substitutions and waivers of admissions requirements, and substitutions and waivers of graduation requirements are available through the program or unit directly.

The University of Scranton
Center for Teaching and Learning Excellence

800 Linden Street

Scranton, PA 18510

http://www.scranton.edu/ctle

Contact: Mrs. Mary Ellen Pichiarello, MS, CRC, Learning Enrichment Specialist. Phone: 570-941-4038. Fax: 570-941-4154. E-mail: pichiarellm2@scranton.edu.

Center for Teaching and Learning Excellence Approximately 60 registered undergraduate students were served during 2006–07. The program or unit includes 7 full-time staff members and 1 part-time staff member. Remediation/learning specialists and other are provided through the program or unit. Academic advisers, counselors, remediation/learning specialists, skill tutors, strategy tutors, and other are provided collaboratively through on-campus or off-campus services.

Unique Aids and Services Aids, services, or accommodations include priority registration.

Assistive Technology Assistive technology is located in the DSS office, a special lab and includes learning support software, scanning, and Kurzweil, Inspiration. Technology training is provided to incoming students.

The University of Scranton (continued)

Subject-Area Tutoring Tutoring is offered one-on-one, in small groups, and in class-size groups for most subjects. Tutoring is provided through the program or unit via graduate assistants/students, LD specialists, and trained peer tutors. Tutoring is also provided collaboratively through on-campus or off-campus services via graduate assistants/students, LD specialists, and trained peer tutors.

Basic Skills Remediation Remediation is offered one-on-one for learning strategies, math, reading, study skills, and time management. Remediation is provided through the program or unit via graduate assistants/students, LD specialists, trained peer tutors, and other. Remediation is also provided collaboratively through on-campus or off-campus services via graduate assistants/students, LD specialists, trained peer tutors, and other.

Enrichment Enrichment programs are available through the program or unit for learning strategies, math, reading, self-advocacy, study skills, test taking, time management, and written composition skills. Programs for college survival skills, health and nutrition, learning strategies, math, reading, self-advocacy, stress management, study skills, test taking, time management, and written composition skills are provided collaboratively through on-campus or off-campus services.

Application For admittance to the program or unit, students are required to apply to the program directly, provide a psychoeducational report (3 years old or less), and provide documentation of high school services. Upon application, materials documenting need for services should be sent only to admissions with institutional application materials. Upon acceptance, documentation of need for services should be sent only to the LD program or unit. *Application deadline (institutional):* 3/1. *Application deadline (LD program):* 8/25 for fall. 1/20 for spring.

Written Policies Written policies regarding course substitutions, general/basic LD accommodations, grade forgiveness, reduced course loads, substitutions and waivers of admissions requirements, and substitutions and waivers of graduation requirements are available on the program Web site. Written policies regarding course substitutions, general/basic LD accommodations, grade forgiveness, reduced course loads, substitutions and waivers of admissions requirements, and substitutions and waivers of graduation requirements are outlined in the school's catalog/handbook. Written policy regarding general/basic LD accommodations is available through the program or unit directly.

University of South Carolina Beaufort
Disability Services

801 Carteret Street

Beaufort, SC 29902-4601

http://www.uscb.edu

Contact: Ms. Gail A. Quick, Vice Chancellor for Student Development. Phone: 843-208-8256. Fax: 843-208-8290. E-mail: quick@gwm.sc.edu.

Disability Services Approximately 24 registered undergraduate students were served during 2006–07. The program or unit includes 1 full-time staff member.

Unique Aids and Services Aids, services, or accommodations include advocates and personal coach.

Subject-Area Tutoring Tutoring is offered one-on-one for some subjects. Tutoring is provided collaboratively through on-campus or off-campus services via professional tutors.

Application For admittance to the program or unit, students are required to apply to the program directly, provide a psychoeducational report (3 years old or less), and provide documentation of high school services. Upon application, materials documenting need for services should be sent only to the LD program or unit. Upon acceptance, documentation of need for services should be sent to both admissions and the LD program or unit. *Application deadline (institutional):* Continuous. *Application deadline (LD program):* Rolling/continuous for fall and rolling/continuous for spring.

Written Policies Written policies regarding course substitutions, general/basic LD accommodations, grade forgiveness, reduced course loads, substitutions and waivers of admissions requirements, and substitutions and waivers of graduation requirements are available on the program Web site.

University of South Carolina Upstate
Disability Services

800 University Way

Spartanburg, SC 29303-4999

http://www.uscupstate.edu/campus_life/student_dev/disability/

Contact: Margaret M. Camp, Student Services Coordinator. Phone: 864-503-5195. Fax: 864-503-5358. E-mail: mcamp@uscupstate.edu.

Disability Services Approximately 60 registered undergraduate students were served during 2006–07. The program or unit includes 2 full-time staff members. Academic advisers, counselors, regular education teachers, skill tutors, strategy tutors, and trained peer tutors are provided collaboratively through on-campus or off-campus services.

Unique Aids and Services Aids, services, or accommodations include personal coach, priority registration, note-taking services, alternative test administration.

Assistive Technology Assistive technology is located in the DSS office, a special lab and includes digital textbooks/e-text, learning support software, and scanning.

Subject-Area Tutoring Tutoring is offered one-on-one, in small groups, and in class-size groups for most subjects. Tutoring is provided collaboratively through on-campus or off-campus services via professional tutors and trained peer tutors.

Enrichment Programs for career planning, college survival skills, learning strategies, self-advocacy, stress management, study skills, test taking, time management, and written composition skills are provided collaboratively through on-campus or off-campus services.

Student Organization Special Education Club consists of 10 members.

Application For admittance to the program or unit, students are required to apply to the program directly and provide a psychoeducational report (3 years old or less). It is recommended that students provide documentation of high school services. Upon application, materials documenting need for services should be sent only to the LD program or unit. Upon acceptance, documentation of need for services should be sent only to the LD program or unit. *Application deadline (LD program):* Rolling/continuous for fall and rolling/continuous for spring.

Written Policies Written policy regarding general/basic LD accommodations is available on the program Web site. Written policies regarding course substitutions, grade forgiveness, reduced course loads, substitutions and waivers of admissions requirements, and substitutions and waivers of graduation requirements are outlined in the school's catalog/handbook. Written policy regarding general/basic LD accommodations is available through the program or unit directly.

University of Southern Indiana
Counseling Center

8600 University Boulevard

Evansville, IN 47712-3590

http://www.usi.edu/cou/index.asp

Contact: Mrs. Leslie M. Smith, Assistant Director of Counseling. Phone: 812-464-1961. Fax: 812-461-5288. E-mail: lmsmith@usi.edu. Head of LD Program: Mr. James W. Browning, Director of Counseling. Phone: 812-464-1867. Fax: 812-461-5288. E-mail: jwbrowni@usi.edu.

Counseling Center Approximately 118 registered undergraduate students were served during 2006–07. The program or unit includes 3 part-time staff members. Counselors are provided through the program or unit. Academic advisers, coaches, regular education teachers, remediation/learning specialists, skill tutors, strategy tutors, and trained peer tutors are provided collaboratively through on-campus or off-campus services.

Unique Aids and Services Aids, services, or accommodations include career counseling and priority registration.

Assistive Technology Assistive technology is located in the classroom, per individual request.

Subject-Area Tutoring Tutoring is offered in small groups for some subjects. Tutoring is provided collaboratively through on-campus or off-campus services via computer-based instruction and trained peer tutors.

Basic Skills Remediation Remediation is offered in class-size groups for learning strategies, math, reading, spelling, study skills, time management, and written language. Remediation is provided collaboratively through on-campus or off-campus services via regular education teachers.

Enrichment Programs for career planning, college survival skills, health and nutrition, learning strategies, math, oral communication skills, practical computer skills, reading, stress management, study skills, test taking, time management, vocabulary development, and written composition skills are provided collaboratively through on-campus or off-campus services. Credit is offered for career planning, college survival skills, health and nutrition, math, oral communication skills, practical computer skills, reading, study skills, vocabulary development, and written composition skills.

Application For admittance to the program or unit, students are required to apply to the program directly, provide a psychoeducational report (3 years old or less), and provide Disability Verification Form. Upon application, materials documenting need for services should be sent only to the LD program or unit. Upon acceptance, documentation of need for services should be sent only to the LD program or unit. *Application deadline (institutional):* 8/15. *Application deadline (LD program):* Rolling/continuous for fall and rolling/continuous for spring.

Written Policies Written policies regarding general/basic LD accommodations and grade forgiveness are outlined in the school's catalog/handbook.

The University of Tampa
Academic Center for Excellence

401 West Kennedy Boulevard

Tampa, FL 33606-1490

http://static.ut.edu/currentstudents/dean/Disability-Information.cfm

Contact: Dr. Keith C. Pounds, Associate Director, Academic Center for Excellence. Phone: 813-258-7251. Fax: 813-259-7331. E-mail: kpounds@ut.edu.

Academic Center for Excellence Approximately 130 registered undergraduate students were served during 2006–07. The program or unit includes 1 full-time staff member. Skill tutors, strategy tutors, and other are provided through the program or unit.

Assistive Technology Assistive technology includes digital textbooks/e-text.

Basic Skills Remediation Remediation is offered one-on-one for learning strategies, study skills, and time management. Remediation is provided through the program or unit.

Enrichment Programs for career planning, college survival skills, learning strategies, math, stress management, study skills, test taking, and time management are provided collaboratively through on-campus or off-campus services.

Application For admittance to the program or unit, students are required to provide a psychoeducational report (3 years old or less). Upon acceptance, documentation of need for services should be sent only to the LD program or unit. *Application deadline (institutional):* Continuous. *Application deadline (LD program):* Rolling/continuous for fall and rolling/continuous for spring.

Written Policies Written policy regarding general/basic LD accommodations is available on the program Web site. Written policy regarding general/basic LD accommodations is outlined in the school's catalog/handbook.

The University of Tennessee
Office of Disability Services

Knoxville, TN 37996

http://ods.utk.edu

Contact: Ms. Shannon Crabtree, LD Coordinator. Phone: 865-974-3873. Fax: 865-974-9552. E-mail: ods@tennessee.edu.

The University of Tennessee (continued)

Office of Disability Services Approximately 700 registered undergraduate students were served during 2006–07. The program or unit includes 2 full-time staff members. LD specialists are provided through the program or unit. Academic advisers, coaches, counselors, diagnostic specialists, graduate assistants/students, professional tutors, regular education teachers, remediation/learning specialists, skill tutors, special education teachers, strategy tutors, teacher trainees, trained peer tutors, and other are provided collaboratively through on-campus or off-campus services.

Unique Aids and Services Aids, services, or accommodations include career counseling, faculty training, and priority registration.

Assistive Technology Assistive technology is located in campus labs, the DSS office and includes digital textbooks/e-text, learning support software, and scanning. Technology training is provided to incoming students.

Subject-Area Tutoring Tutoring is offered one-on-one and in class-size groups for some subjects. Tutoring is provided collaboratively through on-campus or off-campus services via trained peer tutors.

Enrichment Enrichment programs are available through the program or unit for career planning, learning strategies, self-advocacy, study skills, test taking, and time management. Programs for college survival skills, health and nutrition, learning strategies, math, practical computer skills, stress management, study skills, test taking, time management, and written composition skills are provided collaboratively through on-campus or off-campus services. Credit is offered for college survival skills, study skills, and written composition skills.

Student Organization Ability United consists of 10 members.

Application For admittance to the program or unit, students are required to provide a psychoeducational report (3 years old or less). It is recommended that students provide documentation of high school services. Upon application, materials documenting need for services should be sent only to the LD program or unit. Upon acceptance, documentation of need for services should be sent only to the LD program or unit. *Application deadline (institutional):* 2/1. *Application deadline (LD program):* Rolling/continuous for fall and rolling/continuous for spring.

Written Policies Written policy regarding general/basic LD accommodations is available on the program Web site. Written policies regarding course substitutions, general/basic LD accommodations, reduced course loads, and substitutions and waivers of graduation requirements are available through the program or unit directly.

The University of Tennessee at Martin

Program Access for College Enhancement (PACE)

University Street

Martin, TN 38238-1000

http://www.utm.edu/departments/success/disability.php

Contact: Ms. Stephanie Mueller, PACE Coordinator. Phone: 731-881-7605. E-mail: smueller@utm.edu.

Program Access for College Enhancement (PACE) Approximately 50 registered undergraduate students were served during

2006–07. The program or unit includes 2 full-time staff members. Academic advisers, counselors, graduate assistants/students, remediation/learning specialists, skill tutors, strategy tutors, and trained peer tutors are provided through the program or unit. Academic advisers, counselors, remediation/learning specialists, strategy tutors, and trained peer tutors are provided collaboratively through on-campus or off-campus services.

Orientation The program or unit offers a mandatory 2-hour orientation for new students after classes begin and individually by special arrangement.

Unique Aids and Services Aids, services, or accommodations include advocates, faculty training, personal coach, and support groups.

Assistive Technology Assistive technology is located in campus labs, the DSS office and includes digital textbooks/e-text and scanning. Technology training is provided to incoming students.

Subject-Area Tutoring Tutoring is offered one-on-one and in small groups for some subjects. Tutoring is provided through the program or unit via computer-based instruction, graduate assistants/students, LD specialists, and trained peer tutors. Tutoring is also provided collaboratively through on-campus or off-campus services via computer-based instruction and trained peer tutors.

Enrichment Enrichment programs are available through the program or unit for career planning, college survival skills, learning strategies, math, oral communication skills, practical computer skills, reading, self-advocacy, stress management, study skills, test taking, time management, vocabulary development, and written composition skills. Programs for career planning, college survival skills, learning strategies, math, oral communication skills, practical computer skills, reading, self-advocacy, stress management, study skills, test taking, time management, vocabulary development, and written composition skills are provided collaboratively through on-campus or off-campus services.

Application For admittance to the program or unit, students are required to provide a psychoeducational report (3 years old or less). It is recommended that students provide documentation of high school services. Upon application, materials documenting need for services should be sent only to the LD program or unit. Upon acceptance, documentation of need for services should be sent only to the LD program or unit. *Application deadline (institutional):* Continuous. *Application deadline (LD program):* Rolling/continuous for fall and rolling/continuous for spring.

Written Policies Written policy regarding general/basic LD accommodations is available on the program Web site. Written policy regarding general/basic LD accommodations is outlined in the school's catalog/handbook.

The University of Texas at Austin

Services for Students with Disabilities

Austin, TX 78712-1111

http://deanofstudents.utexas.edu/ssd/

Contact: Student Affairs Administrator. Phone: 512-471-6259. Fax: 512-475-7730. E-mail: ssd@uts.cc.utexas.edu.

Services for Students with Disabilities Approximately 170 registered undergraduate students were served during 2006–07. The program or unit includes 3 full-time staff members. Diagnostic specialists, graduate assistants/students, and LD specialists are provided through the program or unit. Academic advisers, coaches, counselors, diagnostic specialists, graduate assistants/students, remediation/learning specialists, skill tutors, strategy tutors, and trained peer tutors are provided collaboratively through on-campus or off-campus services.

Unique Aids and Services Aids, services, or accommodations include faculty training, priority registration, and support groups.

Assistive Technology Assistive technology is located in campus labs, the DSS office and includes digital textbooks/e-text, learning support software, and scanning. Technology training is provided to incoming students.

Subject-Area Tutoring Tutoring is offered one-on-one, in small groups, and in class-size groups for some subjects. Tutoring is provided collaboratively through on-campus or off-campus services via computer-based instruction, graduate assistants/students, professional tutors, and trained peer tutors.

Basic Skills Remediation Remediation is offered one-on-one, in small groups, and in class-size groups for learning strategies, math, reading, study skills, time management, and written language. Remediation is provided collaboratively through on-campus or off-campus services via computer-based instruction, graduate assistants/students, professional tutors, and trained peer tutors.

Enrichment Enrichment programs are available through the program or unit for self-advocacy. Programs for career planning, college survival skills, health and nutrition, learning strategies, math, medication management, reading, stress management, study skills, test taking, time management, and written composition skills are provided collaboratively through on-campus or off-campus services.

Application For admittance to the program or unit, students are required to provide a psychoeducational report (3 years old or less). It is recommended that students provide documentation of high school services. Upon application, materials documenting need for services should be sent only to the LD program or unit. Upon acceptance, documentation of need for services should be sent only to the LD program or unit. *Application deadline (institutional): 2/1. Application deadline (LD program):* Rolling/continuous for fall and rolling/continuous for spring.

Written Policies Written policies regarding general/basic LD accommodations and reduced course loads are available through the program or unit directly.

The University of Texas at El Paso
Disabled Student Services

500 West University Avenue
El Paso, TX 79968-0001
http://www.utep.edu/dsso

Contact: James B. Saunders, Director. Phone: 915-747-5148. Fax: 915-747-8712. E-mail: dss@utep.edu.

Disabled Student Services Approximately 60 registered undergraduate students were served during 2006–07. The program or unit includes 4 full-time and 4 part-time staff members. Academic advisers, counselors, and diagnostic specialists are provided collaboratively through on-campus or off-campus services.

Unique Aids and Services Aids, services, or accommodations include priority registration.

Assistive Technology Assistive technology is located in campus labs, the DSS office and includes digital textbooks/e-text, learning support software, and scanning. Technology training is provided to incoming students.

Subject-Area Tutoring Tutoring is offered in small groups for some subjects. Tutoring is provided collaboratively through on-campus or off-campus services via computer-based instruction and trained peer tutors.

Diagnostic Testing Testing for auditory processing, intelligence, math, motor skills, reading, spelling, spoken language, visual processing, and written language is provided collaboratively through on-campus or off-campus services.

Basic Skills Remediation Remediation is offered in class-size groups for learning strategies, math, reading, study skills, time management, and written language. Remediation is provided collaboratively through on-campus or off-campus services via computer-based instruction, regular education teachers, and trained peer tutors.

Enrichment Programs for career planning, health and nutrition, learning strategies, math, reading, stress management, study skills, test taking, time management, and written composition skills are provided collaboratively through on-campus or off-campus services.

Application For admittance to the program or unit, students are required to provide a psychoeducational report (5 years old or less). Upon application, materials documenting need for services should be sent only to the LD program or unit. Upon acceptance, documentation of need for services should be sent only to the LD program or unit. *Application deadline (institutional): 7/31. Application deadline (LD program):* Rolling/continuous for fall and rolling/continuous for spring.

Written Policies Written policy regarding general/basic LD accommodations is available on the program Web site. Written policy regarding general/basic LD accommodations is available through the program or unit directly.

The University of Texas at San Antonio
Disability Services

6900 North Loop 1604 West
San Antonio, TX 78249-0617
http://www.utsa.edu/disability

Contact: Lorraine Harrison, Director of Disability Services. Phone: 210-458-4157. Fax: 210-458-4980. E-mail: lharrison@utsa.edu.

Disability Services Approximately 156 registered undergraduate students were served during 2006–07. The program or unit includes 2 full-time staff members. Graduate assistants/students and other are provided through the program or unit. Academic advisers, coaches, diagnostic specialists, and skill tutors are provided collaboratively through on-campus or off-campus services.

Assistive Technology Assistive technology is located in campus labs and includes digital textbooks/e-text and scanning.

Subject-Area Tutoring Tutoring is offered in small groups for some subjects. Tutoring is provided collaboratively through on-campus or off-campus services via computer-based instruction and trained peer tutors.

The University of Texas at San Antonio (continued)

Diagnostic Testing Testing for auditory processing, intelligence, math, personality, reading, spelling, spoken language, visual processing, and written language is provided collaboratively through on-campus or off-campus services.

Basic Skills Remediation Remediation is offered in small groups and in class-size groups for learning strategies, math, reading, study skills, time management, and written language. Remediation is provided collaboratively through on-campus or off-campus services via regular education teachers and trained peer tutors.

Enrichment Enrichment programs are available through the program or unit for self-advocacy. Programs for career planning, college survival skills, health and nutrition, learning strategies, math, practical computer skills, reading, stress management, study skills, test taking, time management, and written composition skills are provided collaboratively through on-campus or off-campus services. Credit is offered for college survival skills.

Fees *Diagnostic Testing* fee is $50.

Application For admittance to the program or unit, students are required to provide a psychoeducational report (3 years old or less). Upon application, materials documenting need for services should be sent only to the LD program or unit. Upon acceptance, documentation of need for services should be sent only to the LD program or unit. *Application deadline (institutional): 7/1. Application deadline (LD program):* Rolling/continuous for fall and rolling/continuous for spring.

Written Policies Written policy regarding general/basic LD accommodations is available on the program Web site. Written policy regarding general/basic LD accommodations is available through the program or unit directly.

The University of the Arts
Disability Services

320 South Broad Street

Philadelphia, PA 19102-4944

http://www.uarts.edu/

Contact: Ms. Neila Douglas, Director of Disability Services. Phone: 215-717-6616. Fax: 215-717-6611. E-mail: ndouglas@uarts.edu.

Disability Services Approximately 75 registered undergraduate students were served during 2006–07. The program or unit includes 1 part-time staff member. LD specialists are provided through the program or unit. Academic advisers, counselors, professional tutors, and trained peer tutors are provided collaboratively through on-campus or off-campus services.

Subject-Area Tutoring Tutoring is offered one-on-one for most subjects. Tutoring is provided collaboratively through on-campus or off-campus services via professional tutors and trained peer tutors.

Diagnostic Testing Testing is provided through the program or unit for learning styles.

Application For admittance to the program or unit, students are required to provide a psychoeducational report (3 years old or less). It is recommended that students provide documentation of high school services. Upon application, materials documenting need for services should be sent only to the LD program or unit. Upon acceptance, documentation of need for services should be sent only

to the LD program or unit. *Application deadline (institutional):* Continuous. *Application deadline (LD program):* Rolling/continuous for fall and rolling/continuous for spring.

Written Policies Written policy regarding general/basic LD accommodations is available on the program Web site. Written policy regarding general/basic LD accommodations is outlined in the school's catalog/handbook. Written policies regarding general/basic LD accommodations and reduced course loads are available through the program or unit directly.

University of the District of Columbia
Disability Resource Center

4200 Connecticut Avenue, NW

Washington, DC 20008-1175

http://www.udc.edu/

Contact: Jamal Reed, Assistant Director. Phone: 202-274-6152. Fax: 202-274-5016. E-mail: ajreed@udc.edu.

Disability Resource Center Approximately 289 registered undergraduate students were served during 2006–07. The program or unit includes 7 full-time and 2 part-time staff members. Counselors, LD specialists, trained peer tutors, and other are provided through the program or unit.

Orientation The program or unit offers a mandatory 1-day orientation for new students during registration.

Unique Aids and Services Aids, services, or accommodations include advocates, career counseling, workshops.

Assistive Technology Assistive technology is located in campus labs, the DSS office, a special lab and includes digital textbooks/e-text and learning support software. Technology training is provided to incoming students.

Subject-Area Tutoring Tutoring is offered one-on-one and in small groups for some subjects. Tutoring is provided through the program or unit via trained peer tutors. Tutoring is also provided collaboratively through on-campus or off-campus services via computer-based instruction and LD specialists.

Diagnostic Testing Testing for auditory processing, intelligence, math, motor skills, neuropsychological, reading, written language, and other services is provided collaboratively through on-campus or off-campus services.

Basic Skills Remediation Remediation is offered one-on-one for math and reading. Remediation is provided collaboratively through on-campus or off-campus services via LD specialists and trained peer tutors.

Enrichment Programs for career planning, college survival skills, health and nutrition, math, medication management, oral communication skills, practical computer skills, reading, self-advocacy, stress management, study skills, test taking, time management, vocabulary development, written composition skills, and other are provided collaboratively through on-campus or off-campus services.

Student Organization Conceive and Achieve It Club consists of 30 members.

Application It is recommended that students apply to the program directly and provide a psychoeducational report. Upon application, materials documenting need for services should be sent only to the LD program or unit. Upon acceptance, documentation of need for services should be sent only to the LD program or unit. *Application deadline (institutional):* 8/1. *Application deadline (LD program):* Rolling/continuous for fall and rolling/continuous for spring.

Written Policies Written policy regarding general/basic LD accommodations is available on the program Web site. Written policy regarding general/basic LD accommodations is outlined in the school's catalog/handbook. Written policies regarding course substitutions, general/basic LD accommodations, grade forgiveness, reduced course loads, substitutions and waivers of admissions requirements, and substitutions and waivers of graduation requirements are available through the program or unit directly.

University of the Incarnate Word
Student Disabilities Services

4301 Broadway

San Antonio, TX 78209-6397

http://www.uiw.edu/sds/

Contact: Ms. Ada Soto, Academic Counselor. Phone: 210-805-5813. Fax: 210-805-5895. E-mail: soto@uiwtx.edu. Head of LD Program: Dr. Rhonda H. Rapp, Director, Student Disability Services & Student Success Program. Phone: 210-829-3938. Fax: 210-805-5895. E-mail: rapp@uiwtx.edu.

Student Disabilities Services Approximately 75 registered undergraduate students were served during 2006–07. The program or unit includes 1 full-time and 2 part-time staff members. Services are provided through the program or unit.

Orientation The program or unit offers an optional 1-day orientation for new students before classes begin.

Unique Aids and Services Aids, services, or accommodations include career counseling.

Assistive Technology Assistive technology is located in the DSS office, the library and includes digital textbooks/e-text, learning support software, and scanning. Technology training is provided to incoming students.

Basic Skills Remediation Remediation is offered in class-size groups for math, reading, and written language. Remediation is provided through the program or unit.

Enrichment Programs for career planning, college survival skills, health and nutrition, learning strategies, stress management, study skills, test taking, and time management are provided collaboratively through on-campus or off-campus services.

Application For admittance to the program or unit, students are required to apply to the program directly and provide a psychoeducational report. It is recommended that students provide documentation of high school services. Upon application, materials documenting need for services should be sent only to the LD program or unit. Upon acceptance, documentation of need for services should be sent only to the LD program or unit. *Application deadline (institutional):* Continuous. *Application deadline (LD program):* Rolling/continuous for fall and rolling/continuous for spring.

Written Policies Written policies regarding general/basic LD accommodations and substitutions and waivers of admissions requirements are available on the program Web site. Written policy regarding general/basic LD accommodations is outlined in the school's catalog/handbook. Written policy regarding general/basic LD accommodations is available through the program or unit directly.

University of the Pacific
Office of Services for Students with Disabilities (SSD)

3601 Pacific Avenue

Stockton, CA 95211-0197

http://www.pacific.edu/education/ssd

Contact: Daniel Nuss, Coordinator. Phone: 209-946-2458. Fax: 209-946-2278. E-mail: ssd@uop.edu.

Office of Services for Students with Disabilities (SSD) Approximately 140 registered undergraduate students were served during 2006–07. The program or unit includes 1 full-time and 10 part-time staff members. Remediation/learning specialists and other are provided through the program or unit. Academic advisers, counselors, diagnostic specialists, remediation/learning specialists, skill tutors, trained peer tutors, and other are provided collaboratively through on-campus or off-campus services.

Orientation The program or unit offers an optional orientation for new students individually by special arrangement and during the summer orientation programs.

Unique Aids and Services Aids, services, or accommodations include advocates, faculty training, priority registration.

Subject-Area Tutoring Tutoring is offered one-on-one and in small groups for most subjects. Tutoring is provided through the program or unit via computer-based instruction, graduate assistants/students, trained peer tutors, and other. Tutoring is also provided collaboratively through on-campus or off-campus services via graduate assistants/students, trained peer tutors, and other.

Basic Skills Remediation Remediation is offered in class-size groups for math, reading, and written language. Remediation is provided through the program or unit via regular education teachers and trained peer tutors. Remediation is also provided collaboratively through on-campus or off-campus services via regular education teachers and trained peer tutors.

Enrichment Enrichment programs are available through the program or unit for math, reading, self-advocacy, written composition skills, and other. Programs for career planning, health and nutrition, learning strategies, math, medication management, oral communication skills, practical computer skills, reading, stress management, study skills, test taking, time management, and written composition skills are provided collaboratively through on-campus or off-campus services. Credit is offered for career planning, math, reading, and written composition skills.

Application For admittance to the program or unit, students are required to apply to the program directly and provide a psychoeducational report. It is recommended that students provide documentation of high school services. Upon acceptance, documentation of need for services should be sent only to the LD program or unit. *Application deadline (institutional):* 1/15. *Application deadline (LD program):* Rolling/continuous for fall and rolling/continuous for spring.

University of the Pacific (continued)

Written Policies Written policy regarding general/basic LD accommodations is available on the program Web site. Written policy regarding general/basic LD accommodations is outlined in the school's catalog/handbook. Written policy regarding general/basic LD accommodations is available through the program or unit directly.

University of Toronto
Accessibility Services, Programs and Services for Students with a Disability

Toronto, ON M5S 1A1

Canada

http://disability.sa.utoronto.ca

Contact: Dr. Pearl Levey, Learning Disability Specialist. Phone: 416-978-1724. Fax: 416-978-8246. E-mail: pearl.levey@utoronto.ca.

Accessibility Services, Programs and Services for Students with a Disability Approximately 600 registered undergraduate students were served during 2006–07. The program or unit includes 1 full-time and 8 part-time staff members. Coaches, counselors, diagnostic specialists, LD specialists, remediation/learning specialists, strategy tutors, and trained peer tutors are provided through the program or unit. Academic advisers, coaches, counselors, diagnostic specialists, professional tutors, remediation/learning specialists, and skill tutors are provided collaboratively through on-campus or off-campus services.

Orientation The program or unit offers an optional orientation for new students.

Summer Program To help prepare for the demands of college, there is an optional 1-week summer program prior to entering the school available to high school graduates that focuses on self-advocacy, study skills, test-taking skills, and time management. The program accepts students from out-of-state.

Unique Aids and Services Aids, services, or accommodations include advocates, career counseling, parent workshops, personal coach, support groups, adaptive skills for students on the autism spectrum.

Assistive Technology Assistive technology is located in campus labs, the Adaptive Technology Resource Centre and includes digital textbooks/e-text, learning support software, and scanning. Technology training is provided to incoming students.

Subject-Area Tutoring Tutoring is offered one-on-one for most subjects. Tutoring is provided through the program or unit via LD specialists and trained peer tutors. Tutoring is also provided collaboratively through on-campus or off-campus services via graduate assistants/students and professional tutors.

Diagnostic Testing Testing is provided through the program or unit for auditory processing, intelligence, learning strategies, learning styles, math, motor skills, reading, social skills, spelling, spoken language, study skills, visual processing, and written language. Testing for handwriting, motor skills, neuropsychological, personality, social skills, spoken language, study skills, visual processing, and written language is provided collaboratively through on-campus or off-campus services.

Basic Skills Remediation Remediation is offered one-on-one and in small groups for auditory processing, computer skills, learning strategies, math, reading, social skills, spelling, spoken lan-

guage, study skills, time management, visual processing, written language, and second-language learning. Remediation is provided through the program or unit via LD specialists and trained peer tutors. Remediation is also provided collaboratively through on-campus or off-campus services via professional tutors and other.

Enrichment Enrichment programs are available through the program or unit for college survival skills, learning strategies, math, oral communication skills, practical computer skills, reading, self-advocacy, stress management, study skills, test taking, time management, vocabulary development, and written composition skills. Programs for career planning, college survival skills, health and nutrition, learning strategies, math, medication management, oral communication skills, practical computer skills, reading, self-advocacy, stress management, study skills, test taking, time management, vocabulary development, and written composition skills are provided collaboratively through on-campus or off-campus services.

Fees *Diagnostic Testing* fee is $1200.

Application For admittance to the program or unit, students are required to apply to the program directly and provide a psychoeducational report (3 years old or less). It is recommended that students provide documentation of high school services. Upon application, materials documenting need for services should be sent only to the LD program or unit. Upon acceptance, documentation of need for services should be sent only to the LD program or unit. *Application deadline (institutional):* 3/1. *Application deadline (LD program):* Rolling/continuous for fall and rolling/continuous for spring.

Written Policies Written policies regarding general/basic LD accommodations and reduced course loads are available on the program Web site. Written policy regarding general/basic LD accommodations is outlined in the school's catalog/handbook. Written policies regarding general/basic LD accommodations and reduced course loads are available through the program or unit directly.

University of Vermont
Accommodation, Consultation, Collaboration and Educational Support Services (ACCESS)

Burlington, VT 05405

http://www.uvm.edu/~access/

Contact: Marsha E. Camp, Assistant Director of Academic Support Programs/ACCESS. Phone: 802-656-7753. Fax: 802-656-0739. E-mail: marsha.camp@uvm.edu.

Accommodation, Consultation, Collaboration and Educational Support Services (ACCESS) Approximately 700 registered undergraduate students were served during 2006–07. The program or unit includes 8 full-time and 2 part-time staff members. LD specialists, remediation/learning specialists, skill tutors, and strategy tutors are provided through the program or unit. Academic advisers, coaches, counselors, diagnostic specialists, graduate assistants/students, professional tutors, remediation/learning specialists, skill tutors, strategy tutors, and trained peer tutors are provided collaboratively through on-campus or off-campus services.

Orientation The program or unit offers an optional 1- to 2-hour orientation for new students before registration, before classes begin, during summer prior to enrollment, during registration, after classes begin, and individually by special arrangement.

Unique Aids and Services Aids, services, or accommodations include career counseling, faculty training, parent workshops, priority registration, regular meetings with specialist or study skills tutor.

Assistive Technology Assistive technology is located in the university library and includes digital textbooks/e-text, scanning, and speech-to-text, text-to-speech. Technology training is provided to incoming students.

Subject-Area Tutoring Tutoring is offered one-on-one and in small groups for most subjects. Tutoring is provided collaboratively through on-campus or off-campus services via graduate assistants/students, professional tutors, and trained peer tutors.

Diagnostic Testing Testing for auditory processing, handwriting, intelligence, learning strategies, learning styles, math, motor skills, neuropsychological, personality, reading, social skills, spelling, spoken language, study skills, visual processing, and written language is provided collaboratively through on-campus or off-campus services.

Basic Skills Remediation Remediation is offered one-on-one, in small groups, and in class-size groups for learning strategies, math, reading, spelling, study skills, time management, and written language. Remediation is provided through the program or unit via LD specialists. Remediation is also provided collaboratively through on-campus or off-campus services via graduate assistants/students, LD specialists, professional tutors, trained peer tutors, and other.

Enrichment Enrichment programs are available through the program or unit for college survival skills, learning strategies, self-advocacy, stress management, study skills, test taking, and time management. Programs for career planning, college survival skills, health and nutrition, learning strategies, math, medication management, oral communication skills, practical computer skills, reading, self-advocacy, stress management, study skills, test taking, time management, vocabulary development, and written composition skills are provided collaboratively through on-campus or off-campus services. Credit is offered for college survival skills, learning strategies, self-advocacy, stress management, study skills, test taking, and time management.

Student Organization PALS, Soupy Tuesday.

Fees *Diagnostic Testing* fee is applicable.

Application For admittance to the program or unit, students are required to provide a psychoeducational report (3 years old or less). It is recommended that students provide documentation of high school services and provide a letter from student and/or educational support services professional addressing impact of the LD. Upon application, materials documenting need for services should be sent only to the LD program or unit. Upon acceptance, documentation of need for services should be sent only to the LD program or unit. *Application deadline (institutional):* 1/15. *Application deadline (LD program):* Rolling/continuous for fall and rolling/continuous for spring.

Written Policies Written policies regarding course substitutions, general/basic LD accommodations, reduced course loads, substitutions and waivers of admissions requirements, and substitutions and waivers of graduation requirements are available on the program Web site. Written policies regarding course substitutions, general/basic LD accommodations, reduced course loads, and substitutions and waivers of graduation requirements are outlined in the school's catalog/handbook. Written policies regarding course substitutions, general/basic LD accommodations, reduced course loads, substitutions and waivers of admissions requirements, and substitutions and waivers of graduation requirements are available through the program or unit directly.

University of Virginia
Learning Needs and Evaluation Center (LNEC)

Charlottesville, VA 22903

http://www.virginia.edu/studenthealth/lnec.html

Contact: Dr. Allison Anderson, Director. Phone: 434-243-5180. Fax: 434-243-5188. E-mail: aea3f@virginia.edu.

Learning Needs and Evaluation Center (LNEC) Approximately 325 registered undergraduate students were served during 2006–07. Diagnostic specialists are provided through the program or unit. Coaches and diagnostic specialists are provided collaboratively through on-campus or off-campus services.

Unique Aids and Services Aids, services, or accommodations include career counseling and personal coach.

Assistive Technology Assistive technology is located in campus labs, the DSS office, the library and includes learning support software and hardware (available for loan as needed).

Diagnostic Testing Testing is provided through the program or unit for auditory processing, handwriting, intelligence, learning strategies, learning styles, math, motor skills, neuropsychological, personality, reading, social skills, spelling, spoken language, study skills, visual processing, written language, and other services. Testing for auditory processing, handwriting, intelligence, learning strategies, learning styles, math, motor skills, neuropsychological, personality, reading, social skills, spelling, spoken language, study skills, visual processing, written language, and other services is provided collaboratively through on-campus or off-campus services.

Application For admittance to the program or unit, students are required to provide full psychoeducational testing (use LNEC or AHEAD guidelines). It is recommended that students provide documentation of high school services. *Application deadline (institutional):* 1/2.

Written Policies Written policies regarding course substitutions and general/basic LD accommodations are available on the program Web site. Written policies regarding course substitutions and general/basic LD accommodations are outlined in the school's catalog/handbook. Written policy regarding general/basic LD accommodations is available through the program or unit directly.

The University of Virginia's College at Wise
Disability Services

1 College Avenue

Wise, VA 24293

http://www.uvawise.edu/ada

Contact: Ms. Narda N. Porter, ADA Coordinator. Phone: 276-328-0177. Fax: 276-376-1076. E-mail: nnb3h@uvawise.edu.

Disability Services Approximately 60 registered undergraduate students were served during 2006–07. The program or unit includes 1 full-time and 1 part-time staff member. Academic advisers, coaches, counselors, graduate assistants/students, professional tutors, remediation/

The University of Virginia's College at Wise (continued)
learning specialists, skill tutors, strategy tutors, trained peer tutors, and other are provided through the program or unit. Academic advisers, counselors, graduate assistants/students, skill tutors, strategy tutors, trained peer tutors, and other are provided collaboratively through on-campus or off-campus services.

Unique Aids and Services Aids, services, or accommodations include priority registration.

Assistive Technology Assistive technology is located in campus labs, the DSS office and includes digital textbooks/e-text, learning support software, and scanning.

Subject-Area Tutoring Tutoring is offered one-on-one and in small groups for most subjects. Tutoring is provided through the program or unit via computer-based instruction, trained peer tutors, and other.

Basic Skills Remediation Remediation is offered one-on-one, in small groups, and in class-size groups for computer skills, learning strategies, math, reading, spelling, study skills, time management, visual processing, and written language. Remediation is provided through the program or unit via trained peer tutors. Remediation is also provided collaboratively through on-campus or off-campus services via regular education teachers.

Enrichment Enrichment programs are available through the program or unit for career planning, college survival skills, learning strategies, math, oral communication skills, self-advocacy, stress management, study skills, test taking, time management, vocabulary development, and written composition skills. Programs for career planning, college survival skills, health and nutrition, learning strategies, math, oral communication skills, practical computer skills, reading, vocabulary development, and written composition skills are provided collaboratively through on-campus or off-campus services. Credit is offered for health and nutrition, math, oral communication skills, practical computer skills, reading, vocabulary development, and written composition skills.

Application For admittance to the program or unit, students are required to provide a psychoeducational report (3 years old or less). It is recommended that students apply to the program directly and provide documentation of high school services. Upon application, materials documenting need for services should be sent only to the LD program or unit. Upon acceptance, documentation of need for services should be sent only to the LD program or unit. *Application deadline (institutional): 8/1. Application deadline (LD program):* Rolling/continuous for fall and rolling/continuous for spring.

Written Policies Written policy regarding general/basic LD accommodations is available on the program Web site. Written policies regarding course substitutions, general/basic LD accommodations, and reduced course loads are available through the program or unit directly.

University of Washington
Disability Resources for Students

Seattle, WA 98195

http://www.washington.edu/

Contact: Ms. Dyane Haynes, Director, Disability Resources for Students. Phone: 206-543-8924. Fax: 206-616-8379. E-mail: dyane@u.washington.edu.

Disability Resources for Students Approximately 275 registered undergraduate students were served during 2006–07. The program or unit includes 1 part-time staff member. Counselors and LD specialists are provided through the program or unit. Academic advisers, counselors, diagnostic specialists, and LD specialists are provided collaboratively through on-campus or off-campus services.

Summer Program To help prepare for the demands of college, there is summer program prior to entering the school.

Unique Aids and Services Aids, services, or accommodations include faculty training, priority registration, note-taking services, exam accommodations.

Assistive Technology Assistive technology is located in campus labs, the DSS office, a special lab and includes digital textbooks/e-text, learning support software, and scanning.

Enrichment Enrichment programs are available through the program or unit for college survival skills, learning strategies, oral communication skills, self-advocacy, stress management, study skills, test taking, time management, written composition skills, and other. Programs for career planning, college survival skills, health and nutrition, learning strategies, oral communication skills, practical computer skills, stress management, study skills, test taking, time management, and written composition skills are provided collaboratively through on-campus or off-campus services.

Student Organization Disability Advocacy Student Alliance consists of 10 members.

Application For admittance to the program or unit, students are required to provide a psychoeducational report. Upon application, materials documenting need for services should be sent only to the LD program or unit. Upon acceptance, documentation of need for services should be sent only to the LD program or unit. *Application deadline (institutional): 1/15. Application deadline (LD program):* Rolling/continuous for fall and rolling/continuous for spring.

Written Policies Written policies regarding course substitutions, general/basic LD accommodations, substitutions and waivers of admissions requirements, and substitutions and waivers of graduation requirements are available on the program Web site. Written policies regarding course substitutions, general/basic LD accommodations, substitutions and waivers of admissions requirements, and substitutions and waivers of graduation requirements are outlined in the school's catalog/handbook. Written policies regarding course substitutions, general/basic LD accommodations, reduced course loads, substitutions and waivers of admissions requirements, and substitutions and waivers of graduation requirements are available through the program or unit directly.

University of West Georgia
Disability Services

1601 Maple Street

Carrollton, GA 30118

http://www.westga.edu/~dserve

Contact: Dr. Ann Phillips, Coordinator. Phone: 678-839-6428. Fax: 678-839-6429. E-mail: aphillip@westga.edu.

Disability Services Approximately 500 registered undergraduate students were served during 2006–07. The program or unit includes 1 part-time staff member. Academic advisers, counselors, diagnostic specialists, skill tutors, and strategy tutors are provided through the program or unit. Academic advisers, counselors, diagnostic specialists, and remediation/learning specialists are provided collaboratively through on-campus or off-campus services.

Unique Aids and Services Aids, services, or accommodations include career counseling, priority registration, individualized special accommodations report.

Assistive Technology Assistive technology is located in the library and includes digital textbooks/e-text, scanning, and books on audio CD or tape.

Subject-Area Tutoring Tutoring is offered one-on-one for some subjects. Tutoring is provided collaboratively through on-campus or off-campus services via graduate assistants/students and trained peer tutors.

Diagnostic Testing Testing for auditory processing, intelligence, learning styles, neuropsychological, personality, reading, spelling, and written language is provided collaboratively through on-campus or off-campus services.

Basic Skills Remediation Remediation is offered in class-size groups for math, reading, and written language. Remediation is provided collaboratively through on-campus or off-campus services via regular education teachers.

Enrichment Programs for career planning, college survival skills, health and nutrition, oral communication skills, practical computer skills, reading, stress management, study skills, test taking, time management, and written composition skills are provided collaboratively through on-campus or off-campus services. Credit is offered for health and nutrition, oral communication skills, practical computer skills, reading, and written composition skills.

Fees *Diagnostic Testing* fee is $500.

Application For admittance to the program or unit, students are required to apply to the program directly, provide a psychoeducational report (3 years old or less), provide documentation of high school services, and provide other documentation. Upon application, materials documenting need for services should be sent only to the LD program or unit. Upon acceptance, documentation of need for services should be sent only to the LD program or unit. *Application deadline (institutional):* 7/1. *Application deadline (LD program):* Rolling/continuous for fall and rolling/continuous for spring.

Written Policies Written policy regarding general/basic LD accommodations is available on the program Web site. Written policy regarding general/basic LD accommodations is outlined in the school's catalog/handbook. Written policies regarding course substitutions, general/basic LD accommodations, and reduced course loads are available through the program or unit directly.

University of Wisconsin–Eau Claire
Services for Students with Disabilities

PO Box 4004
Eau Claire, WI 54702-4004
http://www.uwec.edu/ssd

Contact: Kathleen S. Hurley, Director of Services for Students with Disabilities. Phone: 715-836-4542. Fax: 715-836-3712. E-mail: hurleyks@uwec.edu.

Services for Students with Disabilities Approximately 50 registered undergraduate students were served during 2006–07. The program or unit includes 2 part-time staff members. Counselors are provided through the program or unit. Academic advisers, counselors, diagnostic specialists, remediation/learning specialists, skill tutors, strategy tutors, and trained peer tutors are provided collaboratively through on-campus or off-campus services.

Unique Aids and Services Aids, services, or accommodations include career counseling and priority registration.

Assistive Technology Assistive technology includes digital textbooks/e-text and scanning. Technology training is provided to incoming students.

Subject-Area Tutoring Tutoring is offered one-on-one and in small groups for most subjects. Tutoring is provided collaboratively through on-campus or off-campus services via trained peer tutors.

Diagnostic Testing Testing for learning strategies, learning styles, math, reading, study skills, and written language is provided collaboratively through on-campus or off-campus services.

Basic Skills Remediation Remediation is offered one-on-one and in small groups for learning strategies, math, reading, study skills, time management, and written language. Remediation is provided collaboratively through on-campus or off-campus services via trained peer tutors.

Enrichment Enrichment programs are available through the program or unit for college survival skills, self-advocacy, study skills, test taking, and time management. Programs for career planning, college survival skills, health and nutrition, learning strategies, medication management, self-advocacy, stress management, study skills, test taking, time management, and written composition skills are provided collaboratively through on-campus or off-campus services. Credit is offered for college survival skills, learning strategies, self-advocacy, study skills, test taking, and time management.

Application For admittance to the program or unit, students are required to apply to the program directly and provide a psychoeducational report (3 years old or less). It is recommended that students provide documentation of high school services. Upon application, materials documenting need for services should be sent only to the LD program or unit. Upon acceptance, documentation of need for services should be sent only to the LD program or unit. *Application deadline (institutional):* Continuous. *Application deadline (LD program):* Rolling/continuous for fall and rolling/continuous for spring.

Written Policies Written policies regarding course substitutions, general/basic LD accommodations, grade forgiveness, reduced course loads, substitutions and waivers of admissions requirements, and substitutions and waivers of graduation requirements are available on the program Web site. Written policies regarding course substitutions, general/basic LD accommodations, grade forgiveness, reduced course loads, substitutions and waivers of admissions requirements, and substitutions and waivers of graduation requirements are outlined in the school's catalog/handbook. Written policies regarding course substitutions, general/basic LD accommodations, reduced course loads, substitutions and waivers of admissions requirements, and substitutions and waivers of graduation requirements are available through the program or unit directly.

University of Wisconsin–Green Bay

Disability Services Office

2420 Nicolet Drive

Green Bay, WI 54311-7001

http://www.uwgb.edu/ds

Contact: Mrs. Lynn Niemi, Coordinator of Disability Services. Phone: 920-465-2841. Fax: 920-465-2954. E-mail: niemil@uwgb.edu.

Disability Services Office Approximately 50 registered undergraduate students were served during 2006–07. The program or unit includes 2 part-time staff members. Academic advisers are provided collaboratively through on-campus or off-campus services.

Assistive Technology Assistive technology is located in campus labs, the DSS office, a special lab and includes digital textbooks/e-text. Technology training is provided to incoming students.

Subject-Area Tutoring Tutoring is offered in small groups for some subjects. Tutoring is provided collaboratively through on-campus or off-campus services via trained peer tutors.

Basic Skills Remediation Remediation is offered in class-size groups for math, reading, and written language. Remediation is provided collaboratively through on-campus or off-campus services via regular education teachers.

Enrichment Programs for career planning, study skills, and test taking are provided collaboratively through on-campus or off-campus services. Credit is offered for career planning.

Application For admittance to the program or unit, students are required to provide a psychoeducational report. It is recommended that students provide documentation of high school services. Upon application, materials documenting need for services should be sent only to the LD program or unit. Upon acceptance, documentation of need for services should be sent only to the LD program or unit. *Application deadline (LD program):* Rolling/continuous for fall and rolling/continuous for spring.

Written Policies Written policies regarding general/basic LD accommodations and reduced course loads are available on the program Web site. Written policies regarding course substitutions, general/basic LD accommodations, and substitutions and waivers of graduation requirements are available through the program or unit directly.

University of Wisconsin–La Crosse

Disability Resource Services

1725 State Street

La Crosse, WI 54601-3742

http://www.uwlax.edu/drs

Contact: Ms. June A. Reinert, Director of Disability Resource Services. Phone: 608-785-6900. Fax: 608-785-6910. E-mail: reinert.june@uwlax.edu.

Disability Resource Services Approximately 65 registered undergraduate students were served during 2006–07. The program or unit includes 1 full-time and 2 part-time staff members. Academic advisers, counselors, LD specialists, and remediation/learning specialists are provided collaboratively through on-campus or off-campus services.

Orientation The program or unit offers a mandatory 2-hour orientation for new students before classes begin and during registration.

Unique Aids and Services Aids, services, or accommodations include faculty training, priority registration, and support groups.

Assistive Technology Assistive technology is located in campus labs, the DSS office and includes digital textbooks/e-text. Technology training is provided to incoming students.

Subject-Area Tutoring Tutoring is offered in small groups for most subjects. Tutoring is provided collaboratively through on-campus or off-campus services via computer-based instruction.

Student Organization Students Advocating Potential Ability consists of 19 members.

Application For admittance to the program or unit, students are required to apply to the program directly and provide a psychoeducational report (3 years old or less). It is recommended that students provide documentation of high school services and provide WAIS, Woodcock Johnson. Upon acceptance, documentation of need for services should be sent only to the LD program or unit. *Application deadline (institutional):* Continuous. *Application deadline (LD program):* Rolling/continuous for spring.

Written Policies Written policies regarding course substitutions, general/basic LD accommodations, reduced course loads, and substitutions and waivers of graduation requirements are available on the program Web site. Written policy regarding grade forgiveness is available through the program or unit directly.

University of Wisconsin–Madison

McBurney Disability Resource Center

500 Lincoln Drive

Madison, WI 53706-1380

http://www.mcburney.wisc.edu/

Contact: McBurney Disability Resource Center. Phone: 608-263-2741. Fax: 608-265-2998. E-mail: mcburney@odos.wisc.edu. Head of LD Program: Diane Woodbridge, Accommodation Specialist: Learning Disorders. Phone: 608-263-2741. Fax: 608-265-2998. E-mail: woodbridge@odos.wisc.edu.

McBurney Disability Resource Center Approximately 360 registered undergraduate students were served during 2006–07. The program or unit includes 1 full-time and 1 part-time staff member. Academic advisers, counselors, graduate assistants/students, LD specialists, skill tutors, strategy tutors, and trained peer tutors are provided through the program or unit. Academic advisers, counselors, diagnostic specialists, graduate assistants/students, professional tutors, remediation/learning specialists, skill tutors, strategy tutors, and trained peer tutors are provided collaboratively through on-campus or off-campus services.

Orientation The program or unit offers a mandatory 1- to 4-hour orientation for new students before classes begin.

Assistive Technology Assistive technology is located in campus labs, the DSS office and includes digital textbooks/e-text, learning support software, scanning, and voice-recognition software, audio CD. Technology training is provided to incoming students.

Subject-Area Tutoring Tutoring is offered one-on-one, in small groups, and in class-size groups for some subjects. Tutoring is provided collaboratively through on-campus or off-campus services via graduate assistants/students, professional tutors, and trained peer tutors.

Diagnostic Testing Testing for auditory processing, handwriting, intelligence, math, reading, spelling, spoken language, visual processing, written language, and other services is provided collaboratively through on-campus or off-campus services.

Enrichment Enrichment programs are available through the program or unit for self-advocacy and study skills. Programs for career planning, college survival skills, learning strategies, math, medication management, stress management, study skills, time management, vocabulary development, and written composition skills are provided collaboratively through on-campus or off-campus services. Credit is offered for learning strategies and study skills.

Fees *Diagnostic Testing* fee is $200.

Application For admittance to the program or unit, students are required to provide a psychoeducational report (3 years old or less). It is recommended that students apply to the program directly and provide documentation of high school services. Upon application, materials documenting need for services should be sent only to the LD program or unit. Upon acceptance, documentation of need for services should be sent only to the LD program or unit. *Application deadline (institutional):* 2/1. *Application deadline (LD program):* Rolling/continuous for fall and rolling/continuous for spring.

Written Policies Written policies regarding course substitutions, general/basic LD accommodations, and substitutions and waivers of graduation requirements are available on the program Web site. Written policies regarding course substitutions and substitutions and waivers of graduation requirements are outlined in the school's catalog/handbook. Written policy regarding substitutions and waivers of graduation requirements is available through the program or unit directly.

University of Wisconsin–Platteville
Services for Students with Disabilities

1 University Plaza
Platteville, WI 53818-3099
http://www.uwplatt.edu/disability/

Contact: Ms. Rebecca L. Peters, Coordinator of Services for Students with Disabilities. Phone: 608-342-1818. Fax: 608-342-1918. E-mail: petersre@uwplatt.edu.

Services for Students with Disabilities Approximately 115 registered undergraduate students were served during 2006–07. The program or unit includes 1 full-time and 1 part-time staff member. LD specialists are provided through the program or unit. Academic advisers, counselors, diagnostic specialists, remediation/learning specialists, skill tutors, and trained peer tutors are provided collaboratively through on-campus or off-campus services.

Unique Aids and Services Aids, services, or accommodations include support groups.

Assistive Technology Assistive technology is located in the DSS office, a special lab and includes digital textbooks/e-text. Technology training is provided to incoming students.

Subject-Area Tutoring Tutoring is offered one-on-one and in small groups for most subjects. Tutoring is provided collaboratively through on-campus or off-campus services via trained peer tutors.

Basic Skills Remediation Remediation is offered one-on-one, in small groups, and in class-size groups for computer skills, learning strategies, reading, study skills, and time management. Remediation is provided collaboratively through on-campus or off-campus services via computer-based instruction, regular education teachers, and trained peer tutors.

Enrichment Programs for career planning, college survival skills, learning strategies, reading, stress management, study skills, test taking, time management, and written composition skills are provided collaboratively through on-campus or off-campus services. Credit is offered for career planning and college survival skills.

Student Organization Students Planning for Success consists of 15 members.

Application For admittance to the program or unit, students are required to provide a psychoeducational report (3 years old or less) and provide documentation of high school services. Upon application, materials documenting need for services should be sent to both admissions and the LD program or unit. Upon acceptance, documentation of need for services should be sent only to the LD program or unit. *Application deadline (institutional):* Continuous. *Application deadline (LD program):* Rolling/continuous for fall and rolling/continuous for spring.

Written Policies Written policies regarding course substitutions, general/basic LD accommodations, reduced course loads, substitutions and waivers of admissions requirements, and substitutions and waivers of graduation requirements are available through the program or unit directly.

University of Wisconsin–Stevens Point
Office of Disability Services

2100 Main Street
Stevens Point, WI 54481-3897
http://www.uwsp.edu/special/disability/

Contact: James Joque, Disability Services Coordinator. Phone: 715-346-3365. Fax: 715-346-2558. E-mail: jjoque@uwsp.edu.

Office of Disability Services Approximately 105 registered undergraduate students were served during 2006–07. Academic advisers, counselors, and trained peer tutors are provided collaboratively through on-campus or off-campus services.

Unique Aids and Services Aids, services, or accommodations include standard test and classroom accomodations.

Assistive Technology Assistive technology is located in the library (library AT also provides training) and includes digital textbooks/e-text, scanning, and text-to-voice.

University of Wisconsin–Stevens Point (continued)

Subject-Area Tutoring Tutoring is offered one-on-one, in small groups, and in class-size groups. Tutoring is provided collaboratively through on-campus or off-campus services via trained peer tutors.

Basic Skills Remediation Remediation is offered one-on-one for math, reading, study skills, and written language. Remediation is provided collaboratively through on-campus or off-campus services via professional tutors and trained peer tutors.

Enrichment Programs for career planning, reading, study skills, and written composition skills are provided collaboratively through on-campus or off-campus services. Credit is offered for study skills.

Application For admittance to the program or unit, students are required to provide a psychoeducational report (3 years old or less). It is recommended that students provide documentation of high school services. Upon application, materials documenting need for services should be sent only to the LD program or unit. *Application deadline (institutional):* Continuous. *Application deadline (LD program):* Rolling/continuous for fall and rolling/continuous for spring.

Written Policies Written policy regarding general/basic LD accommodations is available on the program Web site. Written policy regarding course substitutions is outlined in the school's catalog/handbook. Written policy regarding general/basic LD accommodations is available through the program or unit directly.

University of Wisconsin–Stout

Menomonie, WI 54751

http://www.uwstout.edu/

Contact: Ms. Debra Joan Shefchik, Director of Disability Services. Phone: 715-232-2995. Fax: 715-232-2996. E-mail: shefchikd@uwstout.edu.

The program or unit includes 3 part-time staff members. Academic advisers, LD specialists, and other are provided through the program or unit.

Orientation The program or unit offers a mandatory 1-hour orientation for new students before classes begin, after classes begin, and individually by special arrangement.

Unique Aids and Services Aids, services, or accommodations include advocates, career counseling, personal coach, priority registration, test accommodations, peer note-takers.

Assistive Technology Assistive technology is located in the DSS office, the library and includes digital textbooks/e-text and scanning.

Subject-Area Tutoring Tutoring is offered one-on-one and in small groups for some subjects. Tutoring is provided collaboratively through on-campus or off-campus services via trained peer tutors and other.

Diagnostic Testing Testing for auditory processing, intelligence, learning styles, math, motor skills, neuropsychological, personality, reading, spelling, visual processing, and written language is provided collaboratively through on-campus or off-campus services.

Basic Skills Remediation Remediation is offered in class-size groups for math and written language. Remediation is provided collaboratively through on-campus or off-campus services via regular education teachers and trained peer tutors.

Enrichment Enrichment programs are available through the program or unit for career planning, college survival skills, learning strategies, reading, self-advocacy, stress management, study skills, test taking, time management, and written composition skills. Programs for career planning, math, stress management, study skills, test taking, time management, and written composition skills are provided collaboratively through on-campus or off-campus services.

Fees *Diagnostic Testing* fee is $100.

Application For admittance to the program or unit, students are required to provide a psychoeducational report (3 years old or less) and provide documentation of high school services. Upon acceptance, documentation of need for services should be sent only to the LD program or unit. *Application deadline (LD program):* Rolling/continuous for fall and rolling/continuous for spring.

Written Policies Written policy regarding general/basic LD accommodations is available on the program Web site. Written policies regarding course substitutions and general/basic LD accommodations are outlined in the school's catalog/handbook. Written policies regarding course substitutions and general/basic LD accommodations are available through the program or unit directly.

University of Wyoming
Disability Support Services

Laramie, WY 82070

http://www.uwyo.edu/udss

Contact: Ms. Chris Primus, Director of University Disability Support Services. Phone: 307-766-6189. Fax: 307-766-4010. E-mail: cfprimus@uwyo.edu.

Disability Support Services Approximately 95 registered undergraduate students were served during 2006–07. The program or unit includes 4 full-time and 25 part-time staff members. Counselors are provided through the program or unit. Academic advisers, counselors, diagnostic specialists, graduate assistants/students, skill tutors, strategy tutors, and trained peer tutors are provided collaboratively through on-campus or off-campus services.

Orientation The program or unit offers an optional half-day orientation for new students before classes begin and individually by special arrangement.

Unique Aids and Services Aids, services, or accommodations include advocates and priority registration.

Assistive Technology Assistive technology is located in campus labs, the DSS office, a special lab and includes digital textbooks/e-text, learning support software, scanning, and voice recognition software, scan and read software. Technology training is provided to incoming students.

Subject-Area Tutoring Tutoring is offered one-on-one and in small groups for most subjects. Tutoring is provided collaboratively through on-campus or off-campus services via computer-based instruction, graduate assistants/students, and trained peer tutors.

Diagnostic Testing Testing for auditory processing, intelligence, learning styles, math, neuropsychological, personality, reading, spelling, spoken language, visual processing, and written language is provided collaboratively through on-campus or off-campus services.

Basic Skills Remediation Remediation is offered one-on-one and in small groups for learning strategies, math, reading, study skills, time management, and written language. Remediation is provided collaboratively through on-campus or off-campus services via computer-based instruction, graduate assistants/students, and trained peer tutors.

Enrichment Enrichment programs are available through the program or unit for self-advocacy. Programs for career planning, college survival skills, health and nutrition, learning strategies, math, oral communication skills, practical computer skills, reading, stress management, study skills, test taking, time management, and written composition skills are provided collaboratively through on-campus or off-campus services.

Student Organization WyoACCESS consists of 15 members.

Fees *Diagnostic Testing* fee is applicable.

Application For admittance to the program or unit, students are required to apply to the program directly and provide a psychoeducational report. It is recommended that students provide documentation of high school services. Upon application, materials documenting need for services should be sent only to the LD program or unit. Upon acceptance, documentation of need for services should be sent only to the LD program or unit. *Application deadline (institutional):* 8/10. *Application deadline (LD program):* Rolling/continuous for fall and rolling/continuous for spring.

Written Policies Written policies regarding course substitutions, general/basic LD accommodations, and substitutions and waivers of graduation requirements are available on the program Web site. Written policies regarding course substitutions, reduced course loads, substitutions and waivers of admissions requirements, and substitutions and waivers of graduation requirements are outlined in the school's catalog/handbook. Written policies regarding course substitutions, general/basic LD accommodations, and substitutions and waivers of graduation requirements are available through the program or unit directly.

Upper Iowa University
Office of Student Development

605 Washington Street, Box 1857

Fayette, IA 52142-1857

http://www.uiu.edu/

Contact: Laurie Kirkpatrick, Assistant Dean/Director of Counseling Services. Phone: 563-425-5786. E-mail: kirkpatrickl@uiu.edu.

Office of Student Development Approximately 26 registered undergraduate students were served during 2006–07. The program or unit includes 2 full-time staff members. Counselors and other are provided through the program or unit. Academic advisers, professional tutors, and regular education teachers are provided collaboratively through on-campus or off-campus services.

Assistive Technology Assistive technology is located in the DSS office and includes digital textbooks/e-text, learning support software, and scanning.

Subject-Area Tutoring Tutoring is offered one-on-one for some subjects. Tutoring is provided collaboratively through on-campus or off-campus services via graduate assistants/students, professional tutors, and trained peer tutors.

Basic Skills Remediation Remediation is offered in class-size groups for math and written language. Remediation is provided collaboratively through on-campus or off-campus services via regular education teachers.

Enrichment Programs for career planning, health and nutrition, math, self-advocacy, stress management, study skills, test taking, time management, and written composition skills are provided collaboratively through on-campus or off-campus services.

Application For admittance to the program or unit, students are required to apply to the program directly and provide documentation of high school services. It is recommended that students provide a psychoeducational report (3 years old or less). Upon acceptance, documentation of need for services should be sent only to the LD program or unit. *Application deadline (institutional):* Continuous. *Application deadline (LD program):* Rolling/continuous for fall and rolling/continuous for spring.

Written Policies Written policy regarding general/basic LD accommodations is available on the program Web site. Written policies regarding general/basic LD accommodations and substitutions and waivers of admissions requirements are outlined in the school's catalog/handbook. Written policies regarding course substitutions, grade forgiveness, reduced course loads, and substitutions and waivers of graduation requirements are available through the program or unit directly.

Urbana University
Office of Disability Services

579 College Way

Urbana, OH 43078-2091

http://www.urbana.edu/

Contact: Ms. Shawna Benson, Director of Disability Services. Phone: 937-484-1286. Fax: 937-484-1365. E-mail: sbenson@urbana.edu. Head of LD Program: Dr. Denise Boldman, Dean, College of Education and Allied Professions. Phone: 937-484-1286. Fax: 937-484-1365. E-mail: dboldman@urbana.edu.

Office of Disability Services Approximately 40 registered undergraduate students were served during 2006–07. The program or unit includes 1 part-time staff member. Academic advisers, coaches, counselors, diagnostic specialists, graduate assistants/students, LD specialists, professional tutors, regular education teachers, remediation/learning specialists, special education teachers, and trained peer tutors are provided collaboratively through on-campus or off-campus services.

Orientation The program or unit offers an optional orientation for new students individually by special arrangement.

Subject-Area Tutoring Tutoring is offered one-on-one and in small groups for most subjects. Tutoring is provided collaboratively through on-campus or off-campus services via graduate assistants/students, LD specialists, and trained peer tutors.

Diagnostic Testing Testing for auditory processing, handwriting, intelligence, learning strategies, learning styles, math, reading, spelling, spoken language, study skills, visual processing, and written language is provided collaboratively through on-campus or off-campus services.

Urbana University (continued)

Basic Skills Remediation Remediation is offered one-on-one, in small groups, and in class-size groups for learning strategies, math, reading, social skills, study skills, time management, and written language. Remediation is provided through the program or unit via LD specialists and special education teachers. Remediation is also provided collaboratively through on-campus or off-campus services via regular education teachers.

Enrichment Enrichment programs are available through the program or unit for learning strategies and test taking. Programs for career planning, college survival skills, health and nutrition, math, oral communication skills, practical computer skills, reading, stress management, study skills, and written composition skills are provided collaboratively through on-campus or off-campus services. Credit is offered for health and nutrition, math, oral communication skills, practical computer skills, reading, and written composition skills.

Fees *Diagnostic Testing* fee is $350 to $450.

Application For admittance to the program or unit, students are required to provide a psychoeducational report (1 year old or less). It is recommended that students provide documentation of high school services. Upon application, materials documenting need for services should be sent to both admissions and the LD program or unit. Upon acceptance, documentation of need for services should be sent only to the LD program or unit. *Application deadline (institutional):* Continuous. *Application deadline (LD program):* Rolling/continuous for fall and rolling/continuous for spring.

Written Policies Written policy regarding general/basic LD accommodations is outlined in the school's catalog/handbook.

Utica College
Learning Services Office/Academic Support Services Center

1600 Burrstone Road

Utica, NY 13502-4892

http://www.utica.edu/

Contact: Mrs. Kateri Teresa Henkel, Coordinator of Learning Services. Phone: 315-792-3032. Fax: 315-792-3292. E-mail: khenkel@utica.edu. Head of LD Program: Mrs. Kateri Teresa Henkel, Director of Learning Services. Phone: 315-792-3032. Fax: 315-223-2504. E-mail: khenkel@utica.edu.

Learning Services Office/Academic Support Services Center Approximately 125 registered undergraduate students were served during 2006–07. The program or unit includes 1 full-time and 1 part-time staff member. Academic advisers, LD specialists, and professional tutors are provided through the program or unit. Academic advisers, counselors, diagnostic specialists, LD specialists, professional tutors, skill tutors, strategy tutors, and trained peer tutors are provided collaboratively through on-campus or off-campus services.

Unique Aids and Services Aids, services, or accommodations include advocates, career counseling, and priority registration.

Assistive Technology Assistive technology is located in the DSS office, the library and includes digital textbooks/e-text and screen reading software. Technology training is provided to incoming students.

Subject-Area Tutoring Tutoring is offered one-on-one and in small groups for most subjects. Tutoring is provided through the program or unit via professional tutors. Tutoring is also provided collaboratively through on-campus or off-campus services via professional tutors and trained peer tutors.

Basic Skills Remediation Remediation is offered one-on-one and in small groups for computer skills, learning strategies, study skills, and time management. Remediation is provided through the program or unit via LD specialists. Remediation is also provided collaboratively through on-campus or off-campus services.

Enrichment Enrichment programs are available through the program or unit for self-advocacy, study skills, test taking, and time management. Programs for career planning, college survival skills, health and nutrition, learning strategies, math, oral communication skills, practical computer skills, stress management, study skills, test taking, time management, and written composition skills are provided collaboratively through on-campus or off-campus services. Credit is offered for college survival skills.

Application For admittance to the program or unit, students are required to provide a psychoeducational report (3 years old or less). It is recommended that students provide documentation of high school services. Upon application, materials documenting need for services should be sent only to admissions with institutional application materials. Upon acceptance, documentation of need for services should be sent only to the LD program or unit. *Application deadline (institutional):* Continuous. *Application deadline (LD program):* Rolling/continuous for fall and rolling/continuous for spring.

Written Policies Written policies regarding course substitutions and general/basic LD accommodations are available through the program or unit directly.

Valdosta State University
Access Office for Students with Disabilities

1500 North Patterson Street

Valdosta, GA 31698

http://www.valdosta.edu/access/

Contact: Kimberly Ann Tanner, Director, Access Office for Students with Disabilities. Phone: 229-245-2498. Fax: 229-245-3788. E-mail: katanner@valdosta.edu.

Access Office for Students with Disabilities Approximately 70 registered undergraduate students were served during 2006–07. The program or unit includes 4 full-time and 3 part-time staff members. Academic advisers, graduate assistants/students, and LD specialists are provided through the program or unit. Academic advisers, coaches, counselors, diagnostic specialists, graduate assistants/students, professional tutors, regular education teachers, remediation/learning specialists, skill tutors, strategy tutors, and trained peer tutors are provided collaboratively through on-campus or off-campus services.

Summer Program To help prepare for the demands of college, there is an optional (collaboratively with the Department of Labor Vocational Rehabilitation Program) 3-day summer program prior to entering the school available to rising juniors, rising seniors that focuses on computing skills, life skills and/or college life adjustment, self-advocacy, study skills, and time management. The program is available to students attending other colleges.

Unique Aids and Services Aids, services, or accommodations include career counseling, faculty training, and priority registration.

Assistive Technology Assistive technology is located in campus labs, the DSS office, a special lab, the library and includes digital textbooks/e-text, scanning, and adaptive software. Technology training is provided to incoming students.

Subject-Area Tutoring Tutoring is offered one-on-one, in small groups, and in class-size groups for all subjects. Tutoring is provided collaboratively through on-campus or off-campus services via computer-based instruction, graduate assistants/students, and trained peer tutors.

Basic Skills Remediation Remediation is offered in class-size groups for math, reading, and written language. Remediation is provided collaboratively through on-campus or off-campus services via regular education teachers.

Enrichment Programs for career planning, college survival skills, health and nutrition, learning strategies, math, oral communication skills, practical computer skills, reading, self-advocacy, stress management, study skills, test taking, time management, vocabulary development, written composition skills, and other are provided collaboratively through on-campus or off-campus services. Credit is offered for college survival skills.

Student Organization Student Advocacy Association.

Application For admittance to the program or unit, students are required to provide a psychoeducational report (3 years old or less). It is recommended that students provide documentation of high school services. Upon application, materials documenting need for services should be sent only to the LD program or unit. Upon acceptance, documentation of need for services should be sent only to the LD program or unit. *Application deadline (institutional):* 7/1. *Application deadline (LD program):* Rolling/continuous for fall and rolling/continuous for spring.

Written Policies Written policies regarding general/basic LD accommodations, reduced course loads, and substitutions and waivers of admissions requirements are available on the program Web site. Written policies regarding course substitutions and substitutions and waivers of graduation requirements are outlined in the school's catalog/handbook. Written policies regarding general/basic LD accommodations, reduced course loads, and substitutions and waivers of admissions requirements are available through the program or unit directly.

Vanguard University of Southern California
Learning Assistance

55 Fair Drive

Costa Mesa, CA 92626-9601

http://www.vanguard.edu/

Contact: Mrs. Barbi Ann Rouse, Director of Learning Skills. Phone: 714-556-3610 Ext. 227. Fax: 714-662-5222. E-mail: brouse@vanguard.edu.

Learning Assistance Approximately 31 registered undergraduate students were served during 2006–07. The program or unit

includes 1 full-time and 1 part-time staff member. Academic advisers, regular education teachers, skill tutors, strategy tutors, and other are provided through the program or unit. Academic advisers, counselors, regular education teachers, and trained peer tutors are provided collaboratively through on-campus or off-campus services.

Unique Aids and Services Aids, services, or accommodations include career counseling, appointments with Director of Learning Skills.

Subject-Area Tutoring Tutoring is offered one-on-one, in small groups, and in class-size groups for most subjects. Tutoring is provided collaboratively through on-campus or off-campus services via graduate assistants/students and trained peer tutors.

Basic Skills Remediation Remediation is offered in class-size groups for learning strategies, reading, study skills, time management, and editing. Remediation is provided collaboratively through on-campus or off-campus services via regular education teachers and trained peer tutors.

Enrichment Enrichment programs are available through the program or unit for college survival skills, learning strategies, stress management, study skills, test taking, time management, and written composition skills. Programs for career planning, learning strategies, reading, study skills, test taking, and time management are provided collaboratively through on-campus or off-campus services. Credit is offered for college survival skills, learning strategies, reading, study skills, test taking, and time management.

Application For admittance to the program or unit, students are required to apply to the program directly, provide a psychoeducational report (3 years old or less), provide documentation of high school services, and provide medical doctor verification in some cases. Upon application, materials documenting need for services should be sent only to admissions with institutional application materials. Upon acceptance, documentation of need for services should be sent to both admissions and the LD program or unit. *Application deadline (institutional):* 12/1. *Application deadline (LD program):* Rolling/continuous for fall and rolling/continuous for spring.

Written Policies Written policy regarding general/basic LD accommodations is available through the program or unit directly.

Vassar College
Office of Disability Support Services

124 Raymond Avenue

Poughkeepsie, NY 12604

http://disabilityandsupportservices.vassar.edu/

Contact: Belinda M. Guthrie, Associate Dean of the College/Director of Equal Opportunity. Phone: 845-437-7584. Fax: 845-437-5715. E-mail: guthrie@vassar.edu.

Office of Disability Support Services Approximately 89 registered undergraduate students were served during 2006–07. The program or unit includes 1 full-time and 2 part-time staff members. Coaches, LD specialists, and strategy tutors are provided through the program or unit. Academic advisers, counselors, skill tutors, strategy tutors, and trained peer tutors are provided collaboratively through on-campus or off-campus services.

Unique Aids and Services Aids, services, or accommodations include faculty training, personal coach, priority registration, support groups, and weekly meetings with faculty.

Vassar College (continued)

Assistive Technology Assistive technology is located in campus labs, the DSS office and includes digital textbooks/e-text, learning support software, and scanning. Technology training is provided to incoming students.

Subject-Area Tutoring Tutoring is offered one-on-one and in small groups for some subjects. Tutoring is provided collaboratively through on-campus or off-campus services via trained peer tutors.

Enrichment Enrichment programs are available through the program or unit for college survival skills, learning strategies, reading, self-advocacy, study skills, test taking, and time management. Programs for career planning, college survival skills, health and nutrition, learning strategies, math, practical computer skills, reading, stress management, study skills, test taking, time management, and written composition skills are provided collaboratively through on-campus or off-campus services. Credit is offered for oral communication skills.

Application For admittance to the program or unit, students are required to provide a psychoeducational report (3 years old or less). Upon application, materials documenting need for services should be sent only to the LD program or unit. Upon acceptance, documentation of need for services should be sent only to the LD program or unit. *Application deadline (institutional): 1/1. Application deadline (LD program): 6/1 for fall. 1/30 for spring.*

Written Policies Written policies regarding course substitutions, general/basic LD accommodations, and reduced course loads are available on the program Web site. Written policies regarding general/basic LD accommodations and reduced course loads are outlined in the school's catalog/handbook. Written policies regarding course substitutions, general/basic LD accommodations, and reduced course loads are available through the program or unit directly.

Vermont Technical College
Academic Support Services

PO Box 500

Randolph Center, VT 05061-0500

http://www.vtc.edu/section_academic_programs/academic_programs_acadserv-disserv.asp

Contact: Robin C. Goodall, Learning Specialist. Phone: 802-728-1278. Fax: 802-728-1260. E-mail: rgoodall@vtc.edu.

Academic Support Services Approximately 75 registered undergraduate students were served during 2006–07. The program or unit includes 1 full-time staff member. Counselors, LD specialists, skill tutors, and strategy tutors are provided through the program or unit. Academic advisers, counselors, LD specialists, professional tutors, skill tutors, strategy tutors, and trained peer tutors are provided collaboratively through on-campus or off-campus services.

Summer Program To help prepare for the demands of college, there is an optional 1-day summer program prior to entering the school available to rising seniors, high school graduates that focuses on computing skills, life skills and/or college life adjustment, and time management. The program accepts students from out-of-state.

Unique Aids and Services Aids, services, or accommodations include career counseling, personal coach, and weekly meetings with faculty.

Assistive Technology Assistive technology is located in campus labs, the DSS office, the Writing and Communication Center and includes digital textbooks/e-text, learning support software, and scanning. Technology training is provided to incoming students.

Subject-Area Tutoring Tutoring is offered one-on-one, in small groups, and in class-size groups for all subjects. Tutoring is provided through the program or unit via computer-based instruction, LD specialists, professional tutors, and trained peer tutors. Tutoring is also provided collaboratively through on-campus or off-campus services via computer-based instruction, professional tutors, and trained peer tutors.

Basic Skills Remediation Remediation is offered one-on-one for computer skills, learning strategies, math, study skills, time management, and written language. Remediation is provided collaboratively through on-campus or off-campus services via computer-based instruction, professional tutors, and trained peer tutors.

Enrichment Programs for career planning, college survival skills, learning strategies, self-advocacy, study skills, test taking, time management, and written composition skills are provided collaboratively through on-campus or off-campus services.

Application For admittance to the program or unit, students are required to provide a psychoeducational report (3 years old or less). It is recommended that students provide documentation of high school services. Upon application, materials documenting need for services should be sent only to the LD program or unit. Upon acceptance, documentation of need for services should be sent only to the LD program or unit. *Application deadline (institutional):* Continuous. *Application deadline (LD program):* Rolling/continuous for fall and rolling/continuous for spring.

Written Policies Written policies regarding course substitutions, general/basic LD accommodations, reduced course loads, and substitutions and waivers of admissions requirements are available on the program Web site. Written policies regarding course substitutions, general/basic LD accommodations, reduced course loads, and substitutions and waivers of admissions requirements are outlined in the school's catalog/handbook. Written policy regarding general/basic LD accommodations is available through the program or unit directly.

Villanova University
Learning Support Services

800 Lancaster Avenue

Villanova, PA 19085-1699

http://learningsupportservices.villanova.edu

Contact: Dr. Nancy M. Mott, Director of Learning Support Services. Phone: 610-591-5636. Fax: 610-519-8015. E-mail: nancy.mott@villanova.edu.

Learning Support Services Approximately 200 registered undergraduate students were served during 2006–07. The program or unit includes 1 full-time staff member. Coaches, graduate assistants/students, LD specialists, remediation/learning specialists, skill tutors, strategy tutors, and trained peer tutors are provided through the program or unit. Academic advisers, counselors, graduate assistants/students, regular education teachers, skill tutors, strategy tutors, and trained peer tutors are provided collaboratively through on-campus or off-campus services.

Unique Aids and Services Aids, services, or accommodations include career counseling, personal coach, and support groups.

Assistive Technology Assistive technology is located in campus labs, the DSS office and includes digital textbooks/e-text, learning support software, and scanning. Technology training is provided to incoming students.

Subject-Area Tutoring Tutoring is offered one-on-one, in small groups, and in class-size groups for most subjects. Tutoring is provided through the program or unit via computer-based instruction, graduate assistants/students, LD specialists, and trained peer tutors. Tutoring is also provided collaboratively through on-campus or off-campus services via computer-based instruction, graduate assistants/students, and trained peer tutors.

Diagnostic Testing Testing is provided through the program or unit for study skills. Testing for study skills is provided collaboratively through on-campus or off-campus services.

Enrichment Enrichment programs are available through the program or unit for college survival skills, learning strategies, self-advocacy, stress management, study skills, test taking, and time management. Programs for career planning, health and nutrition, learning strategies, math, stress management, study skills, test taking, time management, and written composition skills are provided collaboratively through on-campus or off-campus services. Credit is offered for learning strategies, self-advocacy, stress management, study skills, test taking, and time management.

Application For admittance to the program or unit, students are required to provide a psychoeducational report. It is recommended that students provide documentation of high school services. Upon acceptance, documentation of need for services should be sent only to the LD program or unit. *Application deadline (institutional):* 1/7. *Application deadline (LD program):* Rolling/continuous for fall and rolling/continuous for spring.

Written Policies Written policies regarding general/basic LD accommodations, reduced course loads, and substitutions and waivers of graduation requirements are available on the program Web site. Written policies regarding general/basic LD accommodations and substitutions and waivers of graduation requirements are outlined in the school's catalog/handbook. Written policies regarding course substitutions, general/basic LD accommodations, reduced course loads, and substitutions and waivers of graduation requirements are available through the program or unit directly.

Virginia Intermont College
Student Support Services

1013 Moore Street
Bristol, VA 24201-4298

http://www.vic.edu/

Contact: Ms. Talmage A. Dobbins, Director of Student Support Services. Phone: 276-466-7907. Fax: 276-645-6493. E-mail: talmagedobbins@vic.edu.

Student Support Services Approximately 31 registered undergraduate students were served during 2006–07. The program or unit includes 3 full-time staff members. Academic advisers, counselors, diagnostic specialists, and LD specialists are provided through the program or unit. Academic advisers, coaches, and trained peer tutors are provided collaboratively through on-campus or off-campus services.

Unique Aids and Services Aids, services, or accommodations include advocates, faculty training, support groups, academic advising.

Subject-Area Tutoring Tutoring is offered one-on-one and in small groups for most subjects. Tutoring is provided through the program or unit via trained peer tutors.

Diagnostic Testing Testing is provided through the program or unit for auditory processing, intelligence, learning strategies, learning styles, math, motor skills, reading, spelling, spoken language, study skills, visual processing, and written language.

Basic Skills Remediation Remediation is offered in small groups for learning strategies, math, reading, study skills, and time management. Remediation is provided through the program or unit via computer-based instruction, LD specialists, and trained peer tutors. Remediation is also provided collaboratively through on-campus or off-campus services via regular education teachers.

Enrichment Enrichment programs are available through the program or unit for college survival skills, learning strategies, stress management, study skills, test taking, and time management. Programs for career planning, health and nutrition, math, and written composition skills are provided collaboratively through on-campus or off-campus services. Credit is offered for study skills, test taking, and time management.

Application For admittance to the program or unit, students are required to provide a psychoeducational report (5 years old or less). It is recommended that students provide documentation of high school services. Upon acceptance, documentation of need for services should be sent only to the LD program or unit. *Application deadline (institutional):* Continuous. *Application deadline (LD program):* Rolling/continuous for fall and rolling/continuous for spring.

Written Policies Written policy regarding general/basic LD accommodations is available on the program Web site. Written policy regarding general/basic LD accommodations is outlined in the school's catalog/handbook. Written policies regarding course substitutions, general/basic LD accommodations, reduced course loads, and substitutions and waivers of graduation requirements are available through the program or unit directly.

Virginia Military Institute
Disabilities Services

Lexington, VA 24450

http://www.vmi.edu/show.asp?durki=1969

Contact: Dr. Mollie J. Messimer. Fax: 540-464-7798. E-mail: messimermj@vmi.edu.

Disabilities Services Approximately 35 registered undergraduate students were served during 2006–07. The program or unit includes 1 full-time staff member. Special education teachers, strategy tutors, and trained peer tutors are provided through the program or unit. Academic advisers, coaches, counselors, and professional tutors are provided collaboratively through on-campus or off-campus services.

Summer Program To help prepare for the demands of college, there is an optional 1-month summer program prior to entering the school available to high school graduates that focuses on specific subject tutoring. Degree credit will be earned. The program accepts students from out-of-state.

Virginia Military Institute (continued)

Unique Aids and Services Aids, services, or accommodations include faculty training, parent workshops, and support groups.

Assistive Technology Assistive technology is located in the DSS office, the student's personal laptop computer and includes digital textbooks/e-text and scanning.

Subject-Area Tutoring Tutoring is offered one-on-one and in small groups for some subjects. Tutoring is provided through the program or unit via computer-based instruction, graduate assistants/ students, and trained peer tutors. Tutoring is also provided collaboratively through on-campus or off-campus services via professional tutors.

Diagnostic Testing Testing is provided through the program or unit for intelligence and neuropsychological.

Enrichment Enrichment programs are available through the program or unit for learning strategies, math, self-advocacy, study skills, test taking, and time management. Programs for career planning, medication management, stress management, and written composition skills are provided collaboratively through on-campus or off-campus services.

Fees *Diagnostic Testing* fee is applicable.

Application For admittance to the program or unit, students are required to apply to the program directly. It is recommended that students provide a psychoeducational report and provide documentation of high school services. Upon application, materials documenting need for services should be sent only to the LD program or unit. Upon acceptance, documentation of need for services should be sent only to the LD program or unit. *Application deadline (LD program):* Rolling/continuous for fall and rolling/continuous for spring.

Written Policies Written policy regarding general/basic LD accommodations is available on the program Web site. Written policies regarding course substitutions and general/basic LD accommodations are available through the program or unit directly.

Wake Forest University
Learning Assistance Center

Reynolda Station
Winston-Salem, NC 27109
http://www.wfu.edu/lac/
Contact: Dr. Van D. Westervelt, Director of Learning Assistance Center. Phone: 336-758-5929. Fax: 336-758-1991.

Learning Assistance Center Approximately 227 registered undergraduate students were served during 2006–07. The program or unit includes 3 full-time and 3 part-time staff members. Counselors, graduate assistants/students, strategy tutors, and trained peer tutors are provided through the program or unit. Counselors are provided collaboratively through on-campus or off-campus services.

Subject-Area Tutoring Tutoring is offered one-on-one and in small groups for some subjects. Tutoring is provided through the program or unit via graduate assistants/students and trained peer tutors.

Enrichment Enrichment programs are available through the program or unit for learning strategies, self-advocacy, study skills, test taking, and time management. Program for written composition skills is provided collaboratively through on-campus or off-campus services.

Application For admittance to the program or unit, students are required to provide a psychoeducational report (3 years old or less). It is recommended that students provide documentation of high school services. Upon acceptance, documentation of need for services should be sent only to the LD program or unit. *Application deadline (institutional):* 1/15. *Application deadline (LD program):* Rolling/continuous for fall and rolling/continuous for spring.

Written Policies Written policy regarding general/basic LD accommodations is available on the program Web site. Written policy regarding reduced course loads is available through the program or unit directly.

Washburn University
Student Services

1700 SW College Avenue
Topeka, KS 66621
http://www.washburn.edu/studentlife/stuservices/
Contact: Mrs. Jeannene D. Kessler, Director of Student Services. Phone: 785-670-1629. E-mail: student-services@washburn.edu.

Student Services Approximately 25 registered undergraduate students were served during 2006–07.

Assistive Technology Assistive technology is located in the university library and includes screen reader, voice recognition software.

Application For admittance to the program or unit, students are required to provide a psychoeducational report. Upon acceptance, documentation of need for services should be sent only to the LD program or unit. *Application deadline (institutional):* 8/1.

Written Policies Written policy regarding general/basic LD accommodations is available on the program Web site. Written policy regarding general/basic LD accommodations is outlined in the school's catalog/handbook. Written policies regarding general/basic LD accommodations and substitutions and waivers of graduation requirements are available through the program or unit directly.

Washington & Jefferson College
Office of Academic Advising/Academic Affairs

60 South Lincoln Street
Washington, PA 15301
http://www.washjeff.edu/disability
Contact: Catherine Sherman, Director, Academic Advising. Phone: 724-223-6008. Fax: 724-250-3463. E-mail: csherman@washjeff.edu.

Office of Academic Advising/Academic Affairs Approximately 20 registered undergraduate students were served during 2006–07. The program or unit includes 1 full-time staff member. Academic advisers, skill tutors, and trained peer tutors are provided through the program or unit. Academic advisers are provided collaboratively through on-campus or off-campus services.

Orientation The program or unit offers an optional orientation for new students individually by special arrangement.

Unique Aids and Services Aids, services, or accommodations include weekly meetings with faculty.

Subject-Area Tutoring Tutoring is offered one-on-one and in small groups for some subjects. Tutoring is provided through the program or unit via trained peer tutors. Tutoring is also provided collaboratively through on-campus or off-campus services via trained peer tutors.

Basic Skills Remediation Remediation is offered one-on-one for learning strategies, math, spoken language, study skills, time management, and written language. Remediation is provided through the program or unit via trained peer tutors and other.

Enrichment Enrichment programs are available through the program or unit for learning strategies, reading, self-advocacy, stress management, study skills, test taking, and time management. Programs for career planning, math, oral communication skills, and written composition skills are provided collaboratively through on-campus or off-campus services.

Application For admittance to the program or unit, students are required to apply to the program directly and provide a psychoeducational report (3 years old or less). It is recommended that students provide documentation of high school services. Upon acceptance, documentation of need for services should be sent to both admissions and the LD program or unit. *Application deadline (institutional):* 3/1. *Application deadline (LD program):* Rolling/continuous for fall and rolling/continuous for spring.

Written Policies Written policies regarding course substitutions, general/basic LD accommodations, and substitutions and waivers of graduation requirements are available through the program or unit directly.

Washington and Lee University

Lexington, VA 24450-0303

http://www.wlu.edu/

Contact: Dr. Janet Ikeda, Associate Dean of the College. Phone: 540-458-8746. Fax: 540-458-8945. E-mail: ikedaj@wlu.edu.

Approximately 60 registered undergraduate students were served during 2006–07. The program or unit includes 2 part-time staff members. Academic advisers, counselors, and other are provided collaboratively through on-campus or off-campus services.

Subject-Area Tutoring Tutoring is offered one-on-one for most subjects. Tutoring is provided collaboratively through on-campus or off-campus services via trained peer tutors and other.

Enrichment Programs for career planning, college survival skills, health and nutrition, learning strategies, medication management, practical computer skills, stress management, study skills, time management, and written composition skills are provided collaboratively through on-campus or off-campus services.

Application For admittance to the program or unit, students are required to apply to the program directly, provide a psychoeducational report (2 years old or less), and provide a meeting with Associate Dean. It is recommended that students provide documentation of high school services. Upon application, materials documenting need for services should be sent only to the LD program or unit. Upon acceptance, documentation of need for services should be sent only to the LD program or unit. *Application deadline (institutional):* 1/15. *Application deadline (LD program):* Rolling/continuous for fall and rolling/continuous for spring.

Written Policies Written policy regarding general/basic LD accommodations is available on the program Web site.

Watkins College of Art and Design
Office of Student Life

2298 MetroCenter Boulevard

Nashville, TN 37228

http://www.watkins.edu/

Contact: Melissa Winter Means, Director of Student Life. Phone: 615-383-4848 Ext. 7406. Fax: 615-383-4849. E-mail: mmeans@watkins.edu.

Office of Student Life Approximately 4 registered undergraduate students were served during 2006–07. The program or unit includes 1 full-time staff member. Academic advisers and trained peer tutors are provided through the program or unit. Trained peer tutors are provided collaboratively through on-campus or off-campus services.

Unique Aids and Services Aids, services, or accommodations include advocates.

Subject-Area Tutoring Tutoring is offered one-on-one for some subjects. Tutoring is provided through the program or unit via trained peer tutors. Tutoring is also provided collaboratively through on-campus or off-campus services via trained peer tutors.

Basic Skills Remediation Remediation is available for auditory processing, learning strategies, spelling, and written language. Remediation is provided through the program or unit via trained peer tutors. Remediation is also provided collaboratively through on-campus or off-campus services via trained peer tutors.

Enrichment Enrichment programs are available through the program or unit for written composition skills. Program for written composition skills is provided collaboratively through on-campus or off-campus services.

Application It is recommended that students apply to the program directly, provide a psychoeducational report, and provide documentation from doctor visit/diagnosis. Upon application, materials documenting need for services should be sent to both admissions and the LD program or unit. Upon acceptance, documentation of need for services should be sent only to the LD program or unit. *Application deadline (institutional):* 6/1. *Application deadline (LD program):* Rolling/continuous for fall and rolling/continuous for spring.

Written Policies Written policy regarding general/basic LD accommodations is outlined in the school's catalog/handbook. Written policy regarding general/basic LD accommodations is available through the program or unit directly.

Wayne State College
Disability Services

1111 Main Street

Wayne, NE 68787

http://www.wsc.edu/

Contact: Ms. Jamie L. Mackling, Counselor. Phone: 402-375-7321. Fax: 402-375-7058. E-mail: jamackl1@wsc.edu.

Disability Services Approximately 25 registered undergraduate students were served during 2006–07. The program or unit includes 1 full-time staff member. Counselors and graduate assistants/students are provided through the program or unit. Academic advisers, counselors, diagnostic specialists, LD specialists, regular education teachers, and trained peer tutors are provided collaboratively through on-campus or off-campus services.

Unique Aids and Services Aids, services, or accommodations include advocates and priority registration.

Assistive Technology Assistive technology is located in the DSS office and includes learning support software.

Subject-Area Tutoring Tutoring is offered one-on-one, in small groups, and in class-size groups for most subjects. Tutoring is provided collaboratively through on-campus or off-campus services via graduate assistants/students and trained peer tutors.

Diagnostic Testing Testing for auditory processing, intelligence, math, neuropsychological, personality, reading, spelling, spoken language, and written language is provided collaboratively through on-campus or off-campus services.

Enrichment Enrichment programs are available through the program or unit for self-advocacy. Programs for career planning, college survival skills, health and nutrition, learning strategies, stress management, study skills, test taking, time management, vocabulary development, and written composition skills are provided collaboratively through on-campus or off-campus services. Credit is offered for college survival skills, health and nutrition, and stress management.

Student Organization Able Capable and Equal (ACE).

Application For admittance to the program or unit, students are required to provide a psychoeducational report (3 years old or less). It is recommended that students provide documentation of high school services. Upon application, materials documenting need for services should be sent only to the LD program or unit. Upon acceptance, documentation of need for services should be sent only to the LD program or unit. *Application deadline (institutional):* Continuous. *Application deadline (LD program):* Rolling/continuous for fall and rolling/continuous for spring.

Written Policies Written policy regarding general/basic LD accommodations is available on the program Web site. Written policy regarding general/basic LD accommodations is outlined in the school's catalog/handbook.

Wayne State University
Educational Accessibility Services, Academic Success Center

656 West Kirby Street

Detroit, MI 48202

http://www.eas.wayne.edu

Contact: Ms. Jane DePriester-Morandini, Interim Director of Educational Accessibility Services. Phone: 313-577-1851. Fax: 313-577-4898. E-mail: jdeprie@wayne.edu.

Educational Accessibility Services, Academic Success Center Approximately 70 registered undergraduate students were served during 2006–07. The program or unit includes 3 full-time and 6 part-time staff members. Counselors, diagnostic specialists, graduate assistants/students, professional tutors, remediation/learning specialists, skill tutors, and strategy tutors are provided through the program or unit. Academic advisers, coaches, LD specialists, regular education teachers, special education teachers, teacher trainees, trained peer tutors, and other are provided collaboratively through on-campus or off-campus services.

Unique Aids and Services Aids, services, or accommodations include advocates, faculty training, priority registration, alternative testing.

Assistive Technology Assistive technology is located in the DSS office, libraries, Extension Center and includes digital textbooks/e-text.

Subject-Area Tutoring Tutoring is offered one-on-one and in small groups for most subjects. Tutoring is provided through the program or unit via LD specialists. Tutoring is also provided collaboratively through on-campus or off-campus services via computer-based instruction, graduate assistants/students, professional tutors, and trained peer tutors.

Diagnostic Testing Testing is provided through the program or unit for learning strategies, learning styles, reading, spoken language, study skills, and written language. Testing for auditory processing, handwriting, intelligence, learning strategies, learning styles, math, motor skills, neuropsychological, personality, reading, social skills, spelling, study skills, and visual processing is provided collaboratively through on-campus or off-campus services.

Basic Skills Remediation Remediation is offered one-on-one and in small groups for auditory processing, computer skills, learning strategies, math, reading, spelling, study skills, time management, visual processing, and written language. Remediation is provided through the program or unit via computer-based instruction, graduate assistants/students, LD specialists, professional tutors, regular education teachers, special education teachers, teacher trainees, and trained peer tutors.

Enrichment Enrichment programs are available through the program or unit for career planning, health and nutrition, learning strategies, self-advocacy, stress management, study skills, test taking, time management, vocabulary development, and written composition skills. Programs for career planning, college survival skills, learning strategies, math, oral communication skills, practical computer skills, reading, stress management, study skills, test taking, time management, vocabulary development, and written composition skills are provided collaboratively through on-campus or off-campus services.

Student Organization Abled Student Organization consists of 10 members.

Fees *Diagnostic Testing* fee is applicable.

Application For admittance to the program or unit, students are required to apply to the program directly, provide a psychoeducational report (3 years old or less), and provide a medical report. It is recommended that students provide documentation of high school services. Upon application, materials documenting need for services should be sent only to the LD program or unit. Upon acceptance, documentation of need for services should be sent only to the LD program or unit. *Application deadline (institutional): 8/1. Application deadline (LD program):* Rolling/continuous for fall and rolling/continuous for spring.

Written Policies Written policy regarding general/basic LD accommodations is available on the program Web site. Written policies regarding general/basic LD accommodations, reduced course loads, substitutions and waivers of admissions requirements, and substitutions and waivers of graduation requirements are available through the program or unit directly.

Wellesley College
Disability Services

106 Central Street

Wellesley, MA 02481

http://www.wellesley.edu/DisabilityServices/DShome.html

Contact: Jim Wice, Director, Disability Services. Phone: 781-283-2434. E-mail: jwice@wellesley.edu. Head of LD Program: Jim Wice. Phone: 781-283-1000. Fax: 781-283-3678.

Disability Services Approximately 80 registered undergraduate students were served during 2006–07.

Assistive Technology Assistive technology is located in a special lab and includes digital textbooks/e-text, learning support software, and books on tape. Technology training is provided to incoming students.

Subject-Area Tutoring Tutoring is offered one-on-one for most subjects. Tutoring is provided collaboratively through on-campus or off-campus services via other.

Diagnostic Testing Testing for auditory processing, handwriting, intelligence, learning strategies, learning styles, math, motor skills, neuropsychological, personality, reading, social skills, spelling, spoken language, study skills, visual processing, and written language is provided collaboratively through on-campus or off-campus services.

Enrichment Programs for learning strategies, oral communication skills, time management, and written composition skills are provided collaboratively through on-campus or off-campus services.

Fees *Diagnostic Testing* fee is applicable.

Application For admittance to the program or unit, students are required to provide a psychoeducational report (3 years old or less). It is recommended that students provide documentation of high school services. Upon acceptance, documentation of need for services should be sent only to the LD program or unit. *Application deadline (institutional): 1/15. Application deadline (LD program):* Rolling/continuous for fall and rolling/continuous for spring.

Written Policies Written policies regarding course substitutions, general/basic LD accommodations, reduced course loads, and substitutions and waivers of graduation requirements are available on the program Web site. Written policies regarding course substitutions, general/basic LD accommodations, and substitutions and waivers of graduation requirements are outlined in the school's catalog/handbook. Written policies regarding course substitutions, general/basic LD accommodations, reduced course loads, and substitutions and waivers of graduation requirements are available through the program or unit directly.

Wells College
Disabilities Specialist Office

170 Main Street

Aurora, NY 13026

http://www.wells.edu/

Contact: Diane Kay Koester, Associate Dean for Academic and Learning Resources. Phone: 315-364-3241. Fax: 315-364-3383. E-mail: dkoester@wells.edu. Head of LD Program: Kathleen DeSanctis, Disabilities Specialist. Phone: 315-364-3432. Fax: 315-364-3423. E-mail: kdesanctis@wells.edu.

Disabilities Specialist Office Approximately 15 registered undergraduate students were served during 2006–07. The program or unit includes 1 part-time staff member. Academic advisers, coaches, counselors, regular education teachers, strategy tutors, and trained peer tutors are provided collaboratively through on-campus or off-campus services.

Assistive Technology Assistive technology is located in campus labs and includes learning support software.

Subject-Area Tutoring Tutoring is offered one-on-one and in small groups for some subjects. Tutoring is provided collaboratively through on-campus or off-campus services via trained peer tutors.

Enrichment Programs for career planning, learning strategies, math, study skills, test taking, time management, and written composition skills are provided collaboratively through on-campus or off-campus services. Credit is offered for college survival skills and health and nutrition.

Application For admittance to the program or unit, students are required to apply to the program directly, provide a psychoeducational report, and provide documentation of high school services. Upon acceptance, documentation of need for services should be sent only to the LD program or unit. *Application deadline (institutional): 3/1. Application deadline (LD program):* Rolling/continuous for fall and rolling/continuous for spring.

Written Policies Written policy regarding general/basic LD accommodations is outlined in the school's catalog/handbook.

Wesley College
Disability Support Services

120 North State Street

Dover, DE 19901-3875

http://www.wesley.edu/

Contact: Ms. Christine M. McDermott, Assistant Director, Student Support Services. Phone: 302-736-2491. Fax: 302-736-2301. E-mail: mcdermch@wesley.edu.

Wesley College (continued)

Disability Support Services Approximately 50 registered undergraduate students were served during 2006–07. The program or unit includes 1 full-time staff member. LD specialists and trained peer tutors are provided through the program or unit.

Assistive Technology Assistive technology includes books on tape.

Subject-Area Tutoring Tutoring is offered one-on-one and in small groups for most subjects. Tutoring is provided through the program or unit via LD specialists and trained peer tutors.

Basic Skills Remediation Remediation is offered in class-size groups for math, reading, and written language. Remediation is provided through the program or unit via regular education teachers. Remediation is also provided collaboratively through on-campus or off-campus services via regular education teachers.

Enrichment Enrichment programs are available through the program or unit for career planning, college survival skills, learning strategies, self-advocacy, study skills, test taking, and time management. Program for career planning is provided collaboratively through on-campus or off-campus services.

Application For admittance to the program or unit, students are required to provide a psychoeducational report (3 years old or less). Upon acceptance, documentation of need for services should be sent only to the LD program or unit. *Application deadline (institutional):* Continuous. *Application deadline (LD program):* Rolling/continuous for fall and rolling/continuous for spring.

Written Policies Written policy regarding general/basic LD accommodations is outlined in the school's catalog/handbook. Written policy regarding general/basic LD accommodations is available through the program or unit directly.

West Chester University of Pennsylvania
Office of Services for Students with Disabilities (OSSD)

University Avenue and High Street

West Chester, PA 19383

http://www.wcupa.edu/

Contact: Dr. Martin Patwell, Director, OSSD. Phone: 610-436-3217. E-mail: mpatwell@wcupa.edu.

Office of Services for Students with Disabilities (OSSD) Approximately 350 registered undergraduate students were served during 2006–07. The program or unit includes 3 full-time and 10 part-time staff members. Coaches, diagnostic specialists, graduate assistants/students, LD specialists, professional tutors, remediation/learning specialists, skill tutors, and strategy tutors are provided through the program or unit. Academic advisers, counselors, and regular education teachers are provided collaboratively through on-campus or off-campus services.

Orientation The program or unit offers an optional orientation for new students before classes begin.

Unique Aids and Services Aids, services, or accommodations include career counseling, faculty training, personal coach, priority registration, and support groups.

Assistive Technology Assistive technology is located in the DSS office, the library and includes digital textbooks/e-text and learning support software. Technology training is provided to incoming students.

Subject-Area Tutoring Tutoring is offered one-on-one and in small groups for some subjects. Tutoring is provided through the program or unit via graduate assistants/students, LD specialists, and professional tutors. Tutoring is also provided collaboratively through on-campus or off-campus services via trained peer tutors.

Basic Skills Remediation Remediation is offered one-on-one and in class-size groups for computer skills, learning strategies, math, reading, study skills, time management, and written language. Remediation is provided through the program or unit via graduate assistants/students and LD specialists. Remediation is also provided collaboratively through on-campus or off-campus services via regular education teachers.

Enrichment Enrichment programs are available through the program or unit for learning strategies, math, reading, self-advocacy, study skills, test taking, time management, and written composition skills. Programs for college survival skills, health and nutrition, oral communication skills, stress management, and written composition skills are provided collaboratively through on-campus or off-campus services. Credit is offered for college survival skills and reading.

Application For admittance to the program or unit, students are required to provide a psychoeducational report. Upon acceptance, documentation of need for services should be sent only to the LD program or unit. *Application deadline (institutional):* Continuous. *Application deadline (LD program):* Rolling/continuous for fall and rolling/continuous for spring.

Written Policies Written policy regarding general/basic LD accommodations is available on the program Web site. Written policy regarding general/basic LD accommodations is outlined in the school's catalog/handbook. Written policies regarding course substitutions and substitutions and waivers of admissions requirements are available through the program or unit directly.

Western Connecticut State University
Office of Disability Services

181 White Street

Danbury, CT 06810-6885

http://www.wcsu.edu/

Contact: Prof. Jack Sikora, Coordinator Disability Services. Phone: 203-837-8946. Fax: 203-837-8848.

Office of Disability Services Approximately 100 registered undergraduate students were served during 2006–07. The program or unit includes 1 full-time and 1 part-time staff member. Academic advisers, LD specialists, professional tutors, and skill tutors are provided through the program or unit. Academic advisers and counselors are provided collaboratively through on-campus or off-campus services.

Unique Aids and Services Aids, services, or accommodations include advocates, career counseling, faculty training, priority registration, and support groups.

Assistive Technology Assistive technology is located in campus labs, the DSS office, the library and includes learning support software and scanning.

Subject-Area Tutoring Tutoring is offered one-on-one for most subjects. Tutoring is provided through the program or unit via LD specialists and professional tutors. Tutoring is also provided collaboratively through on-campus or off-campus services via professional tutors.

Basic Skills Remediation Remediation is offered in class-size groups for learning strategies, math, reading, study skills, time management, and written language. Remediation is provided collaboratively through on-campus or off-campus services via computer-based instruction and regular education teachers.

Enrichment Enrichment programs are available through the program or unit for college survival skills, learning strategies, self-advocacy, study skills, time management, and written composition skills. Programs for career planning, college survival skills, health and nutrition, math, oral communication skills, stress management, vocabulary development, and written composition skills are provided collaboratively through on-campus or off-campus services.

Student Organization Student Success Group consists of 20 members.

Application For admittance to the program or unit, students are required to apply to the program directly, provide a psychoeducational report, provide documentation of high school services, and provide results of assessments. Upon acceptance, documentation of need for services should be sent only to the LD program or unit. *Application deadline (institutional): 5/1. Application deadline (LD program):* Rolling/continuous for fall and rolling/continuous for spring.

Written Policies Written policy regarding general/basic LD accommodations is outlined in the school's catalog/handbook. Written policy regarding general/basic LD accommodations is available through the program or unit directly.

Western New England College
Student Disability Services

1215 Wilbraham Road

Springfield, MA 01119

http://www1.wnec.edu/academicaffairs/
index.cfm?selection=doc.2987

Contact: Dr. Bonni Alpert, Director of Student Disability Services. Phone: 413-782-1257. Fax: 413-782-1746. E-mail: balpert@wnec.edu.

Student Disability Services Approximately 150 registered undergraduate students were served during 2006–07. The program or unit includes 2 full-time staff members. LD specialists, skill tutors, and strategy tutors are provided through the program or unit. Academic advisers, counselors, professional tutors, and trained peer tutors are provided collaboratively through on-campus or off-campus services.

Orientation The program or unit offers an optional orientation for new students individually by special arrangement and during new student orientation.

Summer Program an optional summer program prior to entering the school.

Unique Aids and Services Aids, services, or accommodations include advocates, career counseling, faculty training, personal coach, priority registration, tutoring.

Assistive Technology Assistive technology is located in the DSS office, the library and includes digital textbooks/e-text, learning support software, and scanning. Technology training is provided to incoming students.

Subject-Area Tutoring Tutoring is offered one-on-one for most subjects. Tutoring is provided through the program or unit via graduate assistants/students and LD specialists. Tutoring is also provided collaboratively through on-campus or off-campus services via computer-based instruction, professional tutors, trained peer tutors, and other.

Basic Skills Remediation Remediation is offered in class-size groups for math, reading, and written language. Remediation is provided through the program or unit via graduate assistants/students. Remediation is also provided collaboratively through on-campus or off-campus services via computer-based instruction, professional tutors, regular education teachers, trained peer tutors, and other.

Enrichment Programs for career planning, college survival skills, health and nutrition, learning strategies, math, medication management, oral communication skills, practical computer skills, reading, self-advocacy, stress management, study skills, test taking, time management, vocabulary development, written composition skills, and other are provided collaboratively through on-campus or off-campus services.

Application For admittance to the program or unit, students are required to apply to the program directly, provide a psychoeducational report, and provide medical documentation. It is recommended that students provide documentation of high school services. Upon application, materials documenting need for services should be sent only to the LD program or unit. *Application deadline (institutional):* Continuous. *Application deadline (LD program):* Rolling/continuous for fall and rolling/continuous for spring.

Written Policies Written policy regarding general/basic LD accommodations is outlined in the school's catalog/handbook.

Western Oregon University
Office of Disability Services

345 North Monmouth Avenue

Monmouth, OR 97361-1394

http://www.wou.edu/student/disability/

Contact: Mr. Phillip A. Pownall, Director. Phone: 503-838-8250. Fax: 503-838-8721. E-mail: ods@wou.edu.

Office of Disability Services Approximately 95 registered undergraduate students were served during 2006–07. The program or unit includes 2 full-time staff members. Counselors are provided through the program or unit. Academic advisers, counselors, diagnostic specialists, and trained peer tutors are provided collaboratively through on-campus or off-campus services.

Unique Aids and Services Aids, services, or accommodations include advocates, career counseling, priority registration, limited academic coaching.

Assistive Technology Assistive technology is located in the DSS office and includes digital textbooks/e-text, learning support software, and scanning. Technology training is provided to incoming students.

Western Oregon University (continued)

Subject-Area Tutoring Tutoring is offered one-on-one and in small groups for most subjects. Tutoring is provided collaboratively through on-campus or off-campus services via graduate assistants/students, trained peer tutors, and other.

Diagnostic Testing Testing for auditory processing, intelligence, learning strategies, learning styles, math, neuropsychological, personality, reading, spelling, study skills, visual processing, written language, and other services is provided collaboratively through on-campus or off-campus services.

Fees *Diagnostic Testing* fee is $800.

Application For admittance to the program or unit, students are required to apply to the program directly and provide a psychoeducational report (3 years old or less). It is recommended that students provide documentation of high school services. Upon application, materials documenting need for services should be sent only to the LD program or unit. Upon acceptance, documentation of need for services should be sent only to the LD program or unit. *Application deadline (institutional):* Continuous. *Application deadline (LD program):* Rolling/continuous for fall and rolling/continuous for spring.

Written Policies Written policy regarding general/basic LD accommodations is available on the program Web site. Written policies regarding course substitutions, general/basic LD accommodations, and substitutions and waivers of admissions requirements are available through the program or unit directly.

West Liberty State College
Center for Student Success

PO Box 295
West Liberty, WV 26074
http://www.westliberty.edu/Students/DisabilityServices.asp
Contact: Mrs. Traci Jordan, Developmental Advising Specialist. Phone: 304-336-8216. Fax: 304-336-8398. E-mail: tjordan@westliberty.edu.

Center for Student Success Approximately 15 registered undergraduate students were served during 2006–07. The program or unit includes 1 full-time staff member. Services are provided through the program or unit. Academic advisers, regular education teachers, trained peer tutors, and other are provided collaboratively on-campus or off-campus services.

Assistive Technology Assistive technology is located in the DSS office, a special lab and includes digital textbooks/e-text, learning support software, and scanning.

Subject-Area Tutoring Tutoring is offered one-on-one and in small groups for most subjects. Tutoring is provided collaboratively through on-campus or off-campus services via trained peer tutors.

Diagnostic Testing Testing for auditory processing, intelligence, learning styles, math, motor skills, neuropsychological, personality, reading, social skills, spelling, spoken language, visual processing, written language, and other services is provided collaboratively through on-campus or off-campus services.

Enrichment Programs for career planning, college survival skills, health and nutrition, learning strategies, stress management, study skills, test taking, and time management are provided collaboratively through on-campus or off-campus services.

Application For admittance to the program or unit, students are required to provide a psychoeducational report (5 years old or less) and provide psychological report only if psychoeducational report is not available. It is recommended that students apply to the program directly. Upon application, materials documenting need for services should be sent only to the LD program or unit. Upon acceptance, documentation of need for services should be sent only to the LD program or unit. *Application deadline (LD program):* 8/31 for fall. 1/31 for spring.

Written Policies Written policy regarding general/basic LD accommodations is available through the program or unit directly.

Westminster College
Office of Disability Support Services

319 South Market Street
New Wilmington, PA 16172-0001
http://www.westminster.edu/student/disability_support/
Contact: Mrs. Yvonne (Bonnie) A. Van Bruggen, Director of the Office of Disability Support Services. Phone: 724-946-7192. Fax: 724-946-6140. E-mail: vanbruggenya@westminster.edu.

Office of Disability Support Services Approximately 45 registered undergraduate students were served during 2006–07. The program or unit includes 1 full-time and 1 part-time staff member. Counselors, LD specialists, and special education teachers are provided through the program or unit. Academic advisers, counselors, diagnostic specialists, regular education teachers, and trained peer tutors are provided collaboratively through on-campus or off-campus services.

Unique Aids and Services Aids, services, or accommodations include career counseling, personal coach.

Assistive Technology Assistive technology is located in campus labs, the Learning Center and includes scanning and Kurzweil, coordination with Recording for the Blind and Dyslexic. Technology training is provided to incoming students.

Subject-Area Tutoring Tutoring is offered one-on-one and in small groups for most subjects. Tutoring is provided through the program or unit via LD specialists and trained peer tutors. Tutoring is also provided collaboratively through on-campus or off-campus services via computer-based instruction, graduate assistants/students, trained peer tutors, and other.

Basic Skills Remediation Remediation is offered one-on-one and in class-size groups for learning strategies, reading, study skills, time management, written language, and others. Remediation is provided collaboratively through on-campus or off-campus services via trained peer tutors and other.

Enrichment Enrichment programs are available through the program or unit for self-advocacy, study skills, and time management. Programs for career planning, college survival skills, health and nutrition, learning strategies, math, medication management, oral communication skills, practical computer skills, reading, stress management, study skills, test taking, time management, written composition skills, and other are provided collaboratively through on-campus or off-campus services.

Application For admittance to the program or unit, students are required to apply to the program directly and provide a psychoeducational report (3 years old or less). It is recommended that students

provide documentation of high school services and provide documentation from Office of Vocational Rehabilitation. Upon application, materials documenting need for services should be sent only to the LD program or unit. Upon acceptance, documentation of need for services should be sent only to the LD program or unit. *Application deadline (institutional):* 5/1. *Application deadline (LD program):* Rolling/continuous for fall and rolling/continuous for spring.
Written Policies Written policy regarding general/basic LD accommodations is available on the program Web site. Written policy regarding general/basic LD accommodations is outlined in the school's catalog/handbook. Written policies regarding course substitutions, general/basic LD accommodations, reduced course loads, and substitutions and waivers of graduation requirements are available through the program or unit directly.

Westminster College
Disability Services Program

1840 South 1300 East
Salt Lake City, UT 84105-3697
http://www.westminstercollege.edu/start_center/
Contact: Ms. Ginny DeWitt, Associate Director of START Center and Coordinator of DS Program. Phone: 801-832-2280. Fax: 801-832-3101. E-mail: gdewitt@westminstercollege.edu.

Disability Services Program Approximately 55 registered undergraduate students were served during 2006–07. The program or unit includes 1 full-time staff member. Diagnostic specialists are provided through the program or unit. Academic advisers, counselors, diagnostic specialists, and regular education teachers are provided collaboratively through on-campus or off-campus services.
Unique Aids and Services Aids, services, or accommodations include priority registration.
Assistive Technology Assistive technology is located in the library and includes learning support software and scanning.
Subject-Area Tutoring Tutoring is offered one-on-one for most subjects. Tutoring is provided collaboratively through on-campus or off-campus services via trained peer tutors.
Basic Skills Remediation Remediation is offered one-on-one for computer skills, learning strategies, math, study skills, time management, and written language. Remediation is provided through the program or unit. Remediation is also provided collaboratively through on-campus or off-campus services via trained peer tutors and other.
Enrichment Programs for career planning, college survival skills, learning strategies, practical computer skills, self-advocacy, stress management, study skills, test taking, time management, and written composition skills are provided collaboratively through on-campus or off-campus services. Credit is offered for college survival skills and practical computer skills.
Application For admittance to the program or unit, students are required to provide a psychoeducational report (4 years old or less). It is recommended that students provide documentation of high school services. Upon acceptance, documentation of need for services should be sent only to the LD program or unit. *Application deadline (institutional):* Continuous. *Application deadline (LD program):* Rolling/continuous for fall and rolling/continuous for spring.

Written Policies Written policy regarding general/basic LD accommodations is available on the program Web site. Written policies regarding general/basic LD accommodations and reduced course loads are available through the program or unit directly.

West Texas A&M University
Student Disability Services

2501 4th Avenue
Canyon, TX 79016-0001
http://www.wtamu.edu/
Contact: Montana Hisel, Coordinator of Student Disability Services. Phone: 806-651-2335. Fax: 806-651-2362. E-mail: mhisel@mail.wtamu.edu.

Student Disability Services Approximately 105 registered undergraduate students were served during 2006–07. The program or unit includes 3 full-time staff members and 1 part-time staff member. Academic advisers, counselors, and strategy tutors are provided through the program or unit. Academic advisers, counselors, professional tutors, regular education teachers, remediation/learning specialists, skill tutors, special education teachers, teacher trainees, and trained peer tutors are provided collaboratively through on-campus or off-campus services.
Unique Aids and Services Aids, services, or accommodations include advocates and career counseling.
Assistive Technology Assistive technology is located in campus labs, the DSS office and includes learning support software and scanning. Technology training is provided to incoming students.
Subject-Area Tutoring Tutoring is offered one-on-one and in small groups for most subjects. Tutoring is provided collaboratively through on-campus or off-campus services via graduate assistants/students, professional tutors, and trained peer tutors.
Diagnostic Testing Testing for auditory processing, intelligence, learning strategies, learning styles, math, motor skills, neuropsychological, reading, spelling, spoken language, visual processing, and written language is provided collaboratively through on-campus or off-campus services.
Basic Skills Remediation Remediation is offered in class-size groups for auditory processing, learning strategies, math, reading, spoken language, study skills, time management, and written language. Remediation is provided collaboratively through on-campus or off-campus services via professional tutors, regular education teachers, and trained peer tutors.
Fees *Diagnostic Testing* fee is $0 to $300.
Application For admittance to the program or unit, students are required to provide a psychoeducational report (5 years old or less). It is recommended that students provide documentation of high school services. Upon application, materials documenting need for services should be sent only to admissions with institutional application materials. Upon acceptance, documentation of need for services should be sent only to the LD program or unit. *Application deadline (institutional):* Continuous. *Application deadline (LD program):* Rolling/continuous for fall and rolling/continuous for spring.
Written Policies Written policies regarding general/basic LD accommodations and substitutions and waivers of admissions requirements are available on the program Web site. Written policies regarding course substitutions, general/basic LD accommodations,

West Texas A&M University (continued)
grade forgiveness, reduced course loads, substitutions and waivers of admissions requirements, and substitutions and waivers of graduation requirements are outlined in the school's catalog/handbook.

West Virginia State University
Disability Services Office

Post Office Box 1000

Institute, WV 25112-1000

http://www.wvstateu.edu/collegiate_support_counseling/default.aspx

Contact: Ms. Carla Blankenbuehler, Disability Services Counselor. Phone: 304-766-3083. Fax: 304-766-4168. E-mail: blankenc@wvstateu.edu.

Disability Services Office Approximately 40 registered undergraduate students were served during 2006–07. The program or unit includes 1 full-time staff member.

Subject-Area Tutoring Tutoring is offered one-on-one and in small groups for most subjects. Tutoring is provided collaboratively through on-campus or off-campus services via graduate assistants/students.

Diagnostic Testing Testing is provided through the program or unit for intelligence and other services.

Application It is recommended that students provide a psychoeducational report (5 years old or less) and provide documentation of high school services. Upon application, materials documenting need for services should be sent only to the LD program or unit. Upon acceptance, documentation of need for services should be sent only to the LD program or unit. *Application deadline (institutional):* 8/11. *Application deadline (LD program):* Rolling/continuous for fall and rolling/continuous for spring.

Written Policies Written policy regarding general/basic LD accommodations is available on the program Web site. Written policy regarding general/basic LD accommodations is available through the program or unit directly.

Wheaton College

501 East College Avenue

Wheaton, IL 60187-5593

http://www.wheaton.edu/

Contact: Paul Johnson, Registrar. Phone: 630-752-5246. Fax: 630-752-5245. E-mail: paul.e.johnson@wheaton.edu.

Approximately 19 registered undergraduate students were served during 2006–07. The program or unit includes 1 part-time staff member. Academic advisers, coaches, counselors, diagnostic specialists, and trained peer tutors are provided collaboratively through on-campus or off-campus services.

Unique Aids and Services Aids, services, or accommodations include personal coach and support groups.

Assistive Technology Assistive technology is located in a special lab and includes digital textbooks/e-text and scanning.

Subject-Area Tutoring Tutoring is offered one-on-one for some subjects. Tutoring is provided collaboratively through on-campus or off-campus services via trained peer tutors and other.

Diagnostic Testing Testing for auditory processing, intelligence, learning strategies, learning styles, neuropsychological, personality, reading, social skills, study skills, visual processing, and written language is provided collaboratively through on-campus or off-campus services.

Enrichment Programs for career planning, health and nutrition, learning strategies, medication management, self-advocacy, stress management, study skills, test taking, time management, and written composition skills are provided collaboratively through on-campus or off-campus services.

Application For admittance to the program or unit, students are required to apply to the program directly and provide a psychoeducational report (3 years old or less). It is recommended that students provide documentation of high school services. Upon acceptance, documentation of need for services should be sent to both admissions and the LD program or unit. *Application deadline (institutional):* 1/10. *Application deadline (LD program):* Rolling/continuous for fall and rolling/continuous for spring.

Written Policies Written policy regarding general/basic LD accommodations is available on the program Web site. Written policy regarding general/basic LD accommodations is outlined in the school's catalog/handbook.

Whitman College
Academic Resources

345 Boyer Avenue

Walla Walla, WA 99362-2083

http://www.whitman.edu/academic_resources/disability_services

Contact: Ms. Clare Carson, Associate Dean of Students. Phone: 509-527-5213. Fax: 509-522-4415. E-mail: arc@whitman.edu.

Academic Resources Approximately 95 registered undergraduate students were served during 2006–07. The program or unit includes 2 full-time staff members and 1 part-time staff member. Academic advisers, skill tutors, strategy tutors, and trained peer tutors are provided through the program or unit. Academic advisers, coaches, counselors, diagnostic specialists, LD specialists, regular education teachers, and trained peer tutors are provided collaboratively through on-campus or off-campus services.

Unique Aids and Services Aids, services, or accommodations include career counseling, faculty training, support groups, notetakers, peer tutors.

Assistive Technology Assistive technology is located in the DSS office, a special lab and includes digital textbooks/e-text, learning support software, scanning, and books on tape and CD, CCTV. Technology training is provided to incoming students.

Subject-Area Tutoring Tutoring is offered one-on-one and in small groups for all subjects. Tutoring is provided through the program or unit via trained peer tutors. Tutoring is also provided collaboratively through on-campus or off-campus services via trained peer tutors.

Diagnostic Testing Testing is provided through the program or unit for learning styles. Testing for auditory processing, math, neuropsychological, reading, spoken language, visual processing, and written language is provided collaboratively through on-campus or off-campus services.

Basic Skills Remediation Remediation is offered one-on-one and in small groups for learning strategies, reading, study skills, time management, and written language. Remediation is provided through the program or unit via professional tutors and trained peer tutors.

Enrichment Enrichment programs are available through the program or unit for college survival skills, learning strategies, reading, stress management, study skills, test taking, time management, and written composition skills. Program for career planning is provided collaboratively through on-campus or off-campus services.

Student Organization Learning Styles Coalition consists of 22 members.

Application For admittance to the program or unit, students are required to provide a psychoeducational report (3 years old or less). It is recommended that students provide documentation of high school services. Upon acceptance, documentation of need for services should be sent only to the LD program or unit. *Application deadline (institutional):* 1/15. *Application deadline (LD program):* Rolling/continuous for fall and rolling/continuous for spring.

Written Policies Written policy regarding general/basic LD accommodations is available on the program Web site. Written policy regarding general/basic LD accommodations is available through the program or unit directly.

Wichita State University
Office of Disability Services

1845 North Fairmount
Wichita, KS 67260
http://webs.wichita.edu/disserv

Contact: Mr. Grady L. Landrum, Director. Phone: 316-978-6970. Fax: 316-978-3114. E-mail: grady.landrum@wichita.edu.

Office of Disability Services Approximately 60 registered undergraduate students were served during 2006–07. The program or unit includes 4 full-time staff members. Academic advisers, counselors, graduate assistants/students, and skill tutors are provided collaboratively through on-campus or off-campus services.

Unique Aids and Services Aids, services, or accommodations include career counseling.

Assistive Technology Assistive technology is located in the DSS office and includes digital textbooks/e-text and learning support software. Technology training is provided to incoming students.

Diagnostic Testing Testing for auditory processing, intelligence, learning strategies, learning styles, math, neuropsychological, personality, reading, visual processing, and written language is provided collaboratively through on-campus or off-campus services.

Enrichment Programs for career planning, college survival skills, learning strategies, practical computer skills, reading, self-advocacy, stress management, study skills, test taking, time management, vocabulary development, and written composition skills are provided collaboratively through on-campus or off-campus services. Credit is offered for college survival skills and practical computer skills.

Student Organization Disability Support Services Student Organization.

Fees *Diagnostic Testing* fee is $250.

Application For admittance to the program or unit, students are required to provide a psychoeducational report (5 years old or less). It is recommended that students provide documentation of high school services and provide psychoeducational report/tests administered by trained psychologist. Upon acceptance, documentation of need for services should be sent only to the LD program or unit. *Application deadline (institutional):* Continuous. *Application deadline (LD program):* 7/30 for fall. 1/15 for spring.

Written Policies Written policy regarding general/basic LD accommodations is available on the program Web site. Written policy regarding general/basic LD accommodations is outlined in the school's catalog/handbook. Written policy regarding general/basic LD accommodations is available through the program or unit directly.

Widener University
Disabilities Services

One University Place
Chester, PA 19013-5792

http://www.widener.edu/disabilitiesserv/

Contact: Mrs. Susan Cortese, Secretary, Academic Support Services. Phone: 610-499-1266. Fax: 610-499-1192. E-mail: smcortese@mail.widener.edu. Head of LD Program: Dr. Cynthia Burch Simonds, Director of Disabilities Services. Phone: 610-499-4179. Fax: 610-499-1192. E-mail: csimonds@mail.widener.edu.

Disabilities Services Approximately 220 registered undergraduate students were served during 2006–07. The program or unit includes 2 full-time and 3 part-time staff members. Coaches, counselors, graduate assistants/students, and LD specialists are provided through the program or unit. Counselors, professional tutors, skill tutors, strategy tutors, and trained peer tutors are provided collaboratively through on-campus or off-campus services.

Unique Aids and Services Aids, services, or accommodations include advocates and personal coach.

Subject-Area Tutoring Tutoring is offered one-on-one and in small groups for most subjects. Tutoring is provided collaboratively through on-campus or off-campus services via graduate assistants/students, professional tutors, and trained peer tutors.

Basic Skills Remediation Remediation is offered one-on-one and in small groups for learning strategies, math, reading, study skills, time management, and written language. Remediation is provided collaboratively through on-campus or off-campus services via graduate assistants/students, professional tutors, and regular education teachers.

Application For admittance to the program or unit, students are required to provide a psychoeducational report (3 years old or less) and provide Request for Accommodation form (needed for accommodations; not needed for academic coaching). Upon acceptance, documentation of need for services should be sent only to the LD program or unit. *Application deadline (institutional):* Continuous. *Application deadline (LD program):* Rolling/continuous for fall and rolling/continuous for spring.

Widener University (continued)

Written Policies Written policies regarding course substitutions, general/basic LD accommodations, and reduced course loads are available on the program Web site. Written policy regarding general/basic LD accommodations is outlined in the school's catalog/handbook. Written policies regarding course substitutions, general/basic LD accommodations, and reduced course loads are available through the program or unit directly.

Wilfrid Laurier University
Accessible Learning Centre

75 University Avenue West

Waterloo, ON N2L 3C5

Canada

http://www.mylaurier.ca/accessible

Contact: MaryBeth Phillips, Intake Coordinator. Phone: 519-884-0710 Ext. 3638. Fax: 519-884-6570. E-mail: mphillips@wlu.ca. Head of LD Program: Ms. Gwen A. Page, Manager. Phone: 519-884-0710 Ext. 3783. Fax: 519-884-6570. E-mail: gpage@wlu.ca.

Accessible Learning Centre Approximately 182 registered undergraduate students were served during 2006–07. The program or unit includes 7 full-time and 7 part-time staff members. Graduate assistants/students, LD specialists, professional tutors, skill tutors, strategy tutors, and trained peer tutors are provided through the program or unit. Academic advisers, counselors, and diagnostic specialists are provided collaboratively through on-campus or off-campus services.

Orientation The program or unit offers an optional half-day and full-day (linked with University Head Start Program) orientation for new students during summer prior to enrollment.

Unique Aids and Services Aids, services, or accommodations include career counseling, faculty training, parent workshops, and personal coach.

Assistive Technology Assistive technology is located in campus labs, the DSS office, a special lab and includes digital textbooks/e-text, learning support software, and scanning. Technology training is provided to incoming students.

Subject-Area Tutoring Tutoring is offered one-on-one for most subjects. Tutoring is provided through the program or unit via graduate assistants/students and trained peer tutors.

Basic Skills Remediation Remediation is offered one-on-one and in small groups for learning strategies, reading, social skills, study skills, time management, and written language. Remediation is provided through the program or unit via LD specialists and trained peer tutors.

Enrichment Enrichment programs are available through the program or unit for college survival skills, learning strategies, oral communication skills, practical computer skills, reading, self-advocacy, stress management, study skills, test taking, time management, and written composition skills.

Application For admittance to the program or unit, students are required to apply to the program directly, provide a psychoeducational report, provide documentation of high school services, and provide psychoeducational assessment with recommendation for post secondary environment. Upon acceptance, documentation of need for services should be sent only to the LD program or unit. *Application deadline (institutional):* 5/1. *Application deadline (LD program):* Rolling/continuous for fall and rolling/continuous for spring.

Written Policies Written policies regarding general/basic LD accommodations and reduced course loads are available on the program Web site. Written policies regarding general/basic LD accommodations and reduced course loads are available through the program or unit directly.

Wilkes University
University College Disability Support Services

84 West South Street

Wilkes-Barre, PA 18766-0002

http://www.wilkes.edu/pages/375.asp

Contact: Mr. Thomas James Thomas, Executive Director, University College. Phone: 570-408-4150. Fax: 570-408-4907. E-mail: thomas.thomas@wilkes.edu.

University College Disability Support Services Approximately 30 registered undergraduate students were served during 2006–07. The program or unit includes 2 full-time and 3 part-time staff members. Academic advisers, LD specialists, professional tutors, remediation/learning specialists, skill tutors, and strategy tutors are provided through the program or unit.

Unique Aids and Services Aids, services, or accommodations include advocates, career counseling, personal coach, and priority registration.

Assistive Technology Assistive technology is located in the DSS office and includes digital textbooks/e-text and scanning.

Subject-Area Tutoring Tutoring is offered one-on-one and in small groups for most subjects. Tutoring is provided through the program or unit via LD specialists and professional tutors. Tutoring is also provided collaboratively through on-campus or off-campus services via computer-based instruction, professional tutors, and trained peer tutors.

Diagnostic Testing Testing is provided through the program or unit for learning strategies, learning styles, and study skills. Testing for intelligence, learning styles, math, neuropsychological, personality, reading, social skills, visual processing, and written language is provided collaboratively through on-campus or off-campus services.

Basic Skills Remediation Remediation is offered one-on-one, in small groups, and in class-size groups for learning strategies, math, study skills, time management, and written language. Remediation is provided through the program or unit via LD specialists and professional tutors. Remediation is also provided collaboratively through on-campus or off-campus services via computer-based instruction, professional tutors, regular education teachers, and trained peer tutors.

Enrichment Enrichment programs are available through the program or unit for career planning, college survival skills, learning strategies, self-advocacy, study skills, test taking, and time management. Programs for health and nutrition, math, medication management, oral communication skills, practical computer skills, reading, stress management, vocabulary development, and written composition skills are provided collaboratively through on-campus or off-campus services. Credit is offered for learning strategies, math, oral communication skills, practical computer skills, and written composition skills.

Application For admittance to the program or unit, students are required to provide a psychoeducational report (2 years old or less). It is recommended that students provide documentation of high school services. Upon application, materials documenting need for services should be sent only to the LD program or unit. Upon acceptance, documentation of need for services should be sent only to the LD program or unit. *Application deadline (institutional):* Continuous. *Application deadline (LD program):* Rolling/continuous for fall and rolling/continuous for spring.

Written Policies Written policy regarding general/basic LD accommodations is available on the program Web site. Written policy regarding general/basic LD accommodations is outlined in the school's catalog/handbook. Written policies regarding course substitutions, reduced course loads, and substitutions and waivers of graduation requirements are available through the program or unit directly.

William Jewell College
Disability Services

500 College Hill

Liberty, MO 64068-1843

http://www.jewell.edu/

Contact: Dr. Richard P. Winslow, Vice President for Student Affairs. Phone: 816-415-5963. Fax: 816-415-5031. E-mail: winslowr@william.jewell.edu. Head of LD Program: Dr. Beth Gentry-Epley, Director of Counseling Services. Phone: 816-415-5946. Fax: 816-415-5031. E-mail: gentry-epleyb@william.jewell.edu.

Disability Services Approximately 9 registered undergraduate students were served during 2006–07. The program or unit includes 1 full-time and 1 part-time staff member. Academic advisers, counselors, graduate assistants/students, professional tutors, skill tutors, and trained peer tutors are provided collaboratively through on-campus or off-campus services.

Orientation The program or unit offers an optional orientation for new students individually by special arrangement.

Unique Aids and Services Aids, services, or accommodations include advocates, faculty training, regularly scheduled meetings with faculty/staff.

Subject-Area Tutoring Tutoring is offered one-on-one for most subjects. Tutoring is provided collaboratively through on-campus or off-campus services via graduate assistants/students, professional tutors, and trained peer tutors.

Basic Skills Remediation Remediation is offered one-on-one for learning strategies, study skills, and written language. Remediation is provided collaboratively through on-campus or off-campus services via computer-based instruction, professional tutors, and trained peer tutors.

Enrichment Programs for career planning, self-advocacy, study skills, test taking, time management, and written composition skills are provided collaboratively through on-campus or off-campus services.

Application It is recommended that students apply to the program directly, provide a psychoeducational report (3 years old or less), and provide documentation of high school services. Upon application, materials documenting need for services should be sent only to admissions with institutional application materials. Upon accep-

tance, documentation of need for services should be sent only to the LD program or unit. *Application deadline (institutional):* 8/15. *Application deadline (LD program):* Rolling/continuous for fall and rolling/continuous for spring.

Written Policies Written policy regarding general/basic LD accommodations is available on the program Web site. Written policy regarding general/basic LD accommodations is outlined in the school's catalog/handbook. Written policy regarding general/basic LD accommodations is available through the program or unit directly.

Wilson College
Learning Resource Center

1015 Philadelphia Avenue

Chambersburg, PA 17201-1285

http://www.wilson.edu/wilson/asp/content.asp?id=221

Contact: Accommodations Coordinator. E-mail: lrc@wilson.edu. Head of LD Program: Vickie Locke, Director, Learning Resource Center. Phone: 717-264-4141 Ext. 3349. E-mail: vlocke@wilson.edu.

Learning Resource Center Approximately 18 registered undergraduate students were served during 2006–07. The program or unit includes 1 full-time and 1 part-time staff member. LD specialists, skill tutors, strategy tutors, and trained peer tutors are provided through the program or unit. Academic advisers, counselors, and regular education teachers are provided collaboratively through on-campus or off-campus services.

Unique Aids and Services Aids, services, or accommodations include career counseling, support groups, weekly meetings with faculty, tutoring, note-taking.

Assistive Technology Assistive technology is located in the Learning Resource Center and includes digital textbooks/e-text. Technology training is provided to incoming students.

Subject-Area Tutoring Tutoring is offered one-on-one and in small groups for most subjects. Tutoring is provided through the program or unit via computer-based instruction, LD specialists, and trained peer tutors. Tutoring is also provided collaboratively through on-campus or off-campus services via other.

Basic Skills Remediation Remediation is offered one-on-one and in small groups for computer skills, learning strategies, math, spoken language, study skills, and time management. Remediation is provided through the program or unit via computer-based instruction, LD specialists, and trained peer tutors.

Enrichment Enrichment programs are available through the program or unit for college survival skills, learning strategies, math, oral communication skills, practical computer skills, reading, self-advocacy, stress management, study skills, test taking, time management, vocabulary development, and written composition skills. Programs for career planning, college survival skills, health and nutrition, medication management, oral communication skills, self-advocacy, and stress management are provided collaboratively through on-campus or off-campus services.

Application For admittance to the program or unit, students are required to provide a psychoeducational report (1 year old or less). It is recommended that students provide documentation of high school services. Upon acceptance, documentation of need for ser-

Wilson College (continued)

vices should be sent only to the LD program or unit. *Application deadline (institutional):* Continuous. *Application deadline (LD program):* Rolling/continuous for fall and rolling/continuous for spring.

Written Policies Written policy regarding general/basic LD accommodations is available on the program Web site. Written policy regarding general/basic LD accommodations is available through the program or unit directly.

Wofford College
Disability Services

429 North Church Street

Spartanburg, SC 29303-3663

http://www.wofford.edu

Contact: Dean Elizabeth Dashiell Wallace, Associate Dean of Students. Phone: 864-597-4371. E-mail: wallaceed@ wofford.edu.

Disability Services Approximately 60 registered undergraduate students were served during 2006–07. The program or unit includes 1 part-time staff member. Academic advisers, coaches, counselors, diagnostic specialists, and LD specialists are provided collaboratively through on-campus or off-campus services.

Orientation The program or unit offers an optional 1-hour orientation for new students during new student orientation.

Unique Aids and Services Aids, services, or accommodations include advocates, career counseling, weekly meetings with faculty, counseling.

Assistive Technology Assistive technology includes books on tape.

Subject-Area Tutoring Tutoring is offered one-on-one for all subjects. Tutoring is provided collaboratively through on-campus or off-campus services via trained peer tutors.

Enrichment Programs for career planning, college survival skills, health and nutrition, learning strategies, math, medication management, oral communication skills, practical computer skills, self-advocacy, stress management, study skills, test taking, time management, and written composition skills are provided collaboratively through on-campus or off-campus services.

Application For admittance to the program or unit, students are required to provide a psychoeducational report (3 years old or less). It is recommended that students apply to the program directly. Upon application, materials documenting need for services should be sent only to the LD program or unit. Upon acceptance, documentation of need for services should be sent only to the LD program or unit. *Application deadline (institutional):* 2/1. *Application deadline (LD program):* Rolling/continuous for fall.

Written Policies Written policy regarding general/basic LD accommodations is available on the program Web site. Written policy regarding general/basic LD accommodations is outlined in the school's catalog/handbook. Written policies regarding course substitutions, general/basic LD accommodations, and reduced course loads are available through the program or unit directly.

Worcester State College

486 Chandler Street

Worcester, MA 01602-2597

http://www.worcester.edu/

Contact: Dennis L. Lindblom, Director, Disability Services Office. Phone: 508-929-8733. Fax: 508-929-8011. E-mail: dlindblom@worcester.edu.

The program or unit includes 1 full-time staff member. LD specialists are provided through the program or unit.

Unique Aids and Services Aids, services, or accommodations include career counseling, priority registration, and support groups.

Assistive Technology Assistive technology is located in the DSS office, a special lab and includes digital textbooks/e-text and Kurzweil (site license for 5 users).

Basic Skills Remediation Remediation is offered one-on-one for learning strategies, reading, social skills, study skills, time management, and written language. Remediation is provided through the program or unit via LD specialists.

Enrichment Enrichment programs are available through the program or unit for college survival skills, learning strategies, practical computer skills, reading, self-advocacy, study skills, test taking, time management, and written composition skills.

Application For admittance to the program or unit, students are required to apply to the program directly and provide a psychoeducational report (3 years old or less). It is recommended that students provide documentation of high school services. Upon application, materials documenting need for services should be sent only to admissions with institutional application materials. Upon acceptance, documentation of need for services should be sent only to the LD program or unit. *Application deadline (institutional):* 6/1. *Application deadline (LD program):* Rolling/continuous for fall and rolling/continuous for spring.

Written Policies Written policies regarding general/basic LD accommodations and substitutions and waivers of admissions requirements are available on the program Web site. Written policies regarding general/basic LD accommodations and substitutions and waivers of admissions requirements are outlined in the school's catalog/handbook. Written policies regarding general/basic LD accommodations and reduced course loads are available through the program or unit directly.

Wright State University
Office of Disability Services

3640 Colonel Glenn Highway

Dayton, OH 45435

http://www.wright.edu

Contact: Ms. Cassandra Mitchell, Assistant Director, Academic Support. Phone: 937-775-5680. Fax: 937-775-5699. E-mail: disability_services@wright.edu. Head of LD Program: Mr. Jeffrey Vernooy, Director. Phone: 937-775-5680. Fax: 937-775-5795. E-mail: disability_services@wright.edu.

Office of Disability Services Approximately 225 registered undergraduate students were served during 2006–07. The program or unit includes 8 full-time and 2 part-time staff members. LD specialists and trained peer tutors are provided through the program or unit. Academic advisers, counselors, diagnostic specialists, graduate assistants/students, skill tutors, and trained peer tutors are provided collaboratively through on-campus or off-campus services.

Orientation The program or unit offers an optional 4-hour orientation for new students before classes begin.

Unique Aids and Services Aids, services, or accommodations include advocates, career counseling, faculty training, personal coach, support groups, and weekly meetings with faculty.

Assistive Technology Assistive technology is located in the DSS office, a special lab and includes digital textbooks/e-text, learning support software, and scanning. Technology training is provided to incoming students.

Subject-Area Tutoring Tutoring is offered one-on-one and in small groups for all subjects. Tutoring is provided through the program or unit via graduate assistants/students and trained peer tutors. Tutoring is also provided collaboratively through on-campus or off-campus services via graduate assistants/students and trained peer tutors.

Diagnostic Testing Testing is provided through the program or unit for auditory processing, intelligence, math, personality, reading, spelling, written language, and other services. Testing for auditory processing, intelligence, math, neuropsychological, personality, reading, spelling, written language, and other services is provided collaboratively through on-campus or off-campus services.

Basic Skills Remediation Remediation is offered in class-size groups for math, reading, and written language. Remediation is provided through the program or unit via graduate assistants/students and LD specialists. Remediation is also provided collaboratively through on-campus or off-campus services via graduate assistants/students, regular education teachers, and trained peer tutors.

Enrichment Enrichment programs are available through the program or unit for career planning, college survival skills, health and nutrition, learning strategies, practical computer skills, self-advocacy, study skills, test taking, and time management. Programs for career planning, college survival skills, health and nutrition, learning strategies, practical computer skills, stress management, study skills, and time management are provided collaboratively through on-campus or off-campus services. Credit is offered for career planning, college survival skills, health and nutrition, learning strategies, practical computer skills, self-advocacy, stress management, study skills, and time management.

Student Organization Abilities United consists of 10 members.

Fees *LD Program or Service* fee is $6 (fee varies according to level/tier of service).

Application For admittance to the program or unit, students are required to apply to the program directly, provide a psychoeducational report (5 years old or less), and provide comprehensive psychoeducational report that includes a diagnosis, a summary of the assessment. It is recommended that students provide documentation of high school services. Upon application, materials documenting need for services should be sent only to the LD program or unit. Upon acceptance, documentation of need for services should be sent only to the LD program or unit. *Application deadline (institutional):* Continuous. *Application deadline (LD program):* Rolling/continuous for fall and rolling/continuous for spring.

Written Policies Written policies regarding course substitutions, general/basic LD accommodations, grade forgiveness, substitutions and waivers of admissions requirements, and substitutions and waivers of graduation requirements are available on the program Web site. Written policies regarding course substitutions, grade forgiveness, substitutions and waivers of admissions requirements, and

substitutions and waivers of graduation requirements are outlined in the school's catalog/handbook. Written policy regarding general/basic LD accommodations is available through the program or unit directly.

Xavier University
Learning Assistance Center

3800 Victory Parkway

Cincinnati, OH 45207

http://www.xavier.edu/lac

Contact: Dr. Ann Dinan, Director, Learning Assistance Center. Phone: 513-745-3280. Fax: 513-745-3877. E-mail: dinan@xavier.edu.

Learning Assistance Center Approximately 280 registered undergraduate students were served during 2006–07. The program or unit includes 3 full-time and 43 part-time staff members. Coaches, graduate assistants/students, LD specialists, skill tutors, strategy tutors, and trained peer tutors are provided through the program or unit. Academic advisers, counselors, diagnostic specialists, professional tutors, and regular education teachers are provided collaboratively through on-campus or off-campus services.

Unique Aids and Services Aids, services, or accommodations include career counseling.

Subject-Area Tutoring Tutoring is offered one-on-one and in small groups for most subjects. Tutoring is provided through the program or unit via trained peer tutors. Tutoring is also provided collaboratively through on-campus or off-campus services via trained peer tutors.

Diagnostic Testing Testing is provided through the program or unit for learning strategies, learning styles, and study skills. Testing for auditory processing, intelligence, learning strategies, learning styles, personality, reading, social skills, study skills, visual processing, and written language is provided collaboratively through on-campus or off-campus services.

Basic Skills Remediation Remediation is offered one-on-one for learning strategies, math, reading, study skills, and time management. Remediation is provided through the program or unit via trained peer tutors. Remediation is also provided collaboratively through on-campus or off-campus services via trained peer tutors.

Enrichment Enrichment programs are available through the program or unit for learning strategies, study skills, test taking, and time management. Programs for career planning, college survival skills, learning strategies, stress management, study skills, and time management are provided collaboratively through on-campus or off-campus services. Credit is offered for college survival skills.

Application For admittance to the program or unit, students are required to provide a psychoeducational report (3 years old or less). It is recommended that students provide documentation of high school services. Upon acceptance, documentation of need for services should be sent only to the LD program or unit. *Application deadline (institutional):* 2/1. *Application deadline (LD program):* Rolling/continuous for fall.

Written Policies Written policies regarding course substitutions, general/basic LD accommodations, and substitutions and waivers of graduation requirements are available on the program Web site. Written policy regarding general/basic LD accommodations is out-

Xavier University (continued)

lined in the school's catalog/handbook. Written policies regarding course substitutions and substitutions and waivers of graduation requirements are available through the program or unit directly.

Yale University
Resource Office on Disabilities

New Haven, CT 06520

http://www.yale.edu/rod

Contact: Judy York, Director of Resource Office on Disabilities. Phone: 203-432-2324. Fax: 203-432-7884. E-mail: judith.york@yale.edu.

Resource Office on Disabilities Approximately 115 registered undergraduate students were served during 2006–07. The program or unit includes 2 full-time staff members. Academic advisers, graduate assistants/students, and trained peer tutors are provided collaboratively through on-campus or off-campus services.

Unique Aids and Services Aids, services, or accommodations include extended time on tests, note-takers.

Assistive Technology Assistive technology is located in campus labs, the DSS office, the student's personal system and includes digital textbooks/e-text.

Subject-Area Tutoring Tutoring is offered one-on-one for most subjects. Tutoring is provided collaboratively through on-campus or off-campus services via trained peer tutors.

Enrichment Programs for career planning, health and nutrition, and written composition skills are provided collaboratively through on-campus or off-campus services.

Application For admittance to the program or unit, students are required to apply to the program directly and provide a psychoeducational report (5 years old or less). It is recommended that students provide documentation of high school services. Upon acceptance, documentation of need for services should be sent only to the LD program or unit. *Application deadline (institutional):* 12/31. *Application deadline (LD program):* Rolling/continuous for fall and rolling/continuous for spring.

Written Policies Written policy regarding substitutions and waivers of graduation requirements is outlined in the school's catalog/handbook. Written policy regarding general/basic LD accommodations is available through the program or unit directly.

Yeshiva University
Office of Disability Services

500 West 185th Street

New York, NY 10033-3201

http://www.yu.edu

Contact: Mrs. Abigail Kelsen, Coordinator of Disability Services, Wilf Campus. Phone: 646-685-0118. E-mail: akelsen@yu.edu. Head of LD Program: Dr. Rochelle Kohn, Director of Disability Services, Manhattan Campuses. Phone: 917-326-4828. E-mail: rkohn1@yu.edu.

Office of Disability Services Approximately 125 registered undergraduate students were served during 2006–07. The program or unit includes 2 full-time staff members. LD specialists are provided through the program or unit. Academic advisers, counselors, LD specialists, remediation/learning specialists, and trained peer tutors are provided collaboratively through on-campus or off-campus services.

Unique Aids and Services Aids, services, or accommodations include faculty training.

Assistive Technology Assistive technology is located in campus labs, the DSS office and includes digital textbooks/e-text, learning support software, and scanning. Technology training is provided to incoming students.

Basic Skills Remediation Remediation is offered one-on-one and in small groups for learning strategies, study skills, time management, and written language. Remediation is provided collaboratively through on-campus or off-campus services.

Enrichment Programs for career planning, learning strategies, study skills, test taking, and time management are provided collaboratively through on-campus or off-campus services.

Application For admittance to the program or unit, students are required to provide a psychoeducational report (3 years old or less). It is recommended that students provide documentation of high school services. Upon acceptance, documentation of need for services should be sent only to the LD program or unit. *Application deadline (LD program):* Rolling/continuous for fall and rolling/continuous for spring.

Written Policies Written policy regarding general/basic LD accommodations is available on the program Web site. Written policy regarding general/basic LD accommodations is outlined in the school's catalog/handbook. Written policies regarding course substitutions, general/basic LD accommodations, grade forgiveness, reduced course loads, and substitutions and waivers of graduation requirements are available through the program or unit directly.

TWO-YEAR COLLEGES WITH STRUCTURED/PROACTIVE PROGRAMS

Calhoun Community College
Services for Special Student Populations

PO Box 2216

Decatur, AL 35609-2216

http://www.calhoun.edu/Student_Affairs/disabilities.html

Contact: Mrs. Dawn M. Hale, Administrative Secretary. Phone: 256-306-2630. E-mail: dmh@calhoun.edu. Head of LD Program: Dr. Kermit L. Carter, Dean of Student Affairs and 504 Coordinator. Phone: 256-306-2613. E-mail: klc@calhoun.edu.

Services for Special Student Populations Approximately 50 registered undergraduate students were served during 2006–07. The program or unit includes 2 full-time staff members. Services are provided through the program or unit. Academic advisers, counselors, regular education teachers, and trained peer tutors are provided collaboratively through on-campus or off-campus services.

Orientation The program or unit offers a mandatory orientation for new students.

Unique Aids and Services Aids, services, or accommodations include career counseling, priority registration, meetings as needed.

Assistive Technology Assistive technology is located in campus labs, the DSS office, the library and includes digital textbooks/e-text, scanning, and TestTalker Software for test-taking (oral testing). Technology training is provided to incoming students.

Subject-Area Tutoring Tutoring is offered one-on-one for some subjects. Tutoring is provided collaboratively through on-campus or off-campus services via trained peer tutors.

Basic Skills Remediation Remediation is offered one-on-one for computer skills, math, written language, and all courses (if tutor is available). Remediation is provided through the program or unit via trained peer tutors. Remediation is also provided collaboratively through on-campus or off-campus services via trained peer tutors.

Enrichment Enrichment programs are available through the program or unit for career planning, college survival skills, practical computer skills, self-advocacy, stress management, and time management. Programs for career planning, college survival skills, math, practical computer skills, study skills, test taking, time management, and vocabulary development are provided collaboratively through on-campus or off-campus services.

Application For admittance to the program or unit, students are required to apply to the program directly and provide a psychoeducational report (3 years old or less). Upon application, materials documenting need for services should be sent only to the LD program or unit. Upon acceptance, documentation of need for services should be sent only to the LD program or unit. *Application deadline (institutional):* Continuous. *Application deadline (LD program):* Rolling/continuous for fall and rolling/continuous for spring.

Written Policies Written policy regarding general/basic LD accommodations is available on the program Web site. Written policies regarding course substitutions, grade forgiveness, substitutions and waivers of admissions requirements, and substitutions and waivers of graduation requirements are outlined in the school's catalog/handbook. Written policy regarding general/basic LD accommodations is available through the program or unit directly.

Community College of Allegheny County
Supportive Services

800 Allegheny Avenue

Pittsburgh, PA 15233-1894

http://www.ccac.edu/default.aspx?id=137533

Contact: Ms. Marilyn Gleser, LD Coordinator. Phone: 412-237-4613. Fax: 412-237-2721. E-mail: mgleser@ccac.edu.

Supportive Services Approximately 275 registered undergraduate students were served during 2006–07. The program or unit includes 2 full-time and 4 part-time staff members. Academic advisers, counselors, LD specialists, remediation/learning specialists, strategy tutors, and trained peer tutors are provided through the program or unit. Professional tutors, regular education teachers, remediation/learning specialists, skill tutors, strategy tutors, and trained peer tutors are provided collaboratively through on-campus or off-campus services.

Orientation The program or unit offers an optional 3-hour orientation for new students before classes begin.

Summer Program To help prepare for the demands of college, there is an optional 4-week summer program prior to entering the school available to rising seniors, high school graduates that focuses on life skills and/or college life adjustment, self-advocacy, study skills, test-taking skills, and time management. Degree credit will be earned. The program accepts students from out-of-state and is available to students attending other colleges.

Unique Aids and Services Aids, services, or accommodations include career counseling, faculty training, priority registration, and weekly meetings with faculty.

Assistive Technology Assistive technology is located in campus labs, the DSS office and includes digital textbooks/e-text and scanning. Technology training is provided to incoming students.

Subject-Area Tutoring Tutoring is offered one-on-one and in small groups for most subjects. Tutoring is provided through the program or unit via trained peer tutors. Tutoring is also provided collaboratively through on-campus or off-campus services via professional tutors and trained peer tutors.

Basic Skills Remediation Remediation is offered in class-size groups for learning strategies, math, reading, study skills, time management, and written language. Remediation is provided through the program or unit via LD specialists and special education teachers. Remediation is also provided collaboratively through on-campus or off-campus services via LD specialists, regular education teachers, and special education teachers.

Enrichment Enrichment programs are available through the program or unit for career planning, college survival skills, learning strategies, math, reading, self-advocacy, study skills, test taking, time management, vocabulary development, and written composition skills. Programs for career planning, learning strategies, math, reading, study skills, vocabulary development, and written composition skills are provided collaboratively through on-campus or off-campus services. Credit is offered for career planning, college survival skills, learning strategies, math, reading, self-advocacy, study skills, vocabulary development, and written composition skills.

Student Organization Using Personal Potential Student Club consists of 15 members.

Community College of Allegheny County (continued)
Application For admittance to the program or unit, students are required to apply to the program directly and provide a psychoeducational report. It is recommended that students provide documentation of high school services. Upon application, materials documenting need for services should be sent only to the LD program or unit. *Application deadline (institutional):* Continuous. *Application deadline (LD program):* Rolling/continuous for fall and rolling/continuous for spring.
Written Policies Written policy regarding general/basic LD accommodations is available on the program Web site. Written policy regarding general/basic LD accommodations is outlined in the school's catalog/handbook. Written policies regarding course substitutions and substitutions and waivers of graduation requirements are available through the program or unit directly.

Dean College
Arch Program
99 Main Street
Franklin, MA 02038-1994
http://www.dean.edu/
Contact: Larry Walter Thode, Assistant Director of Admissions. Phone: 508-541-1510. Fax: 508-541-8726. E-mail: lthode@dean.edu. Head of LD Program: Erin Lowery-Corkran, Director of Arch Program and Disabilities Support Services. Phone: 508-541-1768. Fax: 508-541-8726. E-mail: elowery-corkran@dean.edu.

Arch Program Approximately 50 registered undergraduate students were served during 2006–07. The program or unit includes 7 full-time and 10 part-time staff members. Academic advisers, coaches, counselors, LD specialists, professional tutors, strategy tutors, and trained peer tutors are provided through the program or unit. Regular education teachers are provided collaboratively through on-campus or off-campus services.
Unique Aids and Services Aids, services, or accommodations include career counseling, faculty training, personal coach, support groups, and weekly meetings with faculty.
Assistive Technology Assistive technology is located in a special lab and includes digital textbooks/e-text and scanning. Technology training is provided to incoming students.
Subject-Area Tutoring Tutoring is offered in small groups for most subjects. Tutoring is provided through the program or unit via professional tutors.
Basic Skills Remediation Remediation is offered in small groups and in class-size groups for auditory processing, computer skills, learning strategies, math, reading, study skills, time management, visual processing, and written language. Remediation is provided collaboratively through on-campus or off-campus services via regular education teachers and special education teachers.
Enrichment Enrichment programs are available through the program or unit for self-advocacy, study skills, test taking, time management, and written composition skills. Programs for career planning, college survival skills, health and nutrition, learning strategies, math, practical computer skills, reading, and stress management are provided collaboratively through on-campus or off-campus services. Credit is offered for career planning, college survival skills, health and nutrition, learning strategies, math, practical computer skills, and reading.

Fees *LD Program or Service* fee is $3500.
Application For admittance to the program or unit, students are required to apply to the program directly, provide a psychoeducational report (3 years old or less), and provide WISC-WAIS. Upon application, materials documenting need for services should be sent only to the LD program or unit. *Application deadline (institutional):* Continuous. *Application deadline (LD program):* Rolling/continuous for fall and rolling/continuous for spring.
Written Policies Written policies regarding course substitutions, general/basic LD accommodations, reduced course loads, and substitutions and waivers of admissions requirements are outlined in the school's catalog/handbook.

Eastern New Mexico University–Roswell
Special Services Occupational Training Program
PO Box 6000
Roswell, NM 88202-6000
http://www.roswell.enmu.edu
Contact: Denise McGhee, Director of Special Services. Phone: 505-624-7286. Fax: 505-624-7350. E-mail: denise.mcghee@roswell.enmu.edu.

Special Services Occupational Training Program Approximately 30 registered undergraduate students were served during 2006–07. The program or unit includes 8 full-time and 15 part-time staff members. Counselors, regular education teachers, skill tutors, special education teachers, and other are provided through the program or unit.
Orientation The program or unit offers a mandatory 3-day orientation for new students before classes begin and during registration.
Unique Aids and Services Aids, services, or accommodations include priority registration and weekly meetings with faculty.
Assistive Technology Assistive technology is located in campus labs, the DSS office and includes digital textbooks/e-text, learning support software, and scanning. Technology training is provided to incoming students.
Subject-Area Tutoring Tutoring is offered one-on-one and in small groups for all subjects. Tutoring is provided through the program or unit via graduate assistants/students and professional tutors.
Basic Skills Remediation Remediation is offered one-on-one and in small groups for computer skills, reading, social skills, study skills, and time management. Remediation is provided through the program or unit via graduate assistants/students and professional tutors.
Enrichment Enrichment programs are available through the program or unit for career planning, health and nutrition, oral communication skills, self-advocacy, stress management, and time management.
Fees *LD Program or Service* fee varies according to academic program.
Application For admittance to the program or unit, students are required to apply to the program directly. It is recommended that students provide a psychoeducational report (2 years old or less), provide documentation of high school services, and provide any additional testing that provides relevant information on functioning

level. Upon application, materials documenting need for services should be sent only to the LD program or unit. Upon acceptance, documentation of need for services should be sent only to the LD program or unit. *Application deadline (institutional):* Continuous. *Application deadline (LD program):* 7/31 for fall. 11/30 for spring.
Written Policies Written policy regarding general/basic LD accommodations is available on the program Web site. Written policies regarding course substitutions, general/basic LD accommodations, reduced course loads, substitutions and waivers of admissions requirements, and substitutions and waivers of graduation requirements are outlined in the school's catalog/handbook.

Fresno City College
Disabled Students Programs and Services

1101 East University Avenue

Fresno, CA 93741-0002

http://www.sccd.com

Contact: Ms. Linda Lee Kane, Learning Disability Specialist. Phone: 559-442-8237. Fax: 559-485-7304. E-mail: linda.kane@scccd.com. Head of LD Program: Dr. Janice Emerzian, Director. Phone: 559-442-8237. Fax: 559-485-7304. E-mail: emerzian@scccd.com.

Disabled Students Programs and Services Approximately 780 registered undergraduate students were served during 2006–07. The program or unit includes 1 full-time and 3 part-time staff members. Academic advisers, counselors, diagnostic specialists, graduate assistants/students, LD specialists, professional tutors, and regular education teachers are provided collaboratively through on-campus or off-campus services.
Orientation The program or unit offers an optional 1-hour orientation for new students before registration, before classes begin, during summer prior to enrollment, during registration, after classes begin, and individually by special arrangement.
Summer Program To help prepare for the demands of college, there is an optional 6-week summer program prior to entering the school available to rising juniors, high school graduates that focuses on computing skills. The program accepts students from out-of-state.
Unique Aids and Services Aids, services, or accommodations include career counseling, priority registration, and support groups.
Assistive Technology Assistive technology is located in a special lab and includes digital textbooks/e-text, learning support software, and scanning. Technology training is provided to incoming students.
Subject-Area Tutoring Tutoring is offered in small groups for most subjects. Tutoring is provided collaboratively through on-campus or off-campus services via trained peer tutors.
Diagnostic Testing Testing is provided through the program or unit for auditory processing, intelligence, learning strategies, learning styles, math, reading, spelling, spoken language, study skills, visual processing, and written language.
Basic Skills Remediation Remediation is offered in small groups and in class-size groups for auditory processing, computer skills, learning strategies, math, reading, social skills, spelling, study skills, time management, visual processing, and written language. Reme-

diation is provided collaboratively through on-campus or off-campus services via computer-based instruction, regular education teachers, and special education teachers.
Enrichment Programs for career planning, college survival skills, learning strategies, math, oral communication skills, practical computer skills, reading, self-advocacy, stress management, study skills, test taking, time management, vocabulary development, and written composition skills are provided collaboratively through on-campus or off-campus services.
Fees *Summer Program* fee is $33.
Application For admittance to the program or unit, students are required to apply to the program directly and provide a psychoeducational report (3 years old or less). It is recommended that students provide documentation of high school services. Upon application, materials documenting need for services should be sent only to the LD program or unit. Upon acceptance, documentation of need for services should be sent only to the LD program or unit. *Application deadline (institutional):* Continuous. *Application deadline (LD program):* Rolling/continuous for fall and rolling/continuous for spring.
Written Policies Written policies regarding general/basic LD accommodations, substitutions and waivers of admissions requirements, and substitutions and waivers of graduation requirements are available on the program Web site. Written policies regarding course substitutions, general/basic LD accommodations, reduced course loads, substitutions and waivers of admissions requirements, and substitutions and waivers of graduation requirements are outlined in the school's catalog/handbook. Written policies regarding course substitutions, general/basic LD accommodations, grade forgiveness, reduced course loads, substitutions and waivers of admissions requirements, and substitutions and waivers of graduation requirements are available through the program or unit directly.

Heartland Community College
Disability Support Services

1500 West Raab Road

Normal, IL 61761

http://www.heartland.edu/

Contact: Director of Disability Support Services. Phone: 309-268-8249. Fax: 309-268-7986. E-mail: anita.moore@heartland.edu.

Disability Support Services Approximately 60 registered undergraduate students were served during 2006–07. The program or unit includes 2 full-time staff members and 1 part-time staff member. Academic advisers, counselors, and professional tutors are provided collaboratively through on-campus or off-campus services.
Assistive Technology Assistive technology is located in campus labs, a special lab and includes digital textbooks/e-text, learning support software, and scanning. Technology training is provided to incoming students.
Subject-Area Tutoring Tutoring is offered one-on-one. Tutoring is provided collaboratively through on-campus or off-campus services via professional tutors and trained peer tutors.

Heartland Community College (continued)

Basic Skills Remediation Remediation is offered in class-size groups for math, reading, and written language. Remediation is provided collaboratively through on-campus or off-campus services.

Enrichment Enrichment programs are available through the program or unit for college survival skills, learning strategies, math, reading, study skills, test taking, time management, and written composition skills. Programs for math, practical computer skills, reading, and written composition skills are provided collaboratively through on-campus or off-campus services. Credit is offered for math, reading, and written composition skills.

Application It is recommended that students provide a psychoeducational report and provide documentation of high school services. Upon application, materials documenting need for services should be sent only to the LD program or unit. Upon acceptance, documentation of need for services should be sent only to the LD program or unit. *Application deadline (institutional):* Continuous. *Application deadline (LD program):* Rolling/continuous for fall and rolling/continuous for spring.

Written Policies Written policy regarding general/basic LD accommodations is available on the program Web site. Written policies regarding general/basic LD accommodations and reduced course loads are available through the program or unit directly.

Landmark College

River Road South

Putney, VT 05346

http://www.landmark.edu

Contact: Ben Mitchell, Director of Admissions. Phone: 802-387-1647. Fax: 802-387-6868. E-mail: bmitchell@landmark.edu.

Approximately 480 registered undergraduate students were served during 2006–07. The program or unit includes 125 full-time staff members. Academic advisers, coaches, counselors, diagnostic specialists, LD specialists, regular education teachers, remediation/learning specialists, and other are provided collaboratively through on-campus or off-campus services.

Orientation The program or unit offers 3-day orientation for new students before classes begin.

Summer Program To help prepare for the demands of college, there is an optional 3-week summer program prior to entering the school available to rising seniors, high school graduates that focuses on study skills and time management. The program accepts students from out-of-state and is available to students attending other colleges.

Unique Aids and Services Aids, services, or accommodations include career counseling, faculty training, parent workshops, and weekly meetings with faculty.

Assistive Technology Assistive technology is located in various locations throughout campus and includes digital textbooks/e-text, learning support software, and scanning. Technology training is provided to incoming students.

Basic Skills Remediation Remediation is offered one-on-one, in small groups, and in class-size groups for computer skills, learning strategies, math, reading, social skills, spelling, spoken language, study skills, time management, and written language. Remediation is provided collaboratively through on-campus or off-campus services via LD specialists and regular education teachers.

Enrichment Programs for career planning, college survival skills, learning strategies, medication management, oral communication skills, practical computer skills, reading, self-advocacy, stress management, study skills, time management, vocabulary development, and written composition skills are provided collaboratively through on-campus or off-campus services.

Student Organization Student Governance Association consists of 20 members.

Fees *Summer Program* fee is $8300.

Application For admittance to the program or unit, students are required to provide a psychoeducational report (3 years old or less) and provide transcripts. It is recommended that students provide documentation of high school services. Upon application, materials documenting need for services should be sent only to admissions with institutional application materials. Upon acceptance, documentation of need for services should be sent only to admissions. *Application deadline (institutional):* Continuous. *Application deadline (LD program):* Rolling/continuous for fall and rolling/continuous for spring.

Written Policies Written policy regarding general/basic LD accommodations is available on the program Web site. Written policy regarding general/basic LD accommodations is outlined in the school's catalog/handbook.

Lewis and Clark Community College
Student Development and Counseling

5800 Godfrey Road

Godfrey, IL 62035-2466

http://www.lc.edu/

Contact: Ms. Kathy Haberer, Director, Student Development and Counseling. Phone: 618-468-4126. Fax: 618-468-7257. E-mail: khaberer@lc.edu.

Student Development and Counseling Approximately 125 registered undergraduate students were served during 2006–07. The program or unit includes 4 full-time and 11 part-time staff members. Academic advisers, counselors, diagnostic specialists, LD specialists, professional tutors, regular education teachers, remediation/learning specialists, skill tutors, special education teachers, strategy tutors, teacher trainees, and trained peer tutors are provided through the program or unit. Coaches, regular education teachers, and remediation/learning specialists are provided collaboratively through on-campus or off-campus services.

Orientation The program or unit offers an optional 2-hour orientation for new students before registration, before classes begin, and individually by special arrangement.

Unique Aids and Services Aids, services, or accommodations include career counseling, faculty training, parent workshops, priority registration, support groups.

Assistive Technology Assistive technology is located in campus labs, the DSS office, a special lab and includes digital textbooks/e-text, scanning, and writing organization software. Technology training is provided to incoming students.

Subject-Area Tutoring Tutoring is offered one-on-one and in small groups for most subjects. Tutoring is provided through the program or unit via computer-based instruction, LD specialists, professional tutors, and trained peer tutors. Tutoring is also provided collaboratively through on-campus or off-campus services via computer-based instruction, professional tutors, and trained peer tutors.

Diagnostic Testing Testing is provided through the program or unit for auditory processing, learning strategies, learning styles, math, motor skills, reading, social skills, spelling, spoken language, study skills, visual processing, and written language. Testing for intelligence, neuropsychological, personality, and reading is provided collaboratively through on-campus or off-campus services.

Basic Skills Remediation Remediation is offered one-on-one, in small groups, and in class-size groups for auditory processing, computer skills, learning strategies, math, reading, social skills, spelling, spoken language, study skills, time management, visual processing, and written language. Remediation is provided through the program or unit via computer-based instruction, LD specialists, professional tutors, regular education teachers, special education teachers, and trained peer tutors. Remediation is also provided collaboratively through on-campus or off-campus services via computer-based instruction, professional tutors, regular education teachers, special education teachers, and trained peer tutors.

Enrichment Enrichment programs are available through the program or unit for career planning, college survival skills, health and nutrition, learning strategies, math, oral communication skills, practical computer skills, reading, self-advocacy, stress management, study skills, test taking, time management, vocabulary development, written composition skills, and other. Programs for career planning, college survival skills, health and nutrition, learning strategies, math, oral communication skills, practical computer skills, reading, self-advocacy, stress management, study skills, test taking, time management, vocabulary development, written composition skills, and other are provided collaboratively through on-campus or off-campus services. Credit is offered for career planning, college survival skills, health and nutrition, learning strategies, math, oral communication skills, practical computer skills, reading, self-advocacy, study skills, test taking, time management, vocabulary development, written composition skills, and other.

Student Organization People First consists of 30 members.

Fees *LD Program or Service* fee is $0 to $900 (fee varies according to academic program, disability, course level, and level/tier of service).

Application For admittance to the program or unit, students are required to apply to the program directly and provide a psychoeducational report (5 years old or less). It is recommended that students provide documentation of high school services and provide summary of performance, physician statement. Upon application, materials documenting need for services should be sent only to the LD program or unit. Upon acceptance, documentation of need for services should be sent only to the LD program or unit. *Application deadline (LD program):* Rolling/continuous for fall and rolling/continuous for spring.

Written Policies Written policy regarding general/basic LD accommodations is available on the program Web site. Written policy regarding general/basic LD accommodations is outlined in the school's catalog/handbook.

Metropolitan Community College–Longview
Academic Bridges to Learning Effectiveness (ABLE)

500 Southwest Longview Road

Lee's Summit, MO 64081-2105

http://mcckc.edu/
home.asp?qlinks=ABLE+Program+at+Longview&C=2

Contact: Dr. Joan E. Bergstrom, ABLE Program Director. Phone: 816-672-2053. Fax: 816-672-2025. E-mail: joan.bergstrom@mcckc.edu.

Academic Bridges to Learning Effectiveness (ABLE) Approximately 90 registered undergraduate students were served during 2006–07. The program or unit includes 2 full-time and 15 part-time staff members. Academic advisers, counselors, graduate assistants/students, LD specialists, remediation/learning specialists, and special education teachers are provided through the program or unit.

Orientation The program or unit offers a mandatory 2½-hour orientation for new students before classes begin.

Unique Aids and Services Aids, services, or accommodations include advocates, career counseling, support groups, weekly meetings with faculty, parent support groups.

Assistive Technology Assistive technology includes books on tape.

Subject-Area Tutoring Tutoring is offered in small groups for most subjects. Tutoring is provided through the program or unit via graduate assistants/students, LD specialists, and trained peer tutors. Tutoring is also provided collaboratively through on-campus or off-campus services via graduate assistants/students, LD specialists, and trained peer tutors.

Basic Skills Remediation Remediation is offered in small groups for auditory processing, learning strategies, math, reading, social skills, spelling, spoken language, study skills, time management, visual processing, and written language. Remediation is provided through the program or unit via graduate assistants/students, LD specialists, regular education teachers, special education teachers, and trained peer tutors. Remediation is also provided collaboratively through on-campus or off-campus services via graduate assistants/students, LD specialists, regular education teachers, special education teachers, and trained peer tutors.

Enrichment Programs for career planning, college survival skills, learning strategies, math, oral communication skills, reading, self-advocacy, stress management, study skills, test taking, time management, vocabulary development, and written composition skills are provided collaboratively through on-campus or off-campus services. Credit is offered for career planning, college survival skills, learning strategies, math, oral communication skills, reading, self-advocacy, stress management, study skills, test taking, time management, vocabulary development, and written composition skills.

Fees *LD Program or Service* fee is $35 (fee varies according to academic program).

Application For admittance to the program or unit, students are required to apply to the program directly and provide a psychoeducational report. It is recommended that students provide documentation of high school services and provide neuropsychological report. Upon application, materials documenting need for services should

Metropolitan Community College–Longview (continued)
be sent only to the LD program or unit. Upon acceptance, documentation of need for services should be sent to both admissions and the LD program or unit. *Application deadline (institutional):* Continuous. *Application deadline (LD program):* 7/15 for fall. 12/21 for spring.

Written Policies Written policies regarding course substitutions, general/basic LD accommodations, substitutions and waivers of admissions requirements, and substitutions and waivers of graduation requirements are outlined in the school's catalog/handbook. Written policy regarding reduced course loads is available through the program or unit directly.

Metropolitan Community College–Penn Valley

3201 Southwest Trafficway

Kansas City, MO 64111

http://www.mcckc.edu

Contact: Ms. Pat Goodwin, Director, ABLE Program. Phone: 816-759-4717. Fax: 816-759-4169. E-mail: patricia.goodwin@mcckc.edu.

The program or unit includes 1 full-time and 5 part-time staff members. Counselors, remediation/learning specialists, and trained peer tutors are provided through the program or unit.

Orientation The program or unit offers an optional 3-hour orientation for new students before classes begin.

Unique Aids and Services Aids, services, or accommodations include faculty training, parent workshops, and support groups.

Assistive Technology Assistive technology is located in campus labs, the DSS office and includes digital textbooks/e-text, scanning, and word prediction and dictation software. Technology training is provided to incoming students.

Subject-Area Tutoring Tutoring is offered one-on-one and in small groups for some subjects. Tutoring is provided through the program or unit via LD specialists and trained peer tutors.

Basic Skills Remediation Remediation is offered in class-size groups for math, reading, and written language. Remediation is provided collaboratively through on-campus or off-campus services via regular education teachers.

Enrichment Enrichment programs are available through the program or unit for career planning, college survival skills, learning strategies, self-advocacy, stress management, and study skills. Programs for career planning and college survival skills are provided collaboratively through on-campus or off-campus services. Credit is offered for career planning, college survival skills, self-advocacy, stress management, and study skills.

Fees *LD Program or Service* fee is $35 to $350 (fee varies according to level/tier of service).

Application For admittance to the program or unit, students are required to apply to the program directly and provide a psychoeducational report (3 years old or less). It is recommended that students provide documentation of high school services. Upon application, materials documenting need for services should be sent only to the LD program or unit. Upon acceptance, documentation of need for

services should be sent only to the LD program or unit. *Application deadline (institutional):* Continuous. *Application deadline (LD program):* Rolling/continuous for fall and rolling/continuous for spring.

Written Policies Written policy regarding general/basic LD accommodations is available on the program Web site.

Miami Dade College
ACCESS

300 Northeast Second Avenue

Miami, FL 33132-2296

http://www.mdc.edu/

Contact: Dr. Bruce Smitley, LD Specialist. Phone: 305-237-3072. Fax: 305-237-3464. E-mail: bsmitley@mddc.edu.

ACCESS Approximately 140 registered undergraduate students were served during 2006–07. The program or unit includes 3 full-time and 15 part-time staff members. Academic advisers, diagnostic specialists, LD specialists, professional tutors, remediation/learning specialists, skill tutors, and strategy tutors are provided through the program or unit.

Unique Aids and Services Aids, services, or accommodations include advocates, career counseling, faculty training, personal coach, and priority registration.

Subject-Area Tutoring Tutoring is offered one-on-one and in small groups for most subjects. Tutoring is provided through the program or unit via LD specialists and professional tutors.

Diagnostic Testing Testing is provided through the program or unit for auditory processing, math, reading, spelling, spoken language, visual processing, and written language.

Basic Skills Remediation Remediation is offered one-on-one and in small groups for computer skills, math, reading, spelling, time management, and written language. Remediation is provided through the program or unit via computer-based instruction, LD specialists, and professional tutors.

Enrichment Enrichment programs are available through the program or unit for practical computer skills, reading, and written composition skills.

Application For admittance to the program or unit, students are required to apply to the program directly and provide a psychoeducational report (3 years old or less). It is recommended that students provide documentation of high school services. Upon application, materials documenting need for services should be sent only to the LD program or unit. Upon acceptance, documentation of need for services should be sent only to the LD program or unit. *Application deadline (institutional):* Continuous. *Application deadline (LD program):* Rolling/continuous for fall and rolling/continuous for spring.

Written Policies Written policies regarding course substitutions, general/basic LD accommodations, reduced course loads, substitutions and waivers of admissions requirements, and substitutions and waivers of graduation requirements are available on the program Web site. Written policies regarding course substitutions, general/basic LD accommodations, reduced course loads, substitutions and waivers of admissions requirements, and substitutions and waivers of graduation requirements are available through the program or unit directly.

Middlesex County College
Project Connections

2600 Woodbridge Avenue, PO Box 3050

Edison, NJ 08818-3050

http://www.middlesexcc.edu/acadsupport/control.cfm/ID/74

Contact: Project Connections. Phone: 732-906-2507. Fax: 732-906-7767. Head of LD Program: Ms. Mary Jane E. Warshaw, Director of Project Connections. Phone: 732-906-2507. Fax: 732-906-7767. E-mail: mwarshaw@ middlesexcc.edu.

Project Connections Approximately 160 registered undergraduate students were served during 2006–07. The program or unit includes 7 full-time and 2 part-time staff members. Counselors, diagnostic specialists, LD specialists, professional tutors, remediation/ learning specialists, and strategy tutors are provided through the program or unit. Counselors and diagnostic specialists are provided collaboratively through on-campus or off-campus services.

Orientation The program or unit offers a mandatory 2-day orientation for new students during summer prior to enrollment.

Unique Aids and Services Aids, services, or accommodations include career counseling, faculty training, parent workshops, and priority registration.

Assistive Technology Assistive technology is located in a special lab and includes digital textbooks/e-text and scanning. Technology training is provided to incoming students.

Subject-Area Tutoring Tutoring is offered one-on-one, in small groups, and in class-size groups for most subjects. Tutoring is provided through the program or unit via LD specialists and professional tutors.

Diagnostic Testing Testing is provided through the program or unit for auditory processing, intelligence, math, reading, spelling, spoken language, visual processing, and written language.

Basic Skills Remediation Remediation is offered in class-size groups for math, reading, study skills, and written language. Remediation is provided collaboratively through on-campus or off-campus services via regular education teachers.

Enrichment Enrichment programs are available through the program or unit for career planning, college survival skills, self-advocacy, and time management. Programs for college survival skills, health and nutrition, math, oral communication skills, practical computer skills, reading, stress management, study skills, test taking, time management, vocabulary development, and written composition skills are provided collaboratively through on-campus or off-campus services. Credit is offered for college survival skills, health and nutrition, math, oral communication skills, practical computer skills, time management, and written composition skills.

Student Organization Advocates for Students with Learning Differences consists of 40 members.

Application For admittance to the program or unit, students are required to apply to the program directly, provide a psychoeducational report (3 years old or less), provide documentation of high school services, and provide school evaluation. Upon application, materials documenting need for services should be sent only to the LD program or unit. *Application deadline (institutional):* Continuous. *Application deadline (LD program):* 2/15 for fall.

Written Policies Written policy regarding general/basic LD accommodations is available through the program or unit directly.

Spencerian College– Lexington
Academic Department

2355 Harrodsburg Road

Lexington, KY 40504

http://www.spencerian.edu/

Contact: Karen S. Whalen, Director of Education. Phone: 859-223-9608 Ext. 5430. Fax: 859-977-5408. E-mail: kwhalen@spencerian.edu.

Academic Department Approximately 15 registered undergraduate students were served during 2006–07. The program or unit includes 10 full-time and 5 part-time staff members. Academic advisers, counselors, regular education teachers, skill tutors, trained peer tutors, and other are provided through the program or unit. Diagnostic specialists are provided collaboratively through on-campus or off-campus services.

Orientation The program or unit offers an optional orientation for new students individually by special arrangement.

Unique Aids and Services Aids, services, or accommodations include advocates, career counseling, faculty training, and personal coach.

Subject-Area Tutoring Tutoring is offered one-on-one, in small groups, and in class-size groups for all subjects. Tutoring is provided through the program or unit via computer-based instruction, professional tutors, trained peer tutors, and other. Tutoring is also provided collaboratively through on-campus or off-campus services via computer-based instruction, professional tutors, trained peer tutors, and other.

Diagnostic Testing Testing is provided through the program or unit for math, personality, reading, and written language.

Basic Skills Remediation Remediation is offered one-on-one for computer skills, learning strategies, math, reading, study skills, time management, and written language. Remediation is provided through the program or unit via computer-based instruction, professional tutors, and regular education teachers. Remediation is also provided collaboratively through on-campus or off-campus services via computer-based instruction, professional tutors, and regular education teachers.

Enrichment Enrichment programs are available through the program or unit for career planning, college survival skills, learning strategies, math, practical computer skills, reading, stress management, study skills, test taking, time management, and written composition skills. Programs for career planning, college survival skills, learning strategies, math, practical computer skills, reading, stress management, study skills, test taking, time management, and written composition skills are provided collaboratively through on-campus or off-campus services. Credit is offered for career planning, math, practical computer skills, and written composition skills.

Application It is recommended that students provide a psychoeducational report (2 years old or less) and provide documentation of high school services. Upon application, materials documenting need for services should be sent to both admissions and the LD program or unit. Upon acceptance, documentation of need for services should be sent to both admissions and the LD program or unit. *Application deadline (LD program):* Rolling/continuous for fall and rolling/ continuous for spring.

Written Policies Written policy regarding general/basic LD accommodations is outlined in the school's catalog/handbook.

Vincennes University
Office of Disability Services, COPE Student Support Services, STEP Students Transition into Educational Programs

1002 North First Street
Vincennes, IN 47591-5202
http://www.vinu.edu/

Contact: Mrs. Lynn Linkon-McCormick, Coordinator, Office of Disability Services. Phone: 812-888-4501. Fax: 812-888-2087. E-mail: llinkonmccormick@vinu.edu. Head of LD Program: Mrs. Hope Lynn Clausman, Director, Summer Bridge Program. Phone: 812-888-4149. Fax: 812-888-5128. E-mail: hclausman@vinu.edu.

Office of Disability Services, COPE Student Support Services, STEP Students Transition into Educational Programs Approximately 350 registered undergraduate students were served during 2006–07. The program or unit includes 8 part-time staff members. Academic advisers, coaches, counselors, graduate assistants/students, LD specialists, professional tutors, regular education teachers, remediation/learning specialists, skill tutors, special education teachers, strategy tutors, teacher trainees, trained peer tutors, and other are provided through the program or unit. Academic advisers, coaches, counselors, graduate assistants/students, LD specialists, professional tutors, regular education teachers, remediation/learning specialists, skill tutors, special education teachers, strategy tutors, teacher trainees, trained peer tutors, and other are provided collaboratively through on-campus or off-campus services.

Orientation The program or unit offers an optional 5-week orientation for new students before registration, before classes begin, during summer prior to enrollment, during registration, after classes begin, individually by special arrangement, and during Summer Bridge Program.

Summer Program To help prepare for the demands of college, there is an optional 5-week summer program prior to entering the school available to high school graduates that focuses on life skills and/or college life adjustment, self-advocacy, specific subject tutoring, study skills, test-taking skills, and time management. Degree credit will be earned. The program accepts students from out-of-state.

Unique Aids and Services Aids, services, or accommodations include advocates, career counseling, and support groups.

Assistive Technology Assistive technology is located in campus labs and includes learning support software.

Subject-Area Tutoring Tutoring is offered one-on-one, in small groups, and in class-size groups for most subjects. Tutoring is provided through the program or unit via computer-based instruction, graduate assistants/students, LD specialists, professional tutors, and trained peer tutors. Tutoring is also provided collaboratively through on-campus or off-campus services via computer-based instruction, graduate assistants/students, LD specialists, professional tutors, and trained peer tutors.

Diagnostic Testing Testing is provided through the program or unit for learning strategies, learning styles, math, reading, study skills, and written language. Testing for learning strategies, learning styles, math, reading, study skills, and written language is provided collaboratively through on-campus or off-campus services.

Basic Skills Remediation Remediation is offered one-on-one, in small groups, and in class-size groups for learning strategies, math, reading, spelling, spoken language, study skills, time management, and written language. Remediation is provided through the program or unit via computer-based instruction, graduate assistants/students, LD specialists, professional tutors, regular education teachers, special education teachers, and trained peer tutors. Remediation is also provided collaboratively through on-campus or off-campus services via computer-based instruction, graduate assistants/students, LD specialists, professional tutors, regular education teachers, special education teachers, and trained peer tutors.

Enrichment Enrichment programs are available through the program or unit for career planning, college survival skills, health and nutrition, learning strategies, math, oral communication skills, practical computer skills, reading, self-advocacy, stress management, study skills, test taking, time management, vocabulary development, and written composition skills. Programs for career planning, college survival skills, health and nutrition, learning strategies, math, oral communication skills, practical computer skills, reading, self-advocacy, stress management, study skills, test taking, time management, vocabulary development, and written composition skills are provided collaboratively through on-campus or off-campus services. Credit is offered for career planning, college survival skills, health and nutrition, learning strategies, math, oral communication skills, practical computer skills, reading, self-advocacy, stress management, study skills, test taking, time management, vocabulary development, and written composition skills.

Student Organization Barrier Breakers.

Fees *Summer Program* fee is $3500 to $4500.

Application For admittance to the program or unit, students are required to apply to the program directly, provide a psychoeducational report (3 years old or less), and provide documentation of high school services. Upon application, materials documenting need for services should be sent to both admissions and the LD program or unit. Upon acceptance, documentation of need for services should be sent only to the LD program or unit. *Application deadline (LD program):* Rolling/continuous for fall and rolling/continuous for spring.

Written Policies Written policy regarding general/basic LD accommodations is available on the program Web site. Written policy regarding general/basic LD accommodations is outlined in the school's catalog/handbook.

Two-Year Colleges with Structured/Intrusive Programs

TWO-YEAR COLLEGES WITH SELF-DIRECTED/DECENTRALIZED PROGRAMS

Abraham Baldwin Agricultural College
Student Development Center

2802 Moore Highway

Tifton, GA 31793

http://www.abac.edu

Contact: Dr. Maggie A. Martin, Director of Student Development. Phone: 229-391-5135. Fax: 229-391-5136. E-mail: mmartin@abac.edu. Head of LD Program: Ms. Annie R Sims, Career & Personal Counselor. Phone: 229-391-5135. Fax: 229-391-5136. E-mail: asims@abac.edu.

Student Development Center Approximately 100 registered undergraduate students were served during 2006–07. The program or unit includes 2 full-time staff members. Counselors and other are provided through the program or unit. Academic advisers, counselors, diagnostic specialists, trained peer tutors, and other are provided collaboratively through on-campus or off-campus services.
Orientation The program or unit offers an optional 30-minute orientation for new students during new student orientation.
Unique Aids and Services Aids, services, or accommodations include career counseling and priority registration.
Assistive Technology Assistive technology is located in campus labs, the DSS office, the library and includes digital textbooks/e-text. Technology training is provided to incoming students.
Subject-Area Tutoring Tutoring is offered one-on-one and in small groups for all subjects. Tutoring is provided collaboratively through on-campus or off-campus services via computer-based instruction, trained peer tutors, and other.
Diagnostic Testing Testing for auditory processing, intelligence, learning strategies, math, motor skills, neuropsychological, reading, spelling, spoken language, visual processing, and written language is provided collaboratively through on-campus or off-campus services.
Basic Skills Remediation Remediation is offered in class-size groups for computer skills, learning strategies, math, reading, study skills, time management, and written language. Remediation is provided collaboratively through on-campus or off-campus services via computer-based instruction, regular education teachers, and trained peer tutors.
Enrichment Enrichment programs are available through the program or unit for career planning, college survival skills, learning strategies, self-advocacy, stress management, study skills, test taking, time management, and other. Programs for career planning, college survival skills, health and nutrition, learning strategies, math, medication management, practical computer skills, reading, stress management, study skills, test taking, time management, and other are provided collaboratively through on-campus or off-campus services.
Fees *Diagnostic Testing* fee is $500.
Application For admittance to the program or unit, students are required to provide a psychoeducational report (3 years old or less). It is recommended that students provide documentation of high school services. Upon application, materials documenting need for services should be sent only to the LD program or unit. Upon acceptance, documentation of need for services should be sent only to the LD program or unit. *Application deadline (LD program):* Rolling/continuous for fall and rolling/continuous for spring.

Written Policies Written policies regarding course substitutions and general/basic LD accommodations are available on the program Web site. Written policy regarding general/basic LD accommodations is outlined in the school's catalog/handbook. Written policies regarding course substitutions, general/basic LD accommodations, substitutions and waivers of admissions requirements, and substitutions and waivers of graduation requirements are available through the program or unit directly.

Aims Community College
Disability Access Center

Box 69

5401 West 20th Street

Greeley, CO 80632-0069

http://www.aims.edu/

Contact: Disability Access Center. Phone: 970-339-6388. Fax: 970-506-6937. E-mail: disabilities@aims.edu.

Disability Access Center Approximately 30 registered undergraduate students were served during 2006–07. The program or unit includes 1 full-time and 10 part-time staff members. Academic advisers, counselors, professional tutors, regular education teachers, remediation/learning specialists, skill tutors, and trained peer tutors are provided collaboratively through on-campus or off-campus services.
Assistive Technology Assistive technology is located in the DSS office and includes digital textbooks/e-text and scanning.
Subject-Area Tutoring Tutoring is offered one-on-one, in small groups, and in class-size groups for most subjects. Tutoring is provided collaboratively through on-campus or off-campus services via computer-based instruction, professional tutors, and trained peer tutors.
Basic Skills Remediation Remediation is offered one-on-one, in small groups, and in class-size groups for learning strategies, math, reading, spelling, study skills, time management, and written language. Remediation is provided collaboratively through on-campus or off-campus services via computer-based instruction and regular education teachers.
Enrichment Programs for career planning, college survival skills, health and nutrition, learning strategies, math, oral communication skills, practical computer skills, reading, stress management, study skills, test taking, time management, vocabulary development, and written composition skills are provided collaboratively through on-campus or off-campus services. Credit is offered for career planning, college survival skills, health and nutrition, learning strategies, math, oral communication skills, practical computer skills, reading, stress management, study skills, test taking, time management, vocabulary development, and written composition skills.
Application For admittance to the program or unit, students are required to provide appropriate tests by appropriate person with recommendations. It is recommended that students provide documentation of high school services. Upon application, materials documenting need for services should be sent only to the LD program or unit. Upon acceptance, documentation of need for services should be sent only to the LD program or unit. *Application deadline (institutional):* Continuous. *Application deadline (LD program):* Rolling/continuous for fall and rolling/continuous for spring.

Alabama Southern Community College
Disability Services

PO Box 2000

Monroeville, AL 36461

http://www.ascc.edu/

Contact: Mrs. Mary Beth Brasell, ADA Coordinator. Phone: 334-636-9642 Ext. 613. Fax: 334-636-1380. E-mail: mbbrasell@ascc.edu. Head of LD Program: Ms. Ann Clanton, Dean of Students. Phone: 334-636-9642 Ext. 639. Fax: 334-636-1380.

Disability Services Approximately 8 registered undergraduate students were served during 2006–07. The program or unit includes 4 part-time staff members. Services are provided collaboratively through on-campus or off-campus services.

Unique Aids and Services Aids, services, or accommodations include career counseling, faculty training, and priority registration.

Subject-Area Tutoring Tutoring is offered one-on-one for all subjects. Tutoring is provided collaboratively through on-campus or off-campus services via computer-based instruction, graduate assistants/students, and trained peer tutors.

Diagnostic Testing Testing for learning strategies, learning styles, math, and reading is provided collaboratively through on-campus or off-campus services.

Basic Skills Remediation Remediation is offered in class-size groups for computer skills, learning strategies, math, reading, study skills, time management, and written language. Remediation is provided collaboratively through on-campus or off-campus services via computer-based instruction and regular education teachers.

Enrichment Programs for career planning, college survival skills, health and nutrition, learning strategies, math, practical computer skills, reading, stress management, study skills, test taking, time management, and written composition skills are provided collaboratively through on-campus or off-campus services. Credit is offered for career planning, college survival skills, health and nutrition, learning strategies, math, practical computer skills, reading, stress management, study skills, test taking, time management, and written composition skills.

Application It is recommended that students apply to the program directly, provide a psychoeducational report (2 years old or less), and provide documentation of high school services. Upon application, materials documenting need for services should be sent only to the LD program or unit. Upon acceptance, documentation of need for services should be sent only to the LD program or unit. *Application deadline (LD program):* Rolling/continuous for fall and rolling/continuous for spring.

Written Policies Written policy regarding general/basic LD accommodations is outlined in the school's catalog/handbook. Written policy regarding general/basic LD accommodations is available through the program or unit directly.

Alexandria Technical College
Support Services Department

1601 Jefferson Street

Alexandria, MN 56308-3707

http://www.alextech.org/CollegeServices.htm

Contact: Ms. Mary J. Ackerman, Support Services Coordinator. Phone: 320-762-4673. Fax: 320-762-4501. E-mail: marya@alextech.edu.

Support Services Department Approximately 275 registered undergraduate students were served during 2006–07. The program or unit includes 3 part-time staff members. Academic advisers, counselors, graduate assistants/students, professional tutors, regular education teachers, skill tutors, and trained peer tutors are provided collaboratively through on-campus or off-campus services.

Unique Aids and Services Aids, services, or accommodations include career counseling and parent workshops.

Assistive Technology Assistive technology is located in the DSS office and includes digital textbooks/e-text and learning support software. Technology training is provided to incoming students.

Subject-Area Tutoring Tutoring is offered one-on-one and in small groups for most subjects. Tutoring is provided through the program or unit via graduate assistants/students, professional tutors, and trained peer tutors.

Diagnostic Testing Testing is provided through the program or unit for learning styles. Testing for math, reading, and written language is provided collaboratively through on-campus or off-campus services.

Basic Skills Remediation Remediation is offered in class-size groups for math and written language. Remediation is provided collaboratively through on-campus or off-campus services via computer-based instruction and regular education teachers.

Enrichment Enrichment programs are available through the program or unit for learning strategies, math, oral communication skills, practical computer skills, self-advocacy, stress management, study skills, test taking, time management, vocabulary development, and written composition skills. Program for career planning is provided collaboratively through on-campus or off-campus services.

Application For admittance to the program or unit, students are required to provide a psychoeducational report (3 years old or less), provide documentation of high school services, and provide assessment summary report. Upon application, materials documenting need for services should be sent only to the LD program or unit. Upon acceptance, documentation of need for services should be sent only to the LD program or unit. *Application deadline (institutional):* Continuous. *Application deadline (LD program):* Rolling/continuous for fall and rolling/continuous for spring.

Written Policies Written policy regarding general/basic LD accommodations is available on the program Web site. Written policy regarding general/basic LD accommodations is outlined in the school's catalog/handbook. Written policy regarding general/basic LD accommodations is available through the program or unit directly.

Allegany College of Maryland
Disabled Student Services

12401 Willowbrook Road, SE

Cumberland, MD 21502-2596

http://www.allegany.edu

Contact: Ms. Carol Ann Davis, Coordinator of Special Populations. Phone: 301-784-5355. Fax: 301-784-5060. E-mail: cdavis@allegany.edu. Head of LD Program: Ms. Carol Ann Davis, Coordinator of Services for Students with Disabilities. Phone: 301-784-5355. Fax: 301-784-5060.

Disabled Student Services Approximately 35 registered undergraduate students were served during 2006–07. The program or unit includes 1 full-time staff member. Academic advisers, counselors, professional tutors, remediation/learning specialists, and trained peer tutors are provided through the program or unit. Academic advisers, professional tutors, remediation/learning specialists, and trained peer tutors are provided collaboratively through on-campus or off-campus services.

Unique Aids and Services Aids, services, or accommodations include advocates and career counseling.

Assistive Technology Assistive technology is located in the DSS office and includes learning support software and scanning. Technology training is provided to incoming students.

Subject-Area Tutoring Tutoring is offered one-on-one and in small groups for all subjects. Tutoring is provided through the program or unit via professional tutors and trained peer tutors.

Basic Skills Remediation Remediation is offered one-on-one and in small groups for computer skills, learning strategies, math, reading, study skills, time management, and written language. Remediation is provided through the program or unit via computer-based instruction, professional tutors, and trained peer tutors.

Enrichment Enrichment programs are available through the program or unit for career planning, college survival skills, learning strategies, math, reading, self-advocacy, stress management, study skills, test taking, time management, vocabulary development, and written composition skills.

Application For admittance to the program or unit, students are required to provide a psychoeducational report (3 years old or less). It is recommended that students provide documentation of high school services. Upon application, materials documenting need for services should be sent only to the LD program or unit. Upon acceptance, documentation of need for services should be sent only to the LD program or unit. *Application deadline (institutional):* Continuous. *Application deadline (LD program):* Rolling/continuous for fall and rolling/continuous for spring.

Written Policies Written policy regarding general/basic LD accommodations is available through the program or unit directly.

Altamaha Technical College
Student Services

1777 West Cherry Street

Jesup, GA 31545

http://www.altamahatech.edu/

Contact: Tracy Lynn Evans, Special Needs Coordinator. Phone: 912-427-5861. Fax: 912-427-1901. E-mail: tevans@altamahatech.edu.

Student Services Approximately 3 registered undergraduate students were served during 2006–07. The program or unit includes 1 full-time staff member. Academic advisers are provided through the program or unit. Diagnostic specialists, regular education teachers, and remediation/learning specialists are provided collaboratively through on-campus or off-campus services.

Unique Aids and Services Aids, services, or accommodations include career counseling and faculty training.

Subject-Area Tutoring Tutoring is offered one-on-one and in small groups for some subjects. Tutoring is provided collaboratively through on-campus or off-campus services via computer-based instruction, trained peer tutors, and other.

Basic Skills Remediation Remediation is offered one-on-one, in small groups, and in class-size groups for auditory processing, handwriting, learning strategies, math, reading, spelling, study skills, time management, visual processing, and written language. Remediation is provided through the program or unit. Remediation is also provided collaboratively through on-campus or off-campus services via computer-based instruction, regular education teachers, and trained peer tutors.

Application For admittance to the program or unit, students are required to apply to the program directly and provide a psychoeducational report (3 years old or less). It is recommended that students provide documentation of high school services. Upon application, materials documenting need for services should be sent only to the LD program or unit. Upon acceptance, documentation of need for services should be sent only to the LD program or unit. *Application deadline (LD program):* Rolling/continuous for fall and rolling/continuous for spring.

Written Policies Written policies regarding course substitutions, general/basic LD accommodations, grade forgiveness, reduced course loads, substitutions and waivers of admissions requirements, and substitutions and waivers of graduation requirements are available through the program or unit directly.

Alvin Community College
Office of Disability Services

3110 Mustang Road

Alvin, TX 77511-4898

http://www.alvincollege.edu

Contact: Ms. Eileen Cross, ADA Counselor. Phone: 281-756-3531. Fax: 281-756-3843. E-mail: ecross@alvin.cc.tx.us.

Office of Disability Services Approximately 70 registered undergraduate students were served during 2006–07. The program or unit includes 1 full-time and 1 part-time staff member. Academic advisers, counselors, and LD specialists are provided through the program or unit. Professional tutors, regular education teachers, and remediation/learning specialists are provided collaboratively through on-campus or off-campus services.

Unique Aids and Services Aids, services, or accommodations include career counseling, faculty training, and priority registration.

Alvin Community College (continued)

Assistive Technology Assistive technology is located in campus labs, a special lab, laptops for loan and includes digital textbooks/e-text, learning support software, scanning, and books on tape. Technology training is provided to incoming students.

Subject-Area Tutoring Tutoring is offered one-on-one and in small groups for some subjects. Tutoring is provided collaboratively through on-campus or off-campus services via computer-based instruction, professional tutors, and trained peer tutors.

Diagnostic Testing Testing is provided through the program or unit for learning strategies, learning styles, and study skills.

Basic Skills Remediation Remediation is offered one-on-one and in small groups for math, reading, and written language. Remediation is provided collaboratively through on-campus or off-campus services via computer-based instruction, professional tutors, and trained peer tutors.

Enrichment Programs for career planning, college survival skills, learning strategies, math, stress management, study skills, test taking, and time management are provided collaboratively through on-campus or off-campus services.

Student Organization Student Organization for Disability Awareness (SODA) consists of 4 members.

Application For admittance to the program or unit, students are required to apply to the program directly, provide a psychoeducational report (5 years old or less), and provide documentation of high school services. It is recommended that students provide documentation of professional testing. Upon application, materials documenting need for services should be sent only to the LD program or unit. Upon acceptance, documentation of need for services should be sent only to the LD program or unit. *Application deadline (LD program):* Rolling/continuous for fall and rolling/continuous for spring.

Written Policies Written policy regarding general/basic LD accommodations is available on the program Web site. Written policy regarding general/basic LD accommodations is outlined in the school's catalog/handbook. Written policy regarding general/basic LD accommodations is available through the program or unit directly.

Ancilla College
Services for Students with Disabilities

Union Road, PO Box 1

Donaldson, IN 46513

http://www.ancilla.edu

Contact: Ms. D. Pratt, ADA Coordinator. Phone: 574-936-8898 Ext. 366. E-mail: dpratt@ancilla.edu.

Services for Students with Disabilities Approximately 25 registered undergraduate students were served during 2006–07. The program or unit includes 2 full-time staff members. Coaches, professional tutors, regular education teachers, remediation/learning specialists, skill tutors, strategy tutors, trained peer tutors, and other are provided collaboratively through on-campus or off-campus services.

Summer Program To help prepare for the demands of college, there is an optional 3-day/2-night summer program prior to entering the school available to high school graduates that focuses on computing skills, life skills and/or college life adjustment, self-advocacy, study skills, test-taking skills, and time management. The program accepts students from out-of-state.

Unique Aids and Services Aids, services, or accommodations include career counseling, faculty training, and weekly meetings with faculty.

Assistive Technology Assistive technology is located in a special lab and includes digital textbooks/e-text, learning support software, and scanning. Technology training is provided to incoming students.

Subject-Area Tutoring Tutoring is offered one-on-one, in small groups, and in class-size groups for all subjects. Tutoring is provided collaboratively through on-campus or off-campus services via computer-based instruction, professional tutors, trained peer tutors, and other.

Diagnostic Testing Testing is provided through the program or unit for learning strategies, learning styles, math, personality, reading, study skills, and written language.

Basic Skills Remediation Remediation is offered one-on-one and in class-size groups for computer skills, learning strategies, math, reading, spelling, spoken language, study skills, time management, written language, and others. Remediation is provided collaboratively through on-campus or off-campus services via computer-based instruction, professional tutors, regular education teachers, and trained peer tutors.

Enrichment Programs for career planning, college survival skills, health and nutrition, learning strategies, math, medication management, oral communication skills, practical computer skills, reading, self-advocacy, stress management, study skills, test taking, time management, vocabulary development, written composition skills, and other are provided collaboratively through on-campus or off-campus services. Credit is offered for career planning, college survival skills, health and nutrition, learning strategies, math, oral communication skills, practical computer skills, reading, self-advocacy, stress management, study skills, test taking, time management, vocabulary development, written composition skills, and other.

Fees *Diagnostic Testing* fee is $0 to $15.

Application It is recommended that students provide a psychoeducational report, provide documentation of high school services, and provide other documentation. Upon application, materials documenting need for services should be sent only to the LD program or unit. Upon acceptance, documentation of need for services should be sent only to the LD program or unit. *Application deadline (institutional):* Continuous. *Application deadline (LD program):* Rolling/continuous for fall and rolling/continuous for spring.

Written Policies Written policies regarding course substitutions, general/basic LD accommodations, grade forgiveness, reduced course loads, substitutions and waivers of admissions requirements, and substitutions and waivers of graduation requirements are available through the program or unit directly.

Arkansas State University–Newport
Student Affairs Office

7648 Victory Boulevard

Newport, AR 72112

http://www.asun.edu/

Contact: Dr. Mary Robertson, Vice Chancellor for Student Affairs. Phone: 870-512-7812. Fax: 870-512-7835. E-mail: mrobertson@asun.edu.

Student Affairs Office Approximately 4 registered undergraduate students were served during 2006–07. The program or unit includes 1 full-time staff member. Counselors, regular education teachers, remediation/learning specialists, and skill tutors are provided collaboratively through on-campus or off-campus services.
Unique Aids and Services Aids, services, or accommodations include career counseling, faculty training, and priority registration.
Assistive Technology Assistive technology is located in the DSS office and includes digital textbooks/e-text, learning support software, and scanning. Technology training is provided to incoming students.
Subject-Area Tutoring Tutoring is offered one-on-one, in small groups, and in class-size groups for some subjects. Tutoring is provided collaboratively through on-campus or off-campus services via computer-based instruction, professional tutors, and other.
Diagnostic Testing Testing for math, reading, spelling, and written language is provided collaboratively through on-campus or off-campus services.
Basic Skills Remediation Remediation is offered one-on-one, in small groups, and in class-size groups for computer skills, learning strategies, math, reading, spelling, study skills, time management, and written language. Remediation is provided collaboratively through on-campus or off-campus services via computer-based instruction, professional tutors, regular education teachers, and trained peer tutors.
Enrichment Programs for career planning, college survival skills, health and nutrition, learning strategies, math, oral communication skills, practical computer skills, reading, stress management, study skills, test taking, time management, vocabulary development, and written composition skills are provided collaboratively through on-campus or off-campus services. Credit is offered for college survival skills, learning strategies, math, oral communication skills, practical computer skills, reading, stress management, study skills, test taking, time management, and written composition skills.
Fees *Diagnostic Testing* fee is $30.
Application For admittance to the program or unit, students are required to apply to the program directly. It is recommended that students provide documentation of high school services. Upon application, materials documenting need for services should be sent only to the LD program or unit. Upon acceptance, documentation of need for services should be sent only to the LD program or unit. *Application deadline (LD program):* Rolling/continuous for fall and rolling/continuous for spring.
Written Policies Written policies regarding general/basic LD accommodations and reduced course loads are available through the program or unit directly.

The Art Institute of New York City
Disability Services

75 Varick Street, 16th Floor

New York, NY 10013

http://www.ainyc.aii.edu/

Contact: Ms. Laurie Vesalo, Counselor. Phone: 212-226-5500 Ext. 6700. E-mail: lvesalo@aii.edu.

Disability Services Approximately 15 registered undergraduate students were served during 2006–07. The program or unit includes 1 full-time staff member. Counselors are provided through the program or unit. Academic advisers and regular education teachers are provided collaboratively through on-campus or off-campus services.
Unique Aids and Services Aids, services, or accommodations include career counseling and faculty training.
Assistive Technology Assistive technology is located in campus labs and includes digital textbooks/e-text and learning support software.
Subject-Area Tutoring Tutoring is offered one-on-one, in small groups, and in class-size groups.
Basic Skills Remediation Remediation is offered one-on-one, in small groups, and in class-size groups for math, reading, study skills, and time management. Remediation is provided collaboratively through on-campus or off-campus services via regular education teachers, trained peer tutors, and other.
Enrichment Enrichment programs are available through the program or unit for health and nutrition, math, oral communication skills, practical computer skills, stress management, study skills, and time management. Programs for career planning, college survival skills, learning strategies, study skills, test taking, and time management are provided collaboratively through on-campus or off-campus services. Credit is offered for health and nutrition, math, oral communication skills, and practical computer skills.
Application For admittance to the program or unit, students are required to apply to the program directly, provide a psychoeducational report (5 years old or less), and provide documentation completed by an appropriate professional relevant to the disability. Upon application, materials documenting need for services should be sent only to the LD program or unit. Upon acceptance, documentation of need for services should be sent only to the LD program or unit. *Application deadline (institutional):* Continuous. *Application deadline (LD program):* Rolling/continuous for fall and rolling/continuous for spring.
Written Policies Written policies regarding general/basic LD accommodations and substitutions and waivers of graduation requirements are available on the program Web site. Written policies regarding general/basic LD accommodations and substitutions and waivers of graduation requirements are outlined in the school's catalog/handbook. Written policies regarding general/basic LD accommodations, substitutions and waivers of admissions requirements, and substitutions and waivers of graduation requirements are available through the program or unit directly.

The Art Institute of Ohio–Cincinnati
Disability Services

1011 Glendale Milford Road

Cincinnati, OH 45215

http://www.aiohc.aii.edu

Contact: Dr. Jerry Nuesell, Dean of Student Affairs. Phone: 513-833-2391. Fax: 513-833-2411. E-mail: nusellj@aii.edu.

Disability Services Approximately 10 registered undergraduate students were served during 2006–07. The program or unit includes 1 full-time staff member. Counselors are provided through the program or unit. Academic advisers, regular education teachers, and trained peer tutors are provided collaboratively through on-campus or off-campus services.

Unique Aids and Services Aids, services, or accommodations include personal coach.

Subject-Area Tutoring Tutoring is offered one-on-one, in small groups, and in class-size groups for some subjects. Tutoring is provided collaboratively through on-campus or off-campus services via trained peer tutors and other.

Basic Skills Remediation Remediation is offered one-on-one and in small groups for math, study skills, and time management. Remediation is provided through the program or unit. Remediation is also provided collaboratively through on-campus or off-campus services via regular education teachers and trained peer tutors.

Enrichment Programs for career planning, learning strategies, math, stress management, study skills, test taking, and time management are provided collaboratively through on-campus or off-campus services.

Application For admittance to the program or unit, students are required to provide documentation of disability from qualified service provider. It is recommended that students provide a psychoeducational report (3 years old or less) and provide documentation of high school services. Upon application, materials documenting need for services should be sent to both admissions and the LD program or unit. Upon acceptance, documentation of need for services should be sent only to the LD program or unit. *Application deadline (institutional):* 10/8. *Application deadline (LD program):* Rolling/continuous for fall and rolling/continuous for spring.

Written Policies Written policy regarding general/basic LD accommodations is outlined in the school's catalog/handbook.

Asheville-Buncombe Technical Community College
Disability Services Office

340 Victoria Road

Asheville, NC 28801-4897

http://www.abtech.edu/Student_Services/counseling/disability/default.asp

Contact: Annie Clingenpeel, Disability Services Coordinator and Counselor. Phone: 828-254-1921 Ext. 141. Fax: 828-281-9704. E-mail: aclingenpeel@abtech.edu.

Disability Services Office Approximately 84 registered undergraduate students were served during 2006–07. The program or unit includes 1 full-time and 1 part-time staff member. Counselors are provided through the program or unit. Academic advisers, remediation/learning specialists, skill tutors, and trained peer tutors are provided collaboratively through on-campus or off-campus services.

Orientation The program or unit offers an optional 1-hour orientation for new students individually by special arrangement.

Unique Aids and Services Aids, services, or accommodations include career counseling, faculty training, priority registration, meetings with faculty.

Assistive Technology Assistive technology is located in the DSS office, locations as needed by the student and includes scanning and JAWS.

Subject-Area Tutoring Tutoring is offered in class-size groups for some subjects. Tutoring is provided collaboratively through on-campus or off-campus services via professional tutors, trained peer tutors, and other.

Basic Skills Remediation Remediation is offered in class-size groups for math, reading, and written language. Remediation is provided collaboratively through on-campus or off-campus services via computer-based instruction, professional tutors, regular education teachers, special education teachers, and teacher trainees.

Enrichment Enrichment programs are available through the program or unit for learning strategies, self-advocacy, stress management, study skills, test taking, time management, and other. Programs for career planning, college survival skills, health and nutrition, learning strategies, math, oral communication skills, practical computer skills, reading, stress management, study skills, time management, vocabulary development, and written composition skills are provided collaboratively through on-campus or off-campus services. Credit is offered for college survival skills, health and nutrition, learning strategies, math, oral communication skills, practical computer skills, reading, stress management, study skills, time management, and written composition skills.

Application For admittance to the program or unit, students are required to provide a psychoeducational report (5 years old or less). It is recommended that students apply to the program directly and provide documentation of high school services. Upon application, materials documenting need for services should be sent only to the LD program or unit. Upon acceptance, documentation of need for services should be sent only to the LD program or unit. *Application deadline (institutional):* Continuous. *Application deadline (LD program):* Rolling/continuous for fall and rolling/continuous for spring.

Written Policies Written policy regarding general/basic LD accommodations is available on the program Web site. Written policies regarding course substitutions, general/basic LD accommodations, reduced course loads, and substitutions and waivers of graduation requirements are available through the program or unit directly.

Ashland Community and Technical College
Disability Services

1400 College Drive

Ashland, KY 41101-3683

http://www.ashland.kctcs.edu/

Contact: Ms. Heather Leigh Shelton, Manager of Disability Services. Phone: 606-326-2051. Fax: 606-326-2192. E-mail: heather.shelton@kctcs.edu.

Disability Services Approximately 50 registered undergraduate students were served during 2006–07. The program or unit includes 1 full-time staff member. Academic advisers, counselors, and regular education teachers are provided through the program or unit. Academic advisers, counselors, professional tutors, regular education teachers, and trained peer tutors are provided collaboratively through on-campus or off-campus services.

Orientation The program or unit offers an optional orientation for new students individually by special arrangement.

Unique Aids and Services Aids, services, or accommodations include advocates, career counseling, faculty training, and priority registration.

Assistive Technology Assistive technology is located in the DSS office, the library and includes digital textbooks/e-text, learning support software, and scanning. Technology training is provided to incoming students.

Subject-Area Tutoring Tutoring is offered one-on-one and in small groups for most subjects. Tutoring is provided through the program or unit via computer-based instruction. Tutoring is also provided collaboratively through on-campus or off-campus services via computer-based instruction and trained peer tutors.

Basic Skills Remediation Remediation is offered in class-size groups for learning strategies, math, reading, spelling, study skills, time management, and written language. Remediation is provided through the program or unit via computer-based instruction. Remediation is also provided collaboratively through on-campus or off-campus services via computer-based instruction, regular education teachers, trained peer tutors, and other.

Enrichment Enrichment programs are available through the program or unit for career planning. Programs for career planning, college survival skills, learning strategies, math, reading, stress management, study skills, test taking, time management, vocabulary development, and written composition skills are provided collaboratively through on-campus or off-campus services. Credit is offered for learning strategies, reading, vocabulary development, and written composition skills.

Application For admittance to the program or unit, students are required to apply to the program directly and provide a psychoeducational report (5 years old or less). It is recommended that students provide documentation of high school services. Upon application, materials documenting need for services should be sent only to the LD program or unit. Upon acceptance, documentation of need for services should be sent only to the LD program or unit. *Application deadline (institutional):* 8/20. *Application deadline (LD program):* Rolling/continuous for fall and rolling/continuous for spring.

Written Policies Written policies regarding course substitutions, general/basic LD accommodations, reduced course loads, substitutions and waivers of admissions requirements, and substitutions and waivers of graduation requirements are outlined in the school's catalog/handbook. Written policies regarding course substitutions, general/basic LD accommodations, substitutions and waivers of admissions requirements, and substitutions and waivers of graduation requirements are available through the program or unit directly.

Asnuntuck Community College
Student Services

170 Elm Street

Enfield, CT 06082-3800

http://www.acc.commnet.edu

Contact: P. Maki McHenry, Counselor and Accommodations Coordinator. Phone: 860-253-3021. Fax: 860-253-3029. E-mail: mmchenry@acc.commnet.edu.

Student Services Approximately 35 registered undergraduate students were served during 2006–07. The program or unit includes 1 part-time staff member. Academic advisers, counselors, skill tutors, and strategy tutors are provided collaboratively through on-campus or off-campus services.

Unique Aids and Services Aids, services, or accommodations include advocates, career counseling, faculty training, personal coach, priority registration, support groups.

Assistive Technology Assistive technology is located in campus labs, a special lab and includes digital textbooks/e-text, learning support software, and scanning.

Subject-Area Tutoring Tutoring is offered one-on-one, in small groups, and in class-size groups for some subjects. Tutoring is provided collaboratively through on-campus or off-campus services via computer-based instruction, professional tutors, trained peer tutors, and other.

Basic Skills Remediation Remediation is offered one-on-one, in small groups, and in class-size groups for computer skills, learning strategies, math, reading, social skills, spelling, study skills, time management, and written language. Remediation is provided collaboratively through on-campus or off-campus services via computer-based instruction, professional tutors, regular education teachers, trained peer tutors, and other.

Enrichment Programs for career planning, college survival skills, health and nutrition, learning strategies, math, oral communication skills, practical computer skills, reading, self-advocacy, stress management, study skills, test taking, time management, vocabulary development, and written composition skills are provided collaboratively through on-campus or off-campus services. Credit is offered for career planning, college survival skills, health and nutrition, learning strategies, math, oral communication skills, practical computer skills, reading, study skills, test taking, time management, vocabulary development, and written composition skills.

Application For admittance to the program or unit, students are required to provide a psychoeducational report (7 years old or less). It is recommended that students provide documentation of high school services. Upon application, materials documenting need for services should be sent to both admissions and the LD program or unit. Upon acceptance, documentation of need for services should be sent only to the LD program or unit. *Application deadline (institutional):* Continuous. *Application deadline (LD program):* Rolling/continuous for fall and rolling/continuous for spring.

Asnuntuck Community College (continued)

Written Policies Written policies regarding course substitutions, general/basic LD accommodations, grade forgiveness, reduced course loads, substitutions and waivers of admissions requirements, and substitutions and waivers of graduation requirements are available on the program Web site. Written policies regarding course substitutions, general/basic LD accommodations, grade forgiveness, reduced course loads, substitutions and waivers of admissions requirements, and substitutions and waivers of graduation requirements are outlined in the school's catalog/handbook. Written policies regarding course substitutions, general/basic LD accommodations, grade forgiveness, reduced course loads, substitutions and waivers of admissions requirements, and substitutions and waivers of graduation requirements are available through the program or unit directly.

Bainbridge College

2500 East Shotwell Street
Bainbridge, GA 39819
http://www.bainbridge.edu/

Contact: Mrs. Jessica A. Long, Disabilities Service Provider. Phone: 229-248-2579. Fax: 229-248-2589. E-mail: jlong@bainbridge.edu.

The program or unit includes 2 full-time staff members. Counselors and LD specialists are provided through the program or unit. Academic advisers and remediation/learning specialists are provided collaboratively through on-campus or off-campus services.

Unique Aids and Services Aids, services, or accommodations include career counseling, faculty training, personal coach, and priority registration.

Assistive Technology Assistive technology is located in the DSS office, the library and includes digital textbooks/e-text, learning support software, and scanning. Technology training is provided to incoming students.

Subject-Area Tutoring Tutoring is offered one-on-one, in small groups, and in class-size groups for all subjects. Tutoring is provided collaboratively through on-campus or off-campus services via computer-based instruction and trained peer tutors.

Basic Skills Remediation Remediation is offered one-on-one, in small groups, and in class-size groups for math, reading, and written language. Remediation is provided collaboratively through on-campus or off-campus services via computer-based instruction, regular education teachers, and trained peer tutors.

Enrichment Enrichment programs are available through the program or unit for career planning, learning strategies, stress management, study skills, test taking, and time management. Programs for college survival skills, health and nutrition, math, practical computer skills, reading, vocabulary development, and written composition skills are provided collaboratively through on-campus or off-campus services.

Application For admittance to the program or unit, students are required to provide a psychoeducational report (3 years old or less). It is recommended that students provide documentation of high school services. Upon application, materials documenting need for services should be sent only to the LD program or unit. Upon acceptance, documentation of need for services should be sent only to the LD program or unit. *Application deadline (institutional):* 8/1. *Application deadline (LD program):* Rolling/continuous for fall and rolling/continuous for spring.

Written Policies Written policies regarding course substitutions, general/basic LD accommodations, and substitutions and waivers of admissions requirements are available on the program Web site. Written policies regarding course substitutions, general/basic LD accommodations, and substitutions and waivers of admissions requirements are outlined in the school's catalog/handbook. Written policies regarding course substitutions, general/basic LD accommodations, and substitutions and waivers of admissions requirements are available through the program or unit directly.

Blackhawk Technical College

PO Box 5009
Janesville, WI 53547-5009
http://www.blackhawk.edu/

Contact: Ms. Christine A. Flottum, Instructor and Program Coordinator. Phone: 608-757-7796. Fax: 608-757-7752. E-mail: cflottum@blackhawk.edu.

Approximately 95 registered undergraduate students were served during 2006–07. The program or unit includes 2 full-time and 4 part-time staff members. LD specialists, professional tutors, remediation/learning specialists, skill tutors, special education teachers, strategy tutors, and trained peer tutors are provided through the program or unit. Academic advisers, counselors, and regular education teachers are provided collaboratively through on-campus or off-campus services.

Orientation The program or unit offers an optional orientation for new students during summer prior to enrollment and individually by special arrangement.

Summer Program To help prepare for the demands of college, there is an optional 1-week summer program prior to entering the school available to high school graduates that focuses on life skills and/or college life adjustment, self-advocacy, study skills, test-taking skills, and time management. The program accepts students from out-of-state and is available to students attending other colleges.

Unique Aids and Services Aids, services, or accommodations include career counseling and priority registration.

Assistive Technology Assistive technology is located in campus labs, the DSS office, a special lab and includes digital textbooks/e-text, learning support software, and scanning. Technology training is provided to incoming students.

Subject-Area Tutoring Tutoring is offered one-on-one and in small groups for most subjects. Tutoring is provided through the program or unit via computer-based instruction, LD specialists, professional tutors, and trained peer tutors. Tutoring is also provided collaboratively through on-campus or off-campus services via computer-based instruction and trained peer tutors.

Diagnostic Testing Testing is provided through the program or unit for learning strategies, learning styles, math, reading, spelling, study skills, and written language.

Basic Skills Remediation Remediation is offered in small groups and in class-size groups for computer skills, learning strategies, math, reading, spelling, study skills, time management, and written language. Remediation is provided collaboratively through on-campus or off-campus services via computer-based instruction, professional tutors, regular education teachers, and trained peer tutors.

Enrichment Enrichment programs are available through the program or unit for college survival skills, learning strategies, self-advocacy, study skills, test taking, time management, and written composition skills. Programs for career planning, college survival skills, learning strategies, math, practical computer skills, reading, study skills, test taking, time management, vocabulary development, and written composition skills are provided collaboratively through on-campus or off-campus services.

Application For admittance to the program or unit, students are required to provide a psychoeducational report and provide documentation of high school services. Upon application, materials documenting need for services should be sent only to the LD program or unit. Upon acceptance, documentation of need for services should be sent only to the LD program or unit. *Application deadline (LD program):* Rolling/continuous for fall and rolling/continuous for spring.

Written Policies Written policy regarding general/basic LD accommodations is outlined in the school's catalog/handbook. Written policy regarding general/basic LD accommodations is available through the program or unit directly.

Blinn College
Office of Disability Services

902 College Avenue

Brenham, TX 77833-4049

http://www.blinn.edu/disability.htm

Contact: Ms. Patricia E. Moran, Director of Disability Services. Phone: 979-830-4157. Fax: 979-830-4410. E-mail: pmoran@blinn.edu.

Office of Disability Services Approximately 550 registered undergraduate students were served during 2006–07. The program or unit includes 6 full-time staff members and 1 part-time staff member. Academic advisers, counselors, and LD specialists are provided through the program or unit. Coaches, professional tutors, regular education teachers, remediation/learning specialists, and skill tutors are provided collaboratively through on-campus or off-campus services.

Unique Aids and Services Aids, services, or accommodations include one-on-one counseling on disability-related issues.

Assistive Technology Assistive technology is located in campus labs, the DSS office and includes scanning and text-to-audio software.

Subject-Area Tutoring Tutoring is offered in small groups for most subjects. Tutoring is provided collaboratively through on-campus or off-campus services via computer-based instruction, trained peer tutors, and other.

Basic Skills Remediation Remediation is offered in small groups and in class-size groups for learning strategies, math, reading, study skills, and written language. Remediation is provided collaboratively through on-campus or off-campus services via computer-based instruction, regular education teachers, and trained peer tutors.

Enrichment Programs for career planning, college survival skills, learning strategies, math, practical computer skills, reading, stress management, study skills, test taking, time management, and written composition skills are provided collaboratively through on-campus or off-campus services. Credit is offered for learning strategies, math, practical computer skills, reading, study skills, and written composition skills.

Application For admittance to the program or unit, students are required to provide a psychoeducational report (5 years old or less). It is recommended that students provide documentation of high school services. Upon application, materials documenting need for services should be sent only to the LD program or unit. Upon acceptance, documentation of need for services should be sent only to the LD program or unit. *Application deadline (institutional):* Continuous. *Application deadline (LD program):* Rolling/continuous for fall and rolling/continuous for spring.

Written Policies Written policies regarding course substitutions, substitutions and waivers of admissions requirements, and substitutions and waivers of graduation requirements are outlined in the school's catalog/handbook. Written policies regarding course substitutions, general/basic LD accommodations, substitutions and waivers of admissions requirements, and substitutions and waivers of graduation requirements are available through the program or unit directly.

Blue Mountain Community College
Services for Students with Disabilities

2411 Northwest Carden Avenue

PO Box 100

Pendleton, OR 97801-1000

http://www.bluecc.edu/admissions/disability.html

Contact: Amy Spiegel, Coordinator of Services for Students with Disabilities. Phone: 541-278-5807. Fax: 541-278-5885. E-mail: aspiegel@bluecc.edu.

Services for Students with Disabilities Approximately 73 registered undergraduate students were served during 2006–07. The program or unit includes 1 part-time staff member. Academic advisers, coaches, counselors, regular education teachers, remediation/learning specialists, skill tutors, and trained peer tutors are provided collaboratively through on-campus or off-campus services.

Orientation The program or unit offers an optional varying length orientation for new students before registration, before classes begin, during summer prior to enrollment, during registration, after classes begin, and individually by special arrangement.

Unique Aids and Services Aids, services, or accommodations include advocates, career counseling, faculty training, support groups, and weekly meetings with faculty.

Assistive Technology Assistive technology is located in campus labs, the DSS office, the library and includes digital textbooks/e-text, learning support software, scanning, and screen magnification, voice input. Technology training is provided to incoming students.

Subject-Area Tutoring Tutoring is offered one-on-one and in small groups for all subjects. Tutoring is provided collaboratively through on-campus or off-campus services via computer-based instruction and trained peer tutors.

Diagnostic Testing Testing for learning strategies and learning styles is provided collaboratively through on-campus or off-campus services.

Basic Skills Remediation Remediation is offered one-on-one, in small groups, and in class-size groups for computer skills, learning strategies, math, reading, social skills, spelling, spoken language,

Blue Mountain Community College (continued)
study skills, time management, visual processing, and written language. Remediation is provided collaboratively through on-campus or off-campus services via computer-based instruction, regular education teachers, and trained peer tutors.
Enrichment Programs for career planning, college survival skills, health and nutrition, learning strategies, math, oral communication skills, practical computer skills, reading, self-advocacy, stress management, study skills, test taking, time management, vocabulary development, and written composition skills are provided collaboratively through on-campus or off-campus services. Credit is offered for career planning, college survival skills, health and nutrition, math, oral communication skills, practical computer skills, reading, stress management, study skills, test taking, time management, vocabulary development, and written composition skills.
Application For admittance to the program or unit, students are required to apply to the program directly and provide a psychoeducational report (3 years old or less). Upon application, materials documenting need for services should be sent to both admissions and the LD program or unit. Upon acceptance, documentation of need for services should be sent only to the LD program or unit. *Application deadline (LD program):* Rolling/continuous for fall and rolling/continuous for spring.
Written Policies Written policies regarding course substitutions, general/basic LD accommodations, reduced course loads, and substitutions and waivers of admissions requirements are available on the program Web site. Written policies regarding course substitutions, general/basic LD accommodations, reduced course loads, and substitutions and waivers of admissions requirements are outlined in the school's catalog/handbook. Written policies regarding course substitutions, general/basic LD accommodations, reduced course loads, substitutions and waivers of admissions requirements, and substitutions and waivers of graduation requirements are available through the program or unit directly.

Blue Ridge Community College
Disability Support Services

PO Box 80

Weyers Cave, VA 24486-0080

http://www.brcc.edu/services/disability

Contact: Ms. Beth Gibson, Disability Services Coordinator. Phone: 540-453-2298. Fax: 540-453-2437. E-mail: gibsonb@brcc.edu.

Disability Support Services Approximately 80 registered undergraduate students were served during 2006–07. The program or unit includes 1 full-time staff member. Academic advisers are provided through the program or unit.
Assistive Technology Assistive technology is located in campus labs, a special lab and includes digital textbooks/e-text, learning support software, and scanning.
Subject-Area Tutoring Tutoring is offered one-on-one for most subjects. Tutoring is provided collaboratively through on-campus or off-campus services via trained peer tutors.

Basic Skills Remediation Remediation is offered in class-size groups for math, reading, study skills, time management, and written language. Remediation is provided collaboratively through on-campus or off-campus services via regular education teachers.
Enrichment Programs for career planning, college survival skills, health and nutrition, learning strategies, math, oral communication skills, practical computer skills, reading, stress management, study skills, test taking, time management, vocabulary development, and written composition skills are provided collaboratively through on-campus or off-campus services. Credit is offered for career planning, college survival skills, health and nutrition, learning strategies, oral communication skills, practical computer skills, reading, stress management, study skills, test taking, time management, and vocabulary development.
Application For admittance to the program or unit, students are required to provide a psychoeducational report (3 years old or less). It is recommended that students apply to the program directly and provide documentation of high school services. Upon application, materials documenting need for services should be sent only to the LD program or unit. Upon acceptance, documentation of need for services should be sent only to the LD program or unit. *Application deadline (institutional):* Continuous. *Application deadline (LD program):* Rolling/continuous for fall and rolling/continuous for spring.
Written Policies Written policy regarding general/basic LD accommodations is available on the program Web site. Written policy regarding general/basic LD accommodations is outlined in the school's catalog/handbook. Written policies regarding course substitutions, general/basic LD accommodations, reduced course loads, substitutions and waivers of admissions requirements, and substitutions and waivers of graduation requirements are available through the program or unit directly.

Brevard Community College
Office for Students with Disabilities

1519 Clearlake Road

Cocoa, FL 32922-6597

http://www.brevardcc.edu/osd

Contact: Dr. Lyndi Kolack Fertel, Director of Office for Students with Disabilities. Phone: 321-433-5598. Fax: 321-433-5679. E-mail: fertell@brevardcc.edu.

Office for Students with Disabilities Approximately 300 registered undergraduate students were served during 2006–07. The program or unit includes 9 part-time staff members. LD specialists, professional tutors, and remediation/learning specialists are provided through the program or unit.
Unique Aids and Services Aids, services, or accommodations include advocates, career counseling, and faculty training.
Assistive Technology Assistive technology is located in the DSS office and includes learning support software and scanning. Technology training is provided to incoming students.
Subject-Area Tutoring Tutoring is offered one-on-one for some subjects. Tutoring is provided through the program or unit via LD specialists and professional tutors. Tutoring is also provided collaboratively through on-campus or off-campus services via computer-based instruction, graduate assistants/students, professional tutors, and trained peer tutors.

Diagnostic Testing Testing is provided through the program or unit for auditory processing, learning strategies, learning styles, math, motor skills, reading, spelling, study skills, visual processing, and written language.

Basic Skills Remediation Remediation is offered in small groups for computer skills, learning strategies, math, reading, spelling, study skills, time management, and written language. Remediation is provided through the program or unit via LD specialists and professional tutors. Remediation is also provided collaboratively through on-campus or off-campus services via computer-based instruction, regular education teachers, and trained peer tutors.

Enrichment Enrichment programs are available through the program or unit for math and practical computer skills. Programs for career planning, college survival skills, learning strategies, math, oral communication skills, practical computer skills, reading, self-advocacy, study skills, test taking, time management, and written composition skills are provided collaboratively through on-campus or off-campus services. Credit is offered for college survival skills, health and nutrition, learning strategies, math, oral communication skills, reading, study skills, test taking, time management, and written composition skills.

Application For admittance to the program or unit, students are required to provide a psychoeducational report (3 years old or less). It is recommended that students provide documentation of high school services. Upon application, materials documenting need for services should be sent only to the LD program or unit. *Application deadline (institutional):* Continuous. *Application deadline (LD program):* Rolling/continuous for fall and rolling/continuous for spring.

Written Policies Written policies regarding course substitutions, general/basic LD accommodations, grade forgiveness, substitutions and waivers of admissions requirements, and substitutions and waivers of graduation requirements are available on the program Web site. Written policy regarding general/basic LD accommodations is outlined in the school's catalog/handbook. Written policies regarding course substitutions, general/basic LD accommodations, grade forgiveness, reduced course loads, substitutions and waivers of admissions requirements, and substitutions and waivers of graduation requirements are available through the program or unit directly.

Orientation The program or unit offers an optional 3-hour orientation for new students before classes begin.

Unique Aids and Services Aids, services, or accommodations include personal coach, priority registration, tutoring.

Assistive Technology Assistive technology is located in campus labs, the DSS office, a special lab, the library and includes digital textbooks/e-text, learning support software, and scanning. Technology training is provided to incoming students.

Subject-Area Tutoring Tutoring is offered one-on-one and in small groups for all subjects. Tutoring is provided through the program or unit via LD specialists. Tutoring is also provided collaboratively through on-campus or off-campus services via professional tutors and trained peer tutors.

Diagnostic Testing Testing is provided through the program or unit for auditory processing, intelligence, learning styles, math, reading, spelling, study skills, visual processing, and written language.

Basic Skills Remediation Remediation is offered one-on-one for learning strategies, math, reading, social skills, study skills, time management, and written language. Remediation is provided through the program or unit via computer-based instruction and LD specialists.

Enrichment Enrichment programs are available through the program or unit for learning strategies, math, reading, self-advocacy, stress management, study skills, test taking, time management, and written composition skills. Programs for career planning, college survival skills, math, practical computer skills, reading, stress management, study skills, test taking, time management, and written composition skills are provided collaboratively through on-campus or off-campus services.

Application For admittance to the program or unit, students are required to provide a psychoeducational report (3 years old or less). It is recommended that students provide documentation of high school services and provide report from physician, community agency. Upon application, materials documenting need for services should be sent only to the LD program or unit. Upon acceptance, documentation of need for services should be sent only to the LD program or unit. *Application deadline (institutional):* Continuous. *Application deadline (LD program):* Rolling/continuous for fall and rolling/continuous for spring.

Written Policies Written policy regarding general/basic LD accommodations is available on the program Web site. Written policies regarding course substitutions, general/basic LD accommodations, and substitutions and waivers of graduation requirements are available through the program or unit directly.

Broome Community College
Learning Disabilities Program

PO Box 1017

Binghamton, NY 13902-1017

http://web.sunybroome.edu/~learnassist/learndisabilities.html

Contact: Bruce Pomeroy, Director, Student Support Services Program. Phone: 607-778-5150. Fax: 607-778-5562. E-mail: pomeroy_b@sunybroome.edu. Head of LD Program: Lisa Hughes, Learning Disabilities Specialist. Phone: 607-778-5316. Fax: 607-778-5488. E-mail: hughes_l@sunybroome.edu.

Learning Disabilities Program Approximately 250 registered undergraduate students were served during 2006–07. The program or unit includes 1 full-time and 1 part-time staff member. Coaches and LD specialists are provided through the program or unit. Professional tutors and trained peer tutors are provided collaboratively through on-campus or off-campus services.

Broward Community College
Office of Disability Services

225 East Las Olas Boulevard

Fort Lauderdale, FL 33301-2298

http://www.broward.edu/

Contact: Mrs. Beverly A. Cranmer, Coordinator of Disability Services. Phone: 954-201-7655. Fax: 954-201-7492. E-mail: bcranmer@broward.edu.

Office of Disability Services Approximately 134 registered undergraduate students were served during 2006–07. The program or unit includes 7 full-time and 5 part-time staff members. LD specialists

Broward Community College (continued)

are provided through the program or unit. Academic advisers, counselors, professional tutors, regular education teachers, remediation/learning specialists, and trained peer tutors are provided collaboratively through on-campus or off-campus services.

Unique Aids and Services Aids, services, or accommodations include career counseling, faculty training, support groups, isolated testing, extended time on projects and testing.

Assistive Technology Assistive technology is located in campus labs, the DSS office and includes digital textbooks/e-text, learning support software, and tape recorder.

Subject-Area Tutoring Tutoring is offered in small groups and in class-size groups for some subjects. Tutoring is provided collaboratively through on-campus or off-campus services via computer-based instruction, graduate assistants/students, professional tutors, and trained peer tutors.

Basic Skills Remediation Remediation is offered in small groups and in class-size groups for math, reading, and written language. Remediation is provided collaboratively through on-campus or off-campus services via computer-based instruction and regular education teachers.

Enrichment Enrichment programs are available through the program or unit for learning strategies, self-advocacy, study skills, test taking, and time management. Programs for career planning, college survival skills, health and nutrition, learning strategies, math, practical computer skills, reading, stress management, study skills, test taking, time management, and written composition skills are provided collaboratively through on-campus or off-campus services. Credit is offered for college survival skills, health and nutrition, practical computer skills, and reading.

Application For admittance to the program or unit, students are required to apply to the program directly and provide a psychoeducational report (3 years old or less). It is recommended that students provide documentation of high school services. Upon application, materials documenting need for services should be sent only to the LD program or unit. Upon acceptance, documentation of need for services should be sent only to the LD program or unit. *Application deadline (LD program):* Rolling/continuous for fall and rolling/continuous for spring.

Written Policies Written policies regarding course substitutions, general/basic LD accommodations, and substitutions and waivers of graduation requirements are available on the program Web site. Written policies regarding course substitutions, general/basic LD accommodations, and substitutions and waivers of graduation requirements are outlined in the school's catalog/handbook. Written policies regarding course substitutions, general/basic LD accommodations, and substitutions and waivers of graduation requirements are available through the program or unit directly.

Brown Mackie College–Salina
Student Services

2106 South 9th Street

Salina, KS 67401-2810

http://www.brownmackie.edu/locations.asp?locid=13

Contact: Ms. Cindy Allegree, Student Adviser. Phone: 785-823-4620. Fax: 785-827-7623. E-mail: callegree@edmc.edu.

Student Services Approximately 10 registered undergraduate students were served during 2006–07. The program or unit includes 1 full-time and 3 part-time staff members. Academic advisers, graduate assistants/students, LD specialists, professional tutors, remediation/learning specialists, special education teachers, and trained peer tutors are provided through the program or unit. Academic advisers, graduate assistants/students, LD specialists, professional tutors, remediation/learning specialists, special education teachers, trained peer tutors, and other are provided collaboratively through on-campus or off-campus services.

Unique Aids and Services Aids, services, or accommodations include career counseling, personal coach, support groups, and weekly meetings with faculty.

Assistive Technology Assistive technology is located in the DSS office, local organizations and includes digital textbooks/e-text, learning support software, and screen filters.

Subject-Area Tutoring Tutoring is offered one-on-one for most subjects. Tutoring is provided through the program or unit via computer-based instruction, graduate assistants/students, LD specialists, professional tutors, trained peer tutors, and other. Tutoring is also provided collaboratively through on-campus or off-campus services via other.

Basic Skills Remediation Remediation is offered one-on-one for computer skills, learning strategies, math, reading, spelling, spoken language, study skills, time management, written language, and others. Remediation is provided through the program or unit via computer-based instruction, LD specialists, professional tutors, special education teachers, trained peer tutors, and other. Remediation is also provided collaboratively through on-campus or off-campus services.

Enrichment Enrichment programs are available through the program or unit for practical computer skills, reading, study skills, vocabulary development, and written composition skills. Programs for career planning, college survival skills, learning strategies, math, practical computer skills, reading, stress management, study skills, test taking, time management, vocabulary development, and written composition skills are provided collaboratively through on-campus or off-campus services.

Application For admittance to the program or unit, students are required to provide a psychoeducational report (3 years old or less). It is recommended that students provide documentation of high school services. Upon application, materials documenting need for services should be sent only to the LD program or unit. Upon acceptance, documentation of need for services should be sent only to the LD program or unit. *Application deadline (institutional):* Continuous. *Application deadline (LD program):* Rolling/continuous for fall and rolling/continuous for spring.

Written Policies Written policies regarding general/basic LD accommodations and substitutions and waivers of admissions requirements are available on the program Web site. Written policies regarding course substitutions, general/basic LD accommodations, and substitutions and waivers of admissions requirements are outlined in the school's catalog/handbook. Written policies regarding general/basic LD accommodations and substitutions and waivers of admissions requirements are available through the program or unit directly.

Bryant and Stratton College

150 Bellwood Drive

Rochester, NY 14606

http://www.bryantstratton.edu/

Contact: Ms. Jessica Strollo. E-mail: jastrollo@bryantstratton.edu.

Approximately 35 registered undergraduate students were served during 2006–07. The program or unit includes 2 full-time staff members. Academic advisers are provided through the program or unit. Academic advisers are provided collaboratively through on-campus or off-campus services.

Unique Aids and Services Aids, services, or accommodations include career counseling.

Subject-Area Tutoring Tutoring is offered one-on-one for most subjects. Tutoring is provided through the program or unit via computer-based instruction and trained peer tutors. Tutoring is also provided collaboratively through on-campus or off-campus services via computer-based instruction and trained peer tutors.

Basic Skills Remediation Remediation is offered one-on-one for math and written language. Remediation is provided through the program or unit via computer-based instruction and trained peer tutors. Remediation is also provided collaboratively through on-campus or off-campus services via computer-based instruction and trained peer tutors.

Application It is recommended that students provide documentation of high school services. Upon acceptance, documentation of need for services should be sent only to admissions. *Application deadline (institutional):* Continuous. *Application deadline (LD program):* Rolling/continuous for fall.

Written Policies Written policy regarding general/basic LD accommodations is available on the program Web site. Written policy regarding general/basic LD accommodations is outlined in the school's catalog/handbook.

Bucks County Community College
Disability Services Office

275 Swamp Road

Newtown, PA 18940-1525

http://www.bucks.edu/disability

Contact: Ms. Marge Zipin, Learning Disabilities Specialist. Phone: 215-968-8465. Fax: 215-968-8464. E-mail: zipinm@bucks.edu.

Disability Services Office Approximately 120 registered undergraduate students were served during 2006–07. The program or unit includes 1 full-time staff member. Academic advisers and LD specialists are provided through the program or unit. Counselors, diagnostic specialists, remediation/learning specialists, skill tutors, and trained peer tutors are provided collaboratively through on-campus or off-campus services.

Orientation The program or unit offers an optional 3-day orientation for new students before classes begin, during summer prior to enrollment, and during registration.

Unique Aids and Services Aids, services, or accommodations include career counseling, faculty training, and priority registration.

Assistive Technology Assistive technology is located in campus labs, the DSS office, a special lab, portable computers and includes digital textbooks/e-text, learning support software, and scanning. Technology training is provided to incoming students.

Subject-Area Tutoring Tutoring is offered one-on-one for some subjects. Tutoring is provided through the program or unit via computer-based instruction and LD specialists. Tutoring is also provided collaboratively through on-campus or off-campus services via professional tutors and trained peer tutors.

Basic Skills Remediation Remediation is offered one-on-one and in class-size groups for computer skills, learning strategies, math, reading, spelling, study skills, time management, and written language. Remediation is provided through the program or unit via computer-based instruction and LD specialists. Remediation is also provided collaboratively through on-campus or off-campus services via regular education teachers and trained peer tutors.

Enrichment Enrichment programs are available through the program or unit for self-advocacy, test taking, time management, and written composition skills. Programs for career planning, college survival skills, health and nutrition, learning strategies, math, practical computer skills, reading, stress management, study skills, test taking, time management, vocabulary development, and written composition skills are provided collaboratively through on-campus or off-campus services. Credit is offered for health and nutrition, learning strategies, math, practical computer skills, reading, stress management, study skills, vocabulary development, and written composition skills.

Application For admittance to the program or unit, students are required to provide a psychoeducational report. Upon application, materials documenting need for services should be sent only to the LD program or unit. Upon acceptance, documentation of need for services should be sent only to the LD program or unit. *Application deadline (LD program):* Rolling/continuous for fall and rolling/continuous for spring.

Written Policies Written policy regarding general/basic LD accommodations is available on the program Web site. Written policies regarding general/basic LD accommodations and reduced course loads are available through the program or unit directly.

Bunker Hill Community College
Office for Students with Disabilities

250 New Rutherford Avenue

Boston, MA 02129-2925

http://www.bhcc.mass.edu/

Contact: Ms. Andrea F. Schwartz, Coordinator of Disability Support Services. Phone: 617-228-3415. Fax: 617-228-2331. E-mail: aschwartz@bhcc.mass.edu.

Office for Students with Disabilities Approximately 450 registered undergraduate students were served during 2006–07. The program or unit includes 2 full-time and 3 part-time staff members. Academic advisers, coaches, counselors, graduate assistants/students, LD specialists, professional tutors, regular education teachers, remediation/learning specialists, skill tutors, special education teach-

Bunker Hill Community College (continued)

ers, strategy tutors, teacher trainees, and trained peer tutors are provided through the program or unit. Diagnostic specialists, LD specialists, and remediation/learning specialists are provided collaboratively through on-campus or off-campus services.

Orientation The program or unit offers an optional orientation for new students individually by special arrangement.

Unique Aids and Services Aids, services, or accommodations include career counseling, faculty training, priority registration, and support groups.

Assistive Technology Assistive technology is located in campus labs, the DSS office and includes digital textbooks/e-text and scanning. Technology training is provided to incoming students.

Subject-Area Tutoring Tutoring is offered one-on-one and in small groups for some subjects. Tutoring is provided through the program or unit via graduate assistants/students, LD specialists, professional tutors, and trained peer tutors.

Basic Skills Remediation Remediation is offered one-on-one and in small groups for learning strategies, math, reading, social skills, study skills, time management, and written language. Remediation is provided through the program or unit via computer-based instruction, graduate assistants/students, LD specialists, and trained peer tutors.

Enrichment Enrichment programs are available through the program or unit for career planning, college survival skills, learning strategies, math, reading, and self-advocacy. Programs for career planning, stress management, study skills, test taking, time management, and written composition skills are provided collaboratively through on-campus or off-campus services.

Application For admittance to the program or unit, students are required to provide a psychoeducational report (5 years old or less). It is recommended that students provide documentation of high school services. Upon application, materials documenting need for services should be sent only to the LD program or unit. Upon acceptance, documentation of need for services should be sent only to the LD program or unit. *Application deadline (institutional):* Continuous. *Application deadline (LD program):* Rolling/continuous for fall and rolling/continuous for spring.

Written Policies Written policy regarding general/basic LD accommodations is available on the program Web site. Written policy regarding general/basic LD accommodations is outlined in the school's catalog/handbook. Written policies regarding course substitutions, general/basic LD accommodations, grade forgiveness, reduced course loads, substitutions and waivers of admissions requirements, and substitutions and waivers of graduation requirements are available through the program or unit directly.

Burlington County College
Special Populations Program

Route 530

Pemberton, NJ 08068-1599

http://www.bcc.edu/

Contact: William Murphy, Learning Disabilities Specialist. Phone: 609-894-9311 Ext. 1789. Fax: 609-894-0764. E-mail: wmurphy@bcc.edu. Head of LD Program: Barbara Ericson, Coordinator of Special Populations. Phone: 609-894-9311 Ext. 1208. Fax: 609-894-0764. E-mail: ericson@bcc.edu.

Special Populations Program Approximately 243 registered undergraduate students were served during 2006–07. The program or unit includes 1 full-time and 1 part-time staff member. Academic advisers, counselors, LD specialists, remediation/learning specialists, and strategy tutors are provided through the program or unit. Academic advisers, counselors, professional tutors, trained peer tutors, and other are provided collaboratively through on-campus or off-campus services.

Unique Aids and Services Aids, services, or accommodations include career counseling, faculty training, priority registration.

Assistive Technology Assistive technology is located in campus labs, a special lab and includes learning support software.

Subject-Area Tutoring Tutoring is offered one-on-one for most subjects. Tutoring is provided through the program or unit via LD specialists. Tutoring is also provided collaboratively through on-campus or off-campus services via computer-based instruction, professional tutors, and trained peer tutors.

Basic Skills Remediation Remediation is offered one-on-one for computer skills, learning strategies, math, reading, study skills, and written language. Remediation is provided through the program or unit via LD specialists. Remediation is also provided collaboratively through on-campus or off-campus services via computer-based instruction, professional tutors, regular education teachers, and trained peer tutors.

Enrichment Enrichment programs are available through the program or unit for learning strategies and self-advocacy. Programs for career planning, college survival skills, and study skills are provided collaboratively through on-campus or off-campus services. Credit is offered for college survival skills and study skills.

Application For admittance to the program or unit, students are required to provide a psychoeducational report (3 years old or less). It is recommended that students provide documentation of high school services. Upon acceptance, documentation of need for services should be sent only to the LD program or unit. *Application deadline (institutional):* Continuous. *Application deadline (LD program):* Rolling/continuous for fall and rolling/continuous for spring.

Written Policies Written policy regarding general/basic LD accommodations is available on the program Web site. Written policy regarding general/basic LD accommodations is outlined in the school's catalog/handbook. Written policy regarding general/basic LD accommodations is available through the program or unit directly.

Caldwell Community College and Technical Institute
Disability Services

2855 Hickory Boulevard

Hudson, NC 28638-2397

http://www.cccti.edu/

Contact: Ms. Teena McRary, Disability Services. Phone: 828-726-2200 Ext. 2724. E-mail: tmcrary@cccti.edu. Head of LD Program: Ms. Nancy C. Leonard, Director, Disability Services. Phone: 828-265-2595 Ext. 5239. Fax: 828-297-4174. E-mail: nleonard@cccti.edu.

Disability Services Approximately 125 registered undergraduate students were served during 2006–07. The program or unit includes 2 full-time staff members. Counselors and LD specialists are provided through the program or unit.

Unique Aids and Services Aids, services, or accommodations include career counseling, priority registration, counseling.

Assistive Technology Assistive technology is located in the DSS office, a special lab and includes digital textbooks/e-text, learning support software, scanning, and Braille. Technology training is provided to incoming students.

Subject-Area Tutoring Tutoring is offered in small groups for some subjects. Tutoring is provided collaboratively through on-campus or off-campus services via computer-based instruction, trained peer tutors, and other.

Basic Skills Remediation Remediation is offered one-on-one and in small groups for computer skills, math, reading, written language, and history. Remediation is provided collaboratively through on-campus or off-campus services via computer-based instruction, regular education teachers, trained peer tutors, and other.

Enrichment Programs for career planning, college survival skills, learning strategies, stress management, study skills, test taking, time management, and written composition skills are provided collaboratively through on-campus or off-campus services.

Application For admittance to the program or unit, students are required to provide a psychoeducational report (3 years old or less). Upon acceptance, documentation of need for services should be sent only to the LD program or unit. *Application deadline (institutional):* Continuous. *Application deadline (LD program):* Rolling/continuous for fall and rolling/continuous for spring.

Written Policies Written policy regarding general/basic LD accommodations is available on the program Web site. Written policy regarding general/basic LD accommodations is available through the program or unit directly.

Camden County College
Program for the Academically Challenged Student (PACS)

PO Box 200

Blackwood, NJ 08012-0200

http://www.camdencc.edu

Contact: Ms. Joanne Kinzy, Director. Phone: 856-227-7200 Ext. 4430. Fax: 856-374-4975. E-mail: jkinzy@camdencc.edu.

Program for the Academically Challenged Student (PACS) Approximately 400 registered undergraduate students were served during 2006–07. The program or unit includes 2 full-time staff members. LD specialists, professional tutors, and other are provided through the program or unit.

Orientation The program or unit offers an optional half-day orientation for new students during summer prior to enrollment.

Summer Program To help prepare for the demands of college, there is an optional 6-week summer program prior to entering the school available to high school graduates that focuses on computing skills, life skills and/or college life adjustment, self-advocacy, study skills, test-taking skills, and time management. Degree credit will be earned. The program accepts students from out-of-state and is available to students attending other colleges.

Unique Aids and Services Aids, services, or accommodations include advocates, career counseling, priority registration, extended time on tests.

Assistive Technology Assistive technology is located in the library and includes digital textbooks/e-text and scanning.

Subject-Area Tutoring Tutoring is offered one-on-one and in small groups for most subjects. Tutoring is provided collaboratively through on-campus or off-campus services via professional tutors and trained peer tutors.

Basic Skills Remediation Remediation is offered in class-size groups for learning strategies, math, reading, study skills, time management, and written language. Remediation is provided through the program or unit via regular education teachers. Remediation is also provided collaboratively through on-campus or off-campus services via regular education teachers.

Application For admittance to the program or unit, students are required to provide a psychoeducational report (3 years old or less) and provide documentation of high school services. Upon application, materials documenting need for services should be sent only to the LD program or unit. *Application deadline (LD program):* Rolling/continuous for fall and rolling/continuous for spring.

Written Policies Written policies regarding general/basic LD accommodations and grade forgiveness are available on the program Web site. Written policies regarding general/basic LD accommodations and grade forgiveness are outlined in the school's catalog/handbook. Written policy regarding course substitutions is available through the program or unit directly.

Cape Cod Community College
Learning Disabilities Support Services Program

2240 Iyanough Road

West Barnstable, MA 02668-1599

http://www.capecod.edu

Contact: Dr. Richard H. Sommers, Learning Disabilities Specialist. Phone: 508-362-2131 Ext. 4317. Fax: 508-375-4020. E-mail: rsommers@capecod.edu.

Learning Disabilities Support Services Program Approximately 200 registered undergraduate students were served during 2006–07. The program or unit includes 1 full-time and 1 part-time staff member. Academic advisers, LD specialists, and strategy tutors are provided through the program or unit. Academic advisers, coaches, counselors, professional tutors, skill tutors, and strategy tutors are provided collaboratively through on-campus or off-campus services.

Orientation The program or unit offers an optional half-day orientation for new students before classes begin and individually by special arrangement.

Unique Aids and Services Aids, services, or accommodations include career counseling, faculty training, priority registration, and support groups.

Assistive Technology Assistive technology is located in the DSS office and includes digital textbooks/e-text, learning support software, and scanning. Technology training is provided to incoming students.

Cape Cod Community College (continued)

Subject-Area Tutoring Tutoring is offered one-on-one and in small groups for most subjects. Tutoring is provided collaboratively through on-campus or off-campus services via computer-based instruction, professional tutors, and trained peer tutors.

Basic Skills Remediation Remediation is offered in class-size groups for math, reading, study skills, and written language. Remediation is provided collaboratively through on-campus or off-campus services via computer-based instruction and regular education teachers.

Enrichment Programs for career planning, college survival skills, learning strategies, math, study skills, and written composition skills are provided collaboratively through on-campus or off-campus services. Credit is offered for college survival skills, learning strategies, math, study skills, and written composition skills.

Student Organization Academic Support Team.

Application For admittance to the program or unit, students are required to provide a psychoeducational report (4 years old or less). It is recommended that students provide documentation of high school services. Upon application, materials documenting need for services should be sent only to the LD program or unit. Upon acceptance, documentation of need for services should be sent only to the LD program or unit. *Application deadline (institutional):* 8/10. *Application deadline (LD program):* Rolling/continuous for fall and rolling/continuous for spring.

Written Policies Written policy regarding general/basic LD accommodations is available on the program Web site. Written policies regarding course substitutions, general/basic LD accommodations, and substitutions and waivers of graduation requirements are outlined in the school's catalog/handbook. Written policies regarding course substitutions, general/basic LD accommodations, and substitutions and waivers of graduation requirements are available through the program or unit directly.

Carl Sandburg College

2400 Tom L. Wilson Boulevard

Galesburg, IL 61401-9576

http://www.sandburg.edu/

Contact: Ms. Carol Ann Crouch, Coordinator of Academic Support Services. Phone: 309-341-5262. E-mail: ccrouch@sandburg.edu.

The program or unit includes 1 full-time and 1 part-time staff member. Academic advisers, professional tutors, regular education teachers, and other are provided through the program or unit. Academic advisers, coaches, counselors, diagnostic specialists, and regular education teachers are provided collaboratively through on-campus or off-campus services.

Unique Aids and Services Aids, services, or accommodations include career counseling.

Assistive Technology Assistive technology is located in campus labs, the DSS office, a special lab and includes digital textbooks/e-text, learning support software, and scanning. Technology training is provided to incoming students.

Subject-Area Tutoring Tutoring is offered one-on-one and in small groups for all subjects. Tutoring is provided through the program or unit via professional tutors. Tutoring is also provided collaboratively through on-campus or off-campus services via computer-based instruction and professional tutors.

Diagnostic Testing Testing for auditory processing, intelligence, learning styles, math, motor skills, neuropsychological, personality, reading, social skills, spelling, spoken language, visual processing, and written language is provided collaboratively through on-campus or off-campus services.

Basic Skills Remediation Remediation is offered one-on-one, in small groups, and in class-size groups for computer skills, math, reading, spelling, and written language. Remediation is provided through the program or unit via professional tutors. Remediation is also provided collaboratively through on-campus or off-campus services via professional tutors and regular education teachers.

Enrichment Enrichment programs are available through the program or unit for math. Programs for career planning, college survival skills, health and nutrition, learning strategies, math, medication management, oral communication skills, practical computer skills, reading, self-advocacy, stress management, study skills, test taking, time management, vocabulary development, and written composition skills are provided collaboratively through on-campus or off-campus services. Credit is offered for career planning, college survival skills, health and nutrition, math, oral communication skills, practical computer skills, reading, vocabulary development, and written composition skills.

Application For admittance to the program or unit, students are required to provide a psychoeducational report (3 years old or less) and provide documentation of high school services. Upon application, materials documenting need for services should be sent only to the LD program or unit. Upon acceptance, documentation of need for services should be sent only to the LD program or unit. *Application deadline (LD program):* Rolling/continuous for fall and rolling/continuous for spring.

Written Policies Written policy regarding general/basic LD accommodations is available on the program Web site. Written policy regarding general/basic LD accommodations is outlined in the school's catalog/handbook. Written policy regarding general/basic LD accommodations is available through the program or unit directly.

Cedar Valley College
Disability Services Office

3030 North Dallas Avenue

Lancaster, TX 75134-3799

http://www.cedarvalleycollege.edu/studentservices.html

Contact: Mrs. Keysha McCloud, Senior Rehabilitation Specialist. Phone: 972-860-8182. E-mail: kmccloud@dcccd.edu. Head of LD Program: Mrs. Grenna Rollings, Director, Special Populations. Phone: 972-860-8181. E-mail: grollings@dcccd.edu.

Disability Services Office Approximately 148 registered undergraduate students were served during 2006–07. The program or unit includes 3 full-time staff members. Academic advisers, counselors, LD specialists, and professional tutors are provided through the program or unit. Academic advisers, counselors, LD specialists, and professional tutors are provided collaboratively through on-campus or off-campus services.

Orientation The program or unit offers a mandatory 2-hour orientation for new students during registration and individually by special arrangement.

Unique Aids and Services Aids, services, or accommodations include advocates, career counseling, and priority registration.

Assistive Technology Assistive technology is located in campus labs and includes digital textbooks/e-text, learning support software, and scanning.

Subject-Area Tutoring Tutoring is offered one-on-one for most subjects. Tutoring is provided collaboratively through on-campus or off-campus services via computer-based instruction and professional tutors.

Diagnostic Testing Testing for auditory processing, handwriting, intelligence, learning strategies, learning styles, math, motor skills, neuropsychological, personality, reading, social skills, spelling, spoken language, study skills, visual processing, and written language is provided collaboratively through on-campus or off-campus services.

Basic Skills Remediation Remediation is offered in class-size groups for math, reading, spelling, study skills, and time management. Remediation is provided collaboratively through on-campus or off-campus services via computer-based instruction and professional tutors.

Application For admittance to the program or unit, students are required to apply to the program directly and provide a psychoeducational report (5 years old or less). It is recommended that students provide documentation of high school services. Upon application, materials documenting need for services should be sent only to the LD program or unit. Upon acceptance, documentation of need for services should be sent only to the LD program or unit. *Application deadline (institutional):* Continuous. *Application deadline (LD program):* Rolling/continuous for fall and rolling/continuous for spring.

Written Policies Written policy regarding grade forgiveness is outlined in the school's catalog/handbook. Written policies regarding course substitutions, general/basic LD accommodations, substitutions and waivers of admissions requirements, and substitutions and waivers of graduation requirements are available through the program or unit directly.

Central Arizona College
Special Needs Office

8470 North Overfield Road

Coolidge, AZ 85228-9779

http://www.centralaz.edu/

Contact: Special Needs Coordinator. Phone: 520-494-5410. Fax: 520-494-5027.

Special Needs Office Approximately 110 registered undergraduate students were served during 2006–07. The program or unit includes 1 full-time and 1 part-time staff member. LD specialists are provided through the program or unit.

Assistive Technology Assistive technology is located in the DSS office, the Learning Center and includes learning support software and scanning. Technology training is provided to incoming students.

Subject-Area Tutoring Tutoring is offered one-on-one and in small groups for most subjects. Tutoring is provided collaboratively through on-campus or off-campus services via professional tutors and trained peer tutors.

Basic Skills Remediation Remediation is offered in class-size groups for math, reading, and written language. Remediation is provided collaboratively through on-campus or off-campus services via regular education teachers.

Application For admittance to the program or unit, students are required to apply to the program directly, provide a psychoeducational report (3 years old or less), and provide documentation by specialist with terminal degree. It is recommended that students provide documentation of high school services. Upon application, materials documenting need for services should be sent only to the LD program or unit. Upon acceptance, documentation of need for services should be sent only to the LD program or unit. *Application deadline (institutional):* Continuous. *Application deadline (LD program):* 8/1 for fall. 12/1 for spring.

Written Policies Written policies regarding course substitutions and general/basic LD accommodations are available through the program or unit directly.

Central Florida Community College
Access Services

PO Box 1388

Ocala, FL 34478-1388

http://www.cf.edu/departments/sa/access/index.htm

Contact: Access Services Access Services. Phone: 352-854-2322 Ext. 1580. Fax: 352-873-5882.

Access Services Approximately 30 registered undergraduate students were served during 2006–07. The program or unit includes 1 full-time staff member. Academic advisers and other are provided collaboratively through on-campus or off-campus services.

Assistive Technology Assistive technology is located in campus labs and includes digital textbooks/e-text, learning support software, and scanning. Technology training is provided to incoming students.

Subject-Area Tutoring Tutoring is offered one-on-one and in small groups for some subjects. Tutoring is provided collaboratively through on-campus or off-campus services via computer-based instruction and trained peer tutors.

Basic Skills Remediation Remediation is offered one-on-one and in small groups for computer skills, math, reading, and written language. Remediation is provided collaboratively through on-campus or off-campus services via computer-based instruction and trained peer tutors.

Enrichment Programs for career planning and college survival skills are provided collaboratively through on-campus or off-campus services. Credit is offered for career planning and college survival skills.

Application For admittance to the program or unit, students are required to provide a psychoeducational report (3 years old or less). It is recommended that students provide documentation of high school services. Upon acceptance, documentation of need for services should be sent only to the LD program or unit. *Application deadline (institutional):* Continuous. *Application deadline (LD program):* Rolling/continuous for fall and rolling/continuous for spring.

Central Florida Community College (continued)

Written Policies Written policies regarding course substitutions, substitutions and waivers of admissions requirements, and substitutions and waivers of graduation requirements are outlined in the school's catalog/handbook. Written policies regarding course substitutions, general/basic LD accommodations, grade forgiveness, reduced course loads, substitutions and waivers of admissions requirements, and substitutions and waivers of graduation requirements are available through the program or unit directly.

Central Lakes College
Academic Center for Enrichment (ACE)

501 West College Drive

Brainerd, MN 56401-3904

http://www.clcmn.edu/disabilityservices/

Contact: Judy Richer, Disability Coordinator. Phone: 218-855-8128. Fax: 218-894-5149. E-mail: jricher@clcmn.edu. Head of LD Program: Diane Woullet, Disability Services-Staples Campus. Phone: 218-894-5182. Fax: 218-894-5149. E-mail: dwoullet@clcmn.edu.

Academic Center for Enrichment (ACE) Approximately 300 registered undergraduate students were served during 2006–07. The program or unit includes 2 full-time staff members. Academic advisers, coaches, counselors, graduate assistants/students, LD specialists, professional tutors, regular education teachers, skill tutors, strategy tutors, and trained peer tutors are provided through the program or unit. Academic advisers, coaches, counselors, and regular education teachers are provided collaboratively through on-campus or off-campus services.

Orientation The program or unit offers an optional 1-hour orientation for new students before registration, before classes begin, during registration, after classes begin, and individually by special arrangement.

Summer Program To help prepare for the demands of college, there is an optional up to 3-week summer program prior to entering the school available to high school graduates that focuses on specific subject tutoring, study skills, test-taking skills, time management, and vocational skills. The program accepts students from out-of-state.

Unique Aids and Services Aids, services, or accommodations include career counseling, faculty training, priority registration.

Assistive Technology Assistive technology is located in campus labs, the DSS office, a special lab and includes digital textbooks/e-text, learning support software, and scanning. Technology training is provided to incoming students.

Subject-Area Tutoring Tutoring is offered one-on-one and in small groups for most subjects. Tutoring is provided through the program or unit via computer-based instruction, graduate assistants/students, professional tutors, and trained peer tutors. Tutoring is also provided collaboratively through on-campus or off-campus services via computer-based instruction, professional tutors, and trained peer tutors.

Basic Skills Remediation Remediation is offered one-on-one for learning strategies, math, reading, study skills, and written language. Remediation is provided through the program or unit via computer-based instruction, professional tutors, and trained peer tutors.

Enrichment Enrichment programs are available through the program or unit for college survival skills, learning strategies, math, practical computer skills, reading, self-advocacy, study skills, test taking, vocabulary development, and written composition skills. Programs for career planning, college survival skills, health and nutrition, math, practical computer skills, self-advocacy, stress management, study skills, test taking, and time management are provided collaboratively through on-campus or off-campus services. Credit is offered for career planning and college survival skills.

Fees *Diagnostic Testing* fee is applicable.

Application For admittance to the program or unit, students are required to apply to the program directly and provide a psychoeducational report (3 years old or less). It is recommended that students provide documentation of high school services and provide medical and vocational rehabilitation reports. Upon application, materials documenting need for services should be sent only to the LD program or unit. Upon acceptance, documentation of need for services should be sent only to the LD program or unit. *Application deadline (institutional):* Continuous. *Application deadline (LD program):* Rolling/continuous for fall and rolling/continuous for spring.

Written Policies Written policies regarding general/basic LD accommodations and substitutions and waivers of admissions requirements are available on the program Web site. Written policies regarding course substitutions, general/basic LD accommodations, substitutions and waivers of admissions requirements, and substitutions and waivers of graduation requirements are outlined in the school's catalog/handbook. Written policies regarding course substitutions, general/basic LD accommodations, reduced course loads, substitutions and waivers of admissions requirements, and substitutions and waivers of graduation requirements are available through the program or unit directly.

Central Ohio Technical College
Office for Disability Services

1179 University Drive

Newark, OH 43055-1767

http://www.newarkcampus.org/studentlife/Disability_Services/

Contact: Ms. Connie S. Zang, Director, Office for Disability Services. Phone: 740-366-9441. Fax: 740-364-9646. E-mail: czang@cotc.edu.

Office for Disability Services The program or unit includes 5 full-time staff members. LD specialists, remediation/learning specialists, and trained peer tutors are provided through the program or unit. Academic advisers, counselors, graduate assistants/students, professional tutors, and regular education teachers are provided collaboratively through on-campus or off-campus services.

Summer Program To help prepare for the demands of college, there is an optional 3-day summer program prior to entering the school.

Unique Aids and Services Aids, services, or accommodations include career counseling and personal coach.

Assistive Technology Assistive technology is located in the DSS office and includes digital textbooks/e-text and scanning. Technology training is provided to incoming students.

Subject-Area Tutoring Tutoring is offered one-on-one and in small groups for some subjects. Tutoring is provided through the program or unit via trained peer tutors. Tutoring is also provided collaboratively through on-campus or off-campus services via computer-based instruction.

Diagnostic Testing Testing is provided through the program or unit for learning styles.

Enrichment Enrichment programs are available through the program or unit for career planning, college survival skills, learning strategies, practical computer skills, reading, stress management, study skills, test taking, and time management. Credit is offered for college survival skills, practical computer skills, and reading.

Application For admittance to the program or unit, students are required to provide a psychoeducational report (3 years old or less). It is recommended that students provide documentation of high school services. Upon acceptance, documentation of need for services should be sent only to the LD program or unit. *Application deadline (institutional):* Continuous. *Application deadline (LD program):* Rolling/continuous for fall and rolling/continuous for spring.

Written Policies Written policies regarding course substitutions, general/basic LD accommodations, grade forgiveness, reduced course loads, substitutions and waivers of admissions requirements, and substitutions and waivers of graduation requirements are available on the program Web site. Written policies regarding course substitutions, grade forgiveness, reduced course loads, substitutions and waivers of admissions requirements, and substitutions and waivers of graduation requirements are outlined in the school's catalog/handbook. Written policy regarding general/basic LD accommodations is available through the program or unit directly.

Central Piedmont Community College
Disability Services

PO Box 35009

Charlotte, NC 28235-5009

http://www.cpcc.edu/disabilities/

Contact: Mrs. Pat G. Adams, Counselor. Phone: 704-330-6556. Fax: 704-330-6230. E-mail: patricia.adams@cpcc.edu.

Disability Services Approximately 160 registered undergraduate students were served during 2006–07. The program or unit includes 2 full-time and 5 part-time staff members. Academic advisers, counselors, LD specialists, professional tutors, and skill tutors are provided through the program or unit. Academic advisers, counselors, diagnostic specialists, professional tutors, regular education teachers, skill tutors, and trained peer tutors are provided collaboratively through on-campus or off-campus services.

Orientation The program or unit offers an optional orientation for new students individually by special arrangement.

Unique Aids and Services Aids, services, or accommodations include advocates, career counseling, and faculty training.

Assistive Technology Assistive technology is located in campus labs, the DSS office and includes learning support software.

Subject-Area Tutoring Tutoring is offered one-on-one and in small groups for most subjects. Tutoring is provided collaboratively through on-campus or off-campus services via computer-based instruction, professional tutors, and trained peer tutors.

Basic Skills Remediation Remediation is offered in class-size groups for learning strategies, math, reading, study skills, and time management. Remediation is provided collaboratively through on-campus or off-campus services via computer-based instruction and regular education teachers.

Application For admittance to the program or unit, students are required to provide a psychoeducational report (3 years old or less) and provide psychological evaluation results. It is recommended that students provide documentation of high school services. Upon application, materials documenting need for services should be sent only to the LD program or unit. Upon acceptance, documentation of need for services should be sent only to the LD program or unit. *Application deadline (institutional):* Continuous. *Application deadline (LD program):* Rolling/continuous for fall and rolling/continuous for spring.

Written Policies Written policy regarding general/basic LD accommodations is available on the program Web site. Written policy regarding general/basic LD accommodations is outlined in the school's catalog/handbook. Written policy regarding general/basic LD accommodations is available through the program or unit directly.

Central Wyoming College
Disabilities Assistance Office

2660 Peck Avenue

Riverton, WY 82501-2273

http://www.cwc.edu/

Contact: Dr. Mohammed Waheed, Dean, Student Services. Phone: 307-855-2186. Fax: 307-855-2155. E-mail: mwaheed@cwc.edu.

Disabilities Assistance Office Approximately 40 registered undergraduate students were served during 2006–07. The program or unit includes 1 part-time staff member. Academic advisers, counselors, diagnostic specialists, professional tutors, regular education teachers, skill tutors, and trained peer tutors are provided collaboratively through on-campus or off-campus services.

Orientation The program or unit offers an optional orientation for new students individually by special arrangement.

Unique Aids and Services Aids, services, or accommodations include career counseling, individual academic accommodations.

Subject-Area Tutoring Tutoring is offered one-on-one and in small groups for most subjects. Tutoring is provided collaboratively through on-campus or off-campus services via computer-based instruction, professional tutors, and trained peer tutors.

Diagnostic Testing Testing for intelligence, learning strategies, learning styles, math, reading, spelling, spoken language, visual processing, and written language is provided collaboratively through on-campus or off-campus services.

Basic Skills Remediation Remediation is offered one-on-one for learning strategies, math, reading, spelling, study skills, and written language. Remediation is provided collaboratively through on-campus or off-campus services via professional tutors.

Central Wyoming College (continued)

Enrichment Enrichment programs are available through the program or unit for career planning, learning strategies, math, reading, and written composition skills. Programs for career planning, college survival skills, learning strategies, math, reading, stress management, study skills, and written composition skills are provided collaboratively through on-campus or off-campus services. Credit is offered for study skills.

Application For admittance to the program or unit, students are required to apply to the program directly, provide a psychoeducational report (5 years old or less), provide documentation of high school services, and provide new evaluation if no records are obtainable. Upon application, materials documenting need for services should be sent only to the LD program or unit. Upon acceptance, documentation of need for services should be sent only to the LD program or unit. *Application deadline (institutional):* Continuous. *Application deadline (LD program):* Rolling/continuous for fall and rolling/continuous for spring.

Written Policies Written policy regarding general/basic LD accommodations is outlined in the school's catalog/handbook. Written policy regarding general/basic LD accommodations is available through the program or unit directly.

Chattahoochee Technical College
Disability Services

980 South Cobb Drive

Marietta, GA 30060

http://www.chattcollege.com

Contact: Ms. Mary Frances Bernard, Disability Services Coordinator. Phone: 770-528-4529. Fax: 770-528-5818. E-mail: mfbernard@chattcollege.com.

Disability Services Approximately 146 registered undergraduate students were served during 2006–07. The program or unit includes 1 full-time staff member. Counselors are provided through the program or unit.

Unique Aids and Services Aids, services, or accommodations include advocates, career counseling, faculty training, priority registration.

Assistive Technology Assistive technology is located in campus labs, the DSS office, the library, Learning Centers and includes digital textbooks/e-text, learning support software, and scanning. Technology training is provided to incoming students.

Subject-Area Tutoring Tutoring is offered one-on-one for some subjects. Tutoring is provided collaboratively through on-campus or off-campus services via computer-based instruction and professional tutors.

Basic Skills Remediation Remediation is offered one-on-one for math, reading, spelling, study skills, and written language. Remediation is provided collaboratively through on-campus or off-campus services via computer-based instruction and regular education teachers.

Enrichment Programs for career planning, college survival skills, learning strategies, practical computer skills, and study skills are provided collaboratively through on-campus or off-campus services. Credit is offered for practical computer skills and study skills.

Application For admittance to the program or unit, students are required to apply to the program directly and provide a psychoeducational report (5 years old or less). It is recommended that students provide documentation of high school services. Upon application, materials documenting need for services should be sent only to the LD program or unit. Upon acceptance, documentation of need for services should be sent only to the LD program or unit. *Application deadline (LD program):* Rolling/continuous for fall and rolling/continuous for spring.

Written Policies Written policy regarding general/basic LD accommodations is outlined in the school's catalog/handbook. Written policy regarding general/basic LD accommodations is available through the program or unit directly.

Chattanooga State Technical Community College
Disabilities Support Services

4501 Amnicola Highway

Chattanooga, TN 37406-1097

http://www.chattanoogastate.edu/Student_Services/disability/dimain.asp

Contact: Ms. Wanda Gocher Johnson, Learning Disabilities Specialist. Phone: 423-697-2436. Fax: 423-697-2693. E-mail: wanda.gocher@chattanoogastate.edu.

Disabilities Support Services Approximately 175 registered undergraduate students were served during 2006–07. The program or unit includes 5 full-time staff members. Academic advisers and LD specialists are provided through the program or unit. Academic advisers, counselors, professional tutors, regular education teachers, and trained peer tutors are provided collaboratively through on-campus or off-campus services.

Summer Program To help prepare for the demands of college, there is an optional 1-day summer program prior to entering the school that focuses on life skills and/or college life adjustment, self-advocacy, study skills, test-taking skills, and time management. The program accepts students from out-of-state.

Unique Aids and Services Aids, services, or accommodations include career counseling and support groups.

Assistive Technology Assistive technology is located in campus labs, the DSS office, the library and includes digital textbooks/e-text, learning support software, and scanning.

Subject-Area Tutoring Tutoring is offered in small groups for some subjects. Tutoring is provided collaboratively through on-campus or off-campus services via computer-based instruction, professional tutors, and trained peer tutors.

Basic Skills Remediation Remediation is available for learning strategies, math, reading, and written language. Remediation is provided collaboratively through on-campus or off-campus services via computer-based instruction, professional tutors, regular education teachers, and trained peer tutors.

Enrichment Enrichment programs are available through the program or unit for study skills, test taking, and time management. Programs for career planning, health and nutrition, learning strategies, math, reading, stress management, study skills, test taking, time management, and written composition skills are provided collaboratively through on-campus or off-campus services.

Application For admittance to the program or unit, students are required to provide a psychoeducational report (4 years old or less). Upon application, materials documenting need for services should be sent only to the LD program or unit. Upon acceptance, documentation of need for services should be sent only to the LD program or unit. *Application deadline (institutional):* Continuous. *Application deadline (LD program):* Rolling/continuous for fall and rolling/continuous for spring.

Written Policies Written policies regarding course substitutions and general/basic LD accommodations are available on the program Web site. Written policies regarding course substitutions and general/basic LD accommodations are outlined in the school's catalog/handbook. Written policies regarding course substitutions and general/basic LD accommodations are available through the program or unit directly.

Chesapeake College

PO Box 8

Wye Mills, MD 21679-0008

http://www.chesapeake.edu/

Contact: Ms. Judy Gordon, Developmental Studies Case Manager/ADA Coordinator. Phone: 410-827-5805. Fax: 410-827-5322. E-mail: jgordon@chesapeake.edu.

Approximately 60 registered undergraduate students were served during 2006–07. The program or unit includes 1 full-time staff member. Academic advisers, coaches, counselors, professional tutors, regular education teachers, skill tutors, strategy tutors, and trained peer tutors are provided through the program or unit. Academic advisers, coaches, counselors, professional tutors, regular education teachers, skill tutors, strategy tutors, and trained peer tutors are provided collaboratively through on-campus or off-campus services.

Unique Aids and Services Aids, services, or accommodations include personal coach.

Assistive Technology Assistive technology is located in the DSS office and includes learning support software and scanning.

Subject-Area Tutoring Tutoring is offered one-on-one and in small groups for all subjects. Tutoring is provided through the program or unit via professional tutors and trained peer tutors. Tutoring is also provided collaboratively through on-campus or off-campus services via professional tutors and trained peer tutors.

Basic Skills Remediation Remediation is offered in class-size groups for handwriting, math, reading, and spelling. Remediation is provided through the program or unit via regular education teachers. Remediation is also provided collaboratively through on-campus or off-campus services via regular education teachers.

Enrichment Programs for career planning, college survival skills, health and nutrition, math, oral communication skills, practical computer skills, reading, stress management, study skills, test taking, time management, and written composition skills are provided collaboratively through on-campus or off-campus services. Credit is offered for career planning, college survival skills, health and nutrition, math, oral communication skills, practical computer skills, reading, stress management, study skills, test taking, time management, and written composition skills.

Application For admittance to the program or unit, students are required to apply to the program directly and provide a psychoeducational report. Upon application, materials documenting need for services should be sent only to the LD program or unit. Upon acceptance, documentation of need for services should be sent to both admissions and the LD program or unit. *Application deadline (institutional):* Continuous. *Application deadline (LD program):* Rolling/continuous for fall and rolling/continuous for spring.

Written Policies Written policies regarding general/basic LD accommodations and substitutions and waivers of admissions requirements are available on the program Web site. Written policies regarding course substitutions, general/basic LD accommodations, grade forgiveness, reduced course loads, substitutions and waivers of admissions requirements, and substitutions and waivers of graduation requirements are outlined in the school's catalog/handbook. Written policies regarding course substitutions, general/basic LD accommodations, grade forgiveness, reduced course loads, substitutions and waivers of admissions requirements, and substitutions and waivers of graduation requirements are available through the program or unit directly.

Citrus College
Disabled Students Programs and Services (DSP&S)

1000 West Foothill Boulevard

Glendora, CA 91741-1899

http://www.citruscollege.edu/dsps

Contact: Audrey Abas, Learning Disabilities Specialist. Phone: 626-914-8573. Fax: 626-857-0687. E-mail: aabas@citruscollege.edu. Head of LD Program: Jennifer McLeod, Coordinator/Counselor. Phone: 626-914-8677. Fax: 626-857-0687. E-mail: jmcleod@citruscollege.edu.

Disabled Students Programs and Services (DSP&S) Approximately 630 registered undergraduate students were served during 2006–07. The program or unit includes 7 full-time and 4 part-time staff members. Academic advisers, counselors, and LD specialists are provided through the program or unit. Academic advisers, coaches, counselors, regular education teachers, skill tutors, and trained peer tutors are provided collaboratively through on-campus or off-campus services.

Orientation The program or unit offers an optional 1-hour orientation for new students before classes begin, individually by special arrangement, and in groups and individually by appointment.

Summer Program To help prepare for the demands of college, there is an optional 6-week summer program prior to entering the school that focuses on computing skills, life skills and/or college life adjustment, self-advocacy, study skills, test-taking skills, and time management. The program accepts students from out-of-state and is available to students attending other colleges.

Unique Aids and Services Aids, services, or accommodations include career counseling, priority registration, support groups.

Assistive Technology Assistive technology is located in campus labs, the DSS office, a special lab, the library and includes digital textbooks/e-text, learning support software, and scanning. Technology training is provided to incoming students.

Citrus College (continued)

Subject-Area Tutoring Tutoring is offered one-on-one for some subjects. Tutoring is provided collaboratively through on-campus or off-campus services via computer-based instruction and trained peer tutors.

Diagnostic Testing Testing is provided through the program or unit for auditory processing, intelligence, learning strategies, learning styles, math, reading, spelling, visual processing, and written language. Testing for learning strategies and learning styles is provided collaboratively through on-campus or off-campus services.

Enrichment Enrichment programs are available through the program or unit for college survival skills, health and nutrition, learning strategies, practical computer skills, self-advocacy, stress management, study skills, test taking, and time management. Programs for career planning, college survival skills, health and nutrition, learning strategies, math, oral communication skills, practical computer skills, reading, stress management, study skills, test taking, time management, vocabulary development, and written composition skills are provided collaboratively through on-campus or off-campus services. Credit is offered for career planning, college survival skills, health and nutrition, learning strategies, math, oral communication skills, practical computer skills, reading, self-advocacy, stress management, study skills, test taking, time management, vocabulary development, and written composition skills.

Fees *Diagnostic Testing* fee is $10.

Application For admittance to the program or unit, students are required to apply to the program directly. It is recommended that students provide a psychoeducational report and provide documentation of high school services. Upon application, materials documenting need for services should be sent only to the LD program or unit. Upon acceptance, documentation of need for services should be sent only to the LD program or unit. *Application deadline (LD program):* Rolling/continuous for fall and rolling/continuous for spring.

City Colleges of Chicago, Richard J. Daley College
Special Needs Office

7500 South Pulaski Road
Chicago, IL 60652-1242

http://daley.ccc.edu/studentservices/special.shtml

Contact: Karen Barnett-Lee, Special Needs Coordinator. Phone: 773-838-7578. Fax: 773-838-7524. E-mail: kbarnett@ccc.edu.

Special Needs Office Approximately 50 registered undergraduate students were served during 2006–07. The program or unit includes 1 full-time and 1 part-time staff member. Academic advisers, counselors, and graduate assistants/students are provided through the program or unit. Academic advisers, counselors, graduate assistants/students, professional tutors, regular education teachers, skill tutors, and strategy tutors are provided collaboratively through on-campus or off-campus services.

Orientation The program or unit offers an optional orientation for new students before registration, before classes begin, during registration, after classes begin, and individually by special arrangement.

Unique Aids and Services Aids, services, or accommodations include faculty training.

Assistive Technology Assistive technology is located in campus labs, the DSS office and includes digital textbooks/e-text, learning support software, and scanning. Technology training is provided to incoming students.

Subject-Area Tutoring Tutoring is offered one-on-one and in small groups for all subjects. Tutoring is provided through the program or unit via computer-based instruction and graduate assistants/students. Tutoring is also provided collaboratively through on-campus or off-campus services via computer-based instruction and professional tutors.

Basic Skills Remediation Remediation is offered one-on-one, in small groups, and in class-size groups for computer skills, learning strategies, math, reading, study skills, and written language. Remediation is provided through the program or unit via computer-based instruction and graduate assistants/students. Remediation is also provided collaboratively through on-campus or off-campus services via computer-based instruction, professional tutors, and regular education teachers.

Student Organization Club Successability consists of 20 members.

Application For admittance to the program or unit, students are required to provide a psychoeducational report (3 years old or less) and provide documentation of high school services. Upon application, materials documenting need for services should be sent only to the LD program or unit. Upon acceptance, documentation of need for services should be sent only to the LD program or unit. *Application deadline (institutional):* Continuous. *Application deadline (LD program):* Rolling/continuous for fall and rolling/continuous for spring.

Written Policies Written policies regarding general/basic LD accommodations, substitutions and waivers of admissions requirements, and substitutions and waivers of graduation requirements are available on the program Web site. Written policies regarding general/basic LD accommodations, substitutions and waivers of admissions requirements, and substitutions and waivers of graduation requirements are outlined in the school's catalog/handbook. Written policies regarding general/basic LD accommodations and substitutions and waivers of admissions requirements are available through the program or unit directly.

Coahoma Community College

3240 Friars Point Road
Clarksdale, MS 38614-9799

http://www.ccc.cc.ms.us/

Contact: Ms. Evelyn Carol Washington, Academic Counselor/ADA/504. Phone: 662-621-4148 Ext. N/A. Fax: 662-624-4965 Ext. N/A. E-mail: ewashington@coahomacc.edu.

Counselors are provided collaboratively through on-campus or off-campus services.

Unique Aids and Services Aids, services, or accommodations include career counseling, faculty training, and priority registration.

Subject-Area Tutoring Tutoring is offered one-on-one for some subjects. Tutoring is provided collaboratively through on-campus or off-campus services via other.

Basic Skills Remediation Remediation is offered in class-size groups for math, reading, written language, and biological courses. Remediation is provided collaboratively through on-campus or off-campus services via regular education teachers.

Enrichment Programs for career planning, college survival skills, health and nutrition, math, oral communication skills, practical computer skills, reading, stress management, study skills, test taking, time management, and written composition skills are provided collaboratively through on-campus or off-campus services. Credit is offered for health and nutrition, math, oral communication skills, practical computer skills, reading, and written composition skills.

Application For admittance to the program or unit, students are required to provide documentation of high school services and provide report from medical doctor, psychological report, or vocational rehabilitation report. Upon acceptance, documentation of need for services should be sent only to the LD program or unit. *Application deadline (institutional):* Continuous. *Application deadline (LD program):* Rolling/continuous for fall and rolling/continuous for spring.

Written Policies Written policies regarding course substitutions, general/basic LD accommodations, reduced course loads, substitutions and waivers of admissions requirements, and substitutions and waivers of graduation requirements are available through the program or unit directly.

College of The Albemarle
Disability Support Services

PO Box 2327

Elizabeth City, NC 27906-2327

http://www.albemarle.edu

Contact: Ms. Andrea C. Temple, Director of Disability Support Services. Phone: 252-335-0821 Ext. 2277. Fax: 252-335-2011. E-mail: atemple@albemarle.edu.

Disability Support Services Approximately 5 registered undergraduate students were served during 2006–07. The program or unit includes 1 full-time staff member. Services are provided collaboratively through on-campus or off-campus services.

Orientation The program or unit offers an optional orientation for new students individually by special arrangement.

Unique Aids and Services Aids, services, or accommodations include career counseling, faculty training, and priority registration.

Assistive Technology Assistive technology is located in a special lab.

Subject-Area Tutoring Tutoring is offered one-on-one.

Basic Skills Remediation Remediation is offered one-on-one.

Enrichment Programs for career planning, college survival skills, learning strategies, math, oral communication skills, practical computer skills, reading, self-advocacy, stress management, study skills, test taking, and time management are provided collaboratively through on-campus or off-campus services.

Application For admittance to the program or unit, students are required to apply to the program directly and provide a psychoeducational report (3 years old or less). It is recommended that students provide documentation of high school services. Upon acceptance, documentation of need for services should be sent to both admis-

sions and the LD program or unit. *Application deadline (institutional):* Continuous. *Application deadline (LD program):* Rolling/continuous for fall and rolling/continuous for spring.

Written Policies Written policy regarding general/basic LD accommodations is available on the program Web site. Written policy regarding general/basic LD accommodations is outlined in the school's catalog/handbook. Written policy regarding general/basic LD accommodations is available through the program or unit directly.

College of the Canyons
Disabled Students Programs & Services (DSPS)

26455 Rockwell Canyon Road

Santa Clarita, CA 91355-1803

http://www.canyons.edu/offices/dsps

Contact: Dr. Christi Franklin, LD Specialist. Phone: 661-362-3341. Fax: 661-254-5716. E-mail: christi.franklin@canyons.edu.

Disabled Students Programs & Services (DSPS) Approximately 175 registered undergraduate students were served during 2006–07. The program or unit includes 5 full-time and 6 part-time staff members. Academic advisers, counselors, LD specialists, professional tutors, skill tutors, and trained peer tutors are provided through the program or unit. Academic advisers, counselors, professional tutors, regular education teachers, skill tutors, and trained peer tutors are provided collaboratively through on-campus or off-campus services.

Orientation The program or unit offers a mandatory 1-hour orientation for new students before registration, before classes begin, during summer prior to enrollment, during registration, after classes begin, and individually by special arrangement.

Summer Program To help prepare for the demands of college, there is an optional summer program prior to entering the school. Degree credit will be earned.

Unique Aids and Services Aids, services, or accommodations include career counseling, faculty training, and priority registration.

Assistive Technology Assistive technology is located in the DSS office and includes digital textbooks/e-text and learning support software. Technology training is provided to incoming students.

Subject-Area Tutoring Tutoring is offered in small groups for some subjects. Tutoring is provided through the program or unit via computer-based instruction, professional tutors, and trained peer tutors.

Diagnostic Testing Testing is provided through the program or unit for intelligence, learning strategies, learning styles, math, reading, spelling, visual processing, and written language.

Enrichment Enrichment programs are available through the program or unit for college survival skills. Programs for career planning and college survival skills are provided collaboratively through on-campus or off-campus services. Credit is offered for career planning and college survival skills.

Fees *Diagnostic Testing* fee is $10.

Application For admittance to the program or unit, students are required to apply to the program directly. It is recommended that students provide a psychoeducational report (3 years old or less), provide documentation of high school services, and provide assessment results. Upon application, materials documenting need for

College of the Canyons (continued)

services should be sent only to the LD program or unit. Upon acceptance, documentation of need for services should be sent only to the LD program or unit. *Application deadline (institutional):* 8/22. *Application deadline (LD program):* Rolling/continuous for fall and rolling/continuous for spring.

Written Policies Written policy regarding general/basic LD accommodations is available on the program Web site. Written policy regarding general/basic LD accommodations is outlined in the school's catalog/handbook. Written policy regarding general/basic LD accommodations is available through the program or unit directly.

College of the Desert
Disabled Students Programs & Services (DSPS)

43-500 Monterey Avenue

Palm Desert, CA 92260-9305

http://desert.cc.ca.us/

Contact: Mr. Paul Magg, Alternative Media Specialist and Counselor. Phone: 760-773-2534. Fax: 760-776-2598. E-mail: pmaag@collegeofthedesert.edu. Head of LD Program: Mr. Michael James O'Neill Jr., Coordinator and Learning Disability Specialist. Phone: 760-773-2534. Fax: 760-776-0198. E-mail: moneill@collegeofthedesert.edu.

Disabled Students Programs & Services (DSPS) Approximately 287 registered undergraduate students were served during 2006–07. The program or unit includes 1 full-time and 2 part-time staff members. Counselors, diagnostic specialists, LD specialists, remediation/learning specialists, and trained peer tutors are provided through the program or unit.

Orientation The program or unit offers an optional 2-hour orientation for new students before classes begin and individually by special arrangement.

Unique Aids and Services Aids, services, or accommodations include priority registration.

Assistive Technology Assistive technology is located in campus labs, the DSS office, a special lab and includes digital textbooks/e-text, learning support software, and scanning. Technology training is provided to incoming students.

Subject-Area Tutoring Tutoring is offered one-on-one for all subjects. Tutoring is provided collaboratively through on-campus or off-campus services via computer-based instruction, trained peer tutors, and other.

Diagnostic Testing Testing is provided through the program or unit for auditory processing, intelligence, learning strategies, learning styles, math, reading, spelling, spoken language, visual processing, and written language.

Basic Skills Remediation Remediation is offered in class-size groups for computer skills, learning strategies, math, reading, spelling, study skills, time management, visual processing, and written language. Remediation is provided through the program or unit via computer-based instruction, LD specialists, and special education teachers. Remediation is also provided collaboratively through on-campus or off-campus services via computer-based instruction.

Enrichment Enrichment programs are available through the program or unit for career planning, learning strategies, math, practical computer skills, reading, self-advocacy, study skills, test taking,

time management, vocabulary development, and written composition skills. Programs for career planning, college survival skills, health and nutrition, learning strategies, math, oral communication skills, practical computer skills, reading, self-advocacy, study skills, test taking, time management, vocabulary development, and written composition skills are provided collaboratively through on-campus or off-campus services.

Application For admittance to the program or unit, students are required to apply to the program directly. It is recommended that students provide a psychoeducational report (3 years old or less) and provide documentation of high school services. Upon application, materials documenting need for services should be sent only to the LD program or unit. Upon acceptance, documentation of need for services should be sent only to the LD program or unit. *Application deadline (institutional):* Continuous. *Application deadline (LD program):* Rolling/continuous for fall and rolling/continuous for spring.

Written Policies Written policies regarding course substitutions, general/basic LD accommodations, and substitutions and waivers of graduation requirements are available through the program or unit directly.

College of the Sequoias
Disability Resource Center

915 South Mooney Boulevard

Visalia, CA 93277-2234

http://www.cos.edu/
view_page.asp?nodeid=1298&parentid=1279&moduleid=5

Contact: Ms. Kathleen Conway, Learning Specialist. Phone: 559-730-3805. Fax: 559-730-3803. E-mail: kathc@cos.edu.

Disability Resource Center Approximately 300 registered undergraduate students were served during 2006–07. The program or unit includes 6 full-time and 11 part-time staff members. Academic advisers, counselors, diagnostic specialists, graduate assistants/students, LD specialists, professional tutors, remediation/learning specialists, skill tutors, strategy tutors, and trained peer tutors are provided through the program or unit. Academic advisers, coaches, counselors, professional tutors, regular education teachers, remediation/learning specialists, and trained peer tutors are provided collaboratively through on-campus or off-campus services.

Orientation The program or unit offers individually by special arrangement.

Unique Aids and Services Aids, services, or accommodations include career counseling, faculty training, and priority registration.

Assistive Technology Assistive technology is located in campus labs, a special lab and includes digital textbooks/e-text and scanning. Technology training is provided to incoming students.

Subject-Area Tutoring Tutoring is offered one-on-one and in small groups for most subjects. Tutoring is provided through the program or unit via computer-based instruction, graduate assistants/students, LD specialists, and trained peer tutors. Tutoring is also provided collaboratively through on-campus or off-campus services via graduate assistants/students and trained peer tutors.

Diagnostic Testing Testing is provided through the program or unit for auditory processing, intelligence, learning strategies, learning styles, math, motor skills, reading, spelling, spoken language, visual processing, and written language.

Basic Skills Remediation Remediation is offered one-on-one and in small groups for learning strategies, math, reading, spelling, study skills, time management, and written language. Remediation is provided through the program or unit via computer-based instruction, LD specialists, and trained peer tutors.

Enrichment Enrichment programs are available through the program or unit for college survival skills, learning strategies, study skills, test taking, time management, vocabulary development, and written composition skills. Programs for career planning, college survival skills, learning strategies, study skills, test taking, time management, vocabulary development, and written composition skills are provided collaboratively through on-campus or off-campus services.

Application For admittance to the program or unit, students are required to apply to the program directly and provide completed eligibility components for the CCC LD Model. It is recommended that students provide a psychoeducational report (3 years old or less) and provide documentation of high school services. Upon application, materials documenting need for services should be sent to both admissions and the LD program or unit. Upon acceptance, documentation of need for services should be sent to both admissions and the LD program or unit. *Application deadline (LD program):* Rolling/continuous for fall and rolling/continuous for spring.

Written Policies Written policy regarding general/basic LD accommodations is available on the program Web site. Written policy regarding general/basic LD accommodations is outlined in the school's catalog/handbook. Written policies regarding course substitutions, general/basic LD accommodations, and substitutions and waivers of graduation requirements are available through the program or unit directly.

The College of Westchester
The Learning Center

325 Central Avenue, PO Box 710

White Plains, NY 10602

http://www.cw.edu/

Contact: Dean Jean Carlson, Dean of Student Academic Services. Phone: 914-831-0416. Fax: 914-428-0081. E-mail: jcarlson@cw.edu.

The Learning Center Approximately 60 registered undergraduate students were served during 2006–07. The program or unit includes 2 full-time and 7 part-time staff members. Academic advisers, counselors, professional tutors, and trained peer tutors are provided collaboratively through on-campus or off-campus services.

Unique Aids and Services Aids, services, or accommodations include career counseling, success coaches for new students.

Subject-Area Tutoring Tutoring is offered one-on-one and in small groups for most subjects. Tutoring is provided collaboratively through on-campus or off-campus services via computer-based instruction, professional tutors, and trained peer tutors.

Basic Skills Remediation Remediation is offered in small groups and in class-size groups for math, reading, study skills, and written language. Remediation is provided collaboratively through on-campus or off-campus services via professional tutors and regular education teachers.

Enrichment Programs for career planning, college survival skills, math, oral communication skills, practical computer skills, reading, study skills, test taking, time management, vocabulary development, and written composition skills are provided collaboratively through on-campus or off-campus services. Credit is offered for career planning, college survival skills, math, oral communication skills, practical computer skills, and written composition skills.

Application For admittance to the program or unit, students are required to provide documentation of high school services. It is recommended that students provide a psychoeducational report (3 years old or less). Upon application, materials documenting need for services should be sent only to admissions with institutional application materials. Upon acceptance, documentation of need for services should be sent only to admissions. *Application deadline (institutional):* Continuous. *Application deadline (LD program):* Rolling/continuous for fall and rolling/continuous for spring.

Written Policies Written policy regarding general/basic LD accommodations is outlined in the school's catalog/handbook.

Colorado Mountain College, Alpine Campus
Disability Services

1330 Bob Adams Drive

Steamboat Springs, CO 80487

http://www.coloradomtn.edu/services/disabilitysvcs/spalpine.html

Contact: Ms. Debra Farmer, Disability Services Coordinator. Phone: 970-870-4450. Fax: 970-870-0485. E-mail: dfarmer@coloradomtn.edu.

Disability Services Approximately 100 registered undergraduate students were served during 2006–07. The program or unit includes 1 full-time staff member. LD specialists are provided through the program or unit. Academic advisers, counselors, professional tutors, regular education teachers, remediation/learning specialists, skill tutors, strategy tutors, and trained peer tutors are provided collaboratively through on-campus or off-campus services.

Summer Program To help prepare for the demands of college, there is an optional 4-week summer program prior to entering the school available to high school graduates that focuses on computing skills, life skills and/or college life adjustment, self-advocacy, specific subject tutoring, study skills, test-taking skills, and time management. Degree credit will be earned. The program accepts students from out-of-state and is available to students attending other colleges.

Unique Aids and Services Aids, services, or accommodations include career counseling and priority registration.

Assistive Technology Assistive technology is located in the DSS office, a special lab and includes digital textbooks/e-text, learning support software, and scanning. Technology training is provided to incoming students.

Subject-Area Tutoring Tutoring is offered one-on-one and in small groups for most subjects. Tutoring is provided through the program or unit via computer-based instruction and LD specialists. Tutoring is also provided collaboratively through on-campus or off-campus services via computer-based instruction, professional tutors, and trained peer tutors.

Colorado Mountain College, Alpine Campus (continued)

Basic Skills Remediation Remediation is offered one-on-one, in small groups, and in class-size groups for computer skills, learning strategies, math, reading, spelling, study skills, time management, and written language. Remediation is provided collaboratively through on-campus or off-campus services via computer-based instruction, professional tutors, and regular education teachers.

Enrichment Enrichment programs are available through the program or unit for self-advocacy. Programs for career planning, college survival skills, health and nutrition, learning strategies, math, practical computer skills, reading, stress management, study skills, test taking, time management, vocabulary development, and written composition skills are provided collaboratively through on-campus or off-campus services. Credit is offered for career planning, college survival skills, health and nutrition, learning strategies, math, practical computer skills, reading, stress management, study skills, test taking, time management, and written composition skills.

Fees *Summer Program* fee is $1500 to $3200.

Application For admittance to the program or unit, students are required to apply to the program directly and provide a psychoeducational report (3 years old or less). Upon application, materials documenting need for services should be sent only to the LD program or unit. Upon acceptance, documentation of need for services should be sent only to the LD program or unit. *Application deadline (institutional):* Continuous. *Application deadline (LD program):* Rolling/continuous for fall and rolling/continuous for spring.

Written Policies Written policy regarding general/basic LD accommodations is available on the program Web site. Written policies regarding course substitutions, general/basic LD accommodations, grade forgiveness, reduced course loads, and substitutions and waivers of graduation requirements are outlined in the school's catalog/handbook. Written policies regarding course substitutions, general/basic LD accommodations, and substitutions and waivers of graduation requirements are available through the program or unit directly.

Columbus State Community College

Box 1609

Columbus, OH 43216-1609

http://www.cscc.edu/

Contact: Mr. Ron Lofton, LD Specialist. Phone: 614-287-5396. Fax: 614-287-6054. E-mail: rlofton@ cscc.edu. Head of LD Program: Mr. Wayne Cocchi, Director. Phone: 614-287-2629. Fax: 614-287-6054. E-mail: wcocchi@cscc.edu.

Approximately 375 registered undergraduate students were served during 2006–07. The program or unit includes 2 full-time staff members. Counselors, LD specialists, and remediation/learning specialists are provided through the program or unit. Academic advisers, regular education teachers, remediation/learning specialists, and trained peer tutors are provided collaboratively through on-campus or off-campus services.

Unique Aids and Services Aids, services, or accommodations include note-taking, extra time on exams, reader, scribe.

Assistive Technology Assistive technology is located in campus labs, the DSS office and includes digital textbooks/e-text, learning support software, and scanning.

Subject-Area Tutoring Tutoring is offered one-on-one for some subjects. Tutoring is provided through the program or unit via LD specialists. Tutoring is also provided collaboratively through on-campus or off-campus services via trained peer tutors.

Basic Skills Remediation Remediation is offered one-on-one for computer skills, learning strategies, math, reading, social skills, study skills, time management, and written language. Remediation is provided through the program or unit via LD specialists and professional tutors. Remediation is also provided collaboratively through on-campus or off-campus services via trained peer tutors.

Enrichment Enrichment programs are available through the program or unit for oral communication skills, self-advocacy, time management, and written composition skills. Programs for career planning, college survival skills, math, oral communication skills, practical computer skills, and reading are provided collaboratively through on-campus or off-campus services. Credit is offered for college survival skills.

Application For admittance to the program or unit, students are required to provide a psychoeducational report (5 years old or less) and provide multifactored evaluation (assessment of disability conducted by the secondary school psychologist). It is recommended that students provide documentation of high school services. Upon application, materials documenting need for services should be sent only to the LD program or unit. Upon acceptance, documentation of need for services should be sent only to the LD program or unit. *Application deadline (LD program):* Rolling/continuous for fall and rolling/continuous for spring.

Written Policies Written policy regarding general/basic LD accommodations is available on the program Web site. Written policies regarding general/basic LD accommodations and reduced course loads are available through the program or unit directly.

Commonwealth Technical Institute

727 Goucher Street

Johnstown, PA 15905-3092

http://www.hgac.org/

Contact: Mr. Jack B. Demuth, Education Director. Phone: 814-255-8321. Fax: 814-255-5709. E-mail: jademuth@ state.pa.us.

Academic advisers, counselors, professional tutors, trained peer tutors, and other are provided collaboratively through on-campus or off-campus services.

Subject-Area Tutoring Tutoring is provided collaboratively through on-campus or off-campus services via professional tutors and trained peer tutors.

Basic Skills Remediation Remediation is offered in small groups and in class-size groups for computer skills, math, reading, social skills, spoken language, time management, and written language. Remediation is provided collaboratively through on-campus or off-campus services via professional tutors, regular education teachers, trained peer tutors, and other.

Enrichment Programs for college survival skills, learning strategies, oral communication skills, time management, and other are provided collaboratively through on-campus or off-campus services.
Application *Application deadline (institutional):* Continuous.

Community College of Aurora
Accessibility Services Office

16000 East Centre Tech Parkway
Aurora, CO 80011-9036
http://www.ccaurora.edu/students/academic/accessibility/index.shtml

Contact: Ms. Reniece A. Jones, Accessibility Services Office Director. Phone: 303-361-7395. Fax: 303-340-7551. E-mail: reniece.jones@ccaurora.edu.

Accessibility Services Office Approximately 125 registered undergraduate students were served during 2006–07. The program or unit includes 2 full-time and 3 part-time staff members. Academic advisers, graduate assistants/students, professional tutors, regular education teachers, remediation/learning specialists, skill tutors, and strategy tutors are provided collaboratively through on-campus or off-campus services.
Orientation The program or unit offers an optional orientation for new students individually by special arrangement.
Unique Aids and Services Aids, services, or accommodations include advocates, faculty training, and personal coach.
Assistive Technology Assistive technology is located in campus labs, the DSS office, a special lab and includes digital textbooks/e-text, scanning, and JAWS, ZoomText, Dragon Naturally Speaking. Technology training is provided to incoming students.
Subject-Area Tutoring Tutoring is offered one-on-one and in small groups for some subjects. Tutoring is provided collaboratively through on-campus or off-campus services via computer-based instruction, graduate assistants/students, professional tutors, and trained peer tutors.
Diagnostic Testing Testing for math, reading, and written language is provided collaboratively through on-campus or off-campus services.
Basic Skills Remediation Remediation is offered one-on-one and in small groups for computer skills, handwriting, learning strategies, math, reading, spelling, study skills, time management, and written language. Remediation is provided collaboratively through on-campus or off-campus services via computer-based instruction, graduate assistants/students, professional tutors, regular education teachers, and trained peer tutors.
Enrichment Enrichment programs are available through the program or unit for self-advocacy and other. Programs for career planning, college survival skills, health and nutrition, learning strategies, math, oral communication skills, practical computer skills, reading, stress management, study skills, test taking, time management, vocabulary development, and written composition skills are provided collaboratively through on-campus or off-campus services. Credit is offered for college survival skills, health and nutrition, learning strategies, math, oral communication skills, practical computer skills, reading, stress management, study skills, test taking, time management, vocabulary development, and written composition skills.

Student Organization Equality for All.
Application For admittance to the program or unit, students are required to apply to the program directly and provide a psychoeducational report. It is recommended that students provide documentation of high school services and provide documentation of other disabilities. Upon application, materials documenting need for services should be sent only to the LD program or unit. Upon acceptance, documentation of need for services should be sent only to the LD program or unit. *Application deadline (institutional):* Continuous. *Application deadline (LD program):* Rolling/continuous for fall and rolling/continuous for spring.
Written Policies Written policies regarding general/basic LD accommodations and grade forgiveness are available on the program Web site. Written policies regarding general/basic LD accommodations and grade forgiveness are outlined in the school's catalog/handbook. Written policy regarding general/basic LD accommodations is available through the program or unit directly.

The Community College of Baltimore County

800 South Rolling Road
Baltimore, MD 21228-5381
http://www.ccbcmd.edu/

Contact: Ms. Marian T. Herb, Coordinator of Disability Services. Phone: 410-780-6741. Fax: 410-780-6849. E-mail: mherb@ccbcmd.edu.

The program or unit includes 1 full-time staff member. Academic advisers and LD specialists are provided through the program or unit. Trained peer tutors are provided collaboratively through on-campus or off-campus services.
Orientation The program or unit offers an optional 2-hour orientation for new students before classes begin.
Assistive Technology Assistive technology is located in campus labs, the DSS office and includes digital textbooks/e-text, learning support software, and scanning. Technology training is provided to incoming students.
Subject-Area Tutoring Tutoring is offered one-on-one and in small groups for some subjects. Tutoring is provided collaboratively through on-campus or off-campus services via computer-based instruction and trained peer tutors.
Basic Skills Remediation Remediation is offered one-on-one and in class-size groups for math, reading, study skills, time management, and written language. Remediation is provided through the program or unit via LD specialists. Remediation is also provided collaboratively through on-campus or off-campus services via computer-based instruction, regular education teachers, trained peer tutors, and other.
Enrichment Programs for career planning and college survival skills are provided collaboratively through on-campus or off-campus services. Credit is offered for college survival skills.
Application For admittance to the program or unit, students are required to provide a psychoeducational report. It is recommended that students provide documentation of high school services. Upon application, materials documenting need for services should be sent only to the LD program or unit. *Application deadline (LD program):* Rolling/continuous for fall and rolling/continuous for spring.

The Community College of Baltimore County (continued)

Written Policies Written policy regarding general/basic LD accommodations is available on the program Web site. Written policies regarding course substitutions, general/basic LD accommodations, and substitutions and waivers of graduation requirements are available through the program or unit directly.

Community College of Beaver County
Supportive Services Office

One Campus Drive

Monaca, PA 15061-2588

http://www.ccbc.edu/

Contact: Cheryl Herrington, Manager, Learning Resources. Phone: 724-775-8561 Ext. 161. Fax: 724-775-2495. E-mail: cheryl.herrington@ccbc.edu.

Supportive Services Office Approximately 100 registered undergraduate students were served during 2006–07. The program or unit includes 1 full-time and 3 part-time staff members. Skill tutors, strategy tutors, and trained peer tutors are provided through the program or unit. Academic advisers, counselors, graduate assistants/students, professional tutors, regular education teachers, remediation/learning specialists, skill tutors, strategy tutors, and trained peer tutors are provided collaboratively through on-campus or off-campus services.

Orientation The program or unit offers an optional orientation for new students individually by special arrangement.

Unique Aids and Services Aids, services, or accommodations include career counseling, support groups, testing accommodations.

Assistive Technology Assistive technology is located in the DSS office and includes learning support software and test reader software, voice recognition software. Technology training is provided to incoming students.

Subject-Area Tutoring Tutoring is offered one-on-one and in small groups for most subjects. Tutoring is provided through the program or unit via graduate assistants/students and trained peer tutors. Tutoring is also provided collaboratively through on-campus or off-campus services via computer-based instruction, graduate assistants/students, professional tutors, and trained peer tutors.

Diagnostic Testing Testing is provided through the program or unit for learning styles and study skills.

Basic Skills Remediation Remediation is offered in class-size groups for math, reading, and written language. Remediation is provided collaboratively through on-campus or off-campus services via regular education teachers.

Enrichment Enrichment programs are available through the program or unit for college survival skills, learning strategies, self-advocacy, stress management, study skills, test taking, and time management. Programs for career planning, college survival skills, math, practical computer skills, reading, vocabulary development, and written composition skills are provided collaboratively through on-campus or off-campus services.

Student Organization TRI-C's consists of 8 members.

Application For admittance to the program or unit, students are required to apply to the program directly and provide a psychoeducational report (3 years old or less). Upon application, materials

documenting need for services should be sent only to the LD program or unit. Upon acceptance, documentation of need for services should be sent only to the LD program or unit. *Application deadline (institutional):* Continuous. *Application deadline (LD program):* 8/11 for fall. 12/8 for spring.

Written Policies Written policy regarding general/basic LD accommodations is available on the program Web site. Written policy regarding general/basic LD accommodations is outlined in the school's catalog/handbook. Written policy regarding general/basic LD accommodations is available through the program or unit directly.

Connors State College
Student Services

Route 1 Box 1000

Warner, OK 74469-9700

http://www.connorsstate.edu/

Contact: Mr. Brett Bright, Vice President for Student Services. Phone: 918-463-6245. Fax: 918-463-6272.

Student Services Approximately 12 registered undergraduate students were served during 2006–07. The program or unit includes 2 full-time staff members. Academic advisers, counselors, regular education teachers, and remediation/learning specialists are provided collaboratively through on-campus or off-campus services.

Unique Aids and Services Aids, services, or accommodations include weekly meetings with faculty.

Assistive Technology Assistive technology is located in campus labs and includes learning support software and scanning.

Enrichment Programs for health and nutrition, oral communication skills, study skills, test taking, and time management are provided collaboratively through on-campus or off-campus services.

Application For admittance to the program or unit, students are required to provide a psychoeducational report (3 years old or less). It is recommended that students provide documentation of high school services. Upon application, materials documenting need for services should be sent only to admissions with institutional application materials. Upon acceptance, documentation of need for services should be sent only to admissions. *Application deadline (LD program):* Rolling/continuous for fall and rolling/continuous for spring.

Written Policies Written policies regarding general/basic LD accommodations and substitutions and waivers of admissions requirements are available on the program Web site. Written policies regarding general/basic LD accommodations and substitutions and waivers of admissions requirements are outlined in the school's catalog/handbook. Written policies regarding general/basic LD accommodations, reduced course loads, and substitutions and waivers of admissions requirements are available through the program or unit directly.

Coosa Valley Technical College

One Maurice Culberson Drive

Rome, GA 30161

http://www.coosavalleytech.edu/

Contact: Sheila Parker, ADA Coordinator. Phone: 706-295-6517. Fax: 706-295-6888. E-mail: sparker@coosavalleytech.edu.

Orientation The program or unit offers a mandatory orientation for new students before classes begin and individually by special arrangement.

Assistive Technology Assistive technology is located in campus labs and includes digital textbooks/e-text, learning support software, and scanning. Technology training is provided to incoming students.

Subject-Area Tutoring Tutoring is offered one-on-one for some subjects. Tutoring is provided collaboratively through on-campus or off-campus services via computer-based instruction and professional tutors.

Basic Skills Remediation Remediation is offered in class-size groups for math, reading, study skills, time management, and written language. Remediation is provided collaboratively through on-campus or off-campus services via computer-based instruction, professional tutors, and regular education teachers.

Enrichment Programs for career planning, college survival skills, learning strategies, math, practical computer skills, reading, and written composition skills are provided collaboratively through on-campus or off-campus services. Credit is offered for college survival skills, math, practical computer skills, reading, and written composition skills.

Application It is recommended that students provide documentation of high school services. Upon application, materials documenting need for services should be sent only to the LD program or unit. Upon acceptance, documentation of need for services should be sent only to the LD program or unit. *Application deadline (LD program):* Rolling/continuous for fall and rolling/continuous for spring.

Written Policies Written policy regarding general/basic LD accommodations is available on the program Web site. Written policy regarding general/basic LD accommodations is outlined in the school's catalog/handbook. Written policy regarding general/basic LD accommodations is available through the program or unit directly.

Copper Mountain College
Disabled Student Program and Services

6162 Rotary Way

Joshua Tree, CA 92252

http://www.cmccd.cc.ca.us/

Contact: Ms. Carolyn Beaver, LD Specialist. Phone: 760-366-3791. Fax: 760-366-1299. E-mail: cbeaver@cmccd.edu. Head of LD Program: Mrs. Jacquelin Ann Hanselman, DSPS Coordinator. Phone: 760-366-3791 Ext. 5286. E-mail: jhanselman@cmccd.edu.

Disabled Student Program and Services Approximately 50 registered undergraduate students were served during 2006–07. The program or unit includes 8 part-time staff members. Diagnostic specialists, remediation/learning specialists, skill tutors, special education teachers, and other are provided through the program or unit. Academic advisers, counselors, diagnostic specialists, professional tutors, regular education teachers, and skill tutors are provided collaboratively through on-campus or off-campus services.

Orientation The program or unit offers a mandatory 2-hour orientation for new students during summer prior to enrollment and after classes begin.

Summer Program To help prepare for the demands of college, there is an optional 5-week summer program prior to entering the school available to high school graduates that focuses on computing skills, life skills and/or college life adjustment, self-advocacy, study skills, test-taking skills, and time management. The program accepts students from out-of-state and is available to students attending other colleges.

Unique Aids and Services Aids, services, or accommodations include advocates, career counseling, faculty training, priority registration.

Assistive Technology Assistive technology is located in campus labs, the DSS office, a special lab and includes digital textbooks/e-text, learning support software, and scanning. Technology training is provided to incoming students.

Subject-Area Tutoring Tutoring is offered one-on-one and in small groups for some subjects. Tutoring is provided through the program or unit via computer-based instruction, graduate assistants/students, LD specialists, trained peer tutors, and other. Tutoring is also provided collaboratively through on-campus or off-campus services via computer-based instruction and trained peer tutors.

Diagnostic Testing Testing is provided through the program or unit for auditory processing, handwriting, intelligence, learning strategies, math, neuropsychological, personality, reading, spelling, spoken language, study skills, visual processing, written language, and other services. Testing for learning styles is provided collaboratively through on-campus or off-campus services.

Basic Skills Remediation Remediation is offered one-on-one, in small groups, and in class-size groups for computer skills, learning strategies, math, reading, spelling, study skills, time management, and written language. Remediation is provided through the program or unit via computer-based instruction, graduate assistants/students, LD specialists, and special education teachers. Remediation is also provided collaboratively through on-campus or off-campus services via regular education teachers and trained peer tutors.

Enrichment Enrichment programs are available through the program or unit for career planning, college survival skills, learning strategies, math, practical computer skills, reading, self-advocacy, stress management, study skills, test taking, time management, vocabulary development, and written composition skills. Programs for career planning, college survival skills, health and nutrition, learning strategies, math, medication management, oral communication skills, practical computer skills, reading, self-advocacy, stress management, study skills, test taking, time management, vocabulary development, and written composition skills are provided collaboratively through on-campus or off-campus services. Credit is offered for college survival skills, health and nutrition, learning strategies, math, medication management, oral communication skills, practical computer skills, reading, stress management, study skills, time management, vocabulary development, and written composition skills.

Student Organization Abilities Club consists of 10 members.

Copper Mountain College (continued)

Application For admittance to the program or unit, students are required to apply to the program directly, provide a psychoeducational report (5 years old or less), and provide documentation of high school services. Upon application, materials documenting need for services should be sent only to the LD program or unit. Upon acceptance, documentation of need for services should be sent only to the LD program or unit. *Application deadline (LD program):* Rolling/continuous for fall and rolling/continuous for spring.

Written Policies Written policies regarding general/basic LD accommodations, grade forgiveness, and reduced course loads are available on the program Web site. Written policy regarding general/basic LD accommodations is outlined in the school's catalog/handbook. Written policies regarding general/basic LD accommodations, grade forgiveness, and reduced course loads are available through the program or unit directly.

Cosumnes River College
Disabled Students Programs and Services (DSP&S)

8401 Center Parkway
Sacramento, CA 95823-5799
http://www.crc.losrios.edu/studentservices/dsps.htm
Contact: Scott Hamilton. Phone: 916-691-7446. E-mail: hamilts@crc.losrios.edu.

Disabled Students Programs and Services (DSP&S) Approximately 200 registered undergraduate students were served during 2006–07. The program or unit includes 2 full-time and 4 part-time staff members. Counselors, LD specialists, professional tutors, and trained peer tutors are provided collaboratively through on-campus or off-campus services.

Unique Aids and Services Aids, services, or accommodations include priority registration.

Assistive Technology Assistive technology is located in the DSS office and includes digital textbooks/e-text, scanning, and text-to-speech, speech-to-text software. Technology training is provided to incoming students.

Subject-Area Tutoring Tutoring is offered in class-size groups for some subjects. Tutoring is provided collaboratively through on-campus or off-campus services via professional tutors and trained peer tutors.

Diagnostic Testing Testing for auditory processing, intelligence, math, reading, spelling, visual processing, and written language is provided collaboratively through on-campus or off-campus services.

Application For admittance to the program or unit, students are required to apply to the program directly and provide documentation of high school services. It is recommended that students provide a psychoeducational report. Upon application, materials documenting need for services should be sent only to the LD program or unit. Upon acceptance, documentation of need for services should be sent only to the LD program or unit. *Application deadline (institutional):* 8/1. *Application deadline (LD program):* Rolling/continuous for fall and rolling/continuous for spring.

Written Policies Written policies regarding course substitutions and substitutions and waivers of graduation requirements are outlined in the school's catalog/handbook. Written policy regarding general/basic LD accommodations is available through the program or unit directly.

Cottey College
Student Disabilities Services

1000 West Austin
Nevada, MO 64772
http://www.cottey.edu/
Contact: Ms. Mary W. McNerney, Coordinator of Student Disability Services. Phone: 417-667-6333 Ext. 2131. E-mail: mmcnerney@cottey.edu.

Student Disabilities Services Approximately 20 registered undergraduate students were served during 2006–07. The program or unit includes 1 part-time staff member. Academic advisers, counselors, and regular education teachers are provided collaboratively through on-campus or off-campus services.

Unique Aids and Services Aids, services, or accommodations include career counseling and priority registration.

Subject-Area Tutoring Tutoring is offered one-on-one and in small groups for some subjects. Tutoring is provided collaboratively through on-campus or off-campus services via computer-based instruction, professional tutors, and other.

Diagnostic Testing Testing is provided through the program or unit for learning strategies, learning styles, and study skills. Testing for auditory processing, intelligence, neuropsychological, personality, and visual processing is provided collaboratively through on-campus or off-campus services.

Basic Skills Remediation Remediation is available for learning strategies, study skills, and time management. Remediation is provided collaboratively through on-campus or off-campus services via regular education teachers.

Enrichment Programs for career planning, college survival skills, health and nutrition, learning strategies, math, reading, stress management, study skills, test taking, time management, and written composition skills are provided collaboratively through on-campus or off-campus services. Credit is offered for learning strategies and study skills.

Application For admittance to the program or unit, students are required to apply to the program directly, provide a psychoeducational report (3 years old or less), and provide appropriate documentation from the professional making the diagnosis. It is recommended that students provide documentation of high school services. Upon acceptance, documentation of need for services should be sent only to the LD program or unit. *Application deadline (institutional):* Continuous. *Application deadline (LD program):* Rolling/continuous for fall and rolling/continuous for spring.

Written Policies Written policies regarding course substitutions, grade forgiveness, reduced course loads, and substitutions and waivers of graduation requirements are outlined in the school's catalog/handbook. Written policy regarding general/basic LD accommodations is available through the program or unit directly.

County College of Morris
Horizons

214 Center Grove Road
Randolph, NJ 07869-2086
http://www.ccm.edu/horizons/

Contact: Dr. David C. Nast, Director. Phone: 973-328-5274. Fax: 973-328-5286. E-mail: dnast@ccm.edu.

Horizons Approximately 650 registered undergraduate students were served during 2006–07. The program or unit includes 4 full-time and 10 part-time staff members. Academic advisers, counselors, LD specialists, professional tutors, remediation/learning specialists, skill tutors, and strategy tutors are provided through the program or unit. Academic advisers, counselors, professional tutors, and trained peer tutors are provided collaboratively through on-campus or off-campus services.

Orientation The program or unit offers an optional 2-hour orientation for new students before classes begin and during summer prior to enrollment.

Summer Program To help prepare for the demands of college, there is an optional 3-week summer program prior to entering the school available to high school graduates that focuses on life skills and/or college life adjustment, self-advocacy, study skills, test-taking skills, and time management. The program accepts students from out-of-state.

Unique Aids and Services Aids, services, or accommodations include advocates, faculty training, and support groups.

Assistive Technology Assistive technology is located in campus labs, the DSS office and includes digital textbooks/e-text and scanning. Technology training is provided to incoming students.

Subject-Area Tutoring Tutoring is offered one-on-one and in small groups for most subjects. Tutoring is provided collaboratively through on-campus or off-campus services via professional tutors and trained peer tutors.

Basic Skills Remediation Remediation is offered in class-size groups for learning strategies, math, study skills, time management, visual processing, and written language. Remediation is provided through the program or unit via professional tutors. Remediation is also provided collaboratively through on-campus or off-campus services via professional tutors and regular education teachers.

Enrichment Enrichment programs are available through the program or unit for college survival skills, learning strategies, oral communication skills, reading, self-advocacy, stress management, study skills, test taking, time management, and written composition skills. Programs for career planning, math, and written composition skills are provided collaboratively through on-campus or off-campus services. Credit is offered for career planning, college survival skills, learning strategies, oral communication skills, reading, self-advocacy, stress management, study skills, test taking, time management, and written composition skills.

Student Organization Horizons Student Support Group consists of 10 members.

Fees *Summer Program* fee is $330.

Application For admittance to the program or unit, students are required to apply to the program directly, provide a psychoeducational report (3 years old or less), and provide documentation of high school services. Upon application, materials documenting need for services should be sent only to the LD program or unit. *Application deadline (LD program):* 4/15 for fall. 11/15 for spring.

Written Policies Written policy regarding general/basic LD accommodations is available on the program Web site. Written policies regarding course substitutions and general/basic LD accommodations are available through the program or unit directly.

Crafton Hills College
Disabled Students Programs and Services

11711 Sand Canyon Road

Yucaipa, CA 92399-1799

http://www.craftonhills.edu/

Contact: Ms. Milly M. Douthit, Learning Disability Specialist. Phone: 909-389-3578. Fax: 909-794-3684. E-mail: mdouthit@craftonhills.edu.

Disabled Students Programs and Services Approximately 125 registered undergraduate students were served during 2006–07. The program or unit includes 5 full-time and 2 part-time staff members. Academic advisers, counselors, diagnostic specialists, LD specialists, and trained peer tutors are provided through the program or unit. Academic advisers and counselors are provided collaboratively through on-campus or off-campus services.

Orientation The program or unit offers a mandatory orientation for new students individually by special arrangement.

Unique Aids and Services Aids, services, or accommodations include priority registration, academic counseling.

Assistive Technology Assistive technology is located in the DSS office, the Learning Center and includes digital textbooks/e-text, learning support software, and scanning. Technology training is provided to incoming students.

Subject-Area Tutoring Tutoring is offered one-on-one for some subjects. Tutoring is provided through the program or unit via trained peer tutors. Tutoring is also provided collaboratively through on-campus or off-campus services via computer-based instruction, graduate assistants/students, and trained peer tutors.

Diagnostic Testing Testing is provided through the program or unit for auditory processing, handwriting, intelligence, learning strategies, math, reading, spelling, spoken language, visual processing, and written language. Testing for learning strategies, learning styles, math, reading, spelling, spoken language, and study skills is provided collaboratively through on-campus or off-campus services.

Basic Skills Remediation Remediation is offered one-on-one and in class-size groups for learning strategies, math, reading, study skills, time management, and written language. Remediation is provided collaboratively through on-campus or off-campus services via computer-based instruction, regular education teachers, and trained peer tutors.

Enrichment Programs for career planning, college survival skills, health and nutrition, learning strategies, math, reading, study skills, test taking, time management, vocabulary development, and written composition skills are provided collaboratively through on-campus or off-campus services. Credit is offered for career planning, college survival skills, health and nutrition, learning strategies, math, reading, study skills, test taking, time management, vocabulary development, and written composition skills.

Application It is recommended that students provide a psychoeducational report (5 years old or less) and provide documentation of high school services. *Application deadline (institutional):* Continuous. *Application deadline (LD program):* Rolling/continuous for fall and rolling/continuous for spring.

Written Policies Written policy regarding general/basic LD accommodations is available through the program or unit directly.

Craven Community College
Academic Skills Center

800 College Court

New Bern, NC 28562-4984

http://cravencc.edu

Contact: Mr. Frederick E. Cooze, Director of the Academic Skills Center. Phone: 252-638-7294. Fax: 252-672-8020. E-mail: coozef@cravencc.edu.

Academic Skills Center Approximately 20 registered undergraduate students were served during 2006–07. The program or unit includes 1 full-time and 33 part-time staff members. Counselors, diagnostic specialists, professional tutors, remediation/learning specialists, and trained peer tutors are provided collaboratively through on-campus or off-campus services.

Unique Aids and Services Aids, services, or accommodations include support groups.

Assistive Technology Assistive technology is located in Academic Skills Center and includes digital textbooks/e-text, learning support software, and scanning. Technology training is provided to incoming students.

Subject-Area Tutoring Tutoring is offered one-on-one and in small groups for most subjects. Tutoring is provided collaboratively through on-campus or off-campus services via computer-based instruction, graduate assistants/students, LD specialists, professional tutors, trained peer tutors, and other.

Diagnostic Testing Testing is provided through the program or unit for learning strategies, learning styles, math, personality, study skills, and written language. Testing for auditory processing, handwriting, intelligence, math, motor skills, neuropsychological, reading, social skills, spelling, spoken language, and visual processing is provided collaboratively through on-campus or off-campus services.

Basic Skills Remediation Remediation is offered one-on-one for auditory processing, computer skills, learning strategies, math, reading, study skills, time management, and written language. Remediation is provided collaboratively through on-campus or off-campus services via computer-based instruction, graduate assistants/students, professional tutors, regular education teachers, and trained peer tutors.

Enrichment Enrichment programs are available through the program or unit for learning strategies, math, practical computer skills, reading, self-advocacy, study skills, test taking, time management, and written composition skills. Programs for career planning, college survival skills, health and nutrition, learning strategies, math, practical computer skills, reading, self-advocacy, study skills, test taking, time management, vocabulary development, and written composition skills are provided collaboratively through on-campus or off-campus services. Credit is offered for college survival skills, health and nutrition, learning strategies, math, practical computer skills, reading, study skills, test taking, time management, vocabulary development, and written composition skills.

Application For admittance to the program or unit, students are required to provide a psychoeducational report (3 years old or less). It is recommended that students provide documentation of high school services. Upon application, materials documenting need for services should be sent only to the LD program or unit. Upon acceptance, documentation of need for services should be sent only to the LD program or unit. *Application deadline (LD program):* Rolling/continuous for fall and rolling/continuous for spring.

Written Policies Written policy regarding substitutions and waivers of admissions requirements is available on the program Web site. Written policies regarding general/basic LD accommodations and substitutions and waivers of admissions requirements are outlined in the school's catalog/handbook. Written policies regarding general/basic LD accommodations and substitutions and waivers of admissions requirements are available through the program or unit directly.

Cuesta College
Disabled Student Programs and Services (DSPS)

PO Box 8106

San Luis Obispo, CA 93403-8106

http://academic.cuesta.edu/acasupp/dsps/

Contact: Disabled Student Program and Services Department. Phone: 805-546-3148. Fax: 805-546-3930. E-mail: dspsinfo@cuesta.edu. Head of LD Program: Patrick D. Schwab, EdD; Director of Academic Support and Disabled Student Programs and Services. Phone: 805-546-3148. Fax: 805-546-3930. E-mail: pschwab@cuesta.edu.

Disabled Student Programs and Services (DSPS) Approximately 400 registered undergraduate students were served during 2006–07. The program or unit includes 19 full-time and 5 part-time staff members. Academic advisers, counselors, diagnostic specialists, LD specialists, professional tutors, regular education teachers, remediation/learning specialists, skill tutors, special education teachers, and strategy tutors are provided through the program or unit. Coaches, counselors, professional tutors, regular education teachers, skill tutors, strategy tutors, teacher trainees, and trained peer tutors are provided collaboratively through on-campus or off-campus services.

Orientation The program or unit offers an optional 2-day orientation for new students as part of English and math assessment/orientation/registration advising workshop in April.

Unique Aids and Services Aids, services, or accommodations include alternative testing, note-taking assistance, specialized tutoring.

Assistive Technology Assistive technology is located in campus labs, the DSS office, a special lab and includes digital textbooks/e-text and scanning.

Subject-Area Tutoring Tutoring is offered one-on-one and in small groups for most subjects. Tutoring is provided through the program or unit via computer-based instruction, LD specialists, and professional tutors. Tutoring is also provided collaboratively through on-campus or off-campus services via trained peer tutors.

Diagnostic Testing Testing is provided through the program or unit. Testing is provided collaboratively through on-campus or off-campus services.

Basic Skills Remediation Remediation is offered in class-size groups for computer skills, learning strategies, math, reading, spelling, study skills, time management, written language, and test and performance anxiety. Remediation is provided through the program or unit via regular education teachers and special education teachers. Remediation is also provided collaboratively through on-campus or off-campus services via regular education teachers and special education teachers.

Enrichment Enrichment programs are available through the program or unit for college survival skills, math, practical computer skills, reading, vocabulary development, and written composition skills. Programs for career planning, college survival skills, health and nutrition, learning strategies, math, oral communication skills, practical computer skills, reading, stress management, study skills, test taking, time management, and written composition skills are provided collaboratively through on-campus or off-campus services. Credit is offered for career planning, college survival skills, health and nutrition, learning strategies, math, oral communication skills, practical computer skills, reading, stress management, study skills, test taking, time management, vocabulary development, and written composition skills.

Application For admittance to the program or unit, students are required to apply to the program directly, provide a psychoeducational report (3 years old or less), and provide documentation of high school services. Upon application, materials documenting need for services should be sent only to the LD program or unit. Upon acceptance, documentation of need for services should be sent to both admissions and the LD program or unit. *Application deadline (institutional):* Continuous. *Application deadline (LD program):* Rolling/continuous for fall and rolling/continuous for spring.

Written Policies Written policies regarding course substitutions, general/basic LD accommodations, grade forgiveness, reduced course loads, and substitutions and waivers of graduation requirements are available on the program Web site. Written policies regarding course substitutions, general/basic LD accommodations, and substitutions and waivers of graduation requirements are available through the program or unit directly.

Dabney S. Lancaster Community College
Student Support Services Program

100 Dabney Drive, PO Box 1000

Clifton Forge, VA 24422

http://www.dslcc.edu/VPISS/studentservices/acenter/disabilityservices.htm

Contact: Dr. Mary Wilson, Director of Student Services and Research. Phone: 540-863-2830. Fax: 540-863-2915. E-mail: mwilson@dslcc.edu. Head of LD Program: Elizabeth Davis, Director of Student Support Services Program. Phone: 540-863-2860. Fax: 540-863-2915. E-mail: ldavis@dslcc.edu.

Student Support Services Program Approximately 20 registered undergraduate students were served during 2006–07. The program or unit includes 3 full-time and 5 part-time staff members. Academic advisers, professional tutors, and trained peer tutors are provided through the program or unit.

Unique Aids and Services Aids, services, or accommodations include advocates.

Subject-Area Tutoring Tutoring is offered one-on-one and in small groups for most subjects. Tutoring is provided collaboratively through on-campus or off-campus services via professional tutors and trained peer tutors.

Basic Skills Remediation Remediation is offered in class-size groups for math, reading, and written language. Remediation is provided collaboratively through on-campus or off-campus services via regular education teachers.

Enrichment Programs for career planning, college survival skills, learning strategies, self-advocacy, stress management, study skills, test taking, and time management are provided collaboratively through on-campus or off-campus services.

Application For admittance to the program or unit, students are required to provide documentation of high school services. It is recommended that students provide a psychoeducational report (3 years old or less). Upon application, materials documenting need for services should be sent only to the LD program or unit. Upon acceptance, documentation of need for services should be sent only to the LD program or unit. *Application deadline (institutional):* Continuous. *Application deadline (LD program):* Rolling/continuous for fall and rolling/continuous for spring.

Written Policies Written policy regarding general/basic LD accommodations is available on the program Web site. Written policy regarding general/basic LD accommodations is outlined in the school's catalog/handbook.

Darton College
Disability Services

2400 Gillionville Road

Albany, GA 31707-3098

http://www.darton.edu/current/stu_aff/disabilityservices.php

Contact: Ms. Tanya Anderson, Coordinator of Disability Services. Phone: 229-430-6865. Fax: 229-420-1100. E-mail: andersot@darton.edu.

Disability Services Approximately 66 registered undergraduate students were served during 2006–07. The program or unit includes 1 full-time staff member.

Assistive Technology Assistive technology is located in campus labs, the DSS office and includes scanning.

Subject-Area Tutoring Tutoring is offered one-on-one and in small groups for some subjects. Tutoring is provided collaboratively through on-campus or off-campus services via trained peer tutors.

Diagnostic Testing Testing for auditory processing, handwriting, intelligence, math, motor skills, personality, reading, social skills, spelling, spoken language, visual processing, and written language is provided collaboratively through on-campus or off-campus services.

Basic Skills Remediation Remediation is offered in class-size groups for math, reading, and written language. Remediation is provided collaboratively through on-campus or off-campus services via regular education teachers.

Fees *Diagnostic Testing* fee is $400.

Application For admittance to the program or unit, students are required to provide a psychoeducational report (3 years old or less). It is recommended that students provide documentation of high school services. Upon application, materials documenting need for services should be sent only to the LD program or unit. Upon acceptance, documentation of need for services should be sent only to the LD program or unit. *Application deadline (LD program):* Rolling/continuous for fall and rolling/continuous for spring.

Darton College (continued)

Written Policies Written policies regarding course substitutions, general/basic LD accommodations, substitutions and waivers of admissions requirements, and substitutions and waivers of graduation requirements are available on the program Web site. Written policy regarding general/basic LD accommodations is outlined in the school's catalog/handbook. Written policies regarding course substitutions, general/basic LD accommodations, substitutions and waivers of admissions requirements, and substitutions and waivers of graduation requirements are available through the program or unit directly.

Davenport University
ADA Department

3930 Traxler Court

Bay City, MI 48706

http://www.davenport.edu/

Contact: Ms. Angelia Pierson, ADA Dept. Coordinator. Phone: 989-894-8948 Ext. 3806. E-mail: angelia.pierson@davenport.edu.

ADA Department Approximately 2 registered undergraduate students were served during 2006–07. Academic advisers, professional tutors, and regular education teachers are provided through the program or unit.

Assistive Technology Technology training is provided to incoming students.

Subject-Area Tutoring Tutoring is offered one-on-one and in small groups for all subjects. Tutoring is provided through the program or unit via professional tutors and trained peer tutors.

Enrichment Program for career planning is provided collaboratively through on-campus or off-campus services.

Application It is recommended that students provide a psychoeducational report (1 year old or less) and provide documentation specific to disability. Upon application, materials documenting need for services should be sent only to admissions with institutional application materials. Upon acceptance, documentation of need for services should be sent only to the LD program or unit. *Application deadline (LD program):* Rolling/continuous for fall and rolling/continuous for spring.

Written Policies Written policy regarding general/basic LD accommodations is outlined in the school's catalog/handbook.

DeKalb Technical College
Special Services Office

495 North Indian Creek Drive

Clarkston, GA 30021-2397

http://www.dekalbtech.org

Contact: Ms. Paula Greenwood, Special Services Advisor. Phone: 404-297-9522 Ext. 1155. Fax: 404-294-3424. E-mail: greenwop@dekalbtech.edu. Head of LD Program: Ms. Lisa M. Peters, Special Services Director/ADA/504 Coordinator.

Phone: 404-297-9522 Ext. 1154. Fax: 404-294-6496. E-mail: petersl@dekalbtech.edu.

Special Services Office Approximately 42 registered undergraduate students were served during 2006–07. The program or unit includes 1 full-time staff member. Academic advisers are provided through the program or unit. Academic advisers and remediation/learning specialists are provided collaboratively through on-campus or off-campus services.

Unique Aids and Services Aids, services, or accommodations include career counseling, faculty training, and priority registration.

Assistive Technology Assistive technology is located in campus labs, the DSS office and includes digital textbooks/e-text and learning support software.

Subject-Area Tutoring Tutoring is offered in small groups for some subjects. Tutoring is provided collaboratively through on-campus or off-campus services via computer-based instruction and other.

Basic Skills Remediation Remediation is offered in class-size groups for math, reading, and written language. Remediation is provided collaboratively through on-campus or off-campus services via computer-based instruction and regular education teachers.

Enrichment Programs for career planning, learning strategies, math, oral communication skills, practical computer skills, reading, stress management, study skills, test taking, time management, vocabulary development, and written composition skills are provided collaboratively through on-campus or off-campus services. Credit is offered for learning strategies, math, oral communication skills, practical computer skills, reading, stress management, study skills, test taking, time management, vocabulary development, and written composition skills.

Application For admittance to the program or unit, students are required to apply to the program directly and provide a psychoeducational report (3 years old or less). Upon application, materials documenting need for services should be sent only to the LD program or unit. Upon acceptance, documentation of need for services should be sent only to the LD program or unit. *Application deadline (LD program):* Rolling/continuous for fall and rolling/continuous for spring.

Written Policies Written policy regarding general/basic LD accommodations is available on the program Web site. Written policy regarding general/basic LD accommodations is outlined in the school's catalog/handbook. Written policy regarding general/basic LD accommodations is available through the program or unit directly.

Delaware County Community College
Office of Special Needs Services

901 South Media Line Road

Media, PA 19063-1094

http://www.dccc.edu/accom_dis/

Contact: Ms. Ann S. Binder, Director of Special Needs Services. Phone: 610-325-2748. Fax: 610-355-7162. E-mail: abinder@dccc.edu.

Office of Special Needs Services Approximately 360 registered undergraduate students were served during 2006–07. The program or unit includes 1 full-time and 2 part-time staff members. Academic advisers, coaches, and counselors are provided through the program or unit. Academic advisers, counselors, diagnostic specialists, professional tutors, regular education teachers, skill tutors, strategy tutors, and trained peer tutors are provided collaboratively through on-campus or off-campus services.

Orientation The program or unit offers an optional 1-hour orientation for new students individually by special arrangement.

Unique Aids and Services Aids, services, or accommodations include career counseling and priority registration.

Assistive Technology Assistive technology is located in campus labs, the DSS office, the library and includes digital textbooks/e-text.

Subject-Area Tutoring Tutoring is offered one-on-one and in small groups for most subjects. Tutoring is provided collaboratively through on-campus or off-campus services via computer-based instruction, graduate assistants/students, professional tutors, and trained peer tutors.

Basic Skills Remediation Remediation is offered one-on-one, in small groups, and in class-size groups for computer skills, learning strategies, math, reading, spelling, study skills, time management, and written language. Remediation is provided collaboratively through on-campus or off-campus services via computer-based instruction, professional tutors, and regular education teachers.

Enrichment Programs for career planning, college survival skills, health and nutrition, learning strategies, math, medication management, oral communication skills, practical computer skills, reading, self-advocacy, stress management, study skills, test taking, time management, vocabulary development, and written composition skills are provided collaboratively through on-campus or off-campus services. Credit is offered for career planning, college survival skills, math, oral communication skills, practical computer skills, reading, vocabulary development, and written composition skills.

Application For admittance to the program or unit, students are required to provide a psychoeducational report (3 years old or less), provide documentation of high school services, and provide a comprehensive evaluation report. Upon application, materials documenting need for services should be sent only to the LD program or unit. Upon acceptance, documentation of need for services should be sent only to the LD program or unit. *Application deadline (LD program):* Rolling/continuous for fall and rolling/continuous for spring.

Written Policies Written policy regarding general/basic LD accommodations is available on the program Web site. Written policy regarding general/basic LD accommodations is outlined in the school's catalog/handbook.

Delaware Technical & Community College, Jack F. Owens Campus
Office of Student Support Services

PO Box 610
Georgetown, DE 19947
http://www.dtcc.edu/

Contact: Mrs. Heather Statler, Student Enrichment Coordinator. Phone: 302-855-1681. Fax: 302-858-5469. E-mail: hstatler@dtcc.edu.

Office of Student Support Services Approximately 56 registered undergraduate students were served during 2006–07. The program or unit includes 4 full-time staff members and 1 part-time staff member. Counselors, professional tutors, and trained peer tutors are provided through the program or unit. Academic advisers, coaches, counselors, diagnostic specialists, and remediation/learning specialists are provided collaboratively through on-campus or off-campus services.

Orientation The program or unit offers an optional 1-hour orientation for new students individually by special arrangement.

Unique Aids and Services Aids, services, or accommodations include advocates, career counseling, faculty training, personal coach, priority registration, and support groups.

Assistive Technology Assistive technology is located in a special lab and includes learning support software and scanning.

Subject-Area Tutoring Tutoring is offered one-on-one and in small groups for most subjects. Tutoring is provided through the program or unit via trained peer tutors. Tutoring is also provided collaboratively through on-campus or off-campus services via computer-based instruction, professional tutors, and trained peer tutors.

Basic Skills Remediation Remediation is offered in class-size groups for computer skills, learning strategies, math, reading, social skills, study skills, time management, and written language. Remediation is provided through the program or unit via trained peer tutors. Remediation is also provided collaboratively through on-campus or off-campus services via computer-based instruction, professional tutors, regular education teachers, and trained peer tutors.

Enrichment Enrichment programs are available through the program or unit for career planning, college survival skills, learning strategies, self-advocacy, stress management, study skills, test taking, and time management. Programs for career planning, college survival skills, health and nutrition, learning strategies, math, medication management, oral communication skills, practical computer skills, reading, self-advocacy, vocabulary development, and written composition skills are provided collaboratively through on-campus or off-campus services. Credit is offered for college survival skills, math, oral communication skills, practical computer skills, reading, and written composition skills.

Application For admittance to the program or unit, students are required to apply to the program directly and provide a psychoeducational report (3 years old or less). It is recommended that students provide documentation of high school services and provide disability documentation by a licensed professional. Upon application, materials documenting need for services should be sent to both admissions and the LD program or unit. Upon acceptance, documentation of need for services should be sent only to the LD program or unit. *Application deadline (institutional):* Continuous. *Application deadline (LD program):* Rolling/continuous for fall and rolling/continuous for spring.

Written Policies Written policies regarding course substitutions, general/basic LD accommodations, grade forgiveness, and reduced course loads are available on the program Web site. Written policies regarding course substitutions, general/basic LD accommodations, grade forgiveness, and reduced course loads are outlined in the school's catalog/handbook. Written policy regarding general/basic LD accommodations is available through the program or unit directly.

Des Moines Area Community College
Student Support Services, Special Needs Office

2006 South Ankeny Boulevard

Ankeny, IA 50021-8995

http://www.dmacc.edu/student_services/disabilities.asp

Contact: Mrs. Hollie L. Coon, Coordinator of Special Needs. Phone: 515-964-6850. Fax: 515-965-7150. E-mail: hlcoon@dmacc.edu. Head of LD Program: Ms. Sharon G. Bittner, Supervisor of Student Support Services. Phone: 515-964-6857. Fax: 515-965-7150. E-mail: sgbittner@dmacc.edu.

Student Support Services, Special Needs Office Approximately 150 registered undergraduate students were served during 2006–07. The program or unit includes 2 full-time staff members. Academic advisers, counselors, diagnostic specialists, professional tutors, regular education teachers, remediation/learning specialists, skill tutors, strategy tutors, and trained peer tutors are provided collaboratively through on-campus or off-campus services.

Summer Program To help prepare for the demands of college, there is an optional 6- to 8-week summer program prior to entering the school available to high school graduates that focuses on life skills and/or college life adjustment, self-advocacy, study skills, test-taking skills, and time management. The program accepts students from out-of-state and is available to students attending other colleges.

Unique Aids and Services Aids, services, or accommodations include career counseling, testing accommodations.

Assistive Technology Assistive technology is located in the DSS office, the Tutoring Center and includes digital textbooks/e-text and scanning.

Subject-Area Tutoring Tutoring is offered one-on-one and in small groups for most subjects. Tutoring is provided collaboratively through on-campus or off-campus services via trained peer tutors.

Diagnostic Testing Testing for math, reading, and study skills is provided collaboratively through on-campus or off-campus services.

Basic Skills Remediation Remediation is offered in class-size groups for math, reading, and written language. Remediation is provided collaboratively through on-campus or off-campus services via regular education teachers.

Enrichment Programs for career planning, college survival skills, reading, stress management, study skills, test taking, time management, vocabulary development, and written composition skills are provided collaboratively through on-campus or off-campus services. Credit is offered for college survival skills, reading, stress management, study skills, test taking, time management, vocabulary development, and written composition skills.

Fees *Summer Program* fee is $93.

Application For admittance to the program or unit, students are required to apply to the program directly. It is recommended that students provide a psychoeducational report and provide documentation of high school services. Upon application, materials documenting need for services should be sent only to the LD program or unit. Upon acceptance, documentation of need for services should be sent only to the LD program or unit. *Application deadline (LD program):* Rolling/continuous for fall and rolling/continuous for spring.

Written Policies Written policies regarding course substitutions, general/basic LD accommodations, grade forgiveness, substitutions and waivers of admissions requirements, and substitutions and waivers of graduation requirements are available on the program Web site. Written policies regarding course substitutions, general/basic LD accommodations, grade forgiveness, substitutions and waivers of admissions requirements, and substitutions and waivers of graduation requirements are outlined in the school's catalog/handbook. Written policies regarding course substitutions, general/basic LD accommodations, substitutions and waivers of admissions requirements, and substitutions and waivers of graduation requirements are available through the program or unit directly.

Dixie State College of Utah
Disability Resource Center

225 South 700 East

St. George, UT 84770-3876

http://www.dixie.edu/drc

Contact: Mandee Krajnc, Disability Resource Center Coordinator. Phone: 435-652-7516. E-mail: krajnc@dixie.edu.

Disability Resource Center Approximately 150 registered undergraduate students were served during 2006–07. The program or unit includes 1 full-time and 1 part-time staff member. Academic advisers and counselors are provided through the program or unit. Academic advisers, coaches, counselors, diagnostic specialists, professional tutors, regular education teachers, remediation/learning specialists, skill tutors, special education teachers, strategy tutors, teacher trainees, trained peer tutors, and other are provided collaboratively through on-campus or off-campus services.

Orientation The program or unit offers a mandatory 1-hour orientation for new students individually by special arrangement.

Unique Aids and Services Aids, services, or accommodations include advocates, career counseling, faculty training, priority registration, note-takers, readers, scribes.

Assistive Technology Assistive technology is located in the DSS office and includes digital textbooks/e-text, learning support software, scanning, and books on tape, tape recorders.

Subject-Area Tutoring Tutoring is offered in class-size groups for most subjects. Tutoring is provided collaboratively through on-campus or off-campus services via trained peer tutors.

Basic Skills Remediation Remediation is offered in class-size groups for computer skills, learning strategies, math, reading, spelling, study skills, and written language. Remediation is provided collaboratively through on-campus or off-campus services via regular education teachers and trained peer tutors.

Enrichment Enrichment programs are available through the program or unit for college survival skills and time management. Programs for career planning, college survival skills, health and nutrition, learning strategies, math, oral communication skills, practical computer skills, reading, stress management, study skills, test taking, time management, vocabulary development, and written composition skills are provided collaboratively through on-campus or off-campus services. Credit is offered for college survival skills, health and nutrition, math, oral communication skills, practical computer skills, reading, stress management, study skills, vocabulary development, and written composition skills.

Application For admittance to the program or unit, students are required to apply to the program directly. It is recommended that students provide a psychoeducational report (3 years old or less) and provide documentation of high school services. Upon application, materials documenting need for services should be sent only to the LD program or unit. Upon acceptance, documentation of need for services should be sent only to the LD program or unit. *Application deadline (institutional):* Continuous. *Application deadline (LD program):* Rolling/continuous for fall and rolling/continuous for spring.

Written Policies Written policy regarding general/basic LD accommodations is available on the program Web site. Written policy regarding general/basic LD accommodations is available through the program or unit directly.

Duluth Business University

4724 Mike Colalillo Drive

Duluth, MN 55807

http://www.dbumn.edu/

Contact: Ms. Ann Brascugli Sertich, Academic & Distance Learning Advisor. Phone: 218-722-4000. Fax: 218-628-2127. E-mail: asertich@dbumn.edu.

Academic advisers, regular education teachers, and skill tutors are provided collaboratively through on-campus or off-campus services.

Unique Aids and Services Aids, services, or accommodations include weekly meetings with faculty, student success skills course.

Assistive Technology Assistive technology is located in the DSS office and includes digital textbooks/e-text. Technology training is provided to incoming students.

Subject-Area Tutoring Tutoring is offered one-on-one and in small groups for most subjects. Tutoring is provided collaboratively through on-campus or off-campus services via trained peer tutors.

Enrichment Enrichment programs are available through the program or unit for college survival skills, math, study skills, test taking, time management, and written composition skills. Credit is offered for college survival skills, math, study skills, test taking, time management, and written composition skills.

Application For admittance to the program or unit, students are required to provide documentation of high school services and provide test results (5 years old or less). Upon acceptance, documentation of need for services should be sent only to the LD program or unit. *Application deadline (LD program):* Rolling/continuous for fall and rolling/continuous for spring.

Written Policies Written policy regarding general/basic LD accommodations is available through the program or unit directly.

Durham Technical Community College
Disability Services

1637 Lawson Street

Durham, NC 27703-5023

http://www.durhamtech.edu/

Contact: Paula J. Rubio, Counselor, Disability Services. Phone: 919-686-3652. Fax: 919-686-3742. E-mail: rubiop@durhamtech.edu. Head of LD Program: D. Thomas Jaynes, Associate Dean of Counseling and Student Development. Phone: 919-686-3652. Fax: 919-686-3742. E-mail: jaynest@durhamtech.edu.

Disability Services Approximately 120 registered undergraduate students were served during 2006–07. The program or unit includes 2 full-time staff members. Coaches, counselors, LD specialists, skill tutors, and strategy tutors are provided through the program or unit. Academic advisers, diagnostic specialists, professional tutors, regular education teachers, remediation/learning specialists, skill tutors, strategy tutors, and trained peer tutors are provided collaboratively through on-campus or off-campus services.

Unique Aids and Services Aids, services, or accommodations include career counseling, priority registration, mentor program.

Assistive Technology Assistive technology is located in a special lab and includes digital textbooks/e-text and learning support software.

Subject-Area Tutoring Tutoring is offered one-on-one and in small groups for some subjects. Tutoring is provided collaboratively through on-campus or off-campus services via computer-based instruction, professional tutors, and trained peer tutors.

Basic Skills Remediation Remediation is offered in class-size groups for math, reading, and written language. Remediation is provided collaboratively through on-campus or off-campus services via regular education teachers.

Enrichment Enrichment programs are available through the program or unit for learning strategies, stress management, study skills, test taking, and time management. Programs for career planning, college survival skills, health and nutrition, learning strategies, math, oral communication skills, practical computer skills, reading, study skills, test taking, time management, vocabulary development, and written composition skills are provided collaboratively through on-campus or off-campus services. Credit is offered for college survival skills, health and nutrition, learning strategies, math, oral communication skills, practical computer skills, reading, study skills, test taking, time management, vocabulary development, and written composition skills.

Application For admittance to the program or unit, students are required to provide a psychoeducational report (5 years old or less). It is recommended that students provide documentation of high school services. Upon application, materials documenting need for services should be sent only to the LD program or unit. Upon acceptance, documentation of need for services should be sent only to the LD program or unit. *Application deadline (LD program):* Rolling/continuous for fall and rolling/continuous for spring.

Written Policies Written policy regarding general/basic LD accommodations is available on the program Web site. Written policy regarding general/basic LD accommodations is available through the program or unit directly.

Dutchess Community College

53 Pendell Road

Poughkeepsie, NY 12601-1595

http://www.sunydutchess.edu/

Contact: Paula Perez. E-mail: perez@sunydutchess.edu.

Assistive Technology Assistive technology is located in the DSS office, a special lab and includes digital textbooks/e-text, learning support software, and scanning. Technology training is provided to incoming students.

Written Policies Written policy regarding general/basic LD accommodations is available through the program or unit directly.

East Central College
Access Services

1964 Prairie Dell Road

Union, MO 63084

http://www.eastcentral.edu/

Contact: Ms. Wendy J. Pecka, Director, Counseling and Advisement. Phone: 636-583-5195. Fax: 636-583-1011.

Access Services Approximately 40 registered undergraduate students were served during 2006–07.

Unique Aids and Services Aids, services, or accommodations include career counseling.

Subject-Area Tutoring Tutoring is offered one-on-one and in small groups for most subjects. Tutoring is provided collaboratively through on-campus or off-campus services via trained peer tutors.

Basic Skills Remediation Remediation is offered in class-size groups for math, reading, spelling, and study skills. Remediation is provided collaboratively through on-campus or off-campus services via computer-based instruction and regular education teachers.

Enrichment Programs for career planning, college survival skills, and stress management are provided collaboratively through on-campus or off-campus services. Credit is offered for college survival skills.

Application For admittance to the program or unit, students are required to provide a psychoeducational report. It is recommended that students provide documentation of high school services. Upon application, materials documenting need for services should be sent only to the LD program or unit. *Application deadline (institutional):* Continuous. *Application deadline (LD program):* Rolling/continuous for fall and rolling/continuous for spring.

East Central Community College
Office of Vice President for Instruction/ Vice President for Student Services

PO Box 129

Decatur, MS 39327-0129

http://www.eccc.edu

Contact: Dr. Lavinia Sparkman, Vice President for Instruction. Phone: 601-635-2111 Ext. 203. Fax: 601-635-4011. E-mail: lsparkman@eccc.edu.

Office of Vice President for Instruction/Vice President for Student Services Approximately 5 registered undergraduate students were served during 2006–07. Regular education teachers are provided through the program or unit. Regular education teachers are provided collaboratively through on-campus or off-campus services.

Assistive Technology Assistive technology is located in a special lab.

Subject-Area Tutoring Tutoring is offered one-on-one for some subjects. Tutoring is provided collaboratively through on-campus or off-campus services via computer-based instruction and other.

Basic Skills Remediation Remediation is offered in class-size groups for math and reading. Remediation is provided collaboratively through on-campus or off-campus services via regular education teachers and other.

Application It is recommended that students apply to the program directly, provide a psychoeducational report (1 year old or less), and provide documentation of high school services. Upon acceptance, documentation of need for services should be sent only to the LD program or unit. *Application deadline (LD program):* Rolling/continuous for fall and rolling/continuous for spring.

Written Policies Written policy regarding general/basic LD accommodations is available on the program Web site. Written policies regarding general/basic LD accommodations and substitutions and waivers of admissions requirements are outlined in the school's catalog/handbook.

Eastern Idaho Technical College
Disability Resources & Services Office

1600 South 25th East

Idaho Falls, ID 83404-5788

http://www.eitc.edu

Contact: Ms. Irene Jones, Disability Resources & Services Coordinator. Phone: 208-524-3000 Ext. 3376. Fax: 208-524-3007. E-mail: ijones@eitc.edu.

Disability Resources & Services Office Approximately 15 registered undergraduate students were served during 2006–07. The program or unit includes 1 part-time staff member. Academic advisers, counselors, regular education teachers, remediation/learning specialists, and skill tutors are provided collaboratively through on-campus or off-campus services.

Unique Aids and Services Aids, services, or accommodations include advocates, career counseling, faculty training, and support groups.

Assistive Technology Assistive technology is located in campus labs and includes digital textbooks/e-text and Kurzweil. Technology training is provided to incoming students.

Subject-Area Tutoring Tutoring is offered one-on-one and in small groups for some subjects. Tutoring is provided collaboratively through on-campus or off-campus services via computer-based instruction and other.

Diagnostic Testing Testing for math, reading, and written language is provided collaboratively through on-campus or off-campus services.

Basic Skills Remediation Remediation is offered one-on-one and in class-size groups for computer skills, math, reading, spelling, study skills, and written language. Remediation is provided collaboratively through on-campus or off-campus services via computer-based instruction, regular education teachers, and other.

Enrichment Programs for career planning, college survival skills, learning strategies, math, oral communication skills, practical computer skills, reading, self-advocacy, stress management, study skills, test taking, time management, vocabulary development, and written composition skills are provided collaboratively through on-campus or off-campus services. Credit is offered for college survival skills, learning strategies, math, oral communication skills, practical computer skills, stress management, study skills, test taking, time management, and written composition skills.

Application For admittance to the program or unit, students are required to provide a psychoeducational report. It is recommended that students provide documentation of high school services. Upon acceptance, documentation of need for services should be sent only to the LD program or unit. *Application deadline (institutional):* 8/21. *Application deadline (LD program):* Rolling/continuous for fall and rolling/continuous for spring.

Written Policies Written policy regarding general/basic LD accommodations is outlined in the school's catalog/handbook. Written policies regarding course substitutions, general/basic LD accommodations, grade forgiveness, reduced course loads, substitutions and waivers of admissions requirements, and substitutions and waivers of graduation requirements are available through the program or unit directly.

Eastern Oklahoma State College
Dean of Students Office

1301 West Main

Wilburton, OK 74578-4999

http://www.eosc.edu/

Contact: Mr. Brenton Duncan, Dean of Students. Phone: 918-465-1756. E-mail: bduncan@eosc.edu.

Dean of Students Office Approximately 45 registered undergraduate students were served during 2006–07. The program or unit includes 4 full-time and 3 part-time staff members. Academic advisers, counselors, professional tutors, regular education teachers, remediation/learning specialists, skill tutors, and trained peer tutors

are provided through the program or unit. Academic advisers, counselors, regular education teachers, remediation/learning specialists, and trained peer tutors are provided collaboratively through on-campus or off-campus services.

Unique Aids and Services Aids, services, or accommodations include career counseling, study skills.

Assistive Technology Assistive technology is located in Student Support and Dean of Students offices and includes digital textbooks/e-text, scanning, and magnification. Technology training is provided to incoming students.

Subject-Area Tutoring Tutoring is offered one-on-one and in small groups for some subjects. Tutoring is provided through the program or unit via computer-based instruction. Tutoring is also provided collaboratively through on-campus or off-campus services via computer-based instruction, professional tutors, and trained peer tutors.

Diagnostic Testing Testing for intelligence, learning strategies, learning styles, math, reading, spelling, and written language is provided collaboratively through on-campus or off-campus services.

Basic Skills Remediation Remediation is offered in small groups for computer skills, learning strategies, math, reading, and written language. Remediation is provided collaboratively through on-campus or off-campus services via computer-based instruction, professional tutors, and regular education teachers.

Enrichment Programs for career planning, college survival skills, learning strategies, stress management, study skills, and test taking are provided collaboratively through on-campus or off-campus services.

Application For admittance to the program or unit, students are required to apply to the program directly and provide documentation of high school services. Upon application, materials documenting need for services should be sent only to the LD program or unit. Upon acceptance, documentation of need for services should be sent only to the LD program or unit. *Application deadline (LD program):* Rolling/continuous for fall and rolling/continuous for spring.

Written Policies Written policies regarding general/basic LD accommodations and reduced course loads are outlined in the school's catalog/handbook. Written policies regarding general/basic LD accommodations and reduced course loads are available through the program or unit directly.

Eastern West Virginia Community and Technical College
Learner Support Services

HC 65 Box 402

Moorefield, WV 26836

http://www.eastern.wvnet.edu

Contact: Ms. Sharon Bungard, Dean of Learner Support Services. Phone: 304-434-8000. Fax: 304-434-7000. E-mail: sbungard@eastern.wvnet.edu.

Learner Support Services Approximately 10 registered undergraduate students were served during 2006–07. The program or unit includes 5 full-time staff members. Academic advisers, counselors, professional tutors, and trained peer tutors are provided through the

Eastern West Virginia Community and Technical College (continued)
program or unit. Academic advisers, counselors, diagnostic specialists, graduate assistants/students, LD specialists, professional tutors, and regular education teachers are provided collaboratively through on-campus or off-campus services.

Unique Aids and Services Aids, services, or accommodations include faculty training.

Assistive Technology Assistive technology is located in the Workforce WV Office and includes digital textbooks/e-text, learning support software, and scanning.

Subject-Area Tutoring Tutoring is offered one-on-one and in small groups for some subjects. Tutoring is provided through the program or unit via professional tutors and trained peer tutors. Tutoring is also provided collaboratively through on-campus or off-campus services via computer-based instruction and professional tutors.

Basic Skills Remediation Remediation is offered in class-size groups for math, reading, spelling, study skills, time management, and written language. Remediation is provided collaboratively through on-campus or off-campus services via regular education teachers.

Enrichment Enrichment programs are available through the program or unit for career planning, college survival skills, health and nutrition, learning strategies, stress management, study skills, test taking, and time management. Programs for career planning, math, practical computer skills, reading, vocabulary development, and written composition skills are provided collaboratively through on-campus or off-campus services. Credit is offered for college survival skills, math, practical computer skills, reading, vocabulary development, and written composition skills.

Application For admittance to the program or unit, students are required to provide a psychoeducational report (5 years old or less). It is recommended that students provide documentation of high school services. Upon acceptance, documentation of need for services should be sent only to the LD program or unit. *Application deadline (LD program):* Rolling/continuous for fall and rolling/continuous for spring.

Written Policies Written policy regarding general/basic LD accommodations is available on the program Web site. Written policy regarding general/basic LD accommodations is outlined in the school's catalog/handbook.

Eastfield College
Disability Services Office

3737 Motley Drive

Mesquite, TX 75150-2099

http://www.efc.dcccd.edu/SSI/DSO.htm

Contact: Ms. Melissa Gautreau, Senior Rehabilitation Specialist. Phone: 972-860-8348. Fax: 972-860-7622. E-mail: efcdso@dcccd.edu. Head of LD Program: Ms. Bobbi White, Director, Disability Services Office. Phone: 972-860-8348. Fax: 972-860-7622. E-mail: efcdso@dcccd.edu.

Disability Services Office Approximately 150 registered undergraduate students were served during 2006–07. The program or unit includes 3 full-time staff members. Academic advisers and counselors are provided through the program or unit. Counselors are provided collaboratively through on-campus or off-campus services.

Orientation The program or unit offers an optional orientation for new students during registration, after classes begin, and individually by special arrangement.

Unique Aids and Services Aids, services, or accommodations include priority registration.

Assistive Technology Assistive technology is located in campus labs, the DSS office and includes digital textbooks/e-text and scanning.

Subject-Area Tutoring Tutoring is offered in small groups for some subjects. Tutoring is provided collaboratively through on-campus or off-campus services via computer-based instruction, professional tutors, and trained peer tutors.

Basic Skills Remediation Remediation is offered in class-size groups for learning strategies, math, reading, study skills, time management, and written language. Remediation is provided collaboratively through on-campus or off-campus services via computer-based instruction and regular education teachers.

Application For admittance to the program or unit, students are required to provide a psychoeducational report (3 years old or less). It is recommended that students apply to the program directly and provide documentation of high school services. Upon application, materials documenting need for services should be sent only to the LD program or unit. Upon acceptance, documentation of need for services should be sent only to the LD program or unit. *Application deadline (institutional):* Continuous. *Application deadline (LD program):* Rolling/continuous for fall and rolling/continuous for spring.

Written Policies Written policies regarding course substitutions and general/basic LD accommodations are available on the program Web site. Written policy regarding general/basic LD accommodations is outlined in the school's catalog/handbook.

El Camino College
Special Resource Center, Learning Disabilities Program

16007 Crenshaw Boulevard

Torrance, CA 90506-0001

http://www.elcamino.edu

Contact: William Hoanzl, Learning Disabilities Program. Phone: 310-660-3296. Fax: 310-660-3922. E-mail: srchelp@elcamino.edu.

Special Resource Center, Learning Disabilities Program
Approximately 500 registered undergraduate students were served during 2006–07. The program or unit includes 2 full-time staff members. Diagnostic specialists, LD specialists, regular education teachers, remediation/learning specialists, skill tutors, and strategy tutors are provided through the program or unit. Academic advisers, counselors, diagnostic specialists, graduate assistants/students, remediation/learning specialists, skill tutors, and strategy tutors are provided collaboratively through on-campus or off-campus services.

Orientation The program or unit offers a mandatory 1-hour orientation for new students before registration, before classes begin, during registration, after classes begin, and individually by special arrangement.

Summer Program To help prepare for the demands of college, there is an optional summer program prior to entering the school.

Unique Aids and Services Aids, services, or accommodations include priority registration.

Diagnostic Testing Testing is provided through the program or unit for auditory processing, intelligence, learning strategies, learning styles, math, motor skills, neuropsychological, reading, spelling, study skills, visual processing, and written language.

Basic Skills Remediation Remediation is offered in class-size groups for auditory processing, computer skills, learning strategies, math, motor skills, reading, spelling, study skills, time management, visual processing, and written language. Remediation is provided through the program or unit via computer-based instruction, LD specialists, and special education teachers. Remediation is also provided collaboratively through on-campus or off-campus services via graduate assistants/students, professional tutors, regular education teachers, teacher trainees, and trained peer tutors.

Application For admittance to the program or unit, students are required to apply to the program directly and provide documentation of high school services. It is recommended that students provide a psychoeducational report (3 years old or less). Upon application, materials documenting need for services should be sent only to the LD program or unit. Upon acceptance, documentation of need for services should be sent only to the LD program or unit. *Application deadline (institutional):* Continuous. *Application deadline (LD program):* Rolling/continuous for fall and rolling/continuous for spring.

Written Policies Written policy regarding reduced course loads is available on the program Web site. Written policy regarding reduced course loads is outlined in the school's catalog/handbook. Written policies regarding course substitutions, general/basic LD accommodations, grade forgiveness, substitutions and waivers of admissions requirements, and substitutions and waivers of graduation requirements are available through the program or unit directly.

El Centro College
Disability Services Office

801 Main Street
Dallas, TX 75202-3604
http://www.elcentrocollege.edu/StudentServices/disabilityservices/default.asp
Contact: Karin Reed, Disability Services Coordinator. Phone: 214-860-2411. Fax: 214-860-2233. E-mail: karin.reed@dcccd.edu.

Disability Services Office Approximately 200 registered undergraduate students were served during 2006–07. The program or unit includes 2 full-time and 4 part-time staff members. Academic advisers and other are provided through the program or unit. Coaches, counselors, professional tutors, regular education teachers, skill tutors, and strategy tutors are provided collaboratively through on-campus or off-campus services.

Unique Aids and Services Aids, services, or accommodations include advocates and faculty training.

Assistive Technology Assistive technology is located in the Learning Resource Center and includes learning support software and scanning.

Subject-Area Tutoring Tutoring is offered one-on-one and in small groups for most subjects. Tutoring is provided collaboratively through on-campus or off-campus services via professional tutors and trained peer tutors.

Basic Skills Remediation Remediation is offered in class-size groups for computer skills, math, reading, study skills, time management, and written language. Remediation is provided collaboratively through on-campus or off-campus services via computer-based instruction, regular education teachers, and special education teachers.

Enrichment Enrichment programs are available through the program or unit for self-advocacy. Programs for career planning, college survival skills, learning strategies, math, oral communication skills, practical computer skills, reading, stress management, study skills, test taking, time management, and written composition skills are provided collaboratively through on-campus or off-campus services. Credit is offered for career planning, college survival skills, learning strategies, math, oral communication skills, practical computer skills, reading, stress management, study skills, time management, and written composition skills.

Application For admittance to the program or unit, students are required to apply to the program directly and provide a psychoeducational report (5 years old or less). It is recommended that students provide documentation of high school services. Upon application, materials documenting need for services should be sent only to the LD program or unit. Upon acceptance, documentation of need for services should be sent only to the LD program or unit. *Application deadline (institutional):* Continuous. *Application deadline (LD program):* Rolling/continuous for fall and rolling/continuous for spring.

Written Policies Written policies regarding course substitutions, general/basic LD accommodations, and substitutions and waivers of graduation requirements are available through the program or unit directly.

El Paso Community College
Center for Students with Disabilities

PO Box 20500
El Paso, TX 79998-0500
http://www.epcc.edu/csd
Contact: Counselors. Phone: 915-831-2426. Fax: 915-831-2244.

Center for Students with Disabilities Approximately 540 registered undergraduate students were served during 2006–07. The program or unit includes 18 full-time and 80 part-time staff members. Counselors, trained peer tutors, and other are provided through the program or unit.

Orientation The program or unit offers a mandatory orientation for new students.

Summer Program To help prepare for the demands of college, there is summer program prior to entering the school.

Unique Aids and Services Aids, services, or accommodations include career counseling, faculty training, priority registration, academic counseling, limited personal counseling.

Assistive Technology Assistive technology is located in the DSS office and includes learning support software and scanning. Technology training is provided to incoming students.

Subject-Area Tutoring Tutoring is offered one-on-one and in small groups for most subjects. Tutoring is provided through the program or unit via trained peer tutors. Tutoring is also provided collaboratively through on-campus or off-campus services via trained peer tutors.

El Paso Community College (continued)

Basic Skills Remediation Remediation is offered one-on-one and in small groups for computer skills, learning strategies, math, reading, and spelling. Remediation is provided through the program or unit via trained peer tutors. Remediation is also provided collaboratively through on-campus or off-campus services via regular education teachers and trained peer tutors.

Enrichment Enrichment programs are available through the program or unit for career planning, college survival skills, learning strategies, math, practical computer skills, reading, stress management, study skills, test taking, time management, vocabulary development, and written composition skills. Programs for career planning, math, practical computer skills, reading, and study skills are provided collaboratively through on-campus or off-campus services.

Application For admittance to the program or unit, students are required to provide a psychoeducational report (5 years old or less) and provide documentation of high school services. Upon application, materials documenting need for services should be sent only to the LD program or unit. Upon acceptance, documentation of need for services should be sent only to the LD program or unit. *Application deadline (LD program):* Rolling/continuous for fall and rolling/continuous for spring.

Written Policies Written policy regarding general/basic LD accommodations is available on the program Web site. Written policy regarding general/basic LD accommodations is available through the program or unit directly.

Emory University, Oxford College
Office of Disability Services

100 Hamill Street, PO Box 1328

Oxford, GA 30054

http://www.ods.emory.edu

Contact: Jessalyn P. Smiley, Student Coordinator. Phone: 404-727-6016. Fax: 404-727-1126. E-mail: jpsmile@ emory.edu. Head of LD Program: Gloria Y. Weaver, Director. Phone: 404-727-6016. Fax: 404-727-1126. E-mail: gweaver@emory.edu.

Office of Disability Services Approximately 50 registered undergraduate students were served during 2006–07. The program or unit includes 1 full-time and 1 part-time staff member. Academic advisers, coaches, counselors, skill tutors, strategy tutors, teacher trainees, and trained peer tutors are provided collaboratively through on-campus or off-campus services.

Assistive Technology Assistive technology is located in campus labs and includes digital textbooks/e-text and learning support software.

Subject-Area Tutoring Tutoring is offered for most subjects. Tutoring is provided collaboratively through on-campus or off-campus services via trained peer tutors.

Enrichment Programs for career planning, college survival skills, health and nutrition, learning strategies, math, oral communication skills, practical computer skills, reading, stress management, study skills, test taking, time management, and written composition skills are provided collaboratively through on-campus or off-campus services.

Application For admittance to the program or unit, students are required to apply to the program directly and provide a psychoeducational report (3 years old or less). Upon acceptance, documentation of need for services should be sent only to the LD program or unit. *Application deadline (institutional):* 2/1. *Application deadline (LD program):* Rolling/continuous for fall and rolling/continuous for spring.

Written Policies Written policies regarding course substitutions, general/basic LD accommodations, grade forgiveness, reduced course loads, substitutions and waivers of admissions requirements, and substitutions and waivers of graduation requirements are available on the program Web site. Written policies regarding course substitutions, general/basic LD accommodations, grade forgiveness, reduced course loads, substitutions and waivers of admissions requirements, and substitutions and waivers of graduation requirements are outlined in the school's catalog/handbook. Written policy regarding general/basic LD accommodations is available through the program or unit directly.

Feather River College
Disabled Student Programs and Services (DSP&S)

570 Golden Eagle Avenue

Quincy, CA 95971-9124

http://www.frc.edu/

Contact: Terrie Rose-Boehme, Disabled Student Programs and Services Coordinator. Phone: 530-283-0202 Ext. 247. Fax: 530-283-3757. E-mail: trose-boehme@frc.edu. Head of LD Program: Dr. Larry Holcomb, Education Psychologist and LD Specialist. Phone: 530-283-0202 Ext. 263. Fax: 530-283-4759. E-mail: lholcomb@frc.edu.

Disabled Student Programs and Services (DSP&S) Approximately 75 registered undergraduate students were served during 2006–07. The program or unit includes 1 full-time staff member. Academic advisers, counselors, diagnostic specialists, LD specialists, professional tutors, regular education teachers, remediation/learning specialists, skill tutors, and trained peer tutors are provided collaboratively through on-campus or off-campus services.

Orientation The program or unit offers an optional 1-hour orientation for new students after classes begin and individually by special arrangement.

Unique Aids and Services Aids, services, or accommodations include advocates, career counseling, priority registration, and weekly meetings with faculty.

Assistive Technology Assistive technology is located in the DSS office and includes digital textbooks/e-text, learning support software, and scanning.

Subject-Area Tutoring Tutoring is offered one-on-one and in small groups for some subjects. Tutoring is provided collaboratively through on-campus or off-campus services via computer-based instruction, graduate assistants/students, LD specialists, and professional tutors.

Diagnostic Testing Testing is provided through the program or unit for auditory processing, handwriting, intelligence, learning strategies, learning styles, math, personality, reading, social skills, spelling, spoken language, study skills, visual processing, and written language.

Basic Skills Remediation Remediation is offered one-on-one and in small groups for computer skills, handwriting, learning strategies, math, reading, spelling, study skills, time management, visual processing, and written language. Remediation is provided collaboratively through on-campus or off-campus services via computer-based instruction, graduate assistants/students, professional tutors, and regular education teachers.

Enrichment Programs for career planning, college survival skills, learning strategies, math, oral communication skills, practical computer skills, reading, self-advocacy, stress management, study skills, test taking, time management, vocabulary development, and written composition skills are provided collaboratively through on-campus or off-campus services.

Application It is recommended that students apply to the program directly, provide a psychoeducational report, and provide documentation of high school services. Upon application, materials documenting need for services should be sent only to the LD program or unit. Upon acceptance, documentation of need for services should be sent only to the LD program or unit. *Application deadline (LD program):* Rolling/continuous for fall and rolling/continuous for spring.

Written Policies Written policies regarding course substitutions, general/basic LD accommodations, substitutions and waivers of admissions requirements, and substitutions and waivers of graduation requirements are outlined in the school's catalog/handbook. Written policies regarding general/basic LD accommodations, grade forgiveness, and reduced course loads are available through the program or unit directly.

Florida Community College at Jacksonville
Office of Services for Students with Disabilities

501 West State Street
Jacksonville, FL 32202-4030
http://www.fccj.edu/

Contact: Mrs. Denise J. Giarrusso, Director of Services for Students With Disabilities. Phone: 904-632-5007. Fax: 904-633-8110. E-mail: dgiarrus@fccj.edu.

Office of Services for Students with Disabilities Approximately 413 registered undergraduate students were served during 2006–07. The program or unit includes 5 full-time and 4 part-time staff members. Academic advisers, skill tutors, strategy tutors, trained peer tutors, and other are provided through the program or unit. Academic advisers, counselors, diagnostic specialists, professional tutors, regular education teachers, and remediation/learning specialists are provided collaboratively through on-campus or off-campus services.

Orientation The program or unit offers a mandatory 1-hour orientation for new students before classes begin, after classes begin, and individually by special arrangement.

Unique Aids and Services Aids, services, or accommodations include career counseling, faculty training, and priority registration.

Assistive Technology Assistive technology is located in the DSS office, Learning Resource Centers/the library and includes digital textbooks/e-text, learning support software, and scanning. Technology training is provided to incoming students.

Subject-Area Tutoring Tutoring is offered one-on-one and in small groups for all subjects. Tutoring is provided collaboratively through on-campus or off-campus services via computer-based instruction.

Diagnostic Testing Testing for math, reading, spelling, written language, and other services is provided collaboratively through on-campus or off-campus services.

Basic Skills Remediation Remediation is offered one-on-one and in small groups for math, reading, spelling, and written language. Remediation is provided through the program or unit via professional tutors and trained peer tutors. Remediation is also provided collaboratively through on-campus or off-campus services via computer-based instruction.

Enrichment Enrichment programs are available through the program or unit for career planning, learning strategies, math, self-advocacy, study skills, test taking, and time management. Program for career planning is provided collaboratively through on-campus or off-campus services.

Fees *Diagnostic Testing* fee is $15.

Application For admittance to the program or unit, students are required to apply to the program directly, provide a psychoeducational report, and provide 504 plan. It is recommended that students provide documentation of high school services. Upon application, materials documenting need for services should be sent only to the LD program or unit. *Application deadline (institutional):* Continuous. *Application deadline (LD program):* Rolling/continuous for fall and rolling/continuous for spring.

Written Policies Written policies regarding course substitutions, general/basic LD accommodations, reduced course loads, and substitutions and waivers of graduation requirements are available on the program Web site. Written policies regarding course substitutions, general/basic LD accommodations, reduced course loads, and substitutions and waivers of graduation requirements are outlined in the school's catalog/handbook. Written policy regarding general/basic LD accommodations is available through the program or unit directly.

Foothill College
STEP: Student Tutorial Evaluation Program

12345 El Monte Road
Los Altos Hills, CA 94022-4599
http://www.foothill.edu/al

Contact: Janet M. Spybrook, Instructor/Learning Disabilities Specialist. Phone: 650-949-7618. Fax: 650-917-1064. E-mail: spybrookjanet@foothill.edu.

STEP: Student Tutorial Evaluation Program The program or unit includes 4 full-time staff members and 1 part-time staff member. Academic advisers, counselors, diagnostic specialists, LD specialists, remediation/learning specialists, skill tutors, strategy tutors, teacher trainees, and trained peer tutors are provided through the program or unit. Skill tutors are provided collaboratively through on-campus or off-campus services.

Orientation The program or unit offers an optional 2-week orientation for new students before registration, before classes begin, during summer prior to enrollment, and individually by special arrangement.

Foothill College (continued)

Summer Program To help prepare for the demands of college, there is an optional 2-week summer program prior to entering the school available to high school graduates that focuses on life skills and/or college life adjustment, self-advocacy, and study skills. The program accepts students from out-of-state.

Unique Aids and Services Aids, services, or accommodations include faculty training and priority registration.

Assistive Technology Assistive technology is located in the DSS office, a special lab and includes digital textbooks/e-text, learning support software, and scanning. Technology training is provided to incoming students.

Subject-Area Tutoring Tutoring is offered one-on-one and in small groups for some subjects. Tutoring is provided through the program or unit via LD specialists and trained peer tutors.

Diagnostic Testing Testing is provided through the program or unit for auditory processing, intelligence, math, reading, spelling, visual processing, and written language. Testing for learning strategies, learning styles, neuropsychological, social skills, and study skills is provided collaboratively through on-campus or off-campus services.

Basic Skills Remediation Remediation is offered one-on-one and in small groups for learning strategies, math, reading, study skills, and written language. Remediation is provided through the program or unit via computer-based instruction, LD specialists, and trained peer tutors.

Enrichment Enrichment programs are available through the program or unit for college survival skills, learning strategies, math, practical computer skills, self-advocacy, stress management, study skills, test taking, time management, and written composition skills. Program for college survival skills is provided collaboratively through on-campus or off-campus services. Credit is offered for college survival skills, learning strategies, math, practical computer skills, self-advocacy, stress management, study skills, test taking, time management, and written composition skills.

Fees *Diagnostic Testing* fee is applicable.

Application For admittance to the program or unit, students are required to apply to the program directly, provide a psychoeducational report, and provide documentation of high school services. Upon application, materials documenting need for services should be sent only to the LD program or unit. Upon acceptance, documentation of need for services should be sent only to the LD program or unit. *Application deadline (institutional):* 9/15. *Application deadline (LD program):* Rolling/continuous for fall and rolling/continuous for spring.

Written Policies Written policies regarding general/basic LD accommodations and reduced course loads are available on the program Web site. Written policies regarding general/basic LD accommodations and reduced course loads are available through the program or unit directly.

Fort Scott Community College
Counseling Office

2108 South Horton
Fort Scott, KS 66701
http://www.fortscott.edu/

Contact: Janet Fancher, Counselor. Phone: 620-223-2700 Ext. 362. Fax: 620-223-6530. E-mail: janetf@fortscott.edu.

Counseling Office Approximately 20 registered undergraduate students were served during 2006–07. Academic advisers, counselors, professional tutors, and regular education teachers are provided collaboratively through on-campus or off-campus services.

Unique Aids and Services Aids, services, or accommodations include career counseling.

Assistive Technology Assistive technology includes digital textbooks/e-text.

Subject-Area Tutoring Tutoring is offered one-on-one and in small groups for most subjects. Tutoring is provided collaboratively through on-campus or off-campus services via professional tutors and trained peer tutors.

Diagnostic Testing Testing for intelligence, learning strategies, learning styles, math, reading, and written language is provided collaboratively through on-campus or off-campus services.

Basic Skills Remediation Remediation is offered in class-size groups for math, reading, and written language. Remediation is provided collaboratively through on-campus or off-campus services via computer-based instruction and regular education teachers.

Enrichment Programs for career planning, study skills, test taking, and time management are provided collaboratively through on-campus or off-campus services.

Application For admittance to the program or unit, students are required to provide a psychoeducational report (1 year old or less) and provide documentation of high school services. Upon application, materials documenting need for services should be sent only to admissions with institutional application materials. Upon acceptance, documentation of need for services should be sent only to admissions. *Application deadline (LD program):* Rolling/continuous for fall and rolling/continuous for spring.

Written Policies Written policies regarding general/basic LD accommodations, substitutions and waivers of admissions requirements, and substitutions and waivers of graduation requirements are outlined in the school's catalog/handbook. Written policies regarding course substitutions, grade forgiveness, and reduced course loads are available through the program or unit directly.

Frederick Community College
Services for Students with Disabilities Office

7932 Opossumtown Pike
Frederick, MD 21702-2097
http://www.frederick.edu/

Contact: Ms. Kate Kramer-Jefferson, Director, Services for Students with Disabilities. Phone: 301-846-2408. Fax: 301-846-2599. E-mail: kkramerjefferson@frederick.edu.

Services for Students with Disabilities Office Approximately 35 registered undergraduate students were served during 2006–07. The program or unit includes 2 full-time and 2 part-time staff members. Academic advisers and LD specialists are provided through the program or unit. Academic advisers, coaches, counselors, LD specialists, professional tutors, and trained peer tutors are provided collaboratively through on-campus or off-campus services.

Unique Aids and Services Aids, services, or accommodations include career counseling, priority registration, support groups, and weekly meetings with faculty.

Assistive Technology Assistive technology is located in campus labs, the DSS office, a special lab, the Testing Center/Writing Center and includes digital textbooks/e-text, learning support software, and scanning. Technology training is provided to incoming students.

Subject-Area Tutoring Tutoring is offered one-on-one and in small groups for all subjects. Tutoring is provided collaboratively through on-campus or off-campus services via computer-based instruction, professional tutors, and trained peer tutors.

Diagnostic Testing Testing for learning strategies, learning styles, personality, social skills, and study skills is provided collaboratively through on-campus or off-campus services.

Basic Skills Remediation Remediation is offered one-on-one for learning strategies, reading, study skills, and time management. Remediation is provided through the program or unit via LD specialists, professional tutors, and trained peer tutors.

Enrichment Programs for career planning, college survival skills, learning strategies, stress management, study skills, test taking, and time management are provided collaboratively through on-campus or off-campus services. Credit is offered for career planning, college survival skills, and learning strategies.

Application For admittance to the program or unit, students are required to apply to the program directly and provide a psychoeducational report (3 years old or less). It is recommended that students provide documentation of high school services. Upon application, materials documenting need for services should be sent only to the LD program or unit. Upon acceptance, documentation of need for services should be sent only to the LD program or unit. *Application deadline (institutional): 9/1. Application deadline (LD program):* Rolling/continuous for fall and rolling/continuous for spring.

Written Policies Written policy regarding general/basic LD accommodations is available on the program Web site. Written policy regarding general/basic LD accommodations is outlined in the school's catalog/handbook. Written policies regarding course substitutions, general/basic LD accommodations, and reduced course loads are available through the program or unit directly.

Fulton-Montgomery Community College
The Learning Center

2805 State Highway 67
Johnstown, NY 12095-3790
http://www.fmcc.suny.edu/prospective_students/learning_center.cfm

Contact: Mrs. Ellie Fosmire, Learning Disabilities Specialist. Phone: 518-762-4651 Ext. 5502. Fax: 518-762-3834. E-mail: efosmire@fmcc.suny.edu.

The Learning Center Approximately 80 registered undergraduate students were served during 2006–07. The program or unit includes 3 full-time staff members and 1 part-time staff member. Counselors, graduate assistants/students, LD specialists, professional tutors, regular education teachers, remediation/learning specialists, and trained peer tutors are provided through the program or unit.

Orientation The program or unit offers an optional 1 or 2 half-day orientation for new students before classes begin.

Unique Aids and Services Aids, services, or accommodations include faculty training and support groups.

Assistive Technology Assistive technology is located in campus labs, a special lab and includes digital textbooks/e-text and scanning. Technology training is provided to incoming students.

Subject-Area Tutoring Tutoring is offered one-on-one and in small groups for most subjects. Tutoring is provided through the program or unit via computer-based instruction, LD specialists, professional tutors, and trained peer tutors.

Diagnostic Testing Testing is provided through the program or unit for learning strategies and learning styles. Testing for intelligence is provided collaboratively through on-campus or off-campus services.

Basic Skills Remediation Remediation is offered one-on-one and in small groups for computer skills, learning strategies, math, study skills, time management, and written language. Remediation is provided through the program or unit via computer-based instruction, LD specialists, professional tutors, and trained peer tutors.

Enrichment Enrichment programs are available through the program or unit for stress management, study skills, test taking, time management, vocabulary development, and written composition skills. Programs for career planning, college survival skills, stress management, study skills, test taking, time management, vocabulary development, and written composition skills are provided collaboratively through on-campus or off-campus services. Credit is offered for career planning and college survival skills.

Student Organization ABLE Club consists of 10 members.

Application For admittance to the program or unit, students are required to provide a psychoeducational report (3 years old or less) and provide documentation of high school services. Upon application, materials documenting need for services should be sent only to the LD program or unit. Upon acceptance, documentation of need for services should be sent only to the LD program or unit. *Application deadline (institutional): 9/10. Application deadline (LD program):* Rolling/continuous for fall and rolling/continuous for spring.

Written Policies Written policy regarding general/basic LD accommodations is available on the program Web site. Written policy regarding general/basic LD accommodations is outlined in the school's catalog/handbook. Written policies regarding general/basic LD accommodations and reduced course loads are available through the program or unit directly.

Gadsden State Community College
Student Support Services

PO Box 227
Gadsden, AL 35902-0227
http://www.gadsdenstate.edu/

Contact: Dr. Teresa Rhea, Associate Dean of Student Services. Phone: 256-549-8263. Fax: 256-549-8466. E-mail: trhea@gadsdenstate.edu. Head of LD Program: Ms. Dale Hill, Director, Student Support Services. Phone: 256-549-8375. Fax: 256-549-8206. E-mail: dhill@gadsdenstate.edu.

Gadsden State Community College (continued)

Student Support Services Approximately 100 registered undergraduate students were served during 2006–07. The program or unit includes 6 full-time staff members. Academic advisers, counselors, LD specialists, skill tutors, and trained peer tutors are provided through the program or unit. Academic advisers, counselors, diagnostic specialists, LD specialists, regular education teachers, remediation/learning specialists, skill tutors, and trained peer tutors are provided collaboratively through on-campus or off-campus services.

Summer Program To help prepare for the demands of college, there is an optional 2-week summer program prior to entering the school available to high school graduates that focuses on computing skills, life skills and/or college life adjustment, self-advocacy, study skills, test-taking skills, and time management. Degree credit will be earned. The program is available to students attending other colleges.

Unique Aids and Services Aids, services, or accommodations include career counseling and priority registration.

Assistive Technology Assistive technology is located in campus labs, a special lab and includes digital textbooks/e-text, learning support software, scanning, and screen readers, CCTV.

Subject-Area Tutoring Tutoring is offered one-on-one and in small groups for some subjects. Tutoring is provided through the program or unit via trained peer tutors. Tutoring is also provided collaboratively through on-campus or off-campus services via professional tutors and trained peer tutors.

Basic Skills Remediation Remediation is offered one-on-one for computer skills, learning strategies, math, reading, study skills, time management, and written language. Remediation is provided through the program or unit via trained peer tutors. Remediation is also provided collaboratively through on-campus or off-campus services via professional tutors, regular education teachers, and trained peer tutors.

Enrichment Enrichment programs are available through the program or unit for career planning, college survival skills, learning strategies, math, practical computer skills, reading, self-advocacy, stress management, study skills, test taking, time management, and written composition skills. Programs for career planning, college survival skills, learning strategies, math, practical computer skills, study skills, test taking, time management, and written composition skills are provided collaboratively through on-campus or off-campus services.

Application For admittance to the program or unit, students are required to apply to the program directly, provide a psychoeducational report, and provide documentation of disability, learning or other type. It is recommended that students provide documentation of high school services. Upon application, materials documenting need for services should be sent only to the LD program or unit. Upon acceptance, documentation of need for services should be sent only to the LD program or unit. *Application deadline (institutional):* Continuous. *Application deadline (LD program):* Rolling/continuous for fall and rolling/continuous for spring.

Written Policies Written policies regarding general/basic LD accommodations and grade forgiveness are outlined in the school's catalog/handbook. Written policy regarding general/basic LD accommodations is available through the program or unit directly.

Gainesville State College
Disability Services

PO Box 1358
Oakwood, GA 30503-1358
http://www.gsc.edu/studev/disability/
Contact: Mrs. Carolyn Swindle, Coordinator of Disability Services. Phone: 678-717-3855. Fax: 678-717-3745. E-mail: cswindle@gsc.edu.

Disability Services Approximately 180 registered undergraduate students were served during 2006–07. The program or unit includes 3 full-time and 2 part-time staff members. Skill tutors and other are provided through the program or unit. Academic advisers, coaches, counselors, graduate assistants/students, regular education teachers, remediation/learning specialists, skill tutors, and other are provided collaboratively through on-campus or off-campus services.

Unique Aids and Services Aids, services, or accommodations include career counseling, faculty training, priority registration, support groups, skills coach.

Assistive Technology Assistive technology is located in campus labs, the DSS office and includes digital textbooks/e-text and scanning.

Subject-Area Tutoring Tutoring is offered one-on-one for some subjects. Tutoring is provided collaboratively through on-campus or off-campus services via computer-based instruction, professional tutors, trained peer tutors, and other.

Diagnostic Testing Testing for auditory processing, handwriting, intelligence, learning strategies, learning styles, math, motor skills, neuropsychological, personality, reading, social skills, spelling, spoken language, study skills, visual processing, written language, and other services is provided collaboratively through on-campus or off-campus services.

Basic Skills Remediation Remediation is offered in class-size groups for math, reading, spelling, and written language. Remediation is provided collaboratively through on-campus or off-campus services via computer-based instruction, regular education teachers, special education teachers, and other.

Enrichment Enrichment programs are available through the program or unit for learning strategies, math, and self-advocacy. Programs for career planning, learning strategies, math, reading, stress management, study skills, test taking, time management, vocabulary development, written composition skills, and other are provided collaboratively through on-campus or off-campus services.

Student Organization Freedom, Advocacy, Character, Education (FACE) consists of 7 members.

Fees *Diagnostic Testing* fee is $500.

Application For admittance to the program or unit, students are required to apply to the program directly and provide a psychoeducational report (3 years old or less). It is recommended that students provide documentation of high school services. Upon acceptance, documentation of need for services should be sent only to the LD program or unit. *Application deadline (institutional):* 7/1. *Application deadline (LD program):* Rolling/continuous for fall and rolling/continuous for spring.

Written Policies Written policy regarding general/basic LD accommodations is available on the program Web site. Written policies regarding course substitutions, general/basic LD accommodations, grade forgiveness, reduced course loads, substitutions and waivers of admissions requirements, and substitutions and waivers of graduation requirements are available through the program or unit directly.

Galveston College
Special Services

4015 Avenue Q

Galveston, TX 77550-7496

http://www.gc.edu

Contact: Ms. Jayne Withers, Counselor, Special Services. Phone: 409-944-1223. Fax: 409-944-1501. E-mail: jwithers@gc.edu.

Special Services Approximately 100 registered undergraduate students were served during 2006–07. The program or unit includes 1 full-time staff member. Academic advisers, counselors, professional tutors, and skill tutors are provided through the program or unit. Academic advisers, professional tutors, and skill tutors are provided collaboratively through on-campus or off-campus services.

Orientation The program or unit offers an optional varying length orientation for new students before registration, before classes begin, during summer prior to enrollment, during registration, after classes begin, and individually by special arrangement.

Unique Aids and Services Aids, services, or accommodations include career counseling, priority registration, support groups, special services counselor.

Assistive Technology Assistive technology is located in the library, the Resource Center and includes digital textbooks/e-text, learning support software, and scanning.

Subject-Area Tutoring Tutoring is offered one-on-one for most subjects. Tutoring is provided through the program or unit via professional tutors and trained peer tutors. Tutoring is also provided collaboratively through on-campus or off-campus services via professional tutors and trained peer tutors.

Basic Skills Remediation Remediation is offered one-on-one. Remediation is provided through the program or unit via professional tutors and regular education teachers. Remediation is also provided collaboratively through on-campus or off-campus services via professional tutors and regular education teachers.

Enrichment Enrichment programs are available through the program or unit for career planning, college survival skills, learning strategies, math, medication management, oral communication skills, practical computer skills, reading, self-advocacy, stress management, study skills, test taking, time management, vocabulary development, and written composition skills. Programs for career planning, math, medication management, practical computer skills, reading, study skills, test taking, vocabulary development, and written composition skills are provided collaboratively through on-campus or off-campus services.

Application For admittance to the program or unit, students are required to provide a psychoeducational report, provide documentation of high school services, and provide documentation from an institution or professional for verification. Upon acceptance, documentation of need for services should be sent to both admissions and the LD program or unit. *Application deadline (institutional):* Continuous. *Application deadline (LD program):* Rolling/continuous for fall and rolling/continuous for spring.

Written Policies Written policies regarding course substitutions, general/basic LD accommodations, grade forgiveness, reduced course loads, substitutions and waivers of admissions requirements, and substitutions and waivers of graduation requirements are available on the program Web site. Written policies regarding course substitutions, general/basic LD accommodations, grade forgiveness, reduced course loads, substitutions and waivers of admissions requirements, and substitutions and waivers of graduation requirements are outlined in the school's catalog/handbook.

Gaston College
The Counseling Center

201 Highway 321 South

Dallas, NC 28034-1499

http://www.gaston.edu

Contact: Amy A. Davis, Special Needs Counselor. Phone: 704-922-6224. Fax: 704-922-2345. E-mail: davis.amy@gaston.edu.

The Counseling Center Approximately 20 registered undergraduate students were served during 2006–07. The program or unit includes 1 full-time staff member. Academic advisers, counselors, regular education teachers, and remediation/learning specialists are provided through the program or unit. Academic advisers, counselors, regular education teachers, and remediation/learning specialists are provided collaboratively through on-campus or off-campus services.

Unique Aids and Services Aids, services, or accommodations include career counseling and priority registration.

Assistive Technology Assistive technology is located in a special lab and includes digital textbooks/e-text, learning support software, and scanning. Technology training is provided to incoming students.

Subject-Area Tutoring Tutoring is offered one-on-one for most subjects. Tutoring is provided through the program or unit via LD specialists. Tutoring is also provided collaboratively through on-campus or off-campus services via computer-based instruction, graduate assistants/students, LD specialists, trained peer tutors, and other.

Diagnostic Testing Testing is provided through the program or unit for learning styles, math, personality, reading, social skills, written language, and other services. Testing for learning styles, math, personality, reading, social skills, written language, and other services is provided collaboratively through on-campus or off-campus services.

Basic Skills Remediation Remediation is offered one-on-one, in small groups, and in class-size groups for computer skills, learning strategies, math, reading, spoken language, study skills, time management, and written language. Remediation is provided collaboratively through on-campus or off-campus services via computer-based instruction, graduate assistants/students, regular education teachers, and other.

Enrichment Enrichment programs are available through the program or unit for career planning, college survival skills, learning strategies, self-advocacy, stress management, study skills, test taking, time management, written composition skills, and other. Programs for college survival skills, health and nutrition, learning strategies, math, oral communication skills, practical computer skills, reading, study skills, and written composition skills are provided collaboratively through on-campus or off-campus services. Credit is offered for college survival skills, health and nutrition, math, oral communication skills, practical computer skills, reading, study skills, and written composition skills.

Gaston College (continued)

Application For admittance to the program or unit, students are required to provide a psychoeducational report (3 years old or less). Upon application, materials documenting need for services should be sent only to the LD program or unit. Upon acceptance, documentation of need for services should be sent only to the LD program or unit. *Application deadline (institutional):* Continuous. *Application deadline (LD program):* Rolling/continuous for fall and rolling/continuous for spring.

Written Policies Written policies regarding general/basic LD accommodations and grade forgiveness are available on the program Web site. Written policies regarding general/basic LD accommodations and grade forgiveness are outlined in the school's catalog/handbook. Written policy regarding general/basic LD accommodations is available through the program or unit directly.

Georgia Perimeter College
Center for Disability Services

3251 Panthersville Road

Decatur, GA 30034-3897

http://www.gpc.edu/cds

Contact: Ms. Bonnie Shelby Martin, Director, Disability Services. Phone: 404-299-4038. Fax: 404-298-3830. E-mail: bmartin@gpc.edu.

Center for Disability Services Approximately 80 registered undergraduate students were served during 2006–07. The program or unit includes 9 full-time and 5 part-time staff members. Academic advisers, professional tutors, and strategy tutors are provided through the program or unit. Academic advisers, diagnostic specialists, LD specialists, professional tutors, and strategy tutors are provided collaboratively through on-campus or off-campus services.

Unique Aids and Services Aids, services, or accommodations include faculty training and priority registration.

Assistive Technology Assistive technology is located in campus labs, the DSS office, a special lab and includes digital textbooks/e-text, learning support software, scanning, and voice-to-text, text-to-voice. Technology training is provided to incoming students.

Subject-Area Tutoring Tutoring is offered one-on-one for some subjects. Tutoring is provided through the program or unit via professional tutors. Tutoring is also provided collaboratively through on-campus or off-campus services via computer-based instruction and professional tutors.

Diagnostic Testing Testing for auditory processing, handwriting, intelligence, learning strategies, learning styles, math, motor skills, neuropsychological, personality, reading, social skills, spelling, spoken language, study skills, visual processing, written language, and other services is provided collaboratively through on-campus or off-campus services.

Basic Skills Remediation Remediation is offered in class-size groups for math, reading, and written language. Remediation is provided collaboratively through on-campus or off-campus services via computer-based instruction and regular education teachers.

Enrichment Programs for career planning, college survival skills, health and nutrition, learning strategies, oral communication skills, practical computer skills, reading, self-advocacy, stress manage-

ment, study skills, test taking, time management, vocabulary development, written composition skills, and other are provided collaboratively through on-campus or off-campus services.

Fees *LD Program or Service* fee is $500. *Diagnostic Testing* fee is $500.

Application For admittance to the program or unit, students are required to provide a psychoeducational report (3 years old or less). It is recommended that students provide documentation of high school services. Upon acceptance, documentation of need for services should be sent only to the LD program or unit. *Application deadline (LD program):* Rolling/continuous for fall and rolling/continuous for spring.

Written Policies Written policies regarding general/basic LD accommodations and substitutions and waivers of admissions requirements are available on the program Web site. Written policy regarding general/basic LD accommodations is outlined in the school's catalog/handbook. Written policies regarding course substitutions, general/basic LD accommodations, reduced course loads, substitutions and waivers of admissions requirements, and substitutions and waivers of graduation requirements are available through the program or unit directly.

Glendale Community College
Center for Students with Disabilities, Instructional Assistance Center

1500 North Verdugo Road

Glendale, CA 91208-2894

http://www.glendale.edu/

Contact: Ellen Oppenberg, Program Coordinator. Phone: 818-240-1000 Ext. 5529. Fax: 818-551-5283. E-mail: elleno@glendale.edu.

Center for Students with Disabilities, Instructional Assistance Center Approximately 300 registered undergraduate students were served during 2006–07. The program or unit includes 5 full-time and 2 part-time staff members. Academic advisers, counselors, diagnostic specialists, LD specialists, professional tutors, remediation/learning specialists, skill tutors, and strategy tutors are provided through the program or unit. Academic advisers, coaches, counselors, professional tutors, regular education teachers, skill tutors, and strategy tutors are provided collaboratively through on-campus or off-campus services.

Orientation The program or unit offers an optional 16-week orientation for new students after classes begin.

Unique Aids and Services Aids, services, or accommodations include career counseling, faculty training, priority registration, and support groups.

Assistive Technology Assistive technology is located in campus labs, a special lab and includes digital textbooks/e-text. Technology training is provided to incoming students.

Subject-Area Tutoring Tutoring is offered one-on-one for most subjects. Tutoring is provided through the program or unit via LD specialists, professional tutors, and trained peer tutors. Tutoring is also provided collaboratively through on-campus or off-campus services via computer-based instruction, graduate assistants/students, and trained peer tutors.

Diagnostic Testing Testing is provided through the program or unit for auditory processing, intelligence, math, neuropsychological, reading, spelling, spoken language, visual processing, written language, and other services.

Basic Skills Remediation Remediation is offered one-on-one for math, reading, spelling, and written language. Remediation is provided collaboratively through on-campus or off-campus services via computer-based instruction.

Enrichment Enrichment programs are available through the program or unit for college survival skills, learning strategies, study skills, test taking, and time management. Programs for career planning, college survival skills, math, oral communication skills, practical computer skills, reading, vocabulary development, and written composition skills are provided collaboratively through on-campus or off-campus services. Credit is offered for career planning, college survival skills, learning strategies, math, oral communication skills, practical computer skills, reading, study skills, test taking, time management, vocabulary development, and written composition skills.

Student Organization Delta Sigma Omicron consists of 10 members.

Application It is recommended that students provide a psychoeducational report (3 years old or less) and provide documentation of high school services. Upon application, materials documenting need for services should be sent to both admissions and the LD program or unit. *Application deadline (institutional):* Continuous. *Application deadline (LD program):* Rolling/continuous for fall and rolling/continuous for spring.

Written Policies Written policy regarding general/basic LD accommodations is available on the program Web site. Written policy regarding general/basic LD accommodations is outlined in the school's catalog/handbook. Written policies regarding course substitutions, general/basic LD accommodations, reduced course loads, and substitutions and waivers of graduation requirements are available through the program or unit directly.

Gloucester County College

1400 Tanyard Road

Sewell, NJ 08080

http://www.gccnj.edu/

Contact: Mr. Dennis Cook, Director. Phone: 856-415-2281. E-mail: dcook@gccnj.edu.

Approximately 265 registered undergraduate students were served during 2006–07. The program or unit includes 3 full-time staff members and 1 part-time staff member. Counselors and trained peer tutors are provided through the program or unit. Academic advisers, counselors, professional tutors, regular education teachers, and trained peer tutors are provided collaboratively through on-campus or off-campus services.

Orientation The program or unit offers an optional orientation for new students before registration, before classes begin, during summer prior to enrollment, and group information sessions offered throughout the year.

Unique Aids and Services Aids, services, or accommodations include advocates and career counseling.

Assistive Technology Assistive technology is located in the DSS office and includes scanning. Technology training is provided to incoming students.

Subject-Area Tutoring Tutoring is offered one-on-one and in small groups for most subjects. Tutoring is provided through the program or unit via trained peer tutors. Tutoring is also provided collaboratively through on-campus or off-campus services via computer-based instruction, graduate assistants/students, professional tutors, and trained peer tutors.

Basic Skills Remediation Remediation is offered in class-size groups for learning strategies, math, reading, study skills, time management, and written language. Remediation is provided through the program or unit via trained peer tutors. Remediation is also provided collaboratively through on-campus or off-campus services via professional tutors, regular education teachers, and trained peer tutors.

Enrichment Programs for career planning, college survival skills, health and nutrition, learning strategies, math, oral communication skills, practical computer skills, reading, stress management, study skills, test taking, time management, vocabulary development, and written composition skills are provided collaboratively through on-campus or off-campus services. Credit is offered for career planning, college survival skills, health and nutrition, oral communication skills, practical computer skills, study skills, and time management.

Application For admittance to the program or unit, students are required to apply to the program directly, provide documentation of high school services, and provide documentation of any additional disability. It is recommended that students provide a psychoeducational report. Upon application, materials documenting need for services should be sent only to the LD program or unit. Upon acceptance, documentation of need for services should be sent only to the LD program or unit. *Application deadline (institutional):* Continuous. *Application deadline (LD program):* Rolling/continuous for fall and rolling/continuous for spring.

Written Policies Written policy regarding general/basic LD accommodations is available on the program Web site. Written policy regarding general/basic LD accommodations is outlined in the school's catalog/handbook. Written policy regarding general/basic LD accommodations is available through the program or unit directly.

Greenville Technical College
Student Disability Services

PO Box 5616

Greenville, SC 29606-5616

http://www.greenvilletech.com

Contact: Sharon E. Bellwood, Director: Student Disability Services. Phone: 864-250-8408. Fax: 864-250-8990. E-mail: sharon.bellwood@gvltec.edu.

Student Disability Services Approximately 550 registered undergraduate students were served during 2006–07. The program or unit includes 2 full-time and 16 part-time staff members. Academic advisers, coaches, counselors, professional tutors, regular education teachers, skill tutors, and trained peer tutors are provided collaboratively through on-campus or off-campus services.

Unique Aids and Services Aids, services, or accommodations include career counseling, faculty training, and priority registration.

Greenville Technical College (continued)

Assistive Technology Assistive technology is located in campus labs, the DSS office, a special lab and includes digital textbooks/e-text and scanning. Technology training is provided to incoming students.

Subject-Area Tutoring Tutoring is offered one-on-one and in small groups for most subjects. Tutoring is provided through the program or unit via professional tutors, trained peer tutors, and other. Tutoring is also provided collaboratively through on-campus or off-campus services via professional tutors, trained peer tutors, and other.

Basic Skills Remediation Remediation is offered in class-size groups for computer skills, learning strategies, math, reading, social skills, study skills, and time management. Remediation is provided through the program or unit via trained peer tutors and other. Remediation is also provided collaboratively through on-campus or off-campus services via professional tutors and other.

Enrichment Enrichment programs are available through the program or unit for career planning, college survival skills, math, oral communication skills, practical computer skills, reading, self-advocacy, stress management, study skills, test taking, time management, and written composition skills. Programs for career planning, college survival skills, health and nutrition, learning strategies, math, medication management, reading, vocabulary development, and written composition skills are provided collaboratively through on-campus or off-campus services. Credit is offered for college survival skills, math, oral communication skills, practical computer skills, reading, and written composition skills.

Application For admittance to the program or unit, students are required to apply to the program directly and provide a psychoeducational report. It is recommended that students provide documentation of high school services. Upon application, materials documenting need for services should be sent only to the LD program or unit. Upon acceptance, documentation of need for services should be sent only to the LD program or unit. *Application deadline (institutional):* Continuous. *Application deadline (LD program):* Rolling/continuous for fall and rolling/continuous for spring.

Written Policies Written policies regarding course substitutions, general/basic LD accommodations, grade forgiveness, reduced course loads, substitutions and waivers of admissions requirements, and substitutions and waivers of graduation requirements are outlined in the school's catalog/handbook. Written policies regarding course substitutions, general/basic LD accommodations, reduced course loads, substitutions and waivers of admissions requirements, and substitutions and waivers of graduation requirements are available through the program or unit directly.

Gretna Career College
Disabled Student Services

1415 Whitney Avenue
Gretna, LA 70053-5835
http://www.gretnacareercollege.com/

Contact: Ms. Ava Himes, Director of Admissions. Phone: 504-366-5409. Fax: 504-366-1004. E-mail: admission@gretnacareercollege.edu. Head of LD Program: Ms. Andrea Randazzo, Dean of Education/Campus Director. Phone: 504-366-5409. Fax: 504-366-1294.

Disabled Student Services Approximately 12 registered undergraduate students were served during 2006–07. The program or unit includes 2 full-time staff members. Academic advisers, regular education teachers, skill tutors, strategy tutors, and trained peer tutors are provided through the program or unit. Counselors and diagnostic specialists are provided collaboratively through on-campus or off-campus services.

Unique Aids and Services Aids, services, or accommodations include career counseling, faculty training, and weekly meetings with faculty.

Assistive Technology Assistive technology is located in campus labs and includes learning support software.

Subject-Area Tutoring Tutoring is offered one-on-one and in small groups for all subjects. Tutoring is provided through the program or unit via computer-based instruction, trained peer tutors, and other.

Diagnostic Testing Testing is provided through the program or unit for math, motor skills, reading, spelling, and written language. Testing for auditory processing, handwriting, intelligence, learning strategies, learning styles, math, motor skills, personality, reading, social skills, spelling, study skills, visual processing, and written language is provided collaboratively through on-campus or off-campus services.

Basic Skills Remediation Remediation is offered one-on-one for learning strategies, study skills, and written language. Remediation is provided through the program or unit via regular education teachers and trained peer tutors.

Enrichment Programs for career planning, health and nutrition, oral communication skills, practical computer skills, vocabulary development, written composition skills, and other are provided collaboratively through on-campus or off-campus services. Credit is offered for career planning, health and nutrition, oral communication skills, practical computer skills, vocabulary development, written composition skills, and other.

Application It is recommended that students provide a psychoeducational report (3 years old or less). Upon application, materials documenting need for services should be sent to both admissions and the LD program or unit. Upon acceptance, documentation of need for services should be sent to both admissions and the LD program or unit. *Application deadline (LD program):* Rolling/continuous for fall and rolling/continuous for spring.

Written Policies Written policy regarding general/basic LD accommodations is outlined in the school's catalog/handbook.

Grossmont College
Disabled Students Programs and Services

8800 Grossmont College Drive
El Cajon, CA 92020-1799
http://www.grossmont.edu/dsps/

Contact: Carl Fielden, LD Specialist/Assistive Technology Coordinator. Phone: 619-644-7112. Fax: 619-644-7980. E-mail: carl.fielden@gcccd.edu.

Disabled Students Programs and Services Approximately 350 registered undergraduate students were served during 2006–07. The program or unit includes 2 full-time and 2 part-time staff members. LD specialists and strategy tutors are provided through the program or unit. LD specialists and strategy tutors are provided collaboratively through on-campus or off-campus services.

Orientation The program or unit offers an optional 1-hour orientation for new students before registration, before classes begin, during registration, after classes begin, individually by special arrangement, and twice weekly (students are asked to attend only one).

Unique Aids and Services Aids, services, or accommodations include career counseling, faculty training, parent workshops, and priority registration.

Assistive Technology Assistive technology is located in campus labs, the DSS office, a special lab and includes digital textbooks/e-text, learning support software, and scanning. Technology training is provided to incoming students.

Subject-Area Tutoring Tutoring is offered for most subjects. Tutoring is provided collaboratively through on-campus or off-campus services via computer-based instruction, graduate assistants/students, and trained peer tutors.

Diagnostic Testing Testing is provided through the program or unit for auditory processing, intelligence, math, motor skills, reading, spelling, visual processing, and written language. Testing for learning strategies, learning styles, and study skills is provided collaboratively through on-campus or off-campus services.

Basic Skills Remediation Remediation is offered in small groups for computer skills, learning strategies, math, study skills, time management, and written language. Remediation is provided through the program or unit via computer-based instruction, LD specialists, and trained peer tutors.

Enrichment Enrichment programs are available through the program or unit for learning strategies, math, oral communication skills, practical computer skills, study skills, test taking, time management, and written composition skills. Programs for career planning, college survival skills, health and nutrition, learning strategies, math, stress management, study skills, time management, and written composition skills are provided collaboratively through on-campus or off-campus services. Credit is offered for career planning, college survival skills, learning strategies, math, study skills, test taking, time management, and written composition skills.

Fees *Diagnostic Testing* fee is $10.

Application For admittance to the program or unit, students are required to apply to the program directly, provide a psychoeducational report (3 years old or less), and provide documentation of high school services. Upon application, materials documenting need for services should be sent only to the LD program or unit. Upon acceptance, documentation of need for services should be sent only to the LD program or unit. *Application deadline (institutional):* 8/12. *Application deadline (LD program):* Rolling/continuous for fall and rolling/continuous for spring.

Written Policies Written policies regarding course substitutions and general/basic LD accommodations are available on the program Web site. Written policies regarding course substitutions, general/basic LD accommodations, and substitutions and waivers of admissions requirements are available through the program or unit directly.

Gulf Coast Community College
Disability Support Services

5230 West Highway 98

Panama City, FL 32401-1058

http://www.gulfcoast.edu

Contact: Mrs. Linda B. Van Dalen, Coordinator of Disability Support Services. Phone: 850-872-3834. Fax: 850-913-3273. E-mail: lvandalen@gulfcoast.edu.

Disability Support Services Approximately 150 registered undergraduate students were served during 2006–07. The program or unit includes 5 full-time and 5 part-time staff members. Academic advisers, coaches, counselors, diagnostic specialists, LD specialists, professional tutors, regular education teachers, remediation/learning specialists, skill tutors, strategy tutors, and trained peer tutors are provided through the program or unit. Coaches, counselors, and diagnostic specialists are provided collaboratively through on-campus or off-campus services.

Unique Aids and Services Aids, services, or accommodations include advocates, career counseling, faculty training, priority registration, and support groups.

Assistive Technology Assistive technology is located in campus labs, the DSS office, a special lab and includes learning support software and scanning. Technology training is provided to incoming students.

Subject-Area Tutoring Tutoring is offered one-on-one and in small groups for most subjects. Tutoring is provided through the program or unit via computer-based instruction, graduate assistants/students, LD specialists, professional tutors, and trained peer tutors. Tutoring is also provided collaboratively through on-campus or off-campus services via computer-based instruction.

Basic Skills Remediation Remediation is offered one-on-one, in small groups, and in class-size groups for computer skills, learning strategies, math, reading, social skills, study skills, time management, and written language. Remediation is provided through the program or unit via computer-based instruction, graduate assistants/students, LD specialists, professional tutors, and trained peer tutors. Remediation is also provided collaboratively through on-campus or off-campus services via computer-based instruction and regular education teachers.

Enrichment Enrichment programs are available through the program or unit for career planning, college survival skills, learning strategies, math, practical computer skills, reading, self-advocacy, stress management, study skills, test taking, time management, vocabulary development, and written composition skills. Programs for career planning, college survival skills, learning strategies, math, oral communication skills, practical computer skills, reading, stress management, study skills, test taking, time management, vocabulary development, and written composition skills are provided collaboratively through on-campus or off-campus services. Credit is offered for college survival skills, oral communication skills, practical computer skills, and reading.

Application For admittance to the program or unit, students are required to apply to the program directly and provide a psychoeducational report (3 years old or less). It is recommended that students provide documentation of high school services. Upon application, materials documenting need for services should be sent only to the

Gulf Coast Community College (continued)

LD program or unit. Upon acceptance, documentation of need for services should be sent only to the LD program or unit. *Application deadline (LD program):* Rolling/continuous for fall and rolling/continuous for spring.

Written Policies Written policy regarding general/basic LD accommodations is available on the program Web site. Written policies regarding course substitutions, general/basic LD accommodations, reduced course loads, and substitutions and waivers of graduation requirements are outlined in the school's catalog/handbook. Written policies regarding course substitutions, general/basic LD accommodations, and substitutions and waivers of graduation requirements are available through the program or unit directly.

Hagerstown Community College
Disability Services

11400 Robinwood Drive

Hagerstown, MD 21742-6590

http://www.hagerstowncc.edu/

Contact: Jaime L. Bachtell, Coordinator of Disability Services. Phone: 301-790-2800 Ext. 273. Fax: 301-791-9165. E-mail: bachtellj@hagerstowncc.edu.

Disability Services Approximately 150 registered undergraduate students were served during 2006–07. The program or unit includes 1 full-time staff member. Academic advisers, graduate assistants/students, LD specialists, professional tutors, remediation/learning specialists, skill tutors, strategy tutors, trained peer tutors, and other are provided through the program or unit. Coaches, counselors, diagnostic specialists, graduate assistants/students, professional tutors, regular education teachers, remediation/learning specialists, skill tutors, special education teachers, strategy tutors, teacher trainees, trained peer tutors, and other are provided collaboratively through on-campus or off-campus services.

Unique Aids and Services Aids, services, or accommodations include career counseling, personal coach, and priority registration.

Subject-Area Tutoring Tutoring is offered one-on-one and in small groups for most subjects. Tutoring is provided through the program or unit via computer-based instruction, LD specialists, professional tutors, and trained peer tutors. Tutoring is also provided collaboratively through on-campus or off-campus services via computer-based instruction, professional tutors, and trained peer tutors.

Basic Skills Remediation Remediation is offered one-on-one, in small groups, and in class-size groups for auditory processing, computer skills, learning strategies, math, reading, social skills, spelling, spoken language, study skills, time management, visual processing, and written language. Remediation is provided through the program or unit via LD specialists, professional tutors, regular education teachers, special education teachers, and trained peer tutors. Remediation is also provided collaboratively through on-campus or off-campus services via computer-based instruction, LD specialists, professional tutors, regular education teachers, special education teachers, and trained peer tutors.

Enrichment Enrichment programs are available through the program or unit for career planning, college survival skills, learning strategies, oral communication skills, self-advocacy, stress management, study skills, test taking, and time management. Programs for career planning, college survival skills, health and nutrition, learning strategies, math, medication management, oral communication skills, practical computer skills, reading, self-advocacy, stress management, study skills, test taking, time management, vocabulary development, and written composition skills are provided collaboratively through on-campus or off-campus services. Credit is offered for career planning, college survival skills, health and nutrition, learning strategies, math, oral communication skills, practical computer skills, reading, study skills, vocabulary development, and written composition skills.

Application For admittance to the program or unit, students are required to apply to the program directly. It is recommended that students provide a psychoeducational report (3 years old or less) and provide documentation of high school services. Upon application, materials documenting need for services should be sent only to the LD program or unit. Upon acceptance, documentation of need for services should be sent only to the LD program or unit. *Application deadline (institutional):* Continuous. *Application deadline (LD program):* Rolling/continuous for fall and rolling/continuous for spring.

Written Policies Written policy regarding general/basic LD accommodations is available on the program Web site. Written policies regarding general/basic LD accommodations and reduced course loads are available through the program or unit directly.

Harrisburg Area Community College
Office for Disability Services

1 HACC Drive

Harrisburg, PA 17110-2999

http://www.hacc.edu/index.cfm?fuseaction=studentServices.Disability%20Services&id=540

Contact: Ms. Carole L. Kerper, Director of Disability Services. Phone: 717-780-2614. Fax: 717-780-1115. E-mail: clkerper@hacc.edu.

Office for Disability Services Approximately 180 registered undergraduate students were served during 2006–07. The program or unit includes 2 full-time and 10 part-time staff members. LD specialists are provided through the program or unit. Academic advisers, counselors, professional tutors, skill tutors, strategy tutors, and trained peer tutors are provided collaboratively through on-campus or off-campus services.

Assistive Technology Assistive technology is located in campus labs, the DSS office and includes digital textbooks/e-text, learning support software, and scanning. Technology training is provided to incoming students.

Subject-Area Tutoring Tutoring is offered in small groups for most subjects. Tutoring is provided collaboratively through on-campus or off-campus services via professional tutors and trained peer tutors.

Diagnostic Testing Testing is provided through the program or unit for learning styles. Testing for math, reading, study skills, and written language is provided collaboratively through on-campus or off-campus services.

Basic Skills Remediation Remediation is offered in class-size groups for learning strategies, math, reading, and written language. Remediation is provided collaboratively through on-campus or off-campus services via computer-based instruction and regular education teachers.

Enrichment Programs for career planning, college survival skills, learning strategies, math, reading, stress management, study skills, test taking, time management, and written composition skills are provided collaboratively through on-campus or off-campus services. Credit is offered for career planning, college survival skills, learning strategies, math, reading, study skills, and written composition skills.

Application For admittance to the program or unit, students are required to provide a psychoeducational report (3 years old or less). It is recommended that students provide documentation of high school services. Upon application, materials documenting need for services should be sent only to the LD program or unit. Upon acceptance, documentation of need for services should be sent only to the LD program or unit. *Application deadline (institutional):* Continuous. *Application deadline (LD program):* Rolling/continuous for fall and rolling/continuous for spring.

Written Policies Written policy regarding general/basic LD accommodations is available on the program Web site. Written policy regarding general/basic LD accommodations is outlined in the school's catalog/handbook. Written policy regarding general/basic LD accommodations is available through the program or unit directly.

Hawaii Community College
Ha'awi Kokua Program

200 West Kawili Street

Hilo, HI 96720-4091

http://www.hawcc.hawaii.edu/

Contact: Karen Kane, Counselor and Coordinator. Phone: 808-933-0702. Fax: 808-974-7692. E-mail: kkane@hawaii.edu.

Ha'awi Kokua Program Approximately 60 registered undergraduate students were served during 2006–07. The program or unit includes 1 full-time and 12 part-time staff members. Counselors are provided collaboratively through on-campus or off-campus services.

Unique Aids and Services Aids, services, or accommodations include faculty training, support groups, mid-term monitoring of academic progress (MAP).

Assistive Technology Assistive technology is located in a special lab and includes scanning and Dragon Dictate, Kurzweil Screen Reader. Technology training is provided to incoming students.

Subject-Area Tutoring Tutoring is offered one-on-one for some subjects. Tutoring is provided through the program or unit via trained peer tutors.

Basic Skills Remediation Remediation is offered one-on-one for reading and written language. Remediation is provided collaboratively through on-campus or off-campus services via computer-based instruction.

Enrichment Enrichment programs are available through the program or unit for practical computer skills, reading, self-advocacy, stress management, study skills, test taking, and time management. Programs for career planning, learning strategies, practical computer skills, reading, stress management, study skills, test taking, time management, vocabulary development, and written composition skills are provided collaboratively through on-campus or off-campus services. Credit is offered for college survival skills, learning strategies, math, oral communication skills, practical computer skills, reading, study skills, vocabulary development, and written composition skills.

Student Organization Kokua Ohana consists of 20 members.

Application For admittance to the program or unit, students are required to provide a psychoeducational report. It is recommended that students provide documentation of high school services and provide DVR reports or medical/psychiatric report. Upon application, materials documenting need for services should be sent only to the LD program or unit. Upon acceptance, documentation of need for services should be sent only to the LD program or unit. *Application deadline (LD program):* Rolling/continuous for fall and rolling/continuous for spring.

Written Policies Written policy regarding general/basic LD accommodations is available through the program or unit directly.

Herkimer County Community College
Services for Students with Disabilities

Reservoir Road

Herkimer, NY 13350

http://www.herkimer.edu/studentservices/learning/disabilities/index.htm

Contact: Ms. Leslie Cornish, Special Services Coordinator. Phone: 315-866-0300 Ext. 8331. Fax: 315-866-6957. E-mail: cornishld@herkimer.edu.

Services for Students with Disabilities Approximately 200 registered undergraduate students were served during 2006–07. The program or unit includes 1 full-time and 2 part-time staff members. LD specialists are provided through the program or unit. Academic advisers, coaches, counselors, professional tutors, regular education teachers, remediation/learning specialists, skill tutors, strategy tutors, and trained peer tutors are provided collaboratively through on-campus or off-campus services.

Unique Aids and Services Aids, services, or accommodations include career counseling and faculty training.

Assistive Technology Assistive technology is located in campus labs, the DSS office and includes digital textbooks/e-text, learning support software, scanning, and Dragon Dictate, Kurzweil, Premier. Technology training is provided to incoming students.

Subject-Area Tutoring Tutoring is offered one-on-one, in small groups, and in class-size groups for most subjects. Tutoring is provided through the program or unit via LD specialists. Tutoring is also provided collaboratively through on-campus or off-campus services via computer-based instruction, professional tutors, and trained peer tutors.

Herkimer County Community College (continued)

Basic Skills Remediation Remediation is offered one-on-one, in small groups, and in class-size groups for learning strategies, math, reading, spelling, study skills, time management, and written language. Remediation is provided through the program or unit via LD specialists. Remediation is also provided collaboratively through on-campus or off-campus services via computer-based instruction, professional tutors, regular education teachers, and trained peer tutors.

Enrichment Enrichment programs are available through the program or unit for college survival skills, learning strategies, self-advocacy, stress management, study skills, test taking, and time management. Programs for career planning, college survival skills, learning strategies, math, medication management, oral communication skills, practical computer skills, reading, self-advocacy, stress management, study skills, test taking, time management, vocabulary development, and written composition skills are provided collaboratively through on-campus or off-campus services.

Application For admittance to the program or unit, students are required to provide a psychoeducational report (3 years old or less) and provide documentation of high school services. Upon acceptance, documentation of need for services should be sent only to the LD program or unit.

Written Policies Written policy regarding general/basic LD accommodations is available on the program Web site. Written policies regarding course substitutions and general/basic LD accommodations are outlined in the school's catalog/handbook.

Basic Skills Remediation Remediation is offered in class-size groups for math, reading, spoken language, and written language. Remediation is provided collaboratively through on-campus or off-campus services via computer-based instruction and regular education teachers.

Enrichment Enrichment programs are available through the program or unit for career planning, college survival skills, learning strategies, stress management, study skills, test taking, and time management. Programs for health and nutrition, math, oral communication skills, practical computer skills, reading, vocabulary development, and written composition skills are provided collaboratively through on-campus or off-campus services. Credit is offered for college survival skills, health and nutrition, learning strategies, math, oral communication skills, practical computer skills, reading, stress management, study skills, test taking, time management, vocabulary development, and written composition skills.

Application For admittance to the program or unit, students are required to apply to the program directly and provide a psychoeducational report (5 years old or less). It is recommended that students provide documentation of high school services. Upon application, materials documenting need for services should be sent only to the LD program or unit. Upon acceptance, documentation of need for services should be sent only to the LD program or unit. *Application deadline (LD program):* 10/1 for fall. 2/18 for spring.

Written Policies Written policy regarding general/basic LD accommodations is available on the program Web site. Written policy regarding general/basic LD accommodations is outlined in the school's catalog/handbook.

Hill College of the Hill Junior College District
Counseling Center

PO Box 619

Hillsboro, TX 76645-0619

http://www.hillcollege.edu/StudentServices

Contact: Ms. Lisa Sims, SSS Learning Specialist. Phone: 254-582-2555 Ext. 238. Fax: 254-582-7591. E-mail: lsims@hillcollege.edu. Head of LD Program: Ms. Jessica Shelton, Director of Counseling. Phone: 254-582-2555 Ext. 287. Fax: 254-582-7591. E-mail: jshelton@hillcollege.edu.

Counseling Center Approximately 40 registered undergraduate students were served during 2006–07. The program or unit includes 10 full-time staff members. Counselors and remediation/learning specialists are provided through the program or unit. Regular education teachers and skill tutors are provided collaboratively through on-campus or off-campus services.

Unique Aids and Services Aids, services, or accommodations include advocates, career counseling, and weekly meetings with faculty.

Assistive Technology Assistive technology is located in the DSS office and includes digital textbooks/e-text and learning support software. Technology training is provided to incoming students.

Subject-Area Tutoring Tutoring is offered one-on-one and in small groups for most subjects. Tutoring is provided collaboratively through on-campus or off-campus services via computer-based instruction, trained peer tutors, and other.

Hillsborough Community College
Disability Services

PO Box 31127

Tampa, FL 33631-3127

http://www.hccfl.edu/Student/services/disabilities/index.html

Contact: Ms. Linda Kay Freeman, Learning Disability Specialist. Phone: 813-253-7514. Fax: 813-253-7336. E-mail: lfreeman7@hccfl.edu. Head of LD Program: Ms. Alison Guest, Coordinator of Office for Students with Disabilities. Phone: 813-259-6035. Fax: 813-253-7336. E-mail: aguest@hccfl.edu.

Disability Services Approximately 800 registered undergraduate students were served during 2006–07. The program or unit includes 3 full-time and 35 part-time staff members. LD specialists, professional tutors, remediation/learning specialists, skill tutors, strategy tutors, trained peer tutors, and other are provided through the program or unit. Academic advisers and counselors are provided collaboratively through on-campus or off-campus services.

Unique Aids and Services Aids, services, or accommodations include advocates.

Assistive Technology Assistive technology is located in campus labs, the DSS office and includes learning support software. Technology training is provided to incoming students.

Subject-Area Tutoring Tutoring is offered one-on-one for most subjects. Tutoring is provided through the program or unit via LD specialists. Tutoring is also provided collaboratively through on-campus or off-campus services via professional tutors and trained peer tutors.

Basic Skills Remediation Remediation is offered one-on-one for auditory processing, computer skills, learning strategies, math, reading, social skills, spelling, spoken language, study skills, time management, visual processing, and written language. Remediation is provided through the program or unit via LD specialists. Remediation is also provided collaboratively through on-campus or off-campus services via professional tutors and trained peer tutors.

Enrichment Enrichment programs are available through the program or unit for learning strategies, oral communication skills, self-advocacy, stress management, study skills, test taking, time management, and vocabulary development. Programs for career planning, college survival skills, health and nutrition, math, oral communication skills, practical computer skills, reading, self-advocacy, stress management, study skills, test taking, time management, vocabulary development, and written composition skills are provided collaboratively through on-campus or off-campus services. Credit is offered for career planning, college survival skills, health and nutrition, math, oral communication skills, practical computer skills, reading, stress management, study skills, test taking, time management, vocabulary development, and written composition skills.

Application For admittance to the program or unit, students are required to apply to the program directly and provide a psychoeducational report. It is recommended that students provide documentation of high school services. Upon application, materials documenting need for services should be sent only to the LD program or unit. Upon acceptance, documentation of need for services should be sent only to the LD program or unit. *Application deadline (institutional):* Continuous. *Application deadline (LD program):* Rolling/continuous for fall and rolling/continuous for spring.

Written Policies Written policies regarding course substitutions, general/basic LD accommodations, and substitutions and waivers of admissions requirements are available on the program Web site. Written policies regarding course substitutions, general/basic LD accommodations, and substitutions and waivers of admissions requirements are outlined in the school's catalog/handbook.

Hinds Community College
Disability Support Services

PO Box 1100

Raymond, MS 39154-1100

http://www.hindscc.edu

Contact: Mr. Jamy Dickson, Coordinator of Disability Support Services. Phone: 601-857-3310. Fax: 601-857-3482. E-mail: jedickson@hindscc.edu.

Disability Support Services Approximately 40 registered undergraduate students were served during 2006–07. The program or unit includes 10 full-time and 8 part-time staff members. Academic advisers, counselors, diagnostic specialists, professional tutors, and trained peer tutors are provided collaboratively through on-campus or off-campus services.

Unique Aids and Services Aids, services, or accommodations include priority registration.

Assistive Technology Assistive technology is located in the DSS office and includes digital textbooks/e-text and scanning.

Subject-Area Tutoring Tutoring is offered one-on-one for all subjects. Tutoring is provided through the program or unit via professional tutors and trained peer tutors. Tutoring is also provided collaboratively through on-campus or off-campus services via computer-based instruction.

Application For admittance to the program or unit, students are required to apply to the program directly, provide a psychoeducational report (5 years old or less), and provide psychological evaluation for learning disability. Upon application, materials documenting need for services should be sent only to the LD program or unit. Upon acceptance, documentation of need for services should be sent only to the LD program or unit. *Application deadline (LD program):* Rolling/continuous for fall and rolling/continuous for spring.

Written Policies Written policies regarding course substitutions, general/basic LD accommodations, and reduced course loads are available on the program Web site. Written policy regarding general/basic LD accommodations is outlined in the school's catalog/handbook. Written policies regarding course substitutions, general/basic LD accommodations, and reduced course loads are available through the program or unit directly.

Hocking College
Access Center, Office of Disability Services

3301 Hocking Parkway

Nelsonville, OH 45764-9588

http://www.hocking.edu/

Contact: Ms. Kim Forbes Powell, Education Coordinator for Students with Disabilities. Phone: 740-753-7107. Fax: 740-753-7039. E-mail: forbes_k@hocking.edu.

Access Center, Office of Disability Services Approximately 200 registered undergraduate students were served during 2006–07. The program or unit includes 2 full-time staff members and 1 part-time staff member. LD specialists, professional tutors, and special education teachers are provided through the program or unit. Academic advisers, counselors, remediation/learning specialists, skill tutors, special education teachers, and strategy tutors are provided collaboratively through on-campus or off-campus services.

Unique Aids and Services Aids, services, or accommodations include priority registration.

Assistive Technology Assistive technology is located in the DSS office and includes scanning.

Subject-Area Tutoring Tutoring is offered one-on-one and in small groups for most subjects. Tutoring is provided through the program or unit via computer-based instruction, LD specialists, and professional tutors. Tutoring is also provided collaboratively through on-campus or off-campus services via computer-based instruction and trained peer tutors.

Diagnostic Testing Testing for learning styles, math, personality, reading, and written language is provided collaboratively through on-campus or off-campus services.

Hocking College (continued)

Basic Skills Remediation Remediation is offered one-on-one, in small groups, and in class-size groups for computer skills, learning strategies, math, reading, social skills, spelling, study skills, time management, and written language. Remediation is provided through the program or unit via special education teachers. Remediation is also provided collaboratively through on-campus or off-campus services via computer-based instruction, regular education teachers, and special education teachers.

Enrichment Enrichment programs are available through the program or unit for practical computer skills and reading. Programs for career planning, college survival skills, learning strategies, math, oral communication skills, practical computer skills, reading, stress management, study skills, test taking, time management, vocabulary development, and written composition skills are provided collaboratively through on-campus or off-campus services. Credit is offered for college survival skills, learning strategies, math, oral communication skills, practical computer skills, reading, stress management, study skills, test taking, time management, vocabulary development, and written composition skills.

Application For admittance to the program or unit, students are required to provide documentation of high school services and provide documentation from BVR, MD, psychiatrist/psychologist, audiologist, ophthalmologist/optometrist. It is recommended that students provide a psychoeducational report. Upon application, materials documenting need for services should be sent only to the LD program or unit. Upon acceptance, documentation of need for services should be sent only to the LD program or unit. *Application deadline (institutional):* Continuous. *Application deadline (LD program):* Rolling/continuous for fall and rolling/continuous for spring.

Written Policies Written policy regarding general/basic LD accommodations is available on the program Web site. Written policy regarding general/basic LD accommodations is outlined in the school's catalog/handbook. Written policy regarding general/basic LD accommodations is available through the program or unit directly.

Orientation The program or unit offers an optional 1-hour orientation for new students during summer prior to enrollment, individually by special arrangement, and as part of new student orientation.

Summer Program an optional summer program prior to entering the school. Degree credit will be earned.

Unique Aids and Services Aids, services, or accommodations include note-taking services, testing accommodations.

Assistive Technology Assistive technology is located in campus labs, the DSS office, various locations on campus and includes digital textbooks/e-text and scanning.

Subject-Area Tutoring Tutoring is offered for some subjects.

Basic Skills Remediation Remediation is offered one-on-one and in small groups for learning strategies, math, reading, spelling, and study skills. Remediation is provided collaboratively through on-campus or off-campus services via trained peer tutors.

Enrichment Enrichment programs are available through the program or unit for career planning, college survival skills, self-advocacy, stress management, study skills, test taking, and time management. Programs for career planning, college survival skills, health and nutrition, math, medication management, oral communication skills, practical computer skills, reading, stress management, study skills, test taking, time management, and written composition skills are provided collaboratively through on-campus or off-campus services. Credit is offered for career planning, learning strategies, and study skills.

Application For admittance to the program or unit, students are required to apply to the program directly, provide a psychoeducational report (3 years old or less), and provide reports that document LD, including testing, from a licensed practitioner. It is recommended that students provide documentation of high school services. Upon application, materials documenting need for services should be sent only to the LD program or unit. *Application deadline (LD program):* Rolling/continuous for fall and rolling/continuous for spring.

Written Policies Written policy regarding general/basic LD accommodations is available through the program or unit directly.

Honolulu Community College
Student ACCESS

874 Dillingham Boulevard

Honolulu, HI 96817-4598

http://honolulu.hawaii.edu/disability

Contact: Mrs. Libby Jakubowski, Educational Specialist. Phone: 808-844-2392. Fax: 808-844-2391. E-mail: access@hcc.hawaii.edu. Head of LD Program: Mr. Wayne Sunahara, Disability Specialist. Phone: 808-844-2392. Fax: 808-844-2391. E-mail: access@hcc.hawaii.edu.

Student ACCESS Approximately 30 registered undergraduate students were served during 2006–07. The program or unit includes 2 full-time staff members. Academic advisers and LD specialists are provided through the program or unit. Academic advisers, counselors, professional tutors, remediation/learning specialists, skill tutors, strategy tutors, and trained peer tutors are provided collaboratively through on-campus or off-campus services.

Hopkinsville Community College
Disability Services

PO Box 2100

Hopkinsville, KY 42241-2100

http://www.hopkinsville.kctcs.edu/disabilitysvs/index.htm

Contact: C.J. Newcomb, Senior Administrative Assistant. Phone: 270-707-3802. Fax: 270-886-0237. E-mail: carol.newcomb@kctcs.edu. Head of LD Program: Jason Warren, Disability Services Coordinator. Phone: 270-707-3802. Fax: 270-886-0237. E-mail: jason.warren@kctcs.edu.

Disability Services Approximately 31 registered undergraduate students were served during 2006–07. The program or unit includes 1 part-time staff member. Services are provided collaboratively through on-campus or off-campus services.

Orientation The program or unit offers an optional orientation for new students individually by special arrangement.

Assistive Technology Assistive technology is located in the DSS office and includes Read & Write Gold.

Basic Skills Remediation Remediation is available for math and reading. Remediation is provided collaboratively through on-campus or off-campus services.

Application For admittance to the program or unit, students are required to provide request for accommodation, documentation. Upon application, materials documenting need for services should be sent only to the LD program or unit. *Application deadline (institutional):* Continuous. *Application deadline (LD program):* Rolling/continuous for fall and rolling/continuous for spring.

Written Policies Written policy regarding general/basic LD accommodations is available on the program Web site.

Housatonic Community College
Disability Support Services (DSS)

900 Lafayette Boulevard

Bridgeport, CT 06604-4704

http://www.hctc.commnet.edu/

Contact: Lynne Langella, Director of Disability Support Services. Phone: 203-332-5018. Fax: 203-332-5123. E-mail: llangella@hcc.commnet.edu.

Disability Support Services (DSS) Approximately 200 registered undergraduate students were served during 2006–07. The program or unit includes 1 full-time staff member. Academic advisers, counselors, professional tutors, regular education teachers, skill tutors, trained peer tutors, and other are provided collaboratively through on-campus or off-campus services.

Orientation The program or unit offers a mandatory orientation for new students individually by special arrangement.

Unique Aids and Services Aids, services, or accommodations include faculty training, parent workshops, priority registration, personal counseling as it relates to school success.

Assistive Technology Assistive technology is located in the DSS office, the library, computer lab and includes digital textbooks/e-text, learning support software, and scanning.

Subject-Area Tutoring Tutoring is offered one-on-one, in small groups, and in class-size groups for most subjects. Tutoring is provided collaboratively through on-campus or off-campus services via computer-based instruction, graduate assistants/students, LD specialists, professional tutors, trained peer tutors, and other.

Basic Skills Remediation Remediation is offered one-on-one, in small groups, and in class-size groups for math, reading, study skills, and written language. Remediation is provided collaboratively through on-campus or off-campus services via computer-based instruction, graduate assistants/students, professional tutors, regular education teachers, and trained peer tutors.

Enrichment Programs for college survival skills, health and nutrition, learning strategies, math, practical computer skills, reading, stress management, study skills, test taking, time management, and written composition skills are provided collaboratively through on-campus or off-campus services. Credit is offered for college survival skills, health and nutrition, learning strategies, math, reading, study skills, test taking, time management, and written composition skills.

Application For admittance to the program or unit, students are required to apply to the program directly, provide a psychoeducational report (3 years old or less), provide documentation of high school services, and provide results of testing done outside of high school. Upon acceptance, documentation of need for services should be sent only to the LD program or unit. *Application deadline (institutional):* Continuous. *Application deadline (LD program):* Rolling/continuous for fall and rolling/continuous for spring.

Written Policies Written policy regarding general/basic LD accommodations is available on the program Web site. Written policy regarding general/basic LD accommodations is available through the program or unit directly.

Houston Community College System
Disability Student Services

3100 Main Street

PO Box 667517

Houston, TX 77266-7517

http://hccs.edu

Contact: Ms. Donna B. Price, ADA Coordinator. Phone: 713-718-5165. E-mail: donna.price@hccs.edu. Head of LD Program: John Reno, Lead ADA Counselor. Phone: 713-718-6165. Fax: 713-718-6165. E-mail: john.reno@hccs.edu.

Disability Student Services Approximately 9000 registered undergraduate students were served during 2006–07. The program or unit includes 9 full-time and 7 part-time staff members. Coaches, counselors, professional tutors, remediation/learning specialists, skill tutors, and trained peer tutors are provided through the program or unit. Academic advisers, special education teachers, and teacher trainees are provided collaboratively through on-campus or off-campus services.

Summer Program available to high school graduates.

Unique Aids and Services Aids, services, or accommodations include advocates, career counseling, and priority registration.

Assistive Technology Assistive technology is located in campus labs, the DSS office, a special lab and includes digital textbooks/e-text, learning support software, and scanning. Technology training is provided to incoming students.

Subject-Area Tutoring Tutoring is offered in class-size groups. Tutoring is provided through the program or unit via professional tutors and trained peer tutors.

Enrichment Programs for career planning, college survival skills, health and nutrition, learning strategies, math, medication management, oral communication skills, practical computer skills, reading, self-advocacy, stress management, study skills, test taking, time management, vocabulary development, written composition skills, and other are provided collaboratively through on-campus or off-campus services.

Student Organization Eagles Club consists of 65 members.

Application For admittance to the program or unit, students are required to provide a psychoeducational report (5 years old or less) and provide documentation of high school services. It is recommended that students apply to the program directly. Upon application, materials documenting need for services should be sent only to

Houston Community College System (continued)
the LD program or unit. Upon acceptance, documentation of need for services should be sent only to the LD program or unit. *Application deadline (institutional):* Continuous. *Application deadline (LD program):* Rolling/continuous for fall and rolling/continuous for spring.

Written Policies Written policy regarding general/basic LD accommodations is available on the program Web site. Written policies regarding general/basic LD accommodations and substitutions and waivers of admissions requirements are outlined in the school's catalog/handbook. Written policies regarding course substitutions, general/basic LD accommodations, reduced course loads, substitutions and waivers of admissions requirements, and substitutions and waivers of graduation requirements are available through the program or unit directly.

Howard Community College
Disability Support Services

10901 Little Patuxent Parkway

Columbia, MD 21044-3197

http://www.howardcc.edu/students/
academic_support_services/disability_support_services/
index.html

Contact: Ms. Kathy McSweeney, Disability Support Services Counselor. Phone: 410-772-4606. Fax: 410-772-4499. E-mail: kmcsweeney@howardcc.edu.

Disability Support Services Approximately 135 registered undergraduate students were served during 2006–07. The program or unit includes 2 full-time and 4 part-time staff members. Academic advisers, coaches, counselors, diagnostic specialists, LD specialists, and remediation/learning specialists are provided through the program or unit. Coaches, counselors, professional tutors, regular education teachers, remediation/learning specialists, skill tutors, strategy tutors, and trained peer tutors are provided collaboratively through on-campus or off-campus services.

Orientation The program or unit offers an optional half-day orientation for new students before classes begin and during registration.

Summer Program To help prepare for the demands of college, there is an optional 4-week summer program prior to entering the school available to rising sophomores, rising juniors, rising seniors that focuses on computing skills, life skills and/or college life adjustment, self-advocacy, specific subject tutoring, study skills, and time management. The program accepts students from out-of-state and is available to students attending other colleges.

Unique Aids and Services Aids, services, or accommodations include career counseling, faculty training, parent workshops, personal coach.

Assistive Technology Assistive technology is located in campus labs, a special lab and includes digital textbooks/e-text, learning support software, scanning, and Dragon Naturally Speaking. Technology training is provided to incoming students.

Subject-Area Tutoring Tutoring is offered one-on-one and in small groups for most subjects. Tutoring is provided through the program or unit via LD specialists. Tutoring is also provided collaboratively through on-campus or off-campus services via computer-based instruction, graduate assistants/students, professional tutors, trained peer tutors, and other.

Basic Skills Remediation Remediation is offered one-on-one and in small groups for computer skills, learning strategies, math, reading, study skills, time management, and written language. Remediation is provided through the program or unit via LD specialists. Remediation is also provided collaboratively through on-campus or off-campus services via computer-based instruction, graduate assistants/students, professional tutors, regular education teachers, and trained peer tutors.

Enrichment Programs for career planning, college survival skills, health and nutrition, learning strategies, math, oral communication skills, practical computer skills, reading, self-advocacy, stress management, study skills, test taking, time management, vocabulary development, and written composition skills are provided collaboratively through on-campus or off-campus services. Credit is offered for career planning, college survival skills, health and nutrition, learning strategies, math, oral communication skills, practical computer skills, reading, study skills, vocabulary development, and written composition skills.

Student Organization Leadership Club.

Fees *Summer Program* fee is $450.

Application For admittance to the program or unit, students are required to provide a psychoeducational report. It is recommended that students apply to the program directly and provide documentation of high school services. Upon acceptance, documentation of need for services should be sent only to the LD program or unit. *Application deadline (institutional):* Continuous. *Application deadline (LD program):* Rolling/continuous for fall and rolling/continuous for spring.

Written Policies Written policies regarding course substitutions, general/basic LD accommodations, reduced course loads, substitutions and waivers of admissions requirements, and substitutions and waivers of graduation requirements are available on the program Web site. Written policy regarding general/basic LD accommodations is outlined in the school's catalog/handbook. Written policies regarding course substitutions, general/basic LD accommodations, reduced course loads, substitutions and waivers of admissions requirements, and substitutions and waivers of graduation requirements are available through the program or unit directly.

Hudson Valley Community College
Learning Assistance Center/ Learning Disabilities Office

80 Vandenburgh Avenue

Troy, NY 12180-6096

https://www.hvcc.edu/lac/ld/index.html

Contact: Mrs. Jennifer Miller, Assistant Professor/Learning Disabilities Specialist. Phone: 518-629-7552. E-mail: millejen@hvcc.edu.

Learning Assistance Center/ Learning Disabilities Office Approximately 410 registered undergraduate students were served during 2006–07. The program or unit includes 2 full-time staff members. LD specialists are provided through the program or unit. Academic advisers, coaches, counselors, professional tutors, regular education teachers, remediation/learning specialists, skill tutors, strategy tutors, and trained peer tutors are provided collaboratively through on-campus or off-campus services.

Orientation The program or unit offers an optional 1-hour orientation for new students individually by special arrangement.

Summer Program To help prepare for the demands of college, there is an optional 2-week summer program prior to entering the school available to rising seniors, high school graduates that focuses on computing skills, life skills and/or college life adjustment, self-advocacy, study skills, test-taking skills, and time management. The program is available to students attending other colleges.

Unique Aids and Services Aids, services, or accommodations include career counseling and weekly meetings with faculty.

Assistive Technology Assistive technology is located in campus labs, the DSS office, the LD office and includes digital textbooks/e-text, scanning, and voice recognition. Technology training is provided to incoming students.

Subject-Area Tutoring Tutoring is offered one-on-one, in small groups, and in class-size groups for some subjects. Tutoring is provided through the program or unit via LD specialists. Tutoring is also provided collaboratively through on-campus or off-campus services via professional tutors, trained peer tutors, and other.

Basic Skills Remediation Remediation is offered one-on-one, in small groups, and in class-size groups for computer skills, learning strategies, math, reading, study skills, time management, and written language. Remediation is provided through the program or unit via LD specialists. Remediation is also provided collaboratively through on-campus or off-campus services via professional tutors, regular education teachers, trained peer tutors, and other.

Enrichment Enrichment programs are available through the program or unit for college survival skills, learning strategies, self-advocacy, study skills, test taking, and time management. Programs for career planning, college survival skills, learning strategies, math, practical computer skills, reading, study skills, test taking, time management, and written composition skills are provided collaboratively through on-campus or off-campus services. Credit is offered for career planning and reading.

Student Organization Not a Bit of Difference Club.

Fees *Summer Program* fee is $75 to $800.

Application For admittance to the program or unit, students are required to apply to the program directly, provide a psychoeducational report (3 years old or less), and provide documentation of AD/HD. It is recommended that students provide documentation of high school services. Upon application, materials documenting need for services should be sent only to the LD program or unit. Upon acceptance, documentation of need for services should be sent only to the LD program or unit. *Application deadline (institutional):* Continuous. *Application deadline (LD program):* Rolling/continuous for fall and rolling/continuous for spring.

Written Policies Written policy regarding general/basic LD accommodations is available on the program Web site. Written policy regarding general/basic LD accommodations is available through the program or unit directly.

Illinois Valley Community College
Disability Services Office

815 North Orlando Smith Avenue

Oglesby, IL 61348-9692

http://www.ivcc.edu/disability

Contact: Tina Hardy, Disability Services Coordinator. Phone: 815-224-0284. Fax: 815-224-3033. E-mail: tina_hardy@ivcc.edu.

Disability Services Office Approximately 85 registered undergraduate students were served during 2006–07. The program or unit includes 2 part-time staff members. Diagnostic specialists, LD specialists, remediation/learning specialists, and strategy tutors are provided through the program or unit. Academic advisers, counselors, diagnostic specialists, graduate assistants/students, LD specialists, regular education teachers, remediation/learning specialists, and trained peer tutors are provided collaboratively through on-campus or off-campus services.

Orientation The program or unit offers an optional 2-hour orientation for new students before registration and individually by special arrangement.

Unique Aids and Services Aids, services, or accommodations include faculty training.

Assistive Technology Assistive technology is located in campus labs, the DSS office and includes digital textbooks/e-text and learning support software. Technology training is provided to incoming students.

Subject-Area Tutoring Tutoring is offered one-on-one for most subjects. Tutoring is provided through the program or unit via LD specialists. Tutoring is also provided collaboratively through on-campus or off-campus services via trained peer tutors.

Diagnostic Testing Testing is provided through the program or unit for auditory processing, intelligence, learning strategies, learning styles, math, neuropsychological, reading, spelling, spoken language, study skills, visual processing, and written language. Testing for auditory processing, intelligence, learning styles, neuropsychological, reading, spelling, spoken language, visual processing, and written language is provided collaboratively through on-campus or off-campus services.

Basic Skills Remediation Remediation is offered in class-size groups for learning strategies, math, reading, study skills, time management, and written language. Remediation is provided through the program or unit via special education teachers. Remediation is also provided collaboratively through on-campus or off-campus services via regular education teachers.

Enrichment Enrichment programs are available through the program or unit for learning strategies, study skills, test taking, and time management. Programs for career planning, college survival skills, health and nutrition, learning strategies, practical computer skills, reading, vocabulary development, and written composition skills are provided collaboratively through on-campus or off-campus services. Credit is offered for college survival skills, health and nutrition, practical computer skills, reading, vocabulary development, and written composition skills.

Application For admittance to the program or unit, students are required to apply to the program directly, provide a psychoeducational report (3 years old or less), and provide documentation of high school services. Upon application, materials documenting need for

Illinois Valley Community College (continued)

services should be sent only to the LD program or unit. Upon acceptance, documentation of need for services should be sent only to the LD program or unit. *Application deadline (institutional):* Continuous. *Application deadline (LD program):* Rolling/continuous for fall.

Written Policies Written policy regarding general/basic LD accommodations is available through the program or unit directly.

Irvine Valley College
Disabled Student Programs and Services

5500 Irvine Center Drive

Irvine, CA 92618

http://www.ivc.edu

Contact: Julie Willard, Learning Disabilities Specialist. Phone: 949-451-5357. Fax: 949-451-5270. E-mail: jwillard@ivc.edu.

Disabled Student Programs and Services Approximately 75 registered undergraduate students were served during 2006–07. The program or unit includes 4 full-time staff members and 1 part-time staff member. Academic advisers, counselors, LD specialists, skill tutors, and trained peer tutors are provided through the program or unit.

Orientation The program or unit offers an optional 3-hour orientation for new students individually by special arrangement and during Transition Day in the spring prior to fall enrollment.

Unique Aids and Services Aids, services, or accommodations include priority registration, extended test time, note-takers.

Assistive Technology Assistive technology is located in campus labs, the DSS office, a special lab and includes digital textbooks/e-text, learning support software, and scanning. Technology training is provided to incoming students.

Subject-Area Tutoring Tutoring is offered one-on-one for most subjects. Tutoring is provided through the program or unit via LD specialists. Tutoring is also provided collaboratively through on-campus or off-campus services via computer-based instruction and trained peer tutors.

Diagnostic Testing Testing is provided through the program or unit for auditory processing, intelligence, math, motor skills, neuropsychological, reading, spelling, spoken language, visual processing, and written language.

Basic Skills Remediation Remediation is offered one-on-one and in small groups for math, reading, spelling, and written language. Remediation is provided through the program or unit via LD specialists. Remediation is also provided collaboratively through on-campus or off-campus services via computer-based instruction, regular education teachers, and trained peer tutors.

Enrichment Enrichment programs are available through the program or unit for learning strategies, math, oral communication skills, practical computer skills, reading, study skills, test taking, vocabulary development, and written composition skills. Programs for career planning, college survival skills, health and nutrition, medication management, practical computer skills, reading, self-advocacy, stress management, study skills, test taking, time management, vocabulary development, and written composition skills are provided collaboratively through on-campus or off-campus services. Credit is offered for career planning, college survival

skills, health and nutrition, math, oral communication skills, practical computer skills, reading, stress management, study skills, test taking, time management, vocabulary development, and written composition skills.

Application For admittance to the program or unit, students are required to apply to the program directly and provide a psychoeducational report (3 years old or less). It is recommended that students provide documentation of high school services. Upon application, materials documenting need for services should be sent only to the LD program or unit. Upon acceptance, documentation of need for services should be sent only to the LD program or unit. *Application deadline (institutional):* Continuous. *Application deadline (LD program):* Rolling/continuous for fall and rolling/continuous for spring.

Written Policies Written policy regarding general/basic LD accommodations is outlined in the school's catalog/handbook. Written policies regarding course substitutions, grade forgiveness, reduced course loads, substitutions and waivers of admissions requirements, and substitutions and waivers of graduation requirements are available through the program or unit directly.

Itasca Community College
Office for Students with Disabilities

1851 Highway 169 East

Grand Rapids, MN 55744

http://www.itascacc.net/studentservices/disability.asp

Contact: Mrs. Ann Marie Vidovic, Director of Disability Services. Phone: 218-327-4167. Fax: 218-327-4299. E-mail: avidovic@itascacc.edu.

Office for Students with Disabilities Approximately 40 registered undergraduate students were served during 2006–07. The program or unit includes 1 full-time staff member. Academic advisers, coaches, counselors, LD specialists, professional tutors, remediation/learning specialists, skill tutors, strategy tutors, and trained peer tutors are provided collaboratively through on-campus or off-campus services.

Orientation The program or unit offers an optional 1- to 3-hour orientation for new students before registration, before classes begin, during summer prior to enrollment, during registration, after classes begin, and individually by special arrangement.

Summer Program To help prepare for the demands of college, there is an optional summer program prior to entering the school available to high school graduates that focuses on self-advocacy, specific subject tutoring, study skills, test-taking skills, and time management. The program accepts students from out-of-state and is available to students attending other colleges.

Unique Aids and Services Aids, services, or accommodations include advocates, career counseling, and priority registration.

Assistive Technology Assistive technology is located in campus labs, the DSS office and includes digital textbooks/e-text and scanning. Technology training is provided to incoming students.

Subject-Area Tutoring Tutoring is offered one-on-one, in small groups, and in class-size groups for most subjects. Tutoring is provided collaboratively through on-campus or off-campus services via computer-based instruction, graduate assistants/students, LD specialists, professional tutors, and trained peer tutors.

Diagnostic Testing Testing for learning strategies, learning styles, math, reading, study skills, and written language is provided collaboratively through on-campus or off-campus services.

Basic Skills Remediation Remediation is offered one-on-one, in small groups, and in class-size groups for auditory processing, computer skills, learning strategies, math, reading, social skills, spelling, spoken language, study skills, time management, and written language. Remediation is provided collaboratively through on-campus or off-campus services via computer-based instruction, graduate assistants/students, LD specialists, professional tutors, and trained peer tutors.

Enrichment Programs for career planning, college survival skills, health and nutrition, learning strategies, math, oral communication skills, practical computer skills, reading, self-advocacy, stress management, study skills, test taking, time management, and written composition skills are provided collaboratively through on-campus or off-campus services. Credit is offered for career planning, college survival skills, health and nutrition, learning strategies, math, oral communication skills, practical computer skills, reading, self-advocacy, stress management, study skills, test taking, time management, and written composition skills.

Application For admittance to the program or unit, students are required to provide a psychoeducational report (3 years old or less). It is recommended that students provide documentation of high school services. Upon application, materials documenting need for services should be sent only to the LD program or unit. *Application deadline (institutional): 9/4. Application deadline (LD program):* Rolling/continuous for fall and rolling/continuous for spring.

Written Policies Written policies regarding course substitutions, general/basic LD accommodations, reduced course loads, substitutions and waivers of admissions requirements, and substitutions and waivers of graduation requirements are available on the program Web site. Written policies regarding course substitutions, general/basic LD accommodations, reduced course loads, substitutions and waivers of admissions requirements, and substitutions and waivers of graduation requirements are outlined in the school's catalog/handbook. Written policies regarding general/basic LD accommodations and reduced course loads are available through the program or unit directly.

Unique Aids and Services Aids, services, or accommodations include advocates and career counseling.

Assistive Technology Assistive technology is located in LRC and includes digital textbooks/e-text and ZoomText Xtra, JAWS. Technology training is provided to incoming students.

Subject-Area Tutoring Tutoring is offered one-on-one and in small groups for some subjects. Tutoring is provided collaboratively through on-campus or off-campus services via computer-based instruction, LD specialists, professional tutors, and trained peer tutors.

Basic Skills Remediation Remediation is offered in class-size groups for math, reading, and written language. Remediation is provided collaboratively through on-campus or off-campus services via computer-based instruction and regular education teachers.

Enrichment Enrichment programs are available through the program or unit for self-advocacy, study skills, test taking, and time management. Programs for career planning, college survival skills, health and nutrition, learning strategies, math, medication management, oral communication skills, practical computer skills, reading, self-advocacy, stress management, study skills, test taking, time management, vocabulary development, and written composition skills are provided collaboratively through on-campus or off-campus services. Credit is offered for math.

Application For admittance to the program or unit, students are required to apply to the program directly and provide a psychoeducational report (5 years old or less). It is recommended that students provide documentation of high school services and provide exit case conference report. Upon application, materials documenting need for services should be sent only to the LD program or unit. Upon acceptance, documentation of need for services should be sent only to the LD program or unit. *Application deadline (institutional):* Continuous. *Application deadline (LD program):* Rolling/continuous for fall and rolling/continuous for spring.

Written Policies Written policies regarding general/basic LD accommodations and grade forgiveness are available on the program Web site. Written policies regarding general/basic LD accommodations, grade forgiveness, and substitutions and waivers of graduation requirements are outlined in the school's catalog/handbook. Written policy regarding general/basic LD accommodations is available through the program or unit directly.

Ivy Tech Community College–Kokomo
Disability Support Services (DSS)

1815 East Morgan St, PO Box 1373
Kokomo, IN 46903-1373
http://www.ivytech.edu/

Contact: Ms. Cheryl Locke, Assistant Director of Student Support and Development. Phone: 765-459-0561 Ext. 504. Fax: 765-454-5745. E-mail: clocke@ivytech.edu.

Disability Support Services (DSS) Approximately 70 registered undergraduate students were served during 2006–07. The program or unit includes 3 full-time staff members and 1 part-time staff member. LD specialists, professional tutors, and strategy tutors are provided through the program or unit. Academic advisers, diagnostic specialists, regular education teachers, and skill tutors are provided collaboratively through on-campus or off-campus services.

Ivy Tech Community College–Southwest
Lamkin Student Success Center

3501 First Avenue
Evansville, IN 47710-3398
http://www.ivytech.edu/

Contact: Ms. Cyndi L. Cates, Disability Services Advisor. Phone: 812-429-1386. Fax: 812-429-9834. E-mail: ccates@ivytech.edu.

Lamkin Student Success Center Approximately 40 registered undergraduate students were served during 2006–07. The program or unit includes 1 full-time and 1 part-time staff member. LD specialists and trained peer tutors are provided through the program or unit. Counselors, diagnostic specialists, and LD specialists are provided collaboratively through on-campus or off-campus services.

Ivy Tech Community College–Southwest (continued)

Orientation The program or unit offers a mandatory 30-minute to 1-hour orientation for new students before registration, before classes begin, during summer prior to enrollment, during registration, after classes begin, and individually by special arrangement.

Unique Aids and Services Aids, services, or accommodations include advocates, career counseling, and faculty training.

Assistive Technology Assistive technology is located in the DSS office, the Workforce Certification Center and includes digital textbooks/e-text, learning support software, scanning, and Kurzweil 3000. Technology training is provided to incoming students.

Subject-Area Tutoring Tutoring is offered one-on-one and in small groups for most subjects. Tutoring is provided through the program or unit via computer-based instruction and LD specialists. Tutoring is also provided collaboratively through on-campus or off-campus services via computer-based instruction, graduate assistants/students, professional tutors, and trained peer tutors.

Basic Skills Remediation Remediation is offered in small groups and in class-size groups for learning strategies, math, reading, spelling, study skills, time management, and written language. Remediation is provided through the program or unit via computer-based instruction and trained peer tutors. Remediation is also provided collaboratively through on-campus or off-campus services via computer-based instruction, regular education teachers, and trained peer tutors.

Enrichment Enrichment programs are available through the program or unit for career planning, college survival skills, learning strategies, practical computer skills, reading, self-advocacy, study skills, test taking, time management, vocabulary development, and written composition skills. Programs for career planning, college survival skills, health and nutrition, learning strategies, math, oral communication skills, practical computer skills, reading, self-advocacy, stress management, study skills, test taking, time management, and written composition skills are provided collaboratively through on-campus or off-campus services. Credit is offered for college survival skills, learning strategies, math, oral communication skills, practical computer skills, reading, study skills, test taking, time management, and written composition skills.

Application For admittance to the program or unit, students are required to provide a psychoeducational report (3 years old or less) and provide at least a month's notice for some services. It is recommended that students provide documentation of high school services. Upon application, materials documenting need for services should be sent only to the LD program or unit. Upon acceptance, documentation of need for services should be sent only to the LD program or unit. *Application deadline (institutional):* Continuous. *Application deadline (LD program):* Rolling/continuous for fall and rolling/continuous for spring.

Written Policies Written policy regarding general/basic LD accommodations is available on the program Web site. Written policy regarding general/basic LD accommodations is outlined in the school's catalog/handbook. Written policies regarding course substitutions and general/basic LD accommodations are available through the program or unit directly.

Ivy Tech Community College–Wabash Valley
Disability Support Services

7999 US Highway 41, South

Terre Haute, IN 47802

http://www.goivytech.net

Contact: Mrs. Jaime M. Frey, Disability Support Services Advisor. Phone: 812-298-2282. Fax: 812-298-2291. E-mail: jfrey@ivytech.edu.

Disability Support Services Approximately 106 registered undergraduate students were served during 2006–07. The program or unit includes 1 full-time and 7 part-time staff members. Academic advisers, counselors, LD specialists, professional tutors, strategy tutors, trained peer tutors, and other are provided through the program or unit. Academic advisers, counselors, LD specialists, professional tutors, trained peer tutors, and other are provided collaboratively through on-campus or off-campus services.

Assistive Technology Assistive technology is located in the library and includes digital textbooks/e-text, learning support software, and scanning. Technology training is provided to incoming students.

Subject-Area Tutoring Tutoring is offered one-on-one for most subjects.

Basic Skills Remediation Remediation is offered in class-size groups for computer skills, learning strategies, math, reading, spelling, study skills, time management, and written language.

Enrichment Enrichment programs are available through the program or unit for learning strategies, stress management, study skills, test taking, and time management. Programs for career planning, college survival skills, learning strategies, math, reading, stress management, study skills, test taking, time management, and written composition skills are provided collaboratively through on-campus or off-campus services. Credit is offered for college survival skills, learning strategies, math, reading, study skills, test taking, and time management.

Application For admittance to the program or unit, students are required to provide a psychoeducational report (3 years old or less). It is recommended that students provide documentation of high school services. Upon application, materials documenting need for services should be sent only to the LD program or unit. Upon acceptance, documentation of need for services should be sent only to the LD program or unit. *Application deadline (institutional):* Continuous. *Application deadline (LD program):* Rolling/continuous for fall and rolling/continuous for spring.

Written Policies Written policies regarding general/basic LD accommodations and grade forgiveness are outlined in the school's catalog/handbook. Written policy regarding general/basic LD accommodations is available through the program or unit directly.

James H. Faulkner State Community College
Student Development

1900 Highway 31 South
Bay Minette, AL 36507
http://www.faulknerstate.edu

Contact: Dr. Brenda J. Kennedy, Dean of Student Development. Phone: 251-580-2180. Fax: 251-580-2226. E-mail: bkennedy@faulknerstate.edu.

Student Development Approximately 150 registered undergraduate students were served during 2006–07. The program or unit includes 4 full-time staff members. Regular education teachers and trained peer tutors are provided collaboratively through on-campus or off-campus services.
Orientation The program or unit offers a mandatory varying length orientation for new students individually by special arrangement.
Unique Aids and Services Aids, services, or accommodations include advocates, career counseling, and faculty training.
Subject-Area Tutoring Tutoring is offered one-on-one and in small groups for some subjects. Tutoring is provided collaboratively through on-campus or off-campus services via trained peer tutors.
Basic Skills Remediation Remediation is offered in class-size groups for math, reading, study skills, and time management. Remediation is provided collaboratively through on-campus or off-campus services via regular education teachers and trained peer tutors.
Application For admittance to the program or unit, students are required to provide a psychoeducational report (3 years old or less). It is recommended that students provide documentation of high school services. Upon application, materials documenting need for services should be sent only to the LD program or unit. Upon acceptance, documentation of need for services should be sent only to the LD program or unit. *Application deadline (institutional):* Continuous. *Application deadline (LD program):* Rolling/continuous for fall and rolling/continuous for spring.
Written Policies Written policy regarding general/basic LD accommodations is available on the program Web site. Written policy regarding general/basic LD accommodations is outlined in the school's catalog/handbook.

Jamestown Community College
Disability Support Services

525 Falconer Street
Jamestown, NY 14701-1999
http://www.sunyjcc.edu/college-wide/disabl-support.html

Contact: Nancy Callahan, ADA Coordinator/Disability Support Services. Phone: 716-338-1251. Fax: 716-338-1467. E-mail: nancycallahan@mail.sunyjcc.edu.

Disability Support Services The program or unit includes 1 full-time and 1 part-time staff member. Academic advisers and counselors are provided through the program or unit. Academic

advisers, coaches, counselors, diagnostic specialists, professional tutors, regular education teachers, remediation/learning specialists, skill tutors, strategy tutors, and trained peer tutors are provided collaboratively through on-campus or off-campus services.
Orientation The program or unit offers an optional 2- to 3-hour orientation for new students individually by special arrangement.
Unique Aids and Services Aids, services, or accommodations include advocates, career counseling, and priority registration.
Assistive Technology Assistive technology is located in campus labs, the DSS office, a special lab and includes digital textbooks/e-text and learning support software. Technology training is provided to incoming students.
Subject-Area Tutoring Tutoring is offered one-on-one and in small groups for most subjects. Tutoring is provided collaboratively through on-campus or off-campus services via computer-based instruction, professional tutors, and trained peer tutors.
Basic Skills Remediation Remediation is offered one-on-one, in small groups, and in class-size groups for computer skills, learning strategies, math, reading, social skills, study skills, time management, and written language. Remediation is provided collaboratively through on-campus or off-campus services via professional tutors, regular education teachers, and trained peer tutors.
Application For admittance to the program or unit, students are required to provide a psychoeducational report (3 years old or less) and provide documentation of high school services. Upon application, materials documenting need for services should be sent only to the LD program or unit. Upon acceptance, documentation of need for services should be sent only to the LD program or unit. *Application deadline (institutional):* Continuous. *Application deadline (LD program):* Rolling/continuous for fall and rolling/continuous for spring.
Written Policies Written policies regarding course substitutions, general/basic LD accommodations, and substitutions and waivers of graduation requirements are available on the program Web site. Written policy regarding general/basic LD accommodations is outlined in the school's catalog/handbook. Written policies regarding course substitutions, general/basic LD accommodations, and substitutions and waivers of graduation requirements are available through the program or unit directly.

Jefferson Community and Technical College
Access*Ability Resource Center (ARC)

109 East Broadway
Louisville, KY 40202-2005
http://www.jctc.kctcs.edu/

Contact: Ms. Terri F. Martin, Disability Resource Manager. Phone: 502-213-2449. Fax: 502-213-2479. E-mail: terrif.martin@kctcs.edu.

Access*Ability Resource Center (ARC) Approximately 250 registered undergraduate students were served during 2006–07. The program or unit includes 2 full-time staff members. Academic advisers, counselors, graduate assistants/students, regular education teachers, skill tutors, and strategy tutors are provided collaboratively through on-campus or off-campus services.

Jefferson Community and Technical College (continued)

Unique Aids and Services Aids, services, or accommodations include career counseling, faculty training, and priority registration.

Assistive Technology Assistive technology is located in campus labs, the DSS office, the library and includes digital textbooks/e-text, learning support software, scanning, and speech-to-text software, enlargement software, software that reads to the student. Technology training is provided to incoming students.

Subject-Area Tutoring Tutoring is offered one-on-one and in small groups. Tutoring is provided collaboratively through on-campus or off-campus services via computer-based instruction, graduate assistants/students, and trained peer tutors.

Basic Skills Remediation Remediation is offered one-on-one, in small groups, and in class-size groups for computer skills, math, reading, spelling, study skills, time management, and written language. Remediation is provided collaboratively through on-campus or off-campus services via computer-based instruction, graduate assistants/students, professional tutors, regular education teachers, and trained peer tutors.

Enrichment Enrichment programs are available through the program or unit for career planning, college survival skills, practical computer skills, and self-advocacy. Programs for career planning, college survival skills, health and nutrition, learning strategies, math, oral communication skills, practical computer skills, reading, stress management, study skills, test taking, time management, vocabulary development, and written composition skills are provided collaboratively through on-campus or off-campus services. Credit is offered for career planning, college survival skills, health and nutrition, math, oral communication skills, practical computer skills, reading, vocabulary development, and written composition skills.

Student Organization Disability Awareness Organization consists of 15 members.

Application For admittance to the program or unit, students are required to provide a psychoeducational report (3 years old or less) and provide current psychological evaluation. Upon application, materials documenting need for services should be sent only to the LD program or unit. Upon acceptance, documentation of need for services should be sent only to the LD program or unit. *Application deadline (institutional):* Continuous. *Application deadline (LD program):* Rolling/continuous for fall and rolling/continuous for spring.

Written Policies Written policies regarding course substitutions, general/basic LD accommodations, grade forgiveness, reduced course loads, substitutions and waivers of admissions requirements, and substitutions and waivers of graduation requirements are available on the program Web site. Written policies regarding course substitutions, general/basic LD accommodations, grade forgiveness, reduced course loads, substitutions and waivers of admissions requirements, and substitutions and waivers of graduation requirements are outlined in the school's catalog/handbook. Written policies regarding course substitutions, general/basic LD accommodations, grade forgiveness, reduced course loads, substitutions and waivers of admissions requirements, and substitutions and waivers of graduation requirements are available through the program or unit directly.

Jefferson Community College
Learning Skills Lab

4000 Sunset Boulevard

Steubenville, OH 43952-3598

http://www.jcc.edu

Contact: Ms. Ella Paulman, Director of Learning Skills Lab. Phone: 740-264-5591 Ext. 214. Fax: 740-264-1338. E-mail: epaulman@jcc.edu.

Learning Skills Lab Approximately 23 registered undergraduate students were served during 2006–07. The program or unit includes 1 full-time and 3 part-time staff members. Academic advisers, professional tutors, remediation/learning specialists, skill tutors, and trained peer tutors are provided through the program or unit.

Subject-Area Tutoring Tutoring is offered one-on-one and in small groups for most subjects. Tutoring is provided through the program or unit via professional tutors and trained peer tutors.

Diagnostic Testing Testing is provided through the program or unit for math, reading, and written language.

Basic Skills Remediation Remediation is offered in class-size groups for math, reading, study skills, and written language. Remediation is provided through the program or unit via regular education teachers.

Application For admittance to the program or unit, students are required to provide documentation of high school services. It is recommended that students provide a psychoeducational report (5 years old or less). Upon application, materials documenting need for services should be sent only to the LD program or unit. Upon acceptance, documentation of need for services should be sent only to the LD program or unit. *Application deadline (institutional):* 8/20. *Application deadline (LD program):* Rolling/continuous for fall and rolling/continuous for spring.

Written Policies Written policies regarding course substitutions, general/basic LD accommodations, substitutions and waivers of admissions requirements, and substitutions and waivers of graduation requirements are available on the program Web site. Written policies regarding course substitutions, general/basic LD accommodations, substitutions and waivers of admissions requirements, and substitutions and waivers of graduation requirements are outlined in the school's catalog/handbook.

Kalamazoo Valley Community College
Special Services

PO Box 4070

Kalamazoo, MI 49003-4070

http://www.kvcc.edu/services/Learnctr/SpecialServices.htm

Contact: Lois M. Baldwin, Special Services Advisor. Phone: 269-488-4384. Fax: 269-488-4657. E-mail: lbaldwin@kvcc.edu.

Special Services Approximately 250 registered undergraduate students were served during 2006–07. The program or unit includes

2 full-time staff members and 1 part-time staff member. Counselors are provided through the program or unit. Academic advisers, counselors, professional tutors, skill tutors, strategy tutors, and trained peer tutors are provided collaboratively through on-campus or off-campus services.

Unique Aids and Services Aids, services, or accommodations include advocates and career counseling.

Assistive Technology Assistive technology is located in campus labs, the DSS office, a special lab and includes digital textbooks/e-text, learning support software, and scanning.

Subject-Area Tutoring Tutoring is offered one-on-one, in small groups, and in class-size groups for most subjects. Tutoring is provided collaboratively through on-campus or off-campus services via computer-based instruction, professional tutors, and trained peer tutors.

Basic Skills Remediation Remediation is offered in class-size groups for learning strategies, math, reading, spelling, study skills, time management, and written language. Remediation is provided collaboratively through on-campus or off-campus services via computer-based instruction, professional tutors, regular education teachers, and trained peer tutors.

Enrichment Programs for career planning, college survival skills, health and nutrition, learning strategies, math, medication management, oral communication skills, practical computer skills, reading, self-advocacy, stress management, study skills, test taking, time management, vocabulary development, written composition skills, and other are provided collaboratively through on-campus or off-campus services.

Application For admittance to the program or unit, students are required to provide a psychoeducational report and provide documentation of high school services. Upon application, materials documenting need for services should be sent only to the LD program or unit. Upon acceptance, documentation of need for services should be sent only to the LD program or unit. *Application deadline (LD program):* Rolling/continuous for fall and rolling/continuous for spring.

Written Policies Written policy regarding grade forgiveness is outlined in the school's catalog/handbook. Written policy regarding general/basic LD accommodations is available through the program or unit directly.

Kapiolani Community College

4303 Diamond Head Road

Honolulu, HI 96816-4421

http://www.kcc.hawaii.edu/

Contact: Disability Support Services Office. Phone: 808-734-9552. Fax: 808-734-9456. E-mail: kapdss@hawaii.edu.

The program or unit includes 2 full-time staff members. Academic advisers and counselors are provided collaboratively through on-campus or off-campus services.

Orientation The program or unit offers individually by special arrangement.

Unique Aids and Services Aids, services, or accommodations include career counseling and priority registration.

Assistive Technology Assistive technology is located in campus labs, the DSS office and includes digital textbooks/e-text, learning support software, and scanning.

Application It is recommended that students provide a psychoeducational report and provide documentation of high school services. *Application deadline (institutional):* 7/1. *Application deadline (LD program):* Rolling/continuous for fall and rolling/continuous for spring.

Written Policies Written policies regarding general/basic LD accommodations and substitutions and waivers of admissions requirements are available through the program or unit directly.

Kellogg Community College
Support Services Department/Disability Services

450 North Avenue

Battle Creek, MI 49017-3397

http://www.kellogg.edu/studserv/supportserv.html

Contact: Ms. Holly McKee, Director of Support Services. Phone: 269-965-3931 Ext. 2629. Fax: 269-965-8850. E-mail: mckeeh@kellogg.edu.

Support Services Department/Disability Services Approximately 100 registered undergraduate students were served during 2006–07. The program or unit includes 3 full-time and 5 part-time staff members. Academic advisers, LD specialists, professional tutors, skill tutors, strategy tutors, and trained peer tutors are provided through the program or unit. Academic advisers, coaches, LD specialists, professional tutors, regular education teachers, remediation/learning specialists, skill tutors, and strategy tutors are provided collaboratively through on-campus or off-campus services.

Orientation The program or unit offers an optional 20- to 30-minute orientation for new students before registration, before classes begin, during summer prior to enrollment, during registration, after classes begin, and individually by special arrangement.

Unique Aids and Services Aids, services, or accommodations include advocates and faculty training.

Subject-Area Tutoring Tutoring is offered one-on-one, in small groups, and in class-size groups for most subjects. Tutoring is provided collaboratively through on-campus or off-campus services via computer-based instruction, LD specialists, professional tutors, trained peer tutors, and other.

Diagnostic Testing Testing for learning styles, math, reading, study skills, and written language is provided collaboratively through on-campus or off-campus services.

Basic Skills Remediation Remediation is offered in small groups and in class-size groups for math, study skills, and written language. Remediation is provided collaboratively through on-campus or off-campus services via computer-based instruction, regular education teachers, and other.

Enrichment Programs for career planning, college survival skills, health and nutrition, learning strategies, math, oral communication skills, practical computer skills, reading, self-advocacy, study skills, test taking, vocabulary development, written composition skills, and other are provided collaboratively through on-campus or off-campus services.

Kellogg Community College (continued)

Application For admittance to the program or unit, students are required to apply to the program directly, provide a psychoeducational report (3 years old or less), and provide documentation of high school services. Upon application, materials documenting need for services should be sent only to the LD program or unit. Upon acceptance, documentation of need for services should be sent only to the LD program or unit. *Application deadline (institutional):* 8/30. *Application deadline (LD program):* Rolling/continuous for fall and rolling/continuous for spring.

Written Policies Written policy regarding general/basic LD accommodations is available on the program Web site. Written policy regarding general/basic LD accommodations is outlined in the school's catalog/handbook. Written policy regarding general/basic LD accommodations is available through the program or unit directly.

Kingsborough Community College of the City University of New York
Access-Ability Center

2001 Oriental Blvd, Manhattan Beach
Brooklyn, NY 11235
http://www.kbcc.cuny.edu/

Contact: Dr. A. Colarossi, Director of Special Services Program. Phone: 718-368-5175. Fax: 718-368-4782. E-mail: acolarossi@kbcc.cuny.edu.

Access-Ability Center Approximately 500 registered undergraduate students were served during 2006–07. The program or unit includes 4 full-time and 10 part-time staff members. Academic advisers, counselors, diagnostic specialists, graduate assistants/ students, LD specialists, professional tutors, remediation/learning specialists, skill tutors, and strategy tutors are provided through the program or unit.

Orientation The program or unit offers a mandatory 4- to 5-hour orientation for new students before registration, before classes begin, and individually by special arrangement.

Assistive Technology Assistive technology is located in M126. Technology training is provided to incoming students.

Subject-Area Tutoring Tutoring is offered one-on-one and in small groups for most subjects. Tutoring is provided through the program or unit via graduate assistants/students, LD specialists, and professional tutors. Tutoring is also provided collaboratively through on-campus or off-campus services via computer-based instruction.

Basic Skills Remediation Remediation is offered one-on-one and in small groups for computer skills, learning strategies, math, reading, social skills, study skills, time management, and written language.

Enrichment Enrichment programs are available through the program or unit for career planning, college survival skills, learning strategies, practical computer skills, self-advocacy, stress management, and study skills. Programs for health and nutrition, math, oral communication skills, practical computer skills, and reading are provided collaboratively through on-campus or off-campus services. Credit is offered for career planning, college survival skills, learning strategies, practical computer skills, and study skills.

Application For admittance to the program or unit, students are required to provide a psychoeducational report and provide psychological evaluation and educational evaluation. It is recommended that students provide documentation of high school services. Upon acceptance, documentation of need for services should be sent only to the LD program or unit. *Application deadline (institutional):* 8/15. *Application deadline (LD program):* Rolling/continuous for fall and rolling/continuous for spring.

Written Policies Written policy regarding general/basic LD accommodations is outlined in the school's catalog/handbook. Written policy regarding course substitutions is available through the program or unit directly.

Lackawanna College
Developmental Education

501 Vine Street
Scranton, PA 18509
http://www.lackawanna.edu/

Contact: Ms. Deborah Hartzell, Director of Academic Development. Phone: 570-961-7821. E-mail: hartzelld@ lackawanna.edu.

Developmental Education The program or unit includes 2 full-time staff members. LD specialists and remediation/learning specialists are provided collaboratively through on-campus or off-campus services.

Summer Program To help prepare for the demands of college, there is a mandatory summer program prior to entering the school. The program accepts students from out-of-state and is available to students attending other colleges.

Application *Application deadline (institutional):* Continuous.

Lake City Community College
Disabled Student Services

Route 19, Box 1030
Lake City, FL 32025-8703
http://www.lakecitycc.edu/disabled-student-services.aspx

Contact: Ms. Janice Irwin, Coordinator, Disabled Student Services. Phone: 386-754-4393. Fax: 386-754-4715. E-mail: irwinj@lakecitycc.edu.

Disabled Student Services Approximately 300 registered undergraduate students were served during 2006–07. The program or unit includes 1 full-time and 1 part-time staff member. Academic advisers, counselors, skill tutors, and trained peer tutors are provided through the program or unit. Coaches and regular education teachers are provided collaboratively through on-campus or off-campus services.

Orientation The program or unit offers an optional 1-hour orientation for new students individually by special arrangement.

Unique Aids and Services Aids, services, or accommodations include career counseling, faculty training, personal coach, and priority registration.

Assistive Technology Assistive technology is located in campus labs, the DSS office and includes digital textbooks/e-text and learning support software. Technology training is provided to incoming students.

Subject-Area Tutoring Tutoring is offered one-on-one for some subjects. Tutoring is provided through the program or unit via trained peer tutors. Tutoring is also provided collaboratively through on-campus or off-campus services via computer-based instruction.

Basic Skills Remediation Remediation is offered in small groups for math and study skills. Remediation is provided collaboratively through on-campus or off-campus services via computer-based instruction and trained peer tutors.

Enrichment Enrichment programs are available through the program or unit for learning strategies, self-advocacy, stress management, and time management. Programs for career planning, college survival skills, math, study skills, and test taking are provided collaboratively through on-campus or off-campus services. Credit is offered for college survival skills.

Application For admittance to the program or unit, students are required to apply to the program directly and provide a psychoeducational report (7 years old or less). Upon application, materials documenting need for services should be sent only to the LD program or unit. Upon acceptance, documentation of need for services should be sent only to the LD program or unit. *Application deadline (institutional):* Continuous. *Application deadline (LD program):* Rolling/continuous for fall and rolling/continuous for spring.

Written Policies Written policy regarding general/basic LD accommodations is outlined in the school's catalog/handbook. Written policies regarding course substitutions, general/basic LD accommodations, grade forgiveness, reduced course loads, substitutions and waivers of admissions requirements, and substitutions and waivers of graduation requirements are available through the program or unit directly.

Lake-Sumter Community College
Office for Students with Disabilities

9501 US Highway 441

Leesburg, FL 34788-8751

http://www.lscc.edu/admissions/osd.aspx

Contact: Ms. Raelynn Poole, Senior Manager, Office for Students with Disabilities. Phone: 352-365-3574. Fax: 352-365-3553. E-mail: pooler@lscc.edu.

Office for Students with Disabilities Approximately 40 registered undergraduate students were served during 2006–07. The program or unit includes 1 full-time and 2 part-time staff members. Counselors are provided through the program or unit. Academic advisers, counselors, professional tutors, regular education teachers, skill tutors, and trained peer tutors are provided collaboratively through on-campus or off-campus services.

Unique Aids and Services Aids, services, or accommodations include career counseling, meetings with OSD Manager (upon student request).

Assistive Technology Assistive technology is located in campus labs, the DSS office, a special lab and includes digital textbooks/e-text, learning support software, and scanning.

Subject-Area Tutoring Tutoring is offered one-on-one and in small groups for some subjects. Tutoring is provided collaboratively through on-campus or off-campus services via computer-based instruction, professional tutors, and trained peer tutors.

Basic Skills Remediation Remediation is offered one-on-one, in small groups, and in class-size groups for math, reading, and written language. Remediation is provided collaboratively through on-campus or off-campus services via computer-based instruction, professional tutors, regular education teachers, and trained peer tutors.

Enrichment Programs for career planning, college survival skills, learning strategies, oral communication skills, reading, stress management, study skills, test taking, time management, vocabulary development, and written composition skills are provided collaboratively through on-campus or off-campus services. Credit is offered for career planning, college survival skills, learning strategies, oral communication skills, reading, stress management, study skills, test taking, time management, vocabulary development, and written composition skills.

Application For admittance to the program or unit, students are required to apply to the program directly, provide a psychoeducational report (3 years old or less), and provide official diagnosis by licensed psychomotrist. It is recommended that students provide documentation of high school services. Upon application, materials documenting need for services should be sent only to the LD program or unit. Upon acceptance, documentation of need for services should be sent only to the LD program or unit. *Application deadline (institutional):* Continuous. *Application deadline (LD program):* Rolling/continuous for fall and rolling/continuous for spring.

Written Policies Written policies regarding general/basic LD accommodations, grade forgiveness, and substitutions and waivers of graduation requirements are available on the program Web site. Written policies regarding general/basic LD accommodations, grade forgiveness, and substitutions and waivers of graduation requirements are outlined in the school's catalog/handbook. Written policies regarding course substitutions, general/basic LD accommodations, reduced course loads, substitutions and waivers of admissions requirements, and substitutions and waivers of graduation requirements are available through the program or unit directly.

Lamar Institute of Technology

855 East Lavaca

Beaumont, TX 77705

http://www.lit.edu/

Contact: Mrs. Jamie Lynn Fox, Special Populations Coordinator. Phone: 409-880-1737. Fax: 409-880-1711. E-mail: jamie.fox@lit.edu.

The program or unit includes 1 full-time and 1 part-time staff member. Academic advisers, counselors, diagnostic specialists, LD specialists, professional tutors, and regular education teachers are provided through the program or unit. Services are provided collaboratively through on-campus or off-campus services.

Lamar Institute of Technology (continued)

Unique Aids and Services Aids, services, or accommodations include career counseling, faculty training, and priority registration.

Assistive Technology Assistive technology is located in campus labs, a special lab and includes digital textbooks/e-text, learning support software, and scanning. Technology training is provided to incoming students.

Subject-Area Tutoring Tutoring is offered one-on-one, in small groups, and in class-size groups for some subjects. Tutoring is provided collaboratively through on-campus or off-campus services via computer-based instruction, professional tutors, and trained peer tutors.

Basic Skills Remediation Remediation is offered in class-size groups for math, reading, study skills, and time management. Remediation is provided collaboratively through on-campus or off-campus services via computer-based instruction, professional tutors, regular education teachers, and trained peer tutors.

Enrichment Enrichment programs are available through the program or unit for self-advocacy. Programs for career planning, reading, stress management, and written composition skills are provided collaboratively through on-campus or off-campus services. Credit is offered for college survival skills, study skills, test taking, and time management.

Application For admittance to the program or unit, students are required to apply to the program directly, provide a psychoeducational report (5 years old or less), provide documentation of high school services, and provide psychological evaluation if not diagnosed in high school or older than 5 years. Upon application, materials documenting need for services should be sent only to the LD program or unit. Upon acceptance, documentation of need for services should be sent only to the LD program or unit. *Application deadline (LD program):* Rolling/continuous for fall and rolling/continuous for spring.

Written Policies Written policy regarding general/basic LD accommodations is available on the program Web site. Written policy regarding general/basic LD accommodations is outlined in the school's catalog/handbook. Written policies regarding course substitutions, general/basic LD accommodations, and substitutions and waivers of graduation requirements are available through the program or unit directly.

Lamar State College–Orange
Disability Support Services (DSS)

410 Front Street

Orange, TX 77630-5802

http://www.lsco.edu

Contact: Laure Marcantel, Coordinator of Services for Students with Disabilities. Phone: 409-882-3370. Fax: 409-882-3049. E-mail: laurie.marcantel@lsco.edu. Head of LD Program: Frances Ahearn, Director of Advising, Counseling and Testing. Phone: 409-882-3387. Fax: 409-882-3049. E-mail: Frances.Ahearn@lsco.edu.

Disability Support Services (DSS) Approximately 30 registered undergraduate students were served during 2006–07. The program or unit includes 4 full-time staff members. Academic advis-

ers and counselors are provided through the program or unit. Diagnostic specialists, professional tutors, regular education teachers, and remediation/learning specialists are provided collaboratively through on-campus or off-campus services.

Unique Aids and Services Aids, services, or accommodations include career counseling, faculty training, parent workshops, priority registration, representatives from institution at graduate ARD meetings.

Assistive Technology Assistive technology is located in campus labs, the DSS office, a special lab and includes digital textbooks/e-text and learning support software. Technology training is provided to incoming students.

Subject-Area Tutoring Tutoring is offered for most subjects. Tutoring is provided collaboratively through on-campus or off-campus services via professional tutors and trained peer tutors.

Basic Skills Remediation Remediation is offered one-on-one and in class-size groups for computer skills, handwriting, learning strategies, math, reading, spelling, study skills, time management, and written language. Remediation is provided collaboratively through on-campus or off-campus services via computer-based instruction, professional tutors, and regular education teachers.

Enrichment Enrichment programs are available through the program or unit for career planning, college survival skills, health and nutrition, learning strategies, oral communication skills, self-advocacy, stress management, study skills, test taking, time management, and other. Programs for career planning, college survival skills, health and nutrition, learning strategies, math, oral communication skills, practical computer skills, reading, self-advocacy, stress management, study skills, test taking, time management, vocabulary development, written composition skills, and other are provided collaboratively through on-campus or off-campus services. Credit is offered for health and nutrition, math, oral communication skills, practical computer skills, reading, written composition skills, and other.

Application For admittance to the program or unit, students are required to apply to the program directly and provide a psychoeducational report (3 years old or less). Upon application, materials documenting need for services should be sent only to the LD program or unit. Upon acceptance, documentation of need for services should be sent only to the LD program or unit. *Application deadline (institutional):* Continuous. *Application deadline (LD program):* Rolling/continuous for fall and rolling/continuous for spring.

Written Policies Written policy regarding general/basic LD accommodations is available on the program Web site. Written policy regarding general/basic LD accommodations is outlined in the school's catalog/handbook. Written policy regarding general/basic LD accommodations is available through the program or unit directly.

Laredo Community College
Disability Resource Center

West End Washington Street

Laredo, TX 78040-4395

http://www.laredo.edu/

Contact: Mr. Luis A. Garza, Counselor/Coordinator. Phone: 956-721-5137. Fax: 956-721-5838. E-mail: lgarza@laredo.edu.

Disability Resource Center Approximately 200 registered undergraduate students were served during 2006–07. The program or unit includes 1 full-time staff member. Counselors are provided through the program or unit. Academic advisers, counselors, regular education teachers, skill tutors, strategy tutors, and trained peer tutors are provided collaboratively through on-campus or off-campus services.

Unique Aids and Services Aids, services, or accommodations include advocates, career counseling, and priority registration.

Assistive Technology Assistive technology is located in campus labs, the library, the Learning Center and includes digital textbooks/e-text, learning support software, and scanning.

Subject-Area Tutoring Tutoring is offered one-on-one for some subjects. Tutoring is provided through the program or unit via other.

Basic Skills Remediation Remediation is offered in class-size groups for math, reading, and written language. Remediation is provided collaboratively through on-campus or off-campus services via regular education teachers.

Application For admittance to the program or unit, students are required to apply to the program directly, provide a psychoeducational report (3 years old or less), and provide documentation of high school services. Upon application, materials documenting need for services should be sent only to the LD program or unit. Upon acceptance, documentation of need for services should be sent only to the LD program or unit. *Application deadline (institutional):* Continuous. *Application deadline (LD program):* Rolling/continuous for fall and rolling/continuous for spring.

Written Policies Written policy regarding general/basic LD accommodations is available on the program Web site. Written policy regarding general/basic LD accommodations is outlined in the school's catalog/handbook. Written policy regarding general/basic LD accommodations is available through the program or unit directly.

Lassen Community College District
Disabled Students Programs and Services

Highway 139

PO Box 3000

Susanville, CA 96130

http://www.lassencollege.edu/

Contact: Ms. Cindy Howe, Learning Disabilities Specialist. Phone: 530-251-8867. Fax: 530-257-6181 Ext. 8914.

Disabled Students Programs and Services Approximately 147 registered undergraduate students were served during 2006–07. The program or unit includes 2 full-time staff members and 1 part-time staff member. Diagnostic specialists, LD specialists, professional tutors, remediation/learning specialists, skill tutors, special education teachers, and strategy tutors are provided through the program or unit. Academic advisers, coaches, counselors, professional tutors, regular education teachers, and trained peer tutors are provided collaboratively through on-campus or off-campus services.

Orientation The program or unit offers an optional 1-hour orientation for new students individually by special arrangement.

Unique Aids and Services Aids, services, or accommodations include career counseling.

Assistive Technology Assistive technology is located in a special lab and includes digital textbooks/e-text and learning support software. Technology training is provided to incoming students.

Subject-Area Tutoring Tutoring is offered one-on-one and in small groups for some subjects. Tutoring is provided through the program or unit via computer-based instruction, LD specialists, professional tutors, and trained peer tutors. Tutoring is also provided collaboratively through on-campus or off-campus services via computer-based instruction and trained peer tutors.

Diagnostic Testing Testing is provided through the program or unit for auditory processing, intelligence, learning strategies, learning styles, math, reading, spelling, visual processing, and written language. Testing for learning styles, math, reading, and written language is provided collaboratively through on-campus or off-campus services.

Basic Skills Remediation Remediation is offered in class-size groups for computer skills, learning strategies, math, reading, spelling, study skills, time management, and written language. Remediation is provided through the program or unit via computer-based instruction, LD specialists, professional tutors, special education teachers, and trained peer tutors. Remediation is also provided collaboratively through on-campus or off-campus services via computer-based instruction, regular education teachers, and trained peer tutors.

Enrichment Enrichment programs are available through the program or unit for learning strategies, math, practical computer skills, reading, study skills, test taking, vocabulary development, and written composition skills. Programs for career planning, college survival skills, health and nutrition, learning strategies, math, oral communication skills, practical computer skills, reading, stress management, study skills, test taking, time management, and written composition skills are provided collaboratively through on-campus or off-campus services. Credit is offered for career planning, college survival skills, health and nutrition, learning strategies, math, oral communication skills, practical computer skills, reading, stress management, study skills, test taking, time management, vocabulary development, and written composition skills.

Fees *Diagnostic Testing* fee is $30.

Application For admittance to the program or unit, students are required to apply to the program directly and provide a psychoeducational report (3 years old or less). It is recommended that students provide documentation of high school services and provide school psychologist's report. Upon application, materials documenting need for services should be sent only to the LD program or unit. Upon acceptance, documentation of need for services should be sent only to the LD program or unit. *Application deadline (institutional):* Continuous. *Application deadline (LD program):* Rolling/continuous for fall and rolling/continuous for spring.

Written Policies Written policy regarding grade forgiveness is outlined in the school's catalog/handbook. Written policies regarding general/basic LD accommodations and reduced course loads are available through the program or unit directly.

Lee College
Office of Disability Services

PO Box 818

Baytown, TX 77522-0818

http://www.lee.edu/counseling/#dis

Lee College (continued)

Contact: JoAnn Szabo, Counselor for Students with Disabilities. Phone: 281-425-6384. Fax: 832-556-4004. E-mail: jszabo@lee.edu.

Office of Disability Services Approximately 50 registered undergraduate students were served during 2006–07. The program or unit includes 1 full-time and 3 part-time staff members. Counselors, skill tutors, and other are provided collaboratively through on-campus or off-campus services.

Unique Aids and Services Aids, services, or accommodations include career counseling, faculty training, and priority registration.

Assistive Technology Assistive technology is located in campus labs, the DSS office and includes digital textbooks/e-text and learning support software.

Subject-Area Tutoring Tutoring is offered one-on-one and in small groups for most subjects. Tutoring is provided collaboratively through on-campus or off-campus services via computer-based instruction and trained peer tutors.

Basic Skills Remediation Remediation is offered in class-size groups for math, reading, study skills, and written language. Remediation is provided collaboratively through on-campus or off-campus services via computer-based instruction and regular education teachers.

Enrichment Programs for career planning, college survival skills, learning strategies, math, practical computer skills, reading, study skills, test taking, time management, and written composition skills are provided collaboratively through on-campus or off-campus services.

Application For admittance to the program or unit, students are required to provide a psychoeducational report (5 years old or less). It is recommended that students provide documentation of high school services. Upon application, materials documenting need for services should be sent only to the LD program or unit. Upon acceptance, documentation of need for services should be sent only to the LD program or unit. *Application deadline (institutional):* Continuous. *Application deadline (LD program):* Rolling/continuous for fall and rolling/continuous for spring.

Written Policies Written policy regarding general/basic LD accommodations is available on the program Web site. Written policy regarding general/basic LD accommodations is outlined in the school's catalog/handbook.

Lincoln Land Community College
Special Needs Office

5250 Shepherd Road
PO Box 19256
Springfield, IL 62794-9256
http://www.llcc.edu/

Contact: Ms. Linda D. Chriswell, Special Needs Professional. Phone: 217-786-2828. Fax: 217-786-2310. E-mail: linda.chriswell@llcc.edu.

Special Needs Office Approximately 300 registered undergraduate students were served during 2006–07. The program or unit includes 2 full-time staff members. Academic advisers, counselors, diagnostic specialists, professional tutors, skill tutors, strategy tutors,

and trained peer tutors are provided through the program or unit. Academic advisers, counselors, professional tutors, regular education teachers, remediation/learning specialists, skill tutors, strategy tutors, and trained peer tutors are provided collaboratively through on-campus or off-campus services.

Orientation The program or unit offers an optional 3- to 4-hour orientation for new students before registration, before classes begin, during summer prior to enrollment, during registration, after classes begin, and individually by special arrangement.

Unique Aids and Services Aids, services, or accommodations include career counseling, faculty training, and priority registration.

Subject-Area Tutoring Tutoring is offered one-on-one and in small groups for all subjects. Tutoring is provided through the program or unit via computer-based instruction, professional tutors, and trained peer tutors. Tutoring is also provided collaboratively through on-campus or off-campus services via computer-based instruction, professional tutors, and trained peer tutors.

Diagnostic Testing Testing is provided through the program or unit for math, reading, spelling, and written language. Testing for learning strategies, learning styles, math, and study skills is provided collaboratively through on-campus or off-campus services.

Basic Skills Remediation Remediation is offered one-on-one and in class-size groups for computer skills, learning strategies, math, reading, spelling, study skills, time management, and written language. Remediation is provided through the program or unit via computer-based instruction, professional tutors, and trained peer tutors. Remediation is also provided collaboratively through on-campus or off-campus services via professional tutors, regular education teachers, and trained peer tutors.

Enrichment Enrichment programs are available through the program or unit for career planning, learning strategies, self-advocacy, stress management, and study skills. Programs for career planning, college survival skills, learning strategies, math, practical computer skills, reading, stress management, study skills, test taking, time management, vocabulary development, and written composition skills are provided collaboratively through on-campus or off-campus services. Credit is offered for college survival skills, learning strategies, math, reading, study skills, test taking, time management, vocabulary development, and written composition skills.

Application For admittance to the program or unit, students are required to apply to the program directly and provide a psychoeducational report (3 years old or less). It is recommended that students provide documentation of high school services. Upon application, materials documenting need for services should be sent only to the LD program or unit. Upon acceptance, documentation of need for services should be sent only to the LD program or unit. *Application deadline (institutional):* Continuous. *Application deadline (LD program):* Rolling/continuous for fall and rolling/continuous for spring.

Written Policies Written policies regarding course substitutions, general/basic LD accommodations, grade forgiveness, and substitutions and waivers of admissions requirements are outlined in the school's catalog/handbook. Written policies regarding general/basic LD accommodations and substitutions and waivers of admissions requirements are available through the program or unit directly.

Linn State Technical College

One Technology Drive
Linn, MO 65051-9606
http://www.linnstate.edu/

Contact: Mr. Jason Hoffmeyer, Clinical Counselor/Vocational Resource Educator. Phone: 800-743-8324. Fax: 573-897-5049. Head of LD Program: Mrs. Judy Robinett, Director of Student Support Services. Phone: 800-743-8324. Fax: 573-897-5049. E-mail: judy.robinett@linnstate.edu.

Approximately 7 registered undergraduate students were served during 2006–07. The program or unit includes 3 full-time staff members. Academic advisers, counselors, diagnostic specialists, professional tutors, regular education teachers, skill tutors, strategy tutors, and trained peer tutors are provided collaboratively through on-campus or off-campus services.

Summer Program To help prepare for the demands of college, there is an optional 8-week summer program prior to entering the school available to high school graduates that focuses on computing skills and specific subject tutoring. The program accepts students from out-of-state and is available to students attending other colleges.

Unique Aids and Services Aids, services, or accommodations include advocates, career counseling, and weekly meetings with faculty.

Assistive Technology Assistive technology is located in the Academic Resource Center, any computer lab and includes learning support software and scanning.

Subject-Area Tutoring Tutoring is offered one-on-one and in small groups for all subjects. Tutoring is provided collaboratively through on-campus or off-campus services via computer-based instruction, professional tutors, and trained peer tutors.

Diagnostic Testing Testing for auditory processing, handwriting, intelligence, learning strategies, learning styles, math, motor skills, neuropsychological, personality, reading, social skills, spelling, spoken language, study skills, visual processing, and written language is provided collaboratively through on-campus or off-campus services.

Basic Skills Remediation Remediation is offered in class-size groups for math and written language. Remediation is provided collaboratively through on-campus or off-campus services via computer-based instruction, professional tutors, regular education teachers, and trained peer tutors.

Enrichment Programs for career planning, college survival skills, health and nutrition, learning strategies, math, medication management, oral communication skills, practical computer skills, reading, self-advocacy, stress management, study skills, test taking, time management, vocabulary development, and written composition skills are provided collaboratively through on-campus or off-campus services.

Fees *Diagnostic Testing* fee is $80.

Application For admittance to the program or unit, students are required to provide a psychoeducational report (5 years old or less). It is recommended that students provide documentation of high school services. Upon application, materials documenting need for services should be sent only to admissions with institutional application materials. Upon acceptance, documentation of need for services should be sent to both admissions and the LD program or unit.

Written Policies Written policy regarding general/basic LD accommodations is available on the program Web site. Written policy regarding general/basic LD accommodations is outlined in the school's catalog/handbook. Written policies regarding general/basic LD accommodations and substitutions and waivers of admissions requirements are available through the program or unit directly.

Long Beach City College
Disabled Students Programs and Services

4901 East Carson Street
Long Beach, CA 90808-1780
http://www.lbcc.edu

Contact: Mr. Dan Hansch, Learning Disabilities Specialist and Counselor. Phone: 562-938-4491. Fax: 562-938-4457. E-mail: dhansch@lbcc.edu.

Disabled Students Programs and Services Approximately 130 registered undergraduate students were served during 2006–07. The program or unit includes 2 full-time and 2 part-time staff members. Academic advisers, counselors, diagnostic specialists, LD specialists, remediation/learning specialists, skill tutors, special education teachers, strategy tutors, and trained peer tutors are provided through the program or unit. Academic advisers, counselors, skill tutors, strategy tutors, and trained peer tutors are provided collaboratively through on-campus or off-campus services.

Orientation The program or unit offers an optional 2-hour orientation for new students before registration.

Unique Aids and Services Aids, services, or accommodations include career counseling, faculty training, and priority registration.

Assistive Technology Assistive technology is located in campus labs, the DSS office, a special lab and includes digital textbooks/e-text, learning support software, and scanning. Technology training is provided to incoming students.

Subject-Area Tutoring Tutoring is offered one-on-one and in small groups for some subjects. Tutoring is provided through the program or unit via computer-based instruction, graduate assistants/students, LD specialists, and trained peer tutors. Tutoring is also provided collaboratively through on-campus or off-campus services via computer-based instruction and trained peer tutors.

Diagnostic Testing Testing is provided through the program or unit for auditory processing, intelligence, neuropsychological, reading, spelling, visual processing, and written language.

Basic Skills Remediation Remediation is offered one-on-one, in small groups, and in class-size groups for math, reading, study skills, time management, and written language. Remediation is provided through the program or unit via LD specialists, special education teachers, and trained peer tutors. Remediation is also provided collaboratively through on-campus or off-campus services via computer-based instruction, graduate assistants/students, regular education teachers, and trained peer tutors.

Enrichment Enrichment programs are available through the program or unit for career planning, college survival skills, learning strategies, math, practical computer skills, reading, self-advocacy, stress management, study skills, test taking, time management, vocabulary development, and written composition skills. Programs for career planning, college survival skills, health and nutrition, learning strategies, math, oral communication skills, practical computer skills, reading, self-advocacy, stress management, study skills, test taking, time management, vocabulary development, and written composition skills are provided collaboratively through on-campus or off-campus services. Credit is offered for career planning, col-

Long Beach City College (continued)

lege survival skills, health and nutrition, learning strategies, math, oral communication skills, practical computer skills, reading, study skills, test taking, time management, vocabulary development, and written composition skills.

Student Organization Students for Disability Rights consists of 20 members.

Application For admittance to the program or unit, students are required to apply to the program directly and provide a psychoeducational report (3 years old or less). It is recommended that students provide documentation of high school services. Upon application, materials documenting need for services should be sent only to the LD program or unit. Upon acceptance, documentation of need for services should be sent only to the LD program or unit. *Application deadline (institutional):* Continuous. *Application deadline (LD program):* Rolling/continuous for fall and rolling/continuous for spring.

Written Policies Written policy regarding general/basic LD accommodations is available on the program Web site. Written policies regarding course substitutions and general/basic LD accommodations are outlined in the school's catalog/handbook. Written policy regarding substitutions and waivers of graduation requirements is available through the program or unit directly.

Luna Community College
Disability Support Services

PO Box 1510

Las Vegas, NM 87701

http://www.luna.cc.nm.us/

Contact: Ms. Cynthia Renee Branch, Adaptive Education Specialist. Phone: 505-454-5303 Ext. 1211. Fax: 505-454-2588. E-mail: cbranch@luna.edu.

Disability Support Services Approximately 15 registered undergraduate students were served during 2006–07. The program or unit includes 1 full-time staff member. Academic advisers, counselors, diagnostic specialists, regular education teachers, skill tutors, strategy tutors, teacher trainees, and trained peer tutors are provided collaboratively through on-campus or off-campus services.

Orientation The program or unit offers an optional 1-day orientation for new students before classes begin.

Summer Program To help prepare for the demands of college, there is an optional 2-month summer program prior to entering the school available to rising sophomores, high school graduates that focuses on specific subject tutoring and study skills. The program accepts students from out-of-state and is available to students attending other colleges.

Unique Aids and Services Aids, services, or accommodations include advocates, career counseling, and faculty training.

Assistive Technology Assistive technology is located in campus labs, the DSS office and includes learning support software and scanning. Technology training is provided to incoming students.

Subject-Area Tutoring Tutoring is offered one-on-one for most subjects. Tutoring is provided collaboratively through on-campus or off-campus services via computer-based instruction and trained peer tutors.

Basic Skills Remediation Remediation is offered in small groups for auditory processing, computer skills, learning strategies, math, reading, social skills, spelling, and time management. Remediation is provided collaboratively through on-campus or off-campus services via teacher trainees and trained peer tutors.

Enrichment Programs for career planning, college survival skills, learning strategies, math, test taking, time management, vocabulary development, and written composition skills are provided collaboratively through on-campus or off-campus services.

Application It is recommended that students provide a psychoeducational report (3 years old or less) and provide documentation of high school services. Upon application, materials documenting need for services should be sent only to the LD program or unit. Upon acceptance, documentation of need for services should be sent only to the LD program or unit. *Application deadline (LD program):* Rolling/continuous for fall and rolling/continuous for spring.

Written Policies Written policy regarding general/basic LD accommodations is available on the program Web site. Written policies regarding general/basic LD accommodations, substitutions and waivers of admissions requirements, and substitutions and waivers of graduation requirements are outlined in the school's catalog/handbook. Written policies regarding general/basic LD accommodations, substitutions and waivers of admissions requirements, and substitutions and waivers of graduation requirements are available through the program or unit directly.

Macomb Community College
Special Services

14500 East Twelve Mile Road

Warren, MI 48088-3896

http://www.macomb.edu/SpecialServices/

Contact: Ms. Dina Aiuto, Counselor. Phone: 586-445-7420. Fax: 586-445-7223. E-mail: aiutod@macomb.edu. Head of LD Program: Ms. Susan R. Boyd, Director of Student Development and Special Services. Phone: 586-286-2220. Fax: 586-286-2295. E-mail: boyds@macomb.edu.

Special Services Approximately 600 registered undergraduate students were served during 2006–07. The program or unit includes 6 full-time and 6 part-time staff members. Counselors are provided through the program or unit. Academic advisers, coaches, counselors, diagnostic specialists, graduate assistants/students, LD specialists, professional tutors, regular education teachers, and special education teachers are provided collaboratively through on-campus or off-campus services.

Orientation The program or unit offers a mandatory 3-hour orientation for new students before registration, before classes begin, during summer prior to enrollment, during registration, after classes begin, and individually by special arrangement.

Unique Aids and Services Aids, services, or accommodations include advocates, career counseling, personal coach, priority registration, and support groups.

Assistive Technology Assistive technology is located in campus labs and includes learning support software.

Subject-Area Tutoring Tutoring is offered one-on-one, in small groups, and in class-size groups for some subjects. Tutoring is provided collaboratively through on-campus or off-campus services via trained peer tutors.

Enrichment Programs for career planning, college survival skills, health and nutrition, learning strategies, math, oral communication skills, practical computer skills, reading, stress management, study skills, test taking, time management, and written composition skills are provided collaboratively through on-campus or off-campus services. Credit is offered for career planning, college survival skills, health and nutrition, learning strategies, math, oral communication skills, practical computer skills, reading, and written composition skills.

Application For admittance to the program or unit, students are required to apply to the program directly, provide a psychoeducational report (2 years old or less), provide documentation of high school services, and provide medical documentation or documentation for mental illness. Upon application, materials documenting need for services should be sent only to the LD program or unit. Upon acceptance, documentation of need for services should be sent only to the LD program or unit. *Application deadline (institutional):* Continuous. *Application deadline (LD program):* Rolling/continuous for fall and rolling/continuous for spring.

Written Policies Written policy regarding general/basic LD accommodations is available on the program Web site. Written policy regarding general/basic LD accommodations is outlined in the school's catalog/handbook. Written policies regarding course substitutions, general/basic LD accommodations, reduced course loads, substitutions and waivers of admissions requirements, and substitutions and waivers of graduation requirements are available through the program or unit directly.

Madisonville Community College
Disability Resource Office

2000 College Drive
Madisonville, KY 42431-9185
http://www.madisonville.kctcs.edu/disability/index.html
Contact: Ms. Valerie J. Wolfe, Disability Resource Coordinator. Phone: 270-821-2250 Ext. 41708. Fax: 270-824-1869. E-mail: valerie.wolfe@kctcs.edu.

Disability Resource Office Approximately 35 registered undergraduate students were served during 2006–07.
Unique Aids and Services Aids, services, or accommodations include advocates, career counseling, and faculty training.
Assistive Technology Assistive technology is located in campus labs, the DSS office and includes learning support software and scanning.
Subject-Area Tutoring Tutoring is offered one-on-one and in small groups for some subjects. Tutoring is provided collaboratively through on-campus or off-campus services via trained peer tutors.
Basic Skills Remediation Remediation is offered one-on-one and in small groups for computer skills, learning strategies, math, reading, spelling, study skills, time management, and written language. Remediation is provided collaboratively through on-campus or off-campus services via regular education teachers and trained peer tutors.

Enrichment Programs for career planning, learning strategies, practical computer skills, and stress management are provided collaboratively through on-campus or off-campus services. Credit is offered for college survival skills, math, oral communication skills, reading, study skills, test taking, time management, vocabulary development, and written composition skills.
Application It is recommended that students provide a psychoeducational report (5 years old or less). Upon acceptance, documentation of need for services should be sent only to the LD program or unit. *Application deadline (institutional):* Continuous. *Application deadline (LD program):* Rolling/continuous for fall and rolling/continuous for spring.
Written Policies Written policies regarding course substitutions, general/basic LD accommodations, grade forgiveness, reduced course loads, substitutions and waivers of admissions requirements, and substitutions and waivers of graduation requirements are available on the program Web site. Written policies regarding course substitutions, general/basic LD accommodations, grade forgiveness, reduced course loads, substitutions and waivers of admissions requirements, and substitutions and waivers of graduation requirements are outlined in the school's catalog/handbook.

Massasoit Community College
Disability Services

1 Massasoit Boulevard
Brockton, MA 02302-3996
http://www.massasoit.mass.edu/
Contact: Andrea Henry. Phone: 508-588-9100. E-mail: ahenry@massasoit.mass.edu.

Disability Services Approximately 250 registered undergraduate students were served during 2006–07. The program or unit includes 2 full-time staff members and 1 part-time staff member. Academic advisers and counselors are provided through the program or unit. Academic advisers, counselors, LD specialists, professional tutors, regular education teachers, skill tutors, strategy tutors, and trained peer tutors are provided collaboratively through on-campus or off-campus services.
Summer Program To help prepare for the demands of college, there is an optional half-day summer program prior to entering the school.
Unique Aids and Services Aids, services, or accommodations include career counseling.
Assistive Technology Assistive technology is located in campus labs, a special lab and includes digital textbooks/e-text and scanning. Technology training is provided to incoming students.
Subject-Area Tutoring Tutoring is offered one-on-one and in small groups for most subjects. Tutoring is provided collaboratively through on-campus or off-campus services via computer-based instruction, LD specialists, professional tutors, and trained peer tutors.
Basic Skills Remediation Remediation is offered one-on-one for computer skills, learning strategies, math, reading, study skills, time management, written language, and others. Remediation is provided collaboratively through on-campus or off-campus services via LD specialists, professional tutors, regular education teachers, and trained peer tutors.

Massasoit Community College (continued)

Student Organization Helping Hands consists of 10 members.

Application For admittance to the program or unit, students are required to provide a psychoeducational report (3 years old or less). It is recommended that students provide documentation of high school services. Upon application, materials documenting need for services should be sent only to the LD program or unit. Upon acceptance, documentation of need for services should be sent only to the LD program or unit. *Application deadline (institutional):* Continuous. *Application deadline (LD program):* Rolling/continuous for fall.

Written Policies Written policy regarding general/basic LD accommodations is outlined in the school's catalog/handbook. Written policies regarding course substitutions, general/basic LD accommodations, reduced course loads, substitutions and waivers of admissions requirements, and substitutions and waivers of graduation requirements are available through the program or unit directly.

Maui Community College

310 Kaahumanu Avenue

Kahului, HI 96732

http://www.maui.hawaii.edu

Contact: Ms. Lisa Deneen, Disabilities Coordinator/ Counselor. Phone: 808-984-3327. Fax: 808-242-9618. E-mail: ldeneen@hawaii.edu.

Approximately 25 registered undergraduate students were served during 2006–07. The program or unit includes 1 part-time staff member. Academic advisers, counselors, remediation/learning specialists, and trained peer tutors are provided collaboratively through on-campus or off-campus services.

Unique Aids and Services Aids, services, or accommodations include advocates, career counseling, faculty training, and priority registration.

Assistive Technology Assistive technology is located in campus labs and includes digital textbooks/e-text, learning support software, and scanning. Technology training is provided to incoming students.

Subject-Area Tutoring Tutoring is offered one-on-one for some subjects. Tutoring is provided collaboratively through on-campus or off-campus services via computer-based instruction, professional tutors, and trained peer tutors.

Basic Skills Remediation Remediation is offered one-on-one and in class-size groups for computer skills, learning strategies, math, reading, spelling, study skills, time management, and written language. Remediation is provided collaboratively through on-campus or off-campus services via computer-based instruction, professional tutors, regular education teachers, and trained peer tutors.

Enrichment Programs for career planning, college survival skills, learning strategies, math, oral communication skills, practical computer skills, reading, stress management, study skills, test taking, time management, vocabulary development, and written composition skills are provided collaboratively through on-campus or off-campus services. Credit is offered for career planning, college survival skills, learning strategies, math, oral communication skills, practical computer skills, reading, study skills, test taking, time management, vocabulary development, and written composition skills.

Application For admittance to the program or unit, students are required to provide a psychoeducational report (3 years old or less). It is recommended that students provide documentation of high school services. Upon application, materials documenting need for services should be sent only to the LD program or unit. Upon acceptance, documentation of need for services should be sent only to the LD program or unit. *Application deadline (institutional):* Continuous. *Application deadline (LD program):* Rolling/continuous for fall and rolling/continuous for spring.

Written Policies Written policy regarding general/basic LD accommodations is outlined in the school's catalog/handbook.

Mayland Community College
SOAR Program

PO Box 547

Spruce Pine, NC 28777-0547

http://www.mayland.edu

Contact: Nancy Godwin, Director of the SOAR Program. Phone: 828-765-7351 Ext. 232. E-mail: ngodwin@mayland.edu.

SOAR Program Approximately 21 registered undergraduate students were served during 2006–07. The program or unit includes 4 full-time and 2 part-time staff members. Academic advisers, counselors, LD specialists, professional tutors, regular education teachers, remediation/learning specialists, skill tutors, strategy tutors, and trained peer tutors are provided through the program or unit. Academic advisers, counselors, professional tutors, regular education teachers, remediation/learning specialists, skill tutors, strategy tutors, and trained peer tutors are provided collaboratively through on-campus or off-campus services.

Orientation The program or unit offers a mandatory 1-hour orientation for new students individually by special arrangement.

Unique Aids and Services Aids, services, or accommodations include advocates, career counseling, and faculty training.

Assistive Technology Assistive technology is located in campus labs and includes digital textbooks/e-text. Technology training is provided to incoming students.

Subject-Area Tutoring Tutoring is offered one-on-one and in small groups for most subjects. Tutoring is provided through the program or unit via computer-based instruction, LD specialists, professional tutors, and trained peer tutors. Tutoring is also provided collaboratively through on-campus or off-campus services via trained peer tutors.

Diagnostic Testing Testing is provided through the program or unit for learning strategies, learning styles, and study skills. Testing for intelligence and neuropsychological is provided collaboratively through on-campus or off-campus services.

Basic Skills Remediation Remediation is offered one-on-one and in small groups for computer skills, learning strategies, math, reading, study skills, time management, and written language. Remediation is provided through the program or unit via computer-based instruction, LD specialists, professional tutors, and trained peer tutors. Remediation is also provided collaboratively through on-campus or off-campus services via trained peer tutors.

Enrichment Enrichment programs are available through the program or unit for learning strategies, math, oral communication skills, practical computer skills, reading, self-advocacy, stress management, study skills, test taking, time management, and written composition skills. Programs for career planning, health and nutrition, math, reading, study skills, test taking, time management, vocabulary development, and written composition skills are provided collaboratively through on-campus or off-campus services. Credit is offered for math, oral communication skills, practical computer skills, reading, stress management, study skills, test taking, time management, vocabulary development, and written composition skills.

Application For admittance to the program or unit, students are required to apply to the program directly, provide a psychoeducational report (3 years old or less), and provide documentation of high school services. Upon application, materials documenting need for services should be sent only to the LD program or unit. *Application deadline (LD program):* Rolling/continuous for fall and rolling/continuous for spring.

Written Policies Written policy regarding general/basic LD accommodations is available through the program or unit directly.

Middle Georgia Technical College

80 Cohen Walker Drive

Warner Robbins, GA 31088

http://middlegatech.edu

Contact: Mr. Mark E. Jones, Special Needs Coordinator. Phone: 478-988-6800 Ext. 4013. Fax: 478-988-6813. E-mail: mjones@middlegatech.edu.

Approximately 150 registered undergraduate students were served during 2006–07. The program or unit includes 1 part-time staff member. Academic advisers, counselors, professional tutors, regular education teachers, and remediation/learning specialists are provided collaboratively through on-campus or off-campus services.

Unique Aids and Services Aids, services, or accommodations include career counseling and faculty training.

Assistive Technology Assistive technology is located in campus labs, various classrooms depending on the technology and includes digital textbooks/e-text, learning support software, and scanning. Technology training is provided to incoming students.

Subject-Area Tutoring Tutoring is offered one-on-one for some subjects. Tutoring is provided collaboratively through on-campus or off-campus services via computer-based instruction and professional tutors.

Diagnostic Testing Testing for auditory processing, handwriting, intelligence, learning strategies, learning styles, math, motor skills, neuropsychological, personality, reading, social skills, spelling, spoken language, study skills, visual processing, and written language is provided collaboratively through on-campus or off-campus services.

Basic Skills Remediation Remediation is offered one-on-one, in small groups, and in class-size groups for learning strategies, math, reading, spelling, study skills, time management, and written language. Remediation is provided collaboratively through on-campus or off-campus services via computer-based instruction, professional tutors, and regular education teachers.

Fees *Diagnostic Testing* fee is applicable.

Application For admittance to the program or unit, students are required to provide a psychoeducational report and provide full evaluation/assessment with diagnoses. It is recommended that students provide documentation of high school services. Upon application, materials documenting need for services should be sent only to the LD program or unit. Upon acceptance, documentation of need for services should be sent only to the LD program or unit. *Application deadline (LD program):* Rolling/continuous for fall and rolling/continuous for spring.

Written Policies Written policies regarding general/basic LD accommodations, substitutions and waivers of admissions requirements, and substitutions and waivers of graduation requirements are outlined in the school's catalog/handbook. Written policies regarding general/basic LD accommodations and substitutions and waivers of admissions requirements are available through the program or unit directly.

Middlesex Community College

100 Training Hill Road

Middletown, CT 06457-4889

http://www.mxcc.commnet.edu/

Contact: Mrs. Diane von Hardenberg, Learning Specialist. Phone: 860-343-5879. Fax: 860-343-5735. E-mail: dvonhardenberg@mxcc.commnet.edu.

Approximately 125 registered undergraduate students were served during 2006–07. The program or unit includes 1 part-time staff member. LD specialists, remediation/learning specialists, and trained peer tutors are provided through the program or unit. Academic advisers and counselors are provided collaboratively through on-campus or off-campus services.

Unique Aids and Services Aids, services, or accommodations include advocates, career counseling, faculty training, priority registration, and support groups.

Subject-Area Tutoring Tutoring is offered one-on-one and in small groups for most subjects. Tutoring is provided through the program or unit via LD specialists. Tutoring is also provided collaboratively through on-campus or off-campus services via computer-based instruction and trained peer tutors.

Basic Skills Remediation Remediation is offered one-on-one for learning strategies, social skills, spoken language, study skills, time management, and written language. Remediation is provided through the program or unit via LD specialists.

Enrichment Enrichment programs are available through the program or unit for learning strategies, self-advocacy, stress management, study skills, test taking, and time management. Programs for career planning, math, reading, and written composition skills are provided collaboratively through on-campus or off-campus services.

Application For admittance to the program or unit, students are required to provide a psychoeducational report (5 years old or less). It is recommended that students provide documentation of high school services. Upon application, materials documenting need for services should be sent only to the LD program or unit. Upon acceptance, documentation of need for services should be sent only to the LD program or unit. *Application deadline (institutional):* Continuous.

Middlesex Community College (continued)

Written Policies Written policy regarding general/basic LD accommodations is outlined in the school's catalog/handbook. Written policy regarding general/basic LD accommodations is available through the program or unit directly.

Middlesex Community College
Disability Support Services

Springs Road

Bedford, MA 01730-1655

http://www.middlesex.mass.edu/DisabilitySupport/

Contact: Ms. Susan B. Woods, Director, Disability Support Services & The Transition Program. Phone: 781-280-3641. Fax: 781-275-7126. E-mail: woodss@middlesex.mass.edu.

Disability Support Services Approximately 730 registered undergraduate students were served during 2006–07. The program or unit includes 3 full-time and 3 part-time staff members. Academic advisers, counselors, LD specialists, professional tutors, remediation/learning specialists, skill tutors, and strategy tutors are provided through the program or unit. Academic advisers, counselors, diagnostic specialists, professional tutors, regular education teachers, remediation/learning specialists, skill tutors, and strategy tutors are provided collaboratively through on-campus or off-campus services.
Summer Program To help prepare for the demands of college, there is an optional 1-week summer program prior to entering the school.
Unique Aids and Services Aids, services, or accommodations include advocates, career counseling, faculty training, and weekly meetings with faculty.
Assistive Technology Assistive technology is located in campus labs, the DSS office and includes digital textbooks/e-text.
Subject-Area Tutoring Tutoring is offered one-on-one, in small groups, and in class-size groups for most subjects. Tutoring is provided through the program or unit via LD specialists. Tutoring is also provided collaboratively through on-campus or off-campus services via computer-based instruction, professional tutors, and trained peer tutors.
Basic Skills Remediation Remediation is offered in class-size groups for auditory processing, computer skills, learning strategies, math, motor skills, reading, social skills, spelling, spoken language, study skills, time management, visual processing, and written language. Remediation is provided through the program or unit via LD specialists. Remediation is also provided collaboratively through on-campus or off-campus services via computer-based instruction, LD specialists, professional tutors, regular education teachers, and other.
Enrichment Enrichment programs are available through the program or unit for career planning, college survival skills, learning strategies, oral communication skills, reading, self-advocacy, stress management, study skills, test taking, time management, vocabulary development, written composition skills, and other. Programs for career planning, college survival skills, health and nutrition, learning strategies, math, medication management, oral communication skills, practical computer skills, reading, self-advocacy, stress

management, study skills, test taking, time management, vocabulary development, written composition skills, and other are provided collaboratively through on-campus or off-campus services.
Application For admittance to the program or unit, students are required to apply to the program directly and provide a psychoeducational report (3 years old or less). It is recommended that students provide documentation of high school services. Upon application, materials documenting need for services should be sent only to the LD program or unit. *Application deadline (LD program):* Rolling/continuous for fall.
Written Policies Written policies regarding general/basic LD accommodations and reduced course loads are available through the program or unit directly.

Midland College
Students with Disabilities Office

3600 North Garfield

Midland, TX 79705-6399

http://www.midland.edu/

Contact: Mr. Dale Edward Williams, Counselor/Disability Specialist. Phone: 915-685-5598. Fax: 915-685-4623. E-mail: dewilliams@midland.edu.

Students with Disabilities Office Approximately 30 registered undergraduate students were served during 2006–07. The program or unit includes 1 full-time staff member. Academic advisers, counselors, and skill tutors are provided through the program or unit.
Unique Aids and Services Aids, services, or accommodations include career counseling, priority registration, and weekly meetings with faculty.
Assistive Technology Assistive technology is located in the DSS office and includes digital textbooks/e-text.
Subject-Area Tutoring Tutoring is offered one-on-one for all subjects. Tutoring is provided through the program or unit via graduate assistants/students and trained peer tutors.
Basic Skills Remediation Remediation is offered one-on-one and in class-size groups for math, reading, spelling, study skills, and time management. Remediation is provided collaboratively through on-campus or off-campus services via regular education teachers.
Enrichment Enrichment programs are available through the program or unit for career planning, college survival skills, learning strategies, math, reading, stress management, study skills, test taking, and time management.
Application For admittance to the program or unit, students are required to provide a psychoeducational report (5 years old or less). Upon application, materials documenting need for services should be sent only to the LD program or unit. Upon acceptance, documentation of need for services should be sent only to the LD program or unit. *Application deadline (institutional):* Continuous. *Application deadline (LD program):* Rolling/continuous for fall and rolling/continuous for spring.
Written Policies Written policy regarding general/basic LD accommodations is available on the program Web site. Written policy regarding general/basic LD accommodations is outlined in the school's catalog/handbook. Written policies regarding course substitutions, general/basic LD accommodations, grade forgiveness,

reduced course loads, substitutions and waivers of admissions requirements, and substitutions and waivers of graduation requirements are available through the program or unit directly.

Mid Michigan Community College
Disability Services

1375 South Clare Avenue
Harrison, MI 48625-9447
http://www.midmich.cc.mi.us/

Contact: Ms. Susan M. Cobb, Special Populations Coordinator/Counselor. Phone: 989-386-6636. Fax: 989-386-2411. E-mail: scobb@midmich.edu.

Disability Services Approximately 40 registered undergraduate students were served during 2006–07. The program or unit includes 1 full-time and 3 part-time staff members. Counselors are provided through the program or unit. Academic advisers, professional tutors, remediation/learning specialists, skill tutors, and trained peer tutors are provided collaboratively through on-campus or off-campus services.

Orientation The program or unit offers an optional orientation for new students individually by special arrangement.

Unique Aids and Services Aids, services, or accommodations include advocates and career counseling.

Assistive Technology Assistive technology is located in campus labs and includes digital textbooks/e-text.

Subject-Area Tutoring Tutoring is offered one-on-one and in small groups for most subjects. Tutoring is provided collaboratively through on-campus or off-campus services via computer-based instruction, professional tutors, and trained peer tutors.

Diagnostic Testing Testing for learning strategies, learning styles, math, personality, and reading is provided collaboratively through on-campus or off-campus services.

Basic Skills Remediation Remediation is offered in small groups for computer skills, math, reading, study skills, time management, and written language. Remediation is provided collaboratively through on-campus or off-campus services via computer-based instruction, regular education teachers, and trained peer tutors.

Enrichment Programs for career planning, learning strategies, math, practical computer skills, reading, stress management, study skills, test taking, time management, and written composition skills are provided collaboratively through on-campus or off-campus services. Credit is offered for math, practical computer skills, reading, stress management, and written composition skills.

Application For admittance to the program or unit, students are required to apply to the program directly and provide a psychoeducational report (3 years old or less). It is recommended that students provide documentation of high school services. Upon application, materials documenting need for services should be sent only to the LD program or unit. Upon acceptance, documentation of need for services should be sent only to the LD program or unit. *Application deadline (LD program):* 6/1 for fall. 11/1 for spring.

Written Policies Written policy regarding general/basic LD accommodations is available on the program Web site. Written policy regarding general/basic LD accommodations is outlined in the school's catalog/handbook.

Mid-South Community College
Office of Student Disability Services

2000 West Broadway
West Memphis, AR 72301
http://www.midsouthcc.edu

Contact: Miss Elise May, Student Disability Counselor. Phone: 870-733-6829. E-mail: emay@midsouthcc.edu. Head of LD Program: Ms. Dorothy Gautreaux, Dean of Learning Support. Phone: 870-733-6770. Fax: 870-733-6719. E-mail: dgautreaux@midsouthcc.edu.

Office of Student Disability Services Approximately 40 registered undergraduate students were served during 2006–07. The program or unit includes 2 part-time staff members. Academic advisers, coaches, counselors, remediation/learning specialists, skill tutors, and other are provided collaboratively through on-campus or off-campus services.

Unique Aids and Services Aids, services, or accommodations include faculty training and personal coach.

Assistive Technology Assistive technology is located in campus labs and includes digital textbooks/e-text and learning support software. Technology training is provided to incoming students.

Subject-Area Tutoring Tutoring is offered one-on-one, in small groups, and in class-size groups for most subjects. Tutoring is provided collaboratively through on-campus or off-campus services via computer-based instruction, professional tutors, and trained peer tutors.

Diagnostic Testing Testing for learning strategies, learning styles, reading, study skills, and written language is provided collaboratively through on-campus or off-campus services.

Basic Skills Remediation Remediation is offered in small groups and in class-size groups for math, reading, and written language. Remediation is provided collaboratively through on-campus or off-campus services via computer-based instruction, regular education teachers, and trained peer tutors.

Enrichment Programs for career planning, college survival skills, health and nutrition, learning strategies, math, oral communication skills, practical computer skills, reading, self-advocacy, stress management, study skills, test taking, time management, and written composition skills are provided collaboratively through on-campus or off-campus services. Credit is offered for college survival skills, learning strategies, math, oral communication skills, practical computer skills, reading, study skills, and written composition skills.

Fees *Diagnostic Testing* fee is $5.

Application For admittance to the program or unit, students are required to apply to the program directly and provide a psychoeducational report (5 years old or less). It is recommended that students provide documentation of high school services. Upon application, materials documenting need for services should be sent only to the LD program or unit. Upon acceptance, documentation of need for services should be sent only to the LD program or unit. *Application deadline (institutional):* Continuous. *Application deadline (LD program):* 8/25 for fall. 1/22 for spring.

Written Policies Written policies regarding course substitutions, general/basic LD accommodations, grade forgiveness, reduced course loads, substitutions and waivers of admissions requirements, and substitutions and waivers of graduation requirements are available on the program Web site. Written policies regarding course substi-

Mid-South Community College (continued)
tutions, general/basic LD accommodations, grade forgiveness, reduced course loads, substitutions and waivers of admissions requirements, and substitutions and waivers of graduation requirements are outlined in the school's catalog/handbook. Written policy regarding general/basic LD accommodations is available through the program or unit directly.

Mineral Area College
ACCESS Office

PO Box 1000

Park Hills, MO 63601-1000

http://www.mineralarea.edu/students/studentResources/
disabilitySupportServices.aspx

Contact: Ms. Lisa Leftridge, ACCESS Director. Phone: 573-518-2152. E-mail: lleftrid@mineralarea.edu.

ACCESS Office Approximately 25 registered undergraduate students were served during 2006–07. The program or unit includes 1 full-time and 1 part-time staff member. Academic advisers and graduate assistants/students are provided through the program or unit. Academic advisers, counselors, diagnostic specialists, graduate assistants/students, professional tutors, regular education teachers, and trained peer tutors are provided collaboratively through on-campus or off-campus services.
Unique Aids and Services Aids, services, or accommodations include career counseling, out-of-class testing, readers or writers for tests.
Assistive Technology Assistive technology is located in the DSS office and includes scanning. Technology training is provided to incoming students.
Subject-Area Tutoring Tutoring is offered one-on-one and in small groups for some subjects. Tutoring is provided collaboratively through on-campus or off-campus services via professional tutors, trained peer tutors, and other.
Basic Skills Remediation Remediation is offered one-on-one for math, reading, study skills, and written language. Remediation is provided collaboratively through on-campus or off-campus services via professional tutors and regular education teachers.
Enrichment Enrichment programs are available through the program or unit for learning strategies, self-advocacy, stress management, study skills, test taking, time management, and other. Programs for career planning, college survival skills, health and nutrition, learning strategies, math, medication management, oral communication skills, practical computer skills, reading, vocabulary development, and written composition skills are provided collaboratively through on-campus or off-campus services. Credit is offered for career planning, college survival skills, oral communication skills, and practical computer skills.
Application For admittance to the program or unit, students are required to apply to the program directly and provide a psychoeducational report (5 years old or less). It is recommended that students provide documentation of high school services and provide updated evaluation with adult norms. Upon application, materials documenting need for services should be sent only to the LD program or unit. Upon acceptance, documentation of need for services should be sent only to the LD program or unit.

Written Policies Written policy regarding general/basic LD accommodations is available on the program Web site. Written policies regarding general/basic LD accommodations and substitutions and waivers of graduation requirements are outlined in the school's catalog/handbook. Written policy regarding general/basic LD accommodations is available through the program or unit directly.

Minnesota School of Business–St. Cloud

1201 2nd Street South

Waite Park, MN 56387

http://www.msbcollege.edu/

Contact: Mr. Erik Engberg, Dean of Students. Phone: 320-257-2040. Fax: 320-257-0131. E-mail: eengberg@ msbcollege.edu.

Approximately 6 registered undergraduate students were served during 2006–07. The program or unit includes 1 full-time staff member. Academic advisers, regular education teachers, and other are provided collaboratively through on-campus or off-campus services.
Assistive Technology Assistive technology includes audio books.
Subject-Area Tutoring Tutoring is offered one-on-one and in small groups for all subjects. Tutoring is provided through the program or unit via trained peer tutors and other.
Basic Skills Remediation Remediation is offered in class-size groups for math, reading, and written language. Remediation is provided through the program or unit via regular education teachers.
Application For admittance to the program or unit, students are required to apply to the program directly. It is recommended that students provide a psychoeducational report (4 years old or less) and provide documentation of high school services. Upon application, materials documenting need for services should be sent only to the LD program or unit. Upon acceptance, documentation of need for services should be sent only to the LD program or unit. *Application deadline (institutional):* 10/6. *Application deadline (LD program):* Rolling/continuous for fall and rolling/continuous for spring.
Written Policies Written policies regarding general/basic LD accommodations and substitutions and waivers of admissions requirements are outlined in the school's catalog/handbook. Written policies regarding general/basic LD accommodations and substitutions and waivers of admissions requirements are available through the program or unit directly.

Minnesota State College– Southeast Technical
Learning Resource Center

1250 Homer Road, PO Box 409

Winona, MN 55987

http://www.southeastmn.edu/ss/disableStudent.html

Contact: Mr. Steve Zmyewski, Director of Learning Resources. Phone: 507-453-2410. Fax: 507-453-2715. E-mail: szmyewski@southeastmn.edu.

Learning Resource Center Approximately 20 registered undergraduate students were served during 2006–07. The program or unit includes 1 full-time and 6 part-time staff members. LD specialists, professional tutors, skill tutors, and trained peer tutors are provided through the program or unit. Academic advisers, counselors, LD specialists, regular education teachers, and remediation/learning specialists are provided collaboratively through on-campus or off-campus services.

Orientation The program or unit offers an optional orientation for new students before registration, before classes begin, during summer prior to enrollment, and individually by special arrangement.

Unique Aids and Services Aids, services, or accommodations include advocates, career counseling, priority registration, and weekly meetings with faculty.

Subject-Area Tutoring Tutoring is offered one-on-one and in small groups for all subjects. Tutoring is provided through the program or unit via LD specialists, professional tutors, and trained peer tutors. Tutoring is also provided collaboratively through on-campus or off-campus services via LD specialists and trained peer tutors.

Basic Skills Remediation Remediation is offered one-on-one and in small groups for computer skills, learning strategies, math, reading, spelling, and written language. Remediation is provided through the program or unit via LD specialists, professional tutors, and trained peer tutors. Remediation is also provided collaboratively through on-campus or off-campus services via LD specialists, regular education teachers, and trained peer tutors.

Enrichment Enrichment programs are available through the program or unit for math, oral communication skills, practical computer skills, reading, vocabulary development, and written composition skills. Programs for career planning, college survival skills, health and nutrition, learning strategies, self-advocacy, stress management, study skills, test taking, and time management are provided collaboratively through on-campus or off-campus services.

Application For admittance to the program or unit, students are required to provide a psychoeducational report (2 years old or less). It is recommended that students apply to the program directly, provide documentation of high school services, and provide physiological evaluations. Upon application, materials documenting need for services should be sent only to admissions with institutional application materials. Upon acceptance, documentation of need for services should be sent only to admissions. *Application deadline (institutional):* Continuous. *Application deadline (LD program):* Rolling/continuous for fall and rolling/continuous for spring.

Written Policies Written policies regarding course substitutions, general/basic LD accommodations, and substitutions and waivers of admissions requirements are available on the program Web site. Written policies regarding course substitutions, general/basic LD accommodations, and substitutions and waivers of admissions requirements are outlined in the school's catalog/handbook.

Minnesota State Community and Technical College–Wadena
Learning Services Center
405 Colfax Avenue, SW
PO Box 566
Wadena, MN 56482
http://www.minnesota.edu/
Contact: Michael F. Heino, Learning Services Coordinator. Phone: 218-631-7870 Ext. 7870. Fax: 218-631-7901. E-mail: mike.heino@minnesota.edu.

Learning Services Center Approximately 25 registered undergraduate students were served during 2006–07. The program or unit includes 1 full-time and 1 part-time staff member. Professional tutors, remediation/learning specialists, skill tutors, and strategy tutors are provided through the program or unit. Counselors, LD specialists, regular education teachers, and remediation/learning specialists are provided collaboratively through on-campus or off-campus services.

Unique Aids and Services Aids, services, or accommodations include advocates, career counseling, and priority registration.

Assistive Technology Assistive technology is located in campus labs, the DSS office and includes digital textbooks/e-text and scanning.

Subject-Area Tutoring Tutoring is offered one-on-one, in small groups, and in class-size groups for all subjects. Tutoring is provided through the program or unit via computer-based instruction and professional tutors.

Diagnostic Testing Testing is provided through the program or unit for math, reading, and written language. Testing for math, reading, and written language is provided collaboratively through on-campus or off-campus services.

Basic Skills Remediation Remediation is offered one-on-one, in small groups, and in class-size groups for learning strategies, math, reading, spelling, study skills, time management, and written language. Remediation is provided through the program or unit via computer-based instruction, professional tutors, and regular education teachers. Remediation is also provided collaboratively through on-campus or off-campus services via computer-based instruction and regular education teachers.

Enrichment Enrichment programs are available through the program or unit for career planning, college survival skills, math, practical computer skills, self-advocacy, stress management, study skills, test taking, time management, and written composition skills. Programs for career planning, health and nutrition, reading, self-advocacy, stress management, test taking, time management, and vocabulary development are provided collaboratively through on-campus or off-campus services.

Student Organization Student Senate consists of 15 members.

Application For admittance to the program or unit, students are required to provide documentation of high school services. It is recommended that students provide a psychoeducational report (3 years old or less). Upon application, materials documenting need for services should be sent to both admissions and the LD program or unit. Upon acceptance, documentation of need for services should be sent only to the LD program or unit. *Application deadline (LD program):* Rolling/continuous for fall and rolling/continuous for spring.

Minnesota State Community and Technical College–Wadena (continued)

Written Policies Written policies regarding course substitutions and general/basic LD accommodations are outlined in the school's catalog/handbook. Written policies regarding general/basic LD accommodations and reduced course loads are available through the program or unit directly.

MiraCosta College
Disabled Students Programs and Services

One Barnard Drive

Oceanside, CA 92056-3899

http://www.miracosta.edu/studentservices/dsps

Contact: Ms. Nancy Klump Schaefer, Learning Disabilities Specialist. Phone: 760-795-6658. Fax: 760-795-6604. E-mail: nschaefer@miracosta.edu. Head of LD Program: Ms. Connie Wilbur, DSPS Coordinator. Phone: 760-795-6658. Fax: 760-795-6604. E-mail: cwilbur@miracosta.edu.

Disabled Students Programs and Services Approximately 250 registered undergraduate students were served during 2006–07. The program or unit includes 7 full-time staff members and 1 part-time staff member. Academic advisers, counselors, diagnostic specialists, LD specialists, remediation/learning specialists, and special education teachers are provided through the program or unit. Academic advisers, counselors, professional tutors, regular education teachers, and trained peer tutors are provided collaboratively through on-campus or off-campus services.

Orientation The program or unit offers an optional orientation for new students individually by special arrangement.

Unique Aids and Services Aids, services, or accommodations include career counseling, priority registration, and support groups.

Assistive Technology Assistive technology is located in campus labs, a special lab and includes digital textbooks/e-text and scanning. Technology training is provided to incoming students.

Subject-Area Tutoring Tutoring is offered one-on-one and in small groups for most subjects. Tutoring is provided collaboratively through on-campus or off-campus services via computer-based instruction, graduate assistants/students, and trained peer tutors.

Diagnostic Testing Testing is provided through the program or unit for auditory processing, intelligence, learning strategies, learning styles, math, reading, spelling, study skills, visual processing, and written language.

Basic Skills Remediation Remediation is offered in class-size groups for computer skills, learning strategies, math, reading, study skills, time management, and written language. Remediation is provided through the program or unit via LD specialists, special education teachers, and trained peer tutors. Remediation is also provided collaboratively through on-campus or off-campus services via computer-based instruction, regular education teachers, and trained peer tutors.

Enrichment Enrichment programs are available through the program or unit for practical computer skills. Programs for career planning, college survival skills, health and nutrition, learning strategies, math, oral communication skills, practical computer skills, reading, study skills, and written composition skills are provided collaboratively through on-campus or off-campus services. Credit is offered for career planning, college survival skills, health and nutrition, learning strategies, math, oral communication skills, practical computer skills, reading, study skills, and written composition skills.

Fees *LD Program or Service* fee is $10 (fee varies according to course level). *Diagnostic Testing* fee is $10.

Application For admittance to the program or unit, students are required to apply to the program directly, provide a psychoeducational report (3 years old or less), and provide documentation of high school services. Upon application, materials documenting need for services should be sent only to the LD program or unit. Upon acceptance, documentation of need for services should be sent only to the LD program or unit. *Application deadline (institutional):* Continuous. *Application deadline (LD program):* Rolling/continuous for fall and rolling/continuous for spring.

Written Policies Written policies regarding course substitutions, general/basic LD accommodations, and substitutions and waivers of graduation requirements are available on the program Web site. Written policies regarding course substitutions, general/basic LD accommodations, and substitutions and waivers of graduation requirements are outlined in the school's catalog/handbook. Written policies regarding course substitutions, general/basic LD accommodations, reduced course loads, and substitutions and waivers of graduation requirements are available through the program or unit directly.

Missouri State University– West Plains
Student Advisement & Academic Support Center

128 Garfield

West Plains, MO 65775

http://www.wp.missouristate.edu

Contact: Mrs. Janice F. Johnson, Student Advisement & Academic Support Coordinator. Phone: 417-255-7943. Fax: 417-255-7974. E-mail: janicejohnson@missouristate.edu.

Student Advisement & Academic Support Center Approximately 25 registered undergraduate students were served during 2006–07. The program or unit includes 4 full-time and 8 part-time staff members. Academic advisers, diagnostic specialists, LD specialists, remediation/learning specialists, skill tutors, strategy tutors, and trained peer tutors are provided through the program or unit. Academic advisers, coaches, and regular education teachers are provided collaboratively through on-campus or off-campus services.

Subject-Area Tutoring Tutoring is offered in small groups for some subjects. Tutoring is provided through the program or unit via computer-based instruction and trained peer tutors. Tutoring is also provided collaboratively through on-campus or off-campus services via computer-based instruction, trained peer tutors, and other.

Diagnostic Testing Testing for auditory processing, handwriting, intelligence, learning strategies, learning styles, math, motor skills, neuropsychological, personality, reading, social skills, spelling, spoken language, study skills, visual processing, and written language is provided collaboratively through on-campus or off-campus services.

Basic Skills Remediation Remediation is offered one-on-one for auditory processing, reading, study skills, time management, and visual processing. Remediation is provided through the program or unit via computer-based instruction and professional tutors.

Fees *Diagnostic Testing* fee is $0 to $700.

Application For admittance to the program or unit, students are required to apply to the program directly and provide a psychoeducational report (3 years old or less). It is recommended that students provide documentation of high school services and provide documentation from a psychologist. Upon application, materials documenting need for services should be sent only to the LD program or unit. Upon acceptance, documentation of need for services should be sent only to the LD program or unit. *Application deadline (institutional):* Continuous. *Application deadline (LD program):* Rolling/continuous for fall.

Written Policies Written policy regarding general/basic LD accommodations is available on the program Web site. Written policy regarding general/basic LD accommodations is outlined in the school's catalog/handbook.

Mohawk Valley Community College
Office for Services to Students with Disabilities

1101 Sherman Drive

Utica, NY 13501-5394

http://www.mvcc.edu/students/disabilities/index.cfm

Contact: Ms. Tasha Peterson, Learning Disabilities Specialist. Phone: 315-731-5702. Fax: 315-731-5868. E-mail: vcandeloro@mvcc.edu. Head of LD Program: Ms. Lynn Igoe, Coordinator of Office for Services to Students with Disabilities. Phone: 315-792-5423. Fax: 315-731-5868. E-mail: ligoe@mvcc.edu.

Office for Services to Students with Disabilities Approximately 220 registered undergraduate students were served during 2006–07. The program or unit includes 1 full-time and 2 part-time staff members. LD specialists are provided through the program or unit. Academic advisers, counselors, and professional tutors are provided collaboratively through on-campus or off-campus services.

Orientation The program or unit offers an optional 5- to 6-hour orientation for new students before classes begin.

Unique Aids and Services Aids, services, or accommodations include priority registration and support groups.

Assistive Technology Assistive technology is located in campus labs, the DSS office and includes digital textbooks/e-text, learning support software, scanning, and reading, and voice command software. Technology training is provided to incoming students.

Subject-Area Tutoring Tutoring is offered one-on-one and in small groups for most subjects. Tutoring is provided collaboratively through on-campus or off-campus services via computer-based instruction, professional tutors, and trained peer tutors.

Basic Skills Remediation Remediation is offered in class-size groups for handwriting, math, reading, study skills, time management, and written language. Remediation is provided collaboratively through on-campus or off-campus services via professional tutors and trained peer tutors.

Application For admittance to the program or unit, students are required to provide a psychoeducational report and provide documentation of high school services. Upon application, materials documenting need for services should be sent only to the LD program or

unit. Upon acceptance, documentation of need for services should be sent only to the LD program or unit. *Application deadline (institutional):* Continuous. *Application deadline (LD program):* Rolling/continuous for fall and rolling/continuous for spring.

Written Policies Written policies regarding course substitutions, general/basic LD accommodations, grade forgiveness, reduced course loads, substitutions and waivers of admissions requirements, and substitutions and waivers of graduation requirements are outlined in the school's catalog/handbook. Written policies regarding course substitutions, general/basic LD accommodations, grade forgiveness, reduced course loads, substitutions and waivers of admissions requirements, and substitutions and waivers of graduation requirements are available through the program or unit directly.

Montana State University– Great Falls College of Technology
Disability Services

2100 16th Avenue, South

Great Falls, MT 59405

http://www.msugf.edu/studentlife/DisabilityServices

Contact: Jill M. Davis, Director of Disability and Learning Support Services. Phone: 406-771-4311. Fax: 406-771-4342. E-mail: jdavis@msugf.edu.

Disability Services Approximately 45 registered undergraduate students were served during 2006–07. The program or unit includes 1 full-time staff member. Counselors, diagnostic specialists, and strategy tutors are provided through the program or unit. Academic advisers, counselors, professional tutors, regular education teachers, remediation/learning specialists, skill tutors, and trained peer tutors are provided collaboratively through on-campus or off-campus services.

Unique Aids and Services Aids, services, or accommodations include faculty training.

Assistive Technology Assistive technology is located in campus labs, the Learning Center and includes digital textbooks/e-text, learning support software, scanning, and voice recognition software, screen readers. Technology training is provided to incoming students.

Subject-Area Tutoring Tutoring is offered one-on-one for most subjects. Tutoring is provided through the program or unit via LD specialists. Tutoring is also provided collaboratively through on-campus or off-campus services via computer-based instruction, professional tutors, and trained peer tutors.

Basic Skills Remediation Remediation is offered in class-size groups for math, reading, study skills, time management, and written language. Remediation is provided collaboratively through on-campus or off-campus services via regular education teachers and trained peer tutors.

Enrichment Enrichment programs are available through the program or unit for college survival skills, learning strategies, practical computer skills, self-advocacy, stress management, study skills, test taking, and time management. Programs for career planning, college survival skills, learning strategies, math, practical computer skills, reading, stress management, study skills, test taking, time management, and written composition skills are provided collabo-

Montana State University–Great Falls College of Technology (continued)

ratively through on-campus or off-campus services. Credit is offered for college survival skills, learning strategies, math, practical computer skills, reading, stress management, study skills, test taking, time management, and written composition skills.

Application For admittance to the program or unit, students are required to apply to the program directly and provide a psychoeducational report (3 years old or less). It is recommended that students provide documentation of high school services. Upon application, materials documenting need for services should be sent only to the LD program or unit. Upon acceptance, documentation of need for services should be sent only to the LD program or unit. *Application deadline (LD program):* Rolling/continuous for fall and rolling/continuous for spring.

Written Policies Written policies regarding course substitutions, general/basic LD accommodations, and substitutions and waivers of graduation requirements are available on the program Web site. Written policies regarding course substitutions, general/basic LD accommodations, and substitutions and waivers of graduation requirements are outlined in the school's catalog/handbook.

Moorpark College
ACCESS (Accessibility Coordination Center and Educational Support Services)

7075 Campus Road

Moorpark, CA 93021-1695

http://www.moorparkcollege.edu/access/

Contact: Ms. Melanie Masters, LD Specialist. Phone: 805-378-1461. Fax: 805-378-1598. E-mail: mmasters@vcccd.net. Head of LD Program: Ms. Sherry D'Attile, Director. Phone: 805-378-1513. Fax: 805-378-1594. E-mail: sdattile@vcccd.edu.

ACCESS (Accessibility Coordination Center and Educational Support Services) Approximately 400 registered undergraduate students were served during 2006–07. The program or unit includes 12 full-time and 3 part-time staff members. Academic advisers, counselors, diagnostic specialists, graduate assistants/students, LD specialists, professional tutors, remediation/learning specialists, and special education teachers are provided through the program or unit. Academic advisers, counselors, diagnostic specialists, graduate assistants/students, LD specialists, professional tutors, regular education teachers, remediation/learning specialists, skill tutors, special education teachers, and trained peer tutors are provided collaboratively through on-campus or off-campus services.

Orientation The program or unit offers a mandatory 1- to 2-hour orientation for new students before registration, before classes begin, during summer prior to enrollment, and individually by special arrangement.

Summer Program To help prepare for the demands of college, there is an optional 4-week summer program prior to entering the school that focuses on study skills, test-taking skills, and time management. Degree credit will be earned. The program accepts students from out-of-state and is available to students attending other colleges.

Unique Aids and Services Aids, services, or accommodations include advocates, career counseling, faculty training, priority registration, support groups, and weekly meetings with faculty.

Assistive Technology Assistive technology is located in campus labs, the DSS office, a special lab and includes digital textbooks/e-text, learning support software, and scanning. Technology training is provided to incoming students.

Subject-Area Tutoring Tutoring is offered in small groups for some subjects. Tutoring is provided through the program or unit via LD specialists and professional tutors. Tutoring is also provided collaboratively through on-campus or off-campus services via computer-based instruction, graduate assistants/students, and professional tutors.

Diagnostic Testing Testing is provided through the program or unit for auditory processing, intelligence, learning strategies, learning styles, math, motor skills, neuropsychological, reading, spelling, spoken language, study skills, visual processing, and written language. Testing for math and written language is provided collaboratively through on-campus or off-campus services.

Basic Skills Remediation Remediation is offered in small groups and in class-size groups for auditory processing, computer skills, learning strategies, math, reading, study skills, time management, visual processing, and written language. Remediation is provided through the program or unit via computer-based instruction, LD specialists, and special education teachers. Remediation is also provided collaboratively through on-campus or off-campus services via computer-based instruction and regular education teachers.

Enrichment Enrichment programs are available through the program or unit for career planning, college survival skills, health and nutrition, learning strategies, math, practical computer skills, reading, self-advocacy, stress management, study skills, test taking, time management, vocabulary development, and written composition skills. Programs for career planning, college survival skills, health and nutrition, learning strategies, math, oral communication skills, practical computer skills, reading, stress management, study skills, test taking, time management, vocabulary development, and written composition skills are provided collaboratively through on-campus or off-campus services. Credit is offered for career planning, college survival skills, health and nutrition, learning strategies, math, practical computer skills, reading, stress management, study skills, test taking, time management, vocabulary development, and written composition skills.

Fees *Diagnostic Testing* fee is $20.

Application For admittance to the program or unit, students are required to apply to the program directly. It is recommended that students provide a psychoeducational report (3 years old or less) and provide documentation of high school services. Upon application, materials documenting need for services should be sent only to the LD program or unit. Upon acceptance, documentation of need for services should be sent only to the LD program or unit. *Application deadline (institutional):* Continuous. *Application deadline (LD program):* Rolling/continuous for fall and rolling/continuous for spring.

Written Policies Written policies regarding course substitutions, general/basic LD accommodations, and substitutions and waivers of graduation requirements are available on the program Web site. Written policies regarding course substitutions, general/basic LD accommodations, and substitutions and waivers of graduation requirements are outlined in the school's catalog/handbook. Written policies regarding general/basic LD accommodations and reduced course loads are available through the program or unit directly.

Morton College

3801 South Central Avenue

Cicero, IL 60804-4398

http://www.morton.edu/

Contact: Ms. Christine T. Martin, Academic Advisor (for students with Special Needs). Phone: 708-656-8000 Ext. 153. Fax: 708-656-9592. E-mail: christine.martin@ morton.edu. Head of LD Program: Ms. Lizette Urbina, Director of Student Development. Phone: 708-656-8000 Ext. 151. Fax: 708-656-9592. E-mail: lizette.urbina@morton.edu.

Approximately 70 registered undergraduate students were served during 2006–07. The program or unit includes 2 full-time staff members. Academic advisers, diagnostic specialists, professional tutors, and regular education teachers are provided collaboratively through on-campus or off-campus services.
Unique Aids and Services Aids, services, or accommodations include career counseling.
Assistive Technology Assistive technology is located in Academic Adviser's Office and includes learning support software.
Subject-Area Tutoring Tutoring is offered one-on-one and in small groups for some subjects. Tutoring is provided collaboratively through on-campus or off-campus services via computer-based instruction and professional tutors.
Basic Skills Remediation Remediation is offered one-on-one and in small groups for computer skills, learning strategies, math, reading, spoken language, study skills, time management, and written language. Remediation is provided collaboratively through on-campus or off-campus services via computer-based instruction and professional tutors.
Enrichment Programs for career planning, college survival skills, learning strategies, math, reading, stress management, study skills, test taking, time management, and written composition skills are provided collaboratively through on-campus or off-campus services. Credit is offered for career planning.
Application For admittance to the program or unit, students are required to provide documentation of high school services. It is recommended that students provide a psychoeducational report (3 years old or less). Upon application, materials documenting need for services should be sent only to the LD program or unit. Upon acceptance, documentation of need for services should be sent only to the LD program or unit. *Application deadline (institutional):* Continuous. *Application deadline (LD program):* Rolling/continuous for fall and rolling/continuous for spring.
Written Policies Written policy regarding general/basic LD accommodations is available on the program Web site. Written policy regarding general/basic LD accommodations is outlined in the school's catalog/handbook. Written policies regarding general/basic LD accommodations and reduced course loads are available through the program or unit directly.

Mountain Empire Community College
Student Services

PO Drawer 700

Big Stone Gap, VA 24219-0700

http://www.mecc.edu

Contact: Ms. Lisa Butcher, Director of Student Services. Phone: 276-523-2400 Ext. 251. Fax: 276-523-8297. E-mail: lbutcher@me.vccs.edu.

Student Services Approximately 10 registered undergraduate students were served during 2006–07. Services are provided through the program or unit. Services are provided collaboratively through on-campus or off-campus services.
Subject-Area Tutoring Tutoring is offered one-on-one and in small groups for most subjects. Tutoring is provided collaboratively through on-campus or off-campus services via trained peer tutors.
Basic Skills Remediation Remediation is offered in class-size groups for math, reading, and spelling. Remediation is provided collaboratively through on-campus or off-campus services via regular education teachers.
Application For admittance to the program or unit, students are required to apply to the program directly and provide testing results that led to diagnosis. It is recommended that students provide a psychoeducational report (3 years old or less) and provide documentation of high school services. Upon application, materials documenting need for services should be sent only to the LD program or unit. Upon acceptance, documentation of need for services should be sent to both admissions and the LD program or unit. *Application deadline (LD program):* Rolling/continuous for fall and rolling/continuous for spring.
Written Policies Written policy regarding general/basic LD accommodations is available on the program Web site. Written policy regarding general/basic LD accommodations is outlined in the school's catalog/handbook.

Muscatine Community College
Disability Services

152 Colorado Street

Muscatine, IA 52761-5396

http://www.eicc.edu/

Contact: Kathryn Trosen, Disability Support Provider. Phone: 563-288-6013. Fax: 563-288-6104. E-mail: ktrosen@ eicc.edu.

Disability Services Approximately 50 registered undergraduate students were served during 2006–07. The program or unit includes 1 full-time staff member. LD specialists are provided through the program or unit. Academic advisers, regular education teachers, remediation/learning specialists, skill tutors, strategy tutors, and trained peer tutors are provided collaboratively through on-campus or off-campus services.

Muscatine Community College (continued)

Unique Aids and Services Aids, services, or accommodations include advocates, career counseling, faculty training, and priority registration.

Assistive Technology Assistive technology is located in campus labs and includes learning support software and scanning. Technology training is provided to incoming students.

Subject-Area Tutoring Tutoring is offered one-on-one for most subjects. Tutoring is provided through the program or unit via LD specialists. Tutoring is also provided collaboratively through on-campus or off-campus services via trained peer tutors.

Basic Skills Remediation Remediation is offered in class-size groups for learning strategies, math, reading, study skills, time management, and grammar/writing. Remediation is provided collaboratively through on-campus or off-campus services via regular education teachers and trained peer tutors.

Enrichment Programs for career planning, college survival skills, health and nutrition, learning strategies, practical computer skills, reading, study skills, test taking, and time management are provided collaboratively through on-campus or off-campus services. Credit is offered for career planning, college survival skills, health and nutrition, learning strategies, practical computer skills, reading, study skills, test taking, and time management.

Application For admittance to the program or unit, students are required to provide a psychoeducational report (5 years old or less). It is recommended that students provide documentation of high school services. Upon acceptance, documentation of need for services should be sent only to the LD program or unit. *Application deadline (institutional):* Continuous. *Application deadline (LD program):* Rolling/continuous for fall and rolling/continuous for spring.

Written Policies Written policies regarding course substitutions, general/basic LD accommodations, and substitutions and waivers of graduation requirements are available through the program or unit directly.

Nassau Community College
Center for Students with Disabilities

1 Education Drive

Garden City, NY 11530-6793

http://www.ncc.edu

Contact: Prof. Richard Ashker, Chairman, Student Personnel Services. Phone: 516-572-7241. Fax: 516-572-9874. E-mail: richard.ashker@ncc.edu.

Center for Students with Disabilities Approximately 543 registered undergraduate students were served during 2006–07. The program or unit includes 7 full-time and 2 part-time staff members. Academic advisers, counselors, LD specialists, professional tutors, remediation/learning specialists, skill tutors, special education teachers, strategy tutors, trained peer tutors, and other are provided through the program or unit. Professional tutors, regular education teachers, and remediation/learning specialists are provided collaboratively through on-campus or off-campus services.

Orientation The program or unit offers an optional 1-day orientation for new students during summer prior to enrollment.

Unique Aids and Services Aids, services, or accommodations include advocates, career counseling, faculty training, parent workshops, priority registration, and support groups.

Subject-Area Tutoring Tutoring is offered one-on-one and in small groups for some subjects. Tutoring is provided through the program or unit via computer-based instruction, LD specialists, professional tutors, trained peer tutors, and other. Tutoring is also provided collaboratively through on-campus or off-campus services via computer-based instruction.

Basic Skills Remediation Remediation is offered one-on-one and in small groups for computer skills, learning strategies, math, reading, social skills, study skills, time management, and written language. Remediation is provided through the program or unit via computer-based instruction, LD specialists, professional tutors, special education teachers, and trained peer tutors. Remediation is also provided collaboratively through on-campus or off-campus services via computer-based instruction and trained peer tutors.

Enrichment Enrichment programs are available through the program or unit for career planning, college survival skills, learning strategies, math, practical computer skills, reading, self-advocacy, study skills, test taking, time management, vocabulary development, and written composition skills. Programs for career planning, college survival skills, health and nutrition, learning strategies, math, practical computer skills, reading, stress management, study skills, test taking, time management, vocabulary development, and written composition skills are provided collaboratively through on-campus or off-campus services. Credit is offered for career planning, college survival skills, health and nutrition, practical computer skills, reading, vocabulary development, and written composition skills.

Student Organization Access Club consists of 45 members.

Application For admittance to the program or unit, students are required to provide a psychoeducational report (3 years old or less) and provide documentation of high school services. Upon acceptance, documentation of need for services should be sent only to the LD program or unit. *Application deadline (institutional):* 8/1. *Application deadline (LD program):* Rolling/continuous for fall and rolling/continuous for spring.

Written Policies Written policy regarding general/basic LD accommodations is available through the program or unit directly.

New Hampshire Community Technical College, Nashua/Claremont

505 Amherst Street

Nashua, NH 03063-1026

http://www.ncctc.edu/

Contact: Mary Oswald, Disability Coordinator. Phone: 603-882-6923 Ext. 1451. Fax: 603-882-8690. E-mail: moswald@nhctc.edu.

Approximately 37 registered undergraduate students were served during 2006–07. The program or unit includes 1 full-time staff member. Academic advisers and LD specialists are provided through the program or unit.

Subject-Area Tutoring Tutoring is offered one-on-one and in small groups for some subjects. Tutoring is provided through the program or unit via computer-based instruction, professional tutors, and trained peer tutors.

Application For admittance to the program or unit, students are required to apply to the program directly and provide a psychoeducational report (3 years old or less). It is recommended that students provide documentation of high school services. Upon application, materials documenting need for services should be sent only to the LD program or unit. Upon acceptance, documentation of need for services should be sent only to the LD program or unit. *Application deadline (institutional):* Continuous. *Application deadline (LD program):* Rolling/continuous for fall and rolling/continuous for spring.

Written Policies Written policy regarding general/basic LD accommodations is available on the program Web site. Written policy regarding general/basic LD accommodations is available through the program or unit directly.

New Mexico Junior College
Special Needs Services

5317 Lovington Highway

Hobbs, NM 88240-9123

http://www.nmjc.edu

Contact: Kristine L. Saucer, Counselor/Special Needs Coordinator. Phone: 505-492-2576. Fax: 505-392-0322. E-mail: ksaucer@nmjc.edu.

Special Needs Services Approximately 50 registered undergraduate students were served during 2006–07. The program or unit includes 1 full-time staff member. Academic advisers, counselors, LD specialists, strategy tutors, and other are provided through the program or unit. Academic advisers, coaches, diagnostic specialists, graduate assistants/students, LD specialists, professional tutors, regular education teachers, remediation/learning specialists, skill tutors, strategy tutors, trained peer tutors, and other are provided collaboratively through on-campus or off-campus services.

Unique Aids and Services Aids, services, or accommodations include career counseling, priority registration, and weekly meetings with faculty.

Assistive Technology Assistive technology is located in campus labs, the individual student's computer and includes digital textbooks/e-text, learning support software, and scanning. Technology training is provided to incoming students.

Basic Skills Remediation Remediation is offered in class-size groups for auditory processing, computer skills, handwriting, learning strategies, math, motor skills, reading, spelling, spoken language, study skills, time management, visual processing, and written language. Remediation is provided collaboratively through on-campus or off-campus services via computer-based instruction, professional tutors, and regular education teachers.

Enrichment Enrichment programs are available through the program or unit for career planning, learning strategies, math, oral communication skills, reading, self-advocacy, stress management, study skills, test taking, and time management. Programs for career planning, college survival skills, health and nutrition, learning strategies, math, medication management, oral communication skills, practical computer skills, reading, self-advocacy, stress management, study skills, test taking, time management, vocabulary development, and written composition skills are provided collaboratively through on-campus or off-campus services.

Application For admittance to the program or unit, students are required to apply to the program directly. It is recommended that students provide a psychoeducational report (10 years old or less) and provide documentation of high school services. Upon application, materials documenting need for services should be sent only to the LD program or unit. Upon acceptance, documentation of need for services should be sent only to the LD program or unit. *Application deadline (institutional):* Continuous. *Application deadline (LD program):* Rolling/continuous for fall and rolling/continuous for spring.

Written Policies Written policy regarding general/basic LD accommodations is outlined in the school's catalog/handbook. Written policies regarding course substitutions, general/basic LD accommodations, grade forgiveness, substitutions and waivers of admissions requirements, and substitutions and waivers of graduation requirements are available through the program or unit directly.

New River Community College
LEAP Center

PO Box 1127

Dublin, VA 24084-1127

http://www.nr.cc.va.us/

Contact: Ms. Jeananne F. Dixon, Coordinator. Phone: 540-674-3600 Ext. 4358. Fax: 540-674-3644. E-mail: nrdixoj@nr.edu.

LEAP Center Approximately 150 registered undergraduate students were served during 2006–07. The program or unit includes 1 full-time and 1 part-time staff member. Academic advisers, counselors, graduate assistants/students, and LD specialists are provided through the program or unit. Coaches, diagnostic specialists, professional tutors, skill tutors, strategy tutors, and trained peer tutors are provided collaboratively through on-campus or off-campus services.

Summer Program To help prepare for the demands of college, there is an optional half-day and/or 3-day/2-night summer program prior to entering the school.

Unique Aids and Services Aids, services, or accommodations include career counseling, priority registration, and support groups.

Assistive Technology Assistive technology is located in the DSS office and includes digital textbooks/e-text, learning support software, and scanning. Technology training is provided to incoming students.

Subject-Area Tutoring Tutoring is offered one-on-one and in small groups for most subjects. Tutoring is provided through the program or unit via LD specialists. Tutoring is also provided collaboratively through on-campus or off-campus services via computer-based instruction, LD specialists, professional tutors, and trained peer tutors.

Basic Skills Remediation Remediation is offered in class-size groups for computer skills, learning strategies, math, reading, study skills, time management, visual processing, and written language. Remediation is provided collaboratively through on-campus or off-campus services via computer-based instruction, professional tutors, teacher trainees, and trained peer tutors.

New River Community College (continued)

Enrichment Enrichment programs are available through the program or unit for learning strategies, medication management, self-advocacy, stress management, study skills, test taking, and time management. Programs for career planning, college survival skills, math, practical computer skills, and reading are provided collaboratively through on-campus or off-campus services. Credit is offered for health and nutrition, oral communication skills, vocabulary development, and written composition skills.

Student Organization Leap consists of 30 members.

Application For admittance to the program or unit, students are required to apply to the program directly, provide a psychoeducational report (3 years old or less), and provide documentation of high school services. Upon application, materials documenting need for services should be sent only to the LD program or unit. Upon acceptance, documentation of need for services should be sent only to the LD program or unit. *Application deadline (institutional):* Continuous. *Application deadline (LD program):* Rolling/continuous for fall and rolling/continuous for spring.

Written Policies Written policies regarding course substitutions, general/basic LD accommodations, reduced course loads, and substitutions and waivers of admissions requirements are available on the program Web site. Written policies regarding course substitutions, general/basic LD accommodations, reduced course loads, and substitutions and waivers of admissions requirements are available through the program or unit directly.

New York City College of Technology of the City University of New York

300 Jay Street
Brooklyn, NY 11201-2983
http://www.citytech.cuny.edu/

Contact: Ms. Faith Fogelman, Director of Student Support. Phone: 718-260-5143. Fax: 718-254-8539. E-mail: ffogelman@citytech.cuny.edu.

The program or unit includes 5 full-time and 10 part-time staff members. Academic advisers, counselors, diagnostic specialists, professional tutors, remediation/learning specialists, and skill tutors are provided through the program or unit. Diagnostic specialists are provided collaboratively through on-campus or off-campus services.

Orientation The program or unit offers an optional 1-day orientation for new students after classes begin.

Summer Program To help prepare for the demands of college, there is an optional 3-month summer program prior to entering the school available to high school graduates that focuses on computing skills and specific subject tutoring. Degree credit will be earned. The program accepts students from out-of-state.

Unique Aids and Services Aids, services, or accommodations include career counseling and priority registration.

Assistive Technology Assistive technology is located in the DSS office and includes digital textbooks/e-text and scanning. Technology training is provided to incoming students.

Subject-Area Tutoring Tutoring is offered one-on-one and in small groups for some subjects. Tutoring is provided through the program or unit via computer-based instruction, LD specialists, and

professional tutors. Tutoring is also provided collaboratively through on-campus or off-campus services via computer-based instruction, LD specialists, and professional tutors.

Basic Skills Remediation Remediation is offered one-on-one and in small groups for math, reading, and written language. Remediation is provided through the program or unit via LD specialists. Remediation is also provided collaboratively through on-campus or off-campus services via regular education teachers.

Enrichment Enrichment programs are available through the program or unit for career planning, college survival skills, learning strategies, math, practical computer skills, reading, self-advocacy, stress management, study skills, test taking, time management, and written composition skills. Programs for career planning, college survival skills, learning strategies, math, oral communication skills, practical computer skills, reading, vocabulary development, and written composition skills are provided collaboratively through on-campus or off-campus services. Credit is offered for math, oral communication skills, reading, vocabulary development, and written composition skills.

Application For admittance to the program or unit, students are required to apply to the program directly and provide documentation of high school services. It is recommended that students provide a psychoeducational report (3 years old or less). Upon application, materials documenting need for services should be sent only to the LD program or unit. Upon acceptance, documentation of need for services should be sent only to the LD program or unit. *Application deadline (institutional):* 3/15. *Application deadline (LD program):* 12/15 for fall. 5/15 for spring.

Written Policies Written policy regarding general/basic LD accommodations is available on the program Web site. Written policy regarding general/basic LD accommodations is outlined in the school's catalog/handbook. Written policy regarding general/basic LD accommodations is available through the program or unit directly.

North Central Missouri College
Disability Services

1301 Main Street
Trenton, MO 64683-1824
http://www.ncmissouri.edu/

Contact: Linda Flentje, Counselor. Phone: 660-359-3948 Ext. 404. Fax: 660-359-2211. E-mail: lflentje@mail.ncmissouri.edu.

Disability Services Approximately 15 registered undergraduate students were served during 2006–07. The program or unit includes 1 part-time staff member. Counselors and professional tutors are provided through the program or unit.

Unique Aids and Services Aids, services, or accommodations include priority registration.

Assistive Technology Assistive technology is located in various locations as needed and includes CCTV, adaptive keyboards. Technology training is provided to incoming students.

Subject-Area Tutoring Tutoring is offered in small groups for most subjects. Tutoring is provided collaboratively through on-campus or off-campus services via professional tutors and trained peer tutors.

Basic Skills Remediation Remediation is offered in class-size groups for math, reading, and written language. Remediation is provided collaboratively through on-campus or off-campus services via regular education teachers.

Application It is recommended that students provide documentation of high school services. Upon application, materials documenting need for services should be sent only to the LD program or unit. Upon acceptance, documentation of need for services should be sent only to the LD program or unit. *Application deadline (institutional):* Continuous. *Application deadline (LD program):* Rolling/continuous for fall.

Written Policies Written policy regarding general/basic LD accommodations is available on the program Web site. Written policy regarding general/basic LD accommodations is outlined in the school's catalog/handbook. Written policies regarding course substitutions, grade forgiveness, reduced course loads, substitutions and waivers of admissions requirements, and substitutions and waivers of graduation requirements are available through the program or unit directly.

North Central State College
Office of Specialized Supportive Services

2441 Kenwood Circle, PO Box 698

Mansfield, OH 44901-0698

http://www.ncstatecollege.edu/

Contact: Mrs. Sandra Luckie, Coordinator of Specialized Supportive Services. Phone: 419-755-4727. Fax: 419-755-4750. E-mail: sluckie@ncstatecollege.edu.

Office of Specialized Supportive Services Approximately 100 registered undergraduate students were served during 2006–07. The program or unit includes 1 full-time and 1 part-time staff member. Services are provided through the program or unit. Academic advisers, trained peer tutors, and other are provided collaboratively through on-campus or off-campus services.

Assistive Technology Assistive technology is located in campus labs, the DSS office and includes digital textbooks/e-text, learning support software, and scanning.

Subject-Area Tutoring Tutoring is offered one-on-one, in small groups, and in class-size groups for some subjects. Tutoring is provided collaboratively through on-campus or off-campus services via trained peer tutors and other.

Basic Skills Remediation Remediation is offered in class-size groups for computer skills, learning strategies, math, reading, study skills, time management, and written language. Remediation is provided collaboratively through on-campus or off-campus services.

Application For admittance to the program or unit, students are required to provide a psychoeducational report (3 years old or less) and provide multi-factored team report. It is recommended that students provide documentation of high school services. Upon application, materials documenting need for services should be sent only to the LD program or unit. Upon acceptance, documentation of need for services should be sent only to the LD program or unit. *Application deadline (LD program):* Rolling/continuous for fall and rolling/continuous for spring.

Written Policies Written policy regarding general/basic LD accommodations is available on the program Web site. Written policy regarding general/basic LD accommodations is outlined in the school's catalog/handbook. Written policy regarding general/basic LD accommodations is available through the program or unit directly.

North Central Texas College
Academic and Student Support Services

1525 West California Street

Gainesville, TX 76240-4699

http://www.nctc.edu

Contact: Ms. Robin Truhe, ACCESS Department Coordinator. Phone: 940-498-6207. Fax: 940-497-8000. E-mail: rtruhe@nctc.edu.

Academic and Student Support Services Approximately 125 registered undergraduate students were served during 2006–07. The program or unit includes 3 full-time and 10 part-time staff members. Counselors, LD specialists, professional tutors, and trained peer tutors are provided through the program or unit. Counselors, professional tutors, and trained peer tutors are provided collaboratively through on-campus or off-campus services.

Orientation The program or unit offers a mandatory orientation for new students individually by special arrangement.

Unique Aids and Services Aids, services, or accommodations include advocates, career counseling, faculty training, priority registration, and weekly meetings with faculty.

Assistive Technology Assistive technology is located in a special lab and includes digital textbooks/e-text, learning support software, and scanning.

Subject-Area Tutoring Tutoring is offered one-on-one, in small groups, and in class-size groups for most subjects. Tutoring is provided through the program or unit via graduate assistants/students, professional tutors, and trained peer tutors. Tutoring is also provided collaboratively through on-campus or off-campus services via graduate assistants/students, professional tutors, and trained peer tutors.

Basic Skills Remediation Remediation is offered in class-size groups for math, reading, spelling, and study skills. Remediation is provided through the program or unit via professional tutors and regular education teachers. Remediation is also provided collaboratively through on-campus or off-campus services via professional tutors and regular education teachers.

Enrichment Enrichment programs are available through the program or unit for career planning. Programs for career planning, college survival skills, stress management, test taking, and time management are provided collaboratively through on-campus or off-campus services.

Application For admittance to the program or unit, students are required to apply to the program directly. It is recommended that students provide a psychoeducational report (3 years old or less). Upon application, materials documenting need for services should be sent only to the LD program or unit. Upon acceptance, documentation of need for services should be sent only to the LD program or unit. *Application deadline (institutional):* Continuous.

North Central Texas College (continued)

Written Policies Written policies regarding general/basic LD accommodations and reduced course loads are available on the program Web site. Written policies regarding general/basic LD accommodations and reduced course loads are outlined in the school's catalog/handbook.

Northeast Kansas Technical College
Learning Resource Center

1501 West Riley Street

Atchison, KS 66002

http://www.nektc.net/

Contact: Ms. Phyllis J. Schrader, Learning Resource Coordinator. Phone: 913-367-6204. Fax: 913-367-3107. E-mail: pschrader@nekatech.net.

Learning Resource Center Approximately 125 registered undergraduate students were served during 2006–07. The program or unit includes 1 full-time and 1 part-time staff member. Academic advisers, counselors, and remediation/learning specialists are provided through the program or unit. Academic advisers, counselors, and remediation/learning specialists are provided collaboratively through on-campus or off-campus services.

Summer Program available to rising sophomores, rising juniors, rising seniors, high school graduates.

Unique Aids and Services Aids, services, or accommodations include career counseling.

Assistive Technology Assistive technology is located in campus labs, a special lab and includes learning support software.

Subject-Area Tutoring Tutoring is provided collaboratively through on-campus or off-campus services via computer-based instruction and other.

Diagnostic Testing Testing for handwriting, learning strategies, learning styles, math, reading, and written language is provided collaboratively through on-campus or off-campus services.

Basic Skills Remediation Remediation is offered one-on-one, in small groups, and in class-size groups for math, reading, study skills, time management, and written language. Remediation is provided collaboratively through on-campus or off-campus services via computer-based instruction, regular education teachers, and special education teachers.

Enrichment Credit is offered for college survival skills, math, oral communication skills, practical computer skills, reading, stress management, study skills, test taking, time management, vocabulary development, and written composition skills.

Application It is recommended that students provide a psychoeducational report (5 years old or less) and provide documentation of high school services. Upon application, materials documenting need for services should be sent to both admissions and the LD program or unit. Upon acceptance, documentation of need for services should be sent to both admissions and the LD program or unit.

Written Policies Written policies regarding general/basic LD accommodations and substitutions and waivers of admissions requirements are outlined in the school's catalog/handbook.

North Florida Community College
Student Disability Services

1000 Turner Davis Drive

Madison, FL 32340-1602

http://www.nfcc.edu/

Contact: Ms. Stevie Fenton, Coordinator, Disability Services. Phone: 850-973-9484 Ext. V. E-mail: fentons@nfcc.edu.

Student Disability Services Approximately 25 registered undergraduate students were served during 2006–07. The program or unit includes 2 full-time staff members and 1 part-time staff member. Academic advisers, counselors, diagnostic specialists, professional tutors, regular education teachers, skill tutors, and strategy tutors are provided collaboratively through on-campus or off-campus services.

Orientation The program or unit offers an optional orientation for new students before classes begin.

Unique Aids and Services Aids, services, or accommodations include personal coach, priority registration, and weekly meetings with faculty.

Assistive Technology Assistive technology is located in the DSS office and includes digital textbooks/e-text, learning support software, and scanning. Technology training is provided to incoming students.

Basic Skills Remediation Remediation is offered one-on-one for computer skills, learning strategies, study skills, time management, and organizational skills. Remediation is provided through the program or unit via computer-based instruction, trained peer tutors, and other.

Enrichment Enrichment programs are available through the program or unit for learning strategies, self-advocacy, stress management, study skills, test taking, and time management. Programs for career planning, college survival skills, learning strategies, oral communication skills, practical computer skills, reading, study skills, and test taking are provided collaboratively through on-campus or off-campus services. Credit is offered for college survival skills, learning strategies, oral communication skills, practical computer skills, reading, and study skills.

Application For admittance to the program or unit, students are required to apply to the program directly and provide a psychoeducational report (5 years old or less). It is recommended that students provide documentation of high school services and provide reports from specialized training with learning specialists, counselors, and other service providers. Upon application, materials documenting need for services should be sent only to the LD program or unit. Upon acceptance, documentation of need for services should be sent only to the LD program or unit. *Application deadline (LD program):* Rolling/continuous for fall and rolling/continuous for spring.

Written Policies Written policies regarding course substitutions, general/basic LD accommodations, substitutions and waivers of admissions requirements, and substitutions and waivers of graduation requirements are available on the program Web site. Written policies regarding course substitutions, general/basic LD accommodations, substitutions and waivers of admissions requirements, and substitutions and waivers of graduation requirements are outlined in the school's catalog/handbook. Written policies regarding course substitutions, general/basic LD accommodations, grade forgiveness, reduced course loads, substitutions and waivers of admissions requirements, and substitutions and waivers of graduation requirements are available through the program or unit directly.

Northland Community and Technical College–Thief River Falls
The Learning Center

1101 Highway One East

Thief River Falls, MN 56701

http://www.northlandcollege.edu

Contact: Mr. Dean L. Dalen, Director of the Learning Center. Phone: 218-681-0835. Fax: 218-681-0811. E-mail: dean.dalen@northlandcollege.edu.

The Learning Center Approximately 30 registered undergraduate students were served during 2006–07. The program or unit includes 5 full-time staff members. Professional tutors, remediation/learning specialists, skill tutors, and trained peer tutors are provided through the program or unit.

Orientation The program or unit offers an optional orientation for new students individually by special arrangement.

Assistive Technology Assistive technology is located in the DSS office and includes digital textbooks/e-text. Technology training is provided to incoming students.

Subject-Area Tutoring Tutoring is offered one-on-one and in small groups for most subjects. Tutoring is provided through the program or unit via computer-based instruction, graduate assistants/students, professional tutors, and trained peer tutors. Tutoring is also provided collaboratively through on-campus or off-campus services via computer-based instruction and graduate assistants/students.

Basic Skills Remediation Remediation is offered one-on-one, in small groups, and in class-size groups for computer skills, learning strategies, math, reading, spelling, spoken language, study skills, time management, and written language. Remediation is provided through the program or unit via computer-based instruction, graduate assistants/students, professional tutors, and trained peer tutors. Remediation is also provided collaboratively through on-campus or off-campus services via computer-based instruction, graduate assistants/students, regular education teachers, and trained peer tutors.

Enrichment Enrichment programs are available through the program or unit for college survival skills, learning strategies, math, oral communication skills, practical computer skills, reading, self-advocacy, study skills, test taking, time management, vocabulary development, and written composition skills. Programs for career planning and health and nutrition are provided collaboratively through on-campus or off-campus services. Credit is offered for college survival skills, learning strategies, math, oral communication skills, practical computer skills, reading, study skills, vocabulary development, and written composition skills.

Application It is recommended that students provide a psychoeducational report (5 years old or less) and provide documentation of high school services. Upon application, materials documenting need for services should be sent only to the LD program or unit. Upon acceptance, documentation of need for services should be sent only to the LD program or unit. *Application deadline (institutional):* 8/31. *Application deadline (LD program):* Rolling/continuous for fall and rolling/continuous for spring.

Written Policies Written policies regarding course substitutions, general/basic LD accommodations, reduced course loads, and substitutions and waivers of graduation requirements are available on the program Web site. Written policies regarding course substitutions, general/basic LD accommodations, reduced course loads, and substitutions and waivers of graduation requirements are outlined in the school's catalog/handbook. Written policy regarding reduced course loads is available through the program or unit directly.

North Metro Technical College
Disability Resources

5198 Ross Road

Acworth, GA 30102

http://www.northmetrotech.edu/disability.asp

Contact: Kim Duff, Disablity Counselor. Phone: 770-975-4099. Fax: 770-975-4142. E-mail: kduff@northmetrotech.edu. Head of LD Program: Cheri L. Mattox, Director of Student Support Services. Phone: 770-975-4152. Fax: 770-975-4142. E-mail: cmattox@northmetrotech.edu.

Disability Resources Approximately 100 registered undergraduate students were served during 2006–07. The program or unit includes 1 full-time staff member. Counselors are provided through the program or unit. Counselors are provided collaboratively through on-campus or off-campus services.

Orientation The program or unit offers an optional 1-hour orientation for new students before classes begin.

Unique Aids and Services Aids, services, or accommodations include advocates, career counseling, priority registration, one-on-one counseling services.

Assistive Technology Assistive technology is located in campus labs, the DSS office, individual classrooms and includes digital textbooks/e-text, learning support software, scanning, and dyslexia overlays, reading software.

Subject-Area Tutoring Tutoring is offered one-on-one and in small groups for some subjects. Tutoring is provided collaboratively through on-campus or off-campus services via computer-based instruction, graduate assistants/students, professional tutors, and trained peer tutors.

Diagnostic Testing Testing is provided through the program or unit for learning strategies and learning styles. Testing for learning strategies, learning styles, math, personality, reading, and written language is provided collaboratively through on-campus or off-campus services.

Basic Skills Remediation Remediation is offered in class-size groups for math, reading, and English. Remediation is provided collaboratively through on-campus or off-campus services via computer-based instruction and other.

Enrichment Enrichment programs are available through the program or unit for stress management, study skills, test taking, and time management. Programs for career planning, health and nutri-

North Metro Technical College (continued)

tion, learning strategies, stress management, study skills, test taking, and time management are provided collaboratively through on-campus or off-campus services.

Application For admittance to the program or unit, students are required to apply to the program directly and provide a psychoeducational report (3 years old or less). It is recommended that students provide documentation of high school services and provide vocational rehabilitation assessments. Upon application, materials documenting need for services should be sent only to the LD program or unit. *Application deadline (LD program):* Rolling/continuous for fall and rolling/continuous for spring.

Written Policies Written policy regarding general/basic LD accommodations is available on the program Web site. Written policy regarding general/basic LD accommodations is outlined in the school's catalog/handbook. Written policy regarding reduced course loads is available through the program or unit directly.

Northwestern Michigan College
Tutoring and Support Services

1701 East Front Street

Traverse City, MI 49686-3061

http://www.nmc.edu/tss

Contact: Ms. Denyse Everett, Disabilities Specialist. Phone: 231-995-1139. Fax: 231-995-1253. E-mail: deverett@nmc.edu.

Tutoring and Support Services Approximately 35 registered undergraduate students were served during 2006–07. The program or unit includes 3 full-time staff members. Services are provided through the program or unit.

Assistive Technology Assistive technology is located in campus labs, the DSS office. Technology training is provided to incoming students.

Subject-Area Tutoring Tutoring is offered in small groups for some subjects. Tutoring is provided collaboratively through on-campus or off-campus services via trained peer tutors.

Basic Skills Remediation Remediation is offered in class-size groups for math, reading, and written language. Remediation is provided collaboratively through on-campus or off-campus services via regular education teachers.

Enrichment Programs for career planning, learning strategies, math, oral communication skills, practical computer skills, reading, and written composition skills are provided collaboratively through on-campus or off-campus services. Credit is offered for career planning, learning strategies, oral communication skills, practical computer skills, reading, and written composition skills.

Application For admittance to the program or unit, students are required to provide a psychoeducational report (3 years old or less). It is recommended that students provide documentation of high school services. Upon application, materials documenting need for services should be sent only to the LD program or unit. Upon acceptance, documentation of need for services should be sent only to the LD program or unit. *Application deadline (LD program):* Rolling/continuous for fall and rolling/continuous for spring.

Written Policies Written policy regarding general/basic LD accommodations is available on the program Web site. Written policy regarding general/basic LD accommodations is outlined in the school's catalog/handbook. Written policy regarding general/basic LD accommodations is available through the program or unit directly.

Northwest State Community College
Accessibility Services

22-600 State Route 34

Archbold, OH 43502-9542

http://www.northweststate.edu/Web_pages/?id=20051028155215

Contact: Mr. Dave Donaldson, Accessibility Services. Phone: 419-267-1265. Fax: 419-267-3688. E-mail: ddonaldson@northweststate.edu.

Accessibility Services Approximately 115 registered undergraduate students were served during 2006–07. The program or unit includes 2 part-time staff members. Academic advisers, graduate assistants/students, regular education teachers, skill tutors, and strategy tutors are provided collaboratively through on-campus or off-campus services.

Assistive Technology Assistive technology includes digital textbooks/e-text and learning support software. Technology training is provided to incoming students.

Subject-Area Tutoring Tutoring is offered one-on-one, in small groups, and in class-size groups for most subjects. Tutoring is provided through the program or unit via computer-based instruction, professional tutors, and trained peer tutors. Tutoring is also provided collaboratively through on-campus or off-campus services via computer-based instruction, professional tutors, and trained peer tutors.

Basic Skills Remediation Remediation is offered one-on-one, in small groups, and in class-size groups for math, reading, spelling, and written language. Remediation is provided collaboratively through on-campus or off-campus services.

Enrichment Programs for career planning, college survival skills, health and nutrition, learning strategies, math, oral communication skills, practical computer skills, reading, stress management, study skills, test taking, time management, vocabulary development, and written composition skills are provided collaboratively through on-campus or off-campus services. Credit is offered for career planning, college survival skills, health and nutrition, learning strategies, math, oral communication skills, practical computer skills, reading, stress management, study skills, test taking, time management, vocabulary development, and written composition skills.

Application For admittance to the program or unit, students are required to apply to the program directly. It is recommended that students provide a psychoeducational report (3 years old or less) and provide documentation of high school services. Upon application, materials documenting need for services should be sent only to the LD program or unit. Upon acceptance, documentation of need for services should be sent only to the LD program or unit. *Application deadline (LD program):* 5/23 for fall. 9/15 for spring.

Written Policies Written policies regarding general/basic LD accommodations and grade forgiveness are outlined in the school's catalog/handbook. Written policy regarding general/basic LD accommodations is available through the program or unit directly.

Ocean County College
Disability Services/Project Academic Skills Support

College Drive, PO Box 2001

Toms River, NJ 08754-2001

http://www.ocean.edu/campus/student_services/drc/pass.htm

Contact: Ms. Judith Corby, Secretary. Phone: 732-255-0456. Fax: 732-255-0458. E-mail: jcorby@ocean.edu.

Disability Services/Project Academic Skills Support Approximately 385 registered undergraduate students were served during 2006–07. The program or unit includes 4 full-time staff members and 1 part-time staff member. Academic advisers, counselors, diagnostic specialists, LD specialists, professional tutors, regular education teachers, remediation/learning specialists, skill tutors, and strategy tutors are provided through the program or unit. Counselors, professional tutors, regular education teachers, remediation/learning specialists, skill tutors, and strategy tutors are provided collaboratively through on-campus or off-campus services.
Orientation The program or unit offers an optional 3-hour orientation for new students before classes begin.
Unique Aids and Services Aids, services, or accommodations include career counseling, faculty training, parent workshops, priority registration, and support groups.
Assistive Technology Assistive technology is located in the DSS office, a special lab and includes digital textbooks/e-text, learning support software, and scanning. Technology training is provided to incoming students.
Subject-Area Tutoring Tutoring is offered one-on-one for most subjects. Tutoring is provided through the program or unit via professional tutors.
Diagnostic Testing Testing is provided through the program or unit for auditory processing, intelligence, learning strategies, learning styles, math, reading, spelling, spoken language, study skills, visual processing, written language, and other services.
Basic Skills Remediation Remediation is offered one-on-one and in class-size groups for auditory processing, computer skills, learning strategies, math, reading, spoken language, study skills, time management, visual processing, and written language. Remediation is provided through the program or unit via computer-based instruction, LD specialists, professional tutors, and regular education teachers. Remediation is also provided collaboratively through on-campus or off-campus services via computer-based instruction, LD specialists, professional tutors, and regular education teachers.
Enrichment Enrichment programs are available through the program or unit for career planning, college survival skills, health and nutrition, learning strategies, math, oral communication skills, practical computer skills, reading, self-advocacy, stress management, study skills, test taking, time management, and written composition skills. Programs for career planning, college survival skills, health and nutrition, learning strategies, math, oral communication skills, practical computer skills, reading, self-advocacy, stress manage-

ment, study skills, test taking, time management, and written composition skills are provided collaboratively through on-campus or off-campus services. Credit is offered for career planning, college survival skills, health and nutrition, learning strategies, oral communication skills, self-advocacy, stress management, study skills, test taking, and time management.
Fees *Diagnostic Testing* fee is $575.
Application For admittance to the program or unit, students are required to provide a psychoeducational report (3 years old or less), provide documentation of high school services, and provide medical documentation if no IEP is available. Upon application, materials documenting need for services should be sent only to the LD program or unit. Upon acceptance, documentation of need for services should be sent only to the LD program or unit. *Application deadline (institutional):* Continuous. *Application deadline (LD program):* 7/15 for fall. 12/15 for spring.
Written Policies Written policy regarding general/basic LD accommodations is available on the program Web site. Written policy regarding general/basic LD accommodations is outlined in the school's catalog/handbook. Written policy regarding general/basic LD accommodations is available through the program or unit directly.

Odessa College
Student Development Center

201 West University Avenue

Odessa, TX 79764-7127

http://www.odessa.edu/dept/counseling/disabilities.htm

Contact: Ms. Becky Rivera Weiss, Enrollment Specialist. Phone: 432-335-6861. Fax: 432-335-6553. E-mail: brivera@odessa.edu. Head of LD Program: Ms. Martha Kunkel, Director of Counseling and Recruiting. Phone: 432-335-6346. Fax: 432-335-6553. E-mail: mkunkel@odessa.edu.

Student Development Center Approximately 50 registered undergraduate students were served during 2006–07. The program or unit includes 1 full-time staff member. Academic advisers, counselors, regular education teachers, trained peer tutors, and other are provided collaboratively through on-campus or off-campus services.
Unique Aids and Services Aids, services, or accommodations include career counseling, priority registration, copies of notes and handouts, tutoring and study management.
Assistive Technology Assistive technology is located in campus labs, a special lab and includes learning support software and sign language support, enlarged text support, books on tape.
Subject-Area Tutoring Tutoring is offered one-on-one, in small groups, and in class-size groups for all subjects. Tutoring is provided collaboratively through on-campus or off-campus services via computer-based instruction, trained peer tutors, and other.
Basic Skills Remediation Remediation is offered in class-size groups for math, reading, and written language. Remediation is provided collaboratively through on-campus or off-campus services via computer-based instruction, regular education teachers, and trained peer tutors.
Enrichment Programs for career planning, college survival skills, learning strategies, math, reading, stress management, study skills, test taking, and time management are provided collaboratively through on-campus or off-campus services.

Odessa College (continued)

Application For admittance to the program or unit, students are required to apply to the program directly, provide a psychoeducational report (3 years old or less), and provide documentation of high school services. Upon acceptance, documentation of need for services should be sent only to the LD program or unit. *Application deadline (institutional):* Continuous. *Application deadline (LD program):* Rolling/continuous for fall and rolling/continuous for spring.

Written Policies Written policy regarding general/basic LD accommodations is available on the program Web site. Written policy regarding general/basic LD accommodations is outlined in the school's catalog/handbook. Written policy regarding general/basic LD accommodations is available through the program or unit directly.

Ozarks Technical Community College
Disability Support Services

PO Box 5958

1001 East Chestnut Expressway

Springfield, MO 65801

http://www.otc.edu/

Contact: Ms. Julia M. Bunch, Assistant Dean, Disability Support Services. Phone: 417-447-8188. Fax: 417-447-8194. E-mail: bunchj@otc.edu.

Disability Support Services Approximately 350 registered undergraduate students were served during 2006–07. The program or unit includes 6 full-time and 2 part-time staff members. Counselors, remediation/learning specialists, and other are provided collaboratively through on-campus or off-campus services.

Unique Aids and Services Aids, services, or accommodations include advocates and career counseling.

Assistive Technology Assistive technology is located in the DSS office and includes digital textbooks/e-text, learning support software, and scanning. Technology training is provided to incoming students.

Subject-Area Tutoring Tutoring is offered one-on-one, in small groups, and in class-size groups for some subjects. Tutoring is provided collaboratively through on-campus or off-campus services via trained peer tutors.

Basic Skills Remediation Remediation is offered in class-size groups for learning strategies, math, reading, and written language. Remediation is provided collaboratively through on-campus or off-campus services via computer-based instruction and trained peer tutors.

Enrichment Programs for career planning, health and nutrition, learning strategies, math, reading, stress management, study skills, test taking, time management, vocabulary development, and written composition skills are provided collaboratively through on-campus or off-campus services. Credit is offered for health and nutrition, math, and reading.

Application For admittance to the program or unit, students are required to provide documentation of high school services. It is recommended that students provide a psychoeducational report (3 years old or less). Upon application, materials documenting need for services should be sent only to the LD program or unit. Upon

acceptance, documentation of need for services should be sent only to the LD program or unit. *Application deadline (LD program):* Rolling/continuous for fall and rolling/continuous for spring.

Written Policies Written policies regarding general/basic LD accommodations and substitutions and waivers of admissions requirements are available on the program Web site. Written policies regarding general/basic LD accommodations and substitutions and waivers of admissions requirements are outlined in the school's catalog/handbook.

Paris Junior College
Counseling/Advising Office

2400 Clarksville Street

Paris, TX 75460-6298

http://www.parisjc.edu/

Contact: Ms. Barbara O. Thomas, Director of Counseling/Advising. Phone: 903-782-0426. Fax: 903-782-0796. E-mail: bthomas@parisjc.edu.

Counseling/Advising Office Approximately 25 registered undergraduate students were served during 2006–07. The program or unit includes 2 part-time staff members. Academic advisers, counselors, and trained peer tutors are provided through the program or unit. Academic advisers and counselors are provided collaboratively through on-campus or off-campus services.

Unique Aids and Services Aids, services, or accommodations include career counseling and faculty training.

Assistive Technology Assistive technology is located in campus labs, the DSS office and includes digital textbooks/e-text, learning support software, and scanning.

Subject-Area Tutoring Tutoring is offered one-on-one and in small groups for most subjects. Tutoring is provided through the program or unit via trained peer tutors. Tutoring is also provided collaboratively through on-campus or off-campus services via computer-based instruction.

Basic Skills Remediation Remediation is offered in class-size groups for learning strategies, math, reading, study skills, and written language. Remediation is provided collaboratively through on-campus or off-campus services via computer-based instruction, professional tutors, and regular education teachers.

Enrichment Programs for career planning, learning strategies, math, reading, study skills, and written composition skills are provided collaboratively through on-campus or off-campus services.

Application For admittance to the program or unit, students are required to apply to the program directly and provide a psychoeducational report. It is recommended that students provide documentation of high school services. Upon application, materials documenting need for services should be sent only to the LD program or unit. Upon acceptance, documentation of need for services should be sent only to the LD program or unit. *Application deadline (institutional):* Continuous. *Application deadline (LD program):* Rolling/continuous for fall and rolling/continuous for spring.

Written Policies Written policies regarding general/basic LD accommodations and substitutions and waivers of admissions requirements are available on the program Web site. Written policies regarding general/basic LD accommodations and substitutions and waivers of admissions requirements are outlined in the school's catalog/handbook. Written policies regarding course substitutions, general/basic LD accommodations, reduced course loads, and substitutions and waivers of graduation requirements are available through the program or unit directly.

Penn State DuBois
Office of Disability Services, Learning Center

College Place
DuBois, PA 15801-3199
http://www.equity.psu.edu/ods

Contact: Diana Kreydt, Coordinator of Disability Services. Phone: 814-372-3037. Fax: 814-372-3039. E-mail: dlk34@psu.edu.

Office of Disability Services, Learning Center Approximately 20 registered undergraduate students were served during 2006–07. The program or unit includes 1 full-time and 5 part-time staff members. Academic advisers, counselors, LD specialists, professional tutors, remediation/learning specialists, skill tutors, strategy tutors, and trained peer tutors are provided through the program or unit. Academic advisers, counselors, diagnostic specialists, graduate assistants/students, LD specialists, professional tutors, regular education teachers, remediation/learning specialists, skill tutors, strategy tutors, and trained peer tutors are provided collaboratively through on-campus or off-campus services.

Orientation The program or unit offers an optional 1-day orientation for new students before classes begin, during summer prior to enrollment, after classes begin, and individually by special arrangement.

Unique Aids and Services Aids, services, or accommodations include faculty training, priority registration, weekly meetings with faculty.

Assistive Technology Assistive technology is located in a special lab and includes digital textbooks/e-text, learning support software, and scanning. Technology training is provided to incoming students.

Subject-Area Tutoring Tutoring is offered one-on-one, in small groups, and in class-size groups for most subjects. Tutoring is provided through the program or unit via computer-based instruction, LD specialists, professional tutors, and trained peer tutors. Tutoring is also provided collaboratively through on-campus or off-campus services via computer-based instruction, LD specialists, professional tutors, and trained peer tutors.

Basic Skills Remediation Remediation is offered one-on-one, in small groups, and in class-size groups for auditory processing, computer skills, handwriting, learning strategies, math, motor skills, reading, social skills, spelling, spoken language, study skills, time management, visual processing, and written language. Remediation is provided through the program or unit via computer-based instruction, LD specialists, professional tutors, regular education teachers, and trained peer tutors. Remediation is also provided collaboratively through on-campus or off-campus services via computer-based instruction, LD specialists, professional tutors, regular education teachers, and trained peer tutors.

Enrichment Enrichment programs are available through the program or unit for career planning, college survival skills, learning strategies, oral communication skills, reading, self-advocacy, stress management, study skills, test taking, and time management. Programs for career planning, college survival skills, health and nutrition, learning strategies, math, oral communication skills, reading, self-advocacy, stress management, study skills, test taking, time management, and written composition skills are provided collaboratively through on-campus or off-campus services.

Student Organization The Lion CUBS consists of 5 members.

Application For admittance to the program or unit, students are required to apply to the program directly and provide a psychoeducational report (3 years old or less). It is recommended that students provide documentation of high school services. Upon application, materials documenting need for services should be sent only to the LD program or unit. Upon acceptance, documentation of need for services should be sent only to the LD program or unit. *Application deadline (institutional):* Continuous. *Application deadline (LD program):* Rolling/continuous for fall and rolling/continuous for spring.

Written Policies Written policies regarding course substitutions, general/basic LD accommodations, grade forgiveness, reduced course loads, substitutions and waivers of admissions requirements, and substitutions and waivers of graduation requirements are available on the program Web site. Written policies regarding course substitutions, grade forgiveness, reduced course loads, substitutions and waivers of admissions requirements, and substitutions and waivers of graduation requirements are outlined in the school's catalog/handbook. Written policies regarding course substitutions, general/basic LD accommodations, reduced course loads, substitutions and waivers of admissions requirements, and substitutions and waivers of graduation requirements are available through the program or unit directly.

Penn State Fayette, The Eberly Campus
Disabled Student Services

1 University Drive, PO Box 519
Uniontown, PA 15401-0519
http://www.fe.psu.edu/

Contact: Tammy Henderson, Coordinator for Disability Services. Phone: 724-430-4531. Fax: 724-430-4184. E-mail: tlk196@psu.edu.

Disabled Student Services The program or unit includes 2 part-time staff members. Counselors and other are provided collaboratively through on-campus or off-campus services.

Unique Aids and Services Aids, services, or accommodations include faculty training.

Subject-Area Tutoring Tutoring is offered one-on-one for most subjects. Tutoring is provided collaboratively through on-campus or off-campus services via graduate assistants/students, professional tutors, and trained peer tutors.

Basic Skills Remediation Remediation is offered in class-size groups for learning strategies, math, study skills, time management, and written language. Remediation is provided collaboratively through on-campus or off-campus services via regular education teachers.

Application For admittance to the program or unit, students are required to provide documentation of high school services. Upon acceptance, documentation of need for services should be sent only

Penn State Fayette, The Eberly Campus (continued)
to the LD program or unit. *Application deadline (institutional):* Continuous. *Application deadline (LD program):* Rolling/continuous for fall and rolling/continuous for spring.
Written Policies Written policy regarding general/basic LD accommodations is outlined in the school's catalog/handbook.

Penn State Mont Alto
The Student Success Center

Campus Drive

Mont Alto, PA 17237-9703

http://www.ma.psu.edu/StudentServices/disabled.htm?cn265

Contact: Mr. Jack M. Ebersole, Director of Student Success. Phone: 717-749-6045. Fax: 717-749-6119. E-mail: jme25@psu.edu.

The Student Success Center Approximately 33 registered undergraduate students were served during 2006–07. The program or unit includes 1 full-time and 5 part-time staff members. LD specialists, professional tutors, skill tutors, strategy tutors, and trained peer tutors are provided through the program or unit.
Unique Aids and Services Aids, services, or accommodations include career counseling and priority registration.
Assistive Technology Assistive technology is located in campus labs, the DSS office and includes digital textbooks/e-text, learning support software, and scanning. Technology training is provided to incoming students.
Subject-Area Tutoring Tutoring is offered one-on-one, in small groups, and in class-size groups for most subjects. Tutoring is provided through the program or unit via computer-based instruction, LD specialists, professional tutors, and trained peer tutors. Tutoring is also provided collaboratively through on-campus or off-campus services via computer-based instruction, professional tutors, and trained peer tutors.
Basic Skills Remediation Remediation is offered one-on-one and in small groups for computer skills, learning strategies, math, reading, spelling, study skills, time management, and written language. Remediation is provided through the program or unit via computer-based instruction, LD specialists, and professional tutors. Remediation is also provided collaboratively through on-campus or off-campus services via computer-based instruction, professional tutors, and trained peer tutors.
Enrichment Enrichment programs are available through the program or unit for self-advocacy. Programs for career planning, college survival skills, health and nutrition, learning strategies, math, oral communication skills, practical computer skills, reading, stress management, study skills, test taking, time management, vocabulary development, and written composition skills are provided collaboratively through on-campus or off-campus services. Credit is offered for career planning, college survival skills, health and nutrition, math, oral communication skills, practical computer skills, reading, and written composition skills.
Application For admittance to the program or unit, students are required to provide a psychoeducational report (3 years old or less). It is recommended that students provide documentation of high school services. Upon acceptance, documentation of need for ser-

vices should be sent only to the LD program or unit. *Application deadline (institutional):* Continuous. *Application deadline (LD program):* Rolling/continuous for fall and rolling/continuous for spring.
Written Policies Written policies regarding course substitutions, general/basic LD accommodations, grade forgiveness, reduced course loads, substitutions and waivers of admissions requirements, and substitutions and waivers of graduation requirements are available on the program Web site. Written policy regarding general/basic LD accommodations is outlined in the school's catalog/handbook. Written policies regarding course substitutions, general/basic LD accommodations, grade forgiveness, reduced course loads, substitutions and waivers of admissions requirements, and substitutions and waivers of graduation requirements are available through the program or unit directly.

Penn State Wilkes-Barre
Learning Center

PO PSU

Lehman, PA 18627-0217

http://www.wb.psu.edu/StudentServices/

Contact: Ms. Walteen Grady Truely, Disability Contact Liaison. Phone: 570-675-9217. E-mail: wpt2@psu.edu.

Learning Center The program or unit includes 1 full-time and 1 part-time staff member. Academic advisers, coaches, professional tutors, remediation/learning specialists, skill tutors, and strategy tutors are provided collaboratively through on-campus or off-campus services.
Orientation The program or unit offers a mandatory orientation for new students individually by special arrangement.
Unique Aids and Services Aids, services, or accommodations include personal coach.
Assistive Technology Assistive technology is located in campus labs, a special lab, the library and includes learning support software and scanning.
Subject-Area Tutoring Tutoring is offered one-on-one and in small groups for most subjects. Tutoring is provided collaboratively through on-campus or off-campus services via computer-based instruction and professional tutors.
Basic Skills Remediation Remediation is offered one-on-one and in class-size groups for learning strategies, math, reading, study skills, and time management. Remediation is provided collaboratively through on-campus or off-campus services via computer-based instruction, professional tutors, and regular education teachers.
Enrichment Programs for career planning, college survival skills, health and nutrition, learning strategies, math, reading, stress management, study skills, test taking, time management, vocabulary development, and written composition skills are provided collaboratively through on-campus or off-campus services. Credit is offered for math, reading, stress management, and time management.
Application For admittance to the program or unit, students are required to provide a psychoeducational report (2 years old or less) and provide accommodations recommended by managing physician/clinician. It is recommended that students provide documentation of high school services. Upon acceptance, documentation of need for

services should be sent to both admissions and the LD program or unit. *Application deadline (institutional):* Continuous. *Application deadline (LD program):* Rolling/continuous for fall and rolling/continuous for spring.

Written Policies Written policy regarding general/basic LD accommodations is available on the program Web site.

Pensacola Junior College
Disability Support Services

1000 College Boulevard

Pensacola, FL 32504-8998

http://www.pjc.edu/

Contact: Dr. James L. Nickles, Director. Phone: 850-484-1637. Fax: 850-484-2049. E-mail: jnickles@pjc.edu.

Disability Support Services Approximately 450 registered undergraduate students were served during 2006–07. The program or unit includes 4 full-time and 2 part-time staff members. Academic advisers, counselors, and LD specialists are provided through the program or unit.

Summer Program To help prepare for the demands of college, there is an optional summer program prior to entering the school available to high school graduates. The program accepts students from out-of-state.

Unique Aids and Services Aids, services, or accommodations include career counseling and priority registration.

Assistive Technology Assistive technology is located in the DSS office and includes digital textbooks/e-text and scanning. Technology training is provided to incoming students.

Subject-Area Tutoring Tutoring is provided collaboratively through on-campus or off-campus services via computer-based instruction and trained peer tutors.

Application For admittance to the program or unit, students are required to apply to the program directly, provide a psychoeducational report, and provide documentation of high school services. Upon application, materials documenting need for services should be sent only to the LD program or unit. Upon acceptance, documentation of need for services should be sent only to the LD program or unit. *Application deadline (LD program):* Rolling/continuous for fall and rolling/continuous for spring.

Written Policies Written policy regarding general/basic LD accommodations is available on the program Web site. Written policies regarding course substitutions, grade forgiveness, reduced course loads, substitutions and waivers of admissions requirements, and substitutions and waivers of graduation requirements are outlined in the school's catalog/handbook.

Phoenix College
Disability Resource Center

1202 West Thomas Road

Phoenix, AZ 85013-4234

http://www.phoenixcollege.edu/drc

Contact: Mr. Gene W. Heppard, Manager, Disability Resource Center. Phone: 602-285-7477. Fax: 602-285-7663. E-mail: gene.heppard@pcmail.maricopa.edu.

Disability Resource Center Approximately 150 registered undergraduate students were served during 2006–07. The program or unit includes 3 full-time staff members. Academic advisers, counselors, diagnostic specialists, and LD specialists are provided through the program or unit. Coaches, graduate assistants/students, professional tutors, regular education teachers, remediation/learning specialists, skill tutors, and trained peer tutors are provided collaboratively through on-campus or off-campus services.

Orientation The program or unit offers an optional 2-hour orientation for new students before classes begin, during registration, and individually by special arrangement.

Unique Aids and Services Aids, services, or accommodations include career counseling.

Assistive Technology Assistive technology is located in campus labs, the DSS office, the library and includes digital textbooks/e-text, learning support software, and FM systems, digital recorders. Technology training is provided to incoming students.

Subject-Area Tutoring Tutoring is offered one-on-one and in small groups for most subjects. Tutoring is provided collaboratively through on-campus or off-campus services via computer-based instruction, graduate assistants/students, professional tutors, and trained peer tutors.

Enrichment Enrichment programs are available through the program or unit for career planning. Programs for career planning, college survival skills, health and nutrition, learning strategies, math, oral communication skills, practical computer skills, reading, self-advocacy, stress management, study skills, test taking, time management, vocabulary development, and written composition skills are provided collaboratively through on-campus or off-campus services. Credit is offered for college survival skills, health and nutrition, learning strategies, math, oral communication skills, practical computer skills, reading, self-advocacy, stress management, study skills, test taking, time management, vocabulary development, and written composition skills.

Application For admittance to the program or unit, students are required to provide a psychoeducational report (5 years old or less). It is recommended that students provide documentation of high school services. Upon application, materials documenting need for services should be sent only to the LD program or unit. Upon acceptance, documentation of need for services should be sent only to the LD program or unit. *Application deadline (institutional):* Continuous. *Application deadline (LD program):* Rolling/continuous for fall and rolling/continuous for spring.

Written Policies Written policies regarding course substitutions, general/basic LD accommodations, reduced course loads, substitutions and waivers of admissions requirements, and substitutions and waivers of graduation requirements are available on the program Web site. Written policies regarding course substitutions, reduced course loads, substitutions and waivers of admissions requirements, and substitutions and waivers of graduation requirements are outlined in the school's catalog/handbook. Written policies regarding general/basic LD accommodations, reduced course loads, and substitutions and waivers of admissions requirements are available through the program or unit directly.

Piedmont Community College
Office of Special Populations

PO Box 1197

Roxboro, NC 27573-1197

http://www.piedmont.cc.nc.us

Contact: Counseling Center. Phone: 336-599-1181 Ext. 272. Fax: 336-598-9283.

Office of Special Populations Approximately 60 registered undergraduate students were served during 2006–07. The program or unit includes 1 full-time staff member. Counselors, trained peer tutors, and other are provided collaboratively through on-campus or off-campus services.

Subject-Area Tutoring Tutoring is offered one-on-one and in small groups for some subjects. Tutoring is provided collaboratively through on-campus or off-campus services via trained peer tutors and other.

Basic Skills Remediation Remediation is offered in small groups for math, reading, and written language. Remediation is provided collaboratively through on-campus or off-campus services.

Enrichment Programs for career planning, college survival skills, health and nutrition, learning strategies, practical computer skills, reading, stress management, study skills, test taking, time management, and other are provided collaboratively through on-campus or off-campus services.

Application For admittance to the program or unit, students are required to provide a psychoeducational report (3 years old or less). It is recommended that students provide documentation of high school services. Upon acceptance, documentation of need for services should be sent only to the LD program or unit. *Application deadline (LD program):* Rolling/continuous for fall and rolling/continuous for spring.

Written Policies Written policy regarding general/basic LD accommodations is available through the program or unit directly.

Pierpont Community and Technical College of Fairmont State University
Office of Disability Issues and Psychological Services

1201 Locust Avenue

Fairmont, WV 26554

http://www.fairmontstate.edu/studentlife/disabilityservices/default.asp

Contact: Mrs. Andrea Pammer, Director of Student Disability Services. Phone: 304-367-4686. Fax: 304-367-4406. E-mail: apammer@fairmontstate.edu.

Office of Disability Issues and Psychological Services Approximately 180 registered undergraduate students were served during 2006–07. The program or unit includes 1 full-time and 2 part-time staff members. Academic advisers, counselors, diagnostic specialists, and graduate assistants/students are provided through the program or unit. Academic advisers, graduate assistants/students, and trained peer tutors are provided collaboratively through on-campus or off-campus services.

Unique Aids and Services Aids, services, or accommodations include career counseling, faculty training, and priority registration.

Assistive Technology Assistive technology is located in campus labs, the DSS office, a special lab and includes digital textbooks/e-text, learning support software, and scanning. Technology training is provided to incoming students.

Subject-Area Tutoring Tutoring is offered one-on-one, in small groups, and in class-size groups for most subjects. Tutoring is provided collaboratively through on-campus or off-campus services via trained peer tutors.

Diagnostic Testing Testing is provided through the program or unit for auditory processing, intelligence, learning styles, motor skills, personality, reading, spoken language, visual processing, and written language.

Basic Skills Remediation Remediation is offered one-on-one, in small groups, and in class-size groups for learning strategies, math, reading, study skills, and written language. Remediation is provided collaboratively through on-campus or off-campus services.

Fees *Diagnostic Testing* fee is $250.

Application For admittance to the program or unit, students are required to apply to the program directly and provide a psychoeducational report. Upon acceptance, documentation of need for services should be sent only to the LD program or unit. *Application deadline (LD program):* Rolling/continuous for fall and rolling/continuous for spring.

Written Policies Written policies regarding course substitutions, general/basic LD accommodations, and substitutions and waivers of graduation requirements are available on the program Web site. Written policies regarding course substitutions, general/basic LD accommodations, and substitutions and waivers of graduation requirements are outlined in the school's catalog/handbook. Written policy regarding general/basic LD accommodations is available through the program or unit directly.

Pikes Peak Community College
Office of Accommodative Services and Instructional Support (OASIS)

5675 South Academy Boulevard

Colorado Springs, CO 80906-5498

http://www.ppcc.edu/StudentServices/AccommodativeServicesAndInstructionalSupport/

Contact: Mrs. Judy Kort, Learning Disability Specialist. Phone: 719-502-3024. Fax: 719-502-3334. E-mail: judy.kort@ppcc.edu.

Office of Accommodative Services and Instructional Support (OASIS) Approximately 165 registered undergraduate students were served during 2006–07. The program or unit includes 2 full-time staff members. LD specialists, skill tutors, and other are provided collaboratively through on-campus or off-campus services.

Orientation The program or unit offers an optional 2.5- to 3-hour orientation for new students before classes begin.

Summer Program To help prepare for the demands of college, there is an optional 2½- to 3-hour summer program prior to entering the school.

Unique Aids and Services Aids, services, or accommodations include career counseling, faculty training, and personal coach.

Assistive Technology Assistive technology is located in campus labs, the DSS office, a special lab and includes digital textbooks/e-text.

Subject-Area Tutoring Tutoring is offered one-on-one, in small groups, and in class-size groups for all subjects. Tutoring is provided through the program or unit via computer-based instruction. Tutoring is also provided collaboratively through on-campus or off-campus services via professional tutors, trained peer tutors, and other.

Basic Skills Remediation Remediation is offered in class-size groups for computer skills, learning strategies, math, reading, study skills, time management, and written language. Remediation is provided collaboratively through on-campus or off-campus services via computer-based instruction, regular education teachers, and trained peer tutors.

Enrichment Programs for career planning, college survival skills, learning strategies, math, oral communication skills, practical computer skills, self-advocacy, stress management, study skills, test taking, time management, vocabulary development, and written composition skills are provided collaboratively through on-campus or off-campus services.

Student Organization Disabled Students Club consists of 5 members.

Application For admittance to the program or unit, students are required to apply to the program directly and provide a psychoeducational report (5 years old or less). It is recommended that students provide documentation of high school services. Upon application, materials documenting need for services should be sent only to the LD program or unit. Upon acceptance, documentation of need for services should be sent only to the LD program or unit. *Application deadline (LD program):* Rolling/continuous for fall and rolling/continuous for spring.

Written Policies Written policy regarding general/basic LD accommodations is available on the program Web site. Written policy regarding general/basic LD accommodations is outlined in the school's catalog/handbook. Written policy regarding general/basic LD accommodations is available through the program or unit directly.

Pima Community College
Disabled Student Resources (DSR)

4905 East Broadway
Tucson, AZ 85709-1010
http://www.pima.edu/dsr/

Contact: Ms. Jane Irey, Disability Specialist. Phone: 520-206-7699. Fax: 520-206-7635. E-mail: jirey@pima.edu. Head of LD Program: Dean Nancee Sorenson, Dean of Student Development. Phone: 520-206-6939. Fax: 520-206-6071. E-mail: nsorenson@pima.edu.

Disabled Student Resources (DSR) Approximately 350 registered undergraduate students were served during 2006–07. The program or unit includes 7 full-time staff members. LD specialists

are provided through the program or unit. Academic advisers, counselors, LD specialists, regular education teachers, and trained peer tutors are provided collaboratively through on-campus or off-campus services.

Unique Aids and Services Aids, services, or accommodations include career counseling and priority registration.

Assistive Technology Assistive technology is located in campus labs, the DSS office, the library and includes digital textbooks/e-text, scanning, and audio books. Technology training is provided to incoming students.

Subject-Area Tutoring Tutoring is offered one-on-one and in small groups for most subjects. Tutoring is provided collaboratively through on-campus or off-campus services via trained peer tutors.

Basic Skills Remediation Remediation is offered one-on-one, in small groups, and in class-size groups for math, reading, spelling, study skills, time management, and written language. Remediation is provided collaboratively through on-campus or off-campus services via regular education teachers and trained peer tutors.

Enrichment Programs for career planning, math, reading, stress management, study skills, test taking, time management, vocabulary development, and written composition skills are provided collaboratively through on-campus or off-campus services. Credit is offered for career planning, math, reading, stress management, study skills, test taking, time management, vocabulary development, and written composition skills.

Application For admittance to the program or unit, students are required to provide a psychoeducational report and provide documentation of high school services. Upon application, materials documenting need for services should be sent only to the LD program or unit. Upon acceptance, documentation of need for services should be sent only to the LD program or unit. *Application deadline (institutional):* Continuous. *Application deadline (LD program):* Rolling/continuous for fall and rolling/continuous for spring.

Written Policies Written policies regarding course substitutions and general/basic LD accommodations are available on the program Web site. Written policies regarding course substitutions and general/basic LD accommodations are available through the program or unit directly.

Prince George's Community College
Disability Support Services (DSS)

301 Largo Road
Largo, MD 20774-2199
http://www.pgcc.edu/

Contact: Ms. Lisa A. Britt, Retention Specialist. Phone: 301-322-0123. Fax: 301-386-7542. E-mail: brittla@pgcc.edu. Head of LD Program: Mr. Thomas Oliver Mays, Manager of Disability Support Services. Phone: 301-322-0838. Fax: 301-386-7542. E-mail: maysto@pgcc.edu.

Disability Support Services (DSS) Approximately 200 registered undergraduate students were served during 2006–07. The program or unit includes 2 full-time staff members and 1 part-time staff member. Academic advisers, counselors, and trained peer tutors are provided collaboratively through on-campus or off-campus services.

Prince George's Community College (continued)

Unique Aids and Services Aids, services, or accommodations include career counseling, priority registration, retention services program.

Assistive Technology Assistive technology is located in campus labs, the DSS office and includes digital textbooks/e-text.

Subject-Area Tutoring Tutoring is offered one-on-one and in small groups for all subjects. Tutoring is provided through the program or unit via professional tutors. Tutoring is also provided collaboratively through on-campus or off-campus services via computer-based instruction and trained peer tutors.

Diagnostic Testing Testing is provided through the program or unit for learning strategies, learning styles, and study skills. Testing for auditory processing, handwriting, intelligence, math, motor skills, neuropsychological, personality, reading, social skills, spelling, spoken language, visual processing, and written language is provided collaboratively through on-campus or off-campus services.

Basic Skills Remediation Remediation is offered one-on-one, in small groups, and in class-size groups for auditory processing, computer skills, learning strategies, math, reading, study skills, time management, and written language. Remediation is provided collaboratively through on-campus or off-campus services via computer-based instruction, regular education teachers, special education teachers, and trained peer tutors.

Enrichment Enrichment programs are available through the program or unit for self-advocacy, stress management, study skills, test taking, and time management. Programs for career planning, college survival skills, learning strategies, math, oral communication skills, practical computer skills, reading, self-advocacy, stress management, study skills, test taking, time management, vocabulary development, and written composition skills are provided collaboratively through on-campus or off-campus services. Credit is offered for career planning, college survival skills, math, oral communication skills, practical computer skills, reading, study skills, vocabulary development, and written composition skills.

Fees *Diagnostic Testing* fee is $400 to $2000.

Application For admittance to the program or unit, students are required to provide a psychoeducational report (3 years old or less). It is recommended that students provide documentation of high school services and provide other documentation. Upon application, materials documenting need for services should be sent to both admissions and the LD program or unit. Upon acceptance, documentation of need for services should be sent only to the LD program or unit. *Application deadline (LD program):* Rolling/continuous for fall and rolling/continuous for spring.

Written Policies Written policy regarding general/basic LD accommodations is available on the program Web site. Written policies regarding general/basic LD accommodations and grade forgiveness are outlined in the school's catalog/handbook. Written policy regarding general/basic LD accommodations is available through the program or unit directly.

Pueblo Community College
Disability Resources

900 West Orman Avenue

Pueblo, CO 81004-1499

http://www.pueblocc.edu/

Contact: Mrs. Nancy E. Hunt, Disability Resources Adviser. Phone: 719-549-3044. Fax: 719-549-3445. E-mail: nancy.hunt@pueblocc.edu. Head of LD Program: Mrs. Bonnie Clark, Coordinator of Disability Resources. Phone: 719-549-3449. Fax: 719-549-3445. E-mail: bonnie.clark@pueblocc.edu.

Disability Resources Approximately 153 registered undergraduate students were served during 2006–07. The program or unit includes 2 full-time staff members. Academic advisers, counselors, professional tutors, regular education teachers, trained peer tutors, and other are provided collaboratively through on-campus or off-campus services.

Assistive Technology Assistive technology is located in the Disability Resources Center and includes digital textbooks/e-text and Dragon Naturally Speaking. Technology training is provided to incoming students.

Subject-Area Tutoring Tutoring is offered one-on-one and in small groups for all subjects. Tutoring is provided collaboratively through on-campus or off-campus services via computer-based instruction, professional tutors, and trained peer tutors.

Basic Skills Remediation Remediation is offered one-on-one, in small groups, and in class-size groups for computer skills, learning strategies, math, reading, study skills, time management, and written language. Remediation is provided collaboratively through on-campus or off-campus services via computer-based instruction, professional tutors, regular education teachers, and trained peer tutors.

Application It is recommended that students provide documentation of high school services. Upon application, materials documenting need for services should be sent only to the LD program or unit. Upon acceptance, documentation of need for services should be sent only to the LD program or unit. *Application deadline (institutional):* Continuous. *Application deadline (LD program):* Rolling/continuous for fall and rolling/continuous for spring.

Written Policies Written policy regarding general/basic LD accommodations is available on the program Web site. Written policy regarding general/basic LD accommodations is available through the program or unit directly.

Quincy College
Student Support Services

34 Coddington Street

Quincy, MA 02169-4522

http://www.quincycollege.edu/

Contact: Ms. Susan Bossa, Executive Director, Student Support Services/ADA Coordinator. Phone: 617-984-1656. Fax: 617-984-1792. E-mail: sbossa@quincycollege.edu.

Student Support Services Approximately 30 registered undergraduate students were served during 2006–07. The program or unit includes 1 full-time and 3 part-time staff members. Professional tutors, remediation/learning specialists, skill tutors, and trained peer tutors are provided through the program or unit. Academic advisers, counselors, and regular education teachers are provided collaboratively through on-campus or off-campus services.

Assistive Technology Assistive technology is located in the Learning Center and includes learning support software and scanning.

Subject-Area Tutoring Tutoring is offered one-on-one and in small groups for most subjects. Tutoring is provided through the program or unit via computer-based instruction, professional tutors, and trained peer tutors. Tutoring is also provided collaboratively through on-campus or off-campus services via computer-based instruction.

Basic Skills Remediation Remediation is available for computer skills, math, study skills, and time management. Remediation is provided through the program or unit via computer-based instruction, professional tutors, and trained peer tutors.

Enrichment Enrichment programs are available through the program or unit for learning strategies, math, practical computer skills, study skills, test taking, time management, and written composition skills. Programs for career planning and college survival skills are provided collaboratively through on-campus or off-campus services. Credit is offered for college survival skills.

Application For admittance to the program or unit, students are required to provide a psychoeducational report. It is recommended that students provide documentation of high school services. Upon application, materials documenting need for services should be sent only to the LD program or unit. Upon acceptance, documentation of need for services should be sent only to the LD program or unit. *Application deadline (institutional):* Continuous. *Application deadline (LD program):* Rolling/continuous for fall and rolling/continuous for spring.

Written Policies Written policy regarding general/basic LD accommodations is available on the program Web site. Written policy regarding general/basic LD accommodations is outlined in the school's catalog/handbook. Written policy regarding general/basic LD accommodations is available through the program or unit directly.

Reading Area Community College
Center for Academic Success

PO Box 1706

Reading, PA 19603-1706

http://racc.edu

Contact: Ms. Tomma Lee Furst, Assistant Director for Academic Support. Phone: 610-372-4721 Ext. 5069. Fax: 610-607-6257. E-mail: tfurst@racc.edu. Head of LD Program: Ms. Stephanie Giddens, Special Populations Coordinator. Phone: 610-372-4721 Ext. 5070. Fax: 610-607-6257. E-mail: sgiddens@racc.edu.

Center for Academic Success Approximately 75 registered undergraduate students were served during 2006–07. The program or unit includes 3 full-time staff members and 1 part-time staff member. Academic advisers, counselors, professional tutors, remediation/learning specialists, and trained peer tutors are provided through the program or unit.

Unique Aids and Services Aids, services, or accommodations include career counseling, workshops on various topics.

Assistive Technology Assistive technology is located in the DSS office, the library and includes digital textbooks/e-text, learning support software, and scanning. Technology training is provided to incoming students.

Subject-Area Tutoring Tutoring is offered one-on-one and in small groups for most subjects. Tutoring is provided collaboratively through on-campus or off-campus services via professional tutors and trained peer tutors.

Application For admittance to the program or unit, students are required to provide a psychoeducational report (3 years old or less). It is recommended that students provide documentation of high school services and provide evaluation report. Upon application, materials documenting need for services should be sent only to the LD program or unit. Upon acceptance, documentation of need for services should be sent only to the LD program or unit. *Application deadline (LD program):* Rolling/continuous for fall and rolling/continuous for spring.

Written Policies Written policy regarding general/basic LD accommodations is available on the program Web site. Written policies regarding course substitutions, general/basic LD accommodations, and substitutions and waivers of admissions requirements are outlined in the school's catalog/handbook. Written policy regarding general/basic LD accommodations is available through the program or unit directly.

Reedley College
Disabled Students Programs and Services (DSP&S)

995 North Reed Avenue

Reedley, CA 93654-2099

http://www.reedleycollege.edu/services/dsp/

Contact: Mrs. Linda Reither, Learning Disability Specialist. Phone: 559-638-0332 Ext. 3183. Fax: 559-638-0382. E-mail: linda.reither@reedleycollege.edu. Head of LD Program: Dr. Janice M. Emerzian, District Director Disabled Students Programs and Services. Phone: 559-442-8237. Fax: 559-485-7304. E-mail: janice.emerzian@scccd.com.

Disabled Students Programs and Services (DSP&S) Approximately 120 registered undergraduate students were served during 2006–07. The program or unit includes 1 full-time and 1 part-time staff member. Academic advisers, counselors, diagnostic specialists, LD specialists, remediation/learning specialists, and strategy tutors are provided through the program or unit. Academic advisers, coaches, counselors, regular education teachers, skill tutors, special education teachers, strategy tutors, and trained peer tutors are provided collaboratively through on-campus or off-campus services.

Orientation The program or unit offers an optional orientation for new students individually by special arrangement.

Summer Program To help prepare for the demands of college, there is an optional 1-day summer program prior to entering the school available to high school graduates that focuses on life skills and/or college life adjustment.

Unique Aids and Services Aids, services, or accommodations include career counseling, faculty training, priority registration, and support groups.

Assistive Technology Assistive technology is located in campus labs, the DSS office, a special lab, the library and includes digital textbooks/e-text, learning support software, and spell-checkers.

Subject-Area Tutoring Tutoring is offered one-on-one, in small groups, and in class-size groups for most subjects. Tutoring is provided through the program or unit via computer-based instruc-

Reedley College (continued)

tion and LD specialists. Tutoring is also provided collaboratively through on-campus or off-campus services via computer-based instruction and trained peer tutors.

Diagnostic Testing Testing is provided through the program or unit for auditory processing, intelligence, learning strategies, learning styles, math, reading, spelling, spoken language, study skills, visual processing, and written language. Testing for study skills is provided collaboratively through on-campus or off-campus services.

Basic Skills Remediation Remediation is offered one-on-one, in small groups, and in class-size groups for auditory processing, computer skills, learning strategies, math, reading, social skills, spelling, spoken language, study skills, time management, visual processing, and written language. Remediation is provided through the program or unit via LD specialists and special education teachers. Remediation is also provided collaboratively through on-campus or off-campus services via computer-based instruction, regular education teachers, special education teachers, and trained peer tutors.

Enrichment Enrichment programs are available through the program or unit for college survival skills, learning strategies, math, oral communication skills, practical computer skills, self-advocacy, study skills, test taking, time management, vocabulary development, and written composition skills. Programs for career planning, college survival skills, health and nutrition, learning strategies, math, medication management, oral communication skills, practical computer skills, reading, study skills, test taking, time management, and written composition skills are provided collaboratively through on-campus or off-campus services. Credit is offered for college survival skills, health and nutrition, learning strategies, math, oral communication skills, practical computer skills, reading, self-advocacy, study skills, test taking, time management, vocabulary development, and written composition skills.

Student Organization Students with Disabilities Club consists of 30 members.

Application For admittance to the program or unit, students are required to provide a meeting with DSP&S counselor, who will refer the student to the LD specialist. It is recommended that students provide a psychoeducational report (3 years old or less) and provide documentation of high school services. Upon application, materials documenting need for services should be sent only to the LD program or unit. Upon acceptance, documentation of need for services should be sent only to the LD program or unit. *Application deadline (institutional):* Continuous. *Application deadline (LD program):* Rolling/continuous for fall and rolling/continuous for spring.

Written Policies Written policies regarding course substitutions, general/basic LD accommodations, grade forgiveness, reduced course loads, substitutions and waivers of admissions requirements, and substitutions and waivers of graduation requirements are outlined in the school's catalog/handbook. Written policies regarding general/basic LD accommodations, substitutions and waivers of admissions requirements, and substitutions and waivers of graduation requirements are available through the program or unit directly.

Richard Bland College of The College of William and Mary
Disability Support Services

11301 Johnson Road

Petersburg, VA 23805-7100

http://www.rbc.edu/disability_support_services.pdf

Contact: Mrs. Evanda Shentelle Watts-Martinez, Director of Student Services. Phone: 804-862-6263. E-mail: ewatts@rbc.edu.

Disability Support Services Approximately 35 registered undergraduate students were served during 2006–07. The program or unit includes 1 full-time staff member. LD specialists are provided through the program or unit. Academic advisers, counselors, professional tutors, and trained peer tutors are provided collaboratively through on-campus or off-campus services.

Unique Aids and Services Aids, services, or accommodations include advocates, career counseling, and personal coach.

Assistive Technology Assistive technology is located in the DSS office and includes learning support software.

Subject-Area Tutoring Tutoring is offered one-on-one, in small groups, and in class-size groups for all subjects. Tutoring is provided collaboratively through on-campus or off-campus services via computer-based instruction, trained peer tutors, and other.

Basic Skills Remediation Remediation is offered one-on-one, in small groups, and in class-size groups for auditory processing, computer skills, learning strategies, math, spoken language, study skills, time management, visual processing, and written language. Remediation is provided collaboratively through on-campus or off-campus services via computer-based instruction, regular education teachers, trained peer tutors, and other.

Enrichment Enrichment programs are available through the program or unit for self-advocacy and stress management. Programs for career planning, college survival skills, health and nutrition, learning strategies, math, oral communication skills, practical computer skills, self-advocacy, stress management, study skills, test taking, time management, and written composition skills are provided collaboratively through on-campus or off-campus services. Credit is offered for learning strategies, math, oral communication skills, practical computer skills, stress management, study skills, test taking, time management, and written composition skills.

Student Organization RBC Academic Support Group consists of 30 members.

Fees *LD Program or Service* fee is $1322 (fee varies according to academic program).

Application For admittance to the program or unit, students are required to provide a psychoeducational report (3 years old or less) and provide documentation of high school services. Upon acceptance, documentation of need for services should be sent only to the LD program or unit. *Application deadline (institutional):* 8/15. *Application deadline (LD program):* 8/16 for fall. Rolling/continuous for spring.

Written Policies Written policies regarding course substitutions, general/basic LD accommodations, grade forgiveness, reduced course loads, substitutions and waivers of admissions requirements, and substitutions and waivers of graduation requirements are outlined in the school's catalog/handbook. Written policies regarding general/basic LD accommodations and substitutions and waivers of admissions requirements are available through the program or unit directly.

Richland Community College
Learning Accommodation Services

One College Park

Decatur, IL 62521-8513

http://www.richland.edu/

Contact: Mary Atkins, Director. Phone: 217-875-7211 Ext. 362. Fax: 217-875-2762. E-mail: matkins@richland.edu.

Learning Accommodation Services Approximately 100 registered undergraduate students were served during 2006–07. The program or unit includes 2 full-time and 2 part-time staff members. Academic advisers, counselors, diagnostic specialists, graduate assistants/students, LD specialists, professional tutors, regular education teachers, remediation/learning specialists, skill tutors, special education teachers, strategy tutors, and trained peer tutors are provided through the program or unit. Academic advisers, counselors, graduate assistants/students, professional tutors, regular education teachers, remediation/learning specialists, skill tutors, and trained peer tutors are provided collaboratively through on-campus or off-campus services.

Orientation The program or unit offers an optional 2-hour orientation for new students before classes begin.

Summer Program To help prepare for the demands of college, there is an optional 1-day summer program prior to entering the school available to high school graduates that focuses on life skills and/or college life adjustment, self-advocacy, study skills, test-taking skills, and time management. The program accepts students from out-of-state.

Unique Aids and Services Aids, services, or accommodations include career counseling and support groups.

Assistive Technology Assistive technology is located in campus labs, the DSS office and includes digital textbooks/e-text, learning support software, and scanning. Technology training is provided to incoming students.

Subject-Area Tutoring Tutoring is offered one-on-one and in small groups for all subjects. Tutoring is provided through the program or unit via computer-based instruction, graduate assistants/students, LD specialists, professional tutors, and trained peer tutors. Tutoring is also provided collaboratively through on-campus or off-campus services via graduate assistants/students, professional tutors, and trained peer tutors.

Diagnostic Testing Testing is provided through the program or unit for auditory processing, learning strategies, learning styles, math, reading, social skills, spelling, study skills, visual processing, and written language. Testing for learning strategies, learning styles, math, reading, social skills, spelling, study skills, and written language is provided collaboratively through on-campus or off-campus services.

Basic Skills Remediation Remediation is offered one-on-one, in small groups, and in class-size groups for auditory processing, computer skills, learning strategies, math, reading, social skills, spelling, study skills, time management, visual processing, and written language. Remediation is provided through the program or unit via computer-based instruction, LD specialists, professional tutors, regular education teachers, special education teachers, and trained peer tutors. Remediation is also provided collaboratively through on-campus or off-campus services via computer-based instruction, professional tutors, regular education teachers, and trained peer tutors.

Enrichment Enrichment programs are available through the program or unit for career planning, college survival skills, health and nutrition, learning strategies, math, practical computer skills, reading, self-advocacy, stress management, study skills, test taking, time management, vocabulary development, and written composition skills. Programs for career planning, college survival skills, learning strategies, math, practical computer skills, reading, stress management, study skills, test taking, time management, vocabulary development, and written composition skills are provided collaboratively through on-campus or off-campus services. Credit is offered for career planning and learning strategies.

Application For admittance to the program or unit, students are required to apply to the program directly, provide a psychoeducational report, and provide documentation of high school services. Upon application, materials documenting need for services should be sent only to the LD program or unit. Upon acceptance, documentation of need for services should be sent only to the LD program or unit. *Application deadline (institutional):* Continuous. *Application deadline (LD program):* Rolling/continuous for fall and rolling/continuous for spring.

Written Policies Written policy regarding general/basic LD accommodations is available on the program Web site. Written policy regarding general/basic LD accommodations is outlined in the school's catalog/handbook. Written policies regarding course substitutions, general/basic LD accommodations, and reduced course loads are available through the program or unit directly.

Richmond Community College
Special Populations Office

PO Box 1189

Hamlet, NC 28345-1189

http://www.richmondcc.edu

Contact: Dr. John Wester, VP for Student Development / ADA Student Coordinator. Phone: 910-410-1730. Fax: 910-582-7102. E-mail: johnw@richmondcc.edu.

Special Populations Office Approximately 15 registered undergraduate students were served during 2006–07. The program or unit includes 2 part-time staff members. Services are provided through the program or unit. Academic advisers, counselors, and other are provided collaboratively through on-campus or off-campus services.

Subject-Area Tutoring Tutoring is offered one-on-one and in small groups for some subjects. Tutoring is provided collaboratively through on-campus or off-campus services via computer-based instruction and other.

Basic Skills Remediation Remediation is offered in small groups and in class-size groups for math, reading, and written language. Remediation is provided collaboratively through on-campus or off-campus services via regular education teachers and other.

Richmond Community College (continued)

Enrichment Programs for career planning, college survival skills, health and nutrition, learning strategies, math, oral communication skills, practical computer skills, reading, stress management, study skills, test taking, time management, vocabulary development, written composition skills, and other are provided collaboratively through on-campus or off-campus services. Credit is offered for health and nutrition, math, oral communication skills, practical computer skills, reading, vocabulary development, written composition skills, and other.

Application For admittance to the program or unit, students are required to apply to the program directly and provide assessment and diagnostic documentation. It is recommended that students provide a psychoeducational report (5 years old or less) and provide documentation of high school services. Upon application, materials documenting need for services should be sent only to the LD program or unit. Upon acceptance, documentation of need for services should be sent only to the LD program or unit. *Application deadline (institutional):* Continuous. *Application deadline (LD program):* Rolling/continuous for fall and rolling/continuous for spring.

Written Policies Written policies regarding course substitutions, general/basic LD accommodations, reduced course loads, substitutions and waivers of admissions requirements, and substitutions and waivers of graduation requirements are available on the program Web site. Written policies regarding general/basic LD accommodations, substitutions and waivers of admissions requirements, and substitutions and waivers of graduation requirements are outlined in the school's catalog/handbook. Written policies regarding course substitutions, general/basic LD accommodations, grade forgiveness, reduced course loads, substitutions and waivers of admissions requirements, and substitutions and waivers of graduation requirements are available through the program or unit directly.

Rockingham Community College

PO Box 38

Wentworth, NC 27375-0038

http://www.rockinghamcc.edu/pages/
disability_services.php?n=S

Contact: Ms. LaVonne Waugh James, Counselor. Phone: 336-342-4261 Ext. 2243. Fax: 336-342-1809. E-mail: jamesl@rockinghamcc.edu. Head of LD Program: Mr. Terry Kent, Counselor. Phone: 336-342-4261 Ext. 2127. Fax: 336-342-1809. E-mail: kentt@rockinghamcc.edu.

Approximately 50 registered undergraduate students were served during 2006–07. The program or unit includes 2 part-time staff members. Academic advisers, coaches, counselors, and trained peer tutors are provided collaboratively through on-campus or off-campus services.

Assistive Technology Assistive technology is located in campus labs and includes digital textbooks/e-text.

Subject-Area Tutoring Tutoring is offered one-on-one and in small groups for some subjects. Tutoring is provided collaboratively through on-campus or off-campus services via trained peer tutors and other.

Basic Skills Remediation Remediation is offered in class-size groups for computer skills, math, reading, and written language. Remediation is provided collaboratively through on-campus or off-campus services via regular education teachers.

Enrichment Programs for college survival skills, math, practical computer skills, reading, study skills, test taking, time management, vocabulary development, and written composition skills are provided collaboratively through on-campus or off-campus services. Credit is offered for college survival skills, study skills, test taking, and time management.

Application Upon acceptance, documentation of need for services should be sent only to the LD program or unit. *Application deadline (institutional):* Continuous. *Application deadline (LD program):* Rolling/continuous for fall and rolling/continuous for spring.

Rockland Community College

145 College Road

Suffern, NY 10901-3699

http://www.sunyrockland.edu/

Contact: Ms. Marge Zemek, Learning Disabilities Specialist. Phone: 845-574-4316. Fax: 845-574-4594. E-mail: mzemek@sunyrockland.edu.

The program or unit includes 2 full-time and 2 part-time staff members. Academic advisers, counselors, LD specialists, and remediation/learning specialists are provided through the program or unit. Academic advisers, counselors, professional tutors, regular education teachers, remediation/learning specialists, and skill tutors are provided collaboratively through on-campus or off-campus services.

Summer Program To help prepare for the demands of college, there is an optional 4-week summer program prior to entering the school available to high school graduates that focuses on life skills and/or college life adjustment, study skills, test-taking skills, and time management. Degree credit will be earned. The program accepts students from out-of-state.

Unique Aids and Services Aids, services, or accommodations include advocates and priority registration.

Assistive Technology Assistive technology is located in campus labs, a special lab and includes digital textbooks/e-text, learning support software, and scanning.

Subject-Area Tutoring Tutoring is offered one-on-one for most subjects. Tutoring is provided collaboratively through on-campus or off-campus services via computer-based instruction, graduate assistants/students, professional tutors, and trained peer tutors.

Basic Skills Remediation Remediation is offered in class-size groups for computer skills, math, reading, and written language. Remediation is provided through the program or unit via LD specialists. Remediation is also provided collaboratively through on-campus or off-campus services via computer-based instruction, regular education teachers, and special education teachers.

Enrichment Programs for career planning, math, stress management, study skills, test taking, and written composition skills are provided collaboratively through on-campus or off-campus services.

Application For admittance to the program or unit, students are required to provide documentation of high school services. Upon application, materials documenting need for services should be sent only to the LD program or unit. Upon acceptance, documentation of need for services should be sent only to the LD program or unit. *Application deadline (LD program):* Rolling/continuous for fall and rolling/continuous for spring.

Written Policies Written policy regarding general/basic LD accommodations is available on the program Web site. Written policies regarding general/basic LD accommodations and grade forgiveness are outlined in the school's catalog/handbook. Written policies regarding course substitutions, general/basic LD accommodations, substitutions and waivers of admissions requirements, and substitutions and waivers of graduation requirements are available through the program or unit directly.

Rose State College
Disability Services and Resources

6420 Southeast 15th Street

Midwest City, OK 73110-2799

http://www.rose.edu/cstudent/stuserv/disable.htm

Contact: Ms. Janet Griffith, Coordinator. Phone: 405-733-7407. Fax: 405-733-7549. E-mail: jgriffith@rose.edu.

Disability Services and Resources Approximately 50 registered undergraduate students were served during 2006–07. The program or unit includes 1 full-time staff member. Academic advisers, counselors, and strategy tutors are provided through the program or unit. Academic advisers, counselors, professional tutors, and trained peer tutors are provided collaboratively through on-campus or off-campus services.

Unique Aids and Services Aids, services, or accommodations include career counseling.

Subject-Area Tutoring Tutoring is offered one-on-one and in small groups for some subjects. Tutoring is provided collaboratively through on-campus or off-campus services via computer-based instruction, professional tutors, and trained peer tutors.

Basic Skills Remediation Remediation is offered one-on-one, in small groups, and in class-size groups for learning strategies, math, reading, study skills, time management, written language, and science. Remediation is provided collaboratively through on-campus or off-campus services via computer-based instruction, professional tutors, and trained peer tutors.

Enrichment Enrichment programs are available through the program or unit for career planning, college survival skills, and self-advocacy. Programs for career planning, college survival skills, learning strategies, math, reading, study skills, test taking, time management, and written composition skills are provided collaboratively through on-campus or off-campus services.

Student Organization Abled Disabled Association consists of 4 members.

Application For admittance to the program or unit, students are required to apply to the program directly, provide a psychoeducational report, and provide documentation relating to disability and impact on classroom activities. Upon application, materials documenting need for services should be sent only to the LD program or unit. Upon acceptance, documentation of need for services should be sent only to the LD program or unit. *Application deadline (institutional):* Continuous. *Application deadline (LD program):* Rolling/continuous for fall and rolling/continuous for spring.

Written Policies Written policies regarding general/basic LD accommodations and grade forgiveness are outlined in the school's catalog/handbook.

Roxbury Community College

1234 Columbus Avenue

Roxbury Crossing, MA 02120-3400

http://www.rcc.mass.edu/

Contact: Ms. Linda B. O'Connor, Counselor for Students with Disabilities. Phone: 617-427-0060 Ext. 5006. Fax: 617-541-5371. E-mail: loconn@rcc.mass.edu.

Approximately 25 registered undergraduate students were served during 2006–07. The program or unit includes 1 part-time staff member. Academic advisers, skill tutors, and trained peer tutors are provided through the program or unit.

Unique Aids and Services Aids, services, or accommodations include career counseling and priority registration.

Assistive Technology Assistive technology is located in a special lab and includes digital textbooks/e-text and learning support software. Technology training is provided to incoming students.

Subject-Area Tutoring Tutoring is offered one-on-one and in small groups for most subjects. Tutoring is provided through the program or unit via LD specialists. Tutoring is also provided collaboratively through on-campus or off-campus services via computer-based instruction and professional tutors.

Diagnostic Testing Testing for learning styles, math, reading, and spelling is provided collaboratively through on-campus or off-campus services.

Basic Skills Remediation Remediation is offered in class-size groups for computer skills, learning strategies, math, reading, spelling, study skills, time management, and written language. Remediation is provided collaboratively through on-campus or off-campus services via computer-based instruction, professional tutors, regular education teachers, and trained peer tutors.

Enrichment Programs for career planning, college survival skills, health and nutrition, learning strategies, math, practical computer skills, reading, self-advocacy, study skills, test taking, time management, vocabulary development, and written composition skills are provided collaboratively through on-campus or off-campus services. Credit is offered for career planning, college survival skills, health and nutrition, learning strategies, math, practical computer skills, reading, study skills, test taking, time management, vocabulary development, and written composition skills.

Application For admittance to the program or unit, students are required to provide a psychoeducational report (3 years old or less). It is recommended that students provide documentation of high school services. Upon application, materials documenting need for services should be sent only to the LD program or unit. Upon acceptance, documentation of need for services should be sent only to the LD program or unit. *Application deadline (institutional):* Continuous. *Application deadline (LD program):* Rolling/continuous for fall and rolling/continuous for spring.

Written Policies Written policy regarding general/basic LD accommodations is outlined in the school's catalog/handbook. Written policies regarding general/basic LD accommodations and reduced course loads are available through the program or unit directly.

St. Cloud Technical College

1540 Northway Drive
St. Cloud, MN 56303-1240
http://www.sctc.edu/

Contact: Judy Jacobson Berg, Counselor for Students with Disabilities. Phone: 320-308-5096. Fax: 320-308-5981. E-mail: jjacobsonberg@sctc.edu.

Approximately 50 registered undergraduate students were served during 2006–07. Academic advisers, counselors, professional tutors, remediation/learning specialists, and skill tutors are provided collaboratively through on-campus or off-campus services.

Assistive Technology Assistive technology is located in a special lab and includes digital textbooks/e-text and scanning. Technology training is provided to incoming students.

Subject-Area Tutoring Tutoring is offered one-on-one, in small groups, and in class-size groups for most subjects. Tutoring is provided collaboratively through on-campus or off-campus services via computer-based instruction, professional tutors, and trained peer tutors.

Basic Skills Remediation Remediation is offered in class-size groups for math, reading, and written language. Remediation is provided collaboratively through on-campus or off-campus services via computer-based instruction and regular education teachers.

Enrichment Programs for career planning, study skills, test taking, vocabulary development, and written composition skills are provided collaboratively through on-campus or off-campus services. Credit is offered for career planning, math, vocabulary development, and written composition skills.

Application For admittance to the program or unit, students are required to provide a psychoeducational report (3 years old or less). It is recommended that students provide documentation of high school services. Upon application, materials documenting need for services should be sent only to the LD program or unit. Upon acceptance, documentation of need for services should be sent only to the LD program or unit. *Application deadline (institutional):* Continuous. *Application deadline (LD program):* Rolling/continuous for fall and rolling/continuous for spring.

Written Policies Written policy regarding general/basic LD accommodations is available on the program Web site. Written policy regarding general/basic LD accommodations is outlined in the school's catalog/handbook.

St. Louis Community College at Florissant Valley

Access Office, Services for Students with Disabilities

3400 Pershall Road
St. Louis, MO 63135-1499
http://www.stlcc.edu/access/

Contact: Ms. Mary S. Wagner, LD Specialist. Phone: 314-513-4188. Fax: 314-513-487676. E-mail: mwagner@stlcc.edu. Head of LD Program: Ms. Suelaine M. Matthews, Manager. Phone: 314-513-4549. Fax: 314-513-4876. E-mail: smatthews@stlcc.edu.

Access Office, Services for Students with Disabilities
Approximately 80 registered undergraduate students were served during 2006–07. The program or unit includes 2 full-time and 2 part-time staff members. Academic advisers, counselors, and LD specialists are provided through the program or unit. Academic advisers, counselors, regular education teachers, remediation/learning specialists, skill tutors, strategy tutors, and trained peer tutors are provided collaboratively through on-campus or off-campus services.

Orientation The program or unit offers an optional 1-day orientation for new students before classes begin.

Unique Aids and Services Aids, services, or accommodations include career counseling and faculty training.

Assistive Technology Assistive technology is located in campus labs, the DSS office and includes digital textbooks/e-text, learning support software, and scanning. Technology training is provided to incoming students.

Subject-Area Tutoring Tutoring is offered one-on-one and in small groups for most subjects. Tutoring is provided collaboratively through on-campus or off-campus services via computer-based instruction and trained peer tutors.

Basic Skills Remediation Remediation is offered one-on-one, in small groups, and in class-size groups for computer skills, learning strategies, math, reading, study skills, time management, and written language. Remediation is provided collaboratively through on-campus or off-campus services via computer-based instruction, regular education teachers, and trained peer tutors.

Enrichment Enrichment programs are available through the program or unit for career planning, college survival skills, self-advocacy, stress management, study skills, test taking, and time management. Programs for career planning, college survival skills, health and nutrition, learning strategies, math, oral communication skills, practical computer skills, reading, stress management, study skills, test taking, time management, vocabulary development, and written composition skills are provided collaboratively through on-campus or off-campus services.

Application For admittance to the program or unit, students are required to provide a psychoeducational report (5 years old or less). It is recommended that students provide documentation of high school services. Upon application, materials documenting need for services should be sent only to the LD program or unit. Upon acceptance, documentation of need for services should be sent only to the LD program or unit. *Application deadline (institutional):* 8/19. *Application deadline (LD program):* Rolling/continuous for fall and rolling/continuous for spring.

Written Policies Written policies regarding general/basic LD accommodations and reduced course loads are available on the program Web site. Written policies regarding course substitutions, grade forgiveness, and substitutions and waivers of graduation requirements are outlined in the school's catalog/handbook. Written policies regarding general/basic LD accommodations and reduced course loads are available through the program or unit directly.

St. Louis Community College at Forest Park
Access Office/disAbility Support Services

5600 Oakland Avenue

St. Louis, MO 63110-1316

http://www.stlcc.edu/access/

Contact: Mrs. Deborah S. Carter, Manager. Phone: 314-644-9039. Fax: 314-951-9439. E-mail: fpaccess@stlcc.edu.

Access Office/disAbility Support Services The program or unit includes 2 full-time and 11 part-time staff members. Counselors, LD specialists, and other are provided collaboratively through on-campus or off-campus services.

Orientation The program or unit offers an optional 3-hour orientation for new students before classes begin and once a year in August.

Unique Aids and Services Aids, services, or accommodations include career counseling.

Assistive Technology Assistive technology is located in campus labs, the DSS office and includes digital textbooks/e-text, learning support software, and scanning.

Subject-Area Tutoring Tutoring is offered one-on-one, in small groups, and in class-size groups for some subjects. Tutoring is provided collaboratively through on-campus or off-campus services via computer-based instruction and trained peer tutors.

Basic Skills Remediation Remediation is offered in class-size groups for computer skills, math, reading, study skills, time management, and written language. Remediation is provided collaboratively through on-campus or off-campus services via computer-based instruction, regular education teachers, and trained peer tutors.

Enrichment Programs for career planning, math, practical computer skills, reading, stress management, study skills, test taking, time management, and written composition skills are provided collaboratively through on-campus or off-campus services.

Application For admittance to the program or unit, students are required to provide a psychoeducational report (5 years old or less). It is recommended that students provide documentation of high school services. Upon application, materials documenting need for services should be sent only to the LD program or unit. Upon acceptance, documentation of need for services should be sent only to the LD program or unit. *Application deadline (LD program):* Rolling/continuous for fall and rolling/continuous for spring.

Written Policies Written policies regarding course substitutions, general/basic LD accommodations, reduced course loads, and substitutions and waivers of graduation requirements are available on the program Web site. Written policies regarding course substitutions, general/basic LD accommodations, reduced course loads, and substitutions and waivers of graduation requirements are available through the program or unit directly.

St. Philip's College
Special Needs Services

1801 Martin Luther King Drive

San Antonio, TX 78203-2098

http://www.accd.edu/spc/admin/ess/special_needs.htm

Contact: Mrs. Donna McPeek, Learning Disabilities Specialist. Phone: 210-531-3512. Fax: 210-531-3513. E-mail: dmcpeek@mail.accd.edu.

Special Needs Services Approximately 600 registered undergraduate students were served during 2006–07. The program or unit includes 3 full-time and 40 part-time staff members. Academic advisers, counselors, diagnostic specialists, LD specialists, professional tutors, skill tutors, and trained peer tutors are provided through the program or unit. Academic advisers, counselors, regular education teachers, and remediation/learning specialists are provided collaboratively through on-campus or off-campus services.

Unique Aids and Services Aids, services, or accommodations include career counseling, faculty training, priority registration, extended test time, readers, testing in a non-distracting environment.

Assistive Technology Assistive technology is located in campus labs, a special lab and includes digital textbooks/e-text, learning support software, and scanning. Technology training is provided to incoming students.

Subject-Area Tutoring Tutoring is offered one-on-one and in small groups for all subjects. Tutoring is provided through the program or unit via professional tutors and trained peer tutors. Tutoring is also provided collaboratively through on-campus or off-campus services via computer-based instruction, professional tutors, and trained peer tutors.

Diagnostic Testing Testing is provided through the program or unit for auditory processing, intelligence, math, motor skills, neuropsychological, reading, spelling, visual processing, written language, and other services.

Basic Skills Remediation Remediation is offered one-on-one and in small groups for auditory processing, math, reading, social skills, and English. Remediation is provided through the program or unit via LD specialists and professional tutors. Remediation is also provided collaboratively through on-campus or off-campus services via computer-based instruction, professional tutors, regular education teachers, and trained peer tutors.

Enrichment Enrichment programs are available through the program or unit for career planning, college survival skills, learning strategies, math, reading, self-advocacy, stress management, study skills, test taking, time management, and written composition skills. Programs for career planning, college survival skills, learning strategies, math, reading, stress management, study skills, test taking, time management, and written composition skills are provided collaboratively through on-campus or off-campus services. Credit is offered for college survival skills, math, reading, study skills, and written composition skills.

Application For admittance to the program or unit, students are required to provide a psychoeducational report (3 years old or less). It is recommended that students provide documentation of high school services and provide any appropriate medical documentation, if applicable. Upon application, materials documenting need for services should be sent only to the LD program or unit. Upon acceptance, documentation of need for services should be sent only

St. Philip's College (continued)

to the LD program or unit. *Application deadline (institutional):* Continuous. *Application deadline (LD program):* Rolling/continuous for fall and rolling/continuous for spring.

Written Policies Written policy regarding general/basic LD accommodations is available on the program Web site. Written policy regarding general/basic LD accommodations is outlined in the school's catalog/handbook. Written policy regarding general/basic LD accommodations is available through the program or unit directly.

Salem Community College
Center for Student Success

460 Hollywood Avenue

Carneys Point, NJ 08069-2799

http://www.salemcc.edu/departments/student-services/ SuccessCenter/index.htm

Contact: Mrs. Naydeen G. Gonzalez-DeJesus, Director of the Center for Student Success. Phone: 856-351-2759. Fax: 856-351-2763. E-mail: ngonzalez@salemcc.edu.

Center for Student Success Approximately 20 registered undergraduate students were served during 2006–07. The program or unit includes 3 full-time staff members. Coaches and counselors are provided through the program or unit. Academic advisers, professional tutors, regular education teachers, remediation/learning specialists, and trained peer tutors are provided collaboratively through on-campus or off-campus services.

Unique Aids and Services Aids, services, or accommodations include advocates, faculty training, priority registration, note-takers, extended testing time, isolated testing, alternative format testing.

Assistive Technology Assistive technology is located in campus labs and includes learning support software.

Subject-Area Tutoring Tutoring is offered one-on-one and in small groups for most subjects. Tutoring is provided collaboratively through on-campus or off-campus services via graduate assistants/ students, professional tutors, and trained peer tutors.

Diagnostic Testing Testing for math, reading, and written language is provided collaboratively through on-campus or off-campus services.

Basic Skills Remediation Remediation is offered in class-size groups for math, reading, and written language. Remediation is provided collaboratively through on-campus or off-campus services via regular education teachers.

Enrichment Programs for career planning, college survival skills, learning strategies, stress management, study skills, test taking, time management, vocabulary development, and written composition skills are provided collaboratively through on-campus or off-campus services. Credit is offered for college survival skills, learning strategies, stress management, study skills, test taking, time management, vocabulary development, and written composition skills.

Application For admittance to the program or unit, students are required to provide documentation of high school services. Upon application, materials documenting need for services should be sent only to the LD program or unit. Upon acceptance, documentation of need for services should be sent only to the LD program or unit. *Application deadline (institutional):* Continuous. *Application deadline (LD program):* Rolling/continuous for fall and rolling/continuous for spring.

Written Policies Written policy regarding general/basic LD accommodations is available on the program Web site. Written policy regarding general/basic LD accommodations is outlined in the school's catalog/handbook. Written policy regarding general/basic LD accommodations is available through the program or unit directly.

San Diego Mesa College
Disabled Students Programs and Services

7250 Mesa College Drive

San Diego, CA 92111-4998

http://www.sdmesa.edu

Contact: Prof. Jill Jansen, LD Specialist and Counselor. Phone: 619-388-2780. Fax: 619-388-2460. E-mail: jjansen@ sdccd.edu. Head of LD Program: Prof. Gail Conrad, Coordinator of Disabled Students Programs and Services. Phone: 619-388-2780. Fax: 619-388-2460. E-mail: gconrad@sdccd.edu.

Disabled Students Programs and Services Approximately 250 registered undergraduate students were served during 2006–07. The program or unit includes 1 part-time staff member. Academic advisers, counselors, diagnostic specialists, graduate assistants/ students, LD specialists, and remediation/learning specialists are provided through the program or unit. Academic advisers, counselors, diagnostic specialists, graduate assistants/students, professional tutors, skill tutors, and strategy tutors are provided collaboratively through on-campus or off-campus services.

Orientation The program or unit offers a mandatory online orientation for new students at any time after application is received at Disabled Students Programs and Services Office.

Summer Program an optional summer program prior to entering the school.

Unique Aids and Services Aids, services, or accommodations include career counseling, priority registration, accommodations based on disability verification.

Assistive Technology Assistive technology is located in campus labs, a special lab and includes digital textbooks/e-text, learning support software, and scanning.

Subject-Area Tutoring Tutoring is offered one-on-one and in small groups for most subjects. Tutoring is provided through the program or unit via computer-based instruction and graduate assistants/students. Tutoring is also provided collaboratively through on-campus or off-campus services via computer-based instruction, LD specialists, and professional tutors.

Diagnostic Testing Testing is provided through the program or unit for auditory processing, intelligence, learning styles, math, reading, spelling, visual processing, and written language.

Basic Skills Remediation Remediation is offered in small groups for computer skills, learning strategies, math, reading, spelling, study skills, and written language. Remediation is provided through the program or unit via computer-based instruction, graduate assistants/students, LD specialists, and professional tutors.

Enrichment Enrichment programs are available through the program or unit for learning strategies, math, practical computer skills, reading, self-advocacy, stress management, study skills, and written composition skills. Programs for career planning, college survival skills, health and nutrition, learning strategies, math, oral communication skills, practical computer skills, reading, study skills, test taking, time management, and written composition skills are provided collaboratively through on-campus or off-campus services. Credit is offered for career planning, college survival skills, health and nutrition, learning strategies, math, oral communication skills, practical computer skills, reading, study skills, test taking, time management, and written composition skills.

Application For admittance to the program or unit, students are required to apply to the program directly. It is recommended that students provide a psychoeducational report (3 years old or less) and provide documentation of high school services. Upon application, materials documenting need for services should be sent only to the LD program or unit. Upon acceptance, documentation of need for services should be sent only to the LD program or unit. *Application deadline (institutional):* Continuous. *Application deadline (LD program):* Rolling/continuous for fall and rolling/continuous for spring.

Written Policies Written policy regarding general/basic LD accommodations is available on the program Web site. Written policies regarding course substitutions, general/basic LD accommodations, grade forgiveness, substitutions and waivers of admissions requirements, and substitutions and waivers of graduation requirements are outlined in the school's catalog/handbook. Written policy regarding general/basic LD accommodations is available through the program or unit directly.

San Diego Miramar College
Disability Support Programs and Services (DSPS)

10440 Black Mountain Road

San Diego, CA 92126-2999

http://www.miramar.sdccd.cc.ca.us/depts/stusvcs/dsps/

Contact: Ms. Sandra J. Smith, Educational Psychologist and Counselor. Phone: 619-388-7312. Fax: 619-388-7917. E-mail: ssmith@sdccd.net.

Disability Support Programs and Services (DSPS) Approximately 185 registered undergraduate students were served during 2006–07. The program or unit includes 1 full-time and 2 part-time staff members. Academic advisers, diagnostic specialists, LD specialists, remediation/learning specialists, and strategy tutors are provided through the program or unit. Academic advisers, coaches, counselors, professional tutors, regular education teachers, skill tutors, and trained peer tutors are provided collaboratively through on-campus or off-campus services.

Orientation The program or unit offers an optional orientation for new students before registration, before classes begin, during summer prior to enrollment, during registration, after classes begin, individually by special arrangement, and via an online PowerPoint presentation.

Unique Aids and Services Aids, services, or accommodations include career counseling, faculty training, and priority registration.

Assistive Technology Assistive technology is located in campus labs, the DSS office, a special lab and includes digital textbooks/e-text, learning support software, and scanning. Technology training is provided to incoming students.

Subject-Area Tutoring Tutoring is offered one-on-one and in small groups for most subjects. Tutoring is provided through the program or unit via computer-based instruction. Tutoring is also provided collaboratively through on-campus or off-campus services via graduate assistants/students and trained peer tutors.

Diagnostic Testing Testing is provided through the program or unit for auditory processing, intelligence, learning strategies, learning styles, math, motor skills, neuropsychological, reading, social skills, spelling, spoken language, visual processing, and written language. Testing for study skills is provided collaboratively through on-campus or off-campus services.

Basic Skills Remediation Remediation is offered one-on-one, in small groups, and in class-size groups for auditory processing, computer skills, handwriting, learning strategies, math, motor skills, reading, spelling, spoken language, study skills, time management, visual processing, and written language. Remediation is provided through the program or unit via computer-based instruction and LD specialists. Remediation is also provided collaboratively through on-campus or off-campus services via computer-based instruction, regular education teachers, and trained peer tutors.

Enrichment Enrichment programs are available through the program or unit for college survival skills, learning strategies, math, oral communication skills, practical computer skills, reading, self-advocacy, stress management, study skills, test taking, time management, vocabulary development, and written composition skills. Programs for career planning, health and nutrition, learning strategies, and medication management are provided collaboratively through on-campus or off-campus services. Credit is offered for career planning, college survival skills, health and nutrition, learning strategies, math, oral communication skills, practical computer skills, reading, self-advocacy, stress management, study skills, test taking, time management, vocabulary development, and written composition skills.

Application It is recommended that students apply to the program directly, provide a psychoeducational report (5 years old or less), and provide documentation of high school services. Upon application, materials documenting need for services should be sent only to the LD program or unit. Upon acceptance, documentation of need for services should be sent only to the LD program or unit. *Application deadline (LD program):* Rolling/continuous for fall and rolling/continuous for spring.

Written Policies Written policies regarding course substitutions, general/basic LD accommodations, substitutions and waivers of admissions requirements, and substitutions and waivers of graduation requirements are available on the program Web site. Written policies regarding course substitutions, general/basic LD accommodations, grade forgiveness, substitutions and waivers of admissions requirements, and substitutions and waivers of graduation requirements are outlined in the school's catalog/handbook. Written policies regarding course substitutions, general/basic LD accommodations, substitutions and waivers of admissions requirements, and substitutions and waivers of graduation requirements are available through the program or unit directly.

Santa Ana College
Learning Disabilities Program

1530 West 17th Street

Santa Ana, CA 92706-3398

http://www.sac.edu/students/support_services/dsps/
learning_dis_program.htm

Contact: Ms. Mary Kobane, Professor/Learning Disabilities Specialist. Phone: 714-564-6260. Fax: 714-285-9619. E-mail: kobane_mary@sac.edu. Head of LD Program: Ms. Jane Mathis, Associate Dean, Disabled Students Programs & Services. Phone: 714-564-6277. Fax: 714-285-9619. E-mail: mathis_jane@sac.edu.

Learning Disabilities Program Approximately 250 registered undergraduate students were served during 2006–07. The program or unit includes 4 full-time and 10 part-time staff members. Academic advisers, counselors, diagnostic specialists, graduate assistants/students, LD specialists, professional tutors, regular education teachers, skill tutors, and strategy tutors are provided through the program or unit. Academic advisers, coaches, counselors, diagnostic specialists, professional tutors, regular education teachers, remediation/learning specialists, and skill tutors are provided collaboratively through on-campus or off-campus services.

Orientation The program or unit offers an optional 1-hour orientation for new students after classes begin and individually by special arrangement.

Summer Program To help prepare for the demands of college, there is an optional 6- to 8-week summer program prior to entering the school available to high school graduates that focuses on self-advocacy, specific subject tutoring, study skills, test-taking skills, and time management. The program accepts students from out-of-state.

Unique Aids and Services Aids, services, or accommodations include career counseling, faculty training, and priority registration.

Assistive Technology Assistive technology is located in campus labs, the DSS office, the library, the Testing Center and includes digital textbooks/e-text and scanning. Technology training is provided to incoming students.

Subject-Area Tutoring Tutoring is offered one-on-one and in small groups for some subjects. Tutoring is provided through the program or unit via LD specialists, professional tutors, and trained peer tutors. Tutoring is also provided collaboratively through on-campus or off-campus services via professional tutors and trained peer tutors.

Diagnostic Testing Testing is provided through the program or unit for auditory processing, intelligence, learning strategies, learning styles, math, reading, spelling, study skills, visual processing, and written language. Testing for auditory processing, learning strategies, learning styles, math, neuropsychological, personality, reading, spoken language, study skills, visual processing, and written language is provided collaboratively through on-campus or off-campus services.

Basic Skills Remediation Remediation is offered one-on-one, in small groups, and in class-size groups for computer skills, learning strategies, math, reading, spelling, spoken language, study skills, time management, visual processing, and written language. Remediation is provided through the program or unit via computer-based instruction, LD specialists, professional tutors, and trained peer tutors. Remediation is also provided collaboratively through on-campus or off-campus services via computer-based instruction, professional tutors, regular education teachers, and trained peer tutors.

Enrichment Enrichment programs are available through the program or unit for career planning, college survival skills, learning strategies, math, self-advocacy, study skills, test taking, and time management. Programs for career planning, college survival skills, health and nutrition, learning strategies, math, oral communication skills, practical computer skills, reading, self-advocacy, stress management, study skills, test taking, time management, vocabulary development, and written composition skills are provided collaboratively through on-campus or off-campus services. Credit is offered for career planning, college survival skills, health and nutrition, learning strategies, math, oral communication skills, practical computer skills, reading, study skills, test taking, time management, vocabulary development, and written composition skills.

Fees *LD Program or Service* fee varies according to level/tier of service. *Diagnostic Testing* fee is applicable.

Application For admittance to the program or unit, students are required to apply to the program directly, provide a psychoeducational report (5 years old or less), and provide documentation of high school services. Upon application, materials documenting need for services should be sent only to the LD program or unit. Upon acceptance, documentation of need for services should be sent only to the LD program or unit. *Application deadline (institutional):* 8/21. *Application deadline (LD program):* Rolling/continuous for fall and rolling/continuous for spring.

Written Policies Written policy regarding general/basic LD accommodations is available through the program or unit directly.

Santa Barbara City College
Disabled Students Programs and Services (DSPS)

721 Cliff Drive

Santa Barbara, CA 93109-2394

http://www.sbcc.edu/dsps/

Contact: Ms. Gerry A. Lewin, Learning Disabilities Specialist. Phone: 805-965-0581 Ext. 2343. Fax: 805-884-4966. E-mail: lewin@sbcc.edu. Head of LD Program: Ms. Mary D. Lawson, Learning Disabilities Specialist. Phone: 805-965-0581 Ext. 2343. Fax: 805-884-4966. E-mail: lawson@sbcc.edu.

Disabled Students Programs and Services (DSPS) Approximately 410 registered undergraduate students were served during 2006–07. The program or unit includes 8 full-time and 50 part-time staff members. Coaches, counselors, diagnostic specialists, LD specialists, professional tutors, strategy tutors, and trained peer tutors are provided through the program or unit. Academic advisers, regular education teachers, and skill tutors are provided collaboratively through on-campus or off-campus services.

Unique Aids and Services Aids, services, or accommodations include career counseling, faculty training, priority registration, support groups, weekly meetings with faculty, testing accommodations.

Assistive Technology Assistive technology is located in the DSS office and includes digital textbooks/e-text, scanning, and Inspiration, Kurzweil 3000. Technology training is provided to incoming students.

Subject-Area Tutoring Tutoring is offered one-on-one, in small groups, and in class-size groups for most subjects. Tutoring is provided through the program or unit via computer-based instruction, LD specialists, professional tutors, and trained peer tutors. Tutoring is also provided collaboratively through on-campus or off-campus services via computer-based instruction, professional tutors, and trained peer tutors.

Diagnostic Testing Testing is provided through the program or unit for auditory processing, intelligence, learning strategies, math, motor skills, reading, social skills, spelling, spoken language, study skills, visual processing, and written language. Testing for auditory processing, handwriting, intelligence, learning strategies, learning styles, math, motor skills, neuropsychological, personality, reading, social skills, spelling, spoken language, study skills, visual processing, and written language is provided collaboratively through on-campus or off-campus services.

Basic Skills Remediation Remediation is offered in class-size groups for computer skills, learning strategies, math, reading, spelling, study skills, time management, and written language. Remediation is provided through the program or unit via LD specialists, professional tutors, and trained peer tutors. Remediation is also provided collaboratively through on-campus or off-campus services via computer-based instruction, professional tutors, regular education teachers, and trained peer tutors.

Enrichment Enrichment programs are available through the program or unit for learning strategies, math, practical computer skills, reading, self-advocacy, stress management, study skills, test taking, time management, vocabulary development, and written composition skills. Programs for career planning, college survival skills, health and nutrition, learning strategies, math, medication management, oral communication skills, practical computer skills, reading, stress management, study skills, test taking, time management, vocabulary development, and written composition skills are provided collaboratively through on-campus or off-campus services. Credit is offered for career planning, college survival skills, health and nutrition, learning strategies, math, oral communication skills, practical computer skills, reading, study skills, time management, and written composition skills.

Application It is recommended that students provide a psychoeducational report (3 years old or less). Upon application, materials documenting need for services should be sent only to the LD program or unit. *Application deadline (institutional):* 8/22. *Application deadline (LD program):* Rolling/continuous for fall and rolling/continuous for spring.

Written Policies Written policy regarding general/basic LD accommodations is available on the program Web site. Written policies regarding course substitutions, general/basic LD accommodations, and reduced course loads are available through the program or unit directly.

Santa Fe Community College
Counseling and Special Services Department

6401 Richards Avenue
Santa Fe, NM 87508-4887
http://www.sfccnm.edu/

Contact: Mr. Dennis Matsui, Director. Phone: 505-428-1701. Fax: 505-428-1468. E-mail: dmatsui@sfccnm.edu.

Counseling and Special Services Department Approximately 225 registered undergraduate students were served during 2006–07.

Unique Aids and Services Aids, services, or accommodations include career counseling, faculty training, personal coach, priority registration, and support groups.

Assistive Technology Assistive technology is located in the DSS office and includes digital textbooks/e-text, learning support software, scanning, and voice recognition. Technology training is provided to incoming students.

Subject-Area Tutoring Tutoring is offered one-on-one and in small groups for most subjects. Tutoring is provided through the program or unit via computer-based instruction, graduate assistants/students, and trained peer tutors. Tutoring is also provided collaboratively through on-campus or off-campus services via trained peer tutors.

Basic Skills Remediation Remediation is offered one-on-one, in small groups, and in class-size groups for computer skills, learning strategies, math, reading, spelling, study skills, time management, and written language. Remediation is provided through the program or unit via computer-based instruction, graduate assistants/students, and trained peer tutors. Remediation is also provided collaboratively through on-campus or off-campus services via graduate assistants/students, regular education teachers, and trained peer tutors.

Enrichment Enrichment programs are available through the program or unit for career planning, college survival skills, learning strategies, math, medication management, oral communication skills, practical computer skills, reading, self-advocacy, stress management, study skills, test taking, time management, vocabulary development, and written composition skills. Programs for career planning, college survival skills, health and nutrition, learning strategies, math, medication management, oral communication skills, practical computer skills, reading, self-advocacy, stress management, study skills, test taking, time management, vocabulary development, and written composition skills are provided collaboratively through on-campus or off-campus services. Credit is offered for career planning, college survival skills, health and nutrition, learning strategies, math, oral communication skills, practical computer skills, reading, stress management, study skills, test taking, time management, vocabulary development, and written composition skills.

Student Organization Access To Success.

Application For admittance to the program or unit, students are required to apply to the program directly. It is recommended that students provide a psychoeducational report (5 years old or less) and provide documentation of high school services. Upon application, materials documenting need for services should be sent only to the LD program or unit. *Application deadline (LD program):* Rolling/continuous for fall and rolling/continuous for spring.

Written Policies Written policy regarding general/basic LD accommodations is outlined in the school's catalog/handbook. Written policy regarding general/basic LD accommodations is available through the program or unit directly.

Santa Monica College
Learning Disabilities Program

1900 Pico Boulevard

Santa Monica, CA 90405-1628

http://www.smc.edu/disabledstudent/ld/Default.htm

Contact: George Marcopulos, Professor, Learning Disabilities Specialist. Phone: 310-434-4684. Fax: 310-434-3694. E-mail: marcopulos_george@smc.edu.

Learning Disabilities Program Approximately 400 registered undergraduate students were served during 2006–07. The program or unit includes 2 full-time and 6 part-time staff members. Diagnostic specialists, LD specialists, strategy tutors, and trained peer tutors are provided through the program or unit. Counselors and trained peer tutors are provided collaboratively through on-campus or off-campus services.

Orientation The program or unit offers an optional 1-day orientation for new students before classes begin and during registration.

Summer Program To help prepare for the demands of college, there is an optional 6-week summer program prior to entering the school.

Unique Aids and Services Aids, services, or accommodations include faculty training and priority registration.

Assistive Technology Assistive technology includes digital textbooks/e-text.

Subject-Area Tutoring Tutoring is offered one-on-one, in small groups, and in class-size groups for some subjects. Tutoring is provided through the program or unit via computer-based instruction, LD specialists, and trained peer tutors. Tutoring is also provided collaboratively through on-campus or off-campus services via trained peer tutors.

Diagnostic Testing Testing is provided through the program or unit for auditory processing, intelligence, learning strategies, learning styles, math, reading, spelling, spoken language, visual processing, and written language.

Basic Skills Remediation Remediation is offered in class-size groups for computer skills, learning strategies, math, reading, study skills, time management, and written language. Remediation is provided through the program or unit via LD specialists. Remediation is also provided collaboratively through on-campus or off-campus services via computer-based instruction and regular education teachers.

Enrichment Enrichment programs are available through the program or unit for college survival skills, learning strategies, practical computer skills, self-advocacy, study skills, test taking, time management, and vocabulary development. Programs for career planning, college survival skills, learning strategies, math, practical computer skills, reading, study skills, test taking, time management, vocabulary development, and written composition skills are provided collaboratively through on-campus or off-campus services. Credit is offered for career planning, college survival skills, learning strategies, math, practical computer skills, reading, study skills, test taking, time management, vocabulary development, and written composition skills.

Application For admittance to the program or unit, students are required to provide a psychoeducational report (3 years old or less) and provide documentation of high school services. It is recommended that students apply to the program directly and provide results of assessment to determine eligibility under California Community College guidelines. Upon acceptance, documentation of need for services should be sent only to the LD program or unit. *Application deadline (LD program):* Rolling/continuous for fall.

Written Policies Written policy regarding general/basic LD accommodations is outlined in the school's catalog/handbook. Written policy regarding substitutions and waivers of graduation requirements is available through the program or unit directly.

Santa Rosa Junior College
Disability Resources Department

1501 Mendocino Avenue

Santa Rosa, CA 95401-4395

http://online.santarosa.edu/presentation/?4928

Contact: Catherine Reisman, Learning Disabilities Specialist. Phone: 707-527-4279. E-mail: creisman@santarosa.edu.

Disability Resources Department Approximately 500 registered undergraduate students were served during 2006–07. The program or unit includes 3 full-time and 2 part-time staff members. Academic advisers, counselors, diagnostic specialists, LD specialists, professional tutors, skill tutors, special education teachers, and strategy tutors are provided through the program or unit. Academic advisers and counselors are provided collaboratively through on-campus or off-campus services.

Orientation The program or unit offers an optional orientation for new students before registration and individually by special arrangement.

Unique Aids and Services Aids, services, or accommodations include career counseling and priority registration.

Assistive Technology Assistive technology is located in the DSS office and includes digital textbooks/e-text.

Subject-Area Tutoring Tutoring is offered one-on-one and in small groups for most subjects. Tutoring is provided through the program or unit via computer-based instruction and professional tutors. Tutoring is also provided collaboratively through on-campus or off-campus services via computer-based instruction, graduate assistants/students, professional tutors, and trained peer tutors.

Diagnostic Testing Testing is provided through the program or unit for auditory processing, intelligence, learning strategies, math, motor skills, reading, spelling, visual processing, written language, and other services.

Basic Skills Remediation Remediation is offered one-on-one, in small groups, and in class-size groups for auditory processing, learning strategies, math, reading, spelling, study skills, time management, and written language. Remediation is provided through the program or unit via computer-based instruction, LD specialists, and professional tutors. Remediation is also provided collaboratively through on-campus or off-campus services via computer-based instruction, LD specialists, professional tutors, and regular education teachers.

Enrichment Enrichment programs are available through the program or unit for career planning, college survival skills, learning strategies, math, self-advocacy, stress management, study skills, time management, and written composition skills. Programs for career planning, college survival skills, health and nutrition, learning strategies, math, medication management, oral communication skills, practical computer skills, reading, stress management, study skills, test taking, time management, vocabulary development, and written composition skills are provided collaboratively through on-campus or off-campus services. Credit is offered for career planning, college survival skills, health and nutrition, learning strategies, math, oral communication skills, practical computer skills, reading, self-advocacy, stress management, study skills, test taking, time management, vocabulary development, and written composition skills.

Application For admittance to the program or unit, students are required to provide a psychoeducational report (3 years old or less). It is recommended that students apply to the program directly and provide documentation of high school services. Upon application, materials documenting need for services should be sent only to the LD program or unit. *Application deadline (institutional):* Continuous. *Application deadline (LD program):* Rolling/continuous for fall and rolling/continuous for spring.

Written Policies Written policy regarding general/basic LD accommodations is available on the program Web site. Written policy regarding general/basic LD accommodations is outlined in the school's catalog/handbook. Written policies regarding course substitutions, general/basic LD accommodations, and reduced course loads are available through the program or unit directly.

Sauk Valley Community College
Student Needs Office

173 Illinois Route 2

Dixon, IL 61021

http://www.svcc.edu/

Contact: Ms. Deb Kerns, Student Needs Coordinator. Phone: 815-288-5511 Ext. 1220. Fax: 815-288-5571. E-mail: kernsd@svcc.edu.

Student Needs Office Approximately 65 registered undergraduate students were served during 2006–07. The program or unit includes 1 full-time and 8 part-time staff members. Academic advisers, LD specialists, professional tutors, skill tutors, and trained peer tutors are provided through the program or unit. Academic advisers are provided collaboratively through on-campus or off-campus services.

Orientation The program or unit offers an optional 1-day orientation for new students during summer prior to enrollment.

Summer Program To help prepare for the demands of college, there is an optional 1-day summer program prior to entering the school available to high school graduates that focuses on life skills and/or college life adjustment. The program accepts students from out-of-state.

Unique Aids and Services Aids, services, or accommodations include career counseling, faculty training, parent workshops, priority registration, and support groups.

Assistive Technology Assistive technology is located in campus labs, the DSS office and includes digital textbooks/e-text, learning support software, and scanning. Technology training is provided to incoming students.

Subject-Area Tutoring Tutoring is offered one-on-one for most subjects. Tutoring is provided through the program or unit via professional tutors.

Basic Skills Remediation Remediation is offered one-on-one for learning strategies, math, reading, social skills, study skills, and time management. Remediation is provided through the program or unit via professional tutors.

Enrichment Enrichment programs are available through the program or unit for career planning and self-advocacy. Programs for college survival skills, learning strategies, math, reading, stress management, study skills, test taking, vocabulary development, and written composition skills are provided collaboratively through on-campus or off-campus services. Credit is offered for college survival skills, learning strategies, math, reading, vocabulary development, and written composition skills.

Student Organization Students with Unique Abilities consists of 30 members.

Application For admittance to the program or unit, students are required to apply to the program directly, provide a psychoeducational report (5 years old or less), and provide documentation of high school services. Upon application, materials documenting need for services should be sent only to the LD program or unit. Upon acceptance, documentation of need for services should be sent only to the LD program or unit. *Application deadline (institutional):* Continuous. *Application deadline (LD program):* Rolling/continuous for fall and rolling/continuous for spring.

Written Policies Written policies regarding course substitutions, general/basic LD accommodations, reduced course loads, substitutions and waivers of admissions requirements, and substitutions and waivers of graduation requirements are available through the program or unit directly.

Schoolcraft College
Learning Assistance Center

18600 Haggerty Road

Livonia, MI 48152-2696

http://www.schoolcraft.edu/lac/

Contact: Mr. Carl R. Monroe, Equal Access Counselor. Phone: 734-462-4436. Fax: 734-462-4542. E-mail: cmonroe@schoolcraft.edu. Head of LD Program: Dr. Deborah Daiek, Associate Dean Academic and Assessment Services. Phone: 734-462-4436. Fax: 734-462-4542. E-mail: ddaiek@schoolcraft.edu.

Learning Assistance Center Approximately 150 registered undergraduate students were served during 2006–07. The program or unit includes 4 full-time and 6 part-time staff members. Academic advisers, coaches, counselors, LD specialists, skill tutors, trained peer tutors, and other are provided through the program or unit. Professional tutors, regular education teachers, and remediation/learning specialists are provided collaboratively through on-campus or off-campus services.

Orientation The program or unit offers an optional 1-hour orientation for new students individually by special arrangement.

Unique Aids and Services Aids, services, or accommodations include advocates, career counseling, faculty training, and personal coach.

Assistive Technology Assistive technology is located in campus labs, a special lab and includes digital textbooks/e-text, scanning, and speech-to-text. Technology training is provided to incoming students.

Schoolcraft College (continued)

Subject-Area Tutoring Tutoring is offered one-on-one, in small groups, and in class-size groups for most subjects. Tutoring is provided through the program or unit via trained peer tutors. Tutoring is also provided collaboratively through on-campus or off-campus services via LD specialists and professional tutors.

Diagnostic Testing Testing for intelligence, learning strategies, learning styles, math, neuropsychological, personality, reading, social skills, spelling, study skills, visual processing, and written language is provided collaboratively through on-campus or off-campus services.

Basic Skills Remediation Remediation is offered one-on-one, in small groups, and in class-size groups for computer skills, learning strategies, math, reading, study skills, time management, and written language. Remediation is provided through the program or unit via regular education teachers and trained peer tutors. Remediation is also provided collaboratively through on-campus or off-campus services via LD specialists and professional tutors.

Enrichment Enrichment programs are available through the program or unit for college survival skills, learning strategies, math, practical computer skills, reading, self-advocacy, study skills, test taking, time management, and written composition skills. Programs for career planning, learning strategies, math, oral communication skills, practical computer skills, reading, stress management, test taking, time management, vocabulary development, and written composition skills are provided collaboratively through on-campus or off-campus services. Credit is offered for career planning, college survival skills, learning strategies, oral communication skills, practical computer skills, reading, self-advocacy, study skills, time management, and vocabulary development.

Fees *Diagnostic Testing* fee is applicable.

Application For admittance to the program or unit, students are required to apply to the program directly. It is recommended that students provide a psychoeducational report (3 years old or less), provide documentation of high school services, and provide most recent evaluation. Upon application, materials documenting need for services should be sent only to the LD program or unit. Upon acceptance, documentation of need for services should be sent only to the LD program or unit. *Application deadline (institutional):* Continuous. *Application deadline (LD program):* Rolling/continuous for fall and rolling/continuous for spring.

Written Policies Written policy regarding general/basic LD accommodations is available on the program Web site. Written policy regarding general/basic LD accommodations is available through the program or unit directly.

Scottsdale Community College

9000 East Chaparral Road

Scottsdale, AZ 85256-2626

http://www.sc.maricopa.edu/

Contact: Director, Disability Resources & Services. Phone: 480-423-6517. Fax: 480-423-6377. E-mail: donna.young@sccmail.maricopa.edu.

Approximately 85 registered undergraduate students were served during 2006–07. The program or unit includes 3 part-time staff

members. Academic advisers, counselors, diagnostic specialists, skill tutors, and trained peer tutors are provided collaboratively through on-campus or off-campus services.

Unique Aids and Services Aids, services, or accommodations include faculty training, parent workshops, and priority registration.

Assistive Technology Assistive technology is located in the DSS office and includes digital textbooks/e-text, learning support software, and scanning.

Subject-Area Tutoring Tutoring is offered one-on-one for some subjects. Tutoring is provided through the program or unit via trained peer tutors. Tutoring is also provided collaboratively through on-campus or off-campus services via trained peer tutors.

Basic Skills Remediation Remediation is offered in class-size groups for learning strategies, math, reading, social skills, study skills, and time management. Remediation is provided collaboratively through on-campus or off-campus services via regular education teachers.

Enrichment Enrichment programs are available through the program or unit for self-advocacy, study skills, test taking, and time management. Programs for career planning, college survival skills, health and nutrition, learning strategies, math, reading, self-advocacy, stress management, study skills, test taking, time management, and written composition skills are provided collaboratively through on-campus or off-campus services.

Student Organization ADVOCACY@SCC consists of 8 members.

Fees *Diagnostic Testing* fee is $350.

Application For admittance to the program or unit, students are required to apply to the program directly, provide a psychoeducational report (5 years old or less), and provide documentation of high school services. Upon acceptance, documentation of need for services should be sent only to the LD program or unit. *Application deadline (institutional):* Continuous. *Application deadline (LD program):* Rolling/continuous for fall.

Written Policies Written policies regarding course substitutions, general/basic LD accommodations, reduced course loads, and substitutions and waivers of graduation requirements are available on the program Web site. Written policies regarding course substitutions, general/basic LD accommodations, reduced course loads, and substitutions and waivers of graduation requirements are available through the program or unit directly.

Seminole Community College
Disability Support Services

100 Weldon Boulevard

Sanford, FL 32773-6199

http://www.scc-fl.edu/

Contact: Ms. Dottie Paishon, Director of Disability Support Services. Phone: 407-708-2109. Fax: 407-708-2484. E-mail: paishond@scc-fl.edu.

Disability Support Services Approximately 320 registered undergraduate students were served during 2006–07. The program or unit includes 3 full-time and 4 part-time staff members. Diagnostic specialists, LD specialists, regular education teachers, remediation/

learning specialists, skill tutors, and trained peer tutors are provided through the program or unit. Academic advisers and counselors are provided collaboratively through on-campus or off-campus services.

Unique Aids and Services Aids, services, or accommodations include career counseling.

Assistive Technology Assistive technology is located in the DSS office and includes digital textbooks/e-text and scanning. Technology training is provided to incoming students.

Subject-Area Tutoring Tutoring is offered one-on-one for most subjects. Tutoring is provided through the program or unit via professional tutors and trained peer tutors. Tutoring is also provided collaboratively through on-campus or off-campus services via trained peer tutors.

Diagnostic Testing Testing is provided through the program or unit for auditory processing, intelligence, math, neuropsychological, reading, spelling, spoken language, visual processing, and written language. Testing for learning styles is provided collaboratively through on-campus or off-campus services.

Basic Skills Remediation Remediation is offered in class-size groups for math, reading, and written language. Remediation is provided collaboratively through on-campus or off-campus services via regular education teachers.

Enrichment Programs for career planning, college survival skills, study skills, test taking, and written composition skills are provided collaboratively through on-campus or off-campus services. Credit is offered for career planning, college survival skills, and written composition skills.

Student Organization disAbled Students Lead (DSL) consists of 25 members.

Application For admittance to the program or unit, students are required to apply to the program directly and provide a psychoeducational report (3 years old or less). It is recommended that students provide documentation of high school services. Upon application, materials documenting need for services should be sent only to the LD program or unit. Upon acceptance, documentation of need for services should be sent only to the LD program or unit. *Application deadline (institutional):* Continuous. *Application deadline (LD program):* Rolling/continuous for fall and rolling/continuous for spring.

Written Policies Written policies regarding course substitutions, general/basic LD accommodations, and substitutions and waivers of graduation requirements are available on the program Web site.

Shasta College
Disability Services and Programs for Students

PO Box 496006
11555 Old Oregon Trail
Redding, CA 96049-6006
http://www.shastacollege.edu/

Contact: Mr. Kendall Glen Crenshaw, Learning Disability Counselor. Phone: 530-225-3973. Fax: 530-225-4876. E-mail: kcrenshaw@shastacollege.edu. Head of LD Program: Mr. Jeroen Dragten, Director of Disability Services.

Phone: 530-225-3973. Fax: 530-225-4876. E-mail: jdragten@shastacollege.edu.

Disability Services and Programs for Students Approximately 180 registered undergraduate students were served during 2006–07. The program or unit includes 1 full-time and 1 part-time staff member. Counselors, LD specialists, regular education teachers, remediation/learning specialists, skill tutors, special education teachers, and strategy tutors are provided through the program or unit.

Orientation The program or unit offers an optional 3-hour orientation for new students before registration and before classes begin.

Unique Aids and Services Aids, services, or accommodations include career counseling, faculty training, priority registration, support groups, extra time on tests, note-takers, tutoring.

Assistive Technology Assistive technology is located in the DSS office and includes digital textbooks/e-text, learning support software, scanning, and voice recognition word processing, text-to-voice conversion. Technology training is provided to incoming students.

Subject-Area Tutoring Tutoring is offered one-on-one and in small groups for most subjects. Tutoring is provided through the program or unit via LD specialists and trained peer tutors.

Diagnostic Testing Testing is provided through the program or unit for auditory processing, intelligence, math, personality, reading, spelling, visual processing, written language, and other services.

Basic Skills Remediation Remediation is offered in class-size groups for computer skills, handwriting, learning strategies, math, reading, social skills, spelling, study skills, time management, visual processing, and written language. Remediation is provided through the program or unit via LD specialists, regular education teachers, special education teachers, and trained peer tutors.

Enrichment Enrichment programs are available through the program or unit for career planning, college survival skills, learning strategies, math, practical computer skills, reading, self-advocacy, study skills, test taking, and time management. Programs for career planning, college survival skills, health and nutrition, math, study skills, and written composition skills are provided collaboratively through on-campus or off-campus services. Credit is offered for career planning, college survival skills, math, practical computer skills, reading, and written composition skills.

Student Organization Disability Awareness Club consists of 35 members.

Application It is recommended that students provide a psychoeducational report (3 years old or less) and provide documentation of high school services. Upon application, materials documenting need for services should be sent only to the LD program or unit. Upon acceptance, documentation of need for services should be sent only to the LD program or unit. *Application deadline (institutional):* Continuous. *Application deadline (LD program):* Rolling/continuous for fall and rolling/continuous for spring.

Written Policies Written policies regarding course substitutions, general/basic LD accommodations, reduced course loads, substitutions and waivers of admissions requirements, and substitutions and waivers of graduation requirements are available on the program Web site. Written policy regarding grade forgiveness is outlined in the school's catalog/handbook. Written policy regarding general/basic LD accommodations is available through the program or unit directly.

Shawnee Community College

8364 Shawnee College Road

Ullin, IL 62992-2206

http://www.shawneecc.edu/

Contact: Mrs. Annie Hubbard, Special Needs Counselor. Phone: 618-634-3228. Fax: 618-634-3300. E-mail: annieh@shawneecc.edu.

Approximately 35 registered undergraduate students were served during 2006–07. The program or unit includes 1 full-time staff member. Counselors are provided through the program or unit.

Unique Aids and Services Aids, services, or accommodations include career counseling, untimed testing, note-takers, enlarged notes.

Subject-Area Tutoring Tutoring is offered one-on-one, in small groups, and in class-size groups for most subjects. Tutoring is provided collaboratively through on-campus or off-campus services via computer-based instruction, professional tutors, and trained peer tutors.

Diagnostic Testing Testing for math, reading, and written language is provided collaboratively through on-campus or off-campus services.

Basic Skills Remediation Remediation is offered one-on-one, in small groups, and in class-size groups for math, reading, and written language. Remediation is provided collaboratively through on-campus or off-campus services via regular education teachers.

Application For admittance to the program or unit, students are required to apply to the program directly, provide a psychoeducational report (3 years old or less), and provide documentation of high school services. Upon application, materials documenting need for services should be sent only to the LD program or unit. Upon acceptance, documentation of need for services should be sent only to the LD program or unit. *Application deadline (LD program):* Rolling/continuous for fall.

Written Policies Written policies regarding course substitutions, reduced course loads, substitutions and waivers of admissions requirements, and substitutions and waivers of graduation requirements are outlined in the school's catalog/handbook. Written policy regarding general/basic LD accommodations is available through the program or unit directly.

Shelton State Community College

Office of Disability Services

9500 Old Greensboro Road

Tuscaloosa, AL 35405-8522

http://www.sheltonstate.edu

Contact: Ms. Michele Youngblood, Office of Disability Services Director. Phone: 205-391-3958. Fax: 205-391-3946. E-mail: michele.youngblood@sheltonstate.edu.

Office of Disability Services Approximately 25 registered undergraduate students were served during 2006–07. The program or unit includes 2 full-time staff members and 1 part-time staff member. Academic advisers, counselors, regular education teachers, and skill tutors are provided collaboratively through on-campus or off-campus services.

Orientation The program or unit offers a mandatory orientation for new students during other times.

Summer Program To help prepare for the demands of college, there is summer program prior to entering the school.

Assistive Technology Assistive technology is located in the DSS office.

Subject-Area Tutoring Tutoring is offered one-on-one and in small groups for some subjects. Tutoring is provided collaboratively through on-campus or off-campus services via computer-based instruction, graduate assistants/students, professional tutors, and trained peer tutors.

Application For admittance to the program or unit, students are required to apply to the program directly. It is recommended that students provide a psychoeducational report (3 years old or less) and provide documentation of high school services. Upon application, materials documenting need for services should be sent to both admissions and the LD program or unit. Upon acceptance, documentation of need for services should be sent only to the LD program or unit. *Application deadline (institutional):* Continuous. *Application deadline (LD program):* Rolling/continuous for fall and rolling/continuous for spring.

Written Policies Written policy regarding general/basic LD accommodations is available on the program Web site. Written policies regarding general/basic LD accommodations and substitutions and waivers of admissions requirements are outlined in the school's catalog/handbook. Written policy regarding general/basic LD accommodations is available through the program or unit directly.

Sheridan College–Gillette Campus

Enrollment Services, Disabilities Support Services

300 West Sinclair Street

Gillette, WY 82718

http://www.sheridan.edu

Contact: Zane Garstad, Director of Enrollment Services. Phone: 307-674-6446 Ext. 2006. Fax: 307-674-3373. E-mail: zgarstad@sheridan.edu.

Enrollment Services, Disabilities Support Services Approximately 30 registered undergraduate students were served during 2006–07. The program or unit includes 1 full-time staff member. Counselors are provided through the program or unit. Academic advisers, coaches, diagnostic specialists, professional tutors, regular education teachers, remediation/learning specialists, skill tutors, and strategy tutors are provided collaboratively through on-campus or off-campus services.

Assistive Technology Assistive technology is located in campus labs and includes digital textbooks/e-text.

Subject-Area Tutoring Tutoring is offered one-on-one and in small groups for all subjects. Tutoring is provided collaboratively through on-campus or off-campus services via computer-based instruction, professional tutors, and trained peer tutors.

Basic Skills Remediation Remediation is offered one-on-one and in small groups for computer skills, learning strategies, math, reading, spelling, study skills, and time management. Remediation is provided collaboratively through on-campus or off-campus services via computer-based instruction, professional tutors, and trained peer tutors.

Enrichment Programs for career planning, college survival skills, learning strategies, math, practical computer skills, reading, stress management, study skills, test taking, time management, and written composition skills are provided collaboratively through on-campus or off-campus services. Credit is offered for career planning, college survival skills, practical computer skills, reading, stress management, study skills, test taking, time management, and written composition skills.

Application For admittance to the program or unit, students are required to provide a psychoeducational report (3 years old or less). It is recommended that students provide documentation of high school services. Upon application, materials documenting need for services should be sent only to the LD program or unit. Upon acceptance, documentation of need for services should be sent only to the LD program or unit. *Application deadline (LD program):* Rolling/continuous for fall and rolling/continuous for spring.

Written Policies Written policy regarding general/basic LD accommodations is outlined in the school's catalog/handbook.

Skagit Valley College
Disability Support Services

2405 College Way

Mount Vernon, WA 98273-5899

http://www.skagit.edu/news.asp_Q_pagenumber_E_355

Contact: Mr. Eric L. Anderson, Counselor/Coordinator of Disability Support Services. Phone: 360-416-7818. Fax: 360-416-7950. E-mail: eric.anderson@skagit.edu.

Disability Support Services Approximately 140 registered undergraduate students were served during 2006–07. The program or unit includes 2 full-time staff members. Academic advisers and counselors are provided through the program or unit. Regular education teachers, remediation/learning specialists, and trained peer tutors are provided collaboratively through on-campus or off-campus services.

Unique Aids and Services Aids, services, or accommodations include career counseling and priority registration.

Assistive Technology Assistive technology is located in campus labs, a special lab and includes digital textbooks/e-text, learning support software, and scanning. Technology training is provided to incoming students.

Subject-Area Tutoring Tutoring is offered one-on-one and in small groups for most subjects. Tutoring is provided collaboratively through on-campus or off-campus services via trained peer tutors.

Basic Skills Remediation Remediation is offered in class-size groups for computer skills, learning strategies, math, reading, spelling, study skills, time management, and written language. Remediation is provided collaboratively through on-campus or off-campus services via computer-based instruction and regular education teachers.

Enrichment Programs for career planning, college survival skills, health and nutrition, learning strategies, math, practical computer skills, reading, study skills, test taking, time management, vocabulary development, and written composition skills are provided collaboratively through on-campus or off-campus services. Credit is offered for career planning, college survival skills, health and nutrition, learning strategies, math, practical computer skills, reading, study skills, test taking, time management, vocabulary development, and written composition skills.

Application For admittance to the program or unit, students are required to provide a psychoeducational report (5 years old or less). It is recommended that students provide documentation of high school services. Upon application, materials documenting need for services should be sent only to the LD program or unit. Upon acceptance, documentation of need for services should be sent only to the LD program or unit. *Application deadline (institutional):* Continuous. *Application deadline (LD program):* Rolling/continuous for fall and rolling/continuous for spring.

Written Policies Written policies regarding course substitutions, general/basic LD accommodations, substitutions and waivers of admissions requirements, and substitutions and waivers of graduation requirements are available on the program Web site. Written policies regarding course substitutions, general/basic LD accommodations, substitutions and waivers of admissions requirements, and substitutions and waivers of graduation requirements are outlined in the school's catalog/handbook. Written policies regarding course substitutions, general/basic LD accommodations, substitutions and waivers of admissions requirements, and substitutions and waivers of graduation requirements are available through the program or unit directly.

Somerset Christian College
Office of the Registrar

10 College Way

P. O. Box 9188

Zarephath, NJ 08890-9035

http://www.somerset.edu/

Contact: Mrs. Colleen Klein, Registrar. Phone: 732-356-1595. Fax: 732-356-4846. E-mail: admissions@somerset.edu.

Office of the Registrar Academic advisers are provided collaboratively through on-campus or off-campus services.

Application For admittance to the program or unit, students are required to provide documentation of high school services. Upon application, materials documenting need for services should be sent only to admissions with institutional application materials. Upon acceptance, documentation of need for services should be sent only to admissions. *Application deadline (institutional):* Continuous. *Application deadline (LD program):* Rolling/continuous for fall.

Written Policies Written policies regarding course substitutions, general/basic LD accommodations, grade forgiveness, reduced course loads, substitutions and waivers of admissions requirements, and substitutions and waivers of graduation requirements are outlined in the school's catalog/handbook.

Somerset Community College

Disability Services

808 Monticello Street
Somerset, KY 42501-2973
http://www.somerset.kctcs.edu/

Contact: Ms. Mary Petry, Coordinator of Disability Services.
Phone: 606-451-6706. Fax: 606-676-9065. E-mail:
mary.petry@kctcs.edu.

Disability Services Approximately 6 registered undergraduate students were served during 2006–07. The program or unit includes 2 full-time staff members. Academic advisers, counselors, professional tutors, regular education teachers, remediation/learning specialists, and trained peer tutors are provided collaboratively through on-campus or off-campus services.

Unique Aids and Services Aids, services, or accommodations include faculty training, STAR Learning Center.

Assistive Technology Assistive technology is located in the DSS office, STAR Center and includes digital textbooks/e-text, learning support software, and scanning.

Subject-Area Tutoring Tutoring is offered one-on-one and in small groups for most subjects. Tutoring is provided collaboratively through on-campus or off-campus services via computer-based instruction, trained peer tutors, and other.

Basic Skills Remediation Remediation is offered in class-size groups for computer skills, learning strategies, math, reading, study skills, time management, and written language. Remediation is provided collaboratively through on-campus or off-campus services via regular education teachers.

Application For admittance to the program or unit, students are required to provide letter from doctor, vocational rehab or therapist. It is recommended that students provide a psychoeducational report (3 years old or less) and provide documentation of high school services. Upon application, materials documenting need for services should be sent only to the LD program or unit. Upon acceptance, documentation of need for services should be sent only to admissions. *Application deadline (LD program):* Rolling/continuous for fall and rolling/continuous for spring.

Written Policies Written policy regarding general/basic LD accommodations is outlined in the school's catalog/handbook. Written policies regarding general/basic LD accommodations and substitutions and waivers of admissions requirements are available through the program or unit directly.

Southeast Community College, Lincoln Campus

Career Advising/Disability Services

8800 O Street
Lincoln, NE 68520-1299
http://www.southeast.edu/

Contact: Ms. Theresa Webster, Director of Career Advising.

Phone: 402-437-2624. Fax: 402-437-2540. E-mail:
twebster@southeast.edu.

Career Advising/Disability Services Approximately 170 registered undergraduate students were served during 2006–07. The program or unit includes 4 full-time staff members. LD specialists are provided through the program or unit.

Assistive Technology Assistive technology is located in campus labs, the DSS office and includes digital textbooks/e-text and scanning.

Subject-Area Tutoring Tutoring is offered one-on-one for most subjects. Tutoring is provided collaboratively through on-campus or off-campus services via professional tutors and trained peer tutors.

Basic Skills Remediation Remediation is offered in class-size groups for computer skills, learning strategies, math, reading, spelling, study skills, time management, and written language. Remediation is provided collaboratively through on-campus or off-campus services via computer-based instruction and regular education teachers.

Enrichment Enrichment programs are available through the program or unit for career planning, learning strategies, self-advocacy, stress management, study skills, test taking, and time management. Programs for learning strategies, math, oral communication skills, reading, study skills, time management, vocabulary development, and written composition skills are provided collaboratively through on-campus or off-campus services.

Application For admittance to the program or unit, students are required to apply to the program directly and provide documentation of high school services. It is recommended that students provide a psychoeducational report (3 years old or less). Upon application, materials documenting need for services should be sent only to the LD program or unit. Upon acceptance, documentation of need for services should be sent only to the LD program or unit. *Application deadline (LD program):* Rolling/continuous for fall and rolling/continuous for spring.

Written Policies Written policy regarding general/basic LD accommodations is available on the program Web site. Written policy regarding general/basic LD accommodations is outlined in the school's catalog/handbook. Written policies regarding course substitutions, general/basic LD accommodations, reduced course loads, substitutions and waivers of admissions requirements, and substitutions and waivers of graduation requirements are available through the program or unit directly.

Southeast Technical Institute

Disability Services

2320 N. Career Ave.
Sioux Falls, SD 57107-1301
http://www.southeasttech.com/

Contact: Steven Herr, Disability Services Coordinator.
Phone: 605-367-4450. Fax: 605-367-8305. E-mail:
steve.herr@southeasttech.com.

Disability Services Approximately 80 registered undergraduate students were served during 2006–07. The program or unit includes 2 full-time staff members. Counselors are provided through the program or unit. Academic advisers, counselors, graduate assistants/students, regular education teachers, and trained peer tutors are provided collaboratively through on-campus or off-campus services.

Orientation The program or unit offers an optional orientation for new students individually by special arrangement.

Summer Program available to high school graduates.

Assistive Technology Assistive technology is located in campus labs, the DSS office, classrooms as needed and includes digital textbooks/e-text, learning support software, and scanning. Technology training is provided to incoming students.

Subject-Area Tutoring Tutoring is offered one-on-one, in small groups, and in class-size groups for all subjects. Tutoring is provided collaboratively through on-campus or off-campus services via computer-based instruction, graduate assistants/students, professional tutors, and trained peer tutors.

Basic Skills Remediation Remediation is offered in class-size groups for math, written language, and English. Remediation is provided collaboratively through on-campus or off-campus services via regular education teachers and special education teachers.

Application For admittance to the program or unit, students are required to apply to the program directly and provide documentation of high school services. It is recommended that students provide a psychoeducational report. Upon application, materials documenting need for services should be sent only to the LD program or unit. Upon acceptance, documentation of need for services should be sent only to the LD program or unit. *Application deadline (institutional):* Continuous. *Application deadline (LD program):* Rolling/continuous for fall and rolling/continuous for spring.

Written Policies Written policies regarding course substitutions and general/basic LD accommodations are available on the program Web site. Written policy regarding general/basic LD accommodations is outlined in the school's catalog/handbook. Written policies regarding course substitutions and general/basic LD accommodations are available through the program or unit directly.

Southern Maine Community College

Disability Services

2 Fort Road

South Portland, ME 04106

http://www.smccme.edu

Contact: Ms. Sandra E. Lynham, Educational Liaison. Phone: 207-741-5923. Fax: 207-741-5653. E-mail: slynham@smccme.edu.

Disability Services Approximately 150 registered undergraduate students were served during 2006–07. The program or unit includes 1 full-time and 1 part-time staff member. Academic advisers, counselors, skill tutors, and trained peer tutors are provided collaboratively through on-campus or off-campus services.

Assistive Technology Assistive technology is located in the Learning Assistance Center and includes digital textbooks/e-text, learning support software, and scanning.

Subject-Area Tutoring Tutoring is offered one-on-one for most subjects. Tutoring is provided collaboratively through on-campus or off-campus services via computer-based instruction, professional tutors, and trained peer tutors.

Basic Skills Remediation Remediation is offered in class-size groups for math, reading, and written language. Remediation is provided collaboratively through on-campus or off-campus services via regular education teachers.

Application For admittance to the program or unit, students are required to apply to the program directly, provide a psychoeducational report (3 years old or less), and provide medical documentation for chronic health disabilities. It is recommended that students provide documentation of high school services. Upon application, materials documenting need for services should be sent only to the LD program or unit. Upon acceptance, documentation of need for services should be sent only to the LD program or unit. *Application deadline (institutional):* Continuous. *Application deadline (LD program):* Rolling/continuous for fall and rolling/continuous for spring.

Written Policies Written policy regarding general/basic LD accommodations is available on the program Web site. Written policy regarding general/basic LD accommodations is outlined in the school's catalog/handbook. Written policies regarding course substitutions, general/basic LD accommodations, reduced course loads, substitutions and waivers of admissions requirements, and substitutions and waivers of graduation requirements are available through the program or unit directly.

South Piedmont Community College

Disability Services

PO Box 126

Polkton, NC 28135-0126

http://www.spcc.edu

Contact: Mrs. Rhonda Williams Treadaway, Counselor. Phone: 704-272-5345. Fax: 704-272-5350. E-mail: rtreadaway@spcc.edu. Head of LD Program: Mrs. Elaine Clodfelter, Vice President of Student Success. Phone: 704-272-5302. Fax: 704-272-5350. E-mail: eclodfelter@spcc.edu.

Disability Services Approximately 30 registered undergraduate students were served during 2006–07. The program or unit includes 1 full-time staff member. Academic advisers, counselors, diagnostic specialists, regular education teachers, remediation/learning specialists, and trained peer tutors are provided through the program or unit. Academic advisers, counselors, diagnostic specialists, regular education teachers, remediation/learning specialists, and trained peer tutors are provided collaboratively through on-campus or off-campus services.

Unique Aids and Services Aids, services, or accommodations include career counseling and faculty training.

Assistive Technology Assistive technology is located in Learning Resources Center (library) and includes digital textbooks/e-text, learning support software, and scanning. Technology training is provided to incoming students.

Subject-Area Tutoring Tutoring is offered one-on-one and in small groups for all subjects. Tutoring is provided through the program or unit via trained peer tutors. Tutoring is also provided collaboratively through on-campus or off-campus services via computer-based instruction, trained peer tutors, and other.

Basic Skills Remediation Remediation is offered one-on-one, in small groups, and in class-size groups for computer skills, learning strategies, math, reading, study skills, time management, and writ-

South Piedmont Community College (continued)

ten language. Remediation is provided collaboratively through on-campus or off-campus services via computer-based instruction, professional tutors, and regular education teachers.

Enrichment Enrichment programs are available through the program or unit for career planning, math, reading, self-advocacy, study skills, and written composition skills. Programs for career planning, college survival skills, health and nutrition, math, oral communication skills, practical computer skills, reading, and written composition skills are provided collaboratively through on-campus or off-campus services. Credit is offered for college survival skills, health and nutrition, learning strategies, math, oral communication skills, practical computer skills, reading, stress management, study skills, test taking, time management, vocabulary development, and written composition skills.

Application For admittance to the program or unit, students are required to provide a psychoeducational report (3 years old or less). It is recommended that students provide documentation of high school services and provide transition plan from senior year. Upon application, materials documenting need for services should be sent only to the LD program or unit. Upon acceptance, documentation of need for services should be sent only to the LD program or unit. *Application deadline (institutional):* Continuous. *Application deadline (LD program):* Rolling/continuous for fall and rolling/continuous for spring.

Written Policies Written policies regarding course substitutions, general/basic LD accommodations, grade forgiveness, and substitutions and waivers of graduation requirements are outlined in the school's catalog/handbook. Written policies regarding course substitutions, general/basic LD accommodations, and substitutions and waivers of graduation requirements are available through the program or unit directly.

Southwestern Indian Polytechnic Institute
Academic Support Disability Services

9169 Coors, NW, Box 10146

Albuquerque, NM 87184-0146

http://www.sipi.bia.edu/

Contact: Cece Cometsevah, Vocational Rehabilitation Counselor. Phone: 505-346-2319. Fax: 505-346-7726. E-mail: ccometse@sipi.bia.edu.

Academic Support Disability Services Approximately 30 registered undergraduate students were served during 2006–07. The program or unit includes 1 full-time staff member. Academic advisers, counselors, professional tutors, regular education teachers, skill tutors, and special education teachers are provided collaboratively through on-campus or off-campus services.

Unique Aids and Services Aids, services, or accommodations include advocates, career counseling, faculty training, and support groups.

Assistive Technology Assistive technology is located in Academic Support Lab and includes learning support software and scanning.

Subject-Area Tutoring Tutoring is offered one-on-one, in small groups, and in class-size groups for most subjects. Tutoring is provided through the program or unit via computer-based instruction, professional tutors, and trained peer tutors.

Basic Skills Remediation Remediation is offered one-on-one, in small groups, and in class-size groups for computer skills, handwriting, learning strategies, math, reading, social skills, spelling, study skills, time management, visual processing, and written language. Remediation is provided through the program or unit via computer-based instruction, professional tutors, regular education teachers, special education teachers, teacher trainees, and trained peer tutors.

Enrichment Programs for career planning, college survival skills, health and nutrition, learning strategies, math, practical computer skills, reading, stress management, study skills, test taking, time management, vocabulary development, and written composition skills are provided collaboratively through on-campus or off-campus services. Credit is offered for health and nutrition, math, practical computer skills, and written composition skills.

Application For admittance to the program or unit, students are required to apply to the program directly, provide a psychoeducational report (3 years old or less), provide documentation of high school services, and provide other disability community services including tribal, local, state, and federal. Upon application, materials documenting need for services should be sent only to the LD program or unit. Upon acceptance, documentation of need for services should be sent only to the LD program or unit. *Application deadline (institutional):* Continuous. *Application deadline (LD program):* Rolling/continuous for fall and rolling/continuous for spring.

Written Policies Written policy regarding general/basic LD accommodations is outlined in the school's catalog/handbook.

Southwestern Michigan College
Special Populations Office

58900 Cherry Grove Road

Dowagiac, MI 49047-9793

http://www.swmich.edu/spops/index.html

Contact: Mrs. Susan H. Sullivan, Coordinator of Special Populations Services. Phone: 269-687-4801. Fax: 269-684-2281. E-mail: ssullivan@swmich.edu.

Special Populations Office Approximately 35 registered undergraduate students were served during 2006–07. The program or unit includes 2 full-time staff members and 1 part-time staff member. Academic advisers, counselors, professional tutors, regular education teachers, strategy tutors, and trained peer tutors are provided through the program or unit. Academic advisers, counselors, professional tutors, regular education teachers, remediation/learning specialists, skill tutors, strategy tutors, and trained peer tutors are provided collaboratively through on-campus or off-campus services.

Unique Aids and Services Aids, services, or accommodations include advocates, career counseling, faculty training, instructional accommodations.

Assistive Technology Assistive technology is located in campus labs and includes digital textbooks/e-text, learning support software, and scanning. Technology training is provided to incoming students.

Subject-Area Tutoring Tutoring is offered one-on-one, in small groups, and in class-size groups for most subjects. Tutoring is provided through the program or unit via computer-based instruction. Tutoring is also provided collaboratively through on-campus or off-campus services via computer-based instruction, graduate assistants/students, professional tutors, and trained peer tutors.

Diagnostic Testing Testing is provided through the program or unit for learning strategies, learning styles, and study skills. Testing for learning strategies, learning styles, math, reading, study skills, and written language is provided collaboratively through on-campus or off-campus services.

Basic Skills Remediation Remediation is offered in class-size groups for computer skills, learning strategies, math, reading, social skills, study skills, time management, and written language. Remediation is provided collaboratively through on-campus or off-campus services via computer-based instruction, professional tutors, regular education teachers, and trained peer tutors.

Enrichment Enrichment programs are available through the program or unit for career planning, college survival skills, learning strategies, self-advocacy, stress management, study skills, test taking, and time management. Programs for career planning, college survival skills, learning strategies, math, reading, self-advocacy, stress management, study skills, test taking, time management, and written composition skills are provided collaboratively through on-campus or off-campus services.

Application For admittance to the program or unit, students are required to apply to the program directly and provide medical or professional documentation of disability. It is recommended that students provide a psychoeducational report (3 years old or less) and provide documentation of high school services. Upon application, materials documenting need for services should be sent only to the LD program or unit. Upon acceptance, documentation of need for services should be sent only to the LD program or unit. *Application deadline (institutional):* Continuous. *Application deadline (LD program):* Rolling/continuous for fall and rolling/continuous for spring.

Written Policies Written policies regarding general/basic LD accommodations and reduced course loads are available on the program Web site. Written policies regarding course substitutions, general/basic LD accommodations, grade forgiveness, and substitutions and waivers of graduation requirements are outlined in the school's catalog/handbook. Written policy regarding reduced course loads is available through the program or unit directly.

Spokane Community College

Center for Students with Disabilities

1810 North Greene Street

Spokane, WA 99217-5399

http://www.scc.spokane.edu/dss

Contact: Mr. Dennis J. Johnson, Manager, DSS & Testing. Phone: 509-533-7169. Fax: 509-533-8877. E-mail: djjohnson@scc.spokane.edu.

Center for Students with Disabilities Approximately 90 registered undergraduate students were served during 2006–07. The program or unit includes 2 full-time and 2 part-time staff members.

Academic advisers, counselors, professional tutors, and regular education teachers are provided through the program or unit. Academic advisers, counselors, professional tutors, regular education teachers, and trained peer tutors are provided collaboratively through on-campus or off-campus services.

Orientation The program or unit offers an optional orientation for new students individually by special arrangement.

Assistive Technology Assistive technology is located in campus labs, the DSS office and includes digital textbooks/e-text, learning support software, and scanning. Technology training is provided to incoming students.

Subject-Area Tutoring Tutoring is offered one-on-one for some subjects. Tutoring is provided collaboratively through on-campus or off-campus services via trained peer tutors.

Enrichment Programs for career planning, college survival skills, learning strategies, math, stress management, study skills, and test taking are provided collaboratively through on-campus or off-campus services.

Student Organization Disability Awareness League consists of 15 members.

Application For admittance to the program or unit, students are required to apply to the program directly, provide a psychoeducational report (3 years old or less), and provide current evaluation. It is recommended that students provide documentation of high school services. Upon application, materials documenting need for services should be sent only to the LD program or unit. Upon acceptance, documentation of need for services should be sent only to the LD program or unit. *Application deadline (institutional):* Continuous. *Application deadline (LD program):* Rolling/continuous for fall and rolling/continuous for spring.

Written Policies Written policy regarding general/basic LD accommodations is available on the program Web site. Written policies regarding course substitutions, general/basic LD accommodations, grade forgiveness, reduced course loads, substitutions and waivers of admissions requirements, and substitutions and waivers of graduation requirements are available through the program or unit directly.

Spoon River College

Disability Support Services

23235 North County 22

Canton, IL 61520-9801

http://www.spoonrivercollege.com/services/specialneeds.html

Contact: Janet Munson, Student Development Specialist/Disability Support Services. Phone: 309-649-6273. Fax: 309-649-6393. E-mail: jmunson@spoonrivercollege.edu.

Disability Support Services Approximately 25 registered undergraduate students were served during 2006–07. The program or unit includes 1 full-time staff member. Academic advisers, regular education teachers, remediation/learning specialists, trained peer tutors, and other are provided collaboratively through on-campus or off-campus services.

Unique Aids and Services Aids, services, or accommodations include note-takers, readers, testing accommodations.

Assistive Technology Assistive technology is located in a special lab and includes digital textbooks/e-text and learning support software. Technology training is provided to incoming students.

Spoon River College (continued)

Subject-Area Tutoring Tutoring is offered one-on-one and in small groups for most subjects. Tutoring is provided collaboratively through on-campus or off-campus services via computer-based instruction, professional tutors, and trained peer tutors.

Basic Skills Remediation Remediation is offered in class-size groups for learning strategies, math, reading, study skills, time management, and written language. Remediation is provided collaboratively through on-campus or off-campus services via regular education teachers.

Enrichment Enrichment programs are available through the program or unit for self-advocacy. Programs for career planning, college survival skills, learning strategies, study skills, test taking, and time management are provided collaboratively through on-campus or off-campus services.

Application For admittance to the program or unit, students are required to apply to the program directly and provide a psychoeducational report (3 years old or less). It is recommended that students provide documentation of high school services. Upon application, materials documenting need for services should be sent only to the LD program or unit. Upon acceptance, documentation of need for services should be sent only to the LD program or unit. *Application deadline (institutional):* Continuous. *Application deadline (LD program):* Rolling/continuous for fall and rolling/continuous for spring.

Written Policies Written policy regarding general/basic LD accommodations is available on the program Web site. Written policies regarding general/basic LD accommodations and grade forgiveness are outlined in the school's catalog/handbook. Written policy regarding general/basic LD accommodations is available through the program or unit directly.

Basic Skills Remediation Remediation is offered one-on-one for auditory processing, learning strategies, math, reading, social skills, study skills, time management, and written language. Remediation is provided through the program or unit via computer-based instruction, graduate assistants/students, LD specialists, professional tutors, regular education teachers, and trained peer tutors. Remediation is also provided collaboratively through on-campus or off-campus services via regular education teachers.

Enrichment Enrichment programs are available through the program or unit for career planning, college survival skills, learning strategies, math, oral communication skills, practical computer skills, reading, study skills, test taking, time management, and written composition skills. Programs for college survival skills, health and nutrition, math, oral communication skills, stress management, study skills, test taking, and time management are provided collaboratively through on-campus or off-campus services.

Application For admittance to the program or unit, students are required to provide a psychoeducational report (10 years old or less). It is recommended that students provide documentation of high school services. Upon application, materials documenting need for services should be sent to both admissions and the LD program or unit. Upon acceptance, documentation of need for services should be sent only to the LD program or unit. *Application deadline (institutional):* Continuous. *Application deadline (LD program):* Rolling/continuous for fall and rolling/continuous for spring.

Written Policies Written policies regarding course substitutions, general/basic LD accommodations, grade forgiveness, reduced course loads, substitutions and waivers of admissions requirements, and substitutions and waivers of graduation requirements are available on the program Web site. Written policies regarding course substitutions, general/basic LD accommodations, grade forgiveness, reduced course loads, substitutions and waivers of admissions requirements, and substitutions and waivers of graduation requirements are outlined in the school's catalog/handbook.

Springfield College in Illinois
Resource Center

1500 North Fifth Street

Springfield, IL 62702-2694

http://www.sci.edu/resource

Contact: Ms. Joanna Beth Tweedy, Director of the Resource Center. Phone: 217-525-1420 Ext. 239. Fax: 217-525-1497. E-mail: jtweedy@sci.edu.

Resource Center Approximately 4 registered undergraduate students were served during 2006–07. The program or unit includes 1 full-time and 4 part-time staff members. Academic advisers, LD specialists, professional tutors, remediation/learning specialists, skill tutors, strategy tutors, and trained peer tutors are provided through the program or unit. Academic advisers, coaches, counselors, diagnostic specialists, graduate assistants/students, LD specialists, and regular education teachers are provided collaboratively through on-campus or off-campus services.

Subject-Area Tutoring Tutoring is offered one-on-one for most subjects. Tutoring is provided through the program or unit via computer-based instruction, graduate assistants/students, and trained peer tutors. Tutoring is also provided collaboratively through on-campus or off-campus services via professional tutors.

Stark State College of Technology
Disability Support Services

6200 Frank Avenue, NW

North Canton, OH 44720-7299

http://www.starkstate.edu/

Contact: Mrs. Kathryn Ann Bernstein, Coordinator Disability Support Services. Phone: 330-494-6170 Ext. 4423. E-mail: kbernstein@starkstate.edu.

Disability Support Services Approximately 300 registered undergraduate students were served during 2006–07. The program or unit includes 2 full-time staff members. Academic advisers and counselors are provided through the program or unit. Academic advisers, counselors, graduate assistants/students, professional tutors, regular education teachers, remediation/learning specialists, strategy tutors, and trained peer tutors are provided collaboratively through on-campus or off-campus services.

Orientation The program or unit offers an optional 2-hour orientation for new students before classes begin, during summer prior to enrollment, and individually by special arrangement.

Unique Aids and Services Aids, services, or accommodations include career counseling and faculty training.

Assistive Technology Assistive technology is located in campus labs, the DSS office and includes digital textbooks/e-text, learning support software, and scanning. Technology training is provided to incoming students.

Subject-Area Tutoring Tutoring is offered one-on-one and in small groups for most subjects. Tutoring is provided collaboratively through on-campus or off-campus services via computer-based instruction, professional tutors, and trained peer tutors.

Basic Skills Remediation Remediation is offered one-on-one and in class-size groups for computer skills, learning strategies, math, reading, study skills, time management, and written language. Remediation is provided collaboratively through on-campus or off-campus services via computer-based instruction, graduate assistants/students, professional tutors, regular education teachers, and trained peer tutors.

Enrichment Programs for career planning, college survival skills, learning strategies, study skills, test taking, time management, and written composition skills are provided collaboratively through on-campus or off-campus services.

Application For admittance to the program or unit, students are required to apply to the program directly and provide a psychoeducational report (5 years old or less). It is recommended that students provide documentation of high school services. Upon application, materials documenting need for services should be sent only to the LD program or unit. Upon acceptance, documentation of need for services should be sent only to the LD program or unit. *Application deadline (institutional):* Continuous. *Application deadline (LD program):* Rolling/continuous for fall and rolling/continuous for spring.

Written Policies Written policy regarding general/basic LD accommodations is available on the program Web site. Written policy regarding general/basic LD accommodations is outlined in the school's catalog/handbook. Written policy regarding general/basic LD accommodations is available through the program or unit directly.

State University of New York College of Environmental Science & Forestry, Ranger School

PO Box 48, 257 Ranger School Road

Wanakena, NY 13695

http://www.esf.edu/

Contact: Mr. Thomas O. Slocum, Director of Career and Counseling Services. Phone: 315-470-6660. Fax: 315-470-4728. E-mail: toslocum@esf.edu.

The program or unit includes 1 full-time staff member. Diagnostic specialists, LD specialists, professional tutors, remediation/learning specialists, skill tutors, special education teachers, and strategy tutors are provided through the program or unit. Academic advisers, coaches, counselors, diagnostic specialists, graduate assistants/students, regular education teachers, skill tutors, strategy tutors, and trained peer tutors are provided collaboratively through on-campus or off-campus services.

Assistive Technology Assistive technology is located in the DSS office and includes digital textbooks/e-text.

Subject-Area Tutoring Tutoring is offered one-on-one and in small groups for most subjects. Tutoring is provided through the program or unit via LD specialists and professional tutors. Tutoring is also provided collaboratively through on-campus or off-campus services via graduate assistants/students and trained peer tutors.

Basic Skills Remediation Remediation is offered one-on-one and in class-size groups for learning strategies, study skills, time management, and written language. Remediation is provided through the program or unit via LD specialists and professional tutors. Remediation is also provided collaboratively through on-campus or off-campus services via graduate assistants/students, regular education teachers, and trained peer tutors.

Application For admittance to the program or unit, students are required to provide a psychoeducational report (3 years old or less). It is recommended that students provide documentation of high school services. Upon application, materials documenting need for services should be sent only to the LD program or unit. Upon acceptance, documentation of need for services should be sent only to the LD program or unit. *Application deadline (institutional):* Continuous. *Application deadline (LD program):* Rolling/continuous for fall and rolling/continuous for spring.

Written Policies Written policy regarding general/basic LD accommodations is available through the program or unit directly.

State University of New York College of Technology at Alfred
Student Disability Services

Alfred, NY 14802

http://www.alfredstate.edu/

Contact: Heather Meacham, Coordinator of Student Disability Services. Phone: 607-587-4506. Fax: 607-587-3210. E-mail: meachahm@alfredstate.edu.

Student Disability Services Approximately 150 registered undergraduate students were served during 2006–07. The program or unit includes 1 full-time and 2 part-time staff members. Counselors are provided through the program or unit. Counselors are provided collaboratively through on-campus or off-campus services.

Unique Aids and Services Aids, services, or accommodations include advocates.

Assistive Technology Assistive technology is located in the DSS office and includes digital textbooks/e-text, learning support software, scanning, and MP3 players to which tests are scanned. Technology training is provided to incoming students.

Subject-Area Tutoring Tutoring is offered one-on-one and in small groups for most subjects. Tutoring is provided through the program or unit via professional tutors and trained peer tutors. Tutoring is also provided collaboratively through on-campus or off-campus services via professional tutors and trained peer tutors.

Diagnostic Testing Testing is provided through the program or unit for learning styles. Testing for auditory processing, intelligence, learning styles, and visual processing is provided collaboratively through on-campus or off-campus services.

State University of New York College of Technology at Alfred (continued)

Enrichment Programs for career planning, college survival skills, learning strategies, reading, study skills, test taking, time management, and written composition skills are provided collaboratively through on-campus or off-campus services. Credit is offered for college survival skills, reading, and written composition skills.

Application For admittance to the program or unit, students are required to provide a psychoeducational report (3 years old or less) and provide documentation of high school services. Upon application, materials documenting need for services should be sent only to the LD program or unit. Upon acceptance, documentation of need for services should be sent only to the LD program or unit. *Application deadline (institutional):* Continuous. *Application deadline (LD program):* Rolling/continuous for fall and rolling/continuous for spring.

Written Policies Written policies regarding course substitutions, general/basic LD accommodations, grade forgiveness, reduced course loads, substitutions and waivers of admissions requirements, and substitutions and waivers of graduation requirements are available through the program or unit directly.

State University of New York College of Technology at Canton
Office of Accommodative Services

Cornell Drive

Canton, NY 13617

http://www.canton.edu/can/
can_start.taf?page=serve_accomodate

Contact: Ms. M. Veigh Mehan Lee, Coordinator for Accommodative and Tutoring Services. Phone: 315-386-7392. Fax: 315-379-3877. E-mail: leev@canton.edu.

Office of Accommodative Services Approximately 171 registered undergraduate students were served during 2006–07. The program or unit includes 2 full-time staff members and 1 part-time staff member. Academic advisers, counselors, professional tutors, and trained peer tutors are provided collaboratively through on-campus or off-campus services.

Orientation The program or unit offers an optional 30-minute to 1-hour orientation for new students by appointment during summer orientation.

Unique Aids and Services Aids, services, or accommodations include advocates, career counseling, and priority registration.

Assistive Technology Assistive technology is located in the DSS office, the campus library and includes digital textbooks/e-text, learning support software, and scanning. Technology training is provided to incoming students.

Subject-Area Tutoring Tutoring is offered one-on-one, in small groups, and in class-size groups for all subjects. Tutoring is provided collaboratively through on-campus or off-campus services via computer-based instruction, professional tutors, trained peer tutors, and other.

Basic Skills Remediation Remediation is offered one-on-one, in small groups, and in class-size groups for computer skills, learning strategies, math, reading, spelling, study skills, time management, and written language. Remediation is provided collaboratively through on-campus or off-campus services via computer-based instruction, professional tutors, trained peer tutors, and other.

Enrichment Programs for career planning, college survival skills, learning strategies, math, oral communication skills, practical computer skills, reading, self-advocacy, stress management, study skills, test taking, time management, vocabulary development, and written composition skills are provided collaboratively through on-campus or off-campus services.

Application For admittance to the program or unit, students are required to provide a psychoeducational report (3 years old or less). It is recommended that students provide documentation of high school services. Upon acceptance, documentation of need for services should be sent only to the LD program or unit. *Application deadline (institutional):* Continuous. *Application deadline (LD program):* Rolling/continuous for fall.

Written Policies Written policy regarding general/basic LD accommodations is outlined in the school's catalog/handbook. Written policy regarding general/basic LD accommodations is available through the program or unit directly.

Surry Community College
Office of Disability Services

630 South Main Street

PO Box 304

Dobson, NC 27017-8432

http://depts.surry.edu/stud_dev/programs.html

Contact: Laura Bracken, Special Programs and ADA Coordinator. Phone: 336-386-3264. Fax: 336-386-3690. E-mail: brackenl@surry.cc.nc.us.

Office of Disability Services Approximately 83 registered undergraduate students were served during 2006–07. The program or unit includes 1 full-time staff member. Academic advisers, counselors, LD specialists, remediation/learning specialists, trained peer tutors, and other are provided through the program or unit. Academic advisers, counselors, diagnostic specialists, professional tutors, regular education teachers, and skill tutors are provided collaboratively through on-campus or off-campus services.

Unique Aids and Services Aids, services, or accommodations include advocates, priority registration, support services adviser, note-takers.

Assistive Technology Assistive technology is located in the DSS office, the library and includes digital textbooks/e-text.

Subject-Area Tutoring Tutoring is offered one-on-one for all subjects. Tutoring is provided through the program or unit via computer-based instruction, graduate assistants/students, professional tutors, trained peer tutors, and other. Tutoring is also provided collaboratively through on-campus or off-campus services via LD specialists and trained peer tutors.

Diagnostic Testing Testing for learning strategies, learning styles, motor skills, neuropsychological, personality, spoken language, visual processing, and other services is provided collaboratively through on-campus or off-campus services.

Basic Skills Remediation Remediation is offered in class-size groups for handwriting, learning strategies, math, reading, study skills, time management, written language, and developmental courses. Remediation is provided through the program or unit via computer-based instruction, graduate assistants/students, professional tutors, and other. Remediation is also provided collaboratively through on-campus or off-campus services via computer-based instruction, LD specialists, regular education teachers, and teacher trainees.

Enrichment Enrichment programs are available through the program or unit for self-advocacy. Programs for career planning, college survival skills, health and nutrition, learning strategies, math, oral communication skills, practical computer skills, reading, study skills, test taking, time management, vocabulary development, and written composition skills are provided collaboratively through on-campus or off-campus services.

Application For admittance to the program or unit, students are required to apply to the program directly, provide a psychoeducational report (3 years old or less), and provide results of medical, psychological or emotional diagnostic tests or other professional evaluations. It is recommended that students provide documentation of high school services. Upon application, materials documenting need for services should be sent only to the LD program or unit. Upon acceptance, documentation of need for services should be sent only to the LD program or unit. *Application deadline (LD program):* Rolling/continuous for fall and rolling/continuous for spring.

Written Policies Written policy regarding general/basic LD accommodations is available on the program Web site. Written policies regarding general/basic LD accommodations and substitutions and waivers of admissions requirements are outlined in the school's catalog/handbook. Written policies regarding general/basic LD accommodations and reduced course loads are available through the program or unit directly.

Sussex County Community College
Disabilities Assistance Program (DAP)

1 College Hill

Newton, NJ 07860

http://www.sussex.edu/

Contact: Dr. Kathleen Okay, Director of the Learning Center. Phone: 973-300-2153. Fax: 973-300-2156. E-mail: kokay@sussex.edu.

Disabilities Assistance Program (DAP) Approximately 75 registered undergraduate students were served during 2006–07. The program or unit includes 1 full-time and 2 part-time staff members. Counselors are provided through the program or unit. Academic advisers, counselors, professional tutors, strategy tutors, and trained peer tutors are provided collaboratively through on-campus or off-campus services.

Orientation The program or unit offers an optional 45-minute to 1-hour orientation for new students individually by special arrangement.

Unique Aids and Services Aids, services, or accommodations include career counseling, faculty training, and priority registration.

Assistive Technology Assistive technology includes digital textbooks/e-text.

Subject-Area Tutoring Tutoring is offered one-on-one and in small groups for most subjects. Tutoring is provided collaboratively through on-campus or off-campus services via computer-based instruction, professional tutors, and trained peer tutors.

Diagnostic Testing Testing for intelligence is provided collaboratively through on-campus or off-campus services.

Basic Skills Remediation Remediation is offered in class-size groups for learning strategies, math, reading, and written language. Remediation is provided collaboratively through on-campus or off-campus services via regular education teachers and special education teachers.

Enrichment Enrichment programs are available through the program or unit for college survival skills, learning strategies, study skills, test taking, and written composition skills. Programs for career planning, college survival skills, learning strategies, math, reading, study skills, test taking, time management, and written composition skills are provided collaboratively through on-campus or off-campus services. Credit is offered for college survival skills, learning strategies, and math.

Fees *Diagnostic Testing* fee is $150.

Application For admittance to the program or unit, students are required to apply to the program directly and provide a psychoeducational report (5 years old or less). It is recommended that students provide documentation of high school services. Upon application, materials documenting need for services should be sent only to the LD program or unit. *Application deadline (institutional):* Continuous. *Application deadline (LD program):* Rolling/continuous for fall and rolling/continuous for spring.

Written Policies Written policy regarding general/basic LD accommodations is available on the program Web site. Written policies regarding course substitutions, general/basic LD accommodations, substitutions and waivers of admissions requirements, and substitutions and waivers of graduation requirements are outlined in the school's catalog/handbook. Written policies regarding course substitutions, general/basic LD accommodations, substitutions and waivers of admissions requirements, and substitutions and waivers of graduation requirements are available through the program or unit directly.

Tallahassee Community College
Disability Support Services

444 Appleyard Drive

Tallahassee, FL 32304-2895

http://www.tcc.fl.edu/

Contact: Mark J. Linehan, Counselor. Phone: 850-201-8430. Fax: 850-201-8433. E-mail: linehanm@tcc.fl.edu.

Disability Support Services Approximately 800 registered undergraduate students were served during 2006–07. The program or unit includes 5 full-time and 5 part-time staff members. Academic advisers and counselors are provided through the program or unit. Coaches, graduate assistants/students, and regular education teachers are provided collaboratively through on-campus or off-campus services.

Unique Aids and Services Aids, services, or accommodations include career counseling and priority registration.

Tallahassee Community College (continued)

Enrichment Programs for career planning, college survival skills, reading, stress management, study skills, and test taking are provided collaboratively through on-campus or off-campus services. Credit is offered for career planning, college survival skills, and reading.

Application For admittance to the program or unit, students are required to provide a psychoeducational report. It is recommended that students provide documentation of high school services. Upon application, materials documenting need for services should be sent only to the LD program or unit. Upon acceptance, documentation of need for services should be sent only to the LD program or unit. *Application deadline (institutional):* 8/1. *Application deadline (LD program):* Rolling/continuous for fall and rolling/continuous for spring.

Written Policies Written policies regarding course substitutions, general/basic LD accommodations, and substitutions and waivers of admissions requirements are available on the program Web site. Written policies regarding course substitutions, general/basic LD accommodations, and substitutions and waivers of admissions requirements are outlined in the school's catalog/handbook. Written policy regarding substitutions and waivers of graduation requirements is available through the program or unit directly.

TESST College of Technology

4600 Powder Mill Road

Beltsville, MD 20705

http://www.tesst.com/

Contact: Ms. Tara Anne Corona, Library Manager and Student Event Coordinator. Phone: 301-937-8448 Ext. 147. Fax: 301-937-5327. E-mail: tcorona@tesst.com.

Academic advisers, counselors, professional tutors, regular education teachers, skill tutors, and strategy tutors are provided collaboratively through on-campus or off-campus services.

Unique Aids and Services Aids, services, or accommodations include career counseling and personal coach.

Assistive Technology Assistive technology is located in campus labs, Library Resource Center.

Subject-Area Tutoring Tutoring is offered one-on-one, in small groups, and in class-size groups for all subjects. Tutoring is provided collaboratively through on-campus or off-campus services via professional tutors, trained peer tutors, and other.

Diagnostic Testing Testing for intelligence, learning strategies, learning styles, math, reading, spelling, visual processing, and written language is provided collaboratively through on-campus or off-campus services.

Basic Skills Remediation Remediation is offered one-on-one and in small groups for computer skills, learning strategies, math, reading, spelling, study skills, time management, and written language. Remediation is provided collaboratively through on-campus or off-campus services via professional tutors and regular education teachers.

Enrichment Programs for career planning, college survival skills, health and nutrition, learning strategies, math, oral communication skills, practical computer skills, reading, stress management, study skills, test taking, time management, vocabulary development, and written composition skills are provided collaboratively through on-campus or off-campus services. Credit is offered for career planning, oral communication skills, practical computer skills, and written composition skills.

Application For admittance to the program or unit, students are required to provide documentation of high school services. Upon application, materials documenting need for services should be sent only to admissions with institutional application materials. Upon acceptance, documentation of need for services should be sent only to admissions. *Application deadline (LD program):* Rolling/continuous for fall and rolling/continuous for spring.

Written Policies Written policies regarding general/basic LD accommodations and grade forgiveness are outlined in the school's catalog/handbook.

Texas Southmost College
Disability Services

80 Fort Brown

Brownsville, TX 78520-4991

http://www.ability.utb.edu

Contact: Mr. Steve Wilder, Counselor/Coordinator, Disability Services. Phone: 956-882-7374. Fax: 956-882-7861. E-mail: steve.wilder@utb.edu.

Disability Services Approximately 120 registered undergraduate students were served during 2006–07. Academic advisers, counselors, professional tutors, regular education teachers, remediation/learning specialists, skill tutors, and trained peer tutors are provided collaboratively through on-campus or off-campus services.

Unique Aids and Services Aids, services, or accommodations include time and a half on tests, distraction-reduced area.

Assistive Technology Assistive technology is located in the DSS office, a special lab and includes digital textbooks/e-text and scanning. Technology training is provided to incoming students.

Subject-Area Tutoring Tutoring is offered in small groups for some subjects. Tutoring is provided collaboratively through on-campus or off-campus services via trained peer tutors.

Basic Skills Remediation Remediation is offered one-on-one, in small groups, and in class-size groups for learning strategies, math, reading, study skills, time management, and written language. Remediation is provided collaboratively through on-campus or off-campus services via computer-based instruction, professional tutors, regular education teachers, and trained peer tutors.

Enrichment Programs for career planning, college survival skills, learning strategies, math, study skills, test taking, and time management are provided collaboratively through on-campus or off-campus services.

Application For admittance to the program or unit, students are required to provide psychological evaluation with all scores and subtests reported. It is recommended that students provide a psychoeducational report (4 years old or less) and provide documentation of high school services. Upon application, materials documenting need for services should be sent only to the LD program or unit. Upon acceptance, documentation of need for services should be sent only to the LD program or unit.

Written Policies Written policies regarding course substitutions, substitutions and waivers of admissions requirements, and substitutions and waivers of graduation requirements are outlined in the school's catalog/handbook. Written policy regarding general/basic LD accommodations is available through the program or unit directly.

Thaddeus Stevens College of Technology
Counseling/Special Needs Coordinator Office

750 East King Street

Lancaster, PA 17602-3198

http://www.stevenscollege.edu/

Contact: Chris Metzler. Phone: 717-299-7794. E-mail: metzler@stevenscollege.edu. Head of LD Program: Mrs. Debra A. Schuch, Counselor/Special Needs Coordinator. Phone: 717-299-7408. Fax: 717-391-6929. E-mail: schuch@stevenscollege.edu.

Counseling/Special Needs Coordinator Office Approximately 65 registered undergraduate students were served during 2006–07. The program or unit includes 2 full-time staff members. Counselors are provided through the program or unit. Academic advisers, counselors, professional tutors, regular education teachers, remediation/learning specialists, trained peer tutors, and other are provided collaboratively through on-campus or off-campus services.
Summer Program To help prepare for the demands of college, there is a mandatory 5-week summer program prior to entering the school available to high school graduates that focuses on specific subject tutoring, study skills, test-taking skills, and time management.
Unique Aids and Services Aids, services, or accommodations include career counseling and faculty training.
Assistive Technology Assistive technology is located in campus labs, the DSS office, the library and includes books on tape.
Subject-Area Tutoring Tutoring is offered one-on-one and in small groups for most subjects. Tutoring is provided through the program or unit via professional tutors and trained peer tutors. Tutoring is also provided collaboratively through on-campus or off-campus services via professional tutors and trained peer tutors.
Diagnostic Testing Testing for learning strategies, learning styles, math, reading, social skills, spelling, spoken language, study skills, and written language is provided collaboratively through on-campus or off-campus services.
Basic Skills Remediation Remediation is offered one-on-one and in small groups for computer skills, learning strategies, math, reading, social skills, spelling, study skills, and time management. Remediation is provided collaboratively through on-campus or off-campus services via computer-based instruction, professional tutors, regular education teachers, and trained peer tutors.
Enrichment Programs for learning strategies, math, reading, study skills, test taking, time management, and written composition skills are provided collaboratively through on-campus or off-campus services.
Fees *Diagnostic Testing* fee is applicable.
Application For admittance to the program or unit, students are required to provide a psychoeducational report (3 years old or less) and provide documentation of high school services. It is recom-

mended that students provide physician's letter. Upon application, materials documenting need for services should be sent only to the LD program or unit. Upon acceptance, documentation of need for services should be sent only to the LD program or unit. *Application deadline (LD program):* Rolling/continuous for fall. 3/30 for spring.
Written Policies Written policy regarding general/basic LD accommodations is available on the program Web site. Written policy regarding general/basic LD accommodations is outlined in the school's catalog/handbook.

Tidewater Community College
Learning Disabilities Services

121 College Place

Norfolk, VA 23510

http://www.tcc.edu/students/specialized/disabilityservices/index.htm

Contact: Dr. Linda W. Harris, College-Wide Coordinator of Disability Services. Phone: 757-822-1213. Fax: 757-822-1214. E-mail: lharris@tcc.edu.

Learning Disabilities Services Approximately 215 registered undergraduate students were served during 2006–07. The program or unit includes 1 full-time and 3 part-time staff members. Academic advisers, counselors, diagnostic specialists, graduate assistants/students, LD specialists, and regular education teachers are provided through the program or unit. Academic advisers, counselors, professional tutors, regular education teachers, remediation/learning specialists, skill tutors, strategy tutors, and trained peer tutors are provided collaboratively through on-campus or off-campus services.
Unique Aids and Services Aids, services, or accommodations include advocates, career counseling, faculty training, priority registration, and support groups.
Assistive Technology Assistive technology is located in the DSS office and includes digital textbooks/e-text, learning support software, and scanning. Technology training is provided to incoming students.
Subject-Area Tutoring Tutoring is offered one-on-one, in small groups, and in class-size groups for all subjects. Tutoring is provided collaboratively through on-campus or off-campus services via computer-based instruction, graduate assistants/students, trained peer tutors, and other.
Diagnostic Testing Testing is provided through the program or unit for auditory processing, handwriting, intelligence, learning strategies, learning styles, math, motor skills, neuropsychological, reading, spelling, spoken language, study skills, visual processing, written language, and other services. Testing for learning strategies, learning styles, math, reading, and study skills is provided collaboratively through on-campus or off-campus services.
Basic Skills Remediation Remediation is offered one-on-one, in small groups, and in class-size groups for computer skills, learning strategies, math, motor skills, reading, spelling, study skills, time management, and written language. Remediation is provided collaboratively through on-campus or off-campus services via computer-based instruction, graduate assistants/students, regular education teachers, teacher trainees, trained peer tutors, and other.

Tidewater Community College (continued)

Enrichment Enrichment programs are available through the program or unit for college survival skills, learning strategies, practical computer skills, reading, self-advocacy, stress management, study skills, test taking, time management, vocabulary development, and written composition skills. Programs for career planning, college survival skills, health and nutrition, learning strategies, math, practical computer skills, reading, self-advocacy, stress management, study skills, test taking, and time management are provided collaboratively through on-campus or off-campus services. Credit is offered for college survival skills, health and nutrition, math, practical computer skills, reading, stress management, study skills, test taking, time management, vocabulary development, and written composition skills.

Application For admittance to the program or unit, students are required to provide a psychoeducational report (3 years old or less). Upon application, materials documenting need for services should be sent only to the LD program or unit. Upon acceptance, documentation of need for services should be sent only to the LD program or unit. *Application deadline (institutional):* Continuous. *Application deadline (LD program):* Rolling/continuous for fall and rolling/continuous for spring.

Written Policies Written policies regarding course substitutions and general/basic LD accommodations are available on the program Web site. Written policy regarding course substitutions is outlined in the school's catalog/handbook. Written policy regarding general/basic LD accommodations is available through the program or unit directly.

Tri-County Technical College
Disability Services

PO Box 587, 7900 Highway 76

Pendleton, SC 29670-0587

http://www.tctc.edu/prospective_students/student_services/disabilities.html

Contact: Mrs. Carol A. Miller, Disability Services Coordinator. Phone: 864-646-8361 Ext. 1564. Fax: 864-646-1890. E-mail: cmiller4@tctc.edu.

Disability Services Approximately 40 registered undergraduate students were served during 2006–07. The program or unit includes 1 full-time staff member. Counselors are provided through the program or unit. Counselors are provided collaboratively through on-campus or off-campus services.

Unique Aids and Services Aids, services, or accommodations include career counseling and faculty training.

Assistive Technology Assistive technology is located in campus labs, the DSS office, a special lab and includes digital textbooks/e-text, learning support software, and scanning. Technology training is provided to incoming students.

Subject-Area Tutoring Tutoring is offered in small groups for most subjects. Tutoring is provided collaboratively through on-campus or off-campus services via computer-based instruction, trained peer tutors, and other.

Basic Skills Remediation Remediation is offered one-on-one and in class-size groups for math, reading, and written language. Remediation is provided collaboratively through on-campus or off-campus services via computer-based instruction, regular education teachers, and other.

Enrichment Programs for career planning, college survival skills, math, oral communication skills, practical computer skills, reading, and written composition skills are provided collaboratively through on-campus or off-campus services. Credit is offered for college survival skills, oral communication skills, and practical computer skills.

Application For admittance to the program or unit, students are required to provide a psychoeducational report (3 years old or less). Upon application, materials documenting need for services should be sent only to the LD program or unit. Upon acceptance, documentation of need for services should be sent only to the LD program or unit. *Application deadline (LD program):* Rolling/continuous for fall and rolling/continuous for spring.

Written Policies Written policy regarding general/basic LD accommodations is available on the program Web site. Written policy regarding general/basic LD accommodations is outlined in the school's catalog/handbook. Written policies regarding course substitutions, general/basic LD accommodations, and reduced course loads are available through the program or unit directly.

Trocaire College
Palisano Learning Center

360 Choate Avenue

Buffalo, NY 14220-2094

http://www.trocaire.edu/

Contact: Sister Norine M. Truax RSM, Coordinator for Students with Special Needs. Phone: 716-826-1200 Ext. 1321. E-mail: truaxn@trocaire.edu.

Palisano Learning Center Approximately 21 registered undergraduate students were served during 2006–07. The program or unit includes 1 full-time and 2 part-time staff members. LD specialists are provided through the program or unit. LD specialists, professional tutors, regular education teachers, remediation/learning specialists, special education teachers, and trained peer tutors are provided collaboratively through on-campus or off-campus services.

Orientation The program or unit offers a mandatory 1-day orientation for new students during summer prior to enrollment and during registration.

Summer Program To help prepare for the demands of college, there is a mandatory summer program prior to entering the school available to high school graduates that focuses on specific subject tutoring, study skills, and time management. Degree credit will be earned.

Unique Aids and Services Aids, services, or accommodations include faculty training and support groups.

Subject-Area Tutoring Tutoring is offered one-on-one and in small groups for most subjects. Tutoring is provided through the program or unit via professional tutors. Tutoring is also provided collaboratively through on-campus or off-campus services via computer-based instruction, LD specialists, professional tutors, and trained peer tutors.

.

Diagnostic Testing Testing is provided through the program or unit for reading. Testing for learning strategies, learning styles, math, reading, and written language is provided collaboratively through on-campus or off-campus services.
Basic Skills Remediation Remediation is offered in small groups for computer skills, handwriting, math, reading, study skills, time management, and written language. Remediation is provided through the program or unit via LD specialists. Remediation is also provided collaboratively through on-campus or off-campus services via computer-based instruction, professional tutors, and trained peer tutors.
Enrichment Programs for career planning, college survival skills, learning strategies, math, practical computer skills, reading, study skills, test taking, time management, vocabulary development, and written composition skills are provided collaboratively through on-campus or off-campus services.
Fees *Summer Program* fee is $350. *Orientation* fee is $350.
Application For admittance to the program or unit, students are required to apply to the program directly, provide a psychoeducational report (2 years old or less), and provide documentation of high school services. Upon application, materials documenting need for services should be sent to both admissions and the LD program or unit. Upon acceptance, documentation of need for services should be sent only to the LD program or unit. *Application deadline (institutional):* Continuous. *Application deadline (LD program):* Rolling/continuous for fall and rolling/continuous for spring.
Written Policies Written policies regarding course substitutions, general/basic LD accommodations, grade forgiveness, reduced course loads, substitutions and waivers of admissions requirements, and substitutions and waivers of graduation requirements are outlined in the school's catalog/handbook. Written policies regarding course substitutions, general/basic LD accommodations, reduced course loads, substitutions and waivers of admissions requirements, and substitutions and waivers of graduation requirements are available through the program or unit directly.

Truckee Meadows Community College
Disability Resource Center

7000 Dandini Boulevard
Reno, NV 89512-3901
http://www.tmcc.edu/drc/

Contact: Ms. Joanne Ascencio, Adviser. Phone: 775-673-7277. Fax: 775-673-7207. E-mail: jascencio@tmcc.edu.

Disability Resource Center Approximately 300 registered undergraduate students were served during 2006–07. The program or unit includes 3 full-time staff members. LD specialists, skill tutors, and trained peer tutors are provided through the program or unit. Diagnostic specialists are provided collaboratively through on-campus or off-campus services.
Assistive Technology Assistive technology is located in campus labs, the DSS office and includes digital textbooks/e-text.
Subject-Area Tutoring Tutoring is offered one-on-one for all subjects. Tutoring is provided collaboratively through on-campus or off-campus services via trained peer tutors.

Diagnostic Testing Testing for auditory processing, intelligence, math, reading, spelling, visual processing, and written language is provided collaboratively through on-campus or off-campus services.
Basic Skills Remediation Remediation is offered one-on-one for computer skills, math, reading, spelling, study skills, time management, and written language. Remediation is provided collaboratively through on-campus or off-campus services via professional tutors and trained peer tutors.
Enrichment Programs for career planning, college survival skills, learning strategies, math, oral communication skills, practical computer skills, reading, study skills, test taking, time management, vocabulary development, and written composition skills are provided collaboratively through on-campus or off-campus services. Credit is offered for college survival skills, study skills, test taking, time management, vocabulary development, and written composition skills.
Fees *Diagnostic Testing* fee is $175.
Application For admittance to the program or unit, students are required to provide a psychoeducational report (3 years old or less). It is recommended that students provide documentation of high school services. Upon application, materials documenting need for services should be sent only to the LD program or unit. *Application deadline (LD program):* Rolling/continuous for fall and rolling/continuous for spring.
Written Policies Written policies regarding course substitutions, general/basic LD accommodations, reduced course loads, and substitutions and waivers of graduation requirements are available on the program Web site.

Tunxis Community College
Academic Support Center/Disabilities Services

271 Scott Swamp Road
Farmington, CT 06032-3026
http://www.tunxis.commnet.edu

Contact: Ms. Amanda Nicole Testo, Learning Disabilities Specialist. Phone: 860-255-3578. Fax: 860-255-3581. E-mail: atesto@txcc.commnet.edu. Head of LD Program: Cathy Ann Felice, Learning Disabilities Specialist. Phone: 860-255-3572. Fax: 860-255-3581. E-mail: cfelice@txcc.commnet.edu.

Academic Support Center/Disabilities Services Approximately 25 registered undergraduate students were served during 2006–07. The program or unit includes 2 part-time staff members. Academic advisers, LD specialists, professional tutors, remediation/learning specialists, and strategy tutors are provided through the program or unit. Academic advisers, counselors, professional tutors, skill tutors, and trained peer tutors are provided collaboratively through on-campus or off-campus services.
Unique Aids and Services Aids, services, or accommodations include assistance with early registration.
Assistive Technology Assistive technology is located in the DSS office, classroom/s as requested and includes digital textbooks/e-text, learning support software, scanning, and Naturally Speaking voice recognition program.

Tunxis Community College (continued)

Subject-Area Tutoring Tutoring is offered one-on-one and in small groups for most subjects. Tutoring is provided through the program or unit via LD specialists. Tutoring is also provided collaboratively through on-campus or off-campus services via professional tutors and trained peer tutors.

Enrichment Enrichment programs are available through the program or unit for learning strategies, math, self-advocacy, stress management, study skills, test taking, and written composition skills. Programs for career planning, college survival skills, health and nutrition, math, and stress management are provided collaboratively through on-campus or off-campus services.

Application For admittance to the program or unit, students are required to apply to the program directly and provide a psychoeducational report (3 years old or less). It is recommended that students provide documentation of high school services and provide Summary of Performance document. Upon application, materials documenting need for services should be sent only to the LD program or unit. Upon acceptance, documentation of need for services should be sent only to the LD program or unit. *Application deadline (institutional):* Continuous. *Application deadline (LD program):* Rolling/continuous for fall and rolling/continuous for spring.

Written Policies Written policies regarding course substitutions and general/basic LD accommodations are available on the program Web site. Written policy regarding general/basic LD accommodations is available through the program or unit directly.

The University of Akron– Wayne College
Smucker Learning Center

1901 Smucker Road

Orrville, OH 44667-9192

http://www.wayne.uakron.edu/LearCen

Contact: Dr. Patricia A. Collins, Director of Learning Support Services. Phone: 330-684-8765. E-mail: pacolli@ uakron.edu.

Smucker Learning Center Approximately 60 registered undergraduate students were served during 2006–07. The program or unit includes 1 full-time and 10 part-time staff members. Graduate assistants/students, LD specialists, professional tutors, remediation/learning specialists, skill tutors, strategy tutors, and trained peer tutors are provided through the program or unit. Academic advisers, coaches, counselors, diagnostic specialists, regular education teachers, special education teachers, and teacher trainees are provided collaboratively through on-campus or off-campus services.

Unique Aids and Services Aids, services, or accommodations include career counseling and weekly meetings with faculty.

Assistive Technology Assistive technology is located in Smucker Learning Center and includes digital textbooks/e-text, learning support software, and scanning. Technology training is provided to incoming students.

Subject-Area Tutoring Tutoring is offered one-on-one for most subjects. Tutoring is provided through the program or unit via professional tutors and trained peer tutors.

Diagnostic Testing Testing is provided through the program or unit for learning strategies, learning styles, math, reading, study skills, and written language. Testing for auditory processing, intelligence, motor skills, neuropsychological, personality, social skills, spelling, spoken language, and visual processing is provided collaboratively through on-campus or off-campus services.

Basic Skills Remediation Remediation is offered in class-size groups for computer skills, learning strategies, math, reading, spelling, spoken language, study skills, time management, and written language. Remediation is provided through the program or unit via professional tutors, regular education teachers, and trained peer tutors.

Enrichment Enrichment programs are available through the program or unit for career planning, college survival skills, learning strategies, math, oral communication skills, practical computer skills, reading, self-advocacy, stress management, study skills, test taking, time management, vocabulary development, and written composition skills.

Application For admittance to the program or unit, students are required to apply to the program directly and provide a psychoeducational report (3 years old or less). It is recommended that students provide documentation of high school services. Upon application, materials documenting need for services should be sent only to admissions with institutional application materials. Upon acceptance, documentation of need for services should be sent to both admissions and the LD program or unit. *Application deadline (institutional):* 8/30. *Application deadline (LD program):* Rolling/continuous for fall and rolling/continuous for spring.

Written Policies Written policies regarding course substitutions, general/basic LD accommodations, grade forgiveness, and substitutions and waivers of admissions requirements are available on the program Web site. Written policies regarding course substitutions, general/basic LD accommodations, grade forgiveness, and substitutions and waivers of admissions requirements are outlined in the school's catalog/handbook. Written policy regarding general/basic LD accommodations is available through the program or unit directly.

The University of Montana-Helena College of Technology
Office of Disability Services

1115 North Roberts Street

Helena, MT 59601

http://www.umhelena.edu/

Contact: Ms. Cindy M. Yarberry, Director of the Learning Center and Disability Services. Phone: 406-444-6897. Fax: 406-444-7892. E-mail: yarberryc@umh.umt.edu.

Office of Disability Services Approximately 15 registered undergraduate students were served during 2006–07. The program or unit includes 1 full-time staff member. Academic advisers and remediation/learning specialists are provided collaboratively through on-campus or off-campus services.

Assistive Technology Assistive technology is located in campus labs and includes learning support software and scanning. Technology training is provided to incoming students.

Subject-Area Tutoring Tutoring is offered one-on-one for most subjects. Tutoring is provided collaboratively through on-campus or off-campus services via computer-based instruction and trained peer tutors.

Basic Skills Remediation Remediation is offered one-on-one and in class-size groups for math and written language. Remediation is provided collaboratively through on-campus or off-campus services via computer-based instruction and regular education teachers.

Enrichment Programs for career planning, college survival skills, learning strategies, oral communication skills, stress management, study skills, test taking, time management, and written composition skills are provided collaboratively through on-campus or off-campus services. Credit is offered for oral communication skills and written composition skills.

Application It is recommended that students apply to the program directly, provide a psychoeducational report (4 years old or less), and provide documentation of high school services. Upon application, materials documenting need for services should be sent only to the LD program or unit. Upon acceptance, documentation of need for services should be sent only to the LD program or unit. *Application deadline (institutional):* Continuous. *Application deadline (LD program):* Rolling/continuous for fall and rolling/continuous for spring.

Written Policies Written policy regarding general/basic LD accommodations is available on the program Web site. Written policy regarding general/basic LD accommodations is outlined in the school's catalog/handbook.

University of Wisconsin–Manitowoc
Disability Services

705 Viebahn Street

Manitowoc, WI 54220-6699

http://www.uwc.edu/student_services/disability_services.asp

Contact: Dr. Christopher Lewis, Assistant Dean for Student Services. Phone: 920-683-4707. Fax: 920-683-4776. E-mail: christopher.lewis@uwc.edu.

Disability Services Approximately 20 registered undergraduate students were served during 2006–07. The program or unit includes 1 full-time staff member. Academic advisers are provided through the program or unit. Academic advisers and skill tutors are provided collaboratively through on-campus or off-campus services.

Orientation The program or unit offers a mandatory orientation for new students individually by special arrangement.

Assistive Technology Assistive technology is located in the DSS office and includes learning support software. Technology training is provided to incoming students.

Subject-Area Tutoring Tutoring is offered one-on-one, in small groups, and in class-size groups for some subjects. Tutoring is provided collaboratively through on-campus or off-campus services via computer-based instruction and trained peer tutors.

Basic Skills Remediation Remediation is offered one-on-one, in small groups, and in class-size groups for math. Remediation is provided collaboratively through on-campus or off-campus services via trained peer tutors.

Enrichment Programs for career planning, college survival skills, math, oral communication skills, stress management, study skills, test taking, time management, and written composition skills are provided collaboratively through on-campus or off-campus services. Credit is offered for career planning, college survival skills, oral communication skills, and written composition skills.

Application For admittance to the program or unit, students are required to apply to the program directly and provide a psychoeducational report (5 years old or less). It is recommended that students provide documentation of high school services. Upon application, materials documenting need for services should be sent only to the LD program or unit. Upon acceptance, documentation of need for services should be sent only to the LD program or unit. *Application deadline (LD program):* Rolling/continuous for fall.

Written Policies Written policy regarding general/basic LD accommodations is available on the program Web site. Written policy regarding general/basic LD accommodations is outlined in the school's catalog/handbook. Written policy regarding general/basic LD accommodations is available through the program or unit directly.

University of Wisconsin–Richland
Disabilities Services Office

1200 Highway 14 West

Richland Center, WI 53581

http://www.uwc.edu/student_services/disability_services.asp

Contact: John Poole, Assistant Dean for Student Services. Phone: 608-647-8422 Ext. 223. Fax: 608-647-2275. E-mail: john.poole@uwc.edu. Head of LD Program: Brian Schultz, Coordinator of Services for Students with Disabilities. Phone: 608-262-2001. E-mail: brian.schultz@uwc.edu.

Disabilities Services Office Approximately 25 registered undergraduate students were served during 2006–07. The program or unit includes 1 full-time and 1 part-time staff member. Academic advisers, counselors, diagnostic specialists, LD specialists, regular education teachers, skill tutors, and trained peer tutors are provided collaboratively through on-campus or off-campus services.

Unique Aids and Services Aids, services, or accommodations include priority registration.

Assistive Technology Assistive technology is located in the DSS office and includes digital textbooks/e-text, learning support software, and scanning. Technology training is provided to incoming students.

Subject-Area Tutoring Tutoring is offered one-on-one for some subjects. Tutoring is provided collaboratively through on-campus or off-campus services via trained peer tutors.

Basic Skills Remediation Remediation is offered in class-size groups for learning strategies, math, study skills, time management, and written language. Remediation is provided collaboratively through on-campus or off-campus services via regular education teachers.

Enrichment Programs for career planning, college survival skills, learning strategies, medication management, and written composition skills are provided collaboratively through on-campus or off-campus services. Credit is offered for learning strategies, medication management, and written composition skills.

University of Wisconsin–Richland (continued)

Application For admittance to the program or unit, students are required to apply to the program directly, provide a psychoeducational report (3 years old or less), and provide documentation of high school services. Upon acceptance, documentation of need for services should be sent only to the LD program or unit. *Application deadline (institutional):* Continuous. *Application deadline (LD program):* Rolling/continuous for fall and rolling/continuous for spring.

Written Policies Written policy regarding general/basic LD accommodations is available on the program Web site. Written policy regarding general/basic LD accommodations is outlined in the school's catalog/handbook. Written policies regarding course substitutions, general/basic LD accommodations, and substitutions and waivers of graduation requirements are available through the program or unit directly.

Valencia Community College
Office for Students with Disabilities

PO Box 3028

Orlando, FL 32802-3028

http://www.valenciacc.edu/osd

Contact: Dr. Ellen Hart, Counselor, Office for Students with Disabilities. Phone: 407-582-1533. Fax: 407-582-1326. E-mail: ehart4@valenciacc.edu. Head of LD Program: Ms. Jillian Szentmiklosi, Director. Phone: 407-582-2177. Fax: 407-582-8908. E-mail: jszentmiklosi@valenciacc.edu.

Office for Students with Disabilities Approximately 400 registered undergraduate students were served during 2006–07. The program or unit includes 5 full-time staff members. Academic advisers are provided through the program or unit. Counselors and trained peer tutors are provided collaboratively through on-campus or off-campus services.

Orientation The program or unit offers an optional 3-hour orientation for new students before classes begin.

Unique Aids and Services Aids, services, or accommodations include career counseling and priority registration.

Assistive Technology Assistive technology is located in campus labs, the DSS office and includes digital textbooks/e-text, learning support software, and scanning. Technology training is provided to incoming students.

Subject-Area Tutoring Tutoring is offered one-on-one and in small groups for most subjects. Tutoring is provided collaboratively through on-campus or off-campus services via computer-based instruction and trained peer tutors.

Basic Skills Remediation Remediation is offered in class-size groups for math, reading, study skills, and written language. Remediation is provided collaboratively through on-campus or off-campus services via computer-based instruction and regular education teachers.

Enrichment Enrichment programs are available through the program or unit for self-advocacy and study skills. Programs for career planning, health and nutrition, learning strategies, study skills, test

taking, and time management are provided collaboratively through on-campus or off-campus services. Credit is offered for career planning, health and nutrition, and study skills.

Application For admittance to the program or unit, students are required to provide a psychoeducational report (3 years old or less). It is recommended that students provide documentation of high school services. Upon acceptance, documentation of need for services should be sent only to the LD program or unit. *Application deadline (institutional):* 8/10. *Application deadline (LD program):* Rolling/continuous for fall and rolling/continuous for spring.

Written Policies Written policies regarding course substitutions, general/basic LD accommodations, substitutions and waivers of admissions requirements, and substitutions and waivers of graduation requirements are available on the program Web site. Written policies regarding course substitutions, grade forgiveness, and substitutions and waivers of graduation requirements are outlined in the school's catalog/handbook. Written policies regarding course substitutions, general/basic LD accommodations, substitutions and waivers of admissions requirements, and substitutions and waivers of graduation requirements are available through the program or unit directly.

Ventura College
Educational Assistance Center/Learning Skills Program

4667 Telegraph Road

Ventura, CA 93003-3899

http://www.venturacollege.edu/eacenter/

Contact: Dr. Tom Dalton, Learning Disabilities Specialist. Phone: 805-654-6300 Ext. 1244. Fax: 805-648-8915. E-mail: tdalton@vcccd.edu.

Educational Assistance Center/Learning Skills Program Approximately 390 registered undergraduate students were served during 2006–07. Academic advisers, counselors, diagnostic specialists, LD specialists, special education teachers, and trained peer tutors are provided through the program or unit.

Unique Aids and Services Aids, services, or accommodations include priority registration.

Assistive Technology Assistive technology is located in campus labs, a special lab and includes digital textbooks/e-text and scanning. Technology training is provided to incoming students.

Subject-Area Tutoring Tutoring is offered one-on-one and in small groups for most subjects. Tutoring is provided through the program or unit via computer-based instruction, LD specialists, and trained peer tutors.

Diagnostic Testing Testing is provided through the program or unit for intelligence, learning styles, math, reading, spelling, and written language.

Basic Skills Remediation Remediation is offered in class-size groups for computer skills, learning strategies, math, reading, social skills, spelling, study skills, time management, visual processing, and written language. Remediation is provided through the program or unit via computer-based instruction, LD specialists, special education teachers, and trained peer tutors.

Enrichment Enrichment programs are available through the program or unit for career planning, college survival skills, learning strategies, math, practical computer skills, reading, self-advocacy, stress management, study skills, test taking, time management, vocabulary development, and written composition skills.

Student Organization Success Through Diversity consists of 20 members.

Fees *Diagnostic Testing* fee is $10.

Application For admittance to the program or unit, students are required to apply to the program directly. It is recommended that students provide a psychoeducational report, provide documentation of high school services, and provide documentation from other college disabled students program. Upon application, materials documenting need for services should be sent only to the LD program or unit. *Application deadline (LD program):* Rolling/continuous for fall and rolling/continuous for spring.

Written Policies Written policies regarding course substitutions and substitutions and waivers of graduation requirements are outlined in the school's catalog/handbook. Written policies regarding general/basic LD accommodations and reduced course loads are available through the program or unit directly.

Victor Valley College
Disabled Students Programs and Services (DSPS)

18422 Bear Valley Road

Victorville, CA 92392-5849

http://www.vvc.edu/offices/
disabled_student_program_services/index.htm

Contact: Susan Tillman, LD Specialist/ Counselor. Phone: 760-245-4271 Ext. 2430. Fax: 760-951-9225. Head of LD Program: Jeffrey Holmes, Director. Phone: 760-245-4271 Ext. 2212. Fax: 760-951-9225.

Disabled Students Programs and Services (DSPS) Approximately 300 registered undergraduate students were served during 2006–07. The program or unit includes 3 full-time staff members. Counselors, diagnostic specialists, LD specialists, professional tutors, regular education teachers, skill tutors, special education teachers, and other are provided collaboratively through on-campus or off-campus services.

Orientation The program or unit offers a mandatory 3-hour orientation for new students before registration, before classes begin, during summer prior to enrollment, during registration, after classes begin, individually by special arrangement, and through arrangement with local school districts.

Unique Aids and Services Aids, services, or accommodations include priority registration.

Assistive Technology Assistive technology is located in campus labs, the DSS office, a special lab, the library and includes digital textbooks/e-text, learning support software, scanning, and readers. Technology training is provided to incoming students.

Subject-Area Tutoring Tutoring is offered one-on-one, in small groups, and in class-size groups for most subjects. Tutoring is provided collaboratively through on-campus or off-campus services via computer-based instruction, trained peer tutors, and other.

Diagnostic Testing Testing is provided through the program or unit for auditory processing, handwriting, intelligence, learning strategies, learning styles, math, reading, spelling, spoken language, study skills, visual processing, written language, and other services. Testing for learning strategies, learning styles, personality, social skills, and other services is provided collaboratively through on-campus or off-campus services.

Basic Skills Remediation Remediation is offered in small groups and in class-size groups for computer skills, learning strategies, math, reading, spelling, spoken language, study skills, time management, and written language. Remediation is provided through the program or unit. Remediation is also provided collaboratively through on-campus or off-campus services via computer-based instruction, LD specialists, regular education teachers, and other.

Enrichment Programs for career planning, college survival skills, health and nutrition, learning strategies, math, practical computer skills, reading, study skills, test taking, time management, vocabulary development, written composition skills, and other are provided collaboratively through on-campus or off-campus services. Credit is offered for career planning, college survival skills, health and nutrition, learning strategies, math, practical computer skills, reading, vocabulary development, written composition skills, and other.

Application For admittance to the program or unit, students are required to apply to the program directly, provide a psychoeducational report (3 years old or less), provide documentation of high school services, and provide documentation from a clinician. Upon application, materials documenting need for services should be sent only to the LD program or unit. Upon acceptance, documentation of need for services should be sent only to the LD program or unit. *Application deadline (institutional):* Continuous. *Application deadline (LD program):* Rolling/continuous for fall and rolling/continuous for spring.

Written Policies Written policy regarding general/basic LD accommodations is available on the program Web site. Written policies regarding general/basic LD accommodations and reduced course loads are available through the program or unit directly.

Virginia Highlands Community College
Project EXCEL

PO Box 828

100 VHCC Drive Abingdon

Abingdon, VA 24210

http://www.vhcc.edu/projectexcel

Contact: Mrs. Jackie Thayer Craft, Director, Project EXCEL. Phone: 276-739-2561. Fax: 276-739-2589. E-mail: jcraft@vhcc.edu.

Project EXCEL Approximately 30 registered undergraduate students were served during 2006–07. The program or unit includes 2 full-time staff members and 1 part-time staff member. Counselors, professional tutors, and skill tutors are provided collaboratively through on-campus or off-campus services.

Assistive Technology Assistive technology includes digital textbooks/e-text and learning support software.

Virginia Highlands Community College (continued)

Subject-Area Tutoring Tutoring is offered one-on-one and in small groups for most subjects. Tutoring is provided collaboratively through on-campus or off-campus services via computer-based instruction, professional tutors, and trained peer tutors.

Basic Skills Remediation Remediation is offered in class-size groups.

Application For admittance to the program or unit, students are required to apply to the program directly and provide documentation of high school services. Upon application, materials documenting need for services should be sent only to the LD program or unit. *Application deadline (institutional):* Continuous. *Application deadline (LD program):* Rolling/continuous for fall and rolling/continuous for spring.

Written Policies Written policies regarding course substitutions, general/basic LD accommodations, grade forgiveness, reduced course loads, substitutions and waivers of admissions requirements, and substitutions and waivers of graduation requirements are available on the program Web site. Written policies regarding course substitutions, general/basic LD accommodations, grade forgiveness, reduced course loads, substitutions and waivers of admissions requirements, and substitutions and waivers of graduation requirements are outlined in the school's catalog/handbook. Written policy regarding general/basic LD accommodations is available through the program or unit directly.

Waubonsee Community College
Access Center for Students with Disabilities

Route 47 at Waubonsee Drive

Sugar Grove, IL 60554-9799

http://www.waubonsee.edu/

Contact: Iris Hansen, Manager. Phone: 630-466-7900 Ext. 5702. Fax: 630-466-4649. E-mail: ihansen@waubonsee.edu.

Access Center for Students with Disabilities Approximately 200 registered undergraduate students were served during 2006–07. The program or unit includes 5 full-time and 8 part-time staff members. Academic advisers, counselors, diagnostic specialists, LD specialists, professional tutors, remediation/learning specialists, skill tutors, strategy tutors, and other are provided through the program or unit. Academic advisers, coaches, counselors, professional tutors, regular education teachers, and skill tutors are provided collaboratively through on-campus or off-campus services.

Orientation The program or unit offers an optional 1-day orientation for new students before registration, before classes begin, during summer prior to enrollment, during registration, after classes begin, and individually by special arrangement.

Unique Aids and Services Aids, services, or accommodations include advocates, career counseling, faculty training, and priority registration.

Assistive Technology Assistive technology is located in campus labs, the DSS office and includes digital textbooks/e-text, learning support software, and scanning. Technology training is provided to incoming students.

Subject-Area Tutoring Tutoring is offered one-on-one and in small groups for most subjects. Tutoring is provided through the program or unit via computer-based instruction, LD specialists, and professional tutors. Tutoring is also provided collaboratively through on-campus or off-campus services via computer-based instruction, professional tutors, and trained peer tutors.

Basic Skills Remediation Remediation is offered in class-size groups for computer skills, learning strategies, math, reading, spelling, spoken language, study skills, and written language. Remediation is provided collaboratively through on-campus or off-campus services via computer-based instruction, professional tutors, and regular education teachers.

Enrichment Programs for career planning, college survival skills, health and nutrition, learning strategies, math, practical computer skills, reading, self-advocacy, stress management, study skills, test taking, time management, vocabulary development, and written composition skills are provided collaboratively through on-campus or off-campus services.

Application For admittance to the program or unit, students are required to apply to the program directly. It is recommended that students provide a psychoeducational report (3 years old or less) and provide documentation of high school services. Upon application, materials documenting need for services should be sent only to the LD program or unit. Upon acceptance, documentation of need for services should be sent only to the LD program or unit. *Application deadline (institutional):* Continuous. *Application deadline (LD program):* Rolling/continuous for fall and rolling/continuous for spring.

Written Policies Written policy regarding grade forgiveness is outlined in the school's catalog/handbook. Written policy regarding general/basic LD accommodations is available through the program or unit directly.

Waukesha County Technical College
Special Services

800 Main Street

Pewaukee, WI 53072-4601

http://www.wctc.edu

Contact: Deb A. Jilbert, Director of Special Services. Phone: 262-691-5210. Fax: 262-691-5089. E-mail: djilbert@wctc.edu.

Special Services Approximately 200 registered undergraduate students were served during 2006–07. The program or unit includes 4 full-time staff members. Academic advisers, counselors, and LD specialists are provided through the program or unit.

Orientation The program or unit offers an optional orientation for new students before classes begin and individually by special arrangement.

Summer Program To help prepare for the demands of college, there is an optional 1-day summer program prior to entering the school available to high school graduates that focuses on self-advocacy and test-taking skills.

Unique Aids and Services Aids, services, or accommodations include career counseling.

Assistive Technology Assistive technology is located in a special lab and includes scanning.

Subject-Area Tutoring Tutoring is offered in small groups for most subjects. Tutoring is provided through the program or unit via LD specialists.

Basic Skills Remediation Remediation is offered in class-size groups for math, reading, and written language. Remediation is provided collaboratively through on-campus or off-campus services via computer-based instruction and regular education teachers.

Application For admittance to the program or unit, students are required to provide a psychoeducational report (3 years old or less), provide documentation of high school services, and provide an assistive technology evaluation (when appropriate). It is recommended that students apply to the program directly. Upon application, materials documenting need for services should be sent only to the LD program or unit. Upon acceptance, documentation of need for services should be sent only to the LD program or unit. *Application deadline (institutional):* Continuous. *Application deadline (LD program):* Rolling/continuous for fall and rolling/continuous for spring.

Written Policies Written policy regarding course substitutions is outlined in the school's catalog/handbook. Written policies regarding general/basic LD accommodations and reduced course loads are available through the program or unit directly.

Westchester Community College
Services for Students with Disabilities

75 Grasslands Road

Valhalla, NY 10595-1698

http://www.sunywcc.edu/

Contact: Prof. Sharon Massey, Learning Specialist. Phone: 914-606-6626. Fax: 914-606-7893. E-mail: sharon.massey@sunywcc.edu.

Services for Students with Disabilities Approximately 800 registered undergraduate students were served during 2006–07. The program or unit includes 2 full-time and 2 part-time staff members. LD specialists and other are provided through the program or unit. Academic advisers, coaches, counselors, professional tutors, regular education teachers, skill tutors, strategy tutors, and trained peer tutors are provided collaboratively through on-campus or off-campus services.

Orientation The program or unit offers before registration and at the time of placement testing.

Unique Aids and Services Aids, services, or accommodations include faculty training and priority registration.

Assistive Technology Assistive technology is located in the DSS office, the Academic Support Center and includes scanning. Technology training is provided to incoming students.

Subject-Area Tutoring Tutoring is offered in small groups for some subjects. Tutoring is provided collaboratively through on-campus or off-campus services via computer-based instruction, professional tutors, and trained peer tutors.

Basic Skills Remediation Remediation is offered in small groups for learning strategies, math, reading, study skills, time management, and written language. Remediation is provided collaboratively through on-campus or off-campus services via computer-based instruction, professional tutors, and trained peer tutors.

Enrichment Enrichment programs are available through the program or unit for self-advocacy. Programs for career planning, college survival skills, health and nutrition, learning strategies, math, practical computer skills, reading, stress management, study skills, test taking, time management, vocabulary development, and written composition skills are provided collaboratively through on-campus or off-campus services.

Application For admittance to the program or unit, students are required to provide a psychoeducational report (3 years old or less) and provide documentation of high school services. Upon application, materials documenting need for services should be sent only to the LD program or unit. Upon acceptance, documentation of need for services should be sent only to the LD program or unit. *Application deadline (institutional):* Continuous. *Application deadline (LD program):* Rolling/continuous for fall and rolling/continuous for spring.

Written Policies Written policy regarding general/basic LD accommodations is available on the program Web site. Written policy regarding general/basic LD accommodations is outlined in the school's catalog/handbook. Written policy regarding general/basic LD accommodations is available through the program or unit directly.

Western Nebraska Community College
Counseling Office

371 College Drive

Sidney, NE 69162

http://www.wncc.net/students/disability_services/index.html

Contact: Mr. Norman J. Stephenson, Counseling Director. Phone: 800-348-4435 Ext. 6090. Fax: 308-635-6055. E-mail: stephens@wncc.net.

Counseling Office Approximately 30 registered undergraduate students were served during 2006–07. The program or unit includes 1 full-time and 1 part-time staff member. Counselors are provided through the program or unit. Academic advisers, coaches, counselors, diagnostic specialists, LD specialists, professional tutors, regular education teachers, remediation/learning specialists, skill tutors, special education teachers, trained peer tutors, and other are provided collaboratively through on-campus or off-campus services.

Unique Aids and Services Aids, services, or accommodations include career counseling, faculty training, priority registration, and support groups.

Assistive Technology Assistive technology is located in campus labs, a special lab, Information Technology Department and includes digital textbooks/e-text. Technology training is provided to incoming students.

Subject-Area Tutoring Tutoring is offered one-on-one and in small groups for all subjects. Tutoring is provided through the program or unit via LD specialists. Tutoring is also provided collaboratively through on-campus or off-campus services via computer-based instruction, LD specialists, professional tutors, trained peer tutors, and other.

Western Nebraska Community College (continued)

Basic Skills Remediation Remediation is offered one-on-one and in small groups for computer skills, learning strategies, math, reading, spelling, study skills, time management, and written language. Remediation is provided through the program or unit via LD specialists. Remediation is also provided collaboratively through on-campus or off-campus services via computer-based instruction, LD specialists, professional tutors, regular education teachers, special education teachers, teacher trainees, and trained peer tutors.

Enrichment Enrichment programs are available through the program or unit for career planning, medication management, self-advocacy, stress management, study skills, test taking, and time management. Programs for career planning, college survival skills, health and nutrition, learning strategies, math, medication management, oral communication skills, practical computer skills, reading, self-advocacy, stress management, study skills, test taking, time management, vocabulary development, and written composition skills are provided collaboratively through on-campus or off-campus services. Credit is offered for math, oral communication skills, practical computer skills, reading, and vocabulary development.

Application It is recommended that students apply to the program directly, provide a psychoeducational report (3 years old or less), and provide documentation of high school services. Upon application, materials documenting need for services should be sent only to the LD program or unit. Upon acceptance, documentation of need for services should be sent only to the LD program or unit. *Application deadline (institutional):* Continuous. *Application deadline (LD program):* Rolling/continuous for fall and rolling/continuous for spring.

Written Policies Written policy regarding general/basic LD accommodations is available on the program Web site. Written policies regarding course substitutions, general/basic LD accommodations, grade forgiveness, reduced course loads, substitutions and waivers of admissions requirements, and substitutions and waivers of graduation requirements are available through the program or unit directly.

Western Technical College

304 6th Street North

PO Box C-908

La Crosse, WI 54602-0908

http://www.wwtc.edu/

Contact: Kristina Puent, Instructional Support Specialist-Disability Services. Phone: 608-785-9875. E-mail: puentk@westerntc.edu.

The program or unit includes 2 full-time staff members. LD specialists and remediation/learning specialists are provided through the program or unit.

Orientation The program or unit offers an optional orientation for new students individually by special arrangement.

Unique Aids and Services Aids, services, or accommodations include faculty training, priority registration, and weekly meetings with faculty.

Assistive Technology Assistive technology is located in campus labs, the DSS office and includes digital textbooks/e-text, learning support software, and scanning.

Subject-Area Tutoring Tutoring is offered one-on-one and in small groups for most subjects. Tutoring is provided through the program or unit via LD specialists. Tutoring is also provided collaboratively through on-campus or off-campus services via computer-based instruction, graduate assistants/students, professional tutors, and trained peer tutors.

Basic Skills Remediation Remediation is offered in small groups and in class-size groups for math, reading, study skills, and written language. Remediation is provided collaboratively through on-campus or off-campus services via regular education teachers and special education teachers.

Enrichment Enrichment programs are available through the program or unit for self-advocacy, stress management, study skills, test taking, and time management. Programs for career planning, college survival skills, health and nutrition, learning strategies, math, reading, study skills, test taking, time management, and written composition skills are provided collaboratively through on-campus or off-campus services. Credit is offered for college survival skills, health and nutrition, learning strategies, math, reading, study skills, test taking, time management, and written composition skills.

Application For admittance to the program or unit, students are required to apply to the program directly, provide a psychoeducational report (3 years old or less), and provide documentation of disability. It is recommended that students provide documentation of high school services. Upon application, materials documenting need for services should be sent only to the LD program or unit. Upon acceptance, documentation of need for services should be sent only to the LD program or unit. *Application deadline (institutional):* Continuous. *Application deadline (LD program):* Rolling/continuous for fall and rolling/continuous for spring.

Written Policies Written policy regarding general/basic LD accommodations is available on the program Web site.

West Los Angeles College

9000 Overland Avenue

Culver City, CA 90230-3519

http://www.wlac.cc.ca.us/

Contact: Ms. Frances S. Israel, Learning Specialist. Phone: 310-287-4450. Fax: 310-287-4417. Head of LD Program: Ms. Adrienne A. Foster, Disabled Students Programs Director. Phone: 310-287-4450. Fax: 310-287-4417.

The program or unit includes 2 full-time staff members and 1 part-time staff member. Academic advisers, counselors, diagnostic specialists, LD specialists, and remediation/learning specialists are provided through the program or unit. Academic advisers, counselors, diagnostic specialists, LD specialists, remediation/learning specialists, skill tutors, and strategy tutors are provided collaboratively through on-campus or off-campus services.

Unique Aids and Services Aids, services, or accommodations include career counseling and priority registration.

Assistive Technology Assistive technology is located in the DSS office, CAI Center and includes learning support software.

Subject-Area Tutoring Tutoring is offered one-on-one for most subjects. Tutoring is provided through the program or unit via LD specialists. Tutoring is also provided collaboratively through on-campus or off-campus services via computer-based instruction and trained peer tutors.

Diagnostic Testing Testing is provided through the program or unit for auditory processing, intelligence, learning strategies, learning styles, math, reading, spelling, study skills, visual processing, and written language. Testing for auditory processing, learning styles, math, reading, spelling, and study skills is provided collaboratively through on-campus or off-campus services.

Basic Skills Remediation Remediation is offered one-on-one and in small groups for computer skills, math, reading, study skills, and written language. Remediation is provided through the program or unit via LD specialists. Remediation is also provided collaboratively through on-campus or off-campus services via computer-based instruction, regular education teachers, and trained peer tutors.

Enrichment Enrichment programs are available through the program or unit for career planning, college survival skills, learning strategies, reading, self-advocacy, stress management, study skills, test taking, and time management. Programs for career planning, college survival skills, health and nutrition, math, oral communication skills, practical computer skills, reading, study skills, vocabulary development, and written composition skills are provided collaboratively through on-campus or off-campus services. Credit is offered for career planning, college survival skills, health and nutrition, learning strategies, math, oral communication skills, practical computer skills, reading, self-advocacy, stress management, study skills, test taking, time management, vocabulary development, and written composition skills.

Application For admittance to the program or unit, students are required to apply to the program directly and provide documentation of high school services. It is recommended that students provide a psychoeducational report (5 years old or less). Upon application, materials documenting need for services should be sent only to the LD program or unit. Upon acceptance, documentation of need for services should be sent only to the LD program or unit. *Application deadline (institutional):* 8/16. *Application deadline (LD program):* Rolling/continuous for fall and rolling/continuous for spring.

Written Policies Written policies regarding course substitutions, general/basic LD accommodations, reduced course loads, substitutions and waivers of admissions requirements, and substitutions and waivers of graduation requirements are available through the program or unit directly.

Westmoreland County Community College
Student Development Office

400 Armbrust Road

Youngwood, PA 15697-1898

http://www.wccc-pa.edu/

Contact: Mrs. Mary Ellen Beres, Counselor. Phone: 724-925-4189. Fax: 724-925-5802. E-mail: beresm@wccc.edu.

Student Development Office Approximately 50 registered undergraduate students were served during 2006–07. The program or unit includes 1 full-time staff member. Counselors, professional tutors, regular education teachers, remediation/learning specialists, skill tutors, and strategy tutors are provided collaboratively through on-campus or off-campus services.

Unique Aids and Services Aids, services, or accommodations include career counseling.

Assistive Technology Assistive technology is located in campus labs, a special lab and includes digital textbooks/e-text and learning support software.

Subject-Area Tutoring Tutoring is offered one-on-one and in small groups for most subjects. Tutoring is provided collaboratively through on-campus or off-campus services via computer-based instruction, graduate assistants/students, professional tutors, and trained peer tutors.

Basic Skills Remediation Remediation is offered in class-size groups for math, reading, spelling, spoken language, study skills, time management, and written language. Remediation is provided collaboratively through on-campus or off-campus services via regular education teachers.

Enrichment Programs for career planning, college survival skills, learning strategies, self-advocacy, stress management, and time management are provided collaboratively through on-campus or off-campus services. Credit is offered for college survival skills, health and nutrition, learning strategies, math, practical computer skills, reading, self-advocacy, study skills, test taking, time management, vocabulary development, and written composition skills.

Application For admittance to the program or unit, students are required to provide a psychoeducational report. Upon application, materials documenting need for services should be sent only to the LD program or unit. Upon acceptance, documentation of need for services should be sent only to the LD program or unit. *Application deadline (institutional):* Continuous. *Application deadline (LD program):* Rolling/continuous for fall.

Written Policies Written policy regarding general/basic LD accommodations is available on the program Web site. Written policy regarding general/basic LD accommodations is outlined in the school's catalog/handbook.

West Shore Community College
Support, Tutoring, and Resources Services

PO Box 277, 3000 North Stiles Road

Scottville, MI 49454-0277

http://www.westshore.edu/home.php/students/stars

Contact: Ms. Diann Neil Engblade, Director of Special Populations. Phone: 231-845-6211 Ext. 3513. Fax: 231-845-7227. E-mail: dlneilengblade@westshore.edu.

Support, Tutoring, and Resources Services Approximately 25 registered undergraduate students were served during 2006–07. The program or unit includes 2 full-time staff members. Academic advisers, counselors, professional tutors, and trained peer tutors are provided through the program or unit. Academic advisers, counselors, diagnostic specialists, and regular education teachers are provided collaboratively through on-campus or off-campus services.

Orientation The program or unit offers a mandatory 1-hour orientation for new students individually by special arrangement.

Unique Aids and Services Aids, services, or accommodations include advocates, career counseling, professional tutoring, proctored testing, test reading services.

West Shore Community College (continued)

Assistive Technology Assistive technology is located in the DSS office and includes digital textbooks/e-text, scanning, and Kurzweil, Dragon Naturally Speaking. Technology training is provided to incoming students.

Subject-Area Tutoring Tutoring is offered one-on-one, in small groups, and in class-size groups for all subjects. Tutoring is provided through the program or unit via professional tutors, trained peer tutors, and other. Tutoring is also provided collaboratively through on-campus or off-campus services via computer-based instruction.

Diagnostic Testing Testing is provided through the program or unit for learning strategies, learning styles, reading, spelling, study skills, and written language. Testing for auditory processing, handwriting, intelligence, math, motor skills, neuropsychological, personality, social skills, spoken language, and visual processing is provided collaboratively through on-campus or off-campus services.

Basic Skills Remediation Remediation is offered one-on-one and in class-size groups for learning strategies, math, reading, spelling, study skills, and time management. Remediation is provided through the program or unit via professional tutors, regular education teachers, and trained peer tutors. Remediation is also provided collaboratively through on-campus or off-campus services via computer-based instruction.

Enrichment Enrichment programs are available through the program or unit for career planning, college survival skills, learning strategies, math, reading, self-advocacy, stress management, study skills, test taking, time management, vocabulary development, and written composition skills. Programs for career planning, college survival skills, health and nutrition, learning strategies, math, practical computer skills, reading, stress management, study skills, test taking, time management, vocabulary development, and written composition skills are provided collaboratively through on-campus or off-campus services. Credit is offered for career planning, learning strategies, math, practical computer skills, reading, study skills, and written composition skills.

Application For admittance to the program or unit, students are required to apply to the program directly. It is recommended that students provide a psychoeducational report (3 years old or less), provide documentation of high school services, and provide documentation of the disability from a licensed psychologist, psychiatrist, or physician. Upon application, materials documenting need for services should be sent only to the LD program or unit. Upon acceptance, documentation of need for services should be sent only to the LD program or unit. *Application deadline (institutional):* Continuous. *Application deadline (LD program):* Rolling/continuous for fall and rolling/continuous for spring.

Written Policies Written policy regarding general/basic LD accommodations is available on the program Web site. Written policy regarding general/basic LD accommodations is outlined in the school's catalog/handbook. Written policy regarding course substitutions is available through the program or unit directly.

West Virginia Northern Community College
Support Services for Students with Disabilities

1704 Market Street

Wheeling, WV 26003-3699

http://www.northern.wvnet.edu/

Contact: Ms. Denise A. McBride, Student Disability Coordinator. Phone: 304-233-5900 Ext. 4275. Fax: 304-232-8187. E-mail: dmcbride@wvnorthern.edu.

Support Services for Students with Disabilities Approximately 101 registered undergraduate students were served during 2006–07. The program or unit includes 2 full-time staff members. Academic advisers, counselors, and diagnostic specialists are provided through the program or unit. Academic advisers, counselors, and diagnostic specialists are provided collaboratively through on-campus or off-campus services.

Orientation The program or unit offers an optional 2-hour orientation for new students during summer prior to enrollment.

Summer Program To help prepare for the demands of college, there is an optional 10-week early entrance summer program prior to entering the school that focuses on computing skills, specific subject tutoring, and test-taking skills. Degree credit will be earned. The program accepts students from out-of-state and is available to students attending other colleges.

Assistive Technology Assistive technology is located in the DSS office, the Tutoring Center and includes digital textbooks/e-text, learning support software, and scanning. Technology training is provided to incoming students.

Subject-Area Tutoring Tutoring is offered one-on-one for most subjects. Tutoring is provided collaboratively through on-campus or off-campus services via LD specialists and trained peer tutors.

Diagnostic Testing Testing for math, reading, and written language is provided collaboratively through on-campus or off-campus services.

Basic Skills Remediation Remediation is available for math, reading, and written language.

Application For admittance to the program or unit, students are required to provide disability documentation from doctors, etc. It is recommended that students provide documentation of high school services. Upon application, materials documenting need for services should be sent only to the LD program or unit. Upon acceptance, documentation of need for services should be sent only to the LD program or unit. *Application deadline (institutional):* Continuous. *Application deadline (LD program):* Rolling/continuous for fall and rolling/continuous for spring.

Written Policies Written policy regarding general/basic LD accommodations is available on the program Web site. Written policy regarding general/basic LD accommodations is available through the program or unit directly.

West Virginia State Community and Technical College

Thomas W. Cole, Jr., Complex
PO Box 1000
Institute, WV 25112
http://www.wvsctc.edu/

Contact: Ms. Carla Blankenbuehler, Disability Services Counselor. Phone: 304-766-3083. Fax: 304-766-4168. E-mail: blankenc@wvstateu.edu.

Approximately 30 registered undergraduate students were served during 2006–07. The program or unit includes 1 full-time staff member. Counselors are provided through the program or unit.
Subject-Area Tutoring Tutoring is offered one-on-one and in small groups for most subjects. Tutoring is provided collaboratively through on-campus or off-campus services via graduate assistants/students and trained peer tutors.
Diagnostic Testing Testing is provided through the program or unit for intelligence, learning strategies, learning styles, and neuropsychological.
Application For admittance to the program or unit, students are required to apply to the program directly, provide a psychoeducational report, and provide documentation of high school services. Upon acceptance, documentation of need for services should be sent only to the LD program or unit. *Application deadline (LD program):* Rolling/continuous for fall and rolling/continuous for spring.
Written Policies Written policy regarding general/basic LD accommodations is available on the program Web site. Written policy regarding general/basic LD accommodations is available through the program or unit directly.

Whatcom Community College
Disability Support Services

237 West Kellogg Road
Bellingham, WA 98226-8003
http://www.whatcom.ctc.edu/content/ArchivesItem.phtml?art=87&style=4

Contact: Bill Culwell, Director for Disability Support Services. Phone: 360-676-2170. Fax: 360-676-2171. E-mail: bculwell@whatcom.ctc.edu.

Disability Support Services Approximately 250 registered undergraduate students were served during 2006–07. The program or unit includes 2 full-time staff members and 1 part-time staff member. Academic advisers, counselors, and LD specialists are provided through the program or unit. Academic advisers, counselors, LD specialists, professional tutors, regular education teachers, remediation/learning specialists, and skill tutors are provided collaboratively through on-campus or off-campus services.
Orientation The program or unit offers an optional orientation for new students before registration, during registration, and individually by special arrangement.

Unique Aids and Services Aids, services, or accommodations include career counseling and priority registration.
Assistive Technology Assistive technology is located in the DSS office and includes digital textbooks/e-text, learning support software, and scanning. Technology training is provided to incoming students.
Subject-Area Tutoring Tutoring is offered one-on-one and in small groups for most subjects. Tutoring is provided collaboratively through on-campus or off-campus services via computer-based instruction and trained peer tutors.
Basic Skills Remediation Remediation is offered one-on-one, in small groups, and in class-size groups for computer skills, learning strategies, math, reading, spelling, and study skills. Remediation is provided collaboratively through on-campus or off-campus services via regular education teachers, special education teachers, and trained peer tutors.
Enrichment Programs for career planning, college survival skills, health and nutrition, learning strategies, reading, stress management, study skills, test taking, time management, vocabulary development, and written composition skills are provided collaboratively through on-campus or off-campus services. Credit is offered for career planning, college survival skills, health and nutrition, reading, stress management, study skills, test taking, time management, vocabulary development, and written composition skills.
Application For admittance to the program or unit, students are required to provide a psychoeducational report (5 years old or less). It is recommended that students provide documentation of high school services and provide a professional diagnosis of LD. Upon application, materials documenting need for services should be sent only to the LD program or unit. Upon acceptance, documentation of need for services should be sent only to the LD program or unit. *Application deadline (LD program):* Rolling/continuous for fall and rolling/continuous for spring.
Written Policies Written policies regarding substitutions and waivers of admissions requirements and substitutions and waivers of graduation requirements are outlined in the school's catalog/handbook. Written policies regarding course substitutions, general/basic LD accommodations, and substitutions and waivers of graduation requirements are available through the program or unit directly.

Williston State College
Disabilities Support Services

Box 1326
Williston, ND 58802-1326
http://www.wsc.nodak.edu

Contact: Mrs. Janice Marie Hunter, Director. Phone: 701-774-4594. Fax: 701-774-4275. E-mail: jan.hunter@wsc.nodak.edu.

Disabilities Support Services Approximately 25 registered undergraduate students were served during 2006–07. The program or unit includes 2 full-time staff members. Professional tutors, skill tutors, and trained peer tutors are provided through the program or unit. Academic advisers, diagnostic specialists, professional tutors, skill tutors, and trained peer tutors are provided collaboratively through on-campus or off-campus services.
Unique Aids and Services Aids, services, or accommodations include career counseling.

Williston State College (continued)

Assistive Technology Assistive technology is located in the DSS office and includes digital textbooks/e-text and learning support software.

Subject-Area Tutoring Tutoring is offered one-on-one and in small groups for some subjects. Tutoring is provided through the program or unit via graduate assistants/students, professional tutors, and trained peer tutors. Tutoring is also provided collaboratively through on-campus or off-campus services via graduate assistants/students and trained peer tutors.

Diagnostic Testing Testing for math, reading, and written language is provided collaboratively through on-campus or off-campus services.

Basic Skills Remediation Remediation is offered one-on-one and in small groups for computer skills, learning strategies, math, reading, spelling, study skills, and written language. Remediation is provided through the program or unit via computer-based instruction, professional tutors, and trained peer tutors. Remediation is also provided collaboratively through on-campus or off-campus services via computer-based instruction, professional tutors, and trained peer tutors.

Enrichment Programs for career planning, math, practical computer skills, reading, study skills, and written composition skills are provided collaboratively through on-campus or off-campus services. Credit is offered for career planning, math, practical computer skills, reading, study skills, and written composition skills.

Fees *Diagnostic Testing* fee is $25.

Application For admittance to the program or unit, students are required to apply to the program directly and provide documentation of high school services. It is recommended that students provide a psychoeducational report and provide vocational rehab and psychological evaluations. Upon application, materials documenting need for services should be sent only to the LD program or unit. Upon acceptance, documentation of need for services should be sent only to the LD program or unit. *Application deadline (institutional):* Continuous. *Application deadline (LD program):* Rolling/continuous for fall and rolling/continuous for spring.

Written Policies Written policies regarding course substitutions and general/basic LD accommodations are outlined in the school's catalog/handbook. Written policy regarding general/basic LD accommodations is available through the program or unit directly.

INDEXES

MAJORS INDEX

ACCOUNTING

Abilene Christian U, TX
Abraham Baldwin Coll, GA
Adelphi U, NY
Aims Comm Coll, CO
Alabama A&M U, AL
Albany State U, GA
Albertson Coll of Idaho, ID
Albright Coll, PA
Alderson-Broaddus Coll, WV
Alexandria Tech Coll, MN
Alma Coll, MI
Alvernia Coll, PA
American International Coll, MA
Anderson U, IN
Anderson U, SC
Angelo State U, TX
Arizona State U at the West campus, AZ
Asbury Coll, KY
Ashland Comm and Tech Coll, KY
Ashland U, OH
Asnuntuck Comm Coll, CT
Athabasca U, AB, Canada
Athens State U, AL
Auburn U Montgomery, AL
Augsburg Coll, MN
Aurora U, IL
Avila U, MO
Bainbridge Coll, GA
Baker Coll of Allen Park, MI
Ball State U, IN
Barry U, FL
Baylor U, TX
Belmont Abbey Coll, NC
Bemidji State U, MN
Benedictine Coll, KS
Bentley Coll, MA
Bethel Coll, IN
Bishop's U, QC, Canada
Blinn Coll, TX
Bluefield State Coll, WV
Blue Ridge Comm Coll, VA
Boston Coll, MA
Bradley U, IL
Brenau U, GA
Brevard Comm Coll, FL
Brewton-Parker Coll, GA
Briar Cliff U, IA
British Columbia Inst of Technology, BC, Canada
Brock U, ON, Canada
Broward Comm Coll, FL
Bryant and Stratton Coll, Rochester, NY
Bucks County Comm Coll, PA
Buena Vista U, IA
Bunker Hill Comm Coll, MA
Burlington County Coll, NJ
Caldwell Comm Coll and Tech Inst, NC
Calhoun Comm Coll, AL
California State U, Fullerton, CA
California State U, Northridge, CA

California State U, Sacramento, CA
California State U, San Bernardino, CA
Calvin Coll, MI
Cameron U, OK
Cape Breton U, NS, Canada
Cape Cod Comm Coll, MA
Cardinal Stritch U, WI
Carleton U, ON, Canada
Carlow U, PA
Carroll Coll, MT
Carroll Coll, WI
Carson-Newman Coll, TN
Carthage Coll, WI
The Catholic U of America, DC
Cedar Crest Coll, PA
Cedar Valley Coll, TX
Central Arizona Coll, AZ
Central Lakes Coll, MN
Central Ohio Tech Coll, OH
Central Piedmont Comm Coll, NC
Central Wyoming Coll, WY
Charleston Southern U, SC
Chattahoochee Tech Coll, GA
Chattanooga State Tech Comm Coll, TN
Chesapeake Coll, MD
Christopher Newport U, VA
City Colls of Chicago, Richard J. Daley Coll, IL
Claremont McKenna Coll, CA
Clayton State U, GA
Clemson U, SC
Coahoma Comm Coll, MS
Coastal Carolina U, SC
Coe Coll, IA
Coll of Charleston, SC
Coll of Mount St. Joseph, OH
Coll of St. Joseph, VT
Coll of Saint Mary, NE
The Coll of Saint Rose, NY
The Coll of St. Scholastica, MN
Coll of Staten Island of the City U of New York, NY
Coll of the Canyons, CA
The Coll of Westchester, NY
Colorado Mountain Coll, Alpine Campus, CO
Columbus State U, GA
Commonwealth Tech Inst, PA
Comm Coll of Aurora, CO
Comm Coll of Beaver County, PA
Concordia U, NE
Concord U, WV
Coosa Valley Tech Coll, GA
Cornerstone U, MI
Cosumnes River Coll, Sacramento, CA
Crafton Hills Coll, CA
Daemen Coll, NY
Dalhousie U, NS, Canada

Dallas Baptist U, TX
DeKalb Tech Coll, GA
Delaware State U, DE
Delaware Tech & Comm Coll, Jack F. Owens Campus, DE
DePaul U, IL
Dixie State Coll of Utah, UT
Dominican U, IL
Drake U, IA
Drury U, MO
East Carolina U, NC
East Central Coll, MO
Eastern Connecticut State U, CT
Eastern Idaho Tech Coll, ID
Eastern Mennonite U, VA
Eastern Michigan U, MI
Eastfield Coll, TX
El Camino Coll, CA
El Centro Coll, TX
Elmira Coll, NY
Elms Coll, MA
Elon U, NC
Emory U, GA
Fairfield U, CT
Fairleigh Dickinson U, Coll at Florham, NJ
Fairleigh Dickinson U, Metropolitan Campus, NJ
Fayetteville State U, NC
Ferrum Coll, VA
Fitchburg State Coll, MA
Flagler Coll, FL
Florida Atlantic U, FL
Florida Comm Coll at Jacksonville, FL
Florida Gulf Coast U, FL
Florida Inst of Technology, FL
Florida International U, FL
Fontbonne U, MO
Foothill Coll, CA
Fort Hays State U, KS
Framingham State Coll, MA
Franciscan U of Steubenville, OH
Franklin Coll, IN
Franklin Pierce U, NH
Frederick Comm Coll, MD
Freed-Hardeman U, TN
Fresno Pacific U, CA
Fulton-Montgomery Comm Coll, NY
Furman U, SC
Gannon U, PA
Gardner-Webb U, NC
Gaston Coll, NC
Geneva Coll, PA
Georgetown Coll, KY
The George Washington U, DC
Georgia Coll & State U, GA
Georgian Court U, NJ
Glendale Comm Coll, CA
Glenville State Coll, WV
Gloucester County Coll, NJ
Gonzaga U, WA
Gordon Coll, MA
Goshen Coll, IN

Grace Coll, IN
Graceland U, IA
Grambling State U, LA
Greenville Tech Coll, SC
Grossmont Coll, CA
Gustavus Adolphus Coll, MN
Harding U, AR
Harrisburg Area Comm Coll, PA
Hartwick Coll, NY
Henderson State U, AR
High Point U, NC
Hillsborough Comm Coll, FL
Hocking Coll, OH
Hofstra U, NY
Hope Coll, MI
Houghton Coll, NY
Housatonic Comm Coll, CT
Houston Baptist U, TX
Houston Comm Coll System, TX
Howard Comm Coll, MD
Hudson Valley Comm Coll, NY
Hunter Coll of the City U of New York, NY
Huntington U, IN
Husson U, ME
Idaho State U, ID
Illinois State U, IL
Illinois Valley Comm Coll, IL
Illinois Wesleyan U, IL
Immaculata U, PA
Indiana U Bloomington, IN
Indiana U of Pennsylvania, PA
Indiana U–Purdue U Fort Wayne, IN
Iona Coll, NY
Irvine Valley Coll, CA
Itasca Comm Coll, MN
Ithaca Coll, NY
Jacksonville U, FL
Jamestown Comm Coll, NY
Jefferson Comm and Tech Coll, KY
Jefferson Comm Coll, OH
John Brown U, AR
Johnson & Wales U, CO
Johnson & Wales U, FL
Johnson & Wales U, NC
Johnson & Wales U, RI
Johnson State Coll, VT
Kansas State U, KS
Kapiolani Comm Coll, HI
Kellogg Comm Coll, MI
Kennesaw State U, GA
Kentucky Wesleyan Coll, KY
Keuka Coll, NY
Kingsborough Comm Coll of the City U of New York, NY
King's Coll, PA
Kutztown U of Pennsylvania, PA
Kuyper Coll, MI
LaGrange Coll, GA
Lake Erie Coll, OH
Lakeland Coll, WI

Lake Superior State U, MI
Lamar State Coll–Orange, TX
Lamar U, TX
Langston U, OK
Lassen Comm Coll District, CA
Lebanon Valley Coll, PA
Lehigh U, PA
Le Moyne Coll, NY
LeTourneau U, TX
Lewis U, IL
Liberty U, VA
Lincoln U, PA
Lindenwood U, MO
Long Beach City Coll, CA
Long Island U, Brooklyn Campus, NY
Loras Coll, IA
Loyola Marymount U, CA
Loyola U Chicago, IL
Loyola U New Orleans, LA
Lynchburg Coll, VA
MacMurray Coll, IL
Macomb Comm Coll, MI
Madisonville Comm Coll, KY
Manhattan Coll, NY
Marian Coll, IN
Marietta Coll, OH
Marist Coll, NY
Marquette U, WI
Marshall U, WV
Marymount Manhattan Coll, NY
Marymount U, VA
Marywood U, PA
Massachusetts Coll of Liberal Arts, MA
Massasoit Comm Coll, MA
Maui Comm Coll, HI
McNeese State U, LA
Mercyhurst Coll, PA
Metropolitan Comm Coll–Longview, MO
Metropolitan Comm Coll–Penn Valley, MO
Michigan State U, MI
Middle Georgia Tech Coll, GA
Middlesex Comm Coll, CT
Middlesex County Coll, NJ
Middle Tennessee State U, TN
Midland Lutheran Coll, NE
Minnesota School of Business–St. Cloud, MN
Minnesota State Coll–Southeast Tech, MN
Minnesota State U Mankato, MN
Minnesota State U Moorhead, MN
MiraCosta Coll, CA
Missouri State U, MO
Missouri State U–West Plains, MO
Mitchell Coll, CT
Molloy Coll, NY
Monmouth Coll, IL

479

ACCOUNTING AND BUSINESS/MANAGEMENT

ACCOUNTING AND COMPUTER SCIENCE

ACCOUNTING AND FINANCE

ACCOUNTING RELATED

ACCOUNTING TECHNOLOGY AND BOOKKEEPING

Madisonville Comm Coll, KY
Miami Dade Coll, FL
Mohawk Valley Comm Coll, NY
Montana State U–Billings, MT
Nassau Comm Coll, NY
St. Cloud Tech Coll, MN
South Piedmont Comm Coll, NC
Southwestern Michigan Coll, MI
Spokane Comm Coll, WA
Tallahassee Comm Coll, FL
The U of Akron, OH
The U of Akron–Wayne Coll, OH
The U of Montana-Helena Coll of Technology, MT
U of Rio Grande, OH
Waubonsee Comm Coll, IL
West Virginia Northern Comm Coll, WV
Williston State Coll, ND
Wright State U, OH

ACTING
Bard Coll, NY
Barry U, FL
Baylor U, TX
Carroll Coll, MT
Central Wyoming Coll, WY
Coe Coll, IA
Dalhousie U, NS, Canada
DePaul U, IL
Drake U, IA
Ithaca Coll, NY
Johnson State Coll, VT
Marymount Manhattan Coll, NY
Old Dominion U, VA
Penn State Abington, PA
Penn State DuBois, PA
Penn State Fayette, The Eberly Campus, PA
Penn State Mont Alto, PA
Penn State Wilkes-Barre, PA
Ryerson U, ON, Canada
St. Cloud State U, MN
Santa Barbara City Coll, CA
Seton Hill U, PA
State U of New York Coll at Brockport, NY
Syracuse U, NY
Temple U, PA
Trinity U, TX
The U of Akron, OH
U of Connecticut, CT
U of Northern Iowa, IA
The U of the Arts, PA

ACTING/DIRECTING
Framingham State Coll, MA

ACTUARIAL SCIENCE
Ball State U, IN
Bradley U, IL
Carroll Coll, WI
Drake U, IA
Eastern Michigan U, MI
Harrisburg Area Comm Coll, PA
Hofstra U, NY
Lebanon Valley Coll, PA
Lincoln U, PA
New York U, NY
North Central Coll, IL
The Ohio State U, OH
Penn State Abington, PA
Penn State DuBois, PA
Penn State Fayette, The Eberly Campus, PA
Penn State Mont Alto, PA

Penn State Wilkes-Barre, PA
Queens Coll of the City U of New York, NY
Roosevelt U, IL
Seton Hill U, PA
Southern Adventist U, TN
Temple U, PA
Thiel Coll, PA
U at Albany, State U of New York, NY
U of Central Florida, FL
U of Central Oklahoma, OK
U of Connecticut, CT
U of Illinois at Urbana–Champaign, IL
U of Manitoba, MB, Canada
U of Minnesota, Duluth, MN
U of Nebraska–Lincoln, NE
U of Northern Iowa, IA
U of Pennsylvania, PA
U of St. Thomas, MN
The U of Texas at San Antonio, TX
U of Toronto, ON, Canada
U of Wisconsin–Madison, WI
U of Wisconsin–Stevens Point, WI

ADMINISTRATIVE ASSISTANT AND SECRETARIAL SCIENCE
Abraham Baldwin Coll, GA
Aims Comm Coll, CO
Albany State U, GA
Alexandria Tech Coll, MN
Allegany Coll of Maryland, MD
Altamaha Tech Coll, GA
Ashland Comm and Tech Coll, KY
Asnuntuck Comm Coll, CT
Bainbridge Coll, GA
Ball State U, IN
Blinn Coll, TX
Bluefield State Coll, WV
Blue Ridge Comm Coll, VA
British Columbia Inst of Technology, BC, Canada
Broward Comm Coll, FL
Bryant and Stratton Coll, Rochester, NY
Bucks County Comm Coll, PA
Cape Cod Comm Coll, MA
Cedar Valley Coll, TX
Central Arizona Coll, AZ
Central Lakes Coll, MN
Central Ohio Tech Coll, OH
Central Piedmont Comm Coll, NC
Chattahoochee Tech Coll, GA
Chattanooga State Tech Comm Coll, TN
Chesapeake Coll, MD
Citrus Coll, CA
City Colls of Chicago, Richard J. Daley Coll, IL
Clayton State U, GA
Coahoma Comm Coll, MS
Coll of The Albemarle, NC
Coll of the Canyons, CA
Coll of the Desert, CA
The Coll of Westchester, NY
Comm Coll of Allegheny County, PA
Comm Coll of Beaver County, PA
Concordia Coll–New York, NY
Crafton Hills Coll, CA
Cuesta Coll, CA

Dabney S. Lancaster Comm Coll, VA
DeKalb Tech Coll, GA
Delaware Tech & Comm Coll, Jack F. Owens Campus, DE
Dixie State Coll of Utah, UT
East Central Coll, MO
Eastern Idaho Tech Coll, ID
Eastern New Mexico U–Roswell, NM
Eastern West Virginia Comm and Tech Coll, WV
El Camino Coll, CA
El Centro Coll, TX
Feather River Coll, CA
Florida Comm Coll at Jacksonville, FL
Fort Hays State U, KS
Fresno City Coll, CA
Fulton-Montgomery Comm Coll, NY
Gadsden State Comm Coll, AL
Galveston Coll, TX
Glendale Comm Coll, CA
Grace Coll, IN
Greenville Tech Coll, SC
Grossmont Coll, CA
Harrisburg Area Comm Coll, PA
Heartland Comm Coll, IL
Henderson State U, AR
Hillsborough Comm Coll, FL
Hocking Coll, OH
Hofstra U, NY
Hopkinsville Comm Coll, KY
Housatonic Comm Coll, CT
Houston Comm Coll System, TX
Howard Comm Coll, MD
Hudson Valley Comm Coll, NY
Idaho State U, ID
Illinois Valley Comm Coll, IL
Irvine Valley Coll, CA
James H. Faulkner State Comm Coll, AL
Jefferson Comm Coll, OH
Kellogg Comm Coll, MI
Kingsborough Comm Coll of the City U of New York, NY
Kuyper Coll, MI
Lackawanna Coll, PA
Lake City Comm Coll, FL
Lamar Inst of Technology, TX
Lamar State Coll–Orange, TX
Lamar U, TX
Lancaster Bible Coll, PA
Langston U, OK
Laredo Comm Coll, TX
Lassen Comm Coll District, CA
Lee Coll, TX
Lincoln Land Comm Coll, IL
Long Beach City Coll, CA
Macomb Comm Coll, MI
Madisonville Comm Coll, KY
Massasoit Comm Coll, MA
Maui Comm Coll, HI
Mercyhurst Coll, PA
Metropolitan Comm Coll–Longview, MO
Metropolitan Comm Coll–Penn Valley, MO
Miami Dade Coll, FL
Middle Georgia Tech Coll, GA
Middlesex Comm Coll, CT
Middlesex County Coll, NJ

Midland Lutheran Coll, NE
Minnesota School of Business–St. Cloud, MN
Minnesota State Coll–Southeast Tech, MN
MiraCosta Coll, CA
Mohawk Valley Comm Coll, NY
Montana State U–Billings, MT
Montana Tech of The U of Montana, MT
Morton Coll, IL
Murray State U, KY
Muscatine Comm Coll, IA
Nassau Comm Coll, NY
New Mexico Jr Coll, NM
New River Comm Coll, VA
North Central Missouri Coll, MO
North Central Texas Coll, TX
Northern State U, SD
Northland Comm and Tech Coll–Thief River Falls, MN
North Metro Tech Coll, GA
Ocean County Coll, NJ
Odessa Coll, TX
Ozarks Tech Comm Coll, MO
Paul Quinn Coll, TX
Phoenix Coll, AZ
Pima Comm Coll, AZ
Pueblo Comm Coll, CO
Reedley Coll, CA
Richland Comm Coll, IL
Richmond Comm Coll, NC
Rockingham Comm Coll, NC
Rose State Coll, OK
Roxbury Comm Coll, MA
St. Cloud Tech Coll, MN
St. Louis Comm Coll at Florissant Valley, MO
St. Philip's Coll, TX
San Diego Mesa Coll, CA
Santa Ana Coll, CA
Santa Barbara City Coll, CA
Sauk Valley Comm Coll, IL
Schoolcraft Coll, MI
Scottsdale Comm Coll, AZ
Seminole Comm Coll, FL
Shasta Coll, CA
Shelton State Comm Coll, AL
Skagit Valley Coll, WA
Southwestern Indian Polytechnic Inst, NM
Southwestern Michigan Coll, MI
Spokane Comm Coll, WA
Spoon River Coll, IL
Stark State Coll of Technology, OH
Surry Comm Coll, NC
Sussex County Comm Coll, NJ
Tallahassee Comm Coll, FL
Tidewater Comm Coll, VA
Trinity Baptist Coll, FL
Trocaire Coll, NY
Tunxis Comm Coll, CT
The U of Akron, OH
The U of Akron–Wayne Coll, OH
U of Arkansas at Fort Smith, AR
U of Central Missouri, MO
U of Cincinnati, OH
The U of Findlay, OH
U of Rio Grande, OH
U of the District of Columbia, DC
Valdosta State U, GA
Valencia Comm Coll, FL
Victor Valley Coll, CA

Virginia Highlands Comm Coll, VA
Washburn U, KS
Waubonsee Comm Coll, IL
Waukesha County Tech Coll, WI
Westchester Comm Coll, NY
Western Tech Coll, WI
West Los Angeles Coll, CA
Westmoreland County Comm Coll, PA
West Virginia Northern Comm Coll, WV
West Virginia State U, WV
Williston State Coll, ND
Wright State U, OH

ADULT AND CONTINUING EDUCATION
American International Coll, MA
Brock U, ON, Canada
DePaul U, IL
Franklin Pierce U, NH
Massachusetts Coll of Liberal Arts, MA
U of Central Oklahoma, OK
U of New Brunswick Fredericton, NB, Canada
U of New Hampshire, NH
U of San Francisco, CA
U of the Incarnate Word, TX
Urbana U, OH

ADULT AND CONTINUING EDUCATION ADMINISTRATION
Marshall U, WV
Penn State Abington, PA
Penn State DuBois, PA
Penn State Fayette, The Eberly Campus, PA
Penn State Mont Alto, PA
Penn State Wilkes-Barre, PA

ADULT DEVELOPMENT AND AGING
Mount Saint Vincent U, NS, Canada
St. Thomas U, NB, Canada

ADULT HEALTH NURSING
U at Buffalo, the State U of New York, NY
Wright State U, OH

ADVANCED/GRADUATE DENTISTRY AND ORAL SCIENCES RELATED
Dalhousie U, NS, Canada

ADVERTISING
Academy of Art U, CA
The Art Inst of Pittsburgh, PA
Ball State U, IN
Barry U, FL
Bradley U, IL
California State U, Fullerton, CA
Central Piedmont Comm Coll, NC
Chattanooga State Tech Comm Coll, TN
Cosumnes River Coll, Sacramento, CA
DePaul U, IL
Drake U, IA
Drury U, MO
Eastern Nazarene Coll, MA
El Camino Coll, CA

Fashion Inst of Technology, NY
Fontbonne U, MO
Franklin Pierce U, NH
Gannon U, PA
Grossmont Coll, CA
Harding U, AR
The Illinois Inst of Art–Schaumburg, IL
Iona Coll, NY
Johnson & Wales U, CO
Johnson & Wales U, FL
Johnson & Wales U, RI
Long Beach City Coll, CA
Marist Coll, NY
Marquette U, WI
Marywood U, PA
Mercyhurst Coll, PA
Michigan State U, MI
Middlesex County Coll, NJ
Minneapolis Coll of Art and Design, MN
Minnesota State U Moorhead, MN
Mohawk Valley Comm Coll, NY
Northwood U, MI
Northwood U, Florida Campus, FL
Northwood U, Texas Campus, TX
Notre Dame de Namur U, CA
Penn State Abington, PA
Penn State DuBois, PA
Penn State Fayette, The Eberly Campus, PA
Penn State Mont Alto, PA
Penn State Wilkes-Barre, PA
Portland State U, OR
Rochester Inst of Technology, NY
St. Cloud State U, MN
St. Cloud Tech Coll, MN
San Diego State U, CA
Santa Rosa Jr Coll, CA
School of Visual Arts, NY
Southern Adventist U, TN
Surry Comm Coll, NC
Syracuse U, NY
Temple U, PA
Tidewater Comm Coll, VA
The U of Alabama, AL
U of Central Florida, FL
U of Central Oklahoma, OK
U of Colorado at Boulder, CO
U of Illinois at Urbana–Champaign, IL
U of Kentucky, KY
U of Miami, FL
U of Mississippi, MS
U of Missouri–Columbia, MO
U of Nebraska–Lincoln, NE
U of Oregon, OR
U of Southern Indiana, IN
The U of Tennessee, TN
The U of Texas at Austin, TX
U of the District of Columbia, DC
U of Wisconsin–Madison, WI
Wayne State Coll, NE
Western New England Coll, MA
West Texas A&M U, TX
West Virginia State U, WV
Widener U, PA
Xavier U, OH

AERONAUTICAL/ AEROSPACE ENGINEERING TECHNOLOGY

British Columbia Inst of Technology, BC, Canada
Calhoun Comm Coll, AL
Northeastern U, MA
Santa Rosa Jr Coll, CA
U of Central Missouri, MO

AERONAUTICS/ AVIATION/AEROSPACE SCIENCE AND TECHNOLOGY

Augsburg Coll, MN
Caldwell Comm Coll and Tech Inst, NC
Comm Coll of Beaver County, PA
Embry-Riddle Aeronautical U, FL
Henderson State U, AR
Kansas State U, KS
Liberty U, VA
Miami Dade Coll, FL
Middle Tennessee State U, TN
Northland Comm and Tech Coll–Thief River Falls, MN
Oklahoma State U, OK
U of Nebraska at Omaha, NE
U of the District of Columbia, DC

AEROSPACE, AERONAUTICAL AND ASTRONAUTICAL ENGINEERING

Carleton U, ON, Canada
Cornell U, NY
Eastern Nazarene Coll, MA
Embry-Riddle Aeronautical U, FL
Florida Inst of Technology, FL
North Carolina State U, NC
The Ohio State U, OH
Oklahoma State U, OK
Penn State Abington, PA
Penn State DuBois, PA
Penn State Fayette, The Eberly Campus, PA
Penn State Mont Alto, PA
Penn State Wilkes-Barre, PA
Rensselaer Polytechnic Inst, NY
Rochester Inst of Technology, NY
Ryerson U, ON, Canada
San Diego State U, CA
Syracuse U, NY
Texas A&M U, TX
U at Buffalo, the State U of New York, NY
The U of Alabama, AL
The U of Arizona, AZ
U of California, Irvine, CA
U of California, Los Angeles, CA
U of Central Florida, FL
U of Cincinnati, OH
U of Colorado at Boulder, CO
U of Illinois at Urbana–Champaign, IL
U of Kansas, KS
U of Miami, FL
U of Michigan, MI
U of Missouri–Rolla, MO
U of Notre Dame, IN
The U of Tennessee, TN

The U of Texas at Austin, TX
U of Toronto, ON, Canada
U of Virginia, VA
U of Washington, WA
Wichita State U, KS

AEROSPACE SCIENCE

Dallas Baptist U, TX
Florida Inst of Technology, FL

AFRICAN-AMERICAN/ BLACK STUDIES

Amherst Coll, MA
Bates Coll, ME
Brandeis U, MA
Brown U, RI
California State U, Fullerton, CA
California State U, Northridge, CA
Claremont McKenna Coll, CA
Coe Coll, IA
Colby Coll, ME
Colgate U, NY
Coll of Staten Island of the City U of New York, NY
The Coll of William and Mary, VA
Cornell U, NY
DePaul U, IL
Duke U, NC
Earlham Coll, IN
Eastern Michigan U, MI
El Camino Coll, CA
Emory U, GA
Fresno City Coll, CA
Hampshire Coll, MA
Hunter Coll of the City U of New York, NY
Indiana U Bloomington, IN
Kenyon Coll, OH
Lehigh U, PA
Loyola Marymount U, CA
Marquette U, WI
Mercer U, GA
Mount Holyoke Coll, MA
Nassau Comm Coll, NY
New York U, NY
Northeastern U, MA
The Ohio State U, OH
Ohio Wesleyan U, OH
Penn State Abington, PA
Penn State DuBois, PA
Penn State Fayette, The Eberly Campus, PA
Penn State Mont Alto, PA
Penn State Wilkes-Barre, PA
Roosevelt U, IL
Rutgers, The State U of New Jersey, Newark, NJ
San Diego Mesa Coll, CA
San Diego State U, CA
San Francisco State U, CA
Santa Ana Coll, CA
Santa Barbara City Coll, CA
Seton Hall U, NJ
State U of New York Coll at Brockport, NY
State U of New York Coll at Cortland, NY
State U of New York Coll at Geneseo, NY
Syracuse U, NY
Temple U, PA
Tufts U, MA
U at Albany, State U of New York, NY
U at Buffalo, the State U of New York, NY
U of California, Berkeley, CA

U of California, Irvine, CA
U of California, Los Angeles, CA
U of California, Santa Barbara, CA
U of Cincinnati, OH
U of Delaware, DE
U of Kansas, KS
U of Maryland, Baltimore County, MD
U of Massachusetts Amherst, MA
U of Massachusetts Boston, MA
U of Miami, FL
U of Michigan, MI
U of Nebraska at Omaha, NE
U of New Mexico, NM
The U of North Carolina at Chapel Hill, NC
The U of North Carolina at Charlotte, NC
U of Pennsylvania, PA
U of Pittsburgh, PA
U of Virginia, VA
U of Washington, WA
U of Wisconsin–Madison, WI
Wayne State U, MI
Wellesley Coll, MA
Wells Coll, NY
Wright State U, OH
Yale U, CT

AFRICAN LANGUAGES

U of California, Los Angeles, CA
U of Wisconsin–Madison, WI

AFRICAN STUDIES

Bard Coll, NY
Brandeis U, MA
Carleton U, ON, Canada
Colgate U, NY
DePaul U, IL
Emory U, GA
Hamilton Coll, NY
Haverford Coll, PA
Hofstra U, NY
Illinois Wesleyan U, IL
Indiana U Bloomington, IN
Kennesaw State U, GA
Kenyon Coll, OH
MiraCosta Coll, CA
The Ohio State U, OH
Portland State U, OR
Queens Coll of the City U of New York, NY
Rutgers, The State U of New Jersey, Newark, NJ
St. Lawrence U, NY
State U of New York Coll at Brockport, NY
U of California, Los Angeles, CA
U of Kansas, KS
U of Maryland, Baltimore County, MD
U of Pennsylvania, PA
U of Toronto, ON, Canada
U of Wisconsin–Madison, WI
Vassar Coll, NY
Wellesley Coll, MA
Yale U, CT

AGRIBUSINESS

Abilene Christian U, TX
Adams State Coll, CO
Central Wyoming Coll, WY
Illinois State U, IL
Lindenwood U, MO

Middle Tennessee State U, TN
Missouri State U, MO
North Carolina State U, NC
North Dakota State U, ND
Penn State Abington, PA
Penn State DuBois, PA
Penn State Fayette, The Eberly Campus, PA
Penn State Mont Alto, PA
Penn State Wilkes-Barre, PA
Stephen F. Austin State U, TX
Texas A&M U, TX
U of Arkansas, AR
U of Central Missouri, MO
U of Delaware, DE
U of Illinois at Urbana–Champaign, IL
U of Wyoming, WY
Vermont Tech Coll, VT
West Texas A&M U, TX

AGRICULTURAL AND DOMESTIC ANIMALS SERVICES RELATED

Sterling Coll, VT

AGRICULTURAL AND EXTENSION EDUCATION

Cornell U, NY
North Carolina State U, NC
Penn State Abington, PA
Penn State DuBois, PA
Penn State Fayette, The Eberly Campus, PA
Penn State Mont Alto, PA
Penn State Wilkes-Barre, PA

AGRICULTURAL AND FOOD PRODUCTS PROCESSING

Kansas State U, KS
North Carolina State U, NC
The Ohio State U, OH
Texas A&M U, TX

AGRICULTURAL AND HORTICULTURAL PLANT BREEDING

Cornell U, NY
Delaware State U, DE
Sterling Coll, VT

AGRICULTURAL ANIMAL BREEDING

Cornell U, NY
Sterling Coll, VT
Texas A&M U, TX

AGRICULTURAL/ BIOLOGICAL ENGINEERING AND BIOENGINEERING

Clemson U, SC
Cornell U, NY
Dalhousie U, NS, Canada
Kansas State U, KS
Michigan State U, MI
North Carolina State U, NC
North Dakota State U, ND
The Ohio State U, OH
Penn State Abington, PA
Penn State DuBois, PA
Penn State Fayette, The Eberly Campus, PA
Penn State Mont Alto, PA
Penn State Wilkes-Barre, PA
Rutgers, The State U of New Jersey, New Brunswick, NJ
State U of New York Coll of Environmental Science and Forestry, NY
Texas A&M U, TX

The U of Arizona, AZ
U of Arkansas, AR
U of California, Los Angeles, CA
U of Delaware, DE
U of Illinois at Urbana–Champaign, IL
U of Kentucky, KY
U of Manitoba, MB, Canada
U of Missouri–Rolla, MO
U of Nebraska–Lincoln, NE
The U of Tennessee, TN
U of Wisconsin–Madison, WI

AGRICULTURAL BUSINESS AND MANAGEMENT
Abraham Baldwin Coll, GA
Central Wyoming Coll, WY
Clayton State U, GA
Clemson U, SC
Coll of the Desert, CA
Cornell U, NY
Cosumnes River Coll, Sacramento, CA
Delaware State U, DE
Delaware Tech & Comm Coll, Jack F. Owens Campus, DE
Fort Hays State U, KS
Freed-Hardeman U, TN
Harrisburg Area Comm Coll, PA
Illinois Valley Comm Coll, IL
Kansas State U, KS
Lassen Comm Coll District, CA
Michigan State U, MI
Montana State U, MT
Murray State U, KY
North Carolina State U, NC
North Central Missouri Coll, MO
North Dakota State U, ND
Northwestern Oklahoma State U, OK
Nova Scotia Coll, NS, Canada
The Ohio State U, OH
Oklahoma State U, OK
Reedley Coll, CA
Richland Comm Coll, IL
Rocky Mountain Coll, MT
San Diego State U, CA
Santa Rosa Jr Coll, CA
Shasta Coll, CA
Spokane Comm Coll, WA
State U of New York Coll of Technology at Alfred, NY
Sterling Coll, VT
Surry Comm Coll, NC
Texas A&M U, TX
Truman State U, MO
U of Central Missouri, MO
U of Delaware, DE
U of Guelph, ON, Canada
U of Missouri–Columbia, MO
U of Nebraska at Kearney, NE
U of Nebraska–Lincoln, NE
U of New Hampshire, NH
The U of Tennessee at Martin, TN
U of Wisconsin–Madison, WI
U of Wisconsin–Platteville, WI
Upper Iowa U, IA
Wayne State Coll, NE
West Texas A&M U, TX

AGRICULTURAL BUSINESS AND MANAGEMENT RELATED
Penn State Abington, PA
Penn State DuBois, PA
Penn State Fayette, The Eberly Campus, PA
Penn State Mont Alto, PA
Penn State Wilkes-Barre, PA
Sterling Coll, VT
The U of Tennessee, TN

AGRICULTURAL COMMUNICATION/JOURNALISM
Michigan State U, MI
Oklahoma State U, OK
Sterling Coll, VT
U of Arkansas, AR
U of Illinois at Urbana–Champaign, IL
U of Missouri–Columbia, MO
U of Nebraska–Lincoln, NE
U of Wyoming, WY

AGRICULTURAL ECONOMICS
Abraham Baldwin Coll, GA
Alabama A&M U, AL
Clemson U, SC
Cornell U, NY
James H. Faulkner State Comm Coll, AL
Kansas State U, KS
Langston U, OK
Lassen Comm Coll District, CA
Michigan State U, MI
North Carolina State U, NC
North Dakota State U, ND
Nova Scotia Coll, NS, Canada
The Ohio State U, OH
Oklahoma State U, OK
Southern Illinois U Carbondale, IL
Southern U and A&M Coll, LA
Texas A&M U, TX
Truman State U, MO
The U of Arizona, AZ
U of Arkansas, AR
U of Central Missouri, MO
U of Connecticut, CT
U of Delaware, DE
U of Guelph, ON, Canada
U of Hawaii at Manoa, HI
U of Illinois at Urbana–Champaign, IL
U of Kentucky, KY
U of Manitoba, MB, Canada
U of Missouri–Columbia, MO
U of Nebraska–Lincoln, NE
The U of Tennessee, TN
U of Vermont, VT
U of Wisconsin–Madison, WI

AGRICULTURAL/FARM SUPPLIES RETAILING AND WHOLESALING
Muscatine Comm Coll, IA
Texas A&M U, TX

AGRICULTURAL MECHANICS AND EQUIPMENT TECHNOLOGY
Cornell U, NY

AGRICULTURAL MECHANIZATION
Abraham Baldwin Coll, GA
Aims Comm Coll, CO
Clayton State U, GA
Clemson U, SC
Cosumnes River Coll, Sacramento, CA
Cuesta Coll, CA
Kansas State U, KS
Lassen Comm Coll District, CA
Maui Comm Coll, HI
Metropolitan Comm Coll–Longview, MO
Montana State U, MT
North Central Texas Coll, TX
North Dakota State U, ND
Nova Scotia Coll, NS, Canada
Paris Jr Coll, TX
Penn State Abington, PA
Penn State DuBois, PA
Penn State Fayette, The Eberly Campus, PA
Penn State Mont Alto, PA
Penn State Wilkes-Barre, PA
Santa Rosa Jr Coll, CA
Spoon River Coll, IL
Stephen F. Austin State U, TX
U of Illinois at Urbana–Champaign, IL
U of Missouri–Columbia, MO
The U of Montana-Helena Coll of Technology, MT
U of Nebraska–Lincoln, NE
Western Tech Coll, WI

AGRICULTURAL MECHANIZATION RELATED
Reedley Coll, CA

AGRICULTURAL PRODUCTION
Hillsborough Comm Coll, FL
Lincoln Land Comm Coll, IL
Muscatine Comm Coll, IA
Stephen F. Austin State U, TX
Texas A&M U, TX
U of Hawaii at Manoa, HI
The U of Tennessee at Martin, TN

AGRICULTURAL PRODUCTION RELATED
Sterling Coll, VT

AGRICULTURAL PUBLIC SERVICES RELATED
Sterling Coll, VT

AGRICULTURAL SCIENCES
Cameron U, OK
The U of Tennessee at Martin, TN

AGRICULTURAL TEACHER EDUCATION
Clemson U, SC
Cornell U, NY
Langston U, OK
McNeese State U, LA
Missouri State U, MO
Montana State U, MT
Murray State U, KY
North Carolina State U, NC
North Dakota State U, ND
The Ohio State U, OH
Oklahoma State U, OK

Prairie View A&M U, TX
Southern U and A&M Coll, LA
Spoon River Coll, IL
Sterling Coll, VT
The U of Akron, OH
The U of Arizona, AZ
U of Arkansas, AR
U of Connecticut, CT
U of Delaware, DE
U of Illinois at Urbana–Champaign, IL
U of Missouri–Columbia, MO
U of Nebraska–Lincoln, NE
U of New Hampshire, NH
The U of Tennessee, TN
The U of Tennessee at Martin, TN
U of Wisconsin–Madison, WI
U of Wisconsin–Platteville, WI
U of Wyoming, WY
Victor Valley Coll, CA

AGRICULTURE
Abraham Baldwin Coll, GA
Bainbridge Coll, GA
Blinn Coll, TX
Calhoun Comm Coll, AL
California State U, Stanislaus, CA
Central Arizona Coll, AZ
Central Wyoming Coll, WY
Clayton State U, GA
Cornell U, NY
Delaware State U, DE
Dixie State Coll of Utah, UT
Ferrum Coll, VA
Fort Hays State U, KS
Hampshire Coll, MA
Houston Comm Coll System, TX
Illinois State U, IL
Illinois Valley Comm Coll, IL
Lassen Comm Coll District, CA
Macomb Comm Coll, MI
McNeese State U, LA
Miami Dade Coll, FL
Missouri State U, MO
Missouri State U–West Plains, MO
Murray State U, KY
New Mexico Jr Coll, NM
North Carolina State U, NC
North Dakota State U, ND
Northwestern Oklahoma State U, OK
Nova Scotia Coll, NS, Canada
Odessa Coll, TX
Oklahoma State U, OK
Penn State Abington, PA
Penn State DuBois, PA
Penn State Fayette, The Eberly Campus, PA
Penn State Mont Alto, PA
Penn State Wilkes-Barre, PA
Prairie View A&M U, TX
Reedley Coll, CA
Rutgers, The State U of New Jersey, New Brunswick, NJ
Santa Rosa Jr Coll, CA
Skagit Valley Coll, WA
Southern Illinois U Carbondale, IL
Southern Utah U, UT
State U of New York Coll of Technology at Alfred, NY
Stephen F. Austin State U, TX
Sterling Coll, VT

Texas A&M U, TX
Truman State U, MO
The U of Arizona, AZ
U of Connecticut, CT
U of Delaware, DE
U of Guelph, ON, Canada
U of Illinois at Urbana–Champaign, IL
U of Manitoba, MB, Canada
U of Missouri–Columbia, MO
U of Nebraska–Lincoln, NE
U of New Hampshire, NH
The U of Tennessee at Martin, TN
U of Vermont, VT
U of Wisconsin–Madison, WI
Ventura Coll, CA
Western Nebraska Comm Coll, NE
West Texas A&M U, TX
Williston State Coll, ND

AGRICULTURE AND AGRICULTURE OPERATIONS RELATED
Michigan State U, MI
Sterling Coll, VT
U of Kentucky, KY
U of Wyoming, WY

AGRONOMY AND CROP SCIENCE
Cornell U, NY
Cosumnes River Coll, Sacramento, CA
Delaware State U, DE
Fort Hays State U, KS
Kansas State U, KS
Lassen Comm Coll District, CA
Missouri State U, MO
North Carolina State U, NC
The Ohio State U, OH
Penn State DuBois, PA
Penn State Fayette, The Eberly Campus, PA
Penn State Mont Alto, PA
Penn State Wilkes-Barre, PA
Southern Maine Comm Coll, ME
Spokane Comm Coll, WA
Stephen F. Austin State U, TX
Sterling Coll, VT
Texas A&M U, TX
Truman State U, MO
U of Connecticut, CT
U of Delaware, DE
U of Guelph, ON, Canada
U of Illinois at Urbana–Champaign, IL
U of Kentucky, KY
U of Manitoba, MB, Canada
U of Nebraska–Lincoln, NE
U of New Hampshire, NH
The U of Tennessee at Martin, TN
U of Vermont, VT
U of Wisconsin–Madison, WI
U of Wisconsin–Platteville, WI
West Texas A&M U, TX

AIRCRAFT POWERPLANT TECHNOLOGY
British Columbia Inst of Technology, BC, Canada
Embry-Riddle Aeronautical U, FL

Florida Comm Coll at
Jacksonville, FL
Idaho State U, ID
Linn State Tech Coll, MO
Pima Comm Coll, AZ
St. Philip's Coll, TX

AIR FORCE R.O.T.C./AIR SCIENCE
Rensselaer Polytechnic Inst, NY
U of Washington, WA

AIRFRAME MECHANICS AND AIRCRAFT MAINTENANCE TECHNOLOGY
British Columbia Inst of
Technology, BC, Canada
Clayton State U, GA
Eastern New Mexico
U–Roswell, NM
Florida Comm Coll at
Jacksonville, FL
Glendale Comm Coll, CA
Greenville Tech Coll, SC
Ivy Tech Comm Coll–
Wabash Valley, IN
Kansas State U, KS
LeTourneau U, TX
Lewis U, IL
Middle Georgia Tech Coll, GA
Mohawk Valley Comm Coll, NY
New Hampshire Comm
Tech Coll, Nashua/
Claremont, NH
St. Philip's Coll, TX
Southwestern Michigan Coll, MI
U of Alaska Anchorage, AK
The U of Montana-Helena
Coll of Technology, MT
West Los Angeles Coll, CA

AIRLINE FLIGHT ATTENDANT
The U of Akron, OH

AIRLINE PILOT AND FLIGHT CREW
Baylor U, TX
Broward Comm Coll, FL
Chattanooga State Tech
Comm Coll, TN
Comm Coll of Allegheny
County, PA
Comm Coll of Beaver
County, PA
Cornerstone U, MI
Delaware State U, DE
Dixie State Coll of Utah, UT
Eastern Michigan U, MI
Embry-Riddle Aeronautical
U, FL
Farmingdale State Coll, NY
Florida Comm Coll at
Jacksonville, FL
Glendale Comm Coll, CA
Jacksonville U, FL
Jamestown Comm Coll, NY
Kansas State U, KS
LeTourneau U, TX
Lewis U, IL
Long Beach City Coll, CA
Miami Dade Coll, FL
Midland Coll, TX
Rocky Mountain Coll, MT
St. Cloud State U, MN
Southern Illinois U
Carbondale, IL
U of Alaska Anchorage, AK
U of Dubuque, IA

U of Illinois at Urbana–
Champaign, IL
Westminster Coll, UT

AIR TRAFFIC CONTROL
Comm Coll of Beaver
County, PA
Embry-Riddle Aeronautical
U, FL
Miami Dade Coll, FL
St. Cloud State U, MN
U of Alaska Anchorage, AK

ALLIED HEALTH AND MEDICAL ASSISTING SERVICES RELATED
Washburn U, KS

ALLIED HEALTH DIAGNOSTIC, INTERVENTION, AND TREATMENT PROFESSIONS RELATED
British Columbia Inst of
Technology, BC, Canada
Cameron U, OK
Fairleigh Dickinson U, Coll
at Florham, NJ
Ivy Tech Comm Coll–
Wabash Valley, IN
Ramapo Coll of New Jersey, NJ
Rutgers, The State U of New
Jersey, Newark, NJ
The U of Akron, OH
U of Connecticut, CT

ALTERNATIVE AND COMPLEMENTARY MEDICINE RELATED
Everglades U, Sarasota, FL
Johnson State Coll, VT

AMERICAN GOVERNMENT AND POLITICS
Bard Coll, NY
Claremont McKenna Coll, CA
Drury U, MO
Framingham State Coll, MA
North Carolina State U, NC
Quincy Coll, MA
Rivier Coll, NH
The U of Akron, OH

AMERICAN HISTORY
Bard Coll, NY
Bridgewater Coll, VA
Charleston Southern U, SC
Framingham State Coll, MA

AMERICAN INDIAN/ NATIVE AMERICAN STUDIES
Bemidji State U, MN
Brandon U, MB, Canada
Cape Breton U, NS, Canada
Central Wyoming Coll, WY
Colgate U, NY
Cornell U, NY
Fresno City Coll, CA
Itasca Comm Coll, MN
Pima Comm Coll, AZ
Portland State U, OR
St. Thomas U, NB, Canada
Santa Barbara City Coll, CA
Trent U, ON, Canada
U of California, Berkeley, CA
U of California, Los Angeles, CA
U of Minnesota, Duluth, MN
U of the Incarnate Word, TX

U of Toronto, ON, Canada
U of Washington, WA
U of Wisconsin–Eau Claire, WI

AMERICAN LITERATURE
Cornell U, NY
Queens U of Charlotte, NC
St. Lawrence U, NY
State U of New York Coll at
Brockport, NY
U of California, Los Angeles, CA
U of Great Falls, MT

AMERICAN NATIVE/ NATIVE AMERICAN EDUCATION
The Coll of St. Scholastica, MN
Queen's U at Kingston, ON, Canada

AMERICAN NATIVE/ NATIVE AMERICAN LANGUAGES
Bemidji State U, MN
Idaho State U, ID

AMERICAN SIGN LANGUAGE (ASL)
Bethel Coll, IN
Burlington County Coll, NJ
Gardner-Webb U, NC
Idaho State U, ID
Rochester Inst of
Technology, NY

AMERICAN STUDIES
Albion Coll, MI
Albright Coll, PA
American U, DC
Amherst Coll, MA
Arizona State U at the West
campus, AZ
Ashland U, OH
Austin Coll, TX
Bard Coll, NY
Bates Coll, ME
Baylor U, TX
Brandeis U, MA
Brown U, RI
Bucks County Comm Coll, PA
California State U, Fullerton, CA
California State U, San
Bernardino, CA
Claremont McKenna Coll, CA
Coe Coll, IA
Colby Coll, ME
Coll of Saint Elizabeth, NJ
Coll of St. Joseph, VT
The Coll of Saint Rose, NY
Coll of Staten Island of the
City U of New York, NY
The Coll of William and
Mary, VA
Cornell U, NY
Cosumnes River Coll,
Sacramento, CA
DePaul U, IL
Dominican U, IL
Eckerd Coll, FL
El Camino Coll, CA
Elmira Coll, NY
Emory U, GA
Fairfield U, CT
Foothill Coll, CA
Franklin Coll, IN
Franklin Pierce U, NH
Georgetown Coll, KY
The George Washington U, DC

Hamilton Coll, NY
Hampshire Coll, MA
Harding U, AR
High Point U, NC
Hofstra U, NY
Idaho State U, ID
Illinois Wesleyan U, IL
Kenyon Coll, OH
Lebanon Valley Coll, PA
Lee Coll, TX
Lehigh U, PA
Lewis U, IL
Manhattanville Coll, NY
Marist Coll, NY
Miami Dade Coll, FL
Michigan State U, MI
Minnesota State U
Moorhead, MN
Mount Holyoke Coll, MA
Mount Union Coll, OH
Nova Southeastern U, FL
Oakland U, MI
Occidental Coll, CA
Oglethorpe U, GA
Oklahoma State U, OK
Our Lady of the Lake U of
San Antonio, TX
Penn State Abington, PA
Pine Manor Coll, MA
Queens Coll of the City U of
New York, NY
Queens U of Charlotte, NC
Ramapo Coll of New Jersey, NJ
Randolph Coll, VA
Rutgers, The State U of New
Jersey, Newark, NJ
Rutgers, The State U of New
Jersey, New Brunswick, NJ
St. Cloud State U, MN
Salve Regina U, RI
San Diego State U, CA
San Francisco State U, CA
Sewanee: The U of the
South, TN
Southern Nazarene U, OK
Southwestern U, TX
State U of New York at
Fredonia, NY
State U of New York Coll at
Geneseo, NY
Stetson U, FL
Stonehill Coll, MA
Syracuse U, NY
Temple U, PA
Texas A&M U, TX
Trinity Coll, CT
Tufts U, MA
U at Buffalo, the State U of
New York, NY
The U of Alabama, AL
U of Arkansas, AR
U of California, Berkeley, CA
U of California, Los Angeles, CA
U of Connecticut, CT
U of Dayton, OH
U of Hawaii at Manoa, HI
U of Kansas, KS
U of Maryland, Baltimore
County, MD
U of Mary Washington, VA
U of Massachusetts Boston, MA
U of Massachusetts Lowell, MA
U of Miami, FL
U of Michigan, MI
U of Mississippi, MS
U of Missouri–Kansas City, MO
U of New England, ME
U of New Hampshire, NH

U of New Mexico, NM
The U of North Carolina at
Chapel Hill, NC
U of Northern Iowa, IA
U of Notre Dame, IN
U of Pennsylvania, PA
U of Pittsburgh at
Johnstown, PA
U of Rio Grande, OH
The U of Texas at Austin, TX
The U of Texas at San
Antonio, TX
U of Toronto, ON, Canada
U of Wisconsin–Madison, WI
U of Wyoming, WY
Ursuline Coll, OH
Vassar Coll, NY
Wayne State U, MI
Wellesley Coll, MA
Wells Coll, NY
Wesley Coll, DE
West Chester U of
Pennsylvania, PA
Western Connecticut State
U, CT
Yale U, CT

ANATOMY
Duke U, NC
Minnesota State U Mankato, MN
Wright State U, OH

ANCIENT/CLASSICAL GREEK
Amherst Coll, MA
Asbury Coll, KY
Bard Coll, NY
Baylor U, TX
Brandeis U, MA
Brock U, ON, Canada
Bryn Mawr Coll, PA
Duke U, NC
Hampden-Sydney Coll, VA
Hunter Coll of the City U of
New York, NY
Indiana U Bloomington, IN
Kenyon Coll, OH
Lawrence U, WI
Loyola U Chicago, IL
Multnomah Bible Coll and
Biblical Seminary, OR
Queens Coll of the City U of
New York, NY
Randolph Coll, VA
Randolph-Macon Coll, VA
Rice U, TX
Rockford Coll, IL
Rutgers, The State U of New
Jersey, New Brunswick, NJ
Santa Clara U, CA
U of California, Berkeley, CA
U of California, Los Angeles, CA
U of Nebraska–Lincoln, NE
U of Notre Dame, IN
U of St. Thomas, MN
The U of Scranton, PA
The U of Texas at Austin, TX
U of Vermont, VT
U of Washington, WA
Vassar Coll, NY
Wake Forest U, NC
Wellesley Coll, MA
Yale U, CT

ANCIENT NEAR EASTERN AND BIBLICAL LANGUAGES
Baylor U, TX
Bethany U, CA

Carson-Newman Coll, TN
Cornerstone U, MI
Hope Coll, MI
Northwest Nazarene U, ID
Taylor U, IN
U of Toronto, ON, Canada

ANCIENT STUDIES
Michigan State U, MI
Missouri State U, MO
Mount Holyoke Coll, MA
Ohio Wesleyan U, OH
Rockford Coll, IL
Santa Clara U, CA
U of Kansas, KS
U of Maryland, Baltimore
County, MD
The U of Texas at Austin,
TX

ANIMAL BEHAVIOR AND ETHOLOGY
Carroll Coll, WI
Southwestern U, TX
U of Toronto, ON, Canada

ANIMAL GENETICS
Ball State U, IN
Cedar Crest Coll, PA
The Ohio State U, OH
Ohio Wesleyan U, OH
Rutgers, The State U of New
Jersey, New Brunswick, NJ
U of Manitoba, MB, Canada
U of Toronto, ON, Canada
U of Wisconsin–Madison,
WI

ANIMAL HEALTH
Santa Rosa Jr Coll, CA
Sterling Coll, VT

ANIMAL/LIVESTOCK HUSBANDRY AND PRODUCTION
Feather River Coll, CA
Hopkinsville Comm Coll,
KY
North Central Texas Coll, TX
Rutgers, The State U of New
Jersey, New Brunswick, NJ
Sterling Coll, VT
Texas A&M U, TX
U of Connecticut, CT
U of New Hampshire, NH
The U of Tennessee at
Martin, TN

ANIMAL NUTRITION
Sterling Coll, VT

ANIMAL PHYSIOLOGY
Cornell U, NY
Minnesota State U Mankato,
MN
Rutgers, The State U of New
Jersey, New Brunswick, NJ
San Francisco State U, CA
Santa Rosa Jr Coll, CA
The U of Akron, OH
U of California, Santa
Barbara, CA
U of Connecticut, CT
U of New Brunswick
Fredericton, NB, Canada
U of Toronto, ON, Canada

ANIMAL SCIENCES
Abilene Christian U, TX
Abraham Baldwin Coll, GA
Alabama A&M U, AL
Angelo State U, TX
Clemson U, SC
Cornell U, NY

Cosumnes River Coll,
Sacramento, CA
Delaware State U, DE
Fort Hays State U, KS
Kansas State U, KS
Langston U, OK
Michigan State U, MI
Middle Tennessee State U,
TN
Missouri State U, MO
Montana State U, MT
Moorpark Coll, CA
North Carolina State U, NC
North Dakota State U, ND
Nova Scotia Coll, NS,
Canada
The Ohio State U, OH
Oklahoma State U, OK
Penn State Abington, PA
Penn State DuBois, PA
Penn State Fayette, The
Eberly Campus, PA
Penn State Mont Alto, PA
Penn State Wilkes-Barre, PA
Reedley Coll, CA
Rutgers, The State U of New
Jersey, New Brunswick, NJ
Santa Rosa Jr Coll, CA
Shasta Coll, CA
Southern Illinois U
Carbondale, IL
Southern U and A&M Coll,
LA
Southwestern U, TX
State U of New York Coll of
Technology at Alfred, NY
Stephen F. Austin State U,
TX
Sterling Coll, VT
Texas A&M U, TX
Truman State U, MO
The U of Arizona, AZ
U of Arkansas, AR
U of Connecticut, CT
U of Delaware, DE
U of Guelph, ON, Canada
U of Hawaii at Manoa, HI
U of Illinois at Urbana–
Champaign, IL
U of Kentucky, KY
U of Manitoba, MB, Canada
U of Massachusetts Amherst,
MA
U of Missouri–Columbia,
MO
U of Nebraska–Lincoln, NE
U of New Hampshire, NH
U of Rhode Island, RI
The U of Tennessee, TN
The U of Tennessee at
Martin, TN
U of Vermont, VT
U of Wisconsin–Madison,
WI
U of Wisconsin–Platteville,
WI
West Texas A&M U, TX

ANIMAL SCIENCES RELATED
Cornell U, NY
Penn State Abington, PA
Penn State DuBois, PA
Penn State Fayette, The
Eberly Campus, PA
Penn State Mont Alto, PA
Penn State Wilkes-Barre, PA
Southern U and A&M Coll,
LA
Sterling Coll, VT
U of Wyoming, WY

ANIMAL TRAINING
Sterling Coll, VT

ANIMATION, INTERACTIVE TECHNOLOGY, VIDEO GRAPHICS AND SPECIAL EFFECTS
Academy of Art U, CA
The Art Inst of Houston, TX
The Art Inst of New York
City, NY
The Art Inst of Seattle, WA
Hagerstown Comm Coll, MD
The Illinois Inst of Art–
Schaumburg, IL
North Central Coll, IL
Rochester Inst of
Technology, NY
Savannah Coll of Art and
Design, GA
School of the Art Inst of
Chicago, IL
School of Visual Arts, NY
Southern Adventist U, TN
U of Dubuque, IA

ANTHROPOLOGY
Adelphi U, NY
Albertson Coll of Idaho, ID
Albion Coll, MI
Alma Coll, MI
American U, DC
Amherst Coll, MA
Athabasca U, AB, Canada
Ball State U, IN
Bard Coll, NY
Bates Coll, ME
Baylor U, TX
Brandeis U, MA
Brown U, RI
Bryn Mawr Coll, PA
Buffalo State Coll, State U of
New York, NY
California State U, Fullerton,
CA
California State U,
Northridge, CA
California State U,
Sacramento, CA
California State U, San
Bernardino, CA
California State U,
Stanislaus, CA
Cape Breton U, NS, Canada
Carleton U, ON, Canada
The Catholic U of America,
DC
Claremont McKenna Coll,
CA
Colby Coll, ME
Colgate U, NY
Coll of Charleston, SC
Coll of Staten Island of the
City U of New York, NY
Coll of the Desert, CA
The Coll of William and
Mary, VA
Cornell U, NY
Crafton Hills Coll, CA
Dalhousie U, NS, Canada
DePaul U, IL
Drake U, IA
Duke U, NC
East Carolina U, NC
Eastern Michigan U, MI
Eckerd Coll, FL
Edinboro U of Pennsylvania,
PA
El Camino Coll, CA
Elmira Coll, NY
Emory U, GA
Eugene Lang Coll The New
School for Liberal Arts, NY
Florida Atlantic U, FL
Foothill Coll, CA
Framingham State Coll, MA

Franciscan U of
Steubenville, OH
Franklin Pierce U, NH
Fresno City Coll, CA
Gainesville State Coll, GA
The George Washington U,
DC
Green Mountain Coll, VT
Grinnell Coll, IA
Gustavus Adolphus Coll,
MN
Hamilton Coll, NY
Hamline U, MN
Hampshire Coll, MA
Hartwick Coll, NY
Haverford Coll, PA
Hofstra U, NY
Hunter Coll of the City U of
New York, NY
Idaho State U, ID
Illinois State U, IL
Indiana U Bloomington, IN
Indiana U of Pennsylvania,
PA
Indiana U–Purdue U Fort
Wayne, IN
Indiana U–Purdue U
Indianapolis, IN
Ithaca Coll, NY
Johnson State Coll, VT
Kansas State U, KS
Kellogg Comm Coll, MI
Kenyon Coll, OH
Kutztown U of
Pennsylvania, PA
Lawrence U, WI
Lehigh U, PA
Lincoln U, PA
Loyola U Chicago, IL
Macalester Coll, MN
Marquette U, WI
Massachusetts Coll of Liberal
Arts, MA
Mercyhurst Coll, PA
Miami Dade Coll, FL
Michigan State U, MI
Middle Tennessee State U,
TN
Midland Coll, TX
Millersville U of
Pennsylvania, PA
Minnesota State U Mankato,
MN
Minnesota State U
Moorhead, MN
Missouri State U, MO
Monmouth U, NJ
Montana State U, MT
Moorpark Coll, CA
Mount Holyoke Coll, MA
Mount Saint Vincent U, NS,
Canada
National-Louis U, IL
New York U, NY
North Carolina State U, NC
North Central Coll, IL
Northeastern U, MA
Northern Illinois U, IL
Oakland U, MI
Occidental Coll, CA
The Ohio State U, OH
Ohio Wesleyan U, OH
Old Dominion U, VA
Penn State Abington, PA
Penn State DuBois, PA
Penn State Fayette, The
Eberly Campus, PA
Penn State Mont Alto, PA
Penn State Wilkes-Barre, PA
Pima Comm Coll, AZ
Portland State U, OR
Queens Coll of the City U of
New York, NY
Radford U, VA

Rhodes Coll, TN
Rice U, TX
Ripon Coll, WI
Rockford Coll, IL
Rutgers, The State U of New
Jersey, Newark, NJ
Rutgers, The State U of New
Jersey, New Brunswick, NJ
St. Cloud State U, MN
St. Francis Xavier U, NS,
Canada
St. Lawrence U, NY
St. Mary's Coll of Maryland,
MD
St. Thomas U, NB, Canada
Salve Regina U, RI
San Diego State U, CA
San Francisco State U, CA
Santa Ana Coll, CA
Santa Barbara City Coll, CA
Santa Clara U, CA
Santa Rosa Jr Coll, CA
Seton Hall U, NJ
Sewanee: The U of the
South, TN
Skagit Valley Coll, WA
Slippery Rock U of
Pennsylvania, PA
Southern Illinois U
Carbondale, IL
Southern Illinois U
Edwardsville, IL
Southern Oregon U, OR
Southwestern U, TX
State U of New York Coll at
Brockport, NY
State U of New York Coll at
Cortland, NY
State U of New York Coll at
Geneseo, NY
State U of New York Coll at
Potsdam, NY
Sweet Briar Coll, VA
Syracuse U, NY
Temple U, PA
Texas A&M U, TX
Trent U, ON, Canada
Trinity Coll, CT
Trinity U, TX
Tufts U, MA
U at Albany, State U of New
York, NY
U at Buffalo, the State U of
New York, NY
The U of Alabama, AL
U of Alaska Anchorage, AK
The U of Arizona, AZ
U of Arkansas, AR
U of California, Berkeley,
CA
U of California, Irvine, CA
U of California, Los Angeles,
CA
U of California, Santa
Barbara, CA
U of Central Florida, FL
U of Cincinnati, OH
U of Colorado at Boulder,
CO
U of Connecticut, CT
U of Delaware, DE
U of Guelph, ON, Canada
U of Hawaii at Manoa, HI
U of Hawaii–West Oahu, HI
U of Houston, TX
U of Illinois at Urbana–
Champaign, IL
U of Kansas, KS
U of Kentucky, KY
U of Manitoba, MB, Canada
U of Maryland, Baltimore
County, MD
U of Massachusetts Amherst,
MA

U of Massachusetts Boston, MA
U of Miami, FL
U of Michigan, MI
U of Minnesota, Duluth, MN
U of Mississippi, MS
U of Missouri–Columbia, MO
U of Nebraska–Lincoln, NE
U of New Brunswick Fredericton, NB, Canada
U of New Hampshire, NH
U of New Mexico, NM
U of New Orleans, LA
The U of North Carolina at Chapel Hill, NC
The U of North Carolina at Charlotte, NC
U of Northern British Columbia, BC, Canada
U of Northern Iowa, IA
U of North Florida, FL
U of Notre Dame, IN
U of Oregon, OR
U of Pennsylvania, PA
U of Pittsburgh, PA
U of Redlands, CA
U of Rhode Island, RI
U of San Diego, CA
The U of Tennessee, TN
The U of Tennessee at Martin, TN
The U of Texas at Austin, TX
The U of Texas at El Paso, TX
The U of Texas at San Antonio, TX
U of the District of Columbia, DC
U of Toronto, ON, Canada
U of Vermont, VT
U of Virginia, VA
U of Washington, WA
U of West Georgia, GA
U of Wisconsin–Madison, WI
U of Wisconsin–Oshkosh, WI
U of Wyoming, WY
Vanguard U of Southern California, CA
Vassar Coll, NY
Wake Forest U, NC
Washburn U, KS
Washington and Lee U, VA
Wayne State U, MI
Wellesley Coll, MA
Wells Coll, NY
West Chester U of Pennsylvania, PA
Western Connecticut State U, CT
Western Nebraska Comm Coll, NE
Western Oregon U, OR
West Los Angeles Coll, CA
Wheaton Coll, IL
Whitman Coll, WA
Wichita State U, KS
Widener U, PA
Wilfrid Laurier U, ON, Canada
Wright State U, OH
Yale U, CT

ANTHROPOLOGY RELATED
Carnegie Mellon U, PA

APPAREL AND ACCESSORIES MARKETING
Clayton State U, GA
U of Rhode Island, RI

APPAREL AND TEXTILE MANUFACTURING
Fashion Inst of Technology, NY
North Carolina State U, NC

APPAREL AND TEXTILE MARKETING MANAGEMENT
North Carolina State U, NC
Wayne State U, MI

APPAREL AND TEXTILES
Academy of Art U, CA
Albright Coll, PA
Cornell U, NY
East Carolina U, NC
Fashion Inst of Technology, NY
Freed-Hardeman U, TN
Indiana U Bloomington, IN
Kansas State U, KS
Michigan State U, MI
Middle Tennessee State U, TN
Missouri State U, MO
Murray State U, KY
North Dakota State U, ND
Northern Illinois U, IL
The Ohio State U, OH
Seattle Pacific U, WA
Southern Illinois U Carbondale, IL
Syracuse U, NY
The U of Akron, OH
The U of Alabama, AL
U of Arkansas, AR
U of Central Missouri, MO
U of Illinois at Urbana–Champaign, IL
U of Kentucky, KY
U of Missouri–Columbia, MO
U of Nebraska–Lincoln, NE
U of Northern Iowa, IA
U of Rhode Island, RI
The U of Texas at Austin, TX
U of Wisconsin–Stout, WI

APPAREL AND TEXTILES RELATED
California State U, Sacramento, CA
Framingham State Coll, MA

APPLIANCE INSTALLATION AND REPAIR TECHNOLOGY
Mohawk Valley Comm Coll, NY

APPLIED ART
Academy of Art U, CA
The Art Inst of Pittsburgh, PA
Athabasca U, AB, Canada
Bemidji State U, MN
Buffalo State Coll, State U of New York, NY
Central Piedmont Comm Coll, NC
Chattanooga State Tech Comm Coll, TN
Cosumnes River Coll, Sacramento, CA
Cuesta Coll, CA
Daemen Coll, NY
DePaul U, IL
Elms Coll, MA
Franklin Pierce U, NH
Glendale Comm Coll, CA
Hampshire Coll, MA
Howard Comm Coll, MD

Indiana U Bloomington, IN
Kingsborough Comm Coll of the City U of New York, NY
Lamar U, TX
Lassen Comm Coll District, CA
Lindenwood U, MO
Marywood U, PA
McNeese State U, LA
Middlesex County Coll, NJ
Minnesota State U Mankato, MN
Minnesota State U Moorhead, MN
Odessa Coll, TX
Otis Coll of Art and Design, CA
Portland State U, OR
Pratt Inst, NY
Rochester Inst of Technology, NY
St. Cloud State U, MN
Sewanee: The U of the South, TN
Springfield Coll, MA
State U of New York at Fredonia, NY
Syracuse U, NY
Truman State U, MO
Tunxis Comm Coll, CT
The U of Akron, OH
U of Dayton, OH
U of Delaware, DE
U of Oregon, OR
U of Wisconsin–Madison, WI
Westchester Comm Coll, NY

APPLIED ECONOMICS
The Coll of St. Scholastica, MN
Cornell U, NY
Ithaca Coll, NY
Michigan State U, MI
Penn State Abington, PA
Penn State DuBois, PA
Penn State Fayette, The Eberly Campus, PA
Penn State Mont Alto, PA
Penn State Wilkes-Barre, PA
U of Guelph, ON, Canada
U of Northern Iowa, IA
U of Rhode Island, RI
U of San Francisco, CA
U of Vermont, VT
Western New England Coll, MA

APPLIED HORTICULTURE
Comm Coll of Allegheny County, PA
Ferrum Coll, VA
Nova Scotia Coll, NS, Canada
Santa Barbara City Coll, CA
Skagit Valley Coll, WA
Spokane Comm Coll, WA
Stephen F. Austin State U, TX
Sterling Coll, VT
Temple U, PA
Texas A&M U, TX
U of Connecticut, CT
The U of Maine at Augusta, ME
U of Vermont, VT
West Virginia Northern Comm Coll, WV

APPLIED HORTICULTURE/ HORTICULTURAL BUSINESS SERVICES RELATED
U of Massachusetts Amherst, MA
U of Vermont, VT

APPLIED MATHEMATICS
American U, DC
Asbury Coll, KY
Baylor U, TX
Brock U, ON, Canada
Brown U, RI
California State U, Fullerton, CA
Carleton U, ON, Canada
Carnegie Mellon U, PA
Charleston Southern U, SC
Coastal Carolina U, SC
Coll of Mount St. Joseph, OH
Columbus State U, GA
Cornell U, NY
DePaul U, IL
Farmingdale State Coll, NY
Florida Inst of Technology, FL
Florida International U, FL
Fresno Pacific U, CA
Geneva Coll, PA
The George Washington U, DC
Hampden-Sydney Coll, VA
Hofstra U, NY
Indiana U of Pennsylvania, PA
Iona Coll, NY
Ithaca Coll, NY
Lamar U, TX
Le Moyne Coll, NY
Michigan State U, MI
Montana Tech of The U of Montana, MT
Mount Saint Vincent U, NS, Canada
North Carolina State U, NC
North Central Coll, IL
Northern Illinois U, IL
Queens Coll of the City U of New York, NY
Queens U of Charlotte, NC
Rensselaer Polytechnic Inst, NY
Rice U, TX
Rochester Inst of Technology, NY
Rutgers, The State U of New Jersey, Newark, NJ
St. Thomas Aquinas Coll, NY
San Diego State U, CA
San Francisco State U, CA
Texas A&M U, TX
Trent U, ON, Canada
U at Albany, State U of New York, NY
The U of Akron, OH
U of California, Berkeley, CA
U of California, Los Angeles, CA
U of Central Oklahoma, OK
U of Colorado at Boulder, CO
U of Connecticut, CT
U of Houston, TX
U of Manitoba, MB, Canada
U of Maryland, Baltimore County, MD
U of Massachusetts Lowell, MA
U of Michigan, MI

U of Missouri–Rolla, MO
U of New Brunswick Fredericton, NB, Canada
U of New Haven, CT
The U of North Carolina at Chapel Hill, NC
U of Northern Iowa, IA
U of Pittsburgh, PA
U of Pittsburgh at Bradford, PA
The U of Texas at El Paso, TX
U of Toronto, ON, Canada
U of Virginia, VA
U of Washington, WA
U of Wisconsin–Madison, WI
U of Wisconsin–Stout, WI
Valdosta State U, GA
Wayne State Coll, NE
West Virginia State U, WV
Wright State U, OH
Yale U, CT

APPLIED MATHEMATICS RELATED
Carroll Coll, WI
Temple U, PA
The U of Akron, OH
U of Dayton, OH
U of Wyoming, WY

AQUACULTURE
Hillsborough Comm Coll, FL
Texas A&M U, TX
U of New England, ME

AQUATIC BIOLOGY/ LIMNOLOGY
Florida Inst of Technology, FL
Stetson U, FL
U of California, Santa Barbara, CA
U of Northern British Columbia, BC, Canada

ARABIC
Brandeis U, MA
The Ohio State U, OH
U of California, Los Angeles, CA
U of Michigan, MI
U of Notre Dame, IN
The U of Texas at Austin, TX
U of Toronto, ON, Canada

ARCHEOLOGY
Bard Coll, NY
Bates Coll, ME
Baylor U, TX
Brock U, ON, Canada
Brown U, RI
Bryn Mawr Coll, PA
Claremont McKenna Coll, CA
Cornell U, NY
Franklin Pierce U, NH
The George Washington U, DC
Hamilton Coll, NY
Haverford Coll, PA
Hunter Coll of the City U of New York, NY
Lawrence U, WI
Mercyhurst Coll, PA
Minnesota State U Moorhead, MN
New York U, NY
Penn State Abington, PA
Penn State DuBois, PA
Penn State Fayette, The Eberly Campus, PA
Penn State Mont Alto, PA

Penn State Wilkes-Barre, PA
Southern Adventist U, TN
State U of New York Coll at
Potsdam, NY
Tufts U, MA
U of California, Los Angeles,
CA
U of Evansville, IN
U of Missouri–Columbia,
MO
The U of Texas at Austin,
TX
U of Toronto, ON, Canada
U of Wisconsin–La Crosse,
WI
Washington and Lee U, VA
Wellesley Coll, MA
Wheaton Coll, IL
Wilfrid Laurier U, ON,
Canada
Yale U, CT

ARCHITECTURAL DRAFTING
West Virginia State Comm
and Tech Coll, WV

ARCHITECTURAL DRAFTING AND CAD/CADD
The Art Inst of Pittsburgh,
PA
British Columbia Inst of
Technology, BC, Canada
Commonwealth Tech Inst,
PA
Comm Coll of Allegheny
County, PA
Dixie State Coll of Utah, UT
Florida Comm Coll at
Jacksonville, FL
Indiana U–Purdue U
Indianapolis, IN
Lincoln Land Comm Coll, IL
Macomb Comm Coll, MI
Miami Dade Coll, FL
Mohawk Valley Comm Coll,
NY
Montana Tech of The U of
Montana, MT
New York City Coll of
Technology of the City U
of New York, NY
Pima Comm Coll, AZ
St. Cloud Tech Coll, MN
Waukesha County Tech Coll,
WI

ARCHITECTURAL ENGINEERING
Kansas State U, KS
Oklahoma State U, OK
Penn State Abington, PA
Penn State DuBois, PA
Penn State Fayette, The
Eberly Campus, PA
Penn State Mont Alto, PA
Penn State Wilkes-Barre, PA
Tufts U, MA
U of Cincinnati, OH
U of Colorado at Boulder,
CO
U of Kansas, KS
U of Miami, FL
U of Missouri–Rolla, MO
U of Nebraska at Omaha,
NE
U of Nebraska–Lincoln, NE
The U of Texas at Austin,
TX
U of Wyoming, WY

ARCHITECTURAL ENGINEERING TECHNOLOGY
Bluefield State Coll, WV

British Columbia Inst of
Technology, BC, Canada
Broward Comm Coll, FL
Central Piedmont Comm
Coll, NC
Chesapeake Coll, MD
City Colls of Chicago,
Richard J. Daley Coll, IL
Clayton State U, GA
Coll of The Albemarle, NC
Coll of the Desert, CA
Comm Coll of Beaver
County, PA
Cosumnes River Coll,
Sacramento, CA
Delaware Tech & Comm
Coll, Jack F. Owens
Campus, DE
El Camino Coll, CA
Farmingdale State Coll, NY
Fitchburg State Coll, MA
Florida Comm Coll at
Jacksonville, FL
Gaston Coll, NC
Grambling State U, LA
Greenville Tech Coll, SC
Harrisburg Area Comm Coll,
PA
Hillsborough Comm Coll, FL
Indiana U–Purdue U Fort
Wayne, IN
Indiana U–Purdue U
Indianapolis, IN
Lamar State Coll–Orange, TX
Long Beach City Coll, CA
Massasoit Comm Coll, MA
Miami Dade Coll, FL
MiraCosta Coll, CA
New River Comm Coll, VA
Northland Comm and Tech
Coll–Thief River Falls, MN
Penn State Fayette, The
Eberly Campus, PA
Phoenix Coll, AZ
Purdue U North Central, IN
St. Cloud Tech Coll, MN
San Diego Mesa Coll, CA
Seminole Comm Coll, FL
Southeast Tech Inst, SD
Southern Maine Comm Coll,
ME
Spokane Comm Coll, WA
Stark State Coll of
Technology, OH
State U of New York Coll of
Technology at Alfred, NY
U of Alaska Anchorage, AK
U of Cincinnati, OH
U of Hartford, CT
U of the District of
Columbia, DC
Vermont Tech Coll, VT
Western Tech Coll, WI
Westmoreland County
Comm Coll, PA
West Virginia State U, WV

ARCHITECTURAL HISTORY AND CRITICISM
Brown U, RI
Carnegie Mellon U, PA
Cornell U, NY
Mount Holyoke Coll, MA
Savannah Coll of Art and
Design, GA
U of Kansas, KS
U of Virginia, VA

ARCHITECTURAL TECHNOLOGY
Carnegie Mellon U, PA
The U of Maine at Augusta,
ME

ARCHITECTURE
Ball State U, IN
Baylor U, TX
Boston Architectural Coll,
MA
Carleton U, ON, Canada
Carnegie Mellon U, PA
The Catholic U of America,
DC
Clemson U, SC
Coe Coll, IA
Coll of Staten Island of the
City U of New York, NY
Cornell U, NY
Dalhousie U, NS, Canada
Drury U, MO
Eastern Michigan U, MI
Florida Atlantic U, FL
Harrisburg Area Comm Coll,
PA
Hope Coll, MI
Howard Comm Coll, MD
Kansas State U, KS
Lehigh U, PA
North Carolina State U, NC
North Dakota State U, ND
Northeastern U, MA
The Ohio State U, OH
Oklahoma State U, OK
Parsons The New School for
Design, NY
Portland State U, OR
Prairie View A&M U, TX
Pratt Inst, NY
Rensselaer Polytechnic Inst,
NY
Rice U, TX
Ryerson U, ON, Canada
San Diego Mesa Coll, CA
Sauk Valley Comm Coll, IL
Savannah Coll of Art and
Design, GA
Southern Illinois U
Carbondale, IL
Southern U and A&M Coll,
LA
Syracuse U, NY
Temple U, PA
Texas A&M U, TX
U at Buffalo, the State U of
New York, NY
The U of Arizona, AZ
U of Arkansas, AR
U of California, Berkeley,
CA
U of California, Los Angeles,
CA
U of Cincinnati, OH
U of Hawaii at Manoa, HI
U of Houston, TX
U of Kansas, KS
U of Kentucky, KY
U of Manitoba, MB, Canada
U of Miami, FL
U of Michigan, MI
U of Nebraska–Lincoln, NE
U of New Mexico, NM
The U of North Carolina at
Charlotte, NC
U of Notre Dame, IN
U of Oregon, OR
U of Pennsylvania, PA
U of San Francisco, CA
The U of Tennessee, TN
The U of Texas at Austin,
TX
The U of Texas at San
Antonio, TX
U of the District of
Columbia, DC
U of Toronto, ON, Canada
U of Virginia, VA
U of Washington, WA
Wellesley Coll, MA

Yale U, CT

ARCHITECTURE RELATED
Abilene Christian U, TX
Carnegie Mellon U, PA
Cornell U, NY
Florida International U, FL
Rensselaer Polytechnic Inst,
NY
School of the Art Inst of
Chicago, IL
U of Houston, TX
U of Illinois at Urbana–
Champaign, IL

AREA, ETHNIC, CULTURAL, AND GENDER STUDIES RELATED
Bethel U, MN
Brandeis U, MA
Claremont McKenna Coll,
CA
Coe Coll, IA
New York U, NY
Sterling Coll, VT
Syracuse U, NY
U of California, Irvine, CA
U of Maryland, Baltimore
County, MD
The U of North Carolina at
Chapel Hill, NC
The U of North Carolina at
Charlotte, NC
The U of Tennessee, TN
U of the Incarnate Word, TX

AREA STUDIES
Bard Coll, NY
Hope Coll, MI
Millersville U of
Pennsylvania, PA

AREA STUDIES RELATED
Claremont McKenna Coll,
CA
Colby Coll, ME
Gannon U, PA
Hofstra U, NY
Illinois Wesleyan U, IL
Lewis U, IL
Millersville U of
Pennsylvania, PA
U of California, Los Angeles,
CA
U of Illinois at Urbana–
Champaign, IL
U of Virginia, VA
Wright State U, OH

ARMY ROTC/MILITARY SCIENCE
Dallas Baptist U, TX
Minnesota State U Mankato,
MN
Rensselaer Polytechnic Inst,
NY
U of Washington, WA

ART
Abilene Christian U, TX
Abraham Baldwin Coll, GA
Adams State Coll, CO
Albany State U, GA
Albertson Coll of Idaho, ID
Albion Coll, MI
Albright Coll, PA
Alma Coll, MI
American U, DC
Amherst Coll, MA
Ancilla Coll, IN
Anderson U, SC
Angelo State U, TX
Ashland U, OH

Athens State U, AL
Auburn U Montgomery, AL
Augsburg Coll, MN
Austin Coll, TX
Bainbridge Coll, GA
Ball State U, IN
Bard Coll, NY
Bates Coll, ME
Baylor U, TX
Bemidji State U, MN
Benedictine Coll, KS
Bethel Coll, IN
Bethel U, MN
Bishop's U, QC, Canada
Bradley U, IL
Brandeis U, MA
Brevard Coll, NC
Briar Cliff U, IA
Brock U, ON, Canada
Brown U, RI
Bryn Mawr Coll, PA
Bucks County Comm Coll,
PA
Buena Vista U, IA
Buffalo State Coll, State U of
New York, NY
Bunker Hill Comm Coll, MA
Burlington County Coll, NJ
Caldwell Comm Coll and
Tech Inst, NC
California State U, Fullerton,
CA
California State U,
Northridge, CA
California State U,
Sacramento, CA
California State U, San
Bernardino, CA
California State U,
Stanislaus, CA
Calvin Coll, MI
Cameron U, OK
Cape Cod Comm Coll, MA
Cardinal Stritch U, WI
Carlow U, PA
Carnegie Mellon U, PA
Carroll Coll, MT
Carroll Coll, WI
Carson-Newman Coll, TN
The Catholic U of America,
DC
Cedar Crest Coll, PA
Central Piedmont Comm
Coll, NC
Central Wyoming Coll, WY
Chesapeake Coll, MD
Citrus Coll, CA
City Colls of Chicago,
Richard J. Daley Coll, IL
Claremont McKenna Coll,
CA
Clayton State U, GA
Coahoma Comm Coll, MS
Coe Coll, IA
Colby Coll, ME
Colgate U, NY
Coll of Mount St. Joseph,
OH
Coll of Saint Elizabeth, NJ
Coll of Saint Mary, NE
Coll of The Albemarle, NC
Coll of the Atlantic, ME
Coll of the Canyons, CA
Coll of the Desert, CA
The Coll of William and
Mary, VA
Columbus State U, GA
Comm Coll of Allegheny
County, PA
Concordia U, NE
Cornell U, NY
Cosumnes River Coll,
Sacramento, CA
Crafton Hills Coll, CA

Cuesta Coll, CA
Daemen Coll, NY
Dallas Baptist U, TX
Delaware State U, DE
DePaul U, IL
Dixie State Coll of Utah, UT
Drake U, IA
Drury U, MO
Duke U, NC
Earlham Coll, IN
East Carolina U, NC
Eastern Connecticut State U, CT
Eastern Mennonite U, VA
Eastern Michigan U, MI
Edinboro U of Pennsylvania, PA
El Camino Coll, CA
Elmira Coll, NY
Elms Coll, MA
Elon U, NC
Fairfield U, CT
Fayetteville State U, NC
Ferrum Coll, VA
Florida Atlantic U, FL
Fontbonne U, MO
Foothill Coll, CA
Fort Hays State U, KS
Framingham State Coll, MA
Franklin Pierce U, NH
Frederick Comm Coll, MD
Freed-Hardeman U, TN
Fresno City Coll, CA
Fulton-Montgomery Comm Coll, NY
Furman U, SC
Gardner-Webb U, NC
Gaston Coll, NC
The George Washington U, DC
Georgia Coll & State U, GA
Georgian Court U, NJ
Glendale Comm Coll, CA
Gonzaga U, WA
Gordon Coll, MA
Goshen Coll, IN
Grace Coll, IN
Graceland U, IA
Grambling State U, LA
Green Mountain Coll, VT
Grinnell Coll, IA
Grossmont Coll, CA
Gustavus Adolphus Coll, MN
Hamilton Coll, NY
Hamline U, MN
Harrisburg Area Comm Coll, PA
Hartwick Coll, NY
Haverford Coll, PA
Henderson State U, AR
Hillsborough Comm Coll, FL
Houghton Coll, NY
Housatonic Comm Coll, CT
Howard Comm Coll, MD
Hunter Coll of the City U of New York, NY
Huntington U, IN
Idaho State U, ID
Illinois State U, IL
Illinois Wesleyan U, IL
Indiana U Bloomington, IN
Indiana U of Pennsylvania, PA
Indiana U Southeast, IN
Irvine Valley Coll, CA
Ithaca Coll, NY
Jacksonville U, FL
Johnson State Coll, VT
Kansas State U, KS
Kellogg Comm Coll, MI
Kennesaw State U, GA
Kenyon Coll, OH

Kingsborough Comm Coll of the City U of New York, NY
Lake Erie Coll, OH
Lakeland Coll, WI
Lamar U, TX
Langston U, OK
Lassen Comm Coll District, CA
Lee Coll, TX
Lehigh U, PA
Lewis U, IL
Lincoln Land Comm Coll, IL
Lindenwood U, MO
Long Beach City Coll, CA
Long Island U, Brooklyn Campus, NY
Loyola U New Orleans, LA
Lynchburg Coll, VA
MacMurray Coll, IL
Marian Coll, IN
Marietta Coll, OH
Marist Coll, NY
Marshall U, WV
Marymount Manhattan Coll, NY
Massachusetts Coll of Liberal Arts, MA
McDaniel Coll, MD
McNeese State U, LA
Mercer U, GA
Mercyhurst Coll, PA
Miami Dade Coll, FL
Michigan State U, MI
Middlesex County Coll, NJ
Middle Tennessee State U, TN
Midland Coll, TX
Midland Lutheran Coll, NE
Millersville U of Pennsylvania, PA
Minnesota State U Mankato, MN
Minnesota State U Moorhead, MN
MiraCosta Coll, CA
Missouri State U, MO
Mohawk Valley Comm Coll, NY
Molloy Coll, NY
Monmouth Coll, IL
Monmouth U, NJ
Montana State U, MT
Montana State U–Billings, MT
Moorpark Coll, CA
Moravian Coll, PA
Morningside Coll, IA
Morton Coll, IL
Mount St. Mary's U, MD
Mount Union Coll, OH
Mount Vernon Nazarene U, OH
Nassau Comm Coll, NY
National-Louis U, IL
New Jersey City U, NJ
New Mexico Jr Coll, NM
New York U, NY
North Central Coll, IL
North Dakota State U, ND
Northeastern U, MA
Northern Illinois U, IL
Northern Michigan U, MI
Northern State U, SD
North Georgia Coll & State U, GA
Northwest Nazarene U, ID
Notre Dame Coll, OH
NSCAD U, NS, Canada
Odessa Coll, TX
Oglethorpe U, GA
The Ohio State U, OH
Oklahoma State U, OK
Old Dominion U, VA

Otis Coll of Art and Design, CA
Otterbein Coll, OH
Our Lady of the Lake U of San Antonio, TX
Paris Jr Coll, TX
Parsons The New School for Design, NY
Penn State Abington, PA
Penn State DuBois, PA
Penn State Fayette, The Eberly Campus, PA
Penn State Mont Alto, PA
Penn State Wilkes-Barre, PA
Phoenix Coll, AZ
Piedmont Coll, GA
Pittsburg State U, KS
Point Loma Nazarene U, CA
Portland State U, OR
Pratt Inst, NY
Presbyterian Coll, SC
Queens Coll of the City U of New York, NY
Queens U of Charlotte, NC
Radford U, VA
Randolph Coll, VA
Redeemer U Coll, ON, Canada
Reedley Coll, CA
Reinhardt Coll, GA
Rhodes Coll, TN
Rice U, TX
Ripon Coll, WI
Rivier Coll, NH
Rochester Inst of Technology, NY
Rockingham Comm Coll, NC
Rocky Mountain Coll, MT
Roosevelt U, IL
Rose State Coll, OK
Rowan U, NJ
Rutgers, The State U of New Jersey, Newark, NJ
Rutgers, The State U of New Jersey, New Brunswick, NJ
Saginaw Valley State U, MI
St. Cloud State U, MN
St. Gregory's U, OK
Saint John's U, MN
St. Lawrence U, NY
St. Louis Comm Coll at Florissant Valley, MO
St. Mary's Coll of Maryland, MD
St. Norbert Coll, WI
St. Philip's Coll, TX
St. Thomas Aquinas Coll, NY
Saint Xavier U, IL
San Diego Mesa Coll, CA
San Francisco State U, CA
Santa Ana Coll, CA
Santa Rosa Jr Coll, CA
Sauk Valley Comm Coll, IL
School of the Art Inst of Chicago, IL
Seattle Pacific U, WA
Sewanee: The U of the South, TN
Shasta Coll, CA
Shippensburg U of Pennsylvania, PA
Skagit Valley Coll, WA
Slippery Rock U of Pennsylvania, PA
Southern Adventist U, TN
Southern Illinois U Carbondale, IL
Southern Illinois U Edwardsville, IL
Southern Oregon U, OR
Southern U and A&M Coll, LA
Southern Utah U, UT

Southwest Baptist U, MO
Southwestern U, TX
Spoon River Coll, IL
Springfield Coll in Illinois, IL
State U of New York at Fredonia, NY
State U of New York Coll at Brockport, NY
State U of New York Coll at Geneseo, NY
State U of New York Coll at Potsdam, NY
Stephen F. Austin State U, TX
Stetson U, FL
Syracuse U, NY
Taylor U, IN
Temple U, PA
Texas A&M U–Corpus Christi, TX
Thiel Coll, PA
Towson U, MD
Trinity Coll, CT
Trinity U, TX
Troy U, AL
Truman State U, MO
Tunxis Comm Coll, CT
Union Coll, NE
U at Albany, State U of New York, NY
U at Buffalo, the State U of New York, NY
The U of Akron, OH
The U of Alabama in Huntsville, AL
U of Alaska Anchorage, AK
U of Arkansas, AR
U of California, Berkeley, CA
U of California, Irvine, CA
U of California, Los Angeles, CA
U of California, Santa Barbara, CA
U of Central Florida, FL
U of Central Oklahoma, OK
U of Cincinnati, OH
U of Delaware, DE
U of Evansville, IN
The U of Findlay, OH
U of Great Falls, MT
U of Hawaii at Manoa, HI
U of Houston, TX
U of Maine at Machias, ME
U of Manitoba, MB, Canada
U of Mary Hardin-Baylor, TX
U of Maryland, Baltimore County, MD
U of Mary Washington, VA
U of Massachusetts Boston, MA
U of Miami, FL
U of Minnesota, Duluth, MN
U of Mississippi, MS
U of Missouri–Columbia, MO
U of Missouri–Kansas City, MO
U of Nebraska at Kearney, NE
U of Nebraska at Omaha, NE
U of New Hampshire, NH
U of New Mexico, NM
The U of North Carolina at Asheville, NC
The U of North Carolina at Charlotte, NC
U of Northern Iowa, IA
U of North Florida, FL
U of Oregon, OR
U of Rhode Island, RI
U of Rio Grande, OH
U of San Diego, CA

U of San Francisco, CA
U of Southern Indiana, IN
The U of Tampa, FL
The U of Texas at Austin, TX
The U of Texas at San Antonio, TX
U of the District of Columbia, DC
U of the Incarnate Word, TX
U of the Ozarks, AR
U of the Pacific, CA
U of Toronto, ON, Canada
U of Virginia, VA
The U of Virginia's Coll at Wise, VA
U of Washington, WA
U of West Georgia, GA
U of Wisconsin–Eau Claire, WI
U of Wisconsin–Green Bay, WI
U of Wisconsin–La Crosse, WI
U of Wisconsin–Madison, WI
U of Wisconsin–Oshkosh, WI
U of Wisconsin–Platteville, WI
U of Wyoming, WY
Upper Iowa U, IA
Valdosta State U, GA
Victor Valley Coll, CA
Virginia Intermont Coll, VA
Washburn U, KS
Washington & Jefferson Coll, PA
Waubonsee Comm Coll, IL
Wayne State Coll, NE
Wayne State U, MI
Wells Coll, NY
West Chester U of Pennsylvania, PA
Western Nebraska Comm Coll, NE
Western Oregon U, OR
West Los Angeles Coll, CA
Westminster Coll, PA
Westminster Coll, UT
West Texas A&M U, TX
West Virginia State U, WV
West Virginia Wesleyan Coll, WV
Wheaton Coll, IL
Whitman Coll, WA
Wichita State U, KS
Wilfrid Laurier U, ON, Canada
William Jewell Coll, MO
Wilson Coll, PA
Wright State U, OH
Xavier U, OH
Yale U, CT

ART HISTORY, CRITICISM AND CONSERVATION
Adelphi U, NY
American U, DC
Augsburg Coll, MN
Bard Coll, NY
Baylor U, TX
Boston Coll, MA
Bradley U, IL
Brown U, RI
Bryn Mawr Coll, PA
Buffalo State Coll, State U of New York, NY
California State U, Fullerton, CA
California State U, San Bernardino, CA
Calvin Coll, MI

Carleton U, ON, Canada
Carlow U, PA
The Catholic U of America, DC
Claremont McKenna Coll, CA
Clark U, MA
Colby Coll, ME
Colgate U, NY
Coll of Charleston, SC
The Coll of William and Mary, VA
Cornell U, NY
DePaul U, IL
Dixie State Coll of Utah, UT
Dominican U, IL
Drake U, IA
Drury U, MO
Duke U, NC
East Carolina U, NC
Eastern Michigan U, MI
Edinboro U of Pennsylvania, PA
El Camino Coll, CA
Emory U, GA
Fashion Inst of Technology, NY
Florida International U, FL
Foothill Coll, CA
Framingham State Coll, MA
Furman U, SC
The George Washington U, DC
Georgian Court U, NJ
Glendale Comm Coll, CA
Grossmont Coll, CA
Gustavus Adolphus Coll, MN
Hamilton Coll, NY
Hamline U, MN
Hartwick Coll, NY
Haverford Coll, PA
Hofstra U, NY
Hope Coll, MI
Hunter Coll of the City U of New York, NY
Indiana U Bloomington, IN
Indiana U–Purdue U Indianapolis, IN
Ithaca Coll, NY
Jacksonville U, FL
Kenyon Coll, OH
Lawrence U, WI
Lebanon Valley Coll, PA
Lehigh U, PA
Lindenwood U, MO
Loyola Marymount U, CA
Macalester Coll, MN
MacMurray Coll, IL
Manhattanville Coll, NY
Marian Coll, IN
Marist Coll, NY
Marymount Manhattan Coll, NY
McDaniel Coll, MD
Michigan State U, MI
Minnesota State U Mankato, MN
Minnesota State U Moorhead, MN
Moravian Coll, PA
Mount Holyoke Coll, MA
New York U, NY
Northern Illinois U, IL
NSCAD U, NS, Canada
Oakland U, MI
Occidental Coll, CA
Oglethorpe U, GA
The Ohio State U, OH
Ohio Wesleyan U, OH
Old Dominion U, VA
Penn State Abington, PA
Penn State DuBois, PA

Penn State Fayette, The Eberly Campus, PA
Penn State Mont Alto, PA
Penn State Wilkes-Barre, PA
Pine Manor Coll, MA
Portland State U, OR
Pratt Inst, NY
Queens Coll of the City U of New York, NY
Queen's U at Kingston, ON, Canada
Randolph Coll, VA
Randolph-Macon Coll, VA
Rhodes Coll, TN
Rice U, TX
Rockford Coll, IL
Roosevelt U, IL
Rutgers, The State U of New Jersey, New Brunswick, NJ
St. Cloud State U, MN
St. Lawrence U, NY
Salve Regina U, RI
San Diego State U, CA
Santa Barbara City Coll, CA
Santa Clara U, CA
Savannah Coll of Art and Design, GA
School of the Art Inst of Chicago, IL
Seton Hall U, NJ
Seton Hill U, PA
Sewanee: The U of the South, TN
Skagit Valley Coll, WA
Southwestern U, TX
State U of New York at Fredonia, NY
State U of New York Coll at Cortland, NY
State U of New York Coll at Geneseo, NY
State U of New York Coll at Potsdam, NY
Stephen F. Austin State U, TX
Sweet Briar Coll, VA
Syracuse U, NY
Temple U, PA
Trinity Coll, CT
Trinity U, TX
Troy U, AL
Truman State U, MO
Tufts U, MA
U at Albany, State U of New York, NY
U at Buffalo, the State U of New York, NY
The U of Akron, OH
The U of Alabama, AL
The U of Arizona, AZ
U of California, Berkeley, CA
U of California, Irvine, CA
U of California, Los Angeles, CA
U of California, Santa Barbara, CA
U of Cincinnati, OH
U of Connecticut, CT
U of Dayton, OH
U of Delaware, DE
U of Evansville, IN
U of Guelph, ON, Canada
U of Hartford, CT
U of Houston, TX
U of Illinois at Urbana–Champaign, IL
U of Kansas, KS
U of Kentucky, KY
U of Manitoba, MB, Canada
U of Maryland, Baltimore County, MD
U of Mary Washington, VA

U of Massachusetts Amherst, MA
U of Miami, FL
U of Michigan, MI
U of Minnesota, Duluth, MN
U of Mississippi, MS
U of Missouri–Columbia, MO
U of Missouri–Kansas City, MO
U of Nebraska at Omaha, NE
U of Nebraska–Lincoln, NE
U of New Hampshire, NH
U of New Mexico, NM
U of New Orleans, LA
The U of North Carolina at Chapel Hill, NC
U of Northern Iowa, IA
U of Notre Dame, IN
U of Oregon, OR
U of Pennsylvania, PA
U of Pittsburgh, PA
U of Redlands, CA
U of Rhode Island, RI
U of St. Thomas, MN
U of San Francisco, CA
The U of Tennessee, TN
The U of Texas at Austin, TX
The U of Texas at San Antonio, TX
U of the Pacific, CA
U of Toronto, ON, Canada
U of Vermont, VT
U of Washington, WA
U of Wisconsin–Madison, WI
Ursuline Coll, OH
Vassar Coll, NY
Villanova U, PA
Wake Forest U, NC
Washburn U, KS
Washington and Lee U, VA
Wayne State U, MI
Wellesley Coll, MA
Wells Coll, NY
West Virginia Wesleyan Coll, WV
Wichita State U, KS
Wofford Coll, SC
Wright State U, OH
Yale U, CT

ARTIFICIAL INTELLIGENCE AND ROBOTICS

Chattanooga State Tech Comm Coll, TN
Clayton State U, GA
Cuesta Coll, CA
Lamar U, TX
Montana Tech of The U of Montana, MT
New Hampshire Comm Tech Coll, Nashua/Claremont, NH
Southeast Tech Inst, SD
Spokane Comm Coll, WA
U of Cincinnati, OH
Westmoreland County Comm Coll, PA

ARTS MANAGEMENT

Benedictine Coll, KS
Bishop's U, QC, Canada
Brenau U, GA
Buena Vista U, IA
Coll of Charleston, SC
Concordia Coll–New York, NY
Cuesta Coll, CA
Delaware State U, DE
DePaul U, IL

Drury U, MO
Eastern Michigan U, MI
Fashion Inst of Technology, NY
Fontbonne U, MO
Green Mountain Coll, VT
Ithaca Coll, NY
Marywood U, PA
Mercyhurst Coll, PA
North Carolina State U, NC
Randolph-Macon Coll, VA
Seton Hill U, PA
State U of New York at Fredonia, NY
U of Kentucky, KY
U of Portland, OR
U of San Francisco, CA
U of Toronto, ON, Canada
U of Wisconsin–Stevens Point, WI
Upper Iowa U, IA
Wright State U, OH

ART TEACHER EDUCATION

Abilene Christian U, TX
Adelphi U, NY
Albright Coll, PA
Alma Coll, MI
Ancilla Coll, IN
Anderson U, IN
Anderson U, SC
Asbury Coll, KY
Ashland U, OH
Augsburg Coll, MN
Ball State U, IN
Baylor U, TX
Bemidji State U, MN
Bethel U, MN
Bishop's U, QC, Canada
Brenau U, GA
Buena Vista U, IA
Buffalo State Coll, State U of New York, NY
California State U, Fullerton, CA
Calvin Coll, MI
Cardinal Stritch U, WI
Carlow U, PA
Carroll Coll, WI
Carson-Newman Coll, TN
The Catholic U of America, DC
Clayton State U, GA
Coe Coll, IA
Coll of Mount St. Joseph, OH
The Coll of Saint Rose, NY
Columbus State U, GA
Concordia U, NE
Concord U, WV
Daemen Coll, NY
Delaware State U, DE
East Carolina U, NC
Eastern Mennonite U, VA
Eastern Michigan U, MI
Edinboro U of Pennsylvania, PA
Elmira Coll, NY
Flagler Coll, FL
Florida International U, FL
Fontbonne U, MO
Fort Hays State U, KS
Framingham State Coll, MA
Franklin Pierce U, NH
Freed-Hardeman U, TN
Goshen Coll, IN
Grace Coll, IN
Graceland U, IA
Grambling State U, LA
Gustavus Adolphus Coll, MN
Harding U, AR
Henderson State U, AR

High Point U, NC
Hofstra U, NY
Hope Coll, MI
Houghton Coll, NY
Houston Baptist U, TX
Huntington U, IN
Indiana U Bloomington, IN
Indiana U of Pennsylvania, PA
Indiana U–Purdue U Fort Wayne, IN
Indiana U–Purdue U Indianapolis, IN
Ithaca Coll, NY
Johnson State Coll, VT
Kellogg Comm Coll, MI
Kennesaw State U, GA
Kentucky Wesleyan Coll, KY
Kutztown U of Pennsylvania, PA
Lamar U, TX
Langston U, OK
Lawrence U, WI
Lewis U, IL
Lincoln U, PA
Lindenwood U, MO
Long Island U, Brooklyn Campus, NY
Loras Coll, IA
Manhattanville Coll, NY
Marian Coll, IN
Marywood U, PA
McNeese State U, LA
Mercyhurst Coll, PA
Michigan State U, MI
Middle Tennessee State U, TN
Midland Lutheran Coll, NE
Millersville U of Pennsylvania, PA
Minnesota State U Mankato, MN
Minnesota State U Moorhead, MN
Missouri State U, MO
Montana State U–Billings, MT
Moravian Coll, PA
Morningside Coll, IA
Mount Saint Vincent U, NS, Canada
Mount Vernon Nazarene U, OH
Murray State U, KY
New Jersey City U, NJ
New Mexico Jr Coll, NM
North Central Coll, IL
Northern Illinois U, IL
Northern Michigan U, MI
Northern State U, SD
North Georgia Coll & State U, GA
Northwestern Coll, MN
Northwest Nazarene U, ID
Notre Dame Coll, OH
The Ohio State U, OH
Ohio Wesleyan U, OH
Old Dominion U, VA
Oral Roberts U, OK
Otterbein Coll, OH
Parsons The New School for Design, NY
Penn State Abington, PA
Penn State DuBois, PA
Penn State Fayette, The Eberly Campus, PA
Penn State Mont Alto, PA
Penn State Wilkes-Barre, PA
Pittsburg State U, KS
Point Loma Nazarene U, CA
Pratt Inst, NY
Queens Coll of the City U of New York, NY
Rocky Mountain Coll, MT

King's Coll, PA
Lake Superior State U, MI
Liberty U, VA
Lindenwood U, MO
Long Island U, Brooklyn
  Campus, NY
Loras Coll, IA
Lynchburg Coll, VA
Marietta Coll, OH
Marist Coll, NY
Marquette U, WI
Marywood U, PA
Massachusetts Coll of Liberal
  Arts, MA
Mercyhurst Coll, PA
Middle Tennessee State U,
  TN
Midland Lutheran Coll, NE
Minnesota State U Mankato,
  MN
Missouri State U, MO
Mitchell Coll, CT
Mount Union Coll, OH
New Mexico Jr Coll, NM
North Central Coll, IL
North Dakota State U, ND
Northeastern U, MA
Northern Michigan U, MI
Northland Comm and Tech
  Coll–Thief River Falls, MN
Northwest Nazarene U, ID
Nova Southeastern U, FL
Odessa Coll, TX
The Ohio State U, OH
Oklahoma State U, OK
Otterbein Coll, OH
Park U, MO
Point Loma Nazarene U, CA
Radford U, VA
Rocky Mountain Coll, MT
Saginaw Valley State U, MI
Santa Barbara City Coll, CA
Santa Rosa Jr Coll, CA
Sauk Valley Comm Coll, IL
Slippery Rock U of
  Pennsylvania, PA
Southern Nazarene U, OK
Southwest Baptist U, MO
Southwestern Coll, KS
Springfield Coll, MA
State U of New York Coll at
  Brockport, NY
State U of New York Coll at
  Cortland, NY
Taylor U, IN
Tennessee Wesleyan Coll,
  TN
Texas A&M U–Corpus
  Christi, TX
Towson U, MD
Troy U, AL
The U of Akron, OH
The U of Alabama, AL
U of Delaware, DE
U of Evansville, IN
The U of Findlay, OH
U of Illinois at Urbana–
  Champaign, IL
U of Mary Hardin-Baylor, TX
U of Miami, FL
U of Michigan, MI
U of Nebraska–Lincoln, NE
U of New England, ME
U of New Hampshire, NH
U of Northern Iowa, IA
U of Pittsburgh at Bradford,
  PA
The U of Tennessee at
  Martin, TN
The U of Texas at Austin,
  TX
U of the Incarnate Word, TX
U of Vermont, VT

U of Wisconsin–Eau Claire,
  WI
U of Wisconsin–La Crosse,
  WI
U of Wisconsin–Stevens
  Point, WI
Upper Iowa U, IA
Urbana U, OH
Vanguard U of Southern
  California, CA
Washburn U, KS
Wayne State Coll, NE
West Chester U of
  Pennsylvania, PA
West Virginia Wesleyan Coll,
  WV
Xavier U, OH

**ATHLETIC TRAINING/
SPORTS MEDICINE**
Florida Gulf Coast U, FL
Neumann Coll, PA
Southern Nazarene U, OK
The U of North Carolina at
  Charlotte, NC
U of Pittsburgh at Bradford,
  PA
The U of Tennessee at
  Martin, TN
Valdosta State U, GA

**ATMOSPHERIC
SCIENCES AND
METEOROLOGY**
Cornell U, NY
Dalhousie U, NS, Canada
Embry-Riddle Aeronautical
  U, FL
Millersville U of
  Pennsylvania, PA
Northern Illinois U, IL
Penn State Abington, PA
Penn State DuBois, PA
Penn State Fayette, The
  Eberly Campus, PA
Penn State Mont Alto, PA
Penn State Wilkes-Barre, PA
Rutgers, The State U of New
  Jersey, New Brunswick, NJ
St. Cloud State U, MN
San Francisco State U, CA
Santa Rosa Jr Coll, CA
State U of New York Coll at
  Brockport, NY
Texas A&M U, TX
U at Albany, State U of New
  York, NY
The U of Arizona, AZ
U of California, Berkeley,
  CA
U of California, Los Angeles,
  CA
U of Guelph, ON, Canada
U of Kansas, KS
U of Miami, FL
U of Michigan, MI
U of Missouri–Columbia,
  MO
U of Nebraska–Lincoln, NE
The U of North Carolina at
  Asheville, NC
U of Washington, WA
Western Connecticut State
  U, CT

**ATOMIC/MOLECULAR
PHYSICS**
The Catholic U of America,
  DC
San Diego State U, CA
The U of Akron, OH

AUDIO ENGINEERING
American U, DC
The Art Inst of Seattle, WA

State U of New York at
  Fredonia, NY
U of Hartford, CT

**AUDIOLOGY AND
HEARING SCIENCES**
Indiana U Bloomington, IN
Indiana U–Purdue U Fort
  Wayne, IN
Stephen F. Austin State U,
  TX
The U of Akron, OH
The U of Tennessee, TN

**AUDIOLOGY AND
SPEECH-LANGUAGE
PATHOLOGY**
Adelphi U, NY
Ball State U, IN
Buffalo State Coll, State U of
  New York, NY
California State U, Fullerton,
  CA
California State U,
  Sacramento, CA
Calvin Coll, MI
The Coll of Saint Rose, NY
East Carolina U, NC
East Stroudsburg U of
  Pennsylvania, PA
Elmira Coll, NY
Elms Coll, MA
Fontbonne U, MO
Fort Hays State U, KS
Geneva Coll, PA
The George Washington U,
  DC
Hofstra U, NY
Hunter Coll of the City U of
  New York, NY
Idaho State U, ID
Illinois State U, IL
Indiana U Bloomington, IN
Iona Coll, NY
Ithaca Coll, NY
Lamar U, TX
Marquette U, WI
Marymount Manhattan Coll,
  NY
Marywood U, PA
Miami Dade Coll, FL
Michigan State U, MI
Minnesota State U Mankato,
  MN
Minnesota State U
  Moorhead, MN
Missouri State U, MO
Molloy Coll, NY
Murray State U, KY
Northeastern U, MA
Northern Michigan U, MI
Northern State U, SD
The Ohio State U, OH
Old Dominion U, VA
Otterbein Coll, OH
Our Lady of the Lake U of
  San Antonio, TX
The Richard Stockton Coll
  of New Jersey, NJ
St. Cloud State U, MN
San Francisco State U, CA
Southern Illinois U
  Edwardsville, IL
Southern U and A&M Coll,
  LA
State U of New York at
  Fredonia, NY
State U of New York Coll at
  Cortland, NY
Stephen F. Austin State U,
  TX
Syracuse U, NY
Temple U, PA
Thiel Coll, PA

U at Buffalo, the State U of
  New York, NY
The U of Akron, OH
The U of Alabama, AL
U of Central Florida, FL
U of Central Oklahoma, OK
U of Cincinnati, OH
U of Houston, TX
U of Illinois at Urbana–
  Champaign, IL
U of Kentucky, KY
U of Minnesota, Duluth, MN
U of Mississippi, MS
U of New Hampshire, NH
U of New Mexico, NM
U of Oregon, OR
U of Pittsburgh, PA
U of Redlands, CA
The U of Texas at El Paso,
  TX
U of the District of
  Columbia, DC
U of the Pacific, CA
U of Virginia, VA
U of Washington, WA
U of Wisconsin–Oshkosh,
  WI
U of Wisconsin–Stevens
  Point, WI
U of Wyoming, WY
West Chester U of
  Pennsylvania, PA
Wichita State U, KS

AUDITING
Carlow U, PA

**AUTOBODY/COLLISION
AND REPAIR
TECHNOLOGY**
British Columbia Inst of
  Technology, BC, Canada
Coahoma Comm Coll, MS
Dixie State Coll of Utah, UT
Eastfield Coll, TX
Florida Comm Coll at
  Jacksonville, FL
Fresno City Coll, CA
Idaho State U, ID
Linn State Tech Coll, MO
Montana State U–Billings,
  MT
Montana Tech of The U of
  Montana, MT
New Hampshire Comm
  Tech Coll, Nashua/
  Claremont, NH
Ozarks Tech Comm Coll,
  MO
Pueblo Comm Coll, CO
St. Cloud Tech Coll, MN
St. Philip's Coll, TX
Southeast Tech Inst, SD
State U of New York Coll of
  Technology at Alfred, NY
Waubonsee Comm Coll, IL
Waukesha County Tech Coll,
  WI

**AUTOMOBILE/
AUTOMOTIVE
MECHANICS
TECHNOLOGY**
Aims Comm Coll, CO
Allegany Coll of Maryland,
  MD
Asheville-Buncombe Tech
  Comm Coll, NC
Bainbridge Coll, GA
British Columbia Inst of
  Technology, BC, Canada
Broward Comm Coll, FL
Burlington County Coll, NJ
Cedar Valley Coll, TX

Central Arizona Coll, AZ
Central Florida Comm Coll,
  FL
Central Piedmont Comm
  Coll, NC
Central Wyoming Coll, WY
Chattahoochee Tech Coll,
  GA
Chattanooga State Tech
  Comm Coll, TN
Citrus Coll, CA
Coll of the Desert, CA
Cosumnes River Coll,
  Sacramento, CA
Cuesta Coll, CA
DeKalb Tech Coll, GA
Delaware Tech & Comm
  Coll, Jack F. Owens
  Campus, DE
Dixie State Coll of Utah, UT
East Central Coll, MO
Eastern Idaho Tech Coll, ID
Eastern New Mexico
  U–Roswell, NM
Eastfield Coll, TX
El Camino Coll, CA
Florida Comm Coll at
  Jacksonville, FL
Fresno City Coll, CA
Fulton-Montgomery Comm
  Coll, NY
Gaston Coll, NC
Gloucester County Coll, NJ
Greenville Tech Coll, SC
Harrisburg Area Comm Coll,
  PA
Houston Comm Coll System,
  TX
Hudson Valley Comm Coll,
  NY
Idaho State U, ID
Illinois Valley Comm Coll, IL
Ivy Tech Comm Coll–
  Kokomo, IN
Ivy Tech Comm Coll–
  Southwest, IN
Ivy Tech Comm Coll–
  Wabash Valley, IN
Lamar U, TX
Lassen Comm Coll District,
  CA
Lincoln Land Comm Coll, IL
Linn State Tech Coll, MO
Long Beach City Coll, CA
Macomb Comm Coll, MI
Maui Comm Coll, HI
Metropolitan Comm
  Coll–Longview, MO
Middlesex County Coll, NJ
Midland Coll, TX
Minnesota State Coll–
  Southeast Tech, MN
MiraCosta Coll, CA
Montana State U–Billings,
  MT
Montana Tech of The U of
  Montana, MT
Morton Coll, IL
New Hampshire Comm
  Tech Coll, Nashua/
  Claremont, NH
New Mexico Jr Coll, NM
New River Comm Coll, VA
North Central Missouri Coll,
  MO
North Central Texas Coll, TX
Northern Michigan U, MI
Northland Comm and Tech
  Coll–Thief River Falls, MN
Odessa Coll, TX
Ozarks Tech Comm Coll,
  MO
Pima Comm Coll, AZ
Pittsburg State U, KS

Pueblo Comm Coll, CO
Reedley Coll, CA
Richland Comm Coll, IL
St. Cloud Tech Coll, MN
St. Philip's Coll, TX
Santa Ana Coll, CA
Santa Barbara City Coll, CA
Seminole Comm Coll, FL
Shasta Coll, CA
Skagit Valley Coll, WA
Southeast Tech Inst, SD
Southern Adventist U, TN
Southern Maine Comm Coll, ME
Southern Utah U, UT
South Piedmont Comm Coll, NC
Southwestern Michigan Coll, MI
Spokane Comm Coll, WA
Spoon River Coll, IL
Stark State Coll of Technology, OH
State U of New York Coll of Technology at Alfred, NY
State U of New York Coll of Technology at Canton, NY
Surry Comm Coll, NC
Tidewater Comm Coll, VA
U of Alaska Anchorage, AK
The U of Montana-Helena Coll of Technology, MT
Ventura Coll, CA
Victor Valley Coll, CA
Waubonsee Comm Coll, IL
Waukesha County Tech Coll, WI
Westchester Comm Coll, NY
Western Tech Coll, WI
Williston State Coll, ND

AUTOMOTIVE ENGINEERING TECHNOLOGY

Comm Coll of Allegheny County, PA
Farmingdale State Coll, NY
Harrisburg Area Comm Coll, PA
Macomb Comm Coll, MI
Minnesota State U Mankato, MN
Southern Illinois U Carbondale, IL
Sussex County Comm Coll, NJ
The U of Akron, OH
Vermont Tech Coll, VT

AVIATION/AIRWAY MANAGEMENT

Broward Comm Coll, FL
Chattanooga State Tech Comm Coll, TN
Clayton State U, GA
Comm Coll of Allegheny County, PA
Delaware State U, DE
Dixie State Coll of Utah, UT
Eastern Michigan U, MI
Embry-Riddle Aeronautical U, FL
Everglades U, Sarasota, FL
Farmingdale State Coll, NY
Florida Comm Coll at Jacksonville, FL
Florida Inst of Technology, FL
Geneva Coll, PA
Glendale Comm Coll, CA
Jacksonville U, FL
Lewis U, IL
Long Beach City Coll, CA
Marywood U, PA

Miami Dade Coll, FL
Minnesota State U Mankato, MN
Northland Comm and Tech Coll–Thief River Falls, MN
The Ohio State U, OH
Park U, MO
Rocky Mountain Coll, MT
St. Cloud State U, MN
Southern Illinois U Carbondale, IL
Southern Nazarene U, OK
The U of Akron, OH
U of Alaska Anchorage, AK
U of Dubuque, IA
U of Illinois at Urbana–Champaign, IL
U of Nebraska at Kearney, NE
U of the District of Columbia, DC
Westminster Coll, UT

AVIONICS MAINTENANCE TECHNOLOGY

Aims Comm Coll, CO
British Columbia Inst of Technology, BC, Canada
Broward Comm Coll, FL
Chattanooga State Tech Comm Coll, TN
City Colls of Chicago, Richard J. Daley Coll, IL
Clayton State U, GA
Comm Coll of Beaver County, PA
Foothill Coll, CA
Glendale Comm Coll, CA
Greenville Tech Coll, SC
Housatonic Comm Coll, CT
LeTourneau U, TX
Lewis U, IL
Long Beach City Coll, CA
Minnesota State Coll–Southeast Tech, MN
Mohawk Valley Comm Coll, NY
New Hampshire Comm Tech Coll, Nashua/Claremont, NH
Northern Michigan U, MI
Northland Comm and Tech Coll–Thief River Falls, MN
The Ohio State U, OH
Reedley Coll, CA
Rose State Coll, OK
Shasta Coll, CA
Southern Illinois U Carbondale, IL
Spokane Comm Coll, WA
U of Alaska Anchorage, AK
U of the District of Columbia, DC
West Los Angeles Coll, CA

BAKING AND PASTRY ARTS

The Art Inst of Houston, TX
The Art Inst of Pittsburgh, PA
El Centro Coll, TX
Johnson & Wales U, CO
Johnson & Wales U, FL
Johnson & Wales U, NC
Johnson & Wales U, RI
Kendall Coll, IL

BANKING AND FINANCIAL SUPPORT SERVICES

Alexandria Tech Coll, MN
Asnuntuck Comm Coll, CT
Buena Vista U, IA

Comm Coll of Allegheny County, PA
Delaware State U, DE
Eastern New Mexico U–Roswell, NM
Emory U, GA
Florida Comm Coll at Jacksonville, FL
Harrisburg Area Comm Coll, PA
Husson Coll, ME
Lackawanna Coll, PA
Madisonville Comm Coll, KY
Mohawk Valley Comm Coll, NY
Northwood U, MI
Northwood U, Florida Campus, FL
Northwood U, Texas Campus, TX
Pittsburg State U, KS
St. Cloud Tech Coll, MN
Seminole Comm Coll, FL
State U of New York Coll of Technology at Canton, NY
The U of Akron, OH
U of Illinois at Urbana–Champaign, IL
U of Nebraska at Omaha, NE
U of North Florida, FL
Washburn U, KS
Waubonsee Comm Coll, IL
West Liberty State Coll, WV
West Virginia Northern Comm Coll, WV
West Virginia State Comm and Tech Coll, WV

BARBERING

Coahoma Comm Coll, MS

BEHAVIORAL SCIENCES

Ancilla Coll, IN
Athens State U, AL
Augsburg Coll, MN
Bemidji State U, MN
Brown U, RI
Carnegie Mellon U, PA
Cedar Crest Coll, PA
Citrus Coll, CA
Colorado Mountain Coll, Alpine Campus, CO
Concordia U, NE
Freed-Hardeman U, TN
Fulton-Montgomery Comm Coll, NY
Galveston Coll, TX
Glenville State Coll, WV
Irvine Valley Coll, CA
Loyola U New Orleans, LA
Miami Dade Coll, FL
Midland Coll, TX
Midland Lutheran Coll, NE
Minnesota State U Mankato, MN
MiraCosta Coll, CA
Moorpark Coll, CA
National-Louis U, IL
Northeastern U, MA
Northern Michigan U, MI
Notre Dame de Namur U, CA
Phoenix Coll, AZ
Quincy Coll, MA
St. Cloud State U, MN
Santa Rosa Jr Coll, CA
Tennessee Wesleyan Coll, TN
Trevecca Nazarene U, TN
Tufts U, MA
The U of Akron, OH
U of Kansas, KS

U of Maine at Machias, ME
U of Missouri–Columbia, MO
Ursuline Coll, OH
Westminster Coll, PA
West Virginia State Comm and Tech Coll, WV
Widener U, PA
Wilson Coll, PA

BIBLICAL STUDIES

Abilene Christian U, TX
Anderson U, IN
Asbury Coll, KY
The Baptist Coll of Florida, FL
Bethany U, CA
Bethel Coll, IN
Bethel U, MN
Calvin Coll, MI
Carson-Newman Coll, TN
Cincinnati Christian U, OH
Cornerstone U, MI
Dallas Baptist U, TX
Eastern Mennonite U, VA
Florida Coll, FL
Freed-Hardeman U, TN
Fresno Pacific U, CA
Geneva Coll, PA
Goshen Coll, IN
Grace Coll, IN
Heritage Christian U, AL
Houghton Coll, NY
Houston Baptist U, TX
Huntington U, IN
John Brown U, AR
Kuyper Coll, MI
Lancaster Bible Coll, PA
LeTourneau U, TX
Mount Vernon Nazarene U, OH
Multnomah Bible Coll and Biblical Seminary, OR
Northwestern Coll, MN
Oak Hills Christian Coll, MN
Oral Roberts U, OK
Point Loma Nazarene U, CA
Redeemer U Coll, ON, Canada
Somerset Christian Coll, NJ
Southwest Baptist U, MO
Taylor U, IN
Trinity Baptist Coll, FL
U of Evansville, IN
U of Mary Hardin-Baylor, TX
Vanguard U of Southern California, CA
Wheaton Coll, IL

BILINGUAL AND MULTILINGUAL EDUCATION

Calvin Coll, MI
Elms Coll, MA
Fresno Pacific U, CA
Goshen Coll, IN
Houston Baptist U, TX
Indiana U Bloomington, IN
Long Island U, Brooklyn Campus, NY
Texas A&M U–Corpus Christi, TX
The U of Akron, OH
U of Delaware, DE
The U of Findlay, OH
U of Houston, TX
U of San Francisco, CA
U of Washington, WA

BILINGUAL, MULTILINGUAL, AND MULTICULTURAL EDUCATION RELATED

State U of New York Coll at Brockport, NY

BIOCHEMICAL TECHNOLOGY

U at Buffalo, the State U of New York, NY

BIOCHEMISTRY

Abilene Christian U, TX
Adelphi U, NY
Albright Coll, PA
Alma Coll, MI
Alvernia Coll, PA
American International Coll, MA
American U, DC
Angelo State U, TX
Asbury Coll, KY
Austin Coll, TX
Bard Coll, NY
Bates Coll, ME
Baylor U, TX
Benedictine Coll, KS
Bishop's U, QC, Canada
Boston Coll, MA
Bradley U, IL
Brandeis U, MA
Brock U, ON, Canada
Brown U, RI
California State U, Fullerton, CA
California State U, Northridge, CA
California State U, San Bernardino, CA
Calvin Coll, MI
Carleton U, ON, Canada
Carroll Coll, WI
The Catholic U of America, DC
Cedar Crest Coll, PA
Charleston Southern U, SC
Claremont McKenna Coll, CA
Clark U, MA
Clemson U, SC
Coe Coll, IA
Colby Coll, ME
Colgate U, NY
Coll of Charleston, SC
Coll of Mount St. Joseph, OH
Coll of Mount Saint Vincent, NY
Coll of Saint Elizabeth, NJ
The Coll of Saint Rose, NY
The Coll of St. Scholastica, MN
Coll of Staten Island of the City U of New York, NY
Cornell U, NY
Daemen Coll, NY
DePaul U, IL
Dominican U, IL
Drake U, IA
East Carolina U, NC
Eastern Connecticut State U, CT
Eastern Mennonite U, VA
Eastern Michigan U, MI
East Stroudsburg U of Pennsylvania, PA
Edinboro U of Pennsylvania, PA
Elmira Coll, NY
Fairleigh Dickinson U, Metropolitan Campus, NJ
Florida Inst of Technology, FL
Freed-Hardeman U, TN
Furman U, SC
Georgian Court U, NJ
Gonzaga U, WA
Grinnell Coll, IA
Gustavus Adolphus Coll, MN

Hamilton Coll, NY
Hamline U, MN
Hampden-Sydney Coll, VA
Harding U, AR
Hartwick Coll, NY
Haverford Coll, PA
Hofstra U, NY
Idaho State U, ID
Illinois State U, IL
Immaculata U, PA
Indiana U Bloomington, IN
Indiana U of Pennsylvania, PA
Iona Coll, NY
Ithaca Coll, NY
John Brown U, AR
Kansas State U, KS
Kennesaw State U, GA
Kenyon Coll, OH
Keuka Coll, NY
LaGrange Coll, GA
Lakeland Coll, WI
Lawrence U, WI
Lebanon Valley Coll, PA
Lehigh U, PA
Le Moyne Coll, NY
Lewis U, IL
Loras Coll, IA
Loyola Marymount U, CA
Loyola U Chicago, IL
Manhattan Coll, NY
Manhattanville Coll, NY
Marietta Coll, OH
Marist Coll, NY
Marquette U, WI
McDaniel Coll, MD
Mercer U, GA
Mercyhurst Coll, PA
Michigan State U, MI
Minnesota State U Mankato, MN
Monmouth Coll, IL
Moravian Coll, PA
Mount Holyoke Coll, MA
Mount St. Mary's U, MD
New York U, NY
Niagara U, NY
North Carolina State U, NC
North Central Coll, IL
Northeastern U, MA
Northern Michigan U, MI
Northwest Nazarene U, ID
Notre Dame Coll, OH
Notre Dame de Namur U, CA
Oakland U, MI
Occidental Coll, CA
The Ohio State U, OH
Oklahoma State U, OK
Old Dominion U, VA
Oral Roberts U, OK
Otterbein Coll, OH
Penn State Abington, PA
Penn State DuBois, PA
Penn State Fayette, The Eberly Campus, PA
Penn State Mont Alto, PA
Penn State Wilkes-Barre, PA
Point Loma Nazarene U, CA
Portland State U, OR
Queen's U at Kingston, ON, Canada
Queens U of Charlotte, NC
Rensselaer Polytechnic Inst, NY
Rhodes Coll, TN
Rice U, TX
The Richard Stockton Coll of New Jersey, NJ
Ripon Coll, WI
Rochester Inst of Technology, NY
Rockford Coll, IL
Rockhurst U, MO

Rowan U, NJ
Rutgers, The State U of New Jersey, New Brunswick, NJ
Saginaw Valley State U, MI
St. Bonaventure U, NY
Saint John's U, MN
Saint Joseph's Coll, IN
St. Lawrence U, NY
St. Mary's Coll of Maryland, MD
San Francisco State U, CA
Seattle Pacific U, WA
Seton Hall U, NJ
Seton Hill U, PA
Southern Adventist U, TN
Southern Nazarene U, OK
Southern Oregon U, OR
Southwestern Coll, KS
Southwestern U, TX
State U of New York at Fredonia, NY
State U of New York Coll at Brockport, NY
State U of New York Coll at Geneseo, NY
State U of New York Coll of Environmental Science and Forestry, NY
Stetson U, FL
Stonehill Coll, MA
Syracuse U, NY
Temple U, PA
Texas A&M U, TX
Trent U, ON, Canada
Trinity Coll, CT
Trinity U, TX
Union Coll, NE
U at Albany, State U of New York, NY
U at Buffalo, the State U of New York, NY
The U of Arizona, AZ
U of California, Los Angeles, CA
U of California, Santa Barbara, CA
U of Cincinnati, OH
U of Colorado at Boulder, CO
U of Dayton, OH
U of Delaware, DE
U of Evansville, IN
U of Guelph, ON, Canada
U of Houston, TX
U of Illinois at Urbana–Champaign, IL
U of Massachusetts Boston, MA
U of Miami, FL
U of Michigan, MI
U of Minnesota, Duluth, MN
U of Missouri–Columbia, MO
U of Nebraska–Lincoln, NE
U of New Brunswick Fredericton, NB, Canada
U of New England, ME
U of New Hampshire, NH
U of New Mexico, NM
U of Northern Iowa, IA
U of Notre Dame, IN
U of Oregon, OR
U of Pennsylvania, PA
U of St. Thomas, MN
The U of Tampa, FL
The U of Tennessee, TN
The U of Texas at Austin, TX
U of the Pacific, CA
U of Toronto, ON, Canada
U of Vermont, VT
U of Washington, WA
U of Wisconsin–Madison, WI

Vassar Coll, NY
Washington & Jefferson Coll, PA
Washington and Lee U, VA
Wellesley Coll, MA
Wells Coll, NY
West Chester U of Pennsylvania, PA
Whitman Coll, WA
Widener U, PA
Wilkes U, PA
William Jewell Coll, MO
Wright State U, OH

BIOCHEMISTRY/ BIOPHYSICS AND MOLECULAR BIOLOGY
Cornell U, NY
Dalhousie U, NS, Canada
Lebanon Valley Coll, PA
Liberty U, VA
Michigan State U, MI
Monmouth Coll, IL
North Dakota State U, ND
U of Kansas, KS
U of Maryland, Baltimore County, MD
U of Massachusetts Amherst, MA
U of Northern British Columbia, BC, Canada

BIOCHEMISTRY, BIOPHYSICS AND MOLECULAR BIOLOGY RELATED
Mount Union Coll, OH
Oklahoma State U, OK
Ramapo Coll of New Jersey, NJ
Sweet Briar Coll, VA
U of Maryland, Baltimore County, MD

BIOINFORMATICS
Baylor U, TX
Dalhousie U, NS, Canada
Gannon U, PA
Ramapo Coll of New Jersey, NJ
Rensselaer Polytechnic Inst, NY
Rochester Inst of Technology, NY
Rockhurst U, MO
U at Buffalo, the State U of New York, NY
U of Maryland, Baltimore County, MD
U of Northern Iowa, IA
U of Pennsylvania, PA

BIOLOGICAL AND BIOMEDICAL SCIENCES RELATED
Brandeis U, MA
Carnegie Mellon U, PA
Charleston Southern U, SC
Fairleigh Dickinson U, Coll at Florham, NJ
Fairleigh Dickinson U, Metropolitan Campus, NJ
Farmingdale State Coll, NY
Lehigh U, PA
Lynchburg Coll, VA
Monmouth Coll, IL
Park U, MO
Penn State Abington, PA
Penn State DuBois, PA
Penn State Fayette, The Eberly Campus, PA
Penn State Mont Alto, PA
Penn State Wilkes-Barre, PA

Rensselaer Polytechnic Inst, NY
Rochester Inst of Technology, NY
Rutgers, The State U of New Jersey, Newark, NJ
U of Illinois at Urbana–Champaign, IL
U of Kansas, KS
Ursuline Coll, OH

BIOLOGICAL AND PHYSICAL SCIENCES
Abraham Baldwin Coll, GA
Adams State Coll, CO
Alma Coll, MI
Alvernia Coll, PA
Ancilla Coll, IN
Angelo State U, TX
Athabasca U, AB, Canada
Augsburg Coll, MN
Avila U, MO
Bard Coll, NY
Bemidji State U, MN
Bishop's U, QC, Canada
Bluefield State Coll, WV
Brock U, ON, Canada
Buena Vista U, IA
Burlington County Coll, NJ
Caldwell Comm Coll and Tech Inst, NC
Calvin Coll, MI
Cape Breton U, NS, Canada
Cape Cod Comm Coll, MA
Carleton U, ON, Canada
Cedar Crest Coll, PA
Charleston Southern U, SC
Chesapeake Coll, MD
Clayton State U, GA
Coe Coll, IA
Coll of the Atlantic, ME
Coll of the Canyons, CA
Colorado Mountain Coll, Alpine Campus, CO
Comm Coll of Aurora, CO
Cosumnes River Coll, Sacramento, CA
Cottey Coll, MO
Crafton Hills Coll, CA
Dabney S. Lancaster Comm Coll, VA
Eastern Michigan U, MI
Eastern Nazarene Coll, MA
East Stroudsburg U of Pennsylvania, PA
Edinboro U of Pennsylvania, PA
Fairleigh Dickinson U, Metropolitan Campus, NJ
Florida Inst of Technology, FL
Fort Hays State U, KS
Freed-Hardeman U, TN
Fulton-Montgomery Comm Coll, NY
Galveston Coll, TX
Gannon U, PA
Glendale Comm Coll, CA
Heartland Comm Coll, IL
Houghton Coll, NY
Howard Comm Coll, MD
Huntington U, IN
Indiana U of Pennsylvania, PA
Irvine Valley Coll, CA
King's Coll, PA
Kutztown U of Pennsylvania, PA
Lassen Comm Coll District, CA
Lehigh U, PA
Le Moyne Coll, NY
Lincoln Land Comm Coll, IL

Massachusetts Coll of Liberal Arts, MA
Metropolitan Comm Coll–Longview, MO
Metropolitan Comm Coll–Penn Valley, MO
Michigan State U, MI
Middlesex Comm Coll, CT
Middlesex County Coll, NJ
Middle Tennessee State U, TN
Midland Lutheran Coll, NE
Minnesota State U Mankato, MN
Mitchell Coll, CT
Montana Tech of The U of Montana, MT
Morton Coll, IL
Mount Saint Vincent U, NS, Canada
Mount Vernon Nazarene U, OH
National-Louis U, IL
New Mexico Jr Coll, NM
New River Comm Coll, VA
North Central Coll, IL
North Central Texas Coll, TX
Northern State U, SD
Paris Jr Coll, TX
Penn State Abington, PA
Penn State DuBois, PA
Penn State Fayette, The Eberly Campus, PA
Penn State Mont Alto, PA
Penn State Wilkes-Barre, PA
Portland State U, OR
Redeemer U Coll, ON, Canada
Rensselaer Polytechnic Inst, NY
Richland Comm Coll, IL
Rockford Coll, IL
Rockingham Comm Coll, NC
St. Francis Xavier U, NS, Canada
St. Mary's Coll of Maryland, MD
St. Norbert Coll, WI
Saint Xavier U, IL
Salem Comm Coll, NJ
San Francisco State U, CA
Santa Ana Coll, CA
Santa Clara U, CA
Skagit Valley Coll, WA
Spoon River Coll, IL
State U of New York at Fredonia, NY
State U of New York Coll of Environmental Science and Forestry, NY
State U of New York Coll of Technology at Alfred, NY
State U of New York Coll of Technology at Canton, NY
Sterling Coll, VT
Sussex County Comm Coll, NJ
Tidewater Comm Coll, VA
Trent U, ON, Canada
Trevecca Nazarene U, TN
The U of Akron, OH
The U of Alabama, AL
U of Alaska Anchorage, AK
U of Cincinnati, OH
U of Dubuque, IA
The U of Findlay, OH
U of Massachusetts Amherst, MA
U of New Brunswick Fredericton, NB, Canada
U of New Hampshire, NH
U of Northern British Columbia, BC, Canada
U of Northern Iowa, IA

U of North Florida, FL
U of Oregon, OR
U of Pittsburgh, PA
U of Southern Indiana, IN
The U of Texas at San Antonio, TX
U of Toronto, ON, Canada
U of Wisconsin–Platteville, WI
U of Wisconsin–Richland, WI
Upper Iowa U, IA
Vanguard U of Southern California, CA
Victor Valley Coll, CA
Virginia Highlands Comm Coll, VA
Waubonsee Comm Coll, IL
Westchester Comm Coll, NY
Worcester State Coll, MA
Wright State U, OH
Xavier U, OH

BIOLOGICAL SPECIALIZATIONS RELATED
Marywood U, PA

BIOLOGY/BIOLOGICAL SCIENCES
Abilene Christian U, TX
Abraham Baldwin Coll, GA
Acadia U, NS, Canada
Adams State Coll, CO
Adelphi U, NY
Alabama A&M U, AL
Albany State U, GA
Albertson Coll of Idaho, ID
Albion Coll, MI
Albright Coll, PA
Alderson-Broaddus Coll, WV
Alma Coll, MI
Alvernia Coll, PA
American International Coll, MA
American U, DC
Amherst Coll, MA
Ancilla Coll, IN
Anderson U, IN
Anderson U, SC
Angelo State U, TX
Arizona State U at the West campus, AZ
Asbury Coll, KY
Ashland U, OH
Athens State U, AL
Auburn U Montgomery, AL
Augsburg Coll, MN
Aurora U, IL
Austin Coll, TX
Avila U, MO
Bainbridge Coll, GA
Ball State U, IN
Bard Coll, NY
Barry U, FL
Bates Coll, ME
Baylor U, TX
Belmont Abbey Coll, NC
Bemidji State U, MN
Benedictine Coll, KS
Bethel Coll, IN
Bethel U, MN
Bishop's U, QC, Canada
Blinn Coll, TX
Boston Coll, MA
Bradley U, IL
Brandeis U, MA
Brandon U, MB, Canada
Brenau U, GA
Brewton-Parker Coll, GA
Briar Cliff U, IA
Bridgewater Coll, VA
Brock U, ON, Canada
Brown U, RI

Bryn Mawr Coll, PA
Bucks County Comm Coll, PA
Buena Vista U, IA
Buffalo State Coll, State U of New York, NY
Burlington County Coll, NJ
Calhoun Comm Coll, AL
California State U, Fullerton, CA
California State U, Northridge, CA
California State U, Sacramento, CA
California State U, San Bernardino, CA
California State U, Stanislaus, CA
Calvin Coll, MI
Cameron U, OK
Cape Breton U, NS, Canada
Cardinal Stritch U, WI
Carleton U, ON, Canada
Carlow U, PA
Carnegie Mellon U, PA
Carroll Coll, MT
Carroll Coll, WI
Carson-Newman Coll, TN
Carthage Coll, WI
The Catholic U of America, DC
Cedar Crest Coll, PA
Central Piedmont Comm Coll, NC
Central Wyoming Coll, WY
Charleston Southern U, SC
Chattanooga State Tech Comm Coll, TN
Christopher Newport U, VA
Citrus Coll, CA
Claremont McKenna Coll, CA
Clark U, MA
Clayton State U, GA
Clemson U, SC
Coahoma Comm Coll, MS
Coastal Carolina U, SC
Coe Coll, IA
Colby Coll, ME
Colgate U, NY
Coll of Charleston, SC
Coll of Mount St. Joseph, OH
Coll of Mount Saint Vincent, NY
Coll of Saint Elizabeth, NJ
Coll of Saint Mary, NE
The Coll of Saint Rose, NY
The Coll of St. Scholastica, MN
Coll of Staten Island of the City U of New York, NY
Coll of the Atlantic, ME
Coll of the Canyons, CA
Coll of the Desert, CA
The Coll of William and Mary, VA
Colorado Mountain Coll, Alpine Campus, CO
Columbus State U, GA
Comm Coll of Allegheny County, PA
Comm Coll of Beaver County, PA
Concordia Coll–New York, NY
Concordia U, NE
Concordia U Coll of Alberta, AB, Canada
Concord U, WV
Cornell U, NY
Cornerstone U, MI
Cosumnes River Coll, Sacramento, CA

Crafton Hills Coll, CA
Cuesta Coll, CA
Daemen Coll, NY
Dalhousie U, NS, Canada
Dallas Baptist U, TX
Delaware State U, DE
DePaul U, IL
Dixie State Coll of Utah, UT
Dominican U, IL
Drake U, IA
Drury U, MO
Duke U, NC
Earlham Coll, IN
East Carolina U, NC
East Central Coll, MO
Eastern Connecticut State U, CT
Eastern Mennonite U, VA
Eastern Michigan U, MI
Eastern Nazarene Coll, MA
East Stroudsburg U of Pennsylvania, PA
Eckerd Coll, FL
Edinboro U of Pennsylvania, PA
El Camino Coll, CA
Elmira Coll, NY
Elms Coll, MA
Elon U, NC
Emory U, GA
Fairfield U, CT
Fairleigh Dickinson U, Coll at Florham, NJ
Fairleigh Dickinson U, Metropolitan Campus, NJ
Fayetteville State U, NC
Feather River Coll, CA
Ferrum Coll, VA
Fitchburg State Coll, MA
Florida Atlantic U, FL
Florida Inst of Technology, FL
Florida International U, FL
Fontbonne U, MO
Foothill Coll, CA
Fort Hays State U, KS
Framingham State Coll, MA
Franciscan U of Steubenville, OH
Franklin Coll, IN
Franklin Pierce U, NH
Frederick Comm Coll, MD
Freed-Hardeman U, TN
Fresno Pacific U, CA
Fulton-Montgomery Comm Coll, NY
Furman U, SC
Gainesville State Coll, GA
Gannon U, PA
Gardner-Webb U, NC
Geneva Coll, PA
Georgetown Coll, KY
The George Washington U, DC
Georgia Coll & State U, GA
Georgian Court U, NJ
Glenville State Coll, WV
Gloucester County Coll, NJ
Gonzaga U, WA
Gordon Coll, MA
Goshen Coll, IN
Grace Coll, IN
Graceland U, IA
Grambling State U, LA
Green Mountain Coll, VT
Grinnell Coll, IA
Grossmont Coll, CA
Gustavus Adolphus Coll, MN
Hamilton Coll, NY
Hamline U, MN
Hampden-Sydney Coll, VA
Hampshire Coll, MA
Harding U, AR

Harrisburg Area Comm Coll, PA
Hartwick Coll, NY
Haverford Coll, PA
Henderson State U, AR
High Point U, NC
Hofstra U, NY
Hope Coll, MI
Houghton Coll, NY
Houston Baptist U, TX
Hunter Coll of the City U of New York, NY
Huntington U, IN
Husson Coll, ME
Idaho State U, ID
Illinois State U, IL
Illinois Wesleyan U, IL
Immaculata U, PA
Indiana U Bloomington, IN
Indiana U of Pennsylvania, PA
Indiana U–Purdue U Fort Wayne, IN
Indiana U–Purdue U Indianapolis, IN
Indiana U Southeast, IN
Iona Coll, NY
Irvine Valley Coll, CA
Ithaca Coll, NY
Jacksonville U, FL
John Brown U, AR
Johnson State Coll, VT
Kansas State U, KS
Kellogg Comm Coll, MI
Kennesaw State U, GA
Kentucky Wesleyan Coll, KY
Kenyon Coll, OH
Keuka Coll, NY
Kingsborough Comm Coll of the City U of New York, NY
King's Coll, PA
The King's U Coll, AB, Canada
Kutztown U of Pennsylvania, PA
LaGrange Coll, GA
Lake Erie Coll, OH
Lakeland Coll, WI
Lamar U, TX
Langston U, OK
Lassen Comm Coll District, CA
Lawrence U, WI
Lebanon Valley Coll, PA
Lee Coll, TX
Lehigh U, PA
Le Moyne Coll, NY
LeTourneau U, TX
Lewis U, IL
Liberty U, VA
Lincoln U, PA
Lindenwood U, MO
Long Beach City Coll, CA
Long Island U, Brooklyn Campus, NY
Loras Coll, IA
Loyola Marymount U, CA
Loyola U Chicago, IL
Loyola U New Orleans, LA
Lynchburg Coll, VA
Lynn U, FL
Macalester Coll, MN
MacMurray Coll, IL
Macomb Comm Coll, MI
Manhattan Coll, NY
Manhattanville Coll, NY
Marian Coll, IN
Marietta Coll, OH
Marist Coll, NY
Marquette U, WI
Marshall U, WV
Marymount Manhattan Coll, NY

Marymount U, VA
Marywood U, PA
Massachusetts Coll of Liberal Arts, MA
McDaniel Coll, MD
McNeese State U, LA
Mercer U, GA
Mercyhurst Coll, PA
Metropolitan Comm Coll–Longview, MO
Metropolitan Comm Coll–Penn Valley, MO
Miami Dade Coll, FL
Michigan State U, MI
Middlesex County Coll, NJ
Middle Tennessee State U, TN
Midland Coll, TX
Midland Lutheran Coll, NE
Millersville U of Pennsylvania, PA
Minnesota State U Mankato, MN
Minnesota State U Moorhead, MN
MiraCosta Coll, CA
Missouri State U, MO
Molloy Coll, NY
Monmouth Coll, IL
Monmouth U, NJ
Montana State U, MT
Montana State U–Billings, MT
Montana Tech of The U of Montana, MT
Moorpark Coll, CA
Moravian Coll, PA
Morningside Coll, IA
Mount Holyoke Coll, MA
Mount St. Mary's U, MD
Mount Saint Vincent U, NS, Canada
Mount Union Coll, OH
Mount Vernon Nazarene U, OH
Murray State U, KY
National-Louis U, IL
Neumann Coll, PA
New Jersey City U, NJ
New Mexico Jr Coll, NM
New York U, NY
Niagara U, NY
Nipissing U, ON, Canada
North Carolina State U, NC
North Central Coll, IL
North Dakota State U, ND
Northeastern U, MA
Northern Illinois U, IL
Northern Michigan U, MI
Northern State U, SD
North Georgia Coll & State U, GA
Northwestern Coll, MN
Northwestern Oklahoma State U, OK
Northwest Nazarene U, ID
Notre Dame Coll, OH
Notre Dame de Namur U, CA
Nova Southeastern U, FL
Oakland U, MI
Occidental Coll, CA
Odessa Coll, TX
Oglethorpe U, GA
The Ohio State U, OH
The Ohio State U at Lima, OH
Ohio Wesleyan U, OH
Oklahoma State U, OK
Old Dominion U, VA
Oral Roberts U, OK
Otterbein Coll, OH
Our Lady of the Lake U of San Antonio, TX

Park U, MO
Paul Quinn Coll, TX
Penn State Abington, PA
Penn State DuBois, PA
Penn State Fayette, The
  Eberly Campus, PA
Penn State Mont Alto, PA
Penn State Wilkes-Barre, PA
Piedmont Coll, GA
Pine Manor Coll, MA
Pittsburg State U, KS
Point Loma Nazarene U, CA
Portland State U, OR
Prairie View A&M U, TX
Presbyterian Coll, SC
Purdue U North Central, IN
Queens Coll of the City U of
  New York, NY
Queen's U at Kingston, ON,
  Canada
Queens U of Charlotte, NC
Radford U, VA
Ramapo Coll of New Jersey,
  NJ
Randolph Coll, VA
Randolph-Macon Coll, VA
Redeemer U Coll, ON,
  Canada
Reedley Coll, CA
Reinhardt Coll, GA
Rensselaer Polytechnic Inst,
  NY
Rhodes Coll, TN
Rice U, TX
The Richard Stockton Coll
  of New Jersey, NJ
Ripon Coll, WI
Rivier Coll, NH
Rochester Inst of
  Technology, NY
Rockford Coll, IL
Rockhurst U, MO
Rocky Mountain Coll, MT
Roosevelt U, IL
Rose State Coll, OK
Rowan U, NJ
Roxbury Comm Coll, MA
Rutgers, The State U of New
  Jersey, Newark, NJ
Rutgers, The State U of New
  Jersey, New Brunswick, NJ
Ryerson U, ON, Canada
Saginaw Valley State U, MI
St. Bonaventure U, NY
St. Cloud State U, MN
St. Francis Xavier U, NS,
  Canada
St. Gregory's U, OK
Saint John's U, MN
Saint Joseph's Coll, IN
St. Lawrence U, NY
Saint Leo U, FL
St. Mary's Coll of Maryland,
  MD
St. Norbert Coll, WI
St. Philip's Coll, TX
St. Thomas Aquinas Coll,
  NY
Saint Xavier U, IL
Salem Comm Coll, NJ
Salve Regina U, RI
San Diego Mesa Coll, CA
San Diego State U, CA
San Francisco State U, CA
Santa Ana Coll, CA
Santa Barbara City Coll, CA
Santa Clara U, CA
Santa Rosa Jr Coll, CA
Sauk Valley Comm Coll, IL
Seattle Pacific U, WA
Seton Hall U, NJ
Seton Hill U, PA
Sewanee: The U of the
  South, TN

Shippensburg U of
  Pennsylvania, PA
Skagit Valley Coll, WA
Slippery Rock U of
  Pennsylvania, PA
Southern Adventist U, TN
Southern Illinois U
  Carbondale, IL
Southern Illinois U
  Edwardsville, IL
Southern Nazarene U, OK
Southern Oregon U, OR
Southern U and A&M Coll,
  LA
Southern Utah U, UT
Southwest Baptist U, MO
Southwestern Coll, KS
Southwestern U, TX
Spoon River Coll, IL
Springfield Coll, MA
State U of New York at
  Fredonia, NY
State U of New York Coll at
  Brockport, NY
State U of New York Coll at
  Cortland, NY
State U of New York Coll at
  Geneseo, NY
State U of New York Coll at
  Potsdam, NY
State U of New York Coll of
  Environmental Science
  and Forestry, NY
Stephen F. Austin State U,
  TX
Stetson U, FL
Stonehill Coll, MA
Sweet Briar Coll, VA
Syracuse U, NY
Taylor U, IN
Temple U, PA
Tennessee Wesleyan Coll,
  TN
Texas A&M U, TX
Texas A&M U–Corpus
  Christi, TX
Thiel Coll, PA
Towson U, MD
Trent U, ON, Canada
Trevecca Nazarene U, TN
Trinity Coll, CT
Trinity U, TX
Troy U, AL
Truman State U, MO
Tufts U, MA
Union Coll, NE
U at Albany, State U of New
  York, NY
U at Buffalo, the State U of
  New York, NY
The U of Akron, OH
The U of Alabama, AL
The U of Alabama in
  Huntsville, AL
The U of Arizona, AZ
U of Arkansas, AR
U of California, Berkeley,
  CA
U of California, Irvine, CA
U of California, Los Angeles,
  CA
U of California, Santa
  Barbara, CA
U of Central Florida, FL
U of Central Missouri, MO
U of Central Oklahoma, OK
U of Cincinnati, OH
U of Connecticut, CT
U of Dayton, OH
U of Delaware, DE
U of Dubuque, IA
U of Evansville, IN
The U of Findlay, OH
U of Great Falls, MT

U of Guelph, ON, Canada
U of Hartford, CT
U of Hawaii at Manoa, HI
U of Houston, TX
U of Illinois at Urbana–
  Champaign, IL
U of Kansas, KS
U of Kentucky, KY
The U of Maine at Augusta,
  ME
U of Maine at Machias, ME
U of Manitoba, MB, Canada
U of Mary Hardin-Baylor, TX
U of Maryland, Baltimore
  County, MD
U of Mary Washington, VA
U of Massachusetts Amherst,
  MA
U of Massachusetts Boston,
  MA
U of Massachusetts Lowell,
  MA
U of Miami, FL
U of Michigan, MI
U of Minnesota, Duluth, MN
U of Mississippi, MS
U of Missouri–Columbia,
  MO
U of Missouri–Kansas City,
  MO
U of Missouri–Rolla, MO
U of Nebraska at Kearney,
  NE
U of Nebraska at Omaha,
  NE
U of Nebraska–Lincoln, NE
U of New Brunswick
  Fredericton, NB, Canada
U of New England, ME
U of New Hampshire, NH
U of New Hampshire at
  Manchester, NH
U of New Haven, CT
U of New Mexico, NM
U of New Orleans, LA
The U of North Carolina at
  Asheville, NC
The U of North Carolina at
  Chapel Hill, NC
The U of North Carolina at
  Charlotte, NC
U of Northern British
  Columbia, BC, Canada
U of Northern Iowa, IA
U of North Florida, FL
U of Notre Dame, IN
U of Oregon, OR
U of Pennsylvania, PA
U of Pittsburgh, PA
U of Pittsburgh at Bradford,
  PA
U of Pittsburgh at
  Johnstown, PA
U of Portland, OR
U of Redlands, CA
U of Rhode Island, RI
U of Rio Grande, OH
U of St. Thomas, MN
U of St. Thomas, TX
U of San Diego, CA
U of San Francisco, CA
The U of Scranton, PA
U of South Carolina
  Beaufort, SC
U of South Carolina Upstate,
  SC
U of Southern Indiana, IN
The U of Tampa, FL
The U of Tennessee, TN
The U of Tennessee at
  Martin, TN
The U of Texas at Austin,
  TX

The U of Texas at El Paso,
  TX
The U of Texas at San
  Antonio, TX
U of the District of
  Columbia, DC
U of the Incarnate Word, TX
U of the Ozarks, AR
U of the Pacific, CA
U of Toronto, ON, Canada
U of Vermont, VT
U of Virginia, VA
The U of Virginia's Coll at
  Wise, VA
U of Washington, WA
U of West Georgia, GA
U of Wisconsin–Green Bay,
  WI
U of Wisconsin–La Crosse,
  WI
U of Wisconsin–Madison,
  WI
U of Wisconsin–Oshkosh,
  WI
U of Wisconsin–Platteville,
  WI
U of Wisconsin–Stevens
  Point, WI
U of Wyoming, WY
Upper Iowa U, IA
Urbana U, OH
Ursuline Coll, OH
Utica Coll, NY
Valdosta State U, GA
Vanguard U of Southern
  California, CA
Vassar Coll, NY
Ventura Coll, CA
Victor Valley Coll, CA
Villanova U, PA
Virginia Intermont Coll, VA
Wake Forest U, NC
Washburn U, KS
Washington & Jefferson Coll,
  PA
Washington and Lee U, VA
Wayne State Coll, NE
Wayne State U, MI
Wellesley Coll, MA
Wells Coll, NY
Wesley Coll, DE
West Chester U of
  Pennsylvania, PA
Western Connecticut State
  U, CT
Western Nebraska Comm
  Coll, NE
Western New England Coll,
  MA
Western Oregon U, OR
West Liberty State Coll, WV
West Los Angeles Coll, CA
Westminster Coll, PA
Westminster Coll, UT
West Texas A&M U, TX
West Virginia State U, WV
West Virginia Wesleyan Coll,
  WV
Wheaton Coll, IL
Whitman Coll, WA
Wichita State U, KS
Widener U, PA
Wilfrid Laurier U, ON,
  Canada
Wilkes U, PA
William Jewell Coll, MO
Wilson Coll, PA
Wofford Coll, SC
Worcester State Coll, MA
Wright State U, OH
Xavier U, OH
Yale U, CT

**BIOLOGY/
BIOTECHNOLOGY
LABORATORY
TECHNICIAN**
British Columbia Inst of
  Technology, BC, Canada
California State U,
  Sacramento, CA
Carleton U, ON, Canada
Foothill Coll, CA
Gannon U, PA
Hudson Valley Comm Coll,
  NY
Marywood U, PA
Middlesex Comm Coll, CT
Middlesex County Coll, NJ
Minnesota State U Mankato,
  MN
Niagara U, NY
Northeastern U, MA
Penn State Abington, PA
Penn State DuBois, PA
Penn State Fayette, The
  Eberly Campus, PA
Penn State Mont Alto, PA
Penn State Wilkes-Barre, PA
St. Cloud State U, MN
State U of New York at
  Fredonia, NY
State U of New York Coll at
  Brockport, NY
State U of New York Coll of
  Technology at Alfred, NY
U of Delaware, DE
U of New Haven, CT
U of the District of
  Columbia, DC
Westminster Coll, PA

**BIOLOGY TEACHER
EDUCATION**
Abilene Christian U, TX
Alma Coll, MI
Alvernia Coll, PA
Ancilla Coll, IN
Anderson U, SC
Baylor U, TX
Bethel U, MN
Bishop's U, QC, Canada
Brewton-Parker Coll, GA
Buena Vista U, IA
Carroll Coll, MT
Carroll Coll, WI
The Catholic U of America,
  DC
Charleston Southern U, SC
The Coll of Saint Rose, NY
Columbus State U, GA
Concordia U, NE
Cornerstone U, MI
Daemen Coll, NY
Delaware State U, DE
Eastern Mennonite U, VA
Eastern Michigan U, MI
Elmira Coll, NY
Fayetteville State U, NC
Fitchburg State Coll, MA
Florida Inst of Technology,
  FL
Framingham State Coll, MA
Franklin Coll, IN
Freed-Hardeman U, TN
Glenville State Coll, WV
Gustavus Adolphus Coll,
  MN
Harding U, AR
Hofstra U, NY
Hope Coll, MI
Houston Baptist U, TX
Hunter Coll of the City U of
  New York, NY
Husson Coll, ME
Illinois Wesleyan U, IL
Indiana U Bloomington, IN

Indiana U–Purdue U Fort
Wayne, IN
Indiana U Southeast, IN
Iona Coll, NY
Ithaca Coll, NY
John Brown U, AR
Johnson State Coll, VT
Kennesaw State U, GA
Kentucky Wesleyan Coll, KY
Keuka Coll, NY
Lebanon Valley Coll, PA
Le Moyne Coll, NY
Liberty U, VA
Lindenwood U, MO
Manhattanville Coll, NY
Marist Coll, NY
Marywood U, PA
McNeese State U, LA
Mercyhurst Coll, PA
Miami Dade Coll, FL
Minnesota State U
Moorhead, MN
Missouri State U, MO
Molloy Coll, NY
Montana State U–Billings,
MT
Moravian Coll, PA
Murray State U, KY
New York U, NY
Niagara U, NY
North Carolina State U, NC
North Dakota State U, ND
Northwest Nazarene U, ID
Ohio Wesleyan U, OH
Old Dominion U, VA
Pittsburg State U, KS
Rivier Coll, NH
Rocky Mountain Coll, MT
St. Bonaventure U, NY
St. Gregory's U, OK
Saint Xavier U, IL
Salve Regina U, RI
Seattle Pacific U, WA
Seton Hill U, PA
Southern U and A&M Coll,
LA
State U of New York Coll at
Brockport, NY
State U of New York Coll at
Cortland, NY
State U of New York Coll at
Potsdam, NY
State U of New York Coll of
Environmental Science
and Forestry, NY
Syracuse U, NY
Taylor U, IN
Tennessee Wesleyan Coll,
TN
Trevecca Nazarene U, TN
Union Coll, NE
U at Albany, State U of New
York, NY
The U of Akron, OH
The U of Arizona, AZ
U of Arkansas at Fort Smith,
AR
U of Delaware, DE
U of Dubuque, IA
U of Evansville, IN
U of Great Falls, MT
U of Maine at Machias, ME
U of Missouri–Columbia,
MO
U of Nebraska–Lincoln, NE
U of Pittsburgh at
Johnstown, PA
U of Rio Grande, OH
U of St. Thomas, MN
The U of Tennessee at
Martin, TN
U of the Ozarks, AR
U of Washington, WA
U of West Georgia, GA

Utica Coll, NY
Virginia Intermont Coll, VA
Wayne State Coll, NE
West Chester U of
Pennsylvania, PA
Westminster Coll, UT
Widener U, PA
Xavier U, OH

BIOMATHEMATICS AND BIOINFORMATICS RELATED
U of California, Los Angeles,
CA
The U of Scranton, PA

BIOMEDICAL/MEDICAL ENGINEERING
Brown U, RI
Carnegie Mellon U, PA
The Catholic U of America,
DC
Cedar Crest Coll, PA
Clemson U, SC
Dalhousie U, NS, Canada
Duke U, NC
Eastern Nazarene Coll, MA
Florida International U, FL
Hofstra U, NY
Indiana U–Purdue U
Indianapolis, IN
Lehigh U, PA
LeTourneau U, TX
Marquette U, WI
Michigan State U, MI
North Carolina State U, NC
Oklahoma State U, OK
Oral Roberts U, OK
Penn State Abington, PA
Penn State DuBois, PA
Penn State Fayette, The
Eberly Campus, PA
Penn State Mont Alto, PA
Penn State Wilkes-Barre, PA
Rensselaer Polytechnic Inst,
NY
Rice U, TX
Rochester Inst of
Technology, NY
Rutgers, The State U of New
Jersey, New Brunswick, NJ
Syracuse U, NY
Texas A&M U, TX
Trinity Coll, CT
The U of Akron, OH
U of California, Berkeley,
CA
U of California, Irvine, CA
U of California, Los Angeles,
CA
U of Central Oklahoma, OK
U of Connecticut, CT
U of Guelph, ON, Canada
U of Hartford, CT
U of Houston, TX
U of Illinois at Urbana–
Champaign, IL
U of Miami, FL
U of Nebraska–Lincoln, NE
U of Pennsylvania, PA
U of Pittsburgh, PA
U of Rhode Island, RI
The U of Texas at Austin,
TX
U of the Pacific, CA
U of Toronto, ON, Canada
U of Virginia, VA
U of Wisconsin–Madison,
WI
Western New England Coll,
MA
Wright State U, OH
Yale U, CT

BIOMEDICAL SCIENCES
Brock U, ON, Canada
Brown U, RI
Cedar Crest Coll, PA
Emory U, GA
Florida Inst of Technology,
FL
Framingham State Coll, MA
Keuka Coll, NY
Marist Coll, NY
Marquette U, WI
Rutgers, The State U of New
Jersey, New Brunswick, NJ
St. Cloud State U, MN
St. Gregory's U, OK
State U of New York at
Fredonia, NY
Texas A&M U, TX
Texas A&M U–Corpus
Christi, TX
U of Guelph, ON, Canada
U of Michigan, MI
U of Mississippi, MS
U of New England, ME
U of Pennsylvania, PA
U of Wisconsin–Eau Claire,
WI
U of Wisconsin–Green Bay,
WI

BIOMEDICAL TECHNOLOGY
Alvernia Coll, PA
Caldwell Comm Coll and
Tech Inst, NC
Cedar Crest Coll, PA
Chattahoochee Tech Coll,
GA
Florida Comm Coll at
Jacksonville, FL
Hillsborough Comm Coll, FL
Howard Comm Coll, MD
Indiana U–Purdue U
Indianapolis, IN
Madisonville Comm Coll,
KY
Miami Dade Coll, FL
Oral Roberts U, OK
Penn State DuBois, PA
Penn State Fayette, The
Eberly Campus, PA
St. Philip's Coll, TX
Santa Barbara City Coll, CA
Schoolcraft Coll, MI
Southeast Tech Inst, SD
Spokane Comm Coll, WA
Stark State Coll of
Technology, OH
U of New Hampshire, NH
Washburn U, KS
Wright State U, OH

BIOMETRY/BIOMETRICS
Cornell U, NY
Rutgers, The State U of New
Jersey, New Brunswick, NJ

BIOPHYSICS
Brandeis U, MA
Brown U, RI
Carnegie Mellon U, PA
Claremont McKenna Coll,
CA
Cornell U, NY
Freed-Hardeman U, TN
Hampden-Sydney Coll, VA
Haverford Coll, PA
Rensselaer Polytechnic Inst,
NY
St. Bonaventure U, NY
St. Lawrence U, NY
State U of New York Coll at
Geneseo, NY
Syracuse U, NY

Temple U, PA
U at Buffalo, the State U of
New York, NY
U of California, Los Angeles,
CA
U of Connecticut, CT
U of Guelph, ON, Canada
U of Illinois at Urbana–
Champaign, IL
U of Miami, FL
U of Michigan, MI
U of New Brunswick
Fredericton, NB, Canada
U of Pennsylvania, PA
The U of Scranton, PA
U of Southern Indiana, IN
U of Toronto, ON, Canada
Whitman Coll, WA

BIOPSYCHOLOGY
Carnegie Mellon U, PA
The Coll of William and
Mary, VA
Immaculata U, PA
Lehigh U, PA
Morningside Coll, IA
Rochester Inst of
Technology, NY
U of California, Santa
Barbara, CA
U of Pittsburgh at
Johnstown, PA

BIOSTATISTICS
U at Buffalo, the State U of
New York, NY
U of California, Los Angeles,
CA
The U of North Carolina at
Chapel Hill, NC
U of Washington, WA

BIOTECHNOLOGY
British Columbia Inst of
Technology, BC, Canada
Brock U, ON, Canada
Burlington County Coll, NJ
Calvin Coll, MI
Coll of The Albemarle, NC
Delaware State U, DE
Dixie State Coll of Utah, UT
East Stroudsburg U of
Pennsylvania, PA
Fitchburg State Coll, MA
Florida Gulf Coast U, FL
Framingham State Coll, MA
Howard Comm Coll, MD
Lackawanna Coll, PA
Manhattan Coll, NY
Montana State U, MT
North Dakota State U, ND
The Ohio State U, OH
Rochester Inst of
Technology, NY
Roosevelt U, IL
Rutgers, The State U of New
Jersey, New Brunswick, NJ
Santa Barbara City Coll, CA
State U of New York Coll at
Brockport, NY
State U of New York Coll of
Environmental Science
and Forestry, NY
U at Buffalo, the State U of
New York, NY
U of California, Los Angeles,
CA
U of Delaware, DE
U of Illinois at Urbana–
Champaign, IL
U of Nebraska at Omaha,
NE
U of Northern Iowa, IA
Ursuline Coll, OH

West Texas A&M U, TX
Wilfrid Laurier U, ON,
Canada
Worcester State Coll, MA

BIOTECHNOLOGY RESEARCH
El Centro Coll, TX
Hunter Coll of the City U of
New York, NY
Kennesaw State U, GA

BOILERMAKING
Ivy Tech Comm Coll–
Southwest, IN

BOTANY/PLANT BIOLOGY
Ball State U, IN
Brandon U, MB, Canada
Carleton U, ON, Canada
Coll of the Atlantic, ME
Cornell U, NY
Dixie State Coll of Utah, UT
East Central Coll, MO
El Camino Coll, CA
Idaho State U, ID
Lassen Comm Coll District,
CA
Michigan State U, MI
Minnesota State U Mankato,
MN
North Carolina State U, NC
North Dakota State U, ND
Northern Michigan U, MI
The Ohio State U, OH
Ohio Wesleyan U, OH
Oklahoma State U, OK
Rutgers, The State U of New
Jersey, Newark, NJ
St. Cloud State U, MN
Saint Xavier U, IL
San Francisco State U, CA
Santa Rosa Jr Coll, CA
Southern Illinois U
Carbondale, IL
Southern Maine Comm Coll,
ME
Southern Utah U, UT
Spoon River Coll, IL
State U of New York Coll of
Environmental Science
and Forestry, NY
Texas A&M U, TX
The U of Akron, OH
U of California, Berkeley,
CA
U of California, Los Angeles,
CA
U of Delaware, DE
U of Great Falls, MT
U of Hawaii at Manoa, HI
U of Illinois at Urbana–
Champaign, IL
U of Manitoba, MB, Canada
U of Michigan, MI
U of New Brunswick
Fredericton, NB, Canada
U of New Hampshire, NH
U of Northern British
Columbia, BC, Canada
The U of Tennessee, TN
The U of Texas at Austin,
TX
The U of Texas at El Paso,
TX
U of Toronto, ON, Canada
U of Vermont, VT
U of Washington, WA
U of Wisconsin–Madison,
WI
U of Wyoming, WY

Itasca Comm Coll, MN
Ithaca Coll, NY
Ivy Tech Comm Coll–Kokomo, IN
Ivy Tech Comm Coll–Southwest, IN
Ivy Tech Comm Coll–Wabash Valley, IN
Jacksonville U, FL
James H. Faulkner State Comm Coll, AL
Jamestown Comm Coll, NY
Jefferson Comm and Tech Coll, KY
Jefferson Comm Coll, OH
John Brown U, AR
Johnson & Wales U, CO
Johnson & Wales U, FL
Johnson & Wales U, NC
Johnson & Wales U, RI
Johnson State Coll, VT
Kansas State U, KS
Kellogg Comm Coll, MI
Kendall Coll, IL
Kennesaw State U, GA
Kentucky Wesleyan Coll, KY
Keuka Coll, NY
Kingsborough Comm Coll of the City U of New York, NY
King's Coll, PA
The King's U Coll, AB, Canada
Kutztown U of Pennsylvania, PA
Kuyper Coll, MI
Lackawanna Coll, PA
LaGrange Coll, GA
Lake City Comm Coll, FL
Lake Erie Coll, OH
Lakeland Coll, WI
Lake-Sumter Comm Coll, FL
Lake Superior State U, MI
Lamar State Coll–Orange, TX
Lamar U, TX
Langston U, OK
Lassen Comm Coll District, CA
Lebanon Valley Coll, PA
Lee Coll, TX
Lehigh U, PA
Le Moyne Coll, NY
LeTourneau U, TX
Lewis U, IL
Liberty U, VA
Lincoln Land Comm Coll, IL
Lincoln U, PA
Lindenwood U, MO
Long Beach City Coll, CA
Long Island U, Brooklyn Campus, NY
Loras Coll, IA
Loyola Marymount U, CA
Loyola U Chicago, IL
Loyola U New Orleans, LA
Lynchburg Coll, VA
Lynn U, FL
MacMurray Coll, IL
Macomb Comm Coll, MI
Madisonville Comm Coll, KY
Maine Maritime Academy, ME
Manhattanville Coll, NY
Marian Coll, IN
Marietta Coll, OH
Marist Coll, NY
Marquette U, WI
Marshall U, WV
Marymount Manhattan Coll, NY
Marymount U, VA
Marywood U, PA

Massachusetts Coll of Liberal Arts, MA
Massasoit Comm Coll, MA
McDaniel Coll, MD
McNeese State U, LA
Mercyhurst Coll, PA
Metropolitan Coll of New York, NY
Metropolitan Comm Coll–Longview, MO
Metropolitan Comm Coll–Penn Valley, MO
Miami Dade Coll, FL
Michigan State U, MI
Middlesex Comm Coll, CT
Middlesex County Coll, NJ
Middle Tennessee State U, TN
Midland Lutheran Coll, NE
Millersville U of Pennsylvania, PA
Minnesota School of Business–St. Cloud, MN
Minnesota State U Mankato, MN
Minnesota State U Moorhead, MN
MiraCosta Coll, CA
Missouri State U, MO
Missouri State U–West Plains, MO
Mitchell Coll, CT
Mohawk Valley Comm Coll, NY
Molloy Coll, NY
Monmouth Coll, IL
Monmouth U, NJ
Montana State U–Billings, MT
Montana Tech of The U of Montana, MT
Moorpark Coll, CA
Moravian Coll, PA
Morningside Coll, IA
Morton Coll, IL
Mount Saint Vincent U, NS, Canada
Mount Union Coll, OH
Murray State U, KY
Muscatine Comm Coll, IA
Nassau Comm Coll, NY
National-Louis U, IL
Neumann Coll, PA
New Hampshire Comm Tech Coll, Nashua/Claremont, NH
New Jersey City U, NJ
New Mexico Jr Coll, NM
New River Comm Coll, VA
New York U, NY
Niagara U, NY
Nipissing U, ON, Canada
North Carolina State U, NC
North Central Coll, IL
North Central Missouri Coll, MO
North Central Texas Coll, TX
North Dakota State U, ND
Northeastern U, MA
Northern Illinois U, IL
Northern Michigan U, MI
Northern State U, SD
North Georgia Coll & State U, GA
Northland Comm and Tech Coll–Thief River Falls, MN
Northwestern Coll, MN
Northwestern Oklahoma State U, OK
Northwest Nazarene U, ID
Northwood U, MI
Northwood U, Florida Campus, FL

Northwood U, Texas Campus, TX
Notre Dame Coll, OH
Notre Dame de Namur U, CA
Nova Southeastern U, FL
Ocean County Coll, NJ
Odessa Coll, TX
Oglethorpe U, GA
The Ohio State U, OH
The Ohio State U at Lima, OH
Ohio Wesleyan U, OH
Old Dominion U, VA
Oral Roberts U, OK
Oregon Inst of Technology, OR
Otterbein Coll, OH
Our Lady of the Lake U of San Antonio, TX
Ozarks Tech Comm Coll, MO
Paris Jr Coll, TX
Park U, MO
Paul Quinn Coll, TX
Penn State DuBois, PA
Penn State Fayette, The Eberly Campus, PA
Penn State Mont Alto, PA
Penn State Wilkes-Barre, PA
Phoenix Coll, AZ
Piedmont Coll, GA
Pima Comm Coll, AZ
Pine Manor Coll, MA
Pittsburg State U, KS
Point Loma Nazarene U, CA
Portland State U, OR
Prairie View A&M U, TX
Presbyterian Coll, SC
Pueblo Comm Coll, CO
Purdue U North Central, IN
Queens U of Charlotte, NC
Quincy Coll, MA
Ramapo Coll of New Jersey, NJ
Redeemer U Coll, ON, Canada
Reinhardt Coll, GA
Rensselaer Polytechnic Inst, NY
Rhodes Coll, TN
Rice U, TX
The Richard Stockton Coll of New Jersey, NJ
Richland Comm Coll, IL
Richmond Comm Coll, NC
Ripon Coll, WI
Rivier Coll, NH
Rochester Inst of Technology, NY
Rockford Coll, IL
Rockhurst U, MO
Rockingham Comm Coll, NC
Rocky Mountain Coll, MT
Roosevelt U, IL
Rose State Coll, OK
Rowan U, NJ
Roxbury Comm Coll, MA
Rutgers, The State U of New Jersey, Newark, NJ
Rutgers, The State U of New Jersey, New Brunswick, NJ
Ryerson U, ON, Canada
Saginaw Valley State U, MI
St. Bonaventure U, NY
St. Cloud State U, MN
St. Cloud Tech Coll, MN
St. Francis Xavier U, NS, Canada
St. Gregory's U, OK
Saint John's U, MN
Saint Leo U, FL
St. Louis Comm Coll at Florissant Valley, MO

St. Norbert Coll, WI
St. Philip's Coll, TX
St. Thomas Aquinas Coll, NY
Salem Comm Coll, NJ
Salve Regina U, RI
San Diego Mesa Coll, CA
San Diego State U, CA
San Francisco State U, CA
Santa Ana Coll, CA
Santa Barbara City Coll, CA
Santa Rosa Jr Coll, CA
Sauk Valley Comm Coll, IL
Schoolcraft Coll, MI
Scottsdale Comm Coll, AZ
Seattle Pacific U, WA
Seminole Comm Coll, FL
Seton Hall U, NJ
Seton Hill U, PA
Shasta Coll, CA
Shippensburg U of Pennsylvania, PA
Skagit Valley Coll, WA
Slippery Rock U of Pennsylvania, PA
Southeast Tech Inst, SD
Southern Adventist U, TN
Southern Illinois U Carbondale, IL
Southern Illinois U Edwardsville, IL
Southern Maine Comm Coll, ME
Southern Nazarene U, OK
Southern Oregon U, OR
Southern U and A&M Coll, LA
Southern Utah U, UT
South Piedmont Comm Coll, NC
South U, GA
Southwestern Coll, KS
Southwestern Indian Polytechnic Inst, NM
Southwestern Michigan Coll, MI
Southwestern U, TX
Spalding U, KY
Spokane Comm Coll, WA
Spoon River Coll, IL
Springfield Coll, MA
Springfield Coll in Illinois, IL
Stark State Coll of Technology, OH
State U of New York at Fredonia, NY
State U of New York Coll at Brockport, NY
State U of New York Coll at Geneseo, NY
State U of New York Coll at Potsdam, NY
State U of New York Coll of Technology at Alfred, NY
State U of New York Coll of Technology at Canton, NY
Stephen F. Austin State U, TX
Stetson U, FL
Stonehill Coll, MA
Surry Comm Coll, NC
Sussex County Comm Coll, NJ
Syracuse U, NY
Tallahassee Comm Coll, FL
Taylor U, IN
Temple U, PA
Tennessee Wesleyan Coll, TN
Texas A&M U, TX
Texas A&M U–Corpus Christi, TX
Thiel Coll, PA
Tidewater Comm Coll, VA

Towson U, MD
Trent U, ON, Canada
Trevecca Nazarene U, TN
Trinity U, TX
Trocaire Coll, NY
Troy U, AL
Truman State U, MO
Tunxis Comm Coll, CT
Union Coll, NE
U at Albany, State U of New York, NY
U at Buffalo, the State U of New York, NY
The U of Akron, OH
The U of Akron–Wayne Coll, OH
The U of Alabama, AL
The U of Alabama in Huntsville, AL
U of Alaska Anchorage, AK
U of Arkansas, AR
U of Arkansas at Fort Smith, AR
U of Baltimore, MD
U of California, Berkeley, CA
U of California, Los Angeles, CA
U of Central Florida, FL
U of Central Missouri, MO
U of Central Oklahoma, OK
U of Cincinnati, OH
U of Dayton, OH
U of Delaware, DE
U of Dubuque, IA
U of Evansville, IN
The U of Findlay, OH
U of Great Falls, MT
U of Hartford, CT
U of Hawaii–West Oahu, HI
U of Houston, TX
U of Illinois at Urbana–Champaign, IL
The U of Maine at Augusta, ME
U of Maine at Machias, ME
U of Manitoba, MB, Canada
U of Mary Hardin-Baylor, TX
U of Maryland, Baltimore County, MD
U of Mary Washington, VA
U of Massachusetts Amherst, MA
U of Massachusetts Boston, MA
U of Massachusetts Lowell, MA
U of Miami, FL
U of Michigan, MI
U of Minnesota, Duluth, MN
U of Mississippi, MS
U of Missouri–Columbia, MO
U of Missouri–Kansas City, MO
U of Missouri–Rolla, MO
U of Nebraska at Kearney, NE
U of Nebraska at Omaha, NE
U of Nebraska–Lincoln, NE
U of New Brunswick Fredericton, NB, Canada
U of New England, ME
U of New Hampshire, NH
U of New Hampshire at Manchester, NH
U of New Haven, CT
U of New Mexico, NM
U of New Orleans, LA
The U of North Carolina at Asheville, NC
The U of North Carolina at Chapel Hill, NC

BUSINESS/MANAGERIAL ECONOMICS

Alabama A&M U, AL
American International Coll, MA
Anderson U, IN
Auburn U Montgomery, AL
Augsburg Coll, MN
Aurora U, IL
Ball State U, IN
Baylor U, TX
Bentley Coll, MA
Bishop's U, QC, Canada
Bradley U, IL
Brock U, ON, Canada
Buena Vista U, IA
California State U, Fullerton, CA
California State U, San Bernardino, CA
Cape Breton U, NS, Canada
Cardinal Stritch U, WI
Carnegie Mellon U, PA
Carroll Coll, MT
Carson-Newman Coll, TN
Cedar Crest Coll, PA
Charleston Southern U, SC
Christopher Newport U, VA
Coll of Mount Saint Vincent, NY
Coll of the Desert, CA
Columbus State U, GA
Dallas Baptist U, TX
Delaware State U, DE
DePaul U, IL
Eastern Michigan U, MI
Elmira Coll, NY
Emory U, GA
Fairleigh Dickinson U, Coll at Florham, NJ
Fairleigh Dickinson U, Metropolitan Campus, NJ
Fayetteville State U, NC
Fort Hays State U, KS
Framingham State Coll, MA
Freed-Hardeman U, TN
The George Washington U, DC
Georgia Coll & State U, GA
Gonzaga U, WA
Grambling State U, LA
Green Mountain Coll, VT
Gustavus Adolphus Coll, MN
Hampden-Sydney Coll, VA
Hofstra U, NY
Hope Coll, MI
Houston Baptist U, TX
Huntington U, IN
Indiana U Bloomington, IN
Indiana U–Purdue U Fort Wayne, IN
Indiana U Southeast, IN
Ithaca Coll, NY
Kutztown U of Pennsylvania, PA
Lake Superior State U, MI
Lehigh U, PA
Lewis U, IL
Loyola U Chicago, IL
Loyola U New Orleans, LA
Marquette U, WI
Marshall U, WV
Middle Tennessee State U, TN
Montana State U–Billings, MT
New York U, NY
Niagara U, NY
Northern State U, SD
North Georgia Coll & State U, GA
Northwood U, MI

Notre Dame de Namur U, CA
Occidental Coll, CA
Oglethorpe U, GA
The Ohio State U, OH
Ohio Wesleyan U, OH
Oklahoma State U, OK
Old Dominion U, VA
Otterbein Coll, OH
Park U, MO
Penn State Abington, PA
Penn State DuBois, PA
Penn State Fayette, The Eberly Campus, PA
Penn State Mont Alto, PA
Penn State Wilkes-Barre, PA
Randolph-Macon Coll, VA
Roosevelt U, IL
Saginaw Valley State U, MI
St. Bonaventure U, NY
Seton Hall U, NJ
Seton Hill U, PA
Southern Illinois U Carbondale, IL
Southern Illinois U Edwardsville, IL
Southern U and A&M Coll, LA
State U of New York Coll at Potsdam, NY
State U of New York Coll of Technology at Canton, NY
Stephen F. Austin State U, TX
Stetson U, FL
The U of Alabama, AL
U of Alaska Anchorage, AK
The U of Arizona, AZ
U of Arkansas, AR
U of California, Los Angeles, CA
U of California, Santa Barbara, CA
U of Central Florida, FL
U of Central Oklahoma, OK
U of Dayton, OH
U of Delaware, DE
U of Evansville, IN
U of Hartford, CT
U of Hawaii at Manoa, HI
U of Kentucky, KY
U of Manitoba, MB, Canada
U of Miami, FL
U of Mississippi, MS
U of Missouri–Columbia, MO
U of Nebraska at Omaha, NE
U of Nebraska–Lincoln, NE
U of New Brunswick Fredericton, NB, Canada
U of New Haven, CT
U of New Orleans, LA
The U of North Carolina at Charlotte, NC
U of North Florida, FL
U of Pittsburgh at Johnstown, PA
U of San Diego, CA
The U of Tennessee, TN
The U of Tennessee at Martin, TN
The U of Texas at San Antonio, TX
U of West Georgia, GA
U of Wisconsin–Platteville, WI
U of Wyoming, WY
Urbana U, OH
Utica Coll, NY
Valdosta State U, GA
Villanova U, PA
Wayne State Coll, NE

West Chester U of Pennsylvania, PA
West Liberty State Coll, WV
Westminster Coll, UT
West Texas A&M U, TX
West Virginia Wesleyan Coll, WV
Wheaton Coll, IL
Widener U, PA
Wofford Coll, SC
Wright State U, OH
Xavier U, OH

BUSINESS OPERATIONS SUPPORT AND SECRETARIAL SERVICES RELATED

Ancilla Coll, IN
East Central Coll, MO
Hillsborough Comm Coll, FL
The U of Akron, OH

BUSINESS STATISTICS

Alabama A&M U, AL
Baylor U, TX
Southern Oregon U, OR
U of Central Missouri, MO
U of Houston, TX

BUSINESS SYSTEMS NETWORKING/ TELECOMMUNICATIONS

Caldwell Comm Coll and Tech Inst, NC

BUSINESS TEACHER EDUCATION

Albany State U, GA
American International Coll, MA
Bainbridge Coll, GA
Ball State U, IN
Baylor U, TX
Bethel Coll, IN
Buena Vista U, IA
Buffalo State Coll, State U of New York, NY
Carson-Newman Coll, TN
Clayton State U, GA
Concordia Coll–New York, NY
Concordia U, NE
Concord U, WV
Delaware State U, DE
East Carolina U, NC
Eastern Michigan U, MI
Fayetteville State U, NC
Fort Hays State U, KS
Gannon U, PA
Geneva Coll, PA
Glenville State Coll, WV
Goshen Coll, IN
Grambling State U, LA
Harrisburg Area Comm Coll, PA
Henderson State U, AR
Hofstra U, NY
Huntington U, IN
Illinois State U, IL
Indiana U of Pennsylvania, PA
John Brown U, AR
Johnson & Wales U, CO
Lakeland Coll, WI
Liberty U, VA
Lindenwood U, MO
McNeese State U, LA
Mercyhurst Coll, PA
Middle Tennessee State U, TN
Midland Lutheran Coll, NE
Missouri State U, MO
Morningside Coll, IA

Mount Vernon Nazarene U, OH
Murray State U, KY
New Mexico Jr Coll, NM
Niagara U, NY
Northern Michigan U, MI
Northern State U, SD
Northwestern Oklahoma State U, OK
Ohio Wesleyan U, OH
Paris Jr Coll, TX
Southern Utah U, UT
Spoon River Coll, IL
Temple U, PA
Troy U, AL
Union Coll, NE
The U of Akron, OH
U of Central Florida, FL
U of Central Missouri, MO
U of Central Oklahoma, OK
The U of Findlay, OH
U of Illinois at Urbana–Champaign, IL
U of Maine at Machias, ME
U of Missouri–Columbia, MO
U of Nebraska at Kearney, NE
U of Nebraska–Lincoln, NE
U of New Brunswick Fredericton, NB, Canada
U of Northern Iowa, IA
U of Rio Grande, OH
U of Southern Indiana, IN
The U of Tennessee, TN
The U of Tennessee at Martin, TN
U of the District of Columbia, DC
U of the Ozarks, AR
U of West Georgia, GA
Upper Iowa U, IA
Utica Coll, NY
Valdosta State U, GA
Washburn U, KS
Wayne State Coll, NE
West Virginia State U, WV
Wright State U, OH

CABINETMAKING AND MILLWORK

British Columbia Inst of Technology, BC, Canada
Ivy Tech Comm Coll–Kokomo, IN
Ivy Tech Comm Coll–Southwest, IN
Ivy Tech Comm Coll–Wabash Valley, IN
Macomb Comm Coll, MI

CAD/CADD DRAFTING/ DESIGN TECHNOLOGY

Alexandria Tech Coll, MN
The Art Inst of Pittsburgh, PA
Brown Mackie Coll–Salina, KS
Eastern Michigan U, MI
Johnson & Wales U, RI
St. Philip's Coll, TX
Waubonsee Comm Coll, IL
West Virginia State Comm and Tech Coll, WV

CANADIAN STUDIES

Acadia U, NS, Canada
Athabasca U, AB, Canada
Bishop's U, QC, Canada
Brandon U, MB, Canada
Brock U, ON, Canada
Carleton U, ON, Canada
Concordia U Coll of Alberta, AB, Canada

Dalhousie U, NS, Canada
Duke U, NC
Franklin Coll, IN
Queen's U at Kingston, ON, Canada
St. Francis Xavier U, NS, Canada
St. Lawrence U, NY
Sterling Coll, VT
Trent U, ON, Canada
U of Manitoba, MB, Canada
U of New Brunswick Fredericton, NB, Canada
U of Northern British Columbia, BC, Canada
U of Toronto, ON, Canada
U of Vermont, VT
U of Washington, WA
Wilfrid Laurier U, ON, Canada

CARDIOVASCULAR TECHNOLOGY

British Columbia Inst of Technology, BC, Canada
Bunker Hill Comm Coll, MA
Caldwell Comm Coll and Tech Inst, NC
El Centro Coll, TX
Harrisburg Area Comm Coll, PA
Howard Comm Coll, MD
Molloy Coll, NY
Nebraska Methodist Coll, NE
St. Cloud Tech Coll, MN
Southeast Tech Inst, SD
Southern Maine Comm Coll, ME
Valencia Comm Coll, FL

CARIBBEAN STUDIES

Hofstra U, NY
U of Miami, FL

CARPENTRY

Alexandria Tech Coll, MN
British Columbia Inst of Technology, BC, Canada
Coahoma Comm Coll, MS
Comm Coll of Allegheny County, PA
Delaware Tech & Comm Coll, Jack F. Owens Campus, DE
Fresno City Coll, CA
Fulton-Montgomery Comm Coll, NY
Idaho State U, ID
Illinois Valley Comm Coll, IL
Ivy Tech Comm Coll–Southwest, IN
Ivy Tech Comm Coll–Wabash Valley, IN
Lassen Comm Coll District, CA
Long Beach City Coll, CA
Maui Comm Coll, HI
Minnesota State Coll–Southeast Tech, MN
Mohawk Valley Comm Coll, NY
New Mexico Jr Coll, NM
North Central Missouri Coll, MO
Rockingham Comm Coll, NC
St. Cloud Tech Coll, MN
Southern Maine Comm Coll, ME
Southern Utah U, UT
Spokane Comm Coll, WA
State U of New York Coll of Technology at Alfred, NY
State U of New York Coll of Technology at Canton, NY

The U of Montana-Helena Coll of Technology, MT

CARTOGRAPHY
Alexandria Tech Coll, MN
Ball State U, IN
Dixie State Coll of Utah, UT
Houston Comm Coll System, TX
Kennesaw State U, GA
Missouri State U, MO
Queen's U at Kingston, ON, Canada
Texas A&M U, TX
Texas A&M U–Corpus Christi, TX
The U of Akron, OH
U of Wisconsin–Madison, WI
U of Wisconsin–Platteville, WI

CELL AND MOLECULAR BIOLOGY
Marymount U, VA
Missouri State U, MO
Oklahoma State U, OK
State U of New York Coll at Brockport, NY
Texas A&M U, TX
U of California, Berkeley, CA
U of California, Los Angeles, CA
U of Colorado at Boulder, CO
U of Illinois at Urbana–Champaign, IL
The U of Tennessee at Martin, TN

CELL BIOLOGY AND ANATOMICAL SCIENCES RELATED
Brandeis U, MA
Rutgers, The State U of New Jersey, New Brunswick, NJ
U of Arkansas, AR
U of Connecticut, CT
U of Kentucky, KY
Washington & Jefferson Coll, PA
Yale U, CT

CELL BIOLOGY AND ANATOMY
Montana State U, MT

CELL BIOLOGY AND HISTOLOGY
Ball State U, IN
Colby Coll, ME
The Coll of Saint Rose, NY
Cornell U, NY
Lindenwood U, MO
Rutgers, The State U of New Jersey, New Brunswick, NJ
San Francisco State U, CA
State U of New York Coll at Brockport, NY
The U of Arizona, AZ
U of California, Santa Barbara, CA
U of Illinois at Urbana–Champaign, IL
U of Michigan, MI
U of Minnesota, Duluth, MN
U of New Hampshire, NH
U of Washington, WA
U of Wisconsin–Madison, WI
William Jewell Coll, MO

CELTIC LANGUAGES
U of California, Berkeley, CA

CERAMIC ARTS AND CERAMICS
Anderson U, SC
Ball State U, IN
California State U, Fullerton, CA
The Cleveland Inst of Art, OH
Coe Coll, IA
Coll of the Atlantic, ME
Concord U, WV
Dixie State Coll of Utah, UT
Franklin Pierce U, NH
Glendale Comm Coll, CA
Grossmont Coll, CA
Hofstra U, NY
Indiana U Bloomington, IN
Lassen Comm Coll District, CA
Maine Coll of Art, ME
McNeese State U, LA
Minnesota State U Mankato, MN
Minnesota State U Moorhead, MN
Northwest Nazarene U, ID
NSCAD U, NS, Canada
The Ohio State U, OH
Pratt Inst, NY
Rochester Inst of Technology, NY
Rutgers, The State U of New Jersey, New Brunswick, NJ
St. Cloud State U, MN
Salve Regina U, RI
School of the Art Inst of Chicago, IL
Seton Hill U, PA
State U of New York Coll at Brockport, NY
Syracuse U, NY
Temple U, PA
The U of Akron, OH
U of Hartford, CT
U of Kansas, KS
U of Miami, FL
U of Michigan, MI
U of Oregon, OR
The U of Texas at El Paso, TX
U of the District of Columbia, DC
U of Washington, WA
Ventura Coll, CA
West Virginia Wesleyan Coll, WV

CERAMIC SCIENCES AND ENGINEERING
Clemson U, SC
Hocking Coll, OH
The Ohio State U, OH
Rutgers, The State U of New Jersey, New Brunswick, NJ
U of Missouri–Rolla, MO
U of Washington, WA

CHEMICAL ENGINEERING
Ball State U, IN
Bethel Coll, IN
Brevard Comm Coll, FL
Brown U, RI
Burlington County Coll, NJ
Calvin Coll, MI
Carlow U, PA
Carnegie Mellon U, PA
Chattanooga State Tech Comm Coll, TN
Clemson U, SC

Cornell U, NY
Dalhousie U, NS, Canada
Delaware Tech & Comm Coll, Jack F. Owens Campus, DE
Florida Inst of Technology, FL
Florida International U, FL
Geneva Coll, PA
Gloucester County Coll, NJ
Itasca Comm Coll, MN
Kansas State U, KS
Lamar U, TX
Lehigh U, PA
Manhattan Coll, NY
Michigan State U, MI
Montana State U, MT
Murray State U, KY
North Carolina State U, NC
Northeastern U, MA
The Ohio State U, OH
Oklahoma State U, OK
Penn State Abington, PA
Penn State DuBois, PA
Penn State Fayette, The Eberly Campus, PA
Penn State Mont Alto, PA
Penn State Wilkes-Barre, PA
Prairie View A&M U, TX
Queen's U at Kingston, ON, Canada
Rensselaer Polytechnic Inst, NY
Rice U, TX
Rowan U, NJ
Rutgers, The State U of New Jersey, New Brunswick, NJ
Ryerson U, ON, Canada
St. Louis Comm Coll at Florissant Valley, MO
State U of New York Coll of Environmental Science and Forestry, NY
Syracuse U, NY
Texas A&M U, TX
Thiel Coll, PA
Tufts U, MA
U at Buffalo, the State U of New York, NY
The U of Akron, OH
The U of Alabama, AL
The U of Alabama in Huntsville, AL
The U of Arizona, AZ
U of Arkansas, AR
U of California, Berkeley, CA
U of California, Irvine, CA
U of California, Los Angeles, CA
U of California, Santa Barbara, CA
U of Cincinnati, OH
U of Colorado at Boulder, CO
U of Connecticut, CT
U of Dayton, OH
U of Delaware, DE
U of Guelph, ON, Canada
U of Houston, TX
U of Illinois at Urbana–Champaign, IL
U of Kansas, KS
U of Kentucky, KY
U of Maryland, Baltimore County, MD
U of Massachusetts Amherst, MA
U of Massachusetts Lowell, MA
U of Michigan, MI
U of Minnesota, Duluth, MN
U of Mississippi, MS

U of Missouri–Columbia, MO
U of Missouri–Rolla, MO
U of Nebraska–Lincoln, NE
U of New Brunswick Fredericton, NB, Canada
U of New Hampshire, NH
U of New Haven, CT
U of New Mexico, NM
U of Notre Dame, IN
U of Pennsylvania, PA
U of Pittsburgh, PA
U of Rhode Island, RI
The U of Tennessee, TN
The U of Texas at Austin, TX
U of the District of Columbia, DC
U of Toronto, ON, Canada
U of Virginia, VA
U of Washington, WA
U of Wisconsin–Madison, WI
U of Wyoming, WY
Villanova U, PA
Washington and Lee U, VA
Wayne State U, MI
Westchester Comm Coll, NY
West Virginia State U, WV
Widener U, PA
Xavier U, OH
Yale U, CT

CHEMICAL PHYSICS
Carnegie Mellon U, PA
Michigan State U, MI
Saginaw Valley State U, MI

CHEMICAL TECHNOLOGY
British Columbia Inst of Technology, BC, Canada
Burlington County Coll, NJ
Cape Breton U, NS, Canada
Comm Coll of Allegheny County, PA
Hudson Valley Comm Coll, NY
Indiana U–Purdue U Fort Wayne, IN
Kellogg Comm Coll, MI
Lamar Inst of Technology, TX
Millersville U of Pennsylvania, PA
Mohawk Valley Comm Coll, NY
Murray State U, KY
New York City Coll of Technology of the City U of New York, NY
The U of Akron, OH
West Virginia State Comm and Tech Coll, WV

CHEMISTRY
Abilene Christian U, TX
Abraham Baldwin Coll, GA
Acadia U, NS, Canada
Adams State Coll, CO
Adelphi U, NY
Alabama A&M U, AL
Albany State U, GA
Albertson Coll of Idaho, ID
Albion Coll, MI
Albright Coll, PA
Alma Coll, MI
Alvernia Coll, PA
American International Coll, MA
American U, DC
Amherst Coll, MA
Ancilla Coll, IN
Anderson U, IN

Angelo State U, TX
Asbury Coll, KY
Ashland U, OH
Athens State U, AL
Augsburg Coll, MN
Aurora U, IL
Austin Coll, TX
Avila U, MO
Bainbridge Coll, GA
Ball State U, IN
Bard Coll, NY
Barry U, FL
Bates Coll, ME
Baylor U, TX
Bemidji State U, MN
Benedictine Coll, KS
Bethel Coll, IN
Bethel U, MN
Bishop's U, QC, Canada
Blinn Coll, TX
Boston Coll, MA
Bradley U, IL
Brandeis U, MA
Brandon U, MB, Canada
Briar Cliff U, IA
Bridgewater Coll, VA
Brock U, ON, Canada
Brown U, RI
Bryn Mawr Coll, PA
Bucks County Comm Coll, PA
Buena Vista U, IA
Buffalo State Coll, State U of New York, NY
Bunker Hill Comm Coll, MA
Burlington County Coll, NJ
California State U, Fullerton, CA
California State U, Northridge, CA
California State U, Sacramento, CA
California State U, San Bernardino, CA
California State U, Stanislaus, CA
Calvin Coll, MI
Cameron U, OK
Cape Breton U, NS, Canada
Cardinal Stritch U, WI
Carleton U, ON, Canada
Carlow U, PA
Carnegie Mellon U, PA
Carroll Coll, MT
Carroll Coll, WI
Carson-Newman Coll, TN
Carthage Coll, WI
The Catholic U of America, DC
Cedar Crest Coll, PA
Charleston Southern U, SC
Chattanooga State Tech Comm Coll, TN
Christopher Newport U, VA
Claremont McKenna Coll, CA
Clark U, MA
Clayton State U, GA
Clemson U, SC
Coahoma Comm Coll, MS
Coastal Carolina U, SC
Coe Coll, IA
Colby Coll, ME
Colgate U, NY
Coll of Charleston, SC
Coll of Mount St. Joseph, OH
Coll of Mount Saint Vincent, NY
Coll of Saint Elizabeth, NJ
Coll of Saint Mary, NE
The Coll of Saint Rose, NY
The Coll of St. Scholastica, MN

Coll of Staten Island of the City U of New York, NY
Coll of the Canyons, CA
Coll of the Desert, CA
The Coll of William and Mary, VA
Columbus State U, GA
Comm Coll of Allegheny County, PA
Concordia U, NE
Concordia U Coll of Alberta, AB, Canada
Concord U, WV
Cornell U, NY
Crafton Hills Coll, CA
Cuesta Coll, CA
Dalhousie U, NS, Canada
Delaware State U, DE
DePaul U, IL
Dixie State Coll of Utah, UT
Dominican U, IL
Drake U, IA
Drury U, MO
Duke U, NC
Earlham Coll, IN
East Carolina U, NC
East Central Coll, MO
Eastern Mennonite U, VA
Eastern Michigan U, MI
Eastern Nazarene Coll, MA
East Stroudsburg U of Pennsylvania, PA
Eckerd Coll, FL
Edinboro U of Pennsylvania, PA
El Camino Coll, CA
Elmira Coll, NY
Elms Coll, MA
Elon U, NC
Emory U, GA
Fairfield U, CT
Fairleigh Dickinson U, Coll at Florham, NJ
Fairleigh Dickinson U, Metropolitan Campus, NJ
Fayetteville State U, NC
Ferrum Coll, VA
Florida Atlantic U, FL
Florida Inst of Technology, FL
Florida International U, FL
Foothill Coll, CA
Fort Hays State U, KS
Framingham State Coll, MA
Franciscan U of Steubenville, OH
Franklin Coll, IN
Frederick Comm Coll, MD
Freed-Hardeman U, TN
Fresno Pacific U, CA
Furman U, SC
Gainesville State Coll, GA
Gannon U, PA
Gardner-Webb U, NC
Geneva Coll, PA
Georgetown Coll, KY
The George Washington U, DC
Georgia Coll & State U, GA
Georgian Court U, NJ
Glenville State Coll, WV
Gloucester County Coll, NJ
Gonzaga U, WA
Gordon Coll, MA
Goshen Coll, IN
Graceland U, IA
Grambling State U, LA
Grinnell Coll, IA
Grossmont Coll, CA
Gustavus Adolphus Coll, MN
Hamilton Coll, NY
Hamline U, MN
Hampden-Sydney Coll, VA

Hampshire Coll, MA
Harding U, AR
Harrisburg Area Comm Coll, PA
Hartwick Coll, NY
Haverford Coll, PA
Henderson State U, AR
High Point U, NC
Hofstra U, NY
Hope Coll, MI
Houghton Coll, NY
Houston Baptist U, TX
Hunter Coll of the City U of New York, NY
Huntington U, IN
Idaho State U, ID
Illinois State U, IL
Illinois Wesleyan U, IL
Immaculata U, PA
Indiana U Bloomington, IN
Indiana U of Pennsylvania, PA
Indiana U–Purdue U Fort Wayne, IN
Indiana U–Purdue U Indianapolis, IN
Indiana U Southeast, IN
Iona Coll, NY
Ithaca Coll, NY
Jacksonville U, FL
John Brown U, AR
Kansas State U, KS
Kellogg Comm Coll, MI
Kennesaw State U, GA
Kentucky Wesleyan Coll, KY
Kenyon Coll, OH
Kingsborough Comm Coll of the City U of New York, NY
King's Coll, PA
The King's U Coll, AB, Canada
Kutztown U of Pennsylvania, PA
LaGrange Coll, GA
Lake Erie Coll, OH
Lakeland Coll, WI
Lake Superior State U, MI
Lamar U, TX
Langston U, OK
Lassen Comm Coll District, CA
Lawrence U, WI
Lebanon Valley Coll, PA
Lee Coll, TX
Lehigh U, PA
Le Moyne Coll, NY
LeTourneau U, TX
Lewis U, IL
Lincoln U, PA
Lindenwood U, MO
Long Island U, Brooklyn Campus, NY
Loras Coll, IA
Loyola Marymount U, CA
Loyola U Chicago, IL
Loyola U New Orleans, LA
Lynchburg Coll, VA
Macalester Coll, MN
MacMurray Coll, IL
Macomb Comm Coll, MI
Manhattan Coll, NY
Manhattanville Coll, NY
Marian Coll, IN
Marietta Coll, OH
Marist Coll, NY
Marquette U, WI
Marshall U, WV
Massachusetts Coll of Liberal Arts, MA
McDaniel Coll, MD
McNeese State U, LA
Mercer U, GA
Mercyhurst Coll, PA

Metropolitan Comm Coll–Longview, MO
Metropolitan Comm Coll–Penn Valley, MO
Miami Dade Coll, FL
Michigan State U, MI
Middlesex County Coll, NJ
Middle Tennessee State U, TN
Midland Coll, TX
Midland Lutheran Coll, NE
Millersville U of Pennsylvania, PA
Minnesota State U Mankato, MN
Minnesota State U Moorhead, MN
MiraCosta Coll, CA
Missouri State U, MO
Monmouth Coll, IL
Monmouth U, NJ
Montana State U, MT
Montana State U–Billings, MT
Montana Tech of The U of Montana, MT
Moorpark Coll, CA
Moravian Coll, PA
Morningside Coll, IA
Mount Holyoke Coll, MA
Mount St. Mary's U, MD
Mount Saint Vincent U, NS, Canada
Mount Union Coll, OH
Mount Vernon Nazarene U, OH
Murray State U, KY
New Jersey City U, NJ
New Mexico Jr Coll, NM
New York U, NY
Niagara U, NY
North Carolina State U, NC
North Central Coll, IL
North Dakota State U, ND
Northeastern U, MA
Northern Illinois U, IL
Northern Michigan U, MI
Northern State U, SD
North Georgia Coll & State U, GA
Northwestern Oklahoma State U, OK
Northwest Nazarene U, ID
Notre Dame Coll, OH
Oakland U, MI
Occidental Coll, CA
Odessa Coll, TX
Oglethorpe U, GA
The Ohio State U, OH
Ohio Wesleyan U, OH
Oklahoma State U, OK
Old Dominion U, VA
Oral Roberts U, OK
Otterbein Coll, OH
Our Lady of the Lake U of San Antonio, TX
Park U, MO
Penn State Abington, PA
Penn State DuBois, PA
Penn State Fayette, The Eberly Campus, PA
Penn State Mont Alto, PA
Penn State Wilkes-Barre, PA
Piedmont Coll, GA
Pittsburg State U, KS
Point Loma Nazarene U, CA
Portland State U, OR
Prairie View A&M U, TX
Presbyterian Coll, SC
Purdue U North Central, IN
Queens Coll of the City U of New York, NY
Queen's U at Kingston, ON, Canada

Radford U, VA
Ramapo Coll of New Jersey, NJ
Randolph Coll, VA
Randolph-Macon Coll, VA
Rensselaer Polytechnic Inst, NY
Rhodes Coll, TN
Rice U, TX
The Richard Stockton Coll of New Jersey, NJ
Ripon Coll, WI
Rivier Coll, NH
Rochester Inst of Technology, NY
Rockford Coll, IL
Rockhurst U, MO
Rocky Mountain Coll, MT
Roosevelt U, IL
Rose State Coll, OK
Rowan U, NJ
Rutgers, The State U of New Jersey, Newark, NJ
Rutgers, The State U of New Jersey, New Brunswick, NJ
Ryerson U, ON, Canada
Saginaw Valley State U, MI
St. Bonaventure U, NY
St. Cloud State U, MN
St. Francis Xavier U, NS, Canada
St. Gregory's U, OK
Saint John's U, MN
Saint Joseph's Coll, IN
St. Lawrence U, NY
St. Mary's Coll of Maryland, MD
St. Norbert Coll, WI
St. Philip's Coll, TX
Saint Xavier U, IL
Salem Comm Coll, NJ
Salve Regina U, RI
San Diego Mesa Coll, CA
San Diego State U, CA
San Francisco State U, CA
Santa Ana Coll, CA
Santa Barbara City Coll, CA
Santa Clara U, CA
Santa Rosa Jr Coll, CA
Sauk Valley Comm Coll, IL
Seattle Pacific U, WA
Seton Hall U, NJ
Seton Hill U, PA
Sewanee: The U of the South, TN
Shippensburg U of Pennsylvania, PA
Skagit Valley Coll, WA
Slippery Rock U of Pennsylvania, PA
Southern Adventist U, TN
Southern Illinois U Carbondale, IL
Southern Illinois U Edwardsville, IL
Southern Nazarene U, OK
Southern Oregon U, OR
Southern U and A&M Coll, LA
Southern Utah U, UT
Southwest Baptist U, MO
Southwestern Coll, KS
Southwestern U, TX
Spoon River Coll, IL
State U of New York at Fredonia, NY
State U of New York Coll at Brockport, NY
State U of New York Coll at Cortland, NY
State U of New York Coll at Geneseo, NY
State U of New York Coll at Potsdam, NY

State U of New York Coll of Environmental Science and Forestry, NY
Stephen F. Austin State U, TX
Stetson U, FL
Stonehill Coll, MA
Sweet Briar Coll, VA
Syracuse U, NY
Taylor U, IN
Temple U, PA
Tennessee Wesleyan Coll, TN
Texas A&M U, TX
Texas A&M U–Corpus Christi, TX
Thiel Coll, PA
Towson U, MD
Trent U, ON, Canada
Trevecca Nazarene U, TN
Trinity Coll, CT
Trinity U, TX
Troy U, AL
Truman State U, MO
Tufts U, MA
Union Coll, NE
U at Albany, State U of New York, NY
U at Buffalo, the State U of New York, NY
The U of Akron, OH
The U of Alabama, AL
The U of Alabama in Huntsville, AL
U of Alaska Anchorage, AK
The U of Arizona, AZ
U of Arkansas, AR
U of California, Berkeley, CA
U of California, Irvine, CA
U of California, Los Angeles, CA
U of California, Santa Barbara, CA
U of Central Florida, FL
U of Central Missouri, MO
U of Central Oklahoma, OK
U of Cincinnati, OH
U of Colorado at Boulder, CO
U of Connecticut, CT
U of Dayton, OH
U of Delaware, DE
U of Evansville, IN
U of Great Falls, MT
U of Guelph, ON, Canada
U of Hartford, CT
U of Hawaii at Manoa, HI
U of Houston, TX
U of Illinois at Urbana–Champaign, IL
U of Kansas, KS
U of Kentucky, KY
U of Manitoba, MB, Canada
U of Mary Hardin-Baylor, TX
U of Maryland, Baltimore County, MD
U of Mary Washington, VA
U of Massachusetts Amherst, MA
U of Massachusetts Boston, MA
U of Massachusetts Lowell, MA
U of Miami, FL
U of Michigan, MI
U of Minnesota, Duluth, MN
U of Mississippi, MS
U of Missouri–Columbia, MO
U of Missouri–Kansas City, MO
U of Missouri–Rolla, MO

U of Nebraska at Kearney, NE
U of Nebraska at Omaha, NE
U of Nebraska–Lincoln, NE
U of New Brunswick Fredericton, NB, Canada
U of New England, ME
U of New Hampshire, NH
U of New Haven, CT
U of New Mexico, NM
U of New Orleans, LA
The U of North Carolina at Asheville, NC
The U of North Carolina at Chapel Hill, NC
The U of North Carolina at Charlotte, NC
U of Northern British Columbia, BC, Canada
U of Northern Iowa, IA
U of North Florida, FL
U of Notre Dame, IN
U of Oregon, OR
U of Pennsylvania, PA
U of Pittsburgh, PA
U of Pittsburgh at Bradford, PA
U of Pittsburgh at Johnstown, PA
U of Portland, OR
U of Redlands, CA
U of Rhode Island, RI
U of Rio Grande, OH
U of St. Thomas, MN
U of St. Thomas, TX
U of San Diego, CA
U of San Francisco, CA
The U of Scranton, PA
U of South Carolina Upstate, SC
U of Southern Indiana, IN
The U of Tampa, FL
The U of Tennessee, TN
The U of Tennessee at Martin, TN
The U of Texas at Austin, TX
The U of Texas at El Paso, TX
The U of Texas at San Antonio, TX
U of the District of Columbia, DC
U of the Incarnate Word, TX
U of the Ozarks, AR
U of the Pacific, CA
U of Toronto, ON, Canada
U of Vermont, VT
U of Virginia, VA
The U of Virginia's Coll at Wise, VA
U of Washington, WA
U of West Georgia, GA
U of Wisconsin–Eau Claire, WI
U of Wisconsin–Green Bay, WI
U of Wisconsin–La Crosse, WI
U of Wisconsin–Madison, WI
U of Wisconsin–Oshkosh, WI
U of Wisconsin–Stevens Point, WI
U of Wyoming, WY
Upper Iowa U, IA
Urbana U, OH
Utica Coll, NY
Valdosta State U, GA
Vanguard U of Southern California, CA
Vassar Coll, NY

Villanova U, PA
Wake Forest U, NC
Washburn U, KS
Washington & Jefferson Coll, PA
Washington and Lee U, VA
Wayne State Coll, NE
Wayne State U, MI
Wellesley Coll, MA
Wells Coll, NY
West Chester U of Pennsylvania, PA
Western Connecticut State U, CT
Western Nebraska Comm Coll, NE
Western New England Coll, MA
Western Oregon U, OR
West Liberty State Coll, WV
West Los Angeles Coll, CA
Westminster Coll, PA
Westminster Coll, UT
West Texas A&M U, TX
West Virginia State U, WV
West Virginia Wesleyan Coll, WV
Wheaton Coll, IL
Whitman Coll, WA
Wichita State U, KS
Widener U, PA
Wilfrid Laurier U, ON, Canada
Wilkes U, PA
William Jewell Coll, MO
Wilson Coll, PA
Wofford Coll, SC
Worcester State Coll, MA
Wright State U, OH
Xavier U, OH
Yale U, CT

CHEMISTRY RELATED
California State U, Sacramento, CA
Carnegie Mellon U, PA
Cornell U, NY
Edinboro U of Pennsylvania, PA
Lehigh U, PA
Saginaw Valley State U, MI
San Diego State U, CA
Towson U, MD
U of California, Berkeley, CA
U of Miami, FL
U of Northern Iowa, IA
U of Notre Dame, IN
The U of Scranton, PA
U of the Incarnate Word, TX
U of the Pacific, CA
U of Wisconsin–Eau Claire, WI
Washington & Jefferson Coll, PA

CHEMISTRY TEACHER EDUCATION
Alma Coll, MI
Alvernia Coll, PA
Ancilla Coll, IN
Baylor U, TX
Bethel U, MN
Bishop's U, QC, Canada
Buena Vista U, IA
Carroll Coll, WI
The Catholic U of America, DC
The Coll of Saint Rose, NY
Columbus State U, GA
Concordia U, NE
Delaware State U, DE
Eastern Mennonite U, VA
Eastern Michigan U, MI

Elmira Coll, NY
Florida Inst of Technology, FL
Framingham State Coll, MA
Franklin Coll, IN
Glenville State Coll, WV
Gustavus Adolphus Coll, MN
Hofstra U, NY
Hope Coll, MI
Illinois Wesleyan U, IL
Indiana U Bloomington, IN
Indiana U–Purdue U Fort Wayne, IN
Ithaca Coll, NY
John Brown U, AR
Kennesaw State U, GA
Kentucky Wesleyan Coll, KY
Lebanon Valley Coll, PA
Le Moyne Coll, NY
Lindenwood U, MO
Long Island U, Brooklyn Campus, NY
Manhattanville Coll, NY
Marist Coll, NY
McNeese State U, LA
Mercyhurst Coll, PA
Miami Dade Coll, FL
Michigan State U, MI
Minnesota State U Moorhead, MN
Missouri State U, MO
Montana State U–Billings, MT
Moravian Coll, PA
Murray State U, KY
New York U, NY
Niagara U, NY
North Carolina State U, NC
North Dakota State U, ND
Northwest Nazarene U, ID
Ohio Wesleyan U, OH
Old Dominion U, VA
Pittsburg State U, KS
Rivier Coll, NH
Rocky Mountain Coll, MT
St. Bonaventure U, NY
Seton Hill U, PA
Southern U and A&M Coll, LA
Southwest Baptist U, MO
State U of New York Coll at Brockport, NY
State U of New York Coll at Cortland, NY
State U of New York Coll at Potsdam, NY
State U of New York Coll of Environmental Science and Forestry, NY
Syracuse U, NY
Taylor U, IN
Tennessee Wesleyan Coll, TN
Trevecca Nazarene U, TN
Union Coll, NE
U at Albany, State U of New York, NY
The U of Akron, OH
The U of Arizona, AZ
U of Delaware, DE
U of Evansville, IN
U of Great Falls, MT
U of Illinois at Urbana–Champaign, IL
U of Mary Hardin-Baylor, TX
U of Missouri–Columbia, MO
U of Nebraska–Lincoln, NE
U of New Hampshire, NH
The U of North Carolina at Charlotte, NC
U of Pittsburgh at Johnstown, PA

U of St. Thomas, MN
The U of Tennessee at Martin, TN
U of West Georgia, GA
Utica Coll, NY
Wayne State Coll, NE
West Chester U of Pennsylvania, PA
Westminster Coll, UT
Widener U, PA
Xavier U, OH

CHILD CARE AND SUPPORT SERVICES MANAGEMENT
Alexandria Tech Coll, MN
Asheville-Buncombe Tech Comm Coll, NC
The Baptist Coll of Florida, FL
Broome Comm Coll, NY
Calhoun Comm Coll, AL
Cameron U, OK
Central Wyoming Coll, WY
Dixie State Coll of Utah, UT
Eastern New Mexico U–Roswell, NM
Eastfield Coll, TX
Feather River Coll, CA
Florida Comm Coll at Jacksonville, FL
Gadsden State Comm Coll, AL
Hagerstown Comm Coll, MD
Henderson State U, AR
Hopkinsville Comm Coll, KY
Houston Comm Coll System, TX
Idaho State U, ID
Ivy Tech Comm Coll–Kokomo, IN
Ivy Tech Comm Coll–Southwest, IN
Ivy Tech Comm Coll–Wabash Valley, IN
Jefferson Comm Coll, OH
Lamar Inst of Technology, TX
Macomb Comm Coll, MI
Massasoit Comm Coll, MA
MiraCosta Coll, CA
Mount Vernon Nazarene U, OH
Muscatine Comm Coll, IA
Ocean County Coll, NJ
Pima Comm Coll, AZ
Reedley Coll, CA
Richmond Comm Coll, NC
Ryerson U, ON, Canada
St. Cloud Tech Coll, MN
Santa Barbara City Coll, CA
Schoolcraft Coll, MI
Seton Hill U, PA
Southwestern Michigan Coll, MI
U of the Incarnate Word, TX
Victor Valley Coll, CA

CHILD CARE/GUIDANCE
Caldwell Comm Coll and Tech Inst, NC
Feather River Coll, CA

CHILD-CARE PROVIDER
Lamar Inst of Technology, TX

CHILD-CARE PROVISION
Alexandria Tech Coll, MN
Comm Coll of Allegheny County, PA
Crafton Hills Coll, CA
Eastern West Virginia Comm and Tech Coll, WV

Florida Comm Coll at Jacksonville, FL
Heartland Comm Coll, IL
Lincoln Land Comm Coll, IL
Massasoit Comm Coll, MA
Metropolitan Comm Coll–Penn Valley, MO
Midland Coll, TX
Murray State U, KY
Northland Comm and Tech Coll–Thief River Falls, MN
Pima Comm Coll, AZ
San Diego Mesa Coll, CA
Surry Comm Coll, NC
Waubonsee Comm Coll, IL
Wayne State Coll, NE
Westchester Comm Coll, NY
Western Tech Coll, WI

CHILD-CARE SERVICES MANAGEMENT
Cameron U, OK

CHILD DEVELOPMENT
Abraham Baldwin Coll, GA
Aims Comm Coll, CO
Altamaha Tech Coll, GA
Ashland U, OH
Broward Comm Coll, FL
California State U, Northridge, CA
Carleton U, ON, Canada
Carson-Newman Coll, TN
Central Arizona Coll, AZ
Central Piedmont Comm Coll, NC
Chattahoochee Tech Coll, GA
Chattanooga State Tech Comm Coll, TN
City Colls of Chicago, Richard J. Daley Coll, IL
Coll of the Canyons, CA
Comm Coll of Allegheny County, PA
Coosa Valley Tech Coll, GA
Cosumnes River Coll, Sacramento, CA
Crafton Hills Coll, CA
Cuesta Coll, CA
Delaware Tech & Comm Coll, Jack F. Owens Campus, DE
East Carolina U, NC
Foothill Coll, CA
Franciscan U of Steubenville, OH
Frederick Comm Coll, MD
Freed-Hardeman U, TN
Glendale Comm Coll, CA
Goshen Coll, IN
Grambling State U, LA
Grossmont Coll, CA
Heartland Comm Coll, IL
Hillsborough Comm Coll, FL
Hocking Coll, OH
Housatonic Comm Coll, CT
Houston Baptist U, TX
Houston Comm Coll System, TX
Howard Comm Coll, MD
Illinois Valley Comm Coll, IL
Indiana U Bloomington, IN
Jefferson Comm and Tech Coll, KY
Kansas State U, KS
Kuyper Coll, MI
Lamar U, TX
Laredo Comm Coll, TX
Miami Dade Coll, FL
Michigan State U, MI

Middle Georgia Tech Coll, GA
Middlesex County Coll, NJ
Minnesota State Coll–Southeast Tech, MN
Minnesota State U Mankato, MN
Mitchell Coll, CT
Mount Saint Vincent U, NS, Canada
New Hampshire Comm Tech Coll, Nashua/Claremont, NH
New River Comm Coll, VA
Northern Michigan U, MI
Northland Comm and Tech Coll–Thief River Falls, MN
North Metro Tech Coll, GA
Odessa Coll, TX
Pacific Oaks Coll, CA
Pittsburg State U, KS
Point Loma Nazarene U, CA
Portland State U, OR
Richland Comm Coll, IL
Rockingham Comm Coll, NC
St. Cloud State U, MN
St. Cloud Tech Coll, MN
St. Louis Comm Coll at Florissant Valley, MO
San Diego State U, CA
Seminole Comm Coll, FL
Seton Hill U, PA
Skagit Valley Coll, WA
Southern Maine Comm Coll, ME
Southern Utah U, UT
Spoon River Coll, IL
Stark State Coll of Technology, OH
Syracuse U, NY
Trevecca Nazarene U, TN
Tufts U, MA
The U of Akron, OH
U of Arkansas at Fort Smith, AR
U of Central Oklahoma, OK
U of Cincinnati, OH
U of Delaware, DE
U of Guelph, ON, Canada
U of Illinois at Urbana–Champaign, IL
U of Manitoba, MB, Canada
U of New Hampshire, NH
U of Pittsburgh, PA
The U of Tennessee at Martin, TN
U of the District of Columbia, DC
U of Wisconsin–Madison, WI
Victor Valley Coll, CA
Westchester Comm Coll, NY
Western Tech Coll, WI
Westmoreland County Comm Coll, PA

CHILD GUIDANCE
Blinn Coll, TX
Lassen Comm Coll District, CA
Lincoln Land Comm Coll, IL
Santa Rosa Jr Coll, CA
U of Central Oklahoma, OK
The U of North Carolina at Charlotte, NC

CHINESE
Bard Coll, NY
Bates Coll, ME
Carnegie Mellon U, PA
Claremont McKenna Coll, CA
Colgate U, NY
Cornell U, NY

Emory U, GA
The George Washington U, DC
Grinnell Coll, IA
Hunter Coll of the City U of New York, NY
Indiana U Bloomington, IN
Lawrence U, WI
Lincoln U, PA
The Ohio State U, OH
Portland State U, OR
Rutgers, The State U of New Jersey, New Brunswick, NJ
San Francisco State U, CA
Trinity U, TX
Tufts U, MA
U at Albany, State U of New York, NY
U of California, Berkeley, CA
U of California, Irvine, CA
U of California, Los Angeles, CA
U of California, Santa Barbara, CA
U of Colorado at Boulder, CO
U of Hawaii at Manoa, HI
U of Massachusetts Amherst, MA
U of Michigan, MI
U of Notre Dame, IN
U of Oregon, OR
U of Pittsburgh, PA
U of Washington, WA
U of Wisconsin–Madison, WI
Vassar Coll, NY
Wellesley Coll, MA
Yale U, CT

CHINESE STUDIES
Claremont McKenna Coll, CA

CHIROPRACTIC ASSISTANT
Sauk Valley Comm Coll, IL

CHRISTIAN STUDIES
Bethel Coll, IN
Dallas Baptist U, TX
Gordon Coll, MA
Harding U, AR
Houston Baptist U, TX
Lindenwood U, MO
Mercer U, GA
Seton Hall U, NJ
U of Mary Hardin-Baylor, TX
Ursuline Coll, OH

CINEMATOGRAPHY AND FILM/VIDEO PRODUCTION
Academy of Art U, CA
American U, DC
The Art Inst of New York City, NY
The Art Inst of Pittsburgh, PA
The Art Inst of Seattle, WA
Bard Coll, NY
Bucks County Comm Coll, PA
California State U, Northridge, CA
Coll of Staten Island of the City U of New York, NY
Coll of the Canyons, CA
Fitchburg State Coll, MA
Hunter Coll of the City U of New York, NY
Ithaca Coll, NY
Loyola Marymount U, CA

Miami Dade Coll, FL
Minneapolis Coll of Art and Design, MN
Montana State U, MT
New York U, NY
North Carolina School of the Arts, NC
Pratt Inst, NY
Rochester Inst of Technology, NY
Ryerson U, ON, Canada
St. Louis Comm Coll at Florissant Valley, MO
Savannah Coll of Art and Design, GA
School of the Art Inst of Chicago, IL
School of Visual Arts, NY
Southern Adventist U, TN
Southern Illinois U Carbondale, IL
Southern Maine Comm Coll, ME
Syracuse U, NY
U of Central Florida, FL
U of Hartford, CT
U of Miami, FL
The U of the Arts, PA
Valencia Comm Coll, FL
Vanguard U of Southern California, CA
Wayne State U, MI

CITY/URBAN, COMMUNITY AND REGIONAL PLANNING
Alabama A&M U, AL
Ball State U, IN
Buffalo State Coll, State U of New York, NY
Carleton U, ON, Canada
Cornell U, NY
Dalhousie U, NS, Canada
DePaul U, IL
East Carolina U, NC
Eastern Michigan U, MI
Florida Atlantic U, FL
Framingham State Coll, MA
Indiana U Bloomington, IN
Indiana U of Pennsylvania, PA
Michigan State U, MI
Minnesota State U Mankato, MN
Missouri State U, MO
New York U, NY
The Ohio State U, OH
Portland State U, OR
Ryerson U, ON, Canada
St. Cloud State U, MN
State U of New York Coll of Environmental Science and Forestry, NY
Temple U, PA
The U of Arizona, AZ
U of California, Los Angeles, CA
U of Cincinnati, OH
U of Illinois at Urbana–Champaign, IL
U of New Hampshire, NH
U of Oregon, OR
U of San Francisco, CA
U of the District of Columbia, DC
U of Virginia, VA
U of Washington, WA
West Chester U of Pennsylvania, PA
Wright State U, OH

CIVIL DRAFTING AND CAD/CADD
British Columbia Inst of Technology, BC, Canada

Comm Coll of Allegheny County, PA
Montana Tech of The U of Montana, MT

CIVIL ENGINEERING
Alabama A&M U, AL
Bradley U, IL
Brown U, RI
California State U, Fullerton, CA
Calvin Coll, MI
Carleton U, ON, Canada
Carnegie Mellon U, PA
Carroll Coll, MT
The Catholic U of America, DC
Clemson U, SC
Cornell U, NY
Dalhousie U, NS, Canada
Delaware State U, DE
Duke U, NC
Florida Atlantic U, FL
Florida Inst of Technology, FL
Florida International U, FL
The George Washington U, DC
Gonzaga U, WA
Hofstra U, NY
Idaho State U, ID
Itasca Comm Coll, MN
Kansas State U, KS
Lamar U, TX
Lehigh U, PA
Loyola Marymount U, CA
Manhattan Coll, NY
Marquette U, WI
Michigan State U, MI
Minnesota State U Mankato, MN
Montana State U, MT
Montana Tech of The U of Montana, MT
North Carolina State U, NC
North Dakota State U, ND
Northeastern U, MA
The Ohio State U, OH
Oklahoma State U, OK
Old Dominion U, VA
Oregon Inst of Technology, OR
Penn State Abington, PA
Penn State DuBois, PA
Penn State Fayette, The Eberly Campus, PA
Penn State Mont Alto, PA
Penn State Wilkes-Barre, PA
Portland State U, OR
Prairie View A&M U, TX
Queen's U at Kingston, ON, Canada
Rensselaer Polytechnic Inst, NY
Rice U, TX
Rowan U, NJ
Rutgers, The State U of New Jersey, New Brunswick, NJ
Ryerson U, ON, Canada
San Diego State U, CA
San Francisco State U, CA
Santa Clara U, CA
Santa Rosa Jr Coll, CA
Southern Illinois U Carbondale, IL
Southern Illinois U Edwardsville, IL
Southern U and A&M Coll, LA
Syracuse U, NY
Temple U, PA
Texas A&M U, TX
Tidewater Comm Coll, VA
Tufts U, MA

U at Buffalo, the State U of New York, NY
The U of Akron, OH
The U of Alabama, AL
The U of Alabama in Huntsville, AL
U of Alaska Anchorage, AK
The U of Arizona, AZ
U of Arkansas, AR
U of California, Berkeley, CA
U of California, Irvine, CA
U of California, Los Angeles, CA
U of Central Florida, FL
U of Cincinnati, OH
U of Colorado at Boulder, CO
U of Connecticut, CT
U of Dayton, OH
U of Delaware, DE
U of Evansville, IN
U of Hartford, CT
U of Hawaii at Manoa, HI
U of Houston, TX
U of Illinois at Urbana–Champaign, IL
U of Kansas, KS
U of Kentucky, KY
U of Manitoba, MB, Canada
U of Massachusetts Amherst, MA
U of Massachusetts Lowell, MA
U of Miami, FL
U of Michigan, MI
U of Mississippi, MS
U of Missouri–Columbia, MO
U of Missouri–Kansas City, MO
U of Missouri–Rolla, MO
U of Nebraska at Omaha, NE
U of Nebraska–Lincoln, NE
U of New Brunswick Fredericton, NB, Canada
U of New Hampshire, NH
U of New Haven, CT
U of New Mexico, NM
U of New Orleans, LA
The U of North Carolina at Charlotte, NC
U of North Florida, FL
U of Notre Dame, IN
U of Pittsburgh, PA
U of Portland, OR
U of Rhode Island, RI
The U of Tennessee, TN
The U of Texas at Austin, TX
The U of Texas at El Paso, TX
The U of Texas at San Antonio, TX
U of the District of Columbia, DC
U of the Pacific, CA
U of Toronto, ON, Canada
U of Vermont, VT
U of Virginia, VA
U of Washington, WA
U of Wisconsin–Madison, WI
U of Wisconsin–Platteville, WI
U of Wyoming, WY
Villanova U, PA
Wayne State U, MI
Widener U, PA

CIVIL ENGINEERING RELATED
Bradley U, IL

California State U,
Sacramento, CA
Embry-Riddle Aeronautical
U, FL

CIVIL ENGINEERING TECHNOLOGY

Alabama A&M U, AL
Asheville-Buncombe Tech
Comm Coll, NC
Bluefield State Coll, WV
British Columbia Inst of
Technology, BC, Canada
Broome Comm Coll, NY
Broward Comm Coll, FL
Burlington County Coll, NJ
Central Arizona Coll, AZ
Central Piedmont Comm
Coll, NC
Chattahoochee Tech Coll,
GA
Chattanooga State Tech
Comm Coll, TN
Comm Coll of Allegheny
County, PA
Delaware Tech & Comm
Coll, Jack F. Owens
Campus, DE
Fairleigh Dickinson U,
Metropolitan Campus, NJ
Florida Comm Coll at
Jacksonville, FL
Fontbonne U, MO
Gadsden State Comm Coll,
AL
Gaston Coll, NC
Gloucester County Coll, NJ
Harrisburg Area Comm Coll,
PA
Houston Comm Coll System,
TX
Hudson Valley Comm Coll,
NY
Idaho State U, ID
Indiana U–Purdue U Fort
Wayne, IN
Indiana U–Purdue U
Indianapolis, IN
Linn State Tech Coll, MO
Macomb Comm Coll, MI
Miami Dade Coll, FL
Middlesex County Coll, NJ
Mohawk Valley Comm Coll,
NY
Murray State U, KY
Nassau Comm Coll, NY
New York City Coll of
Technology of the City U
of New York, NY
Ocean County Coll, NJ
Old Dominion U, VA
Phoenix Coll, AZ
Pueblo Comm Coll, CO
Purdue U North Central, IN
Rochester Inst of
Technology, NY
St. Cloud Tech Coll, MN
St. Louis Comm Coll at
Florissant Valley, MO
Seminole Comm Coll, FL
Shasta Coll, CA
Southeast Tech Inst, SD
Southwestern Indian
Polytechnic Inst, NM
Spokane Comm Coll, WA
Stark State Coll of
Technology, OH
State U of New York Coll of
Technology at Alfred, NY
State U of New York Coll of
Technology at Canton, NY
Tallahassee Comm Coll, FL
Temple U, PA
U of Cincinnati, OH

U of Houston, TX
U of Massachusetts Lowell,
MA
U of New Hampshire, NH
The U of North Carolina at
Charlotte, NC
U of Pittsburgh at
Johnstown, PA
U of the District of
Columbia, DC
Valencia Comm Coll, FL
Vermont Tech Coll, VT
Westchester Comm Coll, NY

CLASSICAL, ANCIENT MEDITERRANEAN AND NEAR EASTERN STUDIES AND ARCHAEOLOGY

Bates Coll, ME
U of California, Berkeley,
CA
U of California, Irvine, CA
U of California, Los Angeles,
CA
U of Toronto, ON, Canada

CLASSICS

Emory U, GA
Furman U, SC
Hunter Coll of the City U of
New York, NY
Rockford Coll, IL
Southwestern U, TX
The U of Arizona, AZ
U of Hawaii at Manoa, HI
Washington and Lee U, VA

CLASSICS AND CLASSICAL LANGUAGES RELATED

Austin Coll, TX
Brandeis U, MA
Bryn Mawr Coll, PA
The Catholic U of America,
DC
Lawrence U, WI
Rutgers, The State U of New
Jersey, Newark, NJ
St. Bonaventure U, NY
U of California, Los Angeles,
CA
U of St. Thomas, MN

CLASSICS AND LANGUAGES, LITERATURES AND LINGUISTICS

Acadia U, NS, Canada
Amherst Coll, MA
Asbury Coll, KY
Austin Coll, TX
Ball State U, IN
Bard Coll, NY
Baylor U, TX
Bishop's U, QC, Canada
Boston Coll, MA
Brock U, ON, Canada
Brown U, RI
Bryn Mawr Coll, PA
Calvin Coll, MI
Carleton U, ON, Canada
Carthage Coll, WI
The Catholic U of America,
DC
Claremont McKenna Coll,
CA
Clark U, MA
Coe Coll, IA
Colby Coll, ME
Colgate U, NY
Coll of Charleston, SC
The Coll of William and
Mary, VA

Cornell U, NY
Dalhousie U, NS, Canada
Duke U, NC
Earlham Coll, IN
Elmira Coll, NY
Emory U, GA
Foothill Coll, CA
Franciscan U of
Steubenville, OH
The George Washington U,
DC
Grinnell Coll, IA
Gustavus Adolphus Coll,
MN
Hamilton Coll, NY
Hampden-Sydney Coll, VA
Haverford Coll, PA
Hofstra U, NY
Hope Coll, MI
Hunter Coll of the City U of
New York, NY
Illinois Wesleyan U, IL
Indiana U Bloomington, IN
Kenyon Coll, OH
Lawrence U, WI
Lehigh U, PA
Loyola Marymount U, CA
Loyola U Chicago, IL
Loyola U New Orleans, LA
Macalester Coll, MN
Manhattan Coll, NY
Manhattanville Coll, NY
Marquette U, WI
Mercer U, GA
Monmouth Coll, IL
Moravian Coll, PA
Mount Holyoke Coll, MA
New York U, NY
Nipissing U, ON, Canada
North Central Coll, IL
North Dakota State U, ND
The Ohio State U, OH
Ohio Wesleyan U, OH
Penn State Abington, PA
Penn State DuBois, PA
Penn State Fayette, The
Eberly Campus, PA
Penn State Mont Alto, PA
Penn State Wilkes-Barre, PA
Randolph Coll, VA
Randolph-Macon Coll, VA
Rhodes Coll, TN
Rice U, TX
Rockford Coll, IL
Rutgers, The State U of New
Jersey, Newark, NJ
Rutgers, The State U of New
Jersey, New Brunswick, NJ
St. Bonaventure U, NY
St. Francis Xavier U, NS,
Canada
Saint John's U, MN
San Diego State U, CA
San Francisco State U, CA
Santa Clara U, CA
Seattle Pacific U, WA
Seton Hall U, NJ
Sewanee: The U of the
South, TN
Southern Illinois U
Carbondale, IL
Sweet Briar Coll, VA
Syracuse U, NY
Temple U, PA
Trent U, ON, Canada
Trinity Coll, CT
Trinity U, TX
Truman State U, MO
Tufts U, MA
U at Albany, State U of New
York, NY
U at Buffalo, the State U of
New York, NY
The U of Akron, OH

The U of Alabama, AL
U of Arkansas, AR
U of California, Berkeley,
CA
U of California, Irvine, CA
U of California, Los Angeles,
CA
U of California, Santa
Barbara, CA
U of Cincinnati, OH
U of Colorado at Boulder,
CO
U of Connecticut, CT
U of Delaware, DE
U of Evansville, IN
U of Guelph, ON, Canada
U of Houston, TX
U of Illinois at Urbana–
Champaign, IL
U of Kansas, KS
U of Kentucky, KY
U of Manitoba, MB, Canada
U of Maryland, Baltimore
County, MD
U of Mary Washington, VA
U of Massachusetts Amherst,
MA
U of Massachusetts Boston,
MA
U of Michigan, MI
U of Mississippi, MS
U of Missouri–Columbia,
MO
U of Nebraska–Lincoln, NE
U of New Brunswick
Fredericton, NB, Canada
U of New Hampshire, NH
U of New Mexico, NM
The U of North Carolina at
Asheville, NC
The U of North Carolina at
Chapel Hill, NC
U of Notre Dame, IN
U of Oregon, OR
U of Pennsylvania, PA
U of Pittsburgh, PA
U of Rhode Island, RI
U of St. Thomas, MN
The U of Tennessee, TN
The U of Texas at Austin,
TX
The U of Texas at San
Antonio, TX
U of the Pacific, CA
U of Toronto, ON, Canada
U of Vermont, VT
U of Virginia, VA
U of Washington, WA
U of Wisconsin–Madison,
WI
Vassar Coll, NY
Villanova U, PA
Wake Forest U, NC
Wayne State U, MI
Wellesley Coll, MA
Westminster Coll, PA
Whitman Coll, WA
Wilfrid Laurier U, ON,
Canada
Wright State U, OH
Xavier U, OH
Yale U, CT

CLINICAL LABORATORY SCIENCE/MEDICAL TECHNOLOGY

Abilene Christian U, TX
Alvernia Coll, PA
American International Coll,
MA
Anderson U, IN
Angelo State U, TX
Aurora U, IL
Ball State U, IN

Barry U, FL
Baylor U, TX
Belmont Abbey Coll, NC
Bemidji State U, MN
Bradley U, IL
Bridgewater Coll, VA
Broward Comm Coll, FL
Cameron U, OK
Carroll Coll, MT
Carroll Coll, WI
Carson-Newman Coll, TN
The Catholic U of America,
DC
Cedar Crest Coll, PA
Central Piedmont Comm
Coll, NC
City Colls of Chicago,
Richard J. Daley Coll, IL
Clayton State U, GA
Coahoma Comm Coll, MS
Coll of Mount St. Joseph,
OH
Coll of Saint Mary, NE
The Coll of Saint Rose, NY
Coll of Staten Island of the
City U of New York, NY
Concord U, WV
DePaul U, IL
Dominican U, IL
East Carolina U, NC
Eastern Mennonite U, VA
Eastern Michigan U, MI
East Stroudsburg U of
Pennsylvania, PA
El Centro Coll, TX
Elmira Coll, NY
Elon U, NC
Fairleigh Dickinson U, Coll
at Florham, NJ
Fairleigh Dickinson U,
Metropolitan Campus, NJ
Ferrum Coll, VA
Florida Atlantic U, FL
Fort Hays State U, KS
Gannon U, PA
Gardner-Webb U, NC
The George Washington U,
DC
Graceland U, IA
Grossmont Coll, CA
Harding U, AR
Hartwick Coll, NY
Henderson State U, AR
High Point U, NC
Houghton Coll, NY
Howard Comm Coll, MD
Idaho State U, ID
Illinois State U, IL
Indiana U of Pennsylvania,
PA
Indiana U–Purdue U Fort
Wayne, IN
Indiana U–Purdue U
Indianapolis, IN
Indiana U Southeast, IN
Iona Coll, NY
Kansas State U, KS
Kentucky Wesleyan Coll, KY
Keuka Coll, NY
King's Coll, PA
Kutztown U of
Pennsylvania, PA
Lake Superior State U, MI
Lamar U, TX
Langston U, OK
Lewis U, IL
Lindenwood U, MO
Long Island U, Brooklyn
Campus, NY
Loras Coll, IA
Marist Coll, NY
Marshall U, WV
Marywood U, PA

Massachusetts Coll of Liberal
Arts, MA
McNeese State U, LA
Mercyhurst Coll, PA
Michigan State U, MI
Minnesota State U Mankato,
MN
Minnesota State U
Moorhead, MN
Missouri State U, MO
Monmouth U, NJ
Moravian Coll, PA
Morningside Coll, IA
Mount Vernon Nazarene U,
OH
Murray State U, KY
National-Louis U, IL
North Dakota State U, ND
Northern Illinois U, IL
Northern State U, SD
The Ohio State U, OH
Old Dominion U, VA
Phoenix Coll, AZ
Prairie View A&M U, TX
Radford U, VA
Ramapo Coll of New Jersey,
NJ
Rochester Inst of
Technology, NY
Roosevelt U, IL
Rutgers, The State U of New
Jersey, Newark, NJ
Rutgers, The State U of New
Jersey, New Brunswick, NJ
Saginaw Valley State U, MI
St. Cloud State U, MN
Saint Joseph's Coll, IN
Saint Leo U, FL
St. Thomas Aquinas Coll,
NY
Salve Regina U, RI
Seton Hill U, PA
Southern Adventist U, TN
Southwest Baptist U, MO
State U of New York at
Fredonia, NY
State U of New York Coll at
Brockport, NY
Stephen F. Austin State U,
TX
Stetson U, FL
Taylor U, IN
Texas A&M U–Corpus
Christi, TX
Thiel Coll, PA
Trevecca Nazarene U, TN
Union Coll, NE
U at Buffalo, the State U of
New York, NY
The U of Arizona, AZ
U of Central Florida, FL
U of Central Missouri, MO
U of Central Oklahoma, OK
U of Cincinnati, OH
U of Connecticut, CT
U of Delaware, DE
The U of Findlay, OH
U of Hartford, CT
U of Houston, TX
U of Kansas, KS
U of Kentucky, KY
U of Mary Hardin-Baylor, TX
U of Massachusetts Boston,
MA
U of Massachusetts Lowell,
MA
U of Michigan, MI
U of Mississippi, MS
U of New England, ME
U of New Orleans, LA
The U of North Carolina at
Chapel Hill, NC
The U of North Carolina at
Charlotte, NC

U of Pittsburgh, PA
U of Rhode Island, RI
U of Rio Grande, OH
The U of Scranton, PA
The U of Tennessee, TN
The U of Texas at Austin,
TX
The U of Texas at El Paso,
TX
The U of Texas at San
Antonio, TX
U of the District of
Columbia, DC
U of the Incarnate Word, TX
U of Vermont, VT
The U of Virginia's Coll at
Wise, VA
U of Washington, WA
U of Wisconsin–La Crosse,
WI
U of Wisconsin–Madison,
WI
U of Wisconsin–Oshkosh,
WI
U of Wisconsin–Stevens
Point, WI
Wake Forest U, NC
Wayne State Coll, NE
Wayne State U, MI
Wesley Coll, DE
Westchester Comm Coll, NY
Western Connecticut State
U, CT
Western Nebraska Comm
Coll, NE
West Liberty State Coll, WV
West Texas A&M U, TX
Wichita State U, KS
Wilkes U, PA
William Jewell Coll, MO
Wright State U, OH
Xavier U, OH

**CLINICAL/MEDICAL
LABORATORY
ASSISTANT**
Allegany Coll of Maryland,
MD
Argosy U, Twin Cities,
Eagan, MN
Harrisburg Area Comm Coll,
PA
Northern Michigan U, MI
The U of Maine at Augusta,
ME

**CLINICAL/MEDICAL
LABORATORY SCIENCE
AND ALLIED
PROFESSIONS RELATED**
Hunter Coll of the City U of
New York, NY
Lebanon Valley Coll, PA
Roosevelt U, IL
The U of Akron, OH

**CLINICAL/MEDICAL
LABORATORY
TECHNOLOGY**
Alexandria Tech Coll, MN
Allegany Coll of Maryland,
MD
Asheville-Buncombe Tech
Comm Coll, NC
Barry U, FL
Brevard Comm Coll, FL
British Columbia Inst of
Technology, BC, Canada
Broome Comm Coll, NY
Broward Comm Coll, FL
Cameron U, OK
Central Piedmont Comm
Coll, NC
Clayton State U, GA

Coll of Staten Island of the
City U of New York, NY
Comm Coll of Allegheny
County, PA
Comm Coll of Beaver
County, PA
DeKalb Tech Coll, GA
Delaware Tech & Comm
Coll, Jack F. Owens
Campus, DE
DePaul U, IL
Edinboro U of Pennsylvania,
PA
El Centro Coll, TX
Farmingdale State Coll, NY
Gadsden State Comm Coll,
AL
Gardner-Webb U, NC
The George Washington U,
DC
Greenville Tech Coll, SC
Harrisburg Area Comm Coll,
PA
Housatonic Comm Coll, CT
Houston Comm Coll System,
TX
Ivy Tech Comm Coll–
Wabash Valley, IN
Jamestown Comm Coll, NY
Kapiolani Comm Coll, HI
Kellogg Comm Coll, MI
Lake City Comm Coll, FL
Lamar State Coll–Orange, TX
Laredo Comm Coll, TX
Marquette U, WI
Marshall U, WV
Massachusetts Coll of Liberal
Arts, MA
Miami Dade Coll, FL
Middlesex County Coll, NJ
Nassau Comm Coll, NY
New Mexico Jr Coll, NM
Northeastern U, MA
Northern Michigan U, MI
Northern State U, SD
Ocean County Coll, NJ
Odessa Coll, TX
Oral Roberts U, OK
Penn State DuBois, PA
Phoenix Coll, AZ
Pittsburg State U, KS
Rose State Coll, OK
St. Philip's Coll, TX
St. Thomas Aquinas Coll,
NY
San Diego Mesa Coll, CA
Slippery Rock U of
Pennsylvania, PA
Southeast Tech Inst, SD
Stark State Coll of
Technology, OH
State U of New York Coll of
Technology at Canton, NY
U of Alaska Anchorage, AK
U of Cincinnati, OH
U of Missouri–Kansas City,
MO
U of New Hampshire, NH
U of New Mexico, NM
U of Rio Grande, OH
U of the District of
Columbia, DC
Westchester Comm Coll, NY
Western Tech Coll, WI

**CLINICAL/MEDICAL
SOCIAL WORK**
Slippery Rock U of
Pennsylvania, PA
U of St. Thomas, MN

CLINICAL NUTRITION
Framingham State Coll, MA

West Chester U of
Pennsylvania, PA

CLINICAL PSYCHOLOGY
California State U, Fullerton,
CA
Eastern Nazarene Coll, MA
Fairfield U, CT
Florida Inst of Technology,
FL
Franklin Pierce U, NH
Husson Coll, ME
Lamar U, TX
Moravian Coll, PA
U of New Brunswick
Fredericton, NB, Canada

CLOTHING/TEXTILES
Delaware State U, DE
El Centro Coll, TX
Framingham State Coll, MA
Indiana U Bloomington, IN
Mercyhurst Coll, PA
Minnesota State U Mankato,
MN
The Ohio State U, OH
San Francisco State U, CA
Syracuse U, NY
The U of Akron, OH
U of Central Oklahoma, OK
U of Manitoba, MB, Canada
U of the District of
Columbia, DC
U of Wisconsin–Madison,
WI

**COGNITIVE
PSYCHOLOGY AND
PSYCHOLINGUISTICS**
Brown U, RI
California State U,
Stanislaus, CA
Carleton U, ON, Canada
Indiana U Bloomington, IN
Lawrence U, WI
Occidental Coll, CA
U of Kansas, KS
Vassar Coll, NY
Wellesley Coll, MA
Wilfrid Laurier U, ON,
Canada
Yale U, CT

COGNITIVE SCIENCE
Carnegie Mellon U, PA
Hampshire Coll, MA
Lawrence U, WI
Queen's U at Kingston, ON,
Canada
U of California, Berkeley,
CA
U of California, Los Angeles,
CA
U of Connecticut, CT
U of Evansville, IN
U of Pennsylvania, PA

**COLLEGE STUDENT
COUNSELING AND
PERSONNEL SERVICES**
Kutztown U of
Pennsylvania, PA

**COMMERCIAL AND
ADVERTISING ART**
Abilene Christian U, TX
Academy of Art U, CA
Aims Comm Coll, CO
Alexandria Tech Coll, MN
Anderson U, IN
Anderson U, SC
The Art Inst of Pittsburgh,
PA
Ashland U, OH
Ball State U, IN

Bemidji State U, MN
Brenau U, GA
British Columbia Inst of
Technology, BC, Canada
Bucks County Comm Coll,
PA
Buena Vista U, IA
Buffalo State Coll, State U of
New York, NY
Burlington County Coll, NJ
California State U, Fullerton,
CA
Cardinal Stritch U, WI
Carroll Coll, WI
Carson-Newman Coll, TN
Central Piedmont Comm
Coll, NC
Chattanooga State Tech
Comm Coll, TN
Clark U, MA
The Cleveland Inst of Art,
OH
The Coll of Saint Rose, NY
Comm Coll of Allegheny
County, PA
Comm Coll of Aurora, CO
Concordia U, NE
Concord U, WV
DePaul U, IL
Dixie State Coll of Utah, UT
Dominican U, IL
Drake U, IA
East Central Coll, MO
Fashion Inst of Technology,
NY
Florida Comm Coll at
Jacksonville, FL
Fontbonne U, MO
Fort Hays State U, KS
Franklin Pierce U, NH
Freed-Hardeman U, TN
Fresno City Coll, CA
Fulton-Montgomery Comm
Coll, NY
Glendale Comm Coll, CA
Grace Coll, IN
Graceland U, IA
Hagerstown Comm Coll, MD
Harrisburg Area Comm Coll,
PA
Hillsborough Comm Coll, FL
Housatonic Comm Coll, CT
Houston Comm Coll System,
TX
Huntington U, IN
Indiana U Bloomington, IN
Indiana U–Purdue U Fort
Wayne, IN
James H. Faulkner State
Comm Coll, AL
Jefferson Comm and Tech
Coll, KY
Kellogg Comm Coll, MI
Kingsborough Comm Coll of
the City U of New York,
NY
Kutztown U of
Pennsylvania, PA
Lake-Sumter Comm Coll, FL
Lamar U, TX
Lassen Comm Coll District,
CA
Lewis U, IL
Loyola U New Orleans, LA
Macomb Comm Coll, MI
Marietta Coll, OH
Metropolitan Comm
Coll–Penn Valley, MO
Miami Dade Coll, FL
Middlesex Comm Coll, CT
Middlesex County Coll, NJ
Midland Coll, TX
Minneapolis Coll of Art and
Design, MN

Colleges for Students with Learning Disabilities or AD/HD

Minnesota State U Mankato, MN
Minnesota State U Moorhead, MN
Mitchell Coll, CT
Mohawk Valley Comm Coll, NY
Moorpark Coll, CA
Morningside Coll, IA
Nassau Comm Coll, NY
New Mexico Jr Coll, NM
New York City Coll of Technology of the City U of New York, NY
Northeastern U, MA
Northern Michigan U, MI
Northern State U, SD
Northwest Nazarene U, ID
Notre Dame de Namur U, CA
NSCAD U, NS, Canada
Ocean County Coll, NJ
The Ohio State U, OH
Oral Roberts U, OK
Otis Coll of Art and Design, CA
Parsons The New School for Design, NY
Portland State U, OR
Pratt Inst, NY
Reedley Coll, CA
Rivier Coll, NH
Rutgers, The State U of New Jersey, New Brunswick, NJ
St. Louis Comm Coll at Florissant Valley, MO
St. Norbert Coll, WI
St. Thomas Aquinas Coll, NY
Santa Ana Coll, CA
Santa Barbara City Coll, CA
Schoolcraft Coll, MI
School of the Art Inst of Chicago, IL
Seton Hall U, NJ
Seton Hill U, PA
Skagit Valley Coll, WA
Southeast Tech Inst, SD
South Piedmont Comm Coll, NC
Southwest Baptist U, MO
Southwestern Indian Polytechnic Inst, NM
State U of New York at Fredonia, NY
Surry Comm Coll, NC
Sussex County Comm Coll, NJ
Syracuse U, NY
Taylor U, IN
Tidewater Comm Coll, VA
Truman State U, MO
Tunxis Comm Coll, CT
Union Coll, NE
The U of Akron, OH
U of Central Missouri, MO
U of Central Oklahoma, OK
U of Cincinnati, OH
U of Dayton, OH
U of Delaware, DE
U of Miami, FL
U of Michigan, MI
U of Minnesota, Duluth, MN
U of New Haven, CT
U of Oregon, OR
The U of Tennessee, TN
The U of Tennessee at Martin, TN
The U of Texas at El Paso, TX
U of the District of Columbia, DC
U of the Incarnate Word, TX
U of the Pacific, CA

U of Washington, WA
U of Wisconsin–Platteville, WI
U of Wisconsin–Stevens Point, WI
Upper Iowa U, IA
Valencia Comm Coll, FL
Ventura Coll, CA
Virginia Intermont Coll, VA
Western Connecticut State U, CT
Western Tech Coll, WI
West Liberty State Coll, WV
Westmoreland County Comm Coll, PA
West Texas A&M U, TX
West Virginia Wesleyan Coll, WV
Wichita State U, KS

COMMERCIAL PHOTOGRAPHY

The Art Inst of Pittsburgh, PA
Fashion Inst of Technology, NY
Harrington Coll of Design, IL
Houston Comm Coll System, TX
Minnesota State U Moorhead, MN
Mohawk Valley Comm Coll, NY
Rochester Inst of Technology, NY
The U of Akron, OH

COMMUNICATION AND JOURNALISM RELATED

Abilene Christian U, TX
Bradley U, IL
Clemson U, SC
Dalhousie U, NS, Canada
Flagler Coll, FL
Framingham State Coll, MA
Ithaca Coll, NY
Lehigh U, PA
Loyola U Chicago, IL
Marquette U, WI
Mercer U, GA
Notre Dame de Namur U, CA
The Ohio State U, OH
Old Dominion U, VA
Penn State Abington, PA
Penn State DuBois, PA
Penn State Fayette, The Eberly Campus, PA
Penn State Mont Alto, PA
Penn State Wilkes-Barre, PA
Radford U, VA
San Diego State U, CA
Springfield Coll, MA
State U of New York Coll at Brockport, NY
Syracuse U, NY
The U of Akron, OH
U of Illinois at Urbana–Champaign, IL
U of Miami, FL
The U of the Arts, PA
U of Wisconsin–Green Bay, WI

COMMUNICATION AND MEDIA RELATED

Alma Coll, MI
Asnuntuck Comm Coll, CT
Athabasca U, AB, Canada
Carnegie Mellon U, PA
Clayton State U, GA
Fitchburg State Coll, MA
Framingham State Coll, MA

Harding U, AR
Hofstra U, NY
Houston Baptist U, TX
Indiana U–Purdue U Fort Wayne, IN
King's Coll, PA
Lynn U, FL
Rochester Inst of Technology, NY
St. Gregory's U, OK
Southwestern Coll, KS
State U of New York Coll at Brockport, NY
U of Central Missouri, MO
The U of the Arts, PA

COMMUNICATION DISORDERS

Baylor U, TX
Brock U, ON, Canada
California State U, Fullerton, CA
California State U, Northridge, CA
The Coll of Saint Rose, NY
Edinboro U of Pennsylvania, PA
Harding U, AR
Kansas State U, KS
Marshall U, WV
Minnesota State U Mankato, MN
Northern Illinois U, IL
Oklahoma State U, OK
Penn State Abington, PA
Penn State DuBois, PA
Penn State Fayette, The Eberly Campus, PA
Penn State Mont Alto, PA
Penn State Wilkes-Barre, PA
Queens Coll of the City U of New York, NY
St. Cloud State U, MN
San Diego State U, CA
Southern Illinois U Carbondale, IL
Springfield Coll, MA
State U of New York at Fredonia, NY
Truman State U, MO
The U of Akron, OH
The U of Arizona, AZ
U of Houston, TX
U of Kansas, KS
U of Massachusetts Amherst, MA
U of Nebraska at Kearney, NE
U of Oregon, OR
U of Rhode Island, RI
The U of Texas at Austin, TX
U of Vermont, VT
U of Virginia, VA
U of Wisconsin–Eau Claire, WI
West Texas A&M U, TX
Worcester State Coll, MA

COMMUNICATION DISORDERS SCIENCES AND SERVICES RELATED

Long Island U, Brooklyn Campus, NY
Radford U, VA
St. Cloud State U, MN
U of Missouri–Columbia, MO

COMMUNICATION/ SPEECH COMMUNICATION AND RHETORIC

Adams State Coll, CO
Albright Coll, PA
Alvernia Coll, PA
Angelo State U, TX
Arizona State U at the West campus, AZ
Auburn U Montgomery, AL
Aurora U, IL
Austin Coll, TX
Avila U, MO
Barry U, FL
Baylor U, TX
Bethel Coll, IN
Bethel U, MN
Bradley U, IL
Brewton-Parker Coll, GA
Brock U, ON, Canada
Broome Comm Coll, NY
Buena Vista U, IA
Buffalo State Coll, State U of New York, NY
Bunker Hill Comm Coll, MA
California State U, Fullerton, CA
California State U, Sacramento, CA
California State U, Stanislaus, CA
Calvin Coll, MI
Cameron U, OK
Cape Breton U, NS, Canada
Cardinal Stritch U, WI
Carlow U, PA
Carroll Coll, MT
Carroll Coll, WI
Carthage Coll, WI
The Catholic U of America, DC
Cedar Crest Coll, PA
Christopher Newport U, VA
Coll of Charleston, SC
Coll of Mount St. Joseph, OH
Coll of Saint Elizabeth, NJ
Coll of St. Joseph, VT
The Coll of Saint Rose, NY
The Coll of St. Scholastica, MN
Coll of Staten Island of the City U of New York, NY
Concordia U, NE
Cornell U, NY
Dallas Baptist U, TX
Dean Coll, MA
DePaul U, IL
Dixie State Coll of Utah, UT
Drury U, MO
East Carolina U, NC
Eastern Connecticut State U, CT
Eastern Mennonite U, VA
East Stroudsburg U of Pennsylvania, PA
Eckerd Coll, FL
Edinboro U of Pennsylvania, PA
Elon U, NC
Embry-Riddle Aeronautical U, FL
Fairleigh Dickinson U, Coll at Florham, NJ
Fairleigh Dickinson U, Metropolitan Campus, NJ
Florida Inst of Technology, FL
Florida International U, FL
Fontbonne U, MO
Framingham State Coll, MA
Franciscan U of Steubenville, OH

Furman U, SC
Geneva Coll, PA
Georgian Court U, NJ
Gloucester County Coll, NJ
Gordon Coll, MA
Green Mountain Coll, VT
Harding U, AR
Hofstra U, NY
Hope Coll, MI
Houston Baptist U, TX
Huntington U, IN
Idaho State U, ID
Immaculata U, PA
Indiana U Bloomington, IN
Indiana U of Pennsylvania, PA
Indiana U–Purdue U Indianapolis, IN
Indiana U Southeast, IN
Iona Coll, NY
Jacksonville U, FL
Jamestown Comm Coll, NY
Kansas State U, KS
Kellogg Comm Coll, MI
Kennesaw State U, GA
Kentucky Wesleyan Coll, KY
Keuka Coll, NY
Kuyper Coll, MI
Lackawanna Coll, PA
Lee Coll, TX
Le Moyne Coll, NY
Liberty U, VA
Lincoln U, PA
Long Island U, Brooklyn Campus, NY
Loyola U Chicago, IL
Loyola U New Orleans, LA
Lynchburg Coll, VA
Macalester Coll, MN
Macomb Comm Coll, MI
Marietta Coll, OH
Marquette U, WI
Marymount U, VA
McDaniel Coll, MD
Michigan State U, MI
Millersville U of Pennsylvania, PA
Missouri State U, MO
Molloy Coll, NY
Monmouth U, NJ
Montana Tech of The U of Montana, MT
Mount St. Mary's U, MD
Mount Union Coll, OH
Mount Vernon Nazarene U, OH
Multnomah Bible Coll and Biblical Seminary, OR
Nassau Comm Coll, NY
Neumann Coll, PA
New Jersey City U, NJ
New York U, NY
North Carolina State U, NC
Northeastern U, MA
Northern Illinois U, IL
Northern Michigan U, MI
Northwestern Coll, MN
Northwest Nazarene U, ID
Notre Dame Coll, OH
Notre Dame de Namur U, CA
Oakland U, MI
Oglethorpe U, GA
The Ohio State U, OH
Oral Roberts U, OK
Oregon Inst of Technology, OR
Our Lady of the Lake U of San Antonio, TX
Park U, MO
Penn State Abington, PA
Penn State DuBois, PA
Penn State Fayette, The Eberly Campus, PA

Penn State Mont Alto, PA
Penn State Wilkes-Barre, PA
Pine Manor Coll, MA
Pittsburg State U, KS
Point Loma Nazarene U, CA
Ramapo Coll of New Jersey, NJ
Randolph Coll, VA
Rensselaer Polytechnic Inst, NY
The Richard Stockton Coll of New Jersey, NJ
Ripon Coll, WI
Rivier Coll, NH
Rockhurst U, MO
Rocky Mountain Coll, MT
Roosevelt U, IL
Rowan U, NJ
Rutgers, The State U of New Jersey, New Brunswick, NJ
Saginaw Valley State U, MI
St. Norbert Coll, WI
Saint Xavier U, IL
Santa Ana Coll, CA
Santa Barbara City Coll, CA
Santa Clara U, CA
Santa Rosa Jr Coll, CA
Sauk Valley Comm Coll, IL
Seattle Pacific U, WA
Seton Hall U, NJ
Seton Hill U, PA
Slippery Rock U of Pennsylvania, PA
Southern Nazarene U, OK
Southern Oregon U, OR
Southern U and A&M Coll, LA
Southwest Baptist U, MO
Southwestern U, TX
State U of New York Coll at Brockport, NY
State U of New York Coll at Cortland, NY
State U of New York Coll at Geneseo, NY
Stephen F. Austin State U, TX
Stetson U, FL
Stonehill Coll, MA
Syracuse U, NY
Taylor U, IN
Texas A&M U–Corpus Christi, TX
Thiel Coll, PA
Towson U, MD
Trevecca Nazarene U, TN
Trinity U, TX
Truman State U, MO
U at Buffalo, the State U of New York, NY
The U of Akron, OH
The U of Alabama, AL
The U of Arizona, AZ
U of Arkansas, AR
U of California, Los Angeles, CA
U of California, Santa Barbara, CA
U of Central Oklahoma, OK
U of Colorado at Boulder, CO
U of Connecticut, CT
U of Delaware, DE
U of Evansville, IN
U of Hartford, CT
U of Hawaii at Manoa, HI
U of Houston, TX
U of Kentucky, KY
U of Mary Hardin-Baylor, TX
U of Massachusetts Amherst, MA
U of Miami, FL
U of Missouri–Columbia, MO

U of Missouri–Kansas City, MO
U of Nebraska at Omaha, NE
U of Nebraska–Lincoln, NE
U of New Haven, CT
U of New Orleans, LA
The U of North Carolina at Chapel Hill, NC
The U of North Carolina at Charlotte, NC
U of Northern Iowa, IA
U of North Florida, FL
U of Pennsylvania, PA
U of Pittsburgh, PA
U of Rhode Island, RI
U of Rio Grande, OH
U of St. Thomas, MN
U of St. Thomas, TX
U of San Francisco, CA
The U of Scranton, PA
U of South Carolina Upstate, SC
U of Southern Indiana, IN
The U of Texas at Austin, TX
The U of Texas at San Antonio, TX
The U of the Arts, PA
U of the Incarnate Word, TX
U of the Ozarks, AR
U of the Pacific, CA
The U of Virginia's Coll at Wise, VA
U of Washington, WA
U of Wisconsin–Eau Claire, WI
U of Wisconsin–La Crosse, WI
U of Wisconsin–Stevens Point, WI
U of Wyoming, WY
Utica Coll, NY
Valdosta State U, GA
Vanguard U of Southern California, CA
Wake Forest U, NC
Washburn U, KS
Waubonsee Comm Coll, IL
Wayne State U, MI
West Chester U of Pennsylvania, PA
Western New England Coll, MA
Westminster Coll, UT
West Virginia State U, WV
West Virginia Wesleyan Coll, WV
Wheaton Coll, IL
Wichita State U, KS
Wilkes U, PA
Wright State U, OH

COMMUNICATIONS SYSTEMS INSTALLATION AND REPAIR TECHNOLOGY
Broome Comm Coll, NY
Idaho State U, ID
Mohawk Valley Comm Coll, NY

COMMUNICATIONS TECHNOLOGIES AND SUPPORT SERVICES RELATED
Comm Coll of Allegheny County, PA
The U of Scranton, PA
Western Tech Coll, WI

COMMUNICATIONS TECHNOLOGY
Allegany Coll of Maryland, MD

Bluefield State Coll, WV
Burlington County Coll, NJ
The Coll of Saint Rose, NY
Comm Coll of Beaver County, PA
Eastern Michigan U, MI
East Stroudsburg U of Pennsylvania, PA
Lackawanna Coll, PA
Lassen Comm Coll District, CA
Ocean County Coll, NJ
St. Philip's Coll, TX
Salve Regina U, RI
Southern Maine Comm Coll, ME

COMMUNITY HEALTH AND PREVENTIVE MEDICINE
Hofstra U, NY
Tufts U, MA
U of California, Los Angeles, CA
U of Illinois at Urbana–Champaign, IL
U of Massachusetts Lowell, MA

COMMUNITY HEALTH LIAISON
Delaware State U, DE

COMMUNITY HEALTH SERVICES COUNSELING
Bethel U, MN
California State U, Sacramento, CA
Comm Coll of Allegheny County, PA
Indiana U–Purdue U Fort Wayne, IN
Kingsborough Comm Coll of the City U of New York, NY
Minnesota State U Moorhead, MN
Prairie View A&M U, TX
Seton Hill U, PA
Stephen F. Austin State U, TX
Texas A&M U, TX
U of Houston, TX
U of Kansas, KS
U of Nebraska at Omaha, NE
U of Nebraska–Lincoln, NE
U of Northern Iowa, IA
U of Pennsylvania, PA

COMMUNITY ORGANIZATION AND ADVOCACY
Bemidji State U, MN
Cape Breton U, NS, Canada
Cornell U, NY
Crafton Hills Coll, CA
Eastern Michigan U, MI
High Point U, NC
Marywood U, PA
Mercer U, GA
Midland Lutheran Coll, NE
Mohawk Valley Comm Coll, NY
New River Comm Coll, VA
Northern State U, SD
Rockhurst U, MO
Roosevelt U, IL
Saint Leo U, FL
The U of Akron, OH
U of Baltimore, MD
U of Delaware, DE
The U of Findlay, OH

U of Massachusetts Boston, MA
U of New Hampshire, NH
U of New Mexico, NM
U of Oregon, OR
The U of Texas at El Paso, TX

COMMUNITY PSYCHOLOGY
Montana State U–Billings, MT
Seton Hill U, PA
Western Nebraska Comm Coll, NE
Wilfrid Laurier U, ON, Canada
Wright State U, OH

COMPARATIVE LITERATURE
Bard Coll, NY
Brandeis U, MA
Brown U, RI
Bryn Mawr Coll, PA
California State U, Fullerton, CA
Carleton U, ON, Canada
Clark U, MA
Cornell U, NY
DePaul U, IL
Eckerd Coll, FL
Emory U, GA
Hamilton Coll, NY
Hampshire Coll, MA
Haverford Coll, PA
Hofstra U, NY
Hunter Coll of the City U of New York, NY
Indiana U Bloomington, IN
New York U, NY
Oakland U, MI
Occidental Coll, CA
The Ohio State U, OH
Penn State Abington, PA
Penn State DuBois, PA
Penn State Fayette, The Eberly Campus, PA
Penn State Mont Alto, PA
Penn State Wilkes-Barre, PA
Queens Coll of the City U of New York, NY
Ramapo Coll of New Jersey, NJ
Roosevelt U, IL
Rutgers, The State U of New Jersey, New Brunswick, NJ
St. Cloud State U, MN
San Diego State U, CA
San Francisco State U, CA
Sewanee: The U of the South, TN
State U of New York Coll at Geneseo, NY
Trinity Coll, CT
U of California, Berkeley, CA
U of California, Irvine, CA
U of California, Los Angeles, CA
U of California, Santa Barbara, CA
U of Cincinnati, OH
U of Delaware, DE
U of Illinois at Urbana–Champaign, IL
U of Massachusetts Amherst, MA
U of Michigan, MI
U of New Brunswick Fredericton, NB, Canada
U of New Mexico, NM
The U of North Carolina at Chapel Hill, NC

U of Oregon, OR
U of Pennsylvania, PA
U of Rhode Island, RI
U of Virginia, VA
U of Washington, WA
U of Wisconsin–Madison, WI
Wellesley Coll, MA
West Chester U of Pennsylvania, PA

COMPUTATIONAL MATHEMATICS
Carnegie Mellon U, PA
Indiana U–Purdue U Fort Wayne, IN
Marist Coll, NY
Marquette U, WI
Michigan State U, MI
Northern Illinois U, IL
Southwestern U, TX
U of California, Los Angeles, CA

COMPUTER AND INFORMATION SCIENCES
Adelphi U, NY
Alabama A&M U, AL
Albany State U, GA
Alexandria Tech Coll, MN
Angelo State U, TX
Arizona State U at the West campus, AZ
Asnuntuck Comm Coll, CT
Athabasca U, AB, Canada
Aurora U, IL
Avila U, MO
Baker Coll of Allen Park, MI
Bentley Coll, MA
Bethel Coll, IN
Bethel U, MN
Bishop's U, QC, Canada
Bluefield State Coll, WV
Bradley U, IL
Brewton-Parker Coll, GA
Broome Comm Coll, NY
Brown Mackie Coll–Salina, KS
Bucks County Comm Coll, PA
Calhoun Comm Coll, AL
California State U, Sacramento, CA
California State U, San Bernardino, CA
California State U, Stanislaus, CA
Cameron U, OK
Cape Breton U, NS, Canada
Carroll Coll, WI
Cedar Crest Coll, PA
Central Arizona Coll, AZ
Christopher Newport U, VA
Claremont McKenna Coll, CA
Clemson U, SC
Coastal Carolina U, SC
Coll of Charleston, SC
The Coll of Saint Rose, NY
The Coll of St. Scholastica, MN
Coll of Staten Island of the City U of New York, NY
The Coll of William and Mary, VA
Comm Coll of Beaver County, PA
Concordia U, NE
Cornell U, NY
Dallas Baptist U, TX
Delaware State U, DE
DePaul U, IL
Drury U, MO

Eastern Connecticut State U, CT
Eastern Michigan U, MI
Eastern New Mexico U–Roswell, NM
East Stroudsburg U of Pennsylvania, PA
Edinboro U of Pennsylvania, PA
Fairleigh Dickinson U, Coll at Florham, NJ
Fairleigh Dickinson U, Metropolitan Campus, NJ
Florida Atlantic U, FL
Florida Comm Coll at Jacksonville, FL
Florida Gulf Coast U, FL
Florida International U, FL
Franciscan U of Steubenville, OH
Franklin Coll, IN
Freed-Hardeman U, TN
Fresno Pacific U, CA
Gadsden State Comm Coll, AL
Gannon U, PA
Georgetown Coll, KY
The George Washington U, DC
Georgia Coll & State U, GA
Georgian Court U, NJ
Hagerstown Comm Coll, MD
Harding U, AR
Harrisburg Area Comm Coll, PA
Hartwick Coll, NY
Heartland Comm Coll, IL
Henderson State U, AR
High Point U, NC
Houston Baptist U, TX
Houston Comm Coll System, TX
Idaho State U, ID
Indiana U Bloomington, IN
Indiana U of Pennsylvania, PA
Indiana U–Purdue U Indianapolis, IN
Ithaca Coll, NY
Ivy Tech Comm Coll–Kokomo, IN
Ivy Tech Comm Coll–Southwest, IN
Ivy Tech Comm Coll–Wabash Valley, IN
Jacksonville U, FL
James H. Faulkner State Comm Coll, AL
Jamestown Comm Coll, NY
Johnson & Wales U, RI
Kansas State U, KS
Kennesaw State U, GA
Kentucky Wesleyan Coll, KY
Kingsborough Comm Coll of the City U of New York, NY
King's Coll, PA
Kuyper Coll, MI
Lackawanna Coll, PA
LaGrange Coll, GA
Lancaster Bible Coll, PA
Liberty U, VA
Lincoln U, PA
Loyola U New Orleans, LA
Marshall U, WV
Marymount U, VA
Marywood U, PA
Massachusetts Coll of Liberal Arts, MA
Massasoit Comm Coll, MA
McDaniel Coll, MD
Mercyhurst Coll, PA
Michigan State U, MI
Mid-South Comm Coll, AR

Millersville U of Pennsylvania, PA
Minnesota State U Moorhead, MN
Mohawk Valley Comm Coll, NY
Monmouth U, NJ
Montana State U–Billings, MT
Montana Tech of The U of Montana, MT
Mount St. Mary's U, MD
Mount Saint Vincent U, NS, Canada
Mount Vernon Nazarene U, OH
Murray State U, KY
Nassau Comm Coll, NY
Neumann Coll, PA
Neumont U, UT
New Hampshire Comm Tech Coll, Nashua/Claremont, NH
New Jersey City U, NJ
New York U, NY
Northern Michigan U, MI
North Georgia Coll & State U, GA
Northwood U, MI
Northwood U, Florida Campus, FL
Northwood U, Texas Campus, TX
Nova Southeastern U, FL
Ocean County Coll, NJ
Odessa Coll, TX
The Ohio State U, OH
Old Dominion U, VA
Oregon Inst of Technology, OR
Park U, MO
Penn State Abington, PA
Penn State DuBois, PA
Penn State Fayette, The Eberly Campus, PA
Penn State Mont Alto, PA
Penn State Wilkes-Barre, PA
Phoenix Coll, AZ
Pima Comm Coll, AZ
Portland State U, OR
Ramapo Coll of New Jersey, NJ
Reedley Coll, CA
Rensselaer Polytechnic Inst, NY
Rice U, TX
The Richard Stockton Coll of New Jersey, NJ
Rochester Inst of Technology, NY
Rowan U, NJ
Rutgers, The State U of New Jersey, Newark, NJ
Saginaw Valley State U, MI
St. Francis Xavier U, NS, Canada
Saint Joseph's Coll, IN
St. Mary's Coll of Maryland, MD
St. Norbert Coll, WI
Saint Xavier U, IL
Salem Comm Coll, NJ
San Diego Mesa Coll, CA
Seton Hall U, NJ
Shippensburg U of Pennsylvania, PA
Skagit Valley Coll, WA
Slippery Rock U of Pennsylvania, PA
State U of New York Coll at Potsdam, NY
State U of New York Coll of Technology at Alfred, NY

Stephen F. Austin State U, TX
Sussex County Comm Coll, NJ
Syracuse U, NY
Tallahassee Comm Coll, FL
Temple U, PA
Trinity U, TX
Troy U, AL
U at Albany, State U of New York, NY
The U of Alabama, AL
The U of Alabama in Huntsville, AL
U of Alaska Anchorage, AK
The U of Arizona, AZ
U of Arkansas, AR
U of Arkansas at Fort Smith, AR
U of Baltimore, MD
U of California, Irvine, CA
U of Central Florida, FL
U of Central Missouri, MO
U of Cincinnati, OH
U of Delaware, DE
U of Dubuque, IA
U of Evansville, IN
U of Great Falls, MT
U of Guelph, ON, Canada
U of Hartford, CT
U of Hawaii at Manoa, HI
U of Houston, TX
U of Kansas, KS
U of Kentucky, KY
The U of Maine at Augusta, ME
U of Mary Hardin-Baylor, TX
U of Miami, FL
U of Mississippi, MS
U of Missouri–Columbia, MO
U of Nebraska at Kearney, NE
U of Nebraska–Lincoln, NE
U of New Haven, CT
U of New Mexico, NM
U of Northern British Columbia, BC, Canada
U of North Florida, FL
U of Notre Dame, IN
U of Oregon, OR
U of Rhode Island, RI
U of St. Thomas, MN
U of San Francisco, CA
U of South Carolina Upstate, SC
U of Southern Indiana, IN
The U of Texas at Austin, TX
U of Vermont, VT
U of Virginia, VA
The U of Virginia's Coll at Wise, VA
U of Washington, WA
U of West Georgia, GA
U of Wisconsin–Eau Claire, WI
U of Wisconsin–La Crosse, WI
U of Wisconsin–Stevens Point, WI
Utica Coll, NY
Valdosta State U, GA
Vassar Coll, NY
Ventura Coll, CA
Victor Valley Coll, CA
Virginia Intermont Coll, VA
Wake Forest U, NC
Washburn U, KS
Washington and Lee U, VA
Waubonsee Comm Coll, IL
Wayne State Coll, NE
Wayne State U, MI
Westchester Comm Coll, NY

West Chester U of Pennsylvania, PA
Western Nebraska Comm Coll, NE
Westmoreland County Comm Coll, PA
West Texas A&M U, TX
West Virginia Wesleyan Coll, WV
Wichita State U, KS
Widener U, PA
Wilkes U, PA
Worcester State Coll, MA
Wright State U, OH
Yale U, CT

COMPUTER AND INFORMATION SCIENCES AND SUPPORT SERVICES RELATED

Bunker Hill Comm Coll, MA
Coll of Mount St. Joseph, OH
Coll of Staten Island of the City U of New York, NY
Fairleigh Dickinson U, Metropolitan Campus, NJ
Gretna Career Coll, LA
Harrisburg Area Comm Coll, PA
Lehigh U, PA
Massasoit Comm Coll, MA
Mohawk Valley Comm Coll, NY
Montana State U–Billings, MT
Park U, MO
U of Arkansas at Fort Smith, AR
U of California, Irvine, CA
U of Evansville, IN
U of Great Falls, MT
U of Missouri–Rolla, MO
U of Northern Iowa, IA
U of Notre Dame, IN
U of Pittsburgh, PA
The U of Scranton, PA
Waukesha County Tech Coll, WI
Williston State Coll, ND

COMPUTER AND INFORMATION SCIENCES RELATED

Bucks County Comm Coll, PA
Cape Cod Comm Coll, MA
Citrus Coll, CA
Coll of the Canyons, CA
Coll of the Desert, CA
The Coll of Westchester, NY
DePaul U, IL
Eastfield Coll, TX
Florida Comm Coll at Jacksonville, FL
Galveston Coll, TX
Glendale Comm Coll, CA
Heartland Comm Coll, IL
Howard Comm Coll, MD
Jamestown Comm Coll, NY
Lake-Sumter Comm Coll, FL
Lamar Inst of Technology, TX
Massasoit Comm Coll, MA
Metropolitan Comm Coll–Longview, MO
Metropolitan Comm Coll–Penn Valley, MO
Missouri State U–West Plains, MO
Nassau Comm Coll, NY
Neumont U, UT

Northland Comm and Tech Coll–Thief River Falls, MN
Richland Comm Coll, IL
Santa Ana Coll, CA
Sauk Valley Comm Coll, IL
Seminole Comm Coll, FL
Southeast Tech Inst, SD
Southwestern Michigan Coll, MI
Stark State Coll of Technology, OH
U of Great Falls, MT
U of Northern Iowa, IA
Washburn U, KS
Waubonsee Comm Coll, IL
Westchester Comm Coll, NY
Wilfrid Laurier U, ON, Canada

COMPUTER AND INFORMATION SYSTEMS SECURITY

Chattahoochee Tech Coll, GA
East Stroudsburg U of Pennsylvania, PA
Florida Comm Coll at Jacksonville, FL
Jamestown Comm Coll, NY
Rochester Inst of Technology, NY
St. Philip's Coll, TX
Seminole Comm Coll, FL
U of Great Falls, MT

COMPUTER ENGINEERING

Brown U, RI
California State U, Sacramento, CA
Carleton U, ON, Canada
The Catholic U of America, DC
Christopher Newport U, VA
Clemson U, SC
Dalhousie U, NS, Canada
Dominican U, IL
Eastern Nazarene Coll, MA
Embry-Riddle Aeronautical U, FL
Florida Atlantic U, FL
Florida Inst of Technology, FL
Florida International U, FL
The George Washington U, DC
Gonzaga U, WA
Harding U, AR
Hofstra U, NY
Indiana U–Purdue U Fort Wayne, IN
Indiana U–Purdue U Indianapolis, IN
Itasca Comm Coll, MN
Johnson & Wales U, RI
Kansas State U, KS
Lehigh U, PA
LeTourneau U, TX
Loyola Marymount U, CA
Manhattan Coll, NY
Marquette U, WI
Michigan State U, MI
Minnesota State U Mankato, MN
Montana State U, MT
Montana Tech of The U of Montana, MT
North Carolina State U, NC
North Dakota State U, ND
Northeastern U, MA
Oakland U, MI
The Ohio State U, OH
Old Dominion U, VA
Oral Roberts U, OK

Penn State Abington, PA
Penn State DuBois, PA
Penn State Fayette, The
  Eberly Campus, PA
Penn State Mont Alto, PA
Penn State Wilkes-Barre, PA
Portland State U, OR
Queen's U at Kingston, ON,
  Canada
Rensselaer Polytechnic Inst,
  NY
Rice U, TX
Rochester Inst of
  Technology, NY
Rutgers, The State U of New
  Jersey, New Brunswick, NJ
Ryerson U, ON, Canada
St. Cloud State U, MN
San Diego State U, CA
Santa Barbara City Coll, CA
Santa Clara U, CA
Southern Illinois U
  Carbondale, IL
Southern Illinois U
  Edwardsville, IL
Stonehill Coll, MA
Syracuse U, NY
Taylor U, IN
Texas A&M U, TX
Trinity Coll, CT
Tufts U, MA
U at Buffalo, the State U of
  New York, NY
The U of Akron, OH
The U of Alabama in
  Huntsville, AL
The U of Arizona, AZ
U of Arkansas, AR
U of California, Irvine, CA
U of California, Los Angeles,
  CA
U of California, Santa
  Barbara, CA
U of Central Florida, FL
U of Cincinnati, OH
U of Colorado at Boulder,
  CO
U of Connecticut, CT
U of Dayton, OH
U of Delaware, DE
U of Evansville, IN
U of Hartford, CT
U of Houston, TX
U of Illinois at Urbana–
  Champaign, IL
U of Kansas, KS
U of Manitoba, MB, Canada
U of Maryland, Baltimore
  County, MD
U of Massachusetts Amherst,
  MA
U of Massachusetts Lowell,
  MA
U of Miami, FL
U of Michigan, MI
U of Minnesota, Duluth, MN
U of Missouri–Columbia,
  MO
U of Missouri–Rolla, MO
U of Nebraska at Omaha,
  NE
U of Nebraska–Lincoln, NE
U of New Brunswick
  Fredericton, NB, Canada
U of New Hampshire, NH
U of New Haven, CT
U of New Mexico, NM
The U of North Carolina at
  Charlotte, NC
U of Notre Dame, IN
U of Pennsylvania, PA
U of Pittsburgh, PA
U of Portland, OR
U of Rhode Island, RI

The U of Scranton, PA
The U of Tennessee, TN
The U of Texas at San
  Antonio, TX
U of the Pacific, CA
U of Toronto, ON, Canada
U of Virginia, VA
U of Washington, WA
U of Wisconsin–Madison,
  WI
U of Wyoming, WY
Villanova U, PA
Wichita State U, KS
Wright State U, OH

**COMPUTER
ENGINEERING RELATED**
Carnegie Mellon U, PA
Coll of the Canyons, CA
Glendale Comm Coll, CA
Itasca Comm Coll, MN
Jefferson Comm Coll, OH
Seminole Comm Coll, FL
Stark State Coll of
  Technology, OH
Surry Comm Coll, NC

**COMPUTER
ENGINEERING
TECHNOLOGIES
RELATED**
Old Dominion U, VA

**COMPUTER
ENGINEERING
TECHNOLOGY**
Abraham Baldwin Coll, GA
Allegany Coll of Maryland,
  MD
Brevard Comm Coll, FL
Brock U, ON, Canada
Broome Comm Coll, NY
Broward Comm Coll, FL
Bucks County Comm Coll,
  PA
Central Piedmont Comm
  Coll, NC
Chattanooga State Tech
  Comm Coll, TN
Chesapeake Coll, MD
Clayton State U, GA
Coll of The Albemarle, NC
Colorado Mountain Coll,
  Alpine Campus, CO
Comm Coll of Allegheny
  County, PA
Cuesta Coll, CA
DeKalb Tech Coll, GA
East Carolina U, NC
Eastern Michigan U, MI
Eastfield Coll, TX
Farmingdale State Coll, NY
Florida Comm Coll at
  Jacksonville, FL
Frederick Comm Coll, MD
Fulton-Montgomery Comm
  Coll, NY
Glendale Comm Coll, CA
Heartland Comm Coll, IL
Hillsborough Comm Coll, FL
Hocking Coll, OH
Houston Comm Coll System,
  TX
Indiana U–Purdue U Fort
  Wayne, IN
Irvine Valley Coll, CA
Jamestown Comm Coll, NY
Johnson & Wales U, RI
Kellogg Comm Coll, MI
Lake Superior State U, MI
LeTourneau U, TX
Marshall U, WV
Miami Dade Coll, FL
Middlesex County Coll, NJ

Minnesota State Coll–
  Southeast Tech, MN
Minnesota State U Mankato,
  MN
MiraCosta Coll, CA
Murray State U, KY
New Hampshire Comm
  Tech Coll, Nashua/
  Claremont, NH
New River Comm Coll, VA
North Central Missouri Coll,
  MO
North Central Texas Coll, TX
Northeastern U, MA
Oregon Inst of Technology,
  OR
Paris Jr Coll, TX
Pima Comm Coll, AZ
Purdue U North Central, IN
Richmond Comm Coll, NC
Rochester Inst of
  Technology, NY
St. Louis Comm Coll at
  Florissant Valley, MO
Seminole Comm Coll, FL
Skagit Valley Coll, WA
Southern Maine Comm Coll,
  ME
State U of New York Coll of
  Technology at Alfred, NY
Surry Comm Coll, NC
U of Cincinnati, OH
U of Dayton, OH
U of Hartford, CT
U of Houston, TX
U of the District of
  Columbia, DC
Vermont Tech Coll, VT
Westmoreland County
  Comm Coll, PA

COMPUTER GRAPHICS
Academy of Art U, CA
The Art Inst of Pittsburgh,
  PA
Burlington County Coll, NJ
Calhoun Comm Coll, AL
Cape Cod Comm Coll, MA
Coll of the Atlantic, ME
Coll of the Desert, CA
The Coll of Westchester, NY
DePaul U, IL
Florida Comm Coll at
  Jacksonville, FL
Gloucester County Coll, NJ
Hampshire Coll, MA
Howard Comm Coll, MD
John Brown U, AR
Johnson & Wales U, RI
Kellogg Comm Coll, MI
Miami Dade Coll, FL
Middlesex County Coll, NJ
Missouri State U–West
  Plains, MO
Nassau Comm Coll, NY
New Mexico Jr Coll, NM
New River Comm Coll, VA
North Central Texas Coll, TX
Northland Comm and Tech
  Coll–Thief River Falls, MN
Phoenix Coll, AZ
Pratt Inst, NY
Pueblo Comm Coll, CO
Richland Comm Coll, IL
Rochester Inst of
  Technology, NY
Savannah Coll of Art and
  Design, GA
School of the Art Inst of
  Chicago, IL
School of Visual Arts, NY
Seminole Comm Coll, FL
Southeast Tech Inst, SD
Southern Adventist U, TN

Springfield Coll, MA
State U of New York at
  Fredonia, NY
State U of New York Coll of
  Technology at Alfred, NY
Syracuse U, NY
Tallahassee Comm Coll, FL
Taylor U, IN
U of Dubuque, IA
U of Great Falls, MT
U of Mary Hardin-Baylor, TX
U of Pennsylvania, PA
The U of Tampa, FL
U of the Incarnate Word, TX
Westmoreland County
  Comm Coll, PA

**COMPUTER HARDWARE
ENGINEERING**
Abilene Christian U, TX
Cuesta Coll, CA
Eastfield Coll, TX
Florida Comm Coll at
  Jacksonville, FL
Lake City Comm Coll, FL
Seminole Comm Coll, FL
Stark State Coll of
  Technology, OH
State U of New York Coll of
  Technology at Alfred, NY

**COMPUTER/
INFORMATION
TECHNOLOGY SERVICES
ADMINISTRATION
RELATED**
Brevard Comm Coll, FL
Bucks County Comm Coll,
  PA
Clayton State U, GA
The Coll of Westchester, NY
Dalhousie U, NS, Canada
Eastfield Coll, TX
El Centro Coll, TX
Florida Comm Coll at
  Jacksonville, FL
Howard Comm Coll, MD
Johnson & Wales U, RI
Lindenwood U, MO
Muscatine Comm Coll, IA
North Central Texas Coll, TX
Queens U of Charlotte, NC
St. Cloud Tech Coll, MN
Seattle Pacific U, WA
Seminole Comm Coll, FL
Southeast Tech Inst, SD
Stark State Coll of
  Technology, OH
State U of New York Coll of
  Technology at Alfred, NY
State U of New York Coll of
  Technology at Canton, NY
The U of Akron, OH
U of Great Falls, MT

**COMPUTER
INSTALLATION AND
REPAIR TECHNOLOGY**
Coahoma Comm Coll, MS
Harrisburg Area Comm Coll,
  PA
State U of New York Coll of
  Technology at Alfred, NY
Waukesha County Tech Coll,
  WI

**COMPUTER
MAINTENANCE
TECHNOLOGY**
St. Philip's Coll, TX

**COMPUTER
MANAGEMENT**
Cosumnes River Coll,
  Sacramento, CA

Grossmont Coll, CA
Midland Coll, TX
National-Louis U, IL
New Hampshire Comm
  Tech Coll, Nashua/
  Claremont, NH
North Central Texas Coll, TX
Northwood U, MI
Northwood U, Florida
  Campus, FL
Oklahoma State U, OK
Shasta Coll, CA
Southern Maine Comm Coll,
  ME
U of Cincinnati, OH
U of Great Falls, MT
U of the Incarnate Word, TX

**COMPUTER
PROGRAMMING**
Abraham Baldwin Coll, GA
Altamaha Tech Coll, GA
Ancilla Coll, IN
Asheville-Buncombe Tech
  Comm Coll, NC
Bishop's U, QC, Canada
Brevard Comm Coll, FL
Brock U, ON, Canada
Broward Comm Coll, FL
Bucks County Comm Coll,
  PA
Bunker Hill Comm Coll, MA
Carleton U, ON, Canada
Cedar Valley Coll, TX
Central Ohio Tech Coll, OH
Central Piedmont Comm
  Coll, NC
Charleston Southern U, SC
Chattahoochee Tech Coll,
  GA
Chattanooga State Tech
  Comm Coll, TN
Chesapeake Coll, MD
Clemson U, SC
Coll of Staten Island of the
  City U of New York, NY
Coll of The Albemarle, NC
The Coll of Westchester, NY
Comm Coll of Beaver
  County, PA
Coosa Valley Tech Coll, GA
Cosumnes River Coll,
  Sacramento, CA
Dabney S. Lancaster Comm
  Coll, VA
DeKalb Tech Coll, GA
Delaware Tech & Comm
  Coll, Jack F. Owens
  Campus, DE
DePaul U, IL
Eastfield Coll, TX
El Centro Coll, TX
Farmingdale State Coll, NY
Florida Comm Coll at
  Jacksonville, FL
Framingham State Coll, MA
Franklin Pierce U, NH
Gannon U, PA
Gaston Coll, NC
Greenville Tech Coll, SC
Grossmont Coll, CA
Heartland Comm Coll, IL
Hillsborough Comm Coll, FL
Hocking Coll, OH
Husson Coll, ME
Illinois Valley Comm Coll, IL
Johnson & Wales U, RI
Kellogg Comm Coll, MI
Lake City Comm Coll, FL
Lamar U, TX
Laredo Comm Coll, TX
Lee Coll, TX
Linn State Tech Coll, MO
Long Beach City Coll, CA

Macomb Comm Coll, MI
Massasoit Comm Coll, MA
Metropolitan Comm
Coll–Longview, MO
Miami Dade Coll, FL
Middlesex Comm Coll, CT
Middlesex County Coll, NJ
Midland Lutheran Coll, NE
Minnesota State Coll–
Southeast Tech, MN
Minnesota State U Mankato,
MN
Mohawk Valley Comm Coll,
NY
Montana Tech of The U of
Montana, MT
Neumont U, UT
New Mexico Jr Coll, NM
New York U, NY
North Central Texas Coll, TX
Ocean County Coll, NJ
Oregon Inst of Technology,
OR
Purdue U North Central, IN
Rockhurst U, MO
St. Cloud Tech Coll, MN
St. Louis Comm Coll at
Florissant Valley, MO
Schoolcraft Coll, MI
Seminole Comm Coll, FL
Southeast Tech Inst, SD
Southwestern Coll, KS
Southwestern Michigan Coll,
MI
Spokane Comm Coll, WA
Stark State Coll of
Technology, OH
Surry Comm Coll, NC
Tallahassee Comm Coll, FL
Taylor U, IN
Tidewater Comm Coll, VA
U of Cincinnati, OH
U of Great Falls, MT
The U of Montana-Helena
Coll of Technology, MT
The U of Tampa, FL
Valencia Comm Coll, FL
Waukesha County Tech Coll,
WI
Western Tech Coll, WI
West Los Angeles Coll, CA
West Virginia Northern
Comm Coll, WV
West Virginia State U, WV
Wilfrid Laurier U, ON,
Canada

**COMPUTER
PROGRAMMING
RELATED**
Bucks County Comm Coll,
PA
Coll of the Desert, CA
The Coll of Westchester, NY
Eastfield Coll, TX
Farmingdale State Coll, NY
Florida Comm Coll at
Jacksonville, FL
Glendale Comm Coll, CA
Laredo Comm Coll, TX
Neumont U, UT
North Central Texas Coll, TX
St. Cloud Tech Coll, MN
San Diego Mesa Coll, CA
Santa Ana Coll, CA
Seminole Comm Coll, FL
Southeast Tech Inst, SD
Stark State Coll of
Technology, OH
Surry Comm Coll, NC
Valencia Comm Coll, FL

**COMPUTER
PROGRAMMING
(SPECIFIC
APPLICATIONS)**
Alexandria Tech Coll, MN
Brevard Comm Coll, FL
Bucks County Comm Coll,
PA
Bunker Hill Comm Coll, MA
Caldwell Comm Coll and
Tech Inst, NC
Cedar Valley Coll, TX
Central Piedmont Comm
Coll, NC
Coll of The Albemarle, NC
The Coll of Westchester, NY
DePaul U, IL
Florida Comm Coll at
Jacksonville, FL
Glendale Comm Coll, CA
Heartland Comm Coll, IL
Hudson Valley Comm Coll,
NY
Husson Coll, ME
Idaho State U, ID
Kellogg Comm Coll, MI
Lake City Comm Coll, FL
Lincoln Land Comm Coll, IL
Macomb Comm Coll, MI
Midland Coll, TX
Missouri State U–West
Plains, MO
Neumont U, UT
North Central Texas Coll, TX
Richland Comm Coll, IL
St. Cloud Tech Coll, MN
San Diego Mesa Coll, CA
Seminole Comm Coll, FL
Southeast Tech Inst, SD
South Piedmont Comm Coll,
NC
Stark State Coll of
Technology, OH
Tallahassee Comm Coll, FL
Valencia Comm Coll, FL
Victor Valley Coll, CA
Waubonsee Comm Coll, IL

**COMPUTER
PROGRAMMING
(VENDOR/PRODUCT
CERTIFICATION)**
The Coll of Westchester, NY
Florida Comm Coll at
Jacksonville, FL
Heartland Comm Coll, IL
Lake City Comm Coll, FL
Neumont U, UT
North Central Texas Coll, TX
Seminole Comm Coll, FL
Southeast Tech Inst, SD
Stark State Coll of
Technology, OH

COMPUTER SCIENCE
Abilene Christian U, TX
Abraham Baldwin Coll, GA
Acadia U, NS, Canada
Albion Coll, MI
Albright Coll, PA
Alderson-Broaddus Coll, WV
Alma Coll, MI
American U, DC
Amherst Coll, MA
Anderson U, IN
Ashland U, OH
Athens State U, AL
Augsburg Coll, MN
Austin Coll, TX
Baker Coll of Allen Park, MI
Ball State U, IN
Bard Coll, NY
Barry U, FL
Baylor U, TX

Bemidji State U, MN
Benedictine Coll, KS
Bethel Coll, IN
Bishop's U, QC, Canada
Blinn Coll, TX
Boston Coll, MA
Brandeis U, MA
Brandon U, MB, Canada
Bridgewater Coll, VA
British Columbia Inst of
Technology, BC, Canada
Brock U, ON, Canada
Broward Comm Coll, FL
Brown U, RI
Bucks County Comm Coll,
PA
Buena Vista U, IA
Bunker Hill Comm Coll, MA
Burlington County Coll, NJ
California State U, Fullerton,
CA
California State U,
Northridge, CA
California State U, San
Bernardino, CA
Calvin Coll, MI
Cape Breton U, NS, Canada
Cape Cod Comm Coll, MA
Cardinal Stritch U, WI
Carleton U, ON, Canada
Carlow U, PA
Carnegie Mellon U, PA
Carroll Coll, MT
Carroll Coll, WI
Carson-Newman Coll, TN
Carthage Coll, WI
The Catholic U of America,
DC
Central Arizona Coll, AZ
Central Piedmont Comm
Coll, NC
Central Wyoming Coll, WY
Charleston Southern U, SC
Chattanooga State Tech
Comm Coll, TN
Chesapeake Coll, MD
Christopher Newport U, VA
Citrus Coll, CA
Claremont McKenna Coll,
CA
Clark U, MA
Clayton State U, GA
Clemson U, SC
Coahoma Comm Coll, MS
Coe Coll, IA
Colby Coll, ME
Colgate U, NY
Coll of Mount St. Joseph,
OH
Coll of Mount Saint Vincent,
NY
Coll of Saint Elizabeth, NJ
Coll of the Canyons, CA
Coll of the Desert, CA
Columbus State U, GA
Commonwealth Tech Inst,
PA
Concordia U, NE
Concord U, WV
Cornell U, NY
Crafton Hills Coll, CA
Cuesta Coll, CA
Dalhousie U, NS, Canada
Dallas Baptist U, TX
Delaware State U, DE
DePaul U, IL
Dixie State Coll of Utah, UT
Dominican U, IL
Drake U, IA
Drury U, MO
Duke U, NC
Earlham Coll, IN
East Carolina U, NC
Eastern Mennonite U, VA

Eastern Michigan U, MI
Eastern Nazarene Coll, MA
Eckerd Coll, FL
El Centro Coll, TX
Elms Coll, MA
Elon U, NC
Emory U, GA
Fairfield U, CT
Farmingdale State Coll, NY
Fayetteville State U, NC
Ferrum Coll, VA
Fitchburg State Coll, MA
Florida Inst of Technology,
FL
Florida International U, FL
Fontbonne U, MO
Framingham State Coll, MA
Franciscan U of
Steubenville, OH
Franklin Coll, IN
Franklin Pierce U, NH
Frederick Comm Coll, MD
Freed-Hardeman U, TN
Fulton-Montgomery Comm
Coll, NY
Furman U, SC
Gainesville State Coll, GA
Galveston Coll, TX
Gardner-Webb U, NC
Geneva Coll, PA
The George Washington U,
DC
Glendale Comm Coll, CA
Glenville State Coll, WV
Gloucester County Coll, NJ
Gonzaga U, WA
Gordon Coll, MA
Goshen Coll, IN
Graceland U, IA
Grambling State U, LA
Grinnell Coll, IA
Grossmont Coll, CA
Gustavus Adolphus Coll,
MN
Hamilton Coll, NY
Hampden-Sydney Coll, VA
Hampshire Coll, MA
Harding U, AR
Hartwick Coll, NY
Haverford Coll, PA
Heartland Comm Coll, IL
High Point U, NC
Hocking Coll, OH
Hofstra U, NY
Hope Coll, MI
Houghton Coll, NY
Houston Baptist U, TX
Houston Comm Coll System,
TX
Howard Comm Coll, MD
Hunter Coll of the City U of
New York, NY
Huntington U, IN
Illinois Wesleyan U, IL
Immaculata U, PA
Indiana U–Purdue U Fort
Wayne, IN
Indiana U Southeast, IN
Iona Coll, NY
Ithaca Coll, NY
Jamestown Comm Coll, NY
Kennesaw State U, GA
Kentucky Wesleyan Coll, KY
Kingsborough Comm Coll of
the City U of New York,
NY
King's Coll, PA
The King's U Coll, AB,
Canada
LaGrange Coll, GA
Lakeland Coll, WI
Lake-Sumter Comm Coll, FL
Lake Superior State U, MI
Lamar State Coll–Orange, TX

Lamar U, TX
Langston U, OK
Lassen Comm Coll District,
CA
Lawrence U, WI
Lebanon Valley Coll, PA
Lehigh U, PA
LeTourneau U, TX
Lewis U, IL
Lindenwood U, MO
Long Island U, Brooklyn
Campus, NY
Loras Coll, IA
Loyola Marymount U, CA
Loyola U Chicago, IL
Lynchburg Coll, VA
Macalester Coll, MN
Manhattan Coll, NY
Manhattanville Coll, NY
Marietta Coll, OH
Marist Coll, NY
Marquette U, WI
Marymount U, VA
Massachusetts Coll of Liberal
Arts, MA
Mercer U, GA
Mercyhurst Coll, PA
Metropolitan Comm
Coll–Longview, MO
Metropolitan Comm
Coll–Penn Valley, MO
Miami Dade Coll, FL
Middlesex County Coll, NJ
Middle Tennessee State U,
TN
Midland Lutheran Coll, NE
Millersville U of
Pennsylvania, PA
Minnesota State U Mankato,
MN
Minnesota State U
Moorhead, MN
Missouri State U, MO
Molloy Coll, NY
Monmouth Coll, IL
Montana State U, MT
Montana Tech of The U of
Montana, MT
Moorpark Coll, CA
Moravian Coll, PA
Morningside Coll, IA
Mount Holyoke Coll, MA
Mount Union Coll, OH
Nassau Comm Coll, NY
Neumont U, UT
New Hampshire Comm
Tech Coll, Nashua/
Claremont, NH
New Mexico Jr Coll, NM
New York City Coll of
Technology of the City U
of New York, NY
New York U, NY
Niagara U, NY
Nipissing U, ON, Canada
North Carolina State U, NC
North Central Coll, IL
North Central Texas Coll, TX
North Dakota State U, ND
Northeastern U, MA
Northern Illinois U, IL
Northern Michigan U, MI
North Georgia Coll & State
U, GA
Northland Comm and Tech
Coll–Thief River Falls, MN
Northwestern Oklahoma
State U, OK
Northwest Nazarene U, ID
Notre Dame de Namur U,
CA
Nova Southeastern U, FL
Oakland U, MI
Odessa Coll, TX

Oglethorpe U, GA
The Ohio State U, OH
Ohio Wesleyan U, OH
Oklahoma State U, OK
Oral Roberts U, OK
Otterbein Coll, OH
Park U, MO
Paul Quinn Coll, TX
Piedmont Coll, GA
Pittsburg State U, KS
Point Loma Nazarene U, CA
Portland State U, OR
Prairie View A&M U, TX
Presbyterian Coll, SC
Queens Coll of the City U of New York, NY
Queen's U at Kingston, ON, Canada
Radford U, VA
Randolph-Macon Coll, VA
Redeemer U Coll, ON, Canada
Rensselaer Polytechnic Inst, NY
Rhodes Coll, TN
The Richard Stockton Coll of New Jersey, NJ
Ripon Coll, WI
Rivier Coll, NH
Rochester Inst of Technology, NY
Rockford Coll, IL
Rockhurst U, MO
Rocky Mountain Coll, MT
Roosevelt U, IL
Rowan U, NJ
Rutgers, The State U of New Jersey, New Brunswick, NJ
Ryerson U, ON, Canada
St. Bonaventure U, NY
St. Cloud State U, MN
Saint John's U, MN
St. Lawrence U, NY
St. Louis Comm Coll at Florissant Valley, MO
Saint Xavier U, IL
San Diego Mesa Coll, CA
San Diego State U, CA
San Francisco State U, CA
Santa Ana Coll, CA
Santa Barbara City Coll, CA
Santa Clara U, CA
Santa Rosa Jr Coll, CA
Seattle Pacific U, WA
Seton Hill U, PA
Sewanee: The U of the South, TN
Skagit Valley Coll, WA
Southern Adventist U, TN
Southern Illinois U Carbondale, IL
Southern Illinois U Edwardsville, IL
Southern Oregon U, OR
Southern U and A&M Coll, LA
Southern Utah U, UT
Southwest Baptist U, MO
Southwestern Coll, KS
Southwestern Indian Polytechnic Inst, NM
Southwestern U, TX
Springfield Coll, MA
Springfield Coll in Illinois, IL
State U of New York at Fredonia, NY
State U of New York Coll at Brockport, NY
State U of New York Coll at Geneseo, NY
State U of New York Coll of Technology at Alfred, NY
Stetson U, FL
Stonehill Coll, MA

Sweet Briar Coll, VA
Taylor U, IN
Texas A&M U, TX
Texas A&M U–Corpus Christi, TX
Thiel Coll, PA
Trent U, ON, Canada
Trinity Coll, CT
Truman State U, MO
Tufts U, MA
Union Coll, NE
U at Albany, State U of New York, NY
U at Buffalo, the State U of New York, NY
The U of Akron, OH
The U of Akron–Wayne Coll, OH
U of Alaska Anchorage, AK
U of California, Berkeley, CA
U of California, Irvine, CA
U of California, Los Angeles, CA
U of California, Santa Barbara, CA
U of Central Oklahoma, OK
U of Cincinnati, OH
U of Colorado at Boulder, CO
U of Connecticut, CT
U of Dayton, OH
U of Delaware, DE
U of Dubuque, IA
The U of Findlay, OH
U of Great Falls, MT
U of Guelph, ON, Canada
U of Hawaii at Manoa, HI
U of Illinois at Urbana–Champaign, IL
U of Manitoba, MB, Canada
U of Mary Hardin-Baylor, TX
U of Maryland, Baltimore County, MD
U of Mary Washington, VA
U of Massachusetts Amherst, MA
U of Massachusetts Boston, MA
U of Massachusetts Lowell, MA
U of Miami, FL
U of Michigan, MI
U of Minnesota, Duluth, MN
U of Missouri–Columbia, MO
U of Missouri–Kansas City, MO
U of Missouri–Rolla, MO
U of Nebraska at Omaha, NE
U of New Brunswick Fredericton, NB, Canada
U of New Hampshire, NH
U of New Haven, CT
U of New Orleans, LA
The U of North Carolina at Asheville, NC
The U of North Carolina at Chapel Hill, NC
The U of North Carolina at Charlotte, NC
U of Northern British Columbia, BC, Canada
U of Northern Iowa, IA
U of Oregon, OR
U of Pittsburgh, PA
U of Pittsburgh at Bradford, PA
U of Pittsburgh at Johnstown, PA
U of Portland, OR
U of Redlands, CA
U of Rio Grande, OH

U of San Diego, CA
U of San Francisco, CA
The U of Scranton, PA
The U of Tennessee, TN
The U of Tennessee at Martin, TN
The U of Texas at El Paso, TX
U of the District of Columbia, DC
U of the Pacific, CA
U of Toronto, ON, Canada
U of Vermont, VT
U of Washington, WA
U of Wisconsin–Green Bay, WI
U of Wisconsin–Madison, WI
U of Wisconsin–Oshkosh, WI
U of Wisconsin–Platteville, WI
U of Wyoming, WY
Valdosta State U, GA
Victor Valley Coll, CA
Villanova U, PA
Washington and Lee U, VA
Wellesley Coll, MA
Wells Coll, NY
Westchester Comm Coll, NY
Western Connecticut State U, CT
Western New England Coll, MA
Western Oregon U, OR
Westminster Coll, PA
Westminster Coll, UT
Westmoreland County Comm Coll, PA
West Virginia State Comm and Tech Coll, WV
West Virginia State U, WV
West Virginia Wesleyan Coll, WV
Wheaton Coll, IL
Widener U, PA
Wilfrid Laurier U, ON, Canada
William Jewell Coll, MO
Wofford Coll, SC
Wright State U, OH
Xavier U, OH

COMPUTER SOFTWARE AND MEDIA APPLICATIONS RELATED
Ancilla Coll, IN
Brevard Comm Coll, FL
Brown Mackie Coll–Salina, KS
Carleton U, ON, Canada
The Coll of Westchester, NY
Florida Comm Coll at Jacksonville, FL
Glendale Comm Coll, CA
Indiana–Purdue U Fort Wayne, IN
Kellogg Comm Coll, MI
Laredo Comm Coll, TX
Neumont U, UT
Northland Comm and Tech Coll–Thief River Falls, MN
San Diego Mesa Coll, CA
Seminole Comm Coll, FL
Southeast Tech Inst, SD
Stark State Coll of Technology, OH
U of Great Falls, MT

COMPUTER SOFTWARE ENGINEERING
Brock U, ON, Canada
Carroll Coll, WI
Dalhousie U, NS, Canada

Embry-Riddle Aeronautical U, FL
Fairfield U, CT
Florida Comm Coll at Jacksonville, FL
Florida Inst of Technology, FL
Lake City Comm Coll, FL
Monmouth U, NJ
Notre Dame de Namur U, CA
Rochester Inst of Technology, NY
Seminole Comm Coll, FL
Southeast Tech Inst, SD
Stark State Coll of Technology, OH
U of Toronto, ON, Canada
U of Wisconsin–Platteville, WI
Vermont Tech Coll, VT

COMPUTER SOFTWARE TECHNOLOGY
Miami Dade Coll, FL
U of New Hampshire, NH

COMPUTER SYSTEMS ANALYSIS
Brevard Comm Coll, FL
British Columbia Inst of Technology, BC, Canada
Eastern Mennonite U, VA
Florida Comm Coll at Jacksonville, FL
Lee Coll, TX
Linn State Tech Coll, MO
Montana Tech of The U of Montana, MT
Mount Saint Vincent U, NS, Canada
Pima Comm Coll, AZ
Richmond Comm Coll, NC
Rochester Inst of Technology, NY
Seattle Pacific U, WA
Shippensburg U of Pennsylvania, PA
South Piedmont Comm Coll, NC
The U of Akron, OH
U of Great Falls, MT
U of Houston, TX
U of Miami, FL
U of Vermont, VT
Waukesha County Tech Coll, WI

COMPUTER SYSTEMS NETWORKING AND TELECOMMUNICATIONS
Alexandria Tech Coll, MN
Altamaha Tech Coll, GA
Ancilla Coll, IN
Asheville-Buncombe Tech Comm Coll, NC
Aurora U, IL
Baker Coll of Allen Park, MI
Blinn Coll, TX
Blue Ridge Comm Coll, VA
Brevard Comm Coll, FL
Brown Mackie Coll–Salina, KS
Bunker Hill Comm Coll, MA
Cape Cod Comm Coll, MA
Central Wyoming Coll, WY
Chattahoochee Tech Coll, GA
The Coll of Westchester, NY
Comm Coll of Allegheny County, PA
Cuesta Coll, CA
DeKalb Tech Coll, GA
DePaul U, IL

East Central Coll, MO
Eastern Idaho Tech Coll, ID
Eastfield Coll, TX
Florida Comm Coll at Jacksonville, FL
Harrisburg Area Comm Coll, PA
Heartland Comm Coll, IL
Hillsborough Comm Coll, FL
Howard Comm Coll, MD
Illinois Valley Comm Coll, IL
Iona Coll, NY
Laredo Comm Coll, TX
Lincoln Land Comm Coll, IL
Middle Georgia Tech Coll, GA
Middlesex County Coll, NJ
Minnesota School of Business–St. Cloud, MN
Nassau Comm Coll, NY
Northern Michigan U, MI
Northland Comm and Tech Coll–Thief River Falls, MN
North Metro Tech Coll, GA
Northwestern Oklahoma State U, OK
Odessa Coll, TX
Our Lady of the Lake U of San Antonio, TX
Ozarks Tech Comm Coll, MO
Pima Comm Coll, AZ
Rochester Inst of Technology, NY
Roosevelt U, IL
St. Cloud Tech Coll, MN
St. Philip's Coll, TX
Salem Comm Coll, NJ
Seminole Comm Coll, FL
Southeast Tech Inst, SD
South Piedmont Comm Coll, NC
Stark State Coll of Technology, OH
Surry Comm Coll, NC
Tallahassee Comm Coll, FL
TESST Coll of Technology, Beltsville, MD
The U of Akron–Wayne Coll, OH
The U of Findlay, OH
U of Great Falls, MT
U of Pennsylvania, PA
U of Toronto, ON, Canada
U of Wisconsin–Stout, WI
Waukesha County Tech Coll, WI
Westchester Comm Coll, NY

COMPUTER TEACHER EDUCATION
Alma Coll, MI
Baylor U, TX
Bishop's U, QC, Canada
Buena Vista U, IA
Concordia U, NE
Eastern Michigan U, MI
Immaculata U, PA
Liberty U, VA
Long Island U, Brooklyn Campus, NY
Southern U and A&M Coll, LA
Texas A&M U–Corpus Christi, TX
Union Coll, NE
The U of Akron, OH
U of Nebraska–Lincoln, NE
Utica Coll, NY
Wright State U, OH

COMPUTER/TECHNICAL SUPPORT
Coll of the Desert, CA
The Coll of Westchester, NY

Cuesta Coll, CA
Florida Comm Coll at
Jacksonville, FL
Galveston Coll, TX
Glendale Comm Coll, CA
Heartland Comm Coll, IL
Massasoit Comm Coll, MA
North Central Texas Coll, TX
Northland Comm and Tech
Coll–Thief River Falls, MN
Quincy Coll, MA
St. Cloud Tech Coll, MN
Seminole Comm Coll, FL
Southeast Tech Inst, SD
Stark State Coll of
Technology, OH
State U of New York Coll of
Technology at Alfred, NY

**COMPUTER
TECHNOLOGY/
COMPUTER SYSTEMS
TECHNOLOGY**
Alexandria Tech Coll, MN
Arkansas State U–Newport,
AR
Central Wyoming Coll, WY
Comm Coll of Allegheny
County, PA
Lamar Inst of Technology,
TX
Madisonville Comm Coll,
KY
Miami Dade Coll, FL
Pima Comm Coll, AZ
Prairie View A&M U, TX
Schoolcraft Coll, MI
Southeast Tech Inst, SD
Southwestern Coll, KS
U of Central Florida, FL
Wayne State U, MI

**COMPUTER
TYPOGRAPHY AND
COMPOSITION
EQUIPMENT
OPERATION**
Abraham Baldwin Coll, GA
Coll of the Desert, CA
The Coll of Westchester, NY
Comm Coll of Beaver
County, PA
Fresno City Coll, CA
Fulton-Montgomery Comm
Coll, NY
Housatonic Comm Coll, CT
Long Beach City Coll, CA
McNeese State U, LA
Metropolitan Comm
Coll–Longview, MO
Minnesota State Coll–
Southeast Tech, MN
New Mexico Jr Coll, NM
New River Comm Coll, VA
Paris Jr Coll, TX
Spokane Comm Coll, WA
State U of New York Coll of
Technology at Alfred, NY

CONDUCTING
Calvin Coll, MI
Loyola Marymount U, CA
Mannes Coll The New
School for Music, NY
Temple U, PA
U of Miami, FL

**CONSERVATION
BIOLOGY**
California State U,
Sacramento, CA
St. Gregory's U, OK
Sterling Coll, VT

U of Maine at Machias, ME

**CONSTRUCTION
ENGINEERING**
Bradley U, IL
John Brown U, AR
North Carolina State U, NC
North Dakota State U, ND
State U of New York Coll of
Environmental Science
and Forestry, NY
State U of New York Coll of
Technology at Alfred, NY
U of Cincinnati, OH
U of New Brunswick
Fredericton, NB, Canada

**CONSTRUCTION
ENGINEERING
TECHNOLOGY**
Bemidji State U, MN
British Columbia Inst of
Technology, BC, Canada
California State U,
Sacramento, CA
Coll of Staten Island of the
City U of New York, NY
Comm Coll of Allegheny
County, PA
Cosumnes River Coll,
Sacramento, CA
Cuesta Coll, CA
East Central Coll, MO
Eastern Michigan U, MI
El Camino Coll, CA
Fairleigh Dickinson U,
Metropolitan Campus, NJ
Farmingdale State Coll, NY
Feather River Coll, CA
Fitchburg State Coll, MA
Florida Comm Coll at
Jacksonville, FL
Florida Inst of Technology,
FL
Florida International U, FL
Fresno City Coll, CA
Fulton-Montgomery Comm
Coll, NY
Greenville Tech Coll, SC
Harrisburg Area Comm Coll,
PA
Hillsborough Comm Coll, FL
Houston Comm Coll System,
TX
Hudson Valley Comm Coll,
NY
Indiana U–Purdue U Fort
Wayne, IN
Lake Superior State U, MI
Laredo Comm Coll, TX
Lassen Comm Coll District,
CA
Macomb Comm Coll, MI
Maui Comm Coll, HI
Miami Dade Coll, FL
Middlesex County Coll, NJ
Minnesota State U
Moorhead, MN
Montana State U, MT
New Mexico Jr Coll, NM
New York City Coll of
Technology of the City U
of New York, NY
North Central Missouri Coll,
MO
Ocean County Coll, NJ
Odessa Coll, TX
Ozarks Tech Comm Coll,
MO
Phoenix Coll, AZ
Pima Comm Coll, AZ
Pittsburg State U, KS
Purdue U North Central, IN
Richland Comm Coll, IL

Rockingham Comm Coll, NC
St. Cloud Tech Coll, MN
St. Louis Comm Coll at
Florissant Valley, MO
St. Philip's Coll, TX
San Diego Mesa Coll, CA
Seminole Comm Coll, FL
Shasta Coll, CA
Southern Illinois U
Carbondale, IL
Southern Illinois U
Edwardsville, IL
Southern Maine Comm Coll,
ME
Southern Utah U, UT
Spokane Comm Coll, WA
State U of New York Coll of
Technology at Alfred, NY
State U of New York Coll of
Technology at Canton, NY
Surry Comm Coll, NC
Tallahassee Comm Coll, FL
Texas A&M U, TX
The U of Akron, OH
U of Cincinnati, OH
U of Houston, TX
U of Nebraska at Omaha,
NE
U of Nebraska–Lincoln, NE
U of New Hampshire, NH
U of North Florida, FL
U of Wisconsin–Stout, WI
Valencia Comm Coll, FL
Ventura Coll, CA
Vermont Tech Coll, VT
Victor Valley Coll, CA
Wright State U, OH

**CONSTRUCTION/HEAVY
EQUIPMENT/
EARTHMOVING
EQUIPMENT
OPERATION**
Ivy Tech Comm Coll–
Southwest, IN
Ivy Tech Comm Coll–
Wabash Valley, IN

**CONSTRUCTION
MANAGEMENT**
British Columbia Inst of
Technology, BC, Canada
Broward Comm Coll, FL
Clemson U, SC
Coll of the Desert, CA
Cosumnes River Coll,
Sacramento, CA
Delaware Tech & Comm
Coll, Jack F. Owens
Campus, DE
Eastern Michigan U, MI
Everglades U, Sarasota, FL
Farmingdale State Coll, NY
Frederick Comm Coll, MD
Fresno City Coll, CA
John Brown U, AR
Michigan State U, MI
Minnesota State U Mankato,
MN
North Carolina State U, NC
North Dakota State U, ND
Northern Michigan U, MI
Oklahoma State U, OK
Pittsburg State U, KS
Pratt Inst, NY
St. Philip's Coll, TX
Santa Rosa Jr Coll, CA
Seminole Comm Coll, FL
State U of New York Coll of
Environmental Science
and Forestry, NY
U of Cincinnati, OH
U of New Hampshire, NH
U of Northern Iowa, IA

U of the District of
Columbia, DC
U of Washington, WA
U of Wisconsin–Madison,
WI
U of Wisconsin–Platteville,
WI
Vermont Tech Coll, VT
Victor Valley Coll, CA

**CONSTRUCTION
TRADES**
Coll of The Albemarle, NC
East Central Coll, MO
Lassen Comm Coll District,
CA
Northern Michigan U, MI

**CONSTRUCTION
TRADES RELATED**
British Columbia Inst of
Technology, BC, Canada
Comm Coll of Allegheny
County, PA
East Central Coll, MO
Hope Coll, MI
Ivy Tech Comm Coll–
Kokomo, IN

**CONSUMER
ECONOMICS**
Cornell U, NY
Indiana U of Pennsylvania,
PA
The U of Alabama, AL
The U of Arizona, AZ
U of Delaware, DE
U of Rhode Island, RI
The U of Tennessee, TN

**CONSUMER/
HOMEMAKING
EDUCATION**
MiraCosta Coll, CA

**CONSUMER
MERCHANDISING/
RETAILING
MANAGEMENT**
Bucks County Comm Coll,
PA
Central Piedmont Comm
Coll, NC
Chattanooga State Tech
Comm Coll, TN
Colorado Mountain Coll,
Alpine Campus, CO
Delaware Tech & Comm
Coll, Jack F. Owens
Campus, DE
Fontbonne U, MO
Gloucester County Coll, NJ
Grossmont Coll, CA
Harrisburg Area Comm Coll,
PA
Hocking Coll, OH
Howard Comm Coll, MD
Indiana U Bloomington, IN
Jefferson Comm Coll, OH
Johnson & Wales U, RI
Lindenwood U, MO
Long Beach City Coll, CA
Madisonville Comm Coll,
KY
Middlesex County Coll, NJ
Minnesota State Coll–
Southeast Tech, MN
Northland Comm and Tech
Coll–Thief River Falls, MN
St. Cloud Tech Coll, MN
San Francisco State U, CA
Stark State Coll of
Technology, OH

Sussex County Comm Coll,
NJ
Syracuse U, NY
U of Central Oklahoma, OK
Westchester Comm Coll, NY
Western Tech Coll, WI
West Los Angeles Coll, CA
Westmoreland County
Comm Coll, PA

**CONSUMER SERVICES
AND ADVOCACY**
Carson-Newman Coll, TN
Rockingham Comm Coll, NC
Syracuse U, NY
U of Wisconsin–Madison,
WI

**COOKING AND
RELATED CULINARY
ARTS**
The Art Inst of Pittsburgh,
PA
Kendall Coll, IL

CORRECTIONS
Bluefield State Coll, WV
Brevard Comm Coll, FL
Broome Comm Coll, NY
Broward Comm Coll, FL
Bucks County Comm Coll,
PA
Central Arizona Coll, AZ
Central Ohio Tech Coll, OH
Chesapeake Coll, MD
Comm Coll of Allegheny
County, PA
Fresno City Coll, CA
Grossmont Coll, CA
Heartland Comm Coll, IL
Hillsborough Comm Coll, FL
Hocking Coll, OH
Jefferson Comm Coll, OH
Kellogg Comm Coll, MI
Lake Superior State U, MI
Lamar U, TX
Langston U, OK
Lassen Comm Coll District,
CA
Mercyhurst Coll, PA
Metropolitan Comm
Coll–Longview, MO
Metropolitan Comm
Coll–Penn Valley, MO
Middlesex County Coll, NJ
Minnesota State U Mankato,
MN
Moorpark Coll, CA
Northeastern U, MA
Northern Michigan U, MI
Phoenix Coll, AZ
Pueblo Comm Coll, CO
St. Louis Comm Coll at
Florissant Valley, MO
Sauk Valley Comm Coll, IL
Schoolcraft Coll, MI
Spokane Comm Coll, WA
State U of New York Coll at
Brockport, NY
State U of New York Coll of
Technology at Canton, NY
Stephen F. Austin State U,
TX
Troy U, AL
Tunxis Comm Coll, CT
The U of Akron, OH
U of Great Falls, MT
U of New Mexico, NM
U of Pittsburgh, PA
U of the District of
Columbia, DC
Washburn U, KS
Westchester Comm Coll, NY
Western Oregon U, OR

West Shore Comm Coll, MI
Xavier U, OH

CORRECTIONS ADMINISTRATION
U of Great Falls, MT

CORRECTIONS AND CRIMINAL JUSTICE RELATED
Harding U, AR
Mercyhurst Coll, PA
North Dakota State U, ND
Reedley Coll, CA
State U of New York Coll at Brockport, NY
U of Great Falls, MT

COSMETOLOGY
Caldwell Comm Coll and Tech Inst, NC
Citrus Coll, CA
Coahoma Comm Coll, MS
El Camino Coll, CA
Glendale Comm Coll, CA
Lamar U, TX
Lassen Comm Coll District, CA
Minnesota State Coll–Southeast Tech, MN
MiraCosta Coll, CA
New Mexico Jr Coll, NM
Northland Comm and Tech Coll–Thief River Falls, MN
Odessa Coll, TX
Paris Jr Coll, TX
Rockingham Comm Coll, NC
Santa Ana Coll, CA
Santa Barbara City Coll, CA
Spokane Comm Coll, WA
Surry Comm Coll, NC

COSMETOLOGY AND PERSONAL GROOMING ARTS RELATED
Allegany Coll of Maryland, MD
Comm Coll of Allegheny County, PA

COUNSELING PSYCHOLOGY
Grace Coll, IN
Kutztown U of Pennsylvania, PA
Marywood U, PA
Morningside Coll, IA
Oak Hills Christian Coll, MN
Oregon Inst of Technology, OR
Saint Xavier U, IL
U of Great Falls, MT
Wayne State Coll, NE

COUNSELOR EDUCATION/SCHOOL COUNSELING AND GUIDANCE
Brandon U, MB, Canada
Buena Vista U, IA
Clemson U, SC
DePaul U, IL
Franklin Pierce U, NH
Harding U, AR
Houston Baptist U, TX
Kutztown U of Pennsylvania, PA
Lamar U, TX
Lancaster Bible Coll, PA
Marshall U, WV
St. Cloud State U, MN
Texas A&M U–Corpus Christi, TX
U of Central Oklahoma, OK

U of Hawaii at Manoa, HI
U of New Brunswick Fredericton, NB, Canada
Wright State U, OH

COURT REPORTING
Comm Coll of Allegheny County, PA
Gadsden State Comm Coll, AL
Houston Comm Coll System, TX
Miami Dade Coll, FL
Rose State Coll, OK
Stark State Coll of Technology, OH
State U of New York Coll of Technology at Alfred, NY
U of Cincinnati, OH
U of Mississippi, MS

CRAFTS, FOLK ART AND ARTISANRY
The Cleveland Inst of Art, OH
Coll of The Albemarle, NC
Indiana U–Purdue U Fort Wayne, IN
Kutztown U of Pennsylvania, PA
North Georgia Coll & State U, GA
NSCAD U, NS, Canada
Rochester Inst of Technology, NY
School of the Art Inst of Chicago, IL
The U of Akron, OH
U of Illinois at Urbana–Champaign, IL
The U of the Arts, PA

CREATIVE WRITING
Albertson Coll of Idaho, ID
Alderson-Broaddus Coll, WV
Anderson U, SC
Ashland U, OH
Bard Coll, NY
Bethel Coll, IN
Briar Cliff U, IA
Brown U, RI
California State U, San Bernardino, CA
Cardinal Stritch U, WI
Carlow U, PA
Carnegie Mellon U, PA
Carroll Coll, WI
Carson-Newman Coll, TN
Coe Coll, IA
Colby Coll, ME
Columbus State U, GA
Cornell U, NY
Cornerstone U, MI
DePaul U, IL
Drury U, MO
Eastern Michigan U, MI
Eckerd Coll, FL
Emory U, GA
Eugene Lang Coll The New School for Liberal Arts, NY
Fairleigh Dickinson U, Coll at Florham, NJ
Foothill Coll, CA
Framingham State Coll, MA
Franklin Pierce U, NH
Geneva Coll, PA
Georgia Coll & State U, GA
Green Mountain Coll, VT
Grossmont Coll, CA
Hamilton Coll, NY
High Point U, NC
Hofstra U, NY
Houghton Coll, NY

Indiana U–Purdue U Fort Wayne, IN
Irvine Valley Coll, CA
Ithaca Coll, NY
Johnson State Coll, VT
Kenyon Coll, OH
Le Moyne Coll, NY
Loras Coll, IA
Loyola U New Orleans, LA
Lynchburg Coll, VA
Marquette U, WI
Massachusetts Coll of Liberal Arts, MA
Mercyhurst Coll, PA
Minnesota State U Mankato, MN
Moravian Coll, PA
North Carolina State U, NC
North Central Coll, IL
Northern Michigan U, MI
Northwestern Coll, MN
The Ohio State U, OH
Ohio Wesleyan U, OH
Pine Manor Coll, MA
Pratt Inst, NY
Randolph Coll, VA
Rockhurst U, MO
St. Cloud State U, MN
Saint Joseph's Coll, IN
St. Lawrence U, NY
San Diego State U, CA
San Francisco State U, CA
School of the Art Inst of Chicago, IL
Seton Hill U, PA
State U of New York Coll at Brockport, NY
Sweet Briar Coll, VA
Taylor U, IN
Trinity Coll, CT
The U of Arizona, AZ
U of Evansville, IN
The U of Findlay, OH
U of Great Falls, MT
U of Houston, TX
U of Maine at Machias, ME
U of Miami, FL
U of Michigan, MI
U of Nebraska at Omaha, NE
U of Pittsburgh, PA
U of Pittsburgh at Bradford, PA
U of Pittsburgh at Johnstown, PA
U of Redlands, CA
U of St. Thomas, MN
The U of Tampa, FL
The U of Texas at El Paso, TX
U of Washington, WA
Wayne State Coll, NE
Wells Coll, NY
Western New England Coll, MA
Westminster Coll, PA
West Virginia Wesleyan Coll, WV
Wofford Coll, SC

CRIMINAL JUSTICE/LAW ENFORCEMENT ADMINISTRATION
Abraham Baldwin Coll, GA
Adelphi U, NY
Aims Comm Coll, CO
Alvernia Coll, PA
American International Coll, MA
Ancilla Coll, IN
Anderson U, IN
Anderson U, SC
Arizona State U at the West campus, AZ

Arkansas State U–Newport, AR
Ashland U, OH
Athens State U, AL
Aurora U, IL
Bainbridge Coll, GA
Ball State U, IN
Bemidji State U, MN
Blinn Coll, TX
Bradley U, IL
Brevard Comm Coll, FL
Briar Cliff U, IA
Broward Comm Coll, FL
Brown Mackie Coll–Salina, KS
Bucks County Comm Coll, PA
Buffalo State Coll, State U of New York, NY
Bunker Hill Comm Coll, MA
California State U, Fullerton, CA
California State U, Sacramento, CA
California State U, San Bernardino, CA
California State U, Stanislaus, CA
Cape Cod Comm Coll, MA
Carleton U, ON, Canada
Carroll Coll, WI
Carthage Coll, WI
Cedar Valley Coll, TX
Central Arizona Coll, AZ
Central Ohio Tech Coll, OH
Central Piedmont Comm Coll, NC
Central Wyoming Coll, WY
Charleston Southern U, SC
Chattanooga State Tech Comm Coll, TN
Chesapeake Coll, MD
Citrus Coll, CA
Clayton State U, GA
Coahoma Comm Coll, MS
The Coll of Saint Rose, NY
Coll of The Albemarle, NC
Coll of the Canyons, CA
Coll of the Desert, CA
Comm Coll of Aurora, CO
Comm Coll of Beaver County, PA
Cosumnes River Coll, Sacramento, CA
Crafton Hills Coll, CA
Dabney S. Lancaster Comm Coll, VA
Dallas Baptist U, TX
Dean Coll, MA
Delaware State U, DE
Delaware Tech & Comm Coll, Jack F. Owens Campus, DE
Elmira Coll, NY
Farmingdale State Coll, NY
Fayetteville State U, NC
Feather River Coll, CA
Fitchburg State Coll, MA
Florida Comm Coll at Jacksonville, FL
Franklin Pierce U, NH
Frederick Comm Coll, MD
Fresno City Coll, CA
Fulton-Montgomery Comm Coll, NY
Gainesville State Coll, GA
Gaston Coll, NC
The George Washington U, DC
Georgia Coll & State U, GA
Georgian Court U, NJ
Glenville State Coll, WV
Gonzaga U, WA
Grace Coll, IN

Graceland U, IA
Grambling State U, LA
Greenville Tech Coll, SC
Grossmont Coll, CA
Gustavus Adolphus Coll, MN
Hamline U, MN
Harrisburg Area Comm Coll, PA
Hillsborough Comm Coll, FL
Hocking Coll, OH
Housatonic Comm Coll, CT
Howard Comm Coll, MD
Hudson Valley Comm Coll, NY
Illinois Valley Comm Coll, IL
Iona Coll, NY
Irvine Valley Coll, CA
James H. Faulkner State Comm Coll, AL
Johnson & Wales U, CO
Johnson & Wales U, FL
Johnson & Wales U, RI
Keuka Coll, NY
Lake City Comm Coll, FL
Lake-Sumter Comm Coll, FL
Lake Superior State U, MI
Lamar U, TX
Langston U, OK
Lewis U, IL
Liberty U, VA
Lindenwood U, MO
Long Beach City Coll, CA
MacMurray Coll, IL
Macomb Comm Coll, MI
Marist Coll, NY
Marywood U, PA
Maui Comm Coll, HI
Mercyhurst Coll, PA
Metropolitan Comm Coll–Longview, MO
Metropolitan Comm Coll–Penn Valley, MO
Miami Dade Coll, FL
Michigan State U, MI
Middlesex County Coll, NJ
Middle Tennessee State U, TN
Midland Lutheran Coll, NE
MiraCosta Coll, CA
Missouri State U–West Plains, MO
Mitchell Coll, CT
Mohawk Valley Comm Coll, NY
Moorpark Coll, CA
Moravian Coll, PA
Mount Vernon Nazarene U, OH
Nassau Comm Coll, NY
New River Comm Coll, VA
Niagara U, NY
North Central Missouri Coll, MO
North Central Texas Coll, TX
Northern Michigan U, MI
North Georgia Coll & State U, GA
Northland Comm and Tech Coll–Thief River Falls, MN
Odessa Coll, TX
Park U, MO
Paul Quinn Coll, TX
Penn State Abington, PA
Penn State DuBois, PA
Penn State Fayette, The Eberly Campus, PA
Penn State Mont Alto, PA
Penn State Wilkes-Barre, PA
Piedmont Coll, GA
Portland State U, OR
Pueblo Comm Coll, CO
Quincy Coll, MA
Radford U, VA

Richmond Comm Coll, NC
Rochester Inst of
  Technology, NY
Rockingham Comm Coll, NC
Rose State Coll, OK
Roxbury Comm Coll, MA
Rutgers, The State U of New
  Jersey, New Brunswick, NJ
St. Cloud State U, MN
St. Louis Comm Coll at
  Florissant Valley, MO
St. Philip's Coll, TX
St. Thomas Aquinas Coll,
  NY
Salem Comm Coll, NJ
Salve Regina U, RI
San Diego State U, CA
San Francisco State U, CA
Santa Ana Coll, CA
Santa Barbara City Coll, CA
Santa Rosa Jr Coll, CA
Sauk Valley Comm Coll, IL
Scottsdale Comm Coll, AZ
Seminole Comm Coll, FL
Seton Hill U, PA
Shasta Coll, CA
Southern Illinois U
  Carbondale, IL
Southern Maine Comm Coll,
  ME
Southern Utah U, UT
South U, GA
Southwestern Coll, KS
Spoon River Coll, IL
State U of New York at
  Fredonia, NY
State U of New York Coll at
  Brockport, NY
State U of New York Coll of
  Technology at Canton, NY
Surry Comm Coll, NC
Tallahassee Comm Coll, FL
Texas A&M U–Corpus
  Christi, TX
Truman State U, MO
Tunxis Comm Coll, CT
U at Albany, State U of New
  York, NY
The U of Akron, OH
U of Alaska Anchorage, AK
The U of Arizona, AZ
U of Arkansas at Fort Smith,
  AR
U of Baltimore, MD
U of Central Missouri, MO
U of Central Oklahoma, OK
U of Cincinnati, OH
U of Dayton, OH
U of Delaware, DE
U of Dubuque, IA
The U of Findlay, OH
U of Great Falls, MT
U of Guelph, ON, Canada
U of Hawaii–West Oahu, HI
The U of Maine at Augusta,
  ME
U of Mary Hardin-Baylor, TX
U of Massachusetts Lowell,
  MA
U of Missouri–Kansas City,
  MO
U of New Hampshire, NH
U of New Haven, CT
U of Pittsburgh at Bradford,
  PA
U of South Carolina Upstate,
  SC
The U of Tennessee at
  Martin, TN
The U of Texas at El Paso,
  TX
U of the District of
  Columbia, DC
U of Washington, WA

U of Wisconsin–Oshkosh,
  WI
U of Wisconsin–Platteville,
  WI
Urbana U, OH
Utica Coll, NY
Valencia Comm Coll, FL
Ventura Coll, CA
Villanova U, PA
Virginia Intermont Coll, VA
Washburn U, KS
Wayne State Coll, NE
Westchester Comm Coll, NY
Western New England Coll,
  MA
Western Oregon U, OR
West Liberty State Coll, WV
West Los Angeles Coll, CA
Westminster Coll, PA
Westmoreland County
  Comm Coll, PA
West Texas A&M U, TX
West Virginia State U, WV
West Virginia Wesleyan Coll,
  WV
Widener U, PA

CRIMINAL JUSTICE/ POLICE SCIENCE

Abraham Baldwin Coll, GA
Aims Comm Coll, CO
Alexandria Tech Coll, MN
Allegany Coll of Maryland,
  MD
American International Coll,
  MA
Asheville-Buncombe Tech
  Comm Coll, NC
Ashland Comm and Tech
  Coll, KY
Athabasca U, AB, Canada
Bemidji State U, MN
Bluefield State Coll, WV
Brevard Comm Coll, FL
Broome Comm Coll, NY
Broward Comm Coll, FL
Bucks County Comm Coll,
  PA
Calhoun Comm Coll, AL
Cameron U, OK
Carleton U, ON, Canada
Central Ohio Tech Coll, OH
Central Piedmont Comm
  Coll, NC
Citrus Coll, CA
City Colls of Chicago,
  Richard J. Daley Coll, IL
Coll of the Canyons, CA
Coll of the Desert, CA
Comm Coll of Allegheny
  County, PA
Comm Coll of Beaver
  County, PA
Dean Coll, MA
East Central Coll, MO
Edinboro U of Pennsylvania,
  PA
El Camino Coll, CA
El Centro Coll, TX
Florida Comm Coll at
  Jacksonville, FL
Fresno City Coll, CA
Gadsden State Comm Coll,
  AL
Galveston Coll, TX
Glendale Comm Coll, CA
Gloucester County Coll, NJ
Grambling State U, LA
Greenville Tech Coll, SC
Grossmont Coll, CA
Hagerstown Comm Coll, MD
Harrisburg Area Comm Coll,
  PA
Hillsborough Comm Coll, FL

Hocking Coll, OH
Hopkinsville Comm Coll,
  KY
Houston Comm Coll System,
  TX
Husson Coll, ME
Idaho State U, ID
Illinois Valley Comm Coll, IL
Jamestown Comm Coll, NY
Jefferson Comm Coll, OH
Kellogg Comm Coll, MI
Lake Superior State U, MI
Lamar U, TX
Langston U, OK
Laredo Comm Coll, TX
Lassen Comm Coll District,
  CA
Lee Coll, TX
Lincoln Land Comm Coll, IL
MacMurray Coll, IL
Macomb Comm Coll, MI
Madisonville Comm Coll,
  KY
Massasoit Comm Coll, MA
Mercyhurst Coll, PA
Metropolitan Comm
  Coll–Longview, MO
Metropolitan Comm
  Coll–Penn Valley, MO
Miami Dade Coll, FL
Middlesex County Coll, NJ
Middle Tennessee State U,
  TN
Midland Coll, TX
Minnesota State U Mankato,
  MN
MiraCosta Coll, CA
Missouri State U–West
  Plains, MO
Moorpark Coll, CA
Morton Coll, IL
New Mexico Jr Coll, NM
New River Comm Coll, VA
North Central Texas Coll, TX
Northeastern U, MA
Northern Michigan U, MI
Northern State U, SD
Northland Comm and Tech
  Coll–Thief River Falls, MN
Northwestern Oklahoma
  State U, OK
Ocean County Coll, NJ
Odessa Coll, TX
Phoenix Coll, AZ
Pima Comm Coll, AZ
Pueblo Comm Coll, CO
Quincy Coll, MA
Reedley Coll, CA
Richland Comm Coll, IL
Rockingham Comm Coll, NC
Rowan U, NJ
St. Gregory's U, OK
St. Louis Comm Coll at
  Florissant Valley, MO
Santa Ana Coll, CA
Sauk Valley Comm Coll, IL
Schoolcraft Coll, MI
Skagit Valley Coll, WA
Southern Maine Comm Coll,
  ME
Southern U and A&M Coll,
  LA
South Piedmont Comm Coll,
  NC
Spokane Comm Coll, WA
Spoon River Coll, IL
State U of New York Coll at
  Brockport, NY
State U of New York Coll of
  Technology at Canton, NY
Stephen F. Austin State U,
  TX
TESST Coll of Technology,
  Beltsville, MD

Truman State U, MO
The U of Akron, OH
U of Cincinnati, OH
U of Great Falls, MT
U of Hartford, CT
U of New Haven, CT
U of the District of
  Columbia, DC
U of Toronto, ON, Canada
Victor Valley Coll, CA
Virginia Highlands Comm
  Coll, VA
Washburn U, KS
Waubonsee Comm Coll, IL
Waukesha County Tech Coll,
  WI
Wayne State Coll, NE
Westchester Comm Coll, NY
Western Connecticut State
  U, CT
Western Oregon U, OR
Western Tech Coll, WI
West Los Angeles Coll, CA
Westmoreland County
  Comm Coll, PA
West Shore Comm Coll, MI
West Virginia Northern
  Comm Coll, WV
Wright State U, OH

CRIMINAL JUSTICE/ SAFETY

Albany State U, GA
Altamaha Tech Coll, GA
Ancilla Coll, IN
Angelo State U, TX
Asnuntuck Comm Coll, CT
Auburn U Montgomery, AL
Augsburg Coll, MN
Aurora U, IL
Bethel Coll, IN
Bluefield State Coll, WV
Buena Vista U, IA
Charleston Southern U, SC
Chattahoochee Tech Coll,
  GA
Columbus State U, GA
Coosa Valley Tech Coll, GA
DeKalb Tech Coll, GA
Dixie State Coll of Utah, UT
East Carolina U, NC
Eastern New Mexico
  U–Roswell, NM
Eastfield Coll, TX
Edinboro U of Pennsylvania,
  PA
El Centro Coll, TX
Fairleigh Dickinson U,
  Metropolitan Campus, NJ
Ferrum Coll, VA
Florida Atlantic U, FL
Florida Gulf Coast U, FL
Florida International U, FL
Fort Hays State U, KS
Gannon U, PA
Harding U, AR
High Point U, NC
Husson Coll, ME
Idaho State U, ID
Illinois State U, IL
Indiana U Bloomington, IN
Indiana U–Purdue U Fort
  Wayne, IN
Indiana U–Purdue U
  Indianapolis, IN
Ivy Tech Comm Coll–
  Kokomo, IN
Ivy Tech Comm Coll–
  Southwest, IN
Ivy Tech Comm Coll–
  Wabash Valley, IN
Jamestown Comm Coll, NY
Kellogg Comm Coll, MI
Kennesaw State U, GA

Kentucky Wesleyan Coll, KY
King's Coll, PA
Kutztown U of
  Pennsylvania, PA
Lackawanna Coll, PA
Lakeland Coll, WI
Lincoln U, PA
Loras Coll, IA
Loyola U Chicago, IL
Loyola U New Orleans, LA
Lynn U, FL
Marshall U, WV
Marymount U, VA
Marywood U, PA
McNeese State U, LA
Mercer U, GA
Mercyhurst Coll, PA
Michigan State U, MI
Minnesota State U
  Moorhead, MN
Missouri State U, MO
Molloy Coll, NY
Monmouth U, NJ
Mount St. Mary's U, MD
Murray State U, KY
Nassau Comm Coll, NY
Neumann Coll, PA
New Jersey City U, NJ
Northeastern U, MA
North Georgia Coll & State
  U, GA
Northwestern Coll, MN
The Ohio State U, OH
Penn State Abington, PA
Penn State Fayette, The
  Eberly Campus, PA
Penn State Wilkes-Barre, PA
Phoenix Coll, AZ
Pima Comm Coll, AZ
Prairie View A&M U, TX
Rochester Inst of
  Technology, NY
Rutgers, The State U of New
  Jersey, Newark, NJ
Ryerson U, ON, Canada
Saginaw Valley State U, MI
St. Gregory's U, OK
Saint Joseph's Coll, IN
Saint Leo U, FL
Saint Xavier U, IL
Seton Hall U, NJ
Shippensburg U of
  Pennsylvania, PA
Southern Illinois U
  Edwardsville, IL
Southern U and A&M Coll,
  LA
Stephen F. Austin State U,
  TX
Stonehill Coll, MA
Temple U, PA
Thiel Coll, PA
The U of Akron, OH
The U of Alabama, AL
U of Arkansas, AR
U of Central Florida, FL
U of Central Oklahoma, OK
U of Great Falls, MT
The U of Maine at Augusta,
  ME
U of Massachusetts Boston,
  MA
U of Nebraska at Kearney,
  NE
U of Nebraska at Omaha,
  NE
The U of North Carolina at
  Charlotte, NC
U of North Florida, FL
U of Portland, OR
The U of Scranton, PA
The U of Texas at San
  Antonio, TX

The U of Virginia's Coll at Wise, VA
U of Wisconsin–Eau Claire, WI
U of Wyoming, WY
Valdosta State U, GA
Wayne State Coll, NE
Wayne State U, MI
West Chester U of Pennsylvania, PA
Western Nebraska Comm Coll, NE
West Virginia State Comm and Tech Coll, WV
Wichita State U, KS
Wilkes U, PA
Worcester State Coll, MA
Xavier U, OH

CRIMINOLOGY
Albright Coll, PA
Ball State U, IN
Barry U, FL
Carleton U, ON, Canada
Coll of Mount St. Joseph, OH
Dominican U, IL
Drury U, MO
Eastern Michigan U, MI
Husson Coll, ME
Immaculata U, PA
Indiana U of Pennsylvania, PA
Le Moyne Coll, NY
Lindenwood U, MO
Marquette U, WI
Marymount U, VA
Marywood U, PA
Midland Lutheran Coll, NE
Niagara U, NY
North Carolina State U, NC
Northland Comm and Tech Coll–Thief River Falls, MN
The Ohio State U, OH
Old Dominion U, VA
The Richard Stockton Coll of New Jersey, NJ
Rivier Coll, NH
St. Cloud State U, MN
St. Thomas U, NB, Canada
Southern Oregon U, OR
State U of New York Coll at Brockport, NY
State U of New York Coll at Cortland, NY
Stonehill Coll, MA
U of California, Irvine, CA
U of Miami, FL
U of Minnesota, Duluth, MN
U of Missouri–Kansas City, MO
U of Northern Iowa, IA
U of St. Thomas, MN
The U of Tampa, FL
U of the District of Columbia, DC
U of Toronto, ON, Canada
Upper Iowa U, IA
Wright State U, OH

CRITICAL CARE NURSING
British Columbia Inst of Technology, BC, Canada
U at Buffalo, the State U of New York, NY

CROP PRODUCTION
Cornell U, NY
North Dakota State U, ND
Sterling Coll, VT
U of Arkansas, AR
U of Massachusetts Amherst, MA

CULINARY ARTS
Allegany Coll of Maryland, MD
The Art Inst of Houston, TX
The Art Inst of Pittsburgh, PA
The Art Inst of Seattle, WA
Asheville-Buncombe Tech Comm Coll, NC
Brevard Comm Coll, FL
Bucks County Comm Coll, PA
Bunker Hill Comm Coll, MA
Central Piedmont Comm Coll, NC
Chattahoochee Tech Coll, GA
Coll of The Albemarle, NC
Coll of the Desert, CA
Commonwealth Tech Inst, PA
Comm Coll of Allegheny County, PA
Comm Coll of Beaver County, PA
East Central Coll, MO
El Camino Coll, CA
El Centro Coll, TX
Florida Comm Coll at Jacksonville, FL
Galveston Coll, TX
Glendale Comm Coll, CA
Harrisburg Area Comm Coll, PA
Hillsborough Comm Coll, FL
Hocking Coll, OH
Idaho State U, ID
Jefferson Comm and Tech Coll, KY
Johnson & Wales U, CO
Johnson & Wales U, FL
Johnson & Wales U, NC
Johnson & Wales U, RI
Kapiolani Comm Coll, HI
Kendall Coll, IL
Long Beach City Coll, CA
Macomb Comm Coll, MI
Massasoit Comm Coll, MA
Mercyhurst Coll, PA
Middlesex County Coll, NJ
Mohawk Valley Comm Coll, NY
Odessa Coll, TX
Ozarks Tech Comm Coll, MO
Pueblo Comm Coll, CO
St. Philip's Coll, TX
Santa Rosa Jr Coll, CA
Schoolcraft Coll, MI
Scottsdale Comm Coll, AZ
Shasta Coll, CA
Shelton State Comm Coll, AL
Skagit Valley Coll, WA
Southern Maine Comm Coll, ME
Southwestern Indian Polytechnic Inst, NM
Spokane Comm Coll, WA
State U of New York Coll of Technology at Alfred, NY
The U of Akron, OH
U of Alaska Anchorage, AK
U of New Hampshire, NH
Valencia Comm Coll, FL
Virginia Intermont Coll, VA
Westchester Comm Coll, NY
Westmoreland County Comm Coll, PA

CULINARY ARTS RELATED
The Art Inst of Pittsburgh, PA
Hillsborough Comm Coll, FL

Santa Barbara City Coll, CA

CULTURAL RESOURCE MANAGEMENT AND POLICY ANALYSIS
Sterling Coll, VT

CULTURAL STUDIES
Bard Coll, NY
California State U, Fullerton, CA
California State U, Sacramento, CA
Clark U, MA
The Coll of William and Mary, VA
Cosumnes River Coll, Sacramento, CA
Foothill Coll, CA
Fresno City Coll, CA
Grossmont Coll, CA
Houghton Coll, NY
Minnesota State U Mankato, MN
The Ohio State U, OH
Ohio Wesleyan U, OH
Rutgers, The State U of New Jersey, Newark, NJ
Rutgers, The State U of New Jersey, New Brunswick, NJ
St. Francis Xavier U, NS, Canada
Santa Ana Coll, CA
Santa Barbara City Coll, CA
Santa Rosa Jr Coll, CA
Skagit Valley Coll, WA
U of California, Irvine, CA
U of Colorado at Boulder, CO
U of Oregon, OR
The U of Tennessee, TN
U of Toronto, ON, Canada
U of Virginia, VA
U of Washington, WA
Yale U, CT

CURRICULUM AND INSTRUCTION
Sterling Coll, VT
Texas A&M U, TX
Washburn U, KS
Wright State U, OH

CUSTOMER SERVICE MANAGEMENT
U of Wisconsin–Stout, WI

CYTOTECHNOLOGY
Alderson-Broaddus Coll, WV
Anderson U, SC
Barry U, FL
The Coll of Saint Rose, NY
Indiana U–Purdue U Indianapolis, IN
Indiana U Southeast, IN
Long Island U, Brooklyn Campus, NY
Marshall U, WV
Minnesota State U Moorhead, MN
Northern Michigan U, MI
Old Dominion U, VA
Salve Regina U, RI
Slippery Rock U of Pennsylvania, PA
Thiel Coll, PA
U of Connecticut, CT
U of Kansas, KS

CZECH
The U of Texas at Austin, TX

DAIRY HUSBANDRY AND PRODUCTION
Sterling Coll, VT
U of Vermont, VT

DAIRY SCIENCE
Cornell U, NY
Sterling Coll, VT
Texas A&M U, TX
U of New Hampshire, NH
U of Wisconsin–Madison, WI
Vermont Tech Coll, VT

DANCE
Adelphi U, NY
Alma Coll, MI
Amherst Coll, MA
Ball State U, IN
Bard Coll, NY
Brenau U, GA
California State U, Fullerton, CA
California State U, Sacramento, CA
Cedar Crest Coll, PA
Central Piedmont Comm Coll, NC
Citrus Coll, CA
Claremont McKenna Coll, CA
Cornell U, NY
Dean Coll, MA
Dixie State Coll of Utah, UT
East Carolina U, NC
Eastern Michigan U, MI
Elon U, NC
Emory U, GA
Florida International U, FL
The George Washington U, DC
Glendale Comm Coll, CA
Grossmont Coll, CA
Gustavus Adolphus Coll, MN
Hamilton Coll, NY
Hampshire Coll, MA
Hillsborough Comm Coll, FL
Hofstra U, NY
Hope Coll, MI
Hunter Coll of the City U of New York, NY
Indiana U Bloomington, IN
Ithaca Coll, NY
Jacksonville U, FL
Johnson State Coll, VT
Kenyon Coll, OH
Lake Erie Coll, OH
Lamar U, TX
Lindenwood U, MO
Long Beach City Coll, CA
Long Island U, Brooklyn Campus, NY
Loyola Marymount U, CA
Manhattanville Coll, NY
Marymount Manhattan Coll, NY
Mercyhurst Coll, PA
Miami Dade Coll, FL
Middlesex County Coll, NJ
MiraCosta Coll, CA
Missouri State U, MO
Mount Holyoke Coll, MA
Nassau Comm Coll, NY
New York U, NY
North Carolina School of the Arts, NC
Oakland U, MI
The Ohio State U, OH
Old Dominion U, VA
Queens Coll of the City U of New York, NY
Radford U, VA
Randolph Coll, VA

Rutgers, The State U of New Jersey, New Brunswick, NJ
Ryerson U, ON, Canada
St. Gregory's U, OK
San Diego State U, CA
San Francisco State U, CA
Santa Ana Coll, CA
Santa Rosa Jr Coll, CA
Slippery Rock U of Pennsylvania, PA
Southern Utah U, UT
State U of New York at Fredonia, NY
State U of New York Coll at Brockport, NY
State U of New York Coll at Potsdam, NY
Stephen F. Austin State U, TX
Sweet Briar Coll, VA
Temple U, PA
Towson U, MD
Trinity Coll, CT
U at Buffalo, the State U of New York, NY
The U of Akron, OH
The U of Alabama, AL
The U of Arizona, AZ
U of California, Berkeley, CA
U of California, Irvine, CA
U of California, Los Angeles, CA
U of California, Santa Barbara, CA
U of Central Oklahoma, OK
U of Cincinnati, OH
U of Colorado at Boulder, CO
U of Hartford, CT
U of Hawaii at Manoa, HI
U of Illinois at Urbana–Champaign, IL
U of Kansas, KS
U of Maryland, Baltimore County, MD
U of Massachusetts Amherst, MA
U of Miami, FL
U of Michigan, MI
U of Missouri–Kansas City, MO
U of Nebraska–Lincoln, NE
U of New Mexico, NM
The U of North Carolina at Charlotte, NC
U of Oregon, OR
The U of Tennessee at Martin, TN
The U of Texas at Austin, TX
The U of the Arts, PA
U of Washington, WA
U of Wisconsin–Stevens Point, WI
Virginia Intermont Coll, VA
Wayne State U, MI
Wells Coll, NY
Westchester Comm Coll, NY
Western Oregon U, OR
West Texas A&M U, TX
Wright State U, OH

DATA ENTRY/ MICROCOMPUTER APPLICATIONS
Baker Coll of Allen Park, MI
Bunker Hill Comm Coll, MA
Coll of The Albemarle, NC
The Coll of Westchester, NY
Eastfield Coll, TX
Florida Comm Coll at Jacksonville, FL
Galveston Coll, TX

Glendale Comm Coll, CA
Heartland Comm Coll, IL
Howard Comm Coll, MD
Laredo Comm Coll, TX
Northland Comm and Tech
Coll–Thief River Falls, MN
Richland Comm Coll, IL
Roxbury Comm Coll, MA
St. Philip's Coll, TX
Santa Ana Coll, CA
Seminole Comm Coll, FL
Stark State Coll of
Technology, OH
Valencia Comm Coll, FL

**DATA ENTRY/
MICROCOMPUTER
APPLICATIONS RELATED**
Baker Coll of Allen Park, MI
The Coll of Westchester, NY
Colorado Mountain Coll,
Alpine Campus, CO
Florida Comm Coll at
Jacksonville, FL
Glendale Comm Coll, CA
Heartland Comm Coll, IL
Kellogg Comm Coll, MI
Laredo Comm Coll, TX
Northland Comm and Tech
Coll–Thief River Falls, MN
Richland Comm Coll, IL
San Diego Mesa Coll, CA
Santa Ana Coll, CA
Seminole Comm Coll, FL
Southwestern Michigan Coll,
MI
Stark State Coll of
Technology, OH
West Shore Comm Coll, MI

**DATA MODELING/
WAREHOUSING AND
DATABASE
ADMINISTRATION**
Florida Comm Coll at
Jacksonville, FL
Midland Coll, TX
Neumont U, UT
Northland Comm and Tech
Coll–Thief River Falls, MN
Rochester Inst of
Technology, NY
Seminole Comm Coll, FL

**DATA PROCESSING AND
DATA PROCESSING
TECHNOLOGY**
Abraham Baldwin Coll, GA
Bainbridge Coll, GA
Bemidji State U, MN
British Columbia Inst of
Technology, BC, Canada
Broome Comm Coll, NY
Broward Comm Coll, FL
Bucks County Comm Coll,
PA
Cedar Valley Coll, TX
Central Piedmont Comm
Coll, NC
Chattanooga State Tech
Comm Coll, TN
Chesapeake Coll, MD
Citrus Coll, CA
City Colls of Chicago,
Richard J. Daley Coll, IL
Clayton State U, GA
The Coll of Westchester, NY
Comm Coll of Beaver
County, PA
Cuesta Coll, CA
Dabney S. Lancaster Comm
Coll, VA

Delaware Tech & Comm
Coll, Jack F. Owens
Campus, DE
Dixie State Coll of Utah, UT
Eastfield Coll, TX
El Camino Coll, CA
El Centro Coll, TX
Farmingdale State Coll, NY
Frederick Comm Coll, MD
Fulton-Montgomery Comm
Coll, NY
Gaston Coll, NC
Glendale Comm Coll, CA
Gloucester County Coll, NJ
Housatonic Comm Coll, CT
Illinois Valley Comm Coll, IL
Irvine Valley Coll, CA
Jefferson Comm and Tech
Coll, KY
Jefferson Comm Coll, OH
Kapiolani Comm Coll, HI
Kingsborough Comm Coll of
the City U of New York,
NY
Lamar State Coll–Orange, TX
Lamar U, TX
Laredo Comm Coll, TX
Lee Coll, TX
Long Beach City Coll, CA
Metropolitan Comm
Coll–Longview, MO
Metropolitan Comm
Coll–Penn Valley, MO
Miami Dade Coll, FL
Minnesota State U Mankato,
MN
Montana State U–Billings,
MT
Montana Tech of The U of
Montana, MT
Moorpark Coll, CA
Morton Coll, IL
Mount Vernon Nazarene U,
OH
Nassau Comm Coll, NY
New Hampshire Comm
Tech Coll, Nashua/
Claremont, NH
New Mexico Jr Coll, NM
New York City Coll of
Technology of the City U
of New York, NY
North Central Missouri Coll,
MO
North Central Texas Coll, TX
Northern State U, SD
Odessa Coll, TX
Phoenix Coll, AZ
St. Louis Comm Coll at
Florissant Valley, MO
Schoolcraft Coll, MI
Seminole Comm Coll, FL
Southwestern Indian
Polytechnic Inst, NM
Spokane Comm Coll, WA
Stephen F. Austin State U,
TX
Tallahassee Comm Coll, FL
Tunxis Comm Coll, CT
The U of Akron, OH
The U of Akron–Wayne
Coll, OH
U of Cincinnati, OH
U of New Brunswick
Fredericton, NB, Canada
U of Southern Indiana, IN
U of Washington, WA
Virginia Highlands Comm
Coll, VA
Westchester Comm Coll, NY
Western Tech Coll, WI
West Los Angeles Coll, CA
Westmoreland County
Comm Coll, PA

West Shore Comm Coll, MI
Williston State Coll, ND
Wright State U, OH

**DEMOGRAPHY AND
POPULATION**
Hampshire Coll, MA

DENTAL ASSISTING
Calhoun Comm Coll, AL
Citrus Coll, CA
Foothill Coll, CA
James H. Faulkner State
Comm Coll, AL
Jefferson Comm Coll, OH
Massasoit Comm Coll, MA
Pueblo Comm Coll, CO
Reedley Coll, CA
Rose State Coll, OK
St. Cloud Tech Coll, MN
San Diego Mesa Coll, CA
U of Alaska Anchorage, AK
The U of Maine at Augusta,
ME
U of Southern Indiana, IN

DENTAL HYGIENE
Allegany Coll of Maryland,
MD
Argosy U, Twin Cities,
Eagan, MN
Asheville-Buncombe Tech
Comm Coll, NC
Blinn Coll, TX
Brevard Comm Coll, FL
Broome Comm Coll, NY
Broward Comm Coll, FL
Cape Cod Comm Coll, MA
Central Piedmont Comm
Coll, NC
Chattanooga State Tech
Comm Coll, TN
City Colls of Chicago,
Richard J. Daley Coll, IL
Clayton State U, GA
Dalhousie U, NS, Canada
Dixie State Coll of Utah, UT
Farmingdale State Coll, NY
Florida Comm Coll at
Jacksonville, FL
Foothill Coll, CA
Fresno City Coll, CA
Greenville Tech Coll, SC
Harrisburg Area Comm Coll,
PA
Hillsborough Comm Coll, FL
Hudson Valley Comm Coll,
NY
Idaho State U, ID
Indiana U–Purdue U Fort
Wayne, IN
Indiana U–Purdue U
Indianapolis, IN
Kellogg Comm Coll, MI
Lamar Inst of Technology,
TX
Lamar U, TX
Marquette U, WI
Miami Dade Coll, FL
Middle Georgia Tech Coll,
GA
Middlesex County Coll, NJ
Minnesota State U Mankato,
MN
Montana State U–Billings,
MT
New York City Coll of
Technology of the City U
of New York, NY
New York U, NY
Northeastern U, MA
The Ohio State U, OH
Old Dominion U, VA

Oregon Inst of Technology,
OR
Phoenix Coll, AZ
Pima Comm Coll, AZ
Pueblo Comm Coll, CO
Rose State Coll, OK
St. Cloud Tech Coll, MN
Santa Rosa Jr Coll, CA
Shasta Coll, CA
Southern Adventist U, TN
Southern Illinois U
Carbondale, IL
Spokane Comm Coll, WA
Stark State Coll of
Technology, OH
Tallahassee Comm Coll, FL
Tunxis Comm Coll, CT
U of Alaska Anchorage, AK
U of Arkansas at Fort Smith,
AR
U of Hawaii at Manoa, HI
The U of Maine at Augusta,
ME
U of Manitoba, MB, Canada
U of Michigan, MI
U of Missouri–Kansas City,
MO
U of New England, ME
U of New Haven, CT
U of New Mexico, NM
The U of North Carolina at
Chapel Hill, NC
U of Pittsburgh, PA
U of Rhode Island, RI
U of Southern Indiana, IN
U of Washington, WA
U of Wyoming, WY
Valencia Comm Coll, FL
Vermont Tech Coll, VT
Waukesha County Tech Coll,
WI
Western Tech Coll, WI
West Liberty State Coll, WV
West Los Angeles Coll, CA
Westmoreland County
Comm Coll, PA
Wichita State U, KS

**DENTAL LABORATORY
TECHNOLOGY**
Commonwealth Tech Inst,
PA
Idaho State U, ID
Indiana U–Purdue U Fort
Wayne, IN
New York City Coll of
Technology of the City U
of New York, NY
Pima Comm Coll, AZ
Southern Illinois U
Carbondale, IL

**DESIGN AND APPLIED
ARTS RELATED**
Daemen Coll, NY
Harding U, AR
Hofstra U, NY
Lehigh U, PA
Mohawk Valley Comm Coll,
NY
North Carolina State U, NC
NSCAD U, NS, Canada
Pratt Inst, NY
Ringling Coll of Art and
Design, FL
St. Cloud State U, MN
Savannah Coll of Art and
Design, GA
School of the Art Inst of
Chicago, IL
The U of Akron, OH
U of California, Los Angeles,
CA
U of Wisconsin–Stout, WI

**DESIGN AND VISUAL
COMMUNICATIONS**
Albright Coll, PA
Alma Coll, MI
American U, DC
The Art Inst of Pittsburgh,
PA
Bethel Coll, IN
Buffalo State Coll, State U of
New York, NY
Bunker Hill Comm Coll, MA
Carlow U, PA
Drury U, MO
Duke U, NC
Farmingdale State Coll, NY
Florida Comm Coll at
Jacksonville, FL
Framingham State Coll, MA
Fresno City Coll, CA
Harrisburg Area Comm Coll,
PA
The Illinois Inst of Art–
Schaumburg, IL
Ivy Tech Comm Coll–
Southwest, IN
Ivy Tech Comm Coll–
Wabash Valley, IN
Jacksonville U, FL
Lehigh U, PA
Marywood U, PA
Missouri State U, MO
Montana State U, MT
Mount Union Coll, OH
Nassau Comm Coll, NY
North Carolina State U, NC
North Metro Tech Coll, GA
NSCAD U, NS, Canada
The Ohio State U, OH
Pima Comm Coll, AZ
Pueblo Comm Coll, CO
Rochester Inst of
Technology, NY
Saginaw Valley State U, MI
San Diego State U, CA
Savannah Coll of Art and
Design, GA
School of the Art Inst of
Chicago, IL
Shasta Coll, CA
Southern Illinois U
Carbondale, IL
Syracuse U, NY
Truman State U, MO
U of Evansville, IN
U of Kansas, KS
U of Michigan, MI
U of Notre Dame, IN
The U of Tennessee at
Martin, TN
The U of Texas at Austin,
TX
Waubonsee Comm Coll, IL

**DESKTOP PUBLISHING
AND DIGITAL IMAGING
DESIGN**
Eastern Idaho Tech Coll, ID
Glendale Comm Coll, CA
Lee Coll, TX

**DEVELOPMENTAL AND
CHILD PSYCHOLOGY**
California State U, San
Bernardino, CA
Carson-Newman Coll, TN
Central Lakes Coll, MN
City Colls of Chicago,
Richard J. Daley Coll, IL
Coll of the Canyons, CA
Eastern Connecticut State U,
CT
Fitchburg State Coll, MA
Framingham State Coll, MA
Fresno Pacific U, CA

Fulton-Montgomery Comm
Coll, NY
Grossmont Coll, CA
Houston Baptist U, TX
Jefferson Comm Coll, OH
Langston U, OK
Liberty U, VA
Long Beach City Coll, CA
Marywood U, PA
Midland Coll, TX
Minnesota State U Mankato,
MN
MiraCosta Coll, CA
Mitchell Coll, CT
Mount Saint Vincent U, NS,
Canada
Northern Michigan U, MI
Rose State Coll, OK
Tufts U, MA
The U of Akron, OH
U of Delaware, DE
U of New Brunswick
Fredericton, NB, Canada
U of the District of
Columbia, DC
U of the Incarnate Word, TX
U of Wisconsin–Green Bay,
WI
U of Wisconsin–Madison,
WI
Utica Coll, NY
West Los Angeles Coll, CA
Wilfrid Laurier U, ON,
Canada

**DEVELOPMENTAL
BIOLOGY AND
EMBRYOLOGY**
U of Colorado at Boulder,
CO

**DEVELOPMENT
ECONOMICS AND
INTERNATIONAL
DEVELOPMENT**
Brown U, RI
Calvin Coll, MI
Clark U, MA
Dalhousie U, NS, Canada
Eastern Mennonite U, VA
Fitchburg State Coll, MA
The Ohio State U, OH
Point Loma Nazarene U, CA
U of California, Los Angeles,
CA
U of Vermont, VT

**DIAGNOSTIC MEDICAL
SONOGRAPHY AND
ULTRASOUND
TECHNOLOGY**
Argosy U, Twin Cities,
Eagan, MN
Caldwell Comm Coll and
Tech Inst, NC
Central Ohio Tech Coll, OH
Comm Coll of Allegheny
County, PA
Dalhousie U, NS, Canada
El Centro Coll, TX
Florida Comm Coll at
Jacksonville, FL
Foothill Coll, CA
The George Washington U,
DC
Gloucester County Coll, NJ
Hillsborough Comm Coll, FL
Lackawanna Coll, PA
Lamar Inst of Technology,
TX
Miami Dade Coll, FL
Nebraska Methodist Coll, NE
New York U, NY

Rochester Inst of
Technology, NY
St. Cloud Tech Coll, MN
U of Arkansas at Fort Smith,
AR
U of Missouri–Columbia,
MO
Valencia Comm Coll, FL

**DIESEL MECHANICS
TECHNOLOGY**
Alexandria Tech Coll, MN
British Columbia Inst of
Technology, BC, Canada
Dixie State Coll of Utah, UT
Eastern Idaho Tech Coll, ID
Idaho State U, ID
Lamar Inst of Technology,
TX
Massasoit Comm Coll, MA
Montana State U–Billings,
MT
Ozarks Tech Comm Coll,
MO
St. Cloud Tech Coll, MN
St. Philip's Coll, TX
Santa Ana Coll, CA
Shasta Coll, CA
Shelton State Comm Coll, AL
Skagit Valley Coll, WA
Southeast Tech Inst, SD
U of Alaska Anchorage, AK
The U of Montana-Helena
Coll of Technology, MT
Williston State Coll, ND

DIETETICS
Abilene Christian U, TX
Acadia U, NS, Canada
Ashland U, OH
Ball State U, IN
Buffalo State Coll, State U of
New York, NY
California State U, San
Bernardino, CA
Carson-Newman Coll, TN
Central Arizona Coll, AZ
Coll of Saint Elizabeth, NJ
Delaware State U, DE
Dominican U, IL
East Carolina U, NC
Eastern Michigan U, MI
Florida Comm Coll at
Jacksonville, FL
Florida International U, FL
Fontbonne U, MO
Framingham State Coll, MA
Fresno City Coll, CA
Gannon U, PA
Gaston Coll, NC
Grossmont Coll, CA
Harding U, AR
Harrisburg Area Comm Coll,
PA
Hocking Coll, OH
Idaho State U, ID
Immaculata U, PA
Indiana U Bloomington, IN
Indiana U of Pennsylvania,
PA
Kansas State U, KS
Lamar U, TX
Langston U, OK
Long Beach City Coll, CA
Marshall U, WV
Marywood U, PA
Mercyhurst Coll, PA
Miami Dade Coll, FL
Michigan State U, MI
Middlesex County Coll, NJ
Minnesota State U Mankato,
MN
Missouri State U, MO

Mount Saint Vincent U, NS,
Canada
North Dakota State U, ND
The Ohio State U, OH
Point Loma Nazarene U, CA
Rochester Inst of
Technology, NY
Saint John's U, MN
St. Louis Comm Coll at
Florissant Valley, MO
San Francisco State U, CA
Santa Rosa Jr Coll, CA
Seton Hill U, PA
Southern Maine Comm Coll,
ME
Spokane Comm Coll, WA
Syracuse U, NY
The U of Akron, OH
U of Central Missouri, MO
U of Central Oklahoma, OK
U of Connecticut, CT
U of Dayton, OH
U of Delaware, DE
U of Hawaii at Manoa, HI
U of Illinois at Urbana–
Champaign, IL
U of Missouri–Columbia,
MO
U of Nebraska at Kearney,
NE
U of New Hampshire, NH
U of New Haven, CT
U of Pittsburgh, PA
U of Rhode Island, RI
The U of Tennessee at
Martin, TN
U of Vermont, VT
U of Wisconsin–Madison,
WI
U of Wisconsin–Stevens
Point, WI
U of Wisconsin–Stout, WI
Wayne State U, MI
Westchester Comm Coll, NY
West Chester U of
Pennsylvania, PA
Western Nebraska Comm
Coll, NE
Westmoreland County
Comm Coll, PA

DIETETIC TECHNICIAN
Miami Dade Coll, FL
U of New Hampshire, NH

DIETITIAN ASSISTANT
Comm Coll of Allegheny
County, PA
Florida Comm Coll at
Jacksonville, FL

**DIGITAL
COMMUNICATION AND
MEDIA/MULTIMEDIA**
Abilene Christian U, TX
Academy of Art U, CA
The Art Inst of Pittsburgh,
PA
Brevard Comm Coll, FL
California State U,
Sacramento, CA
Calvin Coll, MI
Cameron U, OK
Central Wyoming Coll, WY
Fashion Inst of Technology,
NY
Florida Atlantic U, FL
Harding U, AR
Hillsborough Comm Coll, FL
Huntington U, IN
The Illinois Inst of Art–
Schaumburg, IL
Kutztown U of
Pennsylvania, PA

Lebanon Valley Coll, PA
Lindenwood U, MO
Marist Coll, NY
New York U, NY
Northwestern Coll, MN
Savannah Coll of Art and
Design, GA
School of the Art Inst of
Chicago, IL
Texas A&M U, TX
U of Baltimore, MD
U of Northern Iowa, IA
The U of the Arts, PA
U of Toronto, ON, Canada

**DIRECTING AND
THEATRICAL
PRODUCTION**
Coe Coll, IA
Drake U, IA
Marywood U, PA
Oakland U, MI

DIVINITY/MINISTRY
Bethany U, CA
Bethel Coll, IN
Cardinal Stritch U, WI
Carson-Newman Coll, TN
Cincinnati Christian U, OH
Dallas Baptist U, TX
Fresno Pacific U, CA
Grace Coll, IN
Harding U, AR
Huntington U, IN
John Brown U, AR
Kuyper Coll, MI
Northwest Nazarene U, ID
Oak Hills Christian Coll, MN

**DRAFTING AND DESIGN
TECHNOLOGY**
Bainbridge Coll, GA
Brevard Comm Coll, FL
British Columbia Inst of
Technology, BC, Canada
Burlington County Coll, NJ
Caldwell Comm Coll and
Tech Inst, NC
Calhoun Comm Coll, AL
Cameron U, OK
Central Florida Comm Coll,
FL
Central Ohio Tech Coll, OH
Central Piedmont Comm
Coll, NC
Chattahoochee Tech Coll,
GA
Chattanooga State Tech
Comm Coll, TN
Citrus Coll, CA
City Colls of Chicago,
Richard J. Daley Coll, IL
Clayton State U, GA
Coll of the Canyons, CA
Coll of the Desert, CA
Comm Coll of Allegheny
County, PA
Comm Coll of Beaver
County, PA
Cosumnes River Coll,
Sacramento, CA
Dabney S. Lancaster Comm
Coll, VA
DeKalb Tech Coll, GA
Delaware Tech & Comm
Coll, Jack F. Owens
Campus, DE
East Central Coll, MO
Eastern New Mexico
U–Roswell, NM
Eastfield Coll, TX
El Camino Coll, CA
El Centro Coll, TX

Florida Comm Coll at
Jacksonville, FL
Frederick Comm Coll, MD
Fresno City Coll, CA
Glendale Comm Coll, CA
Gloucester County Coll, NJ
Grambling State U, LA
Greenville Tech Coll, SC
Heartland Comm Coll, IL
Hocking Coll, OH
Houston Comm Coll System,
TX
Idaho State U, ID
Illinois Valley Comm Coll, IL
Ivy Tech Comm Coll–
Kokomo, IN
Jefferson Comm Coll, OH
Kellogg Comm Coll, MI
Lamar U, TX
Langston U, OK
Lassen Comm Coll District,
CA
Lee Coll, TX
LeTourneau U, TX
Linn State Tech Coll, MO
Long Beach City Coll, CA
Macomb Comm Coll, MI
Miami Dade Coll, FL
Middle Georgia Tech Coll,
GA
Middlesex County Coll, NJ
Midland Coll, TX
Minnesota State Coll–
Southeast Tech, MN
MiraCosta Coll, CA
Mohawk Valley Comm Coll,
NY
Montana State U–Billings,
MT
Montana Tech of The U of
Montana, MT
Morton Coll, IL
Murray State U, KY
New Hampshire Comm
Tech Coll, Nashua/
Claremont, NH
New Mexico Jr Coll, NM
New River Comm Coll, VA
New York City Coll of
Technology of the City U
of New York, NY
North Central Missouri Coll,
MO
North Central Texas Coll, TX
Northern Michigan U, MI
Northland Comm and Tech
Coll–Thief River Falls, MN
Odessa Coll, TX
Paris Jr Coll, TX
Phoenix Coll, AZ
Prairie View A&M U, TX
Richland Comm Coll, IL
Rose State Coll, OK
Santa Ana Coll, CA
Santa Barbara City Coll, CA
Schoolcraft Coll, MI
Seminole Comm Coll, FL
Shasta Coll, CA
Shelton State Comm Coll, AL
Southeast Tech Inst, SD
Southern Maine Comm Coll,
ME
Southern Utah U, UT
South Piedmont Comm Coll,
NC
Southwestern Indian
Polytechnic Inst, NM
Southwestern Michigan Coll,
MI
Spokane Comm Coll, WA
Stark State Coll of
Technology, OH
State U of New York Coll of
Technology at Alfred, NY

Colleges for Students with Learning Disabilities or AD/HD

Surry Comm Coll, NC
Tidewater Comm Coll, VA
The U of Akron, OH
U of Alaska Anchorage, AK
U of Central Missouri, MO
U of Cincinnati, OH
U of Houston, TX
U of Rio Grande, OH
Valencia Comm Coll, FL
Virginia Highlands Comm
  Coll, VA
Washburn U, KS
West Los Angeles Coll, CA
Westmoreland County
  Comm Coll, PA
West Virginia State U, WV
Wright State U, OH

**DRAFTING/DESIGN
ENGINEERING
TECHNOLOGIES
RELATED**
Comm Coll of Allegheny
  County, PA
Idaho State U, ID
The U of Akron, OH

**DRAFTING/DESIGN
TECHNOLOGY**
Lamar Inst of Technology,
  TX
U of Arkansas at Fort Smith,
  AR

**DRAMA AND DANCE
TEACHER EDUCATION**
Baylor U, TX
Bishop's U, QC, Canada
Brenau U, GA
The Catholic U of America,
  DC
Concordia U, NE
East Carolina U, NC
Hope Coll, MI
Huntington U, IN
Indiana U–Purdue U Fort
  Wayne, IN
Jacksonville U, FL
Johnson State Coll, VT
Minnesota State U
  Moorhead, MN
The Ohio State U, OH
Ohio Wesleyan U, OH
Old Dominion U, VA
Salve Regina U, RI
The U of Akron, OH
The U of Arizona, AZ
U of Evansville, IN
The U of North Carolina at
  Charlotte, NC
U of St. Thomas, MN
The U of the Arts, PA
Wayne State Coll, NE
Western Nebraska Comm
  Coll, NE
William Jewell Coll, MO

**DRAMATIC/THEATER
ARTS**
Abilene Christian U, TX
Acadia U, NS, Canada
Adams State Coll, CO
Adelphi U, NY
Albertson Coll of Idaho, ID
Albion Coll, MI
Albright Coll, PA
Alderson-Broaddus Coll, WV
Alma Coll, MI
American U, DC
Amherst Coll, MA
Anderson U, IN
Anderson U, SC
Angelo State U, TX
Ashland U, OH

Augsburg Coll, MN
Avila U, MO
Bainbridge Coll, GA
Ball State U, IN
Bard Coll, NY
Barry U, FL
Bates Coll, ME
Baylor U, TX
Bemidji State U, MN
Benedictine Coll, KS
Bethany U, CA
Bethel Coll, IN
Bethel U, MN
Bishop's U, QC, Canada
Blinn Coll, TX
Boston Coll, MA
Bradley U, IL
Brandeis U, MA
Brenau U, GA
Briar Cliff U, IA
Brock U, ON, Canada
Brown U, RI
Bucks County Comm Coll,
  PA
Buffalo State Coll, State U of
  New York, NY
Bunker Hill Comm Coll, MA
Burlington County Coll, NJ
Calhoun Comm Coll, AL
California State U, Fullerton,
  CA
California State U,
  Northridge, CA
California State U,
  Sacramento, CA
California State U, San
  Bernardino, CA
California State U,
  Stanislaus, CA
Calvin Coll, MI
Cape Cod Comm Coll, MA
Cardinal Stritch U, WI
Carleton U, ON, Canada
Carnegie Mellon U, PA
Carroll Coll, MT
Carroll Coll, WI
Carson-Newman Coll, TN
Carthage Coll, WI
The Catholic U of America,
  DC
Cedar Crest Coll, PA
Central Wyoming Coll, WY
Christopher Newport U, VA
Citrus Coll, CA
City Colls of Chicago,
  Richard J. Daley Coll, IL
Claremont McKenna Coll,
  CA
Clark U, MA
Clayton State U, GA
Coastal Carolina U, SC
Coe Coll, IA
Colby Coll, ME
Colgate U, NY
Coll of Charleston, SC
Coll of Staten Island of the
  City U of New York, NY
Coll of The Albemarle, NC
Coll of the Desert, CA
The Coll of William and
  Mary, VA
Columbus State U, GA
Comm Coll of Allegheny
  County, PA
Concordia U, NE
Cornell U, NY
Cosumnes River Coll,
  Sacramento, CA
Crafton Hills Coll, CA
Dalhousie U, NS, Canada
Dean Coll, MA
DePaul U, IL
Dixie State Coll of Utah, UT
Dominican U, IL

Drake U, IA
Drury U, MO
Duke U, NC
Earlham Coll, IN
East Carolina U, NC
Eastern Mennonite U, VA
Eastern Michigan U, MI
Eastern Nazarene Coll, MA
East Stroudsburg U of
  Pennsylvania, PA
Eckerd Coll, FL
Edinboro U of Pennsylvania,
  PA
El Camino Coll, CA
Elmira Coll, NY
Elon U, NC
Emory U, GA
Eugene Lang Coll The New
  School for Liberal Arts, NY
Fairleigh Dickinson U, Coll
  at Florham, NJ
Fairleigh Dickinson U,
  Metropolitan Campus, NJ
Ferrum Coll, VA
Fitchburg State Coll, MA
Flagler Coll, FL
Florida Atlantic U, FL
Florida International U, FL
Fontbonne U, MO
Franciscan U of
  Steubenville, OH
Franklin Coll, IN
Franklin Pierce U, NH
Freed-Hardeman U, TN
Fresno City Coll, CA
Fulton-Montgomery Comm
  Coll, NY
Furman U, SC
Gainesville State Coll, GA
Galveston Coll, TX
Gannon U, PA
Gardner-Webb U, NC
Georgetown Coll, KY
The George Washington U,
  DC
Georgia Coll & State U, GA
Glendale Comm Coll, CA
Gloucester County Coll, NJ
Gonzaga U, WA
Goshen Coll, IN
Graceland U, IA
Grambling State U, LA
Grinnell Coll, IA
Grossmont Coll, CA
Gustavus Adolphus Coll,
  MN
Hamilton Coll, NY
Hamline U, MN
Hampshire Coll, MA
Harding U, AR
Harrisburg Area Comm Coll,
  PA
Hartwick Coll, NY
Henderson State U, AR
High Point U, NC
Hillsborough Comm Coll, FL
Hofstra U, NY
Hope Coll, MI
Houston Comm Coll System,
  TX
Howard Comm Coll, MD
Hunter Coll of the City U of
  New York, NY
Huntington U, IN
Idaho State U, ID
Illinois State U, IL
Illinois Wesleyan U, IL
Indiana U Bloomington, IN
Indiana U of Pennsylvania,
  PA
Indiana U–Purdue U Fort
  Wayne, IN
Iona Coll, NY
Ithaca Coll, NY

Jacksonville U, FL
Johnson State Coll, VT
Kansas State U, KS
Kellogg Comm Coll, MI
Kennesaw State U, GA
Kenyon Coll, OH
Kingsborough Comm Coll of
  the City U of New York,
  NY
King's Coll, PA
Kutztown U of
  Pennsylvania, PA
LaGrange Coll, GA
Lake Erie Coll, OH
Lamar U, TX
Langston U, OK
Lawrence U, WI
Lee Coll, TX
Lehigh U, PA
Le Moyne Coll, NY
Lewis U, IL
Lindenwood U, MO
Long Beach City Coll, CA
Loyola Marymount U, CA
Loyola U Chicago, IL
Loyola U New Orleans, LA
Lynchburg Coll, VA
Macalester Coll, MN
MacMurray Coll, IL
Marietta Coll, OH
Marist Coll, NY
Marquette U, WI
Marymount Manhattan Coll,
  NY
Marywood U, PA
Massachusetts Coll of Liberal
  Arts, MA
Massasoit Comm Coll, MA
McDaniel Coll, MD
McNeese State U, LA
Mercer U, GA
Miami Dade Coll, FL
Michigan State U, MI
Middlesex County Coll, NJ
Middle Tennessee State U,
  TN
Midland Lutheran Coll, NE
Minnesota State U Mankato,
  MN
Minnesota State U
  Moorhead, MN
MiraCosta Coll, CA
Missouri State U, MO
Mohawk Valley Comm Coll,
  NY
Monmouth Coll, IL
Montana State U, MT
Montana State U–Billings,
  MT
Moorpark Coll, CA
Moravian Coll, PA
Morningside Coll, IA
Mount Holyoke Coll, MA
Mount Union Coll, OH
Mount Vernon Nazarene U,
  OH
Murray State U, KY
Naropa U, CO
Nassau Comm Coll, NY
National-Louis U, IL
New Mexico Jr Coll, NM
New York U, NY
Niagara U, NY
North Carolina School of the
  Arts, NC
North Central Coll, IL
North Dakota State U, ND
Northeastern U, MA
Northern Illinois U, IL
Northern Michigan U, MI
Northern State U, SD
Northwestern Coll, MN
Notre Dame de Namur U,
  CA

Nova Southeastern U, FL
Occidental Coll, CA
The Ohio State U, OH
Ohio Wesleyan U, OH
Oklahoma State U, OK
Old Dominion U, VA
Oral Roberts U, OK
Otterbein Coll, OH
Our Lady of the Lake U of
  San Antonio, TX
Park U, MO
Piedmont Coll, GA
Pima Comm Coll, AZ
Point Loma Nazarene U, CA
Portland State U, OR
Prairie View A&M U, TX
Presbyterian Coll, SC
Queens Coll of the City U of
  New York, NY
Queen's U at Kingston, ON,
  Canada
Queens U of Charlotte, NC
Quincy Coll, MA
Radford U, VA
Randolph Coll, VA
Randolph-Macon Coll, VA
Redeemer U Coll, ON,
  Canada
Rhodes Coll, TN
Ripon Coll, WI
Rockford Coll, IL
Rocky Mountain Coll, MT
Roosevelt U, IL
Rose State Coll, OK
Rowan U, NJ
Rutgers, The State U of New
  Jersey, Newark, NJ
Rutgers, The State U of New
  Jersey, New Brunswick, NJ
Saginaw Valley State U, MI
St. Cloud State U, MN
Saint John's U, MN
Saint Joseph's Coll, IN
St. Lawrence U, NY
St. Louis Comm Coll at
  Florissant Valley, MO
St. Mary's Coll of Maryland,
  MD
St. Philip's Coll, TX
Salve Regina U, RI
San Diego State U, CA
San Francisco State U, CA
Santa Ana Coll, CA
Santa Barbara City Coll, CA
Santa Clara U, CA
Santa Rosa Jr Coll, CA
Sauk Valley Comm Coll, IL
Savannah Coll of Art and
  Design, GA
Scottsdale Comm Coll, AZ
Seattle Pacific U, WA
Seton Hill U, PA
Sewanee: The U of the
  South, TN
Shasta Coll, CA
Slippery Rock U of
  Pennsylvania, PA
Southern Illinois U
  Carbondale, IL
Southern Illinois U
  Edwardsville, IL
Southern Oregon U, OR
Southern U and A&M Coll,
  LA
Southern Utah U, UT
Southwest Baptist U, MO
Southwestern U, TX
Spoon River Coll, IL
State U of New York at
  Fredonia, NY
State U of New York Coll at
  Brockport, NY
State U of New York Coll at
  Geneseo, NY

State U of New York Coll at Potsdam, NY
Stephen F. Austin State U, TX
Stetson U, FL
Sweet Briar Coll, VA
Syracuse U, NY
Taylor U, IN
Temple U, PA
Texas A&M U, TX
Texas A&M U–Corpus Christi, TX
Towson U, MD
Trevecca Nazarene U, TN
Trinity Coll, CT
Trinity U, TX
Troy U, AL
Truman State U, MO
Tufts U, MA
U at Albany, State U of New York, NY
U at Buffalo, the State U of New York, NY
The U of Akron, OH
The U of Alabama, AL
U of Alaska Anchorage, AK
The U of Arizona, AZ
U of Arkansas, AR
U of California, Berkeley, CA
U of California, Irvine, CA
U of California, Los Angeles, CA
U of California, Santa Barbara, CA
U of Central Florida, FL
U of Central Missouri, MO
U of Central Oklahoma, OK
U of Cincinnati, OH
U of Colorado at Boulder, CO
U of Connecticut, CT
U of Dayton, OH
U of Evansville, IN
The U of Findlay, OH
U of Guelph, ON, Canada
U of Hartford, CT
U of Hawaii at Manoa, HI
U of Houston, TX
U of Illinois at Urbana–Champaign, IL
U of Kansas, KS
U of Kentucky, KY
U of Maine at Machias, ME
U of Manitoba, MB, Canada
U of Mary Hardin-Baylor, TX
U of Maryland, Baltimore County, MD
U of Mary Washington, VA
U of Massachusetts Amherst, MA
U of Massachusetts Boston, MA
U of Miami, FL
U of Michigan, MI
U of Minnesota, Duluth, MN
U of Mississippi, MS
U of Missouri–Columbia, MO
U of Missouri–Kansas City, MO
U of Nebraska at Kearney, NE
U of Nebraska at Omaha, NE
U of Nebraska–Lincoln, NE
U of New Brunswick Fredericton, NB, Canada
U of New Hampshire, NH
U of New Mexico, NM
The U of North Carolina at Asheville, NC
The U of North Carolina at Chapel Hill, NC

The U of North Carolina at Charlotte, NC
U of Northern Iowa, IA
U of Notre Dame, IN
U of Oregon, OR
U of Pennsylvania, PA
U of Pittsburgh, PA
U of Pittsburgh at Johnstown, PA
U of Portland, OR
U of St. Thomas, MN
U of St. Thomas, TX
U of San Diego, CA
The U of Scranton, PA
U of Southern Indiana, IN
The U of Tampa, FL
The U of Tennessee, TN
The U of Tennessee at Martin, TN
The U of Texas at Austin, TX
The U of Texas at El Paso, TX
The U of the Arts, PA
U of the District of Columbia, DC
U of the Incarnate Word, TX
U of the Ozarks, AR
U of the Pacific, CA
U of Toronto, ON, Canada
U of Vermont, VT
U of Virginia, VA
The U of Virginia's Coll at Wise, VA
U of Washington, WA
U of West Georgia, GA
U of Wisconsin–Eau Claire, WI
U of Wisconsin–Green Bay, WI
U of Wisconsin–La Crosse, WI
U of Wisconsin–Madison, WI
U of Wisconsin–Oshkosh, WI
U of Wisconsin–Stevens Point, WI
U of Wyoming, WY
Valdosta State U, GA
Valencia Comm Coll, FL
Vanguard U of Southern California, CA
Vassar Coll, NY
Ventura Coll, CA
Victor Valley Coll, CA
Virginia Highlands Comm Coll, VA
Virginia Intermont Coll, VA
Wake Forest U, NC
Washburn U, KS
Washington and Lee U, VA
Wayne State Coll, NE
Wayne State U, MI
Wellesley Coll, MA
Wells Coll, NY
West Chester U of Pennsylvania, PA
Western Connecticut State U, CT
Western Oregon U, OR
Westminster Coll, PA
West Texas A&M U, TX
West Virginia Wesleyan Coll, WV
Whitman Coll, WA
Wichita State U, KS
Wilfrid Laurier U, ON, Canada
Wilkes U, PA
William Jewell Coll, MO
Wofford Coll, SC
Wright State U, OH
Yale U, CT

DRAMATIC/THEATER ARTS AND STAGECRAFT RELATED

Brevard Coll, NC
Charleston Southern U, SC
Coastal Carolina U, SC
Dalhousie U, NS, Canada
DePaul U, IL
Drake U, IA
Fayetteville State U, NC
Lehigh U, PA
St. Cloud State U, MN
St. Philip's Coll, TX
Seton Hill U, PA
U at Buffalo, the State U of New York, NY
The U of Akron, OH
U of Connecticut, CT
The U of the Arts, PA

DRAWING

Academy of Art U, CA
Anderson U, SC
Ball State U, IN
Bard Coll, NY
Brock U, ON, Canada
Buffalo State Coll, State U of New York, NY
California State U, Fullerton, CA
Carson-Newman Coll, TN
The Cleveland Inst of Art, OH
Coll of the Atlantic, ME
DePaul U, IL
Dixie State Coll of Utah, UT
Drake U, IA
Grace Coll, IN
Grossmont Coll, CA
Indiana U Bloomington, IN
Indiana U–Purdue U Fort Wayne, IN
Lassen Comm Coll District, CA
Lewis U, IL
Lindenwood U, MO
McNeese State U, LA
Midland Coll, TX
Minneapolis Coll of Art and Design, MN
Minnesota State U Mankato, MN
North Georgia Coll & State U, GA
NSCAD U, NS, Canada
The Ohio State U, OH
Otis Coll of Art and Design, CA
Parsons The New School for Design, NY
Portland State U, OR
Pratt Inst, NY
Rivier Coll, NH
Rutgers, The State U of New Jersey, New Brunswick, NJ
St. Cloud State U, MN
School of the Art Inst of Chicago, IL
School of Visual Arts, NY
Seton Hill U, PA
Sewanee: The U of the South, TN
State U of New York at Fredonia, NY
State U of New York Coll at Brockport, NY
The U of Akron, OH
U of Hartford, CT
U of Michigan, MI
U of Oregon, OR
U of San Francisco, CA
The U of Texas at El Paso, TX

West Virginia Wesleyan Coll, WV
Wright State U, OH

DRIVER AND SAFETY TEACHER EDUCATION

U of Northern Iowa, IA

DUTCH/FLEMISH

U of California, Berkeley, CA

EARLY CHILDHOOD EDUCATION

Alma Coll, MI
Ancilla Coll, IN
Arkansas State U–Newport, AR
Asnuntuck Comm Coll, CT
Baker Coll of Allen Park, MI
Bethel Coll, IN
Bethel U, MN
Brevard Comm Coll, FL
Brewton-Parker Coll, GA
Bunker Hill Comm Coll, MA
California State U, Fullerton, CA
Carroll Coll, WI
Central Florida Comm Coll, FL
Charleston Southern U, SC
Clemson U, SC
Coastal Carolina U, SC
Coll of Charleston, SC
Coll of Saint Mary, NE
Columbus State U, GA
Concordia U, NE
Cornerstone U, MI
Daemen Coll, NY
Dean Coll, MA
Delaware State U, DE
Eastern Connecticut State U, CT
East Stroudsburg U of Pennsylvania, PA
Fitchburg State Coll, MA
Florida Gulf Coast U, FL
Framingham State Coll, MA
Gainesville State Coll, GA
Gannon U, PA
Gardner-Webb U, NC
Georgia Coll & State U, GA
Hagerstown Comm Coll, MD
Harding U, AR
Henderson State U, AR
Hofstra U, NY
Hopkinsville Comm Coll, KY
Houston Baptist U, TX
Hudson Valley Comm Coll, NY
Illinois State U, IL
Indiana U–Purdue U Fort Wayne, IN
Iona Coll, NY
Ivy Tech Comm Coll–Kokomo, IN
John Brown U, AR
Kendall Coll, IL
Kennesaw State U, GA
Kingsborough Comm Coll of the City U of New York, NY
King's Coll, PA
Lackawanna Coll, PA
LaGrange Coll, GA
Lake Superior State U, MI
Lancaster Bible Coll, PA
Loras Coll, IA
McNeese State U, LA
Mercyhurst Coll, PA
Millersville U of Pennsylvania, PA
Missouri State U, MO

Mount Union Coll, OH
Mount Vernon Nazarene U, OH
Murray State U, KY
Naropa U, CO
North Central Missouri Coll, MO
Northern Michigan U, MI
Northwestern Coll, MN
Notre Dame Coll, OH
Ohio Wesleyan U, OH
Oral Roberts U, OK
Park U, MO
Quincy Coll, MA
Ripon Coll, WI
Ryerson U, ON, Canada
St. Bonaventure U, NY
St. Philip's Coll, TX
Salem Comm Coll, NJ
Salve Regina U, RI
San Diego State U, CA
Sauk Valley Comm Coll, IL
Seton Hill U, PA
Southern Illinois U Carbondale, IL
Southern Illinois U Edwardsville, IL
Southern Nazarene U, OK
Southern U and A&M Coll, LA
Southwestern Coll, KS
State U of New York Coll at Brockport, NY
State U of New York Coll at Geneseo, NY
Texas A&M U–Corpus Christi, TX
Towson U, MD
The U of Alabama, AL
The U of Arizona, AZ
U of Arkansas, AR
U of Arkansas at Fort Smith, AR
U of Central Florida, FL
U of Great Falls, MT
U of Hartford, CT
U of Missouri–Columbia, MO
U of Missouri–Kansas City, MO
U of New Mexico, NM
U of New Orleans, LA
The U of North Carolina at Chapel Hill, NC
The U of Scranton, PA
U of Vermont, VT
U of Wisconsin–Stout, WI
Ursuline Coll, OH
Valdosta State U, GA
Washburn U, KS
Waukesha County Tech Coll, WI
Wayne State Coll, NE
Widener U, PA
Wilfrid Laurier U, ON, Canada

EARTH SCIENCES

Florida Inst of Technology, FL
Framingham State Coll, MA
U of Arkansas, AR
The U of North Carolina at Charlotte, NC

EAST ASIAN LANGUAGES

Cornell U, NY
Eckerd Coll, FL
U of California, Los Angeles, CA
U of Kansas, KS
U of Oregon, OR
U of Pennsylvania, PA

The U of Texas at Austin, TX

EAST ASIAN LANGUAGES RELATED
Claremont McKenna Coll, CA
Michigan State U, MI

ECOLOGY
Abraham Baldwin Coll, GA
Ball State U, IN
Bard Coll, NY
Barry U, FL
Bemidji State U, MN
Bradley U, IL
Brevard Coll, NC
Carleton U, ON, Canada
Clark U, MA
Concordia Coll–New York, NY
Dixie State Coll of Utah, UT
Florida Inst of Technology, FL
Franklin Pierce U, NH
Georgetown Coll, KY
Hocking Coll, OH
Idaho State U, ID
Lawrence U, WI
Lehigh U, PA
Minnesota State U Mankato, MN
North Carolina State U, NC
Northern Michigan U, MI
Rice U, TX
Rutgers, The State U of New Jersey, New Brunswick, NJ
St. Cloud State U, MN
San Francisco State U, CA
State U of New York Coll of Environmental Science and Forestry, NY
Sterling Coll, VT
Texas A&M U, TX
Tufts U, MA
Unity Coll, ME
The U of Akron, OH
U of California, Irvine, CA
U of California, Los Angeles, CA
U of California, Santa Barbara, CA
U of Connecticut, CT
U of Delaware, DE
U of Guelph, ON, Canada
U of Illinois at Urbana–Champaign, IL
U of Maine at Machias, ME
U of Manitoba, MB, Canada
U of Miami, FL
U of New Brunswick Fredericton, NB, Canada
U of New Hampshire, NH
U of New Haven, CT
U of Northern Iowa, IA
U of Pittsburgh, PA
U of Pittsburgh at Johnstown, PA
U of Rio Grande, OH
The U of Tennessee, TN
The U of Texas at Austin, TX
U of Toronto, ON, Canada
West Chester U of Pennsylvania, PA
Western Nebraska Comm Coll, NE
Yale U, CT

ECOLOGY, EVOLUTION, SYSTEMATICS AND POPULATION BIOLOGY RELATED
Cornell U, NY
Marywood U, PA

Sterling Coll, VT
U of Colorado at Boulder, CO

E-COMMERCE
Delaware State U, DE
Florida Inst of Technology, FL
Hudson Valley Comm Coll, NY
North Central Missouri Coll, MO
St. Philip's Coll, TX
Southern U and A&M Coll, LA
Stetson U, FL
Temple U, PA
Thiel Coll, PA
U of Pennsylvania, PA
U of Southern Indiana, IN
U of Toronto, ON, Canada

ECONOMETRICS AND QUANTITATIVE ECONOMICS
Hampden-Sydney Coll, VA
Haverford Coll, PA
Hofstra U, NY
U of Guelph, ON, Canada
U of Rhode Island, RI
U of St. Thomas, MN
Wake Forest U, NC

ECONOMICS
Acadia U, NS, Canada
Adelphi U, NY
Alabama A&M U, AL
Albertson Coll of Idaho, ID
Albion Coll, MI
Albright Coll, PA
Alma Coll, MI
American International Coll, MA
American U, DC
Amherst Coll, MA
Ashland U, OH
Augsburg Coll, MN
Aurora U, IL
Austin Coll, TX
Ball State U, IN
Bard Coll, NY
Barry U, FL
Bates Coll, ME
Baylor U, TX
Belmont Abbey Coll, NC
Bemidji State U, MN
Benedictine Coll, KS
Bethel U, MN
Bishop's U, QC, Canada
Boston Coll, MA
Bradley U, IL
Brandeis U, MA
Brandon U, MB, Canada
Bridgewater Coll, VA
Brock U, ON, Canada
Brown U, RI
Bryn Mawr Coll, PA
Buffalo State Coll, State U of New York, NY
California State U, Fullerton, CA
California State U, Northridge, CA
California State U, Sacramento, CA
California State U, San Bernardino, CA
California State U, Stanislaus, CA
Calvin Coll, MI
Cape Breton U, NS, Canada
Carleton U, ON, Canada
Carnegie Mellon U, PA
Carson-Newman Coll, TN

Carthage Coll, WI
The Catholic U of America, DC
Charleston Southern U, SC
Christopher Newport U, VA
Claremont McKenna Coll, CA
Clark U, MA
Clayton State U, GA
Clemson U, SC
Coastal Carolina U, SC
Coe Coll, IA
Colby Coll, ME
Colgate U, NY
Coll of Charleston, SC
Coll of Mount Saint Vincent, NY
Coll of Staten Island of the City U of New York, NY
Coll of the Atlantic, ME
Coll of the Desert, CA
The Coll of William and Mary, VA
Cornell U, NY
Crafton Hills Coll, CA
Dalhousie U, NS, Canada
DePaul U, IL
Dixie State Coll of Utah, UT
Dominican U, IL
Drury U, MO
Duke U, NC
Earlham Coll, IN
East Carolina U, NC
Eastern Connecticut State U, CT
Eastern Mennonite U, VA
Eastern Michigan U, MI
East Stroudsburg U of Pennsylvania, PA
Eckerd Coll, FL
Edinboro U of Pennsylvania, PA
El Camino Coll, CA
Elmira Coll, NY
Elon U, NC
Emory U, GA
Eugene Lang Coll The New School for Liberal Arts, NY
Fairfield U, CT
Fairleigh Dickinson U, Coll at Florham, NJ
Fitchburg State Coll, MA
Florida Atlantic U, FL
Florida International U, FL
Foothill Coll, CA
Fort Hays State U, KS
Framingham State Coll, MA
Franciscan U of Steubenville, OH
Franklin Coll, IN
Franklin Pierce U, NH
Furman U, SC
Georgetown Coll, KY
The George Washington U, DC
Gonzaga U, WA
Gordon Coll, MA
Goshen Coll, IN
Graceland U, IA
Grossmont Coll, CA
Gustavus Adolphus Coll, MN
Hamilton Coll, NY
Hamline U, MN
Hampden-Sydney Coll, VA
Hampshire Coll, MA
Harding U, AR
Hartwick Coll, NY
Haverford Coll, PA
Hofstra U, NY
Hope Coll, MI
Houston Baptist U, TX
Hunter Coll of the City U of New York, NY

Huntington U, IN
Idaho State U, ID
Illinois State U, IL
Illinois Wesleyan U, IL
Immaculata U, PA
Indiana U Bloomington, IN
Indiana U of Pennsylvania, PA
Indiana U–Purdue U Fort Wayne, IN
Indiana U–Purdue U Indianapolis, IN
Indiana U Southeast, IN
Iona Coll, NY
Ithaca Coll, NY
Jacksonville U, FL
Kansas State U, KS
Kennesaw State U, GA
Kenyon Coll, OH
King's Coll, PA
Kutztown U of Pennsylvania, PA
LaGrange Coll, GA
Lamar U, TX
Langston U, OK
Lawrence U, WI
Lebanon Valley Coll, PA
Lee Coll, TX
Le Moyne Coll, NY
Lewis U, IL
Liberty U, VA
Lincoln U, PA
Lindenwood U, MO
Long Island U, Brooklyn Campus, NY
Loras Coll, IA
Loyola Marymount U, CA
Loyola U Chicago, IL
Loyola U New Orleans, LA
Lynchburg Coll, VA
Macalester Coll, MN
Manhattan Coll, NY
Manhattanville Coll, NY
Marietta Coll, OH
Marist Coll, NY
Marquette U, WI
Marshall U, WV
Marymount U, VA
Massachusetts Coll of Liberal Arts, MA
McDaniel Coll, MD
Mercer U, GA
Miami Dade Coll, FL
Michigan State U, MI
Middle Tennessee State U, TN
Midland Coll, TX
Midland Lutheran Coll, NE
Millersville U of Pennsylvania, PA
Minnesota State U Mankato, MN
Minnesota State U Moorhead, MN
MiraCosta Coll, CA
Missouri State U, MO
Monmouth Coll, IL
Montana State U, MT
Moravian Coll, PA
Mount Holyoke Coll, MA
Mount St. Mary's U, MD
Mount Saint Vincent U, NS, Canada
Mount Union Coll, OH
Murray State U, KY
New Jersey City U, NJ
New York U, NY
Niagara U, NY
Nipissing U, ON, Canada
North Carolina State U, NC
North Central Coll, IL
Northeastern U, MA
Northern Illinois U, IL
Northern Michigan U, MI

Northern State U, SD
Oakland U, MI
Occidental Coll, CA
Oglethorpe U, GA
The Ohio State U, OH
Ohio Wesleyan U, OH
Oklahoma State U, OK
Old Dominion U, VA
Otterbein Coll, OH
Park U, MO
Penn State Abington, PA
Penn State DuBois, PA
Penn State Fayette, The Eberly Campus, PA
Penn State Mont Alto, PA
Penn State Wilkes-Barre, PA
Pittsburg State U, KS
Portland State U, OR
Presbyterian Coll, SC
Queens Coll of the City U of New York, NY
Queen's U at Kingston, ON, Canada
Radford U, VA
Ramapo Coll of New Jersey, NJ
Randolph Coll, VA
Randolph-Macon Coll, VA
Rensselaer Polytechnic Inst, NY
Rhodes Coll, TN
Rice U, TX
The Richard Stockton Coll of New Jersey, NJ
Ripon Coll, WI
Rochester Inst of Technology, NY
Rockford Coll, IL
Rockhurst U, MO
Rocky Mountain Coll, MT
Roosevelt U, IL
Rowan U, NJ
Rutgers, The State U of New Jersey, Newark, NJ
Rutgers, The State U of New Jersey, New Brunswick, NJ
Saginaw Valley State U, MI
St. Cloud State U, MN
St. Francis Xavier U, NS, Canada
Saint John's U, MN
Saint Joseph's Coll, IN
St. Lawrence U, NY
St. Mary's Coll of Maryland, MD
St. Norbert Coll, WI
St. Philip's Coll, TX
St. Thomas U, NB, Canada
Salve Regina U, RI
San Diego State U, CA
San Francisco State U, CA
Santa Ana Coll, CA
Santa Barbara City Coll, CA
Santa Clara U, CA
Santa Rosa Jr Coll, CA
Sauk Valley Comm Coll, IL
Seattle Pacific U, WA
Seton Hall U, NJ
Seton Hill U, PA
Sewanee: The U of the South, TN
Shippensburg U of Pennsylvania, PA
Skagit Valley Coll, WA
Slippery Rock U of Pennsylvania, PA
Southern Illinois U Carbondale, IL
Southern Illinois U Edwardsville, IL
Southern Oregon U, OR
Southern Utah U, UT
Southwestern U, TX

State U of New York at
Fredonia, NY
State U of New York Coll at
Brockport, NY
State U of New York Coll at
Cortland, NY
State U of New York Coll at
Geneseo, NY
State U of New York Coll at
Potsdam, NY
Stephen F. Austin State U,
TX
Stetson U, FL
Stonehill Coll, MA
Sweet Briar Coll, VA
Syracuse U, NY
Taylor U, IN
Temple U, PA
Texas A&M U, TX
Texas A&M U–Corpus
Christi, TX
Towson U, MD
Trent U, ON, Canada
Trinity Coll, CT
Trinity U, TX
Truman State U, MO
Tufts U, MA
U at Albany, State U of New
York, NY
U at Buffalo, the State U of
New York, NY
The U of Akron, OH
U of Alaska Anchorage, AK
The U of Arizona, AZ
U of Arkansas, AR
U of Baltimore, MD
U of California, Berkeley,
CA
U of California, Irvine, CA
U of California, Los Angeles,
CA
U of California, Santa
Barbara, CA
U of Central Florida, FL
U of Central Missouri, MO
U of Central Oklahoma, OK
U of Cincinnati, OH
U of Colorado at Boulder,
CO
U of Connecticut, CT
U of Dayton, OH
U of Delaware, DE
U of Evansville, IN
The U of Findlay, OH
U of Guelph, ON, Canada
U of Hartford, CT
U of Hawaii at Manoa, HI
U of Hawaii–West Oahu, HI
U of Houston, TX
U of Illinois at Urbana–
Champaign, IL
U of Kansas, KS
U of Kentucky, KY
U of Manitoba, MB, Canada
U of Mary Hardin-Baylor, TX
U of Maryland, Baltimore
County, MD
U of Mary Washington, VA
U of Massachusetts Amherst,
MA
U of Massachusetts Boston,
MA
U of Massachusetts Lowell,
MA
U of Miami, FL
U of Michigan, MI
U of Minnesota, Duluth, MN
U of Mississippi, MS
U of Missouri–Columbia,
MO
U of Missouri–Kansas City,
MO
U of Missouri–Rolla, MO

U of Nebraska at Kearney,
NE
U of Nebraska–Lincoln, NE
U of New Brunswick
Fredericton, NB, Canada
U of New Hampshire, NH
U of New Mexico, NM
U of New Orleans, LA
The U of North Carolina at
Asheville, NC
The U of North Carolina at
Chapel Hill, NC
The U of North Carolina at
Charlotte, NC
U of Northern British
Columbia, BC, Canada
U of Northern Iowa, IA
U of North Florida, FL
U of Notre Dame, IN
U of Oregon, OR
U of Pennsylvania, PA
U of Pittsburgh, PA
U of Pittsburgh at Bradford,
PA
U of Pittsburgh at
Johnstown, PA
U of Redlands, CA
U of Rhode Island, RI
U of Rio Grande, OH
U of St. Thomas, MN
U of St. Thomas, TX
U of San Diego, CA
U of San Francisco, CA
The U of Scranton, PA
U of Southern Indiana, IN
The U of Tampa, FL
The U of Tennessee, TN
The U of Tennessee at
Martin, TN
The U of Texas at Austin,
TX
The U of Texas at El Paso,
TX
U of the District of
Columbia, DC
U of the Pacific, CA
U of Toronto, ON, Canada
U of Vermont, VT
U of Virginia, VA
The U of Virginia's Coll at
Wise, VA
U of Washington, WA
U of West Georgia, GA
U of Wisconsin–Eau Claire,
WI
U of Wisconsin–Green Bay,
WI
U of Wisconsin–La Crosse,
WI
U of Wisconsin–Oshkosh,
WI
U of Wisconsin–Platteville,
WI
U of Wisconsin–Stevens
Point, WI
Utica Coll, NY
Vassar Coll, NY
Villanova U, PA
Wake Forest U, NC
Washburn U, KS
Washington & Jefferson Coll,
PA
Washington and Lee U, VA
Wayne State U, MI
Wellesley Coll, MA
Wells Coll, NY
Western Connecticut State
U, CT
Western Nebraska Comm
Coll, NE
Western New England Coll,
MA
Western Oregon U, OR
West Los Angeles Coll, CA

Westminster Coll, PA
West Texas A&M U, TX
West Virginia State U, WV
West Virginia Wesleyan Coll,
WV
Wheaton Coll, IL
Whitman Coll, WA
Wichita State U, KS
Widener U, PA
Wilfrid Laurier U, ON,
Canada
William Jewell Coll, MO
Wofford Coll, SC
Worcester State Coll, MA
Wright State U, OH
Xavier U, OH
Yale U, CT

ECONOMICS RELATED
Claremont McKenna Coll,
CA
Eastern Michigan U, MI
Marymount U, VA
Truman State U, MO
The U of Akron, OH
U of Hartford, CT
U of Illinois at Urbana–
Champaign, IL
U of West Georgia, GA
Wright State U, OH

EDUCATION
Abraham Baldwin Coll, GA
Acadia U, NS, Canada
Adelphi U, NY
Albion Coll, MI
Alderson-Broaddus Coll, WV
Alma Coll, MI
Alvernia Coll, PA
American International Coll,
MA
Anderson U, IN
Anderson U, SC
Ashland U, OH
Augsburg Coll, MN
Bainbridge Coll, GA
Ball State U, IN
The Baptist Coll of Florida,
FL
Barry U, FL
Baylor U, TX
Belmont Abbey Coll, NC
Bemidji State U, MN
Bethany U, CA
Bethel Coll, IN
Bishop's U, QC, Canada
Brandon U, MB, Canada
Brenau U, GA
Brevard Coll, NC
Brewton-Parker Coll, GA
Briar Cliff U, IA
Brock U, ON, Canada
Brown U, RI
Bucks County Comm Coll,
PA
Bunker Hill Comm Coll, MA
Burlington County Coll, NJ
Calhoun Comm Coll, AL
Cameron U, OK
Cape Cod Comm Coll, MA
Cardinal Stritch U, WI
Carroll Coll, MT
Carroll Coll, WI
Carson-Newman Coll, TN
The Catholic U of America,
DC
Cedar Crest Coll, PA
Charleston Southern U, SC
Christopher Newport U, VA
Cincinnati Christian U, OH
City Colls of Chicago,
Richard J. Daley Coll, IL
Clark U, MA
Clayton State U, GA

Coe Coll, IA
Colgate U, NY
Coll of Mount Saint Vincent,
NY
Coll of St. Joseph, VT
Coll of Saint Mary, NE
Coll of The Albemarle, NC
Coll of the Atlantic, ME
Coll of the Desert, CA
Comm Coll of Beaver
County, PA
Concordia Coll–New York,
NY
Concordia U, NE
Concordia U Coll of Alberta,
AB, Canada
Concord U, WV
Cornell U, NY
Cornerstone U, MI
Dabney S. Lancaster Comm
Coll, VA
Dallas Baptist U, TX
DePaul U, IL
Drury U, MO
Eastern Nazarene Coll, MA
Elmira Coll, NY
Elms Coll, MA
Elon U, NC
Emory U, GA
Eugene Lang Coll The New
School for Liberal Arts, NY
Fairleigh Dickinson U,
Metropolitan Campus, NJ
Fayetteville State U, NC
Ferrum Coll, VA
Fitchburg State Coll, MA
Fontbonne U, MO
Framingham State Coll, MA
Franklin Pierce U, NH
Frederick Comm Coll, MD
Freed-Hardeman U, TN
Fresno Pacific U, CA
Furman U, SC
Galveston Coll, TX
Gardner-Webb U, NC
Glendale Comm Coll, CA
Glenville State Coll, WV
Gloucester County Coll, NJ
Goshen Coll, IN
Graceland U, IA
Gustavus Adolphus Coll,
MN
Hagerstown Comm Coll, MD
Hamline U, MN
Hampshire Coll, MA
Harrisburg Area Comm Coll,
PA
Haverford Coll, PA
High Point U, NC
Hillsborough Comm Coll, FL
Hofstra U, NY
Houston Baptist U, TX
Huntington U, IN
Illinois Valley Comm Coll, IL
Illinois Wesleyan U, IL
Indiana U Bloomington, IN
Indiana U–Purdue U Fort
Wayne, IN
Indiana U–Purdue U
Indianapolis, IN
Indiana U Southeast, IN
Iona Coll, NY
Itasca Comm Coll, MN
John Brown U, AR
Johnson State Coll, VT
Kendall Coll, IL
Kingsborough Comm Coll of
the City U of New York,
NY
Kutztown U of
Pennsylvania, PA
Lackawanna Coll, PA
LaGrange Coll, GA
Lake Superior State U, MI

Lamar U, TX
Lancaster Bible Coll, PA
Langston U, OK
Lee Coll, TX
Lehigh U, PA
Lewis U, IL
Lincoln U, PA
Lindenwood U, MO
Long Island U, Brooklyn
Campus, NY
Loras Coll, IA
Loyola U New Orleans, LA
Lynchburg Coll, VA
Manhattan Coll, NY
Manhattanville Coll, NY
Marian Coll, IN
Marietta Coll, OH
Marquette U, WI
Massachusetts Coll of Liberal
Arts, MA
McNeese State U, LA
Mercyhurst Coll, PA
Miami Dade Coll, FL
Michigan State U, MI
Middlesex County Coll, NJ
Midland Lutheran Coll, NE
Minnesota State U Mankato,
MN
Molloy Coll, NY
Monmouth Coll, IL
Monmouth U, NJ
Montana State U–Billings,
MT
Moravian Coll, PA
Morningside Coll, IA
Mount Holyoke Coll, MA
Mount Saint Vincent U, NS,
Canada
Mount Vernon Nazarene U,
OH
New Mexico Jr Coll, NM
New River Comm Coll, VA
New York U, NY
Niagara U, NY
Nipissing U, ON, Canada
North Carolina State U, NC
North Central Coll, IL
Northeastern U, MA
Northern Illinois U, IL
Northern Michigan U, MI
Northern State U, SD
North Georgia Coll & State
U, GA
Notre Dame de Namur U,
CA
Odessa Coll, TX
Ohio Wesleyan U, OH
Oklahoma State U, OK
Oral Roberts U, OK
Otterbein Coll, OH
Paris Jr Coll, TX
Paul Quinn Coll, TX
Presbyterian Coll, SC
Queen's U at Kingston, ON,
Canada
Queens U of Charlotte, NC
Redeemer U Coll, ON,
Canada
Reinhardt Coll, GA
Ripon Coll, WI
Rivier Coll, NH
Rockford Coll, IL
Rockhurst U, MO
Rocky Mountain Coll, MT
Roosevelt U, IL
St. Cloud State U, MN
St. Francis Xavier U, NS,
Canada
Saint John's U, MN
St. Philip's Coll, TX
St. Thomas Aquinas Coll,
NY
St. Thomas U, NB, Canada
Salem Comm Coll, NJ

Santa Rosa Jr Coll, CA
Sauk Valley Comm Coll, IL
Schoolcraft Coll, MI
Southern Nazarene U, OK
Southern Utah U, UT
Spalding U, KY
Spoon River Coll, IL
Springfield Coll, MA
Springfield Coll in Illinois, IL
State U of New York at
    Fredonia, NY
State U of New York Coll at
    Brockport, NY
State U of New York Coll at
    Geneseo, NY
Stetson U, FL
Taylor U, IN
Tennessee Wesleyan Coll,
    TN
Tidewater Comm Coll, VA
Trent U, ON, Canada
Trinity Coll, CT
Troy U, AL
Union Coll, NE
The U of Akron, OH
U of Alaska Anchorage, AK
U of California, Los Angeles,
    CA
U of Central Missouri, MO
U of Cincinnati, OH
U of Dayton, OH
U of Delaware, DE
U of Evansville, IN
The U of Findlay, OH
U of Hawaii at Manoa, HI
U of Houston, TX
U of Maine at Machias, ME
U of Manitoba, MB, Canada
U of Mary Hardin-Baylor, TX
U of Miami, FL
U of Michigan, MI
U of Minnesota, Duluth, MN
U of Missouri–Columbia,
    MO
U of New Brunswick
    Fredericton, NB, Canada
U of Oregon, OR
U of Pittsburgh at
    Johnstown, PA
U of Portland, OR
U of Redlands, CA
U of Rio Grande, OH
U of St. Thomas, TX
U of San Francisco, CA
U of South Carolina
    Beaufort, SC
U of Southern Indiana, IN
U of the Incarnate Word, TX
U of the Pacific, CA
U of Toronto, ON, Canada
U of Vermont, VT
U of Washington, WA
U of Wisconsin–Oshkosh,
    WI
U of Wisconsin–Platteville,
    WI
U of Wisconsin–Stevens
    Point, WI
Upper Iowa U, IA
Urbana U, OH
Vanguard U of Southern
    California, CA
Villanova U, PA
Virginia Highlands Comm
    Coll, VA
Virginia Intermont Coll, VA
Washburn U, KS
Washington & Jefferson Coll,
    PA
Wayne State Coll, NE
Wells Coll, NY
Wesley Coll, DE
Western Connecticut State
    U, CT

West Liberty State Coll, WV
West Los Angeles Coll, CA
Westminster Coll, PA
West Virginia State U, WV
West Virginia Wesleyan Coll,
    WV
Wilkes U, PA
William Jewell Coll, MO
Wright State U, OH
Xavier U, OH

**EDUCATIONAL
ADMINISTRATION AND
SUPERVISION RELATED**
Kendall Coll, IL
Le Moyne Coll, NY

**EDUCATIONAL,
INSTRUCTIONAL, AND
CURRICULUM
SUPERVISION**
Sterling Coll, VT
Wright State U, OH

**EDUCATIONAL/
INSTRUCTIONAL MEDIA
DESIGN**
Ball State U, IN
Ithaca Coll, NY
Kutztown U of
    Pennsylvania, PA
Lindenwood U, MO
St. Cloud State U, MN
Seton Hill U, PA
U of Central Oklahoma, OK
Western Oregon U, OR
Widener U, PA

**EDUCATIONAL
LEADERSHIP AND
ADMINISTRATION**
Charleston Southern U, SC
Harding U, AR
Kendall Coll, IL
Lamar U, TX
Lindenwood U, MO
McNeese State U, LA
North Georgia Coll & State
    U, GA
Oral Roberts U, OK
St. Cloud State U, MN
Sterling Coll, VT
U of California, Los Angeles,
    CA
U of Central Oklahoma, OK
U of Oregon, OR
U of San Francisco, CA
Wright State U, OH

**EDUCATIONAL
PSYCHOLOGY**
The Catholic U of America,
    DC
Cornell U, NY
Marymount U, VA
U of Pittsburgh, PA

**EDUCATIONAL SYSTEM
ADMINISTRATION AND
SUPERINTENDENCY**
Le Moyne Coll, NY

EDUCATION (K-12)
Charleston Southern U, SC
Coll of Saint Mary, NE
The Coll of St. Scholastica,
    MN
Columbus State U, GA
Dominican U, IL
Graceland U, IA
Hamline U, MN
Itasca Comm Coll, MN
Ithaca Coll, NY
Lake Erie Coll, OH

Lewis U, IL
Lindenwood U, MO
Midland Lutheran Coll, NE
Ohio Wesleyan U, OH
Redeemer U Coll, ON,
    Canada
Syracuse U, NY
Tennessee Wesleyan Coll,
    TN
Trevecca Nazarene U, TN
U of St. Thomas, MN
The U of Tampa, FL
The U of Tennessee at
    Martin, TN
West Virginia Wesleyan Coll,
    WV

**EDUCATION (MULTIPLE
LEVELS)**
Coll of Saint Elizabeth, NJ
Gannon U, PA
Harding U, AR
Hofstra U, NY
Iona Coll, NY
Ithaca Coll, NY
Lake Superior State U, MI
Liberty U, VA
Manhattan Coll, NY
Ohio Wesleyan U, OH
Oral Roberts U, OK
Queen's U at Kingston, ON,
    Canada
The Richard Stockton Coll
    of New Jersey, NJ
The U of Akron, OH
U of Great Falls, MT
U of Nebraska–Lincoln, NE
U of Rio Grande, OH
U of the Ozarks, AR
U of Washington, WA
Wake Forest U, NC
Wright State U, OH

EDUCATION RELATED
Albany State U, GA
Kendall Coll, IL
Lancaster Bible Coll, PA
Marywood U, PA
McNeese State U, LA
Mercer U, GA
Park U, MO
Roosevelt U, IL
Sterling Coll, VT
Syracuse U, NY
Towson U, MD
The U of Akron, OH
U of Missouri–Columbia,
    MO
Wright State U, OH

**EDUCATION (SPECIFIC
LEVELS AND METHODS)
RELATED**
Comm Coll of Allegheny
    County, PA
Kendall Coll, IL
Rowan U, NJ
St. Cloud State U, MN
The U of Akron, OH
Wright State U, OH
Xavier U, OH

**EDUCATION (SPECIFIC
SUBJECT AREAS)
RELATED**
Avila U, MO
Baylor U, TX
Bradley U, IL
Cameron U, OK
Comm Coll of Allegheny
    County, PA
Henderson State U, AR
Hofstra U, NY
Hope Coll, MI

Marquette U, WI
Marywood U, PA
Miami Dade Coll, FL
Missouri State U, MO
Syracuse U, NY
The U of Akron, OH
The U of Arizona, AZ
U of Central Oklahoma, OK
U of Kentucky, KY
U of Nebraska–Lincoln, NE
U of St. Thomas, MN
U of Wisconsin–Eau Claire,
    WI
Wright State U, OH

**ELECTRICAL AND
ELECTRONIC
ENGINEERING
TECHNOLOGIES
RELATED**
Embry-Riddle Aeronautical
    U, FL
Fitchburg State Coll, MA
Massasoit Comm Coll, MA
Miami Dade Coll, FL
Mohawk Valley Comm Coll,
    NY
Old Dominion U, VA
Southern Illinois U
    Carbondale, IL
Southwestern Michigan Coll,
    MI
West Virginia State Comm
    and Tech Coll, WV

**ELECTRICAL AND
POWER TRANSMISSION
INSTALLATION**
British Columbia Inst of
    Technology, BC, Canada
St. Cloud Tech Coll, MN

**ELECTRICAL AND
POWER TRANSMISSION
INSTALLATION RELATED**
Calhoun Comm Coll, AL

**ELECTRICAL,
ELECTRONIC AND
COMMUNICATIONS
ENGINEERING
TECHNOLOGY**
Aims Comm Coll, CO
Bainbridge Coll, GA
Bluefield State Coll, WV
Blue Ridge Comm Coll, VA
Bradley U, IL
Brevard Comm Coll, FL
British Columbia Inst of
    Technology, BC, Canada
Broome Comm Coll, NY
Broward Comm Coll, FL
Brown Mackie Coll–Salina,
    KS
Buffalo State Coll, State U of
    New York, NY
Burlington County Coll, NJ
Caldwell Comm Coll and
    Tech Inst, NC
Calhoun Comm Coll, AL
Cameron U, OK
Central Ohio Tech Coll, OH
Central Piedmont Comm
    Coll, NC
Chattahoochee Tech Coll,
    GA
Chattanooga State Tech
    Comm Coll, TN
Chesapeake Coll, MD
Citrus Coll, CA
City Colls of Chicago,
    Richard J. Daley Coll, IL
Clayton State U, GA
Coll of the Canyons, CA

Comm Coll of Allegheny
    County, PA
Comm Coll of Beaver
    County, PA
Cosumnes River Coll,
    Sacramento, CA
Cuesta Coll, CA
Dabney S. Lancaster Comm
    Coll, VA
DeKalb Tech Coll, GA
Delaware State U, DE
Delaware Tech & Comm
    Coll, Jack F. Owens
    Campus, DE
East Carolina U, NC
East Central Coll, MO
Eastern Idaho Tech Coll, ID
Eastern Michigan U, MI
Eastfield Coll, TX
Edinboro U of Pennsylvania,
    PA
El Camino Coll, CA
Fairleigh Dickinson U,
    Metropolitan Campus, NJ
Farmingdale State Coll, NY
Florida Comm Coll at
    Jacksonville, FL
Foothill Coll, CA
Frederick Comm Coll, MD
Fulton-Montgomery Comm
    Coll, NY
Gaston Coll, NC
Grambling State U, LA
Greenville Tech Coll, SC
Harrisburg Area Comm Coll,
    PA
Heartland Comm Coll, IL
Hillsborough Comm Coll, FL
Hocking Coll, OH
Hopkinsville Comm Coll,
    KY
Houston Comm Coll System,
    TX
Howard Comm Coll, MD
Hudson Valley Comm Coll,
    NY
Idaho State U, ID
Illinois Valley Comm Coll, IL
Indiana U–Purdue U Fort
    Wayne, IN
Indiana U–Purdue U
    Indianapolis, IN
Ivy Tech Comm Coll–
    Kokomo, IN
Ivy Tech Comm Coll–
    Southwest, IN
Ivy Tech Comm Coll–
    Wabash Valley, IN
Jamestown Comm Coll, NY
Jefferson Comm and Tech
    Coll, KY
Jefferson Comm Coll, OH
Johnson & Wales U, RI
Lake City Comm Coll, FL
Lake Superior State U, MI
Lamar U, TX
Langston U, OK
Laredo Comm Coll, TX
Lee Coll, TX
LeTourneau U, TX
Lincoln Land Comm Coll, IL
Linn State Tech Coll, MO
Long Beach City Coll, CA
Macomb Comm Coll, MI
Madisonville Comm Coll,
    KY
Massasoit Comm Coll, MA
McNeese State U, LA
Miami Dade Coll, FL
Middlesex County Coll, NJ
Midland Coll, TX
Minnesota State Coll–
    Southeast Tech, MN

Western Tech Coll, WI
Wright State U, OH

ELECTRONEURO--DIAGNOSTIC/ELECTRO-ENCEPHALOGRAPHIC TECHNOLOGY
Comm Coll of Allegheny County, PA
Western Tech Coll, WI

ELEMENTARY AND MIDDLE SCHOOL ADMINISTRATION/ PRINCIPALSHIP
Charleston Southern U, SC
Le Moyne Coll, NY
Piedmont Coll, GA

ELEMENTARY EDUCATION
Abilene Christian U, TX
Abraham Baldwin Coll, GA
Acadia U, NS, Canada
Adams State Coll, CO
Alabama A&M U, AL
Albion Coll, MI
Albright Coll, PA
Alderson-Broaddus Coll, WV
Alma Coll, MI
Alvernia Coll, PA
American International Coll, MA
American U, DC
Ancilla Coll, IN
Anderson U, IN
Anderson U, SC
Aquinas Coll, TN
Arizona State U at the West campus, AZ
Asbury Coll, KY
Ashland U, OH
Athens State U, AL
Auburn U Montgomery, AL
Augsburg Coll, MN
Aurora U, IL
Avila U, MO
Bainbridge Coll, GA
Ball State U, IN
The Baptist Coll of Florida, FL
Barry U, FL
Baylor U, TX
Belmont Abbey Coll, NC
Bemidji State U, MN
Benedictine Coll, KS
Bethany U, CA
Bethel Coll, IN
Bethel U, MN
Bishop's U, QC, Canada
Bluefield State Coll, WV
Boston Coll, MA
Bradley U, IL
Brandon U, MB, Canada
Brevard Coll, NC
Briar Cliff U, IA
Brock U, ON, Canada
Broward Comm Coll, FL
Buena Vista U, IA
Buffalo State Coll, State U of New York, NY
Calhoun Comm Coll, AL
Calvin Coll, MI
Cameron U, OK
Cardinal Stritch U, WI
Carlow U, PA
Carroll Coll, MT
Carroll Coll, WI
Carson-Newman Coll, TN
Carthage Coll, WI
The Catholic U of America, DC
Cedar Crest Coll, PA
Central Wyoming Coll, WY

Charleston Southern U, SC
Chesapeake Coll, MD
City Colls of Chicago, Richard J. Daley Coll, IL
Clark U, MA
Clayton State U, GA
Clemson U, SC
Coahoma Comm Coll, MS
Coastal Carolina U, SC
Coe Coll, IA
Coll of Charleston, SC
Coll of Mount Saint Vincent, NY
Coll of St. Joseph, VT
Coll of Saint Mary, NE
The Coll of Saint Rose, NY
The Coll of St. Scholastica, MN
Coll of the Atlantic, ME
Concordia Coll–New York, NY
Concordia U, NE
Concordia U Coll of Alberta, AB, Canada
Concord U, WV
Cornerstone U, MI
Daemen Coll, NY
Dallas Baptist U, TX
Delaware State U, DE
DePaul U, IL
Dixie State Coll of Utah, UT
Dominican U, IL
Drake U, IA
Drury U, MO
East Carolina U, NC
Eastern Connecticut State U, CT
Eastern Mennonite U, VA
Eastern Michigan U, MI
Eastern Nazarene Coll, MA
East Stroudsburg U of Pennsylvania, PA
Edinboro U of Pennsylvania, PA
Elmira Coll, NY
Elms Coll, MA
Elon U, NC
Fayetteville State U, NC
Fitchburg State Coll, MA
Flagler Coll, FL
Florida Atlantic U, FL
Florida Coll, FL
Florida Gulf Coast U, FL
Florida International U, FL
Fontbonne U, MO
Fort Hays State U, KS
Framingham State Coll, MA
Franciscan U of Steubenville, OH
Franklin Coll, IN
Franklin Pierce U, NH
Frederick Comm Coll, MD
Freed-Hardeman U, TN
Fresno Pacific U, CA
Fulton-Montgomery Comm Coll, NY
Furman U, SC
Gainesville State Coll, GA
Gannon U, PA
Gardner-Webb U, NC
Geneva Coll, PA
Georgetown Coll, KY
Georgian Court U, NJ
Glenville State Coll, WV
Gonzaga U, WA
Gordon Coll, MA
Goshen Coll, IN
Grace Coll, IN
Graceland U, IA
Grambling State U, LA
Green Mountain Coll, VT
Gustavus Adolphus Coll, MN
Hagerstown Comm Coll, MD

Hamline U, MN
Harding U, AR
Harrisburg Area Comm Coll, PA
Henderson State U, AR
High Point U, NC
Hillsborough Comm Coll, FL
Hofstra U, NY
Hope Coll, MI
Houghton Coll, NY
Houston Baptist U, TX
Howard Comm Coll, MD
Hunter Coll of the City U of New York, NY
Huntington U, IN
Husson Coll, ME
Idaho State U, ID
Illinois State U, IL
Illinois Valley Comm Coll, IL
Illinois Wesleyan U, IL
Immaculata U, PA
Indiana U Bloomington, IN
Indiana U of Pennsylvania, PA
Indiana U–Purdue U Fort Wayne, IN
Indiana U–Purdue U Indianapolis, IN
Indiana U Southeast, IN
Iona Coll, NY
Jacksonville U, FL
John Brown U, AR
Johnson State Coll, VT
Kansas State U, KS
Kellogg Comm Coll, MI
Kendall Coll, IL
Kennesaw State U, GA
Kentucky Wesleyan Coll, KY
Keuka Coll, NY
Kingsborough Comm Coll of the City U of New York, NY
King's Coll, PA
The King's U Coll, AB, Canada
Kutztown U of Pennsylvania, PA
Kuyper Coll, MI
LaGrange Coll, GA
Lake Erie Coll, OH
Lakeland Coll, WI
Lake Superior State U, MI
Lamar U, TX
Lancaster Bible Coll, PA
Langston U, OK
Lebanon Valley Coll, PA
Le Moyne Coll, NY
LeTourneau U, TX
Lewis U, IL
Liberty U, VA
Lincoln U, PA
Lindenwood U, MO
Long Island U, Brooklyn Campus, NY
Loras Coll, IA
Loyola U Chicago, IL
Loyola U New Orleans, LA
Lynchburg Coll, VA
Lynn U, FL
MacMurray Coll, IL
Manhattan Coll, NY
Manhattanville Coll, NY
Marian Coll, IN
Marietta Coll, OH
Marist Coll, NY
Marquette U, WI
Marshall U, WV
Marywood U, PA
Massachusetts Coll of Liberal Arts, MA
McNeese State U, LA
Mercer U, GA
Mercyhurst Coll, PA
Miami Dade Coll, FL

Michigan State U, MI
Midland Lutheran Coll, NE
Millersville U of Pennsylvania, PA
Minnesota State U Mankato, MN
Minnesota State U Moorhead, MN
Missouri State U, MO
Mohawk Valley Comm Coll, NY
Molloy Coll, NY
Monmouth Coll, IL
Montana State U, MT
Montana State U–Billings, MT
Moravian Coll, PA
Morningside Coll, IA
Mount St. Mary's U, MD
Mount Saint Vincent U, NS, Canada
Mount Vernon Nazarene U, OH
Murray State U, KY
National-Louis U, IL
Neumann Coll, PA
New Jersey City U, NJ
New Mexico Jr Coll, NM
New York U, NY
Niagara U, NY
North Central Coll, IL
North Dakota State U, ND
Northeastern U, MA
Northern Illinois U, IL
Northern Michigan U, MI
Northern State U, SD
North Georgia Coll & State U, GA
Northwestern Coll, MN
Northwestern Oklahoma State U, OK
Northwest Nazarene U, ID
Notre Dame Coll, OH
Notre Dame de Namur U, CA
Nova Southeastern U, FL
Oakland U, MI
The Ohio State U at Lima, OH
Ohio Wesleyan U, OH
Oklahoma State U, OK
Oral Roberts U, OK
Otterbein Coll, OH
Pacific Oaks Coll, CA
Paris Jr Coll, TX
Park U, MO
Paul Quinn Coll, TX
Penn State Abington, PA
Penn State DuBois, PA
Penn State Fayette, The Eberly Campus, PA
Penn State Mont Alto, PA
Penn State Wilkes-Barre, PA
Pima Comm Coll, AZ
Pine Manor Coll, MA
Pittsburg State U, KS
Purdue U North Central, IN
Queens Coll of the City U of New York, NY
Queen's U at Kingston, ON, Canada
Queens U of Charlotte, NC
Quincy Coll, MA
Randolph Coll, VA
Redeemer U Coll, ON, Canada
Ripon Coll, WI
Rivier Coll, NH
Rockford Coll, IL
Rockhurst U, MO
Rocky Mountain Coll, MT
Roosevelt U, IL
Rose State Coll, OK
Rowan U, NJ

Saginaw Valley State U, MI
St. Bonaventure U, NY
St. Cloud State U, MN
St. Francis Xavier U, NS, Canada
Saint John's U, MN
Saint Joseph's Coll, IN
Saint Leo U, FL
St. Louis Comm Coll at Florissant Valley, MO
St. Norbert Coll, WI
St. Thomas Aquinas Coll, NY
Saint Xavier U, IL
Salve Regina U, RI
Sauk Valley Comm Coll, IL
Seton Hall U, NJ
Seton Hill U, PA
Shippensburg U of Pennsylvania, PA
Slippery Rock U of Pennsylvania, PA
Southern Adventist U, TN
Southern Illinois U Carbondale, IL
Southern Illinois U Edwardsville, IL
Southern Nazarene U, OK
Southern U and A&M Coll, LA
Southern Utah U, UT
Southwest Baptist U, MO
Southwestern Coll, KS
Spalding U, KY
Springfield Coll, MA
State U of New York at Fredonia, NY
State U of New York Coll at Brockport, NY
State U of New York Coll at Cortland, NY
State U of New York Coll at Geneseo, NY
State U of New York Coll at Potsdam, NY
Stetson U, FL
Stonehill Coll, MA
Taylor U, IN
Temple U, PA
Tennessee Wesleyan Coll, TN
Thiel Coll, PA
Towson U, MD
Trent U, ON, Canada
Trinity Baptist Coll, FL
Troy U, AL
Tufts U, MA
Union Coll, NE
The U of Akron, OH
The U of Alabama, AL
The U of Alabama in Huntsville, AL
U of Alaska Anchorage, AK
The U of Arizona, AZ
U of Arkansas, AR
U of Central Florida, FL
U of Central Missouri, MO
U of Central Oklahoma, OK
U of Cincinnati, OH
U of Connecticut, CT
U of Dayton, OH
U of Delaware, DE
U of Dubuque, IA
U of Evansville, IN
The U of Findlay, OH
U of Great Falls, MT
U of Hartford, CT
U of Hawaii at Manoa, HI
U of Illinois at Urbana–Champaign, IL
U of Kansas, KS
U of Kentucky, KY
U of Maine at Machias, ME
U of Manitoba, MB, Canada

U of Mary Hardin-Baylor, TX
U of Mary Washington, VA
U of Miami, FL
U of Michigan, MI
U of Minnesota, Duluth, MN
U of Mississippi, MS
U of Missouri–Columbia, MO
U of Missouri–Kansas City, MO
U of Nebraska at Kearney, NE
U of Nebraska at Omaha, NE
U of Nebraska–Lincoln, NE
U of New Brunswick Fredericton, NB, Canada
U of New England, ME
U of New Hampshire, NH
U of New Mexico, NM
U of New Orleans, LA
The U of North Carolina at Chapel Hill, NC
The U of North Carolina at Charlotte, NC
U of Northern British Columbia, BC, Canada
U of Northern Iowa, IA
U of North Florida, FL
U of Pennsylvania, PA
U of Pittsburgh at Johnstown, PA
U of Portland, OR
U of Redlands, CA
U of Rhode Island, RI
U of Rio Grande, OH
U of St. Thomas, MN
U of St. Thomas, TX
U of San Francisco, CA
The U of Scranton, PA
U of South Carolina Upstate, SC
U of Southern Indiana, IN
The U of Tampa, FL
The U of Tennessee at Martin, TN
U of the District of Columbia, DC
U of the Incarnate Word, TX
U of Vermont, VT
U of Washington, WA
U of West Georgia, GA
U of Wisconsin–Eau Claire, WI
U of Wisconsin–Green Bay, WI
U of Wisconsin–La Crosse, WI
U of Wisconsin–Madison, WI
U of Wisconsin–Oshkosh, WI
U of Wisconsin–Platteville, WI
U of Wisconsin–Stevens Point, WI
U of Wyoming, WY
Upper Iowa U, IA
Urbana U, OH
Utica Coll, NY
Villanova U, PA
Virginia Intermont Coll, VA
Washburn U, KS
Wayne State Coll, NE
Wayne State U, MI
Wells Coll, NY
West Chester U of Pennsylvania, PA
Western Connecticut State U, CT
Western Nebraska Comm Coll, NE
Western New England Coll, MA

West Liberty State Coll, WV
Westminster Coll, PA
Westminster Coll, UT
West Virginia State U, WV
West Virginia Wesleyan Coll, WV
Wheaton Coll, IL
Wichita State U, KS
Widener U, PA
Wilkes U, PA
William Jewell Coll, MO
Wilson Coll, PA
Worcester State Coll, MA
Wright State U, OH
Xavier U, OH

EMERGENCY MEDICAL TECHNOLOGY (EMT PARAMEDIC)

Arkansas State U–Newport, AR
Asheville-Buncombe Tech Comm Coll, NC
Ball State U, IN
Brevard Comm Coll, FL
Broome Comm Coll, NY
Broward Comm Coll, FL
Calhoun Comm Coll, AL
Central Arizona Coll, AZ
Central Florida Comm Coll, FL
Chattanooga State Tech Comm Coll, TN
Clayton State U, GA
Comm Coll of Aurora, CO
Cosumnes River Coll, Sacramento, CA
Crafton Hills Coll, CA
Delaware Tech & Comm Coll, Jack F. Owens Campus, DE
Dixie State Coll of Utah, UT
East Central Coll, MO
Eastern New Mexico U–Roswell, NM
El Centro Coll, TX
Florida Comm Coll at Jacksonville, FL
Foothill Coll, CA
Frederick Comm Coll, MD
Gadsden State Comm Coll, AL
Galveston Coll, TX
The George Washington U, DC
Greenville Tech Coll, SC
Hagerstown Comm Coll, MD
Harrisburg Area Comm Coll, PA
Hillsborough Comm Coll, FL
Hocking Coll, OH
Houston Comm Coll System, TX
Howard Comm Coll, MD
Hudson Valley Comm Coll, NY
Idaho State U, ID
Indiana U–Purdue U Indianapolis, IN
Ivy Tech Comm Coll–Kokomo, IN
Ivy Tech Comm Coll–Southwest, IN
Ivy Tech Comm Coll–Wabash Valley, IN
Jefferson Comm Coll, OH
Kellogg Comm Coll, MI
Lackawanna Coll, PA
Lake City Comm Coll, FL
Lake-Sumter Comm Coll, FL
Lamar Inst of Technology, TX
Laredo Comm Coll, TX
Lee Coll, TX

Macomb Comm Coll, MI
Metropolitan Comm Coll–Penn Valley, MO
Miami Dade Coll, FL
Midland Coll, TX
Minnesota State Coll–Southeast Tech, MN
Mohawk Valley Comm Coll, NY
Montana State U–Billings, MT
Muscatine Comm Coll, IA
Nebraska Methodist Coll, NE
New Mexico Jr Coll, NM
North Central Missouri Coll, MO
North Central Texas Coll, TX
Odessa Coll, TX
Ozarks Tech Comm Coll, MO
Phoenix Coll, AZ
Pima Comm Coll, AZ
Quincy Coll, MA
St. Cloud Tech Coll, MN
St. Louis Comm Coll at Florissant Valley, MO
Santa Rosa Jr Coll, CA
Schoolcraft Coll, MI
Scottsdale Comm Coll, AZ
Seminole Comm Coll, FL
Shelton State Comm Coll, AL
Southwest Baptist U, MO
Spalding U, KY
Springfield Coll, MA
Tallahassee Comm Coll, FL
U of Alaska Anchorage, AK
U of Maryland, Baltimore County, MD
U of Pittsburgh at Johnstown, PA
U of the District of Columbia, DC
Valencia Comm Coll, FL
Westchester Comm Coll, NY
West Shore Comm Coll, MI

ENERGY MANAGEMENT AND SYSTEMS TECHNOLOGY

Chattanooga State Tech Comm Coll, TN
Comm Coll of Allegheny County, PA
Fitchburg State Coll, MA
Lamar U, TX
Lassen Comm Coll District, CA
Macomb Comm Coll, MI
Sterling Coll, VT
U of Cincinnati, OH
U of Rio Grande, OH

ENGINEERING

Abilene Christian U, TX
Barry U, FL
Bates Coll, ME
Baylor U, TX
Bethel Coll, IN
Brown U, RI
Bucks County Comm Coll, PA
Buffalo State Coll, State U of New York, NY
Burlington County Coll, NJ
California State U, Fullerton, CA
California State U, Northridge, CA
Calvin Coll, MI
Cape Breton U, NS, Canada
Carleton U, ON, Canada
Carroll Coll, MT
Carthage Coll, WI

The Catholic U of America, DC
Central Arizona Coll, AZ
Citrus Coll, CA
Claremont McKenna Coll, CA
Clark U, MA
Clayton State U, GA
Coll of Staten Island of the City U of New York, NY
Cuesta Coll, CA
Dalhousie U, NS, Canada
Delaware Tech & Comm Coll, Jack F. Owens Campus, DE
Dixie State Coll of Utah, UT
Drury U, MO
East Central Coll, MO
El Camino Coll, CA
Elon U, NC
Florida Inst of Technology, FL
Fontbonne U, MO
Frederick Comm Coll, MD
Fresno City Coll, CA
Geneva Coll, PA
The George Washington U, DC
Gonzaga U, WA
Hagerstown Comm Coll, MD
Harrisburg Area Comm Coll, PA
Heartland Comm Coll, IL
Hillsborough Comm Coll, FL
Hope Coll, MI
Howard Comm Coll, MD
Idaho State U, ID
Indiana U–Purdue U Indianapolis, IN
Itasca Comm Coll, MN
Jamestown Comm Coll, NY
John Brown U, AR
Kellogg Comm Coll, MI
Lake Superior State U, MI
LeTourneau U, TX
Long Beach City Coll, CA
Maine Maritime Academy, ME
Manhattan Coll, NY
Marquette U, WI
McNeese State U, LA
Mercer U, GA
Metropolitan Comm Coll–Longview, MO
Metropolitan Comm Coll–Penn Valley, MO
Miami Dade Coll, FL
Michigan State U, MI
Middlesex County Coll, NJ
Missouri State U–West Plains, MO
Mitchell Coll, CT
Mohawk Valley Comm Coll, NY
Montana Tech of The U of Montana, MT
Moorpark Coll, CA
Nassau Comm Coll, NY
New Mexico Jr Coll, NM
New River Comm Coll, VA
North Carolina State U, NC
North Dakota State U, ND
Northeastern U, MA
Nova Scotia Coll, NS, Canada
Oakland U, MI
Ocean County Coll, NJ
Oklahoma State U, OK
Paris Jr Coll, TX
Queen's U at Kingston, ON, Canada
Rensselaer Polytechnic Inst, NY

Rochester Inst of Technology, NY
Rutgers, The State U of New Jersey, Newark, NJ
St. Cloud State U, MN
St. Louis Comm Coll at Florissant Valley, MO
San Diego Mesa Coll, CA
San Diego State U, CA
Santa Ana Coll, CA
Santa Barbara City Coll, CA
Santa Clara U, CA
Santa Rosa Jr Coll, CA
Schoolcraft Coll, MI
Seton Hill U, PA
Southern Adventist U, TN
Tallahassee Comm Coll, FL
Tidewater Comm Coll, VA
Trinity Coll, CT
Tufts U, MA
Tunxis Comm Coll, CT
Union Coll, NE
The U of Akron, OH
The U of Akron–Wayne Coll, OH
The U of Arizona, AZ
U of California, Los Angeles, CA
U of Cincinnati, OH
U of Delaware, DE
U of Hartford, CT
U of Illinois at Urbana–Champaign, IL
U of Massachusetts Amherst, MA
U of Michigan, MI
U of Mississippi, MS
U of New Brunswick Fredericton, NB, Canada
U of New Haven, CT
U of Pittsburgh, PA
U of Portland, OR
U of Southern Indiana, IN
The U of Tennessee at Martin, TN
U of Toronto, ON, Canada
U of Virginia, VA
U of Washington, WA
U of Wisconsin–Madison, WI
Ventura Coll, CA
Wake Forest U, NC
Waubonsee Comm Coll, IL
Wayne State U, MI
Wells Coll, NY
West Los Angeles Coll, CA
Westmoreland County Comm Coll, PA
Widener U, PA
Wilkes U, PA
Wright State U, OH

ENGINEERING/ INDUSTRIAL MANAGEMENT

Claremont McKenna Coll, CA
Clemson U, SC
Farmingdale State Coll, NY
John Brown U, AR
Lake Superior State U, MI
Middle Tennessee State U, TN
Saginaw Valley State U, MI
The U of Arizona, AZ
U of Evansville, IN
U of Massachusetts Lowell, MA
U of Missouri–Rolla, MO
U of Portland, OR
U of the Pacific, CA
U of Vermont, VT
U of Wisconsin–Stout, WI
Widener U, PA

Wilkes U, PA

ENGINEERING MECHANICS
Clemson U, SC
Lehigh U, PA
Oral Roberts U, OK
U of Cincinnati, OH
U of Illinois at Urbana–Champaign, IL
U of Wisconsin–Madison, WI
West Virginia Wesleyan Coll, WV

ENGINEERING PHYSICS
Abilene Christian U, TX
Aurora U, IL
Bemidji State U, MN
Bradley U, IL
Brandeis U, MA
Brown U, RI
Cornell U, NY
Delaware State U, DE
Eastern Nazarene Coll, MA
Embry-Riddle Aeronautical U, FL
Hope Coll, MI
Jacksonville U, FL
Lehigh U, PA
Loras Coll, IA
Loyola Marymount U, CA
Missouri State U, MO
Morningside Coll, IA
Murray State U, KY
Northwest Nazarene U, ID
The Ohio State U, OH
Point Loma Nazarene U, CA
Queen's U at Kingston, ON, Canada
Randolph Coll, VA
Rensselaer Polytechnic Inst, NY
St. Bonaventure U, NY
Santa Clara U, CA
Southwestern Coll, KS
Syracuse U, NY
Taylor U, IN
Thiel Coll, PA
Tufts U, MA
U at Buffalo, the State U of New York, NY
The U of Akron, OH
The U of Arizona, AZ
U of California, Berkeley, CA
U of Colorado at Boulder, CO
U of Connecticut, CT
U of Illinois at Urbana–Champaign, IL
U of Kansas, KS
U of Massachusetts Boston, MA
U of Michigan, MI
U of Nebraska at Omaha, NE
U of Northern Iowa, IA
U of Pittsburgh, PA
The U of Tennessee, TN
U of the Pacific, CA
U of Wisconsin–Madison, WI
Washington and Lee U, VA
West Virginia Wesleyan Coll, WV
Wright State U, OH
Yale U, CT

ENGINEERING RELATED
British Columbia Inst of Technology, BC, Canada
Carnegie Mellon U, PA
Charleston Southern U, SC

Chattanooga State Tech Comm Coll, TN
Claremont McKenna Coll, CA
Fairfield U, CT
Idaho State U, ID
Itasca Comm Coll, MN
Kentucky Wesleyan Coll, KY
Lehigh U, PA
Loras Coll, IA
Macomb Comm Coll, MI
Marquette U, WI
Miami Dade Coll, FL
Montana State U–Billings, MT
New York U, NY
Ohio Wesleyan U, OH
Park U, MO
Queen's U at Kingston, ON, Canada
Rochester Inst of Technology, NY
Southern Maine Comm Coll, ME
Syracuse U, NY
Tufts U, MA
The U of Alabama in Huntsville, AL
The U of Arizona, AZ
U of Connecticut, CT
U of Nebraska–Lincoln, NE
U of Pennsylvania, PA
U of the Incarnate Word, TX
Wheaton Coll, IL
Wright State U, OH

ENGINEERING-RELATED TECHNOLOGIES
Rochester Inst of Technology, NY

ENGINEERING SCIENCE
Abilene Christian U, TX
Asnuntuck Comm Coll, CT
Bethel U, MN
Broome Comm Coll, NY
Broward Comm Coll, FL
California State U, Fullerton, CA
Claremont McKenna Coll, CA
Fulton-Montgomery Comm Coll, NY
Gloucester County Coll, NJ
Hofstra U, NY
Houston Baptist U, TX
Hudson Valley Comm Coll, NY
Itasca Comm Coll, MN
Kingsborough Comm Coll of the City U of New York, NY
Lamar U, TX
Middlesex Comm Coll, CT
Middlesex County Coll, NJ
Montana Tech of The U of Montana, MT
Ohio Wesleyan U, OH
Penn State Abington, PA
Penn State DuBois, PA
Penn State Fayette, The Eberly Campus, PA
Penn State Mont Alto, PA
Penn State Wilkes-Barre, PA
Rensselaer Polytechnic Inst, NY
Rochester Inst of Technology, NY
Rutgers, The State U of New Jersey, New Brunswick, NJ
St. Louis Comm Coll at Florissant Valley, MO
St. Thomas Aquinas Coll, NY

Seattle Pacific U, WA
State U of New York Coll of Technology at Alfred, NY
State U of New York Coll of Technology at Canton, NY
Sweet Briar Coll, VA
Trinity U, TX
Tufts U, MA
U at Buffalo, the State U of New York, NY
U of California, Berkeley, CA
U of Cincinnati, OH
U of Manitoba, MB, Canada
U of Maryland, Baltimore County, MD
U of Miami, FL
U of Michigan, MI
U of New Mexico, NM
U of New Orleans, LA
U of Portland, OR
The U of Tennessee, TN
U of Toronto, ON, Canada
Westchester Comm Coll, NY
Wright State U, OH
Yale U, CT

ENGINEERING TECHNOLOGIES RELATED
Cameron U, OK
Comm Coll of Allegheny County, PA
East Carolina U, NC
Harrisburg Area Comm Coll, PA
Massasoit Comm Coll, MA
McNeese State U, LA
Old Dominion U, VA
The U of Akron, OH
U of Hartford, CT
U of Southern Indiana, IN

ENGINEERING TECHNOLOGY
Aims Comm Coll, CO
Ashland Comm and Tech Coll, KY
Buffalo State Coll, State U of New York, NY
Central Piedmont Comm Coll, NC
Charleston Southern U, SC
Citrus Coll, CA
Clayton State U, GA
Coll of the Desert, CA
DeKalb Tech Coll, GA
Delaware Tech & Comm Coll, Jack F. Owens Campus, DE
Eastern Michigan U, MI
Florida Comm Coll at Jacksonville, FL
Gainesville State Coll, GA
Harrisburg Area Comm Coll, PA
Houston Comm Coll System, TX
Itasca Comm Coll, MN
John Brown U, AR
Lake Superior State U, MI
Lassen Comm Coll District, CA
LeTourneau U, TX
Maine Maritime Academy, ME
McNeese State U, LA
Miami Dade Coll, FL
Middlesex Comm Coll, CT
Middlesex County Coll, NJ
Middle Tennessee State U, TN
Montana Tech of The U of Montana, MT

Moorpark Coll, CA
Murray State U, KY
New Hampshire Comm Tech Coll, Nashua/Claremont, NH
North Central Texas Coll, TX
Northern Illinois U, IL
Oklahoma State U, OK
Pittsburg State U, KS
Prairie View A&M U, TX
Pueblo Comm Coll, CO
Rochester Inst of Technology, NY
St. Louis Comm Coll at Florissant Valley, MO
Santa Ana Coll, CA
Santa Barbara City Coll, CA
Santa Rosa Jr Coll, CA
Southeast Tech Inst, SD
Southern Illinois U Carbondale, IL
Southwestern Indian Polytechnic Inst, NM
Southwestern Michigan Coll, MI
State U of New York Coll of Technology at Canton, NY
Temple U, PA
Texas A&M U, TX
Texas A&M U–Corpus Christi, TX
Tunxis Comm Coll, CT
The U of Akron, OH
U of Alaska Anchorage, AK
U of Central Florida, FL
U of Hartford, CT
U of Pittsburgh at Johnstown, PA
U of the District of Columbia, DC
U of Wisconsin–Stout, WI
Virginia Highlands Comm Coll, VA
Westchester Comm Coll, NY

ENGLISH
Abilene Christian U, TX
Abraham Baldwin Coll, GA
Acadia U, NS, Canada
Adams State Coll, CO
Adelphi U, NY
Alabama A&M U, AL
Albany State U, GA
Albertson Coll of Idaho, ID
Albion Coll, MI
Albright Coll, PA
Alma Coll, MI
Alvernia Coll, PA
American International Coll, MA
Amherst Coll, MA
Ancilla Coll, IN
Anderson U, IN
Anderson U, SC
Angelo State U, TX
Aquinas Coll, TN
Arizona State U at the West campus, AZ
Asbury Coll, KY
Ashland U, OH
Athabasca U, AB, Canada
Athens State U, AL
Auburn U Montgomery, AL
Augsburg Coll, MN
Aurora U, IL
Austin Coll, TX
Avila U, MO
Bainbridge Coll, GA
Ball State U, IN
Bard Coll, NY
Barry U, FL
Bates Coll, ME
Baylor U, TX
Belmont Abbey Coll, NC

Bemidji State U, MN
Benedictine Coll, KS
Bentley Coll, MA
Bethany U, CA
Bethel Coll, IN
Bethel U, MN
Bishop's U, QC, Canada
Blinn Coll, TX
Boston Coll, MA
Bradley U, IL
Brandeis U, MA
Brandon U, MB, Canada
Brenau U, GA
Brevard Coll, NC
Brewton-Parker Coll, GA
Briar Cliff U, IA
Bridgewater Coll, VA
Brock U, ON, Canada
Brown U, RI
Bryn Mawr Coll, PA
Buena Vista U, IA
Buffalo State Coll, State U of New York, NY
Bunker Hill Comm Coll, MA
Burlington County Coll, NJ
Calhoun Comm Coll, AL
California State U, Fullerton, CA
California State U, Northridge, CA
California State U, Sacramento, CA
California State U, San Bernardino, CA
California State U, Stanislaus, CA
Calvin Coll, MI
Cameron U, OK
Cape Breton U, NS, Canada
Cardinal Stritch U, WI
Carleton U, ON, Canada
Carlow U, PA
Carnegie Mellon U, PA
Carroll Coll, MT
Carroll Coll, WI
Carson-Newman Coll, TN
Carthage Coll, WI
The Catholic U of America, DC
Cedar Crest Coll, PA
Central Wyoming Coll, WY
Charleston Southern U, SC
Christopher Newport U, VA
Citrus Coll, CA
Claremont McKenna Coll, CA
Clark U, MA
Clayton State U, GA
Clemson U, SC
Coahoma Comm Coll, MS
Coastal Carolina U, SC
Coe Coll, IA
Colby Coll, ME
Colgate U, NY
Coll of Charleston, SC
Coll of Mount St. Joseph, OH
Coll of Mount Saint Vincent, NY
Coll of Saint Elizabeth, NJ
Coll of St. Joseph, VT
Coll of Saint Mary, NE
The Coll of Saint Rose, NY
The Coll of St. Scholastica, MN
Coll of Staten Island of the City U of New York, NY
Coll of the Atlantic, ME
Coll of the Canyons, CA
Coll of the Desert, CA
The Coll of William and Mary, VA
Colorado Mountain Coll, Alpine Campus, CO

Columbus State U, GA
Comm Coll of Allegheny County, PA
Concordia Coll–New York, NY
Concordia U, NE
Concordia U Coll of Alberta, AB, Canada
Concord U, WV
Cornell U, NY
Cornerstone U, MI
Crafton Hills Coll, CA
Daemen Coll, NY
Dalhousie U, NS, Canada
Dallas Baptist U, TX
Delaware State U, DE
DePaul U, IL
Dixie State Coll of Utah, UT
Dominican U, IL
Drake U, IA
Drury U, MO
Duke U, NC
Earlham Coll, IN
East Carolina U, NC
Eastern Connecticut State U, CT
Eastern Mennonite U, VA
Eastern Michigan U, MI
Eastern Nazarene Coll, MA
East Stroudsburg U of Pennsylvania, PA
Edinboro U of Pennsylvania, PA
El Camino Coll, CA
Elmira Coll, NY
Elms Coll, MA
Elon U, NC
Emory U, GA
Eugene Lang Coll The New School for Liberal Arts, NY
Fairfield U, CT
Fairleigh Dickinson U, Coll at Florham, NJ
Fairleigh Dickinson U, Metropolitan Campus, NJ
Fayetteville State U, NC
Feather River Coll, CA
Ferrum Coll, VA
Fitchburg State Coll, MA
Flagler Coll, FL
Florida Atlantic U, FL
Florida International U, FL
Fontbonne U, MO
Foothill Coll, CA
Fort Hays State U, KS
Framingham State Coll, MA
Franciscan U of Steubenville, OH
Franklin Coll, IN
Franklin Pierce U, NH
Frederick Comm Coll, MD
Freed-Hardeman U, TN
Fresno Pacific U, CA
Fulton-Montgomery Comm Coll, NY
Furman U, SC
Gainesville State Coll, GA
Galveston Coll, TX
Gardner-Webb U, NC
Geneva Coll, PA
Georgetown Coll, KY
The George Washington U, DC
Georgia Coll & State U, GA
Georgian Court U, NJ
Glendale Comm Coll, CA
Glenville State Coll, WV
Gloucester County Coll, NJ
Gonzaga U, WA
Gordon Coll, MA
Goshen Coll, IN
Grace Coll, IN
Graceland U, IA
Grambling State U, LA

Green Mountain Coll, VT
Grinnell Coll, IA
Grossmont Coll, CA
Gustavus Adolphus Coll, MN
Hamilton Coll, NY
Hamline U, MN
Hampden-Sydney Coll, VA
Hampshire Coll, MA
Harding U, AR
Hartwick Coll, NY
Haverford Coll, PA
Henderson State U, AR
High Point U, NC
Hofstra U, NY
Hope Coll, MI
Houghton Coll, NY
Houston Baptist U, TX
Hunter Coll of the City U of New York, NY
Huntington U, IN
Idaho State U, ID
Illinois State U, IL
Illinois Valley Comm Coll, IL
Illinois Wesleyan U, IL
Immaculata U, PA
Indiana U Bloomington, IN
Indiana U of Pennsylvania, PA
Indiana U–Purdue U Fort Wayne, IN
Indiana U–Purdue U Indianapolis, IN
Indiana U Southeast, IN
Iona Coll, NY
Irvine Valley Coll, CA
Ithaca Coll, NY
Jacksonville U, FL
John Brown U, AR
Johnson State Coll, VT
Kansas State U, KS
Kellogg Comm Coll, MI
Kennesaw State U, GA
Kentucky Wesleyan Coll, KY
Kenyon Coll, OH
Keuka Coll, NY
King's Coll, PA
The King's U Coll, AB, Canada
Kutztown U of Pennsylvania, PA
LaGrange Coll, GA
Lake Erie Coll, OH
Lakeland Coll, WI
Lake Superior State U, MI
Lamar U, TX
Langston U, OK
Lawrence U, WI
Lebanon Valley Coll, PA
Lee Coll, TX
Lehigh U, PA
Le Moyne Coll, NY
LeTourneau U, TX
Lewis U, IL
Liberty U, VA
Lincoln U, PA
Lindenwood U, MO
Long Beach City Coll, CA
Long Island U, Brooklyn Campus, NY
Loras Coll, IA
Loyola Marymount U, CA
Loyola U Chicago, IL
Loyola U New Orleans, LA
Lynchburg Coll, VA
Lynn U, FL
Macalester Coll, MN
MacMurray Coll, IL
Manhattan Coll, NY
Manhattanville Coll, NY
Marian Coll, IN
Marietta Coll, OH
Marist Coll, NY
Marquette U, WI

Marshall U, WV
Marymount Manhattan Coll, NY
Marymount U, VA
Marywood U, PA
Massachusetts Coll of Liberal Arts, MA
McDaniel Coll, MD
McNeese State U, LA
Mercer U, GA
Mercyhurst Coll, PA
Miami Dade Coll, FL
Michigan State U, MI
Middlesex County Coll, NJ
Middle Tennessee State U, TN
Midland Coll, TX
Midland Lutheran Coll, NE
Millersville U of Pennsylvania, PA
Minnesota State U Mankato, MN
Minnesota State U Moorhead, MN
MiraCosta Coll, CA
Missouri State U, MO
Molloy Coll, NY
Monmouth Coll, IL
Monmouth U, NJ
Montana State U, MT
Montana State U–Billings, MT
Moravian Coll, PA
Morningside Coll, IA
Mount Holyoke Coll, MA
Mount St. Mary's U, MD
Mount Saint Vincent U, NS, Canada
Mount Union Coll, OH
Mount Vernon Nazarene U, OH
Murray State U, KY
Naropa U, CO
National-Louis U, IL
Neumann Coll, PA
New Jersey City U, NJ
New Mexico Jr Coll, NM
New York U, NY
Niagara U, NY
Nipissing U, ON, Canada
North Carolina State U, NC
North Central Coll, IL
North Dakota State U, ND
Northeastern U, MA
Northern Illinois U, IL
Northern Michigan U, MI
Northern State U, SD
North Georgia Coll & State U, GA
Northwestern Coll, MN
Northwestern Oklahoma State U, OK
Northwest Nazarene U, ID
Notre Dame Coll, OH
Notre Dame de Namur U, CA
Nova Southeastern U, FL
Oakland U, MI
Odessa Coll, TX
Oglethorpe U, GA
The Ohio State U, OH
The Ohio State U at Lima, OH
Ohio Wesleyan U, OH
Oklahoma State U, OK
Old Dominion U, VA
Oral Roberts U, OK
Otterbein Coll, OH
Our Lady of the Lake U of San Antonio, TX
Park U, MO
Paul Quinn Coll, TX
Penn State Abington, PA
Penn State DuBois, PA

Penn State Fayette, The Eberly Campus, PA
Penn State Mont Alto, PA
Penn State Wilkes-Barre, PA
Piedmont Coll, GA
Pine Manor Coll, MA
Pittsburg State U, KS
Portland State U, OR
Prairie View A&M U, TX
Presbyterian Coll, SC
Purdue U North Central, IN
Queens Coll of the City U of New York, NY
Queen's U at Kingston, ON, Canada
Queens U of Charlotte, NC
Quincy Coll, MA
Radford U, VA
Randolph Coll, VA
Randolph-Macon Coll, VA
Redeemer U Coll, ON, Canada
Reedley Coll, CA
Reinhardt Coll, GA
Rhodes Coll, TN
Rice U, TX
The Richard Stockton Coll of New Jersey, NJ
Ripon Coll, WI
Rivier Coll, NH
Rockford Coll, IL
Rockhurst U, MO
Rocky Mountain Coll, MT
Roosevelt U, IL
Rose State Coll, OK
Rowan U, NJ
Roxbury Comm Coll, MA
Rutgers, The State U of New Jersey, Newark, NJ
Rutgers, The State U of New Jersey, New Brunswick, NJ
Saginaw Valley State U, MI
St. Bonaventure U, NY
St. Cloud State U, MN
St. Francis Xavier U, NS, Canada
St. Gregory's U, OK
Saint John's U, MN
Saint Joseph's Coll, IN
St. Lawrence U, NY
Saint Leo U, FL
St. Mary's Coll of Maryland, MD
St. Norbert Coll, WI
St. Philip's Coll, TX
St. Thomas Aquinas Coll, NY
St. Thomas U, NB, Canada
Saint Xavier U, IL
Salem Comm Coll, NJ
Salve Regina U, RI
San Diego Mesa Coll, CA
San Diego State U, CA
San Francisco State U, CA
Santa Ana Coll, CA
Santa Barbara City Coll, CA
Santa Clara U, CA
Santa Rosa Jr Coll, CA
Sauk Valley Comm Coll, IL
Seattle Pacific U, WA
Seton Hall U, NJ
Seton Hill U, PA
Sewanee: The U of the South, TN
Shippensburg U of Pennsylvania, PA
Skagit Valley Coll, WA
Slippery Rock U of Pennsylvania, PA
Southern Adventist U, TN
Southern Illinois U Carbondale, IL
Southern Illinois U Edwardsville, IL

Southern Nazarene U, OK
Southern Oregon U, OR
Southern U and A&M Coll, LA
Southern Utah U, UT
Southwest Baptist U, MO
Southwestern Coll, KS
Southwestern U, TX
Spalding U, KY
Spoon River Coll, IL
Springfield Coll, MA
State U of New York at Fredonia, NY
State U of New York Coll at Brockport, NY
State U of New York Coll at Cortland, NY
State U of New York Coll at Geneseo, NY
State U of New York Coll at Potsdam, NY
Stephen F. Austin State U, TX
Stetson U, FL
Stonehill Coll, MA
Sussex County Comm Coll, NJ
Sweet Briar Coll, VA
Syracuse U, NY
Taylor U, IN
Temple U, PA
Tennessee Wesleyan Coll, TN
Texas A&M U, TX
Texas A&M U–Corpus Christi, TX
Thiel Coll, PA
Towson U, MD
Trent U, ON, Canada
Trevecca Nazarene U, TN
Trinity Coll, CT
Trinity U, TX
Troy U, AL
Truman State U, MO
Tufts U, MA
Union Coll, NE
U at Albany, State U of New York, NY
U at Buffalo, the State U of New York, NY
The U of Akron, OH
The U of Alabama, AL
The U of Alabama in Huntsville, AL
U of Alaska Anchorage, AK
The U of Arizona, AZ
U of Arkansas, AR
U of Baltimore, MD
U of California, Berkeley, CA
U of California, Irvine, CA
U of California, Los Angeles, CA
U of California, Santa Barbara, CA
U of Central Florida, FL
U of Central Missouri, MO
U of Central Oklahoma, OK
U of Cincinnati, OH
U of Colorado at Boulder, CO
U of Connecticut, CT
U of Dayton, OH
U of Delaware, DE
U of Dubuque, IA
U of Evansville, IN
The U of Findlay, OH
U of Great Falls, MT
U of Guelph, ON, Canada
U of Hartford, CT
U of Hawaii at Manoa, HI
U of Hawaii–West Oahu, HI
U of Houston, TX

U of Illinois at Urbana–
Champaign, IL
U of Kansas, KS
U of Kentucky, KY
U of Maine at Machias, ME
U of Manitoba, MB, Canada
U of Mary Hardin-Baylor, TX
U of Maryland, Baltimore
County, MD
U of Mary Washington, VA
U of Massachusetts Amherst,
MA
U of Massachusetts Boston,
MA
U of Massachusetts Lowell,
MA
U of Miami, FL
U of Michigan, MI
U of Minnesota, Duluth, MN
U of Mississippi, MS
U of Missouri–Columbia,
MO
U of Missouri–Kansas City,
MO
U of Missouri–Rolla, MO
U of Nebraska at Kearney,
NE
U of Nebraska at Omaha,
NE
U of Nebraska–Lincoln, NE
U of New Brunswick
Fredericton, NB, Canada
U of New England, ME
U of New Hampshire, NH
U of New Hampshire at
Manchester, NH
U of New Haven, CT
U of New Mexico, NM
U of New Orleans, LA
The U of North Carolina at
Asheville, NC
The U of North Carolina at
Chapel Hill, NC
The U of North Carolina at
Charlotte, NC
U of Northern British
Columbia, BC, Canada
U of Northern Iowa, IA
U of North Florida, FL
U of Notre Dame, IN
U of Oregon, OR
U of Pennsylvania, PA
U of Pittsburgh, PA
U of Pittsburgh at Bradford,
PA
U of Pittsburgh at
Johnstown, PA
U of Portland, OR
U of Redlands, CA
U of Rhode Island, RI
U of Rio Grande, OH
U of St. Thomas, MN
U of St. Thomas, TX
U of San Diego, CA
U of San Francisco, CA
The U of Scranton, PA
U of South Carolina
Beaufort, SC
U of South Carolina Upstate,
SC
U of Southern Indiana, IN
The U of Tampa, FL
The U of Tennessee, TN
The U of Tennessee at
Martin, TN
The U of Texas at Austin,
TX
The U of Texas at El Paso,
TX
The U of Texas at San
Antonio, TX
U of the District of
Columbia, DC
U of the Incarnate Word, TX

U of the Ozarks, AR
U of the Pacific, CA
U of Toronto, ON, Canada
U of Vermont, VT
U of Virginia, VA
The U of Virginia's Coll at
Wise, VA
U of Washington, WA
U of West Georgia, GA
U of Wisconsin–Eau Claire,
WI
U of Wisconsin–Green Bay,
WI
U of Wisconsin–La Crosse,
WI
U of Wisconsin–Madison,
WI
U of Wisconsin–Oshkosh,
WI
U of Wisconsin–Platteville,
WI
U of Wisconsin–Stevens
Point, WI
U of Wyoming, WY
Upper Iowa U, IA
Urbana U, OH
Ursuline Coll, OH
Utica Coll, NY
Valdosta State U, GA
Vanguard U of Southern
California, CA
Vassar Coll, NY
Villanova U, PA
Virginia Intermont Coll, VA
Wake Forest U, NC
Washburn U, KS
Washington & Jefferson Coll,
PA
Washington and Lee U, VA
Wayne State Coll, NE
Wayne State U, MI
Wellesley Coll, MA
Wells Coll, NY
Wesley Coll, DE
West Chester U of
Pennsylvania, PA
Western Connecticut State
U, CT
Western Nebraska Comm
Coll, NE
Western New England Coll,
MA
Western Oregon U, OR
West Liberty State Coll, WV
West Los Angeles Coll, CA
Westminster Coll, PA
Westminster Coll, UT
West Texas A&M U, TX
West Virginia State U, WV
West Virginia Wesleyan Coll,
WV
Wheaton Coll, IL
Whitman Coll, WA
Wichita State U, KS
Widener U, PA
Wilfrid Laurier U, ON,
Canada
Wilkes U, PA
William Jewell Coll, MO
Wilson Coll, PA
Wofford Coll, SC
Worcester State Coll, MA
Wright State U, OH
Xavier U, OH
Yale U, CT

ENGLISH AS A SECOND/
FOREIGN LANGUAGE
(TEACHING)
Bethel U, MN
Brock U, ON, Canada
Calvin Coll, MI
Carleton U, ON, Canada
Carnegie Mellon U, PA

Carroll Coll, MT
Concordia U, NE
Elms Coll, MA
Goshen Coll, IN
John Brown U, AR
Langston U, OK
Liberty U, VA
Murray State U, KY
Northwestern Coll, MN
Oral Roberts U, OK
Queens Coll of the City U of
New York, NY
The U of Arizona, AZ
U of California, Los Angeles,
CA
U of Delaware, DE
The U of Findlay, OH
U of Hawaii at Manoa, HI
U of Nebraska–Lincoln, NE
U of New Brunswick
Fredericton, NB, Canada
U of Northern Iowa, IA
U of Washington, WA
U of Wisconsin–Oshkosh,
WI
Wright State U, OH

ENGLISH COMPOSITION
Aurora U, IL
Baylor U, TX
Bethel U, MN
Eastern Michigan U, MI
Graceland U, IA
Lakeland Coll, WI
Mount Union Coll, OH
U of Evansville, IN
U of Great Falls, MT
U of Illinois at Urbana–
Champaign, IL

ENGLISH LANGUAGE
AND LITERATURE
RELATED
Hofstra U, NY
Mohawk Valley Comm Coll,
NY
Moravian Coll, PA
Point Loma Nazarene U, CA
St. Gregory's U, OK
U of California, Los Angeles,
CA
U of Great Falls, MT
The U of Maine at Augusta,
ME
U of Pennsylvania, PA

ENGLISH/LANGUAGE
ARTS TEACHER
EDUCATION
Abilene Christian U, TX
Alma Coll, MI
Alvernia Coll, PA
Ancilla Coll, IN
Anderson U, IN
Anderson U, SC
Barry U, FL
Baylor U, TX
Bethel Coll, IN
Bethel U, MN
Bishop's U, QC, Canada
Brewton-Parker Coll, GA
Buena Vista U, IA
Buffalo State Coll, State U of
New York, NY
Carroll Coll, MT
Carroll Coll, WI
The Catholic U of America,
DC
Charleston Southern U, SC
The Coll of Saint Rose, NY
Columbus State U, GA
Concordia U, NE
Cornerstone U, MI
Daemen Coll, NY

Delaware State U, DE
East Carolina U, NC
Eastern Mennonite U, VA
Eastern Michigan U, MI
Elmira Coll, NY
Elms Coll, MA
Fayetteville State U, NC
Fitchburg State Coll, MA
Florida Atlantic U, FL
Florida International U, FL
Framingham State Coll, MA
Franklin Coll, IN
Freed-Hardeman U, TN
Gardner-Webb U, NC
Glenville State Coll, WV
Grace Coll, IN
Grambling State U, LA
Harding U, AR
Hofstra U, NY
Hope Coll, MI
Houston Baptist U, TX
Illinois Wesleyan U, IL
Indiana U Bloomington, IN
Indiana U of Pennsylvania,
PA
Indiana U–Purdue U Fort
Wayne, IN
Indiana U–Purdue U
Indianapolis, IN
Indiana U Southeast, IN
Iona Coll, NY
Ithaca Coll, NY
John Brown U, AR
Johnson State Coll, VT
Kennesaw State U, GA
Kentucky Wesleyan Coll, KY
Keuka Coll, NY
Lebanon Valley Coll, PA
Le Moyne Coll, NY
Liberty U, VA
Lincoln U, PA
Long Island U, Brooklyn
Campus, NY
Manhattanville Coll, NY
Marist Coll, NY
Marquette U, WI
Marywood U, PA
McNeese State U, LA
Mercyhurst Coll, PA
Millersville U of
Pennsylvania, PA
Minnesota State U
Moorhead, MN
Missouri State U, MO
Molloy Coll, NY
Montana State U–Billings,
MT
Mount Vernon Nazarene U,
OH
Murray State U, KY
New York U, NY
North Carolina State U, NC
North Dakota State U, ND
Northern Michigan U, MI
North Georgia Coll & State
U, GA
Northwestern Coll, MN
Northwest Nazarene U, ID
Old Dominion U, VA
Oral Roberts U, OK
Pittsburg State U, KS
Queens U of Charlotte, NC
Rivier Coll, NH
Rocky Mountain Coll, MT
Saginaw Valley State U, MI
St. Bonaventure U, NY
St. Gregory's U, OK
Saint Xavier U, IL
Salve Regina U, RI
Seattle Pacific U, WA
Seton Hill U, PA
Southern Adventist U, TN
Southern Nazarene U, OK

Southern U and A&M Coll,
LA
Southwest Baptist U, MO
State U of New York Coll at
Brockport, NY
State U of New York Coll at
Potsdam, NY
Syracuse U, NY
Temple U, PA
Tennessee Wesleyan Coll,
TN
Trevecca Nazarene U, TN
Union Coll, NE
U at Albany, State U of New
York, NY
The U of Akron, OH
The U of Arizona, AZ
U of Arkansas at Fort Smith,
AR
U of Central Florida, FL
U of Central Oklahoma, OK
U of Delaware, DE
U of Dubuque, IA
U of Evansville, IN
U of Great Falls, MT
U of Illinois at Urbana–
Champaign, IL
U of Maine at Machias, ME
U of Mississippi, MS
U of Nebraska–Lincoln, NE
U of New Hampshire, NH
U of New Orleans, LA
The U of North Carolina at
Charlotte, NC
U of Pittsburgh at
Johnstown, PA
U of Rio Grande, OH
U of St. Thomas, MN
The U of Tennessee at
Martin, TN
U of the Ozarks, AR
U of Vermont, VT
Ursuline Coll, OH
Utica Coll, NY
Virginia Intermont Coll, VA
Wayne State Coll, NE
Wayne State U, MI
West Chester U of
Pennsylvania, PA
West Virginia Wesleyan Coll,
WV
Widener U, PA
Wright State U, OH

ENGLISH LITERATURE
(BRITISH AND
COMMONWEALTH)
Gannon U, PA
Hofstra U, NY
Hunter Coll of the City U of
New York, NY
Indiana U–Purdue U Fort
Wayne, IN
Oral Roberts U, OK
St. Lawrence U, NY
Syracuse U, NY
U of Miami, FL
U of New Hampshire, NH
U of Pittsburgh, PA

ENTOMOLOGY
Cornell U, NY
Michigan State U, MI
The Ohio State U, OH
Oklahoma State U, OK
State U of New York Coll of
Environmental Science
and Forestry, NY
Texas A&M U, TX
U of Delaware, DE
U of Hawaii at Manoa, HI
U of Illinois at Urbana–
Champaign, IL
U of Manitoba, MB, Canada

U of New Brunswick Fredericton, NB, Canada
U of Wisconsin–Madison, WI

ENTREPRENEURIAL AND SMALL BUSINESS RELATED
Kendall Coll, IL
Stetson U, FL
U of Miami, FL
Williston State Coll, ND

ENTREPRENEURSHIP
Baylor U, TX
Bradley U, IL
British Columbia Inst of Technology, BC, Canada
Bucks County Comm Coll, PA
Buena Vista U, IA
Calhoun Comm Coll, AL
California State U, Fullerton, CA
Comm Coll of Allegheny County, PA
Dalhousie U, NS, Canada
Eastern Michigan U, MI
Hofstra U, NY
Houston Baptist U, TX
Johnson & Wales U, CO
Kendall Coll, IL
Missouri State U–West Plains, MO
Mohawk Valley Comm Coll, NY
Nassau Comm Coll, NY
Northeastern U, MA
Northern Michigan U, MI
Northwood U, MI
Northwood U, Texas Campus, TX
Reedley Coll, CA
Reinhardt Coll, GA
Schoolcraft Coll, MI
Seton Hill U, PA
Syracuse U, NY
Temple U, PA
Union Coll, NE
The U of Akron, OH
The U of Arizona, AZ
U of Illinois at Urbana–Champaign, IL
U of Maine at Machias, ME
U of Miami, FL
U of Pittsburgh at Bradford, PA
U of St. Thomas, MN
The U of Scranton, PA
U of Southern Indiana, IN
The U of Texas at San Antonio, TX
U of the District of Columbia, DC
Waubonsee Comm Coll, IL
Wichita State U, KS
Wilkes U, PA
Xavier U, OH

ENVIRONMENTAL BIOLOGY
Bard Coll, NY
Bethel Coll, IN
Carlow U, PA
Cedar Crest Coll, PA
Colgate U, NY
Coll of the Atlantic, ME
Concordia U Coll of Alberta, AB, Canada
Cornerstone U, MI
East Stroudsburg U of Pennsylvania, PA
Framingham State Coll, MA
Franklin Pierce U, NH

Houghton Coll, NY
Iona Coll, NY
Michigan State U, MI
Minnesota State U Mankato, MN
Monmouth U, NJ
Mount Union Coll, OH
Nipissing U, ON, Canada
Otterbein Coll, OH
Queens Coll of the City U of New York, NY
Queens U of Charlotte, NC
St. Cloud State U, MN
State U of New York Coll at Brockport, NY
State U of New York Coll at Cortland, NY
State U of New York Coll of Environmental Science and Forestry, NY
Sterling Coll, VT
Taylor U, IN
Unity Coll, ME
U of Dayton, OH
U of Dubuque, IA
U of Guelph, ON, Canada
U of Pittsburgh at Johnstown, PA
The U of Tampa, FL
The U of Tennessee at Martin, TN
Ursuline Coll, OH

ENVIRONMENTAL CONTROL TECHNOLOGIES RELATED
Florida International U, FL

ENVIRONMENTAL DESIGN/ARCHITECTURE
Abraham Baldwin Coll, GA
Ball State U, IN
Coll of the Atlantic, ME
Cornell U, NY
Cosumnes River Coll, Sacramento, CA
Dalhousie U, NS, Canada
Florida International U, FL
Gainesville State Coll, GA
Hampshire Coll, MA
Montana State U, MT
North Carolina State U, NC
North Dakota State U, ND
Otis Coll of Art and Design, CA
Parsons The New School for Design, NY
Rutgers, The State U of New Jersey, New Brunswick, NJ
Scottsdale Comm Coll, AZ
State U of New York Coll of Environmental Science and Forestry, NY
Sterling Coll, VT
Texas A&M U, TX
U at Buffalo, the State U of New York, NY
U of California, Irvine, CA
U of Colorado at Boulder, CO
U of Houston, TX
U of Manitoba, MB, Canada
U of Massachusetts Amherst, MA
U of New Mexico, NM
U of Pennsylvania, PA

ENVIRONMENTAL EDUCATION
Coll of the Atlantic, ME
Johnson State Coll, VT
New Mexico Jr Coll, NM
The Ohio State U, OH

State U of New York Coll of Environmental Science and Forestry, NY
Unity Coll, ME
U of Maine at Machias, ME

ENVIRONMENTAL ENGINEERING TECHNOLOGY
British Columbia Inst of Technology, BC, Canada
Broward Comm Coll, FL
Cape Breton U, NS, Canada
Cape Cod Comm Coll, MA
Central Piedmont Comm Coll, NC
Chattanooga State Tech Comm Coll, TN
Comm Coll of Allegheny County, PA
Coosa Valley Tech Coll, GA
Cornell U, NY
Cosumnes River Coll, Sacramento, CA
Delaware Tech & Comm Coll, Jack F. Owens Campus, DE
East Carolina U, NC
Gloucester County Coll, NJ
James H. Faulkner State Comm Coll, AL
Lake Superior State U, MI
Miami Dade Coll, FL
Middle Tennessee State U, TN
Murray State U, KY
Muscatine Comm Coll, IA
Pima Comm Coll, AZ
Rose State Coll, OK
Roxbury Comm Coll, MA
Schoolcraft Coll, MI
Skagit Valley Coll, WA
Southern Maine Comm Coll, ME
Sterling Coll, VT
Temple U, PA
Unity Coll, ME
U of Cincinnati, OH
U of Delaware, DE
U of Guelph, ON, Canada
U of the District of Columbia, DC
Valencia Comm Coll, FL
Westchester Comm Coll, NY
Westmoreland County Comm Coll, PA
Wright State U, OH

ENVIRONMENTAL/ ENVIRONMENTAL HEALTH ENGINEERING
Bradley U, IL
British Columbia Inst of Technology, BC, Canada
Carleton U, ON, Canada
Cornell U, NY
Dalhousie U, NS, Canada
Gannon U, PA
The George Washington U, DC
Hofstra U, NY
Lehigh U, PA
Manhattan Coll, NY
Marquette U, WI
Montana Tech of The U of Montana, MT
North Carolina State U, NC
Old Dominion U, VA
Penn State Abington, PA
Penn State DuBois, PA
Penn State Fayette, The Eberly Campus, PA
Penn State Mont Alto, PA
Penn State Wilkes-Barre, PA

Rensselaer Polytechnic Inst, NY
Rice U, TX
Santa Barbara City Coll, CA
State U of New York Coll of Environmental Science and Forestry, NY
Syracuse U, NY
Tufts U, MA
U at Buffalo, the State U of New York, NY
U of California, Berkeley, CA
U of California, Irvine, CA
U of Central Florida, FL
U of Colorado at Boulder, CO
U of Connecticut, CT
U of Delaware, DE
U of Hartford, CT
U of Miami, FL
U of Michigan, MI
U of Missouri–Rolla, MO
U of New Hampshire, NH
U of Northern British Columbia, BC, Canada
U of Notre Dame, IN
U of Pennsylvania, PA
U of Vermont, VT
U of Wisconsin–Madison, WI
U of Wisconsin–Platteville, WI
Wilkes U, PA
Yale U, CT

ENVIRONMENTAL HEALTH
British Columbia Inst of Technology, BC, Canada
California State U, Northridge, CA
Cape Breton U, NS, Canada
Concordia U Coll of Alberta, AB, Canada
East Carolina U, NC
Illinois State U, IL
Indiana U of Pennsylvania, PA
Oakland U, MI
Old Dominion U, VA
The U of Akron, OH
The U of Akron–Wayne Coll, OH
U of California, Los Angeles, CA
The U of North Carolina at Chapel Hill, NC
U of Washington, WA
U of Wisconsin–Eau Claire, WI
West Chester U of Pennsylvania, PA
Wright State U, OH

ENVIRONMENTAL PSYCHOLOGY
Embry-Riddle Aeronautical U, FL

ENVIRONMENTAL SCIENCE
Abilene Christian U, TX
Albright Coll, PA
Bethel U, MN
Brevard Coll, NC
Briar Cliff U, IA
Bridgewater Coll, VA
Brown U, RI
Carroll Coll, WI
Carthage Coll, WI
Central Wyoming Coll, WY
Colby Coll, ME

Concordia U Coll of Alberta, AB, Canada
Cornell U, NY
Dalhousie U, NS, Canada
Delaware State U, DE
Drake U, IA
Eastern Connecticut State U, CT
Eastern Mennonite U, VA
Fitchburg State Coll, MA
Florida Gulf Coast U, FL
Florida Inst of Technology, FL
Framingham State Coll, MA
Gannon U, PA
Georgia Coll & State U, GA
Hartwick Coll, NY
Hunter Coll of the City U of New York, NY
John Brown U, AR
Keuka Coll, NY
King's Coll, PA
Kutztown U of Pennsylvania, PA
Lehigh U, PA
Lincoln U, PA
Lindenwood U, MO
Marietta Coll, OH
Marshall U, WV
Marymount U, VA
Marywood U, PA
McDaniel Coll, MD
McNeese State U, LA
Mercer U, GA
Michigan State U, MI
Monmouth Coll, IL
Montana State U, MT
North Carolina State U, NC
Notre Dame Coll, OH
Nova Southeastern U, FL
Otterbein Coll, OH
Piedmont Coll, GA
Queens Coll of the City U of New York, NY
Queen's U at Kingston, ON, Canada
Ramapo Coll of New Jersey, NJ
Rochester Inst of Technology, NY
Rocky Mountain Coll, MT
St. Norbert Coll, WI
St. Philip's Coll, TX
San Diego State U, CA
Santa Clara U, CA
Santa Rosa Jr Coll, CA
Slippery Rock U of Pennsylvania, PA
State U of New York Coll at Cortland, NY
Sweet Briar Coll, VA
Temple U, PA
Texas A&M U, TX
Texas A&M U–Corpus Christi, TX
Trinity Coll, CT
Troy U, AL
U at Albany, State U of New York, NY
The U of Arizona, AZ
U of Arkansas, AR
U of California, Berkeley, CA
U of California, Los Angeles, CA
U of Dubuque, IA
U of Evansville, IN
U of Hawaii at Manoa, HI
U of Illinois at Urbana–Champaign, IL
U of Maryland, Baltimore County, MD
U of Massachusetts Amherst, MA

U of Massachusetts Lowell, MA
U of New England, ME
U of New Hampshire, NH
U of New Mexico, NM
The U of North Carolina at Chapel Hill, NC
U of Northern British Columbia, BC, Canada
U of Northern Iowa, IA
U of Oregon, OR
U of San Francisco, CA
The U of Texas at San Antonio, TX
U of Vermont, VT
U of Virginia, VA
U of West Georgia, GA
U of Wisconsin–Green Bay, WI
Upper Iowa U, IA
Vassar Coll, NY
Wayne State U, MI
West Texas A&M U, TX
West Virginia Wesleyan Coll, WV
Wright State U, OH

ENVIRONMENTAL STUDIES
Acadia U, NS, Canada
Albion Coll, MI
Alderson-Broaddus Coll, WV
American U, DC
Ashland U, OH
Aurora U, IL
Austin Coll, TX
Ball State U, IN
Bard Coll, NY
Bates Coll, ME
Baylor U, TX
Bemidji State U, MN
Bishop's U, QC, Canada
Boston Coll, MA
Brenau U, GA
Brevard Coll, NC
Brown U, RI
Bucks County Comm Coll, PA
Burlington County Coll, NJ
California State U, Sacramento, CA
California State U, San Bernardino, CA
Calvin Coll, MI
Cape Breton U, NS, Canada
Cape Cod Comm Coll, MA
Carleton U, ON, Canada
Carroll Coll, MT
Carthage Coll, WI
Cedar Crest Coll, PA
Charleston Southern U, SC
Christopher Newport U, VA
Claremont McKenna Coll, CA
Coe Coll, IA
Colby Coll, ME
Colgate U, NY
The Coll of Saint Rose, NY
Coll of the Atlantic, ME
Coll of the Desert, CA
The Coll of William and Mary, VA
Concordia U Coll of Alberta, AB, Canada
Cornell U, NY
Cosumnes River Coll, Sacramento, CA
Dalhousie U, NS, Canada
DePaul U, IL
Dixie State Coll of Utah, UT
Dominican U, IL
Drake U, IA
Drury U, MO
Duke U, NC

Earlham Coll, IN
Eckerd Coll, FL
Edinboro U of Pennsylvania, PA
Elmira Coll, NY
Elon U, NC
Fairleigh Dickinson U, Metropolitan Campus, NJ
Ferrum Coll, VA
Florida International U, FL
Framingham State Coll, MA
Franklin Pierce U, NH
Fulton-Montgomery Comm Coll, NY
Furman U, SC
The George Washington U, DC
Goshen Coll, IN
Green Mountain Coll, VT
Gustavus Adolphus Coll, MN
Hamline U, MN
Hampshire Coll, MA
Harrisburg Area Comm Coll, PA
Hillsborough Comm Coll, FL
Hofstra U, NY
Hope Coll, MI
Housatonic Comm Coll, CT
Howard Comm Coll, MD
Hudson Valley Comm Coll, NY
Illinois Wesleyan U, IL
Immaculata U, PA
Indiana U Bloomington, IN
Indiana U of Pennsylvania, PA
Itasca Comm Coll, MN
Ithaca Coll, NY
Jacksonville U, FL
John Brown U, AR
Johnson State Coll, VT
Kentucky Wesleyan Coll, KY
Kenyon Coll, OH
King's Coll, PA
The King's U Coll, AB, Canada
Kutztown U of Pennsylvania, PA
Lake Erie Coll, OH
Lake Superior State U, MI
Lamar State Coll–Orange, TX
Lamar U, TX
Lawrence U, WI
Lee Coll, TX
Lehigh U, PA
Lewis U, IL
Loyola U Chicago, IL
Lynchburg Coll, VA
Macalester Coll, MN
Marietta Coll, OH
Marist Coll, NY
Massachusetts Coll of Liberal Arts, MA
Mercer U, GA
Michigan State U, MI
Middlesex Comm Coll, CT
Midland Lutheran Coll, NE
Minnesota State U Mankato, MN
Molloy Coll, NY
Montana State U, MT
Montana State U–Billings, MT
Moravian Coll, PA
Mount Holyoke Coll, MA
Naropa U, CO
Neumann Coll, PA
New Mexico Jr Coll, NM
Nipissing U, ON, Canada
North Carolina State U, NC
Northeastern U, MA
Northern Michigan U, MI
Northern State U, SD

Nova Scotia Coll, NS, Canada
Nova Southeastern U, FL
The Ohio State U, OH
Ohio Wesleyan U, OH
Oklahoma State U, OK
Oregon Inst of Technology, OR
Piedmont Coll, GA
Pittsburg State U, KS
Portland State U, OR
Queens Coll of the City U of New York, NY
Ramapo Coll of New Jersey, NJ
Randolph Coll, VA
Randolph-Macon Coll, VA
The Richard Stockton Coll of New Jersey, NJ
Ripon Coll, WI
Rocky Mountain Coll, MT
Rowan U, NJ
Rutgers, The State U of New Jersey, Newark, NJ
Rutgers, The State U of New Jersey, New Brunswick, NJ
St. Bonaventure U, NY
St. Francis Xavier U, NS, Canada
Saint John's U, MN
St. Lawrence U, NY
St. Norbert Coll, WI
San Diego State U, CA
Santa Ana Coll, CA
Santa Barbara City Coll, CA
Santa Rosa Jr Coll, CA
Sewanee: The U of the South, TN
Shippensburg U of Pennsylvania, PA
Slippery Rock U of Pennsylvania, PA
Southern Nazarene U, OK
Southern Oregon U, OR
Southwestern U, TX
Stark State Coll of Technology, OH
State U of New York at Fredonia, NY
State U of New York Coll at Brockport, NY
State U of New York Coll at Cortland, NY
State U of New York Coll of Environmental Science and Forestry, NY
State U of New York Coll of Technology at Alfred, NY
State U of New York Coll of Technology at Canton, NY
Stephen F. Austin State U, TX
Sterling Coll, VT
Stetson U, FL
Sussex County Comm Coll, NJ
Sweet Briar Coll, VA
Taylor U, IN
Temple U, PA
Texas A&M U, TX
Texas A&M U–Corpus Christi, TX
Thiel Coll, PA
Trent U, ON, Canada
Trocaire Coll, NY
Tufts U, MA
Unity Coll, ME
The U of Arizona, AZ
U of California, Berkeley, CA
U of California, Santa Barbara, CA
U of Cincinnati, OH

U of Colorado at Boulder, CO
U of Connecticut, CT
U of Dayton, OH
U of Delaware, DE
U of Dubuque, IA
U of Evansville, IN
The U of Findlay, OH
U of Guelph, ON, Canada
U of Hawaii at Manoa, HI
U of Houston, TX
U of Kansas, KS
U of Maine at Machias, ME
U of Manitoba, MB, Canada
U of Maryland, Baltimore County, MD
U of Mary Washington, VA
U of Miami, FL
U of Michigan, MI
U of Minnesota, Duluth, MN
U of Missouri–Columbia, MO
U of Nebraska at Omaha, NE
U of Nebraska–Lincoln, NE
U of New England, ME
U of New Hampshire, NH
U of New Orleans, LA
The U of North Carolina at Asheville, NC
The U of North Carolina at Chapel Hill, NC
U of Northern British Columbia, BC, Canada
U of Oregon, OR
U of Pennsylvania, PA
U of Pittsburgh at Bradford, PA
U of Pittsburgh at Johnstown, PA
U of Portland, OR
U of Redlands, CA
U of Rhode Island, RI
U of St. Thomas, TX
U of San Diego, CA
U of San Francisco, CA
The U of Tampa, FL
The U of Tennessee at Martin, TN
U of the District of Columbia, DC
U of the Incarnate Word, TX
U of the Ozarks, AR
U of the Pacific, CA
U of Toronto, ON, Canada
U of Vermont, VT
The U of Virginia's Coll at Wise, VA
U of Washington, WA
U of West Georgia, GA
U of Wisconsin–Green Bay, WI
U of Wyoming, WY
Vassar Coll, NY
Virginia Intermont Coll, VA
Wellesley Coll, MA
Wells Coll, NY
Wesley Coll, DE
West Chester U of Pennsylvania, PA
Western Connecticut State U, CT
Westminster Coll, PA
Westminster Coll, UT
Wheaton Coll, IL
Widener U, PA
Wilson Coll, PA
Yale U, CT

ENVIRONMENTAL TOXICOLOGY
Cornell U, NY
U of Guelph, ON, Canada

EPIDEMIOLOGY
U of California, Los Angeles, CA

EQUESTRIAN STUDIES
Central Wyoming Coll, WY
Hocking Coll, OH
Johnson & Wales U, RI
Lake Erie Coll, OH
North Central Texas Coll, TX
North Dakota State U, ND
Otterbein Coll, OH
Rocky Mountain Coll, MT
Rutgers, The State U of New Jersey, New Brunswick, NJ
Scottsdale Comm Coll, AZ
Sterling Coll, VT
Truman State U, MO
The U of Findlay, OH
U of Massachusetts Amherst, MA
U of New Hampshire, NH
Virginia Intermont Coll, VA
West Texas A&M U, TX
Wilson Coll, PA

ETHICS
Carnegie Mellon U, PA
Drake U, IA

ETHNIC, CULTURAL MINORITY, AND GENDER STUDIES RELATED
California State U, Sacramento, CA
Carnegie Mellon U, PA
Claremont McKenna Coll, CA
Kenyon Coll, OH
Lawrence U, WI
Santa Rosa Jr Coll, CA
Sterling Coll, VT
Stonehill Coll, MA
U of California, Berkeley, CA
U of Hawaii at Manoa, HI
U of Oregon, OR
U of Pittsburgh, PA
The U of Texas at Austin, TX
Wellesley Coll, MA
Yale U, CT

EUROPEAN HISTORY
Bard Coll, NY
Carnegie Mellon U, PA
Charleston Southern U, SC
Cornell U, NY
Framingham State Coll, MA

EUROPEAN STUDIES
American U, DC
Amherst Coll, MA
Bard Coll, NY
Brandeis U, MA
Brock U, ON, Canada
Carleton U, ON, Canada
Carnegie Mellon U, PA
Claremont McKenna Coll, CA
The Coll of William and Mary, VA
Dalhousie U, NS, Canada
Elmira Coll, NY
Georgetown Coll, KY
The George Washington U, DC
Hamline U, MN
Loyola Marymount U, CA
Mount Holyoke Coll, MA
New York U, NY
San Diego State U, CA
Seattle Pacific U, WA

Metropolitan Comm
  Coll–Penn Valley, MO
Michigan State U, MI
Middlesex County Coll, NJ
Minnesota State U Mankato,
  MN
Moorpark Coll, CA
Nassau Comm Coll, NY
Otis Coll of Art and Design,
  CA
Parsons The New School for
  Design, NY
Phoenix Coll, AZ
Pratt Inst, NY
Ryerson U, ON, Canada
San Diego Mesa Coll, CA
Santa Ana Coll, CA
Savannah Coll of Art and
  Design, GA
School of the Art Inst of
  Chicago, IL
Syracuse U, NY
U of Cincinnati, OH
U of Delaware, DE
U of Hawaii at Manoa, HI
U of the Incarnate Word, TX
Ursuline Coll, OH
Ventura Coll, CA
Westmoreland County
  Comm Coll, PA

**FASHION
MERCHANDISING**
Abraham Baldwin Coll, GA
Academy of Art U, CA
Alexandria Tech Coll, MN
The Art Inst of Seattle, WA
Ashland U, OH
Ball State U, IN
Baylor U, TX
Brenau U, GA
Buffalo State Coll, State U of
  New York, NY
Carson-Newman Coll, TN
Central Piedmont Comm
  Coll, NC
Clayton State U, GA
Cuesta Coll, CA
Delaware State U, DE
Dominican U, IL
Eastern Michigan U, MI
Fashion Inst of Technology,
  NY
Florida Comm Coll at
  Jacksonville, FL
Fontbonne U, MO
Framingham State Coll, MA
Freed-Hardeman U, TN
Fresno City Coll, CA
Harding U, AR
Houston Comm Coll System,
  TX
Howard Comm Coll, MD
Immaculata U, PA
Indiana U Bloomington, IN
Indiana U of Pennsylvania,
  PA
Johnson & Wales U, CO
Johnson & Wales U, FL
Johnson & Wales U, NC
Johnson & Wales U, RI
Kingsborough Comm Coll of
  the City U of New York,
  NY
Laboratory Inst of
  Merchandising, NY
Lamar U, TX
Laredo Comm Coll, TX
Lee Coll, TX
Liberty U, VA
Lindenwood U, MO
Long Beach City Coll, CA
Marist Coll, NY
Marymount U, VA

Mercyhurst Coll, PA
Metropolitan Comm
  Coll–Penn Valley, MO
Middlesex County Coll, NJ
Nassau Comm Coll, NY
New York City Coll of
  Technology of the City U
  of New York, NY
Northwood U, MI
Northwood U, Texas
  Campus, TX
Odessa Coll, TX
Our Lady of the Lake U of
  San Antonio, TX
Parsons The New School for
  Design, NY
St. Louis Comm Coll at
  Florissant Valley, MO
San Diego Mesa Coll, CA
Santa Ana Coll, CA
Scottsdale Comm Coll, AZ
Stephen F. Austin State U,
  TX
Tunxis Comm Coll, CT
The U of Akron, OH
U of Central Oklahoma, OK
U of Delaware, DE
U of Illinois at Urbana–
  Champaign, IL
The U of Tennessee at
  Martin, TN
U of the District of
  Columbia, DC
U of the Incarnate Word, TX
U of Wisconsin–Madison,
  WI
Ursuline Coll, OH
Wayne State Coll, NE
Western Tech Coll, WI
Westmoreland County
  Comm Coll, PA
West Virginia State U, WV

FASHION MODELING
Fashion Inst of Technology,
  NY

**FIBER, TEXTILE AND
WEAVING ARTS**
Academy of Art U, CA
The Cleveland Inst of Art,
  OH
Mercyhurst Coll, PA
NSCAD U, NS, Canada
Savannah Coll of Art and
  Design, GA
School of the Art Inst of
  Chicago, IL
Syracuse U, NY
Temple U, PA
U of Kansas, KS
U of Michigan, MI
U of Oregon, OR
U of Washington, WA

FILIPINO/TAGALOG
U of Hawaii at Manoa, HI

FILM/CINEMA STUDIES
Academy of Art U, CA
Bard Coll, NY
Bishop's U, QC, Canada
Brock U, ON, Canada
Brown U, RI
California State U,
  Northridge, CA
Calvin Coll, MI
Carleton U, ON, Canada
Carson-Newman Coll, TN
Claremont McKenna Coll,
  CA
Clark U, MA
Cornell U, NY
Eastern Michigan U, MI
Emory U, GA

Framingham State Coll, MA
Hofstra U, NY
Hunter Coll of the City U of
  New York, NY
Huntington U, IN
Ithaca Coll, NY
Long Beach City Coll, CA
Moorpark Coll, CA
Mount Holyoke Coll, MA
New York U, NY
North Carolina School of the
  Arts, NC
North Carolina State U, NC
Northern Michigan U, MI
NSCAD U, NS, Canada
Oral Roberts U, OK
Penn State Abington, PA
Penn State DuBois, PA
Penn State Fayette, The
  Eberly Campus, PA
Penn State Mont Alto, PA
Penn State Wilkes-Barre, PA
Queens Coll of the City U of
  New York, NY
Queen's U at Kingston, ON,
  Canada
Rutgers, The State U of New
  Jersey, New Brunswick, NJ
St. Cloud State U, MN
San Francisco State U, CA
Santa Barbara City Coll, CA
Santa Rosa Jr Coll, CA
School of the Art Inst of
  Chicago, IL
State U of New York at
  Fredonia, NY
Tallahassee Comm Coll, FL
Temple U, PA
U at Buffalo, the State U of
  New York, NY
U of California, Berkeley,
  CA
U of California, Irvine, CA
U of California, Los Angeles,
  CA
U of California, Santa
  Barbara, CA
U of Colorado at Boulder,
  CO
U of Delaware, DE
U of Hartford, CT
U of Manitoba, MB, Canada
U of Maryland, Baltimore
  County, MD
U of Miami, FL
U of Michigan, MI
U of Nebraska–Lincoln, NE
U of New Mexico, NM
U of Pennsylvania, PA
U of Pittsburgh, PA
U of Toronto, ON, Canada
U of Vermont, VT
Vassar Coll, NY
Watkins Coll of Art and
  Design, TN
Wayne State U, MI
Wellesley Coll, MA
Whitman Coll, WA
Wilfrid Laurier U, ON,
  Canada
Wright State U, OH
Yale U, CT

**FILM/VIDEO AND
PHOTOGRAPHIC ARTS
RELATED**
The Art Inst of Pittsburgh,
  PA
Hampshire Coll, MA
Pratt Inst, NY
Ryerson U, ON, Canada
School of the Art Inst of
  Chicago, IL
Syracuse U, NY

The U of the Arts, PA

FINANCE
Abilene Christian U, TX
Adelphi U, NY
Alabama A&M U, AL
Albright Coll, PA
Alderson-Broaddus Coll, WV
American International Coll,
  MA
Anderson U, IN
Anderson U, SC
Angelo State U, TX
Ashland U, OH
Auburn U Montgomery, AL
Augsburg Coll, MN
Aurora U, IL
Avila U, MO
Ball State U, IN
Barry U, FL
Baylor U, TX
Bentley Coll, MA
Bishop's U, QC, Canada
Boston Coll, MA
Bradley U, IL
British Columbia Inst of
  Technology, BC, Canada
Brock U, ON, Canada
Broward Comm Coll, FL
Bunker Hill Comm Coll, MA
California State U, Fullerton,
  CA
California State U,
  Sacramento, CA
California State U, San
  Bernardino, CA
Cape Breton U, NS, Canada
Carleton U, ON, Canada
Carroll Coll, MT
Carroll Coll, WI
The Catholic U of America,
  DC
Central Piedmont Comm
  Coll, NC
Charleston Southern U, SC
Chattanooga State Tech
  Comm Coll, TN
Christopher Newport U, VA
Clayton State U, GA
Clemson U, SC
Coastal Carolina U, SC
Coll of St. Joseph, VT
Columbus State U, GA
Comm Coll of Aurora, CO
Cosumnes River Coll,
  Sacramento, CA
Dalhousie U, NS, Canada
Dallas Baptist U, TX
Delaware State U, DE
DePaul U, IL
Drake U, IA
Drury U, MO
East Carolina U, NC
Eastern Michigan U, MI
El Camino Coll, CA
Emory U, GA
Fairfield U, CT
Fairleigh Dickinson U, Coll
  at Florham, NJ
Fairleigh Dickinson U,
  Metropolitan Campus, NJ
Fayetteville State U, NC
Florida Atlantic U, FL
Florida Gulf Coast U, FL
Florida International U, FL
Fontbonne U, MO
Fort Hays State U, KS
Framingham State Coll, MA
Franklin Pierce U, NH
Frederick Comm Coll, MD
Freed-Hardeman U, TN
Fresno Pacific U, CA
Fulton-Montgomery Comm
  Coll, NY

Gannon U, PA
The George Washington U,
  DC
Glendale Comm Coll, CA
Gloucester County Coll, NJ
Gonzaga U, WA
Hillsborough Comm Coll, FL
Hofstra U, NY
Hopkinsville Comm Coll,
  KY
Houston Baptist U, TX
Houston Comm Coll System,
  TX
Hudson Valley Comm Coll,
  NY
Husson Coll, ME
Idaho State U, ID
Illinois State U, IL
Immaculata U, PA
Indiana U Bloomington, IN
Indiana U of Pennsylvania,
  PA
Indiana U–Purdue U Fort
  Wayne, IN
Iona Coll, NY
Ithaca Coll, NY
Jacksonville U, FL
Jefferson Comm Coll, OH
Johnson & Wales U, RI
Kansas State U, KS
Kennesaw State U, GA
King's Coll, PA
Kutztown U of
  Pennsylvania, PA
Lake Superior State U, MI
Lamar U, TX
Lehigh U, PA
LeTourneau U, TX
Lewis U, IL
Lincoln U, PA
Lindenwood U, MO
Long Island U, Brooklyn
  Campus, NY
Loras Coll, IA
Loyola U Chicago, IL
Loyola U New Orleans, LA
MacMurray Coll, IL
Macomb Comm Coll, MI
Manhattan Coll, NY
Manhattanville Coll, NY
Marian Coll, IN
Marquette U, WI
Marshall U, WV
Marymount U, VA
Massachusetts Coll of Liberal
  Arts, MA
McNeese State U, LA
Mercyhurst Coll, PA
Miami Dade Coll, FL
Michigan State U, MI
Middle Tennessee State U,
  TN
Minnesota State U Mankato,
  MN
Minnesota State U
  Moorhead, MN
Missouri State U, MO
Montana State U–Billings,
  MT
Montana Tech of The U of
  Montana, MT
Morton Coll, IL
Murray State U, KY
New Mexico Jr Coll, NM
New York U, NY
North Carolina State U, NC
North Central Coll, IL
Northeastern U, MA
Northern Illinois U, IL
Northern Michigan U, MI
Northern State U, SD
North Georgia Coll & State
  U, GA
Northwestern Coll, MN

Northwest Nazarene U, ID
Notre Dame de Namur U, CA
Nova Southeastern U, FL
Oakland U, MI
The Ohio State U, OH
Oklahoma State U, OK
Old Dominion U, VA
Oral Roberts U, OK
Otterbein Coll, OH
Penn State Abington, PA
Penn State DuBois, PA
Penn State Fayette, The Eberly Campus, PA
Penn State Mont Alto, PA
Penn State Wilkes-Barre, PA
Phoenix Coll, AZ
Pittsburg State U, KS
Portland State U, OR
Prairie View A&M U, TX
Queens Coll of the City U of New York, NY
Radford U, VA
Rensselaer Polytechnic Inst, NY
Rochester Inst of Technology, NY
Rockford Coll, IL
Roosevelt U, IL
Rutgers, The State U of New Jersey, Newark, NJ
Rutgers, The State U of New Jersey, New Brunswick, NJ
Ryerson U, ON, Canada
Saginaw Valley State U, MI
St. Bonaventure U, NY
St. Cloud State U, MN
St. Cloud Tech Coll, MN
St. Louis Comm Coll at Florissant Valley, MO
St. Thomas Aquinas Coll, NY
Salve Regina U, RI
San Diego State U, CA
San Francisco State U, CA
Santa Barbara City Coll, CA
Santa Clara U, CA
Scottsdale Comm Coll, AZ
Seminole Comm Coll, FL
Seton Hall U, NJ
Seton Hill U, PA
Shippensburg U of Pennsylvania, PA
Southeast Tech Inst, SD
Southern Illinois U Carbondale, IL
Southern Nazarene U, OK
Southern U and A&M Coll, LA
Spoon River Coll, IL
Stark State Coll of Technology, OH
State U of New York at Fredonia, NY
State U of New York Coll at Brockport, NY
State U of New York Coll of Technology at Alfred, NY
Stephen F. Austin State U, TX
Stetson U, FL
Stonehill Coll, MA
Syracuse U, NY
Tallahassee Comm Coll, FL
Taylor U, IN
Temple U, PA
Tennessee Wesleyan Coll, TN
Texas A&M U, TX
Texas A&M U–Corpus Christi, TX
Tidewater Comm Coll, VA
Trinity U, TX
Troy U, AL

Truman State U, MO
The U of Akron, OH
The U of Alabama, AL
The U of Alabama in Huntsville, AL
U of Alaska Anchorage, AK
The U of Arizona, AZ
U of Arkansas, AR
U of Baltimore, MD
U of Central Florida, FL
U of Central Missouri, MO
U of Central Oklahoma, OK
U of Cincinnati, OH
U of Colorado at Boulder, CO
U of Connecticut, CT
U of Dayton, OH
U of Delaware, DE
U of Evansville, IN
U of Hartford, CT
U of Hawaii at Manoa, HI
U of Houston, TX
U of Illinois at Urbana–Champaign, IL
U of Kansas, KS
U of Kentucky, KY
U of Manitoba, MB, Canada
U of Mary Hardin-Baylor, TX
U of Massachusetts Amherst, MA
U of Miami, FL
U of Minnesota, Duluth, MN
U of Mississippi, MS
U of Missouri–Columbia, MO
U of Nebraska at Omaha, NE
U of Nebraska–Lincoln, NE
U of New Brunswick Fredericton, NB, Canada
U of New Hampshire, NH
U of New Haven, CT
U of New Orleans, LA
The U of North Carolina at Charlotte, NC
U of Northern British Columbia, BC, Canada
U of Northern Iowa, IA
U of North Florida, FL
U of Notre Dame, IN
U of Oregon, OR
U of Pennsylvania, PA
U of Pittsburgh, PA
U of Pittsburgh at Johnstown, PA
U of Portland, OR
U of Rhode Island, RI
U of St. Thomas, MN
U of St. Thomas, TX
U of San Francisco, CA
The U of Scranton, PA
U of Southern Indiana, IN
The U of Tampa, FL
The U of Tennessee, TN
The U of Tennessee at Martin, TN
The U of Texas at Austin, TX
The U of Texas at El Paso, TX
The U of Texas at San Antonio, TX
U of the District of Columbia, DC
U of the Incarnate Word, TX
U of Toronto, ON, Canada
U of West Georgia, GA
U of Wisconsin–Eau Claire, WI
U of Wisconsin–La Crosse, WI
U of Wisconsin–Madison, WI

U of Wisconsin–Oshkosh, WI
U of Wyoming, WY
Valdosta State U, GA
Vanguard U of Southern California, CA
Villanova U, PA
Wake Forest U, NC
Washburn U, KS
Wayne State Coll, NE
Wayne State U, MI
Westchester Comm Coll, NY
West Chester U of Pennsylvania, PA
Western Connecticut State U, CT
Western New England Coll, MA
Western Tech Coll, WI
Westminster Coll, UT
Westmoreland County Comm Coll, PA
West Texas A&M U, TX
West Virginia State U, WV
West Virginia Wesleyan Coll, WV
Wichita State U, KS
Wofford Coll, SC
Wright State U, OH
Xavier U, OH

FINANCE AND FINANCIAL MANAGEMENT SERVICES RELATED

British Columbia Inst of Technology, BC, Canada
Johnson & Wales U, CO
Park U, MO
San Diego State U, CA
The U of Akron, OH

FINANCIAL PLANNING AND SERVICES

Baylor U, TX
British Columbia Inst of Technology, BC, Canada
Broome Comm Coll, NY
Howard Comm Coll, MD
Marywood U, PA
Northern Michigan U, MI
The Ohio State U at Lima, OH
The U of Maine at Augusta, ME
Waukesha County Tech Coll, WI
Widener U, PA

FINE ARTS RELATED

Abilene Christian U, TX
Adelphi U, NY
Ancilla Coll, IN
The Catholic U of America, DC
Coll of Staten Island of the City U of New York, NY
Kentucky Wesleyan Coll, KY
Long Island U, Brooklyn Campus, NY
Loyola U Chicago, IL
Monmouth U, NJ
Mount Vernon Nazarene U, OH
Our Lady of the Lake U of San Antonio, TX
Point Loma Nazarene U, CA
Pratt Inst, NY
Reedley Coll, CA
Rutgers, The State U of New Jersey, Newark, NJ
School of the Art Inst of Chicago, IL
Syracuse U, NY

The U of Akron, OH
U of California, Los Angeles, CA
U of Hartford, CT
Widener U, PA

FINE/STUDIO ARTS

Abilene Christian U, TX
Academy of Art U, CA
Alma Coll, MI
American U, DC
Amherst Coll, MA
Ancilla Coll, IN
Anderson U, IN
Anderson U, SC
Angelo State U, TX
Asbury Coll, KY
Ashland U, OH
Asnuntuck Comm Coll, CT
Augsburg Coll, MN
Ball State U, IN
Bard Coll, NY
Baylor U, TX
Bemidji State U, MN
Bishop's U, QC, Canada
Boston Coll, MA
Bradley U, IL
Brandeis U, MA
Brenau U, GA
Bridgewater Coll, VA
Brock U, ON, Canada
Brown U, RI
Buffalo State Coll, State U of New York, NY
California State U, Fullerton, CA
California State U, Stanislaus, CA
Calvin Coll, MI
Cardinal Stritch U, WI
Carroll Coll, WI
Carthage Coll, WI
The Catholic U of America, DC
Cedar Crest Coll, PA
Christopher Newport U, VA
Claremont McKenna Coll, CA
Clark U, MA
Coastal Carolina U, SC
Coe Coll, IA
Colby Coll, ME
Coll of Charleston, SC
Coll of Mount St. Joseph, OH
The Coll of Saint Rose, NY
Colorado Mountain Coll, Alpine Campus, CO
Concordia U, NE
Cornell U, NY
Daemen Coll, NY
DePaul U, IL
Drake U, IA
Drury U, MO
East Carolina U, NC
Edinboro U of Pennsylvania, PA
Elmira Coll, NY
Emory U, GA
Fashion Inst of Technology, NY
Ferrum Coll, VA
Flagler Coll, FL
Florida International U, FL
Fontbonne U, MO
Foothill Coll, CA
Framingham State Coll, MA
Franklin Pierce U, NH
Fulton-Montgomery Comm Coll, NY
Furman U, SC
Gardner-Webb U, NC
Georgetown Coll, KY

The George Washington U, DC
Georgian Court U, NJ
Gloucester County Coll, NJ
Graceland U, IA
Green Mountain Coll, VT
Hamilton Coll, NY
Hamline U, MN
Hampden-Sydney Coll, VA
Hampshire Coll, MA
Harding U, AR
High Point U, NC
Hofstra U, NY
Hope Coll, MI
Houston Baptist U, TX
Hudson Valley Comm Coll, NY
Hunter Coll of the City U of New York, NY
Illinois State U, IL
Indiana U Bloomington, IN
Indiana U–Purdue U Fort Wayne, IN
Indiana U–Purdue U Indianapolis, IN
Indiana U Southeast, IN
Ithaca Coll, NY
Jacksonville U, FL
Jamestown Comm Coll, NY
Johnson State Coll, VT
Kenyon Coll, OH
Kutztown U of Pennsylvania, PA
Lake Erie Coll, OH
Lamar U, TX
Lawrence U, WI
Lebanon Valley Coll, PA
Lewis U, IL
Lindenwood U, MO
Loras Coll, IA
Loyola Marymount U, CA
Macalester Coll, MN
MacMurray Coll, IL
Manhattanville Coll, NY
Marian Coll, IN
Marietta Coll, OH
Marist Coll, NY
Marymount Manhattan Coll, NY
Marymount U, VA
Marywood U, PA
Massasoit Comm Coll, MA
Mercyhurst Coll, PA
Middlesex Comm Coll, CT
Middlesex County Coll, NJ
Midland Coll, TX
Minneapolis Coll of Art and Design, MN
Minnesota State U Mankato, MN
Minnesota State U Moorhead, MN
Missouri State U, MO
Montana State U, MT
Moravian Coll, PA
Morningside Coll, IA
Morton Coll, IL
Mount Holyoke Coll, MA
Mount Saint Vincent U, NS, Canada
Murray State U, KY
Naropa U, CO
New York U, NY
Northern Illinois U, IL
Northwestern Coll, MN
Notre Dame Coll, OH
Notre Dame de Namur U, CA
NSCAD U, NS, Canada
Occidental Coll, CA
The Ohio State U, OH
Ohio Wesleyan U, OH
Old Dominion U, VA
Oral Roberts U, OK

Otis Coll of Art and Design, CA
Park U, MO
Piedmont Coll, GA
Pine Manor Coll, MA
Pratt Inst, NY
Queens Coll of the City U of New York, NY
Queens U of Charlotte, NC
Ramapo Coll of New Jersey, NJ
Randolph Coll, VA
Randolph-Macon Coll, VA
Rhodes Coll, TN
Rice U, TX
Ringling Coll of Art and Design, FL
Rivier Coll, NH
Rochester Inst of Technology, NY
Rowan U, NJ
Saginaw Valley State U, MI
St. Cloud State U, MN
St. Gregory's U, OK
Saint John's U, MN
Saint Joseph's Coll, IN
St. Lawrence U, NY
St. Thomas Aquinas Coll, NY
Salve Regina U, RI
San Diego State U, CA
Santa Barbara City Coll, CA
School of the Art Inst of Chicago, IL
School of Visual Arts, NY
Seton Hill U, PA
Sewanee: The U of the South, TN
Southern Illinois U Carbondale, IL
Southern Illinois U Edwardsville, IL
Southern U and A&M Coll, LA
Southwestern U, TX
State U of New York at Fredonia, NY
State U of New York Coll at Brockport, NY
State U of New York Coll at Cortland, NY
State U of New York Coll at Geneseo, NY
Stonehill Coll, MA
Sussex County Comm Coll, NJ
Sweet Briar Coll, VA
Syracuse U, NY
Texas A&M U–Corpus Christi, TX
Tidewater Comm Coll, VA
Trinity Coll, CT
Troy U, AL
Truman State U, MO
Union Coll, NE
U at Buffalo, the State U of New York, NY
The U of Akron, OH
The U of Alabama, AL
The U of Arizona, AZ
U of California, Irvine, CA
U of California, Santa Barbara, CA
U of Central Florida, FL
U of Central Missouri, MO
U of Colorado at Boulder, CO
U of Connecticut, CT
U of Dayton, OH
U of Great Falls, MT
U of Guelph, ON, Canada
U of Houston, TX
U of Kansas, KS
U of Kentucky, KY

The U of Maine at Augusta, ME
U of Mary Hardin-Baylor, TX
U of Mary Washington, VA
U of Massachusetts Amherst, MA
U of Massachusetts Lowell, MA
U of Miami, FL
U of Minnesota, Duluth, MN
U of Missouri–Kansas City, MO
U of Nebraska at Omaha, NE
U of Nebraska–Lincoln, NE
U of New Hampshire, NH
U of New Hampshire at Manchester, NH
U of New Haven, CT
U of New Orleans, LA
The U of North Carolina at Asheville, NC
The U of North Carolina at Chapel Hill, NC
The U of North Carolina at Charlotte, NC
U of Northern Iowa, IA
U of North Florida, FL
U of Notre Dame, IN
U of Oregon, OR
U of Pennsylvania, PA
U of Pittsburgh, PA
U of Redlands, CA
U of St. Thomas, TX
U of San Francisco, CA
The U of Tennessee, TN
The U of Texas at Austin, TX
The U of Texas at El Paso, TX
U of the District of Columbia, DC
U of the Pacific, CA
U of Toronto, ON, Canada
U of Vermont, VT
U of Wisconsin–Oshkosh, WI
U of Wisconsin–Stevens Point, WI
Ursuline Coll, OH
Vassar Coll, NY
Ventura Coll, CA
Wake Forest U, NC
Washington and Lee U, VA
Watkins Coll of Art and Design, TN
Wellesley Coll, MA
Wells Coll, NY
Westchester Comm Coll, NY
West Chester U of Pennsylvania, PA
West Texas A&M U, TX
West Virginia Wesleyan Coll, WV
Xavier U, OH

FIRE PROTECTION AND SAFETY TECHNOLOGY
British Columbia Inst of Technology, BC, Canada
Bunker Hill Comm Coll, MA
Comm Coll of Allegheny County, PA
Florida Comm Coll at Jacksonville, FL
Kellogg Comm Coll, MI
Lamar Inst of Technology, TX
Lincoln Land Comm Coll, IL
Macomb Comm Coll, MI
Montana State U–Billings, MT
Ocean County Coll, NJ
Oklahoma State U, OK

The U of Akron, OH
U of Cincinnati, OH
U of Nebraska–Lincoln, NE
U of New Haven, CT
Victor Valley Coll, CA
Waubonsee Comm Coll, IL
Waukesha County Tech Coll, WI
Western Tech Coll, WI

FIRE PROTECTION RELATED
Sussex County Comm Coll, NJ
The U of Akron, OH
U of New Haven, CT

FIRE SCIENCE
Aims Comm Coll, CO
Blinn Coll, TX
Brevard Comm Coll, FL
Broome Comm Coll, NY
Broward Comm Coll, FL
Burlington County Coll, NJ
Cape Cod Comm Coll, MA
Central Florida Comm Coll, FL
Central Piedmont Comm Coll, NC
Chattahoochee Tech Coll, GA
Chattanooga State Tech Comm Coll, TN
City Colls of Chicago, Richard J. Daley Coll, IL
Coll of the Desert, CA
Coosa Valley Tech Coll, GA
Cosumnes River Coll, Sacramento, CA
Crafton Hills Coll, CA
East Central Coll, MO
Eastern New Mexico U–Roswell, NM
El Camino Coll, CA
Florida Comm Coll at Jacksonville, FL
Frederick Comm Coll, MD
Fresno City Coll, CA
Gaston Coll, NC
Glendale Comm Coll, CA
Greenville Tech Coll, SC
Harrisburg Area Comm Coll, PA
Hillsborough Comm Coll, FL
Hocking Coll, OH
Houston Comm Coll System, TX
Idaho State U, ID
Lake-Sumter Comm Coll, FL
Lake Superior State U, MI
Lamar U, TX
Laredo Comm Coll, TX
Long Beach City Coll, CA
Massasoit Comm Coll, MA
Maui Comm Coll, HI
Miami Dade Coll, FL
Middlesex County Coll, NJ
Midland Coll, TX
Missouri State U–West Plains, MO
New Mexico Jr Coll, NM
Odessa Coll, TX
Ozarks Tech Comm Coll, MO
Phoenix Coll, AZ
Pima Comm Coll, AZ
Quincy Coll, MA
Richland Comm Coll, IL
St. Louis Comm Coll at Florissant Valley, MO
Santa Ana Coll, CA
Santa Rosa Jr Coll, CA
Schoolcraft Coll, MI
Scottsdale Comm Coll, AZ

Seminole Comm Coll, FL
Shasta Coll, CA
Skagit Valley Coll, WA
Southern Maine Comm Coll, ME
Spokane Comm Coll, WA
Stark State Coll of Technology, OH
U of Alaska Anchorage, AK
U of Cincinnati, OH
The U of Montana-Helena Coll of Technology, MT
U of New Brunswick Fredericton, NB, Canada
U of the District of Columbia, DC
Valencia Comm Coll, FL
Victor Valley Coll, CA
Westmoreland County Comm Coll, PA

FIRE SERVICES ADMINISTRATION
Calhoun Comm Coll, AL
Comm Coll of Aurora, CO
Midland Coll, TX
Southern Illinois U Carbondale, IL
Western Oregon U, OR

FISH/GAME MANAGEMENT
Abraham Baldwin Coll, GA
Chattanooga State Tech Comm Coll, TN
Delaware State U, DE
Hocking Coll, OH
Itasca Comm Coll, MN
Lake Superior State U, MI
Pittsburg State U, KS
State U of New York Coll of Environmental Science and Forestry, NY
U of Minnesota, Duluth, MN
U of Missouri–Columbia, MO
U of New Brunswick Fredericton, NB, Canada

FISHING AND FISHERIES SCIENCES AND MANAGEMENT
Clemson U, SC
Hocking Coll, OH
Murray State U, KY
North Carolina State U, NC
The Ohio State U, OH
Santa Rosa Jr Coll, CA
State U of New York Coll of Environmental Science and Forestry, NY
Sterling Coll, VT
Texas A&M U, TX
Unity Coll, ME
U of Missouri–Columbia, MO
U of Northern British Columbia, BC, Canada
U of Rhode Island, RI
The U of Tennessee at Martin, TN
U of Washington, WA

FLORICULTURE/ FLORISTRY MANAGEMENT
Cornell U, NY
Santa Rosa Jr Coll, CA

FOLKLORE
Indiana U Bloomington, IN
The Ohio State U, OH
U of Oregon, OR

FOOD/NUTRITION
Radford U, VA
Southern Illinois U Carbondale, IL

FOOD PREPARATION
The Art Inst of Pittsburgh, PA

FOODS AND NUTRITION RELATED
Framingham State Coll, MA
Marywood U, PA
San Diego Mesa Coll, CA
U of Wisconsin–Stout, WI

FOOD SCIENCE
Acadia U, NS, Canada
Alabama A&M U, AL
Central Piedmont Comm Coll, NC
Clemson U, SC
Cornell U, NY
Dalhousie U, NS, Canada
Dominican U, IL
El Centro Coll, TX
Framingham State Coll, MA
Hocking Coll, OH
Kansas State U, KS
Lamar U, TX
Miami Dade Coll, FL
Michigan State U, MI
North Carolina State U, NC
North Dakota State U, ND
The Ohio State U, OH
Penn State Abington, PA
Penn State DuBois, PA
Penn State Fayette, The Eberly Campus, PA
Penn State Mont Alto, PA
Penn State Wilkes-Barre, PA
Rutgers, The State U of New Jersey, New Brunswick, NJ
St. Louis Comm Coll at Florissant Valley, MO
Texas A&M U, TX
The U of Akron, OH
U of Arkansas, AR
U of Delaware, DE
U of Guelph, ON, Canada
U of Illinois at Urbana–Champaign, IL
U of Kentucky, KY
U of Manitoba, MB, Canada
U of Massachusetts Amherst, MA
U of Missouri–Columbia, MO
U of Nebraska–Lincoln, NE
The U of Tennessee, TN
U of the District of Columbia, DC
U of Wisconsin–Madison, WI

FOOD SCIENCE AND TECHNOLOGY RELATED
Framingham State Coll, MA

FOOD SCIENCES
U of Illinois at Urbana–Champaign, IL

FOOD SERVICE AND DINING ROOM MANAGEMENT
The Art Inst of Pittsburgh, PA
Johnson & Wales U, CO
Johnson & Wales U, FL
Johnson & Wales U, NC

FOOD SERVICES TECHNOLOGY

Central Piedmont Comm Coll, NC
Chattanooga State Tech Comm Coll, TN
El Centro Coll, TX
Fresno City Coll, CA
Johnson & Wales U, RI
Long Beach City Coll, CA
Maui Comm Coll, HI
Mohawk Valley Comm Coll, NY
Richland Comm Coll, IL
St. Louis Comm Coll at Florissant Valley, MO
Skagit Valley Coll, WA
Southern Maine Comm Coll, ME
Spokane Comm Coll, WA
Stark State Coll of Technology, OH
U of the District of Columbia, DC
Victor Valley Coll, CA
Washburn U, KS
Westchester Comm Coll, NY
Western Tech Coll, WI

FOODSERVICE SYSTEMS ADMINISTRATION

Burlington County Coll, NJ
Comm Coll of Allegheny County, PA
Dominican U, IL
Florida Comm Coll at Jacksonville, FL
Johnson & Wales U, RI
Mohawk Valley Comm Coll, NY
Murray State U, KY
Rochester Inst of Technology, NY
Santa Barbara City Coll, CA
U of New Haven, CT
U of Wisconsin–Stout, WI

FOODS, NUTRITION, AND WELLNESS

Acadia U, NS, Canada
Ashland U, OH
Bridgewater Coll, VA
California State U, San Bernardino, CA
Carson-Newman Coll, TN
Cedar Crest Coll, PA
Cuesta Coll, CA
Delaware State U, DE
Dominican U, IL
Framingham State Coll, MA
Harrisburg Area Comm Coll, PA
Hunter Coll of the City U of New York, NY
Idaho State U, ID
Immaculata U, PA
Indiana U Bloomington, IN
Indiana U of Pennsylvania, PA
Ithaca Coll, NY
Kansas State U, KS
Langston U, OK
Loyola U Chicago, IL
McNeese State U, LA
Middle Tennessee State U, TN
Minnesota State U Mankato, MN
Mount Saint Vincent U, NS, Canada
Murray State U, KY
New York U, NY
Northern Illinois U, IL
The Ohio State U, OH

Point Loma Nazarene U, CA
Prairie View A&M U, TX
St. Francis Xavier U, NS, Canada
Saint John's U, MN
San Diego Mesa Coll, CA
Santa Ana Coll, CA
Seattle Pacific U, WA
Southern Adventist U, TN
Southern Illinois U Carbondale, IL
Stephen F. Austin State U, TX
Syracuse U, NY
Texas A&M U, TX
The U of Akron, OH
The U of Alabama, AL
U of Arkansas, AR
U of Central Oklahoma, OK
U of Cincinnati, OH
U of Dayton, OH
U of Delaware, DE
U of Houston, TX
U of Kentucky, KY
U of Manitoba, MB, Canada
U of Missouri–Columbia, MO
U of Nebraska–Lincoln, NE
U of New Hampshire, NH
U of New Mexico, NM
The U of North Carolina at Chapel Hill, NC
U of Northern Iowa, IA
U of Rhode Island, RI
The U of Tennessee, TN
The U of Texas at Austin, TX
U of the Incarnate Word, TX
U of Toronto, ON, Canada
U of Wisconsin–Madison, WI
Wayne State U, MI

FOREIGN LANGUAGES AND LITERATURES

American U, DC
Auburn U Montgomery, AL
Carnegie Mellon U, PA
Comm Coll of Allegheny County, PA
Concordia U Coll of Alberta, AB, Canada
Dixie State Coll of Utah, UT
Eckerd Coll, FL
Elmira Coll, NY
Elon U, NC
Framingham State Coll, MA
Gainesville State Coll, GA
Gannon U, PA
Glendale Comm Coll, CA
Gordon Coll, MA
Graceland U, IA
Kansas State U, KS
Kenyon Coll, OH
Long Island U, Brooklyn Campus, NY
Marshall U, WV
Mercyhurst Coll, PA
Middle Tennessee State U, TN
Midland Coll, TX
Minnesota State U Moorhead, MN
Monmouth U, NJ
Montana State U, MT
Old Dominion U, VA
Queens U of Charlotte, NC
Radford U, VA
Reedley Coll, CA
The Richard Stockton Coll of New Jersey, NJ
Roosevelt U, IL
Rutgers, The State U of New Jersey, New Brunswick, NJ

St. Lawrence U, NY
St. Mary's Coll of Maryland, MD
Seton Hall U, NJ
Skagit Valley Coll, WA
Southern Adventist U, TN
Southern Illinois U Edwardsville, IL
Stonehill Coll, MA
Sweet Briar Coll, VA
Syracuse U, NY
The U of Alabama in Huntsville, AL
U of Alaska Anchorage, AK
U of Central Florida, FL
U of Delaware, DE
U of Hartford, CT
U of Massachusetts Lowell, MA
U of New Mexico, NM
U of Northern Iowa, IA
The U of Scranton, PA
U of South Carolina Beaufort, SC
The U of Texas at Austin, TX
The U of Virginia's Coll at Wise, VA
Washington and Lee U, VA
Wayne State U, MI
Widener U, PA
Wright State U, OH

FOREIGN LANGUAGES RELATED

Edinboro U of Pennsylvania, PA
Hofstra U, NY
Houston Baptist U, TX
Marquette U, WI
Southern Illinois U Carbondale, IL
U of California, Berkeley, CA
U of California, Los Angeles, CA
U of Northern Iowa, IA
U of St. Thomas, MN
Yale U, CT

FOREIGN LANGUAGE TEACHER EDUCATION

Baylor U, TX
Buffalo State Coll, State U of New York, NY
Carroll Coll, WI
The Catholic U of America, DC
Eastern Michigan U, MI
Elmira Coll, NY
Florida International U, FL
Framingham State Coll, MA
Gannon U, PA
Gardner-Webb U, NC
Hofstra U, NY
Le Moyne Coll, NY
Lincoln U, PA
Marquette U, WI
McNeese State U, LA
Mercyhurst Coll, PA
Millersville U of Pennsylvania, PA
Moravian Coll, PA
Murray State U, KY
New York U, NY
North Carolina State U, NC
Ohio Wesleyan U, OH
Old Dominion U, VA
Oral Roberts U, OK
Penn State Abington, PA
Penn State DuBois, PA
Penn State Fayette, The Eberly Campus, PA
Penn State Mont Alto, PA

Rivier Coll, NH
St. Bonaventure U, NY
Seton Hill U, PA
State U of New York Coll at Brockport, NY
Temple U, PA
U at Albany, State U of New York, NY
The U of Akron, OH
The U of Arizona, AZ
U of Central Florida, FL
U of Delaware, DE
U of Illinois at Urbana–Champaign, IL
U of Nebraska–Lincoln, NE
U of New Orleans, LA
U of Northern Iowa, IA
U of St. Thomas, MN
U of Vermont, VT
Wayne State Coll, NE
West Chester U of Pennsylvania, PA
Wright State U, OH

FORENSIC PSYCHOLOGY

Florida Inst of Technology, FL

FORENSIC SCIENCE AND TECHNOLOGY

Alvernia Coll, PA
Arkansas State U–Newport, AR
Baylor U, TX
British Columbia Inst of Technology, BC, Canada
Buffalo State Coll, State U of New York, NY
Carroll Coll, WI
Cedar Crest Coll, PA
Hudson Valley Comm Coll, NY
Indiana U Bloomington, IN
Loyola U New Orleans, LA
Macomb Comm Coll, MI
Mercyhurst Coll, PA
Mohawk Valley Comm Coll, NY
New River Comm Coll, VA
Northern Michigan U, MI
Northwest Nazarene U, ID
Seton Hill U, PA
Springfield Coll in Illinois, IL
Towson U, MD
Tunxis Comm Coll, CT
U of Arkansas at Fort Smith, AR
U of Baltimore, MD
U of Central Florida, FL
U of Central Oklahoma, OK
U of Great Falls, MT
U of Mississippi, MS
U of New Haven, CT
U of Toronto, ON, Canada
Washburn U, KS

FOREST ENGINEERING

State U of New York Coll of Environmental Science and Forestry, NY
U of New Brunswick Fredericton, NB, Canada
U of Washington, WA

FOREST/FOREST RESOURCES MANAGEMENT

Allegany Coll of Maryland, MD
British Columbia Inst of Technology, BC, Canada
Clemson U, SC
Lake City Comm Coll, FL

North Carolina State U, NC
State U of New York Coll of Environmental Science and Forestry, NY
Stephen F. Austin State U, TX
Sterling Coll, VT
Texas A&M U, TX
U of California, Berkeley, CA
U of Toronto, ON, Canada
U of Washington, WA
Western Nebraska Comm Coll, NE

FOREST PRODUCTS TECHNOLOGY

Pittsburg State U, KS

FOREST RESOURCES PRODUCTION AND MANAGEMENT

Sterling Coll, VT

FORESTRY

Abraham Baldwin Coll, GA
Albright Coll, PA
Bainbridge Coll, GA
Baylor U, TX
Chattanooga State Tech Comm Coll, TN
Clayton State U, GA
Columbus State U, GA
Delaware State U, DE
Dixie State Coll of Utah, UT
Feather River Coll, CA
Gainesville State Coll, GA
Hocking Coll, OH
Itasca Comm Coll, MN
Miami Dade Coll, FL
Michigan State U, MI
The Ohio State U, OH
Oklahoma State U, OK
Saint John's U, MN
Sewanee: The U of the South, TN
Southern Illinois U Carbondale, IL
Spokane Comm Coll, WA
State U of New York Coll of Environmental Science and Forestry, NY
Stephen F. Austin State U, TX
Sterling Coll, VT
Texas A&M U, TX
Unity Coll, ME
U of California, Berkeley, CA
U of Illinois at Urbana–Champaign, IL
U of Massachusetts Amherst, MA
U of Missouri–Columbia, MO
U of New Brunswick Fredericton, NB, Canada
U of New Hampshire, NH
The U of Tennessee, TN
U of the District of Columbia, DC
U of Toronto, ON, Canada
U of Vermont, VT
U of Washington, WA
U of Wisconsin-Madison, WI
U of Wisconsin–Stevens Point, WI

FORESTRY RELATED

Sterling Coll, VT
The U of Tennessee at Martin, TN

FORESTRY TECHNOLOGY
Abraham Baldwin Coll, GA
British Columbia Inst of Technology, BC, Canada
Chattanooga State Tech Comm Coll, TN
Dabney S. Lancaster Comm Coll, VA
El Camino Coll, CA
Glenville State Coll, WV
Hocking Coll, OH
Itasca Comm Coll, MN
Lake City Comm Coll, FL
Penn State Abington, PA
Penn State DuBois, PA
Penn State Fayette, The Eberly Campus, PA
Penn State Mont Alto, PA
Penn State Wilkes-Barre, PA
State U of New York Coll of Environmental Science & Forestry, Ranger School, NY
State U of New York Coll of Technology at Canton, NY
U of New Hampshire, NH

FOREST SCIENCES AND BIOLOGY
Penn State Abington, PA
Penn State DuBois, PA
Penn State Fayette, The Eberly Campus, PA
Penn State Mont Alto, PA
Penn State Wilkes-Barre, PA
State U of New York Coll of Environmental Science and Forestry, NY
Sterling Coll, VT
U of Illinois at Urbana–Champaign, IL
U of Kentucky, KY
U of Northern British Columbia, BC, Canada
U of Washington, WA

FRENCH
Acadia U, NS, Canada
Adelphi U, NY
Albany State U, GA
Albion Coll, MI
Albright Coll, PA
Alma Coll, MI
American U, DC
Anderson U, IN
Angelo State U, TX
Asbury Coll, KY
Ashland U, OH
Athabasca U, AB, Canada
Augsburg Coll, MN
Austin Coll, TX
Ball State U, IN
Bard Coll, NY
Barry U, FL
Bates Coll, ME
Baylor U, TX
Benedictine Coll, KS
Bethel U, MN
Bishop's U, QC, Canada
Blinn Coll, TX
Boston Coll, MA
Bradley U, IL
Brandeis U, MA
Brandon U, MB, Canada
Bridgewater Coll, VA
Brock U, ON, Canada
Brown U, RI
Bryn Mawr Coll, PA
Buffalo State Coll, State U of New York, NY
California State U, Fullerton, CA

California State U, Northridge, CA
California State U, Sacramento, CA
California State U, San Bernardino, CA
California State U, Stanislaus, CA
Calvin Coll, MI
Cape Breton U, NS, Canada
Cardinal Stritch U, WI
Carleton U, ON, Canada
Carnegie Mellon U, PA
Carroll Coll, MT
Carson-Newman Coll, TN
Carthage Coll, WI
The Catholic U of America, DC
Christopher Newport U, VA
Citrus Coll, CA
Claremont McKenna Coll, CA
Clark U, MA
Clayton State U, GA
Coe Coll, IA
Colby Coll, ME
Colgate U, NY
Coll of Charleston, SC
Coll of Mount Saint Vincent, NY
Coll of the Canyons, CA
Coll of the Desert, CA
The Coll of William and Mary, VA
Concordia U Coll of Alberta, AB, Canada
Cornell U, NY
Crafton Hills Coll, CA
Daemen Coll, NY
Dalhousie U, NS, Canada
Delaware State U, DE
DePaul U, IL
Dominican U, IL
Drury U, MO
Duke U, NC
Earlham Coll, IN
East Carolina U, NC
Eastern Mennonite U, VA
Eastern Michigan U, MI
East Stroudsburg U of Pennsylvania, PA
Eckerd Coll, FL
Elmira Coll, NY
Elms Coll, MA
Elon U, NC
Emory U, GA
Fairfield U, CT
Fairleigh Dickinson U, Coll at Florham, NJ
Fairleigh Dickinson U, Metropolitan Campus, NJ
Florida Atlantic U, FL
Florida International U, FL
Fort Hays State U, KS
Framingham State Coll, MA
Franciscan U of Steubenville, OH
Franklin Coll, IN
Furman U, SC
Gardner-Webb U, NC
Georgetown Coll, KY
The George Washington U, DC
Georgia Coll & State U, GA
Gonzaga U, WA
Gordon Coll, MA
Grace Coll, IN
Grambling State U, LA
Grinnell Coll, IA
Grossmont Coll, CA
Gustavus Adolphus Coll, MN
Hamilton Coll, NY
Hamline U, MN

Hampden-Sydney Coll, VA
Harding U, AR
Hartwick Coll, NY
Haverford Coll, PA
High Point U, NC
Hofstra U, NY
Hope Coll, MI
Houghton Coll, NY
Houston Baptist U, TX
Hunter Coll of the City U of New York, NY
Idaho State U, ID
Illinois State U, IL
Illinois Wesleyan U, IL
Immaculata U, PA
Indiana U Bloomington, IN
Indiana U of Pennsylvania, PA
Indiana U–Purdue U Fort Wayne, IN
Indiana U–Purdue U Indianapolis, IN
Indiana U Southeast, IN
Iona Coll, NY
Ithaca Coll, NY
Jacksonville U, FL
Kennesaw State U, GA
Kenyon Coll, OH
King's Coll, PA
Kutztown U of Pennsylvania, PA
Lake Erie Coll, OH
Lamar U, TX
Lawrence U, WI
Lebanon Valley Coll, PA
Lee Coll, TX
Lehigh U, PA
Le Moyne Coll, NY
Lincoln U, PA
Lindenwood U, MO
Long Beach City Coll, CA
Loras Coll, IA
Loyola Marymount U, CA
Loyola U Chicago, IL
Loyola U New Orleans, LA
Lynchburg Coll, VA
Macalester Coll, MN
Manhattan Coll, NY
Manhattanville Coll, NY
Marian Coll, IN
Marist Coll, NY
Marquette U, WI
Marywood U, PA
McDaniel Coll, MD
McNeese State U, LA
Mercer U, GA
Mercyhurst Coll, PA
Miami Dade Coll, FL
Michigan State U, MI
Midland Coll, TX
Millersville U of Pennsylvania, PA
Minnesota State U Mankato, MN
MiraCosta Coll, CA
Missouri State U, MO
Molloy Coll, NY
Monmouth Coll, IL
Moravian Coll, PA
Mount Holyoke Coll, MA
Mount St. Mary's U, MD
Mount Saint Vincent U, NS, Canada
Mount Union Coll, OH
Murray State U, KY
New York U, NY
Niagara U, NY
North Carolina State U, NC
North Central Coll, IL
North Dakota State U, ND
Northeastern U, MA
Northern Illinois U, IL
Northern Michigan U, MI
Northern State U, SD

North Georgia Coll & State U, GA
Oakland U, MI
Occidental Coll, CA
Oglethorpe U, GA
The Ohio State U, OH
Ohio Wesleyan U, OH
Oklahoma State U, OK
Old Dominion U, VA
Oral Roberts U, OK
Otterbein Coll, OH
Penn State Abington, PA
Penn State DuBois, PA
Penn State Fayette, The Eberly Campus, PA
Penn State Mont Alto, PA
Penn State Wilkes-Barre, PA
Pittsburg State U, KS
Portland State U, OR
Presbyterian Coll, SC
Queens Coll of the City U of New York, NY
Queen's U at Kingston, ON, Canada
Randolph Coll, VA
Randolph-Macon Coll, VA
Redeemer U Coll, ON, Canada
Rhodes Coll, TN
Rice U, TX
Ripon Coll, WI
Rivier Coll, NH
Rockford Coll, IL
Rockhurst U, MO
Rutgers, The State U of New Jersey, Newark, NJ
Rutgers, The State U of New Jersey, New Brunswick, NJ
Saginaw Valley State U, MI
St. Bonaventure U, NY
St. Cloud State U, MN
St. Francis Xavier U, NS, Canada
Saint John's U, MN
St. Lawrence U, NY
St. Norbert Coll, WI
St. Thomas U, NB, Canada
Salve Regina U, RI
San Diego Mesa Coll, CA
San Diego State U, CA
San Francisco State U, CA
Santa Barbara City Coll, CA
Santa Clara U, CA
Sauk Valley Comm Coll, IL
Seattle Pacific U, WA
Seton Hall U, NJ
Sewanee: The U of the South, TN
Shippensburg U of Pennsylvania, PA
Slippery Rock U of Pennsylvania, PA
Southern Adventist U, TN
Southern Illinois U Carbondale, IL
Southern Oregon U, OR
Southern U and A&M Coll, LA
Southern Utah U, UT
Southwestern U, TX
State U of New York at Fredonia, NY
State U of New York Coll at Brockport, NY
State U of New York Coll at Cortland, NY
State U of New York Coll at Geneseo, NY
State U of New York Coll at Potsdam, NY
Stephen F. Austin State U, TX
Stetson U, FL
Sweet Briar Coll, VA

Syracuse U, NY
Taylor U, IN
Temple U, PA
Texas A&M U, TX
Towson U, MD
Trent U, ON, Canada
Trinity Coll, CT
Trinity U, TX
Truman State U, MO
Tufts U, MA
Union Coll, NE
U at Albany, State U of New York, NY
U at Buffalo, the State U of New York, NY
The U of Akron, OH
The U of Alabama, AL
The U of Arizona, AZ
U of Arkansas, AR
U of California, Berkeley, CA
U of California, Irvine, CA
U of California, Los Angeles, CA
U of California, Santa Barbara, CA
U of Central Florida, FL
U of Central Missouri, MO
U of Central Oklahoma, OK
U of Cincinnati, OH
U of Colorado at Boulder, CO
U of Connecticut, CT
U of Dayton, OH
U of Delaware, DE
U of Evansville, IN
U of Hawaii at Manoa, HI
U of Houston, TX
U of Illinois at Urbana–Champaign, IL
U of Kansas, KS
U of Kentucky, KY
U of Manitoba, MB, Canada
U of Maryland, Baltimore County, MD
U of Mary Washington, VA
U of Massachusetts Amherst, MA
U of Massachusetts Boston, MA
U of Miami, FL
U of Michigan, MI
U of Mississippi, MS
U of Missouri–Columbia, MO
U of Missouri–Kansas City, MO
U of Nebraska at Kearney, NE
U of Nebraska at Omaha, NE
U of Nebraska–Lincoln, NE
U of New Brunswick Fredericton, NB, Canada
U of New Hampshire, NH
U of New Mexico, NM
U of New Orleans, LA
The U of North Carolina at Asheville, NC
The U of North Carolina at Charlotte, NC
U of Northern Iowa, IA
U of Notre Dame, IN
U of Oregon, OR
U of Pennsylvania, PA
U of Pittsburgh, PA
U of Redlands, CA
U of Rhode Island, RI
U of St. Thomas, MN
U of St. Thomas, TX
U of San Diego, CA
U of San Francisco, CA
The U of Scranton, PA

U of South Carolina Upstate,
SC
U of Southern Indiana, IN
The U of Tennessee, TN
The U of Tennessee at
Martin, TN
The U of Texas at Austin,
TX
The U of Texas at El Paso,
TX
The U of Texas at San
Antonio, TX
U of the District of
Columbia, DC
U of the Pacific, CA
U of Toronto, ON, Canada
U of Vermont, VT
U of Virginia, VA
The U of Virginia's Coll at
Wise, VA
U of Washington, WA
U of West Georgia, GA
U of Wisconsin–Eau Claire,
WI
U of Wisconsin–Green Bay,
WI
U of Wisconsin–La Crosse,
WI
U of Wisconsin–Madison,
WI
U of Wisconsin–Oshkosh,
WI
U of Wisconsin–Stevens
Point, WI
U of Wyoming, WY
Valdosta State U, GA
Vassar Coll, NY
Villanova U, PA
Wake Forest U, NC
Washburn U, KS
Washington & Jefferson Coll,
PA
Washington and Lee U, VA
Wayne State Coll, NE
Wellesley Coll, MA
Wells Coll, NY
West Chester U of
Pennsylvania, PA
Western Nebraska Comm
Coll, NE
West Los Angeles Coll, CA
Westminster Coll, PA
Wheaton Coll, IL
Whitman Coll, WA
Wichita State U, KS
Widener U, PA
Wilfrid Laurier U, ON,
Canada
Wilkes U, PA
William Jewell Coll, MO
Wilson Coll, PA
Wofford Coll, SC
Wright State U, OH
Xavier U, OH
Yale U, CT

**FRENCH AS A SECOND/
FOREIGN LANGUAGE
(TEACHING)**
Bishop's U, QC, Canada
U of Toronto, ON, Canada

**FRENCH LANGUAGE
TEACHER EDUCATION**
Alma Coll, MI
Anderson U, IN
Baylor U, TX
Bethel U, MN
Bishop's U, QC, Canada
Carroll Coll, WI
The Catholic U of America,
DC
Columbus State U, GA
Daemen Coll, NY

Delaware State U, DE
East Carolina U, NC
Eastern Mennonite U, VA
Eastern Michigan U, MI
Elmira Coll, NY
Franklin Coll, IN
Gardner-Webb U, NC
Grace Coll, IN
Grambling State U, LA
Hofstra U, NY
Hope Coll, MI
Illinois Wesleyan U, IL
Indiana U Bloomington, IN
Indiana U–Purdue U Fort
Wayne, IN
Indiana U–Purdue U
Indianapolis, IN
Iona Coll, NY
Ithaca Coll, NY
Lebanon Valley Coll, PA
Le Moyne Coll, NY
Lindenwood U, MO
Manhattanville Coll, NY
Marist Coll, NY
Marywood U, PA
Missouri State U, MO
Molloy Coll, NY
Moravian Coll, PA
Murray State U, KY
New York U, NY
Niagara U, NY
North Carolina State U, NC
North Dakota State U, ND
Northern Michigan U, MI
Ohio Wesleyan U, OH
Old Dominion U, VA
Oral Roberts U, OK
Pittsburg State U, KS
St. Bonaventure U, NY
Salve Regina U, RI
Seton Hill U, PA
Southern U and A&M Coll,
LA
State U of New York Coll at
Brockport, NY
State U of New York Coll at
Cortland, NY
State U of New York Coll at
Potsdam, NY
U at Albany, State U of New
York, NY
The U of Akron, OH
The U of Arizona, AZ
U of Evansville, IN
U of Illinois at Urbana–
Champaign, IL
U of Minnesota, Duluth, MN
U of Nebraska–Lincoln, NE
The U of North Carolina at
Charlotte, NC
The U of Tennessee at
Martin, TN
U of Toronto, ON, Canada
West Chester U of
Pennsylvania, PA
Widener U, PA

FRENCH STUDIES
Brock U, ON, Canada
Brown U, RI
Claremont McKenna Coll,
CA
Coe Coll, IA
Concordia U Coll of Alberta,
AB, Canada
Lake Superior State U, MI
Santa Clara U, CA
The U of Alabama, AL
U of Guelph, ON, Canada
Wilfrid Laurier U, ON,
Canada

**FUNERAL SERVICE AND
MORTUARY SCIENCE**
Gannon U, PA

Hudson Valley Comm Coll,
NY
Lindenwood U, MO
Miami Dade Coll, FL
Nassau Comm Coll, NY
Southern Illinois U
Carbondale, IL
State U of New York Coll of
Technology at Canton, NY
Thiel Coll, PA
U of Central Oklahoma, OK
U of the District of
Columbia, DC
Wayne State U, MI

**FURNITURE DESIGN
AND MANUFACTURING**
Rochester Inst of
Technology, NY

GAY/LESBIAN STUDIES
Cornell U, NY

**GENERAL RETAILING/
WHOLESALING**
Asheville-Buncombe Tech
Comm Coll, NC
Dixie State Coll of Utah, UT
Gadsden State Comm Coll,
AL
Harrisburg Area Comm Coll,
PA
Nassau Comm Coll, NY
St. Cloud Tech Coll, MN

GENERAL STUDIES
Alderson-Broaddus Coll, WV
Anderson U, IN
Angelo State U, TX
Arkansas State U–Newport,
AR
Asnuntuck Comm Coll, CT
Athabasca U, AB, Canada
Avila U, MO
Bluefield State Coll, WV
Brandon U, MB, Canada
Brenau U, GA
Brevard Coll, NC
Brewton-Parker Coll, GA
Buffalo State Coll, State U of
New York, NY
Bunker Hill Comm Coll, MA
Calhoun Comm Coll, AL
Carroll Coll, MT
The Catholic U of America,
DC
Central Wyoming Coll, WY
Coll of Saint Mary, NE
Comm Coll of Allegheny
County, PA
Dallas Baptist U, TX
DePaul U, IL
East Central Coll, MO
Eastern Connecticut State U,
CT
Eastern Mennonite U, VA
Eastern Nazarene Coll, MA
Eastern West Virginia Comm
and Tech Coll, WV
Fairleigh Dickinson U,
Metropolitan Campus, NJ
Fitchburg State Coll, MA
Florida Gulf Coast U, FL
Florida Inst of Technology,
FL
Franciscan U of
Steubenville, OH
Frederick Comm Coll, MD
Gadsden State Comm Coll,
AL
Gainesville State Coll, GA
Harding U, AR
Hope Coll, MI
Howard Comm Coll, MD
Idaho State U, ID

Indiana U Bloomington, IN
Indiana U of Pennsylvania,
PA
Indiana U–Purdue U Fort
Wayne, IN
Indiana U–Purdue U
Indianapolis, IN
Indiana U Southeast, IN
Itasca Comm Coll, MN
Ivy Tech Comm Coll–
Kokomo, IN
James H. Faulkner State
Comm Coll, AL
Johnson State Coll, VT
Kellogg Comm Coll, MI
Kutztown U of
Pennsylvania, PA
Lackawanna Coll, PA
Lebanon Valley Coll, PA
Liberty U, VA
Lincoln Land Comm Coll, IL
Loyola U Chicago, IL
Loyola U New Orleans, LA
Macomb Comm Coll, MI
Marshall U, WV
McNeese State U, LA
Miami Dade Coll, FL
Middlesex County Coll, NJ
MiraCosta Coll, CA
Missouri State U–West
Plains, MO
Mohawk Valley Comm Coll,
NY
Monmouth U, NJ
Montana State U–Billings,
MT
Mount Vernon Nazarene U,
OH
Murray State U, KY
Nassau Comm Coll, NY
New Hampshire Comm
Tech Coll, Nashua/
Claremont, NH
New River Comm Coll, VA
New York U, NY
Northern Michigan U, MI
Oak Hills Christian Coll, MN
Ocean County Coll, NJ
Ohio Wesleyan U, OH
Pima Comm Coll, AZ
Pittsburg State U, KS
Pueblo Comm Coll, CO
Quincy Coll, MA
Radford U, VA
Reedley Coll, CA
Rochester Inst of
Technology, NY
Roxbury Comm Coll, MA
Ryerson U, ON, Canada
Saginaw Valley State U, MI
Seattle Pacific U, WA
Seton Hill U, PA
Southern Adventist U, TN
Southern Maine Comm Coll,
ME
Southwest Baptist U, MO
Southwestern Coll, KS
Southwestern Michigan Coll,
MI
Springfield Coll, MA
Springfield Coll in Illinois, IL
Temple U, PA
Trevecca Nazarene U, TN
The U of Akron–Wayne
Coll, OH
U of Arkansas at Fort Smith,
AR
U of Connecticut, CT
U of Dayton, OH
U of Hartford, CT
U of Illinois at Urbana–
Champaign, IL
The U of Maine at Augusta,
ME

U of Maine at Machias, ME
U of Mary Hardin-Baylor, TX
U of Massachusetts Amherst,
MA
U of Miami, FL
U of Michigan, MI
U of Missouri–Columbia,
MO
The U of Montana-Helena
Coll of Technology, MT
U of Nebraska at Kearney,
NE
U of Nebraska at Omaha,
NE
U of New Hampshire, NH
U of New Haven, CT
U of New Mexico, NM
U of New Orleans, LA
U of Northern British
Columbia, BC, Canada
U of North Florida, FL
U of Rio Grande, OH
U of St. Thomas, TX
U of the Ozarks, AR
U of Washington, WA
U of Wisconsin–Green Bay,
WI
U of Wisconsin–La Crosse,
WI
U of Wisconsin–Stevens
Point, WI
Valdosta State U, GA
Virginia Intermont Coll, VA
Waubonsee Comm Coll, IL
Western Nebraska Comm
Coll, NE
West Texas A&M U, TX
West Virginia State Comm
and Tech Coll, WV

GENETICS
Clemson U, SC
Cornell U, NY
Ohio Wesleyan U, OH

GENETICS RELATED
The George Washington U,
DC

GEOCHEMISTRY
Brown U, RI
State U of New York at
Fredonia, NY
State U of New York Coll at
Cortland, NY
State U of New York Coll at
Geneseo, NY
U of California, Los Angeles,
CA
U of New Brunswick
Fredericton, NB, Canada

GEOGRAPHY
Ball State U, IN
Bemidji State U, MN
Bishop's U, QC, Canada
Brandon U, MB, Canada
Brock U, ON, Canada
Buffalo State Coll, State U of
New York, NY
California State U, Fullerton,
CA
California State U,
Northridge, CA
California State U,
Sacramento, CA
California State U, San
Bernardino, CA
California State U,
Stanislaus, CA
Calvin Coll, MI
Carleton U, ON, Canada
Carthage Coll, WI
Clark U, MA
Colgate U, NY

Coll of the Canyons, CA
Coll of the Desert, CA
Concordia U, NE
Concord U, WV
DePaul U, IL
East Carolina U, NC
Eastern Michigan U, MI
East Stroudsburg U of
Pennsylvania, PA
Edinboro U of Pennsylvania,
PA
El Camino Coll, CA
Fayetteville State U, NC
Fitchburg State Coll, MA
Florida Atlantic U, FL
Florida International U, FL
Framingham State Coll, MA
Gainesville State Coll, GA
The George Washington U,
DC
Grossmont Coll, CA
Gustavus Adolphus Coll,
MN
Hofstra U, NY
Hunter Coll of the City U of
New York, NY
Illinois State U, IL
Indiana U Bloomington, IN
Indiana U of Pennsylvania,
PA
Indiana U–Purdue U
Indianapolis, IN
Indiana U Southeast, IN
Itasca Comm Coll, MN
Jacksonville U, FL
Kansas State U, KS
Kutztown U of
Pennsylvania, PA
Macalester Coll, MN
Marshall U, WV
Michigan State U, MI
Millersville U of
Pennsylvania, PA
Minnesota State U Mankato,
MN
Missouri State U, MO
Mount Holyoke Coll, MA
Murray State U, KY
Nipissing U, ON, Canada
Northern Illinois U, IL
Northern Michigan U, MI
The Ohio State U, OH
Ohio Wesleyan U, OH
Oklahoma State U, OK
Old Dominion U, VA
Park U, MO
Penn State Abington, PA
Penn State DuBois, PA
Penn State Fayette, The
Eberly Campus, PA
Penn State Mont Alto, PA
Penn State Wilkes-Barre, PA
Pittsburg State U, KS
Portland State U, OR
Queen's U at Kingston, ON,
Canada
Radford U, VA
Roosevelt U, IL
Rowan U, NJ
Rutgers, The State U of New
Jersey, New Brunswick, NJ
Ryerson U, ON, Canada
St. Cloud State U, MN
San Diego Mesa Coll, CA
San Diego State U, CA
San Francisco State U, CA
Santa Ana Coll, CA
Santa Barbara City Coll, CA
Santa Rosa Jr Coll, CA
Shippensburg U of
Pennsylvania, PA
Skagit Valley Coll, WA
Slippery Rock U of
Pennsylvania, PA

Southern Illinois U
Carbondale, IL
Southern Illinois U
Edwardsville, IL
Southern Oregon U, OR
State U of New York Coll at
Cortland, NY
State U of New York Coll at
Geneseo, NY
Stephen F. Austin State U,
TX
Stetson U, FL
Syracuse U, NY
Temple U, PA
Texas A&M U, TX
Towson U, MD
Trent U, ON, Canada
U at Albany, State U of New
York, NY
U at Buffalo, the State U of
New York, NY
The U of Akron, OH
The U of Alabama, AL
The U of Arizona, AZ
U of Arkansas, AR
U of California, Berkeley,
CA
U of California, Los Angeles,
CA
U of California, Santa
Barbara, CA
U of Central Missouri, MO
U of Central Oklahoma, OK
U of Cincinnati, OH
U of Colorado at Boulder,
CO
U of Connecticut, CT
U of Delaware, DE
U of Guelph, ON, Canada
U of Hawaii at Manoa, HI
U of Illinois at Urbana–
Champaign, IL
U of Kansas, KS
U of Kentucky, KY
U of Manitoba, MB, Canada
U of Maryland, Baltimore
County, MD
U of Mary Washington, VA
U of Massachusetts Amherst,
MA
U of Massachusetts Boston,
MA
U of Miami, FL
U of Minnesota, Duluth, MN
U of Missouri–Columbia,
MO
U of Missouri–Kansas City,
MO
U of Nebraska at Kearney,
NE
U of Nebraska at Omaha,
NE
U of Nebraska–Lincoln, NE
U of New Hampshire, NH
U of New Mexico, NM
U of New Orleans, LA
The U of North Carolina at
Chapel Hill, NC
The U of North Carolina at
Charlotte, NC
U of Northern British
Columbia, BC, Canada
U of Northern Iowa, IA
U of Oregon, OR
U of Pittsburgh at
Johnstown, PA
U of St. Thomas, MN
The U of Tampa, FL
The U of Tennessee, TN
The U of Tennessee at
Martin, TN
The U of Texas at Austin,
TX

The U of Texas at El Paso,
TX
The U of Texas at San
Antonio, TX
U of the District of
Columbia, DC
U of Toronto, ON, Canada
U of Vermont, VT
U of Washington, WA
U of West Georgia, GA
U of Wisconsin–Eau Claire,
WI
U of Wisconsin–La Crosse,
WI
U of Wisconsin–Madison,
WI
U of Wisconsin–Oshkosh,
WI
U of Wisconsin–Stevens
Point, WI
U of Wyoming, WY
Vassar Coll, NY
Villanova U, PA
Wayne State Coll, NE
Wayne State U, MI
West Chester U of
Pennsylvania, PA
Western Nebraska Comm
Coll, NE
Western Oregon U, OR
West Los Angeles Coll, CA
West Texas A&M U, TX
Wilfrid Laurier U, ON,
Canada
Worcester State Coll, MA
Wright State U, OH

GEOGRAPHY RELATED
Temple U, PA
U of California, Los Angeles,
CA

**GEOGRAPHY TEACHER
EDUCATION**
Bishop's U, QC, Canada
Concordia U, NE
Fitchburg State Coll, MA
Framingham State Coll, MA
Northern Michigan U, MI
U of Evansville, IN
The U of Tennessee at
Martin, TN
Wayne State Coll, NE

**GEOLOGICAL AND
EARTH SCIENCES/
GEOSCIENCES RELATED**
Baylor U, TX
Lehigh U, PA
Penn State Abington, PA
Penn State DuBois, PA
Penn State Fayette, The
Eberly Campus, PA
Penn State Mont Alto, PA
Penn State Wilkes-Barre, PA
Queens Coll of the City U of
New York, NY
State U of New York Coll at
Brockport, NY
Texas A&M U, TX
The U of Akron, OH
U of Arkansas, AR
U of California, Los Angeles,
CA
U of Illinois at Urbana–
Champaign, IL
U of Miami, FL
The U of North Carolina at
Charlotte, NC
U of Northern Iowa, IA
U of Pittsburgh, PA
The U of Texas at Austin,
TX
U of West Georgia, GA

U of Wyoming, WY
Washington and Lee U, VA
Yale U, CT

**GEOLOGICAL
ENGINEERING**
The U of Arizona, AZ
U of Toronto, ON, Canada

**GEOLOGICAL/
GEOPHYSICAL
ENGINEERING**
Cornell U, NY
Montana Tech of The U of
Montana, MT
Queen's U at Kingston, ON,
Canada
Rutgers, The State U of New
Jersey, Newark, NJ
Tufts U, MA
The U of Akron, OH
U of California, Berkeley,
CA
U of California, Los Angeles,
CA
U of Manitoba, MB, Canada
U of Mississippi, MS
U of Missouri–Rolla, MO
U of New Brunswick
Fredericton, NB, Canada

**GEOLOGY/EARTH
SCIENCE**
Acadia U, NS, Canada
Adams State Coll, CO
Albion Coll, MI
Amherst Coll, MA
Ashland U, OH
Ball State U, IN
Bates Coll, ME
Baylor U, TX
Bemidji State U, MN
Boston Coll, MA
Bradley U, IL
Brandon U, MB, Canada
Brock U, ON, Canada
Brown U, RI
Bryn Mawr Coll, PA
Buffalo State Coll, State U of
New York, NY
California State U, Fullerton,
CA
California State U,
Northridge, CA
California State U,
Sacramento, CA
California State U, San
Bernardino, CA
California State U,
Stanislaus, CA
Calvin Coll, MI
Carleton U, ON, Canada
Clark U, MA
Clayton State U, GA
Clemson U, SC
Colby Coll, ME
Colgate U, NY
Coll of Charleston, SC
Coll of the Canyons, CA
Coll of the Desert, CA
The Coll of William and
Mary, VA
Colorado Mountain Coll,
Alpine Campus, CO
Columbus State U, GA
Cornell U, NY
Cosumnes River Coll,
Sacramento, CA
Crafton Hills Coll, CA
Cuesta Coll, CA
Dalhousie U, NS, Canada
Dixie State Coll of Utah, UT
Duke U, NC
Earlham Coll, IN

East Carolina U, NC
Eastern Michigan U, MI
East Stroudsburg U of
Pennsylvania, PA
Edinboro U of Pennsylvania,
PA
El Camino Coll, CA
Fitchburg State Coll, MA
Florida Atlantic U, FL
Florida International U, FL
Fort Hays State U, KS
Framingham State Coll, MA
Furman U, SC
Gainesville State Coll, GA
The George Washington U,
DC
Grossmont Coll, CA
Gustavus Adolphus Coll,
MN
Hamilton Coll, NY
Hampshire Coll, MA
Hartwick Coll, NY
Haverford Coll, PA
Hofstra U, NY
Hope Coll, MI
Idaho State U, ID
Illinois State U, IL
Indiana U Bloomington, IN
Indiana U of Pennsylvania,
PA
Indiana U–Purdue U Fort
Wayne, IN
Indiana U–Purdue U
Indianapolis, IN
Kansas State U, KS
Kutztown U of
Pennsylvania, PA
Lake Superior State U, MI
Lamar U, TX
Lawrence U, WI
Lee Coll, TX
Macalester Coll, MN
Marietta Coll, OH
Marshall U, WV
McNeese State U, LA
Mercyhurst Coll, PA
Miami Dade Coll, FL
Michigan State U, MI
Middle Tennessee State U,
TN
Midland Coll, TX
Millersville U of
Pennsylvania, PA
Minnesota State U Mankato,
MN
Missouri State U, MO
Montana State U, MT
Moorpark Coll, CA
Moravian Coll, PA
Mount Holyoke Coll, MA
Mount Union Coll, OH
Murray State U, KY
New Jersey City U, NJ
North Carolina State U, NC
North Dakota State U, ND
Northeastern U, MA
Northern Illinois U, IL
Northern Michigan U, MI
Occidental Coll, CA
Odessa Coll, TX
The Ohio State U, OH
Ohio Wesleyan U, OH
Oklahoma State U, OK
Old Dominion U, VA
Penn State Abington, PA
Penn State DuBois, PA
Penn State Fayette, The
Eberly Campus, PA
Penn State Mont Alto, PA
Penn State Wilkes-Barre, PA
Piedmont Coll, GA
Portland State U, OR
Queens Coll of the City U of
New York, NY

Queen's U at Kingston, ON, Canada
Radford U, VA
Rensselaer Polytechnic Inst, NY
Rice U, TX
The Richard Stockton Coll of New Jersey, NJ
Rocky Mountain Coll, MT
Rutgers, The State U of New Jersey, Newark, NJ
Rutgers, The State U of New Jersey, New Brunswick, NJ
St. Cloud State U, MN
St. Francis Xavier U, NS, Canada
St. Lawrence U, NY
St. Norbert Coll, WI
St. Philip's Coll, TX
San Diego State U, CA
San Francisco State U, CA
Santa Ana Coll, CA
Santa Barbara City Coll, CA
Santa Rosa Jr Coll, CA
Sewanee: The U of the South, TN
Shippensburg U of Pennsylvania, PA
Skagit Valley Coll, WA
Slippery Rock U of Pennsylvania, PA
Southern Illinois U Carbondale, IL
Southern Oregon U, OR
Southern Utah U, UT
State U of New York at Fredonia, NY
State U of New York Coll at Brockport, NY
State U of New York Coll at Cortland, NY
State U of New York Coll at Geneseo, NY
State U of New York Coll at Potsdam, NY
Stephen F. Austin State U, TX
Syracuse U, NY
Temple U, PA
Texas A&M U, TX
Texas A&M U–Corpus Christi, TX
Towson U, MD
Trinity U, TX
Tufts U, MA
U at Albany, State U of New York, NY
U at Buffalo, the State U of New York, NY
The U of Akron, OH
The U of Alabama, AL
The U of Arizona, AZ
U of Arkansas, AR
U of California, Berkeley, CA
U of California, Irvine, CA
U of California, Los Angeles, CA
U of California, Santa Barbara, CA
U of Central Missouri, MO
U of Cincinnati, OH
U of Colorado at Boulder, CO
U of Connecticut, CT
U of Dayton, OH
U of Delaware, DE
U of Hawaii at Manoa, HI
U of Houston, TX
U of Illinois at Urbana–Champaign, IL
U of Kansas, KS
U of Kentucky, KY
U of Manitoba, MB, Canada

U of Mary Washington, VA
U of Massachusetts Amherst, MA
U of Massachusetts Boston, MA
U of Miami, FL
U of Michigan, MI
U of Minnesota, Duluth, MN
U of Mississippi, MS
U of Missouri–Columbia, MO
U of Missouri–Kansas City, MO
U of Missouri–Rolla, MO
U of Nebraska at Omaha, NE
U of Nebraska–Lincoln, NE
U of New Brunswick Fredericton, NB, Canada
U of New Hampshire, NH
U of New Mexico, NM
U of New Orleans, LA
The U of North Carolina at Chapel Hill, NC
The U of North Carolina at Charlotte, NC
U of Northern Iowa, IA
U of Notre Dame, IN
U of Oregon, OR
U of Pennsylvania, PA
U of Pittsburgh, PA
U of Pittsburgh at Johnstown, PA
U of Rhode Island, RI
U of St. Thomas, MN
U of Southern Indiana, IN
The U of Tennessee, TN
The U of Tennessee at Martin, TN
The U of Texas at Austin, TX
The U of Texas at El Paso, TX
The U of Texas at San Antonio, TX
U of the Pacific, CA
U of Toronto, ON, Canada
U of Vermont, VT
U of Washington, WA
U of West Georgia, GA
U of Wisconsin–Eau Claire, WI
U of Wisconsin–Green Bay, WI
U of Wisconsin–Madison, WI
U of Wisconsin–Oshkosh, WI
U of Wisconsin–Platteville, WI
U of Wyoming, WY
Vassar Coll, NY
Washington and Lee U, VA
Wayne State U, MI
Wellesley Coll, MA
West Chester U of Pennsylvania, PA
Western Connecticut State U, CT
West Los Angeles Coll, CA
West Texas A&M U, TX
Wheaton Coll, IL
Whitman Coll, WA
Wichita State U, KS
Wilkes U, PA
Wright State U, OH

GEOPHYSICS AND SEISMOLOGY
Baylor U, TX
Boston Coll, MA
Brown U, RI
Eastern Michigan U, MI
Hope Coll, MI

Michigan State U, MI
Occidental Coll, CA
Rice U, TX
St. Lawrence U, NY
State U of New York at Fredonia, NY
State U of New York Coll at Geneseo, NY
Texas A&M U, TX
The U of Akron, OH
U of California, Los Angeles, CA
U of California, Santa Barbara, CA
U of Delaware, DE
U of Houston, TX
U of Missouri–Rolla, MO
U of New Brunswick Fredericton, NB, Canada
U of New Orleans, LA
The U of Texas at Austin, TX
The U of Texas at El Paso, TX
U of Toronto, ON, Canada
U of Washington, WA
U of Wisconsin–Madison, WI
Wright State U, OH

GEOTECHNICAL ENGINEERING
Montana Tech of The U of Montana, MT

GERMAN
Albion Coll, MI
Alma Coll, MI
American U, DC
Amherst Coll, MA
Angelo State U, TX
Augsburg Coll, MN
Austin Coll, TX
Ball State U, IN
Bard Coll, NY
Bates Coll, ME
Baylor U, TX
Bemidji State U, MN
Bishop's U, QC, Canada
Blinn Coll, TX
Boston Coll, MA
Bradley U, IL
Brandeis U, MA
Brock U, ON, Canada
Brown U, RI
Bryn Mawr Coll, PA
California State U, Fullerton, CA
California State U, Northridge, CA
Calvin Coll, MI
Carleton U, ON, Canada
Carnegie Mellon U, PA
Carthage Coll, WI
The Catholic U of America, DC
Christopher Newport U, VA
Citrus Coll, CA
Claremont McKenna Coll, CA
Coe Coll, IA
Colby Coll, ME
Colgate U, NY
Coll of Charleston, SC
Coll of the Canyons, CA
The Coll of William and Mary, VA
Cornell U, NY
Dalhousie U, NS, Canada
DePaul U, IL
Drury U, MO
Duke U, NC
Earlham Coll, IN
East Carolina U, NC

Eastern Mennonite U, VA
Eastern Michigan U, MI
Eckerd Coll, FL
Edinboro U of Pennsylvania, PA
El Camino Coll, CA
Emory U, GA
Fairfield U, CT
Florida Atlantic U, FL
Florida International U, FL
Fort Hays State U, KS
Franciscan U of Steubenville, OH
Furman U, SC
Georgetown Coll, KY
The George Washington U, DC
Gonzaga U, WA
Gordon Coll, MA
Grace Coll, IN
Graceland U, IA
Grinnell Coll, IA
Grossmont Coll, CA
Gustavus Adolphus Coll, MN
Hamilton Coll, NY
Hamline U, MN
Hampden-Sydney Coll, VA
Hartwick Coll, NY
Haverford Coll, PA
Hofstra U, NY
Hope Coll, MI
Hunter Coll of the City U of New York, NY
Idaho State U, ID
Illinois State U, IL
Illinois Wesleyan U, IL
Indiana U Bloomington, IN
Indiana U of Pennsylvania, PA
Indiana U–Purdue U Fort Wayne, IN
Indiana U–Purdue U Indianapolis, IN
Indiana U Southeast, IN
Ithaca Coll, NY
Kenyon Coll, OH
Kutztown U of Pennsylvania, PA
Lake Erie Coll, OH
Lakeland Coll, WI
Lawrence U, WI
Lebanon Valley Coll, PA
Lee Coll, TX
Lehigh U, PA
Long Beach City Coll, CA
Loyola U Chicago, IL
Loyola U New Orleans, LA
Marquette U, WI
McDaniel Coll, MD
Mercer U, GA
Mercyhurst Coll, PA
Miami Dade Coll, FL
Michigan State U, MI
Midland Coll, TX
Millersville U of Pennsylvania, PA
Minnesota State U Mankato, MN
Missouri State U, MO
Moravian Coll, PA
Mount Holyoke Coll, MA
Mount St. Mary's U, MD
Mount Saint Vincent U, NS, Canada
Mount Union Coll, OH
Murray State U, KY
New York U, NY
North Central Coll, IL
Northeastern U, MA
Northern Illinois U, IL
Northern State U, SD
Oakland U, MI
The Ohio State U, OH

Ohio Wesleyan U, OH
Oklahoma State U, OK
Old Dominion U, VA
Oral Roberts U, OK
Penn State Abington, PA
Penn State DuBois, PA
Penn State Fayette, The Eberly Campus, PA
Penn State Mont Alto, PA
Penn State Wilkes-Barre, PA
Portland State U, OR
Presbyterian Coll, SC
Queens Coll of the City U of New York, NY
Queen's U at Kingston, ON, Canada
Randolph Coll, VA
Randolph-Macon Coll, VA
Rhodes Coll, TN
Rice U, TX
Ripon Coll, WI
Rutgers, The State U of New Jersey, Newark, NJ
Rutgers, The State U of New Jersey, New Brunswick, NJ
St. Cloud State U, MN
Saint John's U, MN
St. Lawrence U, NY
St. Norbert Coll, WI
San Diego State U, CA
San Francisco State U, CA
Seattle Pacific U, WA
Sewanee: The U of the South, TN
Southern Illinois U Carbondale, IL
Southern Oregon U, OR
Southern Utah U, UT
Southwestern U, TX
State U of New York Coll at Cortland, NY
Stetson U, FL
Sweet Briar Coll, VA
Syracuse U, NY
Temple U, PA
Texas A&M U, TX
Towson U, MD
Trent U, ON, Canada
Trinity Coll, CT
Trinity U, TX
Truman State U, MO
Tufts U, MA
Union Coll, NE
U at Buffalo, the State U of New York, NY
The U of Akron, OH
The U of Alabama, AL
The U of Arizona, AZ
U of Arkansas, AR
U of California, Berkeley, CA
U of California, Irvine, CA
U of California, Los Angeles, CA
U of California, Santa Barbara, CA
U of Central Missouri, MO
U of Central Oklahoma, OK
U of Cincinnati, OH
U of Connecticut, CT
U of Dayton, OH
U of Delaware, DE
U of Evansville, IN
U of Hawaii at Manoa, HI
U of Houston, TX
U of Illinois at Urbana–Champaign, IL
U of Kentucky, KY
U of Manitoba, MB, Canada
U of Maryland, Baltimore County, MD
U of Mary Washington, VA
U of Massachusetts Amherst, MA

U of Massachusetts Boston, MA
U of Miami, FL
U of Michigan, MI
U of Mississippi, MS
U of Missouri–Columbia, MO
U of Missouri–Kansas City, MO
U of Nebraska at Kearney, NE
U of Nebraska at Omaha, NE
U of Nebraska–Lincoln, NE
U of New Brunswick Fredericton, NB, Canada
U of New Hampshire, NH
U of New Mexico, NM
The U of North Carolina at Asheville, NC
The U of North Carolina at Chapel Hill, NC
The U of North Carolina at Charlotte, NC
U of Northern Iowa, IA
U of Notre Dame, IN
U of Oregon, OR
U of Pennsylvania, PA
U of Pittsburgh, PA
U of Redlands, CA
U of Rhode Island, RI
U of St. Thomas, MN
The U of Scranton, PA
U of Southern Indiana, IN
The U of Tennessee, TN
The U of Texas at Austin, TX
The U of Texas at El Paso, TX
U of the Pacific, CA
U of Toronto, ON, Canada
U of Vermont, VT
U of Virginia, VA
U of Washington, WA
U of West Georgia, GA
U of Wisconsin–La Crosse, WI
U of Wisconsin–Madison, WI
U of Wisconsin–Oshkosh, WI
U of Wisconsin–Platteville, WI
U of Wisconsin–Stevens Point, WI
U of Wyoming, WY
Vassar Coll, NY
Villanova U, PA
Wake Forest U, NC
Washburn U, KS
Washington & Jefferson Coll, PA
Washington and Lee U, VA
Wayne State Coll, NE
Wayne State U, MI
Wellesley Coll, MA
West Chester U of Pennsylvania, PA
Western Nebraska Comm Coll, NE
Western Oregon U, OR
Westminster Coll, PA
Wheaton Coll, IL
Whitman Coll, WA
Wilfrid Laurier U, ON, Canada
Wofford Coll, SC
Wright State U, OH
Xavier U, OH
Yale U, CT

GERMANIC LANGUAGES
Claremont McKenna Coll, CA

Eastern Michigan U, MI
U of Colorado at Boulder, CO
U of Kansas, KS
The U of Texas at San Antonio, TX
U of Wisconsin–Eau Claire, WI
U of Wisconsin–Green Bay, WI

GERMANIC LANGUAGES RELATED
Calvin Coll, MI
U of California, Los Angeles, CA

GERMAN LANGUAGE TEACHER EDUCATION
Alma Coll, MI
Baylor U, TX
Carroll Coll, WI
The Catholic U of America, DC
East Carolina U, NC
Eastern Mennonite U, VA
Eastern Michigan U, MI
Grace Coll, IN
Hofstra U, NY
Hope Coll, MI
Hunter Coll of the City U of New York, NY
Indiana U Bloomington, IN
Indiana U–Purdue U Fort Wayne, IN
Indiana U–Purdue U Indianapolis, IN
Ithaca Coll, NY
Lebanon Valley Coll, PA
Missouri State U, MO
Moravian Coll, PA
Murray State U, KY
Ohio Wesleyan U, OH
Old Dominion U, VA
Oral Roberts U, OK
St. Bonaventure U, NY
The U of Akron, OH
The U of Arizona, AZ
U of Evansville, IN
U of Illinois at Urbana–Champaign, IL
U of Minnesota, Duluth, MN
U of Nebraska–Lincoln, NE
The U of North Carolina at Charlotte, NC
The U of Tennessee at Martin, TN

GERMAN STUDIES
Brock U, ON, Canada
Brown U, RI
Claremont McKenna Coll, CA
Coe Coll, IA
Cornell U, NY
Ithaca Coll, NY
Manhattanville Coll, NY
Moravian Coll, PA
Queen's U at Kingston, ON, Canada
Santa Clara U, CA
The U of Alabama, AL
U of California, Irvine, CA
U of Houston, TX
Wilfrid Laurier U, ON, Canada

GERONTOLOGICAL SERVICES
Coll of Mount St. Joseph, OH
Santa Rosa Jr Coll, CA

GERONTOLOGY
Alma Coll, MI
Bishop's U, QC, Canada
California State U, Sacramento, CA
Cedar Crest Coll, PA
Cosumnes River Coll, Sacramento, CA
Dominican U, IL
El Camino Coll, CA
Ithaca Coll, NY
Langston U, OK
Lindenwood U, MO
Mercyhurst Coll, PA
Millersville U of Pennsylvania, PA
Minnesota State U Moorhead, MN
Missouri State U, MO
Mount Saint Vincent U, NS, Canada
National-Louis U, IL
New River Comm Coll, VA
Roosevelt U, IL
St. Cloud State U, MN
St. Thomas U, NB, Canada
San Diego State U, CA
Southern Nazarene U, OK
State U of New York at Fredonia, NY
Stephen F. Austin State U, TX
Towson U, MD
The U of Akron, OH
U of Guelph, ON, Canada
U of Massachusetts Boston, MA
U of Nebraska at Omaha, NE
U of Northern Iowa, IA
The U of Scranton, PA
Washburn U, KS
West Virginia State Comm and Tech Coll, WV
West Virginia State U, WV
Wichita State U, KS

GRAPHIC AND PRINTING EQUIPMENT OPERATION/ PRODUCTION
Ball State U, IN
Burlington County Coll, NJ
Central Piedmont Comm Coll, NC
Chattanooga State Tech Comm Coll, TN
Eastfield Coll, TX
Fresno City Coll, CA
Fulton-Montgomery Comm Coll, NY
Houston Comm Coll System, TX
Idaho State U, ID
Macomb Comm Coll, MI
Moorpark Coll, CA
Murray State U, KY
Ozarks Tech Comm Coll, MO
Pittsburg State U, KS
Southeast Tech Inst, SD
Southwestern Michigan Coll, MI
U of the District of Columbia, DC
Westmoreland County Comm Coll, PA

GRAPHIC COMMUNICATIONS
Academy of Art U, CA
Carroll Coll, WI
Clemson U, SC
Drury U, MO

Lynn U, FL
Minnesota State U Moorhead, MN
New York U, NY
Notre Dame Coll, OH
Pittsburg State U, KS
Point Loma Nazarene U, CA
Rochester Inst of Technology, NY
Ryerson U, ON, Canada
School of the Art Inst of Chicago, IL
U of Houston, TX
U of Northern Iowa, IA
Waukesha County Tech Coll, WI

GRAPHIC COMMUNICATIONS RELATED
U of the District of Columbia, DC

GRAPHIC DESIGN
Academy of Art U, CA
Alma Coll, MI
American U, DC
Ancilla Coll, IN
The Art Inst of Houston, TX
The Art Inst of New York City, NY
The Art Inst of Ohio–Cincinnati, OH
The Art Inst of Pittsburgh, PA
The Art Inst of Seattle, WA
Briar Cliff U, IA
Calhoun Comm Coll, AL
California State U, Fullerton, CA
California State U, Sacramento, CA
Carthage Coll, WI
The Cleveland Inst of Art, OH
Coll of Mount St. Joseph, OH
Daemen Coll, NY
Drake U, IA
Drury U, MO
East Stroudsburg U of Pennsylvania, PA
Fashion Inst of Technology, NY
Fitchburg State Coll, MA
Flagler Coll, FL
Framingham State Coll, MA
Harding U, AR
Huntington U, IN
Indiana U–Purdue U Fort Wayne, IN
Ivy Tech Comm Coll–Southwest, IN
Maine Coll of Art, ME
Marietta Coll, OH
Marymount U, VA
Marywood U, PA
Massasoit Comm Coll, MA
Moravian Coll, PA
Mount Vernon Nazarene U, OH
North Carolina State U, NC
North Central Coll, IL
Northwestern Coll, MN
Northwest Nazarene U, ID
NSCAD U, NS, Canada
Old Dominion U, VA
Park U, MO
Penn State Abington, PA
Penn State DuBois, PA
Penn State Fayette, The Eberly Campus, PA
Penn State Mont Alto, PA
Penn State Wilkes-Barre, PA

Point Loma Nazarene U, CA
Pratt Inst, NY
Ringling Coll of Art and Design, FL
Rochester Inst of Technology, NY
Salve Regina U, RI
San Diego State U, CA
Santa Rosa Jr Coll, CA
Savannah Coll of Art and Design, GA
School of the Art Inst of Chicago, IL
Southern Adventist U, TN
Temple U, PA
Tidewater Comm Coll, VA
Union Coll, NE
U of Arkansas at Fort Smith, AR
U of Evansville, IN
U of Illinois at Urbana–Champaign, IL
U of Kansas, KS
U of Miami, FL
U of Rio Grande, OH
U of San Francisco, CA
The U of Tennessee at Martin, TN
The U of the Arts, PA
Ursuline Coll, OH
Watkins Coll of Art and Design, TN
Waubonsee Comm Coll, IL
Waukesha County Tech Coll, WI
Wayne State Coll, NE

GREENHOUSE MANAGEMENT
Comm Coll of Allegheny County, PA
Sterling Coll, VT

HAZARDOUS MATERIALS MANAGEMENT AND WASTE TECHNOLOGY
Odessa Coll, TX
Rochester Inst of Technology, NY

HEALTH AIDE
Central Arizona Coll, AZ

HEALTH AND MEDICAL ADMINISTRATIVE SERVICES RELATED
British Columbia Inst of Technology, BC, Canada
The U of Akron, OH
U of Baltimore, MD
U of Miami, FL
Ursuline Coll, OH

HEALTH AND PHYSICAL EDUCATION
Abilene Christian U, TX
Alexandria Tech Coll, MN
Anderson U, IN
Angelo State U, TX
Asbury Coll, KY
Baylor U, TX
Bethel Coll, IN
Bethel U, MN
Bridgewater Coll, VA
California State U, Fullerton, CA
California State U, Sacramento, CA
Cameron U, OK
Carroll Coll, WI
Citrus Coll, CA
Comm Coll of Allegheny County, PA

Concordia U, NE
Eastern Michigan U, MI
Edinboro U of Pennsylvania, PA
Freed-Hardeman U, TN
Gardner-Webb U, NC
Gloucester County Coll, NJ
Hamline U, MN
Houghton Coll, NY
Houston Baptist U, TX
Indiana U of Pennsylvania, PA
Ithaca Coll, NY
Johnson State Coll, VT
Lassen Comm Coll District, CA
Liberty U, VA
Lincoln U, PA
Lindenwood U, MO
Loras Coll, IA
Middle Tennessee State U, TN
Minnesota State U Moorhead, MN
Montana State U, MT
Montana State U–Billings, MT
Mount Vernon Nazarene U, OH
Northwestern Coll, MN
Northwest Nazarene U, ID
Pittsburg State U, KS
Point Loma Nazarene U, CA
Queen's U at Kingston, ON, Canada
Radford U, VA
Redeemer U Coll, ON, Canada
Reedley Coll, CA
Salem Comm Coll, NJ
San Diego State U, CA
Slippery Rock U of Pennsylvania, PA
Southern Illinois U Edwardsville, IL
Southwestern Coll, KS
State U of New York Coll at Brockport, NY
Stephen F. Austin State U, TX
Tennessee Wesleyan Coll, TN
Texas A&M U, TX
U of Arkansas, AR
U of Delaware, DE
U of Evansville, IN
U of Great Falls, MT
U of Hawaii at Manoa, HI
U of Houston, TX
U of Kansas, KS
U of Nebraska at Omaha, NE
The U of North Carolina at Chapel Hill, NC
The U of North Carolina at Charlotte, NC
U of Northern Iowa, IA
U of Rio Grande, OH
U of St. Thomas, MN
U of San Francisco, CA
The U of Tennessee at Martin, TN
The U of Texas at Austin, TX
The U of Texas at San Antonio, TX
U of Toronto, ON, Canada
U of Wisconsin–Stevens Point, WI
Vanguard U of Southern California, CA
Virginia Intermont Coll, VA
West Chester U of Pennsylvania, PA

Western Nebraska Comm Coll, NE
West Texas A&M U, TX
West Virginia Wesleyan Coll, WV

HEALTH AND PHYSICAL EDUCATION RELATED
Avila U, MO
Brewton-Parker Coll, GA
California State U, Sacramento, CA
Coe Coll, IA
East Carolina U, NC
East Stroudsburg U of Pennsylvania, PA
Gustavus Adolphus Coll, MN
Hudson Valley Comm Coll, NY
Ithaca Coll, NY
Kingsborough Comm Coll of the City U of New York, NY
Lincoln U, PA
Naropa U, CO
Reinhardt Coll, GA
Rocky Mountain Coll, MT
Santa Rosa Jr Coll, CA
State U of New York Coll at Brockport, NY
Towson U, MD
The U of Akron, OH
U of Central Oklahoma, OK
U of New England, ME

HEALTH/HEALTH CARE ADMINISTRATION
Alvernia Coll, PA
British Columbia Inst of Technology, BC, Canada
Brock U, ON, Canada
Caldwell Comm Coll and Tech Inst, NC
California State U, Sacramento, CA
California State U, San Bernardino, CA
Cedar Crest Coll, PA
Central Piedmont Comm Coll, NC
Clayton State U, GA
Dallas Baptist U, TX
Eastern Michigan U, MI
Florida Atlantic U, FL
Florida International U, FL
Harding U, AR
Houston Comm Coll System, TX
Idaho State U, ID
Immaculata U, PA
Indiana U–Purdue U Indianapolis, IN
Iona Coll, NY
Ithaca Coll, NY
Langston U, OK
Lebanon Valley Coll, PA
Lewis U, IL
Lindenwood U, MO
Marywood U, PA
Mercy Coll of Health Sciences, IA
Minnesota State U Moorhead, MN
Montana State U, MT
Montana State U–Billings, MT
National-Louis U, IL
New York U, NY
Northeastern U, MA
Penn State Abington, PA
Penn State DuBois, PA
Penn State Fayette, The Eberly Campus, PA

Penn State Mont Alto, PA
Penn State Wilkes-Barre, PA
Roosevelt U, IL
Shippensburg U of Pennsylvania, PA
Southern Adventist U, TN
Southern Illinois U Carbondale, IL
South U, GA
Springfield Coll, MA
State U of New York at Fredonia, NY
State U of New York Coll at Brockport, NY
State U of New York Coll of Technology at Canton, NY
Stonehill Coll, MA
Towson U, MD
The U of Arizona, AZ
U of Central Florida, FL
U of Cincinnati, OH
U of Connecticut, CT
U of Evansville, IN
U of Great Falls, MT
U of Kentucky, KY
U of Maryland, Baltimore County, MD
U of New England, ME
U of New Hampshire, NH
The U of North Carolina at Chapel Hill, NC
U of Pennsylvania, PA
U of Rhode Island, RI
The U of Scranton, PA
The U of Texas at El Paso, TX
U of Wisconsin–Eau Claire, WI
Upper Iowa U, IA
Ursuline Coll, OH
West Chester U of Pennsylvania, PA
Wichita State U, KS
Wright State U, OH

HEALTH INFORMATION/ MEDICAL RECORDS ADMINISTRATION
Bunker Hill Comm Coll, MA
Carroll Coll, MT
Central Piedmont Comm Coll, NC
Chattanooga State Tech Comm Coll, TN
Clayton State U, GA
Coll of Saint Mary, NE
The Coll of St. Scholastica, MN
Cosumnes River Coll, Sacramento, CA
Dalhousie U, NS, Canada
East Carolina U, NC
El Centro Coll, TX
Florida Comm Coll at Jacksonville, FL
Florida International U, FL
Fresno City Coll, CA
Glendale Comm Coll, CA
Hagerstown Comm Coll, MD
Harrisburg Area Comm Coll, PA
Hocking Coll, OH
Houston Comm Coll System, TX
Illinois State U, IL
Indiana U–Purdue U Indianapolis, IN
Lake-Sumter Comm Coll, FL
Metropolitan Comm Coll–Penn Valley, MO
Miami Dade Coll, FL
Montana State U–Billings, MT
North Central Texas Coll, TX

Northern Michigan U, MI
The Ohio State U, OH
Park U, MO
Phoenix Coll, AZ
Pueblo Comm Coll, CO
Ryerson U, ON, Canada
San Diego Mesa Coll, CA
Spokane Comm Coll, WA
Stark State Coll of Technology, OH
State U of New York Coll of Technology at Alfred, NY
Temple U, PA
Trocaire Coll, NY
U of Central Florida, FL
U of Kansas, KS
U of Pittsburgh, PA
Westmoreland County Comm Coll, PA

HEALTH INFORMATION/ MEDICAL RECORDS TECHNOLOGY
Blinn Coll, TX
Broome Comm Coll, NY
Burlington County Coll, NJ
Central Florida Comm Coll, FL
Comm Coll of Allegheny County, PA
Houston Comm Coll System, TX
Hudson Valley Comm Coll, NY
Idaho State U, ID
Jefferson Comm and Tech Coll, KY
Lamar Inst of Technology, TX
Lee Coll, TX
Mercyhurst Coll, PA
Midland Coll, TX
Mohawk Valley Comm Coll, NY
Molloy Coll, NY
New York U, NY
Ozarks Tech Comm Coll, MO
St. Philip's Coll, TX
Santa Barbara City Coll, CA
Schoolcraft Coll, MI
South Piedmont Comm Coll, NC
Tallahassee Comm Coll, FL
Washburn U, KS
West Virginia Northern Comm Coll, WV
Williston State Coll, ND

HEALTH/MEDICAL PHYSICS
California State U, Northridge, CA
Ryerson U, ON, Canada

HEALTH/MEDICAL PREPARATORY PROGRAMS RELATED
Abilene Christian U, TX
Ancilla Coll, IN
Arkansas State U–Newport, AR
Asbury Coll, KY
Aurora U, IL
Avila U, MO
Baylor U, TX
Charleston Southern U, SC
Concordia U, NE
Gannon U, PA
Ithaca Coll, NY
Mercer U, GA
Mercyhurst Coll, PA
Miami Dade Coll, FL
Roosevelt U, IL

St. Cloud State U, MN
Union Coll, NE
U of Evansville, IN
U of Miami, FL
U of Missouri–Columbia, MO
Utica Coll, NY
Wheaton Coll, IL
Wright State U, OH

HEALTH/MEDICAL PSYCHOLOGY
Iona Coll, NY

HEALTH OCCUPATIONS TEACHER EDUCATION
Baylor U, TX
North Carolina State U, NC
U of Central Oklahoma, OK

HEALTH PROFESSIONS RELATED
Albany State U, GA
Allegany Coll of Maryland, MD
Bradley U, IL
British Columbia Inst of Technology, BC, Canada
California State U, Fullerton, CA
California State U, Sacramento, CA
Clemson U, SC
Comm Coll of Allegheny County, PA
Dalhousie U, NS, Canada
Dixie State Coll of Utah, UT
East Carolina U, NC
Gannon U, PA
Hofstra U, NY
King's Coll, PA
Lebanon Valley Coll, PA
Long Island U, Brooklyn Campus, NY
Marywood U, PA
Miami Dade Coll, FL
The Ohio State U, OH
Randolph Coll, VA
San Diego State U, CA
Southwestern Michigan Coll, MI
Towson U, MD
The U of Alabama, AL
U of Miami, FL
U of New England, ME
U of Northern Iowa, IA
U of Pennsylvania, PA
U of Pittsburgh, PA
U of Southern Indiana, IN
Worcester State Coll, MA

HEALTH SCIENCE
Alderson-Broaddus Coll, WV
Alma Coll, MI
American U, DC
Athens State U, AL
Ball State U, IN
Bradley U, IL
Brock U, ON, Canada
Bucks County Comm Coll, PA
California State U, Northridge, CA
California State U, San Bernardino, CA
Carlow U, PA
Cedar Crest Coll, PA
Clemson U, SC
Coll of the Canyons, CA
Columbus State U, GA
Dalhousie U, NS, Canada
Drury U, MO
Eastern Nazarene Coll, MA
Florida Atlantic U, FL

Florida International U, FL
Gannon U, PA
Graceland U, IA
Greenville Tech Coll, SC
Johnson State Coll, VT
Kansas State U, KS
Lamar U, TX
Long Island U, Brooklyn
   Campus, NY
Minnesota State U Mankato,
   MN
Montana Tech of The U of
   Montana, MT
Nassau Comm Coll, NY
New Jersey City U, NJ
New Mexico Jr Coll, NM
Northeastern U, MA
Northern Illinois U, IL
Oakland U, MI
Ocean County Coll, NJ
Oklahoma State U, OK
Oral Roberts U, OK
Roosevelt U, IL
San Francisco State U, CA
Spalding U, KY
Spoon River Coll, IL
State U of New York Coll at
   Brockport, NY
State U of New York Coll at
   Cortland, NY
Sussex County Comm Coll,
   NJ
Syracuse U, NY
Tennessee Wesleyan Coll,
   TN
Texas A&M U–Corpus
   Christi, TX
Truman State U, MO
Union Coll, NE
U of Alaska Anchorage, AK
U of Arkansas, AR
U of Central Florida, FL
U of Hartford, CT
U of Maryland, Baltimore
   County, MD
U of New England, ME
U of St. Thomas, MN
The U of Tennessee at
   Martin, TN
The U of Texas at El Paso,
   TX
Wayne State U, MI
West Liberty State Coll, WV

**HEALTH SERVICES
ADMINISTRATION**
East Stroudsburg U of
   Pennsylvania, PA
Freed-Hardeman U, TN
Indiana U–Purdue U Fort
   Wayne, IN
Marywood U, PA
U of California, Los Angeles,
   CA
Ursuline Coll, OH
Washburn U, KS

**HEALTH SERVICES/
ALLIED HEALTH/
HEALTH SCIENCES**
Ancilla Coll, IN
Brevard Coll, NC
California State U,
   Sacramento, CA
The Coll of St. Scholastica,
   MN
Daemen Coll, NY
Dalhousie U, NS, Canada
Florida Atlantic U, FL
Florida Gulf Coast U, FL
Florida International U, FL
Idaho State U, ID
Immaculata U, PA
Lebanon Valley Coll, PA

Liberty U, VA
Marywood U, PA
Nova Southeastern U, FL
The Ohio State U at Lima,
   OH
Old Dominion U, VA
St. Cloud State U, MN
San Diego State U, CA
Stetson U, FL
U of Central Florida, FL
U of North Florida, FL
The U of Texas at Austin,
   TX
The U of Texas at San
   Antonio, TX
U of Wyoming, WY
Ursuline Coll, OH
West Virginia State Comm
   and Tech Coll, WV
Widener U, PA

**HEALTH TEACHER
EDUCATION**
Alma Coll, MI
Ashland U, OH
Augsburg Coll, MN
Bainbridge Coll, GA
Ball State U, IN
Baylor U, TX
Bemidji State U, MN
Bethel U, MN
Bucks County Comm Coll,
   PA
California State U, San
   Bernardino, CA
Carroll Coll, WI
Chesapeake Coll, MD
Clayton State U, GA
Coahoma Comm Coll, MS
Columbus State U, GA
Concordia U, NE
Concord U, WV
DePaul U, IL
East Carolina U, NC
Eastern Mennonite U, VA
East Stroudsburg U of
   Pennsylvania, PA
Elon U, NC
Fayetteville State U, NC
Florida International U, FL
Framingham State Coll, MA
Freed-Hardeman U, TN
Fulton-Montgomery Comm
   Coll, NY
Gardner-Webb U, NC
Georgia Coll & State U, GA
Graceland U, IA
Gustavus Adolphus Coll,
   MN
Hamline U, MN
Harding U, AR
Hofstra U, NY
Howard Comm Coll, MD
Hunter Coll of the City U of
   New York, NY
Idaho State U, ID
Illinois State U, IL
Indiana U–Purdue U
   Indianapolis, IN
Ithaca Coll, NY
John Brown U, AR
Lamar U, TX
Liberty U, VA
Lynchburg Coll, VA
Middle Tennessee State U,
   TN
Minnesota State U Mankato,
   MN
Minnesota State U
   Moorhead, MN
Montana State U–Billings,
   MT
Mount Vernon Nazarene U,
   OH

Murray State U, KY
North Dakota State U, ND
Northern Illinois U, IL
Northern Michigan U, MI
Northern State U, SD
Northwestern Oklahoma
   State U, OK
Ohio Wesleyan U, OH
Otterbein Coll, OH
Pittsburg State U, KS
Portland State U, OR
Rocky Mountain Coll, MT
St. Cloud State U, MN
San Francisco State U, CA
Southern Illinois U
   Carbondale, IL
Southern Illinois U
   Edwardsville, IL
Southern Oregon U, OR
Springfield Coll, MA
State U of New York Coll at
   Brockport, NY
State U of New York Coll at
   Cortland, NY
Temple U, PA
Texas A&M U–Corpus
   Christi, TX
Troy U, AL
The U of Akron, OH
The U of Arizona, AZ
U of Cincinnati, OH
U of Dayton, OH
U of Delaware, DE
U of Great Falls, MT
U of Kentucky, KY
U of Minnesota, Duluth, MN
U of Nebraska–Lincoln, NE
U of New Brunswick
   Fredericton, NB, Canada
U of New Mexico, NM
U of Northern Iowa, IA
U of Rio Grande, OH
U of St. Thomas, MN
The U of Tennessee, TN
U of the District of
   Columbia, DC
U of Toronto, ON, Canada
U of Wisconsin–La Crosse,
   WI
U of Wyoming, WY
Urbana U, OH
Wayne State U, MI
West Chester U of
   Pennsylvania, PA
Western Connecticut State
   U, CT
West Liberty State Coll, WV
Westmoreland County
   Comm Coll, PA
West Virginia State U, WV
West Virginia Wesleyan Coll,
   WV
Wright State U, OH

**HEALTH UNIT
COORDINATOR/WARD
CLERK**
Comm Coll of Allegheny
   County, PA
Southeast Tech Inst, SD

**HEALTH UNIT
MANAGEMENT/WARD
SUPERVISION**
Ryerson U, ON, Canada

**HEATING, AIR
CONDITIONING AND
REFRIGERATION
TECHNOLOGY**
Calhoun Comm Coll, AL
DeKalb Tech Coll, GA
Gadsden State Comm Coll,
   AL

Harrisburg Area Comm Coll,
   PA
Lamar Inst of Technology,
   TX
Macomb Comm Coll, MI
Massasoit Comm Coll, MA
Miami Dade Coll, FL
Mohawk Valley Comm Coll,
   NY
St. Cloud Tech Coll, MN
South Piedmont Comm Coll,
   NC
State U of New York Coll of
   Technology at Alfred, NY

**HEATING, AIR
CONDITIONING,
VENTILATION AND
REFRIGERATION
MAINTENANCE
TECHNOLOGY**
Asheville-Buncombe Tech
   Comm Coll, NC
British Columbia Inst of
   Technology, BC, Canada
Calhoun Comm Coll, AL
Cedar Valley Coll, TX
Chattanooga State Tech
   Comm Coll, TN
Coll of the Desert, CA
Comm Coll of Allegheny
   County, PA
East Central Coll, MO
Eastfield Coll, TX
El Camino Coll, CA
Fresno City Coll, CA
Greenville Tech Coll, SC
Heartland Comm Coll, IL
Hudson Valley Comm Coll,
   NY
Ivy Tech Comm Coll–
   Kokomo, IN
Ivy Tech Comm Coll–
   Southwest, IN
Ivy Tech Comm Coll–
   Wabash Valley, IN
Kellogg Comm Coll, MI
Lamar U, TX
Lee Coll, TX
Linn State Tech Coll, MO
Long Beach City Coll, CA
Macomb Comm Coll, MI
Miami Dade Coll, FL
Midland Coll, TX
Minnesota State Coll–
   Southeast Tech, MN
Mohawk Valley Comm Coll,
   NY
Montana State U–Billings,
   MT
Morton Coll, IL
New York City Coll of
   Technology of the City U
   of New York, NY
Northern Michigan U, MI
Odessa Coll, TX
Ozarks Tech Comm Coll,
   MO
Paris Jr Coll, TX
Rockingham Comm Coll, NC
St. Cloud Tech Coll, MN
St. Philip's Coll, TX
Sauk Valley Comm Coll, IL
Shelton State Comm Coll, AL
Southeast Tech Inst, SD
Southern Maine Comm Coll,
   ME
Spokane Comm Coll, WA
State U of New York Coll of
   Technology at Alfred, NY
State U of New York Coll of
   Technology at Canton, NY
Surry Comm Coll, NC
U of Alaska Anchorage, AK

U of Cincinnati, OH
Virginia Highlands Comm
   Coll, VA
Waubonsee Comm Coll, IL
Western Tech Coll, WI
Westmoreland County
   Comm Coll, PA
West Virginia Northern
   Comm Coll, WV
West Virginia State Comm
   and Tech Coll, WV

**HEAVY EQUIPMENT
MAINTENANCE
TECHNOLOGY**
British Columbia Inst of
   Technology, BC, Canada
Delaware Tech & Comm
   Coll, Jack F. Owens
   Campus, DE
Linn State Tech Coll, MO
Long Beach City Coll, CA
Metropolitan Comm
   Coll–Longview, MO
Mohawk Valley Comm Coll,
   NY
New Hampshire Comm
   Tech Coll, Nashua/
   Claremont, NH
Ozarks Tech Comm Coll,
   MO
Skagit Valley Coll, WA
Spokane Comm Coll, WA
State U of New York Coll of
   Technology at Alfred, NY
U of Alaska Anchorage, AK

**HEAVY/INDUSTRIAL
EQUIPMENT
MAINTENANCE
TECHNOLOGIES
RELATED**
Eastern West Virginia Comm
   and Tech Coll, WV
Southwestern Michigan Coll,
   MI

HEBREW
Bard Coll, NY
Hofstra U, NY
Hunter Coll of the City U of
   New York, NY
Multnomah Bible Coll and
   Biblical Seminary, OR
New York U, NY
The Ohio State U, OH
Queens Coll of the City U of
   New York, NY
Temple U, PA
U of California, Los Angeles,
   CA
U of Illinois at Urbana–
   Champaign, IL
U of Michigan, MI
U of Oregon, OR
The U of Texas at Austin,
   TX
U of Wisconsin–Madison,
   WI

**HIGHER EDUCATION/
HIGHER EDUCATION
ADMINISTRATION**
Wright State U, OH

**HISPANIC-AMERICAN,
PUERTO RICAN, AND
MEXICAN-AMERICAN/
CHICANO STUDIES**
Boston Coll, MA
Brown U, RI
California State U, Fullerton,
   CA

California State U,
Northridge, CA
Claremont McKenna Coll,
CA
Cornell U, NY
Fresno City Coll, CA
Hampshire Coll, MA
Hofstra U, NY
Hunter Coll of the City U of
New York, NY
Loyola Marymount U, CA
Our Lady of the Lake U of
San Antonio, TX
Rutgers, The State U of New
Jersey, Newark, NJ
Rutgers, The State U of New
Jersey, New Brunswick, NJ
San Diego Mesa Coll, CA
San Diego State U, CA
San Francisco State U, CA
Santa Ana Coll, CA
Santa Barbara City Coll, CA
Trent U, ON, Canada
U at Albany, State U of New
York, NY
The U of Arizona, AZ
U of California, Berkeley,
CA
U of California, Irvine, CA
U of California, Los Angeles,
CA
U of California, Santa
Barbara, CA
U of San Diego, CA
The U of Texas at El Paso,
TX
The U of Texas at San
Antonio, TX
U of Washington, WA
U of Wisconsin–Madison,
WI

**HISTOLOGIC
TECHNICIAN**
Miami Dade Coll, FL

**HISTOLOGIC
TECHNOLOGY/
HISTOTECHNOLOGIST**
Argosy U, Twin Cities,
Eagan, MN
Northern Michigan U, MI

**HISTORIC
PRESERVATION AND
CONSERVATION**
Bucks County Comm Coll,
PA
Coll of Charleston, SC
Cornell U, NY
Salve Regina U, RI
Savannah Coll of Art and
Design, GA
U of Delaware, DE
U of Mary Washington, VA
Ursuline Coll, OH

HISTORY
Abilene Christian U, TX
Abraham Baldwin Coll, GA
Acadia U, NS, Canada
Adams State Coll, CO
Adelphi U, NY
Albany State U, GA
Albertson Coll of Idaho, ID
Albion Coll, MI
Albright Coll, PA
Alderson-Broaddus Coll, WV
Alma Coll, MI
Alvernia Coll, PA
American International Coll,
MA
American U, DC
Amherst Coll, MA

Ancilla Coll, IN
Anderson U, IN
Anderson U, SC
Angelo State U, TX
Arizona State U at the West
campus, AZ
Asbury Coll, KY
Ashland U, OH
Athabasca U, AB, Canada
Athens State U, AL
Auburn U Montgomery, AL
Augsburg Coll, MN
Aurora U, IL
Austin Coll, TX
Avila U, MO
Bainbridge Coll, GA
Ball State U, IN
Bard Coll, NY
Barry U, FL
Bates Coll, ME
Baylor U, TX
Belmont Abbey Coll, NC
Bemidji State U, MN
Benedictine Coll, KS
Bentley Coll, MA
Bethel Coll, IN
Bethel U, MN
Bishop's U, QC, Canada
Blinn Coll, TX
Boston Coll, MA
Bradley U, IL
Brandeis U, MA
Brandon U, MB, Canada
Brenau U, GA
Brevard Coll, NC
Brewton-Parker Coll, GA
Briar Cliff U, IA
Bridgewater Coll, VA
Brock U, ON, Canada
Brown U, RI
Bryn Mawr Coll, PA
Buena Vista U, IA
Buffalo State Coll, State U of
New York, NY
Bunker Hill Comm Coll, MA
Burlington County Coll, NJ
California State U, Fullerton,
CA
California State U,
Northridge, CA
California State U,
Sacramento, CA
California State U, San
Bernardino, CA
California State U,
Stanislaus, CA
Calvin Coll, MI
Cameron U, OK
Cape Breton U, NS, Canada
Cape Cod Comm Coll, MA
Cardinal Stritch U, WI
Carleton U, ON, Canada
Carlow U, PA
Carroll Coll, MT
Carroll Coll, WI
Carson-Newman Coll, TN
Carthage Coll, WI
The Catholic U of America,
DC
Cedar Crest Coll, PA
Charleston Southern U, SC
Christopher Newport U, VA
Claremont McKenna Coll,
CA
Clark U, MA
Clayton State U, GA
Clemson U, SC
Coastal Carolina U, SC
Coe Coll, IA
Colby Coll, ME
Colgate U, NY
Coll of Charleston, SC
Coll of Mount St. Joseph,
OH

Coll of Mount Saint Vincent,
NY
Coll of Saint Elizabeth, NJ
Coll of St. Joseph, VT
The Coll of Saint Rose, NY
The Coll of St. Scholastica,
MN
Coll of Staten Island of the
City U of New York, NY
Coll of the Canyons, CA
Coll of the Desert, CA
The Coll of William and
Mary, VA
Columbus State U, GA
Concordia Coll–New York,
NY
Concordia U, NE
Concordia U Coll of Alberta,
AB, Canada
Concord U, WV
Cornell U, NY
Cornerstone U, MI
Crafton Hills Coll, CA
Daemen Coll, NY
Dalhousie U, NS, Canada
Dallas Baptist U, TX
Delaware State U, DE
DePaul U, IL
Dixie State Coll of Utah, UT
Dominican U, IL
Drake U, IA
Drury U, MO
Duke U, NC
Earlham Coll, IN
East Carolina U, NC
Eastern Connecticut State U,
CT
Eastern Mennonite U, VA
Eastern Michigan U, MI
Eastern Nazarene Coll, MA
East Stroudsburg U of
Pennsylvania, PA
Eckerd Coll, FL
Edinboro U of Pennsylvania,
PA
El Camino Coll, CA
Elmira Coll, NY
Elms Coll, MA
Elon U, NC
Emory U, GA
Eugene Lang Coll The New
School for Liberal Arts, NY
Fairfield U, CT
Fairleigh Dickinson U, Coll
at Florham, NJ
Fairleigh Dickinson U,
Metropolitan Campus, NJ
Fayetteville State U, NC
Feather River Coll, CA
Ferrum Coll, VA
Fitchburg State Coll, MA
Flagler Coll, FL
Florida Atlantic U, FL
Florida Inst of Technology,
FL
Florida International U, FL
Fontbonne U, MO
Foothill Coll, CA
Fort Hays State U, KS
Framingham State Coll, MA
Franciscan U of
Steubenville, OH
Franklin Coll, IN
Franklin Pierce U, NH
Freed-Hardeman U, TN
Fresno Pacific U, CA
Fulton-Montgomery Comm
Coll, NY
Furman U, SC
Gainesville State Coll, GA
Galveston Coll, TX
Gannon U, PA
Gardner-Webb U, NC
Geneva Coll, PA

Georgetown Coll, KY
The George Washington U,
DC
Georgia Coll & State U, GA
Georgian Court U, NJ
Glenville State Coll, WV
Gloucester County Coll, NJ
Gonzaga U, WA
Gordon Coll, MA
Goshen Coll, IN
Graceland U, IA
Grambling State U, LA
Green Mountain Coll, VT
Grinnell Coll, IA
Grossmont Coll, CA
Gustavus Adolphus Coll,
MN
Hamilton Coll, NY
Hamline U, MN
Hampden-Sydney Coll, VA
Hampshire Coll, MA
Harding U, AR
Hartwick Coll, NY
Haverford Coll, PA
Henderson State U, AR
High Point U, NC
Hofstra U, NY
Hope Coll, MI
Houghton Coll, NY
Houston Baptist U, TX
Hunter Coll of the City U of
New York, NY
Huntington U, IN
Idaho State U, ID
Illinois State U, IL
Illinois Wesleyan U, IL
Immaculata U, PA
Indiana U Bloomington, IN
Indiana U of Pennsylvania,
PA
Indiana U–Purdue U Fort
Wayne, IN
Indiana U–Purdue U
Indianapolis, IN
Indiana U Southeast, IN
Iona Coll, NY
Irvine Valley Coll, CA
Ithaca Coll, NY
Jacksonville U, FL
John Brown U, AR
Johnson State Coll, VT
Kansas State U, KS
Kellogg Comm Coll, MI
Kennesaw State U, GA
Kentucky Wesleyan Coll, KY
Kenyon Coll, OH
Keuka Coll, NY
King's Coll, PA
The King's U Coll, AB,
Canada
Kutztown U of
Pennsylvania, PA
LaGrange Coll, GA
Lakeland Coll, WI
Lake Superior State U, MI
Lamar U, TX
Langston U, OK
Lassen Comm Coll District,
CA
Lawrence U, WI
Lebanon Valley Coll, PA
Lee Coll, TX
Lehigh U, PA
Le Moyne Coll, NY
LeTourneau U, TX
Lewis U, IL
Liberty U, VA
Lincoln U, PA
Lindenwood U, MO
Long Island U, Brooklyn
Campus, NY
Loras Coll, IA
Loyola Marymount U, CA
Loyola U Chicago, IL

Loyola U New Orleans, LA
Lynchburg Coll, VA
Macalester Coll, MN
MacMurray Coll, IL
Manhattan Coll, NY
Manhattanville Coll, NY
Marian Coll, IN
Marietta Coll, OH
Marist Coll, NY
Marquette U, WI
Marshall U, WV
Marymount Manhattan Coll,
NY
Marymount U, VA
Marywood U, PA
Massachusetts Coll of Liberal
Arts, MA
McDaniel Coll, MD
McNeese State U, LA
Mercer U, GA
Mercyhurst Coll, PA
Miami Dade Coll, FL
Michigan State U, MI
Middlesex County Coll, NJ
Middle Tennessee State U,
TN
Midland Coll, TX
Midland Lutheran Coll, NE
Millersville U of
Pennsylvania, PA
Minnesota State U Mankato,
MN
Minnesota State U
Moorhead, MN
MiraCosta Coll, CA
Missouri State U, MO
Molloy Coll, NY
Monmouth Coll, IL
Monmouth U, NJ
Montana State U, MT
Montana State U–Billings,
MT
Moravian Coll, PA
Morningside Coll, IA
Mount Holyoke Coll, MA
Mount St. Mary's U, MD
Mount Saint Vincent U, NS,
Canada
Mount Union Coll, OH
Mount Vernon Nazarene U,
OH
Multnomah Bible Coll and
Biblical Seminary, OR
Murray State U, KY
New Jersey City U, NJ
New Mexico Jr Coll, NM
New York U, NY
Niagara U, NY
Nipissing U, ON, Canada
North Carolina State U, NC
North Central Coll, IL
North Dakota State U, ND
Northeastern U, MA
Northern Illinois U, IL
Northern Michigan U, MI
Northern State U, SD
North Georgia Coll & State
U, GA
Northwestern Coll, MN
Northwestern Oklahoma
State U, OK
Northwest Nazarene U, ID
Notre Dame Coll, OH
Notre Dame de Namur U,
CA
Nova Southeastern U, FL
Oakland U, MI
Occidental Coll, CA
Odessa Coll, TX
Oglethorpe U, GA
The Ohio State U, OH
The Ohio State U at Lima,
OH
Ohio Wesleyan U, OH

Oklahoma State U, OK
Old Dominion U, VA
Oral Roberts U, OK
Otterbein Coll, OH
Our Lady of the Lake U of San Antonio, TX
Park U, MO
Paul Quinn Coll, TX
Penn State Abington, PA
Penn State DuBois, PA
Penn State Fayette, The Eberly Campus, PA
Penn State Mont Alto, PA
Penn State Wilkes-Barre, PA
Piedmont Coll, GA
Pine Manor Coll, MA
Pittsburg State U, KS
Point Loma Nazarene U, CA
Portland State U, OR
Prairie View A&M U, TX
Presbyterian Coll, SC
Queens Coll of the City U of New York, NY
Queen's U at Kingston, ON, Canada
Queens U of Charlotte, NC
Quincy Coll, MA
Radford U, VA
Ramapo Coll of New Jersey, NJ
Randolph Coll, VA
Randolph-Macon Coll, VA
Redeemer U Coll, ON, Canada
Reinhardt Coll, GA
Rhodes Coll, TN
Rice U, TX
The Richard Stockton Coll of New Jersey, NJ
Ripon Coll, WI
Rivier Coll, NH
Rockford Coll, IL
Rockhurst U, MO
Rocky Mountain Coll, MT
Roosevelt U, IL
Rose State Coll, OK
Rowan U, NJ
Rutgers, The State U of New Jersey, Newark, NJ
Rutgers, The State U of New Jersey, New Brunswick, NJ
Saginaw Valley State U, MI
St. Bonaventure U, NY
St. Cloud State U, MN
St. Francis Xavier U, NS, Canada
St. Gregory's U, OK
Saint John's U, MN
Saint Joseph's Coll, IN
St. Lawrence U, NY
Saint Leo U, FL
St. Mary's Coll of Maryland, MD
St. Norbert Coll, WI
St. Philip's Coll, TX
St. Thomas Aquinas Coll, NY
St. Thomas U, NB, Canada
Saint Xavier U, IL
Salem Comm Coll, NJ
Salve Regina U, RI
San Diego State U, CA
San Francisco State U, CA
Santa Ana Coll, CA
Santa Barbara City Coll, CA
Santa Clara U, CA
Santa Rosa Jr Coll, CA
Sauk Valley Comm Coll, IL
Seattle Pacific U, WA
Seton Hall U, NJ
Seton Hill U, PA
Sewanee: The U of the South, TN

Shippensburg U of Pennsylvania, PA
Skagit Valley Coll, WA
Slippery Rock U of Pennsylvania, PA
Southern Adventist U, TN
Southern Illinois U Carbondale, IL
Southern Illinois U Edwardsville, IL
Southern Nazarene U, OK
Southern Oregon U, OR
Southern U and A&M Coll, LA
Southern Utah U, UT
Southwest Baptist U, MO
Southwestern Coll, KS
Southwestern U, TX
Spalding U, KY
Spoon River Coll, IL
Springfield Coll, MA
State U of New York at Fredonia, NY
State U of New York Coll at Brockport, NY
State U of New York Coll at Cortland, NY
State U of New York Coll at Geneseo, NY
Stephen F. Austin State U, TX
Stetson U, FL
Stonehill Coll, MA
Sweet Briar Coll, VA
Syracuse U, NY
Taylor U, IN
Temple U, PA
Tennessee Wesleyan Coll, TN
Texas A&M U, TX
Texas A&M U–Corpus Christi, TX
Thiel Coll, PA
Towson U, MD
Trent U, ON, Canada
Trevecca Nazarene U, TN
Trinity Coll, CT
Trinity U, TX
Troy U, AL
Truman State U, MO
Tufts U, MA
Union Coll, NE
U at Albany, State U of New York, NY
U at Buffalo, the State U of New York, NY
The U of Akron, OH
The U of Alabama, AL
The U of Alabama in Huntsville, AL
U of Alaska Anchorage, AK
The U of Arizona, AZ
U of Arkansas, AR
U of Arkansas at Fort Smith, AR
U of Baltimore, MD
U of California, Berkeley, CA
U of California, Irvine, CA
U of California, Los Angeles, CA
U of California, Santa Barbara, CA
U of Central Florida, FL
U of Central Missouri, MO
U of Central Oklahoma, OK
U of Cincinnati, OH
U of Colorado at Boulder, CO
U of Connecticut, CT
U of Dayton, OH
U of Delaware, DE
U of Evansville, IN
The U of Findlay, OH

U of Great Falls, MT
U of Guelph, ON, Canada
U of Hartford, CT
U of Hawaii at Manoa, HI
U of Hawaii–West Oahu, HI
U of Houston, TX
U of Illinois at Urbana–Champaign, IL
U of Kansas, KS
U of Kentucky, KY
U of Maine at Machias, ME
U of Manitoba, MB, Canada
U of Mary Hardin-Baylor, TX
U of Maryland, Baltimore County, MD
U of Mary Washington, VA
U of Massachusetts Amherst, MA
U of Massachusetts Boston, MA
U of Massachusetts Lowell, MA
U of Miami, FL
U of Michigan, MI
U of Minnesota, Duluth, MN
U of Mississippi, MS
U of Missouri–Columbia, MO
U of Missouri–Kansas City, MO
U of Missouri–Rolla, MO
U of Nebraska at Kearney, NE
U of Nebraska at Omaha, NE
U of Nebraska–Lincoln, NE
U of New Brunswick Fredericton, NB, Canada
U of New England, ME
U of New Hampshire, NH
U of New Hampshire at Manchester, NH
U of New Haven, CT
U of New Mexico, NM
U of New Orleans, LA
The U of North Carolina at Asheville, NC
The U of North Carolina at Chapel Hill, NC
The U of North Carolina at Charlotte, NC
U of Northern British Columbia, BC, Canada
U of Northern Iowa, IA
U of North Florida, FL
U of Notre Dame, IN
U of Oregon, OR
U of Pennsylvania, PA
U of Pittsburgh, PA
U of Pittsburgh at Bradford, PA
U of Pittsburgh at Johnstown, PA
U of Portland, OR
U of Redlands, CA
U of Rhode Island, RI
U of Rio Grande, OH
U of St. Thomas, MN
U of St. Thomas, TX
U of San Diego, CA
U of San Francisco, CA
The U of Scranton, PA
U of South Carolina Beaufort, SC
U of South Carolina Upstate, SC
U of Southern Indiana, IN
The U of Tampa, FL
The U of Tennessee, TN
The U of Tennessee at Martin, TN
The U of Texas at Austin, TX

The U of Texas at El Paso, TX
The U of Texas at San Antonio, TX
U of the District of Columbia, DC
U of the Incarnate Word, TX
U of the Ozarks, AR
U of the Pacific, CA
U of Toronto, ON, Canada
U of Vermont, VT
U of Virginia, VA
The U of Virginia's Coll at Wise, VA
U of Washington, WA
U of West Georgia, GA
U of Wisconsin–Eau Claire, WI
U of Wisconsin–Green Bay, WI
U of Wisconsin–La Crosse, WI
U of Wisconsin–Madison, WI
U of Wisconsin–Oshkosh, WI
U of Wisconsin–Platteville, WI
U of Wisconsin–Stevens Point, WI
U of Wyoming, WY
Urbana U, OH
Ursuline Coll, OH
Utica Coll, NY
Valdosta State U, GA
Vanguard U of Southern California, CA
Vassar Coll, NY
Villanova U, PA
Virginia Intermont Coll, VA
Wake Forest U, NC
Washburn U, KS
Washington & Jefferson Coll, PA
Washington and Lee U, VA
Wayne State Coll, NE
Wayne State U, MI
Wellesley Coll, MA
Wells Coll, NY
Wesley Coll, DE
West Chester U of Pennsylvania, PA
Western Connecticut State U, CT
Western Nebraska Comm Coll, NE
Western New England Coll, MA
Western Oregon U, OR
West Liberty State Coll, WV
West Los Angeles Coll, CA
Westminster Coll, PA
Westminster Coll, UT
West Texas A&M U, TX
West Virginia State U, WV
West Virginia Wesleyan Coll, WV
Wheaton Coll, IL
Whitman Coll, WA
Wichita State U, KS
Widener U, PA
Wilfrid Laurier U, ON, Canada
Wilkes U, PA
William Jewell Coll, MO
Wofford Coll, SC
Worcester State Coll, MA
Wright State U, OH
Xavier U, OH
Yale U, CT

HISTORY AND PHILOSOPHY OF SCIENCE AND TECHNOLOGY

Bard Coll, NY
Dalhousie U, NS, Canada
Farmingdale State Coll, NY
U of Pennsylvania, PA
U of Pittsburgh, PA
U of Toronto, ON, Canada
U of Washington, WA
U of Wisconsin–Madison, WI

HISTORY OF PHILOSOPHY

Bard Coll, NY
Marquette U, WI
U of Toronto, ON, Canada

HISTORY RELATED

Bard Coll, NY
Bridgewater Coll, VA
Carnegie Mellon U, PA
Hamilton Coll, NY
Marquette U, WI
Mercyhurst Coll, PA
The Ohio State U, OH
Washburn U, KS

HISTORY TEACHER EDUCATION

Abilene Christian U, TX
Alma Coll, MI
Ancilla Coll, IN
Anderson U, SC
Bishop's U, QC, Canada
Brewton-Parker Coll, GA
Buena Vista U, IA
Carroll Coll, MT
Carroll Coll, WI
The Catholic U of America, DC
Charleston Southern U, SC
Columbus State U, GA
Concordia U, NE
Cornerstone U, MI
Eastern Michigan U, MI
Elmira Coll, NY
Fitchburg State Coll, MA
Framingham State Coll, MA
Hope Coll, MI
Illinois Wesleyan U, IL
Ithaca Coll, NY
Johnson State Coll, VT
Liberty U, VA
Lindenwood U, MO
Marist Coll, NY
Marywood U, PA
Missouri State U, MO
Montana State U–Billings, MT
Moravian Coll, PA
Murray State U, KY
North Carolina State U, NC
North Dakota State U, ND
Northern Michigan U, MI
Northwest Nazarene U, ID
Ohio Wesleyan U, OH
Old Dominion U, VA
Pittsburg State U, KS
Rocky Mountain Coll, MT
Saint Xavier U, IL
Salve Regina U, RI
State U of New York Coll at Brockport, NY
Taylor U, IN
Tennessee Wesleyan Coll, TN
Texas A&M U–Corpus Christi, TX
Trevecca Nazarene U, TN
Union Coll, NE
The U of Akron, OH

The U of Arizona, AZ
U of Arkansas at Fort Smith, AR
U of Central Oklahoma, OK
U of Delaware, DE
U of Great Falls, MT
U of Maine at Machias, ME
U of Nebraska–Lincoln, NE
The U of North Carolina at Charlotte, NC
U of Pittsburgh at Johnstown, PA
U of Rio Grande, OH
The U of Tennessee at Martin, TN
Utica Coll, NY
Wayne State Coll, NE
West Chester U of Pennsylvania, PA
Widener U, PA

HOME FURNISHINGS AND EQUIPMENT INSTALLATION
St. Philip's Coll, TX

HORSE HUSBANDRY/ EQUINE SCIENCE AND MANAGEMENT
Central Wyoming Coll, WY
Santa Rosa Jr Coll, CA
Sterling Coll, VT

HORTICULTURAL SCIENCE
Abraham Baldwin Coll, GA
Central Lakes Coll, MN
Central Piedmont Comm Coll, NC
Chattahoochee Tech Coll, GA
Christopher Newport U, VA
City Colls of Chicago, Richard J. Daley Coll, IL
Clemson U, SC
Coll of the Desert, CA
Cornell U, NY
Cosumnes River Coll, Sacramento, CA
El Camino Coll, CA
Ferrum Coll, VA
Houston Comm Coll System, TX
Kansas State U, KS
Long Beach City Coll, CA
Maui Comm Coll, HI
Miami Dade Coll, FL
Michigan State U, MI
MiraCosta Coll, CA
Missouri State U, MO
Montana State U, MT
North Carolina State U, NC
North Dakota State U, ND
North Metro Tech Coll, GA
The Ohio State U, OH
Oklahoma State U, OK
Penn State Abington, PA
Penn State DuBois, PA
Penn State Fayette, The Eberly Campus, PA
Penn State Mont Alto, PA
Penn State Wilkes-Barre, PA
Reedley Coll, CA
Rockingham Comm Coll, NC
Shasta Coll, CA
Southeast Tech Inst, SD
Southern Maine Comm Coll, ME
Stephen F. Austin State U, TX
Sterling Coll, VT
Surry Comm Coll, NC
Temple U, PA
Texas A&M U, TX

Tidewater Comm Coll, VA
Truman State U, MO
U of Arkansas, AR
U of Connecticut, CT
U of Delaware, DE
U of Guelph, ON, Canada
U of Illinois at Urbana–Champaign, IL
U of Nebraska–Lincoln, NE
U of New Hampshire, NH
U of Wisconsin–Madison, WI
Victor Valley Coll, CA
Westmoreland County Comm Coll, PA

HOSPITAL AND HEALTH CARE FACILITIES ADMINISTRATION
Avila U, MO
Carson-Newman Coll, TN
Harrisburg Area Comm Coll, PA
Ithaca Coll, NY
Marywood U, PA
Saint Leo U, FL
The U of Alabama, AL
Ursuline Coll, OH
Western Tech Coll, WI

HOSPITALITY ADMINISTRATION
Abraham Baldwin Coll, GA
Alexandria Tech Coll, MN
Allegany Coll of Maryland, MD
The Art Inst of Pittsburgh, PA
Bucks County Comm Coll, PA
Buffalo State Coll, State U of New York, NY
Bunker Hill Comm Coll, MA
Cape Breton U, NS, Canada
Central Piedmont Comm Coll, NC
Coll of Charleston, SC
Colorado Mountain Coll, Alpine Campus, CO
Concord U, WV
Delaware State U, DE
Delaware Tech & Comm Coll, Jack F. Owens Campus, DE
Eastern Michigan U, MI
East Stroudsburg U of Pennsylvania, PA
El Centro Coll, TX
Florida Atlantic U, FL
Florida Comm Coll at Jacksonville, FL
Florida International U, FL
Green Mountain Coll, VT
Greenville Tech Coll, SC
Hillsborough Comm Coll, FL
Hocking Coll, OH
Husson Coll, ME
Indiana U–Purdue U Fort Wayne, IN
James H. Faulkner State Comm Coll, AL
Johnson & Wales U, FL
Johnson & Wales U, RI
Johnson State Coll, VT
Kendall Coll, IL
Mercyhurst Coll, PA
Miami Dade Coll, FL
Michigan State U, MI
Middlesex County Coll, NJ
Missouri State U, MO
Mount Saint Vincent U, NS, Canada
New York City Coll of Technology of the City U of New York, NY

New York U, NY
North Dakota State U, ND
Northern Michigan U, MI
The Ohio State U, OH
The Ohio State U at Lima, OH
Pima Comm Coll, AZ
Reedley Coll, CA
Rochester Inst of Technology, NY
Roosevelt U, IL
Ryerson U, ON, Canada
Saint Leo U, FL
San Diego State U, CA
San Francisco State U, CA
Scottsdale Comm Coll, AZ
Seton Hill U, PA
Southern Maine Comm Coll, ME
Stephen F. Austin State U, TX
Syracuse U, NY
Temple U, PA
The U of Akron, OH
U of Central Florida, FL
U of Illinois at Urbana–Champaign, IL
U of Kentucky, KY
U of Massachusetts Amherst, MA
U of New Hampshire, NH
U of New Haven, CT
U of New Orleans, LA
U of South Carolina Beaufort, SC
U of the District of Columbia, DC
U of Wisconsin–Stout, WI
Valencia Comm Coll, FL
Waukesha County Tech Coll, WI
Westmoreland County Comm Coll, PA
West Virginia Northern Comm Coll, WV

HOSPITALITY ADMINISTRATION RELATED
The Art Inst of Pittsburgh, PA
Indiana U–Purdue U Indianapolis, IN
Kendall Coll, IL
Lynn U, FL
Niagara U, NY
Penn State Abington, PA
Penn State DuBois, PA
Penn State Fayette, The Eberly Campus, PA
Penn State Mont Alto, PA
Penn State Wilkes-Barre, PA
San Diego State U, CA
U of the District of Columbia, DC
Widener U, PA

HOSPITALITY AND RECREATION MARKETING
Cape Breton U, NS, Canada
Florida Comm Coll at Jacksonville, FL
Gloucester County Coll, NJ
Johnson & Wales U, RI
Kendall Coll, IL
Northern Michigan U, MI
Rochester Inst of Technology, NY
San Diego Mesa Coll, CA
The U of Akron, OH
U of Delaware, DE

HOTEL AND RESTAURANT MANAGEMENT
Johnson & Wales U, CO
Johnson & Wales U, NC

HOTEL/MOTEL ADMINISTRATION
Alexandria Tech Coll, MN
The Art Inst of Pittsburgh, PA
Asheville-Buncombe Tech Comm Coll, NC
Ashland U, OH
Bluefield State Coll, WV
Broome Comm Coll, NY
Broward Comm Coll, FL
Bucks County Comm Coll, PA
Buffalo State Coll, State U of New York, NY
Bunker Hill Comm Coll, MA
Burlington County Coll, NJ
Cape Cod Comm Coll, MA
Central Arizona Coll, AZ
Central Piedmont Comm Coll, NC
Chattanooga State Tech Comm Coll, TN
Coll of the Canyons, CA
Colorado Mountain Coll, Alpine Campus, CO
Comm Coll of Allegheny County, PA
Concord U, WV
Cornell U, NY
Delaware Tech & Comm Coll, Jack F. Owens Campus, DE
East Carolina U, NC
El Centro Coll, TX
Fairleigh Dickinson U, Coll at Florham, NJ
Fairleigh Dickinson U, Metropolitan Campus, NJ
Florida Comm Coll at Jacksonville, FL
Galveston Coll, TX
Glendale Comm Coll, CA
Grambling State U, LA
Harrisburg Area Comm Coll, PA
Hillsborough Comm Coll, FL
Hocking Coll, OH
Houston Comm Coll System, TX
Indiana U of Pennsylvania, PA
Indiana U–Purdue U Indianapolis, IN
Johnson & Wales U, FL
Johnson & Wales U, RI
Kansas State U, KS
Kapiolani Comm Coll, HI
Kendall Coll, IL
Keuka Coll, NY
Langston U, OK
Laredo Comm Coll, TX
Lincoln Land Comm Coll, IL
Long Beach City Coll, CA
Marywood U, PA
Massasoit Comm Coll, MA
Maui Comm Coll, HI
Mercyhurst Coll, PA
Michigan State U, MI
Middlesex County Coll, NJ
MiraCosta Coll, CA
Mohawk Valley Comm Coll, NY
Mount Saint Vincent U, NS, Canada
Nassau Comm Coll, NY
New York U, NY
Niagara U, NY

Northwood U, MI
Northwood U, Florida Campus, FL
Northwood U, Texas Campus, TX
Oklahoma State U, OK
Ozarks Tech Comm Coll, MO
Rochester Inst of Technology, NY
Ryerson U, ON, Canada
St. Philip's Coll, TX
San Diego Mesa Coll, CA
San Diego State U, CA
Santa Barbara City Coll, CA
Santa Rosa Jr Coll, CA
Scottsdale Comm Coll, AZ
Skagit Valley Coll, WA
Southern Maine Comm Coll, ME
Southern Oregon U, OR
Spokane Comm Coll, WA
Trocaire Coll, NY
The U of Akron, OH
U of Central Missouri, MO
U of Central Oklahoma, OK
U of Delaware, DE
The U of Findlay, OH
U of Guelph, ON, Canada
U of Houston, TX
U of Maine at Machias, ME
U of Missouri–Columbia, MO
U of New Hampshire, NH
U of New Haven, CT
U of San Francisco, CA
The U of Tennessee, TN
Westchester Comm Coll, NY
Westmoreland County Comm Coll, PA
West Virginia State U, WV
Widener U, PA

HOUSING AND HUMAN ENVIRONMENTS
Cornell U, NY
Missouri State U, MO
Syracuse U, NY
The U of Akron, OH
U of Missouri–Columbia, MO
U of Nebraska–Lincoln, NE
U of Northern Iowa, IA
U of the Incarnate Word, TX

HOUSING AND HUMAN ENVIRONMENTS RELATED
Comm Coll of Allegheny County, PA

HUMAN DEVELOPMENT AND FAMILY STUDIES
Abilene Christian U, TX
Ashland U, OH
Baylor U, TX
Boston Coll, MA
California State U, San Bernardino, CA
Cornell U, NY
Cuesta Coll, CA
East Carolina U, NC
Eckerd Coll, FL
Geneva Coll, PA
Gloucester County Coll, NJ
Indiana U Bloomington, IN
Indiana U of Pennsylvania, PA
Kansas State U, KS
Liberty U, VA
Mercyhurst Coll, PA
Missouri State U, MO
Mitchell Coll, CT
Montana State U, MT

Murray State U, KY
National-Louis U, IL
North Dakota State U, ND
Northern Illinois U, IL
The Ohio State U, OH
Oklahoma State U, OK
Pacific Oaks Coll, CA
Penn State Abington, PA
Penn State DuBois, PA
Penn State Fayette, The
  Eberly Campus, PA
Penn State Mont Alto, PA
Penn State Wilkes-Barre, PA
Southern Nazarene U, OK
Southern U and A&M Coll,
  LA
Stephen F. Austin State U,
  TX
Syracuse U, NY
The U of Alabama, AL
The U of Arizona, AZ
U of Arkansas, AR
U of Connecticut, CT
U of Delaware, DE
U of Hawaii at Manoa, HI
U of Houston, TX
U of Illinois at Urbana–
  Champaign, IL
U of Missouri–Columbia,
  MO
U of New Mexico, NM
The U of North Carolina at
  Charlotte, NC
U of Rhode Island, RI
The U of Tennessee, TN
The U of Texas at Austin,
  TX
U of Wisconsin–Stout, WI
Wayne State U, MI

**HUMAN DEVELOPMENT
AND FAMILY STUDIES
RELATED**
Comm Coll of Allegheny
  County, PA
Harding U, AR
Park U, MO

HUMAN ECOLOGY
Coll of the Atlantic, ME
Cornell U, NY
Kansas State U, KS
Mercyhurst Coll, PA
Mount Saint Vincent U, NS,
  Canada
Rutgers, The State U of New
  Jersey, New Brunswick, NJ
Sterling Coll, VT
U of California, Irvine, CA
U of Manitoba, MB, Canada

HUMANITIES
Abraham Baldwin Coll, GA
Adelphi U, NY
Alma Coll, MI
Ancilla Coll, IN
Athens State U, AL
Augsburg Coll, MN
Aurora U, IL
Bard Coll, NY
Baylor U, TX
Bemidji State U, MN
Bishop's U, QC, Canada
Bluefield State Coll, WV
Brock U, ON, Canada
Bucks County Comm Coll,
  PA
Buffalo State Coll, State U of
  New York, NY
California State U,
  Northridge, CA
California State U,
  Sacramento, CA

California State U, San
  Bernardino, CA
Carleton U, ON, Canada
Charleston Southern U, SC
Chesapeake Coll, MD
City Colls of Chicago,
  Richard J. Daley Coll, IL
Colgate U, NY
Coll of Saint Mary, NE
The Coll of St. Scholastica,
  MN
Coll of the Canyons, CA
Colorado Mountain Coll,
  Alpine Campus, CO
Comm Coll of Allegheny
  County, PA
Cornell U, NY
Cosumnes River Coll,
  Sacramento, CA
Crafton Hills Coll, CA
Dixie State Coll of Utah, UT
East Stroudsburg U of
  Pennsylvania, PA
Eckerd Coll, FL
Edinboro U of Pennsylvania,
  PA
Elmira Coll, NY
Eugene Lang Coll The New
  School for Liberal Arts, NY
Fairleigh Dickinson U, Coll
  at Florham, NJ
Fairleigh Dickinson U,
  Metropolitan Campus, NJ
Fitchburg State Coll, MA
Florida Inst of Technology,
  FL
Florida International U, FL
Framingham State Coll, MA
Franciscan U of
  Steubenville, OH
Freed-Hardeman U, TN
Fresno City Coll, CA
Fresno Pacific U, CA
Fulton-Montgomery Comm
  Coll, NY
Galveston Coll, TX
The George Washington U,
  DC
Georgian Court U, NJ
Glendale Comm Coll, CA
Hampden-Sydney Coll, VA
Harding U, AR
Hofstra U, NY
Hope Coll, MI
Houghton Coll, NY
Housatonic Comm Coll, CT
Hunter Coll of the City U of
  New York, NY
Irvine Valley Coll, CA
Jacksonville U, FL
Jamestown Comm Coll, NY
Johnson State Coll, VT
Kansas State U, KS
Kenyon Coll, OH
Lackawanna Coll, PA
Lassen Comm Coll District,
  CA
Lee Coll, TX
Long Island U, Brooklyn
  Campus, NY
Loyola Marymount U, CA
Loyola U New Orleans, LA
Macalester Coll, MN
Marshall U, WV
Mercyhurst Coll, PA
Miami Dade Coll, FL
Michigan State U, MI
Midland Lutheran Coll, NE
Minnesota State U Mankato,
  MN
MiraCosta Coll, CA
Mohawk Valley Comm Coll,
  NY
Monmouth Coll, IL

Mount Saint Vincent U, NS,
  Canada
New York U, NY
North Central Coll, IL
North Dakota State U, ND
Nova Southeastern U, FL
The Ohio State U, OH
Ohio Wesleyan U, OH
Portland State U, OR
Quincy Coll, MA
Redeemer U Coll, ON,
  Canada
Rockford Coll, IL
Roxbury Comm Coll, MA
Ryerson U, ON, Canada
St. Gregory's U, OK
Saint John's U, MN
St. Norbert Coll, WI
St. Thomas Aquinas Coll,
  NY
Salem Comm Coll, NJ
San Diego State U, CA
San Francisco State U, CA
Seton Hall U, NJ
Skagit Valley Coll, WA
Spalding U, KY
State U of New York Coll of
  Technology at Alfred, NY
State U of New York Coll of
  Technology at Canton, NY
Stephen F. Austin State U,
  TX
Stetson U, FL
Syracuse U, NY
Trent U, ON, Canada
Trinity U, TX
The U of Akron, OH
U of California, Irvine, CA
U of Central Florida, FL
U of Cincinnati, OH
U of Colorado at Boulder,
  CO
The U of Findlay, OH
U of Hawaii–West Oahu, HI
U of Illinois at Urbana–
  Champaign, IL
U of Kansas, KS
U of Massachusetts Amherst,
  MA
U of Michigan, MI
U of New Hampshire, NH
U of New Hampshire at
  Manchester, NH
U of New Mexico, NM
U of Northern Iowa, IA
U of Oregon, OR
U of Pittsburgh, PA
U of Pittsburgh at
  Johnstown, PA
U of Rio Grande, OH
U of San Diego, CA
The U of Texas at Austin,
  TX
The U of Texas at San
  Antonio, TX
U of Toronto, ON, Canada
U of Washington, WA
U of Wisconsin–Green Bay,
  WI
U of Wyoming, WY
Ursuline Coll, OH
Victor Valley Coll, CA
Washburn U, KS
Westchester Comm Coll, NY
Western Oregon U, OR
Widener U, PA
Wofford Coll, SC
Wright State U, OH
Yale U, CT

**HUMAN/MEDICAL
GENETICS**
Northern Michigan U, MI

U of California, Los Angeles,
  CA

HUMAN NUTRITION
Baylor U, TX
Cornell U, NY
Framingham State Coll, MA
Penn State Abington, PA
Penn State DuBois, PA
Penn State Fayette, The
  Eberly Campus, PA
Penn State Mont Alto, PA
Penn State Wilkes-Barre, PA
Rochester Inst of
  Technology, NY
Ryerson U, ON, Canada
U of Guelph, ON, Canada
U of Houston, TX
U of Massachusetts Amherst,
  MA
U of Missouri–Columbia,
  MO

**HUMAN RESOURCES
DEVELOPMENT**
Clemson U, SC

**HUMAN RESOURCES
MANAGEMENT**
American International Coll,
  MA
Anderson U, SC
Athabasca U, AB, Canada
Athens State U, AL
Auburn U Montgomery, AL
Ball State U, IN
Baylor U, TX
Bishop's U, QC, Canada
Boston Coll, MA
Briar Cliff U, IA
British Columbia Inst of
  Technology, BC, Canada
Brock U, ON, Canada
Buena Vista U, IA
California State U,
  Sacramento, CA
Carleton U, ON, Canada
Carlow U, PA
The Catholic U of America,
  DC
Coll of Saint Elizabeth, NJ
Comm Coll of Allegheny
  County, PA
Delaware State U, DE
DePaul U, IL
Eckerd Coll, FL
Florida Atlantic U, FL
Florida International U, FL
Freed-Hardeman U, TN
The George Washington U,
  DC
Harding U, AR
Houston Comm Coll System,
  TX
Idaho State U, ID
Immaculata U, PA
Indiana U of Pennsylvania,
  PA
King's Coll, PA
Kutztown U of
  Pennsylvania, PA
Lewis U, IL
Lindenwood U, MO
Loras Coll, IA
Loyola U Chicago, IL
Marietta Coll, OH
Marquette U, WI
Mercyhurst Coll, PA
Michigan State U, MI
Montana State U–Billings,
  MT
Montana Tech of The U of
  Montana, MT
Niagara U, NY

North Carolina State U, NC
North Central Coll, IL
Northeastern U, MA
Notre Dame Coll, OH
Oakland U, MI
The Ohio State U, OH
Our Lady of the Lake U of
  San Antonio, TX
Portland State U, OR
Redeemer U Coll, ON,
  Canada
Rockingham Comm Coll, NC
Roosevelt U, IL
St. Cloud State U, MN
Saint Leo U, FL
Salem Comm Coll, NJ
Seton Hill U, PA
Southwestern Coll, KS
Taylor U, IN
Tennessee Wesleyan Coll,
  TN
Troy U, AL
The U of Akron, OH
The U of Arizona, AZ
U of Baltimore, MD
U of Central Missouri, MO
U of Central Oklahoma, OK
The U of Findlay, OH
U of Guelph, ON, Canada
U of Hawaii at Manoa, HI
U of Illinois at Urbana–
  Champaign, IL
U of Miami, FL
U of Minnesota, Duluth, MN
U of Nebraska at Omaha,
  NE
U of New Brunswick
  Fredericton, NB, Canada
The U of North Carolina at
  Chapel Hill, NC
U of Pennsylvania, PA
U of St. Thomas, MN
The U of Scranton, PA
The U of Tennessee at
  Martin, TN
The U of Texas at San
  Antonio, TX
U of the Incarnate Word, TX
Urbana U, OH
Ursuline Coll, OH
Valencia Comm Coll, FL
Western Tech Coll, WI
Westminster Coll, UT
Wichita State U, KS
Wright State U, OH
Xavier U, OH

**HUMAN RESOURCES
MANAGEMENT AND
SERVICES RELATED**
Bryant and Stratton Coll,
  Rochester, NY
Concordia U Coll of Alberta,
  AB, Canada
Niagara U, NY
Park U, MO
U of the District of
  Columbia, DC
Widener U, PA

HUMAN SERVICES
Albion Coll, MI
Alexandria Tech Coll, MN
American International Coll,
  MA
Anderson U, SC
Asnuntuck Comm Coll, CT
Beacon Coll, FL
Bethel Coll, IN
Bunker Hill Comm Coll, MA
Burlington County Coll, NJ
California State U, San
  Bernardino, CA
Carson-Newman Coll, TN

Central Florida Comm Coll, FL
Central Ohio Tech Coll, OH
Central Piedmont Comm Coll, NC
Central Wyoming Coll, WY
Chesapeake Coll, MD
Clayton State U, GA
Coll of St. Joseph, VT
Cornell U, NY
Cosumnes River Coll, Sacramento, CA
Crafton Hills Coll, CA
Cuesta Coll, CA
Delaware Tech & Comm Coll, Jack F. Owens Campus, DE
Eastern New Mexico U–Roswell, NM
Elmira Coll, NY
Elon U, NC
Fitchburg State Coll, MA
Florida Comm Coll at Jacksonville, FL
Florida Gulf Coast U, FL
Fontbonne U, MO
Framingham State Coll, MA
Frederick Comm Coll, MD
Fresno City Coll, CA
Fulton-Montgomery Comm Coll, NY
Geneva Coll, PA
The George Washington U, DC
Graceland U, IA
Harrisburg Area Comm Coll, PA
High Point U, NC
Hillsborough Comm Coll, FL
Hopkinsville Comm Coll, KY
Housatonic Comm Coll, CT
Hudson Valley Comm Coll, NY
Indiana U–Purdue U Fort Wayne, IN
Itasca Comm Coll, MN
Ivy Tech Comm Coll–Kokomo, IN
Jamestown Comm Coll, NY
Kellogg Comm Coll, MI
Kendall Coll, IL
Kentucky Wesleyan Coll, KY
Kingsborough Comm Coll of the City U of New York, NY
LaGrange Coll, GA
Lake Superior State U, MI
Lassen Comm Coll District, CA
Lincoln U, PA
Lindenwood U, MO
Long Beach City Coll, CA
Lynn U, FL
Marywood U, PA
Massasoit Comm Coll, MA
Maui Comm Coll, HI
Mercer U, GA
Metropolitan Coll of New York, NY
Metropolitan Comm Coll–Longview, MO
Miami Dade Coll, FL
Middlesex Comm Coll, CT
Midland Lutheran Coll, NE
Mitchell Coll, CT
Mohawk Valley Comm Coll, NY
Mount Vernon Nazarene U, OH
National-Louis U, IL
New Hampshire Comm Tech Coll, Nashua/Claremont, NH

New York City Coll of Technology of the City U of New York, NY
New York U, NY
North Central Missouri Coll, MO
Northeastern U, MA
Notre Dame de Namur U, CA
Odessa Coll, TX
Pacific Oaks Coll, CA
Park U, MO
Quincy Coll, MA
Richmond Comm Coll, NC
Roosevelt U, IL
Saint Leo U, FL
St. Louis Comm Coll at Florissant Valley, MO
Santa Rosa Jr Coll, CA
Sauk Valley Comm Coll, IL
Seton Hill U, PA
Skagit Valley Coll, WA
Southwest Baptist U, MO
Stark State Coll of Technology, OH
State U of New York Coll at Cortland, NY
State U of New York Coll of Technology at Alfred, NY
Sussex County Comm Coll, NJ
Tennessee Wesleyan Coll, TN
Tunxis Comm Coll, CT
U of Alaska Anchorage, AK
U of Baltimore, MD
U of Cincinnati, OH
U of Great Falls, MT
The U of Maine at Augusta, ME
U of Maine at Machias, ME
U of Massachusetts Boston, MA
U of Oregon, OR
U of Rhode Island, RI
The U of Scranton, PA
U of Wisconsin–Oshkosh, WI
Upper Iowa U, IA
Villanova U, PA
Virginia Highlands Comm Coll, VA
Washburn U, KS
Westchester Comm Coll, NY
Westmoreland County Comm Coll, PA

HYDRAULICS AND FLUID POWER TECHNOLOGY
Alexandria Tech Coll, MN

HYDROLOGY AND WATER RESOURCES SCIENCE
Citrus Coll, CA
Coll of the Canyons, CA
Cornell U, NY
Lake Superior State U, MI
North Carolina State U, NC
Northern Michigan U, MI
Rensselaer Polytechnic Inst, NY
St. Francis Xavier U, NS, Canada
Spokane Comm Coll, WA
State U of New York Coll at Brockport, NY
State U of New York Coll of Environmental Science and Forestry, NY
U of California, Santa Barbara, CA
U of New Hampshire, NH

The U of Texas at Austin, TX
U of the District of Columbia, DC
U of Toronto, ON, Canada
U of Wisconsin–Madison, WI
U of Wisconsin–Stevens Point, WI
Ventura Coll, CA
Wright State U, OH

ILLUSTRATION
Academy of Art U, CA
The Art Inst of Pittsburgh, PA
California State U, Fullerton, CA
The Cleveland Inst of Art, OH
Fashion Inst of Technology, NY
Pratt Inst, NY
Ringling Coll of Art and Design, FL
Rochester Inst of Technology, NY
Savannah Coll of Art and Design, GA
School of the Art Inst of Chicago, IL
School of Visual Arts, NY
Syracuse U, NY
U of Kansas, KS
U of Miami, FL
U of San Francisco, CA
The U of the Arts, PA

INDUSTRIAL AND ORGANIZATIONAL PSYCHOLOGY
Abilene Christian U, TX
Albright Coll, PA
California State U, Sacramento, CA
Eastern Connecticut State U, CT
Fitchburg State Coll, MA
Ithaca Coll, NY
Lincoln U, PA
Marywood U, PA
Middle Tennessee State U, TN
Moravian Coll, PA
Point Loma Nazarene U, CA
Saint Xavier U, IL
U of Illinois at Urbana–Champaign, IL
The U of Tennessee at Martin, TN
Wright State U, OH

INDUSTRIAL ARTS
Ball State U, IN
Bemidji State U, MN
Buffalo State Coll, State U of New York, NY
Comm Coll of Beaver County, PA
El Camino Coll, CA
Fitchburg State Coll, MA
Fort Hays State U, KS
Fresno City Coll, CA
Langston U, OK
Long Beach City Coll, CA
Minnesota State U Mankato, MN
New Mexico Jr Coll, NM
Northern State U, SD
Pittsburg State U, KS
Rockingham Comm Coll, NC
St. Cloud State U, MN
San Francisco State U, CA
Southern Utah U, UT

U of Cincinnati, OH
U of the District of Columbia, DC
U of Wisconsin–Platteville, WI

INDUSTRIAL DESIGN
Academy of Art U, CA
The Art Inst of Pittsburgh, PA
The Art Inst of Seattle, WA
Carleton U, ON, Canada
Carnegie Mellon U, PA
Clemson U, SC
The Cleveland Inst of Art, OH
Fashion Inst of Technology, NY
North Carolina State U, NC
The Ohio State U, OH
Parsons The New School for Design, NY
Pratt Inst, NY
Rochester Inst of Technology, NY
San Francisco State U, CA
Santa Rosa Jr Coll, CA
Savannah Coll of Art and Design, GA
Syracuse U, NY
U of Cincinnati, OH
U of Illinois at Urbana–Champaign, IL
U of Kansas, KS
U of Michigan, MI
The U of the Arts, PA
U of Washington, WA
U of Wisconsin–Platteville, WI

INDUSTRIAL ELECTRONICS TECHNOLOGY
Northland Comm and Tech Coll–Thief River Falls, MN
Shelton State Comm Coll, AL
State U of New York Coll of Technology at Alfred, NY

INDUSTRIAL ENGINEERING
Bradley U, IL
Clemson U, SC
Dalhousie U, NS, Canada
Eastern Nazarene Coll, MA
Gannon U, PA
Hofstra U, NY
Kansas State U, KS
Lamar U, TX
Lehigh U, PA
Marquette U, WI
Montana State U, MT
North Carolina State U, NC
North Dakota State U, ND
Northeastern U, MA
Northern Illinois U, IL
The Ohio State U, OH
Oklahoma State U, OK
Penn State Abington, PA
Penn State DuBois, PA
Penn State Fayette, The Eberly Campus, PA
Penn State Mont Alto, PA
Penn State Wilkes-Barre, PA
Rensselaer Polytechnic Inst, NY
Rochester Inst of Technology, NY
Rutgers, The State U of New Jersey, New Brunswick, NJ
Ryerson U, ON, Canada
St. Cloud State U, MN
Santa Barbara City Coll, CA

Southern Illinois U Edwardsville, IL
Texas A&M U, TX
Tufts U, MA
U at Buffalo, the State U of New York, NY
The U of Alabama, AL
The U of Alabama in Huntsville, AL
U of Arkansas, AR
U of Central Florida, FL
U of Cincinnati, OH
U of Connecticut, CT
U of Houston, TX
U of Illinois at Urbana–Champaign, IL
U of Manitoba, MB, Canada
U of Massachusetts Amherst, MA
U of Miami, FL
U of Michigan, MI
U of Minnesota, Duluth, MN
U of Missouri–Columbia, MO
U of Missouri–Rolla, MO
U of Nebraska–Lincoln, NE
U of Pittsburgh, PA
U of Rhode Island, RI
U of San Diego, CA
The U of Tennessee, TN
The U of Texas at El Paso, TX
U of Toronto, ON, Canada
U of Vermont, VT
U of Washington, WA
U of Wisconsin–Madison, WI
U of Wisconsin–Platteville, WI
Wayne State U, MI
Western New England Coll, MA
Wichita State U, KS

INDUSTRIAL/ MANUFACTURING ENGINEERING
The U of Arizona, AZ

INDUSTRIAL MECHANICS AND MAINTENANCE TECHNOLOGY
British Columbia Inst of Technology, BC, Canada
Calhoun Comm Coll, AL
Coahoma Comm Coll, MS
Harrisburg Area Comm Coll, PA
Heartland Comm Coll, IL
Lamar Inst of Technology, TX
Macomb Comm Coll, MI
North Central Texas Coll, TX
Southwestern Michigan Coll, MI
Waubonsee Comm Coll, IL

INDUSTRIAL PRODUCTION TECHNOLOGIES RELATED
Broome Comm Coll, NY
East Carolina U, NC
Ivy Tech Comm Coll–Southwest, IN
Ivy Tech Comm Coll–Wabash Valley, IN
Millersville U of Pennsylvania, PA
Mohawk Valley Comm Coll, NY
Richmond Comm Coll, NC
Southwestern Coll, KS

The U of Akron, OH
U of Nebraska–Lincoln, NE
U of Wisconsin–Stout, WI
Wayne State Coll, NE
Wayne State U, MI

INDUSTRIAL RADIOLOGIC TECHNOLOGY
Aims Comm Coll, CO
Ball State U, IN
Blinn Coll, TX
Briar Cliff U, IA
Broward Comm Coll, FL
Chattanooga State Tech Comm Coll, TN
Crafton Hills Coll, CA
Fort Hays State U, KS
Fresno City Coll, CA
The George Washington U, DC
Greenville Tech Coll, SC
Hillsborough Comm Coll, FL
Houston Comm Coll System, TX
Jefferson Comm Coll, OH
Kapiolani Comm Coll, HI
Lamar U, TX
Laredo Comm Coll, TX
Long Beach City Coll, CA
Middlesex Comm Coll, CT
National-Louis U, IL
Odessa Coll, TX
Oregon Inst of Technology, OR
Rose State Coll, OK
San Diego Mesa Coll, CA
Sauk Valley Comm Coll, IL
Southern Maine Comm Coll, ME
Trocaire Coll, NY
U of Cincinnati, OH
U of the District of Columbia, DC
Virginia Highlands Comm Coll, VA
Westchester Comm Coll, NY
Widener U, PA

INDUSTRIAL SAFETY TECHNOLOGY
Rochester Inst of Technology, NY

INDUSTRIAL TECHNOLOGY
Alexandria Tech Coll, MN
Asnuntuck Comm Coll, CT
Ball State U, IN
Bemidji State U, MN
Bradley U, IL
British Columbia Inst of Technology, BC, Canada
Buffalo State Coll, State U of New York, NY
Cameron U, OK
Central Arizona Coll, AZ
Central Ohio Tech Coll, OH
Central Piedmont Comm Coll, NC
Comm Coll of Allegheny County, PA
Cuesta Coll, CA
DeKalb Tech Coll, GA
East Carolina U, NC
East Central Coll, MO
Eastern Michigan U, MI
Eastern New Mexico U–Roswell, NM
Edinboro U of Pennsylvania, PA
Fitchburg State Coll, MA
Fresno City Coll, CA
Glendale Comm Coll, CA

Grambling State U, LA
Greenville Tech Coll, SC
Hagerstown Comm Coll, MD
Heartland Comm Coll, IL
Hocking Coll, OH
Hopkinsville Comm Coll, KY
Houston Comm Coll System, TX
Hudson Valley Comm Coll, NY
Illinois State U, IL
Illinois Valley Comm Coll, IL
Indiana U–Purdue U Fort Wayne, IN
Ivy Tech Comm Coll–Kokomo, IN
Ivy Tech Comm Coll–Southwest, IN
Ivy Tech Comm Coll–Wabash Valley, IN
Jefferson Comm Coll, OH
Kellogg Comm Coll, MI
Lackawanna Coll, PA
Lake Superior State U, MI
Lamar U, TX
Langston U, OK
Long Beach City Coll, CA
Macomb Comm Coll, MI
Miami Dade Coll, FL
Middle Tennessee State U, TN
Millersville U of Pennsylvania, PA
Minnesota State Coll–Southeast Tech, MN
Minnesota State U Mankato, MN
Minnesota State U Moorhead, MN
MiraCosta Coll, CA
Missouri State U–West Plains, MO
Murray State U, KY
New Hampshire Comm Tech Coll, Nashua/Claremont, NH
Northern Illinois U, IL
Ozarks Tech Comm Coll, MO
Pittsburg State U, KS
Prairie View A&M U, TX
Purdue U North Central, IN
Richland Comm Coll, IL
Santa Ana Coll, CA
Santa Barbara City Coll, CA
Schoolcraft Coll, MI
Seminole Comm Coll, FL
Southeast Tech Inst, SD
Southern Illinois U Carbondale, IL
Spokane Comm Coll, WA
Spoon River Coll, IL
Stark State Coll of Technology, OH
State U of New York Coll of Technology at Canton, NY
The U of Akron, OH
U of Central Missouri, MO
U of Cincinnati, OH
U of Dayton, OH
U of Houston, TX
U of Massachusetts Lowell, MA
U of Nebraska at Omaha, NE
U of Nebraska–Lincoln, NE
The U of North Carolina at Charlotte, NC
U of Northern Iowa, IA
U of Rio Grande, OH
U of Wisconsin–Platteville, WI
Valencia Comm Coll, FL

Washburn U, KS
Waubonsee Comm Coll, IL
Wayne State U, MI
West Texas A&M U, TX
West Virginia Northern Comm Coll, WV
Wright State U, OH

INFORMATION RESOURCES MANAGEMENT
Mount St. Mary's U, MD
U of Wisconsin–Eau Claire, WI

INFORMATION SCIENCE/STUDIES
Aims Comm Coll, CO
Albright Coll, PA
Altamaha Tech Coll, GA
Alvernia Coll, PA
American International Coll, MA
Anderson U, IN
Ashland Comm and Tech Coll, KY
Ashland U, OH
Athabasca U, AB, Canada
Athens State U, AL
Bainbridge Coll, GA
Ball State U, IN
Barry U, FL
Beacon Coll, FL
Belmont Abbey Coll, NC
Bemidji State U, MN
Blue Ridge Comm Coll, VA
Bradley U, IL
Brewton-Parker Coll, GA
British Columbia Inst of Technology, BC, Canada
Brock U, ON, Canada
Broome Comm Coll, NY
Broward Comm Coll, FL
Bucks County Comm Coll, PA
Buffalo State Coll, State U of New York, NY
California State U, Fullerton, CA
California State U, Northridge, CA
California State U, Stanislaus, CA
Cape Breton U, NS, Canada
Cape Cod Comm Coll, MA
Carleton U, ON, Canada
Carlow U, PA
Carnegie Mellon U, PA
Carroll Coll, WI
Carson-Newman Coll, TN
Cedar Crest Coll, PA
Chattahoochee Tech Coll, GA
Chattanooga State Tech Comm Coll, TN
Christopher Newport U, VA
Clayton State U, GA
Clemson U, SC
Coll of Charleston, SC
Coll of St. Joseph, VT
The Coll of Saint Rose, NY
Coll of Staten Island of the City U of New York, NY
Coll of The Albemarle, NC
Coll of the Canyons, CA
The Coll of Westchester, NY
Columbus State U, GA
Comm Coll of Aurora, CO
Comm Coll of Beaver County, PA
Concord U, WV
Coosa Valley Tech Coll, GA
Cornell U, NY
Cornerstone U, MI

Cosumnes River Coll, Sacramento, CA
Dabney S. Lancaster Comm Coll, VA
DeKalb Tech Coll, GA
Delaware State U, DE
DePaul U, IL
Dominican U, IL
Eastern Michigan U, MI
El Centro Coll, TX
Elmira Coll, NY
Fairfield U, CT
Farmingdale State Coll, NY
Ferrum Coll, VA
Fitchburg State Coll, MA
Florida Comm Coll at Jacksonville, FL
Florida Inst of Technology, FL
Fort Hays State U, KS
Freed-Hardeman U, TN
Fulton-Montgomery Comm Coll, NY
Gaston Coll, NC
Glenville State Coll, WV
Gloucester County Coll, NJ
Gonzaga U, WA
Goshen Coll, IN
Grambling State U, LA
Grossmont Coll, CA
Heartland Comm Coll, IL
High Point U, NC
Hillsborough Comm Coll, FL
Hofstra U, NY
Houston Baptist U, TX
Howard Comm Coll, MD
Husson Coll, ME
Idaho State U, ID
Illinois State U, IL
Immaculata U, PA
Johnson & Wales U, RI
Johnson State Coll, VT
Kansas State U, KS
Lamar State Coll–Orange, TX
Lamar U, TX
Laredo Comm Coll, TX
Lee Coll, TX
Lehigh U, PA
Le Moyne Coll, NY
LeTourneau U, TX
Loyola U New Orleans, LA
MacMurray Coll, IL
Madisonville Comm Coll, KY
Marietta Coll, OH
Marist Coll, NY
Marquette U, WI
Marymount U, VA
Mercer U, GA
Mercyhurst Coll, PA
Miami Dade Coll, FL
Middle Georgia Tech Coll, GA
Middlesex County Coll, NJ
Minnesota State U Mankato, MN
MiraCosta Coll, CA
Montana Tech of The U of Montana, MT
Moorpark Coll, CA
Mount Saint Vincent U, NS, Canada
Mount Union Coll, OH
Murray State U, KY
National-Louis U, IL
New Hampshire Comm Tech Coll, Nashua/Claremont, NH
New River Comm Coll, VA
New York City Coll of Technology of the City U of New York, NY
New York U, NY
Niagara U, NY

North Central Texas Coll, TX
Northeastern U, MA
Northern Michigan U, MI
North Georgia Coll & State U, GA
Northwestern Oklahoma State U, OK
Notre Dame Coll, OH
Ocean County Coll, NJ
Odessa Coll, TX
The Ohio State U, OH
Ozarks Tech Comm Coll, MO
Paris Jr Coll, TX
Penn State Abington, PA
Penn State DuBois, PA
Penn State Fayette, The Eberly Campus, PA
Penn State Mont Alto, PA
Penn State Wilkes-Barre, PA
Phoenix Coll, AZ
Pueblo Comm Coll, CO
Purdue U North Central, IN
Queens U of Charlotte, NC
Radford U, VA
Ramapo Coll of New Jersey, NJ
Reedley Coll, CA
Reinhardt Coll, GA
The Richard Stockton Coll of New Jersey, NJ
Richland Comm Coll, IL
Rivier Coll, NH
Rockingham Comm Coll, NC
Rose State Coll, OK
Roxbury Comm Coll, MA
Rutgers, The State U of New Jersey, Newark, NJ
Rutgers, The State U of New Jersey, New Brunswick, NJ
St. Cloud State U, MN
St. Francis Xavier U, NS, Canada
St. Louis Comm Coll at Florissant Valley, MO
St. Thomas Aquinas Coll, NY
Salve Regina U, RI
San Diego State U, CA
San Francisco State U, CA
Santa Ana Coll, CA
Santa Barbara City Coll, CA
Scottsdale Comm Coll, AZ
Seminole Comm Coll, FL
Southeast Tech Inst, SD
Southern Illinois U Carbondale, IL
Southern Maine Comm Coll, ME
Southern Utah U, UT
Spoon River Coll, IL
State U of New York at Fredonia, NY
State U of New York Coll of Technology at Canton, NY
Surry Comm Coll, NC
Syracuse U, NY
Taylor U, IN
Texas A&M U–Corpus Christi, TX
Thiel Coll, PA
Towson U, MD
Trevecca Nazarene U, TN
Tunxis Comm Coll, CT
Union Coll, NE
U at Albany, State U of New York, NY
U of Alaska Anchorage, AK
U of Baltimore, MD
U of California, Los Angeles, CA
U of Cincinnati, OH
U of Dayton, OH
U of Great Falls, MT

U of Guelph, ON, Canada
U of Houston, TX
U of Mary Hardin-Baylor, TX
U of Maryland, Baltimore County, MD
U of Miami, FL
U of Missouri–Rolla, MO
U of New Brunswick Fredericton, NB, Canada
U of New Haven, CT
The U of North Carolina at Chapel Hill, NC
U of Pittsburgh, PA
U of Pittsburgh at Bradford, PA
U of San Francisco, CA
The U of Scranton, PA
The U of Tampa, FL
The U of Texas at El Paso, TX
U of the District of Columbia, DC
U of the Pacific, CA
U of Vermont, VT
U of Washington, WA
U of Wisconsin–Green Bay, WI
Valdosta State U, GA
Victor Valley Coll, CA
Villanova U, PA
Virginia Highlands Comm Coll, VA
Wayne State Coll, NE
Wayne State U, MI
Westchester Comm Coll, NY
West Liberty State Coll, WV
Westminster Coll, PA
Westmoreland County Comm Coll, PA
West Virginia Wesleyan Coll, WV
Widener U, PA
Wilkes U, PA
William Jewell Coll, MO
Wright State U, OH

INFORMATION TECHNOLOGY

Blue Ridge Comm Coll, VA
Bryant and Stratton Coll, Rochester, NY
Bucks County Comm Coll, PA
Burlington County Coll, NJ
Caldwell Comm Coll and Tech Inst, NC
Cape Cod Comm Coll, MA
Central Florida Comm Coll, FL
Coll of The Albemarle, NC
The Coll of Westchester, NY
Columbus State U, GA
Cuesta Coll, CA
El Centro Coll, TX
Everglades U, Sarasota, FL
Florida Comm Coll at Jacksonville, FL
Florida International U, FL
Framingham State Coll, MA
Frederick Comm Coll, MD
Furman U, SC
Gainesville State Coll, GA
Galveston Coll, TX
Harding U, AR
Harrisburg Area Comm Coll, PA
Heartland Comm Coll, IL
Houghton Coll, NY
Howard Comm Coll, MD
Hudson Valley Comm Coll, NY
Illinois State U, IL
Kutztown U of Pennsylvania, PA

Laredo Comm Coll, TX
Lassen Comm Coll District, CA
Marist Coll, NY
McNeese State U, LA
Minnesota School of Business–St. Cloud, MN
Missouri State U–West Plains, MO
Neumont U, UT
North Carolina State U, NC
Northland Comm and Tech Coll–Thief River Falls, MN
Rensselaer Polytechnic Inst, NY
Rochester Inst of Technology, NY
Rocky Mountain Coll, MT
Ryerson U, ON, Canada
St. Cloud Tech Coll, MN
San Diego State U, CA
Santa Ana Coll, CA
Santa Barbara City Coll, CA
Seminole Comm Coll, FL
Slippery Rock U of Pennsylvania, PA
Southeast Tech Inst, SD
South U, GA
Stark State Coll of Technology, OH
Surry Comm Coll, NC
Temple U, PA
Tidewater Comm Coll, VA
U of Arkansas, AR
U of Central Florida, FL
U of Great Falls, MT
U of Houston, TX
U of Massachusetts Lowell, MA
U of Missouri–Kansas City, MO
U of Rio Grande, OH
U of the Incarnate Word, TX
Valencia Comm Coll, FL
Vermont Tech Coll, VT
Washington & Jefferson Coll, PA
Western Nebraska Comm Coll, NE
West Shore Comm Coll, MI
West Virginia Northern Comm Coll, WV

INSTITUTIONAL FOOD WORKERS

The Art Inst of Pittsburgh, PA
Asheville-Buncombe Tech Comm Coll, NC
Grambling State U, LA
Harrisburg Area Comm Coll, PA
Kendall Coll, IL
Lamar Inst of Technology, TX
MiraCosta Coll, CA
Santa Barbara City Coll, CA
West Virginia Northern Comm Coll, WV

INSTRUMENTATION TECHNOLOGY

Chattanooga State Tech Comm Coll, TN
Clayton State U, GA
DeKalb Tech Coll, GA
Florida Comm Coll at Jacksonville, FL
Idaho State U, ID
Lamar Inst of Technology, TX
Lee Coll, TX
McNeese State U, LA
Nassau Comm Coll, NY

New River Comm Coll, VA
Ozarks Tech Comm Coll, MO
St. Cloud Tech Coll, MN

INSURANCE

Ball State U, IN
Baylor U, TX
Bradley U, IL
Broward Comm Coll, FL
California State U, Sacramento, CA
Central Piedmont Comm Coll, NC
Comm Coll of Allegheny County, PA
Florida Comm Coll at Jacksonville, FL
Florida International U, FL
Gannon U, PA
Houston Comm Coll System, TX
Illinois State U, IL
Illinois Wesleyan U, IL
Mercyhurst Coll, PA
Minnesota State U Mankato, MN
Missouri State U, MO
Nassau Comm Coll, NY
The Ohio State U, OH
Richland Comm Coll, IL
Roosevelt U, IL
St. Cloud State U, MN
Temple U, PA
U of Cincinnati, OH
U of Connecticut, CT
U of Hartford, CT
U of Mississippi, MS
U of Pennsylvania, PA
U of Wisconsin–Madison, WI

INTERCULTURAL/ MULTICULTURAL AND DIVERSITY STUDIES

Immaculata U, PA
Marquette U, WI
Sterling Coll, VT
Western Oregon U, OR

INTERDISCIPLINARY STUDIES

Abilene Christian U, TX
Albright Coll, PA
Alderson-Broaddus Coll, WV
American U, DC
Amherst Coll, MA
Angelo State U, TX
Arizona State U at the West campus, AZ
Augsburg Coll, MN
Bard Coll, NY
Bentley Coll, MA
Bethany U, CA
Bluefield State Coll, WV
Boston Coll, MA
Brevard Coll, NC
Brock U, ON, Canada
California State U, San Bernardino, CA
Calvin Coll, MI
Cardinal Stritch U, WI
Carleton U, ON, Canada
Carson-Newman Coll, TN
The Catholic U of America, DC
Christopher Newport U, VA
Clark U, MA
Coe Coll, IA
Coll of Mount Saint Vincent, NY
The Coll of Saint Rose, NY
Coll of the Atlantic, ME

The Coll of William and Mary, VA
Cornell U, NY
Cornerstone U, MI
Dallas Baptist U, TX
DePaul U, IL
Earlham Coll, IN
Eckerd Coll, FL
Elmira Coll, NY
Elms Coll, MA
Emory U, GA
Eugene Lang Coll The New School for Liberal Arts, NY
Florida Inst of Technology, FL
Freed-Hardeman U, TN
The George Washington U, DC
Grinnell Coll, IA
Gustavus Adolphus Coll, MN
Hope Coll, MI
Houston Baptist U, TX
Hudson Valley Comm Coll, NY
Illinois State U, IL
Illinois Wesleyan U, IL
Iona Coll, NY
Ithaca Coll, NY
Jacksonville U, FL
John Brown U, AR
Kansas State U, KS
Kentucky Wesleyan Coll, KY
Kenyon Coll, OH
Keuka Coll, NY
Lake Superior State U, MI
Lamar U, TX
LeTourneau U, TX
Liberty U, VA
Long Island U, Brooklyn Campus, NY
Macalester Coll, MN
Marquette U, WI
Marywood U, PA
Massachusetts Coll of Liberal Arts, MA
Middle Tennessee State U, TN
Minneapolis Coll of Art and Design, MN
Minnesota State U Moorhead, MN
Molloy Coll, NY
Morningside Coll, IA
Mount Holyoke Coll, MA
Mount Saint Vincent U, NS, Canada
Mount Union Coll, OH
New York U, NY
Nova Southeastern U, FL
Oglethorpe U, GA
Piedmont Coll, GA
Prairie View A&M U, TX
Queens Coll of the City U of New York, NY
Radford U, VA
Ramapo Coll of New Jersey, NJ
Rensselaer Polytechnic Inst, NY
Rhodes Coll, TN
The Richard Stockton Coll of New Jersey, NJ
Ripon Coll, WI
Rochester Inst of Technology, NY
Rocky Mountain Coll, MT
Rutgers, The State U of New Jersey, New Brunswick, NJ
St. Bonaventure U, NY
St. Cloud State U, MN
St. Thomas U, NB, Canada
Santa Clara U, CA
Southern Oregon U, OR

State U of New York at Fredonia, NY
State U of New York Coll at Brockport, NY
State U of New York Coll of Technology at Canton, NY
Stephen F. Austin State U, TX
Syracuse U, NY
Temple U, PA
Tennessee Wesleyan Coll, TN
Texas A&M U, TX
Texas A&M U–Corpus Christi, TX
Towson U, MD
Trent U, ON, Canada
Trinity Coll, CT
Unity Coll, ME
U at Albany, State U of New York, NY
The U of Akron, OH
The U of Akron–Wayne Coll, OH
The U of Alabama, AL
U of Alaska Anchorage, AK
U of Baltimore, MD
U of California, Santa Barbara, CA
U of Hartford, CT
U of Hawaii at Manoa, HI
U of Houston, TX
U of Kentucky, KY
U of Maryland, Baltimore County, MD
U of Mary Washington, VA
U of Massachusetts Boston, MA
U of Michigan, MI
U of Minnesota, Duluth, MN
U of Missouri–Columbia, MO
U of Missouri–Kansas City, MO
U of New Hampshire, NH
U of Pittsburgh, PA
U of Portland, OR
U of Redlands, CA
U of Rhode Island, RI
U of St. Thomas, MN
U of San Francisco, CA
U of South Carolina Upstate, SC
The U of Tennessee at Martin, TN
The U of Texas at El Paso, TX
U of the Incarnate Word, TX
U of the Pacific, CA
U of Vermont, VT
The U of Virginia's Coll at Wise, VA
U of Washington, WA
U of Wisconsin–Green Bay, WI
Vanguard U of Southern California, CA
Vassar Coll, NY
Virginia Intermont Coll, VA
Wayne State Coll, NE
Wayne State U, MI
Western Nebraska Comm Coll, NE
Western Oregon U, OR
West Liberty State Coll, WV
Westminster Coll, PA
West Texas A&M U, TX
William Jewell Coll, MO

INTERIOR ARCHITECTURE

Indiana U of Pennsylvania, PA
Kansas State U, KS

St. Philip's Coll, TX
School of the Art Inst of
Chicago, IL
Stephen F. Austin State U,
TX
Syracuse U, NY
U of Central Missouri, MO
U of Houston, TX
U of Missouri–Columbia,
MO
U of Nebraska–Lincoln, NE
U of New Haven, CT
U of Oregon, OR
The U of Texas at San
Antonio, TX
U of Washington, WA

INTERIOR DESIGN
Abilene Christian U, TX
Academy of Art U, CA
Alexandria Tech Coll, MN
Anderson U, SC
The Art Inst of Houston, TX
The Art Inst of Ohio–
Cincinnati, OH
The Art Inst of Pittsburgh,
PA
The Art Inst of Seattle, WA
Baker Coll of Allen Park, MI
Baylor U, TX
Boston Architectural Coll,
MA
Brenau U, GA
British Columbia Inst of
Technology, BC, Canada
Broward Comm Coll, FL
California State U,
Sacramento, CA
Carson-Newman Coll, TN
Central Piedmont Comm
Coll, NC
The Cleveland Inst of Art,
OH
Coll of Mount St. Joseph,
OH
Coll of the Canyons, CA
Coll of the Desert, CA
Cosumnes River Coll,
Sacramento, CA
Cuesta Coll, CA
Dixie State Coll of Utah, UT
East Carolina U, NC
Eastern Michigan U, MI
El Camino Coll, CA
El Centro Coll, TX
Fashion Inst of Technology,
NY
Florida Comm Coll at
Jacksonville, FL
Florida International U, FL
Harding U, AR
Harrington Coll of Design,
IL
High Point U, NC
Hillsborough Comm Coll, FL
Houston Comm Coll System,
TX
The Illinois Inst of Art–
Schaumburg, IL
Indiana U Bloomington, IN
Indiana U–Purdue U Fort
Wayne, IN
Indiana U–Purdue U
Indianapolis, IN
Ivy Tech Comm Coll–
Southwest, IN
Kansas State U, KS
Lamar U, TX
Long Beach City Coll, CA
Marian Coll, IN
Marymount U, VA
Mercyhurst Coll, PA
Miami Dade Coll, FL
Michigan State U, MI

Middle Tennessee State U,
TN
Minnesota State U Mankato,
MN
Nassau Comm Coll, NY
North Dakota State U, ND
The Ohio State U, OH
Otis Coll of Art and Design,
CA
Park U, MO
Parsons The New School for
Design, NY
Phoenix Coll, AZ
Pratt Inst, NY
Radford U, VA
Ringling Coll of Art and
Design, FL
Rochester Inst of
Technology, NY
Ryerson U, ON, Canada
St. Philip's Coll, TX
San Diego Mesa Coll, CA
San Diego State U, CA
San Francisco State U, CA
Santa Barbara City Coll, CA
Santa Rosa Jr Coll, CA
Savannah Coll of Art and
Design, GA
School of the Art Inst of
Chicago, IL
School of Visual Arts, NY
Scottsdale Comm Coll, AZ
Seminole Comm Coll, FL
Southern Illinois U
Carbondale, IL
Southern Utah U, UT
Syracuse U, NY
Tidewater Comm Coll, VA
The U of Akron, OH
The U of Alabama, AL
U of Arkansas, AR
U of Central Missouri, MO
U of Central Oklahoma, OK
U of Cincinnati, OH
U of Houston, TX
U of Kansas, KS
U of Kentucky, KY
U of Manitoba, MB, Canada
U of Massachusetts Amherst,
MA
U of Northern Iowa, IA
The U of Tennessee, TN
The U of Tennessee at
Martin, TN
The U of Texas at Austin,
TX
The U of Texas at San
Antonio, TX
U of the Incarnate Word, TX
U of Wisconsin–Madison,
WI
U of Wisconsin–Stevens
Point, WI
Ursuline Coll, OH
Valdosta State U, GA
Watkins Coll of Art and
Design, TN
Waukesha County Tech Coll,
WI
Wayne State Coll, NE
Western Tech Coll, WI

**INTERMEDIA/
MULTIMEDIA**
American U, DC
The Art Inst of Pittsburgh,
PA
The Art Inst of Seattle, WA
The Cleveland Inst of Art,
OH
Fitchburg State Coll, MA
Hillsborough Comm Coll, FL
Indiana U of Pennsylvania,
PA

Lewis U, IL
Maine Coll of Art, ME
Middlesex Comm Coll, CT
Minneapolis Coll of Art and
Design, MN
Minnesota School of
Business–St. Cloud, MN
Northern Michigan U, MI
Radford U, VA
Ramapo Coll of New Jersey,
NJ
San Diego Mesa Coll, CA
School of the Art Inst of
Chicago, IL
State U of New York at
Fredonia, NY
U of Central Florida, FL
U of Michigan, MI
U of Oregon, OR

**INTERNATIONAL
AGRICULTURE**
Cornell U, NY
Eastern Mennonite U, VA
Sterling Coll, VT
U of Missouri–Columbia,
MO

**INTERNATIONAL AND
COMPARATIVE
EDUCATION**
Sterling Coll, VT

**INTERNATIONAL
BUSINESS/TRADE/
COMMERCE**
Albertson Coll of Idaho, ID
Albright Coll, PA
Alma Coll, MI
American International Coll,
MA
Arizona State U at the West
campus, AZ
Augsburg Coll, MN
Avila U, MO
Barry U, FL
Baylor U, TX
Belmont Abbey Coll, NC
Bethel Coll, IN
Bishop's U, QC, Canada
Bradley U, IL
Brevard Comm Coll, FL
British Columbia Inst of
Technology, BC, Canada
Brock U, ON, Canada
Buena Vista U, IA
Bunker Hill Comm Coll, MA
California State U,
Sacramento, CA
Cardinal Stritch U, WI
Carleton U, ON, Canada
Carlow U, PA
Christopher Newport U, VA
Claremont McKenna Coll,
CA
Clemson U, SC
Coll of Charleston, SC
The Coll of St. Scholastica,
MN
Dalhousie U, NS, Canada
DePaul U, IL
Dominican U, IL
Drake U, IA
Drury U, MO
Eastern Mennonite U, VA
Eastern Michigan U, MI
Eckerd Coll, FL
Elmira Coll, NY
Florida Atlantic U, FL
Florida Inst of Technology,
FL
Florida International U, FL
Foothill Coll, CA
Framingham State Coll, MA

Frederick Comm Coll, MD
Fresno Pacific U, CA
Gannon U, PA
The George Washington U,
DC
Georgia Coll & State U, GA
Gonzaga U, WA
Grace Coll, IN
Graceland U, IA
Grossmont Coll, CA
Gustavus Adolphus Coll,
MN
Hamline U, MN
Harding U, AR
High Point U, NC
Hofstra U, NY
Houston Baptist U, TX
Husson Coll, ME
Illinois State U, IL
Illinois Wesleyan U, IL
Immaculata U, PA
Indiana U of Pennsylvania,
PA
Iona Coll, NY
Ithaca Coll, NY
Jacksonville U, FL
John Brown U, AR
Johnson & Wales U, CO
King's Coll, PA
Kutztown U of
Pennsylvania, PA
Lake Erie Coll, OH
Lakeland Coll, WI
Laredo Comm Coll, TX
Lee Coll, TX
LeTourneau U, TX
Lewis U, IL
Long Beach City Coll, CA
Loras Coll, IA
Loyola U New Orleans, LA
Maine Maritime Academy,
ME
Marietta Coll, OH
Marquette U, WI
Marymount U, VA
Marywood U, PA
Minnesota State U Mankato,
MN
Minnesota State U
Moorhead, MN
Moravian Coll, PA
Mount Union Coll, OH
Murray State U, KY
National-Louis U, IL
Neumann Coll, PA
New York U, NY
Niagara U, NY
North Central Coll, IL
Northeastern U, MA
Northern State U, SD
Northland Comm and Tech
Coll–Thief River Falls, MN
Northwestern Coll, MN
Northwest Nazarene U, ID
Northwood U, MI
Northwood U, Florida
Campus, FL
Northwood U, Texas
Campus, TX
Notre Dame de Namur U,
CA
The Ohio State U, OH
Ohio Wesleyan U, OH
Old Dominion U, VA
Oral Roberts U, OK
Otterbein Coll, OH
Penn State DuBois, PA
Pima Comm Coll, AZ
Pittsburg State U, KS
Queens Coll of the City U of
New York, NY
Ramapo Coll of New Jersey,
NJ
Rhodes Coll, TN

Rochester Inst of
Technology, NY
Roosevelt U, IL
Roxbury Comm Coll, MA
Saginaw Valley State U, MI
St. Bonaventure U, NY
St. Cloud State U, MN
St. Norbert Coll, WI
Saint Xavier U, IL
San Diego State U, CA
San Francisco State U, CA
Seton Hill U, PA
Southern Adventist U, TN
Stark State Coll of
Technology, OH
State U of New York Coll at
Brockport, NY
Stephen F. Austin State U,
TX
Stetson U, FL
Taylor U, IN
Temple U, PA
Thiel Coll, PA
Trinity U, TX
The U of Akron, OH
U of Arkansas, AR
U of Baltimore, MD
U of Dayton, OH
U of Evansville, IN
The U of Findlay, OH
U of Hawaii at Manoa, HI
U of Miami, FL
U of Mississippi, MS
U of Missouri–Columbia,
MO
U of Nebraska–Lincoln, NE
U of New Brunswick
Fredericton, NB, Canada
U of New Haven, CT
The U of North Carolina at
Charlotte, NC
U of Northern British
Columbia, BC, Canada
U of North Florida, FL
U of Oregon, OR
U of Pennsylvania, PA
U of Portland, OR
U of Rhode Island, RI
U of Rio Grande, OH
U of St. Thomas, MN
U of San Francisco, CA
The U of Scranton, PA
The U of Tampa, FL
The U of Tennessee at
Martin, TN
The U of Texas at San
Antonio, TX
U of the Incarnate Word, TX
U of Washington, WA
U of Wisconsin–La Crosse,
WI
Utica Coll, NY
Vanguard U of Southern
California, CA
Villanova U, PA
Virginia Intermont Coll, VA
Washington & Jefferson Coll,
PA
Westchester Comm Coll, NY
Westminster Coll, PA
Westminster Coll, UT
Wichita State U, KS
Widener U, PA
William Jewell Coll, MO
Wofford Coll, SC
Xavier U, OH

**INTERNATIONAL
ECONOMICS**
Albertson Coll of Idaho, ID
Austin Coll, TX
Bard Coll, NY
Brock U, ON, Canada
Carson-Newman Coll, TN

Carthage Coll, WI
The Catholic U of America, DC
Claremont McKenna Coll, CA
Eastern Michigan U, MI
Hamline U, MN
Lawrence U, WI
Loyola Marymount U, CA
Rhodes Coll, TN
Rockford Coll, IL
Ryerson U, ON, Canada
Taylor U, IN
U of California, Los Angeles, CA
U of Missouri–Columbia, MO
U of St. Thomas, MN
U of West Georgia, GA
Westminster Coll, PA

INTERNATIONAL FINANCE
Broome Comm Coll, NY
The Catholic U of America, DC
The U of Akron, OH

INTERNATIONAL/ GLOBAL STUDIES
Abilene Christian U, TX
Adelphi U, NY
The Coll of St. Scholastica, MN
Framingham State Coll, MA
Hampshire Coll, MA
Harding U, AR
Hope Coll, MI
Illinois Wesleyan U, IL
Iona Coll, NY
Kenyon Coll, OH
Lewis U, IL
Macomb Comm Coll, MI
Marquette U, WI
Michigan State U, MI
Minnesota State U Moorhead, MN
North Dakota State U, ND
Northern Michigan U, MI
Oral Roberts U, OK
Pittsburg State U, KS
Point Loma Nazarene U, CA
Ramapo Coll of New Jersey, NJ
Randolph-Macon Coll, VA
Rockford Coll, IL
St. Lawrence U, NY
State U of New York Coll at Cortland, NY
Sterling Coll, VT
Texas A&M U, TX
U of California, Irvine, CA
U of Colorado at Boulder, CO
U of Nebraska at Omaha, NE
U of New Hampshire, NH
U of New Orleans, LA
U of Northern British Columbia, BC, Canada
U of Pennsylvania, PA

INTERNATIONAL MARKETING
Fashion Inst of Technology, NY
The U of Akron, OH

INTERNATIONAL PUBLIC HEALTH
Clemson U, SC

INTERNATIONAL RELATIONS AND AFFAIRS
Albion Coll, MI
American International Coll, MA
American U, DC
Ashland U, OH
Augsburg Coll, MN
Austin Coll, TX
Bard Coll, NY
Barry U, FL
Baylor U, TX
Bethany U, CA
Bethel U, MN
Bishop's U, QC, Canada
Bradley U, IL
Brenau U, GA
Bridgewater Coll, VA
Brown U, RI
Calvin Coll, MI
Carleton U, ON, Canada
Carnegie Mellon U, PA
Carroll Coll, MT
Carroll Coll, WI
The Catholic U of America, DC
Cedar Crest Coll, PA
Claremont McKenna Coll, CA
Clark U, MA
Colby Coll, ME
Colgate U, NY
Coll of Saint Elizabeth, NJ
Coll of Staten Island of the City U of New York, NY
The Coll of William and Mary, VA
Concordia Coll–New York, NY
Dalhousie U, NS, Canada
DePaul U, IL
Drake U, IA
Duke U, NC
Earlham Coll, IN
Eckerd Coll, FL
Elmira Coll, NY
Elms Coll, MA
Elon U, NC
Emory U, GA
Eugene Lang Coll The New School for Liberal Arts, NY
Fairfield U, CT
Fairleigh Dickinson U, Metropolitan Campus, NJ
Ferrum Coll, VA
Florida International U, FL
The George Washington U, DC
Gonzaga U, WA
Gordon Coll, MA
Graceland U, IA
Hamilton Coll, NY
Hamline U, MN
Hampden-Sydney Coll, VA
Harding U, AR
Harrisburg Area Comm Coll, PA
High Point U, NC
Houghton Coll, NY
Immaculata U, PA
Indiana U of Pennsylvania, PA
Jacksonville U, FL
John Brown U, AR
Kellogg Comm Coll, MI
Kennesaw State U, GA
Kenyon Coll, OH
Lawrence U, WI
Lehigh U, PA
Le Moyne Coll, NY
Lincoln U, PA
Lindenwood U, MO
Loras Coll, IA

Loyola U Chicago, IL
Lynchburg Coll, VA
Lynn U, FL
Macalester Coll, MN
Manhattan Coll, NY
Manhattanville Coll, NY
Marquette U, WI
Marshall U, WV
Marymount Manhattan Coll, NY
Mercer U, GA
Miami Dade Coll, FL
Michigan State U, MI
Middle Tennessee State U, TN
Minnesota State U Mankato, MN
Mount Holyoke Coll, MA
Mount St. Mary's U, MD
Murray State U, KY
New York U, NY
Niagara U, NY
North Central Coll, IL
Northeastern U, MA
Northwest Nazarene U, ID
Occidental Coll, CA
Oglethorpe U, GA
The Ohio State U, OH
Ohio Wesleyan U, OH
Old Dominion U, VA
Oral Roberts U, OK
Otterbein Coll, OH
Penn State Abington, PA
Penn State DuBois, PA
Penn State Fayette, The Eberly Campus, PA
Penn State Mont Alto, PA
Penn State Wilkes-Barre, PA
Portland State U, OR
Queens U of Charlotte, NC
Randolph Coll, VA
Randolph-Macon Coll, VA
Rhodes Coll, TN
Rochester Inst of Technology, NY
Rockhurst U, MO
Roosevelt U, IL
Saginaw Valley State U, MI
St. Cloud State U, MN
Saint Joseph's Coll, IN
Saint Leo U, FL
St. Norbert Coll, WI
Saint Xavier U, IL
San Diego State U, CA
San Francisco State U, CA
Santa Barbara City Coll, CA
Seton Hall U, NJ
Seton Hill U, PA
Sewanee: The U of the South, TN
Southern Nazarene U, OK
Southern Oregon U, OR
Southwestern U, TX
State U of New York Coll at Brockport, NY
State U of New York Coll at Cortland, NY
State U of New York Coll at Geneseo, NY
Stetson U, FL
Stonehill Coll, MA
Sweet Briar Coll, VA
Syracuse U, NY
Taylor U, IN
Towson U, MD
Trent U, ON, Canada
Trinity Coll, CT
Tufts U, MA
Union Coll, NE
The U of Alabama, AL
U of Arkansas, AR
U of Cincinnati, OH
U of Dayton, OH
U of Delaware, DE

U of Evansville, IN
U of Kansas, KS
U of Mary Washington, VA
U of Miami, FL
U of Michigan, MI
U of Minnesota, Duluth, MN
U of Mississippi, MS
U of Nebraska at Kearney, NE
U of Nebraska–Lincoln, NE
U of New Brunswick Fredericton, NB, Canada
U of New Hampshire, NH
U of North Florida, FL
U of Oregon, OR
U of Pennsylvania, PA
U of Redlands, CA
U of St. Thomas, MN
U of St. Thomas, TX
U of San Diego, CA
The U of Scranton, PA
U of Southern Indiana, IN
The U of Tampa, FL
The U of Tennessee at Martin, TN
U of the Pacific, CA
U of Toronto, ON, Canada
U of Virginia, VA
U of Washington, WA
U of West Georgia, GA
U of Wisconsin–Madison, WI
U of Wisconsin–Oshkosh, WI
U of Wisconsin–Platteville, WI
U of Wisconsin–Stevens Point, WI
U of Wyoming, WY
Utica Coll, NY
Vassar Coll, NY
Wellesley Coll, MA
Wells Coll, NY
West Chester U of Pennsylvania, PA
Western New England Coll, MA
Western Oregon U, OR
Westminster Coll, PA
West Virginia Wesleyan Coll, WV
Wheaton Coll, IL
Widener U, PA
Wilfrid Laurier U, ON, Canada
Wilkes U, PA
William Jewell Coll, MO
Wilson Coll, PA
Wofford Coll, SC
Wright State U, OH
Xavier U, OH

IRANIAN/PERSIAN LANGUAGES
The U of Texas at Austin, TX

IRONWORKING
Ivy Tech Comm Coll–Southwest, IN
Ivy Tech Comm Coll–Wabash Valley, IN

ISLAMIC STUDIES
Brandeis U, MA
The Ohio State U, OH
U of California, Los Angeles, CA
U of California, Santa Barbara, CA
U of Michigan, MI
The U of Texas at Austin, TX
U of Toronto, ON, Canada

Wellesley Coll, MA

ITALIAN
Bard Coll, NY
Bishop's U, QC, Canada
Boston Coll, MA
Brock U, ON, Canada
Brown U, RI
Bryn Mawr Coll, PA
Carleton U, ON, Canada
Claremont McKenna Coll, CA
Coll of the Desert, CA
Cornell U, NY
DePaul U, IL
Dominican U, IL
Duke U, NC
El Camino Coll, CA
Emory U, GA
Florida International U, FL
Gonzaga U, WA
Haverford Coll, PA
Hofstra U, NY
Hunter Coll of the City U of New York, NY
Indiana U Bloomington, IN
Iona Coll, NY
Lake Erie Coll, OH
Loyola U Chicago, IL
Miami Dade Coll, FL
Mount Holyoke Coll, MA
New York U, NY
Northeastern U, MA
Oakland U, MI
The Ohio State U, OH
Penn State Abington, PA
Penn State DuBois, PA
Penn State Fayette, The Eberly Campus, PA
Penn State Mont Alto, PA
Penn State Wilkes-Barre, PA
Queens Coll of the City U of New York, NY
Rutgers, The State U of New Jersey, Newark, NJ
Rutgers, The State U of New Jersey, New Brunswick, NJ
San Francisco State U, CA
Santa Clara U, CA
Seton Hall U, NJ
Sweet Briar Coll, VA
Syracuse U, NY
Temple U, PA
Trinity Coll, CT
U at Albany, State U of New York, NY
U at Buffalo, the State U of New York, NY
The U of Arizona, AZ
U of California, Berkeley, CA
U of California, Los Angeles, CA
U of California, Santa Barbara, CA
U of Colorado at Boulder, CO
U of Connecticut, CT
U of Delaware, DE
U of Houston, TX
U of Illinois at Urbana–Champaign, IL
U of Massachusetts Amherst, MA
U of Massachusetts Boston, MA
U of Miami, FL
U of Michigan, MI
U of Notre Dame, IN
U of Oregon, OR
U of Pennsylvania, PA
U of Pittsburgh, PA
U of Rhode Island, RI
The U of Scranton, PA

The U of Tennessee, TN
The U of Texas at Austin, TX
U of Toronto, ON, Canada
U of Virginia, VA
U of Washington, WA
U of Wisconsin–Madison, WI
Vassar Coll, NY
Villanova U, PA
Wellesley Coll, MA
Yale U, CT

ITALIAN STUDIES
Brock U, ON, Canada
Brown U, RI
Dalhousie U, NS, Canada
Santa Clara U, CA
U of Vermont, VT
Wellesley Coll, MA

JAPANESE
Ball State U, IN
Bates Coll, ME
California State U, Fullerton, CA
Carnegie Mellon U, PA
Citrus Coll, CA
Claremont McKenna Coll, CA
Colgate U, NY
DePaul U, IL
Eastern Michigan U, MI
El Camino Coll, CA
Emory U, GA
Gustavus Adolphus Coll, MN
Hope Coll, MI
Indiana U Bloomington, IN
Lawrence U, WI
Lincoln U, PA
MiraCosta Coll, CA
Mount Union Coll, OH
North Central Coll, IL
The Ohio State U, OH
Penn State Abington, PA
Penn State DuBois, PA
Penn State Fayette, The Eberly Campus, PA
Penn State Mont Alto, PA
Penn State Wilkes-Barre, PA
Portland State U, OR
San Diego State U, CA
San Francisco State U, CA
U of California, Berkeley, CA
U of California, Irvine, CA
U of California, Los Angeles, CA
U of California, Santa Barbara, CA
U of Colorado at Boulder, CO
The U of Findlay, OH
U of Hawaii at Manoa, HI
U of Massachusetts Amherst, MA
U of Michigan, MI
U of Notre Dame, IN
U of Oregon, OR
U of Pittsburgh, PA
U of St. Thomas, MN
U of the Pacific, CA
U of Washington, WA
U of Wisconsin–Madison, WI
Vassar Coll, NY
Wellesley Coll, MA
Yale U, CT

JAPANESE STUDIES
Claremont McKenna Coll, CA
Earlham Coll, IN

Gustavus Adolphus Coll, MN
U at Albany, State U of New York, NY
U of San Francisco, CA

JAZZ
Hope Coll, MI
The U of Akron, OH

JAZZ/JAZZ STUDIES
Bard Coll, NY
DePaul U, IL
Drake U, IA
Hofstra U, NY
Hope Coll, MI
Indiana U Bloomington, IN
Ithaca Coll, NY
Johnson State Coll, VT
Lamar U, TX
Long Island U, Brooklyn Campus, NY
Loyola U New Orleans, LA
Michigan State U, MI
North Central Coll, IL
The Ohio State U, OH
Roosevelt U, IL
Rowan U, NJ
Rutgers, The State U of New Jersey, New Brunswick, NJ
St. Cloud State U, MN
St. Francis Xavier U, NS, Canada
Southern U and A&M Coll, LA
Temple U, PA
U of Cincinnati, OH
U of Hartford, CT
U of Michigan, MI
U of Minnesota, Duluth, MN
U of North Florida, FL
U of Oregon, OR

JEWISH/JUDAIC STUDIES
American U, DC
Bard Coll, NY
Brandeis U, MA
Brown U, RI
Clark U, MA
DePaul U, IL
Emory U, GA
Florida Atlantic U, FL
The George Washington U, DC
Hamline U, MN
Hofstra U, NY
Hunter Coll of the City U of New York, NY
Indiana U Bloomington, IN
Mount Holyoke Coll, MA
New York U, NY
The Ohio State U, OH
Penn State Abington, PA
Penn State DuBois, PA
Penn State Fayette, The Eberly Campus, PA
Penn State Mont Alto, PA
Penn State Wilkes-Barre, PA
Queens Coll of the City U of New York, NY
Rutgers, The State U of New Jersey, New Brunswick, NJ
San Diego State U, CA
Temple U, PA
Trinity Coll, CT
Tufts U, MA
U at Albany, State U of New York, NY
The U of Arizona, AZ
U of California, Los Angeles, CA
U of Cincinnati, OH
U of Hartford, CT

U of Manitoba, MB, Canada
U of Massachusetts Amherst, MA
U of Miami, FL
U of Michigan, MI
U of Oregon, OR
U of Pennsylvania, PA
The U of Texas at Austin, TX
U of Toronto, ON, Canada
U of Washington, WA
Vassar Coll, NY
Wellesley Coll, MA
Yale U, CT

JOURNALISM
Abilene Christian U, TX
Abraham Baldwin Coll, GA
American U, DC
Anderson U, SC
Angelo State U, TX
Asbury Coll, KY
Ashland U, OH
Bainbridge Coll, GA
Ball State U, IN
Barry U, FL
Baylor U, TX
Bemidji State U, MN
Bethel Coll, IN
Bradley U, IL
Bucks County Comm Coll, PA
Buffalo State Coll, State U of New York, NY
Burlington County Coll, NJ
California State U, Fullerton, CA
California State U, Northridge, CA
California State U, Sacramento, CA
Carleton U, ON, Canada
Carroll Coll, WI
Carson-Newman Coll, TN
Cincinnati Christian U, OH
Citrus Coll, CA
City Colls of Chicago, Richard J. Daley Coll, IL
Clayton State U, GA
Coll of St. Joseph, VT
Coll of the Canyons, CA
Coll of the Desert, CA
Comm Coll of Allegheny County, PA
Cosumnes River Coll, Sacramento, CA
Cuesta Coll, CA
Delaware State U, DE
Delaware Tech & Comm Coll, Jack F. Owens Campus, DE
Dixie State Coll of Utah, UT
Drake U, IA
Drury U, MO
Eastern Michigan U, MI
Eastern Nazarene Coll, MA
Edinboro U of Pennsylvania, PA
El Camino Coll, CA
Elon U, NC
Emory U, GA
Fitchburg State Coll, MA
Fort Hays State U, KS
Framingham State Coll, MA
Franklin Coll, IN
Franklin Pierce U, NH
Fresno City Coll, CA
Gainesville State Coll, GA
Gardner-Webb U, NC
The George Washington U, DC
Georgia Coll & State U, GA
Glendale Comm Coll, CA
Gonzaga U, WA

Goshen Coll, IN
Grace Coll, IN
Harrisburg Area Comm Coll, PA
Henderson State U, AR
Hofstra U, NY
Houghton Coll, NY
Housatonic Comm Coll, CT
Huntington U, IN
Illinois State U, IL
Illinois Valley Comm Coll, IL
Indiana U Bloomington, IN
Indiana U of Pennsylvania, PA
Indiana U–Purdue U Indianapolis, IN
Indiana U Southeast, IN
Iona Coll, NY
Ithaca Coll, NY
John Brown U, AR
Johnson State Coll, VT
Kansas State U, KS
Kellogg Comm Coll, MI
Kingsborough Comm Coll of the City U of New York, NY
Lamar U, TX
Langston U, OK
Lassen Comm Coll District, CA
Lee Coll, TX
Lehigh U, PA
Lewis U, IL
Lincoln U, PA
Lindenwood U, MO
Long Beach City Coll, CA
Long Island U, Brooklyn Campus, NY
Loras Coll, IA
Loyola U Chicago, IL
Lynchburg Coll, VA
Marietta Coll, OH
Marist Coll, NY
Marquette U, WI
Marshall U, WV
Massachusetts Coll of Liberal Arts, MA
Mercer U, GA
Mercyhurst Coll, PA
Miami Dade Coll, FL
Michigan State U, MI
Middlesex County Coll, NJ
Midland Coll, TX
Midland Lutheran Coll, NE
Minnesota State U Mankato, MN
Minnesota State U Moorhead, MN
MiraCosta Coll, CA
Missouri State U, MO
Moorpark Coll, CA
Mount Vernon Nazarene U, OH
Multnomah Bible Coll and Biblical Seminary, OR
Murray State U, KY
New York U, NY
North Central Coll, IL
Northeastern U, MA
Northern Illinois U, IL
Northwestern Coll, MN
Oakland U, MI
Ocean County Coll, NJ
The Ohio State U, OH
Ohio Wesleyan U, OH
Oklahoma State U, OK
Oral Roberts U, OK
Otterbein Coll, OH
Penn State Abington, PA
Penn State DuBois, PA
Penn State Fayette, The Eberly Campus, PA
Penn State Mont Alto, PA
Penn State Wilkes-Barre, PA

Point Loma Nazarene U, CA
Queens U of Charlotte, NC
Roosevelt U, IL
Rose State Coll, OK
Rutgers, The State U of New Jersey, Newark, NJ
Rutgers, The State U of New Jersey, New Brunswick, NJ
Ryerson U, ON, Canada
St. Bonaventure U, NY
St. Cloud State U, MN
St. Gregory's U, OK
St. Louis Comm Coll at Florissant Valley, MO
St. Thomas Aquinas Coll, NY
St. Thomas U, NB, Canada
Salem Comm Coll, NJ
San Diego State U, CA
San Francisco State U, CA
Santa Ana Coll, CA
Santa Rosa Jr Coll, CA
Seton Hill U, PA
Shasta Coll, CA
Shippensburg U of Pennsylvania, PA
Skagit Valley Coll, WA
Southern Adventist U, TN
Southern Illinois U Carbondale, IL
Southern Nazarene U, OK
State U of New York Coll at Brockport, NY
Stephen F. Austin State U, TX
Sussex County Comm Coll, NJ
Syracuse U, NY
Temple U, PA
Texas A&M U, TX
Troy U, AL
Truman State U, MO
Union Coll, NE
The U of Alabama, AL
U of Alaska Anchorage, AK
The U of Arizona, AZ
U of Arkansas, AR
U of Baltimore, MD
U of California, Irvine, CA
U of Central Florida, FL
U of Central Missouri, MO
U of Central Oklahoma, OK
U of Colorado at Boulder, CO
U of Connecticut, CT
U of Dayton, OH
U of Delaware, DE
The U of Findlay, OH
U of Hawaii at Manoa, HI
U of Houston, TX
U of Illinois at Urbana–Champaign, IL
U of Kansas, KS
U of Kentucky, KY
U of Massachusetts Amherst, MA
U of Miami, FL
U of Mississippi, MS
U of Missouri–Columbia, MO
U of Nebraska at Kearney, NE
U of Nebraska at Omaha, NE
U of New Hampshire, NH
U of New Mexico, NM
U of Oregon, OR
U of Pittsburgh at Johnstown, PA
U of Portland, OR
U of Rhode Island, RI
U of St. Thomas, MN
U of Southern Indiana, IN
The U of Tennessee, TN

The U of Tennessee at Martin, TN

The U of Texas at Austin, TX

The U of Texas at El Paso, TX

U of West Georgia, GA

U of Wisconsin–Eau Claire, WI

U of Wisconsin–Madison, WI

U of Wisconsin–Oshkosh, WI

U of Wyoming, WY

Utica Coll, NY

Ventura Coll, CA

Washington and Lee U, VA

Wayne State Coll, NE

Wayne State U, MI

Western Nebraska Comm Coll, NE

West Los Angeles Coll, CA

West Texas A&M U, TX

JOURNALISM RELATED

Grace Coll, IN

Roosevelt U, IL

U of Nebraska–Lincoln, NE

The U of North Carolina at Asheville, NC

U of St. Thomas, MN

JUDAIC STUDIES

Hampshire Coll, MA

San Diego State U, CA

The U of Arizona, AZ

KINDERGARTEN/ PRESCHOOL EDUCATION

Abraham Baldwin Coll, GA

Aims Comm Coll, CO

Alabama A&M U, AL

Albany State U, GA

Albright Coll, PA

Alma Coll, MI

Alvernia Coll, PA

American International Coll, MA

Anderson U, SC

Ashland U, OH

Athens State U, AL

Augsburg Coll, MN

Bainbridge Coll, GA

Ball State U, IN

Barry U, FL

Baylor U, TX

Bethany U, CA

Boston Coll, MA

Bradley U, IL

Brandon U, MB, Canada

Brenau U, GA

Broward Comm Coll, FL

Bucks County Comm Coll, PA

Buffalo State Coll, State U of New York, NY

Cape Cod Comm Coll, MA

Cardinal Stritch U, WI

Carlow U, PA

Carroll Coll, WI

Carson-Newman Coll, TN

The Catholic U of America, DC

Central Arizona Coll, AZ

Central Ohio Tech Coll, OH

Central Piedmont Comm Coll, NC

Charleston Southern U, SC

Chattanooga State Tech Comm Coll, TN

Chesapeake Coll, MD

Cincinnati Christian U, OH

Clayton State U, GA

Coahoma Comm Coll, MS

Coll of Mount St. Joseph, OH

Coll of St. Joseph, VT

Coll of the Canyons, CA

Coll of the Desert, CA

Comm Coll of Aurora, CO

Concordia U, NE

Concord U, WV

Cosumnes River Coll, Sacramento, CA

Cuesta Coll, CA

Dallas Baptist U, TX

Delaware State U, DE

DePaul U, IL

Dixie State Coll of Utah, UT

East Carolina U, NC

Eastern Connecticut State U, CT

Eastern Mennonite U, VA

Eastern Nazarene Coll, MA

Edinboro U of Pennsylvania, PA

El Camino Coll, CA

Elms Coll, MA

Fayetteville State U, NC

Fontbonne U, MO

Fort Hays State U, KS

Franklin Pierce U, NH

Frederick Comm Coll, MD

Fulton-Montgomery Comm Coll, NY

Furman U, SC

Gardner-Webb U, NC

Gaston Coll, NC

Glenville State Coll, WV

Goshen Coll, IN

Grambling State U, LA

Harding U, AR

Harrisburg Area Comm Coll, PA

Heartland Comm Coll, IL

High Point U, NC

Hopkinsville Comm Coll, KY

Houston Baptist U, TX

Howard Comm Coll, MD

Hunter Coll of the City U of New York, NY

Indiana U Bloomington, IN

Indiana U of Pennsylvania, PA

Indiana U–Purdue U Indianapolis, IN

John Brown U, AR

Kellogg Comm Coll, MI

Kendall Coll, IL

Kutztown U of Pennsylvania, PA

Lakeland Coll, WI

Lamar U, TX

Langston U, OK

Lassen Comm Coll District, CA

Lincoln U, PA

Lindenwood U, MO

Long Beach City Coll, CA

Loras Coll, IA

Lynchburg Coll, VA

Marian Coll, IN

Massachusetts Coll of Liberal Arts, MA

McNeese State U, LA

Metropolitan Comm Coll–Penn Valley, MO

Miami Dade Coll, FL

Middlesex County Coll, NJ

Middle Tennessee State U, TN

Midland Lutheran Coll, NE

Minnesota State Coll–Southeast Tech, MN

Minnesota State U Mankato, MN

Minnesota State U Moorhead, MN

MiraCosta Coll, CA

Mitchell Coll, CT

Moorpark Coll, CA

Mount Saint Vincent U, NS, Canada

Mount Vernon Nazarene U, OH

Nassau Comm Coll, NY

National-Louis U, IL

Neumann Coll, PA

New Hampshire Comm Tech Coll, Nashua/ Claremont, NH

New Jersey City U, NJ

New York U, NY

Northeastern U, MA

Northern Illinois U, IL

North Georgia Coll & State U, GA

Northwestern Oklahoma State U, OK

Notre Dame Coll, OH

Nova Southeastern U, FL

Odessa Coll, TX

Oglethorpe U, GA

Ohio Wesleyan U, OH

Oral Roberts U, OK

Our Lady of the Lake U of San Antonio, TX

Ozarks Tech Comm Coll, MO

Pacific Oaks Coll, CA

Piedmont Coll, GA

Pine Manor Coll, MA

Presbyterian Coll, SC

Pueblo Comm Coll, CO

Reinhardt Coll, GA

Rivier Coll, NH

Roosevelt U, IL

Rose State Coll, OK

Rowan U, NJ

Roxbury Comm Coll, MA

St. Bonaventure U, NY

St. Cloud State U, MN

St. Cloud Tech Coll, MN

St. Thomas Aquinas Coll, NY

Saint Xavier U, IL

Santa Ana Coll, CA

Santa Barbara City Coll, CA

Scottsdale Comm Coll, AZ

Seton Hill U, PA

Shasta Coll, CA

Skagit Valley Coll, WA

Southern Adventist U, TN

Southern Maine Comm Coll, ME

Southern U and A&M Coll, LA

Spalding U, KY

Spoon River Coll, IL

Springfield Coll, MA

State U of New York at Fredonia, NY

State U of New York Coll at Cortland, NY

State U of New York Coll of Technology at Canton, NY

Stonehill Coll, MA

Syracuse U, NY

Tallahassee Comm Coll, FL

Taylor U, IN

Tidewater Comm Coll, VA

Trocaire Coll, NY

Troy U, AL

Tufts U, MA

Tunxis Comm Coll, CT

The U of Akron, OH

The U of Alabama, AL

U of Alaska Anchorage, AK

The U of Arizona, AZ

U of Central Oklahoma, OK

U of Cincinnati, OH

U of Dayton, OH

U of Delaware, DE

U of Great Falls, MT

U of Illinois at Urbana–Champaign, IL

U of Kentucky, KY

U of Manitoba, MB, Canada

U of Mary Hardin-Baylor, TX

U of Minnesota, Duluth, MN

U of Missouri–Columbia, MO

U of New Brunswick Fredericton, NB, Canada

U of New Hampshire, NH

The U of North Carolina at Charlotte, NC

U of Northern Iowa, IA

U of Rio Grande, OH

The U of Scranton, PA

U of South Carolina Upstate, SC

The U of Tennessee at Martin, TN

U of the District of Columbia, DC

U of the Incarnate Word, TX

U of Vermont, VT

U of Wisconsin–Madison, WI

U of Wisconsin–Oshkosh, WI

U of Wisconsin–Platteville, WI

U of Wisconsin–Stevens Point, WI

Victor Valley Coll, CA

Waubonsee Comm Coll, IL

Western Nebraska Comm Coll, NE

West Liberty State Coll, WV

Westminster Coll, UT

West Virginia State U, WV

West Virginia Wesleyan Coll, WV

Widener U, PA

Worcester State Coll, MA

Wright State U, OH

KINESIOLOGY AND EXERCISE SCIENCE

Acadia U, NS, Canada

Adams State Coll, CO

Albertson Coll of Idaho, ID

Alma Coll, MI

Ball State U, IN

Barry U, FL

Bethel Coll, IN

Bethel U, MN

Brevard Coll, NC

Bridgewater Coll, VA

Brock U, ON, Canada

Buffalo State Coll, State U of New York, NY

California State U, Northridge, CA

California State U, Sacramento, CA

Calvin Coll, MI

Carroll Coll, WI

Carson-Newman Coll, TN

Coll of Mount Saint Vincent, NY

Columbus State U, GA

Concordia U, NE

Cornerstone U, MI

Dalhousie U, NS, Canada

Drury U, MO

East Carolina U, NC

East Stroudsburg U of Pennsylvania, PA

Fitchburg State Coll, MA

Florida Atlantic U, FL

Florida Gulf Coast U, FL

Florida International U, FL

Furman U, SC

Gainesville State Coll, GA

Georgetown Coll, KY

The George Washington U, DC

Gloucester County Coll, NJ

Gonzaga U, WA

Gordon Coll, MA

Hamline U, MN

Harding U, AR

High Point U, NC

Hofstra U, NY

Hope Coll, MI

Houston Baptist U, TX

Houston Comm Coll System, TX

Huntington U, IN

Illinois State U, IL

Immaculata U, PA

Ithaca Coll, NY

Jacksonville U, FL

John Brown U, AR

Johnson State Coll, VT

Kansas State U, KS

Kennesaw State U, GA

Lake Superior State U, MI

Lee Coll, TX

Liberty U, VA

Loras Coll, IA

Lynchburg Coll, VA

Marquette U, WI

Marymount U, VA

McDaniel Coll, MD

McNeese State U, LA

Michigan State U, MI

Minnesota State U Moorhead, MN

Mount Union Coll, OH

Mount Vernon Nazarene U, OH

Murray State U, KY

North Central Coll, IL

Northwestern Coll, MN

Northwest Nazarene U, ID

Occidental Coll, CA

The Ohio State U, OH

Old Dominion U, VA

Oral Roberts U, OK

Penn State Abington, PA

Penn State DuBois, PA

Penn State Fayette, The Eberly Campus, PA

Penn State Mont Alto, PA

Penn State Wilkes-Barre, PA

Point Loma Nazarene U, CA

Queens Coll of the City U of New York, NY

Radford U, VA

Redeemer U Coll, ON, Canada

Rice U, TX

Rocky Mountain Coll, MT

Rose State Coll, OK

Rutgers, The State U of New Jersey, New Brunswick, NJ

Saginaw Valley State U, MI

St. Cloud State U, MN

St. Francis Xavier U, NS, Canada

St. Philip's Coll, TX

Salem Comm Coll, NJ

Santa Ana Coll, CA

Santa Barbara City Coll, CA

Seattle Pacific U, WA

Shippensburg U of Pennsylvania, PA

Southern Adventist U, TN

Southern Nazarene U, OK

Southwestern U, TX

Springfield Coll, MA

State U of New York Coll at Brockport, NY

State U of New York Coll at Cortland, NY
Stetson U, FL
Syracuse U, NY
Tennessee Wesleyan Coll, TN
Texas A&M U–Corpus Christi, TX
Towson U, MD
Trevecca Nazarene U, TN
Truman State U, MO
Union Coll, NE
U at Buffalo, the State U of New York, NY
U of Arkansas, AR
U of California, Los Angeles, CA
U of Dayton, OH
U of Delaware, DE
U of Evansville, IN
U of Hawaii at Manoa, HI
U of Houston, TX
U of Illinois at Urbana–Champaign, IL
U of Massachusetts Amherst, MA
U of Massachusetts Lowell, MA
U of Miami, FL
U of Michigan, MI
U of Minnesota, Duluth, MN
U of Mississippi, MS
U of Nebraska–Lincoln, NE
U of New Brunswick Fredericton, NB, Canada
U of New England, ME
U of New Hampshire, NH
The U of Scranton, PA
U of Southern Indiana, IN
The U of Tampa, FL
The U of Tennessee, TN
U of the Pacific, CA
U of Wisconsin–Eau Claire, WI
U of Wisconsin–La Crosse, WI
U of Wyoming, WY
Upper Iowa U, IA
Valdosta State U, GA
Vanguard U of Southern California, CA
Wake Forest U, NC
Wayne State Coll, NE
West Chester U of Pennsylvania, PA
West Liberty State Coll, WV
Wilfrid Laurier U, ON, Canada
Wilson Coll, PA

KOREAN
U of California, Los Angeles, CA
U of Hawaii at Manoa, HI

KOREAN STUDIES
Claremont McKenna Coll, CA

LABOR AND INDUSTRIAL RELATIONS
Athabasca U, AB, Canada
Brock U, ON, Canada
Cape Breton U, NS, Canada
Carleton U, ON, Canada
Cornell U, NY
El Camino Coll, CA
Indiana U Bloomington, IN
Indiana U–Purdue U Indianapolis, IN
Indiana U Southeast, IN
Ithaca Coll, NY

Kingsborough Comm Coll of the City U of New York, NY
Le Moyne Coll, NY
Penn State Abington, PA
Penn State DuBois, PA
Penn State Fayette, The Eberly Campus, PA
Penn State Mont Alto, PA
Penn State Wilkes-Barre, PA
Queens Coll of the City U of New York, NY
Rockingham Comm Coll, NC
Roosevelt U, IL
Rutgers, The State U of New Jersey, New Brunswick, NJ
San Francisco State U, CA
Seton Hall U, NJ
State U of New York at Fredonia, NY
State U of New York Coll at Potsdam, NY
Temple U, PA
The U of Akron, OH
U of Manitoba, MB, Canada
U of Massachusetts Boston, MA
U of Toronto, ON, Canada
U of Wisconsin–Madison, WI
Westminster Coll, PA

LABOR STUDIES
Eastern Michigan U, MI
Hofstra U, NY
Indiana U–Purdue U Fort Wayne, IN
Wayne State U, MI

LANDSCAPE ARCHITECTURE
Ball State U, IN
Clemson U, SC
Coll of the Atlantic, ME
Cornell U, NY
Foothill Coll, CA
Kansas State U, KS
Michigan State U, MI
North Carolina State U, NC
North Dakota State U, ND
The Ohio State U, OH
Oklahoma State U, OK
Penn State Wilkes-Barre, PA
San Diego Mesa Coll, CA
Santa Rosa Jr Coll, CA
State U of New York Coll of Environmental Science and Forestry, NY
Temple U, PA
Texas A&M U, TX
The U of Arizona, AZ
U of Arkansas, AR
U of California, Berkeley, CA
U of Connecticut, CT
U of Guelph, ON, Canada
U of Hawaii at Manoa, HI
U of Illinois at Urbana–Champaign, IL
U of Kentucky, KY
U of Massachusetts Amherst, MA
U of Michigan, MI
U of New Hampshire, NH
U of Oregon, OR
U of Rhode Island, RI
U of Washington, WA
U of Wisconsin–Madison, WI

LANDSCAPING AND GROUNDSKEEPING
Abraham Baldwin Coll, GA

Caldwell Comm Coll and Tech Inst, NC
Central Florida Comm Coll, FL
Comm Coll of Allegheny County, PA
Cosumnes River Coll, Sacramento, CA
Farmingdale State Coll, NY
James H. Faulkner State Comm Coll, AL
Lake City Comm Coll, FL
Lincoln Land Comm Coll, IL
Miami Dade Coll, FL
MiraCosta Coll, CA
North Carolina State U, NC
Penn State Abington, PA
Penn State DuBois, PA
Penn State Fayette, The Eberly Campus, PA
Penn State Mont Alto, PA
Penn State Wilkes-Barre, PA
Santa Barbara City Coll, CA
Southern Maine Comm Coll, ME
Spokane Comm Coll, WA
State U of New York Coll of Technology at Alfred, NY
U of Massachusetts Amherst, MA
U of Nebraska–Lincoln, NE
U of New Hampshire, NH
The U of Tennessee at Martin, TN
Vermont Tech Coll, VT

LAND USE PLANNING AND MANAGEMENT
Hocking Coll, OH
State U of New York Coll of Environmental Science and Forestry, NY
Sterling Coll, VT
U of Northern British Columbia, BC, Canada
U of Wisconsin–Platteville, WI

LASER AND OPTICAL TECHNOLOGY
Idaho State U, ID
Indiana U Bloomington, IN
Linn State Tech Coll, MO
Moorpark Coll, CA
Oregon Inst of Technology, OR
Schoolcraft Coll, MI
Southeast Tech Inst, SD
Southwestern Indian Polytechnic Inst, NM

LATIN
Acadia U, NS, Canada
Amherst Coll, MA
Asbury Coll, KY
Austin Coll, TX
Ball State U, IN
Bard Coll, NY
Baylor U, TX
Brandeis U, MA
Bryn Mawr Coll, PA
Calvin Coll, MI
Carleton U, ON, Canada
Carroll Coll, MT
The Catholic U of America, DC
Claremont McKenna Coll, CA
Colgate U, NY
The Coll of William and Mary, VA
Duke U, NC
Emory U, GA
Furman U, SC

Hamilton Coll, NY
Hampden-Sydney Coll, VA
Haverford Coll, PA
Hofstra U, NY
Hope Coll, MI
Hunter Coll of the City U of New York, NY
Idaho State U, ID
Indiana U Bloomington, IN
Kenyon Coll, OH
Lawrence U, WI
Loyola Marymount U, CA
Loyola U Chicago, IL
Macalester Coll, MN
Mercer U, GA
Missouri State U, MO
Monmouth Coll, IL
New York U, NY
Queens Coll of the City U of New York, NY
Randolph Coll, VA
Randolph-Macon Coll, VA
Rhodes Coll, TN
Rice U, TX
Rockford Coll, IL
Rutgers, The State U of New Jersey, New Brunswick, NJ
Santa Clara U, CA
Seattle Pacific U, WA
Sewanee: The U of the South, TN
Southwestern U, TX
Trent U, ON, Canada
Tufts U, MA
U at Albany, State U of New York, NY
U of California, Berkeley, CA
U of California, Los Angeles, CA
U of Delaware, DE
U of Houston, TX
U of Manitoba, MB, Canada
U of Mary Washington, VA
U of Michigan, MI
U of Missouri–Columbia, MO
U of Nebraska–Lincoln, NE
U of New Brunswick Fredericton, NB, Canada
U of New Hampshire, NH
U of Notre Dame, IN
U of Oregon, OR
U of St. Thomas, MN
The U of Scranton, PA
The U of Texas at Austin, TX
U of Toronto, ON, Canada
U of Vermont, VT
U of Washington, WA
U of Wisconsin–Madison, WI
Vassar Coll, NY
Wake Forest U, NC
Wellesley Coll, MA
West Chester U of Pennsylvania, PA
Westminster Coll, PA
Wichita State U, KS
Wilfrid Laurier U, ON, Canada
Yale U, CT

LATIN AMERICAN STUDIES
Adelphi U, NY
Albright Coll, PA
American U, DC
Austin Coll, TX
Ball State U, IN
Bard Coll, NY
Baylor U, TX
Brandeis U, MA
Brown U, RI

California State U, Fullerton, CA
Carleton U, ON, Canada
Carnegie Mellon U, PA
Claremont McKenna Coll, CA
Colby Coll, ME
Colgate U, NY
Coll of Charleston, SC
The Coll of William and Mary, VA
Cornell U, NY
DePaul U, IL
Earlham Coll, IN
Edinboro U of Pennsylvania, PA
Emory U, GA
Flagler Coll, FL
The George Washington U, DC
Gustavus Adolphus Coll, MN
Hamline U, MN
Hampshire Coll, MA
Haverford Coll, PA
Hofstra U, NY
Hunter Coll of the City U of New York, NY
Illinois Wesleyan U, IL
Indiana U Bloomington, IN
Macalester Coll, MN
Miami Dade Coll, FL
Mount Holyoke Coll, MA
New York U, NY
Oakland U, MI
The Ohio State U, OH
Ohio Wesleyan U, OH
Penn State Abington, PA
Penn State DuBois, PA
Penn State Fayette, The Eberly Campus, PA
Penn State Mont Alto, PA
Penn State Wilkes-Barre, PA
Portland State U, OR
Queens Coll of the City U of New York, NY
Rice U, TX
Ripon Coll, WI
Rutgers, The State U of New Jersey, New Brunswick, NJ
St. Cloud State U, MN
San Diego State U, CA
Santa Rosa Jr Coll, CA
Seattle Pacific U, WA
Southwestern U, TX
State U of New York Coll at Brockport, NY
Stetson U, FL
Syracuse U, NY
Temple U, PA
Trinity U, TX
U at Albany, State U of New York, NY
The U of Alabama, AL
The U of Arizona, AZ
U of California, Berkeley, CA
U of California, Los Angeles, CA
U of California, Santa Barbara, CA
U of Cincinnati, OH
U of Connecticut, CT
U of Delaware, DE
U of Illinois at Urbana–Champaign, IL
U of Kansas, KS
U of Kentucky, KY
U of Miami, FL
U of Michigan, MI
U of Missouri–Columbia, MO
U of Nebraska at Omaha, NE

Colleges for Students with Learning Disabilities or AD/HD

Barry U, FL
Beacon Coll, FL
Bemidji State U, MN
Benedictine Coll, KS
Bentley Coll, MA
Bethany U, CA
Bethel Coll, IN
Bethel U, MN
Bishop's U, QC, Canada
Bluefield State Coll, WV
Bradley U, IL
Brandon U, MB, Canada
Brevard Comm Coll, FL
Briar Cliff U, IA
Bridgewater Coll, VA
Brock U, ON, Canada
Broome Comm Coll, NY
Broward Comm Coll, FL
Bucks County Comm Coll, PA
Buffalo State Coll, State U of New York, NY
Burlington County Coll, NJ
Caldwell Comm Coll and Tech Inst, NC
Calhoun Comm Coll, AL
California State U, Fullerton, CA
California State U, Northridge, CA
California State U, Sacramento, CA
California State U, San Bernardino, CA
California State U, Stanislaus, CA
Cape Breton U, NS, Canada
Cape Cod Comm Coll, MA
Cardinal Stritch U, WI
Carlow U, PA
Carnegie Mellon U, PA
Carson-Newman Coll, TN
Cedar Crest Coll, PA
Cedar Valley Coll, TX
Central Arizona Coll, AZ
Central Florida Comm Coll, FL
Central Lakes Coll, MN
Central Piedmont Comm Coll, NC
Charleston Southern U, SC
Chattanooga State Tech Comm Coll, TN
Chesapeake Coll, MD
Citrus Coll, CA
City Colls of Chicago, Richard J. Daley Coll, IL
Coahoma Comm Coll, MS
Coastal Carolina U, SC
Coe Coll, IA
Coll of Mount St. Joseph, OH
Coll of Mount Saint Vincent, NY
Coll of St. Joseph, VT
The Coll of Saint Rose, NY
The Coll of St. Scholastica, MN
Coll of Staten Island of the City U of New York, NY
Coll of The Albemarle, NC
Coll of the Atlantic, ME
Coll of the Canyons, CA
Coll of the Desert, CA
Colorado Mountain Coll, Alpine Campus, CO
Columbus State U, GA
Comm Coll of Allegheny County, PA
Comm Coll of Aurora, CO
Comm Coll of Beaver County, PA
Concordia Coll–New York, NY

Cornell U, NY
Cosumnes River Coll, Sacramento, CA
Cottey Coll, MO
Crafton Hills Coll, CA
Cuesta Coll, CA
Dabney S. Lancaster Comm Coll, VA
Dallas Baptist U, TX
Dean Coll, MA
Dixie State Coll of Utah, UT
East Carolina U, NC
Eastern Mennonite U, VA
Eastern Nazarene Coll, MA
Eastern New Mexico U–Roswell, NM
Eastern West Virginia Comm and Tech Coll, WV
Eastfield Coll, TX
East Stroudsburg U of Pennsylvania, PA
Edinboro U of Pennsylvania, PA
El Camino Coll, CA
El Centro Coll, TX
Elmira Coll, NY
Elms Coll, MA
Emory U, GA
Emory U, Oxford Coll, GA
Eugene Lang Coll The New School for Liberal Arts, NY
Fairleigh Dickinson U, Metropolitan Campus, NJ
Farmingdale State Coll, NY
Feather River Coll, CA
Ferrum Coll, VA
Fitchburg State Coll, MA
Flagler Coll, FL
Florida Atlantic U, FL
Florida Coll, FL
Florida Comm Coll at Jacksonville, FL
Florida Gulf Coast U, FL
Florida International U, FL
Fontbonne U, MO
Fort Hays State U, KS
Framingham State Coll, MA
Franklin Pierce U, NH
Frederick Comm Coll, MD
Freed-Hardeman U, TN
Fresno City Coll, CA
Fresno Pacific U, CA
Fulton-Montgomery Comm Coll, NY
Gadsden State Comm Coll, AL
Galveston Coll, TX
Gannon U, PA
Georgetown Coll, KY
The George Washington U, DC
Georgian Court U, NJ
Glendale Comm Coll, CA
Glenville State Coll, WV
Gloucester County Coll, NJ
Gonzaga U, WA
Goshen Coll, IN
Graceland U, IA
Green Mountain Coll, VT
Greenville Tech Coll, SC
Grossmont Coll, CA
Hagerstown Comm Coll, MD
Harrisburg Area Comm Coll, PA
Heartland Comm Coll, IL
Hillsborough Comm Coll, FL
Hofstra U, NY
Hope Coll, MI
Hopkinsville Comm Coll, KY
Houghton Coll, NY
Housatonic Comm Coll, CT
Houston Baptist U, TX

Houston Comm Coll System, TX
Howard Comm Coll, MD
Hudson Valley Comm Coll, NY
Husson Coll, ME
Illinois Valley Comm Coll, IL
Iona Coll, NY
Irvine Valley Coll, CA
Itasca Comm Coll, MN
Ithaca Coll, NY
Ivy Tech Comm Coll–Kokomo, IN
Ivy Tech Comm Coll–Southwest, IN
Ivy Tech Comm Coll–Wabash Valley, IN
Jacksonville U, FL
James H. Faulkner State Comm Coll, AL
Jefferson Comm and Tech Coll, KY
John Brown U, AR
Johnson State Coll, VT
Kapiolani Comm Coll, HI
Kellogg Comm Coll, MI
Keuka Coll, NY
Kingsborough Comm Coll of the City U of New York, NY
Kutztown U of Pennsylvania, PA
Kuyper Coll, MI
Lackawanna Coll, PA
LaGrange Coll, GA
Lake City Comm Coll, FL
Lake-Sumter Comm Coll, FL
Lake Superior State U, MI
Lamar State Coll–Orange, TX
Lamar U, TX
Landmark Coll, VT
Langston U, OK
Laredo Comm Coll, TX
Lassen Comm Coll District, CA
Lebanon Valley Coll, PA
Lee Coll, TX
Lewis U, IL
Lincoln Land Comm Coll, IL
Lindenwood U, MO
Long Beach City Coll, CA
Long Island U, Brooklyn Campus, NY
Loras Coll, IA
Loyola Marymount U, CA
Lynn U, FL
MacMurray Coll, IL
Macomb Comm Coll, MI
Manhattan Coll, NY
Marian U, IN
Marietta Coll, OH
Marymount Manhattan Coll, NY
Marymount U, VA
Massasoit Comm Coll, MA
Maui Comm Coll, HI
McNeese State U, LA
Mercer U, GA
Mercyhurst Coll, PA
Metropolitan Comm Coll–Longview, MO
Metropolitan Comm Coll–Penn Valley, MO
Middlesex Comm Coll, CT
Middle Tennessee State U, TN
Midland Coll, TX
Midland Lutheran Coll, NE
Mid-South Comm Coll, AR
Millersville U of Pennsylvania, PA
Minnesota State U Mankato, MN

Minnesota State U Moorhead, MN
MiraCosta Coll, CA
Mitchell Coll, CT
Mohawk Valley Comm Coll, NY
Molloy Coll, NY
Monmouth Coll, IL
Montana State U–Billings, MT
Montana Tech of The U of Montana, MT
Moorpark Coll, CA
Morton Coll, IL
Mount Saint Vincent U, NS, Canada
Murray State U, KY
Muscatine Comm Coll, IA
Nassau Comm Coll, NY
National-Louis U, IL
Neumann Coll, PA
New Hampshire Comm Tech Coll, Nashua/Claremont, NH
New Mexico Jr Coll, NM
New River Comm Coll, VA
New York City Coll of Technology of the City U of New York, NY
New York U, NY
Niagara U, NY
Nipissing U, ON, Canada
North Carolina State U, NC
North Central Coll, IL
North Central Missouri Coll, MO
North Central Texas Coll, TX
Northeastern U, MA
Northern Illinois U, IL
Northern Michigan U, MI
Northern State U, SD
Northland Comm and Tech Coll–Thief River Falls, MN
Northwestern Coll, MN
Northwest Nazarene U, ID
Notre Dame de Namur U, CA
Nova Southeastern U, FL
Ocean County Coll, NJ
Odessa Coll, TX
The Ohio State U at Lima, OH
Oklahoma State U, OK
Oral Roberts U, OK
Oregon Inst of Technology, OR
Our Lady of the Lake U of San Antonio, TX
Ozarks Tech Comm Coll, MO
Paris Jr Coll, TX
Park U, MO
Penn State Abington, PA
Penn State DuBois, PA
Penn State Fayette, The Eberly Campus, PA
Penn State Mont Alto, PA
Penn State Wilkes-Barre, PA
Phoenix Coll, AZ
Pima Comm Coll, AZ
Pine Manor Coll, MA
Point Loma Nazarene U, CA
Portland State U, OR
Pueblo Comm Coll, CO
Purdue U North Central, IN
Quincy Coll, MA
Radford U, VA
Randolph Coll, VA
Redeemer U Coll, ON, Canada
Reedley Coll, CA
Reinhardt Coll, GA

Richard Bland Coll of The Coll of William and Mary, VA
The Richard Stockton Coll of New Jersey, NJ
Richland Comm Coll, IL
Richmond Comm Coll, NC
Rivier Coll, NH
Rockingham Comm Coll, NC
Rocky Mountain Coll, MT
Roosevelt U, IL
Rose State Coll, OK
Rowan U, NJ
Rutgers, The State U of New Jersey, New Brunswick, NJ
St. Cloud State U, MN
St. Francis Xavier U, NS, Canada
St. Gregory's U, OK
Saint Leo U, FL
St. Louis Comm Coll at Florissant Valley, MO
St. Philip's Coll, TX
Saint Xavier U, IL
Salem Comm Coll, NJ
Salve Regina U, RI
San Diego Mesa Coll, CA
San Diego State U, CA
San Francisco State U, CA
Santa Ana Coll, CA
Santa Barbara City Coll, CA
Santa Clara U, CA
Santa Rosa Jr Coll, CA
Sauk Valley Comm Coll, IL
Schoolcraft Coll, MI
Seattle Pacific U, WA
Seminole Comm Coll, FL
Seton Hall U, NJ
Shelton State Comm Coll, AL
Skagit Valley Coll, WA
Southern Illinois U Carbondale, IL
Southern Illinois U Edwardsville, IL
Southern Maine Comm Coll, ME
Southern Nazarene U, OK
Southern Oregon U, OR
South Piedmont Comm Coll, NC
Southwestern Coll, KS
Southwestern Indian Polytechnic Inst, NM
Southwestern Michigan Coll, MI
Spalding U, KY
Spokane Comm Coll, WA
Spoon River Coll, IL
Springfield Coll in Illinois, IL
State U of New York at Fredonia, NY
State U of New York Coll of Technology at Alfred, NY
State U of New York Coll of Technology at Canton, NY
Sterling Coll, VT
Surry Comm Coll, NC
Sussex County Comm Coll, NJ
Sweet Briar Coll, VA
Syracuse U, NY
Tallahassee Comm Coll, FL
Thiel Coll, PA
Tidewater Comm Coll, VA
Trent U, ON, Canada
Trocaire Coll, NY
Troy U, AL
Tunxis Comm Coll, CT
The U of Akron, OH
The U of Akron–Wayne Coll, OH
The U of Arizona, AZ
U of Arkansas at Fort Smith, AR

U of Baltimore, MD
U of California, Los Angeles, CA
U of Central Florida, FL
U of Central Oklahoma, OK
U of Cincinnati, OH
U of Delaware, DE
U of Evansville, IN
U of Hartford, CT
U of Illinois at Urbana–Champaign, IL
U of Kansas, KS
The U of Maine at Augusta, ME
U of Mary Washington, VA
U of Massachusetts Lowell, MA
U of Miami, FL
U of Mississippi, MS
U of Missouri–Kansas City, MO
U of Nebraska–Lincoln, NE
U of New Brunswick Fredericton, NB, Canada
U of New England, ME
U of New Hampshire, NH
U of New Hampshire at Manchester, NH
U of New Haven, CT
U of New Mexico, NM
The U of North Carolina at Asheville, NC
The U of North Carolina at Chapel Hill, NC
U of Northern British Columbia, BC, Canada
U of Northern Iowa, IA
U of North Florida, FL
U of Notre Dame, IN
U of Oregon, OR
U of Pennsylvania, PA
U of Pittsburgh, PA
U of Pittsburgh at Bradford, PA
U of Redlands, CA
U of Rhode Island, RI
U of St. Thomas, TX
U of San Diego, CA
U of San Francisco, CA
U of South Carolina Beaufort, SC
U of Southern Indiana, IN
The U of Tampa, FL
The U of Texas at Austin, TX
U of the Incarnate Word, TX
U of Vermont, VT
U of Virginia, VA
The U of Virginia's Coll at Wise, VA
U of Washington, WA
U of Wisconsin–Eau Claire, WI
U of Wisconsin–Manitowoc, WI
U of Wisconsin–Oshkosh, WI
U of Wisconsin–Platteville, WI
U of Wisconsin–Richland, WI
U of Wisconsin–Stevens Point, WI
Upper Iowa U, IA
Urbana U, OH
Utica Coll, NY
Valdosta State U, GA
Valencia Comm Coll, FL
Ventura Coll, CA
Victor Valley Coll, CA
Villanova U, PA
Virginia Highlands Comm Coll, VA
Virginia Intermont Coll, VA

Washburn U, KS
Washington & Jefferson Coll, PA
Waubonsee Comm Coll, IL
Wesley Coll, DE
Westchester Comm Coll, NY
West Chester U of Pennsylvania, PA
Western Connecticut State U, CT
Western Nebraska Comm Coll, NE
Western New England Coll, MA
Western Oregon U, OR
West Los Angeles Coll, CA
Westmoreland County Comm Coll, PA
West Shore Comm Coll, MI
West Virginia Northern Comm Coll, WV
West Virginia State U, WV
Wichita State U, KS
Wilkes U, PA
Williston State Coll, ND
Wilson Coll, PA
Wright State U, OH
Xavier U, OH

LIBRARY ASSISTANT
Citrus Coll, CA
Ivy Tech Comm Coll–Kokomo, IN
Ivy Tech Comm Coll–Southwest, IN
Ivy Tech Comm Coll–Wabash Valley, IN
The U of Maine at Augusta, ME

LIBRARY SCIENCE
Citrus Coll, CA
Concord U, WV
Cuesta Coll, CA
Fresno City Coll, CA
Hope Coll, MI
Kutztown U of Pennsylvania, PA
Murray State U, KY
Rose State Coll, OK
St. Cloud State U, MN
Santa Ana Coll, CA
The U of Maine at Augusta, ME
U of Nebraska at Omaha, NE
U of the District of Columbia, DC

LIBRARY SCIENCE RELATED
Bethel U, MN
U of California, Los Angeles, CA
U of Great Falls, MT

LINEWORKER
Linn State Tech Coll, MO

LINGUISTIC AND COMPARATIVE LANGUAGE STUDIES RELATED
U of California, Los Angeles, CA

LINGUISTICS
Baylor U, TX
Brandeis U, MA
Brock U, ON, Canada
Brown U, RI
California State U, Fullerton, CA
California State U, Northridge, CA

Carleton U, ON, Canada
The Coll of William and Mary, VA
Cornell U, NY
Dalhousie U, NS, Canada
Duke U, NC
Eastern Michigan U, MI
Florida Atlantic U, FL
Foothill Coll, CA
Hampshire Coll, MA
Indiana U Bloomington, IN
Lawrence U, WI
Macalester Coll, MN
Mount Saint Vincent U, NS, Canada
New York U, NY
Northeastern U, MA
Oakland U, MI
The Ohio State U, OH
Portland State U, OR
Queens Coll of the City U of New York, NY
Queen's U at Kingston, ON, Canada
Rice U, TX
Rutgers, The State U of New Jersey, New Brunswick, NJ
St. Cloud State U, MN
San Diego State U, CA
Southern Illinois U Carbondale, IL
Syracuse U, NY
Temple U, PA
U at Albany, State U of New York, NY
U at Buffalo, the State U of New York, NY
The U of Arizona, AZ
U of California, Berkeley, CA
U of California, Irvine, CA
U of California, Los Angeles, CA
U of California, Santa Barbara, CA
U of Cincinnati, OH
U of Colorado at Boulder, CO
U of Connecticut, CT
U of Delaware, DE
U of Hawaii at Manoa, HI
U of Illinois at Urbana–Champaign, IL
U of Kansas, KS
U of Kentucky, KY
U of Maryland, Baltimore County, MD
U of Massachusetts Amherst, MA
U of Michigan, MI
U of Mississippi, MS
U of Missouri–Columbia, MO
U of New Brunswick Fredericton, NB, Canada
U of New Hampshire, NH
U of New Mexico, NM
U of Oregon, OR
U of Pennsylvania, PA
U of Pittsburgh, PA
The U of Texas at Austin, TX
The U of Texas at El Paso, TX
U of Toronto, ON, Canada
U of Washington, WA
U of Wisconsin–Madison, WI
Wayne State U, MI
Wellesley Coll, MA
Wright State U, OH
Yale U, CT

LITERATURE
Alderson-Broaddus Coll, WV
American U, DC
Bard Coll, NY
Barry U, FL
Bishop's U, QC, Canada
Blinn Coll, TX
Brock U, ON, Canada
Carson-Newman Coll, TN
Christopher Newport U, VA
Claremont McKenna Coll, CA
Coe Coll, IA
Coll of the Atlantic, ME
Columbus State U, GA
Dalhousie U, NS, Canada
DePaul U, IL
Duke U, NC
Elmira Coll, NY
Emory U, GA
Eugene Lang Coll The New School for Liberal Arts, NY
Fitchburg State Coll, MA
Foothill Coll, CA
Franklin Pierce U, NH
Fresno Pacific U, CA
Gonzaga U, WA
Graceland U, IA
High Point U, NC
Houghton Coll, NY
Hunter Coll of the City U of New York, NY
Irvine Valley Coll, CA
Johnson State Coll, VT
Kenyon Coll, OH
Lake Superior State U, MI
Lamar State Coll–Orange, TX
Lincoln Land Comm Coll, IL
Marist Coll, NY
Massachusetts Coll of Liberal Arts, MA
Miami Dade Coll, FL
Midland Coll, TX
Minnesota State U Mankato, MN
Morningside Coll, IA
Mount Saint Vincent U, NS, Canada
Ohio Wesleyan U, OH
Otterbein Coll, OH
Ramapo Coll of New Jersey, NJ
Rockford Coll, IL
Roosevelt U, IL
San Francisco State U, CA
Sewanee: The U of the South, TN
Skagit Valley Coll, WA
Southwestern U, TX
State U of New York Coll at Brockport, NY
Syracuse U, NY
Taylor U, IN
Trent U, ON, Canada
The U of Akron, OH
U of Baltimore, MD
U of California, Irvine, CA
U of Cincinnati, OH
U of New Brunswick Fredericton, NB, Canada
U of New Hampshire, NH
U of Pittsburgh at Johnstown, PA
U of Redlands, CA
U of Toronto, ON, Canada
Wayne State Coll, NE
West Virginia Wesleyan Coll, WV
Yale U, CT

LIVESTOCK MANAGEMENT
Sterling Coll, VT

LOGIC
Carnegie Mellon U, PA
U of Pennsylvania, PA

LOGISTICS AND MATERIALS MANAGEMENT
Chattahoochee Tech Coll, GA
Florida International U, FL
Houston Comm Coll System, TX
Lee Coll, TX
Maine Maritime Academy, ME
Michigan State U, MI
Niagara U, NY
Northeastern U, MA
The Ohio State U, OH
Park U, MO
Penn State Fayette, The Eberly Campus, PA
Portland State U, OR
Syracuse U, NY
The U of Akron, OH
U of Arkansas, AR
The U of Findlay, OH
The U of Tennessee, TN
Waubonsee Comm Coll, IL
Wayne State U, MI
Wright State U, OH

MACHINE SHOP TECHNOLOGY
Comm Coll of Allegheny County, PA
Florida Comm Coll at Jacksonville, FL
Mohawk Valley Comm Coll, NY
North Central Texas Coll, TX
Pima Comm Coll, AZ
Southwestern Michigan Coll, MI

MACHINE TOOL TECHNOLOGY
Alexandria Tech Coll, MN
Altamaha Tech Coll, GA
Asheville-Buncombe Tech Comm Coll, NC
Asnuntuck Comm Coll, CT
British Columbia Inst of Technology, BC, Canada
Calhoun Comm Coll, AL
Central Piedmont Comm Coll, NC
Chattanooga State Tech Comm Coll, TN
City Colls of Chicago, Richard J. Daley Coll, IL
DeKalb Tech Coll, GA
East Central Coll, MO
Fresno City Coll, CA
Glendale Comm Coll, CA
Greenville Tech Coll, SC
Heartland Comm Coll, IL
Idaho State U, ID
Ivy Tech Comm Coll–Kokomo, IN
Ivy Tech Comm Coll–Southwest, IN
Ivy Tech Comm Coll–Wabash Valley, IN
Kellogg Comm Coll, MI
Lamar Inst of Technology, TX
Lamar U, TX
Lee Coll, TX
Linn State Tech Coll, MO
Long Beach City Coll, CA
Macomb Comm Coll, MI
Minnesota State Coll–Southeast Tech, MN

MiraCosta Coll, CA
Muscatine Comm Coll, IA
New Hampshire Comm Tech Coll, Nashua/Claremont, NH
New Mexico Jr Coll, NM
New River Comm Coll, VA
North Central Texas Coll, TX
Odessa Coll, TX
Ozarks Tech Comm Coll, MO
Pueblo Comm Coll, CO
Reedley Coll, CA
Richmond Comm Coll, NC
St. Cloud Tech Coll, MN
Shelton State Comm Coll, AL
Southeast Tech Inst, SD
Southern Maine Comm Coll, ME
South Piedmont Comm Coll, NC
Spokane Comm Coll, WA
State U of New York Coll of Technology at Alfred, NY
Surry Comm Coll, NC
The U of Montana-Helena Coll of Technology, MT
Ventura Coll, CA
Virginia Highlands Comm Coll, VA
Waubonsee Comm Coll, IL
West Shore Comm Coll, MI

MANAGEMENT INFORMATION SYSTEMS
Alderson-Broaddus Coll, WV
Allegany Coll of Maryland, MD
American International Coll, MA
Angelo State U, TX
Aquinas Coll, TN
Ashland Comm and Tech Coll, KY
Auburn U Montgomery, AL
Augsburg Coll, MN
Aurora U, IL
Ball State U, IN
Barry U, FL
Baylor U, TX
Bishop's U, QC, Canada
Boston Coll, MA
Bradley U, IL
Briar Cliff U, IA
Bridgewater Coll, VA
Buena Vista U, IA
Burlington County Coll, NJ
California State U, Sacramento, CA
California State U, San Bernardino, CA
Calvin Coll, MI
Cameron U, OK
Cape Breton U, NS, Canada
Carleton U, ON, Canada
Carson-Newman Coll, TN
Central Wyoming Coll, WY
Charleston Southern U, SC
Clayton State U, GA
Clemson U, SC
The Coll of Westchester, NY
Comm Coll of Allegheny County, PA
Concordia U, NE
Cornerstone U, MI
Cosumnes River Coll, Sacramento, CA
Dallas Baptist U, TX
DePaul U, IL
East Carolina U, NC
Eastern Connecticut State U, CT
Eastern Michigan U, MI
Fairfield U, CT

Florida Atlantic U, FL
Florida Gulf Coast U, FL
Florida Inst of Technology, FL
Florida International U, FL
Fontbonne U, MO
Gannon U, PA
Gardner-Webb U, NC
Grace Coll, IN
Graceland U, IA
Hagerstown Comm Coll, MD
Harrisburg Area Comm Coll, PA
Heartland Comm Coll, IL
Henderson State U, AR
Hofstra U, NY
Hopkinsville Comm Coll, KY
Husson Coll, ME
Indiana U Bloomington, IN
Indiana U of Pennsylvania, PA
Iona Coll, NY
Jacksonville U, FL
Johnson State Coll, VT
Lackawanna Coll, PA
Lake Superior State U, MI
Lehigh U, PA
Le Moyne Coll, NY
LeTourneau U, TX
Lewis U, IL
Liberty U, VA
Lindenwood U, MO
Loras Coll, IA
Loyola U Chicago, IL
MacMurray Coll, IL
Marquette U, WI
Miami Dade Coll, FL
Middle Tennessee State U, TN
Midland Lutheran Coll, NE
Missouri State U, MO
Morningside Coll, IA
Mount Saint Vincent U, NS, Canada
Murray State U, KY
Nassau Comm Coll, NY
New York U, NY
North Central Coll, IL
Northeastern U, MA
Northern Illinois U, IL
Northern Michigan U, MI
Northern State U, SD
Northwestern Coll, MN
Northwood U, MI
Northwood U, Florida Campus, FL
Northwood U, Texas Campus, TX
Oakland U, MI
The Ohio State U, OH
Oklahoma State U, OK
Old Dominion U, VA
Oral Roberts U, OK
Oregon Inst of Technology, OR
Ozarks Tech Comm Coll, MO
Park U, MO
Penn State Abington, PA
Penn State DuBois, PA
Penn State Fayette, The Eberly Campus, PA
Penn State Mont Alto, PA
Penn State Wilkes-Barre, PA
Point Loma Nazarene U, CA
Pueblo Comm Coll, CO
Rensselaer Polytechnic Inst, NY
Rochester Inst of Technology, NY
Rockford Coll, IL
Rocky Mountain Coll, MT
Rose State Coll, OK

St. Francis Xavier U, NS, Canada
St. Gregory's U, OK
Saint Joseph's Coll, IN
Saint Leo U, FL
Salem Comm Coll, NJ
Santa Clara U, CA
Seton Hall U, NJ
Seton Hill U, PA
Shasta Coll, CA
Southern Adventist U, TN
Southern Illinois U Edwardsville, IL
Southern Maine Comm Coll, ME
Southern Nazarene U, OK
Southwestern Coll, KS
Springfield Coll, MA
Tallahassee Comm Coll, FL
Taylor U, IN
Temple U, PA
Texas A&M U–Corpus Christi, TX
Thiel Coll, PA
Troy U, AL
The U of Akron, OH
The U of Akron–Wayne Coll, OH
The U of Alabama, AL
The U of Alabama in Huntsville, AL
U of Alaska Anchorage, AK
The U of Arizona, AZ
U of Baltimore, MD
U of Central Florida, FL
U of Central Missouri, MO
U of Cincinnati, OH
U of Connecticut, CT
U of Dayton, OH
U of Hartford, CT
U of Hawaii at Manoa, HI
U of Houston, TX
U of Mary Hardin-Baylor, TX
U of Mississippi, MS
U of Missouri–Columbia, MO
U of Nebraska at Omaha, NE
U of New Orleans, LA
The U of North Carolina at Charlotte, NC
U of Northern Iowa, IA
U of Notre Dame, IN
U of Pennsylvania, PA
U of Redlands, CA
U of Rhode Island, RI
U of St. Thomas, TX
U of San Francisco, CA
The U of Tennessee at Martin, TN
The U of Texas at Austin, TX
The U of Texas at San Antonio, TX
U of the Incarnate Word, TX
U of Washington, WA
U of West Georgia, GA
U of Wisconsin–La Crosse, WI
U of Wisconsin–Oshkosh, WI
U of Wyoming, WY
Upper Iowa U, IA
Ursuline Coll, OH
Victor Valley Coll, CA
Villanova U, PA
Wake Forest U, NC
Wayne State U, MI
Western Connecticut State U, CT
Western New England Coll, MA
West Texas A&M U, TX
Wichita State U, KS

Wilson Coll, PA
Wright State U, OH
Xavier U, OH

MANAGEMENT INFORMATION SYSTEMS AND SERVICES RELATED
Anderson U, SC
Arkansas State U–Newport, AR
Buena Vista U, IA
Carroll Coll, WI
Cedar Valley Coll, TX
Coll of Mount St. Joseph, OH
Lewis U, IL
Mid-South Comm Coll, AR
Mohawk Valley Comm Coll, NY
Rensselaer Polytechnic Inst, NY
St. Bonaventure U, NY
U of Southern Indiana, IN
Westminster Coll, UT
Widener U, PA

MANAGEMENT SCIENCE
British Columbia Inst of Technology, BC, Canada
Cape Cod Comm Coll, MA
Dalhousie U, NS, Canada
Fitchburg State Coll, MA
Florida Inst of Technology, FL
Harrisburg Area Comm Coll, PA
Le Moyne Coll, NY
Manhattan Coll, NY
Minnesota State U Mankato, MN
Northeastern U, MA
Nova Southeastern U, FL
Oklahoma State U, OK
Oral Roberts U, OK
Phoenix Coll, AZ
Reedley Coll, CA
Rocky Mountain Coll, MT
Roosevelt U, IL
Rutgers, The State U of New Jersey, New Brunswick, NJ
St. Bonaventure U, NY
St. Gregory's U, OK
Santa Ana Coll, CA
Shippensburg U of Pennsylvania, PA
Southern Adventist U, TN
Southern Illinois U Carbondale, IL
Southern Nazarene U, OK
Southwestern Coll, KS
Stetson U, FL
Texas A&M U, TX
Trinity U, TX
The U of Alabama, AL
U of Arkansas, AR
U of Connecticut, CT
U of Great Falls, MT
U of Kentucky, KY
U of Nebraska–Lincoln, NE
The U of Scranton, PA
The U of Tennessee at Martin, TN
The U of Texas at San Antonio, TX
U of the Incarnate Word, TX
U of Washington, WA
U of Wyoming, WY
Wake Forest U, NC
Wright State U, OH

MANAGEMENT SCIENCES AND QUANTITATIVE METHODS RELATED
Rutgers, The State U of New Jersey, New Brunswick, NJ
U of Pennsylvania, PA

MANUFACTURING ENGINEERING
Hofstra U, NY
North Dakota State U, ND
Penn State Fayette, The Eberly Campus, PA
Penn State Wilkes-Barre, PA
Rensselaer Polytechnic Inst, NY
Southern Illinois U Edwardsville, IL
U of California, Berkeley, CA
U of California, Los Angeles, CA
U of Connecticut, CT
U of Missouri–Rolla, MO
U of Toronto, ON, Canada
U of Wisconsin–Stout, WI
Wichita State U, KS

MANUFACTURING TECHNOLOGY
Altamaha Tech Coll, GA
Brevard Comm Coll, FL
East Carolina U, NC
East Central Coll, MO
Eastern Michigan U, MI
Farmingdale State Coll, NY
Fitchburg State Coll, MA
Hopkinsville Comm Coll, KY
Macomb Comm Coll, MI
Murray State U, KY
Northern Michigan U, MI
Rochester Inst of Technology, NY
Southwestern Coll, KS
Texas A&M U, TX
U of Nebraska at Omaha, NE
U of Northern Iowa, IA
Waukesha County Tech Coll, WI

MARINE BIOLOGY
Cornell U, NY
Monmouth U, NJ
U of Hawaii at Manoa, HI

MARINE BIOLOGY AND BIOLOGICAL OCEANOGRAPHY
American U, DC
Ball State U, IN
Barry U, FL
Bemidji State U, MN
Brown U, RI
Coastal Carolina U, SC
Coll of Charleston, SC
Coll of the Atlantic, ME
Dalhousie U, NS, Canada
Dixie State Coll of Utah, UT
East Stroudsburg U of Pennsylvania, PA
Eckerd Coll, FL
Fairleigh Dickinson U, Coll at Florham, NJ
Fairleigh Dickinson U, Metropolitan Campus, NJ
Florida Inst of Technology, FL
Florida International U, FL
Maine Maritime Academy, ME
Mitchell Coll, CT

Northeastern U, MA
Nova Southeastern U, FL
Old Dominion U, VA
The Richard Stockton Coll
of New Jersey, NJ
Rutgers, The State U of New
Jersey, New Brunswick, NJ
San Francisco State U, CA
Southern Maine Comm Coll,
ME
Southwestern Coll, KS
Troy U, AL
Unity Coll, ME
The U of Alabama, AL
U of California, Los Angeles,
CA
U of California, Santa
Barbara, CA
U of Connecticut, CT
U of Maine at Machias, ME
U of Miami, FL
U of New England, ME
U of New Hampshire, NH
U of New Haven, CT
U of Rhode Island, RI

**MARINE MAINTENANCE
AND SHIP REPAIR
TECHNOLOGY**
Alexandria Tech Coll, MN

**MARINE SCIENCE/
MERCHANT MARINE
OFFICER**
American U, DC
Jacksonville U, FL
Maine Maritime Academy,
ME
U of New Hampshire, NH
U of San Diego, CA
The U of Tampa, FL
U of the District of
Columbia, DC

MARINE TECHNOLOGY
Coll of The Albemarle, NC
Kingsborough Comm Coll of
the City U of New York,
NY
Lamar U, TX
Santa Barbara City Coll, CA
Skagit Valley Coll, WA

MARITIME SCIENCE
Coll of the Atlantic, ME

**MARKETING/
MARKETING
MANAGEMENT**
Abilene Christian U, TX
Abraham Baldwin Coll, GA
Aims Comm Coll, CO
Alabama A&M U, AL
Albany State U, GA
Albright Coll, PA
Alderson-Broaddus Coll, WV
Alexandria Tech Coll, MN
Allegany Coll of Maryland,
MD
Alma Coll, MI
Altamaha Tech Coll, GA
Alvernia Coll, PA
American International Coll,
MA
Anderson U, IN
Anderson U, SC
Angelo State U, TX
Ashland U, OH
Athabasca U, AB, Canada
Auburn U Montgomery, AL
Augsburg Coll, MN
Aurora U, IL
Avila U, MO
Bainbridge Coll, GA

Baker Coll of Allen Park, MI
Ball State U, IN
Barry U, FL
Baylor U, TX
Bentley Coll, MA
Bishop's U, QC, Canada
Bluefield State Coll, WV
Boston Coll, MA
Bradley U, IL
Brenau U, GA
Bridgewater Coll, VA
British Columbia Inst of
Technology, BC, Canada
Brock U, ON, Canada
Broward Comm Coll, FL
Bucks County Comm Coll,
PA
Buena Vista U, IA
California State U, Fullerton,
CA
California State U,
Sacramento, CA
California State U, San
Bernardino, CA
Cape Breton U, NS, Canada
Carleton U, ON, Canada
Carroll Coll, WI
Carson-Newman Coll, TN
Carthage Coll, WI
Cedar Valley Coll, TX
Central Arizona Coll, AZ
Central Florida Comm Coll,
FL
Central Lakes Coll, MN
Central Piedmont Comm
Coll, NC
Charleston Southern U, SC
Chattahoochee Tech Coll,
GA
Christopher Newport U, VA
City Colls of Chicago,
Richard J. Daley Coll, IL
Clayton State U, GA
Clemson U, SC
Coastal Carolina U, SC
The Coll of St. Scholastica,
MN
Coll of the Desert, CA
The Coll of Westchester, NY
Colorado Mountain Coll,
Alpine Campus, CO
Columbus State U, GA
Comm Coll of Allegheny
County, PA
Comm Coll of Aurora, CO
Comm Coll of Beaver
County, PA
Coosa Valley Tech Coll, GA
Cornerstone U, MI
Cosumnes River Coll,
Sacramento, CA
Crafton Hills Coll, CA
Cuesta Coll, CA
Dalhousie U, NS, Canada
Dallas Baptist U, TX
DeKalb Tech Coll, GA
Delaware State U, DE
Delaware Tech & Comm
Coll, Jack F. Owens
Campus, DE
DePaul U, IL
Drake U, IA
Drury U, MO
East Carolina U, NC
Eastern Idaho Tech Coll, ID
Eastern Michigan U, MI
El Camino Coll, CA
Elmira Coll, NY
Elms Coll, MA
Emory U, GA
Fairfield U, CT
Fairleigh Dickinson U, Coll
at Florham, NJ
Fayetteville State U, NC

Fitchburg State Coll, MA
Florida Atlantic U, FL
Florida Comm Coll at
Jacksonville, FL
Florida Gulf Coast U, FL
Florida International U, FL
Fontbonne U, MO
Fort Hays State U, KS
Framingham State Coll, MA
Franklin Pierce U, NH
Frederick Comm Coll, MD
Freed-Hardeman U, TN
Fresno Pacific U, CA
Gannon U, PA
The George Washington U,
DC
Georgia Coll & State U, GA
Glenville State Coll, WV
Gloucester County Coll, NJ
Gonzaga U, WA
Grambling State U, LA
Greenville Tech Coll, SC
Grossmont Coll, CA
Harding U, AR
Harrisburg Area Comm Coll,
PA
High Point U, NC
Hillsborough Comm Coll, FL
Hocking Coll, OH
Hofstra U, NY
Houston Baptist U, TX
Houston Comm Coll System,
TX
Hudson Valley Comm Coll,
NY
Husson Coll, ME
Idaho State U, ID
Illinois State U, IL
Illinois Valley Comm Coll, IL
Indiana U Bloomington, IN
Indiana U of Pennsylvania,
PA
Indiana U–Purdue U Fort
Wayne, IN
Iona Coll, NY
Ithaca Coll, NY
Jacksonville U, FL
John Brown U, AR
Johnson & Wales U, CO
Johnson & Wales U, FL
Johnson & Wales U, RI
Johnson State Coll, VT
Kansas State U, KS
Kapiolani Comm Coll, HI
Kendall Coll, IL
Kennesaw State U, GA
Keuka Coll, NY
Kingsborough Comm Coll of
the City U of New York,
NY
King's Coll, PA
Kutztown U of
Pennsylvania, PA
Laboratory Inst of
Merchandising, NY
Lakeland Coll, WI
Lamar U, TX
Laredo Comm Coll, TX
Lehigh U, PA
Le Moyne Coll, NY
LeTourneau U, TX
Lewis U, IL
Lindenwood U, MO
Long Beach City Coll, CA
Long Island U, Brooklyn
Campus, NY
Loras Coll, IA
Loyola U Chicago, IL
Loyola U New Orleans, LA
Lynchburg Coll, VA
MacMurray Coll, IL
Macomb Comm Coll, MI
Manhattan Coll, NY
Marietta Coll, OH

Marquette U, WI
Marshall U, WV
Marymount U, VA
Marywood U, PA
Massachusetts Coll of Liberal
Arts, MA
Massasoit Comm Coll, MA
Maui Comm Coll, HI
McNeese State U, LA
Mercyhurst Coll, PA
Metropolitan Comm
Coll–Longview, MO
Metropolitan Comm
Coll–Penn Valley, MO
Miami Dade Coll, FL
Michigan State U, MI
Middle Georgia Tech Coll,
GA
Middlesex Comm Coll, CT
Middlesex County Coll, NJ
Middle Tennessee State U,
TN
Midland Lutheran Coll, NE
Minnesota State Coll–
Southeast Tech, MN
Minnesota State U Mankato,
MN
Minnesota State U
Moorhead, MN
MiraCosta Coll, CA
Missouri State U, MO
Montana State U–Billings,
MT
Moorpark Coll, CA
Morningside Coll, IA
Morton Coll, IL
Mount Saint Vincent U, NS,
Canada
Mount Vernon Nazarene U,
OH
Murray State U, KY
Nassau Comm Coll, NY
Neumann Coll, PA
New Mexico Jr Coll, NM
New River Comm Coll, VA
New York City Coll of
Technology of the City U
of New York, NY
New York U, NY
Niagara U, NY
North Carolina State U, NC
North Central Coll, IL
North Central Missouri Coll,
MO
Northeastern U, MA
Northern Illinois U, IL
Northern Michigan U, MI
Northern State U, SD
North Georgia Coll & State
U, GA
Northland Comm and Tech
Coll–Thief River Falls, MN
North Metro Tech Coll, GA
Northwestern Coll, MN
Northwest Nazarene U, ID
Northwood U, MI
Northwood U, Florida
Campus, FL
Northwood U, Texas
Campus, TX
Notre Dame Coll, OH
Notre Dame de Namur U,
CA
Nova Southeastern U, FL
Oakland U, MI
The Ohio State U, OH
Oklahoma State U, OK
Old Dominion U, VA
Oral Roberts U, OK
Otterbein Coll, OH
Our Lady of the Lake U of
San Antonio, TX
Park U, MO
Penn State Abington, PA

Penn State DuBois, PA
Penn State Fayette, The
Eberly Campus, PA
Penn State Mont Alto, PA
Penn State Wilkes-Barre, PA
Phoenix Coll, AZ
Pittsburg State U, KS
Portland State U, OR
Prairie View A&M U, TX
Purdue U North Central, IN
Radford U, VA
Rensselaer Polytechnic Inst,
NY
Rochester Inst of
Technology, NY
Rockford Coll, IL
Roosevelt U, IL
Rutgers, The State U of New
Jersey, Newark, NJ
Rutgers, The State U of New
Jersey, New Brunswick, NJ
Ryerson U, ON, Canada
St. Bonaventure U, NY
St. Cloud State U, MN
St. Cloud Tech Coll, MN
St. Gregory's U, OK
St. Thomas Aquinas Coll,
NY
Salem Comm Coll, NJ
San Diego Mesa Coll, CA
San Diego State U, CA
San Francisco State U, CA
Santa Ana Coll, CA
Santa Barbara City Coll, CA
Santa Clara U, CA
Sauk Valley Comm Coll, IL
Schoolcraft Coll, MI
Seminole Comm Coll, FL
Seton Hall U, NJ
Seton Hill U, PA
Shippensburg U of
Pennsylvania, PA
Southeast Tech Inst, SD
Southern Adventist U, TN
Southern Illinois U
Carbondale, IL
Southern Nazarene U, OK
Southern Oregon U, OR
Southern U and A&M Coll,
LA
Southwestern Indian
Polytechnic Inst, NM
Spokane Comm Coll, WA
Stark State Coll of
Technology, OH
State U of New York at
Fredonia, NY
State U of New York Coll at
Brockport, NY
State U of New York Coll of
Technology at Alfred, NY
Stephen F. Austin State U,
TX
Stetson U, FL
Stonehill Coll, MA
Syracuse U, NY
Tallahassee Comm Coll, FL
Taylor U, IN
Temple U, PA
Texas A&M U, TX
Texas A&M U–Corpus
Christi, TX
Tidewater Comm Coll, VA
Trevecca Nazarene U, TN
Trinity U, TX
Trocaire Coll, NY
Tunxis Comm Coll, CT
The U of Akron, OH
The U of Alabama, AL
The U of Alabama in
Huntsville, AL
U of Alaska Anchorage, AK
The U of Arizona, AZ
U of Arkansas, AR

U of Baltimore, MD
U of Central Florida, FL
U of Central Missouri, MO
U of Central Oklahoma, OK
U of Cincinnati, OH
U of Colorado at Boulder, CO
U of Connecticut, CT
U of Dayton, OH
U of Delaware, DE
U of Evansville, IN
The U of Findlay, OH
U of Great Falls, MT
U of Guelph, ON, Canada
U of Hawaii at Manoa, HI
U of Houston, TX
U of Kentucky, KY
U of Maine at Machias, ME
U of Mary Hardin-Baylor, TX
U of Massachusetts Amherst, MA
U of Miami, FL
U of Minnesota, Duluth, MN
U of Mississippi, MS
U of Missouri–Columbia, MO
U of Nebraska at Omaha, NE
U of Nebraska–Lincoln, NE
U of New Brunswick Fredericton, NB, Canada
U of New Haven, CT
U of New Orleans, LA
U of Northern British Columbia, BC, Canada
U of Northern Iowa, IA
U of North Florida, FL
U of Notre Dame, IN
U of Oregon, OR
U of Pennsylvania, PA
U of Pittsburgh, PA
U of Portland, OR
U of Rhode Island, RI
U of Rio Grande, OH
U of St. Thomas, MN
U of St. Thomas, TX
U of San Francisco, CA
The U of Scranton, PA
U of Southern Indiana, IN
The U of Tampa, FL
The U of Tennessee, TN
The U of Tennessee at Martin, TN
The U of Texas at Austin, TX
The U of Texas at El Paso, TX
The U of Texas at San Antonio, TX
U of the District of Columbia, DC
U of the Incarnate Word, TX
U of the Ozarks, AR
U of West Georgia, GA
U of Wisconsin–Eau Claire, WI
U of Wisconsin–La Crosse, WI
U of Wisconsin–Oshkosh, WI
U of Wyoming, WY
Upper Iowa U, IA
Urbana U, OH
Ursuline Coll, OH
Valdosta State U, GA
Valencia Comm Coll, FL
Vanguard U of Southern California, CA
Villanova U, PA
Virginia Intermont Coll, VA
Washburn U, KS
Waukesha County Tech Coll, WI
Wayne State U, MI

Wesley Coll, DE
Westchester Comm Coll, NY
Western Connecticut State U, CT
Western New England Coll, MA
Western Tech Coll, WI
West Liberty State Coll, WV
West Los Angeles Coll, CA
Westminster Coll, UT
Westmoreland County Comm Coll, PA
West Shore Comm Coll, MI
West Texas A&M U, TX
West Virginia State U, WV
West Virginia Wesleyan Coll, WV
Wichita State U, KS
Widener U, PA
Williston State Coll, ND
Wright State U, OH
Xavier U, OH

MARKETING OPERATIONS/ MARKETING AND DISTRIBUTION RELATED
Dalhousie U, NS, Canada

MARKETING RELATED
Clayton State U, GA
Fashion Inst of Technology, NY
Troy U, AL
The U of Akron, OH
U of Illinois at Urbana–Champaign, IL
Western New England Coll, MA
West Virginia State Comm and Tech Coll, WV

MARKETING RESEARCH
Ashland U, OH
Fairleigh Dickinson U, Metropolitan Campus, NJ
Fashion Inst of Technology, NY
Ithaca Coll, NY
Mount Saint Vincent U, NS, Canada
Saginaw Valley State U, MI
San Diego Mesa Coll, CA

MARRIAGE AND FAMILY THERAPY/COUNSELING
Harding U, AR
Seton Hill U, PA

MASONRY
Alexandria Tech Coll, MN
Florida Comm Coll at Jacksonville, FL
Ivy Tech Comm Coll–Southwest, IN
Ivy Tech Comm Coll–Wabash Valley, IN
State U of New York Coll of Technology at Alfred, NY

MASSAGE THERAPY
Minnesota School of Business–St. Cloud, MN
Waubonsee Comm Coll, IL

MASS COMMUNICATION/ MEDIA
Albion Coll, MI
Alderson-Broaddus Coll, WV
American International Coll, MA
American U, DC
Anderson U, IN

Anderson U, SC
Ashland U, OH
Asnuntuck Comm Coll, CT
Augsburg Coll, MN
Barry U, FL
Bemidji State U, MN
Benedictine Coll, KS
Bethel U, MN
Blinn Coll, TX
Boston Coll, MA
Brenau U, GA
Briar Cliff U, IA
Bridgewater Coll, VA
Brock U, ON, Canada
Bucks County Comm Coll, PA
Buena Vista U, IA
Buffalo State Coll, State U of New York, NY
Bunker Hill Comm Coll, MA
California State U, Sacramento, CA
Calvin Coll, MI
Cape Cod Comm Coll, MA
Carleton U, ON, Canada
Carson-Newman Coll, TN
Chattanooga State Tech Comm Coll, TN
City Colls of Chicago, Richard J. Daley Coll, IL
Clark U, MA
Clayton State U, GA
Coll of Mount Saint Vincent, NY
Coll of the Desert, CA
Concordia U, NE
Concord U, WV
Cornerstone U, MI
Cosumnes River Coll, Sacramento, CA
Cuesta Coll, CA
DePaul U, IL
Dominican U, IL
Drake U, IA
Drury U, MO
Eastern Nazarene Coll, MA
Fairfield U, CT
Fort Hays State U, KS
Franklin Pierce U, NH
Frederick Comm Coll, MD
Fresno Pacific U, CA
Fulton-Montgomery Comm Coll, NY
Gainesville State Coll, GA
Gardner-Webb U, NC
Georgetown Coll, KY
The George Washington U, DC
Glendale Comm Coll, CA
Gonzaga U, WA
Goshen Coll, IN
Grace Coll, IN
Grambling State U, LA
Gustavus Adolphus Coll, MN
Hamilton Coll, NY
Hamline U, MN
Hampshire Coll, MA
Harrisburg Area Comm Coll, PA
High Point U, NC
Hillsborough Comm Coll, FL
Hofstra U, NY
Houston Baptist U, TX
Houston Comm Coll System, TX
Hunter Coll of the City U of New York, NY
Huntington U, IN
Idaho State U, ID
Illinois State U, IL
Indiana U Bloomington, IN
Iona Coll, NY
Ithaca Coll, NY

John Brown U, AR
Johnson & Wales U, RI
Lackawanna Coll, PA
Lamar State Coll–Orange, TX
Lamar U, TX
Langston U, OK
Lassen Comm Coll District, CA
Lewis U, IL
Lindenwood U, MO
Loras Coll, IA
Loyola Marymount U, CA
Lynchburg Coll, VA
Lynn U, FL
Marian Coll, IN
Marquette U, WI
Marymount Manhattan Coll, NY
Massachusetts Coll of Liberal Arts, MA
McNeese State U, LA
Mercer U, GA
Mercyhurst Coll, PA
Miami Dade Coll, FL
Michigan State U, MI
Middlesex Comm Coll, CT
Middle Tennessee State U, TN
Midland Coll, TX
Midland Lutheran Coll, NE
Minnesota State U Mankato, MN
Minnesota State U Moorhead, MN
Missouri State U, MO
Montana State U–Billings, MT
Morningside Coll, IA
Mount Union Coll, OH
Murray State U, KY
Nassau Comm Coll, NY
New York U, NY
Niagara U, NY
North Carolina State U, NC
North Dakota State U, ND
Northeastern U, MA
Northern Michigan U, MI
Northland Comm and Tech Coll–Thief River Falls, MN
Northwestern Oklahoma State U, OK
Northwest Nazarene U, ID
Oglethorpe U, GA
Paul Quinn Coll, TX
Phoenix Coll, AZ
Piedmont Coll, GA
Pine Manor Coll, MA
Point Loma Nazarene U, CA
Queens Coll of the City U of New York, NY
Queens U of Charlotte, NC
Reinhardt Coll, GA
Rutgers, The State U of New Jersey, New Brunswick, NJ
St. Bonaventure U, NY
St. Cloud State U, MN
Saint Joseph's Coll, IN
St. Louis Comm Coll at Florissant Valley, MO
St. Thomas Aquinas Coll, NY
San Diego State U, CA
Southern Adventist U, TN
Southern Illinois U Edwardsville, IL
Southern Nazarene U, OK
Southern U and A&M Coll, LA
Southern Utah U, UT
Southwestern U, TX
Spalding U, KY
Spoon River Coll, IL
Springfield Coll in Illinois, IL

State U of New York at Fredonia, NY
State U of New York Coll at Brockport, NY
Taylor U, IN
Thiel Coll, PA
Towson U, MD
Trevecca Nazarene U, TN
Truman State U, MO
U at Albany, State U of New York, NY
U at Buffalo, the State U of New York, NY
The U of Akron, OH
U of Alaska Anchorage, AK
U of Baltimore, MD
U of California, Berkeley, CA
U of Central Florida, FL
U of Cincinnati, OH
U of Dayton, OH
U of Delaware, DE
U of Dubuque, IA
U of Evansville, IN
U of Houston, TX
U of Illinois at Urbana–Champaign, IL
U of Mary Hardin-Baylor, TX
U of Miami, FL
U of Missouri–Columbia, MO
U of Missouri–Kansas City, MO
U of Nebraska at Kearney, NE
U of New Hampshire, NH
U of New Hampshire at Manchester, NH
The U of North Carolina at Chapel Hill, NC
U of Oregon, OR
U of Pittsburgh at Johnstown, PA
U of Portland, OR
U of Rio Grande, OH
U of San Diego, CA
U of San Francisco, CA
The U of Tampa, FL
The U of Texas at El Paso, TX
The U of Texas at San Antonio, TX
U of the District of Columbia, DC
U of the Incarnate Word, TX
U of Toronto, ON, Canada
U of Wisconsin–Eau Claire, WI
U of Wisconsin–Madison, WI
U of Wisconsin–Oshkosh, WI
U of Wisconsin–Platteville, WI
Upper Iowa U, IA
Urbana U, OH
Valdosta State U, GA
Villanova U, PA
Washburn U, KS
Waubonsee Comm Coll, IL
Wayne State Coll, NE
Wesley Coll, DE
Westchester Comm Coll, NY
Western Connecticut State U, CT
Western New England Coll, MA
Western Tech Coll, WI
West Liberty State Coll, WV
Westminster Coll, PA
West Texas A&M U, TX
Widener U, PA
Wilfrid Laurier U, ON, Canada

Wilson Coll, PA
Worcester State Coll, MA
Wright State U, OH

**MASS
COMMUNICATIONS**
Clemson U, SC
James H. Faulkner State
Comm Coll, AL
Saint Leo U, FL
The U of Tennessee at
Martin, TN

**MATERIALS
ENGINEERING**
Brown U, RI
Clemson U, SC
Cornell U, NY
Lehigh U, PA
Montana Tech of The U of
Montana, MT
North Carolina State U, NC
The Ohio State U, OH
Rensselaer Polytechnic Inst,
NY
Rice U, TX
U of California, Irvine, CA
U of California, Los Angeles,
CA
U of Connecticut, CT
U of Kentucky, KY
U of Michigan, MI
U of Missouri–Rolla, MO
U of Pennsylvania, PA
U of Pittsburgh, PA
The U of Tennessee, TN
U of Toronto, ON, Canada
U of Washington, WA
Wright State U, OH

MATERIALS SCIENCE
Carnegie Mellon U, PA
Central Arizona Coll, AZ
Cornell U, NY
Duke U, NC
Greenville Tech Coll, SC
Michigan State U, MI
Montana Tech of The U of
Montana, MT
North Carolina State U, NC
The Ohio State U, OH
Penn State Abington, PA
Penn State DuBois, PA
Penn State Fayette, The
Eberly Campus, PA
Penn State Mont Alto, PA
Penn State Wilkes-Barre, PA
Rice U, TX
The U of Arizona, AZ
U of California, Berkeley,
CA
U of California, Los Angeles,
CA
U of Illinois at Urbana–
Champaign, IL
U of Michigan, MI
U of New Hampshire, NH
U of Pennsylvania, PA
U of Toronto, ON, Canada

**MATERNAL/CHILD
HEALTH AND
NEONATAL NURSING**
U at Buffalo, the State U of
New York, NY
U of Washington, WA

**MATHEMATICAL
STATISTICS AND
PROBABILITY**
Carnegie Mellon U, PA
Northern Illinois U, IL

MATHEMATICS
Abilene Christian U, TX
Abraham Baldwin Coll, GA
Acadia U, NS, Canada
Adams State Coll, CO
Adelphi U, NY
Alabama A&M U, AL
Albany State U, GA
Albertson Coll of Idaho, ID
Albion Coll, MI
Albright Coll, PA
Alderson-Broaddus Coll, WV
Alma Coll, MI
Alvernia Coll, PA
American International Coll,
MA
American U, DC
Amherst Coll, MA
Ancilla Coll, IN
Anderson U, IN
Anderson U, SC
Angelo State U, TX
Asbury Coll, KY
Ashland U, OH
Athens State U, AL
Auburn U Montgomery, AL
Augsburg Coll, MN
Aurora U, IL
Austin Coll, TX
Avila U, MO
Bainbridge Coll, GA
Ball State U, IN
Bard Coll, NY
Barry U, FL
Bates Coll, ME
Baylor U, TX
Bemidji State U, MN
Benedictine Coll, KS
Bentley Coll, MA
Bethel Coll, IN
Bethel U, MN
Bishop's U, QC, Canada
Blinn Coll, TX
Boston Coll, MA
Bradley U, IL
Brandeis U, MA
Brandon U, MB, Canada
Brevard Coll, NC
Brewton-Parker Coll, GA
Briar Cliff U, IA
Bridgewater Coll, VA
Brock U, ON, Canada
Brown U, RI
Bryn Mawr Coll, PA
Bucks County Comm Coll,
PA
Buena Vista U, IA
Buffalo State Coll, State U of
New York, NY
Bunker Hill Comm Coll, MA
Burlington County Coll, NJ
Calhoun Comm Coll, AL
California State U, Fullerton,
CA
California State U,
Northridge, CA
California State U,
Sacramento, CA
California State U, San
Bernardino, CA
California State U,
Stanislaus, CA
Calvin Coll, MI
Cameron U, OK
Cape Breton U, NS, Canada
Cape Cod Comm Coll, MA
Cardinal Stritch U, WI
Carleton U, ON, Canada
Carlow U, PA
Carroll Coll, MT
Carroll Coll, WI
Carson-Newman Coll, TN
Carthage Coll, WI

The Catholic U of America,
DC
Cedar Crest Coll, PA
Charleston Southern U, SC
Chesapeake Coll, MD
Christopher Newport U, VA
Citrus Coll, CA
Claremont McKenna Coll,
CA
Clark U, MA
Clayton State U, GA
Clemson U, SC
Coe Coll, IA
Colby Coll, ME
Colgate U, NY
Coll of Charleston, SC
Coll of Mount St. Joseph,
OH
Coll of Mount Saint Vincent,
NY
Coll of Saint Elizabeth, NJ
Coll of Saint Mary, NE
The Coll of Saint Rose, NY
The Coll of St. Scholastica,
MN
Coll of Staten Island of the
City U of New York, NY
Coll of the Canyons, CA
Coll of the Desert, CA
The Coll of William and
Mary, VA
Colorado Mountain Coll,
Alpine Campus, CO
Columbus State U, GA
Comm Coll of Allegheny
County, PA
Concordia Coll–New York,
NY
Concordia U, NE
Concordia U Coll of Alberta,
AB, Canada
Concord U, WV
Cornell U, NY
Cornerstone U, MI
Cosumnes River Coll,
Sacramento, CA
Crafton Hills Coll, CA
Cuesta Coll, CA
Daemen Coll, NY
Dalhousie U, NS, Canada
Dallas Baptist U, TX
Delaware State U, DE
DePaul U, IL
Dixie State Coll of Utah, UT
Dominican U, IL
Drake U, IA
Drury U, MO
Duke U, NC
Earlham Coll, IN
East Carolina U, NC
Eastern Connecticut State U,
CT
Eastern Mennonite U, VA
Eastern Michigan U, MI
Eastern Nazarene Coll, MA
East Stroudsburg U of
Pennsylvania, PA
Eckerd Coll, FL
Edinboro U of Pennsylvania,
PA
El Camino Coll, CA
Elmira Coll, NY
Elms Coll, MA
Elon U, NC
Emory U, GA
Fairfield U, CT
Fairleigh Dickinson U, Coll
at Florham, NJ
Fairleigh Dickinson U,
Metropolitan Campus, NJ
Fayetteville State U, NC
Feather River Coll, CA
Ferrum Coll, VA
Fitchburg State Coll, MA

Florida Atlantic U, FL
Florida International U, FL
Fontbonne U, MO
Foothill Coll, CA
Fort Hays State U, KS
Framingham State Coll, MA
Franciscan U of
Steubenville, OH
Franklin Coll, IN
Franklin Pierce U, NH
Frederick Comm Coll, MD
Freed-Hardeman U, TN
Fresno Pacific U, CA
Fulton-Montgomery Comm
Coll, NY
Furman U, SC
Gainesville State Coll, GA
Galveston Coll, TX
Gannon U, PA
Gardner-Webb U, NC
Georgetown Coll, KY
The George Washington U,
DC
Georgia Coll & State U, GA
Georgian Court U, NJ
Glendale Comm Coll, CA
Gloucester County Coll, NJ
Gonzaga U, WA
Gordon Coll, MA
Goshen Coll, IN
Grace Coll, IN
Graceland U, IA
Grambling State U, LA
Grinnell Coll, IA
Grossmont Coll, CA
Gustavus Adolphus Coll,
MN
Hamilton Coll, NY
Hamline U, MN
Hampden-Sydney Coll, VA
Hampshire Coll, MA
Harding U, AR
Harrisburg Area Comm Coll,
PA
Hartwick Coll, NY
Haverford Coll, PA
Henderson State U, AR
High Point U, NC
Hofstra U, NY
Hope Coll, MI
Houghton Coll, NY
Housatonic Comm Coll, CT
Houston Baptist U, TX
Hunter Coll of the City U of
New York, NY
Huntington U, IN
Idaho State U, ID
Illinois State U, IL
Illinois Wesleyan U, IL
Immaculata U, PA
Indiana U Bloomington, IN
Indiana U of Pennsylvania,
PA
Indiana U–Purdue U Fort
Wayne, IN
Indiana U–Purdue U
Indianapolis, IN
Indiana U Southeast, IN
Iona Coll, NY
Irvine Valley Coll, CA
Ithaca Coll, NY
Jacksonville U, FL
John Brown U, AR
Johnson State Coll, VT
Kansas State U, KS
Kellogg Comm Coll, MI
Kennesaw State U, GA
Kentucky Wesleyan Coll, KY
Kenyon Coll, OH
Keuka Coll, NY
Kingsborough Comm Coll of
the City U of New York,
NY
King's Coll, PA

Kutztown U of
Pennsylvania, PA
LaGrange Coll, GA
Lake Erie Coll, OH
Lakeland Coll, WI
Lake Superior State U, MI
Lamar State Coll–Orange, TX
Lamar U, TX
Langston U, OK
Lassen Comm Coll District,
CA
Lawrence U, WI
Lebanon Valley Coll, PA
Lee Coll, TX
Lehigh U, PA
Le Moyne Coll, NY
LeTourneau U, TX
Lewis U, IL
Liberty U, VA
Lincoln U, PA
Lindenwood U, MO
Long Beach City Coll, CA
Long Island U, Brooklyn
Campus, NY
Loras Coll, IA
Loyola Marymount U, CA
Loyola U Chicago, IL
Loyola U New Orleans, LA
Lynchburg Coll, VA
Macalester Coll, MN
MacMurray Coll, IL
Macomb Comm Coll, MI
Manhattan Coll, NY
Manhattanville Coll, NY
Marian Coll, IN
Marietta Coll, OH
Marist Coll, NY
Marquette U, WI
Marshall U, WV
Marymount U, VA
Marywood U, PA
Massachusetts Coll of Liberal
Arts, MA
McDaniel Coll, MD
McNeese State U, LA
Mercer U, GA
Mercyhurst Coll, PA
Miami Dade Coll, FL
Michigan State U, MI
Middlesex County Coll, NJ
Middle Tennessee State U,
TN
Midland Coll, TX
Midland Lutheran Coll, NE
Millersville U of
Pennsylvania, PA
Minnesota State U Mankato,
MN
Minnesota State U
Moorhead, MN
MiraCosta Coll, CA
Missouri State U, MO
Molloy Coll, NY
Monmouth Coll, IL
Monmouth U, NJ
Montana State U, MT
Montana State U–Billings,
MT
Montana Tech of The U of
Montana, MT
Moorpark Coll, CA
Moravian Coll, PA
Morningside Coll, IA
Mount Holyoke Coll, MA
Mount St. Mary's U, MD
Mount Saint Vincent U, NS,
Canada
Mount Union Coll, OH
Mount Vernon Nazarene U,
OH
Murray State U, KY
Nassau Comm Coll, NY
National-Louis U, IL
New Jersey City U, NJ

New Mexico Jr Coll, NM
New York U, NY
Niagara U, NY
Nipissing U, ON, Canada
North Carolina State U, NC
North Central Coll, IL
North Dakota State U, ND
Northeastern U, MA
Northern Illinois U, IL
Northern Michigan U, MI
Northern State U, SD
North Georgia Coll & State U, GA
Northwestern Coll, MN
Northwestern Oklahoma State U, OK
Northwest Nazarene U, ID
Notre Dame Coll, OH
Oakland U, MI
Occidental Coll, CA
Odessa Coll, TX
Oglethorpe U, GA
The Ohio State U, OH
The Ohio State U at Lima, OH
Ohio Wesleyan U, OH
Oklahoma State U, OK
Old Dominion U, VA
Oral Roberts U, OK
Otterbein Coll, OH
Our Lady of the Lake U of San Antonio, TX
Paris Jr Coll, TX
Park U, MO
Paul Quinn Coll, TX
Penn State Abington, PA
Penn State DuBois, PA
Penn State Fayette, The Eberly Campus, PA
Penn State Mont Alto, PA
Penn State Wilkes-Barre, PA
Piedmont Coll, GA
Pittsburg State U, KS
Point Loma Nazarene U, CA
Portland State U, OR
Prairie View A&M U, TX
Presbyterian Coll, SC
Purdue U North Central, IN
Queens Coll of the City U of New York, NY
Queen's U at Kingston, ON, Canada
Queens U of Charlotte, NC
Quincy Coll, MA
Radford U, VA
Ramapo Coll of New Jersey, NJ
Randolph Coll, VA
Randolph-Macon Coll, VA
Redeemer U Coll, ON, Canada
Reedley Coll, CA
Rensselaer Polytechnic Inst, NY
Rhodes Coll, TN
Rice U, TX
The Richard Stockton Coll of New Jersey, NJ
Ripon Coll, WI
Rivier Coll, NH
Rochester Inst of Technology, NY
Rockford Coll, IL
Rockhurst U, MO
Rocky Mountain Coll, MT
Roosevelt U, IL
Rose State Coll, OK
Rowan U, NJ
Roxbury Comm Coll, MA
Rutgers, The State U of New Jersey, Newark, NJ
Rutgers, The State U of New Jersey, New Brunswick, NJ
Saginaw Valley State U, MI

St. Bonaventure U, NY
St. Cloud State U, MN
St. Francis Xavier U, NS, Canada
St. Gregory's U, OK
Saint John's U, MN
Saint Joseph's Coll, IN
St. Lawrence U, NY
Saint Leo U, FL
St. Louis Comm Coll at Florissant Valley, MO
St. Mary's Coll of Maryland, MD
St. Norbert Coll, WI
St. Philip's Coll, TX
St. Thomas Aquinas Coll, NY
St. Thomas U, NB, Canada
Saint Xavier U, IL
Salem Comm Coll, NJ
Salve Regina U, RI
San Diego Mesa Coll, CA
San Diego State U, CA
San Francisco State U, CA
Santa Ana Coll, CA
Santa Barbara City Coll, CA
Santa Clara U, CA
Santa Rosa Jr Coll, CA
Sauk Valley Comm Coll, IL
Scottsdale Comm Coll, AZ
Seattle Pacific U, WA
Seton Hall U, NJ
Seton Hill U, PA
Sewanee: The U of the South, TN
Shippensburg U of Pennsylvania, PA
Skagit Valley Coll, WA
Slippery Rock U of Pennsylvania, PA
Southern Adventist U, TN
Southern Illinois U Carbondale, IL
Southern Illinois U Edwardsville, IL
Southern Nazarene U, OK
Southern Oregon U, OR
Southern U and A&M Coll, LA
Southern Utah U, UT
Southwest Baptist U, MO
Southwestern Coll, KS
Southwestern U, TX
Spoon River Coll, IL
Springfield Coll, MA
Springfield Coll in Illinois, IL
State U of New York at Fredonia, NY
State U of New York Coll at Brockport, NY
State U of New York Coll at Cortland, NY
State U of New York Coll at Geneseo, NY
State U of New York Coll at Potsdam, NY
State U of New York Coll of Technology at Alfred, NY
Stephen F. Austin State U, TX
Stetson U, FL
Stonehill Coll, MA
Sweet Briar Coll, VA
Syracuse U, NY
Taylor U, IN
Temple U, PA
Tennessee Wesleyan Coll, TN
Texas A&M U, TX
Texas A&M U–Corpus Christi, TX
Thiel Coll, PA
Towson U, MD
Trent U, ON, Canada

Trevecca Nazarene U, TN
Trinity Coll, CT
Trinity U, TX
Troy U, AL
Truman State U, MO
Tufts U, MA
Union Coll, NE
U at Albany, State U of New York, NY
U at Buffalo, the State U of New York, NY
The U of Akron, OH
The U of Alabama, AL
The U of Alabama in Huntsville, AL
U of Alaska Anchorage, AK
The U of Arizona, AZ
U of Arkansas, AR
U of Arkansas at Fort Smith, AR
U of California, Berkeley, CA
U of California, Irvine, CA
U of California, Los Angeles, CA
U of California, Santa Barbara, CA
U of Central Florida, FL
U of Central Missouri, MO
U of Central Oklahoma, OK
U of Cincinnati, OH
U of Colorado at Boulder, CO
U of Connecticut, CT
U of Dayton, OH
U of Delaware, DE
U of Evansville, IN
The U of Findlay, OH
U of Great Falls, MT
U of Guelph, ON, Canada
U of Hartford, CT
U of Hawaii at Manoa, HI
U of Houston, TX
U of Illinois at Urbana–Champaign, IL
U of Kansas, KS
U of Kentucky, KY
U of Manitoba, MB, Canada
U of Mary Hardin-Baylor, TX
U of Maryland, Baltimore County, MD
U of Mary Washington, VA
U of Massachusetts Amherst, MA
U of Massachusetts Boston, MA
U of Massachusetts Lowell, MA
U of Miami, FL
U of Michigan, MI
U of Minnesota, Duluth, MN
U of Mississippi, MS
U of Missouri–Columbia, MO
U of Missouri–Kansas City, MO
U of Nebraska at Kearney, NE
U of Nebraska at Omaha, NE
U of Nebraska–Lincoln, NE
U of New Brunswick Fredericton, NB, Canada
U of New England, ME
U of New Hampshire, NH
U of New Haven, CT
U of New Mexico, NM
U of New Orleans, LA
The U of North Carolina at Asheville, NC
The U of North Carolina at Chapel Hill, NC
The U of North Carolina at Charlotte, NC

U of Northern British Columbia, BC, Canada
U of Northern Iowa, IA
U of North Florida, FL
U of Notre Dame, IN
U of Oregon, OR
U of Pennsylvania, PA
U of Pittsburgh, PA
U of Pittsburgh at Johnstown, PA
U of Portland, OR
U of Redlands, CA
U of Rhode Island, RI
U of Rio Grande, OH
U of St. Thomas, MN
U of St. Thomas, TX
U of San Diego, CA
U of San Francisco, CA
The U of Scranton, PA
U of South Carolina Upstate, SC
U of Southern Indiana, IN
The U of Tampa, FL
The U of Tennessee, TN
The U of Tennessee at Martin, TN
The U of Texas at Austin, TX
The U of Texas at El Paso, TX
The U of Texas at San Antonio, TX
U of the District of Columbia, DC
U of the Incarnate Word, TX
U of the Ozarks, AR
U of the Pacific, CA
U of Toronto, ON, Canada
U of Vermont, VT
U of Virginia, VA
The U of Virginia's Coll at Wise, VA
U of Washington, WA
U of West Georgia, GA
U of Wisconsin–Eau Claire, WI
U of Wisconsin–Green Bay, WI
U of Wisconsin–La Crosse, WI
U of Wisconsin–Madison, WI
U of Wisconsin–Oshkosh, WI
U of Wisconsin–Platteville, WI
U of Wisconsin–Stevens Point, WI
U of Wyoming, WY
Upper Iowa U, IA
Ursuline Coll, OH
Utica Coll, NY
Valdosta State U, GA
Vanguard U of Southern California, CA
Vassar Coll, NY
Victor Valley Coll, CA
Villanova U, PA
Wake Forest U, NC
Washburn U, KS
Washington & Jefferson Coll, PA
Washington and Lee U, VA
Wayne State Coll, NE
Wayne State U, MI
Wellesley Coll, MA
Wells Coll, NY
West Chester U of Pennsylvania, PA
Western Connecticut State U, CT
Western Nebraska Comm Coll, NE

Western New England Coll, MA
Western Oregon U, OR
West Liberty State Coll, WV
West Los Angeles Coll, CA
Westminster Coll, PA
Westminster Coll, UT
West Texas A&M U, TX
West Virginia State U, WV
West Virginia Wesleyan Coll, WV
Wheaton Coll, IL
Whitman Coll, WA
Wichita State U, KS
Widener U, PA
Wilfrid Laurier U, ON, Canada
Wilkes U, PA
William Jewell Coll, MO
Wilson Coll, PA
Wofford Coll, SC
Worcester State Coll, MA
Wright State U, OH
Xavier U, OH
Yale U, CT

MATHEMATICS AND COMPUTER SCIENCE
Anderson U, IN
Bethel Coll, IN
Brandon U, MB, Canada
Brown U, RI
Cardinal Stritch U, WI
Dean Coll, MA
Fresno City Coll, CA
Hampden-Sydney Coll, VA
Hofstra U, NY
Immaculata U, PA
Ithaca Coll, NY
Lake Superior State U, MI
Lawrence U, WI
Loyola U Chicago, IL
Mount Saint Vincent U, NS, Canada
Piedmont Coll, GA
Rochester Inst of Technology, NY
St. Gregory's U, OK
Saint John's U, MN
Saint Joseph's Coll, IN
St. Lawrence U, NY
Southern Oregon U, OR
U at Albany, State U of New York, NY
The U of Akron, OH
U of Illinois at Urbana–Champaign, IL
U of Northern British Columbia, BC, Canada
U of Oregon, OR
Yale U, CT

MATHEMATICS AND STATISTICS RELATED
Anderson U, IN
Bradley U, IL
Carnegie Mellon U, PA
Hofstra U, NY
New York U, NY
The Ohio State U, OH
Seattle Pacific U, WA
The U of Akron, OH
U of Hartford, CT
U of Miami, FL
U of Pittsburgh, PA
The U of Scranton, PA

MATHEMATICS RELATED
Hofstra U, NY
Lassen Comm Coll District, CA
Seton Hill U, PA

U at Buffalo, the State U of New York, NY
U of California, Los Angeles, CA

MATHEMATICS TEACHER EDUCATION
Abilene Christian U, TX
Alma Coll, MI
Alvernia Coll, PA
Ancilla Coll, IN
Anderson U, IN
Anderson U, SC
Baylor U, TX
Bethel Coll, IN
Bethel U, MN
Bishop's U, QC, Canada
Brewton-Parker Coll, GA
Brock U, ON, Canada
Buena Vista U, IA
Buffalo State Coll, State U of New York, NY
Carroll Coll, MT
Carroll Coll, WI
The Catholic U of America, DC
Charleston Southern U, SC
Clemson U, SC
The Coll of Saint Rose, NY
Columbus State U, GA
Concordia U, NE
Cornell U, NY
Cornerstone U, MI
Daemen Coll, NY
Delaware State U, DE
East Carolina U, NC
Eastern Mennonite U, VA
Eastern Michigan U, MI
Elmira Coll, NY
Elms Coll, MA
Fayetteville State U, NC
Fitchburg State Coll, MA
Florida Atlantic U, FL
Florida Inst of Technology, FL
Florida International U, FL
Framingham State Coll, MA
Franklin Coll, IN
Frederick Comm Coll, MD
Freed-Hardeman U, TN
Gardner-Webb U, NC
Geneva Coll, PA
Glenville State Coll, WV
Grace Coll, IN
Gustavus Adolphus Coll, MN
Harding U, AR
Hofstra U, NY
Hope Coll, MI
Houston Baptist U, TX
Hunter Coll of the City U of New York, NY
Illinois Wesleyan U, IL
Indiana U Bloomington, IN
Indiana U of Pennsylvania, PA
Indiana U–Purdue U Fort Wayne, IN
Indiana U Southeast, IN
Iona Coll, NY
Ithaca Coll, NY
Johnson State Coll, VT
Kennesaw State U, GA
Kentucky Wesleyan Coll, KY
Keuka Coll, NY
Lebanon Valley Coll, PA
Le Moyne Coll, NY
Liberty U, VA
Lincoln U, PA
Lindenwood U, MO
Long Island U, Brooklyn Campus, NY
Manhattanville Coll, NY
Marist Coll, NY

Marquette U, WI
Marywood U, PA
McNeese State U, LA
Mercyhurst Coll, PA
Miami Dade Coll, FL
Millersville U of Pennsylvania, PA
Minnesota State U Moorhead, MN
Missouri State U, MO
Molloy Coll, NY
Montana State U–Billings, MT
Moravian Coll, PA
Mount Vernon Nazarene U, OH
Murray State U, KY
New York U, NY
Niagara U, NY
North Carolina State U, NC
North Dakota State U, ND
Northern Michigan U, MI
North Georgia Coll & State U, GA
Northwestern Coll, MN
Northwest Nazarene U, ID
Oakland U, MI
Ohio Wesleyan U, OH
Old Dominion U, VA
Oral Roberts U, OK
Pittsburg State U, KS
Queens U of Charlotte, NC
Rivier Coll, NH
Rocky Mountain Coll, MT
St. Bonaventure U, NY
St. Gregory's U, OK
Saint Xavier U, IL
Salve Regina U, RI
San Diego State U, CA
Seattle Pacific U, WA
Seton Hill U, PA
Southern Nazarene U, OK
Southern U and A&M Coll, LA
Southwest Baptist U, MO
State U of New York Coll at Brockport, NY
State U of New York Coll at Cortland, NY
State U of New York Coll at Potsdam, NY
Syracuse U, NY
Temple U, PA
Tennessee Wesleyan Coll, TN
Texas A&M U–Corpus Christi, TX
Trevecca Nazarene U, TN
Union Coll, NE
U at Albany, State U of New York, NY
The U of Akron, OH
The U of Arizona, AZ
U of Arkansas at Fort Smith, AR
U of Central Florida, FL
U of Central Oklahoma, OK
U of Delaware, DE
U of Evansville, IN
U of Great Falls, MT
U of Maine at Machias, ME
U of Mary Hardin-Baylor, TX
U of Minnesota, Duluth, MN
U of Mississippi, MS
U of Missouri–Columbia, MO
U of Nebraska–Lincoln, NE
U of New Hampshire, NH
U of New Orleans, LA
The U of North Carolina at Charlotte, NC
U of Northern Iowa, IA
U of North Florida, FL

U of Pittsburgh at Johnstown, PA
U of Rio Grande, OH
U of St. Thomas, MN
The U of Tennessee at Martin, TN
U of the Ozarks, AR
U of Vermont, VT
Ursuline Coll, OH
Utica Coll, NY
Wayne State Coll, NE
Wayne State U, MI
West Chester U of Pennsylvania, PA
West Virginia Wesleyan Coll, WV
Widener U, PA
Wright State U, OH

MECHANICAL DESIGN TECHNOLOGY
Asheville-Buncombe Tech Comm Coll, NC
Blue Ridge Comm Coll, VA
Chattanooga State Tech Comm Coll, TN
Clayton State U, GA
Coll of The Albemarle, NC
Comm Coll of Allegheny County, PA
Dabney S. Lancaster Comm Coll, VA
Heartland Comm Coll, IL
Illinois Valley Comm Coll, IL
Macomb Comm Coll, MI
Minnesota State Coll–Southeast Tech, MN
Mohawk Valley Comm Coll, NY
Phoenix Coll, AZ
St. Cloud Tech Coll, MN
Spokane Comm Coll, WA
State U of New York Coll of Technology at Alfred, NY
Western Tech Coll, WI
Westmoreland County Comm Coll, PA

MECHANICAL DRAFTING
Cameron U, OK

MECHANICAL DRAFTING AND CAD/CADD
Alexandria Tech Coll, MN
British Columbia Inst of Technology, BC, Canada
Cameron U, OK
Commonwealth Tech Inst, PA
Comm Coll of Allegheny County, PA
Dixie State Coll of Utah, UT
Eastern Michigan U, MI
Gaston Coll, NC
Indiana U–Purdue U Indianapolis, IN
Macomb Comm Coll, MI
Mohawk Valley Comm Coll, NY
Montana Tech of The U of Montana, MT
Murray State U, KY
Ozarks Tech Comm Coll, MO
St. Cloud Tech Coll, MN
Waukesha County Tech Coll, WI

MECHANICAL ENGINEERING
Alabama A&M U, AL
Baylor U, TX

Bradley U, IL
Brown U, RI
California State U, Fullerton, CA
California State U, Sacramento, CA
Calvin Coll, MI
Carleton U, ON, Canada
Carnegie Mellon U, PA
The Catholic U of America, DC
Clemson U, SC
Cornell U, NY
Dalhousie U, NS, Canada
Delaware State U, DE
Duke U, NC
Eastern Nazarene Coll, MA
Embry-Riddle Aeronautical U, FL
Fairfield U, CT
Florida Atlantic U, FL
Florida Inst of Technology, FL
Florida International U, FL
Gannon U, PA
The George Washington U, DC
Gonzaga U, WA
Hofstra U, NY
Idaho State U, ID
Indiana U–Purdue U Fort Wayne, IN
Indiana U–Purdue U Indianapolis, IN
Itasca Comm Coll, MN
Jacksonville U, FL
John Brown U, AR
Kansas State U, KS
Lake Superior State U, MI
Lamar U, TX
Lehigh U, PA
LeTourneau U, TX
Loyola Marymount U, CA
Manhattan Coll, NY
Marquette U, WI
Michigan State U, MI
Minnesota State U Mankato, MN
Montana State U, MT
Montana Tech of The U of Montana, MT
Murray State U, KY
North Carolina State U, NC
North Dakota State U, ND
Northeastern U, MA
Northern Illinois U, IL
Oakland U, MI
The Ohio State U, OH
Oklahoma State U, OK
Old Dominion U, VA
Oral Roberts U, OK
Penn State Abington, PA
Penn State DuBois, PA
Penn State Fayette, The Eberly Campus, PA
Penn State Mont Alto, PA
Penn State Wilkes-Barre, PA
Portland State U, OR
Prairie View A&M U, TX
Queen's U at Kingston, ON, Canada
Rensselaer Polytechnic Inst, NY
Rice U, TX
Rochester Inst of Technology, NY
Rowan U, NJ
Rutgers, The State U of New Jersey, New Brunswick, NJ
Ryerson U, ON, Canada
Saginaw Valley State U, MI
St. Cloud State U, MN
San Diego State U, CA
San Francisco State U, CA

Santa Clara U, CA
Southern Illinois U Carbondale, IL
Southern Illinois U Edwardsville, IL
Southern U and A&M Coll, LA
Syracuse U, NY
Temple U, PA
Texas A&M U, TX
Trinity Coll, CT
Tufts U, MA
U at Buffalo, the State U of New York, NY
The U of Akron, OH
The U of Alabama, AL
The U of Alabama in Huntsville, AL
The U of Arizona, AZ
U of Arkansas, AR
U of California, Berkeley, CA
U of California, Irvine, CA
U of California, Los Angeles, CA
U of California, Santa Barbara, CA
U of Central Florida, FL
U of Cincinnati, OH
U of Colorado at Boulder, CO
U of Connecticut, CT
U of Dayton, OH
U of Delaware, DE
U of Evansville, IN
U of Hartford, CT
U of Hawaii at Manoa, HI
U of Houston, TX
U of Illinois at Urbana–Champaign, IL
U of Kansas, KS
U of Kentucky, KY
U of Manitoba, MB, Canada
U of Maryland, Baltimore County, MD
U of Massachusetts Amherst, MA
U of Massachusetts Lowell, MA
U of Miami, FL
U of Michigan, MI
U of Mississippi, MS
U of Missouri–Columbia, MO
U of Missouri–Kansas City, MO
U of Missouri–Rolla, MO
U of Nebraska–Lincoln, NE
U of New Brunswick Fredericton, NB, Canada
U of New Hampshire, NH
U of New Haven, CT
U of New Mexico, NM
U of New Orleans, LA
The U of North Carolina at Charlotte, NC
U of North Florida, FL
U of Notre Dame, IN
U of Pennsylvania, PA
U of Pittsburgh, PA
U of Portland, OR
U of Rhode Island, RI
U of St. Thomas, MN
U of San Diego, CA
The U of Tennessee, TN
The U of Texas at Austin, TX
The U of Texas at El Paso, TX
The U of Texas at San Antonio, TX
U of the District of Columbia, DC
U of the Pacific, CA

U of Toronto, ON, Canada
U of Vermont, VT
U of Virginia, VA
U of Washington, WA
U of Wisconsin–Madison, WI
U of Wisconsin–Platteville, WI
U of Wyoming, WY
Villanova U, PA
Wayne State U, MI
Western New England Coll, MA
West Texas A&M U, TX
Wichita State U, KS
Widener U, PA
Wilkes U, PA
Wright State U, OH
Yale U, CT

MECHANICAL ENGINEERING/ MECHANICAL TECHNOLOGY
Alabama A&M U, AL
Asheville-Buncombe Tech Comm Coll, NC
Bluefield State Coll, WV
British Columbia Inst of Technology, BC, Canada
Broome Comm Coll, NY
Broward Comm Coll, FL
Buffalo State Coll, State U of New York, NY
California State U, Sacramento, CA
Central Ohio Tech Coll, OH
Central Piedmont Comm Coll, NC
Chattanooga State Tech Comm Coll, TN
Citrus Coll, CA
Delaware State U, DE
Eastern Michigan U, MI
Fairleigh Dickinson U, Metropolitan Campus, NJ
Farmingdale State Coll, NY
Gadsden State Comm Coll, AL
Gaston Coll, NC
Greenville Tech Coll, SC
Hagerstown Comm Coll, MD
Harrisburg Area Comm Coll, PA
Hudson Valley Comm Coll, NY
Illinois Valley Comm Coll, IL
Indiana U–Purdue U Fort Wayne, IN
Indiana U–Purdue U Indianapolis, IN
Jamestown Comm Coll, NY
Jefferson Comm and Tech Coll, KY
Jefferson Comm Coll, OH
Lake Superior State U, MI
Lassen Comm Coll District, CA
LeTourneau U, TX
Macomb Comm Coll, MI
Madisonville Comm Coll, KY
Middlesex County Coll, NJ
Mohawk Valley Comm Coll, NY
Montana State U, MT
Murray State U, KY
New York City Coll of Technology of the City U of New York, NY
Northeastern U, MA
Northern Michigan U, MI
Oklahoma State U, OK

Oregon Inst of Technology, OR
Penn State DuBois, PA
Pittsburg State U, KS
Purdue U North Central, IN
Richmond Comm Coll, NC
Rochester Inst of Technology, NY
St. Louis Comm Coll at Florissant Valley, MO
Sauk Valley Comm Coll, IL
Schoolcraft Coll, MI
Southeast Tech Inst, SD
South Piedmont Comm Coll, NC
Spokane Comm Coll, WA
Stark State Coll of Technology, OH
State U of New York Coll of Technology at Alfred, NY
State U of New York Coll of Technology at Canton, NY
Texas A&M U, TX
Texas A&M U–Corpus Christi, TX
The U of Akron, OH
U of Cincinnati, OH
U of Dayton, OH
U of Massachusetts Lowell, MA
U of New Hampshire at Manchester, NH
The U of North Carolina at Charlotte, NC
U of Pittsburgh at Johnstown, PA
U of Rio Grande, OH
U of the District of Columbia, DC
Vermont Tech Coll, VT
Wayne State U, MI
Westchester Comm Coll, NY
Westmoreland County Comm Coll, PA

MECHANICAL ENGINEERING TECHNOLOGIES RELATED
Old Dominion U, VA
U of Central Florida, FL
U of Hartford, CT

MECHANIC AND REPAIR TECHNOLOGIES RELATED
Hope Coll, MI
Ivy Tech Comm Coll–Kokomo, IN
Ivy Tech Comm Coll–Southwest, IN
Macomb Comm Coll, MI

MECHANICS AND REPAIR
Idaho State U, ID
Ivy Tech Comm Coll–Kokomo, IN
Ivy Tech Comm Coll–Southwest, IN
Ivy Tech Comm Coll–Wabash Valley, IN
Santa Rosa Jr Coll, CA

MEDICAL ADMINISTRATIVE ASSISTANT
Minnesota School of Business–St. Cloud, MN

MEDICAL ADMINISTRATIVE ASSISTANT AND MEDICAL SECRETARY
Alexandria Tech Coll, MN
Brevard Comm Coll, FL

British Columbia Inst of Technology, BC, Canada
Broward Comm Coll, FL
Bryant and Stratton Coll, Rochester, NY
Cape Cod Comm Coll, MA
Central Arizona Coll, AZ
Central Lakes Coll, MN
Central Piedmont Comm Coll, NC
Chattanooga State Tech Comm Coll, TN
Chesapeake Coll, MD
City Colls of Chicago, Richard J. Daley Coll, IL
Coll of The Albemarle, NC
The Coll of Westchester, NY
Comm Coll of Allegheny County, PA
Comm Coll of Beaver County, PA
Cosumnes River Coll, Sacramento, CA
Crafton Hills Coll, CA
Dabney S. Lancaster Comm Coll, VA
Delaware Tech & Comm Coll, Jack F. Owens Campus, DE
East Central Coll, MO
El Centro Coll, TX
Frederick Comm Coll, MD
Fresno City Coll, CA
Fulton-Montgomery Comm Coll, NY
Glendale Comm Coll, CA
Gloucester County Coll, NJ
Gretna Career Coll, LA
Grossmont Coll, CA
Hillsborough Comm Coll, FL
Hocking Coll, OH
Houston Comm Coll System, TX
Howard Comm Coll, MD
Jefferson Comm Coll, OH
Kellogg Comm Coll, MI
Lackawanna Coll, PA
Lamar U, TX
Lassen Comm Coll District, CA
Long Beach City Coll, CA
Mercyhurst Coll, PA
Metropolitan Comm Coll–Longview, MO
Metropolitan Comm Coll–Penn Valley, MO
Middlesex Comm Coll, CT
Midland Lutheran Coll, NE
Minnesota State Coll–Southeast Tech, MN
Montana State U–Billings, MT
Montana Tech of The U of Montana, MT
Morton Coll, IL
Nassau Comm Coll, NY
New Mexico Jr Coll, NM
New River Comm Coll, VA
Phoenix Coll, AZ
Pueblo Comm Coll, CO
Richland Comm Coll, IL
Rockingham Comm Coll, NC
Roxbury Comm Coll, MA
St. Cloud Tech Coll, MN
St. Philip's Coll, TX
Scottsdale Comm Coll, AZ
Shasta Coll, CA
Shelton State Comm Coll, AL
Skagit Valley Coll, WA
South Piedmont Comm Coll, NC
Spokane Comm Coll, WA
Spoon River Coll, IL
Surry Comm Coll, NC

Trocaire Coll, NY
Tunxis Comm Coll, CT
The U of Akron, OH
The U of Akron–Wayne Coll, OH
U of Cincinnati, OH
The U of Montana-Helena Coll of Technology, MT
U of Rio Grande, OH
Valencia Comm Coll, FL
Western Tech Coll, WI
West Los Angeles Coll, CA
Westmoreland County Comm Coll, PA
Wright State U, OH

MEDICAL BASIC SCIENCES RELATED
Ramapo Coll of New Jersey, NJ

MEDICAL/CLINICAL ASSISTANT
Argosy U, Twin Cities, Eagan, MN
Baker Coll of Allen Park, MI
Bluefield State Coll, WV
Brevard Comm Coll, FL
Broome Comm Coll, NY
Broward Comm Coll, FL
Brown Mackie Coll–Salina, KS
Bryant and Stratton Coll, Rochester, NY
Bucks County Comm Coll, PA
Central Piedmont Comm Coll, NC
Clayton State U, GA
Coll of the Desert, CA
Comm Coll of Allegheny County, PA
Cosumnes River Coll, Sacramento, CA
Cuesta Coll, CA
DeKalb Tech Coll, GA
Delaware Tech & Comm Coll, Jack F. Owens Campus, DE
Eastern Idaho Tech Coll, ID
El Camino Coll, CA
El Centro Coll, TX
Fresno City Coll, CA
Gaston Coll, NC
Glendale Comm Coll, CA
Gretna Career Coll, LA
Grossmont Coll, CA
Hocking Coll, OH
Idaho State U, ID
Ivy Tech Comm Coll–Kokomo, IN
Ivy Tech Comm Coll–Southwest, IN
Ivy Tech Comm Coll–Wabash Valley, IN
Jefferson Comm Coll, OH
Kapiolani Comm Coll, HI
Laredo Comm Coll, TX
Long Beach City Coll, CA
Macomb Comm Coll, MI
Massasoit Comm Coll, MA
Miami Dade Coll, FL
Mohawk Valley Comm Coll, NY
Montana State U–Billings, MT
New Mexico Jr Coll, NM
North Central Missouri Coll, MO
Ocean County Coll, NJ
Phoenix Coll, AZ
Richmond Comm Coll, NC
Rockingham Comm Coll, NC
San Diego Mesa Coll, CA

Santa Ana Coll, CA
Shasta Coll, CA
Skagit Valley Coll, WA
Southern Maine Comm Coll, ME
South Piedmont Comm Coll, NC
South U, GA
Stark State Coll of Technology, OH
Trocaire Coll, NY
The U of Akron, OH
U of Alaska Anchorage, AK
Ventura Coll, CA
Waubonsee Comm Coll, IL
West Virginia State U, WV

MEDICAL ILLUSTRATION
Alma Coll, MI
Clayton State U, GA
The Cleveland Inst of Art, OH
Rochester Inst of Technology, NY

MEDICAL INFORMATICS
U of Miami, FL

MEDICAL INSURANCE CODING
Alexandria Tech Coll, MN
Baker Coll of Allen Park, MI
Paris Jr Coll, TX

MEDICAL INSURANCE/ MEDICAL BILLING
Baker Coll of Allen Park, MI
Gretna Career Coll, LA

MEDICAL LABORATORY TECHNOLOGY
Abilene Christian U, TX
Argosy U, Twin Cities, Eagan, MN
British Columbia Inst of Technology, BC, Canada
Chattahoochee Tech Coll, GA
DeKalb Tech Coll, GA
Delaware Tech & Comm Coll, Jack F. Owens Campus, DE
Florida Comm Coll at Jacksonville, FL
Frederick Comm Coll, MD
The George Washington U, DC
Mohawk Valley Comm Coll, NY
Oakland U, MI
Phoenix Coll, AZ
Rockhurst U, MO
Roosevelt U, IL
Rose State Coll, OK
Schoolcraft Coll, MI
U of Cincinnati, OH
U of New England, ME

MEDICAL MICROBIOLOGY AND BACTERIOLOGY
Ball State U, IN
Dalhousie U, NS, Canada
Idaho State U, ID
Indiana U Bloomington, IN
Minnesota State U Mankato, MN
Montana State U, MT
Northern Michigan U, MI
The Ohio State U, OH
Ohio Wesleyan U, OH
Penn State Abington, PA
Penn State DuBois, PA

Penn State Fayette, The
Eberly Campus, PA
Penn State Mont Alto, PA
Penn State Wilkes-Barre, PA
Rutgers, The State U of New
Jersey, New Brunswick, NJ
St. Cloud State U, MN
San Francisco State U, CA
The U of Akron, OH
The U of Alabama, AL
U of California, Los Angeles,
CA
U of California, Santa
Barbara, CA
U of Central Florida, FL
U of Cincinnati, OH
U of Manitoba, MB, Canada
U of Miami, FL
U of New Brunswick
Fredericton, NB, Canada
U of New Hampshire, NH
U of Pittsburgh, PA
U of Rhode Island, RI
The U of Tennessee, TN
The U of Texas at El Paso,
TX
U of Toronto, ON, Canada
U of Vermont, VT
U of Washington, WA
U of Wisconsin–Madison,
WI
U of Wisconsin–Oshkosh,
WI

**MEDICAL OFFICE
ASSISTANT**
Asnuntuck Comm Coll, CT
Commonwealth Tech Inst,
PA
Harrisburg Area Comm Coll,
PA
Mercy Coll of Health
Sciences, IA
Sauk Valley Comm Coll, IL

**MEDICAL OFFICE
COMPUTER SPECIALIST**
Baker Coll of Allen Park, MI

**MEDICAL OFFICE
MANAGEMENT**
Brown Mackie Coll–Salina,
KS
Coosa Valley Tech Coll, GA
Eastern New Mexico
U–Roswell, NM
Florida Comm Coll at
Jacksonville, FL
Gaston Coll, NC
St. Cloud Tech Coll, MN
The U of Akron, OH
The U of Akron–Wayne
Coll, OH

**MEDICAL RADIOLOGIC
TECHNOLOGY**
Allegany Coll of Maryland,
MD
Argosy U, Twin Cities,
Eagan, MN
Asheville-Buncombe Tech
Comm Coll, NC
Avila U, MO
Bluefield State Coll, WV
British Columbia Inst of
Technology, BC, Canada
Broome Comm Coll, NY
Bunker Hill Comm Coll, MA
Burlington County Coll, NJ
Caldwell Comm Coll and
Tech Inst, NC
Central Ohio Tech Coll, OH
Chattahoochee Tech Coll,
GA

Chesapeake Coll, MD
Comm Coll of Allegheny
County, PA
El Centro Coll, TX
Fairleigh Dickinson U, Coll
at Florham, NJ
Fairleigh Dickinson U,
Metropolitan Campus, NJ
Florida Comm Coll at
Jacksonville, FL
Foothill Coll, CA
Gadsden State Comm Coll,
AL
Galveston Coll, TX
Gannon U, PA
Hagerstown Comm Coll, MD
Harrisburg Area Comm Coll,
PA
Houston Comm Coll System,
TX
Idaho State U, ID
Indiana U–Purdue U
Indianapolis, IN
Ivy Tech Comm Coll–
Wabash Valley, IN
Jefferson Comm and Tech
Coll, KY
Kellogg Comm Coll, MI
Lamar Inst of Technology,
TX
Lincoln Land Comm Coll, IL
McNeese State U, LA
Mercy Coll of Health
Sciences, IA
Middle Georgia Tech Coll,
GA
Midland Coll, TX
Missouri State U, MO
Mohawk Valley Comm Coll,
NY
Nassau Comm Coll, NY
New York City Coll of
Technology of the City U
of New York, NY
North Central Coll, IL
North Metro Tech Coll, GA
The Ohio State U, OH
Pima Comm Coll, AZ
Pueblo Comm Coll, CO
Roosevelt U, IL
Rose State Coll, OK
St. Philip's Coll, TX
Santa Barbara City Coll, CA
Southern Illinois U
Carbondale, IL
The U of Akron, OH
U of Central Florida, FL
U of Hartford, CT
U of Missouri–Columbia,
MO
U of New Mexico, NM
The U of North Carolina at
Chapel Hill, NC
U of Southern Indiana, IN
U of Vermont, VT
Valencia Comm Coll, FL
Washburn U, KS

MEDICAL RECEPTION
Alexandria Tech Coll, MN

**MEDICAL
TRANSCRIPTION**
Alexandria Tech Coll, MN
Central Arizona Coll, AZ
El Centro Coll, TX
Mercyhurst Coll, PA
Southeast Tech Inst, SD
Ventura Coll, CA
Williston State Coll, ND

**MEDICINAL AND
PHARMACEUTICAL
CHEMISTRY**
U at Buffalo, the State U of
New York, NY

**MEDIEVAL AND
RENAISSANCE STUDIES**
Bard Coll, NY
Brown U, RI
Carleton U, ON, Canada
The Catholic U of America,
DC
The Coll of William and
Mary, VA
Cornell U, NY
Duke U, NC
Emory U, GA
Hamilton Coll, NY
Mount Holyoke Coll, MA
New York U, NY
Ohio Wesleyan U, OH
Penn State Abington, PA
Penn State DuBois, PA
Penn State Fayette, The
Eberly Campus, PA
Penn State Mont Alto, PA
Penn State Wilkes-Barre, PA
Rutgers, The State U of New
Jersey, New Brunswick, NJ
Sewanee: The U of the
South, TN
Syracuse U, NY
U at Albany, State U of New
York, NY
U of California, Santa
Barbara, CA
U of Manitoba, MB, Canada
U of Michigan, MI
U of Nebraska–Lincoln, NE
U of Notre Dame, IN
U of Toronto, ON, Canada
Vassar Coll, NY
Washington and Lee U, VA
Wellesley Coll, MA

**MENTAL AND SOCIAL
HEALTH SERVICES AND
ALLIED PROFESSIONS
RELATED**
Broome Comm Coll, NY
Marymount U, VA
Old Dominion U, VA
The U of Maine at Augusta,
ME
Waukesha County Tech Coll,
WI
Wright State U, OH

**MENTAL HEALTH
COUNSELING**
Florida Gulf Coast U, FL
Marywood U, PA
Washburn U, KS

**MENTAL HEALTH/
REHABILITATION**
Blinn Coll, TX
Brandon U, MB, Canada
Elmira Coll, NY
Glendale Comm Coll, CA
Hopkinsville Comm Coll,
KY
Housatonic Comm Coll, CT
Houston Comm Coll System,
TX
Kingsborough Comm Coll of
the City U of New York,
NY
Lackawanna Coll, PA
Lake Superior State U, MI
Macomb Comm Coll, MI
Middlesex Comm Coll, CT

Mohawk Valley Comm Coll,
NY
St. Cloud State U, MN
Springfield Coll, MA
Tufts U, MA

MERCHANDISING
Clayton State U, GA
Michigan State U, MI
North Central Texas Coll, TX
The U of Akron, OH

**MERCHANDISING,
SALES, AND
MARKETING
OPERATIONS RELATED
(GENERAL)**
Broome Comm Coll, NY
Clayton State U, GA
Eastern Michigan U, MI
Southwestern Michigan Coll,
MI
The U of Akron, OH

**MERCHANDISING,
SALES, AND
MARKETING
OPERATIONS RELATED
(SPECIALIZED)**
Baylor U, TX
Clayton State U, GA
Eastern Michigan U, MI
Gannon U, PA
The U of Akron, OH

**METAL AND JEWELRY
ARTS**
Academy of Art U, CA
The Cleveland Inst of Art,
OH
Coll of The Albemarle, NC
Fashion Inst of Technology,
NY
Hofstra U, NY
Indiana U Bloomington, IN
Maine Coll of Art, ME
NSCAD U, NS, Canada
Paris Jr Coll, TX
Pratt Inst, NY
Pueblo Comm Coll, CO
Rochester Inst of
Technology, NY
Savannah Coll of Art and
Design, GA
School of the Art Inst of
Chicago, IL
Seton Hill U, PA
State U of New York Coll at
Brockport, NY
Syracuse U, NY
Temple U, PA
The U of Akron, OH
U of Kansas, KS
U of Michigan, MI
U of Oregon, OR
U of Washington, WA

**METALLURGICAL
ENGINEERING**
Dalhousie U, NS, Canada
Montana Tech of The U of
Montana, MT
The Ohio State U, OH
The U of Alabama, AL
U of Cincinnati, OH
U of Michigan, MI
U of Missouri–Rolla, MO
U of Pittsburgh, PA
The U of Texas at El Paso,
TX
U of Toronto, ON, Canada
U of Washington, WA
U of Wisconsin–Madison,
WI

**METALLURGICAL
TECHNOLOGY**
Macomb Comm Coll, MI
Mohawk Valley Comm Coll,
NY
Penn State DuBois, PA
Penn State Fayette, The
Eberly Campus, PA
Penn State Wilkes-Barre, PA
Schoolcraft Coll, MI
U of Cincinnati, OH

METEOROLOGY
Dalhousie U, NS, Canada
Florida Inst of Technology,
FL
North Carolina State U, NC
State U of New York Coll at
Brockport, NY
U of Hawaii at Manoa, HI
U of Miami, FL
The U of North Carolina at
Charlotte, NC
West Virginia State Comm
and Tech Coll, WV

**MICROBIOLOGICAL
SCIENCES AND
IMMUNOLOGY RELATED**
Dalhousie U, NS, Canada
U of California, Los Angeles,
CA
Wright State U, OH

MICROBIOLOGY
Clemson U, SC
Cornell U, NY
Idaho State U, ID
Michigan State U, MI
North Carolina State U, NC
North Dakota State U, ND
Northern Michigan U, MI
San Diego State U, CA
Southern Illinois U
Carbondale, IL
Texas A&M U, TX
U of California, Berkeley,
CA
U of California, Irvine, CA
U of California, Santa
Barbara, CA
U of Guelph, ON, Canada
U of Hawaii at Manoa, HI
U of Illinois at Urbana–
Champaign, IL
U of Kansas, KS
U of Massachusetts Amherst,
MA
U of Miami, FL
U of Missouri–Columbia,
MO
U of Northern Iowa, IA
The U of Texas at Austin,
TX
U of Toronto, ON, Canada
U of Wisconsin–La Crosse,
WI
U of Wyoming, WY

**MIDDLE/NEAR EASTERN
AND SEMITIC
LANGUAGES RELATED**
Bryn Mawr Coll, PA
U of California, Los Angeles,
CA
Wayne State U, MI

**MIDDLE SCHOOL
EDUCATION**
Abilene Christian U, TX
Albany State U, GA
American International Coll,
MA

Arkansas State U–Newport, AR
Asbury Coll, KY
Ashland U, OH
Avila U, MO
Bethel Coll, IN
Brandon U, MB, Canada
Brenau U, GA
Brevard Coll, NC
Brewton-Parker Coll, GA
Carroll Coll, WI
Cedar Crest Coll, PA
Christopher Newport U, VA
Clark U, MA
Clayton State U, GA
Coastal Carolina U, SC
Coll of Charleston, SC
Coll of Mount St. Joseph, OH
Coll of the Atlantic, ME
Columbus State U, GA
Concordia Coll–New York, NY
Concordia U, NE
Delaware State U, DE
East Carolina U, NC
Eastern Mennonite U, VA
Eastern Nazarene Coll, MA
Elmira Coll, NY
Elon U, NC
Fayetteville State U, NC
Fitchburg State Coll, MA
Fontbonne U, MO
Gainesville State Coll, GA
Georgetown Coll, KY
Georgia Coll & State U, GA
Gordon Coll, MA
Harding U, AR
Henderson State U, AR
High Point U, NC
Houston Baptist U, TX
Huntington U, IN
Ithaca Coll, NY
John Brown U, AR
Johnson State Coll, VT
Kennesaw State U, GA
Kentucky Wesleyan Coll, KY
LaGrange Coll, GA
Lakeland Coll, WI
Lake Superior State U, MI
Lindenwood U, MO
Manhattan Coll, NY
Marquette U, WI
Massachusetts Coll of Liberal Arts, MA
Mercer U, GA
Miami Dade Coll, FL
Midland Lutheran Coll, NE
Minnesota State U Moorhead, MN
Missouri State U, MO
Mount Union Coll, OH
Mount Vernon Nazarene U, OH
Murray State U, KY
New York U, NY
North Carolina State U, NC
North Georgia Coll & State U, GA
Notre Dame Coll, OH
Oglethorpe U, GA
Ohio Wesleyan U, OH
Otterbein Coll, OH
Piedmont Coll, GA
Presbyterian Coll, SC
Reinhardt Coll, GA
St. Bonaventure U, NY
St. Cloud State U, MN
Saint Leo U, FL
Southern Nazarene U, OK
Southern U and A&M Coll, LA
Southwest Baptist U, MO
Spalding U, KY

Springfield Coll, MA
State U of New York Coll at Brockport, NY
State U of New York Coll at Cortland, NY
Taylor U, IN
The U of Akron, OH
U of Arkansas, AR
U of Arkansas at Fort Smith, AR
U of Central Missouri, MO
U of Delaware, DE
U of Great Falls, MT
U of Kansas, KS
U of Kentucky, KY
U of Mary Hardin-Baylor, TX
U of Minnesota, Duluth, MN
U of Missouri–Columbia, MO
U of Missouri–Kansas City, MO
U of Nebraska–Lincoln, NE
U of New Orleans, LA
The U of North Carolina at Chapel Hill, NC
The U of North Carolina at Charlotte, NC
U of Northern Iowa, IA
U of North Florida, FL
U of St. Thomas, MN
U of the Ozarks, AR
U of Vermont, VT
U of West Georgia, GA
U of Wisconsin–Platteville, WI
Urbana U, OH
Ursuline Coll, OH
Valdosta State U, GA
Wayne State Coll, NE
West Virginia Wesleyan Coll, WV
Wright State U, OH
Xavier U, OH

MILITARY STUDIES
Florida Inst of Technology, FL

MILITARY TECHNOLOGIES
Calhoun Comm Coll, AL
Murray State U, KY
Wright State U, OH

MINING AND MINERAL ENGINEERING
Dalhousie U, NS, Canada
Montana Tech of The U of Montana, MT
Penn State Abington, PA
Penn State DuBois, PA
Penn State Fayette, The Eberly Campus, PA
Penn State Mont Alto, PA
Penn State Wilkes-Barre, PA
Queen's U at Kingston, ON, Canada
Southern Illinois U Carbondale, IL
The U of Arizona, AZ
U of Kentucky, KY
U of Missouri–Rolla, MO
U of Toronto, ON, Canada
U of Wisconsin–Madison, WI

MINING TECHNOLOGY
Bluefield State Coll, WV
British Columbia Inst of Technology, BC, Canada

MISSIONARY STUDIES AND MISSIOLOGY
Abilene Christian U, TX
Asbury Coll, KY

Bethel Coll, IN
Freed-Hardeman U, TN
Gardner-Webb U, NC
Harding U, AR
Huntington U, IN
John Brown U, AR
Kuyper Coll, MI
Lancaster Bible Coll, PA
LeTourneau U, TX
Multnomah Bible Coll and Biblical Seminary, OR
Northwestern Coll, MN
Northwest Nazarene U, ID
Oral Roberts U, OK
Southern Nazarene U, OK
Trinity Baptist Coll, FL
Vanguard U of Southern California, CA

MODERN GREEK
Ball State U, IN
Bard Coll, NY
Calvin Coll, MI
Carleton U, ON, Canada
The Catholic U of America, DC
Claremont McKenna Coll, CA
Colgate U, NY
The Coll of William and Mary, VA
Emory U, GA
Furman U, SC
Hamilton Coll, NY
Haverford Coll, PA
Kenyon Coll, OH
Loyola Marymount U, CA
Macalester Coll, MN
Monmouth Coll, IL
Mount Holyoke Coll, MA
New York U, NY
The Ohio State U, OH
Queens Coll of the City U of New York, NY
Rhodes Coll, TN
Sewanee: The U of the South, TN
Trent U, ON, Canada
Tufts U, MA
U of California, Los Angeles, CA
U of Manitoba, MB, Canada
U of Michigan, MI
U of Missouri–Columbia, MO
U of New Brunswick Fredericton, NB, Canada
U of New Hampshire, NH
U of Oregon, OR
U of Toronto, ON, Canada
U of Wisconsin–Madison, WI
Wilfrid Laurier U, ON, Canada
Wright State U, OH

MODERN LANGUAGES
Albion Coll, MI
Alma Coll, MI
Ball State U, IN
Bard Coll, NY
Bemidji State U, MN
Bishop's U, QC, Canada
Cape Cod Comm Coll, MA
Carleton U, ON, Canada
Citrus Coll, CA
City Colls of Chicago, Richard J. Daley Coll, IL
Claremont McKenna Coll, CA
Clark U, MA
Clemson U, SC
Coll of Mount Saint Vincent, NY

The Coll of William and Mary, VA
Dallas Baptist U, TX
DePaul U, IL
Eckerd Coll, FL
Elmira Coll, NY
Fairfield U, CT
Galveston Coll, TX
Hamilton Coll, NY
Immaculata U, PA
Kennesaw State U, GA
Kenyon Coll, OH
Lake Erie Coll, OH
Long Island U, Brooklyn Campus, NY
Middlesex County Coll, NJ
Midland Coll, TX
Minnesota State U Mankato, MN
Monmouth Coll, IL
Mount Saint Vincent U, NS, Canada
Northeastern U, MA
Odessa Coll, TX
Presbyterian Coll, SC
Rivier Coll, NH
Rose State Coll, OK
St. Bonaventure U, NY
St. Francis Xavier U, NS, Canada
St. Lawrence U, NY
St. Thomas Aquinas Coll, NY
Santa Ana Coll, CA
Slippery Rock U of Pennsylvania, PA
Syracuse U, NY
Trent U, ON, Canada
Trinity Coll, CT
U of Maryland, Baltimore County, MD
U of Mary Washington, VA
U of New Brunswick Fredericton, NB, Canada
U of New Hampshire, NH
U of Toronto, ON, Canada
Wayne State Coll, NE
Westminster Coll, PA
Widener U, PA
Wright State U, OH

MOLECULAR BIOCHEMISTRY
U of California, Irvine, CA
U of California, Los Angeles, CA

MOLECULAR BIOLOGY
Ball State U, IN
Bard Coll, NY
Bethel U, MN
Bradley U, IL
Brown U, RI
California State U, Sacramento, CA
Cedar Crest Coll, PA
Clark U, MA
Coe Coll, IA
Colby Coll, ME
Colgate U, NY
Cornell U, NY
Elms Coll, MA
Florida Inst of Technology, FL
Hamilton Coll, NY
Houston Baptist U, TX
Kenyon Coll, OH
Lehigh U, PA
Marquette U, WI
Missouri State U, MO
Otterbein Coll, OH
Rutgers, The State U of New Jersey, New Brunswick, NJ
San Francisco State U, CA

State U of New York Coll at Brockport, NY
Stetson U, FL
U at Albany, State U of New York, NY
U of California, Los Angeles, CA
U of California, Santa Barbara, CA
U of Guelph, ON, Canada
U of Kansas, KS
U of Maryland, Baltimore County, MD
U of Michigan, MI
U of Minnesota, Duluth, MN
U of New Brunswick Fredericton, NB, Canada
U of New Hampshire, NH
U of Pittsburgh, PA
The U of Texas at Austin, TX
U of Toronto, ON, Canada
U of Vermont, VT
U of Washington, WA
U of Wisconsin–Eau Claire, WI
U of Wisconsin–Madison, WI
U of Wyoming, WY
Wells Coll, NY
West Chester U of Pennsylvania, PA
Western New England Coll, MA
Westminster Coll, PA
Whitman Coll, WA
William Jewell Coll, MO
Yale U, CT

MOLECULAR GENETICS
Texas A&M U, TX
U of Guelph, ON, Canada
U of Vermont, VT

MOLECULAR PHARMACOLOGY
U at Buffalo, the State U of New York, NY
U of California, Los Angeles, CA

MOLECULAR PHYSIOLOGY
U of California, Los Angeles, CA

MOLECULAR TOXICOLOGY
U of California, Los Angeles, CA

MONTESSORI TEACHER EDUCATION
Xavier U, OH

MOVEMENT THERAPY AND MOVEMENT EDUCATION
Brock U, ON, Canada
U of Vermont, VT

MULTI-/ INTERDISCIPLINARY STUDIES RELATED
Abilene Christian U, TX
Adelphi U, NY
Albright Coll, PA
Angelo State U, TX
Arizona State U at the West campus, AZ
Arkansas State U–Newport, AR
Austin Coll, TX
Bates Coll, ME
Baylor U, TX

Bethel U, MN
Brandeis U, MA
Brevard Coll, NC
Buena Vista U, IA
Buffalo State Coll, State U of
New York, NY
California State U,
Stanislaus, CA
Clayton State U, GA
Colby Coll, ME
Coll of Saint Elizabeth, NJ
The Coll of William and
Mary, VA
Cornell U, NY
Cornerstone U, MI
Dalhousie U, NS, Canada
Dallas Baptist U, TX
Eastern Mennonite U, VA
Eastern West Virginia Comm
and Tech Coll, WV
Fairleigh Dickinson U,
Metropolitan Campus, NJ
Florida Inst of Technology,
FL
Gannon U, PA
Georgetown Coll, KY
Glenville State Coll, WV
Hofstra U, NY
Hope Coll, MI
Idaho State U, ID
Ithaca Coll, NY
Kentucky Wesleyan Coll, KY
Kenyon Coll, OH
Lebanon Valley Coll, PA
Liberty U, VA
Long Island U, Brooklyn
Campus, NY
Marquette U, WI
Marshall U, WV
Marywood U, PA
Massachusetts Coll of Liberal
Arts, MA
McDaniel Coll, MD
Mercer U, GA
Mercyhurst Coll, PA
Middle Tennessee State U,
TN
Mid-South Comm Coll, AR
Montana State U–Billings,
MT
Mount St. Mary's U, MD
Naropa U, CO
North Central Coll, IL
North Dakota State U, ND
Notre Dame Coll, OH
Nova Southeastern U, FL
Ohio Wesleyan U, OH
Old Dominion U, VA
Otterbein Coll, OH
Park U, MO
Queens Coll of the City U of
New York, NY
Ramapo Coll of New Jersey,
NJ
Rice U, TX
Rocky Mountain Coll, MT
Rutgers, The State U of New
Jersey, Newark, NJ
Ryerson U, ON, Canada
St. Cloud State U, MN
St. Mary's Coll of Maryland,
MD
San Diego State U, CA
Shippensburg U of
Pennsylvania, PA
Southern Illinois U
Carbondale, IL
Stephen F. Austin State U,
TX
Sterling Coll, VT
Stonehill Coll, MA
Temple U, PA
Texas A&M U, TX

U at Buffalo, the State U of
New York, NY
The U of Akron, OH
The U of Arizona, AZ
U of Arkansas at Fort Smith,
AR
U of California, Berkeley,
CA
U of California, Irvine, CA
U of California, Los Angeles,
CA
U of California, Santa
Barbara, CA
U of Connecticut, CT
U of Evansville, IN
U of Hartford, CT
U of Kentucky, KY
U of Massachusetts Amherst,
MA
U of Nebraska at Omaha,
NE
U of Northern British
Columbia, BC, Canada
U of St. Thomas, MN
The U of Tennessee, TN
The U of Texas at Austin,
TX
U of Virginia, VA
U of Wyoming, WY
Ursuline Coll, OH
Vassar Coll, NY
Washington and Lee U, VA
Waukesha County Tech Coll,
WI
West Texas A&M U, TX
Wheaton Coll, IL
Wilkes U, PA
Williston State Coll, ND
Wright State U, OH
Yale U, CT

MUSEUM STUDIES
Baylor U, TX
Coll of the Atlantic, ME
Randolph Coll, VA
Texas A&M U, TX

MUSIC
Abilene Christian U, TX
Abraham Baldwin Coll, GA
Acadia U, NS, Canada
Adams State Coll, CO
Adelphi U, NY
Albany State U, GA
Albertson Coll of Idaho, ID
Albion Coll, MI
Albright Coll, PA
Alderson-Broaddus Coll, WV
Alma Coll, MI
American U, DC
Amherst Coll, MA
Anderson U, SC
Angelo State U, TX
Asbury Coll, KY
Ashland U, OH
Augsburg Coll, MN
Austin Coll, TX
Ball State U, IN
Bard Coll, NY
Bates Coll, ME
Baylor U, TX
Bemidji State U, MN
Benedictine Coll, KS
Bethel Coll, IN
Bethel U, MN
Bishop's U, QC, Canada
Blinn Coll, TX
Boston Coll, MA
Bradley U, IL
Brandeis U, MA
Brandon U, MB, Canada
Brenau U, GA
Brevard Coll, NC
Brewton-Parker Coll, GA

Briar Cliff U, IA
Brock U, ON, Canada
Brown U, RI
Bryn Mawr Coll, PA
Bucks County Comm Coll,
PA
Buffalo State Coll, State U of
New York, NY
Burlington County Coll, NJ
Caldwell Comm Coll and
Tech Inst, NC
Calhoun Comm Coll, AL
California State U, Fullerton,
CA
California State U,
Northridge, CA
California State U,
Sacramento, CA
California State U, San
Bernardino, CA
California State U,
Stanislaus, CA
Calvin Coll, MI
Cameron U, OK
Cape Cod Comm Coll, MA
Cardinal Stritch U, WI
Carleton U, ON, Canada
Carroll Coll, WI
Carson-Newman Coll, TN
Carthage Coll, WI
The Catholic U of America,
DC
Cedar Crest Coll, PA
Cedar Valley Coll, TX
Central Piedmont Comm
Coll, NC
Central Wyoming Coll, WY
Charleston Southern U, SC
Chesapeake Coll, MD
Christopher Newport U, VA
Citrus Coll, CA
City Colls of Chicago,
Richard J. Daley Coll, IL
Claremont McKenna Coll,
CA
Clark U, MA
Clayton State U, GA
Coastal Carolina U, SC
Coe Coll, IA
Colby Coll, ME
Colgate U, NY
Coll of Charleston, SC
Coll of Mount St. Joseph,
OH
Coll of Saint Elizabeth, NJ
The Coll of Saint Rose, NY
Coll of Staten Island of the
City U of New York, NY
Coll of The Albemarle, NC
Coll of the Atlantic, ME
Coll of the Desert, CA
The Coll of William and
Mary, VA
Columbus State U, GA
Comm Coll of Allegheny
County, PA
Concordia Coll–New York,
NY
Concordia U, NE
Concordia U Coll of Alberta,
AB, Canada
Cornell U, NY
Cornerstone U, MI
Cosumnes River Coll,
Sacramento, CA
Crafton Hills Coll, CA
Dalhousie U, NS, Canada
Dallas Baptist U, TX
Delaware State U, DE
DePaul U, IL
Dixie State Coll of Utah, UT
Drake U, IA
Drury U, MO
Duke U, NC

Earlham Coll, IN
Eastern Mennonite U, VA
Eastern Michigan U, MI
Eastern Nazarene Coll, MA
Eckerd Coll, FL
Edinboro U of Pennsylvania,
PA
El Camino Coll, CA
Elmira Coll, NY
Elon U, NC
Emory U, GA
Florida Atlantic U, FL
Florida International U, FL
Foothill Coll, CA
Fort Hays State U, KS
Franklin Pierce U, NH
Freed-Hardeman U, TN
Fresno Pacific U, CA
Furman U, SC
Gainesville State Coll, GA
Galveston Coll, TX
Geneva Coll, PA
Georgetown Coll, KY
The George Washington U,
DC
Georgia Coll & State U, GA
Georgian Court U, NJ
Glendale Comm Coll, CA
Gonzaga U, WA
Gordon Coll, MA
Goshen Coll, IN
Graceland U, IA
Grinnell Coll, IA
Grossmont Coll, CA
Gustavus Adolphus Coll,
MN
Hamilton Coll, NY
Hamline U, MN
Hampshire Coll, MA
Harding U, AR
Harrisburg Area Comm Coll,
PA
Hartwick Coll, NY
Haverford Coll, PA
Henderson State U, AR
Hillsborough Comm Coll, FL
Hofstra U, NY
Hope Coll, MI
Houghton Coll, NY
Houston Baptist U, TX
Howard Comm Coll, MD
Hunter Coll of the City U of
New York, NY
Huntington U, IN
Idaho State U, ID
Illinois State U, IL
Illinois Wesleyan U, IL
Immaculata U, PA
Indiana U Bloomington, IN
Indiana U of Pennsylvania,
PA
Indiana U–Purdue U Fort
Wayne, IN
Indiana U Southeast, IN
Ithaca Coll, NY
Jacksonville U, FL
John Brown U, AR
Johnson State Coll, VT
Kansas State U, KS
Kellogg Comm Coll, MI
Kennesaw State U, GA
Kenyon Coll, OH
Kingsborough Comm Coll of
the City U of New York,
NY
The King's U Coll, AB,
Canada
Kutztown U of
Pennsylvania, PA
LaGrange Coll, GA
Lake Erie Coll, OH
Lakeland Coll, WI
Lamar U, TX
Langston U, OK

Lawrence U, WI
Lebanon Valley Coll, PA
Lee Coll, TX
Lehigh U, PA
Lewis U, IL
Liberty U, VA
Lincoln Land Comm Coll, IL
Lincoln U, PA
Lindenwood U, MO
Long Beach City Coll, CA
Loras Coll, IA
Loyola Marymount U, CA
Loyola U Chicago, IL
Loyola U New Orleans, LA
Lynchburg Coll, VA
Lynn U, FL
Macalester Coll, MN
MacMurray Coll, IL
Manhattanville Coll, NY
Mannes Coll The New
School for Music, NY
Marian Coll, IN
Marietta Coll, OH
Marywood U, PA
Massachusetts Coll of Liberal
Arts, MA
McDaniel Coll, MD
McNeese State U, LA
Mercer U, GA
Mercyhurst Coll, PA
Miami Dade Coll, FL
Michigan State U, MI
Middlesex County Coll, NJ
Middle Tennessee State U,
TN
Midland Coll, TX
Midland Lutheran Coll, NE
Millersville U of
Pennsylvania, PA
Minnesota State U Mankato,
MN
Minnesota State U
Moorhead, MN
MiraCosta Coll, CA
Missouri State U, MO
Molloy Coll, NY
Monmouth Coll, IL
Monmouth U, NJ
Montana State U, MT
Montana State U–Billings,
MT
Moorpark Coll, CA
Moravian Coll, PA
Morningside Coll, IA
Morton Coll, IL
Mount Holyoke Coll, MA
Mount Union Coll, OH
Mount Vernon Nazarene U,
OH
Murray State U, KY
New Jersey City U, NJ
New Mexico Jr Coll, NM
New York U, NY
North Central Coll, IL
North Dakota State U, ND
Northeastern U, MA
Northern Illinois U, IL
Northern Michigan U, MI
Northern State U, SD
North Georgia Coll & State
U, GA
Northwestern Coll, MN
Northwestern Oklahoma
State U, OK
Northwest Nazarene U, ID
Notre Dame de Namur U,
CA
Oakland U, MI
Occidental Coll, CA
Odessa Coll, TX
The Ohio State U, OH
Ohio Wesleyan U, OH
Oklahoma State U, OK
Old Dominion U, VA

Oral Roberts U, OK
Otterbein Coll, OH
Park U, MO
Penn State DuBois, PA
Penn State Mont Alto, PA
Penn State Wilkes-Barre, PA
Piedmont Coll, GA
Pima Comm Coll, AZ
Pittsburg State U, KS
Point Loma Nazarene U, CA
Portland State U, OR
Prairie View A&M U, TX
Presbyterian Coll, SC
Queen's U at Kingston, ON, Canada
Queens U of Charlotte, NC
Quincy Coll, MA
Radford U, VA
Ramapo Coll of New Jersey, NJ
Randolph-Macon Coll, VA
Redeemer U Coll, ON, Canada
Reinhardt Coll, GA
Rhodes Coll, TN
Rice U, TX
Ripon Coll, WI
Rockford Coll, IL
Roosevelt U, IL
Rose State Coll, OK
Roxbury Comm Coll, MA
Rutgers, The State U of New Jersey, Newark, NJ
Rutgers, The State U of New Jersey, New Brunswick, NJ
Saginaw Valley State U, MI
St. Cloud State U, MN
St. Francis Xavier U, NS, Canada
Saint John's U, MN
St. Lawrence U, NY
St. Louis Comm Coll at Florissant Valley, MO
St. Mary's Coll of Maryland, MD
St. Norbert Coll, WI
St. Philip's Coll, TX
Saint Xavier U, IL
Salve Regina U, RI
San Diego Mesa Coll, CA
San Francisco State U, CA
Santa Ana Coll, CA
Santa Barbara City Coll, CA
Santa Clara U, CA
Santa Rosa Jr Coll, CA
Sauk Valley Comm Coll, IL
Seattle Pacific U, WA
Seton Hall U, NJ
Seton Hill U, PA
Sewanee: The U of the South, TN
Shasta Coll, CA
Skagit Valley Coll, WA
Slippery Rock U of Pennsylvania, PA
Southern Adventist U, TN
Southern Illinois U Carbondale, IL
Southern Illinois U Edwardsville, IL
Southern Oregon U, OR
Southern Utah U, UT
Southwest Baptist U, MO
Southwestern Coll, KS
Southwestern U, TX
State U of New York at Fredonia, NY
State U of New York Coll at Geneseo, NY
Stephen F. Austin State U, TX
Stetson U, FL
Sweet Briar Coll, VA
Syracuse U, NY

Taylor U, IN
Temple U, PA
Tennessee Wesleyan Coll, TN
Texas A&M U, TX
Texas A&M U–Corpus Christi, TX
Tidewater Comm Coll, VA
Towson U, MD
Trevecca Nazarene U, TN
Trinity Coll, CT
Trinity U, TX
Truman State U, MO
Tufts U, MA
Union Coll, NE
U at Albany, State U of New York, NY
U at Buffalo, the State U of New York, NY
The U of Akron, OH
The U of Alabama, AL
The U of Alabama in Huntsville, AL
U of Alaska Anchorage, AK
The U of Arizona, AZ
U of Arkansas, AR
U of Arkansas at Fort Smith, AR
U of California, Berkeley, CA
U of California, Irvine, CA
U of California, Los Angeles, CA
U of California, Santa Barbara, CA
U of Central Missouri, MO
U of Central Oklahoma, OK
U of Cincinnati, OH
U of Colorado at Boulder, CO
U of Connecticut, CT
U of Dayton, OH
U of Delaware, DE
U of Evansville, IN
U of Guelph, ON, Canada
U of Hartford, CT
U of Hawaii at Manoa, HI
U of Houston, TX
U of Illinois at Urbana–Champaign, IL
U of Kansas, KS
The U of Maine at Augusta, ME
U of Maine at Machias, ME
U of Manitoba, MB, Canada
U of Maryland, Baltimore County, MD
U of Mary Washington, VA
U of Massachusetts Amherst, MA
U of Massachusetts Boston, MA
U of Massachusetts Lowell, MA
U of Miami, FL
U of Michigan, MI
U of Minnesota, Duluth, MN
U of Mississippi, MS
U of Missouri–Columbia, MO
U of Missouri–Kansas City, MO
U of Nebraska at Kearney, NE
U of Nebraska at Omaha, NE
U of Nebraska–Lincoln, NE
U of New Hampshire, NH
U of New Haven, CT
U of New Orleans, LA
The U of North Carolina at Asheville, NC
The U of North Carolina at Chapel Hill, NC

The U of North Carolina at Charlotte, NC
U of Northern Iowa, IA
U of North Florida, FL
U of Notre Dame, IN
U of Oregon, OR
U of Pennsylvania, PA
U of Pittsburgh, PA
U of Portland, OR
U of Redlands, CA
U of Rhode Island, RI
U of Rio Grande, OH
U of St. Thomas, MN
U of St. Thomas, TX
U of San Diego, CA
The U of Tampa, FL
The U of Tennessee, TN
The U of Tennessee at Martin, TN
The U of Texas at Austin, TX
The U of Texas at El Paso, TX
The U of Texas at San Antonio, TX
U of the District of Columbia, DC
U of the Incarnate Word, TX
U of the Ozarks, AR
U of the Pacific, CA
U of Toronto, ON, Canada
U of Vermont, VT
U of Virginia, VA
U of Washington, WA
U of Wisconsin–Eau Claire, WI
U of Wisconsin–Green Bay, WI
U of Wisconsin–La Crosse, WI
U of Wisconsin–Madison, WI
U of Wisconsin–Oshkosh, WI
U of Wisconsin–Platteville, WI
U of Wisconsin–Stevens Point, WI
U of Wyoming, WY
Valdosta State U, GA
Vanguard U of Southern California, CA
Vassar Coll, NY
Ventura Coll, CA
Victor Valley Coll, CA
Wake Forest U, NC
Washburn U, KS
Washington & Jefferson Coll, PA
Washington and Lee U, VA
Waubonsee Comm Coll, IL
Wayne State Coll, NE
Wayne State U, MI
Wellesley Coll, MA
Wells Coll, NY
West Chester U of Pennsylvania, PA
Western Connecticut State U, CT
Western Oregon U, OR
West Los Angeles Coll, CA
Westminster Coll, PA
West Texas A&M U, TX
West Virginia Wesleyan Coll, WV
Wheaton Coll, IL
Whitman Coll, WA
Wichita State U, KS
Wilfrid Laurier U, ON, Canada
William Jewell Coll, MO
Wright State U, OH
Xavier U, OH
Yale U, CT

MUSICAL INSTRUMENT FABRICATION AND REPAIR
Ball State U, IN
Indiana U Bloomington, IN
Minnesota State Coll–Southeast Tech, MN
U of Washington, WA

MUSICAL INSTRUMENT TECHNOLOGY
Delaware State U, DE

MUSIC HISTORY, LITERATURE, AND THEORY
Bard Coll, NY
Baylor U, TX
Brandon U, MB, Canada
Bridgewater Coll, VA
California State U, Fullerton, CA
Calvin Coll, MI
The Catholic U of America, DC
Christopher Newport U, VA
Dalhousie U, NS, Canada
Eugene Lang Coll The New School for Liberal Arts, NY
Fairfield U, CT
Hofstra U, NY
Indiana U Bloomington, IN
Loyola Marymount U, CA
Northeastern U, MA
The Ohio State U, OH
Otterbein Coll, OH
Randolph Coll, VA
Rice U, TX
Roosevelt U, IL
St. Cloud State U, MN
Saint Joseph's Coll, IN
Sewanee: The U of the South, TN
State U of New York at Fredonia, NY
Temple U, PA
The U of Akron, OH
U of California, Los Angeles, CA
U of Cincinnati, OH
U of Hartford, CT
U of Illinois at Urbana–Champaign, IL
U of Kentucky, KY
U of Michigan, MI
U of New Hampshire, NH
U of Redlands, CA
The U of Texas at Austin, TX
U of the Pacific, CA
U of Toronto, ON, Canada
U of Vermont, VT
U of Washington, WA
West Chester U of Pennsylvania, PA
Western Connecticut State U, CT
Wheaton Coll, IL
Wright State U, OH

MUSIC MANAGEMENT AND MERCHANDISING
Anderson U, IN
California State U, Sacramento, CA
Dallas Baptist U, TX
DePaul U, IL
Drake U, IA
Geneva Coll, PA
Hofstra U, NY
Houston Comm Coll System, TX
Huntington U, IN
Jacksonville U, FL

Johnson State Coll, VT
Lebanon Valley Coll, PA
Lewis U, IL
Loyola U New Orleans, LA
Middle Tennessee State U, TN
Minnesota State U Mankato, MN
Minnesota State U Moorhead, MN
New York U, NY
Northeastern U, MA
Otterbein Coll, OH
Saint Joseph's Coll, IN
Southern Nazarene U, OK
Southern Oregon U, OR
State U of New York at Fredonia, NY
Syracuse U, NY
Taylor U, IN
Trevecca Nazarene U, TN
U of Evansville, IN
U of Hartford, CT
U of Miami, FL
U of New Haven, CT
The U of Texas at San Antonio, TX
U of the Incarnate Word, TX
U of the Pacific, CA

MUSICOLOGY AND ETHNOMUSICOLOGY
Brown U, RI
Loyola Marymount U, CA
The U of Akron, OH
U of California, Los Angeles, CA
U of Kansas, KS
U of Miami, FL
U of Washington, WA

MUSIC PEDAGOGY
Baylor U, TX
California State U, Sacramento, CA
Columbus State U, GA
Lawrence U, WI
Michigan State U, MI
Roosevelt U, IL
St. Cloud State U, MN
Temple U, PA
The U of Tennessee at Martin, TN

MUSIC PERFORMANCE
Adams State Coll, CO
Alma Coll, MI
Anderson U, IN
Anderson U, SC
Avila U, MO
Bard Coll, NY
Baylor U, TX
Bethel Coll, IN
Bethel U, MN
Bradley U, IL
Brandon U, MB, Canada
Brewton-Parker Coll, GA
Buena Vista U, IA
California State U, Fullerton, CA
California State U, Stanislaus, CA
Calvin Coll, MI
Carnegie Mellon U, PA
The Catholic U of America, DC
Charleston Southern U, SC
Clayton State U, GA
Coe Coll, IA
The Coll of St. Scholastica, MN
Cornerstone U, MI
Dalhousie U, NS, Canada
DePaul U, IL

Drake U, IA
Drury U, MO
East Carolina U, NC
Eastern Michigan U, MI
Eastern Nazarene Coll, MA
Elon U, NC
Fresno City Coll, CA
Gardner-Webb U, NC
Geneva Coll, PA
Gordon Coll, MA
Grambling State U, LA
Henderson State U, AR
Hofstra U, NY
Hope Coll, MI
Houghton Coll, NY
Houston Baptist U, TX
Idaho State U, ID
Illinois State U, IL
Immaculata U, PA
Indiana U of Pennsylvania, PA
Ithaca Coll, NY
Jacksonville U, FL
Johnson State Coll, VT
Lawrence U, WI
Lebanon Valley Coll, PA
Long Island U, Brooklyn Campus, NY
Loyola U New Orleans, LA
Lynchburg Coll, VA
Lynn U, FL
Macomb Comm Coll, MI
Marywood U, PA
McNeese State U, LA
Mercer U, GA
Mercyhurst Coll, PA
Miami Dade Coll, FL
Michigan State U, MI
Missouri State U, MO
Moravian Coll, PA
Mount Union Coll, OH
Naropa U, CO
Nassau Comm Coll, NY
New York U, NY
North Carolina School of the Arts, NC
Northwestern Coll, MN
Northwest Nazarene U, ID
Notre Dame de Namur U, CA
Oakland U, MI
The Ohio State U, OH
Ohio Wesleyan U, OH
Old Dominion U, VA
Oral Roberts U, OK
Otterbein Coll, OH
Piedmont Coll, GA
Point Loma Nazarene U, CA
Queens Coll of the City U of New York, NY
Randolph Coll, VA
Reedley Coll, CA
Rice U, TX
Rockford Coll, IL
Rocky Mountain Coll, MT
Roosevelt U, IL
Rowan U, NJ
St. Cloud State U, MN
Saint Xavier U, IL
Seton Hall U, NJ
Seton Hill U, PA
Slippery Rock U of Pennsylvania, PA
Southern Adventist U, TN
Southern Nazarene U, OK
Southern U and A&M Coll, LA
State U of New York Coll at Potsdam, NY
Stephen F. Austin State U, TX
Stetson U, FL
Syracuse U, NY
Taylor U, IN

Temple U, PA
Trinity U, TX
Truman State U, MO
Union Coll, NE
U at Buffalo, the State U of New York, NY
The U of Akron, OH
U of Alaska Anchorage, AK
The U of Arizona, AZ
U of California, Irvine, CA
U of Central Florida, FL
U of Evansville, IN
U of Hartford, CT
U of Houston, TX
U of Illinois at Urbana–Champaign, IL
U of Kansas, KS
U of Kentucky, KY
U of Mary Hardin-Baylor, TX
U of Massachusetts Amherst, MA
U of Massachusetts Lowell, MA
U of Miami, FL
U of Missouri–Kansas City, MO
U of Nebraska at Omaha, NE
U of New Hampshire, NH
U of New Mexico, NM
The U of North Carolina at Chapel Hill, NC
The U of North Carolina at Charlotte, NC
U of Northern Iowa, IA
U of North Florida, FL
U of Oregon, OR
U of Redlands, CA
U of Rhode Island, RI
The U of Tennessee at Martin, TN
The U of Texas at Austin, TX
The U of Texas at San Antonio, TX
The U of the Arts, PA
U of the Incarnate Word, TX
U of Vermont, VT
U of Washington, WA
U of West Georgia, GA
U of Wyoming, WY
Valdosta State U, GA
West Chester U of Pennsylvania, PA
West Texas A&M U, TX
Wheaton Coll, IL
Wilkes U, PA
William Jewell Coll, MO
Wright State U, OH

MUSIC RELATED

Brenau U, GA
Brown U, RI
California State U, Sacramento, CA
Claremont McKenna Coll, CA
Long Island U, Brooklyn Campus, NY
Mercer U, GA
Minnesota School of Business–St. Cloud, MN
Roosevelt U, IL
San Diego State U, CA
School of the Art Inst of Chicago, IL
The U of Arizona, AZ
U of Hartford, CT
U of Miami, FL
The U of North Carolina at Asheville, NC
U of Wisconsin–Green Bay, WI
Wheaton Coll, IL

MUSIC TEACHER EDUCATION

Abilene Christian U, TX
Acadia U, NS, Canada
Alabama A&M U, AL
Alderson-Broaddus Coll, WV
Alma Coll, MI
Anderson U, IN
Anderson U, SC
Asbury Coll, KY
Ashland U, OH
Augsburg Coll, MN
Ball State U, IN
The Baptist Coll of Florida, FL
Baylor U, TX
Bemidji State U, MN
Benedictine Coll, KS
Bethany U, CA
Bethel Coll, IN
Bethel U, MN
Bishop's U, QC, Canada
Bradley U, IL
Brandon U, MB, Canada
Brenau U, GA
Brewton-Parker Coll, GA
Brock U, ON, Canada
Buena Vista U, IA
Buffalo State Coll, State U of New York, NY
California State U, Fullerton, CA
Calvin Coll, MI
Carroll Coll, WI
Carson-Newman Coll, TN
Carthage Coll, WI
The Catholic U of America, DC
Charleston Southern U, SC
Coe Coll, IA
The Coll of Saint Rose, NY
Columbus State U, GA
Concordia Coll–New York, NY
Concordia U, NE
Concord U, WV
Cornerstone U, MI
Dallas Baptist U, TX
Delaware State U, DE
DePaul U, IL
Drake U, IA
Drury U, MO
East Carolina U, NC
Eastern Mennonite U, VA
Eastern Michigan U, MI
Eastern Nazarene Coll, MA
Elon U, NC
Fayetteville State U, NC
Florida Atlantic U, FL
Florida International U, FL
Fort Hays State U, KS
Frederick Comm Coll, MD
Freed-Hardeman U, TN
Fresno Pacific U, CA
Furman U, SC
Gardner-Webb U, NC
Geneva Coll, PA
Georgetown Coll, KY
Georgia Coll & State U, GA
Glenville State Coll, WV
Gonzaga U, WA
Gordon Coll, MA
Goshen Coll, IN
Grace Coll, IN
Graceland U, IA
Grambling State U, LA
Gustavus Adolphus Coll, MN
Hamline U, MN
Harding U, AR
Hartwick Coll, NY
Henderson State U, AR
Hofstra U, NY
Hope Coll, MI

Houghton Coll, NY
Houston Baptist U, TX
Huntington U, IN
Idaho State U, ID
Illinois State U, IL
Illinois Wesleyan U, IL
Immaculata U, PA
Indiana U Bloomington, IN
Indiana U of Pennsylvania, PA
Indiana U–Purdue U Fort Wayne, IN
Ithaca Coll, NY
Jacksonville U, FL
John Brown U, AR
Johnson State Coll, VT
Kansas State U, KS
Kennesaw State U, GA
Lakeland Coll, WI
Lamar U, TX
Lancaster Bible Coll, PA
Langston U, OK
Lawrence U, WI
Lebanon Valley Coll, PA
Liberty U, VA
Lincoln U, PA
Lindenwood U, MO
Long Island U, Brooklyn Campus, NY
Loyola U New Orleans, LA
MacMurray Coll, IL
Manhattanville Coll, NY
Marian Coll, IN
Marywood U, PA
McNeese State U, LA
Mercer U, GA
Mercyhurst Coll, PA
Miami Dade Coll, FL
Michigan State U, MI
Midland Coll, TX
Midland Lutheran Coll, NE
Millersville U of Pennsylvania, PA
Minnesota State U Mankato, MN
Minnesota State U Moorhead, MN
Missouri State U, MO
Montana State U, MT
Montana State U–Billings, MT
Moravian Coll, PA
Morningside Coll, IA
Mount Union Coll, OH
Mount Vernon Nazarene U, OH
Murray State U, KY
New Jersey City U, NJ
New York U, NY
North Central Coll, IL
North Dakota State U, ND
Northern Illinois U, IL
Northern Michigan U, MI
Northern State U, SD
North Georgia Coll & State U, GA
Northwestern Coll, MN
Northwestern Oklahoma State U, OK
Northwest Nazarene U, ID
Oakland U, MI
The Ohio State U, OH
Ohio Wesleyan U, OH
Oklahoma State U, OK
Old Dominion U, VA
Oral Roberts U, OK
Otterbein Coll, OH
Pittsburg State U, KS
Point Loma Nazarene U, CA
Presbyterian Coll, SC
Queens Coll of the City U of New York, NY
Ripon Coll, WI
Rocky Mountain Coll, MT

Roosevelt U, IL
Rutgers, The State U of New Jersey, New Brunswick, NJ
Saginaw Valley State U, MI
St. Cloud State U, MN
St. Norbert Coll, WI
Saint Xavier U, IL
Salve Regina U, RI
San Diego State U, CA
Schoolcraft Coll, MI
Seattle Pacific U, WA
Seton Hill U, PA
Southern Adventist U, TN
Southern Nazarene U, OK
Southern U and A&M Coll, LA
Southern Utah U, UT
Southwest Baptist U, MO
Southwestern Coll, KS
State U of New York at Fredonia, NY
State U of New York Coll at Potsdam, NY
Stephen F. Austin State U, TX
Stetson U, FL
Syracuse U, NY
Taylor U, IN
Temple U, PA
Tennessee Wesleyan Coll, TN
Texas A&M U–Corpus Christi, TX
Towson U, MD
Trevecca Nazarene U, TN
Troy U, AL
Union Coll, NE
The U of Akron, OH
The U of Alabama, AL
U of Alaska Anchorage, AK
The U of Arizona, AZ
U of Arkansas at Fort Smith, AR
U of Central Florida, FL
U of Central Missouri, MO
U of Central Oklahoma, OK
U of Cincinnati, OH
U of Colorado at Boulder, CO
U of Connecticut, CT
U of Dayton, OH
U of Delaware, DE
U of Evansville, IN
U of Hartford, CT
U of Illinois at Urbana–Champaign, IL
U of Kansas, KS
U of Kentucky, KY
U of Mary Hardin-Baylor, TX
U of Mary Washington, VA
U of Miami, FL
U of Michigan, MI
U of Minnesota, Duluth, MN
U of Missouri–Columbia, MO
U of Missouri–Kansas City, MO
U of Nebraska at Omaha, NE
U of Nebraska–Lincoln, NE
U of New Brunswick Fredericton, NB, Canada
U of New Hampshire, NH
U of New Mexico, NM
U of New Orleans, LA
The U of North Carolina at Charlotte, NC
U of Northern Iowa, IA
U of North Florida, FL
U of Oregon, OR
U of Portland, OR
U of Redlands, CA
U of Rhode Island, RI
U of Rio Grande, OH

U of St. Thomas, MN
U of St. Thomas, TX
The U of Tennessee, TN
The U of Tennessee at
 Martin, TN
U of the District of
 Columbia, DC
U of the Incarnate Word, TX
U of the Pacific, CA
U of Toronto, ON, Canada
U of Vermont, VT
U of Washington, WA
U of West Georgia, GA
U of Wisconsin–Madison,
 WI
U of Wisconsin–Oshkosh,
 WI
U of Wisconsin–Stevens
 Point, WI
U of Wyoming, WY
Valdosta State U, GA
Washburn U, KS
Waubonsee Comm Coll, IL
Wayne State Coll, NE
West Chester U of
 Pennsylvania, PA
Western Connecticut State
 U, CT
Western Nebraska Comm
 Coll, NE
West Liberty State Coll, WV
Westminster Coll, PA
West Virginia State U, WV
West Virginia Wesleyan Coll,
 WV
Wheaton Coll, IL
Wichita State U, KS
Wilkes U, PA
William Jewell Coll, MO
Wright State U, OH
Xavier U, OH

**MUSIC THEORY AND
COMPOSITION**
Bard Coll, NY
Baylor U, TX
Bradley U, IL
Brandon U, MB, Canada
California State U,
 Sacramento, CA
Calvin Coll, MI
Carnegie Mellon U, PA
Carson-Newman Coll, TN
The Catholic U of America,
 DC
Christopher Newport U, VA
Clayton State U, GA
Coe Coll, IA
Cornerstone U, MI
Dalhousie U, NS, Canada
Dallas Baptist U, TX
DePaul U, IL
Drury U, MO
East Carolina U, NC
Hofstra U, NY
Hope Coll, MI
Houghton Coll, NY
Houston Baptist U, TX
Houston Comm Coll System,
 TX
Huntington U, IN
Ithaca Coll, NY
Jacksonville U, FL
Lawrence U, WI
Lehigh U, PA
Long Island U, Brooklyn
 Campus, NY
Loyola Marymount U, CA
Loyola U New Orleans, LA
Lynchburg Coll, VA
Mannes Coll The New
 School for Music, NY
Michigan State U, MI

Minnesota State U
 Moorhead, MN
Missouri State U, MO
Moravian Coll, PA
New York U, NY
Northwestern Coll, MN
Northwest Nazarene U, ID
Oakland U, MI
The Ohio State U, OH
Oral Roberts U, OK
Point Loma Nazarene U, CA
Randolph Coll, VA
Rice U, TX
Roosevelt U, IL
Rowan U, NJ
St. Cloud State U, MN
Seton Hill U, PA
Southern Adventist U, TN
Stetson U, FL
Syracuse U, NY
Temple U, PA
Trinity U, TX
The U of Akron, OH
U of Central Missouri, MO
U of Delaware, DE
U of Hartford, CT
U of Houston, TX
U of Illinois at Urbana–
 Champaign, IL
U of Kansas, KS
U of Mary Hardin-Baylor, TX
U of Miami, FL
U of Michigan, MI
U of Missouri–Kansas City,
 MO
U of Nebraska at Omaha,
 NE
U of Northern Iowa, IA
U of Redlands, CA
U of Rhode Island, RI
The U of Texas at Austin,
 TX
The U of Texas at San
 Antonio, TX
The U of the Arts, PA
U of the Pacific, CA
U of Washington, WA
U of West Georgia, GA
U of Wyoming, WY
West Chester U of
 Pennsylvania, PA
West Texas A&M U, TX
Wheaton Coll, IL
William Jewell Coll, MO
Wright State U, OH

MUSIC THERAPY
Augsburg Coll, MN
Charleston Southern U, SC
East Carolina U, NC
Eastern Michigan U, MI
Georgia Coll & State U, GA
Immaculata U, PA
Indiana U–Purdue U Fort
 Wayne, IN
Marywood U, PA
Michigan State U, MI
Molloy Coll, NY
Queens U of Charlotte, NC
Slippery Rock U of
 Pennsylvania, PA
State U of New York at
 Fredonia, NY
Temple U, PA
U of Dayton, OH
U of Evansville, IN
U of Kansas, KS
U of Miami, FL
U of the Incarnate Word, TX
U of the Pacific, CA
U of Wisconsin–Eau Claire,
 WI
U of Wisconsin–Oshkosh,
 WI

West Texas A&M U, TX
Wilfrid Laurier U, ON,
 Canada

**NATURAL RESOURCE
ECONOMICS**
Cornell U, NY
Michigan State U, MI

**NATURAL RESOURCES
AND CONSERVATION
RELATED**
Penn State Abington, PA
Penn State DuBois, PA
Penn State Fayette, The
 Eberly Campus, PA
Penn State Mont Alto, PA
Penn State Wilkes-Barre, PA
St. Gregory's U, OK
Stephen F. Austin State U,
 TX
Sterling Coll, VT
U of Miami, FL

**NATURAL RESOURCES/
CONSERVATION**
California State U,
 Sacramento, CA
Carroll Coll, WI
Clemson U, SC
Cornell U, NY
Dixie State Coll of Utah, UT
Fulton-Montgomery Comm
 Coll, NY
Hocking Coll, OH
Itasca Comm Coll, MN
Montana State U, MT
Mount Vernon Nazarene U,
 OH
Muscatine Comm Coll, IA
North Carolina State U, NC
Northern Michigan U, MI
Penn State Abington, PA
Penn State DuBois, PA
Penn State Fayette, The
 Eberly Campus, PA
Penn State Mont Alto, PA
Penn State Wilkes-Barre, PA
Rutgers, The State U of New
 Jersey, New Brunswick, NJ
Santa Rosa Jr Coll, CA
Slippery Rock U of
 Pennsylvania, PA
State U of New York Coll of
 Environmental Science
 and Forestry, NY
Sterling Coll, VT
Texas A&M U, TX
Unity Coll, ME
U of California, Berkeley,
 CA
U of Connecticut, CT
U of Illinois at Urbana–
 Champaign, IL
U of Kentucky, KY
U of Missouri–Columbia,
 MO
U of Nebraska–Lincoln, NE
U of New Hampshire, NH
U of Rhode Island, RI
U of Vermont, VT
U of Wisconsin–Stevens
 Point, WI
U of Wyoming, WY
Upper Iowa U, IA

**NATURAL RESOURCES/
CONSERVATION
RELATED**
Sterling Coll, VT
U of Illinois at Urbana–
 Champaign, IL

**NATURAL RESOURCES
MANAGEMENT**
Feather River Coll, CA
Hocking Coll, OH
Moravian Coll, PA
The Ohio State U, OH
Reedley Coll, CA
Rutgers, The State U of New
 Jersey, New Brunswick, NJ
Sterling Coll, VT
Unity Coll, ME
U of Hawaii at Manoa, HI
The U of Tennessee at
 Martin, TN

**NATURAL RESOURCES
MANAGEMENT AND
POLICY**
Albright Coll, PA
Ball State U, IN
Carnegie Mellon U, PA
Charleston Southern U, SC
Clark U, MA
Coll of the Desert, CA
Dixie State Coll of Utah, UT
Fort Hays State U, KS
Green Mountain Coll, VT
Hocking Coll, OH
Huntington U, IN
Itasca Comm Coll, MN
Johnson State Coll, VT
Lake Superior State U, MI
North Carolina State U, NC
North Dakota State U, ND
The Ohio State U, OH
Rochester Inst of
 Technology, NY
Santa Rosa Jr Coll, CA
Sewanee: The U of the
 South, TN
Shasta Coll, CA
Southwestern Indian
 Polytechnic Inst, NM
Spokane Comm Coll, WA
State U of New York Coll of
 Environmental Science
 and Forestry, NY
Sterling Coll, VT
Unity Coll, ME
U of California, Berkeley,
 CA
U of Delaware, DE
U of Guelph, ON, Canada
U of Massachusetts Amherst,
 MA
U of Miami, FL
U of Michigan, MI
U of Nebraska–Lincoln, NE
U of New Hampshire, NH
U of Rhode Island, RI
U of Washington, WA
U of Wisconsin–Madison,
 WI
U of Wisconsin–Stevens
 Point, WI
Ventura Coll, CA

NATURAL SCIENCES
Alderson-Broaddus Coll, WV
Augsburg Coll, MN
Avila U, MO
Bard Coll, NY
Bemidji State U, MN
Benedictine Coll, KS
Bishop's U, QC, Canada
California State U, San
 Bernardino, CA
Calvin Coll, MI
Cameron U, OK
Carthage Coll, WI
Cedar Crest Coll, PA
Charleston Southern U, SC
Citrus Coll, CA
Colgate U, NY

Coll of Mount St. Joseph,
 OH
Coll of Saint Mary, NE
The Coll of St. Scholastica,
 MN
Coll of the Atlantic, ME
Coll of the Canyons, CA
Concordia U, NE
Daemen Coll, NY
Dallas Baptist U, TX
Elms Coll, MA
Fresno Pacific U, CA
Galveston Coll, TX
Georgian Court U, NJ
Goshen Coll, IN
Hofstra U, NY
Houghton Coll, NY
Kenyon Coll, OH
Lassen Comm Coll District,
 CA
Lee Coll, TX
LeTourneau U, TX
Loyola Marymount U, CA
Miami Dade Coll, FL
Midland Lutheran Coll, NE
Minnesota State U Mankato,
 MN
Monmouth Coll, IL
Moorpark Coll, CA
Our Lady of the Lake U of
 San Antonio, TX
Park U, MO
Quincy Coll, MA
Redeemer U Coll, ON,
 Canada
St. Cloud State U, MN
St. Gregory's U, OK
Saint John's U, MN
St. Thomas Aquinas Coll,
 NY
Skagit Valley Coll, WA
Spalding U, KY
State U of New York Coll at
 Geneseo, NY
Sterling Coll, VT
Taylor U, IN
Trent U, ON, Canada
The U of Akron, OH
U of Alaska Anchorage, AK
U of Cincinnati, OH
U of Nebraska at Omaha,
 NE
U of New Hampshire, NH
U of Northern British
 Columbia, BC, Canada
U of Pennsylvania, PA
U of Pittsburgh at
 Johnstown, PA
U of Wisconsin–Stevens
 Point, WI
Victor Valley Coll, CA
Villanova U, PA
Washburn U, KS
Wayne State Coll, NE
Western Oregon U, OR
Xavier U, OH

**NAVAL ARCHITECTURE
AND MARINE
ENGINEERING**
British Columbia Inst of
 Technology, BC, Canada
Maine Maritime Academy,
 ME
U of Michigan, MI
U of New Orleans, LA

**NAVY/MARINE CORPS
ROTC/NAVAL SCIENCE**
Rensselaer Polytechnic Inst,
 NY
U of Washington, WA

Colleges for Students with Learning Disabilities or AD/HD

El Centro Coll, TX
Elmira Coll, NY
Elms Coll, MA
Emory U, GA
Fairfield U, CT
Fairleigh Dickinson U,
  Metropolitan Campus, NJ
Farmingdale State Coll, NY
Fayetteville State U, NC
Fitchburg State Coll, MA
Florida Atlantic U, FL
Florida Comm Coll at
  Jacksonville, FL
Florida Gulf Coast U, FL
Florida International U, FL
Fort Hays State U, KS
Framingham State Coll, MA
Franciscan U of
  Steubenville, OH
Frederick Comm Coll, MD
Fresno City Coll, CA
Fulton-Montgomery Comm
  Coll, NY
Gadsden State Comm Coll,
  AL
Galveston Coll, TX
Gannon U, PA
Gardner-Webb U, NC
Gaston Coll, NC
Georgia Coll & State U, GA
Glendale Comm Coll, CA
Glenville State Coll, WV
Gloucester County Coll, NJ
Gonzaga U, WA
Goshen Coll, IN
Graceland U, IA
Grambling State U, LA
Greenville Tech Coll, SC
Grossmont Coll, CA
Gustavus Adolphus Coll,
  MN
Hagerstown Comm Coll, MD
Harding U, AR
Harrisburg Area Comm Coll,
  PA
Hartwick Coll, NY
Heartland Comm Coll, IL
Henderson State U, AR
Hillsborough Comm Coll, FL
Hocking Coll, OH
Hope Coll, MI
Hopkinsville Comm Coll,
  KY
Housatonic Comm Coll, CT
Houston Baptist U, TX
Houston Comm Coll System,
  TX
Howard Comm Coll, MD
Hudson Valley Comm Coll,
  NY
Hunter Coll of the City U of
  New York, NY
Husson Coll, ME
Idaho State U, ID
Illinois State U, IL
Illinois Valley Comm Coll, IL
Illinois Wesleyan U, IL
Indiana U of Pennsylvania,
  PA
Indiana U–Purdue U Fort
  Wayne, IN
Indiana U–Purdue U
  Indianapolis, IN
Indiana U Southeast, IN
Ivy Tech Comm Coll–
  Southwest, IN
Ivy Tech Comm Coll–
  Wabash Valley, IN
Jacksonville U, FL
James H. Faulkner State
  Comm Coll, AL
Jamestown Comm Coll, NY
Jefferson Comm and Tech
  Coll, KY

Kapiolani Comm Coll, HI
Kellogg Comm Coll, MI
Kennesaw State U, GA
Keuka Coll, NY
Kingsborough Comm Coll of
  the City U of New York,
  NY
Kutztown U of
  Pennsylvania, PA
Kuyper Coll, MI
LaGrange Coll, GA
Lake City Comm Coll, FL
Lake-Sumter Comm Coll, FL
Lake Superior State U, MI
Lamar State Coll–Orange, TX
Lamar U, TX
Langston U, OK
Laredo Comm Coll, TX
Lassen Comm Coll District,
  CA
Lewis U, IL
Liberty U, VA
Lincoln Land Comm Coll, IL
Long Beach City Coll, CA
Long Island U, Brooklyn
  Campus, NY
Loyola U Chicago, IL
Loyola U New Orleans, LA
Lynchburg Coll, VA
MacMurray Coll, IL
Macomb Comm Coll, MI
Madisonville Comm Coll,
  KY
Marian Coll, IN
Marquette U, WI
Marshall U, WV
Marymount U, VA
Marywood U, PA
Massasoit Comm Coll, MA
Maui Comm Coll, HI
McNeese State U, LA
Mercer U, GA
Mercy Coll of Health
  Sciences, IA
Mercyhurst Coll, PA
Metropolitan Comm
  Coll–Penn Valley, MO
Miami Dade Coll, FL
Michigan State U, MI
Middlesex County Coll, NJ
Middle Tennessee State U,
  TN
Midland Coll, TX
Midland Lutheran Coll, NE
Millersville U of
  Pennsylvania, PA
Minnesota State Coll–
  Southeast Tech, MN
Minnesota State U Mankato,
  MN
Minnesota State U
  Moorhead, MN
Missouri State U, MO
Missouri State U–West
  Plains, MO
Mohawk Valley Comm Coll,
  NY
Molloy Coll, NY
Montana State U, MT
Montana Tech of The U of
  Montana, MT
Moorpark Coll, CA
Moravian Coll, PA
Morningside Coll, IA
Morton Coll, IL
Murray State U, KY
Nassau Comm Coll, NY
Nebraska Methodist Coll, NE
Neumann Coll, PA
New Mexico Jr Coll, NM
New York City Coll of
  Technology of the City U
  of New York, NY
New York U, NY

Nipissing U, ON, Canada
North Central Missouri Coll,
  MO
North Central Texas Coll, TX
North Dakota State U, ND
Northern Illinois U, IL
Northern Michigan U, MI
North Georgia Coll & State
  U, GA
Northland Comm and Tech
  Coll–Thief River Falls, MN
Northwestern Oklahoma
  State U, OK
Northwest Nazarene U, ID
Nova Southeastern U, FL
Oakland U, MI
Ocean County Coll, NJ
Odessa Coll, TX
The Ohio State U, OH
Old Dominion U, VA
Oral Roberts U, OK
Otterbein Coll, OH
Paris Jr Coll, TX
Park U, MO
Penn State Abington, PA
Penn State DuBois, PA
Penn State Fayette, The
  Eberly Campus, PA
Penn State Mont Alto, PA
Penn State Wilkes-Barre, PA
Phoenix Coll, AZ
Piedmont Coll, GA
Pima Comm Coll, AZ
Pittsburg State U, KS
Point Loma Nazarene U, CA
Prairie View A&M U, TX
Pueblo Comm Coll, CO
Purdue U North Central, IN
Queen's U at Kingston, ON,
  Canada
Quincy Coll, MA
Radford U, VA
Ramapo Coll of New Jersey,
  NJ
Reinhardt Coll, GA
The Richard Stockton Coll
  of New Jersey, NJ
Richland Comm Coll, IL
Richmond Comm Coll, NC
Rivier Coll, NH
Rockford Coll, IL
Rockhurst U, MO
Rockingham Comm Coll, NC
Rose State Coll, OK
Roxbury Comm Coll, MA
Rutgers, The State U of New
  Jersey, Newark, NJ
Rutgers, The State U of New
  Jersey, New Brunswick, NJ
Ryerson U, ON, Canada
Saginaw Valley State U, MI
St. Cloud State U, MN
St. Francis Xavier U, NS,
  Canada
Saint John's U, MN
Saint Joseph's Coll, IN
St. Louis Comm Coll at
  Florissant Valley, MO
Saint Xavier U, IL
Salve Regina U, RI
San Diego State U, CA
San Francisco State U, CA
Santa Ana Coll, CA
Santa Barbara City Coll, CA
Santa Rosa Jr Coll, CA
Sauk Valley Comm Coll, IL
Schoolcraft Coll, MI
Scottsdale Comm Coll, AZ
Seattle Pacific U, WA
Seminole Comm Coll, FL
Seton Hall U, NJ
Seton Hill U, PA
Shasta Coll, CA
Shelton State Comm Coll, AL

Skagit Valley Coll, WA
Slippery Rock U of
  Pennsylvania, PA
Southern Adventist U, TN
Southern Illinois U
  Edwardsville, IL
Southern Maine Comm Coll,
  ME
Southern Nazarene U, OK
Southern Oregon U, OR
Southern U and A&M Coll,
  LA
Southwest Baptist U, MO
Southwestern Coll, KS
Southwestern Michigan Coll,
  MI
Spalding U, KY
Spokane Comm Coll, WA
Spoon River Coll, IL
Stark State Coll of
  Technology, OH
State U of New York Coll at
  Brockport, NY
State U of New York Coll of
  Technology at Alfred, NY
State U of New York Coll of
  Technology at Canton, NY
Stephen F. Austin State U,
  TX
Surry Comm Coll, NC
Tallahassee Comm Coll, FL
Temple U, PA
Tennessee Wesleyan Coll,
  TN
Texas A&M U–Corpus
  Christi, TX
Tidewater Comm Coll, VA
Towson U, MD
Trent U, ON, Canada
Trocaire Coll, NY
Troy U, AL
Truman State U, MO
Union Coll, NE
U at Buffalo, the State U of
  New York, NY
The U of Akron, OH
The U of Alabama, AL
The U of Alabama in
  Huntsville, AL
U of Alaska Anchorage, AK
The U of Arizona, AZ
U of Arkansas, AR
U of Arkansas at Fort Smith,
  AR
U of California, Los Angeles,
  CA
U of Central Florida, FL
U of Central Missouri, MO
U of Central Oklahoma, OK
U of Cincinnati, OH
U of Connecticut, CT
U of Delaware, DE
U of Dubuque, IA
U of Evansville, IN
U of Hartford, CT
U of Hawaii at Manoa, HI
U of Kentucky, KY
The U of Maine at Augusta,
  ME
U of Manitoba, MB, Canada
U of Mary Hardin-Baylor, TX
U of Massachusetts Amherst,
  MA
U of Massachusetts Boston,
  MA
U of Massachusetts Lowell,
  MA
U of Miami, FL
U of Michigan, MI
U of Missouri–Columbia,
  MO
U of Missouri–Kansas City,
  MO

U of New Brunswick
  Fredericton, NB, Canada
U of New England, ME
U of New Hampshire, NH
U of New Mexico, NM
The U of North Carolina at
  Chapel Hill, NC
The U of North Carolina at
  Charlotte, NC
U of Northern British
  Columbia, BC, Canada
U of North Florida, FL
U of Pennsylvania, PA
U of Pittsburgh, PA
U of Pittsburgh at Bradford,
  PA
U of Portland, OR
U of Rhode Island, RI
U of Rio Grande, OH
U of San Francisco, CA
The U of Scranton, PA
U of South Carolina Upstate,
  SC
U of Southern Indiana, IN
The U of Tampa, FL
The U of Tennessee, TN
The U of Tennessee at
  Martin, TN
The U of Texas at Austin,
  TX
The U of Texas at El Paso,
  TX
U of the District of
  Columbia, DC
U of the Incarnate Word, TX
U of Toronto, ON, Canada
U of Vermont, VT
U of Virginia, VA
U of Washington, WA
U of West Georgia, GA
U of Wisconsin–Eau Claire,
  WI
U of Wisconsin–Madison,
  WI
U of Wisconsin–Oshkosh,
  WI
U of Wyoming, WY
Ursuline Coll, OH
Utica Coll, NY
Valdosta State U, GA
Valencia Comm Coll, FL
Ventura Coll, CA
Vermont Tech Coll, VT
Victor Valley Coll, CA
Villanova U, PA
Virginia Highlands Comm
  Coll, VA
Washburn U, KS
Waubonsee Comm Coll, IL
Waukesha County Tech Coll,
  WI
Wayne State U, MI
Wesley Coll, DE
Westchester Comm Coll, NY
West Chester U of
  Pennsylvania, PA
Western Connecticut State
  U, CT
Western Nebraska Comm
  Coll, NE
Western Tech Coll, WI
West Liberty State Coll, WV
Westminster Coll, UT
Westmoreland County
  Comm Coll, PA
West Shore Comm Coll, MI
West Texas A&M U, TX
West Virginia Northern
  Comm Coll, WV
West Virginia Wesleyan Coll,
  WV
Widener U, PA
Wilkes U, PA
William Jewell Coll, MO

Worcester State Coll, MA
Wright State U, OH

NURSING RELATED
Adelphi U, NY
Avila U, MO
British Columbia Inst of
Technology, BC, Canada
California State U, Fullerton,
CA
Coll of Staten Island of the
City U of New York, NY
Le Moyne Coll, NY
Long Island U, Brooklyn
Campus, NY
Northeastern U, MA
Rowan U, NJ
San Diego State U, CA
Southeast Tech Inst, SD
U at Buffalo, the State U of
New York, NY
The U of Akron, OH
U of California, Los Angeles,
CA
U of Kentucky, KY
U of Pennsylvania, PA
Wright State U, OH

NURSING SCIENCE
Brandon U, MB, Canada
Brock U, ON, Canada
Cedar Crest Coll, PA
Coll of Mount St. Joseph,
OH
Coll of Saint Elizabeth, NJ
Elmira Coll, NY
Fairleigh Dickinson U,
Metropolitan Campus, NJ
Immaculata U, PA
Kutztown U of
Pennsylvania, PA
Mercy Coll of Health
Sciences, IA
Millersville U of
Pennsylvania, PA
Minnesota School of
Business–St. Cloud, MN
Monmouth U, NJ
New Jersey City U, NJ
The Ohio State U, OH
Queens U of Charlotte, NC
The Richard Stockton Coll
of New Jersey, NJ
St. Francis Xavier U, NS,
Canada
Southern Adventist U, TN
The U of Akron, OH
U of Delaware, DE
U of Kansas, KS
U of New Hampshire at
Manchester, NH
U of Wisconsin–Green Bay,
WI
Wichita State U, KS
Xavier U, OH

NUTRITIONAL SCIENCES
Syracuse U, NY

NUTRITION SCIENCES
Cornell U, NY
Edinboro U of Pennsylvania,
PA
Hampshire Coll, MA
Michigan State U, MI
Mohawk Valley Comm Coll,
NY
Mount Saint Vincent U, NS,
Canada
Rutgers, The State U of New
Jersey, New Brunswick, NJ
U at Buffalo, the State U of
New York, NY
The U of Arizona, AZ

U of California, Berkeley,
CA
U of Connecticut, CT
U of Delaware, DE
U of Guelph, ON, Canada
U of Missouri–Columbia,
MO
U of the District of
Columbia, DC
U of the Incarnate Word, TX
U of Vermont, VT
U of Wisconsin–Green Bay,
WI

**OCCUPATIONAL AND
ENVIRONMENTAL
HEALTH NURSING**
British Columbia Inst of
Technology, BC, Canada

**OCCUPATIONAL
HEALTH AND
INDUSTRIAL HYGIENE**
British Columbia Inst of
Technology, BC, Canada
Montana Tech of The U of
Montana, MT
Ryerson U, ON, Canada

**OCCUPATIONAL SAFETY
AND HEALTH
TECHNOLOGY**
Ball State U, IN
Embry-Riddle Aeronautical
U, FL
Houston Comm Coll System,
TX
Indiana U Bloomington, IN
Indiana U of Pennsylvania,
PA
Ivy Tech Comm Coll–
Wabash Valley, IN
Lamar Inst of Technology,
TX
Lamar U, TX
Marshall U, WV
Millersville U of
Pennsylvania, PA
Montana Tech of The U of
Montana, MT
Murray State U, KY
Muscatine Comm Coll, IA
Oakland U, MI
Rochester Inst of
Technology, NY
Slippery Rock U of
Pennsylvania, PA
Southwest Baptist U, MO
The U of Akron–Wayne
Coll, OH
U of Central Missouri, MO
U of Central Oklahoma, OK
U of Cincinnati, OH
U of New Haven, CT
Wright State U, OH

**OCCUPATIONAL
THERAPIST ASSISTANT**
Allegany Coll of Maryland,
MD
Comm Coll of Allegheny
County, PA
Eastern New Mexico
U–Roswell, NM
Hocking Coll, OH
Houston Comm Coll System,
TX
Idaho State U, ID
Jamestown Comm Coll, NY
Lincoln Land Comm Coll, IL
Macomb Comm Coll, MI
Madisonville Comm Coll,
KY

Ozarks Tech Comm Coll,
MO
Penn State DuBois, PA
Penn State Mont Alto, PA
Pueblo Comm Coll, CO
Rockingham Comm Coll, NC
St. Philip's Coll, TX
Schoolcraft Coll, MI
State U of New York Coll of
Technology at Canton, NY
U of Southern Indiana, IN

**OCCUPATIONAL
THERAPY**
Allegany Coll of Maryland,
MD
Alvernia Coll, PA
American International Coll,
MA
Brenau U, GA
Calvin Coll, MI
Carthage Coll, WI
Chattanooga State Tech
Comm Coll, TN
Clayton State U, GA
Dalhousie U, NS, Canada
Drury U, MO
East Carolina U, NC
Eastern Michigan U, MI
Florida Gulf Coast U, FL
Florida International U, FL
Grossmont Coll, CA
Hamline U, MN
Hillsborough Comm Coll, FL
Husson Coll, ME
Indiana U–Purdue U
Indianapolis, IN
Ithaca Coll, NY
Kapiolani Comm Coll, HI
Keuka Coll, NY
Long Island U, Brooklyn
Campus, NY
Metropolitan Comm
Coll–Penn Valley, MO
North Central Texas Coll, TX
The Ohio State U, OH
Ozarks Tech Comm Coll,
MO
Penn State Mont Alto, PA
Pueblo Comm Coll, CO
Queen's U at Kingston, ON,
Canada
Saint John's U, MN
Santa Ana Coll, CA
Sauk Valley Comm Coll, IL
Southern Adventist U, TN
Spalding U, KY
Springfield Coll, MA
Stark State Coll of
Technology, OH
Towson U, MD
U at Buffalo, the State U of
New York, NY
The U of Findlay, OH
U of Hartford, CT
U of Kansas, KS
U of Manitoba, MB, Canada
U of Missouri–Columbia,
MO
U of New England, ME
U of New Hampshire, NH
U of Pittsburgh, PA
U of Southern Indiana, IN
U of Washington, WA
U of Wisconsin–Madison,
WI
Wayne State U, MI
Western Tech Coll, WI
Worcester State Coll, MA
Xavier U, OH

OCEAN ENGINEERING
Florida Atlantic U, FL

Florida Inst of Technology,
FL
Texas A&M U, TX
U of New Hampshire, NH
U of Rhode Island, RI

OCEANOGRAPHY
Coll of the Atlantic, ME
Dalhousie U, NS, Canada
Florida Inst of Technology,
FL

**OCEANOGRAPHY
(CHEMICAL AND
PHYSICAL)**
Kutztown U of
Pennsylvania, PA
Lamar U, TX
Maine Maritime Academy,
ME
Millersville U of
Pennsylvania, PA
North Carolina State U, NC
Old Dominion U, VA
Santa Rosa Jr Coll, CA
Southern Maine Comm Coll,
ME
U of Miami, FL
U of Michigan, MI
U of New Hampshire, NH
U of Washington, WA

OFFICE MANAGEMENT
Alexandria Tech Coll, MN
Calhoun Comm Coll, AL
Central Florida Comm Coll,
FL
Comm Coll of Allegheny
County, PA
Eastern Michigan U, MI
Florida Comm Coll at
Jacksonville, FL
Georgia Coll & State U, GA
Howard Comm Coll, MD
Indiana U of Pennsylvania,
PA
Lake-Sumter Comm Coll, FL
Lake Superior State U, MI
Lee Coll, TX
Mercyhurst Coll, PA
Middle Tennessee State U,
TN
Mohawk Valley Comm Coll,
NY
Murray State U, KY
Park U, MO
St. Cloud Tech Coll, MN
Skagit Valley Coll, WA
State U of New York Coll of
Technology at Canton, NY
Stephen F. Austin State U,
TX
U of Central Missouri, MO
U of Nebraska–Lincoln, NE
U of Southern Indiana, IN
Valencia Comm Coll, FL
Washburn U, KS
Western Tech Coll, WI
Wright State U, OH

**OFFICE OCCUPATIONS
AND CLERICAL
SERVICES**
Alexandria Tech Coll, MN
El Centro Coll, TX
Florida Comm Coll at
Jacksonville, FL
Hillsborough Comm Coll, FL
Mohawk Valley Comm Coll,
NY
Reedley Coll, CA
The U of Montana-Helena
Coll of Technology, MT

The U of Tennessee at
Martin, TN
West Virginia State Comm
and Tech Coll, WV
Wright State U, OH

**OPERATIONS
MANAGEMENT**
Alexandria Tech Coll, MN
Asheville-Buncombe Tech
Comm Coll, NC
Aurora U, IL
Baylor U, TX
British Columbia Inst of
Technology, BC, Canada
Bunker Hill Comm Coll, MA
California State U,
Sacramento, CA
DeKalb Tech Coll, GA
Edinboro U of Pennsylvania,
PA
Farmingdale State Coll, NY
Gaston Coll, NC
Indiana U–Purdue U Fort
Wayne, IN
Indiana U–Purdue U
Indianapolis, IN
Lee Coll, TX
Loyola U Chicago, IL
Macomb Comm Coll, MI
Massasoit Comm Coll, MA
Michigan State U, MI
Northern Illinois U, IL
The Ohio State U, OH
Pittsburg State U, KS
Saginaw Valley State U, MI
San Diego State U, CA
South Piedmont Comm Coll,
NC
Stark State Coll of
Technology, OH
The U of Arizona, AZ
U of Delaware, DE
U of Houston, TX
U of Illinois at Urbana–
Champaign, IL
U of Nebraska at Kearney,
NE
The U of North Carolina at
Asheville, NC
The U of North Carolina at
Charlotte, NC
U of Pennsylvania, PA
U of St. Thomas, MN
The U of Scranton, PA
The U of Tennessee at
Martin, TN
The U of Texas at San
Antonio, TX
U of Wisconsin–Stout, WI
Waubonsee Comm Coll, IL
Waukesha County Tech Coll,
WI
Widener U, PA
Wright State U, OH

OPERATIONS RESEARCH
Boston Coll, MA
California State U, Fullerton,
CA
Carleton U, ON, Canada
Carnegie Mellon U, PA
Cornell U, NY
DePaul U, IL
Long Island U, Brooklyn
Campus, NY
New York U, NY
U of California, Berkeley,
CA
U of Cincinnati, OH
U of New Brunswick
Fredericton, NB, Canada
U of Toronto, ON, Canada

OPHTHALMIC AND OPTOMETRIC SUPPORT SERVICES AND ALLIED PROFESSIONS RELATED

Tennessee Wesleyan Coll, TN

OPHTHALMIC LABORATORY TECHNOLOGY

Abilene Christian U, TX
DeKalb Tech Coll, GA
Hillsborough Comm Coll, FL
Hocking Coll, OH
Indiana U Bloomington, IN
Middlesex Comm Coll, CT
New Hampshire Comm Tech Coll, Nashua/Claremont, NH
New York City Coll of Technology of the City U of New York, NY
Pueblo Comm Coll, CO
Rochester Inst of Technology, NY
Santa Rosa Jr Coll, CA
Spokane Comm Coll, WA
Westmoreland County Comm Coll, PA

OPHTHALMIC/OPTOMETRIC SERVICES

Gannon U, PA
Howard Comm Coll, MD
Indiana U Bloomington, IN

OPHTHALMIC TECHNOLOGY

Miami Dade Coll, FL
Old Dominion U, VA

OPTICAL SCIENCES

Saginaw Valley State U, MI
The U of Arizona, AZ

OPTICIANRY

DeKalb Tech Coll, GA
Harrisburg Area Comm Coll, PA
The U of Akron, OH

OPTOMETRIC TECHNICIAN

Indiana U Bloomington, IN
Sauk Valley Comm Coll, IL
Texas A&M U–Corpus Christi, TX

ORGANIZATIONAL BEHAVIOR

Anderson U, IN
Athabasca U, AB, Canada
Brown U, RI
Cape Breton U, NS, Canada
Carroll Coll, WI
The Coll of St. Scholastica, MN
Florida Inst of Technology, FL
Loyola U Chicago, IL
Manhattan Coll, NY
Penn State Abington, PA
Penn State DuBois, PA
Penn State Fayette, The Eberly Campus, PA
Penn State Mont Alto, PA
Penn State Wilkes-Barre, PA
Temple U, PA
U of Houston, TX
U of Illinois at Urbana–Champaign, IL
U of San Francisco, CA
U of the Incarnate Word, TX
Wayne State U, MI

ORGANIZATIONAL COMMUNICATION

Buena Vista U, IA
California State U, Sacramento, CA
Carroll Coll, WI
Indiana U–Purdue U Fort Wayne, IN
Iona Coll, NY
Lynchburg Coll, VA
Marist Coll, NY
North Central Coll, IL
State U of New York Coll at Brockport, NY
U of Houston, TX
U of Northern Iowa, IA
Wright State U, OH

ORNAMENTAL HORTICULTURE

Abraham Baldwin Coll, GA
Coll of the Desert, CA
Comm Coll of Allegheny County, PA
Cornell U, NY
El Camino Coll, CA
Farmingdale State Coll, NY
Foothill Coll, CA
Hillsborough Comm Coll, FL
Long Beach City Coll, CA
Miami Dade Coll, FL
MiraCosta Coll, CA
Santa Barbara City Coll, CA
Shasta Coll, CA
Spokane Comm Coll, WA
Texas A&M U, TX
U of Arkansas, AR
U of Delaware, DE
U of Illinois at Urbana–Champaign, IL
U of Massachusetts Amherst, MA
The U of Tennessee, TN
U of the District of Columbia, DC
U of Wisconsin–Platteville, WI
Valencia Comm Coll, FL
Victor Valley Coll, CA

ORTHOTICS/PROSTHETICS

Florida International U, FL
U of Washington, WA

PACIFIC AREA/PACIFIC RIM STUDIES

Claremont McKenna Coll, CA
U of Hawaii at Manoa, HI

PAINTING

Academy of Art U, CA
The Art Inst of Pittsburgh, PA
Bard Coll, NY
Buffalo State Coll, State U of New York, NY
California State U, Fullerton, CA
The Catholic U of America, DC
The Cleveland Inst of Art, OH
Coe Coll, IA
Dixie State Coll of Utah, UT
Drake U, IA
Framingham State Coll, MA
Grace Coll, IN
Harding U, AR
Henderson State U, AR
Hofstra U, NY
Indiana U–Purdue U Fort Wayne, IN

Lewis U, IL
Maine Coll of Art, ME
Minneapolis Coll of Art and Design, MN
Minnesota State U Moorhead, MN
Northwest Nazarene U, ID
NSCAD U, NS, Canada
The Ohio State U, OH
Pratt Inst, NY
Rivier Coll, NH
Rutgers, The State U of New Jersey, New Brunswick, NJ
St. Cloud State U, MN
Salve Regina U, RI
Savannah Coll of Art and Design, GA
School of the Art Inst of Chicago, IL
Seton Hill U, PA
State U of New York Coll at Brockport, NY
Syracuse U, NY
Temple U, PA
The U of Akron, OH
U of Hartford, CT
U of Houston, TX
U of Illinois at Urbana–Champaign, IL
U of Kansas, KS
U of Miami, FL
U of Michigan, MI
U of Oregon, OR
U of San Francisco, CA
The U of the Arts, PA
U of Washington, WA
West Virginia Wesleyan Coll, WV

PAINTING AND WALL COVERING

Ivy Tech Comm Coll–Southwest, IN
Ivy Tech Comm Coll–Wabash Valley, IN

PALEONTOLOGY

Mercyhurst Coll, PA
North Carolina State U, NC
U of Delaware, DE
U of Toronto, ON, Canada

PARALEGAL/LEGAL ASSISTANT

Coosa Valley Tech Coll, GA
DeKalb Tech Coll, GA
Elms Coll, MA
Minnesota School of Business–St. Cloud, MN
Tidewater Comm Coll, VA

PARKS, RECREATION AND LEISURE

Arizona State U at the West campus, AZ
Ashland U, OH
Bemidji State U, MN
Brevard Coll, NC
Brock U, ON, Canada
California State U, Northridge, CA
California State U, Sacramento, CA
Calvin Coll, MI
Cape Breton U, NS, Canada
Cape Cod Comm Coll, MA
Carson-Newman Coll, TN
Central Florida Comm Coll, FL
Chesapeake Coll, MD
Clayton State U, GA
Coll of the Desert, CA
Dalhousie U, NS, Canada
East Central Coll, MO

Elon U, NC
Ferrum Coll, VA
Fresno City Coll, CA
Georgia Coll & State U, GA
Glendale Comm Coll, CA
Gordon Coll, MA
Graceland U, IA
Green Mountain Coll, VT
High Point U, NC
Houghton Coll, NY
Huntington U, IN
Indiana U Bloomington, IN
Ithaca Coll, NY
Johnson & Wales U, NC
Johnson & Wales U, RI
Johnson State Coll, VT
Kingsborough Comm Coll of the City U of New York, NY
Lake Superior State U, MI
Marywood U, PA
Miami Dade Coll, FL
Midland Lutheran Coll, NE
Minnesota State U Mankato, MN
Missouri State U, MO
Mitchell Coll, CT
New Mexico Jr Coll, NM
North Dakota State U, ND
Northwest Nazarene U, ID
Radford U, VA
Redeemer U Coll, ON, Canada
St. Thomas Aquinas Coll, NY
San Diego State U, CA
San Francisco State U, CA
Santa Barbara City Coll, CA
Skagit Valley Coll, WA
Southern Illinois U Carbondale, IL
Southwest Baptist U, MO
Springfield Coll, MA
State U of New York Coll at Brockport, NY
State U of New York Coll at Cortland, NY
State U of New York Coll of Environmental Science and Forestry, NY
Sterling Coll, VT
Tallahassee Comm Coll, FL
Temple U, PA
Tennessee Wesleyan Coll, TN
Texas A&M U, TX
Troy U, AL
U of Central Missouri, MO
U of Dubuque, IA
U of Hawaii at Manoa, HI
U of Illinois at Urbana–Champaign, IL
U of Maine at Machias, ME
U of Mary Hardin-Baylor, TX
U of Minnesota, Duluth, MN
U of Mississippi, MS
U of Missouri–Columbia, MO
U of Nebraska at Kearney, NE
U of Nebraska at Omaha, NE
U of New Brunswick Fredericton, NB, Canada
U of New Hampshire, NH
U of New Mexico, NM
U of Northern British Columbia, BC, Canada
U of Northern Iowa, IA
U of the District of Columbia, DC
U of Wisconsin–Madison, WI
Upper Iowa U, IA

Ventura Coll, CA
Wesley Coll, DE
West Virginia State U, WV

PARKS, RECREATION AND LEISURE FACILITIES MANAGEMENT

Abraham Baldwin Coll, GA
Asbury Coll, KY
Ball State U, IN
California State U, Sacramento, CA
Chattahoochee Tech Coll, GA
Clemson U, SC
Coll of St. Joseph, VT
Coll of the Desert, CA
Colorado Mountain Coll, Alpine Campus, CO
Concord U, WV
Cuesta Coll, CA
Delaware State U, DE
East Carolina U, NC
Eastern Michigan U, MI
East Stroudsburg U of Pennsylvania, PA
Feather River Coll, CA
Florida International U, FL
Franklin Pierce U, NH
Green Mountain Coll, VT
Henderson State U, AR
High Point U, NC
Hocking Coll, OH
Illinois State U, IL
Indiana U Bloomington, IN
Indiana U Southeast, IN
James H. Faulkner State Comm Coll, AL
Johnson & Wales U, CO
Johnson & Wales U, FL
Johnson & Wales U, NC
Johnson & Wales U, RI
Kansas State U, KS
Lake Superior State U, MI
Marshall U, WV
Michigan State U, MI
Middle Tennessee State U, TN
Minnesota State U Mankato, MN
Mohawk Valley Comm Coll, NY
Murray State U, KY
North Carolina State U, NC
Northern Michigan U, MI
Old Dominion U, VA
Penn State Abington, PA
Penn State DuBois, PA
Penn State Fayette, The Eberly Campus, PA
Penn State Mont Alto, PA
Penn State Wilkes-Barre, PA
Rose State Coll, OK
Skagit Valley Coll, WA
Slippery Rock U of Pennsylvania, PA
Spokane Comm Coll, WA
Springfield Coll, MA
State U of New York Coll at Cortland, NY
Sterling Coll, VT
Texas A&M U, TX
Unity Coll, ME
U of Connecticut, CT
U of Delaware, DE
U of Maine at Machias, ME
U of Miami, FL
The U of North Carolina at Chapel Hill, NC
U of Northern British Columbia, BC, Canada
The U of Tennessee, TN

The U of Tennessee at
Martin, TN
U of Vermont, VT
U of West Georgia, GA
U of Wisconsin–La Crosse,
WI
U of Wyoming, WY

**PARKS, RECREATION,
AND LEISURE RELATED**
Feather River Coll, CA
Franklin Coll, IN
North Carolina State U, NC
State U of New York Coll at
Brockport, NY

**PARTS, WAREHOUSING,
AND INVENTORY
MANAGEMENT**
Central Wyoming Coll, WY

**PASTORAL COUNSELING
AND SPECIALIZED
MINISTRIES RELATED**
Coll of Mount St. Joseph,
OH
Harding U, AR
Lancaster Bible Coll, PA
Multnomah Bible Coll and
Biblical Seminary, OR
Oak Hills Christian Coll, MN

**PASTORAL STUDIES/
COUNSELING**
Abilene Christian U, TX
The Baptist Coll of Florida,
FL
Bethany U, CA
Bethel Coll, IN
Charleston Southern U, SC
Concordia U, NE
Cornerstone U, MI
Dallas Baptist U, TX
Fresno Pacific U, CA
Gardner-Webb U, NC
Grace Coll, IN
Harding U, AR
Houghton Coll, NY
John Brown U, AR
Kuyper Coll, MI
Lancaster Bible Coll, PA
Lindenwood U, MO
Multnomah Bible Coll and
Biblical Seminary, OR
Northwest Nazarene U, ID
Notre Dame Coll, OH
Oak Hills Christian Coll, MN
Oral Roberts U, OK
St. Gregory's U, OK
Saint Joseph's Coll, IN
Southwest Baptist U, MO
Southwestern Coll, KS
Trinity Baptist Coll, FL
Union Coll, NE
U of Mary Hardin-Baylor, TX
U of St. Thomas, TX
Vanguard U of Southern
California, CA

**PATHOLOGIST
ASSISTANT**
Wayne State U, MI

**PATHOLOGY/
EXPERIMENTAL
PATHOLOGY**
U of California, Los Angeles,
CA
U of Connecticut, CT
The U of North Carolina at
Chapel Hill, NC

**PEACE STUDIES AND
CONFLICT RESOLUTION**
American U, DC
Clark U, MA
Colgate U, NY
Coll of Saint Elizabeth, NJ
Earlham Coll, IN
Eastern Mennonite U, VA
Goshen Coll, IN
Hamline U, MN
Hampshire Coll, MA
Haverford Coll, PA
Le Moyne Coll, NY
Molloy Coll, NY
Mount Saint Vincent U, NS,
Canada
The Ohio State U, OH
Saint John's U, MN
Syracuse U, NY
U of California, Berkeley,
CA
U of Hawaii at Manoa, HI
U of Missouri–Columbia,
MO
The U of North Carolina at
Chapel Hill, NC
U of St. Thomas, MN
U of Toronto, ON, Canada
Wellesley Coll, MA

PEDIATRIC NURSING
British Columbia Inst of
Technology, BC, Canada
U at Buffalo, the State U of
New York, NY

**PERIOPERATIVE/
OPERATING ROOM AND
SURGICAL NURSING**
British Columbia Inst of
Technology, BC, Canada
Comm Coll of Allegheny
County, PA
Murray State U, KY

**PERSONAL AND
CULINARY SERVICES
RELATED**
The Art Inst of Pittsburgh,
PA

**PETROLEUM
ENGINEERING**
Marietta Coll, OH
Montana Tech of The U of
Montana, MT
Penn State Abington, PA
Penn State DuBois, PA
Penn State Fayette, The
Eberly Campus, PA
Penn State Mont Alto, PA
Penn State Wilkes-Barre, PA
Texas A&M U, TX
U of Kansas, KS
U of Missouri–Rolla, MO
The U of Texas at Austin,
TX
U of Toronto, ON, Canada

**PETROLEUM PRODUCTS
RETAILING OPERATIONS**
Cape Breton U, NS, Canada

**PETROLEUM
TECHNOLOGY**
British Columbia Inst of
Technology, BC, Canada
Cape Breton U, NS, Canada
McNeese State U, LA
Mercyhurst Coll, PA
Montana State U–Billings,
MT
Montana Tech of The U of
Montana, MT

New Mexico Jr Coll, NM
Odessa Coll, TX
U of Alaska Anchorage, AK

PHARMACOLOGY
U at Buffalo, the State U of
New York, NY
U of California, Santa
Barbara, CA
U of Cincinnati, OH
U of Toronto, ON, Canada
U of Wisconsin–Madison,
WI

**PHARMACOLOGY AND
TOXICOLOGY**
Wright State U, OH

**PHARMACOLOGY AND
TOXICOLOGY RELATED**
The George Washington U,
DC

PHARMACY
City Colls of Chicago,
Richard J. Daley Coll, IL
Clayton State U, GA
Dalhousie U, NS, Canada
Drake U, IA
Eastern Nazarene Coll, MA
Long Island U, Brooklyn
Campus, NY
North Dakota State U, ND
Northeastern U, MA
The Ohio State U, OH
Rutgers, The State U of New
Jersey, New Brunswick, NJ
U of Cincinnati, OH
U of Connecticut, CT
U of Houston, TX
U of Kansas, KS
U of Manitoba, MB, Canada
U of Michigan, MI
U of Mississippi, MS
U of Missouri–Kansas City,
MO
U of New Mexico, NM
U of Pittsburgh, PA
U of Rhode Island, RI
U of the Pacific, CA
U of Toronto, ON, Canada
U of Washington, WA
U of Wisconsin–Madison,
WI
Wilkes U, PA

**PHARMACY
ADMINISTRATION/
PHARMACEUTICS**
Drake U, IA
U at Buffalo, the State U of
New York, NY

**PHARMACY,
PHARMACEUTICAL
SCIENCES, AND
ADMINISTRATION
RELATED**
Dalhousie U, NS, Canada
U at Buffalo, the State U of
New York, NY
U of Connecticut, CT
Wilkes U, PA

**PHARMACY
TECHNICIAN**
Abraham Baldwin Coll, GA
Comm Coll of Allegheny
County, PA
Harrisburg Area Comm Coll,
PA
Hillsborough Comm Coll, FL
Idaho State U, ID
Muscatine Comm Coll, IA
Pima Comm Coll, AZ

Santa Ana Coll, CA

PHILOSOPHY
Acadia U, NS, Canada
Adelphi U, NY
Albertson Coll of Idaho, ID
Albion Coll, MI
Albright Coll, PA
Alma Coll, MI
Alvernia Coll, PA
American International Coll,
MA
American U, DC
Amherst Coll, MA
Anderson U, IN
Asbury Coll, KY
Ashland U, OH
Augsburg Coll, MN
Aurora U, IL
Austin Coll, TX
Ball State U, IN
Bard Coll, NY
Barry U, FL
Bates Coll, ME
Baylor U, TX
Belmont Abbey Coll, NC
Bemidji State U, MN
Benedictine Coll, KS
Bentley Coll, MA
Bethel Coll, IN
Bethel U, MN
Bishop's U, QC, Canada
Blinn Coll, TX
Boston Coll, MA
Bradley U, IL
Brandeis U, MA
Brandon U, MB, Canada
Brock U, ON, Canada
Brown U, RI
Bryn Mawr Coll, PA
Buffalo State Coll, State U of
New York, NY
Burlington County Coll, NJ
California State U, Fullerton,
CA
California State U,
Northridge, CA
California State U,
Sacramento, CA
California State U, San
Bernardino, CA
California State U,
Stanislaus, CA
Calvin Coll, MI
Cape Breton U, NS, Canada
Cape Cod Comm Coll, MA
Carleton U, ON, Canada
Carlow U, PA
Carnegie Mellon U, PA
Carroll Coll, MT
Carson-Newman Coll, TN
Carthage Coll, WI
The Catholic U of America,
DC
Christopher Newport U, VA
Claremont McKenna Coll,
CA
Clark U, MA
Clayton State U, GA
Clemson U, SC
Coastal Carolina U, SC
Coe Coll, IA
Colby Coll, ME
Colgate U, NY
Coll of Charleston, SC
Coll of Mount Saint Vincent,
NY
Coll of Saint Elizabeth, NJ
Coll of Staten Island of the
City U of New York, NY
Coll of the Atlantic, ME
Coll of the Desert, CA
The Coll of William and
Mary, VA

Concordia U Coll of Alberta,
AB, Canada
Cornell U, NY
Cornerstone U, MI
Crafton Hills Coll, CA
Dalhousie U, NS, Canada
Dallas Baptist U, TX
DePaul U, IL
Dixie State Coll of Utah, UT
Dominican U, IL
Drake U, IA
Drury U, MO
Duke U, NC
Earlham Coll, IN
East Carolina U, NC
East Central Coll, MO
Eastern Michigan U, MI
East Stroudsburg U of
Pennsylvania, PA
Eckerd Coll, FL
Edinboro U of Pennsylvania,
PA
El Camino Coll, CA
Elmira Coll, NY
Elon U, NC
Emory U, GA
Eugene Lang Coll The New
School for Liberal Arts, NY
Fairfield U, CT
Fairleigh Dickinson U, Coll
at Florham, NJ
Fairleigh Dickinson U,
Metropolitan Campus, NJ
Ferrum Coll, VA
Flagler Coll, FL
Florida Atlantic U, FL
Florida International U, FL
Foothill Coll, CA
Fort Hays State U, KS
Franciscan U of
Steubenville, OH
Franklin Coll, IN
Freed-Hardeman U, TN
Furman U, SC
Gannon U, PA
Geneva Coll, PA
Georgetown Coll, KY
The George Washington U,
DC
Gonzaga U, WA
Gordon Coll, MA
Green Mountain Coll, VT
Grinnell Coll, IA
Grossmont Coll, CA
Gustavus Adolphus Coll,
MN
Hamilton Coll, NY
Hamline U, MN
Hampden-Sydney Coll, VA
Hampshire Coll, MA
Hartwick Coll, NY
Haverford Coll, PA
High Point U, NC
Hofstra U, NY
Hope Coll, MI
Houghton Coll, NY
Hunter Coll of the City U of
New York, NY
Huntington U, IN
Idaho State U, ID
Illinois State U, IL
Illinois Wesleyan U, IL
Indiana U Bloomington, IN
Indiana U of Pennsylvania,
PA
Indiana U–Purdue U Fort
Wayne, IN
Indiana U–Purdue U
Indianapolis, IN
Indiana U Southeast, IN
Iona Coll, NY
Ithaca Coll, NY
Jacksonville U, FL
Kansas State U, KS

Colleges for Students with Learning Disabilities or AD/HD

Kellogg Comm Coll, MI
Kentucky Wesleyan Coll, KY
Kenyon Coll, OH
King's Coll, PA
The King's U Coll, AB,
  Canada
Kutztown U of
  Pennsylvania, PA
Lawrence U, WI
Lebanon Valley Coll, PA
Lehigh U, PA
Le Moyne Coll, NY
Lewis U, IL
Liberty U, VA
Lincoln U, PA
Long Island U, Brooklyn
  Campus, NY
Loras Coll, IA
Loyola Marymount U, CA
Loyola U Chicago, IL
Loyola U New Orleans, LA
Lynchburg Coll, VA
Macalester Coll, MN
MacMurray Coll, IL
Manhattan Coll, NY
Manhattanville Coll, NY
Marian Coll, IN
Marietta Coll, OH
Marist Coll, NY
Marquette U, WI
Marymount U, VA
Massachusetts Coll of Liberal
  Arts, MA
McDaniel Coll, MD
Mercer U, GA
Mercyhurst Coll, PA
Miami Dade Coll, FL
Michigan State U, MI
Middle Tennessee State U,
  TN
Millersville U of
  Pennsylvania, PA
Minnesota State U Mankato,
  MN
Minnesota State U
  Moorhead, MN
MiraCosta Coll, CA
Missouri State U, MO
Molloy Coll, NY
Monmouth Coll, IL
Montana State U, MT
Moravian Coll, PA
Morningside Coll, IA
Mount Holyoke Coll, MA
Mount St. Mary's U, MD
Mount Saint Vincent U, NS,
  Canada
Mount Union Coll, OH
Mount Vernon Nazarene U,
  OH
Murray State U, KY
New Jersey City U, NJ
New York U, NY
Niagara U, NY
Nipissing U, ON, Canada
North Carolina State U, NC
North Central Coll, IL
North Dakota State U, ND
Northeastern U, MA
Northern Illinois U, IL
Northern Michigan U, MI
Northwest Nazarene U, ID
Notre Dame de Namur U,
  CA
Oakland U, MI
Occidental Coll, CA
Oglethorpe U, GA
The Ohio State U, OH
Ohio Wesleyan U, OH
Oklahoma State U, OK
Old Dominion U, VA
Oral Roberts U, OK
Otterbein Coll, OH

Our Lady of the Lake U of
  San Antonio, TX
Penn State Abington, PA
Penn State DuBois, PA
Penn State Fayette, The
  Eberly Campus, PA
Penn State Mont Alto, PA
Penn State Wilkes-Barre, PA
Piedmont Coll, GA
Point Loma Nazarene U, CA
Portland State U, OR
Queens Coll of the City U of
  New York, NY
Queen's U at Kingston, ON,
  Canada
Queens U of Charlotte, NC
Randolph Coll, VA
Randolph-Macon Coll, VA
Redeemer U Coll, ON,
  Canada
Rensselaer Polytechnic Inst,
  NY
Rhodes Coll, TN
Rice U, TX
The Richard Stockton Coll
  of New Jersey, NJ
Ripon Coll, WI
Rockford Coll, IL
Rockhurst U, MO
Rocky Mountain Coll, MT
Roosevelt U, IL
Rutgers, The State U of New
  Jersey, Newark, NJ
Rutgers, The State U of New
  Jersey, New Brunswick, NJ
St. Bonaventure U, NY
St. Cloud State U, MN
St. Francis Xavier U, NS,
  Canada
St. Gregory's U, OK
Saint John's U, MN
Saint Joseph's Coll, IN
St. Lawrence U, NY
St. Mary's Coll of Maryland,
  MD
St. Norbert Coll, WI
St. Philip's Coll, TX
St. Thomas Aquinas Coll,
  NY
St. Thomas U, NB, Canada
Saint Xavier U, IL
Salve Regina U, RI
San Diego State U, CA
San Francisco State U, CA
Santa Ana Coll, CA
Santa Barbara City Coll, CA
Santa Clara U, CA
Santa Rosa Jr Coll, CA
Seattle Pacific U, WA
Seton Hall U, NJ
Sewanee: The U of the
  South, TN
Skagit Valley Coll, WA
Slippery Rock U of
  Pennsylvania, PA
Southern Illinois U
  Carbondale, IL
Southern Illinois U
  Edwardsville, IL
Southern Nazarene U, OK
Southwestern U, TX
Spalding U, KY
State U of New York at
  Fredonia, NY
State U of New York Coll at
  Brockport, NY
State U of New York Coll at
  Cortland, NY
State U of New York Coll at
  Geneseo, NY
State U of New York Coll at
  Potsdam, NY
Stetson U, FL
Stonehill Coll, MA

Sweet Briar Coll, VA
Syracuse U, NY
Taylor U, IN
Temple U, PA
Texas A&M U, TX
Thiel Coll, PA
Towson U, MD
Trent U, ON, Canada
Trinity Coll, CT
Trinity U, TX
Truman State U, MO
Tufts U, MA
U at Albany, State U of New
  York, NY
U at Buffalo, the State U of
  New York, NY
The U of Akron, OH
The U of Alabama, AL
The U of Alabama in
  Huntsville, AL
The U of Arizona, AZ
U of Arkansas, AR
U of California, Berkeley,
  CA
U of California, Irvine, CA
U of California, Los Angeles,
  CA
U of California, Santa
  Barbara, CA
U of Central Florida, FL
U of Central Oklahoma, OK
U of Cincinnati, OH
U of Colorado at Boulder,
  CO
U of Connecticut, CT
U of Dayton, OH
U of Delaware, DE
U of Dubuque, IA
U of Evansville, IN
The U of Findlay, OH
U of Guelph, ON, Canada
U of Hartford, CT
U of Hawaii at Manoa, HI
U of Hawaii–West Oahu, HI
U of Houston, TX
U of Illinois at Urbana–
  Champaign, IL
U of Kansas, KS
U of Kentucky, KY
U of Manitoba, MB, Canada
U of Maryland, Baltimore
  County, MD
U of Mary Washington, VA
U of Massachusetts Amherst,
  MA
U of Massachusetts Boston,
  MA
U of Massachusetts Lowell,
  MA
U of Miami, FL
U of Michigan, MI
U of Minnesota, Duluth, MN
U of Mississippi, MS
U of Missouri–Columbia,
  MO
U of Missouri–Kansas City,
  MO
U of Missouri–Rolla, MO
U of Nebraska at Omaha,
  NE
U of Nebraska–Lincoln, NE
U of New Brunswick
  Fredericton, NB, Canada
U of New Hampshire, NH
U of New Mexico, NM
U of New Orleans, LA
The U of North Carolina at
  Asheville, NC
The U of North Carolina at
  Chapel Hill, NC
The U of North Carolina at
  Charlotte, NC
U of Northern Iowa, IA
U of North Florida, FL

U of Notre Dame, IN
U of Oregon, OR
U of Pennsylvania, PA
U of Pittsburgh, PA
U of Portland, OR
U of Redlands, CA
U of Rhode Island, RI
U of St. Thomas, MN
U of St. Thomas, TX
U of San Diego, CA
U of San Francisco, CA
The U of Scranton, PA
U of Southern Indiana, IN
The U of Tampa, FL
The U of Tennessee, TN
The U of Tennessee at
  Martin, TN
The U of Texas at Austin,
  TX
The U of Texas at El Paso,
  TX
The U of Texas at San
  Antonio, TX
U of the District of
  Columbia, DC
U of the Incarnate Word, TX
U of the Pacific, CA
U of Toronto, ON, Canada
U of Vermont, VT
U of Virginia, VA
U of Washington, WA
U of West Georgia, GA
U of Wisconsin–Eau Claire,
  WI
U of Wisconsin–Green Bay,
  WI
U of Wisconsin–La Crosse,
  WI
U of Wisconsin–Madison,
  WI
U of Wisconsin–Oshkosh,
  WI
U of Wisconsin–Platteville,
  WI
U of Wisconsin–Stevens
  Point, WI
U of Wyoming, WY
Urbana U, OH
Ursuline Coll, OH
Utica Coll, NY
Valdosta State U, GA
Vassar Coll, NY
Villanova U, PA
Wake Forest U, NC
Washburn U, KS
Washington & Jefferson Coll,
  PA
Washington and Lee U, VA
Wayne State U, MI
Wellesley Coll, MA
Wells Coll, NY
West Chester U of
  Pennsylvania, PA
Western New England Coll,
  MA
Western Oregon U, OR
West Los Angeles Coll, CA
Westminster Coll, PA
Westminster Coll, UT
West Virginia Wesleyan Coll,
  WV
Wheaton Coll, IL
Whitman Coll, WA
Wichita State U, KS
Wilfrid Laurier U, ON,
  Canada
Wilkes U, PA
William Jewell Coll, MO
Wofford Coll, SC
Wright State U, OH
Xavier U, OH
Yale U, CT

**PHILOSOPHY AND
RELIGIOUS STUDIES
RELATED**
Bridgewater Coll, VA
Buena Vista U, IA
California State U,
  Sacramento, CA
Claremont McKenna Coll,
  CA
Eastern Mennonite U, VA
Graceland U, IA
Point Loma Nazarene U, CA
Radford U, VA
Saint Joseph's Coll, IN
Southwestern Coll, KS
Syracuse U, NY
U of Notre Dame, IN
U of the Ozarks, AR
West Virginia Wesleyan Coll,
  WV
Wilson Coll, PA

PHILOSOPHY RELATED
Claremont McKenna Coll,
  CA
U of Pennsylvania, PA

PHLEBOTOMY
Alexandria Tech Coll, MN

**PHOTOGRAPHIC AND
FILM/VIDEO
TECHNOLOGY**
Calhoun Comm Coll, AL
Dixie State Coll of Utah, UT
Miami Dade Coll, FL
Mohawk Valley Comm Coll,
  NY
Rochester Inst of
  Technology, NY

PHOTOGRAPHY
Academy of Art U, CA
The Art Inst of Pittsburgh,
  PA
The Art Inst of Seattle, WA
Ball State U, IN
Bard Coll, NY
Barry U, FL
Buffalo State Coll, State U of
  New York, NY
California State U, Fullerton,
  CA
California State U,
  Sacramento, CA
Carroll Coll, WI
Carson-Newman Coll, TN
Citrus Coll, CA
City Colls of Chicago,
  Richard J. Daley Coll, IL
The Cleveland Inst of Art,
  OH
Coe Coll, IA
Cosumnes River Coll,
  Sacramento, CA
Dixie State Coll of Utah, UT
Dominican U, IL
El Camino Coll, CA
Fitchburg State Coll, MA
Foothill Coll, CA
Fresno City Coll, CA
Glendale Comm Coll, CA
Grossmont Coll, CA
Harrisburg Area Comm Coll,
  PA
Hofstra U, NY
Howard Comm Coll, MD
Indiana U Bloomington, IN
Indiana U–Purdue U Fort
  Wayne, IN
Ithaca Coll, NY
Lassen Comm Coll District,
  CA
Lee Coll, TX

Long Beach City Coll, CA
Maine Coll of Art, ME
Marywood U, PA
McNeese State U, LA
Miami Dade Coll, FL
Middlesex County Coll, NJ
Minneapolis Coll of Art and
 Design, MN
Moorpark Coll, CA
Morningside Coll, IA
Nassau Comm Coll, NY
New York U, NY
NSCAD U, NS, Canada
Odessa Coll, TX
Otis Coll of Art and Design,
 CA
Parsons The New School for
 Design, NY
Pratt Inst, NY
Ringling Coll of Art and
 Design, FL
Rivier Coll, NH
Rochester Inst of
 Technology, NY
Rutgers, The State U of New
 Jersey, New Brunswick, NJ
Ryerson U, ON, Canada
St. Louis Comm Coll at
 Florissant Valley, MO
Salve Regina U, RI
Santa Ana Coll, CA
Savannah Coll of Art and
 Design, GA
School of the Art Inst of
 Chicago, IL
School of Visual Arts, NY
Scottsdale Comm Coll, AZ
Southern Adventist U, TN
Syracuse U, NY
Temple U, PA
The U of Akron, OH
U of Central Florida, FL
U of Central Missouri, MO
U of Central Oklahoma, OK
U of Dayton, OH
U of Hartford, CT
U of Houston, TX
U of Illinois at Urbana–
 Champaign, IL
The U of Maine at Augusta,
 ME
U of Maryland, Baltimore
 County, MD
U of Miami, FL
U of Michigan, MI
U of Oregon, OR
The U of the Arts, PA
U of Washington, WA
Virginia Intermont Coll, VA
Watkins Coll of Art and
 Design, TN
Westmoreland County
 Comm Coll, PA
Wright State U, OH

PHOTOJOURNALISM
Rochester Inst of
 Technology, NY
St. Gregory's U, OK
U of Missouri–Columbia,
 MO

**PHYSICAL AND
THEORETICAL
CHEMISTRY**
Lehigh U, PA
Michigan State U, MI
Rice U, TX

**PHYSICAL EDUCATION
TEACHING AND
COACHING**
Abilene Christian U, TX
Abraham Baldwin Coll, GA

Adelphi U, NY
Alabama A&M U, AL
Albany State U, GA
Albertson Coll of Idaho, ID
Albion Coll, MI
Alderson-Broaddus Coll, WV
Alma Coll, MI
Anderson U, IN
Anderson U, SC
Asbury Coll, KY
Ashland U, OH
Athens State U, AL
Augsburg Coll, MN
Aurora U, IL
Austin Coll, TX
Ball State U, IN
Barry U, FL
Baylor U, TX
Bemidji State U, MN
Benedictine Coll, KS
Bethel Coll, IN
Bethel U, MN
Blinn Coll, TX
Brewton-Parker Coll, GA
Briar Cliff U, IA
Bridgewater Coll, VA
Brock U, ON, Canada
Bucks County Comm Coll,
 PA
Buena Vista U, IA
California State U, Fullerton,
 CA
California State U, San
 Bernardino, CA
California State U,
 Stanislaus, CA
Calvin Coll, MI
Cape Cod Comm Coll, MA
Carroll Coll, MT
Carroll Coll, WI
Carson-Newman Coll, TN
Carthage Coll, WI
Charleston Southern U, SC
Chesapeake Coll, MD
Citrus Coll, CA
Clayton State U, GA
Coastal Carolina U, SC
Coe Coll, IA
Coll of Charleston, SC
Coll of Mount Saint Vincent,
 NY
Coll of the Canyons, CA
Coll of the Desert, CA
The Coll of William and
 Mary, VA
Columbus State U, GA
Concordia U, NE
Concord U, WV
Cornerstone U, MI
Crafton Hills Coll, CA
Cuesta Coll, CA
Dallas Baptist U, TX
Dean Coll, MA
Delaware State U, DE
DePaul U, IL
Dixie State Coll of Utah, UT
East Carolina U, NC
East Central Coll, MO
Eastern Connecticut State U,
 CT
Eastern Mennonite U, VA
Eastern Michigan U, MI
Eastern Nazarene Coll, MA
East Stroudsburg U of
 Pennsylvania, PA
Edinboro U of Pennsylvania,
 PA
El Camino Coll, CA
Elon U, NC
Fayetteville State U, NC
Ferrum Coll, VA
Florida International U, FL
Foothill Coll, CA
Fort Hays State U, KS

Franklin Coll, IN
Frederick Comm Coll, MD
Freed-Hardeman U, TN
Fresno Pacific U, CA
Fulton-Montgomery Comm
 Coll, NY
Gadsden State Comm Coll,
 AL
Galveston Coll, TX
Gardner-Webb U, NC
Georgia Coll & State U, GA
Glenville State Coll, WV
Gonzaga U, WA
Goshen Coll, IN
Grace Coll, IN
Graceland U, IA
Grambling State U, LA
Gustavus Adolphus Coll,
 MN
Hamline U, MN
Harding U, AR
Harrisburg Area Comm Coll,
 PA
Henderson State U, AR
High Point U, NC
Hillsborough Comm Coll, FL
Hofstra U, NY
Hope Coll, MI
Houghton Coll, NY
Houston Baptist U, TX
Hunter Coll of the City U of
 New York, NY
Huntington U, IN
Husson Coll, ME
Idaho State U, ID
Illinois State U, IL
Indiana U Bloomington, IN
Indiana U of Pennsylvania,
 PA
Indiana U–Purdue U
 Indianapolis, IN
Ithaca Coll, NY
Jacksonville U, FL
Johnson State Coll, VT
Kellogg Comm Coll, MI
Kennesaw State U, GA
Kentucky Wesleyan Coll, KY
Lamar U, TX
Lancaster Bible Coll, PA
Langston U, OK
Lassen Comm Coll District,
 CA
Lee Coll, TX
LeTourneau U, TX
Lewis U, IL
Liberty U, VA
Lindenwood U, MO
Long Beach City Coll, CA
Long Island U, Brooklyn
 Campus, NY
Loras Coll, IA
Lynchburg Coll, VA
MacMurray Coll, IL
Manhattan Coll, NY
Marian Coll, IN
Marshall U, WV
McDaniel Coll, MD
McNeese State U, LA
Miami Dade Coll, FL
Michigan State U, MI
Middlesex County Coll, NJ
Midland Coll, TX
Midland Lutheran Coll, NE
Minnesota State U Mankato,
 MN
Minnesota State U
 Moorhead, MN
Missouri State U, MO
Mitchell Coll, CT
Mohawk Valley Comm Coll,
 NY
Monmouth Coll, IL
Montana State U–Billings,
 MT

Mount Union Coll, OH
Mount Vernon Nazarene U,
 OH
Murray State U, KY
New Mexico Jr Coll, NM
North Central Coll, IL
North Dakota State U, ND
Northern Illinois U, IL
Northern Michigan U, MI
Northern State U, SD
North Georgia Coll & State
 U, GA
Northwestern Coll, MN
Northwestern Oklahoma
 State U, OK
Northwest Nazarene U, ID
Odessa Coll, TX
The Ohio State U, OH
Ohio Wesleyan U, OH
Oklahoma State U, OK
Old Dominion U, VA
Oral Roberts U, OK
Otterbein Coll, OH
Paul Quinn Coll, TX
Pittsburg State U, KS
Queens Coll of the City U of
 New York, NY
Queen's U at Kingston, ON,
 Canada
Radford U, VA
Reinhardt Coll, GA
Ripon Coll, WI
Rockford Coll, IL
Rocky Mountain Coll, MT
Rose State Coll, OK
Rowan U, NJ
Saginaw Valley State U, MI
St. Bonaventure U, NY
St. Cloud State U, MN
St. Francis Xavier U, NS,
 Canada
Saint Joseph's Coll, IN
San Diego Mesa Coll, CA
San Francisco State U, CA
Santa Barbara City Coll, CA
Santa Rosa Jr Coll, CA
Sauk Valley Comm Coll, IL
Seattle Pacific U, WA
Skagit Valley Coll, WA
Southern Adventist U, TN
Southern Illinois U
 Carbondale, IL
Southern Nazarene U, OK
Southern Oregon U, OR
Southern U and A&M Coll,
 LA
Southern Utah U, UT
Southwest Baptist U, MO
Spoon River Coll, IL
Springfield Coll, MA
State U of New York Coll at
 Brockport, NY
State U of New York Coll at
 Cortland, NY
State U of New York Coll at
 Potsdam, NY
Syracuse U, NY
Taylor U, IN
Temple U, PA
Tennessee Wesleyan Coll,
 TN
Texas A&M U–Corpus
 Christi, TX
Towson U, MD
Trevecca Nazarene U, TN
Troy U, AL
Union Coll, NE
The U of Akron, OH
The U of Alabama, AL
U of Alaska Anchorage, AK
The U of Arizona, AZ
U of Central Florida, FL
U of Central Missouri, MO
U of Central Oklahoma, OK

U of Cincinnati, OH
U of Connecticut, CT
U of Dayton, OH
U of Delaware, DE
U of Dubuque, IA
U of Evansville, IN
The U of Findlay, OH
U of Great Falls, MT
U of Hawaii at Manoa, HI
U of Kansas, KS
U of Kentucky, KY
U of Manitoba, MB, Canada
U of Mary Hardin-Baylor, TX
U of Massachusetts Boston,
 MA
U of Michigan, MI
U of Minnesota, Duluth, MN
U of Nebraska at Kearney,
 NE
U of Nebraska at Omaha,
 NE
U of Nebraska–Lincoln, NE
U of New Brunswick
 Fredericton, NB, Canada
U of New Hampshire, NH
U of New Mexico, NM
U of New Orleans, LA
U of Northern Iowa, IA
U of North Florida, FL
U of Pittsburgh, PA
U of Rhode Island, RI
U of Rio Grande, OH
U of St. Thomas, MN
U of San Francisco, CA
U of South Carolina Upstate,
 SC
U of Southern Indiana, IN
The U of Tampa, FL
U of the District of
 Columbia, DC
U of the Incarnate Word, TX
U of the Ozarks, AR
U of Vermont, VT
U of Virginia, VA
U of West Georgia, GA
U of Wisconsin–Madison,
 WI
U of Wisconsin–Oshkosh,
 WI
U of Wisconsin–Stevens
 Point, WI
U of Wyoming, WY
Upper Iowa U, IA
Valdosta State U, GA
Valencia Comm Coll, FL
Vanguard U of Southern
 California, CA
Virginia Intermont Coll, VA
Washburn U, KS
Wayne State Coll, NE
Wayne State U, MI
Wesley Coll, DE
West Chester U of
 Pennsylvania, PA
West Liberty State Coll, WV
West Los Angeles Coll, CA
West Virginia State U, WV
West Virginia Wesleyan Coll,
 WV
Wichita State U, KS
Wilfrid Laurier U, ON,
 Canada
Wright State U, OH

PHYSICAL SCIENCES
Abraham Baldwin Coll, GA
Asbury Coll, KY
Auburn U Montgomery, AL
Bard Coll, NY
Bemidji State U, MN
Brock U, ON, Canada
California State U,
 Sacramento, CA

California State U,
Stanislaus, CA
Calvin Coll, MI
Central Wyoming Coll, WY
Chesapeake Coll, MD
Citrus Coll, CA
Coe Coll, IA
Colgate U, NY
Coll of the Canyons, CA
Colorado Mountain Coll,
Alpine Campus, CO
Concordia U, NE
East Stroudsburg U of
Pennsylvania, PA
El Camino Coll, CA
Feather River Coll, CA
Fort Hays State U, KS
Framingham State Coll, MA
Frederick Comm Coll, MD
Freed-Hardeman U, TN
Fresno City Coll, CA
Fulton-Montgomery Comm
Coll, NY
Goshen Coll, IN
Graceland U, IA
Harrisburg Area Comm Coll,
PA
Howard Comm Coll, MD
Kansas State U, KS
Lassen Comm Coll District,
CA
Lincoln U, PA
Long Beach City Coll, CA
Long Island U, Brooklyn
Campus, NY
Loras Coll, IA
Miami Dade Coll, FL
Michigan State U, MI
Middlesex County Coll, NJ
Midland Lutheran Coll, NE
Minnesota State U Mankato,
MN
MiraCosta Coll, CA
Mitchell Coll, CT
Otterbein Coll, OH
Ozarks Tech Comm Coll,
MO
Radford U, VA
Reedley Coll, CA
Ripon Coll, WI
Rowan U, NJ
Roxbury Comm Coll, MA
St. Bonaventure U, NY
St. Cloud State U, MN
St. Francis Xavier U, NS,
Canada
San Diego Mesa Coll, CA
San Diego State U, CA
San Francisco State U, CA
Santa Rosa Jr Coll, CA
Southern Utah U, UT
Southwestern U, TX
Spoon River Coll, IL
Taylor U, IN
Trent U, ON, Canada
Troy U, AL
U of California, Berkeley,
CA
U of Dayton, OH
U of Guelph, ON, Canada
U of Pittsburgh, PA
U of Pittsburgh at Bradford,
PA
U of Rio Grande, OH
U of the District of
Columbia, DC
U of the Pacific, CA
Ventura Coll, CA
Victor Valley Coll, CA
Wayne State Coll, NE

**PHYSICAL SCIENCES
RELATED**
Charleston Southern U, SC

The Coll of St. Scholastica,
MN
Eastern Michigan U, MI
Schoolcraft Coll, MI
The U of North Carolina at
Chapel Hill, NC
U of Toronto, ON, Canada

**PHYSICAL SCIENCE
TECHNOLOGIES
RELATED**
Missouri State U, MO
The U of Akron, OH

**PHYSICAL THERAPIST
ASSISTANT**
Allegany Coll of Maryland,
MD
Ashland Comm and Tech
Coll, KY
Blinn Coll, TX
Broome Comm Coll, NY
Cape Cod Comm Coll, MA
Central Florida Comm Coll,
FL
Central Ohio Tech Coll, OH
Comm Coll of Allegheny
County, PA
Florida Comm Coll at
Jacksonville, FL
Hocking Coll, OH
Houston Comm Coll System,
TX
Idaho State U, ID
Kellogg Comm Coll, MI
Kingsborough Comm Coll of
the City U of New York,
NY
Lake City Comm Coll, FL
Lincoln Land Comm Coll, IL
Linn State Tech Coll, MO
Macomb Comm Coll, MI
Madisonville Comm Coll,
KY
Mercyhurst Coll, PA
Miami Dade Coll, FL
Nassau Comm Coll, NY
New York U, NY
Ozarks Tech Comm Coll,
MO
Penn State DuBois, PA
Penn State Mont Alto, PA
Pueblo Comm Coll, CO
Rockingham Comm Coll, NC
St. Philip's Coll, TX
San Diego Mesa Coll, CA
Southern Illinois U
Carbondale, IL
South U, GA
State U of New York Coll of
Technology at Canton, NY
U of Evansville, IN
Washburn U, KS
Western Nebraska Comm
Coll, NE
Western Tech Coll, WI
Williston State Coll, ND

PHYSICAL THERAPY
Alvernia Coll, PA
American International Coll,
MA
Bradley U, IL
Broward Comm Coll, FL
Caldwell Comm Coll and
Tech Inst, NC
Central Piedmont Comm
Coll, NC
Chattanooga State Tech
Comm Coll, TN
Clayton State U, GA
Coll of Staten Island of the
City U of New York, NY
Dalhousie U, NS, Canada

Eastern Nazarene Coll, MA
Greenville Tech Coll, SC
Gustavus Adolphus Coll,
MN
Hamline U, MN
Hillsborough Comm Coll, FL
Housatonic Comm Coll, CT
Husson Coll, ME
Indiana U–Purdue U
Indianapolis, IN
Ithaca Coll, NY
Jefferson Comm and Tech
Coll, KY
Kapiolani Comm Coll, HI
Kingsborough Comm Coll of
the City U of New York,
NY
Langston U, OK
Laredo Comm Coll, TX
Long Island U, Brooklyn
Campus, NY
Marquette U, WI
Mercyhurst Coll, PA
Metropolitan Comm
Coll–Penn Valley, MO
Morton Coll, IL
Mount Vernon Nazarene U,
OH
Northeastern U, MA
Northern Illinois U, IL
Northwest Nazarene U, ID
Odessa Coll, TX
The Ohio State U, OH
Queen's U at Kingston, ON,
Canada
Rose State Coll, OK
St. Cloud State U, MN
Saint John's U, MN
Sauk Valley Comm Coll, IL
Seminole Comm Coll, FL
Southern Adventist U, TN
Springfield Coll, MA
Stark State Coll of
Technology, OH
State U of New York Coll of
Environmental Science
and Forestry, NY
Tunxis Comm Coll, CT
U of Cincinnati, OH
U of Connecticut, CT
The U of Findlay, OH
U of Hartford, CT
U of Kentucky, KY
U of Manitoba, MB, Canada
U of New England, ME
U of Washington, WA
U of Wisconsin–La Crosse,
WI
Vanguard U of Southern
California, CA
Virginia Highlands Comm
Coll, VA
Western Nebraska Comm
Coll, NE

PHYSICIAN ASSISTANT
Alderson-Broaddus Coll, WV
Augsburg Coll, MN
Coll of Staten Island of the
City U of New York, NY
Daemen Coll, NY
East Carolina U, NC
Foothill Coll, CA
Gannon U, PA
Gardner-Webb U, NC
The George Washington U,
DC
High Point U, NC
Hofstra U, NY
Le Moyne Coll, NY
Long Island U, Brooklyn
Campus, NY
Marquette U, WI
Marywood U, PA

Minnesota School of
Business–St. Cloud, MN
Nova Southeastern U, FL
Rochester Inst of
Technology, NY
Rocky Mountain Coll, MT
Santa Rosa Jr Coll, CA
Seton Hill U, PA
Southern Adventist U, TN
Southern Illinois U
Carbondale, IL
South U, GA
Springfield Coll, MA
Union Coll, NE
The U of Findlay, OH
U of New England, ME
U of New Mexico, NM
U of Washington, WA
U of Wisconsin–La Crosse,
WI
U of Wisconsin–Madison,
WI
Wake Forest U, NC
Wichita State U, KS

PHYSICS
Abilene Christian U, TX
Acadia U, NS, Canada
Adelphi U, NY
Alabama A&M U, AL
Albertson Coll of Idaho, ID
Albion Coll, MI
Albright Coll, PA
Alma Coll, MI
American U, DC
Amherst Coll, MA
Anderson U, IN
Angelo State U, TX
Ashland U, OH
Athens State U, AL
Augsburg Coll, MN
Austin Coll, TX
Ball State U, IN
Bard Coll, NY
Bates Coll, ME
Baylor U, TX
Bemidji State U, MN
Benedictine Coll, KS
Bethel Coll, IN
Bethel U, MN
Bishop's U, QC, Canada
Blinn Coll, TX
Boston Coll, MA
Bradley U, IL
Brandeis U, MA
Brandon U, MB, Canada
Bridgewater Coll, VA
Brock U, ON, Canada
Brown U, RI
Bryn Mawr Coll, PA
Buena Vista U, IA
Buffalo State Coll, State U of
New York, NY
Bunker Hill Comm Coll, MA
Burlington County Coll, NJ
California State U, Fullerton,
CA
California State U,
Northridge, CA
California State U,
Sacramento, CA
California State U, San
Bernardino, CA
California State U,
Stanislaus, CA
Calvin Coll, MI
Cameron U, OK
Carleton U, ON, Canada
Carnegie Mellon U, PA
Carthage Coll, WI
The Catholic U of America,
DC
Christopher Newport U, VA

Claremont McKenna Coll,
CA
Clark U, MA
Clayton State U, GA
Clemson U, SC
Coastal Carolina U, SC
Coe Coll, IA
Colby Coll, ME
Colgate U, NY
Coll of Charleston, SC
Coll of Mount Saint Vincent,
NY
Coll of Staten Island of the
City U of New York, NY
Coll of the Desert, CA
The Coll of William and
Mary, VA
Comm Coll of Allegheny
County, PA
Cornell U, NY
Crafton Hills Coll, CA
Cuesta Coll, CA
Dalhousie U, NS, Canada
Delaware State U, DE
DePaul U, IL
Dixie State Coll of Utah, UT
Drake U, IA
Drury U, MO
Duke U, NC
Earlham Coll, IN
East Carolina U, NC
East Central Coll, MO
Eastern Michigan U, MI
Eastern Nazarene Coll, MA
East Stroudsburg U of
Pennsylvania, PA
Eckerd Coll, FL
Edinboro U of Pennsylvania,
PA
El Camino Coll, CA
Elon U, NC
Emory U, GA
Fairfield U, CT
Florida Atlantic U, FL
Florida Inst of Technology,
FL
Florida International U, FL
Foothill Coll, CA
Fort Hays State U, KS
Furman U, SC
Gainesville State Coll, GA
Geneva Coll, PA
Georgetown Coll, KY
The George Washington U,
DC
Georgian Court U, NJ
Gonzaga U, WA
Gordon Coll, MA
Goshen Coll, IN
Grambling State U, LA
Grinnell Coll, IA
Grossmont Coll, CA
Gustavus Adolphus Coll,
MN
Hamilton Coll, NY
Hamline U, MN
Hampden-Sydney Coll, VA
Hampshire Coll, MA
Harding U, AR
Hartwick Coll, NY
Haverford Coll, PA
Henderson State U, AR
Hofstra U, NY
Hope Coll, MI
Houghton Coll, NY
Houston Baptist U, TX
Hunter Coll of the City U of
New York, NY
Idaho State U, ID
Illinois State U, IL
Illinois Wesleyan U, IL
Indiana U Bloomington, IN
Indiana U of Pennsylvania,
PA

Indiana U–Purdue U Fort Wayne, IN
Indiana U–Purdue U Indianapolis, IN
Iona Coll, NY
Ithaca Coll, NY
Jacksonville U, FL
Kansas State U, KS
Kellogg Comm Coll, MI
Kentucky Wesleyan Coll, KY
Kenyon Coll, OH
Kingsborough Comm Coll of the City U of New York, NY
Kutztown U of Pennsylvania, PA
Lamar U, TX
Lawrence U, WI
Lebanon Valley Coll, PA
Lee Coll, TX
Lehigh U, PA
Le Moyne Coll, NY
Lewis U, IL
Lincoln U, PA
Long Island U, Brooklyn Campus, NY
Loras Coll, IA
Loyola Marymount U, CA
Loyola U Chicago, IL
Loyola U New Orleans, LA
Lynchburg Coll, VA
Macalester Coll, MN
MacMurray Coll, IL
Manhattan Coll, NY
Manhattanville Coll, NY
Marietta Coll, OH
Marquette U, WI
Marshall U, WV
Massachusetts Coll of Liberal Arts, MA
McDaniel Coll, MD
McNeese State U, LA
Mercer U, GA
Mercyhurst Coll, PA
Miami Dade Coll, FL
Michigan State U, MI
Middlesex County Coll, NJ
Middle Tennessee State U, TN
Midland Coll, TX
Millersville U of Pennsylvania, PA
Minnesota State U Mankato, MN
Minnesota State U Moorhead, MN
MiraCosta Coll, CA
Missouri State U, MO
Monmouth Coll, IL
Montana State U, MT
Moravian Coll, PA
Morningside Coll, IA
Mount Holyoke Coll, MA
Mount Union Coll, OH
Murray State U, KY
New Jersey City U, NJ
New York U, NY
North Carolina State U, NC
North Central Coll, IL
North Dakota State U, ND
Northeastern U, MA
Northern Illinois U, IL
North Georgia Coll & State U, GA
Northwestern Oklahoma State U, OK
Northwest Nazarene U, ID
Oakland U, MI
Occidental Coll, CA
Odessa Coll, TX
Oglethorpe U, GA
The Ohio State U, OH
Ohio Wesleyan U, OH
Oklahoma State U, OK

Old Dominion U, VA
Oral Roberts U, OK
Otterbein Coll, OH
Penn State Abington, PA
Penn State DuBois, PA
Penn State Fayette, The Eberly Campus, PA
Penn State Mont Alto, PA
Penn State Wilkes-Barre, PA
Piedmont Coll, GA
Pittsburg State U, KS
Point Loma Nazarene U, CA
Portland State U, OR
Prairie View A&M U, TX
Presbyterian Coll, SC
Purdue U North Central, IN
Queens Coll of the City U of New York, NY
Queen's U at Kingston, ON, Canada
Ramapo Coll of New Jersey, NJ
Randolph Coll, VA
Randolph-Macon Coll, VA
Rhodes Coll, TN
Rice U, TX
The Richard Stockton Coll of New Jersey, NJ
Rochester Inst of Technology, NY
Rockhurst U, MO
Rose State Coll, OK
Rutgers, The State U of New Jersey, Newark, NJ
Rutgers, The State U of New Jersey, New Brunswick, NJ
Saginaw Valley State U, MI
St. Bonaventure U, NY
St. Cloud State U, MN
St. Francis Xavier U, NS, Canada
Saint John's U, MN
St. Lawrence U, NY
St. Mary's Coll of Maryland, MD
St. Norbert Coll, WI
Salem Comm Coll, NJ
San Diego Mesa Coll, CA
San Diego State U, CA
San Francisco State U, CA
Santa Ana Coll, CA
Santa Barbara City Coll, CA
Santa Clara U, CA
Santa Rosa Jr Coll, CA
Sauk Valley Comm Coll, IL
Seattle Pacific U, WA
Seton Hall U, NJ
Seton Hill U, PA
Sewanee: The U of the South, TN
Shippensburg U of Pennsylvania, PA
Slippery Rock U of Pennsylvania, PA
Southern Adventist U, TN
Southern Illinois U Carbondale, IL
Southern Illinois U Edwardsville, IL
Southern Nazarene U, OK
Southern Oregon U, OR
Southern U and A&M Coll, LA
Southwestern Coll, KS
Southwestern U, TX
Spoon River Coll, IL
State U of New York at Fredonia, NY
State U of New York Coll at Brockport, NY
State U of New York Coll at Cortland, NY
State U of New York Coll at Geneseo, NY

State U of New York Coll at Potsdam, NY
Stephen F. Austin State U, TX
Stetson U, FL
Sweet Briar Coll, VA
Syracuse U, NY
Taylor U, IN
Temple U, PA
Texas A&M U, TX
Thiel Coll, PA
Towson U, MD
Trent U, ON, Canada
Trevecca Nazarene U, TN
Trinity Coll, CT
Trinity U, TX
Truman State U, MO
Tufts U, MA
Union Coll, NE
U at Albany, State U of New York, NY
U at Buffalo, the State U of New York, NY
The U of Akron, OH
The U of Alabama, AL
The U of Alabama in Huntsville, AL
The U of Arizona, AZ
U of Arkansas, AR
U of California, Berkeley, CA
U of California, Irvine, CA
U of California, Los Angeles, CA
U of California, Santa Barbara, CA
U of Central Florida, FL
U of Central Missouri, MO
U of Central Oklahoma, OK
U of Cincinnati, OH
U of Colorado at Boulder, CO
U of Connecticut, CT
U of Dayton, OH
U of Delaware, DE
U of Evansville, IN
U of Guelph, ON, Canada
U of Hartford, CT
U of Hawaii at Manoa, HI
U of Houston, TX
U of Illinois at Urbana–Champaign, IL
U of Kansas, KS
U of Kentucky, KY
U of Manitoba, MB, Canada
U of Maryland, Baltimore County, MD
U of Mary Washington, VA
U of Massachusetts Amherst, MA
U of Massachusetts Boston, MA
U of Massachusetts Lowell, MA
U of Miami, FL
U of Minnesota, Duluth, MN
U of Mississippi, MS
U of Missouri–Columbia, MO
U of Missouri–Kansas City, MO
U of Missouri–Rolla, MO
U of Nebraska at Kearney, NE
U of Nebraska at Omaha, NE
U of Nebraska–Lincoln, NE
U of New Brunswick Fredericton, NB, Canada
U of New Hampshire, NH
U of New Mexico, NM
U of New Orleans, LA
The U of North Carolina at Asheville, NC

The U of North Carolina at Chapel Hill, NC
The U of North Carolina at Charlotte, NC
U of Northern British Columbia, BC, Canada
U of North Florida, FL
U of Notre Dame, IN
U of Oregon, OR
U of Pennsylvania, PA
U of Pittsburgh, PA
U of Portland, OR
U of Redlands, CA
U of Rhode Island, RI
U of St. Thomas, MN
U of San Diego, CA
U of San Francisco, CA
The U of Scranton, PA
The U of Tennessee, TN
The U of Texas at Austin, TX
The U of Texas at El Paso, TX
The U of Texas at San Antonio, TX
U of the District of Columbia, DC
U of the Pacific, CA
U of Toronto, ON, Canada
U of Vermont, VT
U of Virginia, VA
U of Washington, WA
U of West Georgia, GA
U of Wisconsin–Eau Claire, WI
U of Wisconsin–La Crosse, WI
U of Wisconsin–Oshkosh, WI
U of Wisconsin–Stevens Point, WI
U of Wyoming, WY
Utica Coll, NY
Valdosta State U, GA
Vassar Coll, NY
Villanova U, PA
Wake Forest U, NC
Washburn U, KS
Washington & Jefferson Coll, PA
Washington and Lee U, VA
Wayne State U, MI
Wellesley Coll, MA
Wells Coll, NY
West Chester U of Pennsylvania, PA
Western Nebraska Comm Coll, NE
West Los Angeles Coll, CA
Westminster Coll, PA
Westminster Coll, UT
West Texas A&M U, TX
West Virginia Wesleyan Coll, WV
Wheaton Coll, IL
Whitman Coll, WA
Wichita State U, KS
Widener U, PA
Wilfrid Laurier U, ON, Canada
William Jewell Coll, MO
Wofford Coll, SC
Xavier U, OH
Yale U, CT

PHYSICS RELATED

Angelo State U, TX
Bridgewater Coll, VA
Carnegie Mellon U, PA
Embry-Riddle Aeronautical U, FL
Hampden-Sydney Coll, VA
North Carolina State U, NC

Rutgers, The State U of New Jersey, Newark, NJ
State U of New York Coll at Brockport, NY
Syracuse U, NY
U at Buffalo, the State U of New York, NY
The U of Akron, OH
U of Miami, FL
U of Northern Iowa, IA
U of Notre Dame, IN
Wright State U, OH

PHYSICS TEACHER EDUCATION

Alma Coll, MI
Baylor U, TX
Bethel U, MN
Bishop's U, QC, Canada
Buena Vista U, IA
Carroll Coll, WI
Concordia U, NE
Cornell U, NY
Delaware State U, DE
Eastern Michigan U, MI
Florida Inst of Technology, FL
Gustavus Adolphus Coll, MN
Hofstra U, NY
Hope Coll, MI
Illinois Wesleyan U, IL
Indiana U Bloomington, IN
Indiana U–Purdue U Fort Wayne, IN
Ithaca Coll, NY
Lebanon Valley Coll, PA
Le Moyne Coll, NY
Miami Dade Coll, FL
Minnesota State U Moorhead, MN
Missouri State U, MO
Moravian Coll, PA
Murray State U, KY
New York U, NY
North Carolina State U, NC
North Dakota State U, ND
Ohio Wesleyan U, OH
Old Dominion U, VA
Pittsburg State U, KS
St. Bonaventure U, NY
Southern U and A&M Coll, LA
State U of New York Coll at Brockport, NY
State U of New York Coll at Cortland, NY
State U of New York Coll at Potsdam, NY
Syracuse U, NY
Union Coll, NE
The U of Akron, OH
The U of Arizona, AZ
U of Central Missouri, MO
U of Delaware, DE
U of Evansville, IN
U of Missouri–Columbia, MO
U of Nebraska–Lincoln, NE
U of Rio Grande, OH
U of St. Thomas, MN
U of West Georgia, GA
Utica Coll, NY
West Chester U of Pennsylvania, PA
Xavier U, OH

PHYSIOLOGICAL PSYCHOLOGY/ PSYCHOBIOLOGY

Albright Coll, PA
Claremont McKenna Coll, CA
Florida Atlantic U, FL

Hamilton Coll, NY
Lebanon Valley Coll, PA
Lincoln U, PA
Occidental Coll, CA
Ripon Coll, WI
U of California, Los Angeles, CA
U of Evansville, IN
U of Miami, FL
U of New Brunswick Fredericton, NB, Canada
U of New England, ME
Vassar Coll, NY
Westminster Coll, PA
Wilson Coll, PA

PHYSIOLOGY
Michigan State U, MI
Oklahoma State U, OK
Southern Illinois U Carbondale, IL
The U of Arizona, AZ
U of California, Los Angeles, CA
U of California, Santa Barbara, CA
U of Illinois at Urbana–Champaign, IL
U of Oregon, OR

PIANO AND ORGAN
Abilene Christian U, TX
Acadia U, NS, Canada
Ancilla Coll, IN
Ball State U, IN
Barry U, FL
Bethel Coll, IN
Brenau U, GA
California State U, Fullerton, CA
California State U, Sacramento, CA
Calvin Coll, MI
Carnegie Mellon U, PA
Carson-Newman Coll, TN
The Catholic U of America, DC
Cincinnati Christian U, OH
Columbus State U, GA
Concordia U, NE
Dallas Baptist U, TX
DePaul U, IL
Drake U, IA
Fresno City Coll, CA
Furman U, SC
Grace Coll, IN
Hope Coll, MI
Houghton Coll, NY
Huntington U, IN
Illinois Wesleyan U, IL
Indiana U Bloomington, IN
Indiana U–Purdue U Fort Wayne, IN
Ithaca Coll, NY
Lamar U, TX
Lawrence U, WI
Loyola U New Orleans, LA
Mannes Coll The New School for Music, NY
Minnesota State U Mankato, MN
Minnesota State U Moorhead, MN
New York U, NY
North Carolina School of the Arts, NC
Northwestern Coll, MN
Notre Dame de Namur U, CA
The Ohio State U, OH
Otterbein Coll, OH
Prairie View A&M U, TX
Queens U of Charlotte, NC
Roosevelt U, IL

St. Cloud State U, MN
Seton Hill U, PA
Southern Nazarene U, OK
State U of New York at Fredonia, NY
Stetson U, FL
Syracuse U, NY
Taylor U, IN
Temple U, PA
Truman State U, MO
The U of Akron, OH
U of Central Oklahoma, OK
U of Cincinnati, OH
U of Delaware, DE
U of Kansas, KS
U of Miami, FL
U of Michigan, MI
U of Minnesota, Duluth, MN
U of New Hampshire, NH
U of Redlands, CA
The U of Tennessee at Martin, TN
U of the Pacific, CA
U of Washington, WA
West Chester U of Pennsylvania, PA

PIPEFITTING AND SPRINKLER FITTING
British Columbia Inst of Technology, BC, Canada
Ivy Tech Comm Coll–Kokomo, IN
Ivy Tech Comm Coll–Southwest, IN
Ivy Tech Comm Coll–Wabash Valley, IN
Kellogg Comm Coll, MI
St. Cloud Tech Coll, MN
Southern Maine Comm Coll, ME
State U of New York Coll of Technology at Alfred, NY
State U of New York Coll of Technology at Canton, NY

PLANT GENETICS
Cornell U, NY

PLANT NURSERY MANAGEMENT
Comm Coll of Allegheny County, PA
Foothill Coll, CA
Miami Dade Coll, FL

PLANT PATHOLOGY/ PHYTOPATHOLOGY
Cornell U, NY
Dixie State Coll of Utah, UT
Michigan State U, MI
The Ohio State U, OH
State U of New York Coll of Environmental Science and Forestry, NY

PLANT PHYSIOLOGY
State U of New York Coll of Environmental Science and Forestry, NY

PLANT PROTECTION
U of Hawaii at Manoa, HI

PLANT PROTECTION AND INTEGRATED PEST MANAGEMENT
Cornell U, NY
Dixie State Coll of Utah, UT
North Carolina State U, NC
North Dakota State U, ND
State U of New York Coll of Environmental Science and Forestry, NY
Sterling Coll, VT

Texas A&M U, TX
U of Delaware, DE
U of Nebraska–Lincoln, NE
The U of Tennessee, TN
West Texas A&M U, TX

PLANT SCIENCES
Cornell U, NY
Middle Tennessee State U, TN
Montana State U, MT
Nova Scotia Coll, NS, Canada
The Ohio State U, OH
Oklahoma State U, OK
Reedley Coll, CA
Rutgers, The State U of New Jersey, New Brunswick, NJ
Southern Illinois U Carbondale, IL
State U of New York Coll of Environmental Science and Forestry, NY
Sterling Coll, VT
The U of Arizona, AZ
U of California, Los Angeles, CA
U of Massachusetts Amherst, MA
U of Missouri–Columbia, MO
The U of Tennessee, TN
U of Vermont, VT
Ventura Coll, CA

PLANT SCIENCES RELATED
Sterling Coll, VT

PLASTICS ENGINEERING TECHNOLOGY
Ball State U, IN
British Columbia Inst of Technology, BC, Canada
Eastern Michigan U, MI
Kellogg Comm Coll, MI
Macomb Comm Coll, MI
Pittsburg State U, KS

PLAYWRITING AND SCREENWRITING
Bard Coll, NY
DePaul U, IL
Hampshire Coll, MA
Loyola Marymount U, CA
New York U, NY

PLUMBING TECHNOLOGY
Macomb Comm Coll, MI

POLITICAL SCIENCE AND GOVERNMENT
Abilene Christian U, TX
Abraham Baldwin Coll, GA
Acadia U, NS, Canada
Adams State Coll, CO
Adelphi U, NY
Alabama A&M U, AL
Albany State U, AL
Albertson Coll of Idaho, ID
Albion Coll, MI
Albright Coll, PA
Alderson-Broaddus Coll, WV
Alma Coll, MI
Alvernia Coll, PA
American International Coll, MA
American U, DC
Amherst Coll, MA
Anderson U, IN
Angelo State U, TX
Arizona State U at the West campus, AZ
Ashland U, OH

Athabasca U, AB, Canada
Athens State U, AL
Auburn U Montgomery, AL
Augsburg Coll, MN
Aurora U, IL
Austin Coll, TX
Avila U, MO
Bainbridge Coll, GA
Ball State U, IN
Bard Coll, NY
Barry U, FL
Bates Coll, ME
Baylor U, TX
Belmont Abbey Coll, NC
Bemidji State U, MN
Benedictine Coll, KS
Bethel U, MN
Bishop's U, QC, Canada
Boston Coll, MA
Bradley U, IL
Brandeis U, MA
Brandon U, MB, Canada
Brenau U, GA
Brewton-Parker Coll, GA
Briar Cliff U, IA
Bridgewater Coll, VA
Brock U, ON, Canada
Brown U, RI
Bryn Mawr Coll, PA
Buena Vista U, IA
Buffalo State Coll, State U of New York, NY
Burlington County Coll, NJ
California State U, Fullerton, CA
California State U, Northridge, CA
California State U, Sacramento, CA
California State U, San Bernardino, CA
California State U, Stanislaus, CA
Calvin Coll, MI
Cameron U, OK
Cape Breton U, NS, Canada
Cardinal Stritch U, WI
Carleton U, ON, Canada
Carlow U, PA
Carnegie Mellon U, PA
Carroll Coll, MT
Carroll Coll, WI
Carson-Newman Coll, TN
Carthage Coll, WI
The Catholic U of America, DC
Cedar Crest Coll, PA
Charleston Southern U, SC
Christopher Newport U, VA
Claremont McKenna Coll, CA
Clark U, MA
Clayton State U, GA
Clemson U, SC
Coastal Carolina U, SC
Coe Coll, IA
Colby Coll, ME
Colgate U, NY
Coll of Charleston, SC
Coll of St. Joseph, VT
The Coll of Saint Rose, NY
Coll of Staten Island of the City U of New York, NY
Coll of the Canyons, CA
Coll of the Desert, CA
The Coll of William and Mary, VA
Columbus State U, GA
Concordia U Coll of Alberta, AB, Canada
Concord U, WV
Cornell U, NY
Cornerstone U, MI
Crafton Hills Coll, CA

Daemen Coll, NY
Dalhousie U, NS, Canada
Dallas Baptist U, TX
Delaware State U, DE
DePaul U, IL
Dixie State Coll of Utah, UT
Dominican U, IL
Drake U, IA
Drury U, MO
Duke U, NC
Earlham Coll, IN
East Carolina U, NC
East Central Coll, MO
Eastern Connecticut State U, CT
Eastern Michigan U, MI
East Stroudsburg U of Pennsylvania, PA
Eckerd Coll, FL
Edinboro U of Pennsylvania, PA
El Camino Coll, CA
Elmira Coll, NY
Elon U, NC
Emory U, GA
Eugene Lang Coll The New School for Liberal Arts, NY
Fairfield U, CT
Fairleigh Dickinson U, Coll at Florham, NJ
Fairleigh Dickinson U, Metropolitan Campus, NJ
Fayetteville State U, NC
Ferrum Coll, VA
Fitchburg State Coll, MA
Flagler Coll, FL
Florida Atlantic U, FL
Florida Gulf Coast U, FL
Florida International U, FL
Foothill Coll, CA
Fort Hays State U, KS
Framingham State Coll, MA
Franciscan U of Steubenville, OH
Franklin Coll, IN
Franklin Pierce U, NH
Frederick Comm Coll, MD
Fresno Pacific U, CA
Furman U, SC
Gainesville State Coll, GA
Gannon U, PA
Gardner-Webb U, NC
Geneva Coll, PA
Georgetown Coll, KY
The George Washington U, DC
Georgia Coll & State U, GA
Gloucester County Coll, NJ
Gonzaga U, WA
Gordon Coll, MA
Grambling State U, LA
Grinnell Coll, IA
Grossmont Coll, CA
Gustavus Adolphus Coll, MN
Hamilton Coll, NY
Hamline U, MN
Hampden-Sydney Coll, VA
Hampshire Coll, MA
Harding U, AR
Hartwick Coll, NY
Haverford Coll, PA
Henderson State U, AR
High Point U, NC
Hofstra U, NY
Hope Coll, MI
Houghton Coll, NY
Houston Baptist U, TX
Hunter Coll of the City U of New York, NY
Huntington U, IN
Idaho State U, ID
Illinois State U, IL
Illinois Wesleyan U, IL

Indiana U Bloomington, IN
Indiana U of Pennsylvania, PA
Indiana U–Purdue U Fort Wayne, IN
Indiana U–Purdue U Indianapolis, IN
Indiana U Southeast, IN
Iona Coll, NY
Ithaca Coll, NY
Jacksonville U, FL
Johnson State Coll, VT
Kansas State U, KS
Kellogg Comm Coll, MI
Kennesaw State U, GA
Kentucky Wesleyan Coll, KY
Kenyon Coll, OH
King's Coll, PA
Kutztown U of Pennsylvania, PA
LaGrange Coll, GA
Lake Superior State U, MI
Lamar U, TX
Lawrence U, WI
Lebanon Valley Coll, PA
Lee Coll, TX
Lehigh U, PA
Le Moyne Coll, NY
Lewis U, IL
Liberty U, VA
Lincoln U, PA
Lindenwood U, MO
Long Island U, Brooklyn Campus, NY
Loras Coll, IA
Loyola Marymount U, CA
Loyola U Chicago, IL
Loyola U New Orleans, LA
Lynchburg Coll, VA
Macalester Coll, MN
MacMurray Coll, IL
Manhattan Coll, NY
Manhattanville Coll, NY
Marietta Coll, OH
Marist Coll, NY
Marquette U, WI
Marshall U, WV
Marymount Manhattan Coll, NY
Marymount U, VA
McDaniel Coll, MD
McNeese State U, LA
Mercer U, GA
Mercyhurst Coll, PA
Miami Dade Coll, FL
Michigan State U, MI
Middlesex County Coll, NJ
Middle Tennessee State U, TN
Midland Coll, TX
Millersville U of Pennsylvania, PA
Minnesota State U Mankato, MN
Minnesota State U Moorhead, MN
MiraCosta Coll, CA
Missouri State U, MO
Molloy Coll, NY
Monmouth Coll, IL
Monmouth U, NJ
Montana State U, MT
Moravian Coll, PA
Morningside Coll, IA
Mount Holyoke Coll, MA
Mount St. Mary's U, MD
Mount Saint Vincent U, NS, Canada
Mount Union Coll, OH
Murray State U, KY
Neumann Coll, PA
New Jersey City U, NJ
New York U, NY
Niagara U, NY

North Carolina State U, NC
North Central Coll, IL
North Dakota State U, ND
Northeastern U, MA
Northern Illinois U, IL
Northern Michigan U, MI
Northern State U, SD
North Georgia Coll & State U, GA
Northwestern Oklahoma State U, OK
Northwest Nazarene U, ID
Notre Dame Coll, OH
Notre Dame de Namur U, CA
Oakland U, MI
Occidental Coll, CA
Odessa Coll, TX
Oglethorpe U, GA
The Ohio State U, OH
Ohio Wesleyan U, OH
Oklahoma State U, OK
Old Dominion U, VA
Oral Roberts U, OK
Otterbein Coll, OH
Our Lady of the Lake U of San Antonio, TX
Park U, MO
Penn State Abington, PA
Penn State DuBois, PA
Penn State Fayette, The Eberly Campus, PA
Penn State Mont Alto, PA
Penn State Wilkes-Barre, PA
Piedmont Coll, GA
Pima Comm Coll, AZ
Pine Manor Coll, MA
Pittsburg State U, KS
Point Loma Nazarene U, CA
Portland State U, OR
Prairie View A&M U, TX
Presbyterian Coll, SC
Queens Coll of the City U of New York, NY
Queen's U at Kingston, ON, Canada
Queens U of Charlotte, NC
Quincy Coll, MA
Radford U, VA
Ramapo Coll of New Jersey, NJ
Randolph Coll, VA
Randolph-Macon Coll, VA
Redeemer U Coll, ON, Canada
Rhodes Coll, TN
Rice U, TX
The Richard Stockton Coll of New Jersey, NJ
Ripon Coll, WI
Rivier Coll, NH
Rockford Coll, IL
Rockhurst U, MO
Rocky Mountain Coll, MT
Roosevelt U, IL
Rose State Coll, OK
Rowan U, NJ
Rutgers, The State U of New Jersey, Newark, NJ
Rutgers, The State U of New Jersey, New Brunswick, NJ
Saginaw Valley State U, MI
St. Bonaventure U, NY
St. Cloud State U, MN
St. Francis Xavier U, NS, Canada
St. Gregory's U, OK
Saint John's U, MN
Saint Joseph's Coll, IN
St. Lawrence U, NY
Saint Leo U, FL
St. Mary's Coll of Maryland, MD
St. Norbert Coll, WI

St. Philip's Coll, TX
St. Thomas U, NB, Canada
Saint Xavier U, IL
Salem Comm Coll, NJ
Salve Regina U, RI
San Diego State U, CA
San Francisco State U, CA
Santa Ana Coll, CA
Santa Barbara City Coll, CA
Santa Clara U, CA
Santa Rosa Jr Coll, CA
Sauk Valley Comm Coll, IL
Seattle Pacific U, WA
Seton Hall U, NJ
Seton Hill U, PA
Sewanee: The U of the South, TN
Shippensburg U of Pennsylvania, PA
Skagit Valley Coll, WA
Slippery Rock U of Pennsylvania, PA
Southern Illinois U Carbondale, IL
Southern Illinois U Edwardsville, IL
Southern Nazarene U, OK
Southern Oregon U, OR
Southern U and A&M Coll, LA
Southern Utah U, UT
Southwest Baptist U, MO
Southwestern U, TX
Spoon River Coll, IL
State U of New York at Fredonia, NY
State U of New York Coll at Brockport, NY
State U of New York Coll at Cortland, NY
State U of New York Coll at Geneseo, NY
State U of New York Coll at Potsdam, NY
Stephen F. Austin State U, TX
Stetson U, FL
Stonehill Coll, MA
Sweet Briar Coll, VA
Syracuse U, NY
Taylor U, IN
Temple U, PA
Texas A&M U, TX
Texas A&M U–Corpus Christi, TX
Thiel Coll, PA
Towson U, MD
Trent U, ON, Canada
Trinity Coll, CT
Trinity U, TX
Troy U, AL
Truman State U, MO
Tufts U, MA
U at Albany, State U of New York, NY
U at Buffalo, the State U of New York, NY
The U of Akron, OH
The U of Alabama, AL
The U of Alabama in Huntsville, AL
U of Alaska Anchorage, AK
The U of Arizona, AZ
U of Arkansas, AR
U of Baltimore, MD
U of California, Berkeley, CA
U of California, Irvine, CA
U of California, Los Angeles, CA
U of California, Santa Barbara, CA
U of Central Florida, FL
U of Central Missouri, MO

U of Central Oklahoma, OK
U of Cincinnati, OH
U of Colorado at Boulder, CO
U of Connecticut, CT
U of Dayton, OH
U of Delaware, DE
U of Evansville, IN
The U of Findlay, OH
U of Great Falls, MT
U of Guelph, ON, Canada
U of Hartford, CT
U of Hawaii at Manoa, HI
U of Hawaii–West Oahu, HI
U of Houston, TX
U of Illinois at Urbana–Champaign, IL
U of Kansas, KS
U of Kentucky, KY
U of Manitoba, MB, Canada
U of Mary Hardin-Baylor, TX
U of Maryland, Baltimore County, MD
U of Mary Washington, VA
U of Massachusetts Amherst, MA
U of Massachusetts Boston, MA
U of Massachusetts Lowell, MA
U of Miami, FL
U of Michigan, MI
U of Minnesota, Duluth, MN
U of Mississippi, MS
U of Missouri–Columbia, MO
U of Missouri–Kansas City, MO
U of Nebraska at Kearney, NE
U of Nebraska at Omaha, NE
U of Nebraska–Lincoln, NE
U of New Brunswick Fredericton, NB, Canada
U of New England, ME
U of New Hampshire, NH
U of New Haven, CT
U of New Mexico, NM
U of New Orleans, LA
The U of North Carolina at Asheville, NC
The U of North Carolina at Chapel Hill, NC
The U of North Carolina at Charlotte, NC
U of Northern British Columbia, BC, Canada
U of Northern Iowa, IA
U of North Florida, FL
U of Notre Dame, IN
U of Oregon, OR
U of Pennsylvania, PA
U of Pittsburgh, PA
U of Pittsburgh at Bradford, PA
U of Pittsburgh at Johnstown, PA
U of Portland, OR
U of Redlands, CA
U of Rhode Island, RI
U of Rio Grande, OH
U of St. Thomas, MN
U of St. Thomas, TX
U of San Diego, CA
U of San Francisco, CA
The U of Scranton, PA
U of South Carolina Upstate, SC
U of Southern Indiana, IN
The U of Tampa, FL
The U of Tennessee, TN
The U of Tennessee at Martin, TN

The U of Texas at Austin, TX
The U of Texas at El Paso, TX
The U of Texas at San Antonio, TX
U of the District of Columbia, DC
U of the Incarnate Word, TX
U of the Ozarks, AR
U of the Pacific, CA
U of Toronto, ON, Canada
U of Vermont, VT
U of Virginia, VA
The U of Virginia's Coll at Wise, VA
U of Washington, WA
U of West Georgia, GA
U of Wisconsin–Eau Claire, WI
U of Wisconsin–Green Bay, WI
U of Wisconsin–La Crosse, WI
U of Wisconsin–Madison, WI
U of Wisconsin–Oshkosh, WI
U of Wisconsin–Platteville, WI
U of Wisconsin–Stevens Point, WI
U of Wyoming, WY
Utica Coll, NY
Valdosta State U, GA
Vanguard U of Southern California, CA
Vassar Coll, NY
Villanova U, PA
Virginia Intermont Coll, VA
Wake Forest U, NC
Washburn U, KS
Washington & Jefferson Coll, PA
Washington and Lee U, VA
Wayne State Coll, NE
Wayne State U, MI
Wellesley Coll, MA
Wells Coll, NY
Wesley Coll, DE
West Chester U of Pennsylvania, PA
Western Connecticut State U, CT
Western Nebraska Comm Coll, NE
Western New England Coll, MA
Western Oregon U, OR
West Liberty State Coll, WV
West Los Angeles Coll, CA
Westminster Coll, PA
Westminster Coll, UT
West Texas A&M U, TX
West Virginia State U, WV
West Virginia Wesleyan Coll, WV
Wheaton Coll, IL
Whitman Coll, WA
Wichita State U, KS
Widener U, PA
Wilfrid Laurier U, ON, Canada
Wilkes U, PA
William Jewell Coll, MO
Wofford Coll, SC
Wright State U, OH
Xavier U, OH
Yale U, CT

POLITICAL SCIENCE AND GOVERNMENT RELATED
Buena Vista U, IA

Colleges for Students with Learning Disabilities or AD/HD

Columbus State U, GA
Concordia Coll–New York, NY
Concordia U, NE
Cornell U, NY
Cornerstone U, MI
Dalhousie U, NS, Canada
DePaul U, IL
Dixie State Coll of Utah, UT
Dominican U, IL
Drake U, IA
Drury U, MO
Earlham Coll, IN
Eastern Nazarene Coll, MA
Elmira Coll, NY
Elms Coll, MA
Elon U, NC
Fontbonne U, MO
Fort Hays State U, KS
Franklin Pierce U, NH
Fresno Pacific U, CA
Furman U, SC
Gannon U, PA
Gardner-Webb U, NC
The George Washington U, DC
Goshen Coll, IN
Graceland U, IA
Grambling State U, LA
Gustavus Adolphus Coll, MN
Hamline U, MN
Hartwick Coll, NY
Haverford Coll, PA
High Point U, NC
Houghton Coll, NY
Houston Baptist U, TX
Huntington U, IN
Immaculata U, PA
Indiana U Bloomington, IN
Indiana U–Purdue U Indianapolis, IN
Ithaca Coll, NY
Jacksonville U, FL
Kellogg Comm Coll, MI
Kentucky Wesleyan Coll, KY
Kenyon Coll, OH
Keuka Coll, NY
King's Coll, PA
LaGrange Coll, GA
Lake Erie Coll, OH
Lake Superior State U, MI
Langston U, OK
Lawrence U, WI
Lebanon Valley Coll, PA
Le Moyne Coll, NY
LeTourneau U, TX
Lewis U, IL
Lindenwood U, MO
Lynchburg Coll, VA
MacMurray Coll, IL
Marian Coll, IN
Marquette U, WI
Marywood U, PA
Massachusetts Coll of Liberal Arts, MA
Mercyhurst Coll, PA
Michigan State U, MI
Midland Lutheran Coll, NE
Minnesota State U Mankato, MN
Minnesota State U Moorhead, MN
Molloy Coll, NY
Montana State U–Billings, MT
Morningside Coll, IA
Mount Vernon Nazarene U, OH
Niagara U, NY
North Central Coll, IL
Northern Michigan U, MI
Northern State U, SD

Northwestern Oklahoma State U, OK
Northwest Nazarene U, ID
Notre Dame Coll, OH
Notre Dame de Namur U, CA
Nova Southeastern U, FL
Oglethorpe U, GA
Ohio Wesleyan U, OH
Oral Roberts U, OK
Otterbein Coll, OH
Queens U of Charlotte, NC
Redeemer U Coll, ON, Canada
Rensselaer Polytechnic Inst, NY
Ripon Coll, WI
Rivier Coll, NH
Rochester Inst of Technology, NY
Rockford Coll, IL
Roosevelt U, IL
Rutgers, The State U of New Jersey, New Brunswick, NJ
St. Bonaventure U, NY
St. Cloud State U, MN
St. Francis Xavier U, NS, Canada
St. Gregory's U, OK
Saint John's U, MN
St. Philip's Coll, TX
Seattle Pacific U, WA
Seton Hill U, PA
Southern Nazarene U, OK
Southern Oregon U, OR
Springfield Coll, MA
Springfield Coll in Illinois, IL
State U of New York at Fredonia, NY
State U of New York Coll at Brockport, NY
State U of New York Coll at Cortland, NY
State U of New York Coll at Geneseo, NY
State U of New York Coll of Environmental Science and Forestry, NY
Stetson U, FL
Syracuse U, NY
Taylor U, IN
Tennessee Wesleyan Coll, TN
Texas A&M U–Corpus Christi, TX
Thiel Coll, PA
Trinity U, TX
Truman State U, MO
The U of Akron, OH
U of California, Santa Barbara, CA
U of Cincinnati, OH
U of Dayton, OH
The U of Findlay, OH
U of Houston, TX
U of Illinois at Urbana–Champaign, IL
U of Manitoba, MB, Canada
U of Maryland, Baltimore County, MD
U of Mary Washington, VA
U of Minnesota, Duluth, MN
U of Missouri–Rolla, MO
U of New Brunswick Fredericton, NB, Canada
U of Pittsburgh at Johnstown, PA
U of Portland, OR
U of Rio Grande, OH
U of St. Thomas, TX
The U of Tampa, FL
U of the Incarnate Word, TX
U of West Georgia, GA

U of Wisconsin–Oshkosh, WI
Urbana U, OH
Utica Coll, NY
Vanguard U of Southern California, CA
Virginia Intermont Coll, VA
Washburn U, KS
Wells Coll, NY
Western Nebraska Comm Coll, NE
West Liberty State Coll, WV
Westminster Coll, PA
West Texas A&M U, TX
West Virginia Wesleyan Coll, WV
William Jewell Coll, MO
Wofford Coll, SC
Wright State U, OH

PRE-MEDICAL STUDIES

Abilene Christian U, TX
Acadia U, NS, Canada
Adams State Coll, CO
Albertson Coll of Idaho, ID
Albion Coll, MI
Alderson-Broaddus Coll, WV
Alma Coll, MI
Alvernia Coll, PA
American International Coll, MA
Anderson U, IN
Ashland U, OH
Augsburg Coll, MN
Ball State U, IN
Bard Coll, NY
Barry U, FL
Baylor U, TX
Belmont Abbey Coll, NC
Bemidji State U, MN
Bethel Coll, IN
Boston Coll, MA
Brandon U, MB, Canada
Buffalo State Coll, State U of New York, NY
Calhoun Comm Coll, AL
Calvin Coll, MI
Cape Breton U, NS, Canada
Cardinal Stritch U, WI
Carroll Coll, MT
Carroll Coll, WI
Carthage Coll, WI
Cedar Crest Coll, PA
Charleston Southern U, SC
Claremont McKenna Coll, CA
Clark U, MA
Coe Coll, IA
Coll of Charleston, SC
Coll of Mount Saint Vincent, NY
Coll of Saint Mary, NE
Columbus State U, GA
Concordia U, NE
Concord U, WV
Cornerstone U, MI
Dalhousie U, NS, Canada
Dominican U, IL
Drake U, IA
Drury U, MO
Earlham Coll, IN
Eastern Mennonite U, VA
Eastern Nazarene Coll, MA
Elmira Coll, NY
Elms Coll, MA
Elon U, NC
Florida Inst of Technology, FL
Fontbonne U, MO
Franklin Pierce U, NH
Fresno Pacific U, CA
Furman U, SC
Gainesville State Coll, GA
Gannon U, PA

Gardner-Webb U, NC
The George Washington U, DC
Goshen Coll, IN
Graceland U, IA
Gustavus Adolphus Coll, MN
Hamline U, MN
Harding U, AR
Hartwick Coll, NY
Haverford Coll, PA
High Point U, NC
Hofstra U, NY
Houghton Coll, NY
Howard Comm Coll, MD
Huntington U, IN
Indiana U Bloomington, IN
Indiana U–Purdue U Fort Wayne, IN
Indiana U–Purdue U Indianapolis, IN
Ithaca Coll, NY
Jacksonville U, FL
Johnson State Coll, VT
Kansas State U, KS
Kellogg Comm Coll, MI
Kentucky Wesleyan Coll, KY
Kenyon Coll, OH
Keuka Coll, NY
King's Coll, PA
LaGrange Coll, GA
Lake Erie Coll, OH
Langston U, OK
Lawrence U, WI
Lebanon Valley Coll, PA
Lehigh U, PA
Le Moyne Coll, NY
LeTourneau U, TX
Lewis U, IL
Lindenwood U, MO
Lynchburg Coll, VA
MacMurray Coll, IL
Manhattanville Coll, NY
Marian Coll, IN
Marquette U, WI
Mercer U, GA
Mercyhurst Coll, PA
Michigan State U, MI
Midland Lutheran Coll, NE
Minnesota State U Mankato, MN
Minnesota State U Moorhead, MN
Molloy Coll, NY
Montana State U–Billings, MT
Morningside Coll, IA
Mount Vernon Nazarene U, OH
New York U, NY
Niagara U, NY
North Central Coll, IL
Northern Michigan U, MI
Northern State U, SD
North Georgia Coll & State U, GA
Northwestern Oklahoma State U, OK
Northwest Nazarene U, ID
Notre Dame Coll, OH
Notre Dame de Namur U, CA
Nova Southeastern U, FL
Oglethorpe U, GA
Ohio Wesleyan U, OH
Oral Roberts U, OK
Oregon Inst of Technology, OR
Otterbein Coll, OH
Paul Quinn Coll, TX
Penn State Abington, PA
Penn State DuBois, PA
Penn State Fayette, The Eberly Campus, PA

Penn State Mont Alto, PA
Penn State Wilkes-Barre, PA
Queens U of Charlotte, NC
Redeemer U Coll, ON, Canada
Rensselaer Polytechnic Inst, NY
Ripon Coll, WI
Rivier Coll, NH
Rochester Inst of Technology, NY
Rockford Coll, IL
Roosevelt U, IL
Rutgers, The State U of New Jersey, New Brunswick, NJ
St. Bonaventure U, NY
St. Cloud State U, MN
St. Francis Xavier U, NS, Canada
St. Gregory's U, OK
Saint John's U, MN
St. Philip's Coll, TX
St. Thomas Aquinas Coll, NY
Sauk Valley Comm Coll, IL
Seattle Pacific U, WA
Seton Hill U, PA
Southern Nazarene U, OK
Southern Oregon U, OR
Springfield Coll, MA
Springfield Coll in Illinois, IL
State U of New York at Fredonia, NY
State U of New York Coll at Brockport, NY
State U of New York Coll at Cortland, NY
State U of New York Coll at Geneseo, NY
State U of New York Coll of Environmental Science and Forestry, NY
Stetson U, FL
Syracuse U, NY
Taylor U, IN
Tennessee Wesleyan Coll, TN
Texas A&M U–Corpus Christi, TX
Thiel Coll, PA
Trinity U, TX
Troy U, AL
Truman State U, MO
U of Central Missouri, MO
U of Cincinnati, OH
U of Dayton, OH
U of Evansville, IN
The U of Findlay, OH
U of Hartford, CT
U of Houston, TX
U of Maine at Machias, ME
U of Manitoba, MB, Canada
U of Maryland, Baltimore County, MD
U of Mary Washington, VA
U of Massachusetts Amherst, MA
U of Minnesota, Duluth, MN
U of Missouri–Rolla, MO
U of Nebraska–Lincoln, NE
U of New Brunswick Fredericton, NB, Canada
U of New England, ME
U of New Hampshire, NH
U of Notre Dame, IN
U of Oregon, OR
U of Pittsburgh at Johnstown, PA
U of Portland, OR
U of Rio Grande, OH
U of St. Thomas, TX
U of San Diego, CA
U of San Francisco, CA
The U of Tampa, FL

The U of Tennessee at
Martin, TN
U of the Incarnate Word, TX
U of the Ozarks, AR
U of West Georgia, GA
U of Wisconsin–Oshkosh,
WI
Upper Iowa U, IA
Urbana U, OH
Utica Coll, NY
Virginia Intermont Coll, VA
Washburn U, KS
Wayne State Coll, NE
Wells Coll, NY
West Chester U of
Pennsylvania, PA
Western Connecticut State
U, CT
Western Nebraska Comm
Coll, NE
West Liberty State Coll, WV
Westminster Coll, PA
West Virginia State U, WV
West Virginia Wesleyan Coll,
WV
Widener U, PA
William Jewell Coll, MO
Wofford Coll, SC
Wright State U, OH

PRE-NURSING STUDIES
Adams State Coll, CO
Baylor U, TX
Concordia U, NE
Gainesville State Coll, GA
Lindenwood U, MO
Marywood U, PA
Montana State U–Billings,
MT
St. Gregory's U, OK
St. Philip's Coll, TX
Springfield Coll in Illinois, IL

PRE-PHARMACY STUDIES
Abilene Christian U, TX
Adams State Coll, CO
Ashland U, OH
Barry U, FL
Belmont Abbey Coll, NC
Calhoun Comm Coll, AL
Carroll Coll, MT
Carroll Coll, WI
Charleston Southern U, SC
Columbus State U, GA
Concordia U, NE
Dalhousie U, NS, Canada
Drury U, MO
Gainesville State Coll, GA
Gardner-Webb U, NC
Howard Comm Coll, MD
Kellogg Comm Coll, MI
King's Coll, PA
Le Moyne Coll, NY
Montana State U–Billings,
MT
Mount Vernon Nazarene U,
OH
Roosevelt U, IL
Rose State Coll, OK
St. Cloud State U, MN
St. Gregory's U, OK
Saint John's U, MN
St. Philip's Coll, TX
Santa Rosa Jr Coll, CA
Sauk Valley Comm Coll, IL
Southern Nazarene U, OK
Springfield Coll in Illinois, IL
Tennessee Wesleyan Coll,
TN
Truman State U, MO
U of Central Missouri, MO
U of Connecticut, CT
U of Evansville, IN

U of Miami, FL
U of Minnesota, Duluth, MN
U of Nebraska–Lincoln, NE
U of St. Thomas, TX
The U of Tennessee at
Martin, TN
U of the Incarnate Word, TX
Washburn U, KS
Western Nebraska Comm
Coll, NE
West Virginia Wesleyan Coll,
WV
Wright State U, OH

PRE-THEOLOGY/ PRE-MINISTERIAL STUDIES
Alma Coll, MI
Ashland U, OH
Concordia U, NE
Concordia U Coll of Alberta,
AB, Canada
Cornerstone U, MI
Geneva Coll, PA
Kellogg Comm Coll, MI
Kuyper Coll, MI
Loras Coll, IA
Loyola U Chicago, IL
Minnesota State U Mankato,
MN
Northwestern Coll, MN
Ohio Wesleyan U, OH
Point Loma Nazarene U, CA
Redeemer U Coll, ON,
Canada
St. Gregory's U, OK
Saint John's U, MN
Tennessee Wesleyan Coll,
TN
U of Rio Grande, OH
Washburn U, KS

PRE-VETERINARY STUDIES
Abilene Christian U, TX
Acadia U, NS, Canada
Adams State Coll, CO
Albion Coll, MI
Alderson-Broaddus Coll, WV
Alma Coll, MI
American International Coll,
MA
Anderson U, IN
Ashland U, OH
Augsburg Coll, MN
Bard Coll, NY
Barry U, FL
Belmont Abbey Coll, NC
Bemidji State U, MN
Brandon U, MB, Canada
Buffalo State Coll, State U of
New York, NY
Calhoun Comm Coll, AL
Calvin Coll, MI
Cape Breton U, NS, Canada
Cardinal Stritch U, WI
Carroll Coll, MT
Carroll Coll, WI
Carthage Coll, WI
Cedar Crest Coll, PA
Clark U, MA
Coe Coll, IA
Coll of Saint Mary, NE
Coll of the Atlantic, ME
Columbus State U, GA
Concordia U, NE
Concord U, WV
Cornerstone U, MI
Dalhousie U, NS, Canada
Delaware State U, DE
Dominican U, IL
Drake U, IA
Drury U, MO
Eastern Mennonite U, VA

Elmira Coll, NY
Elms Coll, MA
Elon U, NC
Franklin Pierce U, NH
Furman U, SC
Gannon U, PA
Gardner-Webb U, NC
Goshen Coll, IN
Gustavus Adolphus Coll,
MN
Hamline U, MN
Harding U, AR
Hartwick Coll, NY
Haverford Coll, PA
High Point U, NC
Hofstra U, NY
Houghton Coll, NY
Howard Comm Coll, MD
Huntington U, IN
Immaculata U, PA
Indiana U–Purdue U
Indianapolis, IN
Jacksonville U, FL
Kansas State U, KS
Kellogg Comm Coll, MI
Kentucky Wesleyan Coll, KY
Kenyon Coll, OH
Keuka Coll, NY
King's Coll, PA
LaGrange Coll, GA
Lake Erie Coll, OH
Langston U, OK
Lawrence U, WI
Lebanon Valley Coll, PA
Le Moyne Coll, NY
LeTourneau U, TX
Lewis U, IL
Lindenwood U, MO
Lynchburg Coll, VA
MacMurray Coll, IL
Marian Coll, IN
Mercyhurst Coll, PA
Michigan State U, MI
Midland Lutheran Coll, NE
Minnesota State U Mankato,
MN
Minnesota State U
Moorhead, MN
Molloy Coll, NY
Morningside Coll, IA
Mount Vernon Nazarene U,
OH
Niagara U, NY
North Central Coll, IL
Northern Michigan U, MI
North Georgia Coll & State
U, GA
Nova Scotia Coll, NS,
Canada
Oglethorpe U, GA
Ohio Wesleyan U, OH
Oklahoma State U, OK
Otterbein Coll, OH
Queens U of Charlotte, NC
Redeemer U Coll, ON,
Canada
Ripon Coll, WI
Rivier Coll, NH
Rochester Inst of
Technology, NY
Rockford Coll, IL
St. Bonaventure U, NY
St. Cloud State U, MN
St. Francis Xavier U, NS,
Canada
Saint John's U, MN
Sauk Valley Comm Coll, IL
Seton Hill U, PA
Springfield Coll in Illinois, IL
State U of New York at
Fredonia, NY
State U of New York Coll at
Brockport, NY

State U of New York Coll at
Geneseo, NY
State U of New York Coll of
Environmental Science
and Forestry, NY
Stetson U, FL
Syracuse U, NY
Taylor U, IN
Tennessee Wesleyan Coll,
TN
Texas A&M U, TX
Texas A&M U–Corpus
Christi, TX
Thiel Coll, PA
Trinity U, TX
Troy U, AL
Truman State U, MO
The U of Arizona, AZ
U of Central Missouri, MO
U of Cincinnati, OH
U of Delaware, DE
U of Evansville, IN
The U of Findlay, OH
U of Hartford, CT
U of Houston, TX
U of Illinois at Urbana–
Champaign, IL
U of Manitoba, MB, Canada
U of Maryland, Baltimore
County, MD
U of Mary Washington, VA
U of Massachusetts Amherst,
MA
U of Minnesota, Duluth, MN
U of Nebraska–Lincoln, NE
U of New Brunswick
Fredericton, NB, Canada
U of New Hampshire, NH
U of Pittsburgh at
Johnstown, PA
U of Rio Grande, OH
U of St. Thomas, TX
U of San Francisco, CA
The U of Tampa, FL
The U of Tennessee at
Martin, TN
U of the Ozarks, AR
U of West Georgia, GA
U of Wisconsin–Oshkosh,
WI
Upper Iowa U, IA
Urbana U, OH
Utica Coll, NY
Virginia Intermont Coll, VA
Washburn U, KS
Wayne State Coll, NE
Wells Coll, NY
Western Nebraska Comm
Coll, NE
Westminster Coll, PA
West Virginia State U, WV
West Virginia Wesleyan Coll,
WV
Widener U, PA
William Jewell Coll, MO
Wofford Coll, SC
Wright State U, OH

PRINTING MANAGEMENT
Carroll Coll, WI
U of Central Missouri, MO
U of Wisconsin–Stout, WI

PRINTMAKING
Academy of Art U, CA
Ball State U, IN
Buffalo State Coll, State U of
New York, NY
California State U, Fullerton,
CA
The Cleveland Inst of Art,
OH
Dixie State Coll of Utah, UT

Drake U, IA
Florida Comm Coll at
Jacksonville, FL
Framingham State Coll, MA
Indiana U–Purdue U Fort
Wayne, IN
Maine Coll of Art, ME
McNeese State U, LA
Minneapolis Coll of Art and
Design, MN
Minnesota State U
Moorhead, MN
NSCAD U, NS, Canada
The Ohio State U, OH
Pratt Inst, NY
Rutgers, The State U of New
Jersey, New Brunswick, NJ
St. Cloud State U, MN
School of the Art Inst of
Chicago, IL
Seton Hill U, PA
Syracuse U, NY
Temple U, PA
The U of Akron, OH
U of Houston, TX
U of Kansas, KS
U of Miami, FL
U of Michigan, MI
U of Oregon, OR
U of San Francisco, CA
The U of Texas at El Paso,
TX
The U of the Arts, PA
U of Washington, WA

PROFESSIONAL STUDIES
Bemidji State U, MN
Briar Cliff U, IA
U of Dubuque, IA
The U of Tennessee at
Martin, TN

PSYCHIATRIC/MENTAL HEALTH NURSING
Brandon U, MB, Canada
U at Buffalo, the State U of
New York, NY

PSYCHIATRIC/MENTAL HEALTH SERVICES TECHNOLOGY
Allegany Coll of Maryland,
MD
Comm Coll of Allegheny
County, PA
Eastfield Coll, TX
Franciscan U of
Steubenville, OH
Hagerstown Comm Coll, MD
Houston Comm Coll System,
TX
Ivy Tech Comm Coll–
Kokomo, IN
Ivy Tech Comm Coll–
Southwest, IN
Ivy Tech Comm Coll–
Wabash Valley, IN
Kingsborough Comm Coll of
the City U of New York,
NY
Lake Superior State U, MI
Pueblo Comm Coll, CO
South Piedmont Comm Coll,
NC

PSYCHOLOGY
Abilene Christian U, TX
Abraham Baldwin Coll, GA
Acadia U, NS, Canada
Adams State Coll, CO
Adelphi U, NY
Alabama A&M U, AL
Albany State U, GA
Albertson Coll of Idaho, ID

Albion Coll, MI
Albright Coll, PA
Alderson-Broaddus Coll, WV
Alma Coll, MI
Alvernia Coll, PA
American International Coll, MA
American U, DC
Amherst Coll, MA
Anderson U, IN
Anderson U, SC
Angelo State U, TX
Argosy U, Twin Cities, Eagan, MN
Arizona State U at the West campus, AZ
Asbury Coll, KY
Ashland U, OH
Athabasca U, AB, Canada
Athens State U, AL
Auburn U Montgomery, AL
Augsburg Coll, MN
Aurora U, IL
Austin Coll, TX
Avila U, MO
Bainbridge Coll, GA
Ball State U, IN
Bard Coll, NY
Barry U, FL
Bates Coll, ME
Baylor U, TX
Belmont Abbey Coll, NC
Bemidji State U, MN
Benedictine Coll, KS
Bethany U, CA
Bethel Coll, IN
Bethel U, MN
Bishop's U, QC, Canada
Blinn Coll, TX
Bluefield State Coll, WV
Boston Coll, MA
Bradley U, IL
Brandeis U, MA
Brandon U, MB, Canada
Brenau U, GA
Brevard Coll, NC
Brewton-Parker Coll, GA
Briar Cliff U, IA
Bridgewater Coll, VA
Brock U, ON, Canada
Brown U, RI
Bryn Mawr Coll, PA
Bucks County Comm Coll, PA
Buena Vista U, IA
Buffalo State Coll, State U of New York, NY
Bunker Hill Comm Coll, MA
Burlington County Coll, NJ
California State U, Fullerton, CA
California State U, Northridge, CA
California State U, Sacramento, CA
California State U, San Bernardino, CA
California State U, Stanislaus, CA
Calvin Coll, MI
Cameron U, OK
Cape Breton U, NS, Canada
Cape Cod Comm Coll, MA
Cardinal Stritch U, WI
Carleton U, ON, Canada
Carlow U, PA
Carnegie Mellon U, PA
Carroll Coll, MT
Carroll Coll, WI
Carson-Newman Coll, TN
Carthage Coll, WI
The Catholic U of America, DC
Cedar Crest Coll, PA

Central Wyoming Coll, WY
Charleston Southern U, SC
Cincinnati Christian U, OH
Claremont McKenna Coll, CA
Clark U, MA
Clayton State U, GA
Clemson U, SC
Coastal Carolina U, SC
Coe Coll, IA
Colby Coll, ME
Colgate U, NY
Coll of Charleston, SC
Coll of Mount St. Joseph, OH
Coll of Mount Saint Vincent, NY
Coll of Saint Elizabeth, NJ
Coll of St. Joseph, VT
Coll of Saint Mary, NE
The Coll of Saint Rose, NY
The Coll of St. Scholastica, MN
Coll of Staten Island of the City U of New York, NY
Coll of the Atlantic, ME
Coll of the Canyons, CA
Coll of the Desert, CA
The Coll of William and Mary, VA
Columbus State U, GA
Comm Coll of Allegheny County, PA
Concordia U, NE
Concordia U Coll of Alberta, AB, Canada
Concord U, WV
Cornell U, NY
Cornerstone U, MI
Crafton Hills Coll, CA
Cuesta Coll, CA
Daemen Coll, NY
Dalhousie U, NS, Canada
Dallas Baptist U, TX
Delaware State U, DE
DePaul U, IL
Dixie State Coll of Utah, UT
Dominican U, IL
Drake U, IA
Drury U, MO
Duke U, NC
Earlham Coll, IN
East Carolina U, NC
East Central Coll, MO
Eastern Connecticut State U, CT
Eastern Mennonite U, VA
Eastern Michigan U, MI
Eastern Nazarene Coll, MA
East Stroudsburg U of Pennsylvania, PA
Eckerd Coll, FL
Edinboro U of Pennsylvania, PA
El Camino Coll, CA
Elmira Coll, NY
Elms Coll, MA
Elon U, NC
Emory U, GA
Eugene Lang Coll The New School for Liberal Arts, NY
Fairfield U, CT
Fairleigh Dickinson U, Coll at Florham, NJ
Fairleigh Dickinson U, Metropolitan Campus, NJ
Fayetteville State U, NC
Ferrum Coll, VA
Fitchburg State Coll, MA
Flagler Coll, FL
Florida Atlantic U, FL
Florida Inst of Technology, FL
Florida International U, FL

Fontbonne U, MO
Foothill Coll, CA
Fort Hays State U, KS
Framingham State Coll, MA
Franciscan U of Steubenville, OH
Franklin Coll, IN
Franklin Pierce U, NH
Frederick Comm Coll, MD
Freed-Hardeman U, TN
Fresno Pacific U, CA
Fulton-Montgomery Comm Coll, NY
Furman U, SC
Gainesville State Coll, GA
Gannon U, PA
Gardner-Webb U, NC
Geneva Coll, PA
Georgetown Coll, KY
The George Washington U, DC
Georgia Coll & State U, GA
Georgian Court U, NJ
Gloucester County Coll, NJ
Gonzaga U, WA
Gordon Coll, MA
Goshen Coll, IN
Grace Coll, IN
Graceland U, IA
Grambling State U, LA
Green Mountain Coll, VT
Grinnell Coll, IA
Gustavus Adolphus Coll, MN
Hamilton Coll, NY
Hamline U, MN
Hampden-Sydney Coll, VA
Hampshire Coll, MA
Harding U, AR
Harrisburg Area Comm Coll, PA
Hartwick Coll, NY
Haverford Coll, PA
Henderson State U, AR
High Point U, NC
Hofstra U, NY
Hope Coll, MI
Houghton Coll, NY
Houston Baptist U, TX
Howard Comm Coll, MD
Hunter Coll of the City U of New York, NY
Huntington U, IN
Idaho State U, ID
Illinois State U, IL
Illinois Wesleyan U, IL
Immaculata U, PA
Indiana U Bloomington, IN
Indiana U of Pennsylvania, PA
Indiana U-Purdue U Fort Wayne, IN
Indiana U-Purdue U Indianapolis, IN
Indiana U Southeast, IN
Iona Coll, NY
Itasca Comm Coll, MN
Ithaca Coll, NY
Jacksonville U, FL
John Brown U, AR
Johnson State Coll, VT
Kansas State U, KS
Kellogg Comm Coll, MI
Kennesaw State U, GA
Kentucky Wesleyan Coll, KY
Kenyon Coll, OH
Keuka Coll, NY
King's Coll, PA
The King's U Coll, AB, Canada
Kutztown U of Pennsylvania, PA
LaGrange Coll, GA
Lake Erie Coll, OH

Lakeland Coll, WI
Lake Superior State U, MI
Lamar U, TX
Langston U, OK
Lassen Comm Coll District, CA
Lawrence U, WI
Lebanon Valley Coll, PA
Lee Coll, TX
Lehigh U, PA
Le Moyne Coll, NY
LeTourneau U, TX
Lewis U, IL
Liberty U, VA
Lincoln U, PA
Lindenwood U, MO
Long Island U, Brooklyn Campus, NY
Loras Coll, IA
Loyola Marymount U, CA
Loyola U Chicago, IL
Loyola U New Orleans, LA
Lynchburg Coll, VA
Lynn U, FL
Macalester Coll, MN
MacMurray Coll, IL
Manhattan Coll, NY
Manhattanville Coll, NY
Marian Coll, IN
Marietta Coll, OH
Marist Coll, NY
Marquette U, WI
Marshall U, WV
Marymount Manhattan Coll, NY
Marymount U, VA
Marywood U, PA
Massachusetts Coll of Liberal Arts, MA
McDaniel Coll, MD
McNeese State U, LA
Mercer U, GA
Mercyhurst Coll, PA
Miami Dade Coll, FL
Michigan State U, MI
Middlesex County Coll, NJ
Middle Tennessee State U, TN
Midland Coll, TX
Midland Lutheran Coll, NE
Millersville U of Pennsylvania, PA
Minnesota State U Mankato, MN
Minnesota State U Moorhead, MN
MiraCosta Coll, CA
Missouri State U, MO
Mitchell Coll, CT
Molloy Coll, NY
Monmouth Coll, IL
Monmouth U, NJ
Montana State U, MT
Montana State U-Billings, MT
Moravian Coll, PA
Morningside Coll, IA
Mount Holyoke Coll, MA
Mount St. Mary's U, MD
Mount Saint Vincent U, NS, Canada
Mount Union Coll, OH
Mount Vernon Nazarene U, OH
Murray State U, KY
Naropa U, CO
National-Louis U, IL
Neumann Coll, PA
New Jersey City U, NJ
New York U, NY
Niagara U, NY
Nipissing U, ON, Canada
North Carolina State U, NC
North Central Coll, IL

North Dakota State U, ND
Northeastern U, MA
Northern Illinois U, IL
Northern Michigan U, MI
Northern State U, SD
North Georgia Coll & State U, GA
Northwestern Coll, MN
Northwestern Oklahoma State U, OK
Northwest Nazarene U, ID
Notre Dame Coll, OH
Notre Dame de Namur U, CA
Nova Southeastern U, FL
Oakland U, MI
Occidental Coll, CA
Odessa Coll, TX
Oglethorpe U, GA
The Ohio State U, OH
The Ohio State U at Lima, OH
Ohio Wesleyan U, OH
Oklahoma State U, OK
Old Dominion U, VA
Oral Roberts U, OK
Otterbein Coll, OH
Our Lady of the Lake U of San Antonio, TX
Park U, MO
Penn State Abington, PA
Penn State DuBois, PA
Penn State Fayette, The Eberly Campus, PA
Penn State Mont Alto, PA
Penn State Wilkes-Barre, PA
Piedmont Coll, GA
Pine Manor Coll, MA
Pittsburg State U, KS
Point Loma Nazarene U, CA
Portland State U, OR
Prairie View A&M U, TX
Presbyterian Coll, SC
Queens Coll of the City U of New York, NY
Queen's U at Kingston, ON, Canada
Queens U of Charlotte, NC
Quincy Coll, MA
Radford U, VA
Ramapo Coll of New Jersey, NJ
Randolph Coll, VA
Randolph-Macon Coll, VA
Redeemer U Coll, ON, Canada
Reinhardt Coll, GA
Rensselaer Polytechnic Inst, NY
Rhodes Coll, TN
Rice U, TX
The Richard Stockton Coll of New Jersey, NJ
Ripon Coll, WI
Rivier Coll, NH
Rochester Inst of Technology, NY
Rockford Coll, IL
Rockhurst U, MO
Rocky Mountain Coll, MT
Roosevelt U, IL
Rose State Coll, OK
Rowan U, NJ
Rutgers, The State U of New Jersey, Newark, NJ
Rutgers, The State U of New Jersey, New Brunswick, NJ
Ryerson U, ON, Canada
Saginaw Valley State U, MI
St. Bonaventure U, NY
St. Cloud State U, MN
St. Francis Xavier U, NS, Canada
St. Gregory's U, OK

Colleges for Students with Learning Disabilities or AD/HD

PUBLIC ADMINISTRATION AND SOCIAL SERVICE PROFESSIONS RELATED

Cornell U, NY
Eastern Michigan U, MI
Indiana U–Purdue U Fort Wayne, IN
Kentucky Wesleyan Coll, KY
Roosevelt U, IL
Sauk Valley Comm Coll, IL
The U of Akron, OH

PUBLIC/APPLIED HISTORY AND ARCHIVAL ADMINISTRATION

Clayton State U, GA
East Carolina U, NC
U of California, Santa Barbara, CA

PUBLIC HEALTH

Alma Coll, MI
Brock U, ON, Canada
Hampshire Coll, MA
Hunter Coll of the City U of New York, NY
Indiana U Bloomington, IN
Indiana U–Purdue U Indianapolis, IN
Minnesota State U Mankato, MN
The Richard Stockton Coll of New Jersey, NJ
Rutgers, The State U of New Jersey, New Brunswick, NJ
Ryerson U, ON, Canada
Slippery Rock U of Pennsylvania, PA
Springfield Coll, MA
Truman State U, MO
Tufts U, MA
U of Cincinnati, OH
U of Washington, WA
West Chester U of Pennsylvania, PA

PUBLIC HEALTH/ COMMUNITY NURSING

Northern Illinois U, IL
U of Northern British Columbia, BC, Canada
U of Washington, WA
Wright State U, OH

PUBLIC HEALTH EDUCATION AND PROMOTION

American U, DC
Coastal Carolina U, SC
Dalhousie U, NS, Canada
East Carolina U, NC
Ithaca Coll, NY
Liberty U, VA
Oakland U, MI
Temple U, PA
U of St. Thomas, MN
West Chester U of Pennsylvania, PA

PUBLIC HEALTH RELATED

Concordia U Coll of Alberta, AB, Canada
U of California, Berkeley, CA
U of California, Los Angeles, CA
U of Illinois at Urbana–Champaign, IL
West Chester U of Pennsylvania, PA
Western Tech Coll, WI

PUBLIC POLICY ANALYSIS

Albion Coll, MI
Bentley Coll, MA
Carlow U, PA
Carnegie Mellon U, PA
Coll of the Atlantic, ME
The Coll of William and Mary, VA
Cornell U, NY
DePaul U, IL
Duke U, NC
The George Washington U, DC
Hamilton Coll, NY
Houston Baptist U, TX
Immaculata U, PA
Indiana U Bloomington, IN
Indiana U–Purdue U Fort Wayne, IN
Kenyon Coll, OH
North Carolina State U, NC
Occidental Coll, CA
Rice U, TX
Rochester Inst of Technology, NY
St. Cloud State U, MN
St. Mary's Coll of Maryland, MD
Trinity Coll, CT
U at Albany, State U of New York, NY
U of California, Los Angeles, CA
U of Cincinnati, OH
U of Massachusetts Boston, MA
The U of North Carolina at Chapel Hill, NC
U of Oregon, OR
U of Pennsylvania, PA
U of Rhode Island, RI
Washington and Lee U, VA
Wells Coll, NY

PUBLIC RELATIONS

Delaware State U, DE
San Diego State U, CA

PUBLIC RELATIONS, ADVERTISING, AND APPLIED COMMUNICATION RELATED

Buena Vista U, IA
Carroll Coll, WI
The Coll of St. Scholastica, MN
John Brown U, AR
Marietta Coll, OH
Murray State U, KY
Notre Dame Coll, OH
Rochester Inst of Technology, NY
State U of New York Coll at Brockport, NY
Texas A&M U, TX
The U of Akron, OH
U of Vermont, VT

PUBLIC RELATIONS/ IMAGE MANAGEMENT

American U, DC
Anderson U, SC
The Art Inst of Pittsburgh, PA
Ball State U, IN
Barry U, FL
Bradley U, IL
Bridgewater Coll, VA
Buffalo State Coll, State U of New York, NY
California State U, Fullerton, CA

Cardinal Stritch U, WI
Carroll Coll, MT
Coe Coll, IA
Comm Coll of Beaver County, PA
Cosumnes River Coll, Sacramento, CA
Drake U, IA
Drury U, MO
Eastern Michigan U, MI
Fort Hays State U, KS
Freed-Hardeman U, TN
Gonzaga U, WA
Harding U, AR
Hofstra U, NY
Huntington U, IN
Illinois State U, IL
Iona Coll, NY
Ithaca Coll, NY
John Brown U, AR
Johnson & Wales U, CO
Johnson & Wales U, FL
Johnson & Wales U, NC
Johnson & Wales U, RI
Kellogg Comm Coll, MI
Lewis U, IL
Lindenwood U, MO
Loras Coll, IA
Marist Coll, NY
Marquette U, WI
Marywood U, PA
Mercyhurst Coll, PA
Middle Tennessee State U, TN
Minnesota State U Mankato, MN
Minnesota State U Moorhead, MN
Monmouth Coll, IL
Montana State U–Billings, MT
Mount Saint Vincent U, NS, Canada
Murray State U, KY
North Carolina State U, NC
Northern Michigan U, MI
Northwestern Coll, MN
Northwest Nazarene U, ID
Oral Roberts U, OK
Otterbein Coll, OH
Rochester Inst of Technology, NY
Roosevelt U, IL
St. Cloud State U, MN
San Diego State U, CA
Southern Adventist U, TN
State U of New York Coll at Brockport, NY
Syracuse U, NY
Temple U, PA
Union Coll, NE
The U of Alabama, AL
U of Central Missouri, MO
U of Central Oklahoma, OK
U of Dayton, OH
U of Delaware, DE
The U of Findlay, OH
U of Houston, TX
U of Miami, FL
U of Northern Iowa, IA
U of Oregon, OR
U of Pittsburgh at Bradford, PA
U of Rio Grande, OH
U of Southern Indiana, IN
The U of Tennessee at Martin, TN
The U of Texas at Austin, TX
U of Toronto, ON, Canada
U of Wisconsin–Madison, WI
Ursuline Coll, OH
Utica Coll, NY

Wayne State U, MI
Westminster Coll, PA
West Virginia Wesleyan Coll, WV
Xavier U, OH

PUBLISHING

Graceland U, IA
Rochester Inst of Technology, NY
U of Missouri–Columbia, MO
Westmoreland County Comm Coll, PA

PURCHASING, PROCUREMENT/ ACQUISITIONS AND CONTRACTS MANAGEMENT

Mercyhurst Coll, PA
North Georgia Coll & State U, GA
Southwestern Coll, KS
U of the District of Columbia, DC
Washburn U, KS
Wright State U, OH

QUALITY CONTROL AND SAFETY TECHNOLOGIES RELATED

Ivy Tech Comm Coll–Wabash Valley, IN

QUALITY CONTROL TECHNOLOGY

Broome Comm Coll, NY
Coll of the Canyons, CA
Comm Coll of Allegheny County, PA
Heartland Comm Coll, IL
Macomb Comm Coll, MI
New Hampshire Comm Tech Coll, Nashua/Claremont, NH
Santa Ana Coll, CA
U of Cincinnati, OH
Waubonsee Comm Coll, IL

RADIO AND TELEVISION

Academy of Art U, CA
The Art Inst of Pittsburgh, PA
Ashland U, OH
Asnuntuck Comm Coll, CT
Barry U, FL
Baylor U, TX
Bemidji State U, MN
Bradley U, IL
Brevard Comm Coll, FL
Bucks County Comm Coll, PA
Buffalo State Coll, State U of New York, NY
California State U, Fullerton, CA
Chattanooga State Tech Comm Coll, TN
Coahoma Comm Coll, MS
Cosumnes River Coll, Sacramento, CA
Cuesta Coll, CA
Delaware State U, DE
Dixie State Coll of Utah, UT
Drake U, IA
Eastern Nazarene Coll, MA
Foothill Coll, CA
Fort Hays State U, KS
Franklin Pierce U, NH
Freed-Hardeman U, TN
Gannon U, PA

Geneva Coll, PA
The George Washington U, DC
Grossmont Coll, CA
Hillsborough Comm Coll, FL
Hofstra U, NY
Indiana U Bloomington, IN
Iona Coll, NY
Ithaca Coll, NY
John Brown U, AR
Lamar U, TX
Langston U, OK
Lassen Comm Coll District, CA
Lee Coll, TX
Lindenwood U, MO
Long Beach City Coll, CA
Marietta Coll, OH
Marist Coll, NY
Mercyhurst Coll, PA
Miami Dade Coll, FL
Michigan State U, MI
Middlesex Comm Coll, CT
Murray State U, KY
New York U, NY
North Central Coll, IL
Northeastern U, MA
Northland Comm and Tech Coll–Thief River Falls, MN
Northwestern Coll, MN
Odessa Coll, TX
Oral Roberts U, OK
Otterbein Coll, OH
Roosevelt U, IL
Ryerson U, ON, Canada
St. Cloud State U, MN
St. Louis Comm Coll at Florissant Valley, MO
San Diego State U, CA
San Francisco State U, CA
Southern Illinois U Carbondale, IL
State U of New York at Fredonia, NY
State U of New York Coll at Brockport, NY
Stephen F. Austin State U, TX
Syracuse U, NY
Temple U, PA
The U of Alabama, AL
The U of Arizona, AZ
U of Central Florida, FL
U of Central Missouri, MO
U of Central Oklahoma, OK
U of Cincinnati, OH
U of Dayton, OH
U of Kentucky, KY
U of Miami, FL
U of Mississippi, MS
U of Missouri–Columbia, MO
U of Northern Iowa, IA
U of Oregon, OR
U of Southern Indiana, IN
The U of Tennessee, TN
The U of Texas at Austin, TX
U of Wisconsin–Madison, WI
U of Wisconsin–Oshkosh, WI
Vanguard U of Southern California, CA
Washburn U, KS
Wayne State U, MI
Westminster Coll, PA
Xavier U, OH

RADIO AND TELEVISION BROADCASTING TECHNOLOGY
Alabama A&M U, AL
Asbury Coll, KY
British Columbia Inst of Technology, BC, Canada
Cedar Valley Coll, TX
Central Wyoming Coll, WY
Eastern Michigan U, MI
Gadsden State Comm Coll, AL
Gardner-Webb U, NC
Geneva Coll, PA
Hillsborough Comm Coll, FL
Hofstra U, NY
Houston Comm Coll System, TX
Iona Coll, NY
Kellogg Comm Coll, MI
Lewis U, IL
Miami Dade Coll, FL
Northwest Nazarene U, ID
Ozarks Tech Comm Coll, MO
Schoolcraft Coll, MI
Southern Adventist U, TN
Trevecca Nazarene U, TN

RADIOLOGICAL SCIENCE
Alderson-Broaddus Coll, WV
U of Toronto, ON, Canada

RADIOLOGIC TECHNOLOGY/SCIENCE
Brevard Comm Coll, FL
Clayton State U, GA
Dalhousie U, NS, Canada
East Central Coll, MO
El Centro Coll, TX
Foothill Coll, CA
The George Washington U, DC
Hillsborough Comm Coll, FL
Hudson Valley Comm Coll, NY
Indiana U–Purdue U Fort Wayne, IN
Laredo Comm Coll, TX
Madisonville Comm Coll, KY
Manhattan Coll, NY
Massasoit Comm Coll, MA
Miami Dade Coll, FL
Middlesex County Coll, NJ
Midland Coll, TX
Missouri State U, MO
Nebraska Methodist Coll, NE
North Dakota State U, ND
The Ohio State U, OH
Oregon Inst of Technology, OR
Paris Jr Coll, TX
Southern Maine Comm Coll, ME
Trocaire Coll, NY
U of Arkansas at Fort Smith, AR
U of Michigan, MI
U of Missouri–Columbia, MO
U of Pittsburgh at Bradford, PA
U of Rio Grande, OH
Washburn U, KS
Western Nebraska Comm Coll, NE
Western Tech Coll, WI

RADIO, TELEVISION, AND DIGITAL COMMUNICATION RELATED
Dixie State Coll of Utah, UT
Drake U, IA
Hillsborough Comm Coll, FL
John Brown U, AR
State U of New York Coll at Brockport, NY

RADIO/TELEVISION BROADCASTING TECHNOLOGY
Hudson Valley Comm Coll, NY

RANGE SCIENCE AND MANAGEMENT
Central Wyoming Coll, WY
Dixie State Coll of Utah, UT
Fort Hays State U, KS
Montana State U, MT
Sterling Coll, VT
Texas A&M U, TX
U of Nebraska–Lincoln, NE
U of Wyoming, WY

READING TEACHER EDUCATION
Abilene Christian U, TX
Baylor U, TX
Eastern Michigan U, MI
Harding U, AR
Millersville U of Pennsylvania, PA
Mount Saint Vincent U, NS, Canada
Murray State U, KY
North Georgia Coll & State U, GA
Oakland U, MI
St. Cloud State U, MN
State U of New York Coll at Cortland, NY
Texas A&M U–Corpus Christi, TX
U of Central Missouri, MO
U of Central Oklahoma, OK
U of Great Falls, MT
U of Nebraska–Lincoln, NE
U of Northern Iowa, IA
U of the Incarnate Word, TX
Upper Iowa U, IA
Wright State U, OH

REAL ESTATE
Angelo State U, TX
Ashland Comm and Tech Coll, KY
Ball State U, IN
Baylor U, TX
Blinn Coll, TX
British Columbia Inst of Technology, BC, Canada
Calhoun Comm Coll, AL
California State U, Sacramento, CA
Cedar Valley Coll, TX
Central Piedmont Comm Coll, NC
Citrus Coll, CA
Coll of the Canyons, CA
Coll of the Desert, CA
Comm Coll of Allegheny County, PA
Cosumnes River Coll, Sacramento, CA
Cuesta Coll, CA
El Camino Coll, CA
Florida Atlantic U, FL
Florida Comm Coll at Jacksonville, FL
Florida International U, FL

Foothill Coll, CA
Fresno City Coll, CA
Glendale Comm Coll, CA
Harrisburg Area Comm Coll, PA
Houston Comm Coll System, TX
Indiana U Bloomington, IN
Jefferson Comm and Tech Coll, KY
Jefferson Comm Coll, OH
Lamar Inst of Technology, TX
Lamar State Coll–Orange, TX
Lamar U, TX
Laredo Comm Coll, TX
Lassen Comm Coll District, CA
Long Beach City Coll, CA
Madisonville Comm Coll, KY
Minnesota State U Mankato, MN
MiraCosta Coll, CA
Monmouth U, NJ
Morton Coll, IL
Nassau Comm Coll, NY
New Mexico Jr Coll, NM
New York U, NY
North Central Texas Coll, TX
Ocean County Coll, NJ
The Ohio State U, OH
Phoenix Coll, AZ
Pima Comm Coll, AZ
St. Cloud State U, MN
St. Louis Comm Coll at Florissant Valley, MO
San Diego Mesa Coll, CA
San Diego State U, CA
San Francisco State U, CA
Santa Ana Coll, CA
Santa Barbara City Coll, CA
Scottsdale Comm Coll, AZ
Shasta Coll, CA
Temple U, PA
Tidewater Comm Coll, VA
U of Central Oklahoma, OK
U of Cincinnati, OH
U of Connecticut, CT
U of Guelph, ON, Canada
U of Illinois at Urbana–Champaign, IL
U of Mississippi, MS
U of Missouri–Columbia, MO
U of Nebraska at Omaha, NE
U of Northern Iowa, IA
U of Pennsylvania, PA
U of St. Thomas, MN
The U of Texas at El Paso, TX
U of West Georgia, GA
U of Wisconsin–Madison, WI
Ventura Coll, CA
Victor Valley Coll, CA
West Los Angeles Coll, CA
Westmoreland County Comm Coll, PA

RECEPTIONIST
Alexandria Tech Coll, MN
Baker Coll of Allen Park, MI

RECORDING ARTS TECHNOLOGY
Ithaca Coll, NY
Lebanon Valley Coll, PA
Miami Dade Coll, FL
Savannah Coll of Art and Design, GA

RECREATION PRODUCTS/SERVICES MARKETING OPERATIONS
Oral Roberts U, OK
U of Arkansas, AR

REGIONAL STUDIES
Mercer U, GA

REHABILITATION AND THERAPEUTIC PROFESSIONS RELATED
East Stroudsburg U of Pennsylvania, PA
Montana State U–Billings, MT
Penn State Abington, PA
Penn State DuBois, PA
Penn State Fayette, The Eberly Campus, PA
Penn State Mont Alto, PA
Penn State Wilkes-Barre, PA
Southern Illinois U Carbondale, IL
Southern U and A&M Coll, LA
U of Pittsburgh, PA
U of Wisconsin–La Crosse, WI
Wilson Coll, PA

REHABILITATION THERAPY
East Stroudsburg U of Pennsylvania, PA
Ithaca Coll, NY
Montana State U–Billings, MT
Nassau Comm Coll, NY
Northeastern U, MA
Southern U and A&M Coll, LA
Springfield Coll, MA
Stephen F. Austin State U, TX
U of Manitoba, MB, Canada

RELIGIOUS EDUCATION
Asbury Coll, KY
Ashland U, OH
The Baptist Coll of Florida, FL
Cardinal Stritch U, WI
Carroll Coll, MT
The Catholic U of America, DC
Cincinnati Christian U, OH
Coll of Mount St. Joseph, OH
Concordia U, NE
Concordia U Coll of Alberta, AB, Canada
Cornerstone U, MI
Dallas Baptist U, TX
Eastern Nazarene Coll, MA
Franciscan U of Steubenville, OH
Gardner-Webb U, NC
Harding U, AR
Houghton Coll, NY
John Brown U, AR
Kuyper Coll, MI
LaGrange Coll, GA
Lancaster Bible Coll, PA
Loyola U New Orleans, LA
Marian Coll, IN
Marywood U, PA
Mercyhurst Coll, PA
Mount Vernon Nazarene U, OH
Multnomah Bible Coll and Biblical Seminary, OR
Northwestern Coll, MN

Northwest Nazarene U, ID
Oak Hills Christian Coll, MN
St. Bonaventure U, NY
Saint John's U, MN
Seattle Pacific U, WA
Seton Hall U, NJ
Southern Adventist U, TN
Southern Nazarene U, OK
Taylor U, IN
Thiel Coll, PA
Union Coll, NE
U of Dayton, OH
U of the Ozarks, AR
Vanguard U of Southern California, CA
Westminster Coll, PA
West Virginia Wesleyan Coll, WV
Wheaton Coll, IL

RELIGIOUS/SACRED MUSIC
Alderson-Broaddus Coll, WV
Anderson U, IN
Anderson U, SC
The Baptist Coll of Florida, FL
Baylor U, TX
Bethany U, CA
Bethel Coll, IN
Bethel U, MN
Calvin Coll, MI
Charleston Southern U, SC
Cincinnati Christian U, OH
Concordia Coll–New York, NY
Concordia U, NE
Dallas Baptist U, TX
Drake U, IA
Eastern Nazarene Coll, MA
Fresno Pacific U, CA
Furman U, SC
Gardner-Webb U, NC
Gustavus Adolphus Coll, MN
Houston Baptist U, TX
Huntington U, IN
Immaculata U, PA
Kuyper Coll, MI
Lancaster Bible Coll, PA
Loyola U New Orleans, LA
Marywood U, PA
Moravian Coll, PA
Mount Vernon Nazarene U, OH
Multnomah Bible Coll and Biblical Seminary, OR
Northwest Nazarene U, ID
Oral Roberts U, OK
Point Loma Nazarene U, CA
Seton Hill U, PA
Taylor U, IN
Trevecca Nazarene U, TN
U of Mary Hardin-Baylor, TX
Westminster Coll, PA
William Jewell Coll, MO

RELIGIOUS STUDIES
Albertson Coll of Idaho, ID
Albion Coll, MI
Albright Coll, PA
Alderson-Broaddus Coll, WV
Alma Coll, MI
Alvernia Coll, PA
Amherst Coll, MA
Anderson U, IN
Anderson U, SC
Ashland U, OH
Athens State U, AL
Augsburg Coll, MN
Austin Coll, TX
Avila U, MO
Ball State U, IN
Bard Coll, NY

Bates Coll, ME
Baylor U, TX
Bemidji State U, MN
Benedictine Coll, KS
Bishop's U, QC, Canada
Bradley U, IL
Brandon U, MB, Canada
Brevard Coll, NC
Brewton-Parker Coll, GA
Brown U, RI
Bryn Mawr Coll, PA
California State U, Fullerton, CA
California State U, Northridge, CA
Calvin Coll, MI
Cape Breton U, NS, Canada
Cardinal Stritch U, WI
Carleton U, ON, Canada
Carroll Coll, MT
Carroll Coll, WI
Carson-Newman Coll, TN
Carthage Coll, WI
The Catholic U of America, DC
Charleston Southern U, SC
Claremont McKenna Coll, CA
Coe Coll, IA
Colby Coll, ME
Colgate U, NY
Coll of Charleston, SC
Coll of Mount St. Joseph, OH
Coll of Mount Saint Vincent, NY
The Coll of Saint Rose, NY
The Coll of St. Scholastica, MN
The Coll of William and Mary, VA
Concordia Coll–New York, NY
Concordia U Coll of Alberta, AB, Canada
Cornell U, NY
Cornerstone U, MI
Crafton Hills Coll, CA
Daemen Coll, NY
Dalhousie U, NS, Canada
DePaul U, IL
Dominican U, IL
Drake U, IA
Drury U, MO
Duke U, NC
Earlham Coll, IN
East Central Coll, MO
Eastern Nazarene Coll, MA
Eckerd Coll, FL
Elmira Coll, NY
Elms Coll, MA
Elon U, NC
Emory U, GA
Eugene Lang Coll The New School for Liberal Arts, NY
Fairfield U, CT
Ferrum Coll, VA
Florida International U, FL
Fontbonne U, MO
Franklin Coll, IN
Fresno Pacific U, CA
Furman U, SC
Gardner-Webb U, NC
Georgetown Coll, KY
The George Washington U, DC
Georgian Court U, NJ
Gonzaga U, WA
Goshen Coll, IN
Graceland U, IA
Grinnell Coll, IA
Gustavus Adolphus Coll, MN
Hamilton Coll, NY

Hamline U, MN
Hampden-Sydney Coll, VA
Hampshire Coll, MA
Harding U, AR
Hartwick Coll, NY
Haverford Coll, PA
High Point U, NC
Hope Coll, MI
Houghton Coll, NY
Houston Baptist U, TX
Hunter Coll of the City U of New York, NY
Huntington U, IN
Illinois Wesleyan U, IL
Indiana U Bloomington, IN
Indiana U of Pennsylvania, PA
Indiana U–Purdue U Indianapolis, IN
Iona Coll, NY
John Brown U, AR
Kenyon Coll, OH
LaGrange Coll, GA
Lakeland Coll, WI
Lawrence U, WI
Lebanon Valley Coll, PA
Lehigh U, PA
Le Moyne Coll, NY
LeTourneau U, TX
Lewis U, IL
Liberty U, VA
Lincoln U, PA
Lindenwood U, MO
Loras Coll, IA
Loyola U New Orleans, LA
Lynchburg Coll, VA
Macalester Coll, MN
MacMurray Coll, IL
Manhattan Coll, NY
Manhattanville Coll, NY
Marquette U, WI
Marymount U, VA
Marywood U, PA
McDaniel Coll, MD
Mercyhurst Coll, PA
Michigan State U, MI
Midland Lutheran Coll, NE
Missouri State U, MO
Molloy Coll, NY
Monmouth Coll, IL
Moravian Coll, PA
Morningside Coll, IA
Mount Holyoke Coll, MA
Mount Saint Vincent U, NS, Canada
Mount Union Coll, OH
Naropa U, CO
New York U, NY
Niagara U, NY
North Carolina State U, NC
North Central Coll, IL
Northwest Nazarene U, ID
Notre Dame de Namur U, CA
Occidental Coll, CA
The Ohio State U, OH
Ohio Wesleyan U, OH
Oral Roberts U, OK
Otterbein Coll, OH
Our Lady of the Lake U of San Antonio, TX
Paul Quinn Coll, TX
Penn State Abington, PA
Penn State DuBois, PA
Penn State Fayette, The Eberly Campus, PA
Penn State Mont Alto, PA
Penn State Wilkes-Barre, PA
Piedmont Coll, GA
Presbyterian Coll, SC
Queens Coll of the City U of New York, NY
Queen's U at Kingston, ON, Canada

Queens U of Charlotte, NC
Randolph Coll, VA
Randolph-Macon Coll, VA
Redeemer U Coll, ON, Canada
Reinhardt Coll, GA
Rhodes Coll, TN
Rice U, TX
Ripon Coll, WI
Rocky Mountain Coll, MT
Rutgers, The State U of New Jersey, New Brunswick, NJ
St. Francis Xavier U, NS, Canada
St. Lawrence U, NY
St. Mary's Coll of Maryland, MD
St. Norbert Coll, WI
St. Thomas Aquinas Coll, NY
St. Thomas U, NB, Canada
Saint Xavier U, IL
Salve Regina U, RI
San Diego State U, CA
San Francisco State U, CA
Santa Clara U, CA
Seton Hall U, NJ
Seton Hill U, PA
Sewanee: The U of the South, TN
Southern Adventist U, TN
Southwest Baptist U, MO
Southwestern U, TX
Spalding U, KY
Stetson U, FL
Stonehill Coll, MA
Sweet Briar Coll, VA
Syracuse U, NY
Taylor U, IN
Temple U, PA
Tennessee Wesleyan Coll, TN
Thiel Coll, PA
Towson U, MD
Trevecca Nazarene U, TN
Trinity Coll, CT
Trinity U, TX
Truman State U, MO
Union Coll, NE
U at Albany, State U of New York, NY
The U of Alabama, AL
The U of Arizona, AZ
U of California, Berkeley, CA
U of California, Los Angeles, CA
U of California, Santa Barbara, CA
U of Colorado at Boulder, CO
U of Dayton, OH
U of Dubuque, IA
U of Evansville, IN
The U of Findlay, OH
U of Great Falls, MT
U of Hawaii at Manoa, HI
U of Illinois at Urbana–Champaign, IL
U of Kansas, KS
U of Manitoba, MB, Canada
U of Mary Hardin-Baylor, TX
U of Mary Washington, VA
U of Miami, FL
U of Michigan, MI
U of Missouri–Columbia, MO
U of Nebraska at Omaha, NE
U of New Mexico, NM
The U of North Carolina at Chapel Hill, NC
The U of North Carolina at Charlotte, NC

U of Northern Iowa, IA
U of Oregon, OR
U of Pennsylvania, PA
U of Pittsburgh, PA
U of Redlands, CA
U of St. Thomas, MN
U of San Diego, CA
U of San Francisco, CA
The U of Scranton, PA
The U of Tennessee, TN
The U of Texas at Austin, TX
U of the Incarnate Word, TX
U of the Pacific, CA
U of Toronto, ON, Canada
U of Vermont, VT
U of Virginia, VA
U of Washington, WA
U of Wisconsin–Eau Claire, WI
U of Wisconsin–Oshkosh, WI
Urbana U, OH
Vanguard U of Southern California, CA
Vassar Coll, NY
Villanova U, PA
Virginia Intermont Coll, VA
Wake Forest U, NC
Washburn U, KS
Washington and Lee U, VA
Wellesley Coll, MA
Wells Coll, NY
Westminster Coll, PA
West Virginia Wesleyan Coll, WV
Wheaton Coll, IL
Whitman Coll, WA
Wilfrid Laurier U, ON, Canada
William Jewell Coll, MO
Wofford Coll, SC
Wright State U, OH
Yale U, CT

RELIGIOUS STUDIES RELATED
Claremont McKenna Coll, CA
Point Loma Nazarene U, CA
Ursuline Coll, OH

RESORT MANAGEMENT
The Art Inst of Pittsburgh, PA
Coastal Carolina U, SC
Florida Gulf Coast U, FL
Green Mountain Coll, VT
Lakeland Coll, WI
Rochester Inst of Technology, NY

RESPIRATORY CARE THERAPY
Allegany Coll of Maryland, MD
Ashland Comm and Tech Coll, KY
Ball State U, IN
Broward Comm Coll, FL
Cameron U, OK
Central Piedmont Comm Coll, NC
Chattanooga State Tech Comm Coll, TN
Coll of the Desert, CA
Comm Coll of Allegheny County, PA
Crafton Hills Coll, CA
Dalhousie U, NS, Canada
El Camino Coll, CA
El Centro Coll, TX
Florida Comm Coll at Jacksonville, FL

Foothill Coll, CA
Frederick Comm Coll, MD
Fresno City Coll, CA
Gannon U, PA
Gloucester County Coll, NJ
Greenville Tech Coll, SC
Grossmont Coll, CA
Harrisburg Area Comm Coll, PA
Hillsborough Comm Coll, FL
Houston Comm Coll System, TX
Hudson Valley Comm Coll, NY
Indiana U of Pennsylvania, PA
Indiana U–Purdue U Indianapolis, IN
Jefferson Comm and Tech Coll, KY
Jefferson Comm Coll, OH
Kapiolani Comm Coll, HI
Lamar Inst of Technology, TX
Lamar U, TX
Lincoln Land Comm Coll, IL
Long Island U, Brooklyn Campus, NY
Macomb Comm Coll, MI
Madisonville Comm Coll, KY
Massasoit Comm Coll, MA
Metropolitan Comm Coll–Penn Valley, MO
Miami Dade Coll, FL
Middlesex County Coll, NJ
Midland Coll, TX
Midland Lutheran Coll, NE
Missouri State U, MO
Mohawk Valley Comm Coll, NY
Molloy Coll, NY
Nassau Comm Coll, NY
National-Louis U, IL
Nebraska Methodist Coll, NE
North Dakota State U, ND
Odessa Coll, TX
The Ohio State U, OH
Ozarks Tech Comm Coll, MO
Pima Comm Coll, AZ
Pueblo Comm Coll, CO
Rockingham Comm Coll, NC
Rose State Coll, OK
St. Philip's Coll, TX
Seminole Comm Coll, FL
Shelton State Comm Coll, AL
Southern Adventist U, TN
Southern Illinois U Carbondale, IL
Southern Maine Comm Coll, ME
Spokane Comm Coll, WA
Stark State Coll of Technology, OH
Sussex County Comm Coll, NJ
Tallahassee Comm Coll, FL
The U of Akron, OH
U of Arkansas at Fort Smith, AR
U of Central Florida, FL
U of Hartford, CT
U of Kansas, KS
U of Missouri–Columbia, MO
U of Pittsburgh at Johnstown, PA
U of Southern Indiana, IN
U of the District of Columbia, DC
Valencia Comm Coll, FL
Vermont Tech Coll, VT
Victor Valley Coll, CA

Colleges for Students with Learning Disabilities or AD/HD

Washburn U, KS
Westchester Comm Coll, NY
Western Tech Coll, WI

RESPIRATORY THERAPY TECHNICIAN
Coahoma Comm Coll, MS
Coosa Valley Tech Coll, GA
Dalhousie U, NS, Canada
Harrisburg Area Comm Coll, PA
Massasoit Comm Coll, MA
Miami Dade Coll, FL
Missouri State U–West Plains, MO

RESTAURANT, CULINARY, AND CATERING MANAGEMENT
The Art Inst of Houston, TX
The Art Inst of New York City, NY
The Art Inst of Pittsburgh, PA
Central Florida Comm Coll, FL
Coahoma Comm Coll, MS
Comm Coll of Allegheny County, PA
Hillsborough Comm Coll, FL
Johnson & Wales U, FL
Johnson & Wales U, NC
Johnson & Wales U, RI
Kendall Coll, IL
Lindenwood U, MO
Mohawk Valley Comm Coll, NY
Pima Comm Coll, AZ
State U of New York Coll of Technology at Alfred, NY
The U of Akron, OH
U of Illinois at Urbana–Champaign, IL
U of New Hampshire, NH
Virginia Intermont Coll, VA
Waukesha County Tech Coll, WI

RESTAURANT/FOOD SERVICES MANAGEMENT
The Art Inst of Pittsburgh, PA
Cornell U, NY
Johnson & Wales U, CO
Kendall Coll, IL
Massasoit Comm Coll, MA
Niagara U, NY
Rochester Inst of Technology, NY
St. Philip's Coll, TX
Syracuse U, NY
U of Missouri–Columbia, MO
U of New Hampshire, NH
U of San Francisco, CA

RETAILING
Comm Coll of Allegheny County, PA
Florida Comm Coll at Jacksonville, FL
Johnson & Wales U, RI
North Central Texas Coll, TX
Syracuse U, NY
Waubonsee Comm Coll, IL
Waukesha County Tech Coll, WI
Western Tech Coll, WI

ROBOTICS TECHNOLOGY
British Columbia Inst of Technology, BC, Canada

Comm Coll of Allegheny County, PA
Indiana U–Purdue U Indianapolis, IN
Ivy Tech Comm Coll–Southwest, IN
Ivy Tech Comm Coll–Wabash Valley, IN
Kellogg Comm Coll, MI
Lake Superior State U, MI
Macomb Comm Coll, MI
Schoolcraft Coll, MI
U of Rio Grande, OH
Waubonsee Comm Coll, IL

ROMANCE LANGUAGES
Bard Coll, NY
Bryn Mawr Coll, PA
Cameron U, OK
The Catholic U of America, DC
Colgate U, NY
Coll of the Desert, CA
Cornell U, NY
Elmira Coll, NY
Haverford Coll, PA
Hunter Coll of the City U of New York, NY
Kenyon Coll, OH
Manhattanville Coll, NY
Mount Holyoke Coll, MA
New York U, NY
Point Loma Nazarene U, CA
Ripon Coll, WI
Rockford Coll, IL
St. Thomas Aquinas Coll, NY
Tufts U, MA
U at Albany, State U of New York, NY
U of Cincinnati, OH
U of Michigan, MI
U of New Brunswick Fredericton, NB, Canada
U of New Hampshire, NH
The U of North Carolina at Chapel Hill, NC
U of Oregon, OR
U of Toronto, ON, Canada
U of Washington, WA

ROMANCE LANGUAGES RELATED
Houston Baptist U, TX
The U of North Carolina at Chapel Hill, NC
U of Pennsylvania, PA

RUSSIAN
American U, DC
Amherst Coll, MA
Bard Coll, NY
Bates Coll, ME
Baylor U, TX
Boston Coll, MA
Brandeis U, MA
Bryn Mawr Coll, PA
Carleton U, ON, Canada
Claremont McKenna Coll, CA
Colgate U, NY
Dalhousie U, NS, Canada
Duke U, NC
El Camino Coll, CA
Emory U, GA
Ferrum Coll, VA
The George Washington U, DC
Grinnell Coll, IA
Gustavus Adolphus Coll, MN
Haverford Coll, PA
Hofstra U, NY

Hunter Coll of the City U of New York, NY
Indiana U Bloomington, IN
Indiana U of Pennsylvania, PA
Kutztown U of Pennsylvania, PA
Lawrence U, WI
Loyola U New Orleans, LA
Macalester Coll, MN
Michigan State U, MI
New York U, NY
Northeastern U, MA
Northern Illinois U, IL
The Ohio State U, OH
Oklahoma State U, OK
Penn State Abington, PA
Penn State DuBois, PA
Penn State Fayette, The Eberly Campus, PA
Penn State Mont Alto, PA
Penn State Wilkes-Barre, PA
Portland State U, OR
Queens Coll of the City U of New York, NY
Rice U, TX
Rutgers, The State U of New Jersey, New Brunswick, NJ
San Diego State U, CA
San Francisco State U, CA
Seattle Pacific U, WA
Sewanee: The U of the South, TN
Southern Illinois U Carbondale, IL
Syracuse U, NY
Temple U, PA
Texas A&M U, TX
Trinity Coll, CT
Trinity U, TX
Truman State U, MO
Tufts U, MA
U at Albany, State U of New York, NY
The U of Alabama, AL
The U of Arizona, AZ
U of California, Irvine, CA
U of California, Los Angeles, CA
U of Delaware, DE
U of Hawaii at Manoa, HI
U of Illinois at Urbana–Champaign, IL
U of Kentucky, KY
U of Manitoba, MB, Canada
U of Maryland, Baltimore County, MD
U of Massachusetts Boston, MA
U of Michigan, MI
U of Missouri–Columbia, MO
U of Nebraska–Lincoln, NE
U of New Brunswick Fredericton, NB, Canada
U of New Hampshire, NH
U of New Mexico, NM
U of Northern Iowa, IA
U of Notre Dame, IN
U of Oregon, OR
U of Pennsylvania, PA
U of Pittsburgh, PA
U of St. Thomas, MN
The U of Tennessee, TN
The U of Texas at Austin, TX
U of Toronto, ON, Canada
U of Vermont, VT
U of Washington, WA
U of Wisconsin–Madison, WI
U of Wyoming, WY
Vassar Coll, NY
Wake Forest U, NC

Wellesley Coll, MA
West Chester U of Pennsylvania, PA
Yale U, CT

RUSSIAN STUDIES
American U, DC
Bard Coll, NY
Boston Coll, MA
Brandeis U, MA
Brock U, ON, Canada
Brown U, RI
California State U, Fullerton, CA
Carleton U, ON, Canada
Claremont McKenna Coll, CA
Colby Coll, ME
Colgate U, NY
The Coll of William and Mary, VA
Cornell U, NY
Dalhousie U, NS, Canada
The George Washington U, DC
Gustavus Adolphus Coll, MN
Hamilton Coll, NY
Hamline U, MN
Indiana U Bloomington, IN
Lawrence U, WI
Lehigh U, PA
Macalester Coll, MN
Mount Holyoke Coll, MA
The Ohio State U, OH
Randolph Coll, VA
Rhodes Coll, TN
Rice U, TX
Rutgers, The State U of New Jersey, New Brunswick, NJ
San Diego State U, CA
Sewanee: The U of the South, TN
Stetson U, FL
Syracuse U, NY
Tufts U, MA
U at Albany, State U of New York, NY
U of California, Los Angeles, CA
U of Colorado at Boulder, CO
U of Houston, TX
U of Illinois at Urbana–Champaign, IL
U of Kansas, KS
U of Manitoba, MB, Canada
U of Massachusetts Amherst, MA
U of Michigan, MI
U of Missouri–Columbia, MO
U of New Mexico, NM
The U of North Carolina at Chapel Hill, NC
U of Northern Iowa, IA
U of St. Thomas, MN
The U of Texas at Austin, TX
U of Toronto, ON, Canada
U of Vermont, VT
U of Washington, WA
Washington and Lee U, VA
Wellesley Coll, MA
Yale U, CT

SAFETY/SECURITY TECHNOLOGY
Farmingdale State Coll, NY
Lamar U, TX
Macomb Comm Coll, MI
U of Central Oklahoma, OK
U of Cincinnati, OH

SALES AND MARKETING/ MARKETING AND DISTRIBUTION TEACHER EDUCATION
East Carolina U, NC
Eastern Michigan U, MI
Fayetteville State U, NC
Middle Tennessee State U, TN
North Carolina State U, NC
Old Dominion U, VA
U of Nebraska–Lincoln, NE
U of Wisconsin–Stout, WI
Wright State U, OH

SALES, DISTRIBUTION AND MARKETING
Baylor U, TX
Brock U, ON, Canada
Brown Mackie Coll–Salina, KS
Burlington County Coll, NJ
Cape Breton U, NS, Canada
Fairleigh Dickinson U, Coll at Florham, NJ
Harding U, AR
Husson Coll, ME
Johnson & Wales U, NC
Johnson & Wales U, RI
Middle Tennessee State U, TN
North Central Texas Coll, TX
Purdue U North Central, IN
Ryerson U, ON, Canada
Santa Ana Coll, CA
Santa Barbara City Coll, CA
Seton Hill U, PA
State U of New York Coll of Technology at Alfred, NY
Syracuse U, NY
Texas A&M U, TX
U of Baltimore, MD
The U of Findlay, OH
U of Houston, TX
U of Illinois at Urbana–Champaign, IL
U of Pennsylvania, PA
U of Wisconsin–Stout, WI
West Chester U of Pennsylvania, PA
Western Tech Coll, WI
Wichita State U, KS

SANSKRIT AND CLASSICAL INDIAN LANGUAGES
U of Hawaii at Manoa, HI

SCANDINAVIAN LANGUAGES
Augsburg Coll, MN
Gustavus Adolphus Coll, MN
U of California, Berkeley, CA
U of California, Los Angeles, CA
The U of Texas at Austin, TX
U of Washington, WA
U of Wisconsin–Madison, WI

SCANDINAVIAN STUDIES
Gustavus Adolphus Coll, MN
Sterling Coll, VT
U of Michigan, MI
U of Washington, WA

SCHOOL LIBRARIAN/ SCHOOL LIBRARY MEDIA
The Coll of St. Scholastica, MN
U of Great Falls, MT

SCHOOL PSYCHOLOGY
Fort Hays State U, KS
Valdosta State U, GA

SCIENCE TEACHER EDUCATION
Abilene Christian U, TX
Albany State U, GA
Alderson-Broaddus Coll, WV
Alma Coll, MI
Alvernia Coll, PA
Anderson U, IN
Ashland U, OH
Athens State U, AL
Ball State U, IN
Baylor U, TX
Bemidji State U, MN
Bethel Coll, IN
Bethel U, MN
Bishop's U, QC, Canada
Brewton-Parker Coll, GA
Brock U, ON, Canada
Buena Vista U, IA
Buffalo State Coll, State U of New York, NY
Calvin Coll, MI
Cardinal Stritch U, WI
Carroll Coll, WI
Cedar Crest Coll, PA
Charleston Southern U, SC
Clemson U, SC
Coe Coll, IA
Coll of Saint Mary, NE
Coll of the Atlantic, ME
Columbus State U, GA
Concordia Coll–New York, NY
Concordia U, NE
Cornerstone U, MI
Dallas Baptist U, TX
Delaware State U, DE
East Carolina U, NC
Eastern Michigan U, MI
Elmira Coll, NY
Elms Coll, MA
Elon U, NC
Florida Atlantic U, FL
Florida Inst of Technology, FL
Florida International U, FL
Fort Hays State U, KS
Freed-Hardeman U, TN
Fresno Pacific U, CA
Glenville State Coll, WV
Goshen Coll, IN
Grace Coll, IN
Graceland U, IA
Grambling State U, LA
Hamline U, MN
Harding U, AR
Harrisburg Area Comm Coll, PA
Henderson State U, AR
Hofstra U, NY
Hope Coll, MI
Houston Baptist U, TX
Hunter Coll of the City U of New York, NY
Huntington U, IN
Indiana U Bloomington, IN
Indiana U of Pennsylvania, PA
Indiana U–Purdue U Fort Wayne, IN
Indiana U Southeast, IN
Iona Coll, NY
Ithaca Coll, NY

Lakeland Coll, WI
Lebanon Valley Coll, PA
Le Moyne Coll, NY
Lindenwood U, MO
Marquette U, WI
Marywood U, PA
Mercyhurst Coll, PA
Miami Dade Coll, FL
Midland Lutheran Coll, NE
Millersville U of Pennsylvania, PA
Minnesota State U Mankato, MN
Minnesota State U Moorhead, MN
Missouri State U, MO
Montana State U–Billings, MT
Moravian Coll, PA
Morningside Coll, IA
Mount Vernon Nazarene U, OH
Murray State U, KY
Niagara U, NY
North Carolina State U, NC
North Dakota State U, ND
Northern Michigan U, MI
North Georgia Coll & State U, GA
Northwestern Oklahoma State U, OK
Oakland U, MI
Oral Roberts U, OK
Otterbein Coll, OH
Queen's U at Kingston, ON, Canada
Saginaw Valley State U, MI
St. Cloud State U, MN
Seattle Pacific U, WA
Southern Illinois U Edwardsville, IL
Southern Nazarene U, OK
Southern U and A&M Coll, LA
Southwest Baptist U, MO
Southwestern U, TX
Springfield Coll, MA
State U of New York at Fredonia, NY
State U of New York Coll at Brockport, NY
State U of New York Coll at Cortland, NY
State U of New York Coll at Potsdam, NY
State U of New York Coll of Environmental Science and Forestry, NY
Sterling Coll, VT
Taylor U, IN
Temple U, PA
Texas A&M U–Corpus Christi, TX
Troy U, AL
U at Albany, State U of New York, NY
The U of Akron, OH
The U of Arizona, AZ
U of Central Florida, FL
U of Central Oklahoma, OK
U of Cincinnati, OH
U of Dayton, OH
U of Delaware, DE
U of Evansville, IN
The U of Findlay, OH
U of Great Falls, MT
U of Illinois at Urbana–Champaign, IL
U of Kentucky, KY
U of Maine at Machias, ME
U of Manitoba, MB, Canada
U of Mary Hardin-Baylor, TX
U of Minnesota, Duluth, MN
U of Mississippi, MS

U of Missouri–Columbia, MO
U of Nebraska–Lincoln, NE
U of New Brunswick Fredericton, NB, Canada
U of New Hampshire, NH
U of New Orleans, LA
U of Northern Iowa, IA
U of North Florida, FL
U of Notre Dame, IN
U of Pittsburgh at Johnstown, PA
U of Rio Grande, OH
U of St. Thomas, MN
The U of Tennessee at Martin, TN
U of the Ozarks, AR
U of Toronto, ON, Canada
U of Vermont, VT
U of Washington, WA
U of Wisconsin–Eau Claire, WI
U of Wisconsin–La Crosse, WI
U of Wisconsin–Madison, WI
U of Wisconsin–Platteville, WI
Upper Iowa U, IA
Urbana U, OH
Ursuline Coll, OH
Wayne State Coll, NE
Wayne State U, MI
West Chester U of Pennsylvania, PA
West Virginia State U, WV
Wheaton Coll, IL
Wichita State U, KS
Widener U, PA
Wright State U, OH
Xavier U, OH

SCIENCE TECHNOLOGIES RELATED
Athens State U, AL
British Columbia Inst of Technology, BC, Canada
Charleston Southern U, SC
Clemson U, SC
Comm Coll of Allegheny County, PA
Eastern West Virginia Comm and Tech Coll, WV
Hope Coll, MI
Lehigh U, PA
The U of Arizona, AZ
U of Wisconsin–Stout, WI
Victor Valley Coll, CA

SCIENCE, TECHNOLOGY AND SOCIETY
Carnegie Mellon U, PA
Colby Coll, ME
Cornell U, NY
Dalhousie U, NS, Canada
Michigan State U, MI
North Carolina State U, NC
Rensselaer Polytechnic Inst, NY
Rutgers, The State U of New Jersey, Newark, NJ
Slippery Rock U of Pennsylvania, PA
U of Alaska Anchorage, AK
Vassar Coll, NY

SCULPTURE
Academy of Art U, CA
Ball State U, IN
Bard Coll, NY
Buffalo State Coll, State U of New York, NY

California State U, Fullerton, CA
The Catholic U of America, DC
The Cleveland Inst of Art, OH
DePaul U, IL
Dixie State Coll of Utah, UT
Drake U, IA
Framingham State Coll, MA
Grossmont Coll, CA
Indiana U Bloomington, IN
Indiana U–Purdue U Fort Wayne, IN
Maine Coll of Art, ME
Mercyhurst Coll, PA
Minneapolis Coll of Art and Design, MN
Minnesota State U Mankato, MN
Minnesota State U Moorhead, MN
Northwest Nazarene U, ID
NSCAD U, NS, Canada
The Ohio State U, OH
Otis Coll of Art and Design, CA
Parsons The New School for Design, NY
Portland State U, OR
Pratt Inst, NY
Rochester Inst of Technology, NY
Rutgers, The State U of New Jersey, New Brunswick, NJ
St. Cloud State U, MN
School of the Art Inst of Chicago, IL
Seton Hill U, PA
State U of New York Coll at Brockport, NY
Syracuse U, NY
Temple U, PA
The U of Akron, OH
U of Hartford, CT
U of Houston, TX
U of Illinois at Urbana–Champaign, IL
U of Kansas, KS
U of Miami, FL
U of Michigan, MI
U of Oregon, OR
The U of Texas at El Paso, TX
The U of the Arts, PA
U of Washington, WA

SECONDARY EDUCATION
Abilene Christian U, TX
Acadia U, NS, Canada
Adams State Coll, CO
Alabama A&M U, AL
Albion Coll, MI
Albright Coll, PA
Alderson-Broaddus Coll, WV
Alma Coll, MI
American International Coll, MA
American U, DC
Anderson U, SC
Arizona State U at the West campus, AZ
Ashland U, OH
Athens State U, AL
Auburn U Montgomery, AL
Augsburg Coll, MN
Ball State U, IN
Baylor U, TX
Belmont Abbey Coll, NC
Bemidji State U, MN
Benedictine Coll, KS
Bethel Coll, IN
Bishop's U, QC, Canada

Boston Coll, MA
Brevard Coll, NC
Brewton-Parker Coll, GA
Briar Cliff U, IA
Brock U, ON, Canada
Buffalo State Coll, State U of New York, NY
Calhoun Comm Coll, AL
Calvin Coll, MI
Cardinal Stritch U, WI
Carroll Coll, MT
Carroll Coll, WI
Carson-Newman Coll, TN
Carthage Coll, WI
The Catholic U of America, DC
Cedar Crest Coll, PA
Central Wyoming Coll, WY
Charleston Southern U, SC
Clark U, MA
Clemson U, SC
Coastal Carolina U, SC
Coe Coll, IA
Coll of St. Joseph, VT
Coll of Saint Mary, NE
Coll of the Atlantic, ME
Columbus State U, GA
Concordia Coll–New York, NY
Concordia U, NE
Concord U, WV
Cornerstone U, MI
Dallas Baptist U, TX
Delaware State U, DE
DePaul U, IL
Dixie State Coll of Utah, UT
Drake U, IA
Drury U, MO
Eastern Connecticut State U, CT
Eastern Mennonite U, VA
Eastern Nazarene Coll, MA
East Stroudsburg U of Pennsylvania, PA
Elmira Coll, NY
Elms Coll, MA
Elon U, NC
Fairfield U, CT
Fitchburg State Coll, MA
Flagler Coll, FL
Fontbonne U, MO
Framingham State Coll, MA
Franklin Pierce U, NH
Freed-Hardeman U, TN
Fresno Pacific U, CA
Furman U, SC
Gainesville State Coll, GA
Gannon U, PA
Gardner-Webb U, NC
Geneva Coll, PA
Glenville State Coll, WV
Gonzaga U, WA
Goshen Coll, IN
Graceland U, IA
Grambling State U, LA
Green Mountain Coll, VT
Gustavus Adolphus Coll, MN
Hamline U, MN
Harding U, AR
High Point U, NC
Hofstra U, NY
Hope Coll, MI
Houghton Coll, NY
Houston Baptist U, TX
Howard Comm Coll, MD
Hunter Coll of the City U of New York, NY
Huntington U, IN
Idaho State U, ID
Illinois Wesleyan U, IL
Indiana U Bloomington, IN
Indiana U of Pennsylvania, PA

Chesapeake Coll, MD
Citrus Coll, CA
Clayton State U, GA
Colgate U, NY
Coll of Mount Saint Vincent, NY
Coll of Saint Mary, NE
The Coll of St. Scholastica, MN
Coll of the Canyons, CA
Coll of the Desert, CA
Colorado Mountain Coll, Alpine Campus, CO
Comm Coll of Allegheny County, PA
Concordia Coll–New York, NY
Concordia U, NE
Concordia U Coll of Alberta, AB, Canada
Cosumnes River Coll, Sacramento, CA
DePaul U, IL
Dominican U, IL
Eastern Mennonite U, VA
Eastern Michigan U, MI
East Stroudsburg U of Pennsylvania, PA
Edinboro U of Pennsylvania, PA
Elmira Coll, NY
Eugene Lang Coll The New School for Liberal Arts, NY
Feather River Coll, CA
Florida Atlantic U, FL
Fontbonne U, MO
Foothill Coll, CA
Framingham State Coll, MA
Freed-Hardeman U, TN
Fresno City Coll, CA
Fresno Pacific U, CA
Fulton-Montgomery Comm Coll, NY
Galveston Coll, TX
Gardner-Webb U, NC
Glendale Comm Coll, CA
Gloucester County Coll, NJ
Graceland U, IA
Gustavus Adolphus Coll, MN
Hamline U, MN
Harding U, AR
Harrisburg Area Comm Coll, PA
Hofstra U, NY
Hope Coll, MI
Housatonic Comm Coll, CT
Houston Comm Coll System, TX
Howard Comm Coll, MD
Iona Coll, NY
Irvine Valley Coll, CA
Ithaca Coll, NY
Jamestown Comm Coll, NY
John Brown U, AR
Kansas State U, KS
Keuka Coll, NY
The King's U Coll, AB, Canada
Kutztown U of Pennsylvania, PA
Lake Erie Coll, OH
Lake Superior State U, MI
Lamar State Coll–Orange, TX
Laredo Comm Coll, TX
Lassen Comm Coll District, CA
Lehigh U, PA
Liberty U, VA
Long Beach City Coll, CA
Long Island U, Brooklyn Campus, NY
Loyola U New Orleans, LA

Marymount Manhattan Coll, NY
Marywood U, PA
Mercyhurst Coll, PA
Miami Dade Coll, FL
Michigan State U, MI
Middlesex County Coll, NJ
Midland Lutheran Coll, NE
Minnesota State U Mankato, MN
MiraCosta Coll, CA
Moravian Coll, PA
Mount St. Mary's U, MD
Mount Saint Vincent U, NS, Canada
Mount Vernon Nazarene U, OH
National-Louis U, IL
New York U, NY
Niagara U, NY
North Central Coll, IL
North Dakota State U, ND
Northern Michigan U, MI
North Georgia Coll & State U, GA
Northwestern Coll, MN
Northwestern Oklahoma State U, OK
Northwest Nazarene U, ID
Notre Dame de Namur U, CA
Odessa Coll, TX
The Ohio State U, OH
Our Lady of the Lake U of San Antonio, TX
Piedmont Coll, GA
Point Loma Nazarene U, CA
Portland State U, OR
Quincy Coll, MA
Radford U, VA
Ramapo Coll of New Jersey, NJ
Reedley Coll, CA
Rensselaer Polytechnic Inst, NY
Rockford Coll, IL
Rockhurst U, MO
Roosevelt U, IL
Roxbury Comm Coll, MA
St. Bonaventure U, NY
St. Cloud State U, MN
St. Gregory's U, OK
Saint John's U, MN
St. Thomas Aquinas Coll, NY
Saint Xavier U, IL
Salem Comm Coll, NJ
San Diego Mesa Coll, CA
San Diego State U, CA
San Francisco State U, CA
Santa Ana Coll, CA
Santa Rosa Jr Coll, CA
Sewanee: The U of the South, TN
Skagit Valley Coll, WA
Southern Illinois U Carbondale, IL
Southern Oregon U, OR
Southern Utah U, UT
Southwestern U, TX
Spalding U, KY
Spoon River Coll, IL
State U of New York Coll of Technology at Alfred, NY
State U of New York Coll of Technology at Canton, NY
Stephen F. Austin State U, TX
Stetson U, FL
Taylor U, IN
Towson U, MD
Trent U, ON, Canada
Trevecca Nazarene U, TN
Troy U, AL

Union Coll, NE
The U of Akron, OH
U of California, Irvine, CA
U of Central Florida, FL
U of Cincinnati, OH
The U of Findlay, OH
U of Great Falls, MT
U of Hawaii–West Oahu, HI
U of Kentucky, KY
The U of Maine at Augusta, ME
U of Michigan, MI
U of Pittsburgh, PA
U of Pittsburgh at Bradford, PA
U of Pittsburgh at Johnstown, PA
U of Rio Grande, OH
U of St. Thomas, MN
U of South Carolina Beaufort, SC
U of Southern Indiana, IN
The U of Tampa, FL
U of the Ozarks, AR
U of the Pacific, CA
U of Washington, WA
U of Wisconsin–Madison, WI
U of Wisconsin–Platteville, WI
U of Wisconsin–Stevens Point, WI
U of Wyoming, WY
Upper Iowa U, IA
Utica Coll, NY
Victor Valley Coll, CA
Wayne State Coll, NE
Westchester Comm Coll, NY
Western Connecticut State U, CT
Western Oregon U, OR
West Liberty State Coll, WV
Westminster Coll, UT
West Texas A&M U, TX
Widener U, PA
Wilson Coll, PA

SOCIAL SCIENCES RELATED

Abilene Christian U, TX
Adelphi U, NY
Carnegie Mellon U, PA
Eastern Michigan U, MI
Edinboro U of Pennsylvania, PA
Lehigh U, PA
Marywood U, PA
Millersville U of Pennsylvania, PA
Monmouth U, NJ
Queens Coll of the City U of New York, NY
Roosevelt U, IL
Rutgers, The State U of New Jersey, New Brunswick, NJ
The U of Akron, OH
U of California, Berkeley, CA
U of Massachusetts Amherst, MA
U of New England, ME

SOCIAL SCIENCE TEACHER EDUCATION

Alma Coll, MI
Baylor U, TX
Buena Vista U, IA
Carroll Coll, MT
Carroll Coll, WI
Columbus State U, GA
Concordia U, NE
Cornerstone U, MI
Eastern Mennonite U, VA
Eastern Michigan U, MI

East Stroudsburg U of Pennsylvania, PA
Elmira Coll, NY
Elon U, NC
Fayetteville State U, NC
Florida Atlantic U, FL
Florida International U, FL
Grambling State U, LA
Johnson State Coll, VT
Kennesaw State U, GA
Liberty U, VA
Lindenwood U, MO
Marquette U, WI
Mercyhurst Coll, PA
Michigan State U, MI
Montana State U–Billings, MT
Murray State U, KY
North Dakota State U, ND
Northern Michigan U, MI
North Georgia Coll & State U, GA
Northwest Nazarene U, ID
Rivier Coll, NH
Seattle Pacific U, WA
Southern Nazarene U, OK
Southwest Baptist U, MO
Stetson U, FL
Taylor U, IN
Union Coll, NE
U at Albany, State U of New York, NY
The U of Akron, OH
The U of Arizona, AZ
U of Central Florida, FL
U of Evansville, IN
U of Great Falls, MT
U of Maine at Machias, ME
U of Nebraska–Lincoln, NE
U of Northern Iowa, IA
U of Rio Grande, OH
U of Vermont, VT
Upper Iowa U, IA
Utica Coll, NY
Wayne State Coll, NE
Westminster Coll, UT

SOCIAL STUDIES TEACHER EDUCATION

Abilene Christian U, TX
Alma Coll, MI
Anderson U, IN
Baylor U, TX
Bethel Coll, IN
Bethel U, MN
Buffalo State Coll, State U of New York, NY
Carlow U, PA
Carroll Coll, WI
Charleston Southern U, SC
The Coll of Saint Rose, NY
Cornerstone U, MI
Daemen Coll, NY
East Carolina U, NC
Eastern Michigan U, MI
Edinboro U of Pennsylvania, PA
Elmira Coll, NY
Elon U, NC
Franklin Coll, IN
Gannon U, PA
Glenville State Coll, WV
Gustavus Adolphus Coll, MN
Harding U, AR
Hofstra U, NY
Hope Coll, MI
Houston Baptist U, TX
Illinois State U, IL
Indiana U Bloomington, IN
Indiana U of Pennsylvania, PA
Indiana U–Purdue U Fort Wayne, IN

Indiana U–Purdue U Indianapolis, IN
Indiana U Southeast, IN
Iona Coll, NY
Ithaca Coll, NY
John Brown U, AR
Johnson State Coll, VT
Kentucky Wesleyan Coll, KY
Keuka Coll, NY
Lebanon Valley Coll, PA
Le Moyne Coll, NY
Long Island U, Brooklyn Campus, NY
Manhattanville Coll, NY
Marist Coll, NY
Marquette U, WI
McNeese State U, LA
Millersville U of Pennsylvania, PA
Minnesota State U Mankato, MN
Minnesota State U Moorhead, MN
Molloy Coll, NY
Moravian Coll, PA
Mount Vernon Nazarene U, OH
Murray State U, KY
New York U, NY
Niagara U, NY
North Carolina State U, NC
Northwestern Coll, MN
Ohio Wesleyan U, OH
Oral Roberts U, OK
Pittsburg State U, KS
Queens Coll of the City U of New York, NY
Rocky Mountain Coll, MT
St. Bonaventure U, NY
St. Gregory's U, OK
Seton Hill U, PA
Southern Nazarene U, OK
Southern U and A&M Coll, LA
Southwestern U, TX
State U of New York Coll at Brockport, NY
State U of New York Coll at Cortland, NY
State U of New York Coll at Potsdam, NY
Syracuse U, NY
Temple U, PA
Texas A&M U–Corpus Christi, TX
The U of Akron, OH
The U of Arizona, AZ
U of Central Oklahoma, OK
U of Evansville, IN
U of Great Falls, MT
U of Illinois at Urbana–Champaign, IL
U of Mary Hardin-Baylor, TX
U of Minnesota, Duluth, MN
U of Mississippi, MS
U of Missouri–Columbia, MO
U of New Orleans, LA
U of Northern Iowa, IA
U of Pittsburgh at Johnstown, PA
U of St. Thomas, MN
U of the Ozarks, AR
U of Wisconsin–Eau Claire, WI
U of Wisconsin–La Crosse, WI
Ursuline Coll, OH
Utica Coll, NY
Virginia Intermont Coll, VA
Wayne State U, MI
West Chester U of Pennsylvania, PA
Wheaton Coll, IL

Widener U, PA
Wright State U, OH

SOCIAL WORK
Abilene Christian U, TX
Abraham Baldwin Coll, GA
Adelphi U, NY
Alabama A&M U, AL
Albany State U, GA
Alvernia Coll, PA
Anderson U, IN
Arizona State U at the West campus, AZ
Asbury Coll, KY
Asheville-Buncombe Tech Comm Coll, NC
Ashland U, OH
Augsburg Coll, MN
Aurora U, IL
Avila U, MO
Ball State U, IN
Baylor U, TX
Bemidji State U, MN
Bethel U, MN
Bradley U, IL
Briar Cliff U, IA
Bucks County Comm Coll, PA
Buena Vista U, IA
Buffalo State Coll, State U of New York, NY
California State U, Sacramento, CA
California State U, San Bernardino, CA
Calvin Coll, MI
Carleton U, ON, Canada
Carlow U, PA
Carroll Coll, MT
Carthage Coll, WI
The Catholic U of America, DC
Cedar Crest Coll, PA
Central Piedmont Comm Coll, NC
Christopher Newport U, VA
City Colls of Chicago, Richard J. Daley Coll, IL
Coahoma Comm Coll, MS
Coll of Mount St. Joseph, OH
The Coll of Saint Rose, NY
The Coll of St. Scholastica, MN
Coll of Staten Island of the City U of New York, NY
Comm Coll of Allegheny County, PA
Concordia Coll–New York, NY
Concord U, WV
Cornerstone U, MI
Daemen Coll, NY
Dalhousie U, NS, Canada
Delaware State U, DE
Dixie State Coll of Utah, UT
East Carolina U, NC
Eastern Connecticut State U, CT
Eastern Mennonite U, VA
Eastern Michigan U, MI
Eastern Nazarene Coll, MA
Eastern New Mexico U–Roswell, NM
Eastfield Coll, TX
Edinboro U of Pennsylvania, PA
El Camino Coll, CA
Elmira Coll, NY
Elms Coll, MA
Ferrum Coll, VA
Florida Atlantic U, FL
Florida Gulf Coast U, FL
Florida International U, FL

Fort Hays State U, KS
Franciscan U of Steubenville, OH
Franklin Pierce U, NH
Freed-Hardeman U, TN
Fresno Pacific U, CA
Gainesville State Coll, GA
Galveston Coll, TX
Gannon U, PA
Geneva Coll, PA
Georgian Court U, NJ
Gordon Coll, MA
Goshen Coll, IN
Grace Coll, IN
Graceland U, IA
Grambling State U, LA
Harding U, AR
Harrisburg Area Comm Coll, PA
Henderson State U, AR
Hope Coll, MI
Huntington U, IN
Idaho State U, ID
Illinois State U, IL
Immaculata U, PA
Indiana U Bloomington, IN
Indiana U–Purdue U Indianapolis, IN
Iona Coll, NY
Jefferson Comm and Tech Coll, KY
Kansas State U, KS
Kellogg Comm Coll, MI
Kennesaw State U, GA
Keuka Coll, NY
Kutztown U of Pennsylvania, PA
Kuyper Coll, MI
LaGrange Coll, GA
Lamar U, TX
Lancaster Bible Coll, PA
Lewis U, IL
Lindenwood U, MO
Long Island U, Brooklyn Campus, NY
Loras Coll, IA
Loyola U Chicago, IL
MacMurray Coll, IL
Marist Coll, NY
Marquette U, WI
Marshall U, WV
Marywood U, PA
Massachusetts Coll of Liberal Arts, MA
McDaniel Coll, MD
Mercyhurst Coll, PA
Miami Dade Coll, FL
Michigan State U, MI
Middle Tennessee State U, TN
Millersville U of Pennsylvania, PA
Minnesota State U Mankato, MN
Minnesota State U Moorhead, MN
Missouri State U, MO
Molloy Coll, NY
Monmouth U, NJ
Mount Vernon Nazarene U, OH
Murray State U, KY
New Hampshire Comm Tech Coll, Nashua/Claremont, NH
New York U, NY
Niagara U, NY
North Carolina State U, NC
Northern Michigan U, MI
Northern State U, SD
Northwestern Oklahoma State U, OK
Northwest Nazarene U, ID
Ocean County Coll, NJ

Oglethorpe U, GA
The Ohio State U, OH
Oral Roberts U, OK
Our Lady of the Lake U of San Antonio, TX
Paul Quinn Coll, TX
Pittsburg State U, KS
Point Loma Nazarene U, CA
Prairie View A&M U, TX
Quincy Coll, MA
Radford U, VA
Ramapo Coll of New Jersey, NJ
Redeemer U Coll, ON, Canada
The Richard Stockton Coll of New Jersey, NJ
Rockford Coll, IL
Rutgers, The State U of New Jersey, Newark, NJ
Rutgers, The State U of New Jersey, New Brunswick, NJ
Ryerson U, ON, Canada
Saginaw Valley State U, MI
St. Cloud State U, MN
Saint John's U, MN
Saint Joseph's Coll, IN
Saint Leo U, FL
St. Philip's Coll, TX
St. Thomas U, NB, Canada
Salve Regina U, RI
San Diego State U, CA
San Francisco State U, CA
Sauk Valley Comm Coll, IL
Seton Hall U, NJ
Seton Hill U, PA
Shippensburg U of Pennsylvania, PA
Slippery Rock U of Pennsylvania, PA
Southern Adventist U, TN
Southern Illinois U Carbondale, IL
Southern Illinois U Edwardsville, IL
Southern Nazarene U, OK
Southern U and A&M Coll, LA
South Piedmont Comm Coll, NC
Spalding U, KY
Springfield Coll in Illinois, IL
State U of New York at Fredonia, NY
State U of New York Coll at Brockport, NY
State U of New York Coll at Cortland, NY
Stephen F. Austin State U, TX
Syracuse U, NY
Taylor U, IN
Temple U, PA
Troy U, AL
Union Coll, NE
U at Albany, State U of New York, NY
U at Buffalo, the State U of New York, NY
The U of Akron, OH
The U of Akron–Wayne Coll, OH
The U of Alabama, AL
U of Alaska Anchorage, AK
U of Arkansas, AR
U of California, Berkeley, CA
U of California, Los Angeles, CA
U of Central Florida, FL
U of Central Missouri, MO
U of Cincinnati, OH
The U of Findlay, OH
U of Hawaii at Manoa, HI

U of Kansas, KS
U of Kentucky, KY
U of Manitoba, MB, Canada
U of Mary Hardin-Baylor, TX
U of Maryland, Baltimore County, MD
U of Mississippi, MS
U of Missouri–Columbia, MO
U of Nebraska at Kearney, NE
U of Nebraska at Omaha, NE
U of New Hampshire, NH
The U of North Carolina at Charlotte, NC
U of Northern British Columbia, BC, Canada
U of Northern Iowa, IA
U of Pittsburgh, PA
U of Portland, OR
U of Rio Grande, OH
U of St. Thomas, MN
U of Southern Indiana, IN
The U of Tennessee, TN
The U of Tennessee at Martin, TN
The U of Texas at Austin, TX
The U of Texas at El Paso, TX
U of the District of Columbia, DC
U of Vermont, VT
U of Washington, WA
U of Wisconsin–Eau Claire, WI
U of Wisconsin–Green Bay, WI
U of Wisconsin–Madison, WI
U of Wisconsin–Oshkosh, WI
U of Wyoming, WY
Ursuline Coll, OH
Virginia Intermont Coll, VA
Washburn U, KS
Waubonsee Comm Coll, IL
Wayne State U, MI
West Chester U of Pennsylvania, PA
Western Connecticut State U, CT
Western Nebraska Comm Coll, NE
Western New England Coll, MA
West Texas A&M U, TX
West Virginia Northern Comm Coll, WV
West Virginia State U, WV
Wichita State U, KS
Widener U, PA
Wright State U, OH
Xavier U, OH

SOCIAL WORK RELATED
U of Northern British Columbia, BC, Canada

SOCIOBIOLOGY
Tufts U, MA

SOCIOLOGY
Abilene Christian U, TX
Abraham Baldwin Coll, GA
Acadia U, NS, Canada
Adams State Coll, CO
Adelphi U, NY
Alabama A&M U, AL
Albany State U, GA
Albertson Coll of Idaho, ID
Albion Coll, MI
Albright Coll, PA

Alderson-Broaddus Coll, WV
Alma Coll, MI
American International Coll, MA
American U, DC
Amherst Coll, MA
Anderson U, IN
Angelo State U, TX
Arizona State U at the West campus, AZ
Asbury Coll, KY
Ashland U, OH
Athabasca U, AB, Canada
Athens State U, AL
Auburn U Montgomery, AL
Augsburg Coll, MN
Aurora U, IL
Austin Coll, TX
Avila U, MO
Bainbridge Coll, GA
Ball State U, IN
Bard Coll, NY
Barry U, FL
Bates Coll, ME
Baylor U, TX
Belmont Abbey Coll, NC
Bemidji State U, MN
Benedictine Coll, KS
Bethel Coll, IN
Bishop's U, QC, Canada
Boston Coll, MA
Bradley U, IL
Brandeis U, MA
Brandon U, MB, Canada
Brewton-Parker Coll, GA
Bridgewater Coll, VA
Brock U, ON, Canada
Brown U, RI
Bryn Mawr Coll, PA
Buena Vista U, IA
Buffalo State Coll, State U of New York, NY
Bunker Hill Comm Coll, MA
Burlington County Coll, NJ
California State U, Fullerton, CA
California State U, Northridge, CA
California State U, Sacramento, CA
California State U, San Bernardino, CA
California State U, Stanislaus, CA
Calvin Coll, MI
Cameron U, OK
Cape Breton U, NS, Canada
Cardinal Stritch U, WI
Carleton U, ON, Canada
Carlow U, PA
Carroll Coll, MT
Carroll Coll, WI
Carson-Newman Coll, TN
Carthage Coll, WI
The Catholic U of America, DC
Charleston Southern U, SC
Chesapeake Coll, MD
Christopher Newport U, VA
Claremont McKenna Coll, CA
Clark U, MA
Clayton State U, GA
Clemson U, SC
Coastal Carolina U, SC
Coe Coll, IA
Colby Coll, ME
Colgate U, NY
Coll of Charleston, SC
Coll of Mount St. Joseph, OH
Coll of Mount Saint Vincent, NY
Coll of Saint Elizabeth, NJ

The Coll of Saint Rose, NY
Coll of Staten Island of the City U of New York, NY
Coll of the Desert, CA
The Coll of William and Mary, VA
Columbus State U, GA
Comm Coll of Allegheny County, PA
Concordia U, NE
Concordia U Coll of Alberta, AB, Canada
Concord U, WV
Cornell U, NY
Cornerstone U, MI
Crafton Hills Coll, CA
Dalhousie U, NS, Canada
Dallas Baptist U, TX
Delaware State U, DE
DePaul U, IL
Dixie State Coll of Utah, UT
Dominican U, IL
Drake U, IA
Drury U, MO
Duke U, NC
Earlham Coll, IN
East Carolina U, NC
East Central Coll, MO
Eastern Connecticut State U, CT
Eastern Mennonite U, VA
Eastern Michigan U, MI
Eastern Nazarene Coll, MA
East Stroudsburg U of Pennsylvania, PA
Eckerd Coll, FL
Edinboro U of Pennsylvania, PA
El Camino Coll, CA
Elmira Coll, NY
Elms Coll, MA
Elon U, NC
Emory U, GA
Eugene Lang Coll The New School for Liberal Arts, NY
Fairfield U, CT
Fairleigh Dickinson U, Coll at Florham, NJ
Fairleigh Dickinson U, Metropolitan Campus, NJ
Fayetteville State U, NC
Ferrum Coll, VA
Fitchburg State Coll, MA
Flagler Coll, FL
Florida Atlantic U, FL
Florida International U, FL
Foothill Coll, CA
Fort Hays State U, KS
Framingham State Coll, MA
Franciscan U of Steubenville, OH
Franklin Coll, IN
Franklin Pierce U, NH
Fresno Pacific U, CA
Furman U, SC
Gainesville State Coll, GA
Gardner-Webb U, NC
Geneva Coll, PA
Georgetown Coll, KY
The George Washington U, DC
Georgia Coll & State U, GA
Georgian Court U, NJ
Gloucester County Coll, NJ
Gonzaga U, WA
Gordon Coll, MA
Goshen Coll, IN
Grace Coll, IN
Graceland U, IA
Grambling State U, LA
Green Mountain Coll, VT
Grinnell Coll, IA
Gustavus Adolphus Coll, MN

Hamilton Coll, NY
Hamline U, MN
Hampshire Coll, MA
Hartwick Coll, NY
Haverford Coll, PA
Henderson State U, AR
High Point U, NC
Hofstra U, NY
Hope Coll, MI
Houghton Coll, NY
Houston Baptist U, TX
Hunter Coll of the City U of New York, NY
Huntington U, IN
Idaho State U, ID
Illinois State U, IL
Illinois Wesleyan U, IL
Immaculata U, PA
Indiana U Bloomington, IN
Indiana U of Pennsylvania, PA
Indiana U–Purdue U Fort Wayne, IN
Indiana U–Purdue U Indianapolis, IN
Indiana U Southeast, IN
Iona Coll, NY
Ithaca Coll, NY
Jacksonville U, FL
Johnson State Coll, VT
Kansas State U, KS
Kellogg Comm Coll, MI
Kennesaw State U, GA
Kentucky Wesleyan Coll, KY
Kenyon Coll, OH
Keuka Coll, NY
King's Coll, PA
The King's U Coll, AB, Canada
Kutztown U of Pennsylvania, PA
Lake Erie Coll, OH
Lakeland Coll, WI
Lake Superior State U, MI
Lamar U, TX
Langston U, OK
Lebanon Valley Coll, PA
Lee Coll, TX
Lehigh U, PA
Le Moyne Coll, NY
Lewis U, IL
Lincoln U, PA
Lindenwood U, MO
Long Island U, Brooklyn Campus, NY
Loras Coll, IA
Loyola Marymount U, CA
Loyola U Chicago, IL
Loyola U New Orleans, LA
Lynchburg Coll, VA
Macalester Coll, MN
Manhattan Coll, NY
Manhattanville Coll, NY
Marian Coll, IN
Marquette U, WI
Marshall U, WV
Marymount Manhattan Coll, NY
Marymount U, VA
Massachusetts Coll of Liberal Arts, MA
McDaniel Coll, MD
McNeese State U, LA
Mercer U, GA
Mercyhurst Coll, PA
Miami Dade Coll, FL
Michigan State U, MI
Middlesex County Coll, NJ
Middle Tennessee State U, TN
Midland Coll, TX
Midland Lutheran Coll, NE
Millersville U of Pennsylvania, PA

Minnesota State U Mankato, MN
Minnesota State U Moorhead, MN
MiraCosta Coll, CA
Missouri State U, MO
Molloy Coll, NY
Monmouth Coll, IL
Montana State U, MT
Montana State U–Billings, MT
Moravian Coll, PA
Mount Holyoke Coll, MA
Mount St. Mary's U, MD
Mount Saint Vincent U, NS, Canada
Mount Union Coll, OH
Mount Vernon Nazarene U, OH
Murray State U, KY
New Jersey City U, NJ
New York U, NY
Niagara U, NY
Nipissing U, ON, Canada
North Carolina State U, NC
North Central Coll, IL
North Dakota State U, ND
Northeastern U, MA
Northern Illinois U, IL
Northern Michigan U, MI
Northern State U, SD
North Georgia Coll & State U, GA
Northwestern Oklahoma State U, OK
Notre Dame de Namur U, CA
Oakland U, MI
Occidental Coll, CA
Odessa Coll, TX
Oglethorpe U, GA
The Ohio State U, OH
Ohio Wesleyan U, OH
Oklahoma State U, OK
Old Dominion U, VA
Otterbein Coll, OH
Our Lady of the Lake U of San Antonio, TX
Park U, MO
Paul Quinn Coll, TX
Penn State Abington, PA
Penn State DuBois, PA
Penn State Fayette, The Eberly Campus, PA
Penn State Mont Alto, PA
Penn State Wilkes-Barre, PA
Piedmont Coll, GA
Pima Comm Coll, AZ
Pittsburg State U, KS
Point Loma Nazarene U, CA
Portland State U, OR
Prairie View A&M U, TX
Presbyterian Coll, SC
Queens Coll of the City U of New York, NY
Queen's U at Kingston, ON, Canada
Quincy Coll, MA
Radford U, VA
Ramapo Coll of New Jersey, NJ
Randolph Coll, VA
Randolph-Macon Coll, VA
Redeemer U Coll, ON, Canada
Reinhardt Coll, GA
Rhodes Coll, TN
Rice U, TX
The Richard Stockton Coll of New Jersey, NJ
Ripon Coll, WI
Rivier Coll, NH
Rockford Coll, IL
Rockhurst U, MO

Rocky Mountain Coll, MT
Roosevelt U, IL
Rose State Coll, OK
Rowan U, NJ
Rutgers, The State U of New Jersey, Newark, NJ
Rutgers, The State U of New Jersey, New Brunswick, NJ
Ryerson U, ON, Canada
Saginaw Valley State U, MI
St. Bonaventure U, NY
St. Cloud State U, MN
St. Francis Xavier U, NS, Canada
St. Gregory's U, OK
Saint John's U, MN
Saint Joseph's Coll, IN
St. Lawrence U, NY
Saint Leo U, FL
St. Mary's Coll of Maryland, MD
St. Norbert Coll, WI
St. Philip's Coll, TX
St. Thomas U, NB, Canada
Saint Xavier U, IL
Salem Comm Coll, NJ
Salve Regina U, RI
San Diego Mesa Coll, CA
San Diego State U, CA
San Francisco State U, CA
Santa Ana Coll, CA
Santa Barbara City Coll, CA
Santa Clara U, CA
Santa Rosa Jr Coll, CA
Sauk Valley Comm Coll, IL
Seattle Pacific U, WA
Seton Hall U, NJ
Seton Hill U, PA
Shippensburg U of Pennsylvania, PA
Skagit Valley Coll, WA
Slippery Rock U of Pennsylvania, PA
Southern Illinois U Carbondale, IL
Southern Illinois U Edwardsville, IL
Southern Nazarene U, OK
Southern Oregon U, OR
Southern U and A&M Coll, LA
Southern Utah U, UT
Southwest Baptist U, MO
Southwestern U, TX
Spoon River Coll, IL
Springfield Coll, MA
State U of New York at Fredonia, NY
State U of New York Coll at Brockport, NY
State U of New York Coll at Cortland, NY
State U of New York Coll at Geneseo, NY
State U of New York Coll at Potsdam, NY
Stephen F. Austin State U, TX
Stetson U, FL
Stonehill Coll, MA
Sweet Briar Coll, VA
Syracuse U, NY
Taylor U, IN
Temple U, PA
Texas A&M U, TX
Texas A&M U–Corpus Christi, TX
Thiel Coll, PA
Trent U, ON, Canada
Trinity Coll, CT
Trinity U, TX
Troy U, AL
Truman State U, MO
Tufts U, MA

U at Albany, State U of New York, NY
U at Buffalo, the State U of New York, NY
The U of Akron, OH
The U of Alabama, AL
The U of Alabama in Huntsville, AL
U of Alaska Anchorage, AK
The U of Arizona, AZ
U of Arkansas, AR
U of California, Berkeley, CA
U of California, Irvine, CA
U of California, Los Angeles, CA
U of California, Santa Barbara, CA
U of Central Florida, FL
U of Central Missouri, MO
U of Central Oklahoma, OK
U of Cincinnati, OH
U of Colorado at Boulder, CO
U of Connecticut, CT
U of Dayton, OH
U of Delaware, DE
U of Dubuque, IA
U of Evansville, IN
The U of Findlay, OH
U of Great Falls, MT
U of Guelph, ON, Canada
U of Hartford, CT
U of Hawaii at Manoa, HI
U of Hawaii–West Oahu, HI
U of Houston, TX
U of Illinois at Urbana–Champaign, IL
U of Kansas, KS
U of Kentucky, KY
U of Manitoba, MB, Canada
U of Mary Hardin-Baylor, TX
U of Maryland, Baltimore County, MD
U of Mary Washington, VA
U of Massachusetts Amherst, MA
U of Massachusetts Boston, MA
U of Massachusetts Lowell, MA
U of Miami, FL
U of Michigan, MI
U of Minnesota, Duluth, MN
U of Mississippi, MS
U of Missouri–Columbia, MO
U of Missouri–Kansas City, MO
U of Nebraska at Kearney, NE
U of Nebraska at Omaha, NE
U of Nebraska–Lincoln, NE
U of New Brunswick Fredericton, NB, Canada
U of New England, ME
U of New Hampshire, NH
U of New Mexico, NM
U of New Orleans, LA
The U of North Carolina at Asheville, NC
The U of North Carolina at Chapel Hill, NC
The U of North Carolina at Charlotte, NC
U of Northern Iowa, IA
U of North Florida, FL
U of Notre Dame, IN
U of Oregon, OR
U of Pennsylvania, PA
U of Pittsburgh, PA
U of Pittsburgh at Bradford, PA

U of Pittsburgh at
  Johnstown, PA
U of Portland, OR
U of Redlands, CA
U of Rhode Island, RI
U of Rio Grande, OH
U of St. Thomas, MN
U of San Diego, CA
U of San Francisco, CA
The U of Scranton, PA
U of South Carolina Upstate,
  SC
U of Southern Indiana, IN
The U of Tampa, FL
The U of Tennessee, TN
The U of Tennessee at
  Martin, TN
The U of Texas at Austin,
  TX
The U of Texas at El Paso,
  TX
The U of Texas at San
  Antonio, TX
U of the District of
  Columbia, DC
U of the Incarnate Word, TX
U of the Ozarks, AR
U of the Pacific, CA
U of Toronto, ON, Canada
U of Vermont, VT
U of Virginia, VA
The U of Virginia's Coll at
  Wise, VA
U of Washington, WA
U of West Georgia, GA
U of Wisconsin–Eau Claire,
  WI
U of Wisconsin–La Crosse,
  WI
U of Wisconsin–Madison,
  WI
U of Wisconsin–Oshkosh,
  WI
U of Wisconsin–Stevens
  Point, WI
U of Wyoming, WY
Upper Iowa U, IA
Urbana U, OH
Ursuline Coll, OH
Utica Coll, NY
Valdosta State U, GA
Vanguard U of Southern
  California, CA
Vassar Coll, NY
Villanova U, PA
Wake Forest U, NC
Washburn U, KS
Washington & Jefferson Coll,
  PA
Washington and Lee U, VA
Wayne State Coll, NE
Wayne State U, MI
Wellesley Coll, MA
Wells Coll, NY
West Chester U of
  Pennsylvania, PA
Western Connecticut State
  U, CT
Western Nebraska Comm
  Coll, NE
Western New England Coll,
  MA
Western Oregon U, OR
West Liberty State Coll, WV
West Los Angeles Coll, CA
Westminster Coll, PA
Westminster Coll, UT
West Texas A&M U, TX
West Virginia State U, WV
West Virginia Wesleyan Coll,
  WV
Wheaton Coll, IL
Whitman Coll, WA
Wichita State U, KS

Widener U, PA
Wilfrid Laurier U, ON,
  Canada
Wilkes U, PA
Wofford Coll, SC
Worcester State Coll, MA
Wright State U, OH
Xavier U, OH
Yale U, CT

SOIL CONSERVATION
Ball State U, IN
The Ohio State U, OH
U of Delaware, DE
U of New Hampshire, NH
The U of Tennessee at
  Martin, TN
U of Wisconsin–Stevens
  Point, WI

**SOIL SCIENCE AND
AGRONOMY**
Dixie State Coll of Utah, UT
Michigan State U, MI
North Carolina State U, NC
North Dakota State U, ND
Penn State Abington, PA
Penn State DuBois, PA
Penn State Fayette, The
  Eberly Campus, PA
Penn State Mont Alto, PA
Penn State Wilkes-Barre, PA
Sterling Coll, VT
U of Delaware, DE
U of Nebraska–Lincoln, NE

SOIL SCIENCES
The U of Arizona, AZ

**SOIL SCIENCES
RELATED**
Cornell U, NY
Sterling Coll, VT

**SOLAR ENERGY
TECHNOLOGY**
Comm Coll of Allegheny
  County, PA
Sterling Coll, VT

**SOUTH ASIAN
LANGUAGES**
Claremont McKenna Coll,
  CA
Oakland U, MI
Syracuse U, NY
U of Hawaii at Manoa, HI
Yale U, CT

SPANISH
Abilene Christian U, TX
Adams State Coll, CO
Adelphi U, NY
Albany State U, GA
Albertson Coll of Idaho, ID
Albion Coll, MI
Albright Coll, PA
Alma Coll, MI
American International Coll,
  MA
American U, DC
Amherst Coll, MA
Anderson U, IN
Anderson U, SC
Angelo State U, TX
Arizona State U at the West
  campus, AZ
Asbury Coll, KY
Ashland U, OH
Augsburg Coll, MN
Austin Coll, TX
Ball State U, IN
Bard Coll, NY
Barry U, FL
Bates Coll, ME

Baylor U, TX
Bemidji State U, MN
Benedictine Coll, KS
Bethel U, MN
Bishop's U, QC, Canada
Blinn Coll, TX
Bradley U, IL
Brandeis U, MA
Briar Cliff U, IA
Bridgewater Coll, VA
Brock U, ON, Canada
Brown U, RI
Bryn Mawr Coll, PA
Buena Vista U, IA
Buffalo State Coll, State U of
  New York, NY
California State U, Fullerton,
  CA
California State U,
  Northridge, CA
California State U,
  Sacramento, CA
California State U, San
  Bernardino, CA
California State U,
  Stanislaus, CA
Calvin Coll, MI
Cardinal Stritch U, WI
Carleton U, ON, Canada
Carlow U, PA
Carnegie Mellon U, PA
Carroll Coll, MT
Carroll Coll, WI
Carson-Newman Coll, TN
Carthage Coll, WI
The Catholic U of America,
  DC
Cedar Crest Coll, PA
Charleston Southern U, SC
Christopher Newport U, VA
Citrus Coll, CA
Claremont McKenna Coll,
  CA
Clark U, MA
Clayton State U, GA
Coastal Carolina U, SC
Coe Coll, IA
Colby Coll, ME
Colgate U, NY
Coll of Charleston, SC
Coll of Mount Saint Vincent,
  NY
Coll of Saint Elizabeth, NJ
The Coll of Saint Rose, NY
Coll of Staten Island of the
  City U of New York, NY
Coll of the Canyons, CA
The Coll of William and
  Mary, VA
Concordia U, NE
Cornell U, NY
Cornerstone U, MI
Crafton Hills Coll, CA
Daemen Coll, NY
Dalhousie U, NS, Canada
Delaware State U, DE
DePaul U, IL
Dominican U, IL
Drury U, MO
Duke U, NC
Earlham Coll, IN
East Carolina U, NC
Eastern Connecticut State U,
  CT
Eastern Mennonite U, VA
Eastern Michigan U, MI
East Stroudsburg U of
  Pennsylvania, PA
Eckerd Coll, FL
Edinboro U of Pennsylvania,
  PA
El Camino Coll, CA
Elmira Coll, NY
Elms Coll, MA

Elon U, NC
Emory U, GA
Fairfield U, CT
Fairleigh Dickinson U, Coll
  at Florham, NJ
Fairleigh Dickinson U,
  Metropolitan Campus, NJ
Fayetteville State U, NC
Ferrum Coll, VA
Flagler Coll, FL
Florida Atlantic U, FL
Florida International U, FL
Foothill Coll, CA
Fort Hays State U, KS
Framingham State Coll, MA
Franciscan U of
  Steubenville, OH
Franklin Coll, IN
Fresno City Coll, CA
Fresno Pacific U, CA
Furman U, SC
Gardner-Webb U, NC
Geneva Coll, PA
Georgetown Coll, KY
The George Washington U,
  DC
Georgia Coll & State U, GA
Georgian Court U, NJ
Gonzaga U, WA
Gordon Coll, MA
Goshen Coll, IN
Grace Coll, IN
Graceland U, IA
Grambling State U, LA
Grinnell Coll, IA
Grossmont Coll, CA
Gustavus Adolphus Coll,
  MN
Hamilton Coll, NY
Hamline U, MN
Hampden-Sydney Coll, VA
Harding U, AR
Hartwick Coll, NY
Haverford Coll, PA
Henderson State U, AR
High Point U, NC
Hofstra U, NY
Hope Coll, MI
Houghton Coll, NY
Houston Baptist U, TX
Hunter Coll of the City U of
  New York, NY
Idaho State U, ID
Illinois State U, IL
Illinois Wesleyan U, IL
Immaculata U, PA
Indiana U Bloomington, IN
Indiana U of Pennsylvania,
  PA
Indiana U–Purdue U Fort
  Wayne, IN
Indiana U–Purdue U
  Indianapolis, IN
Indiana U Southeast, IN
Iona Coll, NY
Ithaca Coll, NY
Jacksonville U, FL
John Brown U, AR
Kennesaw State U, GA
Kentucky Wesleyan Coll, KY
Kenyon Coll, OH
King's Coll, PA
Kutztown U of
  Pennsylvania, PA
LaGrange Coll, GA
Lake Erie Coll, OH
Lakeland Coll, WI
Lamar U, TX
Lawrence U, WI
Lebanon Valley Coll, PA
Lee Coll, TX
Lehigh U, PA
Le Moyne Coll, NY
Liberty U, VA

Lincoln U, PA
Lindenwood U, MO
Long Beach City Coll, CA
Loras Coll, IA
Loyola Marymount U, CA
Loyola U Chicago, IL
Loyola U New Orleans, LA
Lynchburg Coll, VA
Macalester Coll, MN
MacMurray Coll, IL
Manhattan Coll, NY
Manhattanville Coll, NY
Marian Coll, IN
Marietta Coll, OH
Marist Coll, NY
Marquette U, WI
Marywood U, PA
McDaniel Coll, MD
McNeese State U, LA
Mercer U, GA
Mercyhurst Coll, PA
Miami Dade Coll, FL
Michigan State U, MI
Midland Coll, TX
Millersville U of
  Pennsylvania, PA
Minnesota State U Mankato,
  MN
Minnesota State U
  Moorhead, MN
MiraCosta Coll, CA
Missouri State U, MO
Molloy Coll, NY
Monmouth Coll, IL
Montana State U–Billings,
  MT
Moravian Coll, PA
Morningside Coll, IA
Mount Holyoke Coll, MA
Mount St. Mary's U, MD
Mount Saint Vincent U, NS,
  Canada
Mount Union Coll, OH
Mount Vernon Nazarene U,
  OH
Murray State U, KY
New Jersey City U, NJ
New York U, NY
Niagara U, NY
North Carolina State U, NC
North Central Coll, IL
North Dakota State U, ND
Northeastern U, MA
Northern Illinois U, IL
Northern Michigan U, MI
Northern State U, SD
North Georgia Coll & State
  U, GA
Northwestern Oklahoma
  State U, OK
Northwest Nazarene U, ID
Oakland U, MI
Occidental Coll, CA
Oglethorpe U, GA
The Ohio State U, OH
Ohio Wesleyan U, OH
Oklahoma State U, OK
Old Dominion U, VA
Oral Roberts U, OK
Otterbein Coll, OH
Our Lady of the Lake U of
  San Antonio, TX
Park U, MO
Penn State Abington, PA
Penn State DuBois, PA
Penn State Fayette, The
  Eberly Campus, PA
Penn State Mont Alto, PA
Penn State Wilkes-Barre, PA
Piedmont Coll, GA
Pittsburg State U, KS
Point Loma Nazarene U, CA
Portland State U, OR
Prairie View A&M U, TX

Presbyterian Coll, SC
Queens Coll of the City U of New York, NY
Queen's U at Kingston, ON, Canada
Ramapo Coll of New Jersey, NJ
Randolph Coll, VA
Randolph-Macon Coll, VA
Rhodes Coll, TN
Rice U, TX
Ripon Coll, WI
Rivier Coll, NH
Rockford Coll, IL
Rockhurst U, MO
Roosevelt U, IL
Rowan U, NJ
Rutgers, The State U of New Jersey, Newark, NJ
Rutgers, The State U of New Jersey, New Brunswick, NJ
Saginaw Valley State U, MI
St. Bonaventure U, NY
St. Cloud State U, MN
Saint John's U, MN
St. Lawrence U, NY
St. Norbert Coll, WI
St. Philip's Coll, TX
St. Thomas Aquinas Coll, NY
St. Thomas U, NB, Canada
Saint Xavier U, IL
Salve Regina U, RI
San Diego Mesa Coll, CA
San Diego State U, CA
San Francisco State U, CA
Santa Barbara City Coll, CA
Santa Clara U, CA
Sauk Valley Comm Coll, IL
Seattle Pacific U, WA
Seton Hall U, NJ
Seton Hill U, PA
Sewanee: The U of the South, TN
Shippensburg U of Pennsylvania, PA
Skagit Valley Coll, WA
Slippery Rock U of Pennsylvania, PA
Southern Adventist U, TN
Southern Illinois U Carbondale, IL
Southern Nazarene U, OK
Southern Oregon U, OR
Southern U and A&M Coll, LA
Southern Utah U, UT
Southwest Baptist U, MO
Southwestern U, TX
State U of New York at Fredonia, NY
State U of New York Coll at Brockport, NY
State U of New York Coll at Cortland, NY
State U of New York Coll at Geneseo, NY
State U of New York Coll at Potsdam, NY
Stephen F. Austin State U, TX
Stetson U, FL
Sweet Briar Coll, VA
Syracuse U, NY
Taylor U, IN
Temple U, PA
Texas A&M U, TX
Texas A&M U–Corpus Christi, TX
Thiel Coll, PA
Towson U, MD
Trent U, ON, Canada
Trinity Coll, CT
Trinity U, TX

Truman State U, MO
Tufts U, MA
Union Coll, NE
U at Albany, State U of New York, NY
U at Buffalo, the State U of New York, NY
The U of Akron, OH
The U of Alabama, AL
The U of Arizona, AZ
U of Arkansas, AR
U of California, Berkeley, CA
U of California, Irvine, CA
U of California, Los Angeles, CA
U of California, Santa Barbara, CA
U of Central Florida, FL
U of Central Missouri, MO
U of Central Oklahoma, OK
U of Cincinnati, OH
U of Colorado at Boulder, CO
U of Connecticut, CT
U of Dayton, OH
U of Delaware, DE
U of Evansville, IN
The U of Findlay, OH
U of Guelph, ON, Canada
U of Hawaii at Manoa, HI
U of Houston, TX
U of Illinois at Urbana–Champaign, IL
U of Kansas, KS
U of Kentucky, KY
U of Manitoba, MB, Canada
U of Mary Hardin-Baylor, TX
U of Maryland, Baltimore County, MD
U of Mary Washington, VA
U of Massachusetts Amherst, MA
U of Massachusetts Boston, MA
U of Miami, FL
U of Michigan, MI
U of Minnesota, Duluth, MN
U of Mississippi, MS
U of Missouri–Columbia, MO
U of Missouri–Kansas City, MO
U of Nebraska at Kearney, NE
U of Nebraska at Omaha, NE
U of Nebraska–Lincoln, NE
U of New Brunswick Fredericton, NB, Canada
U of New Hampshire, NH
U of New Mexico, NM
U of New Orleans, LA
The U of North Carolina at Asheville, NC
The U of North Carolina at Charlotte, NC
U of Northern Iowa, IA
U of North Florida, FL
U of Notre Dame, IN
U of Oregon, OR
U of Pennsylvania, PA
U of Pittsburgh, PA
U of Portland, OR
U of Redlands, CA
U of Rhode Island, RI
U of St. Thomas, MN
U of St. Thomas, TX
U of San Diego, CA
U of San Francisco, CA
The U of Scranton, PA
U of South Carolina Upstate, SC
U of Southern Indiana, IN

The U of Tampa, FL
The U of Tennessee, TN
The U of Tennessee at Martin, TN
The U of Texas at Austin, TX
The U of Texas at El Paso, TX
The U of Texas at San Antonio, TX
U of the District of Columbia, DC
U of the Incarnate Word, TX
U of the Pacific, CA
U of Toronto, ON, Canada
U of Vermont, VT
U of Virginia, VA
The U of Virginia's Coll at Wise, VA
U of Washington, WA
U of West Georgia, GA
U of Wisconsin–Eau Claire, WI
U of Wisconsin–Green Bay, WI
U of Wisconsin–La Crosse, WI
U of Wisconsin–Madison, WI
U of Wisconsin–Oshkosh, WI
U of Wisconsin–Platteville, WI
U of Wisconsin–Stevens Point, WI
U of Wyoming, WY
Valdosta State U, GA
Vanguard U of Southern California, CA
Vassar Coll, NY
Villanova U, PA
Wake Forest U, NC
Washburn U, KS
Washington & Jefferson Coll, PA
Washington and Lee U, VA
Wayne State Coll, NE
Wellesley Coll, MA
Wells Coll, NY
West Chester U of Pennsylvania, PA
Western Connecticut State U, CT
Western Nebraska Comm Coll, NE
Western Oregon U, OR
West Los Angeles Coll, CA
Westminster Coll, PA
West Texas A&M U, TX
Wheaton Coll, IL
Whitman Coll, WA
Wichita State U, KS
Widener U, PA
Wilfrid Laurier U, ON, Canada
Wilkes U, PA
William Jewell Coll, MO
Wilson Coll, PA
Wofford Coll, SC
Worcester State Coll, MA
Wright State U, OH
Xavier U, OH
Yale U, CT

SPANISH AND IBERIAN STUDIES

Coe Coll, IA
Santa Clara U, CA
The U of Alabama, AL
U of Houston, TX

SPANISH LANGUAGE TEACHER EDUCATION

Abilene Christian U, TX
Alma Coll, MI

Anderson U, IN
Anderson U, SC
Baylor U, TX
Bethel U, MN
Bishop's U, QC, Canada
Buena Vista U, IA
Carroll Coll, MT
Carroll Coll, WI
The Catholic U of America, DC
Charleston Southern U, SC
The Coll of Saint Rose, NY
Columbus State U, GA
Concordia U, NE
Daemen Coll, NY
Delaware State U, DE
East Carolina U, NC
Eastern Mennonite U, VA
Eastern Michigan U, MI
Elmira Coll, NY
Fayetteville State U, NC
Franklin Coll, IN
Frederick Comm Coll, MD
Grace Coll, IN
Hofstra U, NY
Hope Coll, MI
Illinois Wesleyan U, IL
Indiana U Bloomington, IN
Indiana U–Purdue U Fort Wayne, IN
Indiana U–Purdue U Indianapolis, IN
Iona Coll, NY
Ithaca Coll, NY
Kentucky Wesleyan Coll, KY
Lebanon Valley Coll, PA
Le Moyne Coll, NY
Liberty U, VA
Lindenwood U, MO
Long Island U, Brooklyn Campus, NY
Manhattanville Coll, NY
Marist Coll, NY
Marywood U, PA
Minnesota State U Moorhead, MN
Missouri State U, MO
Molloy Coll, NY
Montana State U–Billings, MT
Moravian Coll, PA
Mount Vernon Nazarene U, OH
Murray State U, KY
Niagara U, NY
North Carolina State U, NC
North Dakota State U, ND
Northern Michigan U, MI
Northwest Nazarene U, ID
Notre Dame Coll, OH
Ohio Wesleyan U, OH
Old Dominion U, VA
Oral Roberts U, OK
Pittsburg State U, KS
St. Bonaventure U, NY
Saint Xavier U, IL
Salve Regina U, RI
Seton Hill U, PA
Southern Nazarene U, OK
Southern U and A&M Coll, LA
State U of New York Coll at Brockport, NY
State U of New York Coll at Cortland, NY
State U of New York Coll at Potsdam, NY
Taylor U, IN
Texas A&M U–Corpus Christi, TX
U at Albany, State U of New York, NY
The U of Akron, OH
The U of Arizona, AZ

U of Evansville, IN
U of Illinois at Urbana–Champaign, IL
U of Minnesota, Duluth, MN
U of Nebraska–Lincoln, NE
The U of North Carolina at Charlotte, NC
The U of Tennessee at Martin, TN
U of the Incarnate Word, TX
West Chester U of Pennsylvania, PA
Widener U, PA

SPECIAL EDUCATION

Abilene Christian U, TX
Alabama A&M U, AL
Albany State U, GA
Albright Coll, PA
American International Coll, MA
Anderson U, SC
Arizona State U at the West campus, AZ
Ashland U, OH
Athens State U, AL
Avila U, MO
Ball State U, IN
Barry U, FL
Baylor U, TX
Benedictine Coll, KS
Boston Coll, MA
Brenau U, GA
Buena Vista U, IA
Buffalo State Coll, State U of New York, NY
Calvin Coll, MI
Cardinal Stritch U, WI
Carlow U, PA
Carson-Newman Coll, TN
Carthage Coll, WI
Clemson U, SC
Coastal Carolina U, SC
Coll of Charleston, SC
Coll of Mount St. Joseph, OH
Coll of Saint Elizabeth, NJ
Coll of St. Joseph, VT
Coll of Saint Mary, NE
The Coll of Saint Rose, NY
Columbus State U, GA
Concordia U, NE
Concord U, WV
Daemen Coll, NY
Delaware State U, DE
Eastern Michigan U, MI
Eastern Nazarene Coll, MA
East Stroudsburg U of Pennsylvania, PA
Edinboro U of Pennsylvania, PA
Elms Coll, MA
Elon U, NC
Fitchburg State Coll, MA
Florida Atlantic U, FL
Florida Gulf Coast U, FL
Fontbonne U, MO
Freed-Hardeman U, TN
Furman U, SC
Gannon U, PA
Geneva Coll, PA
Georgia Coll & State U, GA
Georgian Court U, NJ
Glenville State Coll, WV
Gonzaga U, WA
Gordon Coll, MA
Grace Coll, IN
Grambling State U, LA
Green Mountain Coll, VT
High Point U, NC
Houghton Coll, NY
Houston Baptist U, TX
Huntington U, IN
Idaho State U, ID

Colleges for Students with Learning Disabilities or AD/HD

Monmouth Coll, IL
Murray State U, KY
North Central Coll, IL
North Dakota State U, ND
Northern Michigan U, MI
Northern State U, SD
Northwestern Oklahoma
State U, OK
Odessa Coll, TX
Oklahoma State U, OK
Old Dominion U, VA
Oral Roberts U, OK
Portland State U, OR
Rose State Coll, OK
St. Cloud State U, MN
Saint John's U, MN
St. Philip's Coll, TX
San Diego Mesa Coll, CA
San Diego State U, CA
San Francisco State U, CA
Sauk Valley Comm Coll, IL
Shasta Coll, CA
Shippensburg U of
Pennsylvania, PA
Skagit Valley Coll, WA
Southern Illinois U
Carbondale, IL
Southern Illinois U
Edwardsville, IL
Southern Nazarene U, OK
Southern U and A&M Coll,
LA
Southern Utah U, UT
Spoon River Coll, IL
State U of New York Coll at
Brockport, NY
State U of New York Coll at
Cortland, NY
State U of New York Coll at
Potsdam, NY
Stephen F. Austin State U,
TX
Stonehill Coll, MA
Syracuse U, NY
Temple U, PA
Texas A&M U, TX
Trinity U, TX
Troy U, AL
Truman State U, MO
U at Albany, State U of New
York, NY
The U of Akron, OH
The U of Alabama, AL
The U of Alabama in
Huntsville, AL
U of California, Berkeley,
CA
U of Central Florida, FL
U of Central Missouri, MO
U of Dubuque, IA
U of Hawaii at Manoa, HI
U of Houston, TX
U of Illinois at Urbana–
Champaign, IL
U of Kansas, KS
U of Michigan, MI
U of Nebraska at Kearney,
NE
U of Nebraska at Omaha,
NE
U of New Mexico, NM
U of Northern Iowa, IA
U of Pittsburgh, PA
The U of Tennessee, TN
The U of Texas at El Paso,
TX
U of the Incarnate Word, TX
U of Virginia, VA
U of Washington, WA
U of Wisconsin–Platteville,
WI
Vanguard U of Southern
California, CA
Wayne State Coll, NE

West Chester U of
Pennsylvania, PA
West Los Angeles Coll, CA
West Texas A&M U, TX
West Virginia Wesleyan Coll,
WV
William Jewell Coll, MO

SPEECH-LANGUAGE PATHOLOGY
Abilene Christian U, TX
Crafton Hills Coll, CA
Eastern Michigan U, MI
Elms Coll, MA
Grambling State U, LA
Harding U, AR
Marshall U, WV
Northern Michigan U, MI
Rockhurst U, MO
St. Cloud State U, MN
Saint Xavier U, IL
Santa Rosa Jr Coll, CA
Southern Adventist U, TN
Southwestern U, TX
Towson U, MD
The U of Akron, OH
U of Central Missouri, MO
U of Nebraska–Lincoln, NE
U of Northern Iowa, IA
The U of Tennessee, TN
U of West Georgia, GA
Valdosta State U, GA

SPEECH TEACHER EDUCATION
Anderson U, IN
Baylor U, TX
Buena Vista U, IA
Concordia U, NE
Elmira Coll, NY
Harding U, AR
Indiana U Bloomington, IN
Indiana U–Purdue U Fort
Wayne, IN
Indiana U–Purdue U
Indianapolis, IN
McNeese State U, LA
Minnesota State U
Moorhead, MN
Murray State U, KY
North Dakota State U, ND
Northwestern Oklahoma
State U, OK
Pittsburg State U, KS
Southern Nazarene U, OK
Southwest Baptist U, MO
Taylor U, IN
Texas A&M U–Corpus
Christi, TX
The U of Akron, OH
The U of Arizona, AZ
U of Northern Iowa, IA
U of Rio Grande, OH
Wayne State Coll, NE
William Jewell Coll, MO

SPEECH/THEATER EDUCATION
Bemidji State U, MN
Columbus State U, GA
Graceland U, IA
Grambling State U, LA
Hamline U, MN
Lewis U, IL
Midland Lutheran Coll, NE
Saginaw Valley State U, MI
Texas A&M U–Corpus
Christi, TX
U of St. Thomas, MN

SPEECH THERAPY
Elms Coll, MA
Fontbonne U, MO
Indiana U Bloomington, IN

Lamar U, TX
Murray State U, KY
St. Cloud State U, MN
State U of New York at
Fredonia, NY
State U of New York Coll at
Geneseo, NY
U of New Hampshire, NH
U of Redlands, CA
U of Wisconsin–Madison,
WI

SPORT AND FITNESS ADMINISTRATION/ MANAGEMENT
Abilene Christian U, TX
Albertson Coll of Idaho, ID
Alvernia Coll, PA
Anderson U, SC
Asbury Coll, KY
Ball State U, IN
Barry U, FL
Baylor U, TX
Bemidji State U, MN
Bethel Coll, IN
Brock U, ON, Canada
Bucks County Comm Coll,
PA
Buena Vista U, IA
Calvin Coll, MI
Cape Breton U, NS, Canada
Carroll Coll, MT
Carthage Coll, WI
Coahoma Comm Coll, MS
Concordia U, NE
Cornerstone U, MI
Dean Coll, MA
Delaware State U, DE
Drury U, MO
Eastern Connecticut State U,
CT
Eastern Mennonite U, VA
Edinboro U of Pennsylvania,
PA
Elon U, NC
Ferrum Coll, VA
Fitchburg State Coll, MA
Flagler Coll, FL
Franklin Pierce U, NH
Fresno Pacific U, CA
Gainesville State Coll, GA
Gardner-Webb U, NC
Gonzaga U, WA
Graceland U, IA
Harding U, AR
Henderson State U, AR
High Point U, NC
Howard Comm Coll, MD
Husson Coll, ME
Indiana U Bloomington, IN
Ithaca Coll, NY
Johnson State Coll, VT
Kennesaw State U, GA
Kentucky Wesleyan Coll, KY
Kingsborough Comm Coll of
the City U of New York,
NY
Lake-Sumter Comm Coll, FL
Lake Superior State U, MI
LeTourneau U, TX
Liberty U, VA
Lindenwood U, MO
Loras Coll, IA
Lynchburg Coll, VA
MacMurray Coll, IL
Marymount U, VA
Mercyhurst Coll, PA
Minnesota State U Mankato,
MN
Minnesota State U
Moorhead, MN
Mitchell Coll, CT
Montana State U, MT

Montana State U–Billings,
MT
Mount St. Mary's U, MD
Mount Union Coll, OH
Mount Vernon Nazarene U,
OH
Neumann Coll, PA
New York U, NY
North Carolina State U, NC
North Central Coll, IL
North Dakota State U, ND
Northern Michigan U, MI
Northwood U, MI
Northwood U, Florida
Campus, FL
Northwood U, Texas
Campus, TX
Notre Dame Coll, OH
Nova Southeastern U, FL
Old Dominion U, VA
Otterbein Coll, OH
Reinhardt Coll, GA
Saint Leo U, FL
Seton Hall U, NJ
Southern Adventist U, TN
Southern Nazarene U, OK
Southwest Baptist U, MO
Southwestern Coll, KS
Springfield Coll, MA
State U of New York Coll at
Brockport, NY
State U of New York Coll of
Technology at Alfred, NY
Stetson U, FL
Syracuse U, NY
Taylor U, IN
Tennessee Wesleyan Coll,
TN
Towson U, MD
Troy U, AL
Union Coll, NE
U of Dayton, OH
U of Delaware, DE
U of Mary Hardin-Baylor, TX
U of Massachusetts Amherst,
MA
U of Michigan, MI
U of Nebraska at Kearney,
NE
U of New England, ME
U of Pittsburgh at Bradford,
PA
The U of Tennessee, TN
The U of Tennessee at
Martin, TN
The U of Texas at Austin,
TX
U of the Incarnate Word, TX
Virginia Intermont Coll, VA
Wayne State Coll, NE
Western New England Coll,
MA
West Virginia Wesleyan Coll,
WV
Widener U, PA
Xavier U, OH

STATISTICS
American U, DC
Baylor U, TX
Brock U, ON, Canada
California State U, Fullerton,
CA
Carleton U, ON, Canada
Carnegie Mellon U, PA
Cornell U, NY
Dalhousie U, NS, Canada
DePaul U, IL
Eastern Michigan U, MI
Florida International U, FL
The George Washington U,
DC
Hunter Coll of the City U of
New York, NY

Indiana U–Purdue U Fort
Wayne, IN
Kansas State U, KS
Kenyon Coll, OH
Lehigh U, PA
Loyola U Chicago, IL
Marquette U, WI
Mercyhurst Coll, PA
Michigan State U, MI
Mount Holyoke Coll, MA
Mount Saint Vincent U, NS,
Canada
New York U, NY
North Carolina State U, NC
North Dakota State U, ND
Oakland U, MI
Ohio Wesleyan U, OH
Oklahoma State U, OK
Penn State Abington, PA
Penn State DuBois, PA
Penn State Fayette, The
Eberly Campus, PA
Penn State Mont Alto, PA
Penn State Wilkes-Barre, PA
Purdue U North Central, IN
Queen's U at Kingston, ON,
Canada
Rice U, TX
Rochester Inst of
Technology, NY
Roosevelt U, IL
Rutgers, The State U of New
Jersey, New Brunswick, NJ
St. Cloud State U, MN
San Diego State U, CA
San Francisco State U, CA
The U of Akron, OH
U of California, Berkeley,
CA
U of California, Los Angeles,
CA
U of California, Santa
Barbara, CA
U of Central Florida, FL
U of Connecticut, CT
U of Guelph, ON, Canada
U of Houston, TX
U of Illinois at Urbana–
Champaign, IL
U of Manitoba, MB, Canada
U of Maryland, Baltimore
County, MD
U of Michigan, MI
U of Minnesota, Duluth, MN
U of Missouri–Columbia,
MO
U of Missouri–Kansas City,
MO
U of Nebraska at Kearney,
NE
U of New Brunswick
Fredericton, NB, Canada
U of New Hampshire, NH
U of New Mexico, NM
U of North Florida, FL
U of Pennsylvania, PA
U of Pittsburgh, PA
The U of Tennessee, TN
The U of Tennessee at
Martin, TN
The U of Texas at El Paso,
TX
The U of Texas at San
Antonio, TX
U of Toronto, ON, Canada
U of Vermont, VT
U of Washington, WA
U of Wisconsin–Madison,
WI
U of Wyoming, WY
Wilfrid Laurier U, ON,
Canada
Wright State U, OH

TURKISH
The U of Texas at Austin, TX

URBAN EDUCATION AND LEADERSHIP
U of Missouri–Kansas City, MO

URBAN FORESTRY
Southern U and A&M Coll, LA
Texas A&M U, TX

URBAN STUDIES/ AFFAIRS
Augsburg Coll, MN
Baylor U, TX
Brown U, RI
Bryn Mawr Coll, PA
Buffalo State Coll, State U of New York, NY
California State U, Northridge, CA
Carleton U, ON, Canada
Clayton State U, GA
Coll of Charleston, SC
Coll of Mount Saint Vincent, NY
Cornell U, NY
DePaul U, IL
Eugene Lang Coll The New School for Liberal Arts, NY
Florida International U, FL
Furman U, SC
Hamline U, MN
Hampshire Coll, MA
Haverford Coll, PA
Hunter Coll of the City U of New York, NY
Indiana U Bloomington, IN
Langston U, OK
Lehigh U, PA
Loyola Marymount U, CA
Macalester Coll, MN
Manhattan Coll, NY
Metropolitan Coll of New York, NY
Minnesota State U Mankato, MN
New Jersey City U, NJ
New York U, NY
Oglethorpe U, GA
Ohio Wesleyan U, OH
Portland State U, OR
Queens Coll of the City U of New York, NY
Rhodes Coll, TN
Roosevelt U, IL
Rutgers, The State U of New Jersey, New Brunswick, NJ
Ryerson U, ON, Canada
St. Cloud State U, MN
St. Philip's Coll, TX
San Diego State U, CA
San Francisco State U, CA
Southern Nazarene U, OK
Trinity U, TX
Tufts U, MA
U at Albany, State U of New York, NY
U of California, Berkeley, CA
U of Cincinnati, OH
U of Connecticut, CT
U of Minnesota, Duluth, MN
U of Missouri–Kansas City, MO
U of New Orleans, LA
U of Pennsylvania, PA
U of Pittsburgh, PA
U of San Diego, CA
The U of Tampa, FL

The U of Texas at Austin, TX
U of the District of Columbia, DC
U of Toronto, ON, Canada
U of Wisconsin–Green Bay, WI
U of Wisconsin–Madison, WI
U of Wisconsin–Oshkosh, WI
Vassar Coll, NY
Worcester State Coll, MA
Wright State U, OH

VEHICLE AND VEHICLE PARTS AND ACCESSORIES MARKETING
Northwood U, MI
Northwood U, Florida Campus, FL
Northwood U, Texas Campus, TX

VEHICLE/EQUIPMENT OPERATION
Skagit Valley Coll, WA

VEHICLE MAINTENANCE AND REPAIR TECHNOLOGIES RELATED
British Columbia Inst of Technology, BC, Canada
Massasoit Comm Coll, MA
Victor Valley Coll, CA

VETERINARY/ANIMAL HEALTH TECHNOLOGY
Cedar Valley Coll, TX
Central Florida Comm Coll, FL
Macomb Comm Coll, MI
Michigan State U, MI
Midland Coll, TX
Murray State U, KY
North Dakota State U, ND
Pima Comm Coll, AZ
Sussex County Comm Coll, NJ
The U of Maine at Augusta, ME
U of Nebraska–Lincoln, NE
Wilson Coll, PA

VETERINARY SCIENCES
Clayton State U, GA
Macomb Comm Coll, MI
Rutgers, The State U of New Jersey, New Brunswick, NJ
State U of New York Coll of Technology at Alfred, NY

VETERINARY TECHNOLOGY
Argosy U, Twin Cities, Eagan, MN
Blue Ridge Comm Coll, VA
Brevard Comm Coll, FL
Cosumnes River Coll, Sacramento, CA
Delaware Tech & Comm Coll, Jack F. Owens Campus, DE
Foothill Coll, CA
Gaston Coll, NC
Michigan State U, MI
Midland Coll, TX
Minnesota School of Business–St. Cloud, MN
San Diego Mesa Coll, CA
State U of New York Coll of Technology at Canton, NY

Vermont Tech Coll, VT

VIOLIN, VIOLA, GUITAR AND OTHER STRINGED INSTRUMENTS
Acadia U, NS, Canada
Ball State U, IN
California State U, Fullerton, CA
Carnegie Mellon U, PA
Columbus State U, GA
DePaul U, IL
Hope Coll, MI
Houghton Coll, NY
Illinois Wesleyan U, IL
Lamar U, TX
Lawrence U, WI
Mannes Coll The New School for Music, NY
Minnesota State Coll–Southeast Tech, MN
Notre Dame de Namur U, CA
Otterbein Coll, OH
Roosevelt U, IL
St. Cloud State U, MN
Seton Hill U, PA
State U of New York at Fredonia, NY
Stetson U, FL
Syracuse U, NY
Temple U, PA
The U of Akron, OH
U of Central Oklahoma, OK
U of Cincinnati, OH
U of Kansas, KS
U of Michigan, MI
U of New Hampshire, NH
U of Washington, WA

VISUAL AND PERFORMING ARTS
Alderson-Broaddus Coll, WV
Angelo State U, TX
Arizona State U at the West campus, AZ
Bard Coll, NY
Brown U, RI
Bucks County Comm Coll, PA
Calhoun Comm Coll, AL
Cameron U, OK
Carroll Coll, MT
Citrus Coll, CA
Claremont McKenna Coll, CA
Clemson U, SC
Concordia U Coll of Alberta, AB, Canada
Eastern Connecticut State U, CT
East Stroudsburg U of Pennsylvania, PA
Eckerd Coll, FL
Fairleigh Dickinson U, Coll at Florham, NJ
Fairleigh Dickinson U, Metropolitan Campus, NJ
Gannon U, PA
Green Mountain Coll, VT
Ithaca Coll, NY
Jacksonville U, FL
Johnson State Coll, VT
Kutztown U of Pennsylvania, PA
LaGrange Coll, GA
Lee Coll, TX
Loras Coll, IA
Loyola U New Orleans, LA
Marywood U, PA
Massachusetts Coll of Liberal Arts, MA
Missouri State U, MO
Naropa U, CO

Nassau Comm Coll, NY
North Carolina School of the Arts, NC
Penn State Abington, PA
Penn State DuBois, PA
Penn State Fayette, The Eberly Campus, PA
Penn State Mont Alto, PA
Penn State Wilkes-Barre, PA
Quincy Coll, MA
Ramapo Coll of New Jersey, NJ
The Richard Stockton Coll of New Jersey, NJ
Roxbury Comm Coll, MA
Rutgers, The State U of New Jersey, New Brunswick, NJ
St. Bonaventure U, NY
St. Gregory's U, OK
School of the Art Inst of Chicago, IL
Seton Hall U, NJ
The U of Arizona, AZ
U of Arkansas at Fort Smith, AR
U of Maine at Machias, ME
U of Maryland, Baltimore County, MD
U of Miami, FL
U of Michigan, MI
U of Pennsylvania, PA
U of Rio Grande, OH
U of San Diego, CA
U of San Francisco, CA
The U of Tampa, FL
The U of Tennessee at Martin, TN
The U of Texas at Austin, TX
U of Toronto, ON, Canada
Valdosta State U, GA
Vassar Coll, NY
Wichita State U, KS

VISUAL AND PERFORMING ARTS RELATED
Adelphi U, NY
Claremont McKenna Coll, CA
Clemson U, SC
Comm Coll of Allegheny County, PA
Florida Comm Coll at Jacksonville, FL
Illinois State U, IL
Illinois Wesleyan U, IL
Kutztown U of Pennsylvania, PA
Maine Coll of Art, ME
Marywood U, PA
Rensselaer Polytechnic Inst, NY
Rice U, TX
St. Cloud State U, MN
School of the Art Inst of Chicago, IL
State U of New York Coll at Geneseo, NY
Stetson U, FL
The U of Akron, OH
U of California, Los Angeles, CA
U of New Haven, CT
The U of the Arts, PA

VOCATIONAL REHABILITATION COUNSELING
East Carolina U, NC
U of Illinois at Urbana–Champaign, IL
U of Wisconsin–Stout, WI
Wright State U, OH

VOICE AND OPERA
Abilene Christian U, TX
Acadia U, NS, Canada
Ball State U, IN
Bard Coll, NY
Barry U, FL
Bethel Coll, IN
Brandon U, MB, Canada
Brenau U, GA
California State U, Fullerton, CA
Calvin Coll, MI
Carnegie Mellon U, PA
Carson-Newman Coll, TN
The Catholic U of America, DC
Charleston Southern U, SC
Cincinnati Christian U, OH
Columbus State U, GA
Concordia U, NE
Delaware State U, DE
DePaul U, IL
Drake U, IA
Fresno City Coll, CA
Furman U, SC
Hope Coll, MI
Houghton Coll, NY
Huntington U, IN
Illinois Wesleyan U, IL
Indiana U Bloomington, IN
Indiana U–Purdue U Fort Wayne, IN
Ithaca Coll, NY
Jacksonville U, FL
Lamar U, TX
Langston U, OK
Lawrence U, WI
Lindenwood U, MO
Loyola Marymount U, CA
Mannes Coll The New School for Music, NY
Mercyhurst Coll, PA
Minnesota State U Mankato, MN
Minnesota State U Moorhead, MN
New York U, NY
North Carolina School of the Arts, NC
Northern State U, SD
Northwestern Coll, MN
Notre Dame de Namur U, CA
The Ohio State U, OH
Otterbein Coll, OH
Prairie View A&M U, TX
Queens U of Charlotte, NC
Reedley Coll, CA
Roosevelt U, IL
St. Cloud State U, MN
Seton Hill U, PA
Southern Nazarene U, OK
State U of New York at Fredonia, NY
Stetson U, FL
Syracuse U, NY
Taylor U, IN
Temple U, PA
Trinity U, TX
Truman State U, MO
The U of Akron, OH
U of Central Oklahoma, OK
U of Cincinnati, OH
U of Delaware, DE
U of Illinois at Urbana–Champaign, IL
U of Kansas, KS
U of Miami, FL
U of Michigan, MI
U of Nebraska at Omaha, NE
U of New Hampshire, NH
U of Redlands, CA

St. Francis Xavier U, NS, Canada
San Diego State U, CA
San Francisco State U, CA
Santa Ana Coll, CA
Santa Rosa Jr Coll, CA
Southwestern U, TX
State U of New York at Fredonia, NY
State U of New York Coll at Brockport, NY
Syracuse U, NY
Temple U, PA
Towson U, MD
Trent U, ON, Canada
Trinity Coll, CT
Tufts U, MA
U at Albany, State U of New York, NY
U at Buffalo, the State U of New York, NY
The U of Arizona, AZ
U of California, Berkeley, CA
U of California, Irvine, CA
U of California, Los Angeles, CA
U of California, Santa Barbara, CA
U of Colorado at Boulder, CO
U of Connecticut, CT
U of Delaware, DE
U of Guelph, ON, Canada
U of Hawaii at Manoa, HI
U of Illinois at Urbana–Champaign, IL
U of Kansas, KS
U of Manitoba, MB, Canada
U of Massachusetts Amherst, MA

U of Massachusetts Boston, MA
U of Miami, FL
U of Michigan, MI
U of Minnesota, Duluth, MN
U of Nebraska at Omaha, NE
U of Nebraska–Lincoln, NE
U of New Hampshire, NH
U of New Mexico, NM
U of New Orleans, LA
The U of North Carolina at Asheville, NC
The U of North Carolina at Chapel Hill, NC
U of Northern British Columbia, BC, Canada
U of Oregon, OR
U of Pennsylvania, PA
U of Rhode Island, RI
U of St. Thomas, MN
U of Toronto, ON, Canada
U of Vermont, VT
U of Washington, WA
U of Wisconsin–Madison, WI
U of Wyoming, WY
Vassar Coll, NY
Wellesley Coll, MA
Wells Coll, NY
West Chester U of Pennsylvania, PA
Wichita State U, KS
Wilfrid Laurier U, ON, Canada
Wright State U, OH
Yale U, CT

WOOD SCIENCE AND WOOD PRODUCTS/PULP AND PAPER TECHNOLOGY
Dabney S. Lancaster Comm Coll, VA
North Carolina State U, NC
State U of New York Coll of Environmental Science and Forestry, NY
Sterling Coll, VT
U of Massachusetts Amherst, MA
U of Toronto, ON, Canada
U of Washington, WA
U of Wisconsin–Stevens Point, WI

WOODWORKING
Bucks County Comm Coll, PA

WORD PROCESSING
Baker Coll of Allen Park, MI
Coll of the Desert, CA
The Coll of Westchester, NY
Eastfield Coll, TX
Florida Comm Coll at Jacksonville, FL
Galveston Coll, TX
Kellogg Comm Coll, MI
North Central Texas Coll, TX
Northland Comm and Tech Coll–Thief River Falls, MN
Richland Comm Coll, IL
Santa Ana Coll, CA
Seminole Comm Coll, FL
Stark State Coll of Technology, OH
Tallahassee Comm Coll, FL
Valencia Comm Coll, FL

West Virginia Northern Comm Coll, WV

WORK AND FAMILY STUDIES
Ursuline Coll, OH

YOUTH MINISTRY
Benedictine Coll, KS
Bethel Coll, IN
Bethel U, MN
Charleston Southern U, SC
Gardner-Webb U, NC
Gordon Coll, MA
Harding U, AR
John Brown U, AR
Kuyper Coll, MI
Lancaster Bible Coll, PA
Lindenwood U, MO
Mount Vernon Nazarene U, OH
Multnomah Bible Coll and Biblical Seminary, OR
Northwestern Coll, MN
Oak Hills Christian Coll, MN
Point Loma Nazarene U, CA
Southern Nazarene U, OK
Vanguard U of Southern California, CA

YOUTH SERVICES
Indiana U–Purdue U Fort Wayne, IN
U of Northern British Columbia, BC, Canada

ZOOLOGY/ANIMAL BIOLOGY
Ball State U, IN
Brandon U, MB, Canada
Coll of the Atlantic, ME
Dixie State Coll of Utah, UT
East Central Coll, MO

El Camino Coll, CA
Idaho State U, ID
Michigan State U, MI
North Carolina State U, NC
North Dakota State U, ND
Northern Michigan U, MI
The Ohio State U, OH
Ohio Wesleyan U, OH
Oklahoma State U, OK
Rutgers, The State U of New Jersey, Newark, NJ
San Francisco State U, CA
Southern Illinois U Carbondale, IL
Southern Utah U, UT
Spoon River Coll, IL
State U of New York Coll of Environmental Science and Forestry, NY
Texas A&M U, TX
The U of Akron, OH
U of California, Santa Barbara, CA
U of Guelph, ON, Canada
U of Hawaii at Manoa, HI
U of Manitoba, MB, Canada
U of Michigan, MI
U of New Brunswick Fredericton, NB, Canada
U of New Hampshire, NH
U of Rhode Island, RI
The U of Tennessee, TN
The U of Texas at Austin, TX
The U of Texas at El Paso, TX
U of Toronto, ON, Canada
U of Vermont, VT
U of Washington, WA
U of Wisconsin–Madison, WI
U of Wyoming, WY

ALPHABETICAL INDEX OF COLLEGES

The names of colleges with **structured/ proactive programs** for students with LD are printed in bold-face type; those with self-directed/decentralized services for students with LD are in regular type.

Alphabetical Index of Colleges

GEOGRAPHICAL INDEX OF COLLEGES

The names of colleges with **structured/proactive programs** for students with LD are printed in bold-face type; those with self-directed/decentralized services for students with LD are in regular type.

U.S. AND U.S. TERRITORIES

Union College, Lincoln	253
University of Nebraska at Kearney, Kearney	279
University of Nebraska at Omaha, Omaha	279
University of Nebraska–Lincoln, Lincoln	280
Wayne State College, Wayne	314
Western Nebraska Community College, Sidney	471

NEVADA

Truckee Meadows Community College, Reno	465

NEW HAMPSHIRE

Franklin Pierce University, Rindge	124
New Hampshire Community Technical College, Nashua/Claremont, Nashua	422
Rivier College, Nashua	217
University of New Hampshire, Durham	281
University of New Hampshire at Manchester, Manchester	282

NEW JERSEY

Burlington County College, Pemberton	352
Camden County College, Blackwood	353
College of Saint Elizabeth, Morristown	98
County College of Morris, Randolph	368
Fairleigh Dickinson University, College at Florham, Madison	**34**
Fairleigh Dickinson University, Metropolitan Campus, Teaneck	**34**
Georgian Court University, Lakewood	**36**
Gloucester County College, Sewell	387
Middlesex County College, Edison	**335**
Monmouth University, West Long Branch	177
New Jersey City University, Jersey City	184
Ocean County College, Toms River	429
Ramapo College of New Jersey, Mahwah	213
The Richard Stockton College of New Jersey, Pomona	216
Rowan University, Glassboro	220
Rutgers, The State University of New Jersey, Newark, Newark	221
Rutgers, The State University of New Jersey, New Brunswick, New Brunswick	221
Salem Community College, Carneys Point	444
Seton Hall University, South Orange	231
Somerset Christian College, Zarephath	453
Sussex County Community College, Newton	461
Thomas Edison State College, Trenton	248

NEW MEXICO

Eastern New Mexico University–Roswell, Roswell	**330**
Luna Community College, Las Vegas	410
New Mexico Junior College, Hobbs	423
Santa Fe Community College, Santa Fe	447
Southwestern Indian Polytechnic Institute, Albuquerque	456
University of New Mexico, Albuquerque	283

NEW YORK

Adelphi University, Garden City	**29**
The Art Institute of New York City, New York	343
Bard College, Annandale-on-Hudson	71
Broome Community College, Binghamton	349
Bryant and Stratton College, Rochester	351
Buffalo State College, State University of New York, Buffalo	83
Colgate University, Hamilton	97
College of Mount Saint Vincent, Riverdale	98
The College of Saint Rose, Albany	100
College of Staten Island of the City University of New York, Staten Island	100

The College of Westchester, White Plains	363
Concordia College–New York, Bronxville	**33**
Cornell University, Ithaca	104
Daemen College, Amherst	105
Dutchess Community College, Poughkeepsie	376
Elmira College, Elmira	113
Eugene Lang College The New School for Liberal Arts, New York	115
Farmingdale State College, Farmingdale	116
Fashion Institute of Technology, New York	117
Fulton-Montgomery Community College, Johnstown	383
Hamilton College, Clinton	134
Hartwick College, Oneonta	137
Herkimer County Community College, Herkimer	391
Hofstra University, Hempstead	**37**
Houghton College, Houghton	140
Hudson Valley Community College, Troy	396
Hunter College of the City University of New York, New York	141
Iona College, New Rochelle	**37**
Ithaca College, Ithaca	146
Jamestown Community College, Jamestown	401
Keuka College, Keuka Park	152
Kingsborough Community College of the City University of New York, Brooklyn	404
Laboratory Institute of Merchandising, New York	154
Le Moyne College, Syracuse	160
Long Island University, Brooklyn Campus, Brooklyn	162
Manhattan College, Riverdale	166
Manhattanville College, Purchase	167
Mannes College The New School for Music, New York	167
Marist College, Poughkeepsie	**40**
Marymount Manhattan College, New York	**41**
Metropolitan College of New York, New York	**43**
Mohawk Valley Community College, Utica	419
Molloy College, Rockville Centre	176
Nassau Community College, Garden City	422
The New School: A University, New York	185
New York City College of Technology of the City University of New York, Brooklyn	424
New York University, New York	185
Niagara University, Niagara Falls, Niagara University	186
Parsons The New School for Design, New York	205
Pratt Institute, Brooklyn	209
Queens College of the City University of New York, Flushing	211
Rensselaer Polytechnic Institute, Troy	215
Rochester Institute of Technology, Rochester	218
Rockland Community College, Suffern	440
The Sage Colleges, Troy	222
St. Bonaventure University, St. Bonaventure	223
St. Lawrence University, Canton	225
St. Thomas Aquinas College, Sparkill	**47**
School of Visual Arts, New York	230
State University of New York at Fredonia, Fredonia	240
State University of New York College at Brockport, Brockport	241
State University of New York College at Cortland, Cortland	241

State University of New York College at Geneseo, Geneseo	242
State University of New York College at Potsdam, Potsdam	242
State University of New York College of Environmental Science and Forestry, Syracuse	242
State University of New York College of Environmental Science & Forestry, Ranger School, Wanakena	459
State University of New York College of Technology at Alfred, Alfred	459
State University of New York College of Technology at Canton, Canton	460
Syracuse University, Syracuse	245
Trocaire College, Buffalo	464
University at Albany, State University of New York, Albany	254
University at Buffalo, the State University of New York, Buffalo	254
Utica College, Utica	308
Vassar College, Poughkeepsie	309
Wells College, Aurora	315
Westchester Community College, Valhalla	471
Yeshiva University, New York	326

NORTH CAROLINA

Asheville-Buncombe Technical Community College, Asheville	344
Belmont Abbey College, Belmont	73
Brevard College, Brevard	79
Caldwell Community College and Technical Institute, Hudson	352
Central Piedmont Community College, Charlotte	357
College of The Albemarle, Elizabeth City	361
Craven Community College, New Bern	370
Duke University, Durham	109
Durham Technical Community College, Durham	375
East Carolina University, Greenville	110
Elon University, Elon	114
Fayetteville State University, Fayetteville	117
Gardner-Webb University, Boiling Springs	128
Gaston College, Dallas	385
Greensboro College, Greensboro	133
High Point University, High Point	139
Johnson & Wales University, Charlotte	148
Mayland Community College, Spruce Pine	412
North Carolina School of the Arts, Winston-Salem	187
North Carolina State University, Raleigh	188
Piedmont Community College, Roxboro	434
Queens University of Charlotte, Charlotte	212
Richmond Community College, Hamlet	439
Rockingham Community College, Wentworth	440
South Piedmont Community College, Polkton	455
Surry Community College, Dobson	460
The University of North Carolina at Asheville, Asheville	284
The University of North Carolina at Chapel Hill, Chapel Hill	**50**
The University of North Carolina at Charlotte, Charlotte	284
Wake Forest University, Winston-Salem	312

NORTH DAKOTA

North Dakota State University, Fargo	189
Williston State College, Williston	475

OHIO

The Art Institute of Ohio–Cincinnati, Cincinnati	344
Ashland University, Ashland	67
Central Ohio Technical College, Newark	356
Cincinnati Christian University, Cincinnati	93

Peterson's
Book Satisfaction Survey

Give Us Your Feedback

Thank you for choosing Peterson's as your source for personalized solutions for your education and career achievement. Please take a few minutes to answer the following questions. Your answers will go a long way in helping us to produce the most user-friendly and comprehensive resources to meet your individual needs.

When completed, please tear out this page and mail it to us at:

Publishing Department
Peterson's, a Nelnet company
2000 Lenox Drive
Lawrenceville, NJ 08648

You can also complete this survey online at **www.petersons.com/booksurvey**.

1. **What is the ISBN of the book you have purchased? (The ISBN can be found on the book's back cover in the lower right-hand corner.)** _____

2. **Where did you purchase this book?**
   ❑ Retailer, such as Barnes & Noble
   ❑ Online reseller, such as Amazon.com
   ❑ Petersons.com
   ❑ Other (please specify) _____

3. **If you purchased this book on Petersons.com, please rate the following aspects of your online purchasing experience on a scale of 4 to 1 (4 = Excellent and 1 = Poor).**

	4	3	2	1
Comprehensiveness of Peterson's Online Bookstore page	❑	❑	❑	❑
Overall online customer experience	❑	❑	❑	❑

4. **Which category best describes you?**
   ❑ High school student
   ❑ Parent of high school student
   ❑ College student
   ❑ Graduate/professional student
   ❑ Returning adult student

   ❑ Teacher
   ❑ Counselor
   ❑ Working professional/military
   ❑ Other (please specify) _____

5. **Rate your overall satisfaction with this book.**

Extremely Satisfied	Satisfied	Not Satisfied
❑	❑	❑

6. **Rate each of the following aspects of this book on a scale of 4 to 1 (4 = Excellent and 1 = Poor).**

	4	3	2	1
Comprehensiveness of the information	❏	❏	❏	❏
Accuracy of the information	❏	❏	❏	❏
Usability	❏	❏	❏	❏
Cover design	❏	❏	❏	❏
Book layout	❏	❏	❏	❏
Special features (e.g., CD, flashcards, charts, etc.)	❏	❏	❏	❏
Value for the money	❏	❏	❏	❏

7. **This book was recommended by:**
   - ❏ Guidance counselor
   - ❏ Parent/guardian
   - ❏ Family member/relative
   - ❏ Friend
   - ❏ Teacher
   - ❏ Not recommended by anyone—I found the book on my own
   - ❏ Other (please specify) _____

8. **Would you recommend this book to others?**

Yes	Not Sure	No
❏	❏	❏

9. **Please provide any additional comments.**

_____

_____

_____

_____

_____

Remember, you can tear out this page and mail it to us at:

Publishing Department
Peterson's, a Nelnet company
2000 Lenox Drive
Lawrenceville, NJ 08648

or you can complete the survey online at **www.petersons.com/booksurvey.**

Your feedback is important to us at Peterson's, and we thank you for your time!

If you would like us to keep in touch with you about new products and services, please include your e-mail address here: _____